DISCOVERING BIOLOGICAL PSYCHOLOGY

DISCOVERING BIOLOGICAL PSYCHOLOGY

SECOND EDITION

Laura A. Freberg

CALIFORNIA POLYTECHNIC STATE UNIVERSITY, SAN LUIS OBISPO

Australia • Brazil • Japan • Korea • Mexico • Singapore • Spain • United Kingdom • United States

Discovering Biological Psychology,
Second Edition
Laura A. Freberg

Senior Sponsoring Editor: Jane Potter
Developmental Editor: Mary Falcon
Assistant Editor: Rebecca Rosenberg
Editorial Assistant: Nicolas Albert
Media Editor: Lauren Keyes
Executive Marketing Manager: Kimberly Russell
Marketing Manager: Tierra Morgan
Marketing Assistant: Molly Felz
Executive Marketing Communications Manager: Talia Wise
Senior Content Project Manager: Pat Waldo
Creative Director: Rob Hugel
Art Director: Vernon Boes
Print Buyer: Becky Cross
Rights Acquisitions Account Manager, Text: Katie Huha
Rights Acquisitions Account Manager, Image: Jennifer Meyer Dare
Production Service: Elm Street Publishing Services
Text Designer: Diane Beasley
Photo Researcher: Lisa Jelly
Cover Designer: Marsha Cohen
Cover Image: © Getty Images
Compositor: Integra Software Services Pvt. Ltd.

Library of Congress Control Number: 2008943481

ISBN-13: 978-0-547-17779-3

ISBN-10: 0-547-17779-8

Wadsworth
10 Davis Drive
Belmont, CA 94002-3098
USA

Cengage Learning is a leading provider of customized learning solutions with office locations around the globe, including Singapore, the United Kingdom, Australia, Mexico, Brazil, and Japan. Locate your local office at **www.cengage.com/international.**

Cengage Learning products are represented in Canada by Nelson Education, Ltd.

To learn more about Wadsworth, visit **www.cengage.com/Wadsworth**

Purchase any of our products at your local college store or at our preferred online store **www.ichapters.com.**

Printed in the United States of America
1 2 3 4 5 6 7 13 12 11 10 09

TO MY FAMILY

Roger, Kristin, Karen, and Karla

About the Author

If you have not had the opportunity to write a text yourself, you may find it baffling that others of us engage in such behavior. My route to this project was neither short nor direct. The fact that I ride a 1994 Harley Davidson Fat Boy, listen to vintage Rolling Stones, obsess about college football, and have a weakness for playing *Legend of Zelda* on the Wii may not directly affect the way I describe classical conditioning in sea slugs, but these are important parts of who I am.

I had the very real privilege to study psychology with some of the most gifted faculty in the United States. During the 1970s, the psychology faculty at UCLA read like a who's who in the discipline. My thinking about psychology was shaped by Eric Holman, John Garcia, Ivar Lovaas, Jackson Beatty, John Libeskind, Donald Novin, Frank Krasne, and F. Nowell Jones, to name a few. As a graduate student, I sat in awe as Arnold Scheibel lectured on neuroanatomy for three hours straight without pause, and without ever referring to any notes. Many happy hours were spent in Murray Jarvik's and Ron Siegel's lab, where we watched monkeys apparently hallucinating and discovered that it is virtually impossible to make elephants drunk. As a capstone, I had the very real pleasure to complete my dissertation research under the direction of Robert Rescorla, then at Yale. Bob has a mastery of experimental design that I've never seen equaled by anyone else, and he tolerated my many questions with patience and grace.

With this background, I might have been expected to pursue a career at a research university, but other factors intervened. My youngest daughter, Karla, has autism, and in the interests of finding a reasonable mix between career and family, I opted for a more teaching-oriented career. Beginning with my first class at Pasadena City College, when I was 23, I have spent more than 30 years in front of the classroom. Currently, I serve as a professor of psychology at California Polytechnic State University, located in the beautiful seaside town of San Luis Obispo.

I didn't just sit down to write a textbook. Instead, I found myself getting gradually more involved with the publishing business. Reviewing others' work led to production of test banks, study guides, and instructors' manuals, coauthoring revised editions, and editing collections of readings for psychology. Eventually, curiosity took over, and I wondered what the material would look like if I could write it my way. The text you have in your hands is the end result not only of my personal experience but the sum of many collaborative, thought-provoking discussions with students and faculty colleagues, to whom I am immensely grateful.

It is a privilege to be able to communicate the work of so many gifted scientists to the next generation of students. In 1904, William James predicted that our knowledge and understanding of psychology would achieve meaningful progress only when we possessed the science and technology we needed to understand the underlying biological processes of thought and behavior. James observed that, "Something definite happens when to a certain brain-state a certain 'sciousness' corresponds. A genuine glimpse into what it is would be *the* scientific achievement, before which all past achievements would pale." Who could wish for a better subject about which to write?

Brief Contents

Contents

6 Vision 154

7 Nonvisual Sensation and Perception 188

Preface

In the more than 30 years that I have taught the biological psychology course, the first few minutes of every class have been the same—and I am quite sure that if you are examining this book for adoption in your course, you have had the same experience. I stand there smiling and cheerful as my new students, fear and trepidation written plainly across their faces, file in and take their seats. My first goal, and I'm sure yours as well, has also always been the same: to soften those fearful student eyes as quickly as I can. Also like you, I have never been willing to sacrifice the important content of the course, but over the years I have gotten better at teaching the content in a style and at a pace commensurate with my students' abilities to comprehend it.

My second goal (Isn't it yours as well?) is to get my students not just comfortable in my class but interested! To get those eyes riveted and those heads nodding with flashes of insight. And again, over the years, I have learned to sprinkle my lectures with spicy tidbits like black widow spider venom and hallucinating monkeys and, perhaps more importantly, with answers to the unspoken student questions, "Why do I need to learn this?" and "How does this relate to my life?" Thus, when I opened a fresh, new Word document to begin writing the First Edition of this text, a very important question came to mind. Given the wide range of textbooks in biological psychology, "Why write another one?" My answer was that no existing textbook met the criteria I had set for myself as an instructor—thoroughness balanced by clarity and student appeal. Would it be possible to write a text that effectively combines the rigor of current research with a student-friendly teaching approach appropriate for diverse student needs and abilities?

I believed it was possible, and that was why I decided to write this book. Now, having used the First Edition in my own classes, I believe that it met those goals. But the world of biological psychology refused to stand still just because my First Edition had been published. Every day, news feeds describing exciting new research that challenged and rewrote much of our understanding of brain and behavior crossed my desk. Questions that had to be left unanswered in my First Edition were not only answered, but they were replaced by whole new sets of questions unimagined just a few years earlier. Technology continued to advance at lightning speed. Repeated transcranial magnetic stimulation was so new when the First Edition went to press that I had to rely on my high school Latin and a very good dictionary to struggle through an article written in Portuguese, just so that I might include something about this important technique in my book. Today, only a few years later, a Medline search returns hundreds of pages of articles on rTMS technology (and most, fortunately for me, are in English).

Besides getting very helpful feedback from my own students, I also had the pleasure of hearing from students and instructors from all over the world who were using the book and who took the time to offer many innovative ways it could be improved for their use. These ideas, along with the very helpful formal reviews of the First Edition from my publisher, confirmed my ideas for change and added some exciting new ones. When I finally got the green light to start working on the new edition, I jumped at the opportunity. Looking back at the changes made in the Second Edition, I am amazed at the many accomplishments of scientists in our field over just the past few years, and the opportunity to share this new information is exciting. Even more than the First Edition, this new text synthesizes my experience in conveying the excitement and fascination of biological psychology in a way that I hope will appeal to both my colleagues and our students.

For the Instructor

For the instructor, the ***readability and student appeal*** of this text ***is balanced by accuracy, completeness of coverage, and currency***. Because presenting the most current research and thought is critically important in this field, a very real advantage of a second edition over an eighth or ninth edition is the ability to integrate new findings into a table of contents constructed 5 years, rather than 25 years, earlier. Completeness of coverage is balanced by the recognition that one can cover only so much information in one quarter or semester. Still, faculty will find all of the traditional topics of a biological psychology course, along with a few surprises. For example:

- Chapter 1 features extensive coverage of research methods and technologies in biological psychology including the use of stem cells, accompanied by a careful consideration of research ethics.
- Chapter 2 covers the anatomy of the nervous system and its evolution.
- Chapter 5 offers optional coverage of genetics and heritability not found in many comparable texts.
- Chapter 8 offers current research on mirror neurons, and relevance and student interest are enhanced by the inclusion of discussions of performance-enhancing drugs and gene doping.
- Chapter 10 includes a discussion of attraction and romantic love within the context of sexual behavior. This chapter also offers very current coverage of biological influences on parenting and sexual orientation.
- Chapter 15 tells the story of how research unraveled the mystery of neurological conditions caused by TSEs, such as mad-cow disease, and is unique in its discussion of neurological assessment and rehabilitation.
- Chapter 16 covers a full range of psychological disorders including schizophrenia, mood disorders, ADHD, anxiety disorders, antisocial personality disorder, and autism.

Instructor Ancillaries

To further serve the needs of faculty, I have paid close attention to the production of useful ancillaries. As tempting as it was to farm these out in the interests of time and sanity, I have been personally involved with the production of animations, PowerPoint® presentation materials, and the Instructor's Manual as well as the construction of more than 2,800 questions for the Test Bank. Many of these questions have been piloted in my own classes. My questions reflect past collaboration with consultants who specialize in test construction for higher education, and I think you will find them a refreshing change from the usual test banks supplied with textbooks. The following ancillaries give instructors the tools to present course materials according to individual preference:

- ***Instructor's Resource Manual:*** Save time, streamline your course preparation, and get the most from the text by preparing for class more quickly and effectively. The Instructor's Resource Manual contains sample lecture outlines, ideas for classroom demonstrations and handouts, and suggestions for using outside resources in the classroom.
- ***Test Bank:*** The Test Bank includes more than 2,400 multiple-choice questions and more than 400 true/false, fill-in, short-answer, and essay questions. New to the Second Edition of the Test Bank are novel ***illustration-based test items*** (multiple-choice, fill-in, and short-answer) that contain black and white printable versions of figures in the text.
- ***PowerLecture:*** This one-stop lecture and class preparation tool contains ready-to-use Microsoft® PowerPoint® slides and allows you to assemble, edit, publish, and present custom lectures for your course. PowerLecture lets you bring together text-specific lecture outlines along with videos, animations based on the art program, or your own materials—culminating in a powerful, personalized, media-enhanced presentation. The CD-ROM also includes JoinIn®, an interactive tool that lets you pose book-specific questions and display students' answers seamlessly within the

PowerPoint slides of your own lecture, in conjunction with the "clicker" hardware of your choice, as well as the ExamView® assessment and tutorial system, and guides you step by step through the process of creating tests.

- ***The Instructors' Web Site:*** Log on to the password-protected site to access a wide range of resources such as electronic versions of the instructor's manual, PowerPoint® slides, and more.
- ***Webtutor:*** Jump-start your course with customizable, rich, text-specific content within your Course Management System. Whether you want to Web-enable your class or put an entire course online, WebTutor™ delivers. Visit webtutor.cengage.com to learn more.

For the Student

To meet the needs of students, I have continued in the Second Edition of this text to write in an accessible, readable style that helps them process information. Having taught biological psychology to students majoring not only in the sciences but also in education, the liberal arts, the social sciences, computer science, and engineering, I know where students stumble in this material, and those are the places where I slow down and provide the steps students need to understand a point. By "steps" I mean sequential ideas that build one upon the other. That is the way we learn. I learned about learning when I graduated from high school. Before I could drive my graduation gift, a new (used) car, my Dad opened the hood and pointed to things—that's the carburetor, that's the timing belt, those are the plugs, this here's your battery . . . Got it? Sure Dad, got it. But when the car ran out of oil and broke down, Dad blamed himself. He realized that he had named all the parts to me but had never explained how they worked.

After Dad's second lesson, I took better care of my car and later in life I always taught my children how things worked before they used them. And that is the approach I take to teaching biological psychology. The "how things work" approach is supported by photos and carefully constructed illustrations, all of which are designed to both instruct and grab interest.

Speaking of interest, the other reason Dad's second lesson was more effective than the first was that breaking down in traffic on the interstate *motivated* me to learn how a car works. Although most faculty find biological psychology intrinsically fascinating, I make an extra effort to make topics such as classical conditioning in the sea slug compelling to the average college sophomore. Each chapter of this book is filled with catchy, real-life examples to help keep students motivated to learn the material. As I wrote this book, I paused here and there to address the questions, "Why do we (as a society) need to know this?" and "What can we (students) do with this information?" ***New Directions*** boxed features connect chapter content to current events, controversies, or other real-world issues, such as the possibility of using imaging technologies to "read" minds and the use of virtual reality for rehabilitation following brain injury. In ***Why Does This Matter?*** features, readers will find connections to more directly interesting information, such as the hazards of designer drugs and why little girls like pink. Occassionally in the margin, a pithy ***quotation*** from a well-known person in history, science, or the arts (e.g., *Pain is inevitable. Suffering is optional.* —Dalai Lama) lightens the moment.

Student-focused pedagogy is another essential element of this text. Like architect Frank Lloyd Wright, who argued that "form follows function," I worked to make the form of each chapter fit its teaching function. A ***chapter outline*** and ***learning objectives*** are placed clearly at the beginning of each chapter. Words that are new to a college sophomore's vocabulary are ***defined in the margins***, along with ***pronunciation guides*** for difficult words. My foreign readers have found this feature especially helpful.

Chapter content is reviewed at two or three points within each chapter in ***Interim Summaries*** that include ***summary points*** correlated to the learning objectives, ***summary tables***, that present important information visually, and open-ended ***review questions***. Finally, a ***Chapter Review*** brings it all together for the student with open-ended ***thought questions*** that could form the basis of term papers, class discussions, or projects and an alphbetized list of the ***key terms*** (with page references) of the chapter.

Finally, I hope I have added another "f" to Wright's form and function—fun! Students work very hard to master the concepts in biological psychology, and they need a payoff. Learning about puffer fish (fugu) poisoning and brain worms (yes, they really do exist) lightens an otherwise daunting task.

Student Ancillaries

The ***Study Guide*** for the text provides guided reviews correlated to learning objectives from the text, as well as additional ***self-quizzing materials*** not found on the student Web site, and ***answers*** to the Interim Summary and Chapter Review questions. New to the Second Edition of the Study Guide are ***coloring and labeling exercises*** based on the art in the text.

A comprehensive ***Student Web Site*** incorporates ***animation-based tutorials*** along with self-quizzing, vocabulary review, and other study tools. Selected materials from the Study Guide, such as suggested answers to review questions from the Interim Summaries, are provided on the Web site.

About the Second Edition

As I launched into the writing of the Second Edition I had three major goals: to update and refine the ***content***, enhance the student ***interest*** factor, and augment the student ***learning aids***.

New and Expanded Content

In addition to the usual updates reflecting recent research, I have added new topics and expanded coverage of others. The new edition features nearly 1,000 new references, about half of which are dated 2006 or later. In the Second Edition, users of the First Edition will find new topics, such as:

- mirror neurons and their role in movement, empathy, language, and autism,
- von Economo neurons and their implications for evolution,
- new models of brain development during adolescence and young adulthood, with an emphasis on implications for psychological disorders, decision-making, and the juvenile justice system, and
- the implications of artificial light on sleep, obesity, and health.

Users of the First Edition will also find more coverage of such topics as stem cells, genetics, Alzheimer's disease, oxytocin and social behavior, psychopathy, stress and memory, and decision-making in the Second Edition.

New and Expanded Student Interest Features

In addtion to the continued effort to insert student-engaging tid bits of information throughout the text narrative, I have added and/or expanded the following features:

- **Why Does This Matter?** A new feature in the Second Edition, two WDTM features appear in each chapter and look at such topics as gender and cognitive abilities, daytime sleepiness, does dieting work, and are there "steroids" for improving our minds—to show students why biological psychology research is germaine in their everyday lives.
- **New Directions** As in the First Edition, in each chapter we take a brief detour to explore an especially interesting and timely research study. New ones include: cerebral asymmetry and schizophrenia, light pollution, genetically modified mice and addiction, and neuroscientists' search for self-awareness in the brain.
- **Margin Quotations** Also new to the Second Edition, lively little quotes in the margins (e.g., *Quitting smoking is easy; I have done it thousands of times.* —Mark Twain) help to brighten up the moment for readers.

New and Expanded Student Learning Aids

- **Interim Summary Tables** Because users of the First Edition told me their students found these tables especially helpful, I added many more of them in the Second Edition.
- **Margin Definitions** The standard approach to margin definitions is to provide them only for key terms—the terms students will be held responsible for knowing on exams. But I think it is more helpful to students to define all the technical and medical terms with which the average college sophomore may be unfamiliar.
- **Key Terms List** At the end of each chapter I provide an alphabetized "short list" of the terms (with page references) that students should master in this course.

As the Second Edition goes to press, I feel that I have done everything possible to accomplish the goals I set out to achieve: to update and refine the content, enhance student interest, and augment student learning. Nevertheless, I view this text as a work in progress. Please take a moment to share your thoughts and suggestions with me: lfreberg@calpoly.edu. You can also find me on Facebook and on my blog: http://www.laurafreberg.com/blog.

Acknowledgments

I am enormously grateful for the team that Cengage assembled to help make this book a reality. First, I would like to thank my professional colleagues who reviewed the many drafts of this text, in both editions, during all stages of development:

John Agnew, *University of Colorado at Boulder*
James E. Arruda, *Mercer University*
Giorgio Ascoli, *George Mason University*
Jeffrey S. Bedwell, *University of Central Florida*
Virginia Bridwell, *Bellevue College*
Gayle Brosnan-Watters, *Slippery Rock University*
John P. Bruno, *Ohio State University*
Allen E. Butt, *Indiana State University*
David A. Cater, *John Brown University*
James R. Coleman, *University of South Carolina*
Bob Ferguson, *Buena Vista University*
Aaron Ettenberg, *University of California, Santa Barbara*
Thomas M. Fischer, *Wayne State University*
John P. Galla, *Widener University*
Ben Givens, *Ohio State University*
Karen Glendenning, *Florida State University*
C. Hardy, *Colubia College*
James G. Holland, *University of Pittsburgh*
Richard Howe, *College of the Canyons*
Robert A. Jensen, *Southern Illinois University*
Camille Tessitore King, *Stetson University*
Norman E. Kinney, *Southeast Missouri State University*
Paul J. Kulkosky, *Colorado State University Pueblo*
Gloria Lawrence, *Wayne State College*
Simon LeVay
Charles F. Levinthal, *Hofstra University*
David R. Linden, *West Liberty State College*
Michael R. Markham, *Florida International University*
Richard Mascolo, *El Camino College*
Robert Matchock, *Penn State University, Altoona*
Janice E. McPhee, *Gulf Coast University*
Jody Meerdink, *Nebraska Wesleyan University*
Maura Mitrushina, *California State University Northridge*
Robert R. Mowrer, *Angelo State University*

Mark Nawrot, *North Dakota State University*
David W. Pittman, *Wofford College*
Jerome L. Rekart, *Rivier College*
John C. Ruch, *Mills College*
Lawrence J. Ryan, *Oregon State University*
Carl Samuels, *Glandale Community College*
Anthony C. Santucci, *Manhattanville College*
Virginia F. Saunders, *San Francisco State University*
Sheralee Tershner, *Western New England College*
C. Robin Timmons, *Drew University*
Linda L. Walsh, *University of Northern Iowa*
Frank M. Webbe, *Florida Institute of Technology*
Stephen P. Weinert, *Cuyamaca College*
Margaret H. White, *California State University Fullerton*
Xiojuan Xu, *Grand Valley State University*
Robert M. Zacharko, *Carleton University*
Ronald Baenninger, *Temple University*
Joseph H. Porter, *Virginia Commonwealth University*
Cynthia Gibson, *Creighton University*
Marcello Spinella, *Richard Stockton College of New Jersey*

The many instructors who responded to market research surveys and interviews over the past several years have also contributed greatly to the text and its ancillaries.

I would like to give a special thank you to several colleagues. Simon LeVay is not only a gifted researcher but a truly elegant writer. His careful review of the chapter on sexual behavior is deeply appreciated. Marie Banich at the University of Colorado at Boulder provided her expert opinions on the art program, and Gayle Brosnan-Watters at Slippery Rock University contributed many helpful suggestions as a reviewer and while working with me on the first edition of the Test Bank. John Cacioppo of the University of Chicago generously shared his considerable insight into the social aspects of neuroscience. Larry Butcher of UCLA, one of my former professors, provided valuable assistance in the fine-tuning of one of my figures. Rick Howe and the students and faculty of the psychology department at College of the Canyons in California not only took the time to meet with me to share their reactions to the First Edition, but fed me cookies as well.

At Cengage, Jane Potter, Senior Sponsoring Editor for Psychology, has championed my text through two editions. Mary Falcon, my developmental editor for the Second Edition, was my sounding board and partner every step of the way. Pat Waldo, senior project manager, guided the production of the text and coordinated innumerable aspects of the art and text program. Photo researcher Lisa Jelly Smith tenaciously pursued the photos that enliven the text. Vernon Boes, Art Director, guided our design to new heights in appeal and usability. I would also like to thank the many other capable and creative professionals at Cengage who contributed to this project in ways large and small over the years of its development.

Finally, I would like to thank my family for their patience and support. Roger, my husband of 40 years, read every word, helped me choose photos, and even contributed some of our original sketches when I had trouble articulating what I wanted to show. My daughters, Kristin, Karen, and Karla, frequently offered their encouragement and student perspectives. In particular, I would like to dedicate this edition to two of my former readers who passed away this year: my mother, June Sievers, and my brother, Leroy Sievers, a gifted writer and Emmy-winning news producer. I will miss their advice. I am very much indebted to all.

Laura A. Freberg

DISCOVERING BIOLOGICAL PSYCHOLOGY

1 Introducing Biological Psychology

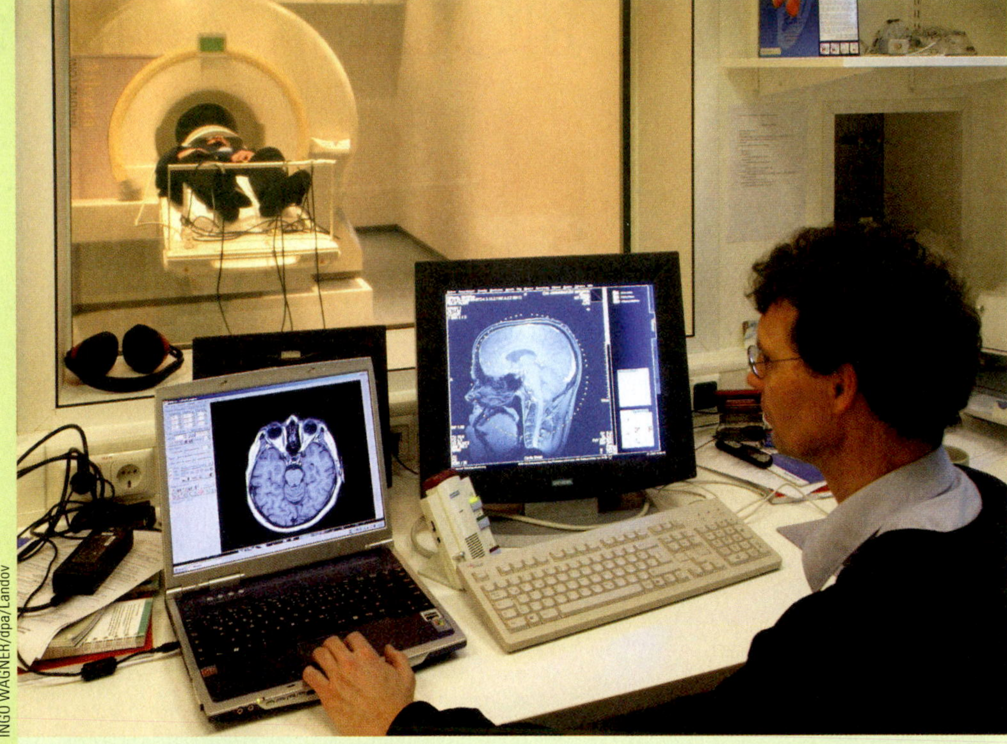
INGO WAGNER/dpa/Landov

▲ **New Technologies Guide the Neurosciences** The history of advances in the neurosciences parallels the development of new technologies, such as this magnetic resonance imaging system.

Introduction

You have probably heard the expression, "You only use 10 percent of your brain." This little bit of misinformation has become part of our popular culture. It certainly would be nice to think that we all had a large chunk of brain awaiting more extensive use, perhaps for use in extrasensory perception (ESP) or in surviving those upcoming final exams.

We're not really sure where the 10 percent myth originated. Some writers blame the work of Pierre Flourens, described later in this chapter. Perhaps by showing that animals could still perform many functions with large parts of their brains surgically removed, Flourens's work could have led to the perception that all those parts really weren't necessary after all. Other authors suggest that misquotes of statements made by Albert Einstein or the philosopher/psychologist William James might be the original source of the myth.

Regardless of the exact origin of the 10 percent myth, we know today that it is categorically false. Some of the new techniques discussed in this chapter for imaging the brain show that separate parts of the brain become more active during different tasks but that each has its particular role to play. From an evolutionary standpoint, it seems unlikely that we would bother to evolve structures that did not contribute directly to our chances of survival. The human brain contains 5 percent of the body's mass, but it consumes 20 percent of its glucose and oxygen. It would be an extravagant waste to use only 10 percent of an organ that used so many resources. Finally, observations of patients with brain damage show that even small injuries, such as those caused by a concussion, can have a detrimental effect on brain functioning. A person who experienced damage to 90 percent of the brain would likely be dead or, at a minimum, unable to emerge from a coma.

Although it may be disappointing to you to see the 10 percent myth debunked, we suspect that this course in biological psychology will leave you with an enormous amount of respect for the real, scientifically demonstrated capacities of this remarkable organ, the human brain.

LEARNING OBJECTIVES

After reading this chapter, you should be able to

LO1 Define biological psychology.

LO2 Trace the major historical highlights in the study of the brain and nervous system.

LO3 Describe the major uses of histological research methods.

LO4 Compare and contrast the imaging techniques of CT, PET, MRI, and fMRI.

LO5 Describe the use of EEG, MEG, evoked potentials, and single cell recording.

LO6 Describe the use of stimulation and lesion methods.

LO7 Summarize the methods used to assess the biochemistry of the nervous system.

LO8 Identify the contributions made by studies involving twins, adoptions, and genetically engineered research animals to our understanding of genetic influences on the nervous system and behavior.

LO9 Compare and contrast the characteristics of stem cells derived from embryos, adult cells, and umbilical cord blood.

LO10 Summarize the major ethical concerns regarding the use of human participants, animal subjects, and emerging technologies in biological psychology research.

Biological Psychology as an Interdisciplinary Field

Biological psychology is defined as "the branch of psychology that studies the biological foundations of behavior, emotions, and mental processes" (Pickett, 2000). Researchers in biological psychology draw techniques and theories from psychology, biology, physiology, biochemistry, the neurosciences, and related fields to identify the relationships between the activity of the nervous system and observable behavior. In this text, the topics explored will range from sleep to sexuality, from emotions to learning, from hunger to psychopathology. In each of the topic areas, you will see that the relationship between biology and behavior is circular. Just as our biology influences our behavior, so does our behavior influence our biology. We suspect that high levels of testosterone are associated with increased aggression (Dabbs, 1990). Biology in this case appears to be driving behavior. At the same time, we know that watching your favorite sports team lose acts to lower your testosterone (Bernhardt, Dabbs, Fielden, & Lutter, 1998). In this case, behavior (watching sports and supporting a team) drives biology (testosterone levels).

biological psychology The branch of psychology in which the biological foundations of behavior, emotions, and mental processes are studied.

Historical Highlights in Biological Psychology

In today's world, we take for granted that the brain and nervous system are the sources of intellect, reason, sensation, and movement. This disarmingly simple fact has not been universally accepted throughout human history. Although some ancient observers came very close to the truth, periods of enlightenment were interspersed with periods of remarkable misunderstanding.

Our earliest ancestors apparently had at least a rudimentary understanding about the brain's essential role in maintaining life. Archaeological evidence of brain surgery suggests that as long as 7,000 years ago, people tried to cure others by drilling holes in the skull. The results of one such operation are shown in Figure 1.1. Because some skulls have been located that show evidence of healing following the drilling procedure, known as trephining or trepanation, we can assume that the patient lived through the procedure and that this was not a postmortem ritual. What is less clear is the intent of such surgeries. Possibly, these early surgeons hoped to release demons or relieve feelings of pressure (Clower & Finger, 2001).

Based on Egyptian texts believed to be at least 5,000 years old, the *Edwin Smith Surgical Papyrus* represents the oldest known medical writing in history (Breasted, 1930). In general, the Egyptians did not seem to view the brain as an important structure. During mummification, the brain was removed through the nostrils and replaced with rosin. Nonetheless, the *Edwin Smith Surgical Papyrus* contains a number of rather modern-sounding observations regarding the structure and function of the brain. The original author discussed the membranes covering the brain, or meninges.

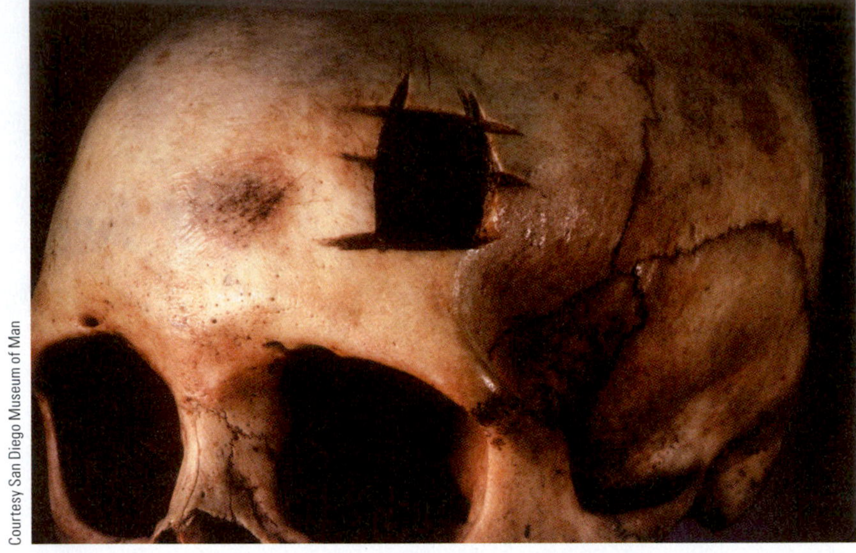
Courtesy San Diego Museum of Man

■ **Figure 1.1**
Prehistoric Brain Surgery
As far back in the past as 7,000 years ago, people used trepanation, the drilling of holes in the head, possibly to cure "afflictions" such as demonic possession. Regrowth around some of the holes indicates that at least some of these patients survived the procedure.

The convolutions of the cerebral cortex were quite accurately compared to the "corrugations which form molten copper." The author clearly understood that paralysis and lack of sensation in the body resulted from nervous system damage. Cases of nervous system damage were usually classified as "an ailment not to be treated," indicating the author's understanding of the relatively permanent damage involved.

Building on the knowledge taken from ancient Egypt, the Greek scholars of the fourth century B.C. proposed that the brain was the organ of sensation. Hippocrates (460–379 B.C.) went further by suggesting that the brain was also the source of intelligence. Hippocrates' observations were quite modern. He correctly identified epilepsy as originating in the brain, although the most obvious outward signs of the disorder were muscular convulsions (see Chapter 15). Not all of the Greeks shared Hippocrates' views, however. Aristotle believed that the heart was the source of intellect, whereas Herophilus, who is often referred to as the father of anatomy, believed that the ventricles (the fluid-filled cavities in the brain) played this important role.

© Bettmann/CORBIS

■ **Figure 1.2**
The Reflex According to Descartes Philosopher René Descartes illustrated his conceptualization of a reflex. When nerves sensed heat or pain, they opened "pores" in the brain. These pores in turn released animal spirits that circulated through hollow tubes in the body. Reservoirs in the muscles would fill with these spirits, causing the foot to pull away from the fire.

Galen (130–200 C.E.), a Greek physician serving the Roman Empire, made careful dissections of animals (and we suspect of the mortally wounded gladiators in his care as well). Although Galen made many accurate observations, one of his errors influenced thinking for nearly 1,500 years. Perhaps due to the influence of Herophilus, Galen believed that the ventricles played an important role in transmitting messages to and from the brain (Aronson, 2007). Fluids flowing within the ventricles were believed to be continuous with fluids in the nerves. This notion of the nervous system as a network of fluid-filled, interconnected tubes and chambers persisted until nearly modern times.

Galen's ideas regarding the ventricles and fluid transmission gained support from the French philosopher René Descartes (1596–1650). Descartes was impressed by the hydraulic statues popular in his day among the wealthy, and he used these statues as his model for how the human body should work. ■ Figure 1.2 shows Descartes's hydraulic, or fluid-driven, model of a simple withdrawal reflex.

In addition to his arguments for the mechanical nature of movement, Descartes is also notable for his support of **mind-body dualism.** According to Descartes, the bodies of both humans and animals worked mechanically. However, Descartes believed that human beings had unique capacities that they did not share with other animals and that these were contained in the mind. For Descartes and other dualists, the mind is neither physical nor accessible to study through the physical sciences. In contrast, the modern neurosciences, including biological psychology, are based on **monism** rather than dualism. The monism perspective proposes that the mind is the result of activity in the brain, which can be studied scientifically. Descartes's ideas were very influential, and even today, some people struggle with the idea that factors such as personality, memory, and logic simply represent the activity of neurons in the brain. Later in the chapter, the discussion of research ethics presents another legacy of Descartes's ideas.

mind-body dualism A philosophical perspective put forward by René Descartes in which the body is mechanistic, whereas the mind is separate and nonphysical.

monism (MOH-nizm) A philosophical perspective characteristic of the neurosciences in which the mind is viewed as the product of activity in the brain and nervous system.

Because many shared his view of animals as mechanical, not sentient, beings, experiments were carried out on animals that often seem barbaric to modern thinkers.

The best scientist is open to experience and begins with romance—the idea that anything is possible.
Ray Bradbury

Between 1500 and 1800, scientists made considerable progress in describing the structure and function of the nervous system. The advent of microscopes, beginning with the work of Anton van Leeuwenhoek in 1674, opened up a whole new level of analysis and understanding. (The various techniques of microscopy used in research will be explored later in this chapter.) With a better understanding of electricity, thanks to observers such as Benjamin Franklin, the Galen-Descartes notion of control via the movement of fluids was finally discarded. Work by Luigi Galvani and Emil du Bois-Reymond established electricity as the mode of communication used by the nervous system. Some of these experiments look quaint by modern standards. Galvani was known to entertain his dinner guests with visits to his basement frog laboratory, depicted in ■ Figure 1.3. Galvani had connected wires from a rooftop antenna to the legs of his frogs, and electrical disturbances in passing clouds would make the frogs twitch in unison. Fortunately for both Galvani and his frogs, there is no record of his having experienced a true thunderstorm during these demonstrations.

Although it was now understood that electrical signals transmitted information to and from the brain, other questions remained. Did these messages share a single pathway, like a two-way street? Scientists knew that when a peripheral nerve in an arm or leg was damaged, both sensation and movement were affected. On the other hand, these peripheral nerves were known to be quite complex, containing many separate nerve fibers. Could sensation and movement have their own designated routes, or one-way streets? The answer was independently provided by British physiologist Charles Bell (1774–1842) and French physiologist François Magendie (1783–1855). These researchers established an important principle that will be revisited in our chapter about the cells of the nervous system. Transmission of information along nerves is typically a one-way street.

While Bell and Magendie were publishing their conclusions regarding the functions of the nervous system, other anatomists were attempting to describe its structure. Resourceful scientists applied dyes designed to stain cloth and chemicals used in photography to nerve tissue and discovered a new world under the microscope. Many scientists, including Italian researcher Camillo Golgi, continued to support the concept of the nervous system as a vast, interconnected network of continuous fibers. Others, including the Spanish anatomist Santiago Ramón y Cajal ■ (Figure 1.4), argued that the nervous system was composed of an array of separate, independent cells. Cajal's concept came to be known as the Neuron Doctrine. Golgi and Cajal shared the Nobel Prize

This "telephone" has too many shortcomings to be seriously considered as a means of communication. The device is inherently of no value to us.
Western Union Internal Memo, 1876

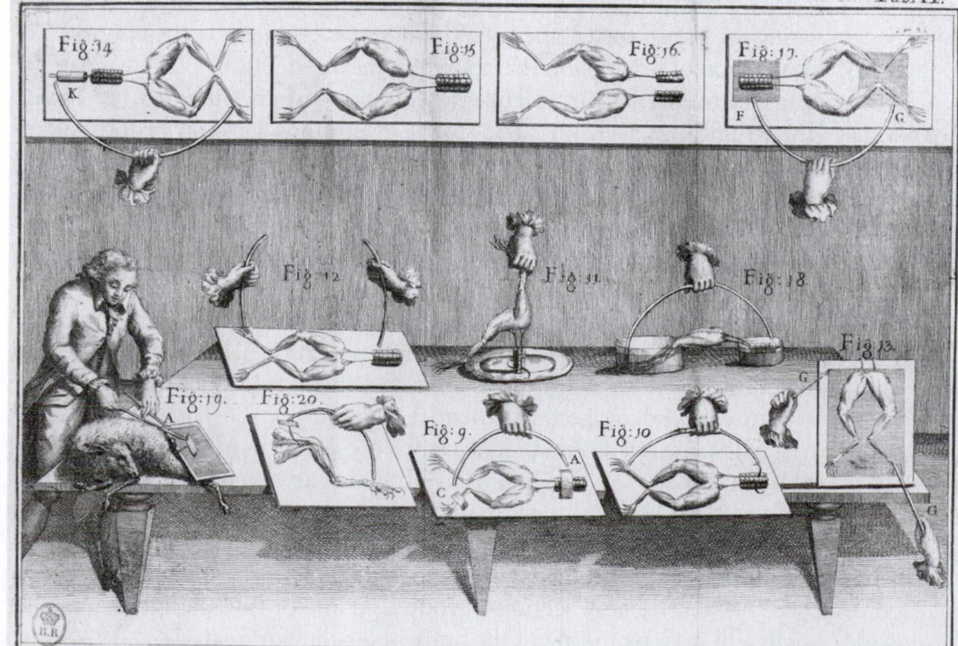

■ **FIGURE 1.3 Luigi Galvani Demonstrated a Role for Electricity in Neural Communication** This engraving illustrates the basement laboratory of Luigi Galvani, where his experiments with frogs helped establish understanding of the electrical nature of neural communication.

■ **Figure 1.4**
Spanish Anatomist Santiago Ramón y Cajal Cajal believed that the nervous system is comprised of a vast array of independent, separate nerve cells, a point of view known today as the Neuron Doctrine. He used a stain developed by his rival Camillo Golgi to prove that Golgi's theory of the nervous system as an interconnected network of fibers was wrong.

for their work in 1906. Each man argued his position in his acceptance speech, but we know today that Cajal's view is correct.

The road to our current understanding of the nervous system has not been without its odd turns and dead ends. The notion that certain body functions are controlled by certain areas of the brain, called localization of function, began with an idea proposed by Franz Josef Gall and elaborated by Johann Casper Spurzheim. These otherwise respectable scientists proposed that the structure of an individual's skull could be correlated with his or her individual personality characteristics and abilities. Their approach was known as **phrenology** (see Chapter 2). ■ Figure 1.5 shows one of the busts used by phrenologists in the process of "reading" a client's skull. Although misguided, Gall and Spurzheim's work did move us away from the metaphysical, nonlocalized view of the brain that had persisted from the time of Descartes. Instead, Gall and Spurzheim proposed a more modern view of the brain as the organ of the mind, composed of interconnected, cooperative, yet relatively independent functional units.

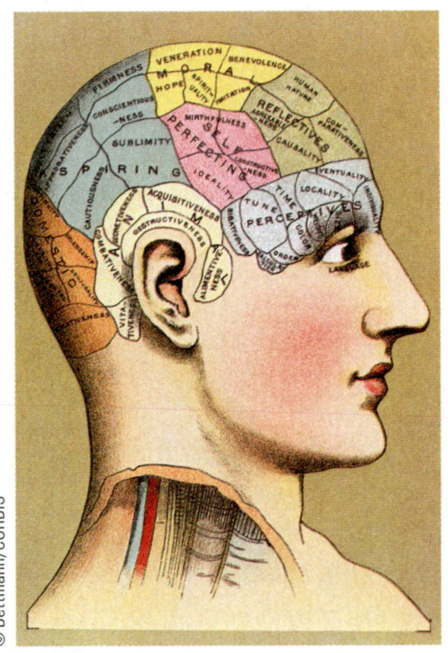

■ **Figure 1.5**
Phrenology Bust Franz Josef Gall and his followers used busts like this one to identify traits located under different parts of the skull. Bumps on the skull were believed to indicate that the underlying trait had been "exercised." Although Gall's system was an example of very bad science, the underlying principle that functions could be localized in the brain turned out to be valuable.

Further evidence in support of localization of function in the brain began to accumulate. In the middle 1800s, Paul Broca correlated the damage he observed in patients with their behavior and concluded that language functions were localized in the brain (see Chapter 13). Gustav Theodor Fritsch and Eduard Hitzig published a remarkable paper, "On the Electrical Excitability of the Cerebrum," in 1870. In this paper, Fritsch and Hitzig (1870/1960) described the results of electrically stimulating the cortex of a rabbit and a dog. By stimulating the motor cortex, they could produce movement on the opposite side of the body. Localization of function in the brain became a generally accepted concept.

The founding of modern neuroscience has often been attributed to the British neurologist John Hughlings Jackson (1835–1911). Hughlings Jackson proposed that the nervous system was organized as a hierarchy, with simpler processing carried out by lower levels and more sophisticated processing carried out by the higher levels, such as the cerebral cortex. We meet Hughlings Jackson again in Chapter 15, in which his contributions to the understanding of epilepsy will be discussed.

Progress in the neurosciences over the past hundred years accelerated rapidly as new methods became available for studying the nervous system. Charles Sherrington not only coined the term "synapse," (the point of communication between two neurons), but also conducted extensive research on reflexes and the motor systems of the brain (see Chapter 8). Otto Loewi demonstrated chemical signaling at the synapse (see Chapter 3), using an elegant research design that he claims came to him while asleep. Sir John Eccles, Bernard Katz, Andrew Huxley, and Alan Hodgkin furthered our understanding of neural communication. You will meet many more contemporary neuroscientists as you read the remainder of this text. The ranks of neuroscientists continue to grow, with the Society for Neuroscience reporting more than 38,000 members as of 2007 (Society for Neuroscience, 2008). The next section introduces some of the methodologies that have made our current understanding of the brain and behavior possible.

phrenology The pseudoscientific notion that skull contours indicate personality and character traits.

INTERIM SUMMARY 1.1

Summary Table: Highlights in the Biological Psychology Timeline

Historical Period	Significant Highlights and Contributions
Ca. 3000 B.C.	• Egyptians discard brain during mummification process; however, published case studies indicate accurate observations of neural disorders.
Ca. 400 B.C.–200 A.D.	• Hippocrates declares that the brain is the source of intellect. • Galen makes accurate observations from dissection; however, believed that fluids transmitted messages.
1600–1800	• René Descartes suggests mind-body dualism; hydraulic transmission. • Anton van Leeuwenhoek invents the light microscope. • Galvani and du Bois-Reymond discover that electricity transmits messages in the nervous system.
1800–1900	• Bell and Magendie determine that neurons communicate in one direction and that sensation and movement are controlled by separate pathways. • Gall and Spurzheim demonstrate that phrenology is inaccurate, but the notion of localization of function in the nervous system is accurate. • Paul Broca discovers localization of speech production. • Fritsch and Hitzig identify localization of motor function in the cerebral cortex.
1900–Present	• Ramón y Cajal declares that the nervous system is composed of separate cells. • John Hughlings Jackson explains brain functions as a hierarchy, with more complicated functions carried out by higher levels of the brain. • Otto Loewi demonstrates chemical signaling at the synapse. • Charles Sherrington coins the term "synapse," wins Nobel Prize in 1932. • Sir John Eccles, Andrew Huxley, and Alan Hodgkin share the 1963 Nobel Prize for their work in advancing our understanding of the way neurons communicate. • Bernard Katz receives the 1970 Nobel Prize for his work on chemical transmission at the synapse. • Society for Neuroscience counts more than 38,000 members in 2007.

Summary Points

1. Biological psychology is defined as "the branch of psychology that studies the biological foundations of behavior, emotions, and mental processes." **(LO1)**
2. Although some periods of enlightenment regarding the relationship between the nervous system and behavior emerged among the Egyptians and Greeks, the major advances in biological psychology have been relatively modern and recent. **(LO2)**
3. Highlights in the timeline of biological psychology include discoveries regarding the electrical nature of neural communication, the control of sensation and motor functions by separate nerves, the role of single cells as building blocks for the nervous system, and the localization of functions in the brain. **(LO2)**

Review Questions

1. How would you describe the goals and methods of the interdisciplinary field of biological psychology?
2. What historical events contributed to our modern understanding of the brain and behavior? Which concepts actually led us in the wrong directions?

Research Methods in Biological Psychology

Imagination is more important than knowledge.
Albert Einstein

The methods described in this section have helped neuroscientists discover the structure, connections, and functions of the nervous system and its components. From the level of single nerve cells to the operation of large parts of the nervous system, we now have the ability to make detailed observations that would likely astonish the early pioneers of neuroscience.

Histology

Histology refers to the study of microscopic structures and tissues. Histological methods provide means for observing the structure, organization, and connections of individual cells. As mentioned earlier, the first investigation of nerve tissue under a microscope was conducted by Anton van Leeuwenhoek in 1674. However, due to the technical challenges of viewing structures as small and complex as those found in the nervous system, most of the advances in microscopy occurred following the development of stronger, clearer lenses during the 1800s.

Tissue to be studied under the microscope must be prepared for viewing in a series of steps. Tissue must be made thin enough to allow light to pass through it. Brain tissue is fragile and somewhat watery, which makes the production of thin enough slices impossible without further treatment. To solve this problem, the first step in the histological process is to "fix" the tissue, either by freezing it or by treating it with formalin, a liquid containing the gas formaldehyde. Formalin not only hardens the tissue, making it possible to produce thin slices, but it also preserves the tissue from breakdown by enzymes or bacteria. Freezing the tissue accomplishes these objectives as well.

Once tissue is fixed, it is sliced by a special machine known as a **microtome.** A microtome typically looks and works like a miniature version of the meat slicers found in most delicatessens. The tissue is pushed forward while a sliding blade moves back and forth across the tissue, producing slices. For viewing tissue under the light microscope, tissue slices between 10 and 80 μm (micrometers) thick are prepared. A micrometer is one one-millionth of a meter or one one-thousandth of a millimeter. Electron microscopes require slices of less than 1 μm. The fragile slices are mounted on slides for viewing. Sectioning a single rat brain produces several thousand slides.

Measure what is measurable, and make measurable what is not so.
Galileo Galilei

Even when fixed and mounted on slides, nerve tissue would appear nearly transparent under the microscope if it were not for a variety of specialized stains. Researchers select particular stains depending on the features they wish to examine. For example, to make a detailed structural analysis of a small number of single cells, the best choice is a **Golgi silver stain,** named after its discoverer, Camillo Golgi. On the other hand, you might be more interested in identifying clusters of cell bodies, the major bulk of the nerve cell, within a sample of tissue. In this case, you would select a **Nissl stain.** **A myelin stain** would allow you to follow pathways carrying information from one part of the brain to another by staining the insulating material that covers many nerve fibers (see Chapter 3). If you know where a pathway ends but would like to discover its point of origin, you should use **horseradish peroxidase.** When this enzyme is injected into the end of a nerve fiber, it travels backward toward the cell body. The use of horseradish peroxidase to trace a pathway from the thalamus, a structure located near the center of the brain, back to the retina of the eye is illustrated in ■ Figure 1.6. Antibodies, proteins normally produced by the immune system to identify invading organisms, can be combined with a variety of dyes to highlight particular proteins found in cells. In particular, antibodies are helpful in identifying the activity of the c-fos gene in the brain, which in turn is a reliable indicator of brain activity in response to a wide variety of stimuli (Herrera & Robertson, 1996).

Once tissue is appropriately prepared, it can be viewed under either a light or electron microscope. Electron microscopes were developed in Germany in the 1930s, and they use short, highly concentrated electron beams rather than light to form images.

histology (his-TALL-oh-jee) The study of cells and tissues on the microscopic level.
microtome (MY-kroh-tome) A device used to make very thin slices of tissue for histology.
Golgi silver stain (GOLE-jee) A stain developed by Camillo Golgi used to observe single neurons.
Nissl stain (NISS-uhl) A stain used to view populations of cell bodies.
myelin stain A stain used to trace neural pathways.
horseradish peroxidase (HORSErad-ish per-OX-i-daze) A stain used to trace axon pathways from their terminals to points of origin.

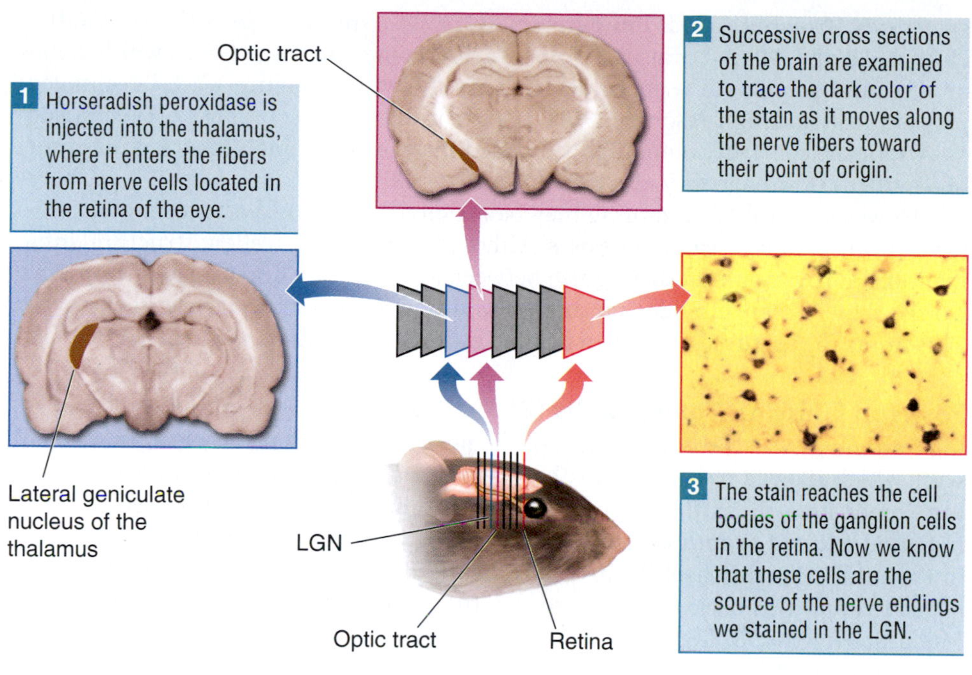

Optic tract
1 Horseradish peroxidase is injected into the thalamus, where it enters the fibers from nerve cells located in the retina of the eye.
2 Successive cross sections of the brain are examined to trace the dark color of the stain as it moves along the nerve fibers toward their point of origin.
Lateral geniculate nucleus of the thalamus
LGN
Optic tract
Retina
3 The stain reaches the cell bodies of the ganglion cells in the retina. Now we know that these cells are the source of the nerve endings we stained in the LGN.

FIGURE 1.6 Horseradish Peroxidase Provides a Method for Identifying Neural Pathways If horseradish peroxidase is infused into an area containing nerve endings in a living animal, the stain will be taken up by nerve fibers and transported retroactively back to the cell body. By tracing this path through successive slices of neural tissue, researchers can identify the cell bodies that are the source of the nerve endings. In this example, horseradish peroxidase is infused into the lateral geniculate nucleus of the thalamus (1). After the animal is sacrificed, successive sections of the optic tract show the pathways of the stained axons (2). Finally, an examination of the ganglion cells of the retina shows that these cells are the source of the stained nerve fibers (3).

Modern electron microscopes produce magnifications of up to 1 million times. Using an electron microscope, Sanford Palay and George Palade (1955) provided clear images of the synapse, a point of communication between two nerve cells (see Chapter 3).

We must recollect that all our provisional ideas in psychology will presumably one day be based on an organic substructure.

Sigmund Freud

Autopsy

Researchers have frequently relied on observations made during an **autopsy,** or examination of the body following death. The word autopsy means "to view for oneself." Although autopsy for research purposes has been largely replaced by modern imaging methods, it remains a useful technique. Simon LeVay (1991) used autopsy to examine an area of the brain known as INAH-3 (see Chapter 10). LeVay believed that the size of INAH-3 might be used to differentiate between homosexual and heterosexual males. Because this structure was too small to see well with existing imaging techniques, LeVay studied the brains of deceased individuals. Autopsies, like other correlational methods, must be interpreted carefully and precisely. Although LeVay's data suggest that differences in brain structure are correlated with sexual orientation, we cannot conclude on the basis of these data that brain structure either causes or is caused by sexual orientation.

Imaging

New imaging techniques provide significant advantages over autopsy. With current imaging technologies, we can watch the living brain as it engages in processes such as reading (Chapter 13) or emotional response (Chapter 14). We can identify differences in the ways the brains of serial murderers function compared with the brains of typical people (Chapter 16).

Computerized Tomography (CT) The groundwork for medical imaging was laid by German physicist Wilhelm Röntgen, who discovered X-rays in 1896. Röntgen was astonished to learn that X-rays could move through the human body and that they would produce a negative photographic image of the body's major structures. The first X-ray ever taken was an image of Röntgen's wife's hand.

Normal X-rays do not do a very good job of imaging soft tissue. If you have ever seen an X-ray of your head taken by your dentist or orthodontist, you probably saw bones and teeth, but not much brain. However, with adaptations made possible by more modern computers, X-rays can be used to image previously unseen anatomical

autopsy (AW-top-see) The examination of body tissues following death.

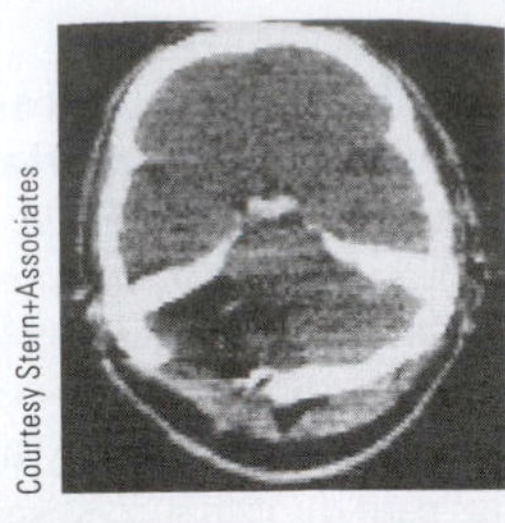
Courtesy Stern+Associates

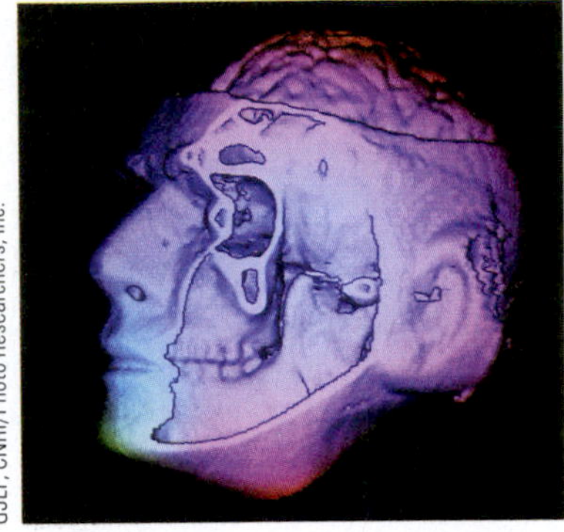
GJLP, CNRI/Photo Researchers, Inc.

■ **FIGURE 1.7**
CT Scans Hounsfield's original machine took several hours to obtain data for a single slice (above). Modern scanning equipment is much faster, and can produce detailed 3-D images (bottom).

structures. **Computerized tomography (CT)** was invented in 1972 by Godfrey Hounsfield and Allan Cormack. "Tomography" comes from the Greek words *tomos*, or slice, and *graphia*, to write or describe. As shown in ■ Figure 1.7, CT technology provided the first high-resolution look at a living brain. More modern CT technology allows for the construction of highly detailed three-dimensional images. An example of a modern CT image may also be seen in Figure 1.7.

However useful CT scanning may be for medical imaging, the technology does have drawbacks for research purposes. Although it provides excellent structural information, a CT scan cannot distinguish between a living brain and a dead one. In other words, the CT scan provides no information regarding activity levels in the brain. This limits the usefulness of CT in helping us answer questions about behavior.

Positron Emission Tomography (PET) The next major breakthrough in imaging technology was the development of the **positron emission tomography,** or **PET,** scan, which allowed researchers to observe brain activity for the first time. PET scans were made possible by the invention of the gamma camera, which is used to detect radiation released by radioactive atoms that were decaying or breaking up. Beginning in the mid-1970s, Michael Phelps and Edward Hoffman of Washington University began to apply this basic technique to the study of brain function (Hoffman, Phelps, Mullani, Higgins, & Ter-Pogossian, 1976; Phelps, Hoffman, Mullani, Higgins, & Ter-Pogossian, 1976).

PET brain studies combine radioactive tracers with a wide variety of molecules, including oxygen, water, and drugs. Each gamma ray resulting from the breakdown of the tracer is recorded by detectors and fed to a computer, by which the data are reconstructed into images. Typically, programmers have assigned red and yellow to areas of high activity and green, blue, and black to areas of low activity. Examples of PET scans appear in ■ Figure 1.8. Newer PET machines can take images of adjacent slices at the same time, which allows for three-dimensional reconstruction of brain activity.

Magnetic Resonance Imaging (MRI) As shown in ■ Figure 1.9, **magnetic resonance imaging, or MRI,** has become a standard medical diagnostic tool and a valuable research asset. Raymond Damadian, Larry Minkoff, and Michael Goldsmith produced the first MRI image in 1977. This imaging technology uses powerful magnets to align hydrogen atoms within a magnetic field. Next, radio frequency (RF) pulses are directed at the part of the body to be imaged, producing "resonance," or spinning, of the hydrogen atoms. When the RF pulses cease, the hydrogen atoms return to their natural alignment within the magnetic field. As the atoms "relax," each becomes a miniature radio transmitter, emitting a characteristic pulse that is detected by the scanner. To construct the image, each small area of tissue is assigned a **voxel,** which is a three-dimensional version of a pixel. The darkness or coloration of each voxel represents the level of pulse activity in an area.

Functional MRI (fMRI) is used to assess brain activity. The first fMRI of the brain was conducted by Belliveau et al. (1991). Functional MRI takes advantage of the fact that active neurons require more oxygen than less active neurons, and that variations in blood flow to a particular area will reflect this need.

The use of fMRI to track blood flow in the brain was previewed in the nineteenth century by William James, who was impressed by the observations of Italian physiologist Angelo Mosso on patients with head injuries. Due to the nature of these injuries, in which some of the patients' skull bones were missing or damaged, Mosso was able to measure and correlate blood flow with the patients' mental activity (Mosso, 1881). James' reflections on Mosso's work sound very contemporary: "Blood very likely may rush to each region of the cortex according as it is most active, but of this we know nothing" (James, 1890, vol. 1, p. 99). Mosso's observations were confirmed by Roy and Sherrington (1890), who reported the existence of "an automatic mechanism by which the blood supply of any part of the cerebral tissue is varied in accordance with the activity of the chemical changes which underlie the functional action of that part" (p. 105).

computerized tomography (CT) An imaging technology in which computers are used to enhance X-ray images.
positron emission tomography (PET) An imaging technique that provides information regarding the localization of brain activity.
magnetic resonance imaging (MRI) An imaging technique that provides very high resolution structural images.
voxel Short for "volume pixel." A pixel is the smallest distinguishable square part of a two-dimensional image. A voxel is the smallest distinguishable box-shaped part of a three-dimensional image.
functional MRI (fMRI) A technology using a series of MRI images taken 1 to 4 seconds apart in order to assess the activity of the brain.

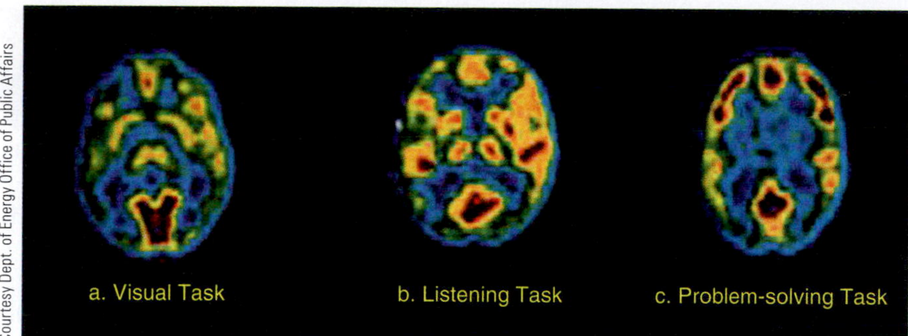

Courtesy Dept. of Energy Office of Public Affairs

■ **FIGURE 1.8**
PET Scans Show Patterns of Brain Activation PET scans do not provide much structural detail, but they do offer a clear picture of brain activity. Red and yellow areas are most active, whereas blue and black areas are least active. These three images show different patterns of brain activity during a visual task, a listening task, and a problem-solving task.

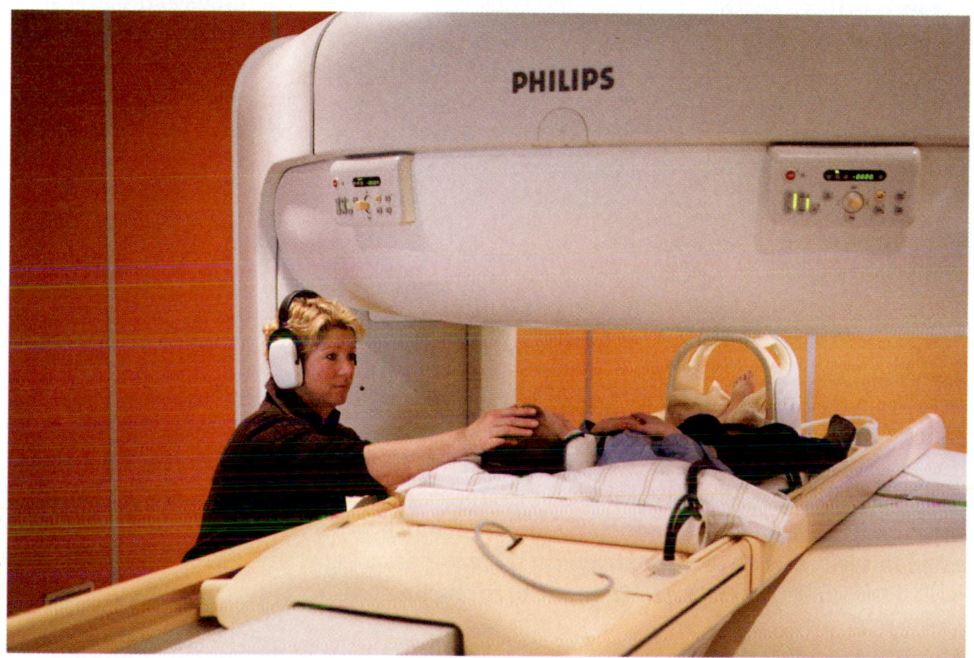

■ **FIGURE 1.9**
Magnetic Resonance Imaging (MRI) Modern MRI equipment uses powerful magnets to obtain high-resolution images of soft tissue, including the brain. The newer, open-style machine shown here is less confining and more comfortable for the patient than the tube-like machine shown at the beginning of this chapter.

How does fMRI track cerebral blood flow? Hemoglobin, the protein molecule that carries oxygen within the blood, has different magnetic properties when combined with oxygen or not (Ogawa, Lee, Kay, & Tank, 1990). Consequently, signals from a voxel will change depending on the oxygenation of the blood in that area, known as the Blood Oxygenation Level Dependent (BOLD) effect. Let's look at an example provided by Hirsch and her colleagues (1994), shown in ■ Figure 1.10. Thirty MRI images of a slice of the brain were taken within a short interval of time. During the middle 10 scans, the participant was touched on the left hand. The resulting image highlights the voxels that showed changes in activity correlated with stimulation. The tracing illustrates the activity changes in one of those voxels as a function of stimulation.

MRI technology has significant advantages over both CT and PET. It can provide images taken at any angle without any movement of the individual. In tracking brain activity, fMRI is considered superior in both spatial and temporal resolution to PET scans (Cohen & Bookheimer, 1994).

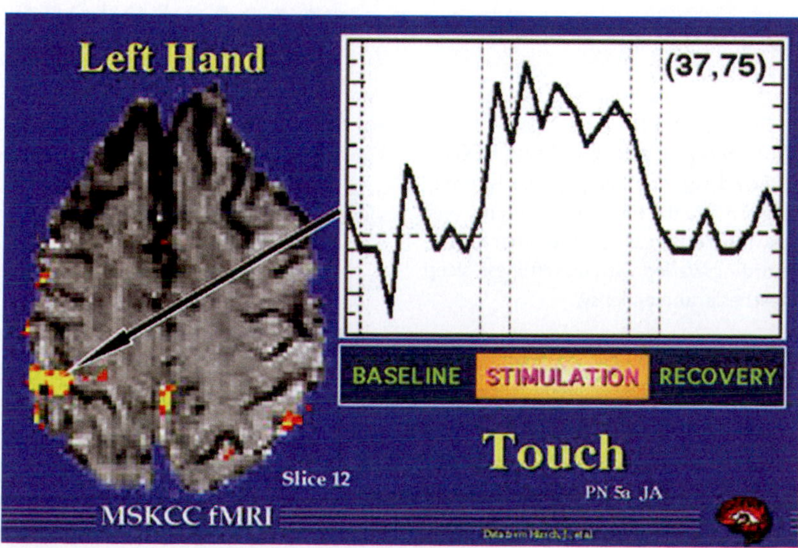

from *Supplement to Investigative Ophthalmology and Visual Science, 35*, 1438/Hirsch, J., De La Paz, R., Relkin, N., Victor, J., Li, T., Kim, K., Olyarchuk, J., & Georgakakos, B. (1994)/Annual Meeting Presentation, Association for Research in Vision and Ophthalmology

■ **FIGURE 1.10**
Functional Magnetic Resonance Imaging (fMRI) Tracks Cerebral Blood Flow This image demonstrates the use of fMRI to identify parts of the brain (the red and yellow areas) that become selectively active when the participant's left hand is touched. The tracing on the right of the figure shows the activity changes in one of those voxels across baseline, touch, and recovery (no touch) trials.

NEW DIRECTIONS

Will Imaging Technologies Allow Us to "Read" People's Minds?

In the 2002 film, *Minority Report*, Tom Cruise plays a police officer who arrests people for crimes they have not yet committed. How close are we to knowing what people are planning to do before they actually do it? Perhaps closer than you think.

John-Dylan Haynes and Geraint Rees (2006) concluded that current imaging technologies, such as fMRI, do not exactly allow us to "read" the human mind, but we are getting ever closer to that ability. For example, O'Craven and Kanwisher (2000) were able to determine, with an 85% accuracy rate, whether a person was imagining a building or a face simply by looking at corresponding fMRI scans of the brain. Imagining a face activated a part of the brain that typically responds when we view a face, the fusiform face area (FFA; see Chapter 2), whereas imagining a building activated a part of the brain that typically responds to places, the parahippocampal place area (PPA).

Of even greater importance for society is the fact that researchers are closing in on the ability to use fMRI to detect deception (Kay, Naselaris, Prenger, & Gallant, 2008; Kozel et al., 2005; Langleben et al., 2005). As we will see in our discussion of emotion in Chapter 14, typical lie detection technologies, which rely on indirect measures of arousal, are so poor that they are not admissible as court evidence in the United States. The ability to detect deception directly through brain scans promises enormous benefits to criminal justice and national security, but raises equally substantial concerns about ethics. Not only can we envision the legislative need to expand our constitutional right to privacy to include "mental privacy," but legislators will also have to consider that the new technology may acquire from brain scans information that is irrelevant to the purpose of the investigation in the first place.

Recording

Although perhaps less dramatic than the imaging techniques, methods that allow researchers to record the electrical and magnetic output from the brain continue to be useful. As we will see in greater detail in Chapter 3, nerve cells are capable of generating small electrical charges across their membranes, much like miniature batteries. Although small in scale, this electrical activity can be recorded using electrodes either on the surface of the skull or imbedded within the brain tissue itself.

The Electroencephalogram (EEG) The first recordings of the human brain's electrical activity, measured through electrodes placed on the scalp, were made by a German psychiatrist, Hans Berger, in 1924. One of Berger's first **electroencephalogram (EEG)** recordings is shown in ■ Figure 1.11. Berger noted that the recordings varied during wakefulness, sleep, anesthesia, and epilepsy. Chapter 11 investigates the relationship between the EEG and states of consciousness in greater detail.

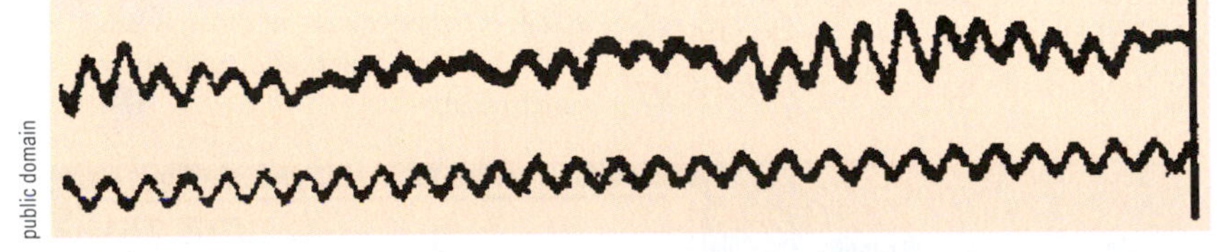

public domain

■ **FIGURE 1.11**
Hans Berger and the First EEG Recording German psychiatrist Hans Berger made the first EEG recording, shown here. Berger observed that his recordings varied with wakefulness, sleep, anesthesia, and epilepsy.

EEG recordings measure the activity of large numbers of cells, known as a field potential. Several factors produce some distortion of the relationship between the actual activity of the brain and the recorded field potentials. Because the recording electrodes are located on the surface of the scalp, the EEG is most highly influenced by the activity of cortical cells closest to the electrodes. Cells from deeper structures in the brain have little, if any, influence on the EEG. The bones and tissue separating the brain from the electrodes substantially reduce the signal reaching the electrodes.

For many years, EEG technology did not change much. Although it was useful in the study of sleep and the diagnosis of epilepsy, EEG did not offer anything further to our understanding of brain function. With the advent of more powerful computers, however, new quantitative methods for analyzing EEG recordings became possible. Computerized EEG brain tomography can be used to generate maps of activity, making it possible to pinpoint the source of abnormal activity. In addition, EEG brain tomography can be used to follow a patient through withdrawal from psychoactive drugs or during a coma. The technique can aid in diagnoses of many disorders,

electroencephalogram (EEG) (eelek-troh-en-SEF-uh-loh-gram) A technology for studying the activity of the brain through recordings from electrodes placed on the scalp.

including schizophrenia, dementias, epilepsy, and attention deficit hyperactivity disorder (see Chapters 5, 15 and 16). Computerized analysis of EEG recordings can be used to generate animations of activity over time and for the construction of three-dimensional maps of brain activity. These analysis tools have breathed new life into EEG technology.

Evoked Potentials An application of basic EEG technology that is used in the assessment of sensory activity is the recording of **evoked potentials.** This technique allows researchers to correlate the activity of cortical sensory neurons recorded through scalp electrodes with stimuli presented to the participant. The brain's electrical activity in response to a stimulus, such as a tone, is quite small compared to the activity normally recorded in an EEG, so responses to many presentations of a stimulus are averaged, as shown in ■ Figure 1.12. This type of analysis can be helpful in cases in which a person's behavior does not provide a clear indication of whether a particular stimulus has been perceived. For example, young children with autism (see Chapter 16) often behave as though their hearing were impaired. When spoken to by parents or others, a child with autism often shows no reaction at all. Through observations of evoked potentials to sound, we can determine whether the child can actually hear.

It is an old maxim of mine that when you have excluded the impossible, whatever remains, however improbable, must be the truth.

Arthur Conan Doyle

Magnetoencephalography (MEG) **Magnetoencephalography** (MEG) allows researchers to record the brain's magnetic activity (Cohen, 1972). Active neurons put out tiny magnetic fields. By "tiny," we mean that the fields generated by neural activity are about 1 billion times smaller than the Earth's magnetic field and about 10,000 times smaller than the field surrounding a typical household electric wire. The major advantage of recording magnetism rather than electrical activity from the brain relates to the interference of the skull bones and other tissues separating the brain from the electrodes. As we noted previously, these tissues prevent a large amount of the brain's electrical activity from being recorded using EEG. In contrast, the skull bones and tissues allow magnetism to pass through without any reduction. In addition, recordings of the magnetic fields produced by the brain can be taken much faster than either fMRI or PET scans, providing a moment-by-moment picture of brain activity. MEG has the added advantage of being silent, as opposed to the loud hammering sound produced by the magnets used in MRI. Consequently, MEG provides researchers with an important technique for studying brain responses to sound.

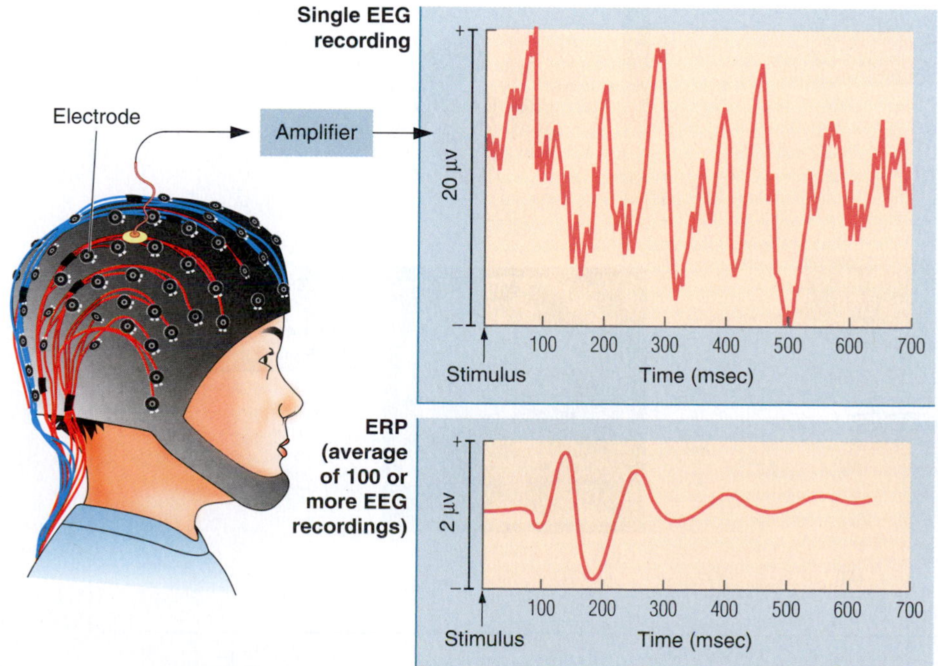

■ **FIGURE 1.12**
Evoked Potentials The analysis of evoked potentials allows researchers to map the brain's EEG response to environmental stimuli. In this example, a characteristic waveform emerges when responses to the presentation of a tone are averaged over 100 trials.

evoked potential (ee-VOKED poh-TEN-shuhl) An alteration in the EEG recording produced in response to the application of a particular stimulus.

magnetoencephalography (MEG) (mag-nee-toh-en-seh-fuhl-AW-graf-ee) A technology for recording the magnetic output of the brain.

MEG utilizes sensors known as superconducting quantum interference devices, or SQUIDs, that convert magnetic energy into electrical impulses that can be recorded and analyzed. Because MEG does not provide any anatomical data, researchers superimpose MEG recordings on three-dimensional images obtained with MRI. This combination provides simultaneous information about brain activity and anatomy. An example of the superimposition of MEG data on an MRI image is illustrated in ■ Figure 1.13. Not only does MEG allow researchers to localize cognitive functions such as language, but it also provides precise localization of the source of the abnormal electrical activity that characterizes a seizure (see Chapter 15).

Single-Cell Recordings Both extracellular and intracellular events from a single neuron can be assessed using tiny microelectrodes surgically implanted in the area of interest. The microelectrodes are made from either fine wires or tiny, fluid-filled micropipettes or glass tubes. These electrodes can identify the occurrence of electrical signals within a single neuron without contamination of activity from adjacent cells. Electrodes can be permanently implanted, allowing animals free range of movement during stimulation ■ (Figure 1.14).

■ **FIGURE 1.13**
Magnetoencephalograpy (MEG) (a) To record the tiny magnetic fields generated by the brain, a series of supercooled sensors known as superconducting quantum interference devices (SQUIDs) are arrayed around the participant's head. (b) This sequence illustrates the process of using MEG to record a participant's response to a tone.

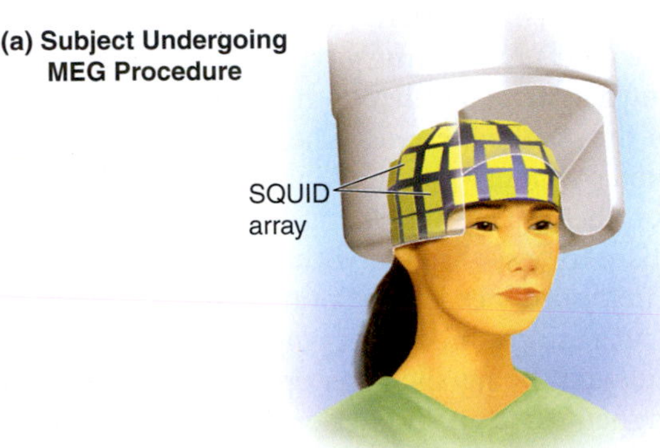
(a) Subject Undergoing MEG Procedure
SQUID array

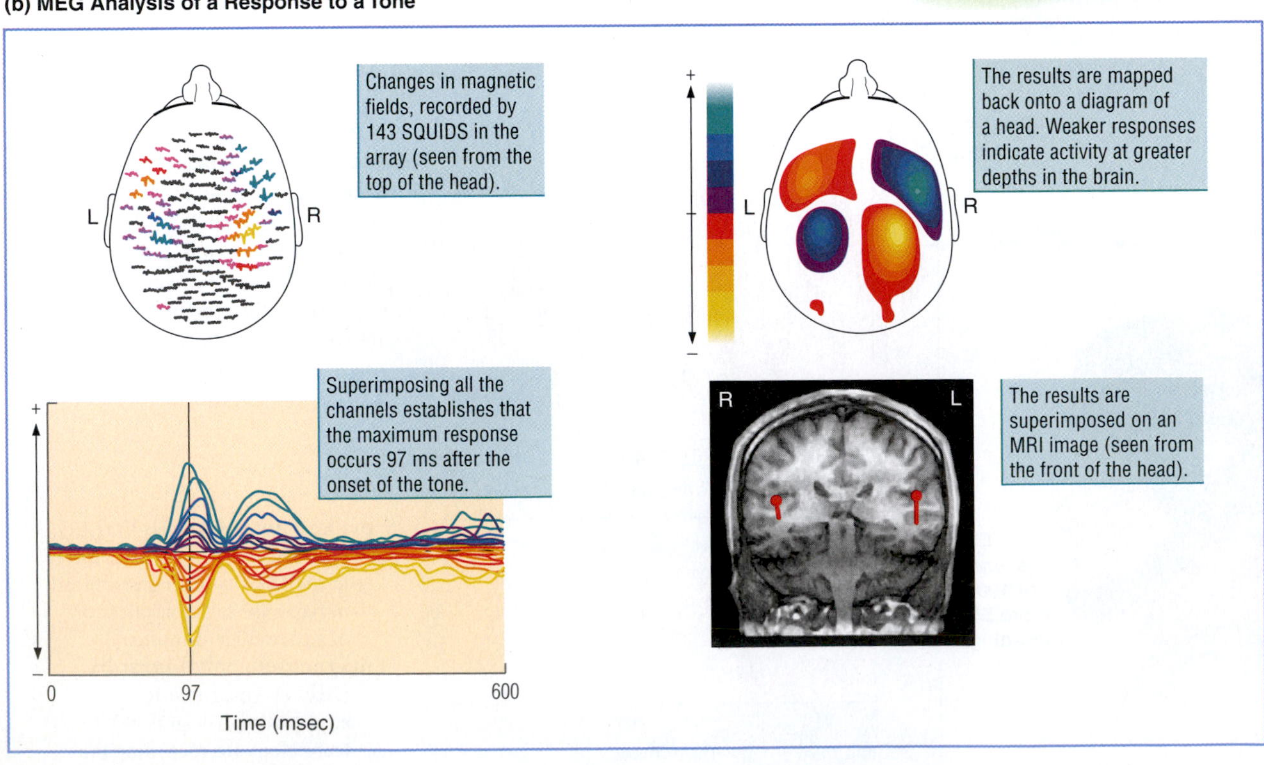
(b) MEG Analysis of a Response to a Tone
Changes in magnetic fields, recorded by 143 SQUIDS in the array (seen from the top of the head).
L
R
+
–
The results are mapped back onto a diagram of a head. Weaker responses indicate activity at greater depths in the brain.
Superimposing all the channels establishes that the maximum response occurs 97 ms after the onset of the tone.
0
97
600
Time (msec)
The results are superimposed on an MRI image (seen from the front of the head).

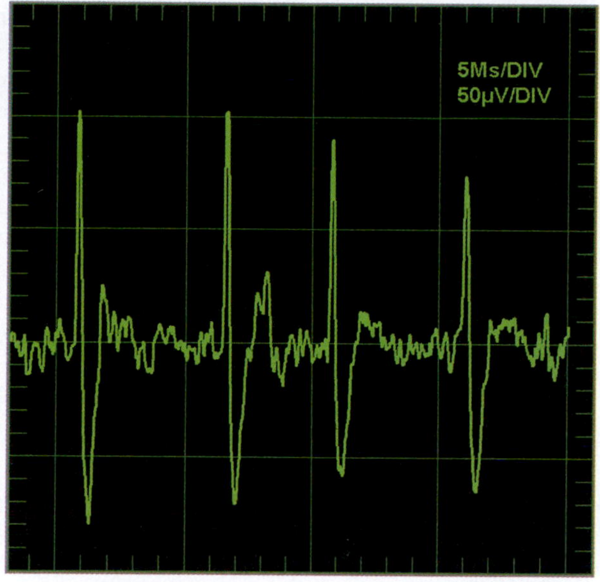

FIGURE 1.14
Recording Electrodes Surgically Implanted in a Rat's Brain Once the animal recovers from the surgery, the activity of single cells can be recorded while the animal moves freely. (a) This rat is searching a space for food while the researchers record activity from brain cells believed to participate in the formation of mental maps of the environment. The white card is a cue that the rat can use to navigate the otherwise uniformly colored space. (b) This recording of the electrical activity of a single cell, taken while the rat searches for food, illustrates the typical "complex burst" pattern that often occurs in the brain's "place cells." Scientists use this type of information to learn about the brain correlates of memory and navigation.

The use of single-cell recordings was pioneered by Vernon Mountcastle, David Hubel, and Torsten Wiesel for use in their investigations of the visual system. As we will see in Chapter 6, these researchers painstakingly mapped the visual cortex by presenting visual stimuli to awake animals. The nature of each stimulus (horizontal line, vertical line, etc.) was correlated with the activity of single neurons. As a result, we know which parts of the visual cortex are responsible for assessing features such as line orientation or movement.

Brain Stimulation

One of the important questions raised in biological psychology relates to the localization of functions within the brain and nervous system. Although this question can be approached with a number of techniques, we can begin by artificially stimulating the area in question and watching for resulting behavior. Interpretation of the results of stimulation research must be done with great caution. Because brain structures are richly connected with other areas of the brain, stimulating one area will also affect other areas to which it is connected.

I hated to serve as a subject. I didn't like the stuffy, artificial instructions given to subjects... With animals I was at home. I felt that, in studying them, I was keeping close to biology with my feet on the ground.

J.B. Watson

Electrical stimulation of the brain can be applied during neurosurgery. As unpleasant as it may sound to you, most neurosurgery is conducted under local, as opposed to general, anesthesia. The tissues of the brain itself lack receptors for pain. Once the bone and the tissues covering the brain are anesthetized, the surgeon can work on the brain of the conscious patient without causing pain. Why would we put people through such an unpleasant experience? Although brains are similar in many ways from person to person, individual differences frequently do occur. As discussed in Chapter 13, individual variations occur in the patterns of localization of many cognitive functions, such as language. Before operating in an area, the surgeon will want to know whether an essential function such as language is being managed by neurons in that area. By stimulating the area in question with a small amount of electricity and assessing any changes in behavior, the surgeon can identify whether the area participates in a particular type of behavior.

Considerable knowledge regarding the mapping of the functions of the cortex has been derived from this technique. Neurosurgeon Wilder Penfield investigated the brains of more than a thousand patients undergoing surgery for the treatment of epilepsy (see Chapter 15). Penfield's work contributed significantly to our understanding of the mapping of motor cortex, memory, and language (Penfield, 1958). Penfield's stimulation was restricted to the surface of the cortex. Others

■ **Figure 1.15 Bullfighting with Electrical Stimulation** Neuroscientist José Delgado faces a fierce fighting bull armed only with a transmitter that can activate electrodes that have been surgically implanted in the bull's brain. Fortunately for Delgado, the experiment was successful.

have investigated stimulation of deeper structures through implanted electrodes. Robert Heath (1963) implanted electrodes in a patient who suffered from the sleep disorder narcolepsy (see Chapter 11), and allowed the patient to push a button that administered a brief electrical stimulus. The patient was able to describe his reactions to stimulation of each of the fourteen electrodes implanted in his brain. One of the electrodes, which the patient activated most frequently, elicited sexual arousal.

For ethical reasons, most stimulation research has been conducted with laboratory animals rather than humans. A classic example of the use of brain stimulation of this type was the work of Olds and Milner (1954). These researchers found that stimulation to certain parts of the brain acted as reinforcement. Rats would press levers or stay in a particular corner of a cage if these behaviors resulted in brain stimulation.

Not all areas of the brain produce pleasant sensations when stimulated, however. Fear, anxiety, rage, or other negative responses are also elicited by electrical stimulation. Probably one of the more bizarre demonstrations of the power of brain stimulation was the work of physiologist José Delgado and his fighting bulls. As shown in ■ Figure 1.15, Delgado would face a bull armed with only a transmitter. When the bull charged, Delgado would activate electrodes implanted in the bull's brain that would stop the bull in its tracks.

Repeated transcranial magnetic stimulation (rTMS) consists of magnetic pulses delivered through a single coil of wire encased in plastic that is placed on the scalp ■ (Figure 1.16). Low frequency rTMS (about one pulse per second) provides an interesting technique for temporarily changing brain activity immediately below the stimulation site (Hoffman et al., 2003). In some cases, rTMS will inhibit a certain function, such as "hearing voices" among some patients with schizophrenia (Hoffman et al., 2005; see Chapter 16). In other cases, rTMS appears to disinhibit behavior, or allow a normally inhibited behavior to be expressed. For example, Snyder et al. (2006) used rTMS to temporarily produce unusual calculation skills, like those occasionally found in people with autism, in their healthy participants. Repeated TMS has also shown promise in treating some cases of depression (Møller, Hjaltason, Ivarsson, & Stefansson, 2006; Ridding & Rothwell, 2007).

Lesion

A **lesion** is an injury to neural tissue and can be either naturally occurring or deliberately produced. As was the case with stimulation, the primary purpose of lesion analysis is to assess the probable function of an area. Behavior observed prior to the lesion can be compared with behavior occurring after the lesion, with changes attributed to the area that was damaged. Once again, interpretation must be done very carefully. Lesions not only damage a particular area of the brain but also damage any nerve fibers passing through that area.

Neuropsychologists evaluate naturally occurring lesions that result from injury or disease, gaining a great deal of information about the function of the brain. Many examples of this type of analysis will be discussed in the remainder of the text. The ability to perform an autopsy allowed Paul Broca to make the previously mentioned correlations between the damage he observed and the clinical observations he made during the patient's lifetime.

Deliberate lesions are generally performed in research using laboratory animals, as opposed to human participants. However, as we will see in Chapter 15, lesions are occasionally used to treat cases of epilepsy that do not respond to medication. The technique of producing deliberate lesions in research animals originated with Pierre Flourens in the 1800s. A classic example of lesion work using animals identified a role for the ventromedial hypothalamus (VMH) in satiety (Hoebel & Teitelbaum, 1966). When this area is electrically stimulated, an animal will stop eating. When this area is lesioned, the animal eats so much that its body weight can double or even triple (see Chapter 9).

repeated transcranial magnetic stimulation (rTMS) A technique for stimulating the cortex at regular intervals by applying a magnetic pulse through a wire coil encased in plastic and placed on the scalp.

lesion (LEE-zhun) Pathological or traumatic damage to tissue.

Deliberate lesions are performed in a number of ways. In some studies, large areas of brain tissue are surgically removed. In this case, we might refer to the procedure as **ablation** rather than lesion. As shown in ■ Figure 1.17, lesions are experimentally produced when an electrode is surgically inserted into the area of interest. The electrode is insulated except at the very tip, to prevent damage to cells lining the entire pathway of the electrode. Heat is generated at the tip of the electrode, effectively killing a small population of cells surrounding the tip. Small lesions can also be produced by applying neurotoxins, chemicals that specifically kill neurons, into the area of interest through a surgically implanted micropipette. Chemically produced lesions have the advantage of harming only the cell bodies of neurons while leaving the nerve fibers traveling through the area intact. Conversely, fiber pathways can be chemically lesioned while sparing adjacent cell bodies. Obviously, both heat-produced and chemically produced lesions result in permanent damage to the brain. A reversible type of lesion can be produced by cooling an area using a probe. When the area is chilled, the neurons are unable to function. However, when the area returns to normal temperatures, normal behavioral function is restored.

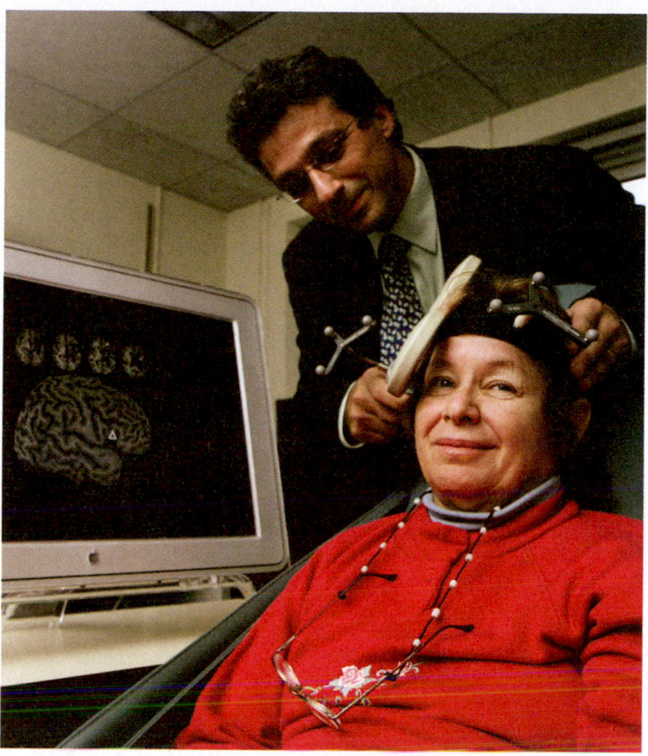

AP Photo/Charles Krupa

■ **Figure 1.16**
Repeated Transcranial Magnetic Stimulation (r TMS) In this procedure, small magnetic pulses are delivered to the brain through a wand held above the scalp. The magnetism temporarily changes the activity of small areas of cortex lying below the wand. This technique shows promise for research as well as for the treatment of depression and hallucination.

Biochemical Methods

As we will see in Chapters 3 and 4, the brain and nervous system are unusually well protected, compared with other organs in the body, from circulating toxins. As a result, if a researcher wishes to investigate the effects of chemical stimulation in the brain, these normal protective mechanisms must be bypassed. Obviously, some chemicals naturally gain access to the brain, resulting in psychoactive effects. Many other chemicals are blocked from exiting the blood supply into neural tissue. For instance, most agents used for cancer chemotherapy simply circulate through the brain without leaving the blood supply, adding to the challenges of treating brain tumors.

Different methods used to administer drugs to a subject include eating, inhaling, chewing, and injecting the drug. These methods result in the delivery of very different concentrations of a drug into the blood supply within a given period. For research purposes, chemicals can be directly administered to the brain through the surgical implantation of micropipettes. This technique allows researchers to observe the effects of chemicals administered in an awake, freely moving animal.

On occasion, it is desirable to be able to identify the chemicals that naturally exist in a particular location. Using the same micropipette implantation technique described previously, small amounts of fluid are filtered from the area of the brain surrounding the

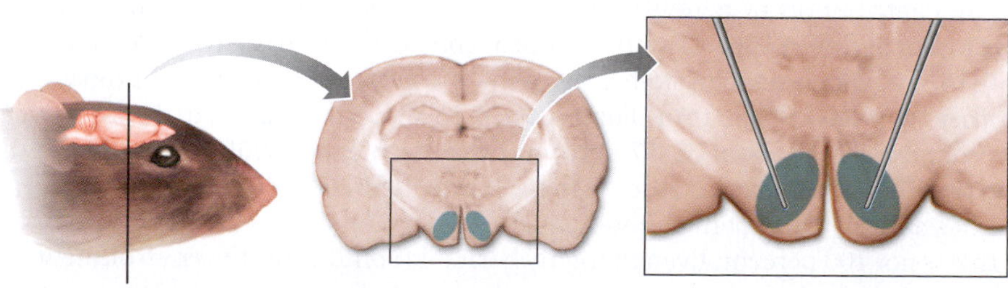

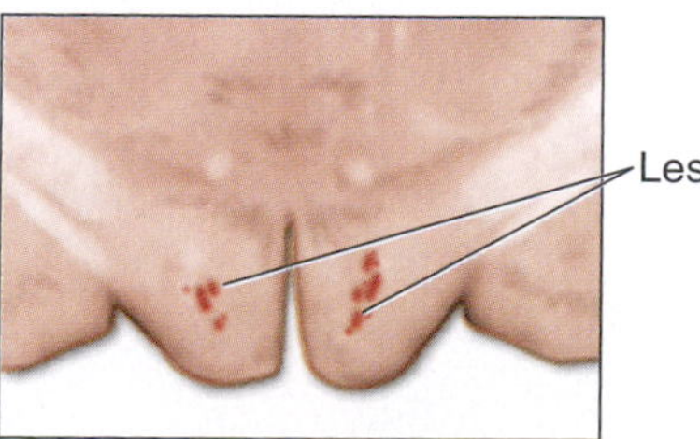

(a) Section of Brain to Be Lesioned (b) Electrodes Inserted (c) Resulting Lesions

■ **Figure 1.17**
Lesion To investigate the function of a particular part of the brain (a), radio frequency current is passed through the tips of insulated electrodes that have been surgically implanted (b). Resulting changes in behavior are correlated with the lesions produced (c).

ablation (uh-BLAY-shun) The surgical removal of tissue.

WHY DOES THIS MATTER?

Nature versus Nurture

Twin and adoption studies allow researchers to estimate the relative contributions of nature (our innate qualities) and nurture (our personal experiences) to human traits and behaviors. These comparisons matter because they help us understand the causes of individual differences in a trait. If we understand the causes of a trait or behavior, we are in a stronger position to bring about positive changes.

Contributions of nature and nurture to a trait or behavior fall along a continuum. Some human traits are virtually all nature. Huntington's disease (HD), an ultimately fatal, degenerative condition characterized by involuntary, jerky movement, is caused by a dominant gene located on the fourth chromosome (see Chapter 8). Any child receiving the HD gene from a parent will inevitably develop the disease. Other behaviors, such as whether one speaks Chinese or English, are purely a matter of nurture. Most traits and behaviors fall somewhere in the middle of the continuum, representing an interaction of nature and nurture. We would expect the child of two professional basketball players to be very tall (nature). However, these parents can increase the likelihood that their child will reach his or her full genetic potential for height by providing their child with a healthy diet (nurture).

tip of the pipette for analysis. This technique is known as **microdialysis.** Microdialysis allows researchers to identify which neurochemicals are active in a precise location, as well as the approximate quantity of these chemicals.

Genetic Methods

Many researchers strive to identify the relative contributions of hereditary and environmental variables on a particular behavior. There are a number of ways to approach this type of question. None of these approaches is completely satisfying, but each has resulted in dramatically furthering our knowledge of the role of heredity in behavior.

Twin Studies One approach to the question of heredity versus environment is to compare the variable of interest by using identical (monozygotic) and fraternal (dizygotic) twins. This natural comparison provides a fair amount of control because we can assume that twins enjoy similar prenatal and postnatal environments. Although twins are not exposed to completely identical environments (parents may treat one twin quite differently from another), the environments experienced by twins are more similar than the environments of nontwin siblings.

Monozygotic twins share an identical set of genes, whereas fraternal twins average about 50 percent of their genes in common, just like any other pair of non-identical siblings. Comparisons between the two types of twins, therefore, provide a sense of the extent of genetic influence on a trait of interest. As is discussed in Chapter 16, some psychological disorders, such as bipolar disorder and schizophrenia, are significantly influenced by heredity. Others, such as major depressive disorder, show some evidence of genetic vulnerability but are also heavily influenced by environmental variables.

The contribution of heredity to these conditions is often stated in the form of a concordance rate, a type of statistical probability. Given the existence of a trait in one twin, the concordance rate for the remaining twin estimates the probability of the other twin having the trait. For instance, in the case of bipolar disorder, we see concordance rates of about 71–77 percent (Edvardsen et al., 2008). This suggests that the heritability of bipolar disorder is high. If one identical twin has the disorder, the other has a 71–77 percent likelihood of also being diagnosed with the disorder. Note that this is not 100 percent. Even in highly heritable conditions, the environment plays an important role. In contrast, the concordance rate for identical twins in regard to major depressive disorder is usually reported to be about 33 percent (Kendler, Gatz, Gardner, & Pedersen, 2006; Wurtman, 2005). This indicates that some heritability for depression does occur but that environmental variables play a more significant role than in the case of bipolar disorder. However, it is important to remember that environmental variables might still include biological components such as prenatal environment and exposure to infection.

microdialysis (my-kroh-die-AL-i-sis) A technique for assessing the chemical composition of a very small area of the brain.

Adoption Studies Another approach to quantifying the influences of heredity and environment is to compare the similarities of an adopted individual to his or her biological and adoptive parents. Similarities to the biological parents suggest a role for heredity, whereas similarities to the adoptive parents suggest a role for the environment. Adoption studies have been used to assess the relative contributions of heredity and environment to such characteristics as intelligence and criminality. Interpretation of such studies remains controversial, because adoptive families are often quite similar to one another, which in turn magnifies genetic influences. **Heritability,** or the amount that a trait varies in a population due to genetics, is still influenced by the environment. For example, if you planted seeds under ideal conditions (good soil, lots of sunlight, regular watering), the differences you observe among your mature plants are largely due to genetics. In contrast, if you planted seeds under more variable conditions, the resulting plants would reflect contributions of both genetic and environmental factors. Like the ideal conditions for our plants, genetic influences may be magnified by the similar environments provided by adoptive parents.

Studies of Genetically-Modified Animals We review a number of studies in this text that use a relatively new genetic technique in which specially engineered, defective versions of genes are inserted into the chromosomes of animals, usually mice. The normal version of these knockout genes encodes for a specific protein. The **knockout genes** take the place of the normal genes but fail to produce the specific protein. By using this method, researchers can assess the roles of particular genes and the proteins they encode.

One example of this method is found in the work of H. W. Matthes and his colleagues (1996) on a type of opiate receptor. As we will see in Chapter 4, many drugs have effects on behavior because they are chemically similar to normally occurring chemicals found in the nervous system. Opiates, such as morphine and heroin, activate receptors for naturally occurring substances known as endorphins. Matthes et al. (1996) bred mice that lacked the genes for producing some of the opiate receptors. Their general behavior seemed unaffected, but they did not experience any pain relief when given morphine. They were incapable of becoming addicted to morphine, and they showed no withdrawal symptoms when morphine administration was discontinued. We can therefore conclude that certain aspects of an animal's normal reaction to morphine are dependent on the existence of opiate receptors. Without these receptors, pain reduction, addiction, and withdrawal do not occur.

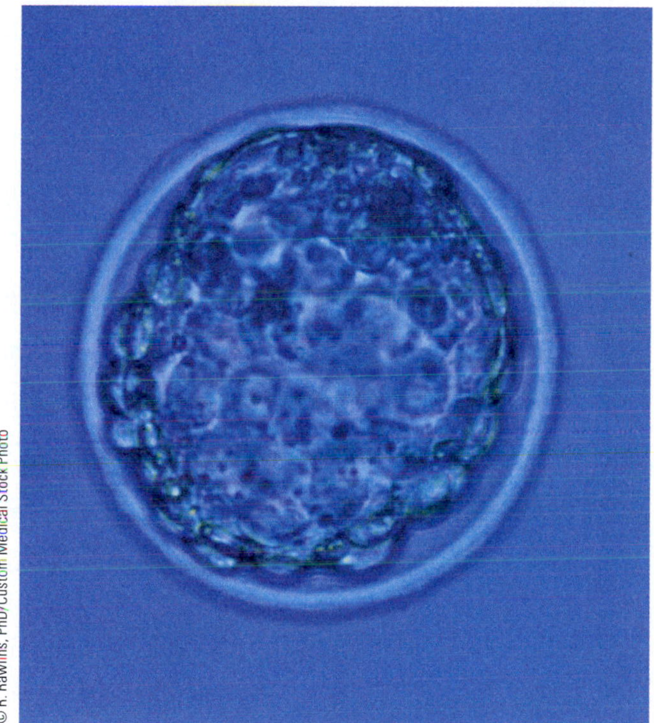

FIGURE 1.18
A Blastocyst Developed Through Assisted Reproduction Considerable controversy surrounds the use of embryonic stem cells for research. These cells are typically obtained from unused embryos developed in fertility clinics for assisted reproduction purposes.

STEM CELLS

One of the most promising approaches to the problem of repairing brain and spinal cord damage is the use of stem cells. A **stem cell** is an undifferentiated cell that can divide and differentiate into other types of cells (see Chapter 5). If provided with the appropriate laboratory environment, a stem cell line, or culture, can replicate indefinitely. Currently, researchers can derive stem cell lines from three sources: adult stem cells, stem cells from umbilical cord blood, and embryonic stem cells.

The various types of stem cells offer different sets of advantages and disadvantages. Embryonic stem cells are usually obtained from embryos in the blastocyst stage, or about 5 days after conception in humans. These cells are pluripotent, meaning that they can differentiate into any type of tissue. In addition, embryonic cells are virtually immortal, as they can divide endlessly in the laboratory. On the other hand, these cells will provoke an immune reaction in a recipient, just like any other transplanted tissue. Adult stem cells have been retrieved from blood, nerve cells, muscle, the cornea and retina of the eye, some internal organs, and skin. Typically, these cells are less flexible than the embryonic cells, and can only differentiate into cells similar to their source. They lack the immortality of the embryonic cells, but are less likely to cause rejection by a tissue recipient.

heritability The amount of variability of a trait in a population that is due to genetics.
knockout genes Genes that take the place of normal genes but that fail to produce the specific protein produced by the normal genes.
stem cell An undifferentiated cell that can divide and differentiate into other types of cells.

Researchers are very excited about the potential of using stem cells to grow replacement tissue. For example, Schultz (2005, p. 63) suggests that the abilities of stem cells to "incorporate into the spinal cord, differentiate, and to improve locomotor recovery hold promise for a cure" for spinal damage. However, stem cell research has been the focus of considerable ethical debate, which we will address in a later section of this chapter.

INTERIM SUMMARY 1.2

Summary Table: Methods in Biological Psychology

Method	Function
Histology	Studying the microscopic structure of the nervous system
Autopsy	Studying the structure of the nervous system following death
Computerized tomography (CT)	Studying structure and diagnosing structural damage
Positron emission tomography (PET)	Studying the relative activity of nervous system structures
Magnetic resonance imaging (MRI)	Studying structure in very fine detail
Functional MRI (fMRI)	Studying the activity of nervous system structures
Electroencephalogram (EEG)	Studying brain activity, primarily during sleep or seizures
Evoked potential recording	An adapted EEG used to study the brain's response to specific stimuli
Magnetoencephalography (MEG)	Studying brain activity
Single-cell recordings	Identifying the stimulus responsible for activating an individual neuron
Electrical stimulation and lesion	Identifying behavior linked to a particular location in the nervous system
Repeated transcranial magnetic stimulation	Producing long-lasting changes in cortical activity, linking behavior to a particular location in the cortex.
Microdialysis	Identifying particular chemicals in a very small location
Twin and adoption studies	Studying contributions of genetic and nongenetic factors to behavior
Genetically-modified animals (knockout genes)	Studying the role of particular genes and the proteins they produce
Stem Cells	Growing replacement tissue for repairing damaged organs, including the brain and spinal cord

Summary Points

1. Improvements in histology provided the means for examining the nervous system at the microscopic level. **(LO3)**
2. Imaging technologies, including CT scans, PET scans, MRI, and fMRI, have built on knowledge gained through autopsy regarding the structure and function of the brain. **(LO4)**
3. Recording techniques include measurements of the brain's overall electrical and magnetic outputs. In addition, recordings can also be made of the activity of single cells. **(LO5)**
4. Stimulation and lesion techniques can be used to assess the function of particular areas of the brain. Magnetic stimulation can enhance or reduce the activity of the brain. **(LO6)**
5. Biochemical methods allow for the artificial stimulation of the nervous system with chemicals as well as the assessment of the biochemical environment in an area of particular interest within the nervous system. **(LO6, LO7)**
6. Genetic methods, including twin studies, adoption studies, and the use of animals bred with knockout genes, allow researchers to assess the role of our genetic inheritance in the relationship between the nervous system and behavior. **(LO8)**
7. Stem cells provide a promising method for repairing brain and spinal cord damage, and can be derived from embryos, umbilical cord blood, and some adult tissues. **(LO9)**

(continued)

INTERIM SUMMARY 1.2 (continued)

Review Questions

1. What are the relative strengths and weaknesses of the major imaging methods?
2. What are the challenges involved with the interpretation of data from stimulation and lesion research?

Research Ethics

The Greek physician and scholar Hippocrates set a standard for ethical behavior in the sciences that has certainly stood the test of time. Hippocrates wrote in *The Epidemics:* "As to diseases, make a habit of two things—to help, or at least do no harm." As you have seen in this chapter, we have developed a wealth of technology in the neurosciences that has moved our understanding forward quite rapidly. In our rush for knowledge, what controls are in place to ensure that Hippocrates' rule of "do no harm" is respected by those entrusted with the lives and welfare of research participants?

Although we have numerous written guidelines in place, ethical issues rarely fall into neat boxes labeled "right" and "wrong." Consider for a moment the common practice of using a double-blind procedure to test the efficacy of an experimental drug. Normally, we would randomly assign participants to a drug condition or a placebo condition, in which the participants would receive an inactive substance instead of a drug. Both the participants and the researchers observing outcomes remain unaware of the participants' group assignments until the data are tabulated. So far, things sound pretty normal. What would you think about this procedure, however, if the participants happen to be children under the age of five suffering from AIDS? In evaluations of ethical issues, what looks easy on paper can become very complicated in real-world applications.

Before discussing the actual provisions that are in place for the protection of human and animal research subjects, it is useful to gain an understanding of the mechanisms for ensuring compliance with written policies. Currently, protection for research subjects in the United States begins with the federal government and the Common Rule. The Common Rule refers to a set of standards shared by seventeen federal agencies (Center for Science, Technology, and Congress, 2001). These standards include many of the provisions discussed in detail later, including the establishment of review boards and guidelines for obtaining informed consent. These standards apply to any researcher obtaining federal funds or conducting research at an institution that receives federal funds. When a researcher applies to an agency for funding for a project, the prospectus for the project will be scrutinized for compliance with federal standards. In addition to the federal standards, professional societies such as the American Psychological Association and the Society for Neuroscience have also developed guidelines specific to their subject matter.

Animals, whom we have made our slaves, we do not like to consider our equals.

Charles Darwin

A second tier of review occurs at the level of the university at which the research is to take place. Each university conducting research, whether by students, faculty or full-time researchers, has separate institutional review boards (IRBs) for human and animal research. The IRBs are composed of faculty members with expertise in the appropriate areas, plus at least one faculty member from a nonscience discipline. In addition, the boards include a community member, so that the university is not simply policing itself behind closed doors.

A final stage occurs when the investigator submits his or her research for publication. Reviewers of the work will also scrutinize the ethics of the work before approving it for publication. Although this stage occurs too late for the protection of the individuals who have already participated in the project, failure to gain publication due to noncompliance with ethical standards will usually be enough of an incentive to prevent further mistakes on the part of that researcher.

Many challenges to ethical research remain. For example, the independence of research partnerships between private corporations and universities is occasionally in doubt. Krimsky, Rothenberg, Stott, and Kyle (1996) surveyed nearly 800 papers published in biology and medical journals and reported that one third of the lead authors had a financial interest in the corporation sponsoring the research. Few of these authors disclosed this personal interest to readers. Mildred Cho (1996) compared drug studies funded by pharmaceutical companies with studies funded by the federal government. Ninety-eight percent of the studies funded by pharmaceutical companies reported that the new drugs were better than existing drugs, whereas only 79 percent of the independent studies reached the same conclusion.

The protections discussed in this section do not extend to privately funded research. The National Bioethics Advisory Commission (NBAC) recommended extending provisions protecting research participants in federal studies to all participants, regardless of funding source. The group called for legislation to be enacted to bring participants in privately funded research under the same federal oversight system, but this has yet to occur.

Human Participants Guidelines

Thinking about the protection of human participants has changed dramatically over the past 30 years. Today's scientific community is far more protective of the safety and well-being of research participants. As an undergraduate student in introductory psychology, I was compelled to serve as a research participant in a fixed number of experiments to pass the course. I found myself acting as the confederate in a Milgram-type obedience experiment in which the real participant was supposed to administer a

WHY DOES THIS MATTER?

The Death of Jesse Gelsinger

Having excellent guidelines in place for the protection of human research participants matters because these situations can literally mean the difference between life and death. While attempting to solve important problems, we cannot lose sight of our responsibility for offering participants the best protection possible. This is the story of one of the cases in which things went terribly wrong.

On September 17, 1999, an exuberant teenager named Jesse Gelsinger became the first person to die from gene therapy. The tragedy of Gelsinger's death was compounded by the fact that he wasn't really sick. Jesse had a rare genetic disorder, a liver condition known as ornithine transcarbamylase deficiency. Ornithine transcarbamylase is an enzyme that metabolizes ammonia produced during the breakdown of proteins. Most patients with this condition die at birth, but Jesse was able to stay healthy with a special diet and medications. His participation in the genetic therapy experiment at the University of Pennsylvania was purely altruistic—he wanted to help people who suffered from the fatal version of his disease (Gelsinger, 2002). Jesse's treatment was a standard example of gene transfer (Wirth & Ylä-Herttuala, 2006). A virus was used to insert a "corrected" gene that would allow him to produce larger quantities of the enzyme. The corrected gene was not a problem, but the virus used to deliver the gene triggered a massive response by Jesse's immune system, leading to organ failure and death.

Gelsinger's death was doubly shocking, as the American public had until that time viewed gene therapy as a safe and promising approach to disease. A variety of irregularities in the approval process for the experiment that killed Jesse surfaced.

FIGURE 1.19 Jesse Gelsinger Teenager Jesse Gelsinger altruistically volunteered to serve as a participant in a gene therapy study that tragically ended his life. Gelsinger's case illustrates many of the ethical dilemmas facing researchers today.

Jesse's father testified that he had been unaware of the risks involved with the procedure, including the fact that identical procedures had resulted in the death of several monkeys. In addition, one of the physicians involved with the trials appeared to have a serious financial conflict of interest in the project. Consequently, the University of Pennsylvania institute performing the research was shut down, and the physicians involved were sanctioned (Smith & Byers, 2002).

punishment to me in the form of increasingly potent electrical shocks. As in Milgram's original experiment (1963), I received no shocks, but the real participant (a girl from my floor in the dorm) believed that I was being shocked. After she "administered" the maximum levels of shock to me, I never quite trusted her again, and she avoided me for the remainder of our undergraduate days.

Today, such a study would be impossible to conduct. Coercing people into serving as research participants, either for course credit or any other incentive, is unacceptable. Although we recognize as psychologists that people who volunteer for research are probably quite different from people who don't volunteer, the resulting limitations on our abilities to generalize are a reasonable price to pay for ethical practice. Coercion of research participants is to be avoided at all costs. Benefits for participation, including money, should not be "excessive or inappropriate" (American Psychological Association, 1992). Participants must be informed at the outset that they can leave the experiment at any point in time without penalty. In this text, you will read about research conducted with human participants who are not able to volunteer freely to participate. For example, individuals may not be capable of fully understanding the nature of the experiment or of their participation due to conditions such as schizophrenia or Alzheimer's disease. In these situations, legal permission must be obtained from a third party. The university-level review boards play an essential role in deciding these gray areas on a case-by-case basis.

To freely volunteer, a participant must be told enough about the experiment to make an informed decision about participating. This disclosure is accomplished through a carefully worded informed consent form prepared by the researchers and reviewed by the campus human participants IRB. The form provides information about the general purpose of the experiment and any risks that may be involved. Participants are provided with contact information in case they have further questions regarding the study. Participants are assured that their data will be confidential and that they can choose to receive information about the outcomes and conclusions of the experiment.

I trust that I shall not be thought rash if I express a belief that experiments on the higher nervous systems of animals will yield not a few directional indications for education and self-education in man.

Ivan Pavlov

Animal Subjects Guidelines

The first provision for the protection of animal subjects relates to necessity. The American Psychological Association (2008) stipulates that animal research should have a clear scientific purpose, such as increasing our knowledge of behavior or improving the health and welfare of humans or other animals. In other words, the research needs to do more than build a scientist's résumé for tenure and promotion. The knowledge gained should balance and justify the use of animals. The species used should be appropriate to the task. If the same questions can be asked without using animals, the alternate method should be used.

A second provision relates to basic care and housing of the animals. When I was a graduate student in the 1970s, a furnished apartment near UCLA cost about $165 per month. In that same period, housing a single rhesus monkey for research purposes cost approximately $650 per month. Regular checkups by veterinarians and inspections occurred. We were extensively trained regarding the typical behavior of the animals (more for our own safety, in this case, as adult rhesus can be quite dangerous to humans).

Finally, experimental procedures should cause as little pain and distress as possible. Consider, however, that animals are generally used when procedures are not acceptable for human participants. The American Psychological Association guidelines include provisions related to the use of pain, surgery, stress, and deprivation with animal subjects, as well as to the termination of the animal's life. Some individuals and groups object to the notion that research that is considered unethical with humans is acceptable when animal subjects are used. Nonetheless, this is the primary rationale for the use of animal subjects, and we can expect a continued lively debate on the topic.

Emerging Issues in Research Ethics

Scientists frequently work to advance technology without taking the time to consider how it might be used. That task is often shifted to the politician, the religious leader, and the philosopher. In many cases, consensus remains elusive.

I hope that posterity will judge me kindly, not only as to the things which I have explained, but also to those which I have intentionally omitted so as to leave to others the pleasure of discovery.
Rene Descartes

The Ethics of Research on the Internet Intrigued by research regarding the preservation of the ability to use profanity in patients who otherwise lose most language capabilities due to stroke, one of my students set out to study the use of profanity by bilingual and multilingual speakers. Our university does not have a significant number of international or bilingual students, so we thought that a survey posted on the Internet might garner a more substantial number of participants. Our research posed a simple survey identical to one we might distribute in person. Internet research similar to ours, as well as studies that mine data from chat rooms and bulletin boards (see Galegher, Sproull, & Kiesler, 1998, for an example), raise new concerns about privacy, confidentiality, and informed consent. Although it's unlikely that any Internet participant will experience physical harm as a result of participation, what special considerations are necessary to protect these participants?

To address these issues, a workshop was convened in June 1999 under the auspices of the U.S. Office for Protection from Research Risks (OPRR) and the Scientific Freedom, Responsibility, and Law Program of the American Association for the Advancement of Science (AAAS; Frankel & Siang, 1999). Workshop participants identified a number of challenges relating to the use of the Internet to conduct research. Privacy issues, obtaining informed consent from participants, and difficulties in debriefing participants are among the many ethical considerations that researchers face.

Although researchers are delighted with the opportunity to reach thousands of participants with very little cost (Kraut et al., 2004), much further discussion is needed to refine these concerns and find solutions.

The Ethics of Stem Cell Research As noted in a previous section, three sources of human stem cells exist: adult stem cells, umbilical cord blood, and embryonic stem cells. Considerable ethical controversy swirls around the latter source. Most of these cells are obtained from unused embryos from fertility clinics. In most cases, a clinic will produce 7 or 8 embryos for couples seeking assisted reproduction when only 2 or 3 will be implanted. The couple must notify the clinic about their wishes for the remaining embryos. In addition to donations for research, the embryos can remain frozen for future use, donated to another couple, or destroyed. The issue of destroying these "extra" embryos for research is divisive. In addition to opposing in vitro fertilization in the first place, the Catholic Church argues that embryonic stem cell research violates the sanctity of life. Others, including former first lady Nancy Reagan, oppose abortion but support embryonic stem cell research.

United States policy on embryonic stem cells reflects the divisive nature of the stem cell debate. In 1995, President Clinton signed the Dickey Amendment, which banned federal funding for the use of destroyed embryos for research. In 2000, a legal challenge from the Department of Health and Human Services argued that federal funding should be available for research with stem cell lines developed from embryos destroyed using private or state funding. Upon taking office in 2001, President Bush closed this loophole by restricting federal funding to stem cell lines from embryos destroyed prior to his administration. These federal policies often required researchers to maintain two laboratories engaged in identical research, one using federal funds with approved cell lines, and one using funds and cell lines from non-federal sources. As this book goes to press in January 2009, President Obama has reversed Bush's decision, but his position regarding the original Dickey Amendment remains unknown.

The United States has not been alone with this controversy. Some nations, including Germany, France, Austria, Ireland, Italy, and Portugal, have outlawed embryonic stem cell research completely. Other European nations (Sweden, Finland, Greece, Great Britain, and the Netherlands) allow it to occur with few restrictions. Japan, India, South Korea, Brazil, South Africa, and China are generally supportive. With the exception of Brazil and South Africa, South American and African countries are restrictive. New Zealand is restrictive, and Australia is mixed. One of the obvious concerns is that further restrictions in the United States will produce a brain drain of scientists seeking more generous funding elsewhere.

More may have been learned about the brain and the mind in the 1990s—the so-called decade of the brain—than during the entire previous history of psychology and neuroscience.
Antonio Damasio

The ability to find other sources for stem cells would go a long way toward resolving ethical dilemmas. Cells that behave in similar fashion to embryonic stem cells have been harvested from umbilical cord blood (McGuckin et al., 2005). In 2007, two laboratories reported successful techniques for producing pluripotent stem cells from adult tissues (Takahashi et al., 2007; Yu et al., 2007). Another solution to ethical objections is the development of stem cells that do not require the destruction of the embryo. Robert Lanza and his colleagues have reported achieving this result (Chung et al., 2008; Klimanskaya, Chung, Becker, Lu, & Lanza, 2006).

INTERIM SUMMARY 1.3

Summary Table: Ethical Principles

Participants	Ethical Principles
Human participants	No coercion Informed consent Confidentiality
Animal subjects	Necessity Excellent food, housing, vet care Avoidance of pain and distress

Summary Points

1. Research ethics agreed upon by government agencies, universities, and individual researchers are designed to protect both human participants and animal subjects from harm. **(LO9)**
2. In addition to being protected from physical and psychological harm, human participants must not be coerced into participation, and their confidentiality must be strictly maintained. **(LO9)**
3. Animal subjects must be protected from unnecessary pain and suffering. Researchers must establish the necessity of using animal subjects and are obligated to provide excellent housing, food, and veterinary care. **(LO9)**
4. Emerging technologies, such as research over the Internet and the use of embryonic stem cells continue to push the boundaries of existing ethical guidelines. **(LO10)**

Review Question

1. What are the major considerations for the protection of human participants and animal research subjects?

CHAPTER REVIEW

THOUGHT QUESTIONS

1. If you were responsible for writing a new policy on the use of stem cells, what guidelines would you include?
2. How have societal factors influenced scientific discovery in the past? What aspects of our current environment act to enhance or hinder scientific understanding?
3. Which of the methods outlined in this chapter have the greatest potential for producing further advancements in our understanding of brain and behavior?

KEY TERMS

ablation (p. 17)
autopsy (p. 9)
biological psychology (p. 3)
computerized tomography (CT) (p. 10)
electroencephalogram (EEG) (p. 12)
evoked potential (p. 13)
functional magnetic resonance imaging (fMRI) (p. 10)
heritability (p. 19)
histology (p. 8)
knockout genes (p. 19)
lesion (p. 16)
magnetic resonance imaging (MRI) (p. 10)
magnetoencephalography (MEG) (p. 13)
microdialysis (p. 18)
mind-body dualism (p. 4)
monism (p. 4)
positron emission tomography (PET) (p. 10)
repeated transcranial magnetic stimulation (rTMS) (p. 16)
stem cell (p. 19)

2 The Anatomy and Evolution of the Nervous System

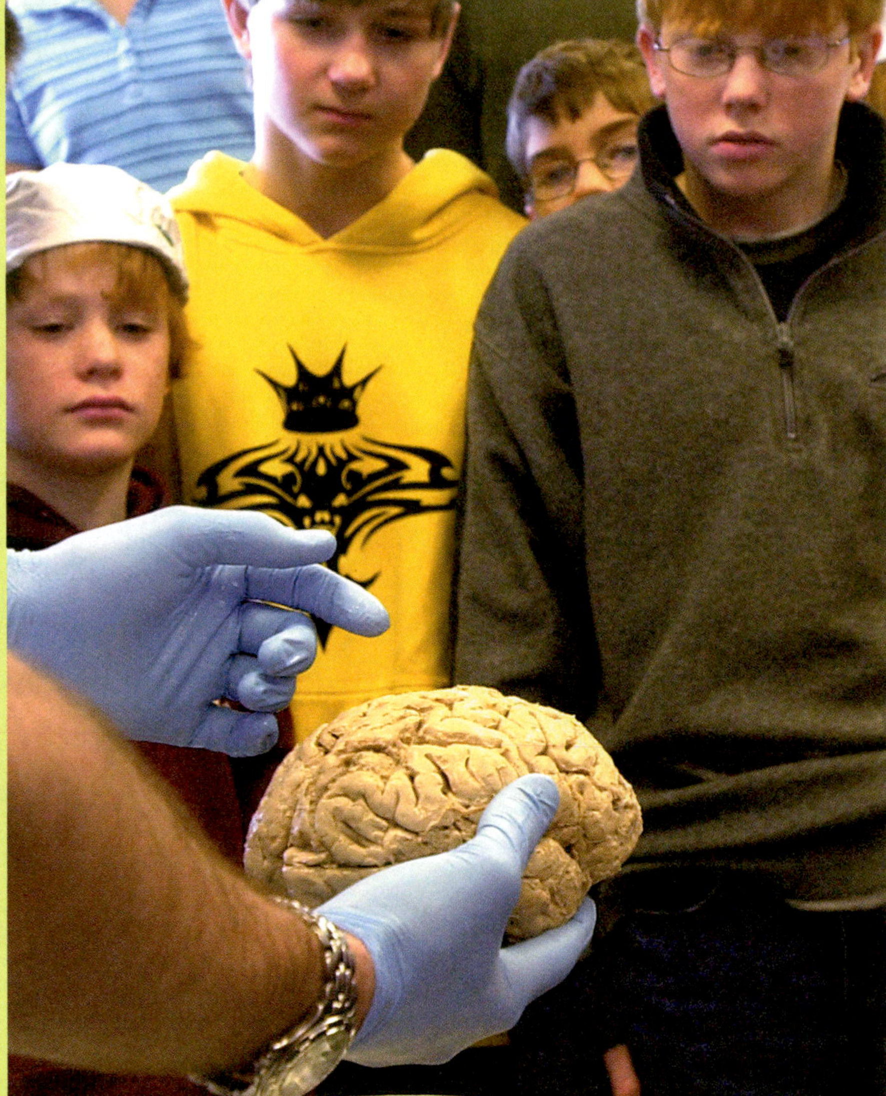

Mesabi Daily News/AP/Wide World

▲ **Four Youngsters and a Brain** No matter our age, we are all fascinated by the organ that makes us "tick."

CHAPTER OUTLINE

Introduction

The road to our current understanding of the structure and function of the nervous system has had its share of twists and turns. Concepts that we now take for granted were not easy to establish. In some cases, students of the brain got a lot of things right, only to undo their credibility by the errors they made. A classic example of the ups and downs of brain science is the work of Franz Joseph Gall (1758–1828), the Austrian physician we met in Chapter 1 as the developer of phrenology. Phrenology was a pseudoscience that argued that a person's character could be determined by feeling the lumps on the skull. Phrenologists reasoned that parts of the brain that were related to a particular trait would be exercised through expression of that trait, leading to increases in brain size reflected in bumps on the skull. Phrenology became wildly popular in Europe and in the United States, and numbered among its fans were such notables as Walt Whitman, Edgar Allan Poe, and Ralph Waldo Emerson. Employers would insist that job candidates undergo a phrenology exam, and engaged couples would consult phrenologists to see whether their characters were compatible. Candidates for public office would challenge their rivals to see which person had the best reading. Today's political debates begin to look better.

Gall actually got a few things right in spite of not subjecting his ideas to controlled experimentation. Gall was correct in assuming that the brain is the organ of the mind, and he was right again in suggesting that the brain was not a single entity but a collection of structures with different functions. Gall was substantially ahead of his time in suggesting that certain functions were localized in the brain. Where Gall fell completely off track was in his suggestion that the external contours of the skull had anything whatsoever to do with the functions of the brain beneath it.

In this chapter, we will preview many topics that will later be explained in greater detail in their own chapters. Feel free to look ahead. Similarly, as you read later chapters, you may find it helpful to return to sections of this chapter as a reminder of how the various parts of this miraculous structure work together. Perhaps 200 years from now, our understanding of brain science will have advanced so far that some of the material in this chapter will seem as wrong as Gall's phrenology. I don't think this will be the case. Our advantage over Gall is the painstaking and carefully controlled research that has pieced together our current understanding of the structures, functions, and evolutionary history of the brain. ■

LEARNING OBJECTIVES

After reading this chapter, you should be able to:

LO1 Identify the major anatomical directional terms and planes of section.

LO2 Describe the three layers of the meninges, the circulation of cerebrospinal fluid, and the major sources of blood supply to the brain.

LO3 Describe the major divisions and functions of the spinal cord.

LO4 Identify the major structures and functions of the hindbrain, midbrain, and forebrain.

LO5 Describe the outer appearance and layered structure of the cerebral cortex and the location and function of the four cortical lobes.

LO6 Differentiate the sensory, motor, and association cortices.

LO7 Describe the structure and function of the cranial and spinal nerves.

LO8 Summarize the major structural and functional features of the peripheral nervous system.

LO9 Trace the evolution of the human nervous system.

Anatomical Directions and Planes of Section

Navigating around the three-dimensional human brain is similar to describing the geography of our three-dimensional world. Without a vocabulary to describe the location of one area relative to others, we would quickly get lost. Instead of north, south, east, or west, anatomists have their own sets of directional terms. Although it might seem to be a lot of work to memorize these terms, the payoff comes when you can locate structures easily by their names. The ventromedial hypothalamus could simply be memorized, but knowing that *ventral* means toward the belly side of an animal and *medial* means toward the midline, you will know exactly where to look in the hypothalamus for this structure.

Because anatomical directions for human beings are complicated by the fact that we walk on two legs, we'll start off with the simpler case of the four-legged animal. Structures that are located toward the head end of the animal are **rostral** or **anterior.** In other words, the head of a dog is rostral to its shoulders. Structures located toward the tail end of the animal are **caudal** or **posterior.** For example, the dog's ears are caudal to its nose, and its hips are caudal to its shoulders. Structures located toward the belly side are **inferior** or **ventral,** whereas structures toward the back are **superior** or **dorsal.** If you have trouble keeping these last two straight, it might help to remember that scary dorsal shark fin cutting through the water in the film *Jaws.* Like geographical terms, these anatomical terms are relative to another place. Just as New York is north of Florida but south of Canada, the dog's ears are caudal to its nose but rostral to its shoulders.

Why are anatomical directions different in people? As shown in ■ Figure 2.1, our two-legged stance puts a 90-degree bend in the **neuraxis,** an imaginary line

rostral / anterior (RAHS-truhl) A directional term meaning toward the head of a four-legged animal.

caudal / posterior (KAW-duhl) A directional term meaning toward the tail of a four-legged animal.

inferior / ventral A directional term meaning toward the belly of a four-legged animal.

superior / dorsal A directional term meaning toward the back of a four legged animal.

neuraxis (ner-AX-is) An imaginary line that runs the length of the spinal cord to the front of the brain.

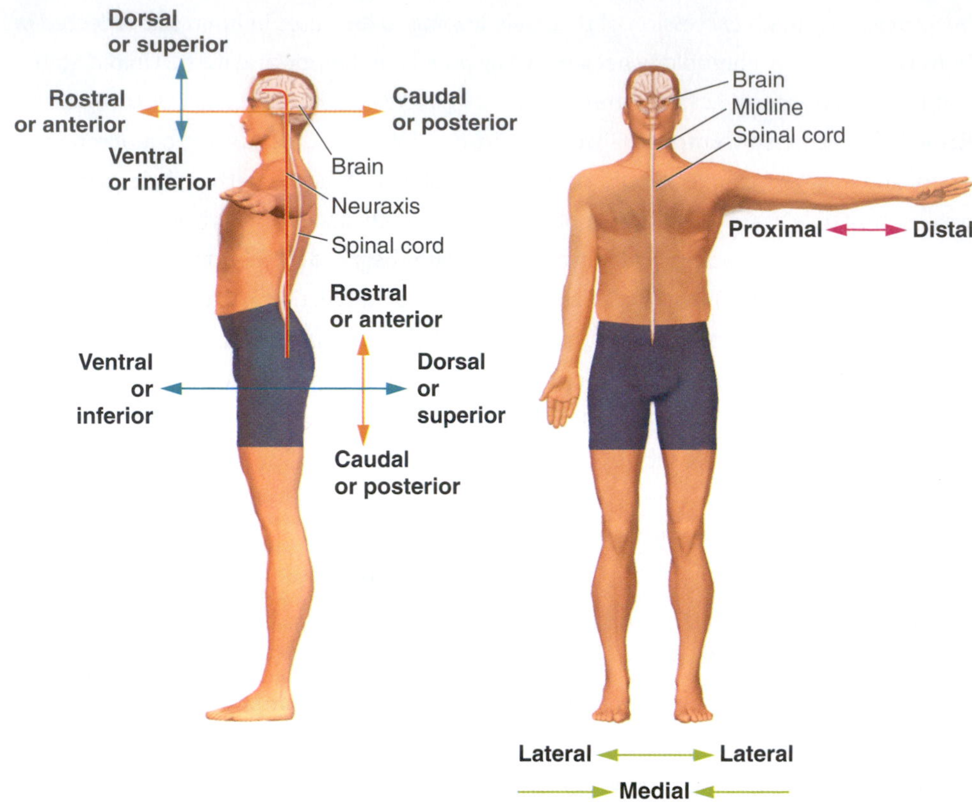

FIGURE 2.1
Anatomical Directions Anatomists use directional terms to name and locate brain structures. Because standing upright puts a 90-degree angle in the human neuraxis, the dorsal surface of the human brain also forms a 90-degree angle with the dorsal spinal cord.

that runs the length of the spinal cord through the brain. In the four-legged animal, the neuraxis forms a straight line running parallel to the ground. The dorsal parts of the animal's brain are in line with the dorsal parts of the spinal cord. In humans, the dorsal parts of our brain form a 90-degree angle with the dorsal parts of the spinal cord.

Additional directional terms refer to the **midline,** an imaginary line that divides us into approximately equal halves. If two structures are **ipsilateral,** they are both on the same side of the midline. My left arm and left leg are ipsilateral. If structures are on opposite sides of the midline, we say they are **contralateral.** My right arm and left leg are contralateral to each other. Structures close to the midline are referred to as **medial,** and structures to the side of the midline are called **lateral.** My heart is medial to my arms, whereas my ears are lateral to my nose. Similar terms include **proximal,** which means close to the center, and **distal,** which means far away from the center. Usually, we use these two terms to refer to limbs. My toes are distal relative to my knees, and my shoulders are proximal relative to my elbows.

Although directional terms help us find our way around the nervous system, we also need a way to view three-dimensional structures as flat images on a page. Anatomists have found it useful to make particular cuts or sections in the nervous system to view the structures in two rather than three dimensions. The choice of how to make the section can be arbitrary. Different structures are often more easily viewed with one section than with others. My graduate neuroanatomy professor, the esteemed Dr. Arnold Scheibel, was fond of using his favorite diagonal cross-sections during exams. Traditionally, we use the *coronal, sagittal,* and *horizontal* sections.

The three major planes of section, along with representative images of brain slices, can be seen in Figure 2.2. **Coronal sections,** also known as frontal sections, divide the nervous system from front to back. In other words, you are looking at the brain in the face. **Sagittal sections** are parallel to the midline, allowing us a side view of brain structures. The special section that divides the brain into two relatively equal halves is known as a **midsagittal section.** The third type of section is the **horizontal** or **axial section,** which divides the brain from top to bottom. You will see many examples of each type of section in this chapter and in the remainder of the text.

midline An imaginary line dividing the body into two equal halves.
ipsilateral A directional term referring to structures on the same side of the midline.
contralateral A directional term referring to structures on opposite sides of the midline.
medial A directional term meaning toward the midline.
lateral A directional term meaning away from the midline.
proximal A directional term that means closer to center; usually applied to limbs; opposite of distal.
distal A directional term meaning farther away from another structure, usually in reference to limbs.
coronal section An anatomical section dividing the brain front to back, parallel to the face. Also known as a frontal section.
sagittal section (SA-ji-tuhl) An anatomical section that is parallel to the midline.
midsagittal section A sagittal section that divides the brain into two approximately equal halves.
horizontal / axial section (AX-ee-uhl) An anatomical section that divides the brain from top to bottom.

■ **FIGURE 2.2**
Planes of Section
Anatomists use the horizontal, coronal, and sagittal sections to view three-dimensional structures as two-dimensional images.

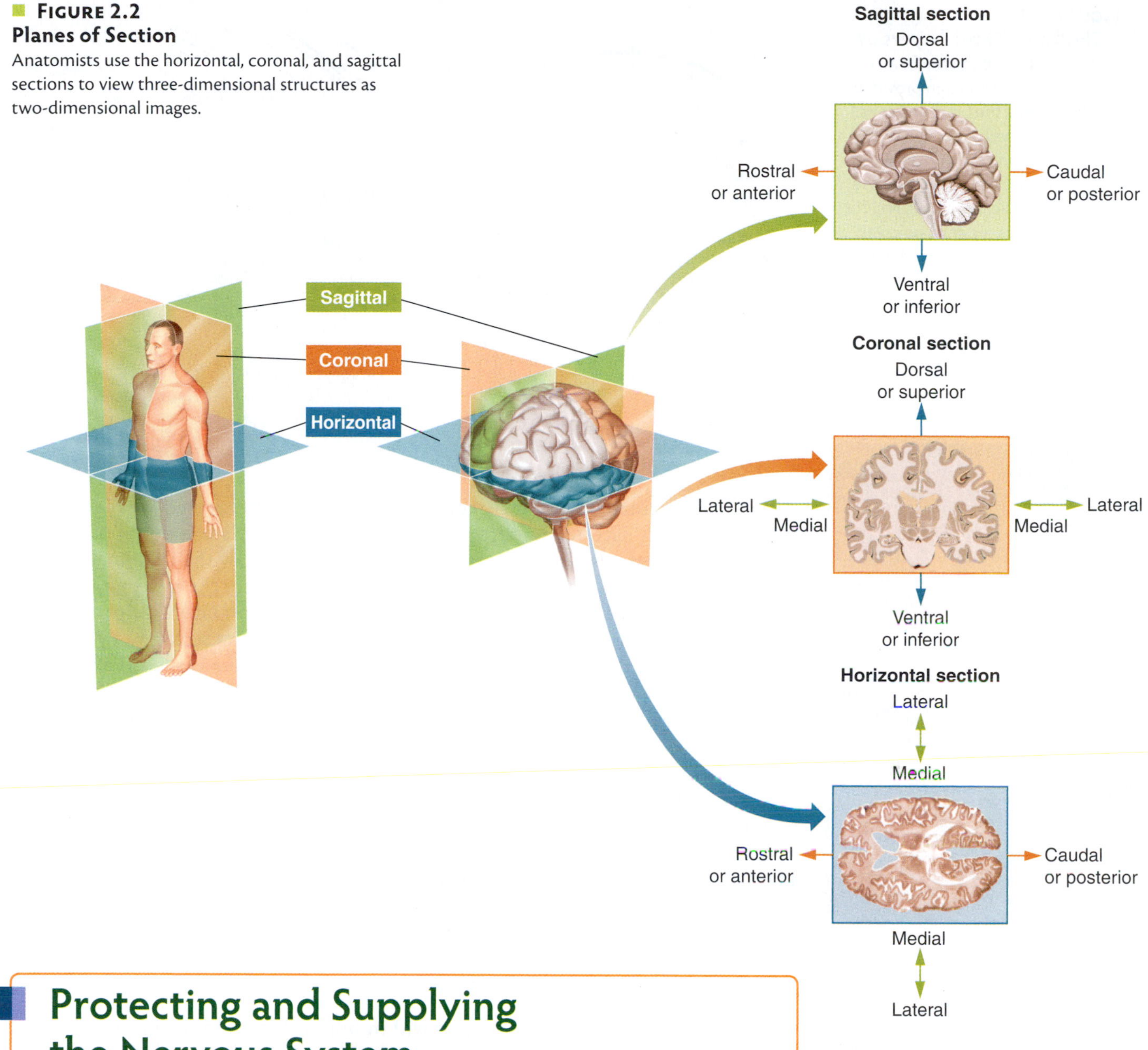

Protecting and Supplying the Nervous System

Because of the obvious importance of the brain, it is one of the most protected organs in your body. The bony skull protects the brain from all but the most serious blows. It is important to note, however, that the skull bones are not fully mature in infants. The infant is born with skull bones that can overlap each other, somewhat like the tectonic plates of the Earth. This design aids the movement of the baby's head through the birth canal. In a young baby with very light or no hair, you can often see a pulse at the top of the head between the skull bones, known as a soft spot, or fontanel. It takes about 18 months for human skull bones to fuse completely.

MENINGES

Although the bones offer the best defense, even the baby with a soft spot enjoys substantial protection of its brain provided by the layers of membranes, or **meninges,** that surround the nervous system.

The three layers of the meninges are illustrated in ■ Figure 2.3. The outermost layer is known as the **dura mater,** which literally means "hard mother" in Latin. Our word *durable* comes from the same root. The reference to "mother"

meninges (meh-NIN-jees) The layers of membranes that cover the central nervous system and the peripheral nerves.

dura mater (DO-ruh MAH-ter) The outermost of the three layers of meninges, found in both the central and peripheral nervous systems.

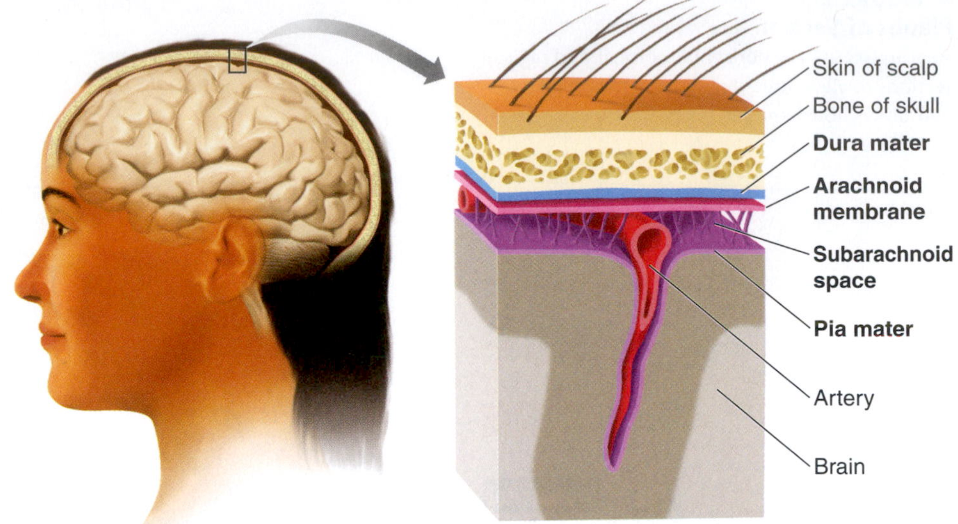

■ **Figure 2.3**
The Skull and Three Layers of Membrane Protect the Brain In addition to the protection provided by the skull bones, the brain and spinal cord are covered with three layers of membranes known as meninges. Going from the skull to the brain, we find the dura mater, the arachnoid layer, and the pia mater. Between the arachnoid and pia mater layers is the subarachnoid space, which contains cerebrospinal fluid. In the peripheral nervous system, only the dura mater and pia mater layers cover the nerves. There is no cerebrospinal fluid in the peripheral nervous system.

might have originated from early comparisons between the protective membranes and the blankets used to swaddle infants. The dura mater is composed of leather-like tissue that follows the outlines of the skull bones. Below the dura mater is the **arachnoid layer.** This more delicate layer gets its name from the fact that its structure looks like a spider's web in cross-section. The innermost layer is the **pia mater,** or "pious mother." This nearly transparent membrane sticks closely to the outside of the brain. Between the arachnoid and pia mater layers is the **subarachnoid space,** with *sub* meaning below. All three of these layers cover the brain and spinal cord. Only the dura mater and pia mater cover nerves that exit the brain and spinal cord. These nerves are referred to as the *peripheral nervous system* (discussed later in this chapter).

When the meninges become infected, the resulting condition is known as **meningitis.** Various viruses and bacteria are responsible for meningitis, which can be a life-threatening disease (see Chapter 15). In ■ Figure 2.4, you can see an example of a brain from a person who died of meningitis. When tumors arise in the tissue of the meninges, they are referred to as *meningiomas,* also discussed in Chapter 15.

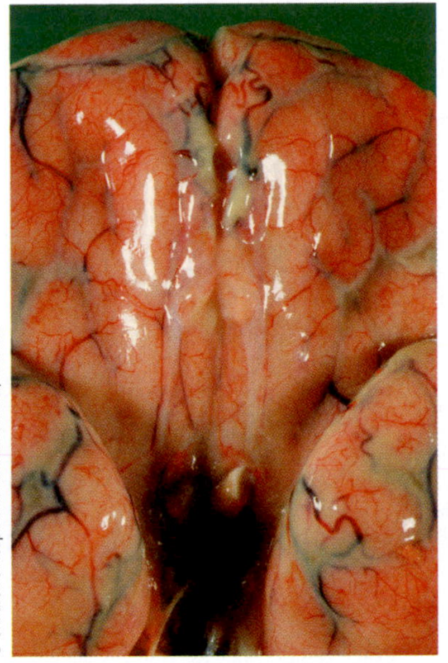

■ **Figure 2.4**
Meningitis Results from Infection of the Meninges Viruses and bacteria can invade the layers of the meninges, causing meningitis. Meningitis causes headache and stiffness of the neck, which can be followed by incoherence, drowsiness, coma, and death. This photo shows a fatal case of meningitis with large areas of pus within the meninges.

Cerebrospinal Fluid

Cerebrospinal fluid (CSF) is secreted within hollow spaces in the brain known as **ventricles.** Within the lining of the ventricles, the **choroid plexus** converts material from the nearby blood supply into cerebrospinal fluid. CSF is very similar in composition to the clear plasma of the blood. Because of its weight and composition, CSF essentially floats the brain within the skull. This has several advantages. If you bump your head, the fluid acts like a cushion to soften the blow to your brain. In addition, neurons respond to appropriate input, not to pressure on the brain. Pressure can often cause neurons to fire in maladaptive ways, such as when a tumor causes seizures by pressing down on a part of the brain. By floating the brain, the cerebrospinal fluid prevents neurons from responding to pressure and providing false information.

CSF circulates through the **central canal** of the spinal cord and four ventricles in the brain: the two lateral ventricles, one in each hemisphere, and the third and fourth ventricles in the brainstem. The fourth ventricle is continuous with the central canal of the spinal cord, which runs the length of the cord at its midline. The ventricles and the circulation of CSF are illustrated in ■ Figure 2.5. Below the fourth ventricle, there is a small opening that allows the CSF to flow into the subarachnoid space that surrounds both the brain and spinal cord. New CSF is made constantly, with the entire supply being turned over about three times per day. The old CSF is reabsorbed into the blood supply at the top of the head.

arachnoid layer (uh-RACK-noid) The middle layer of the meninges covering the central nervous system.
pia mater (PEE-ah MAH-ter) The innermost of the layers of meninges, found in both the central and peripheral nervous systems.
subarachnoid space (sub-uh-RACK-noid) A space filled with cerebrospinal fluid that lies between the arachnoid and pia mater layers of the meninges in the central nervous system.

FIGURE 2.5
Cerebrospinal Fluid Circulates Through the Ventricles, Spinal Cord, and Subarachnoid Space Cerebrospinal fluid (CSF) is produced by the choroid plexus that lines the walls of the ventricles. From the lateral ventricles, the CSF flows through the third and fourth ventricle and into the central canal of the spinal cord. At the base of the cerebellum, CSF exits into the subarachnoid space and is reabsorbed by veins near the top of the head.

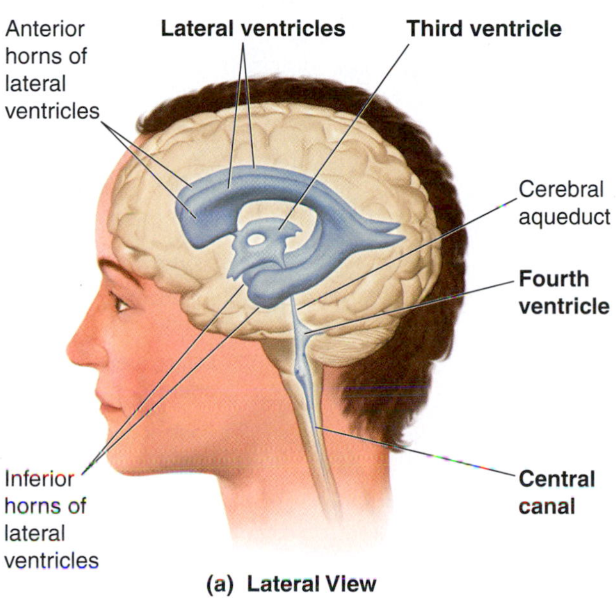

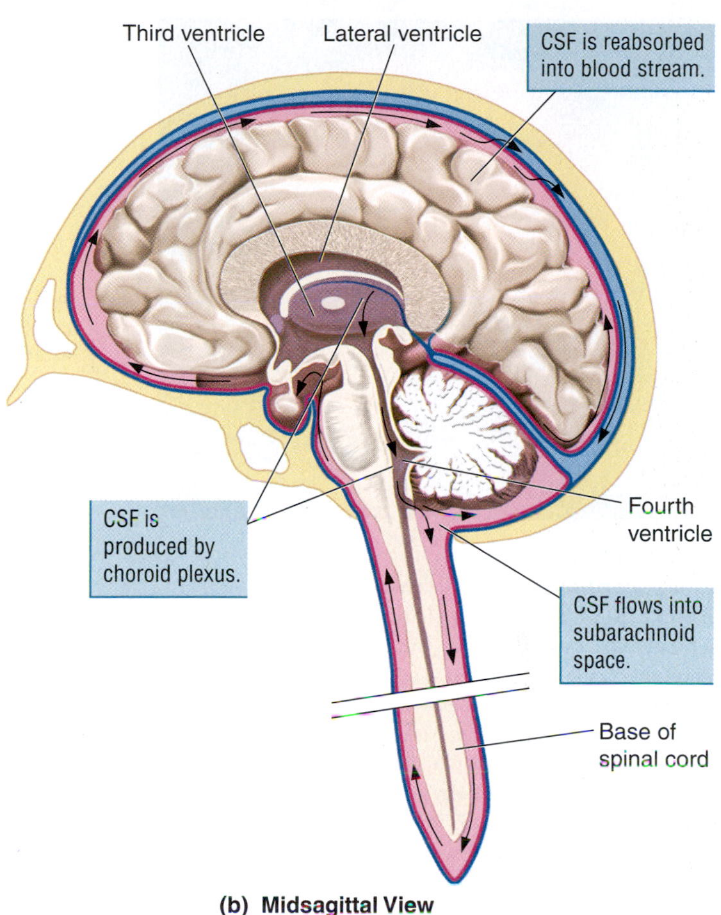

Because there are several narrow sections in this circulation system, blockages sometimes occur. This condition, known as hydrocephalus, is apparent at birth in affected infants, such as the one depicted in Figure 2.6. Hydrocephalus literally means water on the brain. Left untreated, hydrocephalus can cause mental retardation, as the large quantity of CSF prevents the normal growth of the brain. Currently, however, hydrocephalus can be treated by the installation of a shunt to drain off excess fluid. When the baby is old enough, surgery can be used to repair the obstruction. Some adults also experience blockages of the CSF circulatory system. They, too, must be treated with shunts and/or surgery.

CSF moves through a completely self-contained and separate circulation system that never has direct contact with the blood supply. Because the composition of the cerebrospinal fluid is often important in diagnosing diseases, a spinal tap is a common, though extremely unpleasant, procedure. In a spinal tap, the physician withdraws some fluid from the subarachnoid space through a needle.

BLOOD SUPPLY

The brain has enormous energy requirements, so its blood supply is generous. The brain receives its nutrients through the **carotid arteries** on either side of the neck as well as through the **vertebral arteries** that travel up through the back of the skull. Once inside the skull, these major arteries, as shown in Figure 2.7, branch to form the anterior, middle, and posterior cerebral arteries, which serve most of the brain.

Because the brain is unable to store energy, any interruption of the blood supply produces damage very quickly. Significant brain damage occurs less than three minutes after the stopping of a person's heart. Other structures in the body will not be affected so quickly. With life support, other organs are able to continue almost indefinitely. That's why we currently view brain death as our working definition of death.

meningitis (meh-nin-JIE-tis) An infection of the meninges.

cerebrospinal fluid (CSF) (ser-eebroh-SPINE-uhl) The special plasmalike fluid circulating within the ventricles of the brain, the central canal of the spinal cord, and the subarachnoid space.

ventricle One of four hollow spaces within the brain that contain cerebrospinal fluid.

choroid plexus (KOR-oid PLEX-us) The lining of the ventricles, which secretes the cerebrospinal fluid.

central canal The small midline channel in the spinal cord that contains cerebrospinal fluid.

carotid artery (car-AH-tid) One of the two major blood vessels that travel up the sides of the neck to supply the brain.

vertebral artery One of the important blood vessels that enter the brain from the back of the skull.

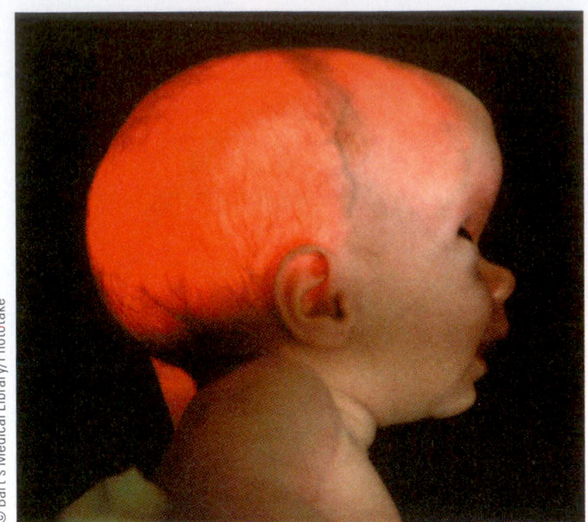

FIGURE 2.6
Hydrocephalus Results from Blockage in the Circulation of Cerebrospinal Fluid This photograph shows a baby born with the condition of hydrocephalus, which results when the normal circulation of cerebrospinal fluid (CSF) is blocked. Note the large size of the baby's head, which has expanded to accommodate all of the CSF. Untreated, hydrocephalus causes mental retardation, but today, shunts installed to drain off the excess fluid can prevent any further damage to the child's brain.

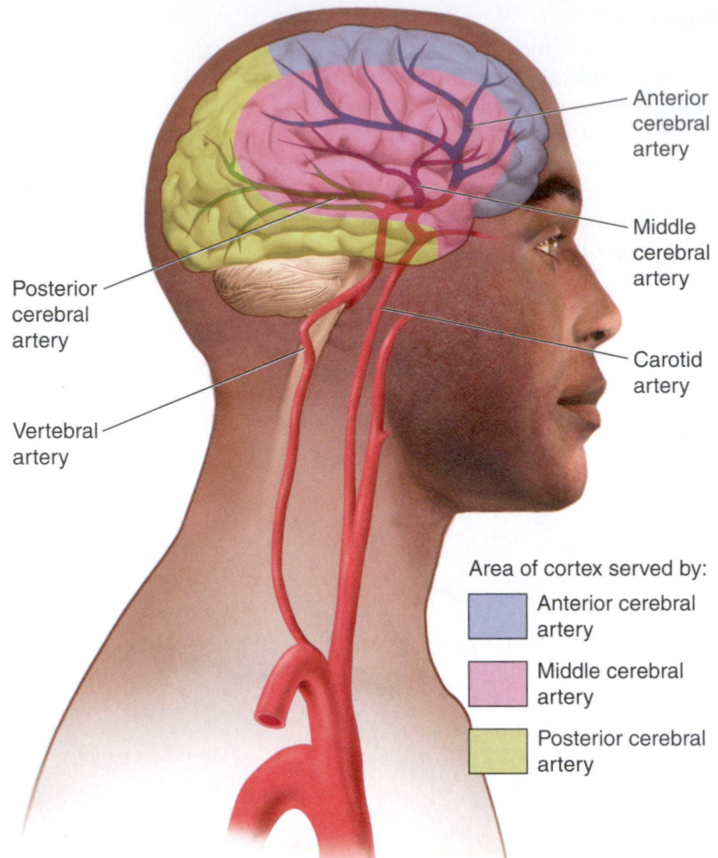

FIGURE 2.7
The Brain Has a Generous Supply of Blood Blood reaches the brain either through the carotid arteries on either side of the neck or through the vertebral arteries entering through the base of the skull. Once in the brain, these arteries branch into the anterior cerebral artery, the middle cerebral artery, and the posterior cerebral artery.

INTERIM SUMMARY 2.1

Summary Points

1. Anatomical directions help us locate structures in the nervous system. In four-legged animals, rostral or anterior structures are located toward the head, caudal or posterior structures are located toward the tail, dorsal or superior structures are located toward the back, and ventral or inferior structures are located toward the belly. In humans, the dorsal parts of our brain form a 90-degree angle with the dorsal parts of the spinal cord. **(LO1)**
2. Ipsilateral structures are on the same side of the midline, and contralateral structures are on opposite sides of the midline. Structures near the midline are medial, and structures away from the midline are lateral. In limbs, proximal structures are closer to the body center, and distal structures are farther away. **(LO1)**
3. Coronal sections divide the brain from front to back. Sagittal sections are parallel to the midline and give us a side view of the brain. Horizontal sections divide the brain from top to bottom. **(LO1)**
4. Three layers of meninges protect the central nervous system: the dura mater, the arachnoid, and the pia mater. Only the dura mater and pia mater layers are present in the peripheral nervous system. Cerebrospinal fluid floats and cushions the brain. Cerebrospinal fluid circulates through the four ventricles of the brain, the central canal of the spinal cord, and the subarachnoid space. **(LO2)**
5. The brain is supplied with blood through the carotid and vertebral arteries. **(LO1)**

Review Questions

1. Which layers of meninges are found in the central and peripheral nervous systems?
2. Why do we have cerebrospinal fluid, and where in the nervous system is it found?

The Central Nervous System

We divide the entire nervous system into two components, the **central nervous system (CNS)** and the **peripheral nervous system (PNS).** The central nervous system includes the brain and **spinal cord.** The peripheral nervous system contains all the nerves that exit the brain and spinal cord, carrying sensory and motor messages to and from the other parts of the body. The tissue of the CNS is encased in bone, but the tissue of the PNS is not. ■ Figure 2.8 summarizes the general organization of the central and peripheral nervous systems.

What we think, we become.
Buddha

Although the neurons in both the CNS and PNS are essentially similar, there are some differences between the two systems. As we saw previously, the CNS is covered by three layers of membranes, whereas the PNS is covered by only two. Cerebrospinal fluid circulates within the layers covering the CNS but not within the PNS. In addition, damage to the CNS is considered permanent, whereas recovery can occur in the PNS.

The Spinal Cord

The spinal cord is a long cylinder of nerve tissue that extends from the medulla, the most caudal structure of the brain, down to the first lumbar vertebra (a bone in the spine, or **vertebral column**). The neurons making up the spinal cord are found in the upper two thirds of the vertebral column. The spinal cord is shorter than the vertebral column because the cord itself stops growing before the bones in the vertebral column do. Running down the center of the spinal cord is the central canal.

As shown in ■ Figure 2.9, the spinal nerves exit between the bones of the vertebral column. The bones are cushioned from one another with disks. If any of these disks

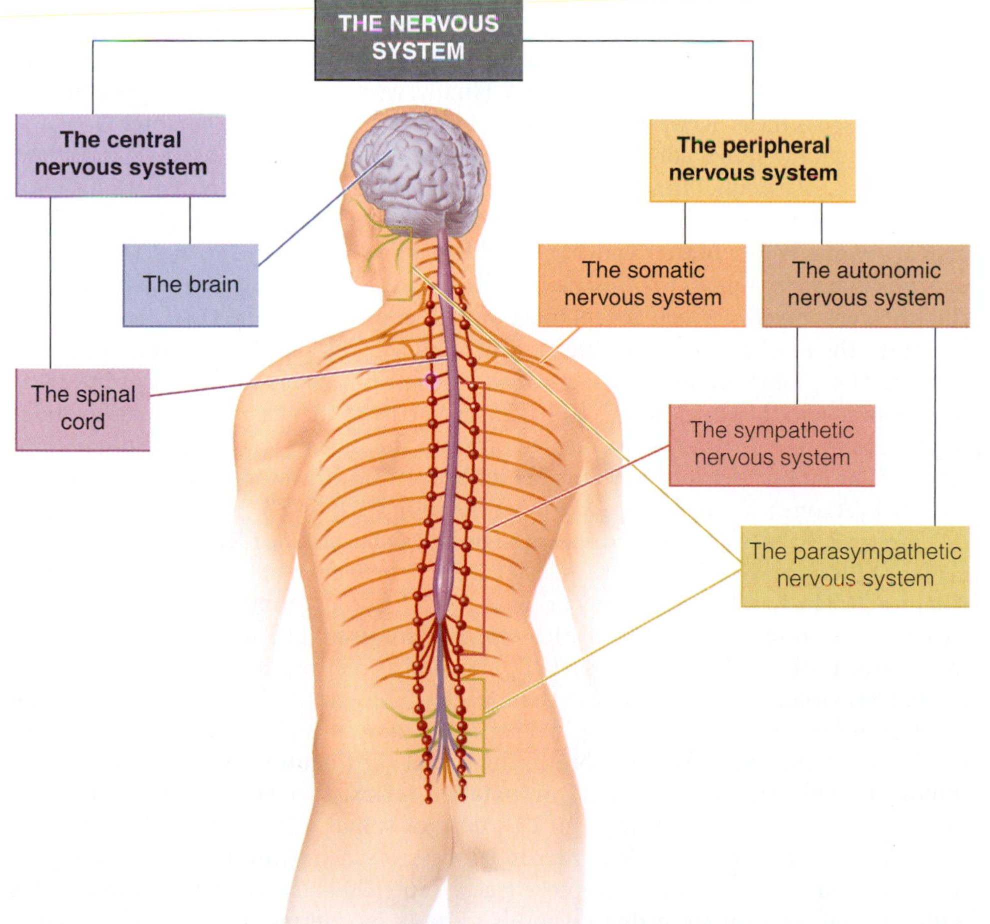

■ **Figure 2.8**
The Organization of the Nervous System The nervous system has two major components, the central nervous system, which includes the brain and spinal cord, and the peripheral nervous system, which contains all the nerves that exit the brain and spinal cord.

central nervous system (CNS) The brain and spinal cord.
peripheral nervous system (PNS) The nerves exiting the brain and spinal cord that serve sensory and motor functions for the rest of the body.
spinal cord A long cylinder of nervous tissue extending from the medulla to the first lumbar vertebra.
vertebral column The bones of the spinal column that protect and enclose the spinal cord.

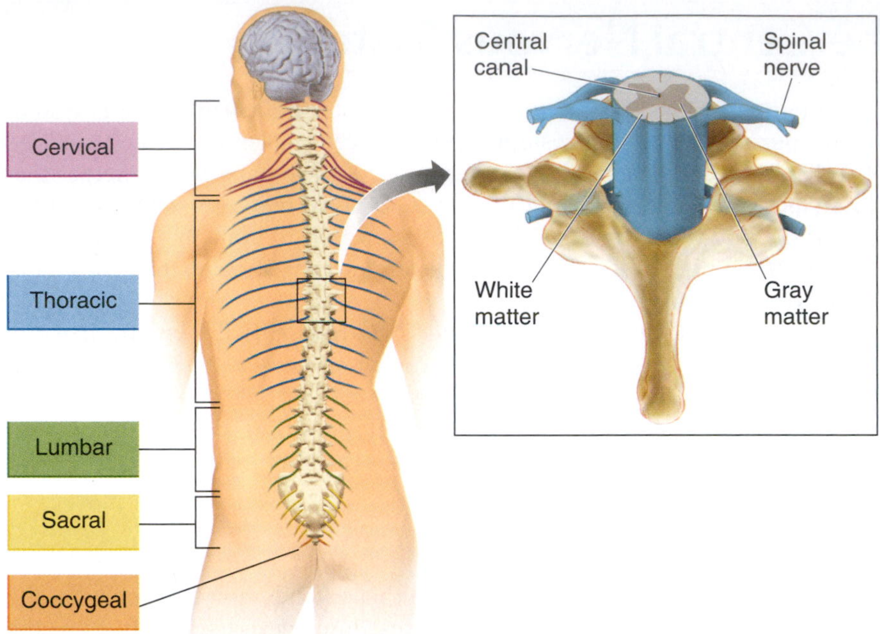

FIGURE 2.9
The Anatomy of the Spinal Cord
The spinal cord is divided into cervical, thoracic, lumbar, sacral, and coccygeal segments. The spinal nerves exit either side of the cord between the surrounding bony vertebrae.

degenerate, pressure is exerted on the adjacent spinal nerves, producing a painful pinched nerve. Based on the points of exit, we divide the spinal cord into 31 segments. Starting closest to the brain, there are eight **cervical nerves** that serve the area of the head, neck, and arms. We refer to the neck brace used after a whiplash injury as a cervical collar. Below the cervical nerves are the 12 **thoracic nerves,** which serve most of the torso. You may have heard the term *thoracic surgeon* used to identify a surgeon who specializes in operations involving the chest, such as heart or lung surgeries. Five **lumbar nerves** come next, serving the lower back and legs. If somebody complains of lower back pain, this means he or she has lumbar problems. The five **sacral nerves** serve the backs of the legs and the genitals. Finally, we have the single **coccygeal nerve.** We will discuss these nerves in greater detail in relation to touch in Chapter 7.

Although the spinal cord weighs only 2 percent as much as the brain, it is responsible for several essential functions. The spinal cord is the original information superhighway. When viewed in a horizontal section, as in Figure 2.9, much of the cord appears white. **White matter** is made up of nerve fibers known as *axons*, the parts of neurons that carry signals to other neurons. The tissue looks white due to a fatty material known as myelin, which covers most human axons. When the tissue is preserved for study, the myelin repels staining and remains white, looking much like the fat on a steak. These large bundles or tracts of axons are responsible for carrying information to and from the brain. Axons from sensory neurons that carry information about touch, position, pain, and temperature travel up the dorsal parts of the spinal cord. Axons from motor neurons, responsible for movement, travel in the ventral parts of the cord. (Axons will be discussed in more detail in Chapter 3.)

Figure 2.9 also shows what appears to be a gray butterfly or letter H shape in the center of the cord. **Gray matter** consists of areas primarily made up of cell bodies (see Chapter 3). The tissue appears gray because the cell bodies absorb some of the chemicals used to preserve the tissue, which stains them gray. The neurons found in the **dorsal horns** of the H receive sensory input, whereas neurons in the **ventral horns** of the H pass motor information on to the muscles. These ventral horn cells participate in either voluntary movement or spinal **reflexes.**

Without any input from the brain, the spinal cord neurons are capable of some important reflexes. The knee jerk, or **patellar reflex,** that your doctor checks by tapping your knee, is an example of one type of spinal reflex. This reflex is managed by only two neurons. One neuron processes sensory information coming to the cord from muscle stretch receptors (see Chapter 8). This neuron communicates with a spinal motor neuron that responds to input by contracting a muscle, causing

cervical nerve (SER-vi-kuhl) One of the first eight spinal nerves that serve the area of the head, neck, and arms.

thoracic nerve (tho-RA-sik) One of twelve pairs of spinal nerves that serve the torso.

lumbar nerve One of the five spinal nerves serving the lower back and legs.

sacral nerve (SAY-kruhl) One of the five spinal nerves that serve the backs of the legs and the genitals.

coccygeal nerve (cock-i-JEE-uhl) The most caudal of the spinal nerves.

white matter An area of neural tissue primarily made up of myelinated axons.

gray matter An area of neural tissue primarily made up of cell bodies.

dorsal horns Gray matter in the spinal cord that contains sensory neurons.

ventral horns Gray matter in the spinal cord that contains motor neurons.

reflex An involuntary action or response.

patellar reflex (puh-TEL-er) The knee-jerk reflex; a spinal reflex in which tapping below the knee produces a reflexive contraction of the quadriceps muscle of the thigh, causing the foot to kick.

your foot to kick. Spinal reflexes also protect us from injury. If you touch something hot or step on something sharp, your spinal cord produces a **withdrawal reflex**. You immediately pull your body away from the source of the pain. This time, three neurons are involved: a sensory neuron, a motor neuron, and an interneuron between them. Because so few neurons are involved, the withdrawal reflex produces very rapid movement. The spinal cord also manages a number of more complex postural reflexes that help us stand and walk. These reflexes allow us to shift our weight automatically from one leg to the other.

Damage to the spinal cord results in loss of sensation (of both the skin and internal organs) and loss of voluntary movement in parts of the body served by nerves located below the damaged area. Some spinal reflexes are usually retained. Muscles can be stimulated, but they are not under voluntary control. A person with cervical damage, such as the late actor Christopher Reeve, is a *quadriplegic* (*quad* meaning "four," indicating loss of control over all four limbs). All sensation and ability to move the arms, legs, and torso are lost. A person with lumbar-level damage is a *paraplegic.* Use of the arms and torso is maintained, but sensation and movement in the lower torso and legs are lost. In all cases of spinal injury, bladder and bowel functions are no longer under voluntary control, as input from the brain to the sphincter muscles does not occur. Currently, spinal damage is considered permanent, but significant progress is being made in repairing the spinal cord (see Chapters 5 and 15).

The Hindbrain

We will begin our exploration of the brain with the hindbrain, which is located just above the spinal cord. Early in embryological development, the brain divides into three parts: the **hindbrain, midbrain** (or **mesencephalon**), and **forebrain.** Together, the hindbrain and midbrain make up the **brainstem.** You can observe the relationship between the brainstem and forebrain in ■ Figure 2.10. Later in embryological development, the midbrain makes no further divisions, but the hindbrain divides into the **myelencephalon,** or **medulla,** and the **metencephalon.** *Cephalon,* by the way, refers to the head.

The Myelencephalon (Medulla)

The gradual swelling of tissue above the cervical spinal cord marks the most caudal portion of the brain, the myelencephalon, or medulla. The medulla, like the spinal cord, contains large quantities of white matter. The vast majority of all information passing to and from higher structures of the brain must still pass through the medulla.

Instead of the butterfly appearance of the gray matter in the spinal cord, the medulla contains a number of **nuclei,** or collections of cell bodies with a shared function. These nuclei are suspended within the white matter of the medulla. Some of these nuclei contain cell bodies whose axons make up several of the cranial nerves serving the head and neck area. Other nuclei manage essential functions such as breathing, heart rate, and blood pressure. Damage to the medulla is typically fatal due to its control over these vital functions.

Along the midline of the upper medulla, we see the caudal portion of a structure known as the **reticular formation.** The reticular formation, shown in Figure 2.10, is a complex collection of nuclei that runs along the midline of the brainstem from the medulla up into the midbrain. The structure gets its name from the Latin *reticulum,* or network. The reticular formation plays an important role in the regulation of sleep and arousal (see Chapter 11).

The Metencephalon

The metencephalon contains two major structures, the **pons** and the **cerebellum.** The pons, which also appears in Figure 2.10, lies immediately rostral to the medulla. *Pons* means "bridge" in Latin, and one of the roles of the pons is to form connections between the medulla and higher brain centers as well as with the cerebellum.

As in the medulla, large fiber pathways with embedded nuclei are found in the pons. Among the important nuclei found at this level of the brainstem are the **cochlear nucleus** and the **vestibular nucleus.** The fibers communicating with these

withdrawal reflex A spinal reflex that pulls a body part away from a source of pain.

hindbrain The most caudal division of the brain, including the medulla, pons, and cerebellum.

midbrain The division of the brain lying between the hindbrain and forebrain.

forebrain The division of the brain containing the diencephalon and the telencephalon.

brainstem The lower two thirds of the brain, including the hindbrain and midbrain.

myelencephalon / medulla (my-len-SEF-ah-lon, muh-DOO-luh) The most caudal part of the hindbrain.

metencephalon (met-en-SEF-uh-lon) The division of the hindbrain containing the pons and cerebellum.

nuclei Collections of cell bodies that share a function.

reticular formation (reh-TIK-you-ler) A collection of brainstem nuclei, located near the midline from the rostral medulla up into the midbrain, that regulate sleep and arousal.

pons A structure located in the metencephalon between the medulla and midbrain; part of the brainstem located in the hindbrain.

cerebellum (sair-uh-BELL-um) A structure located in the metencephalon that participates in balance, muscle tone, muscle coordination, some types of learning, and possibly higher cognitive functions in humans.

cochlear nucleus (KOKE-lee-er) A nucleus found in the pons that receives information about sound from the inner ear.

vestibular nucleus (ves-TIB-you-lar) A group of cell bodies in the pons that receive input about the location and movement of the head from sensory structures in the inner ear.

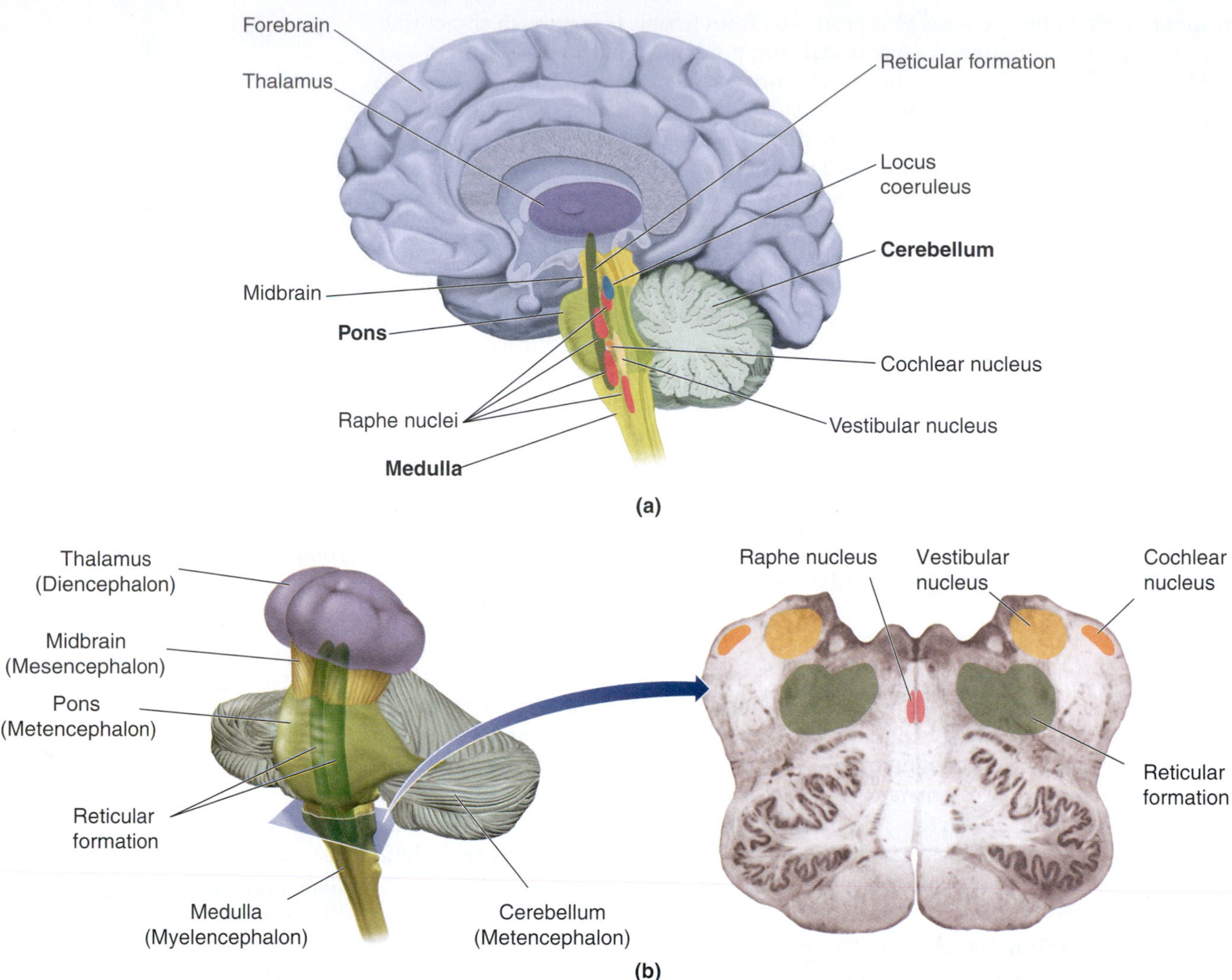

FIGURE 2.10
Structures of the Brainstem (a) This sagittal section displays many of the important structures found in the brainstem. (b) Wih the cerebral hemispheres removed, we can see spatial relationships between the major structures of the brainstem. The key-to-slice allows us to view a horizontal section of the medulla and several of the important structures found at this level of the brain.

nuclei arise in the inner ear (see Chapter 7). The cochlear nucleus receives information about sound, and the vestibular nucleus receives information about the position and movement of the head. This vestibular input helps us keep our balance (or makes us feel motion sickness on occasion).

The reticular formation, which begins in the medulla, extends through the pons and on into the midbrain. The pons contains a number of other important nuclei that have wide-ranging effects on the activity of the rest of the brain. Nuclei located within the pons are necessary for the production of rapid-eye-movement (REM) sleep, which is discussed in greater detail in Chapter 11. The **raphe nuclei** and the **locus coeruleus** project widely to the rest of the brain and influence mood, states of arousal, and sleep.

The second major part of the metencephalon, the cerebellum, is also shown in Figure 2.10. The cerebellum looks almost like a second little brain attached to the dorsal surface of the brainstem. Its name, *cerebellum,* actually means "little brain" in Latin. The use of "little" is misleading because the cerebellum actually contains more nerve cells (neurons) than the rest of the brain combined. When viewed with a sagittal section, the internal structure of the cerebellum resembles a tree. White matter, or axons, forms the trunk and branches, while gray matter, or cell bodies, forms the leaves.

raphe nuclei (RAH-fay) Nuclei located in the pons that participate in the regulation of sleep and arousal.

locus coeruleus (LOW-kuss se-ROOlee-us) A structure in the pons that participates in arousal.

The traditional view of the cerebellum emphasizes its role in coordinating voluntary movements, maintaining muscle tone, and regulating balance. Input from the spinal cord tells the cerebellum about the current location of the body in three-dimensional space. Input from the cerebral cortex, by way of the pons, tells the cerebellum about the movements you intend to make. The cerebellum then processes the sequences and timing of muscle movements required to carry out the plan.

Considerable data support this role for the cerebellum in movement. Damage to the cerebellum affects skilled movements, including speech production. Because the cerebellum is one of the first structures affected by the consumption of alcohol, most sobriety tests, such as walking a straight line or pointing in a particular direction, are actually tests of cerebellar function. Along with the previously mentioned vestibular system, the cerebellum contributes to the experience of motion sickness.

More contemporary views see the cerebellum as responsible for much more than balance and motor coordination. In spite of its lowly position in the hindbrain, the cerebellum is involved in some of our more sophisticated processing of information. In the course of evolution, the size of the cerebellum has kept pace with increases in the size of the cerebral cortex. One of the embedded nuclei of the cerebellum, the dentate nucleus, has become particularly large in monkeys and humans. A part of the dentate nucleus, known as the neodentate, is found only in humans. In addition to language difficulties, patients with cerebellar damage also experience subtle deficits in cognition and perception. As we will see in Chapter 12, the cerebellum also participates in learning (Albus, 1971; Marr, 1969). In cases of autism, a disorder in which language, cognition, and social awareness are severely afflicted, the most reliable anatomical marker is an abnormal cerebellum (Courchesne, 1997). Although neuroscientists do not agree on its exact function, most theories propose a cerebellum that can use past experience to make corrections and automate behaviors, whether they involve motor systems or not.

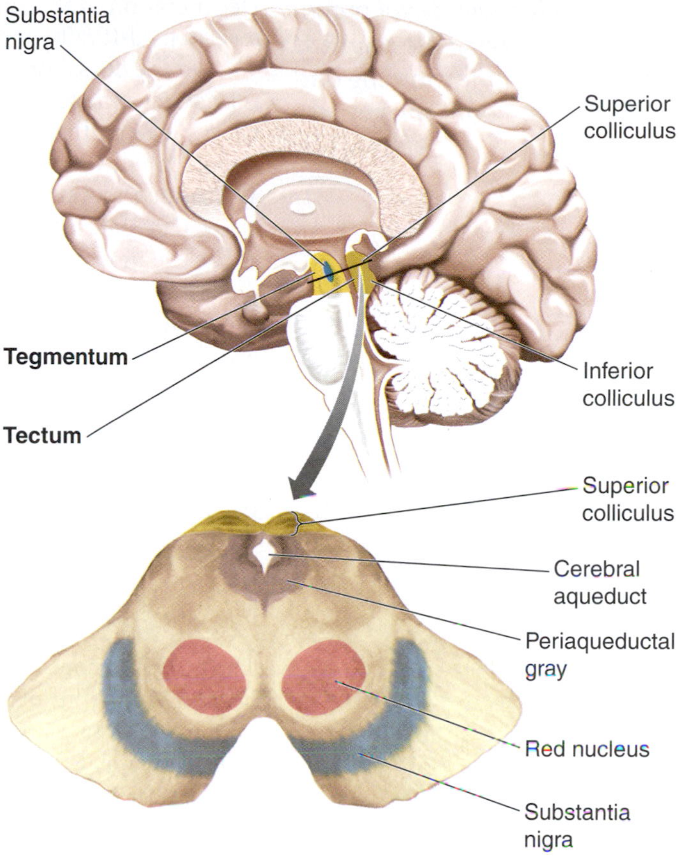

FIGURE 2.11
The Internal Structure of the Midbrain Important structures in the midbrain include the superior colliculi, the cerebral aqueduct, the periaqueductal gray, the substantia nigra, and the red nucleus.

THE MIDBRAIN

The midbrain, or **mesencephalon,** shown in Figure 2.11, has a dorsal or top half known as the **tectum,** or "roof," and a ventral, or bottom half, known as the **tegmentum,** or "covering." In the midbrain, cerebrospinal fluid is contained in a small channel at the midline known as the **cerebral aqueduct.** The cerebral aqueduct separates the tectum from the tegmentum and links the third and fourth ventricles.

Although the midbrain is relatively small compared with the other portions of the brainstem, it still contains a complex array of nuclei. Surrounding the cerebral aqueduct are cell bodies known as **periaqueductal gray** (*peri* means around). Periaqueductal gray appears to play an important role in our perception of pain, discussed more fully in Chapter 7. There are large numbers of receptors in the periaqueductal gray that respond to opiates such as morphine and heroin. Electrical stimulation of this area provides considerable relief from pain.

The midbrain also contains the most rostral portion of the reticular formation and a number of nuclei associated with cranial nerves. Several important motor nuclei are also found at this level of the brainstem, including the **red nucleus** and the **substantia nigra.** The red nucleus, which is located within the reticular formation, communicates motor information between the spinal cord and the cerebellum. The substantia nigra, whose name literally means "black stuff" due to the pigmentation of the structure, is closely connected with the basal ganglia of the forebrain (see the next section).

mesencephalon Another term for midbrain, the division of the brain lying between the hindbrain and forebrain.

tectum The "roof," or dorsal half, of the midbrain.

tegmentum (teg-MEN-tum) The "covering," or ventral half of the midbrain.

cerebral aqueduct (ser-EE-bruhl AHkwi-dukt) The small channel running along the midline of the midbrain that connects the third and fourth ventricles.

periaqueductal gray (pear-ee-AHkweh-duk-tuhl) Gray matter surrounding the cerebral aqueduct of the midbrain that is believed to play a role in the sensation of pain.

The brain is a wonderful organ; it starts working the moment you get up in the morning and does not stop until you get into the office.
Robert Frost

Degeneration of the substantia nigra occurs in Parkinson's disease, which is characterized by difficulty moving.

On the dorsal surface of the midbrain are four prominent bumps. The upper pair is known as the **superior colliculi.** The superior colliculi receive input from the optic nerves leaving the eye. Although the colliculi are part of the visual system, they are unable to tell you what you're seeing. Instead, these structures allow us to make visually guided movements, such as pointing in the direction of a visual stimulus. They also participate in a variety of visual reflexes, including changing the size of the pupils of the eye in response to light conditions (see Chapter 6).

The other pair of bumps is known as the **inferior colliculi.** These structures are involved with hearing, or audition. The inferior colliculi are one stop along the pathway from the ear to the auditory cortex. These structures are involved with auditory reflexes such as turning the head in the direction of a loud noise. The inferior colliculi also appear to participate in the localization of sounds in the environment by comparing the timing of the arrival of sounds at the two ears (see Chapter 7).

Before proceeding to the discussion of the forebrain, you may want to review the important structures and functions of the brainstem that are summarized in Table 2.1.

The Forebrain

The forebrain contains the most advanced and most recently evolved structures of the brain. Like the hindbrain, the forebrain divides again later in embryological development. The two resulting divisions are the **diencephalon** and the **telencephalon.** The diencephalon contains the thalamus and hypothalamus, which are located at the midline just above the mesencephalon or midbrain. The telencephalon contains the bulk of the symmetrical left and right **cerebral hemispheres.**

The Thalamus and Hypothalamus The diencephalon, depicted in Figure 2.12, is located at the rostral end of the brainstem. The upper portion of the diencephalon consists of the **thalamus.** We actually have two thalamic nuclei, one on either side of

red nucleus A structure located within the reticular formation that communicates motor information between the spinal cord and the cerebellum.
substantia nigra (sub-STAN-shuh NIE-gruh) Midbrain nuclei that communicate with the basal ganglia of the forebrain.
superior colliculi (kohl-IK-you-lee) A pair of bumps on the dorsal surface of the midbrain that coordinate visually guided movements and visual reflexes.
inferior colliculi A pair of bumps on the dorsal surface of the midbrain that process auditory information.
diencephalon (die-en-SEF-uh-lon) A division of the forebrain made up of the hypothalamus and the thalamus.
telencephalon (tee-len-SEF-uh-lon) The division of the brain comprising the cerebral hemispheres.
cerebral hemisphere One of the two large, globular structures that make up the telencephalon of the forebrain.
thalamus (THAL-uh-mus) A structure in the diencephalon that processes sensory information, contributes to states of arousal, and participates in learning and memory.

TABLE 2.1 Some Important Structures in the Brainstem

Brainstem Location	Important Structures	Functions
Medulla	Reticular formation Cranial nerve nuclei	Arousal Various
Pons	Reticular formation (continuing) Cranial nerve nuclei Cochlear nucleus Vestibular nucleus Raphe nucleus Locus coeruleus	Arousal Various Audition Balance, position Sleep and arousal Sleep and arousal
Cerebellum		Balance, motor coordination, cognition
Midbrain	Reticular formation (continuing) Cranial nerve nuclei Periaqueductal gray Red nucleus Substantia nigra Superior colliculi Inferior colliculi	Arousal Various Pain Motor Motor Vision Audition

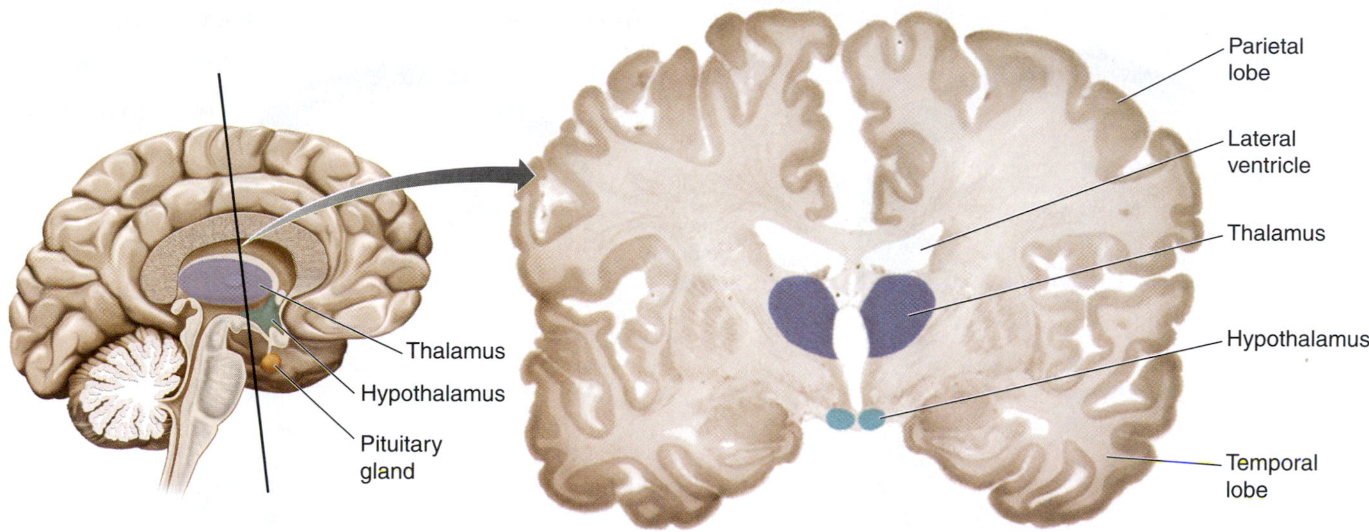

FIGURE 2.12
The Thalamus and Hypothalamus of the Diencephalon

the midline. These structures appear to be just about in the middle of the brain, as viewed in a midsagittal section. Inputs from most of our sensory systems converge on the thalamus, which then forwards the information on to the cerebral cortex for further processing. It appears that the thalamus does not change the nature of the sensory information, so much as it filters the information passed along to the cortex, depending on the organism's state of arousal (Alexander et al., 2006). The cerebral cortex, in turn, forms large numbers of connections with the thalamus. The exact purpose of this cortical input to the thalamus remains a mystery. In addition to its role in sensation, the thalamus is also involved with states of arousal and consciousness (see Chapter 11). Damage to the thalamus typically results in coma, and disturbances in circuits linking the thalamus and cerebral cortex are involved in some seizures (see Chapter 15). The thalamus has also been implicated in learning and memory (see Chapter 12).

Just below the thalamus is the **hypothalamus.** The name *hypothalamus* literally means "below the thalamus." The hypothalamus is a major regulatory center for such behaviors as eating, drinking, sex, biorhythms, and temperature control. Rather than being a single, homogeneous structure, the hypothalamus is a collection of nuclei. For example, the aforementioned *ventromedial nucleus of the hypothalamus (VMH)* participates in the regulation of feeding behavior. The *suprachiasmatic nucleus* receives input from the optic nerve and helps set daily rhythms according to the rising of the sun. The hypothalamus is directly connected to the **pituitary gland,** from which many important hormones are released (see Chapter 10). Finally, the hypothalamus directs the autonomic nervous system, the portion of the peripheral nervous system that controls our glands and organs.

The Basal Ganglia Several nuclei make up the **basal ganglia,** which participate in motor control. A ganglion (*ganglia* is plural) is a general term for a collection of cell bodies. These nuclei, illustrated in Figure 2.13, include the **caudate nucleus,** the **putamen,** the **globus pallidus,** and the **subthalamic nucleus** (which gets its name from its location "sub," or below, the thalamus). Because these structures are so closely connected with the substantia nigra of the midbrain, some anatomists include the substantia nigra as part of the basal ganglia. Also associated with the basal ganglia is the nucleus accumbens, which plays an important role in the experience of reward.

The basal ganglia are an important part of our motor system. Degeneration of the basal ganglia, which occurs in Parkinson's disease and in Huntington's disease, produces characteristic disorders of movement. The basal ganglia have also been implicated

hypothalamus (hie-po-THAL-uh-mus) A structure found in the diencephalon that participates in the regulation of hunger, thirst, sexual behavior, and aggression; part of the limbic system.

pituitary gland (pi-TOO-i-tare-ee) A gland located just above the roof of the mouth that is connected to the hypothalamus and serves as a major source of hormones.

basal ganglia (BAZE-uhl GANG-leeuh) A collection of nuclei within the cerebral hemispheres that participate in the control of movement.

caudate nucleus (KAW-date) One of the major nuclei that make up the basal ganglia.

putamen (pew-TAY-muhn) One of the nuclei contained in the basal ganglia.

globus pallidus (GLOW-bus PAL-i-dus) One of the nuclei making up the basal ganglia.

subthalamic nucleus (SUB-thal-AM-mic) A small nucleus, located ventral to the thalamus, that is part of the basal ganglia.

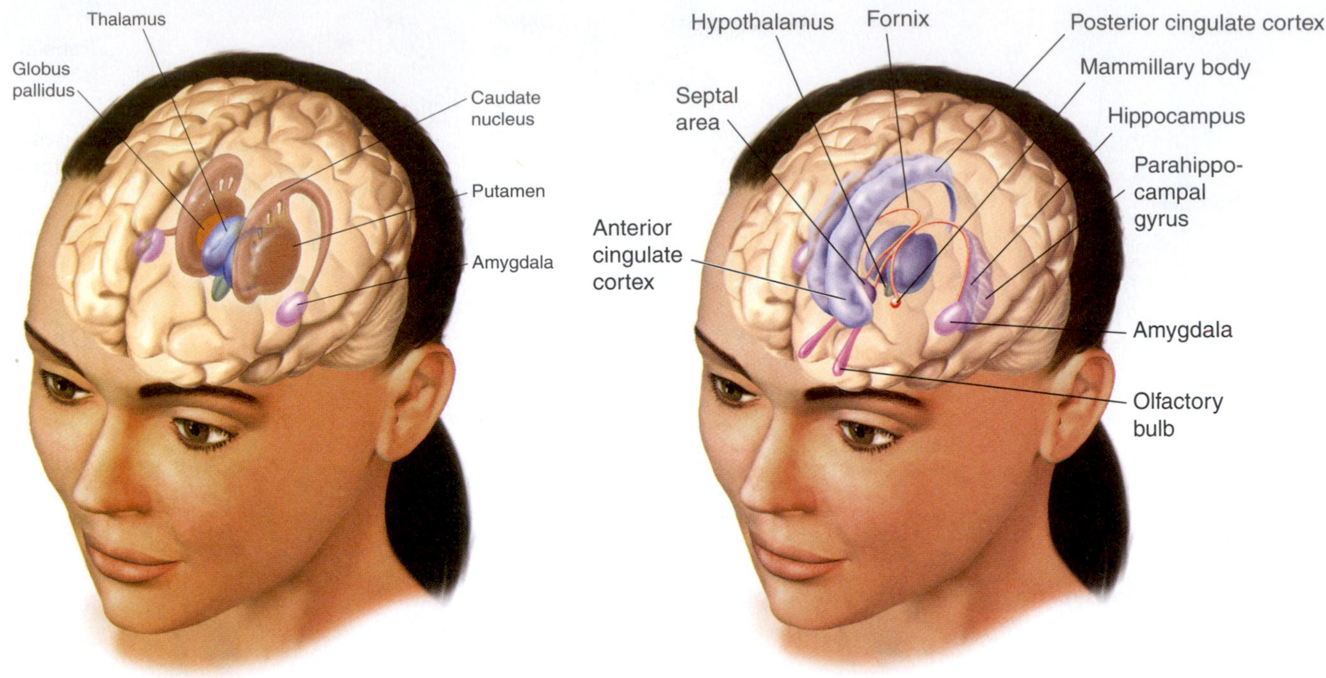

■ **Figure 2.13**
The Basal Ganglia Are Located Deep Within the Cerebral Hemispheres The basal ganglia, including the caudate nucleus, putamen, globus pallidus, and subthalamic nucleus, are found in the forebrain. Many anatomists include the substantia nigra of the midbrain as part of the basal ganglia due to their tight connections.

■ **Figure 2.14**
The Limbic System Participates in Learning and Emotion A number of closely connected forebrain structures are included in the limbic system, which participates in many emotional, learning, and motivational behaviors.

in a number of psychological disorders, including attention deficit/hyperactivity disorder (ADHD) and obsessive-compulsive disorder (OCD; see Chapter 16).

The Limbic System Different anatomists propose different sets of forebrain structures for inclusion in the **limbic system,** illustrated in ■ Figure 2.14. *Limbic* means border and describes the location of these structures on the margins of the cerebral cortex.

I not only use all the brains I have, but all I can borrow.
Woodrow Wilson

The **hippocampus,** named after the Greek word for "seahorse," curves around within the cerebral hemispheres from close to the midline out to the tip of the temporal lobe. The hippocampus participates in learning and memory. Damage to the hippocampus in both hemispheres produces a syndrome known as *anterograde amnesia* (see Chapter 12). People with this type of memory loss have difficulty forming new long-term declarative memories, which are memories for facts, language, and personal experience. In studies of patients with hippocampal damage, it was found that memories formed prior to the damage remained relatively intact; however, the patients were able to learn and remember procedures for solving a puzzle requiring multiple steps, like the Tower of Hanoi (see Chapter 12).

The **amygdala** plays important roles in fear, rage, and aggression (see Chapter 14). In addition, the amygdala interacts with the hippocampus during the encoding and storage of emotional memories (Phelps, 2004). Damage to the amygdala specifically interferes with an organism's ability to respond appropriately to dangerous situations. In laboratory studies, rats with damaged amygdalas were unable to learn to fear tones that reliably predicted electric shock (LeDoux, 2000). Rhesus monkeys with damaged amygdalas were overly friendly with unfamiliar monkeys, a potentially dangerous way to behave in a species that enforces strict social hierarchies (Emery et al., 2001). Stimuli that normally elicit fear in monkeys, such as rubber snakes or unfamiliar humans, failed to do so in monkeys with lesions in their amygdalas (Mason et al., 2006). In humans, autism, which produces either extreme and inappropriate fear and

limbic system (LIM-bik) A collection of forebrain structures that participate in emotional behavior and learning.
hippocampus (hip-oh-KAMP-us) A structure deep within the cerebral hemispheres that is involved with the formation of long-term declarative memories; part of the limbic system.
amygdala (uh-MIG-duh-luh) An almond-shaped structure in the rostral temporal lobes that is part of the limbic system.

anxiety or a complete lack of fear, might involve abnormalities of the amygdala (see Chapter 16).

In very rare cases, abnormalities affecting the amygdala result in irrational violence. Charles Whitman (■ Figure 2.15), the sniper who killed 15 people and wounded 31 from the clock tower at the University of Texas, Austin, in 1966, had a cancerous tumor that was pressing against his amygdala. In a case described by Mark and Ervin (1970), a woman experiencing a seizure originating in her amygdala stabbed another person for simply brushing against her on the way out of a restroom. The controversial solution suggested by these researchers, and agreed to by the woman, was the lesioning of the woman's amygdala, which seemed to reduce her violent behavior. Nonetheless, most cases of human violence are extremely complex, and the number of violent acts resulting from abnormalities of the amygdala is quite small.

Although located in the diencephalon, the hypothalamus is often included in the limbic system. We are obviously emotional when it comes to eating, drinking, and sex. The hypothalamus also produces our so-called fight-or-flight response to emergencies. Electrical stimulation to parts of the hypothalamus can produce pleasure, rage, and fear as well as predatory behavior.

■ **FIGURE 2.15**
Amygdala Abnormalities Can Lead to Irrational Violence
In very rare cases, abnormalities of the amygdala are correlated with uncharacteristic, totally irrational violence. Charles Whitman, who led a previously unremarkable life, killed several family members and then climbed a clock tower at the University of Texas, Austin in 1966. He methodically opened fire on the people below, killing 15 and injuring 31. Whitman, who was killed by police, was later found to have a tumor pressing on his amygdala.

The **cingulate cortex** is a fold of cortical tissue on the inner surface of the cerebral hemispheres. "Cingulum" means "belt" in Latin. The cingulate cortex contains an unusual and possibly recently evolved class of nerve cells known as *Von Economo neurons* (see Chapter 3). Von Economo neurons are found only in the great apes and humans and might, therefore, have considerable significance for the recent evolution of intelligent behavior (Nimchinsky, 1999).

The cingulate cortex is further divided into anterior and posterior sections. The anterior cingulate cortex (ACC) exerts some influence over autonomic functions but has received the greatest attention from neuroscientists for its apparent roles in decision-making, error detection, emotion, anticipation of reward, and empathy. For example, Taylor and her colleagues (2006) found greater ACC activation when participants believed they had lost money while performing a decision task. In addition, the ACC processes information about pain (see Chapter 7). Not only does the ACC respond to physical pain, but it also participates in social pain, such as the negative feelings associated with being socially excluded by others. Naomi Eisenberger and her colleagues (2003) observed the brain activity of participants who were led to believe that they were being left out of a game being played by other participants. These feelings of exclusion experienced by the left-out participants activated the same areas of the cingulate cortex that are normally active when we feel physical pain. This result might reflect the evolution of the physical pain system to manage more complex human social interactions. The posterior cingulate cortex (PCC) participates in a variety of functions, including eye movements, spatial orientation, and memory (Vogt, Finch, & Olson, 1992). The PCC is one of the first structures in the brain to be affected by Alzheimer's disease (Valla, Berndt, & Gonzalez-Lima, 2001).

The **septal area** is located anterior to the thalamus and hypothalamus. Electrical stimulation of this area is usually experienced as pleasurable, whereas lesions in this area produce uncontrollable rage and attack behaviors. On one unforgettable occasion, a rat with a septal lesion jumped at my face when I leaned over to pick it up (my apologies to those of you who are phobic about rodents).

Other structures often included in the limbic system are the **olfactory bulbs,** which are located at the base of the forebrain. These structures receive and process

cingulate cortex (SING-you-let) A segment of older cortex just dorsal to the corpus callosum that is part of the limbic system.

septal area An area anterior to the thalamus and hypothalamus that is often included as part of the limbic system.

olfactory bulb (ole-FAC-to-ree) A structure extending from the ventral surface of the brain that processes the sense of smell; part of the limbic system.

I must have a prodigious quantity of mind; it takes me as much as a week sometimes, to make it up.
Mark Twain

information about smell. If our sense of smell were not at all emotional, the perfume industry would probably go out of business. The **parahippocampal gyrus,** a fold of tissue near the hippocampus, the **mammillary bodies** of the diencephalon, and the **fornix,** a fiber pathway connecting the mammillary bodies and the hippocampus, are also included in many descriptions of the limbic system. These diverse structures are actually tightly connected with one another and participate in memory processes. The structures included in the limbic system and their general functions are summarized in Table 2.2.

The Cortex The outer covering of the cerebral hemispheres is known as the cortex, from the Latin word for "bark." Like the bark of a tree, the cerebral cortex is a thin layer of gray matter that varies from 1.5 mm to 4 mm in thickness in different parts of the brain. Unlike the spinal cord, the cerebral hemispheres are organized with gray matter on the outside and white matter on the inside. Below the thin layers of cortical cell bodies are vast fiber pathways that connect the cortex with the rest of the nervous system.

The cerebral cortex has a wrinkled appearance somewhat like the outside of a walnut. The hills of the cortex are referred to as **gyri** (plural of *gyrus*), and the valleys are known as **sulci** (plural of *sulcus*). A particularly large sulcus is usually called a **fissure.** Why is the cerebral cortex so wrinkled? This feature of the cortex provides more surface area for cortical cells. We have limited space within the skull for brain tissue, and the wrinkled surface of the cortex allows us to pack in more neurons than we could otherwise. If stretched out flat, the human cortex would cover an area of about 2½ square feet. Just as we ball up a piece of paper to save space in our wastebasket, the sulci and gyri of the brain allow us to fit more tissue into our heads. The degree of wrinkling, or convolution, is related to how advanced a species is. As shown in ■ Figure 2.16, our brains are much more convoluted than a sheep's brain, for instance, and the sheep's brain is more convoluted than a rat's brain.

The cells of the cerebral cortex are organized in layers. The number, organization, and size of the layers vary somewhat throughout the cortex. In most parts

parahippocampal gyrus (pear-uh-hip-oh-KAMP-uhl JIE-rus) A fold of tissue near the hippocampus that is often included in the limbic system.
mammillary body (MAM-i-laree) One of two bumps on the ventral surface of the brain that participate in memory and are included in the limbic system.
fornix (FOR-nix) A fiber pathway connecting the hippocampus and mammillary bodies that is often included in the limbic system.
gyrus/gyri (JIE-rus/JIE-ree) One of the "hills" on the convoluted surface of the cerebral cortex.
sulcus/sulci (SULL-kuss/SULL-sie) A "valley" in the convoluted surface of the cerebral cortex.
fissure A large sulcus.
granule cell (GRAN-yule) A small type of cell found in layers II and IV of the cerebral cortex.
pyramidal cell (per-AM-i-duhl) A large, triangular cell found in layers III and V of the cerebral cortex.

TABLE 2.2 Structures of the Limbic System

Structure	Function
Hippocampus	Declarative memory formation
Amygdala	Fear, aggression, memory
Hypothalamus	Aggression; regulation of hunger, thirst, sex, temperature, circadian rhythms, hormones
Anterior cingulate cortex	Decision making, error detection, emotion, anticipation of reward, pain, and empathy
Posterior cingulate cortex	Eye movements, spatial orientation, and memory
Septal area	Reward
Olfactory bulbs	Olfaction (smell)
Parahippocampal gyrus	Memory
Mammillary bodies	Part of the hypothalamus; memory
Fornix	Connects the hippocampus to mammillary bodies and other parts of the brain

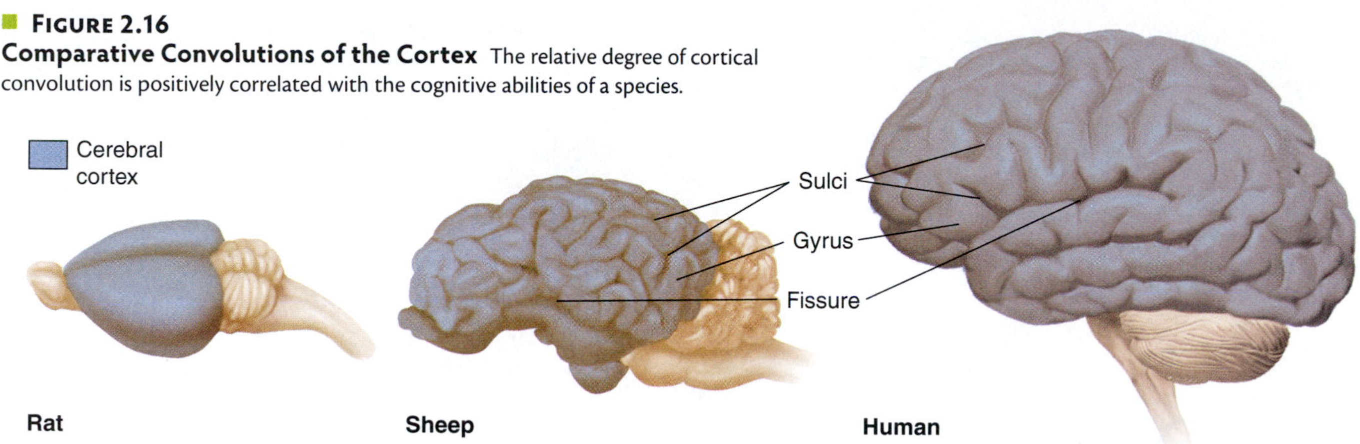

FIGURE 2.16
Comparative Convolutions of the Cortex The relative degree of cortical convolution is positively correlated with the cognitive abilities of a species.

FIGURE 2.17
The Layers of the Cerebral Cortex The cerebral cortex covers the outer surface of the brain. Six distinct layers are apparent in most areas of the cortex. Three different views of these layers are shown here. The Golgi stain highlights entire neurons, and the Nissl stain highlights cell bodies. Note the large pyramidal cells shown by the Nissl stain in layer V. The Weigert stain highlights pathways formed by myelinated axons through the cortex.

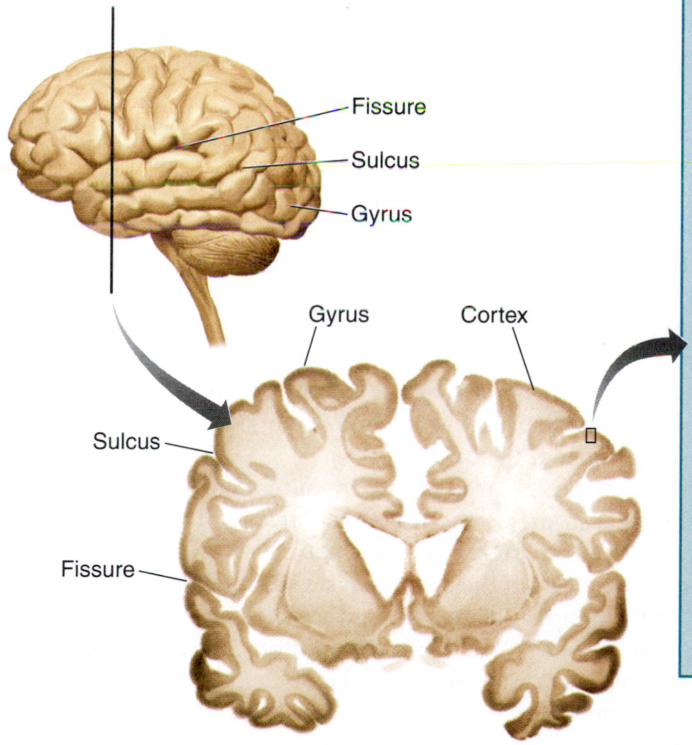

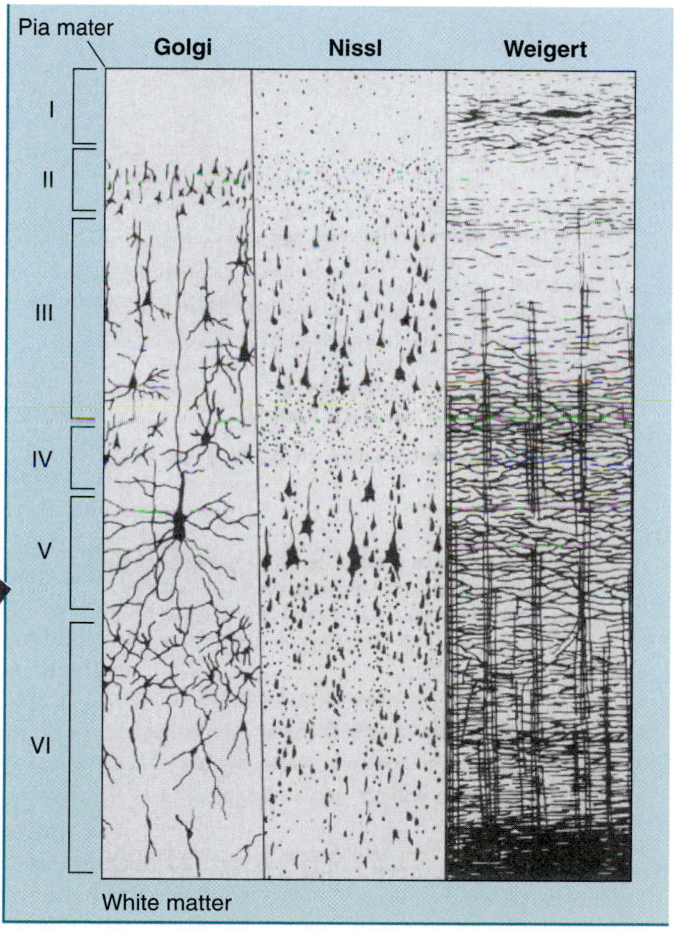

of the cortex, there are six distinct layers, which are numbered from the outermost layer toward the center of the brain. Examples of these layers can be seen in ■ Figure 2.17. Layer I has no cell bodies at all. Instead, it is made up of the nerve fibers of cells forming connections with other layers. Layers II and IV contain large numbers of small cells known as **granule cells.** Layers III and V are characterized by large numbers of the triangular-shaped **pyramidal cells.** These layers usually provide most of the output from an area of cortex to other parts of the nervous system. Layer VI has many types of neurons, which merge into the white matter that lies below the cortical layers.

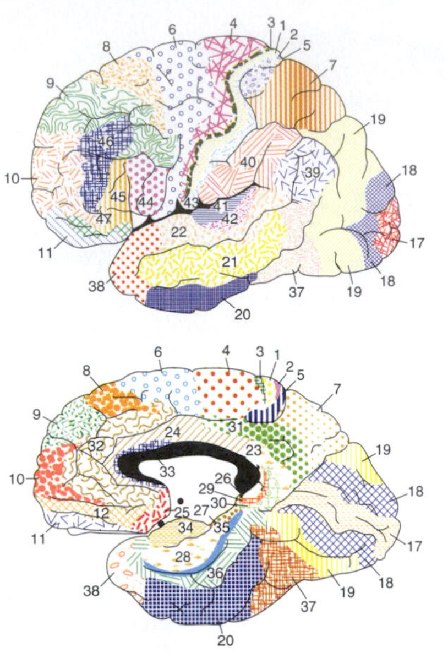

■ **FIGURE 2.18**
Brodmann's Map of the Brain Early twentieth century German neurologist Korbinian Brodmann divided the cerebral cortex into 52 different areas, based on the distribution of cell bodies in each area. One hundred years after Brodmann's system was first published, it remains the most widely used system for describing cortical architecture.

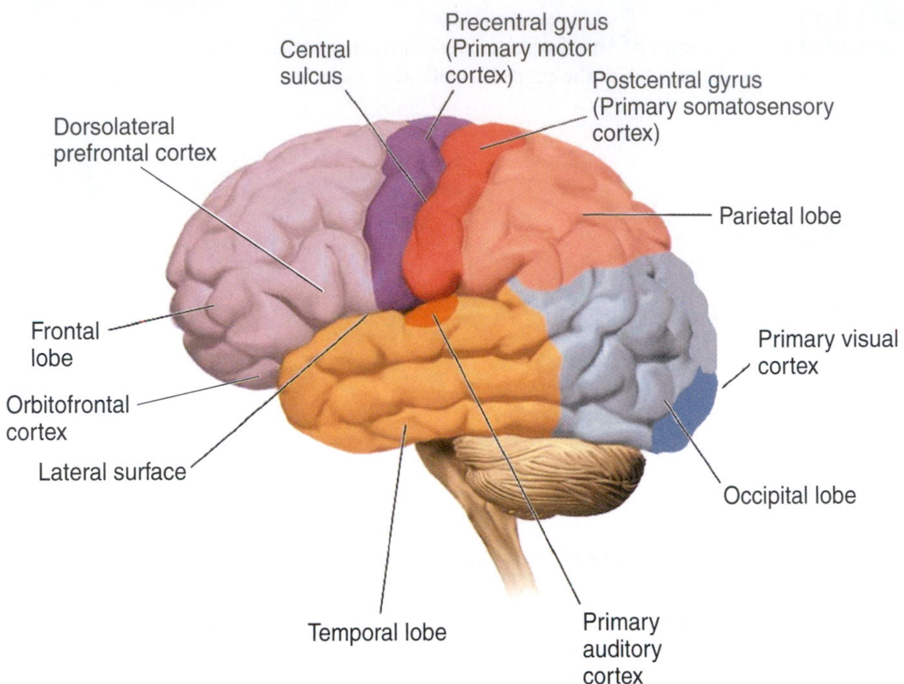

■ **FIGURE 2.19**
The Lobes of the Cerebral Cortex The outer surface of the brain consists of a thin layer of cortex. The cortex is traditionally divided into the frontal, parietal, temporal, and occipital lobes. The hills of the cortex are known as gyri, and the valleys of the cortex are known as sulci, or fissures.

There are a number of systems for dividing the cerebral cortex. As shown in ■ Figure 2.18, Korbinian Brodmann used the distribution of cell bodies within the six layers to distinguish between 52 separate areas of the cortex (Brodmann, 1909/1994). A simpler approach divides the cortex into four sections known as **lobes,** as shown in ■ Figure 2.19. The lobes are actually named after the skull bones that lie above them. The most rostral of the lobes is the **frontal lobe.** The caudal boundary of the frontal lobe is marked by the **central sulcus.** On the other side of the central sulcus, we find the **parietal lobe.** In the ventral direction, the frontal lobe is separated from the **temporal lobe** by the **lateral sulcus.** At the very back of the cortex is the **occipital lobe.** Separating the two cerebral hemispheres along the dorsal midline is the **longitudinal fissure.**

These areas of the cortex are so large that many different functions are located in each lobe. In general, we can divide the functional areas of the cortex into three categories: sensory cortex, motor cortex, and association cortex. The **sensory cortex** processes incoming information from the sensory systems. Different areas of the sensory cortex are found in the occipital, temporal, and parietal lobes. The occipital lobe contains the **primary visual cortex.** The **primary auditory cortex** is located in the temporal lobe. The **postcentral gyrus** of the parietal lobe contains the **primary somatosensory cortex,** which is the highest level of processing for information about touch, pain, position, and temperature. The postcentral gyrus gets its name from its location directly caudal ("post" means after) to the central sulcus, which divides the frontal and parietal lobes. The motor areas of the cortex provide the highest level of command for voluntary movements. The **primary motor cortex** is located in the **precentral gyrus** of the frontal lobe.

Some areas of the cortex have neither specific motor nor specific sensory functions. These areas are known as **association cortex.** *Association* means connection. In other words, these are the areas we have available for connecting and integrating sensory and motor functions.

The right and left cerebral hemispheres are linked by a special branch of white matter known as the **corpus callosum** and by the much smaller **anterior commissure**. These commissures may be seen in ■ Figure 2.20.

lobe One of the four major areas of the cerebral cortex: frontal, parietal, temporal, and occipital.
frontal lobe The most rostral lobe of the cerebral cortex, separated from the parietal lobe by the central sulcus and from the temporal lobe by the lateral sulcus.
central sulcus The fissure separating the frontal and parietal lobes of the cerebral cortex.
parietal lobe (puh-RIE-et-uhl) One of the four lobes of the cerebral cortex; located between the frontal and occipital lobes.
temporal lobe The lobe of the cerebral cortex lying ventral and lateral to the frontal and parietal lobes and rostral to the occipital lobe.
lateral sulcus The fissure separating the temporal and frontal lobes of the cortex.
occipital lobe (ox-SIP-i-tuhl) The most caudal lobe of the cortex; location of primary visual cortex.
longitudinal fissure The major fissure dividing the two cerebral hemispheres on the dorsal side of the brain.
sensory cortex An area of the cortex that is devoted to the processing of sensory information.

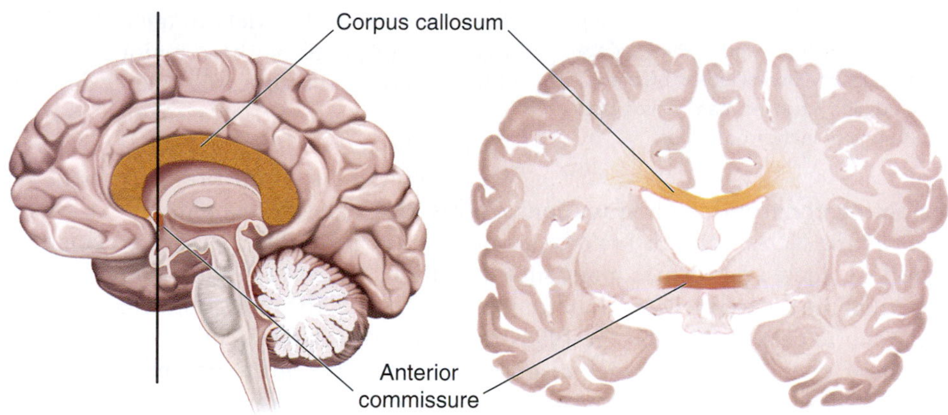

■ **FIGURE 2.20**
The Corpus Callosum and the Anterior Commissure Two fiber bundles, the very large corpus callosum and the much smaller anterior commissure, connect the right and left cerebral hemispheres.

Localization of Function in the Cortex In addition to the sensory and motor functions identified earlier, we can localize a number of specific functions in areas of the cerebral cortex. In many cases, these functions appear to be managed by cortex on either the left or right hemisphere.

In addition to being the location of the primary motor cortex, the frontal lobe participates in a number of higher-level cognitive processes such as the planning of behavior, attention, and judgment (Fuster, 1997). Two important structures within the frontal lobes are the **dorsolateral prefrontal cortex,** located to the top and side of the frontal lobes, and the **orbitofrontal cortex,** located above and behind the eyes. These areas of the frontal lobes, illustrated in Figure 2.19, maintain extensive, reciprocal connections with the limbic system, the basal ganglia, and other parts of the cortex. The dorsolateral prefrontal cortex is involved in executive functions such as attention and working memory and the planning of behavior (see Chapter 12), whereas the orbitofrontal cortex is involved in impulse control.

One of the classical methods for identifying brain functions is to consider cases in which the area of interest has been damaged. Possibly the most dramatic case of frontal lobe damage is that of the unfortunate Phineas Gage, a railroad worker in the middle 1800s. While Gage was preparing to blow up some rock, a spark set off his gunpowder and blew an iron tamping rod through his head, entering below his left eye and exiting through the top of his skull. A reconstruction of the rod's pathway through Gage's skull can be seen in ■ Figure 2.21. Miraculously, Gage survived the accident. He was not the same man, however, according to his friends. Prior to his accident, Gage appears to have been responsible, friendly, and polite. After his accident, Gage had difficulty holding a job and was profane and irritable. His memory and reason were intact, but his personality was greatly changed for the worse.

Gage's results are consistent with modern findings of frontal lobe damage. People with damage to the dorsolateral prefrontal cortex experience apathy, personality change, and the lack of ability to plan. People with damage to the orbitofrontal cortex experience emotional disturbances and impulsivity. As we will see in our discussion of mental disorders (Chapter 16), several types of psychopathology involve the frontal lobes. Some people with schizophrenia show lower than normal activity in the frontal lobe. Because children with attention deficit/hyperactivity disorder are usually very impulsive and have short attention spans, it has been suggested that they, too, suffer from underactivity of the frontal lobes. Finally, people who show extreme antisocial behavior, including serial murderers, frequently show damage to the orbitofrontal cortex.

In 1935, Yale researchers Carlyle Jacobsen and John Fulton reported evidence indicating that chimpanzees with frontal lobe damage experienced a reduction in negative emotions. After listening to a presentation by Fulton, Portuguese neurologist Egaz Moniz advocated the use of **frontal lobotomies** with human patients. During the 1940s and 1950s, more than 10,000 frontal lobotomies were performed

primary visual cortex An area of the sensory cortex located within the occipital lobe that provides the initial cortical processing of visual information.

primary auditory cortex An area of the sensory cortex located within the temporal lobe that provides the initial cortical processing of sound information.

postcentral gyrus The fold of parietal lobe tissue just caudal to the central sulcus; the location of the primary somatosensory cortex.

primary somatosensory cortex (soh-mat-oh-SEN-sor-ee) An area of the sensory cortex located within the parietal lobe that provides the highest level of processing for body senses such as touch, position, temperature, and pain.

primary motor cortex An area of the cortex located within the frontal lobe that provides the highest level of command to the motor systems.

precentral gyrus The fold of frontal lobe tissue just rostral to the central sulcus; the location of the primary motor cortex.

association cortex Areas of the cortex that link and integrate sensory and motor information.

corpus callosum (KOR-pus kall-OH-sum) A wide band of axons connecting the right and left cerebral hemispheres.

anterior commissure A small bundle of axons that connects structures in the right and left cerebral hemispheres.

dorsolateral prefrontal cortex An area located at the top and sides of the frontal lobe that participates in executive functions such as attention and the planning of behavior.

orbitofrontal cortex An area of the frontal lobe located just behind the eyes involved in impulse control; damage to this area can produce some antisocial behavior.

FIGURE 2.21
The Case of Phineas Gage Mid-nineteenth-century railroad worker Phineas Gage suffered an accident in which an iron rod was shot through the frontal lobe of his brain. Although Gage survived, he was described by his friends as a "changed man." Gage's case illustrates the localization of higher-order cognitive functions in the frontal lobe.

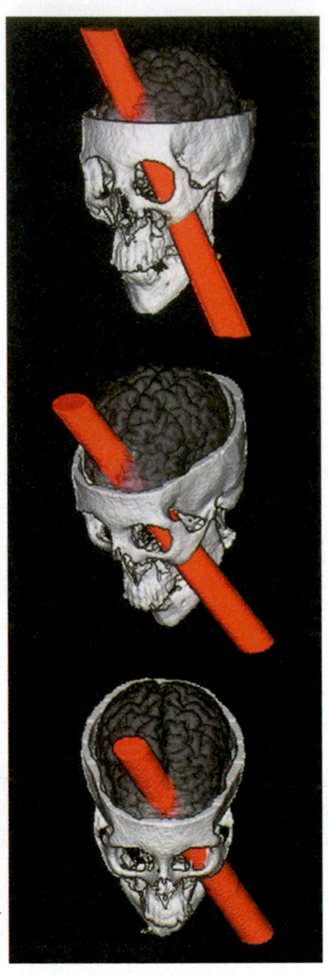
Courtesy Dr. Hanna Damasio

to reduce fear and anxiety in mental patients and in some people without major disorders. The lobotomy, discussed in greater detail in Chapter 14, consisted of a surgical separation of the most rostral parts of the frontal lobe from the rest of the brain. Without any remaining connections, the functions of this area of cortex would be lost. Moniz received the Nobel Prize in 1949 for advocating the procedure. Walter Freeman, an American doctor, performed many such operations, either in his office or even in his car, which he nicknamed his "lobotomobile." Initially, the operation was restricted to psychotic patients, but by the 1950s in the United States, depressed housewives and other people without major disorders were victims of the procedure. I would like to be able to say that physicians stopped doing lobotomies (very few are done today) because they recognized the tremendous negative side effects of the procedure, but that would not be entirely accurate. Lobotomies were largely discontinued when major antipsychotic medications were discovered. With the new drugs, the lobotomies were no longer considered necessary.

The frontal lobe is also home to an important area of the motor cortex known as **Broca's area.** Broca's area is necessary for speech production. Damage to this area produces difficulty speaking but has relatively less effect on a person's understanding or comprehension of speech. For most people, language functions appear to be controlled by cortex on the left hemisphere rather than on the right hemisphere. We will explore the lateralization of the language function in more detail in the chapter on language and cognition (see Chapter 13).

In addition to speech, other cognitive functions appear to show lateralization to one hemisphere or the other. For the vast majority of people, the left hemisphere manages logical thought and basic mathematical computation. You might think of the left hemisphere as the rational, school side of your brain. In contrast, the right hemisphere appears to be more emotional and intuitive. Our appreciation for art and music, as well as our ability to think three-dimensionally, are typically located in the right hemisphere. Please try to forget any pop psychology you have read previously about accessing your right brain to become a better artist. With the corpus callosum constantly relaying messages from one hemisphere to the other, you are already using your right hemisphere as much as you can.

INTERIM SUMMARY 2.2

Summary Table: Major Structures of the Central Nervous System

Division	Major Structures	Functions
Hindbrain	Medulla	Breathing, heart rate, and blood pressure; contains nuclei serving several cranial nerves
	Reticular formation (extends into midbrain)	Arousal and attention
	Pons	Sleep/waking cycles; contains nuclei serving several cranial nerves
	Cerebellum	Motor control, balance, cognition
Midbrain	Superior colliculi	Visual reflexes
	Inferior colliculi	Auditory reflexes
	Substantia nigra	Motor control
	Periaqueductal gray	Pain

(continued)

INTERIM SUMMARY 2.2 (continued)

Forebrain	Thalamus	Sensory processing, states of arousal, memory
	Hypothalamus	Regulation of hunger, thirst, aggression, sexual behavior, and the autonomic nervous system
	Amygdala	Recognition of danger; aggression
	Hippocampus	Memory formation
	Cerebral cortex	Highest level of sensory and motor processing; highest cognitive activity
	Corpus callosum	Connects the two cerebral hemispheres

Summary Points

1. The spinal cord is divided into cervical, thoracic, lumbar, sacral, and coccygeal segments. In addition to carrying messages to and from the brain, the spinal cord provides a variety of protective and motor reflexes. **(LO3)**
2. The hindbrain consists of the medulla, pons, and cerebellum. Running through the medulla and pons at the midline is the reticular formation, which helps control arousal. The midbrain contains the remaining section of the reticular formation, the periaqueductal gray, the red nucleus, the superior colliculi, the inferior colliculi, and the substantia nigra. The forebrain is divided into the diencephalon and the telencephalon. The diencephalon contains the thalamus and hypothalamus. The telencephalon contains the cerebral cortex, basal ganglia, and limbic system structures. **(LO4)**
3. The cerebral cortex is made up of six layers that cover the outer surface of the cerebral hemispheres. The hills of the cortex are referred to as gyri, and the valleys are referred to as sulci or fissures. **(LO5)**
4. The cerebral cortex is divided into four lobes: the frontal lobe, the parietal lobe, the temporal lobe, and the occipital lobe. The cortex also can be divided into sensory, motor, or association cortex based on its function. **(LO5, LO6)**
5. The two cerebral hemispheres are connected by the corpus callosum and the anterior commissure. Some functions, such as language, appear to be localized on one hemisphere or the other. **(LO5)**

Review Questions

1. What are the major structures and functions found in the hindbrain, midbrain, and forebrain?
2. What functions may be localized in particular areas of cortex?

The Peripheral Nervous System

For all its power, the brain still depends on the peripheral nervous system to enable it to perceive the outside world and to tell the body to carry out its commands. The role of the peripheral nervous system is to carry sensory information from the body to the spinal cord and brain and bring back to the body commands for appropriate responses. The peripheral nervous system contains three structural divisions: the cranial nerves, the spinal nerves, and the autonomic nervous system.

Together, the cranial nerves and spinal nerves comprise the **somatic nervous system.** The somatic nervous system brings sensory input to the brain and spinal cord and returns commands to the muscles. The **autonomic nervous system** controls the actions of many glands and organs.

The Cranial Nerves

As shown in ■ Figure 2.22, 12 pairs of **cranial nerves** enter and exit the brain directly to serve the region of the head and neck. Three of the cranial nerves carry only sensory information. These are the **olfactory nerve (I)**, the **optic nerve (II)**, and the **auditory nerve (VIII)**. Five of the nerves carry only motor information. The muscles of the eyes are controlled by the **oculomotor nerve (III)**, the **trochlear nerve (IV)**, and the **abducens nerve (VI)**. The **spinal accessory nerve (XI)** controls the muscles

frontal lobotomy (luh-BOT-oh-mee) A surgical procedure in which a large portion of the frontal lobe is separated from the rest of the brain.

Broca's area (BROH-kuhs) An area near the primary motor cortex in the frontal lobe that participates in speech production.

somatic nervous system (soh-MA-tik) The peripheral nervous system division that brings sensory input to the brain and spinal cord and returns commands to the muscles.

autonomic nervous system (aw-toh-NOM-ik) The division of the peripheral nervous system that directs the activity of the glands, organs, and smooth muscles of the body.

cranial nerves Twelve pairs of nerves that exit the brain as part of the peripheral nervous system.

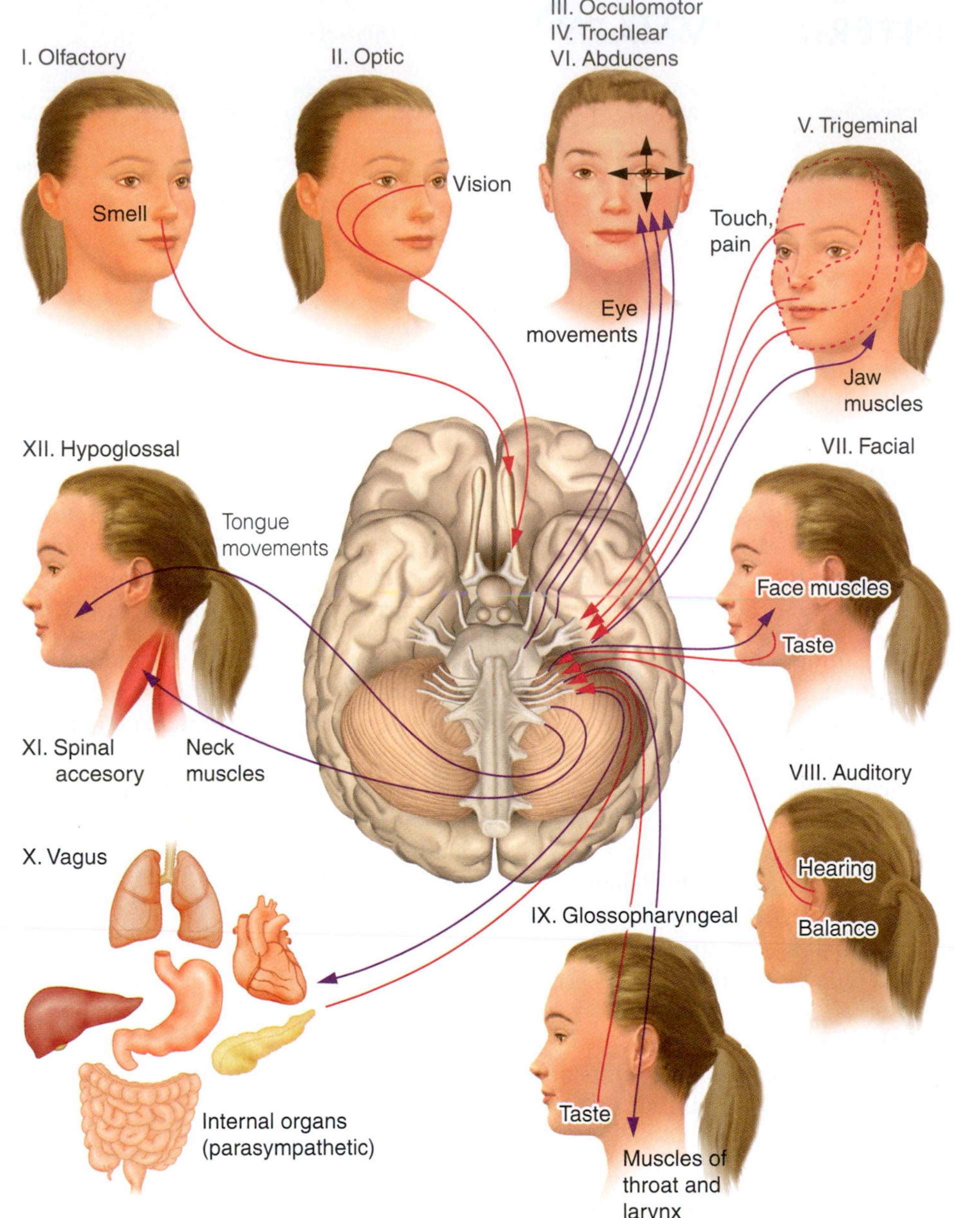

■ **FIGURE 2.22**
The Twelve Pairs of Cranial Nerves Twelve pairs of cranial nerves leave the brain directly to carry sensory and motor information to and from the head and neck areas. The red lines represent sensory functions, and the blue lines show motor control. Some cranial nerves are sensory only, some are motor only, and some are mixed.

olfactory nerve (I) A cranial nerve carrying information about smell to the brain.
optic nerve (II) A cranial nerve carrying information from the eyes to the brain.
auditory nerve (VIII) The cranial nerve that carries information from the inner ear to the brain.
oculomotor nerve (III) (ah-kew-loe-MOE-ter) A cranial nerve that controls muscles of the eye.
trochlear nerve (IV) (TROH-klee-ar) A cranial nerve that controls the muscles of the eye.
abducens nerve (VI) (ab-DOO-sens) A cranial nerve that controls the muscles of the eye.
spinal accessory nerve (XI) A cranial nerve that controls the muscles of the neck.
hypoglossal nerve (XII) (hie-poe-GLOSS-uhl) A cranial nerve responsible for movement of the tongue.
trigeminal nerve (V) (trie-JEM-inuhl) A cranial nerve that controls chewing movements and provides feedback regarding facial expression.
facial nerve (VII) A cranial nerve that produces muscle movement in facial expressions and that carries taste information back to the brain.
glossopharyngeal nerve (IX) (glossoh-far-IN-jee-uhl) A cranial nerve that manages both sensory and motor functions in the throat.
vagus nerve (X) (VAY-guss) A cranial nerve that serves the heart, liver, and digestive tract.
mixed nerves Spinal nerves that carry both sensory and motor information.

of the neck, and the **hypoglossal nerve (XII)** controls movement of the tongue. The remaining nerves have mixed sensory and motor functions. The **trigeminal nerve (V)** controls chewing movements but also provides some feedback regarding facial expression. The **facial nerve (VII)** produces facial expressions and carries the sensation of taste. The **glossopharyngeal nerve (IX)** performs both sensory and motor functions for the throat. Finally, the long-distance fibers of the **vagus nerve (X)** provide input and receive sensation from the heart, liver, and digestive tract.

The Spinal Nerves

As mentioned earlier, 31 pairs of spinal nerves exit the spinal cord to provide sensory and motor pathways to the torso, arms, and legs. Each spinal nerve is also known as a **mixed nerve,** because it contains a sensory, or **afferent,** nerve (*a* means toward the CNS in this case, as in *access*) and a motor, or **efferent,** nerve (*e* means away from the CNS, as in *exit*). The mixed nerves travel together to the part of the body they serve. This makes a great deal of practical sense. The nerves that are bringing you sensory information from your hand are adjacent to the nerves that tell your hand to move. Damage to a mixed nerve is likely to reduce both sensation and motor control for a particular part of the body.

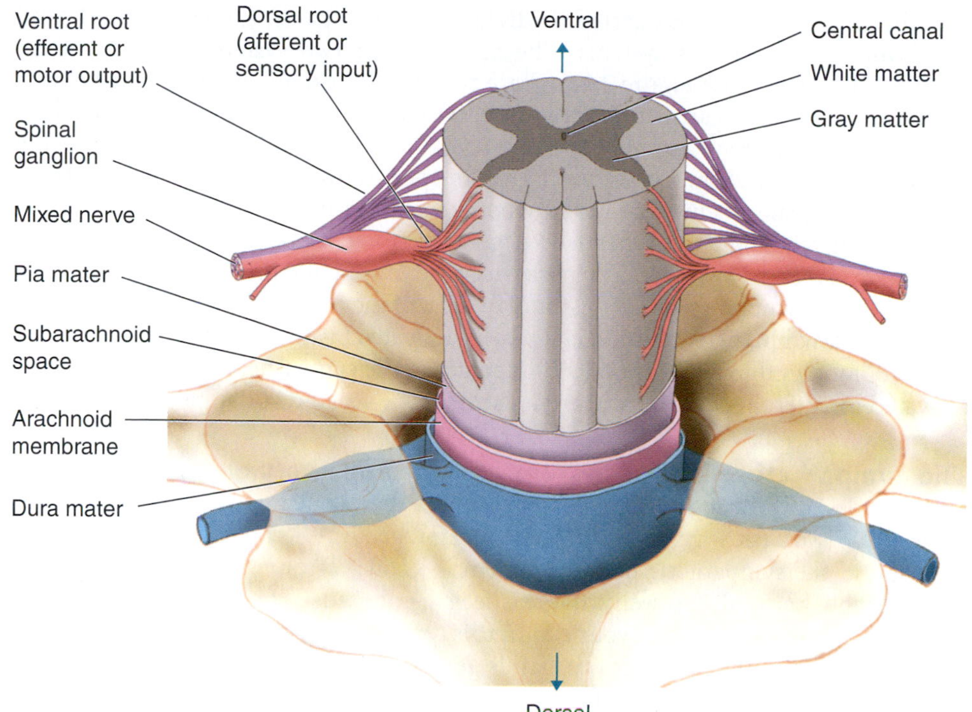

FIGURE 2.23 The Structure of the Spinal Cord This cross-section of the spinal cord shows a number of important anatomical features. Three layers of meninges surround the cord. The gray matter of the cord is located in a butterfly shape near the central canal, which contains cerebrospinal fluid. The dorsal afferent (sensory) nerves join the ventral efferent (motor) nerves beyond the spinal ganglion to form a mixed nerve.

Figure 2.23 shows the spinal nerves exiting a segment of the spinal cord. Upon leaving the spinal cord itself, the spinal nerves enjoy the protection of only two layers of meninges: the dura mater and pia mater. CSF does not surround the spinal nerves. Afferent roots arise from the dorsal part of the spinal cord, whereas efferent roots arise from the ventral part. Once outside the cord, the dorsal afferent root swells into the dorsal **spinal ganglion,** which contains the cell bodies of the afferent nerves that process information about touch, temperature, and other body senses from the periphery. Beyond the dorsal spinal ganglion, the dorsal and ventral roots join to form a mixed nerve.

And of course, the brain is not responsible for any of the sensations at all. The correct view is that the seat and source of sensation is the region of the heart.

Aristotle

Afferent (sensory) nerves contain both myelinated and unmyelinated fibers, whereas efferent (motor) nerves are all myelinated in the adult. As discussed in Chapter 3, myelin is a substance that insulates nerve fibers and increases the speed with which they can transmit messages. Myelinated fibers in both systems tend to be very large and very fast. Among the sensations carried by myelinated afferent fibers is the first, sharp experience of pain. Small unmyelinated afferent fibers are responsible for that dull, achy feeling that follows injury.

THE AUTONOMIC NERVOUS SYSTEM

The autonomic nervous system was first described as "cells and fibers that pass to tissues other than the skeletal muscle" (Langley, 1921). Your heart, lungs, digestive system, and other organs are commanded by the autonomic nervous system. You might think of this system as the automatic, or "cruise control," nervous system. It manages many vital functions without conscious effort or awareness. You wouldn't have much of a social life if you had to consciously command your lungs to inhale and exhale and your heart to beat. This doesn't mean that you are incapable of taking voluntary control of autonomic functions. We do this all the time, but it takes attention. For instance, breathing normally continues whether we are awake or asleep. However, when we swim, it's vital that we take conscious control of our breathing patterns, or we'll end up swallowing a lot of water. Through specialized training in **biofeedback,** people can learn to control a number of autonomic processes, such as lowering blood pressure and reducing blood flow to the brain to avoid migraine headaches. Once they shift attention, however, the effect may not last. The autonomic nervous system participates in a large number of critical regulatory functions, including blood circulation, secretion, digestion, urination, and defecation. In addition, many reflexive behaviors are carried out with the assistance of autonomic neurons. These reflexes include respiration, pupil dilation, sneezing, coughing, swallowing, vomiting, and genital responses.

afferent nerve (AF-er-ent) A nerve that carries sensory information to the CNS.
efferent nerve (EE-fer-ent) A nerve that carries motor commands away from the CNS.
spinal ganglion A collection of cell bodies of afferent nerves located just outside the spinal cord.
biofeedback A set of techniques that enable people to control typically unconscious or involuntary functions such as blood pressure.

My own brain is to me the most unaccountable of machinery—always buzzing, humming, soaring roaring diving, and then buried in mud. And why? What's this passion for?
Virginia Woolf

The autonomic nervous system is divided into two parts, the **sympathetic** and **parasympathetic** nervous systems. The action of the two systems on their target organs is illustrated in ■ Figure 2.24. These two systems usually have opposite effects on the same set of organs, so we traditionally view them as working like a toggle switch. Turning one system on can inhibit the other. It's difficult to imagine being aroused and resting at the same time. Nonetheless, it is overly simplistic to view these systems as mutually exclusive. There are many instances in which both systems operate cooperatively and simultaneously. A good example of the cooperation between the systems is sexual behavior. The parasympathetic system stimulates erection of the penis, and the sympathetic system stimulates ejaculation.

The parasympathetic division is typically activated by internal stimuli such as the arrival of food in the digestive system. In contrast, the sympathetic nervous system is activated by external environmental cues such as the sensing of danger.

The Sympathetic Nervous System The sympathetic nervous system has been elegantly designed to cope with emergencies. It prepares the body for action. Human beings have two basic ways of dealing with an emergency. We can run, or we can fight. As a result, the sympathetic nervous system is known as our *fight-or-flight* system. You probably know all too well what this feels like because you probably have had a close call or two while driving your car. In this type of emergency, our hearts race, our breathing is rapid, the palms of our hands get sweaty, our faces are pale, and we are mentally alert and focused. All of these behaviors have been refined through millions of years of evolution to keep you alive when faced with an emergency.

The sympathetic nervous system prepares the body for fighting or fleeing by shutting down low-priority systems and putting blood and oxygen into the most necessary parts of the body. Salivation and digestion are put on standby. If you're facing a hungry lion on the Serengeti Plain, you don't need to worry about digesting your lunch unless you survive the encounter. Your heart and lungs operate to provide extra oxygen, which is fed to the large-muscle groups. Blood vessels near the skin's surface are constricted to channel blood to the large-muscle groups. Aside from giving you that pale look, you enjoy the added benefit of not bleeding very badly should you be cut. With the increased blood flow to the brain, mental alertness is at a peak.

The sympathetic nervous system is configured for a simultaneous, coordinated response to emergencies. Axons from neurons in the thoracic and lumbar segments of the spinal cord communicate with a series of ganglia just outside the cord known as the **sympathetic chain**. Fibers from cells in the sympathetic chain then communicate with target organs. Because the messages from the spinal neurons reach the sympathetic chain through fibers of equal length, they arrive at about the same time. Consequently, input from the sympathetic chain arrives at all of the target organs simultaneously. This coordinated response is essential for survival. It wouldn't be efficient for the heart to get a delayed message in the case of an emergency.

Because the same organs receive input from both the sympathetic and parasympathetic systems, it is important for the organs to have a way to identify the source of the input. This is accomplished through the types of chemical messengers used by the two systems. Both the sympathetic and parasympathetic systems communicate with cells in ganglia outside the spinal cord, which then form a second connection with a target organ. Both systems use the chemical messenger acetylcholine (ACh) to communicate with their ganglia (see Chapter 3). At the target organ, the parasympathetic nervous system continues to use acetylcholine. The sympathetic nervous system, however, switches to another chemical messenger, norepinephrine, to communicate with target organs. The only exception is the connection between the sympathetic nerves and the sweat glands, where acetylcholine is still used. This system of two chemical messengers provides a clear method of action at the target organ. If the heart, for instance, is stimulated by acetylcholine, it will react by slowing. If it receives stimulation from norepinephrine, it will speed up. Survival depends on not having any ambiguities, mixed messages, or possibility of error.

The Parasympathetic Nervous System During times of sympathetic nervous system activity, the body is expending rather than storing energy. Obviously, the sympathetic

sympathetic nervous system The division of the autonomic nervous system that coordinates arousal.
parasympathetic nervous system (pear-uh-sim-puh-THET-ik) The division of the autonomic nervous system responsible for rest and energy storage.
sympathetic chain A string of cell bodies outside the spinal cord that receive input from sympathetic neurons in the central nervous system and that communicate with target organs.

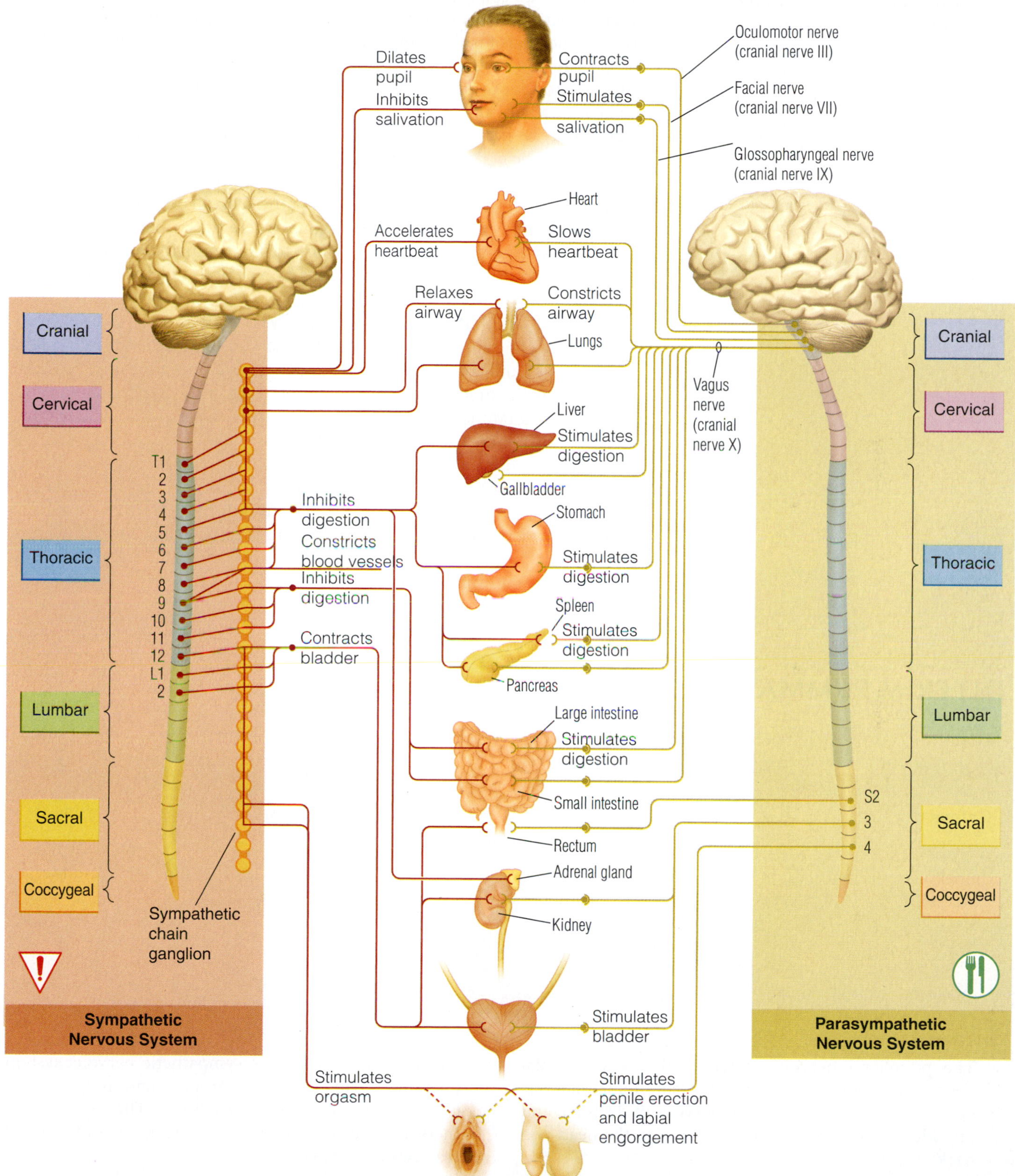

FIGURE 2.24
The Autonomic Nervous System The sympathetic and parasympathetic divisions of the autonomic nervous system often have opposite effects on target organs. To carry out their respective tasks, sympathetic neurons form their first synapse in the sympathetic chain, whereas parasympathetic neurons synapse on ganglia close to the target organs. In addition, the systems use different neurotransmitters at the target organ.

If your head tells you one thing and your heart tells you another, before you do anything, you should first decide whether you have a better head or a better heart.
Marilyn Vos Savant

nervous system can't run continuously, or the body would run out of resources. The job of the parasympathetic nervous system is to provide rest, repair, and energy storage.

Whereas the neurons for the sympathetic nervous system are found in the thoracic and lumbar regions of the spinal cord, the neurons for the parasympathetic nervous system are found above and below these regions, in the brain and sacral divisions of the spinal cord, specifically. This is the origin of the name *parasympathetic. Para* means around, and the neurons of the parasympathetic nervous system are around those of the sympathetic nervous system, like brackets or parentheses.

After exiting the brain and sacral spinal cord, parasympathetic axons do not synapse with a chain, as was the case with the sympathetic axons. Instead, they travel some distance to locations near their target organs, where the parasympathetic ganglia are located. Because timing is not as important to parasympathetic activity as it is to sympathetic activity, the coordination provided by a chain is not necessary.

Central Control of the Autonomic Nervous System The brain structure that plays the greatest role in managing the autonomic nervous system is the hypothalamus. The pathways to and from the hypothalamus are exceedingly complex. Many structures involved with emotion have the potential to affect the hypothalamus and, indirectly then, the autonomic nervous system. As a result, the responses of our internal organs are tightly connected with our emotional behaviors, leading to the many common physical symptoms we experience as a result of our emotions.

The hypothalamus, in turn, connects with the midbrain tegmentum and to the reticular formation in particular. Damage to the midbrain in the vicinity of the red nucleus produces a wide variety of autonomic disturbances, probably due to interruptions to large fiber pathways that descend from these areas to the autonomic neurons of the lower brainstem and spinal cord.

INTERIM SUMMARY 2.3

Summary Table: Major Structures of the Peripheral Nervous System

Structure	Function
Cranial nerves	Carry sensory and motor information between the brain and regions of the head and neck
Spinal nerves: cervical, thoracic, lumbar, sacral, coccygeal	Carry sensory and motor information between the spinal cord and the remainder of the body
Autonomic nervous system Sympathetic division (arousal) Parasympathetic division (resting)	Provides input to the glands and organs

Summary Points

1. The peripheral nervous system includes the cranial nerves, the spinal nerves, and the autonomic nervous system. The 12 pairs of cranial nerves exit the brain and provide sensory and motor functions to the head and neck. **(LO7)**
2. The autonomic nervous system processes sensory and motor information to and from glands, organs, and smooth muscle. The sympathetic nervous system operates during times of arousal and prepares the body for fight-or-flight reactions. The parasympathetic nervous system operates during times of rest and restoration. **(LO8)**

Review Questions

1. How are the spinal nerves organized once they exit the cord?
2. How are the structures of the sympathetic and parasympathetic nervous systems well suited to their functions?

Evolution of the Human Brain and Nervous System

The human genome, the set of DNA instructions for building a human being, is the result of millions of years of evolution. Brains are a relatively recent addition among living things, and our modern *Homo sapiens* brain may be only about 200,000 years old.

Natural Selection and Evolution

The difference in mind between man and the higher animals, great as it is, certainly is one of degree and not of kind.

Charles Darwin

As outlined in his 1859 *On the Origin of the Species,* Charles Darwin proposed that species evolve, or change from one version to the next, in an orderly manner. Modern biologists define evolution as "descent with modification from a common ancestor."

Darwin was well aware of the artificial selection procedures used by farmers to develop animals and plants with particular desirable traits. If a farmer's goal was to raise the strongest oxen, it was advisable to breed the strongest available oxen to each other. In these cases, the farmer makes the determination of which individuals have the opportunity to produce offspring. In **natural selection,** Darwin suggested that the pressures of survival and reproduction in the wild would take the place of the farmer. Natural selection favors the organism with the highest degree of **fitness,** or likelihood of reproducing successfully compared with others of the same species. Fitness is not some static characteristic, such as being strongest or fastest. Instead, fitness describes the successful interaction between an organism's characteristics and the environment in which it exists. An organism that succeeds during an ice age might be at a significant disadvantage during more temperate times.

natural selection The process by which favorable traits would become more common and unfavorable traits would become less common in subsequent generations due to differences among organisms in their ability to reproduce successfully.

Combining our modern understanding of genetics (see Chapter 5) with Darwin's work provides a basis for understanding the progression of species

WHY DOES THIS MATTER?

Is Evolution Still Shaping Human Beings?

The short answer to the question is, Yes. Recognizing that the process of evolution is not something that somehow stopped in the past matters because we can look objectively to current processes that are shaping what human beings and other species will become in the future.

One of the concepts we will explore in greater detail in Chapter 5 is the difference between dominant and recessive genes. A dominant gene from one parent will result in a particular trait, regardless of whether the gene from the other parent is the same or different. A recessive gene, in contrast, will produce a trait only if both parents supply the same gene. Blonde hair, which is the result of inheriting a recessive gene from each parent, first appeared in Europe about 15,000 years ago, probably due to a spontaneous genetic mutation. Peter Frost (2006) suggests that the gene spread quickly due to its novelty. When people have a choice of equally attractive mates, we tend to choose the one that "stands out from the crowd." Some anthropologists now believe that blonde hair is on the endangered list and may disappear from the human population in as little as 200 years.

How can we account for this change? People today are much more mobile than in prehistoric Europe, where geographical boundaries corralled those with the blonde gene, raising the likelihood that two carriers of the recessive gene would mate with one another. With today's global mobility and Internet dating, people with the recessive blonde gene are less likely to mate with each other. Then, of course, we have the ability to dye our hair. Men attracted to blondes may in fact be mating with women who do not carry the blonde gene at all, reducing the advantage previously enjoyed by natural blondes.

Blonde hair provides an admittedly superficial example of how the human genome is currently changing but reminds us that evolution is inevitable and ongoing, potentially affecting other genes that are far more significant to the future of the human species, including those that influence the brain.

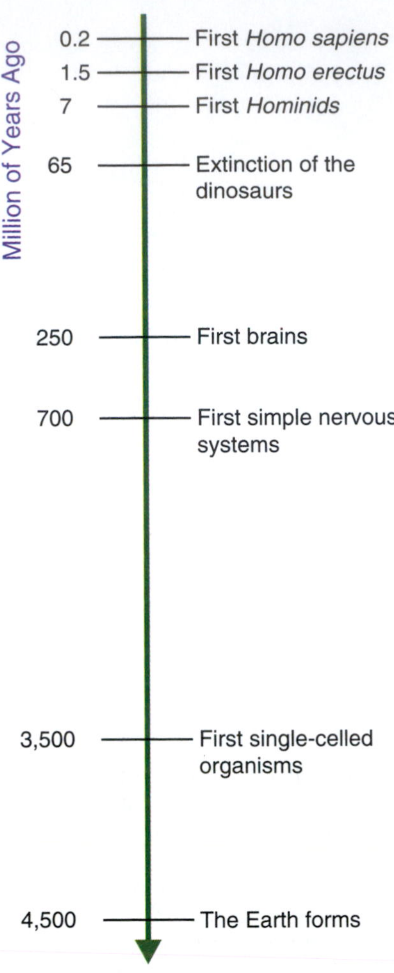

FIGURE 2.25
Timeline for the Evolution of the Brain When compared with the entire time scale of evolution, nervous systems represent a very new development, appearing for the first time in the form of simple neural nets about 700 million years ago. Advanced brains, such as the human brain, are more recent still.

and their behavior. As Richard Dawkins (1982) reminds us, genes can replicate themselves but not without a lot of help from their friends. All genes in a single individual share the same fate. If that individual survives and reproduces, his or her genes will become more frequent in the next generation. At the same time, an individual's ability to survive and reproduce will be a function of the characteristics encoded by his or her genes.

Evolution of the Nervous System

Nervous systems are a rather recent development belonging only to animals. To begin our evolution timeline, illustrated in Figure 2.25, current estimates place the origin of the Earth at about 4.5 billion years ago. Single-cell organisms appeared about 3.5 billion years ago, and animals with very simple nerve nets first developed about 700 million years ago. More complex animals, with the first rudimentary brains, appeared about 250 million years ago, and the first human brain probably appeared about 7 million years ago (Calvin, 2004).

The neural networks that developed early, such as those found in snails, consist of collections of cells, or ganglia, that control certain aspects of the animal's behavior in a particular region of the body. Although some of these ganglia are located in the head, they do not perform the central executive functions we normally attribute to a brain. The abdominal ganglia may perform behaviors that are just as crucial to the animal's survival as behaviors managed by ganglia in the head. In addition, most of these primitive nervous systems are located in the more vulnerable ventral, or belly side, of the animal where they are easily damaged or attacked. Because they lack a spinal column, such animals are referred to by biologists as *invertebrates*.

Animals with spinal columns and real brains are referred to as vertebrates, or **chordates**. As shown in Figure 2.26, brains provide a number of advantages for chordates compared with the neural networks found in more primitive species. Unlike the ganglia of the invertebrate, the brain and spinal cord coordinate all of the animal's activity. The brain exerts this executive control from its vantage point in the head, close to the major sensory systems that provide information from the eyes, ears, nose, and mouth. With its centralized functions and ability to integrate sensory input, the brain of the first chordates to appear on the scene many millions of years ago enabled those animals to respond consistently and rapidly. The brains and spinal cords of the chordates enjoyed much more protection than the ganglia of the invertebrates. Not only were these important structures now encased in bone, but their location on the dorsal, or back, surface of the animal's body was easier to defend.

As shown in Figure 2.27, the brains of chordates continued to develop, culminating in the very large brains found in mammals and birds. Early brains differ

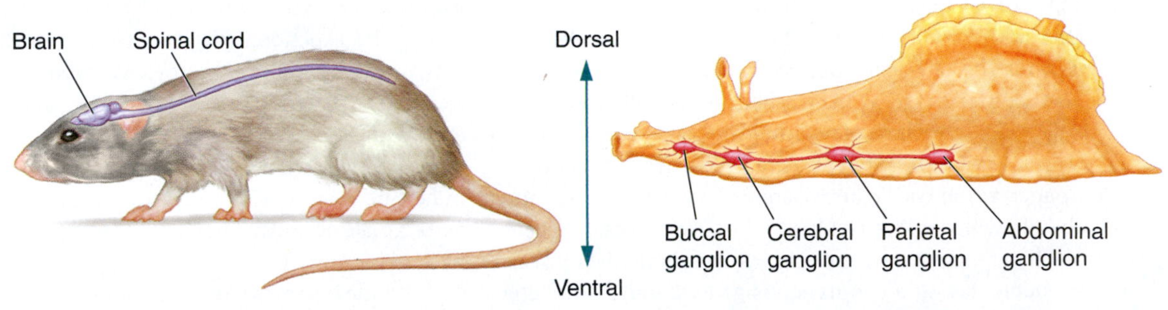

FIGURE 2.26
True Brains Are Found in Chordates Compared with invertebrates, such as the *Aplysia californica* (a type of sea slug) on the right, chordates have true brains as opposed to ganglia. The chordate nervous system runs near the dorsal rather than the ventral surface of the animal's body.

WHY DOES THIS MATTER?

Do Animals Have Minds?

René Descartes postulated that the only species with "mind" was the human. As we observe our dogs "training" us to take them for walks and our cats as they mount strategic military offensives against the innocent songbirds in the garden, we often find Descartes's premise difficult to accept. Although Darwin's Theory of Evolution speaks primarily to the physical progression of species, his later work indicates that he believed that behavior, such as emotion, followed many of the same rules (Darwin, 1872). If we accept Darwin, we must also accept the idea that human-like abilities did not blossom in one species alone.

Understanding the capabilities of other species matters because we not only gain insight into the history of our own species, but we also renew our respect for the species with whom we share the planet. One of the major roadblocks to an understanding of animal ability is finding tasks that provide fair comparisons. What does it mean to be a "smart" dog? In a later chapter, we discuss animal communication and language. Other psychologists are investigating the evolution of a sense of self. Gordon Gallup and his colleagues developed an interesting way to test whether an individual had a sense of self. If you place a dot of red dye on the forehead of a human infant of about 18 months of age, the infant will touch his or her own forehead when looking in the mirror. In other words, infants looking into a mirror understand that they are gazing at an image of themselves. In addition to humans, chimpanzees and orangutans pass the mirror test, but most monkeys do not (Anderson & Gallup, 1999; Gallup, 1977). Joshua Plotnik and his colleagues report that elephants are also capable of self-recognition (Plotnik, de Waal, & Reiss, 2006).

What does this mean for us? Human beings clearly have cognitive advantages over other species, but research on our fellow creatures renews our respect for their capabilities.

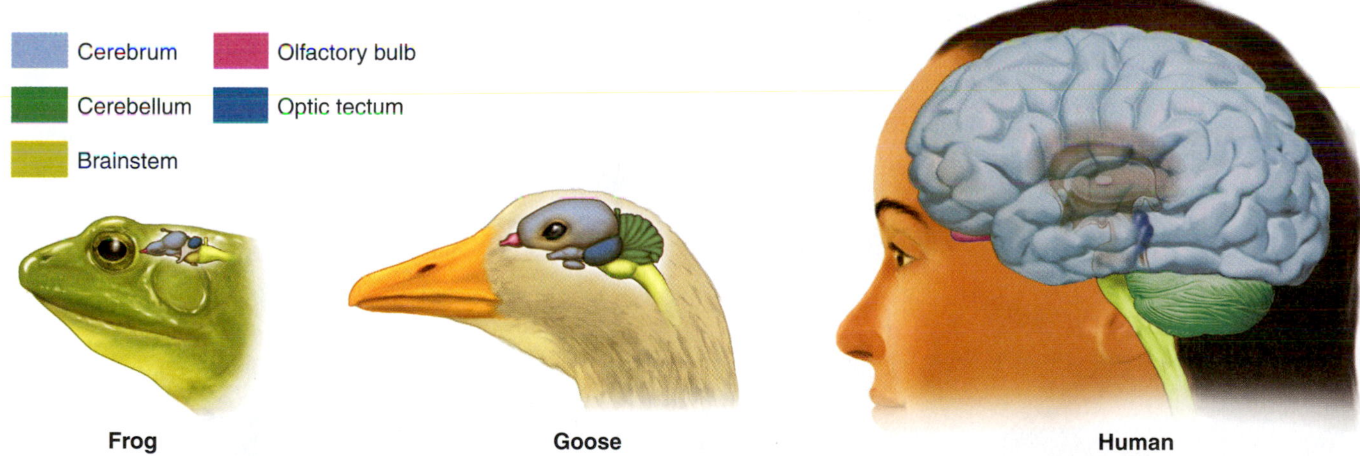

■ **Figure 2.27**
Chordate Brains Continued to Evolve More complex chordate brains feature increased convolutions and larger cerebellums.

from more advanced brains in both size and degree of convolution, or folding, of the cortex. In addition, the size of the cerebellum increased in more advanced chordate species.

Evolution of the Human Brain

Human beings are members of the primate order, a biological category that includes some 275 species of apes, monkeys, lemurs, tarsiers, and marmosets. We are further classified as being in the suborder of apes, the family of **hominids,** and the species of ***Homo sapiens.***

There have been a number of hominid species over the past 7 million years, beginning with *Sahelanthropus tchadensis* and including several *Australopithecus* species. The first *Homo* species, *Homo habilis,* lived about 2 million years ago. Analyses of the fossilized skulls of this hominid suggest a well-developed Broca's area, indicating that speech was a possibility (Corballis, 2003). *Homo erectus,* a species with nearly modern brain size and upright posture, lived from about 1.5 million to perhaps 300,000 years ago. *Homo erectus* showed behavioral signs of improved intellect that corresponded

fitness The ability of an organism with one genetic makeup to reproduce more successfully than organisms with other types of genetic makeup.

chordates The phylum of animals that possess true brains and spinal cords. Also known as vertebrates.

hominid A primate in the family Hominidae, of which *Homo sapiens* is the only surviving member.

Homo sapiens The species of modern humans.

The juvenile sea squirt wanders through the sea searching for a suitable rock or hunk of coral to cling to and make its home for life. For this task it has a rudimentary nervous system. When it finds its spot and takes root, it doesn't need its brain any more so it eats it. It's rather like getting tenure.
Daniel Dennet

with increased brain size, such as advanced tool use and the controlled use of fire. Finally, modern *Homo sapiens* appeared approximately 200,000 years ago. By this point, early humans had migrated extensively throughout Europe and Asia. Their tool use appeared quite sophisticated, they hunted efficiently, and their culture, which included the ritual burial of their dead, was cooperative and social.

The outstanding feature of modern humans is brain size. Within a species, brain size does not correlate well with intelligence. After all, Albert Einstein's brain was, on average, smaller than age-matched controls (Witelson, Kigar, & Harvey, 1999). However, brain size *does* correlate with differences in intelligence between species, although we need to make some adjustments for body size. Elephants have much larger brains than humans, and although elephants are clearly quite intelligent, they're not as smart as people. Jerison (1973) proposed that a ratio of body weight and brain weight be used to predict intelligent behavior between species (see ■ Figure 2.28). This rationale suggests that it takes a certain amount of brain, analogous to the operating system (Windows, Mac OS, Linux, etc.) of your computer, to run a certain size body. The remaining portion of the brain, corresponding to the open hard drive space in your computer, is available for intelligent behavior. Jerison further modified his argument by computing an encephalization quotient (EQ), a ratio of brain size to the expected brain size for a particular size of body. By this measure, human beings clearly stand apart from even their most large-brained fellow creatures.

Among hominid species, brain development appears to have occurred very quickly. The relative skull sizes of representative hominids are shown in ■ Figure 2.29. The early tool-using australopithecines had brains that were about the same size as that of a modern chimpanzee, around 400 cubic cm. *Homo erectus* had a brain of about 700 cubic cm, and modern human brains are around 1,400 cubic cm. Larger brains enabled hominids to adapt to quickly changing climates and food supplies. Others argue that the availability of certain high-protein food sources, such as meat and seafood, made it possible to develop larger brains. Stephen Cunnane (2006) noted

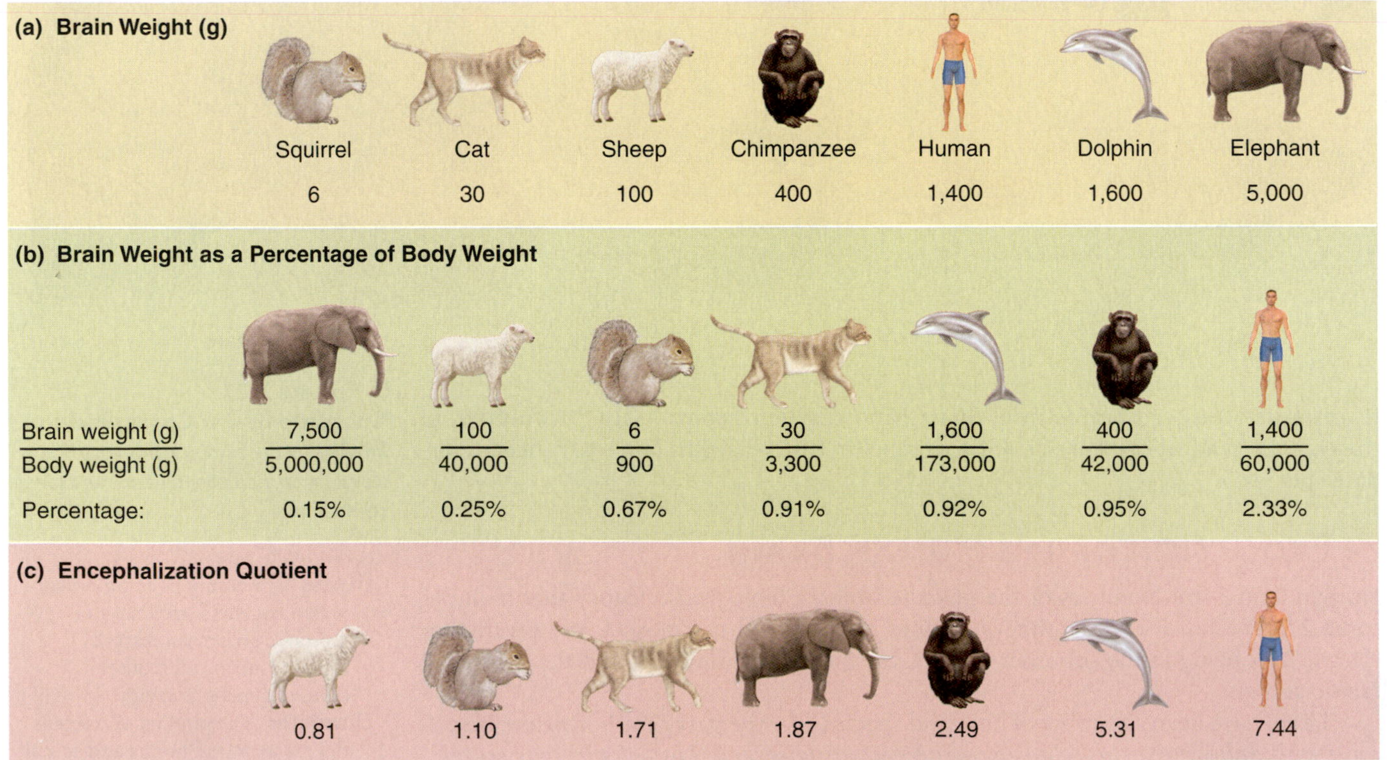

■ **FIGURE 2.28**
Relative Encephalization Quotients Simple brain size, or even a brain-weight-to-body-weight ratio, is not an appropriate method for predicting the intelligence of a species. It is unlikely that shrews are smarter than people. Jerison (1973) proposed the encephalization quotient (EQ), which compares actual brain size to the expected brain size needed to run the body. The application of EQ appears to provide a good fit with the behavioral data regarding the capabilities of each species.

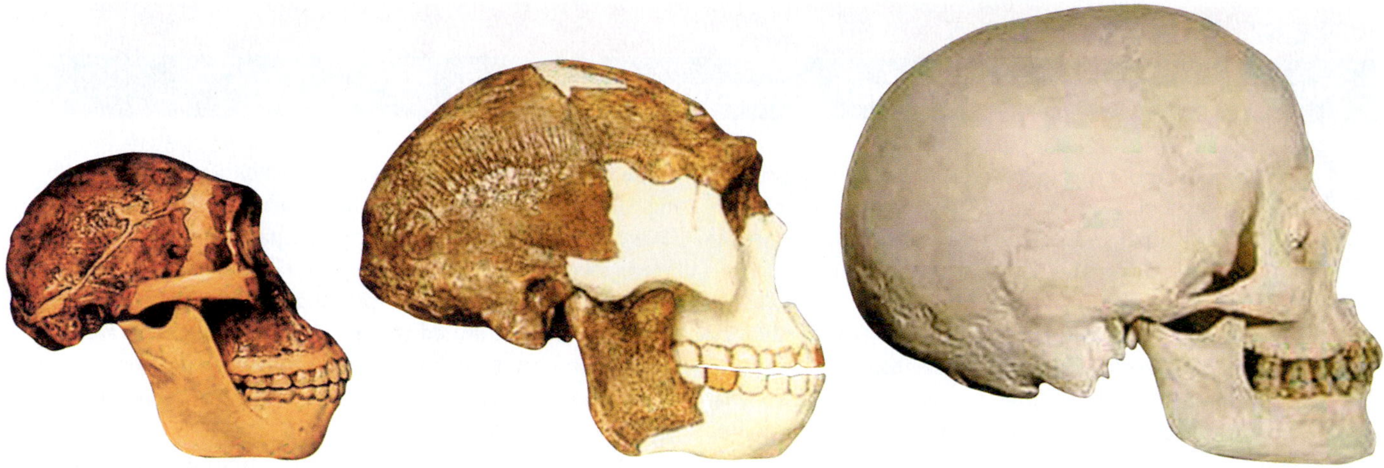

FIGURE 2.29 Human Brain Development Proceeded Swiftly Hominid brains advanced rapidly from those of the early australopithecines, who had brains about the size of modern chimpanzees, to *Homo erectus* (700 cm^3), to *Homo sapiens* (1,400 cm^3). Brain development then appears to have leveled off. You are reading this text with essentially the same brain that has worked for *Homo sapiens* for the past 200,000 years.

that the habitat in which early humans evolved was dominated by wetlands and shorelines, where abundant supplies of seafood, frogs, and bird eggs provided much more reliable and nutritious foods than those that could be found on the savannahs. As pregnant women dined on this rich, year-round source of food, their fetuses accumulated excess fat. Human babies are the only primates that are born with additional fat, a considerable advantage to a species whose newborn brain consumes about 75 percent of its daily energy needs. Possible remnants of our seafood-eating history include our needs for the fatty acid DHA and iodine. Iodine deficiency still plagues the world's inland populations, often resulting in cognitive deficits. Consequently, more than 100 nations currently require the addition of iodine to table salt. Furthermore, the consumption of fish appears to provide some protection from bipolar disorder, which is characterized by extreme mood swings (Noaghiul & Hibbeln, 2003; see Chapter 16).

In addition to improved food supplies, it is likely that new skills such as tool use, language, social behavior, and the ability to plan for the future drove much of the increase in brain size among humans (Finlay & Darlington, 1995). However, since the initial appearance of *Homo sapiens* about 200,000 years ago, brain size has not changed much. What is unclear is why such major cultural changes over the past 200,000 years, such as agriculture, urbanization, and literacy, have not produced additional changes in brain size. Further increases in brain size might simply be too costly in terms of greater difficulties in childbirth and the need for more resources. Unless we experience a reduction in costs or pressure for even greater intelligence, we might have reached a balance between the advantages and disadvantages of large brains.

INTERIM SUMMARY 2.4

Summary Points

1. Charles Darwin proposed his Theory of Evolution to account for the orderly progression of change from one version of a species to the next. Natural selection leads to the reproductive success of organisms with the greatest degree of fitness. **(LO9)**
2. The nervous system is a relatively recent development in the course of evolution. Chordates are the only animals possessing a true spinal cord and brain. As the brain evolved, it became larger and more convoluted. **(LO9)**
3. Human beings have experienced very rapid brain growth, possibly in response to the challenges of using tools, language, social behavior, and learning to plan for the future. **(LO9)**

Review Questions

1. What are the basic principles underlying Darwin's Theory of Evolution?
2. What are the major milestones in the evolution of the nervous system?

NEW DIRECTIONS

Neuroscientists Search for Self-Awareness in the Brain

Questions about the self have fascinated philosophers and psychologists for years. "Who am I?" "When did I begin?" "What happens when I die?" Was Phineas Gage, whose frontal lobe was damaged when an iron rod shot through his head, the same self before and after his accident? Needless to say, these questions extend far beyond biological psychology. Nevertheless, in recent years, neuroscientists have renewed their search for the psychological holy grail—the self. So what can we say about the neuroscience of the self? Is it possible to locate the self in the brain?

In their review of brain correlates of the self, Seth Gillihan and Martha Farah (2005) provide a model for determining whether a certain brain activity is essential to a sense of self. Their approach is to measure activity in different parts of participants' brains while they first do certain things, then watch other people do the same things. For example, if some area of the brain behaves differently when we think about ourselves reading this text as opposed to when we think about our classmates reading the text, we might have located an area in the brain involved with some aspect of self.

Ruby and Decety found distinct patterns of brain activity accompanying consideration of our own actions as opposed to the actions of others. When participants imagined themselves stapling papers or peeling bananas, a different pattern of brain activity occurred than when they imagined the experimenter carrying out the same actions (Ruby & Decety, 2001). In another study, people hearing their own voice while reading aloud showed different patterns of brain activity than people hearing the experimenter's voice (McGuire, Silbersweig, & Frith, 1996).

Other studies have found that activation of our sense of self is not constant over time or situations. We have all experienced that unique sense of "losing ourselves" when engaged in certain tasks such as concentrating hard on a problem, watching a movie, or having sex. Rafael Malach and his colleagues (Hasson et al., 2004) noted that participants viewing a popular movie showed activation of the posterior portions of the brain but very little activity in the frontal areas. Consequently, these researchers hypothesized that it might be possible to activate sensory processing (occurring in the posterior portions of the brain) and self-awareness (occurring in the frontal portions of the brain) selectively and separately.

In a subsequent study by the same group (Goldberg et al., 2006), participants viewed a series of photos or listened to a series of musical clips while undergoing functional MRI. Brain activity patterns were compared over three conditions. In the first, stimuli were presented slowly, and participants pushed a button if an animal appeared in a picture or if a trumpet was heard in a music clip. In the second condition, stimuli were presented three times as rapidly as in the first. In the third condition, participants used buttons to indicate their emotional response to the stimuli. In two of the conditions, the slow presentation of stimuli and the emotional response conditions, frontal lobe activity accompanied activation of sensory cortex. However, in the rapid presentation of stimuli condition, no such frontal activation occurred. The researchers speculated that when faced with demanding sensory tasks, the self part of the brain, represented in the frontal lobe, literally switches off. Ilan Goldberg suggests, "If there is a sudden danger, such as the appearance of a snake, it is not helpful to stand around wondering how one feels about the situation" (Vince, 2006, ¶ 9). These researchers further propose the possibility that errors in this switching process might contribute to the distortions of self that accompany disorders such as autism and schizophrenia (see Chapter 16).

CHAPTER REVIEW

THOUGHT QUESTIONS

1. Given your understanding of the functions of the basal ganglia, why are these structures suspected of playing a role in attention deficit/hyperactivity disorder and obsessive-compulsive disorder?
2. Because the limbic system is often referred to as our emotional brain, what conclusions can you draw about the possibility of conscious, voluntary control over emotion?
3. Given your understanding of frontal lobe functions, what objectionable side effects might result from a frontal lobotomy?
4. Why are suggestions that you "access your right brain" to perform artistically probably not scientifically valid?
5. What types of challenges facing human populations today might result in additional changes to the human genome? What might those changes be?

KEY TERMS

amygdala (p. 40)
anterior (p. 27)
anterior commissure (p. 44)
arachnoid layer (p. 30)
association cortex (p. 44)
autonomic nervous system (p. 47)
axial section (p. 27)
basal ganglia (p. 39)
brainstem (p. 35)
caudal (p. 27)
central canal (p. 30)
central nervous system (CNS) (p. 33)
central sulcus (p. 44)
cerebellum (p. 35)
cerebral aqueduct (p. 37)
cerebral hemispheres (p. 38)
cerebrospinal fluid (CSF) (p. 30)
chordates (p. 54)
cingulate cortex (p. 41)
contralateral (p. 28)
coronal section (p. 28)
corpus callosum (p. 44)
cranial nerves (p. 47)
diencephalon (p. 38)
distal (p. 28)
dorsal (p. 27)
dorsal horns (p. 34)
dorsolateral prefrontal cortex (p. 45)
dura mater (p. 29)
forebrain (p. 35)
frontal lobe (p. 44)
gray matter (p. 34)
gyrus/gyri (p. 42)
hindbrain (p. 35)
hippocampus (p. 40)
hominids (p. 55)
Homo sapiens (p. 55)
horizontal section (p. 28)
hypothalamus (p. 39)
inferior (p. 27)
ipsilateral (p. 28)
lateral (p. 28)
limbic system (p. 40)
locus coeruleus (p. 36)
medial (p. 28)
medulla (p. 35)
meninges (p. 29)
mesencephalon (p. 35)
metencephalon (p. 35)
midbrain (p. 35)
midline (p. 28)
myelencephalon (p. 35)
neuraxis (p. 27)
occipital lobe (p. 44)
oculomotor nerve (p. 47)
parasympathetic nervous system (p. 50)
parietal lobe (p. 44)
peripheral nervous system (PNS) (p. 33)
pia mater (p. 30)
pons (p. 35)
postcentral gyrus (p. 44)
posterior (p. 27)
proximal (p. 28)
raphe nuclei (p. 36)
reflexes (p. 34)
reticular formation (p. 35)
rostral (p. 27)
sagittal section (p. 28)
spinal cord (p. 33)
subarachnoid space (p. 30)
substantia nigra (p. 37)
sulcus/sulci (p. 42)
superior (p. 27)
sympathetic chain (p. 50)
telencephalon (p. 38)
temporal lobe (p. 44)
thalamus (p. 38)
ventral (p. 27)
ventricle (p. 30)
white matter (p. 34)

3 Cells of the Nervous System

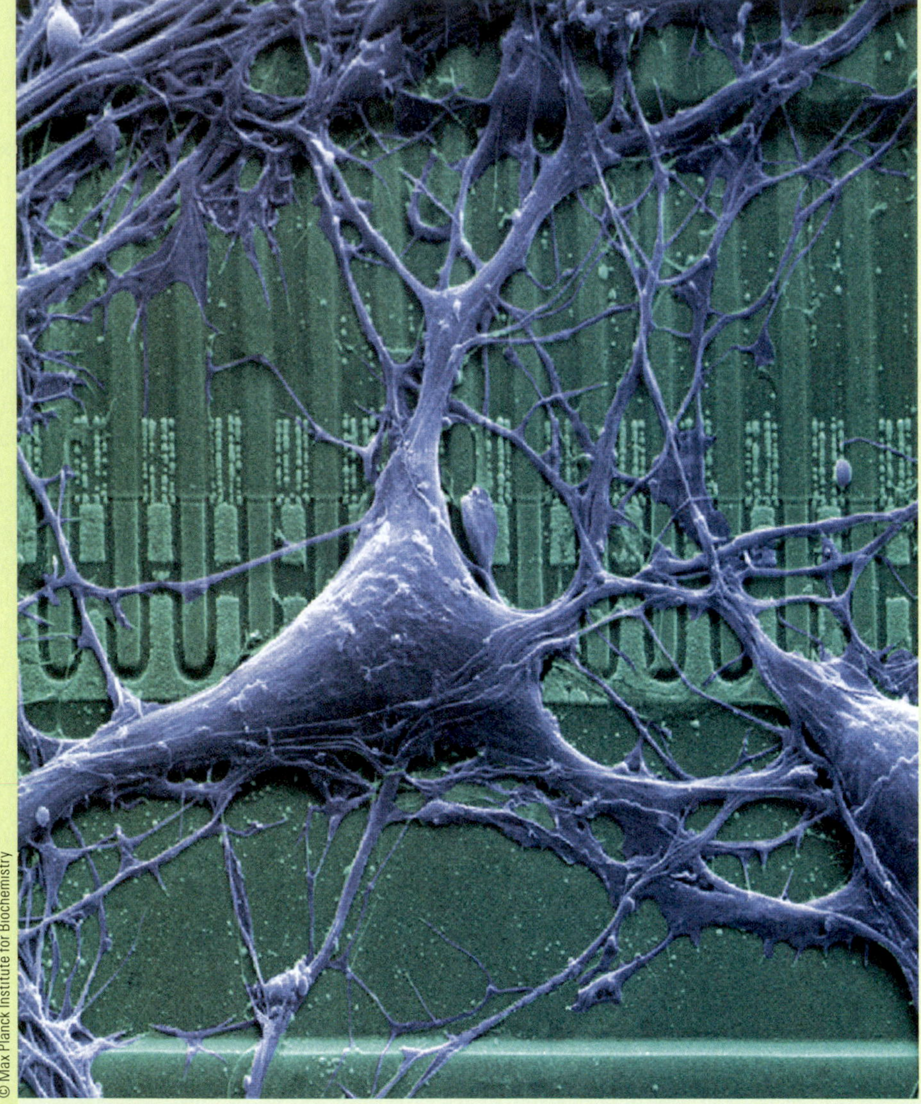

© Max Planck Institute for Biochemistry

▲ **Neuro-semiconductor Interface** Researchers are pushing the boundaries of technology by developing silicon chips that can communicate with living neurons.

CHAPTER OUTLINE

Introduction

Between October and March each year in Japan, hundreds of thousands of pounds of puffer fish (or *fugu* in Japanese) are consumed by delighted gourmets. The fish, shown in ■ Figure 3.1, is prized for its creamy white meat, reminiscent of frog's leg, and it is served in gelatins, as sushi, and as tempura. Eating *fugu* can be risky, however. Despite a tightly controlled and rigorous training program for *fugu* chefs, each year between 100 and 200 Japanese people die from the effects of tetrodotoxin (TTX), the toxin found in the meat and other parts of the puffer fish. An old Japanese folk song captures the dilemma, "I want to eat *fugu*, but I don't want to die" (*Fugu wa kuitashii, inochi wa oshishii.*)

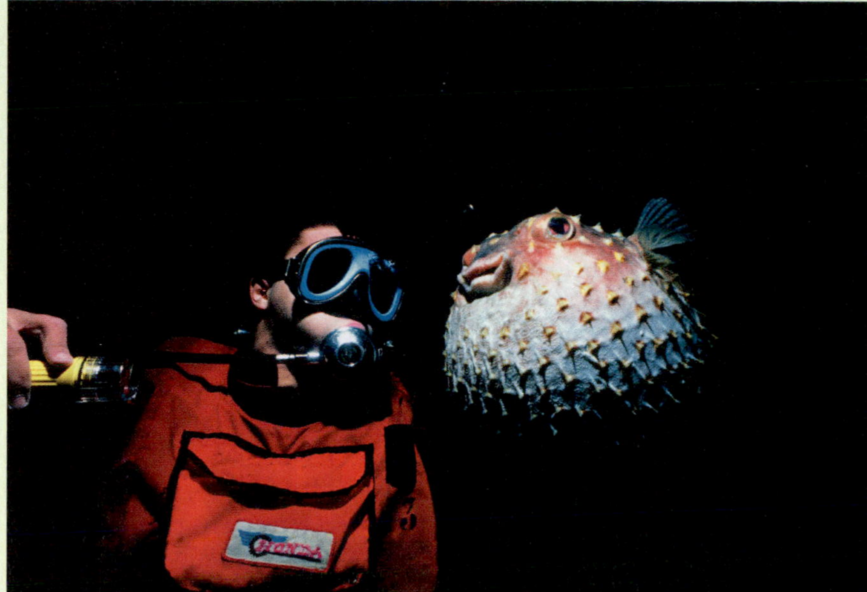

© Jeffrey L. Rotman/CORBIS

Figure 3.1
Hundreds Die Each Year from Puffer Fish Poisoning In spite of their intimidating appearance, hundreds of thousands of pounds of puffer fish, or *fugu,* are consumed each year in Japan. Unfortunately, certain species of puffer contain tetrodotoxin. In very small amounts, tetrodotoxin can cause death by blocking voltage-dependent sodium channels in the membranes of nerve fibers. When sodium is unable to enter the neuron, no signaling can occur, and death soon follows.

What does TTX have to do with a discussion of cells of the nervous system? TTX blocks the formation and transmission of electrical signals, or **action potentials,** within nerve cells. Specifically, TTX blocks the movement of sodium ions across the cell membrane that makes signaling possible. Without signals from the nervous system, lungs and other essential organs don't work. If TTX is so potent, why don't the puffer fish poison themselves? Special adaptations of the puffer fish sodium channel, the pore through which sodium ions cross cell membranes, not only protect the puffer from its own toxin but allow it to feed on other TTX species as well (Venkatesh et al., 2005).

LEARNING OBJECTIVES

After reading this chapter, you should be able to:

LO1 Differentiate between the characteristics of neurons and glia.

LO2 Identify the functions and major structural features of the neural membrane and cytoskeleton.

LO3 Describe the functions of the major organelles found in the cell body.

LO4 Describe the major features of axons and dendrites.

LO5 Differentiate between the structural and functional types of neurons.

LO6 Identify the major structures, types, and functions of the macroglia and microglia.

LO7 Describe events responsible for the resting potential, the action potential, the refractory periods, and the propagation of action potentials down the length of the axon.

LO8 Summarize the events responsible for exocytosis and the deactivation of neurotransmitters.

LO9 Differentiate between EPSPs and IPSPs. Summarize the major features of neural integration.

LO10 Summarize the nervous system's abilities to modulate the effects of chemical messengers.

Neurons and Glia

The nervous system is made up of two types of cells, **neurons** and **glia.** The neuron is specialized to carry out the functions of information processing and communication. The glia, whose name comes from the Greek word for "glue," serve a variety of support functions for neurons. In the human nervous system, there are at least 10 to 50 glia for every neuron.

The neurons and glia cooperate to carry out nervous system functions. First, we will consider the basic structure and function of neurons, followed by a more detailed discussion of the supportive glia.

The Structure of Neurons

All animal cells, including neurons, have membranes, nuclei, and small internal structures known as **organelles.** Many of these structures are found within the main mass of the neuron, known as the **cell body,** or **soma.** Neurons differ structurally from other cells in that they have specialized branches extending from the cell body, known as the **axons** and **dendrites,** which they use to communicate with other cells.

action potential The nerve impulse arising in an axon.

neuron A cell of the nervous system that is specialized for information processing and communication.

glia (GLEE-uh) Cells in the nervous system that support the activities of neurons.

organelle A small structure within a cell that carries out a specific function.

cell body / soma (SOH-muh) The main mass of a neuron, containing the nucleus and many organelles.

axon The branch of a neuron usually responsible for carrying signals to other neurons.

The separation of psychology from the premises of biology is purely artificial, because the human psyche lives in indissoluble union with the body.
Carl Jung

Neuron Membranes The primary task of any cell membrane is to form a boundary between the cell and its external environment. The neural membrane must separate the **intracellular fluid** of the cell's interior from the **extracellular fluid** surrounding the neuron. As we will see later in the chapter, the chemical compositions of these two types of fluids are quite different. Maintaining this difference is essential to the process of generating and sending neural messages.

The neural membrane accomplishes its task by way of its molecular structure. As illustrated in ■ Figure 3.2, the neural membrane is made up of a double layer of phospholipids, fatty molecules that contain phosphate. Because they are fats, phospholipids do not dissolve in water. You have probably observed while cooking or making salad dressing that oil and water do not mix. As a result of its lipid structure, the neural membrane is able to restrain the water-based fluids on either side, maintaining the structural integrity of the cell. Membranes are able to do this in spite of being only two phospholipid molecules wide, with a resulting thickness of only five nanometers (1 nanometer = 1 billionth of a meter, or 10^{-9} meters).

Suspended within this phospholipid membrane are a number of important protein structures that control its **permeability,** the movement of substances across the cell membrane. There are two primary types of protein structures of interest to us in our discussion of neural function, **ion channels** and **ion pumps.** These structures provide pores, or channels, through which specific **ions,** or electrically charged particles, can move into or out of the neuron. Ion channels allow ions to move passively, without the expenditure of energy, whereas ion pumps require energy. Both channels and pumps show ion selectivity, or the ability to let a particular type of ion pass and no others. The amino acids, or protein building blocks, that make up the ion channel or pump determine which ions will be allowed to pass through the membrane.

Ion channels have the ability to open and close in response to stimuli in their immediate vicinity. Some ion channels, known as **voltage-dependent channels,** open and close in response to the electrical status of adjacent areas of membrane. These channels form an important part of our discussion of electrical signaling within

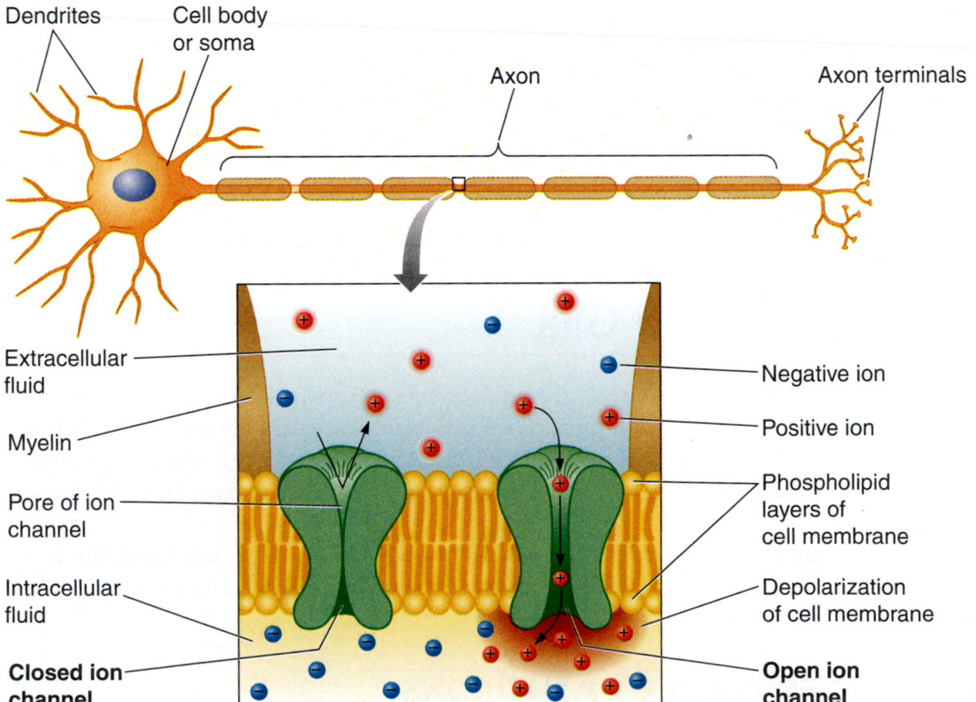

■ **FIGURE 3.2**
The Neural Membrane Neural membranes consist of double layers of phospholipid molecules. Embedded within the lipid layers are proteins that serve as ion channels and ion pumps. These structures open and close, controlling the movement of ions across the neural membrane.

dendrite The branch of a neuron that generally receives information from other neurons.
intracellular fluid The fluid inside a cell.
extracellular fluid The fluid surrounding a cell.
permeability A property of a substance that determines the extent to which other substances may pass through it.
ion channel A protein structure embedded in a cell membrane that allows ions to pass without the use of additional energy.
ion pump A protein structure embedded in a cell membrane that uses energy to move ions across the membrane.
ion An electrically charged particle in solution.
voltage-dependent channel An ion channel that opens or closes in response to the local electrical environment.

the neuron. **Ligand-gated channels** open when they come in contact with specific chemicals. These chemicals are typically our naturally occurring chemical messengers but can be drugs from artificial sources as well (see Chapter 4). Ligand-gated channels become very important as we discuss events taking place at the **synapse,** or the junction between two neurons. The two most important pumps in neurons are the **sodium-potassium pumps** and the **calcium pumps.** Sodium-potassium pumps help maintain the differences in chemical composition between the intracellular and extracellular fluids. Sodium-potassium pumps do a "prisoner exchange" across the neural membrane by sending three sodium ions out of the cell while collecting two potassium ions from the extracellular environment. This process comes at a high cost to the neuron. Possibly as much as 20 to 40 percent of the energy required by the brain is used to run the sodium-potassium pumps (Sheng, 2000). Calcium pumps perform a similar function, although they do not collect another type of ion in exchange for the calcium they pump out of the cell. When we discuss the release of chemical messengers, or **neurotransmitters,** by a neuron, you will see why it is essential to maintain low levels of calcium within the cell.

The Neural Cytoskeleton Having a neural membrane without structural support would be like having skin without bones. The structural support that maintains the shape of the neuron is provided by the **cytoskeleton.** Three types of filament, or fiber, make up the neural cytoskeleton. These structural fibers also move elements within the cell and anchor the various channel and receptor proteins in their appropriate places on the neural membrane.

Largest of the three types of cytoskeleton fibers are the **microtubules,** which are formed in the shape of hollow tubes with a diameter of about 25 nm (nanometers). Microtubules, shown in ■ Figure 3.3, are responsible for the movement of various materials within the cell. Movement along the microtubules from the cell body to the axon terminal is known as **anterograde transport,** and movement back to the cell body from the periphery of the neuron is known as **retrograde transport.** Microtubules have been implicated in the development of Alzheimer's disease (see Chapter 5). This

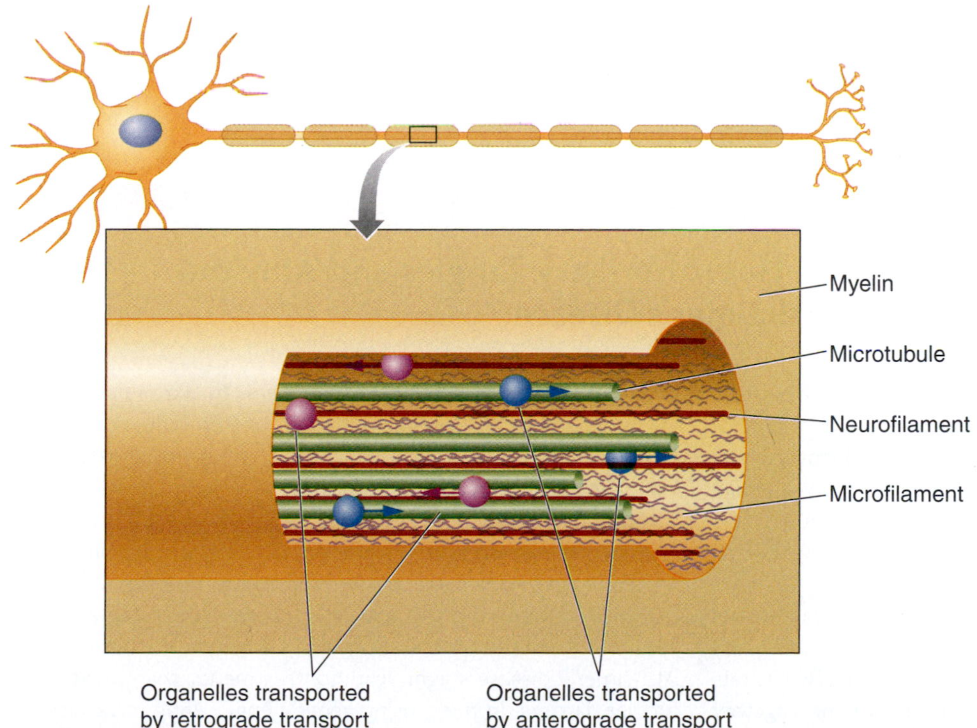

■ **FIGURE 3.3**
Three Fiber Types Compose the Cytoskeleton of Neurons Microtubules provide means for transporting materials within the neuron. Neurofilaments provide structural support, whereas microfilaments may be involved with structural changes associated with learning.

ligand-gated channel (LIE-gend) An ion channel in the neural membrane that responds to chemical messengers.

synapse (SIN-aps) The junction between two neurons at which information is transferred from one to another.

sodium-potassium pump An ion pump that uses energy to transfer three sodium ions to the extracellular fluid for every two potassium ions retrieved from the extracellular fluid.

calcium pump A protein structure embedded in the neural membrane that uses energy to move calcium ions out of the cell.

neurotransmitter A chemical messenger that transfers information across a synapse.

cytoskeleton (sie-toh-SKEL-uh-ton) A network of filaments that provides the internal structure of a neuron.

microtubule The largest fiber in the cell cytoskeleton, responsible for the transport of neurotransmitters and other products to and from the cell body.

anterograde transport Movement of materials from the cell body of a neuron to the axon terminal along the microtubules.

retrograde transport Movement of material from the axon terminal back to the cell body via the cell's system of microtubules.

condition is characterized initially by memory loss, followed by progressive decline in cognitive and physical functions, eventually leading to death. One of the characteristic symptoms of Alzheimer's disease is the presence of neurofibrillary tangles consisting of a protein called *tau*. In a healthy brain, tau connects adjacent microtubules and holds them in place. In Alzheimer's disease, the tau levels become elevated (Baas & Qiang, 2005). In response, an affected neuron adds molecules of phosphate to the tau protein, which causes it to disconnect from the microtubules. As shown in ■ Figure 3.4, the disconnected tau begins to form tangles, hindering the cell's ability to signal and maintain its structure. The neuron folds in on itself and collapses (Brandt, 2001).

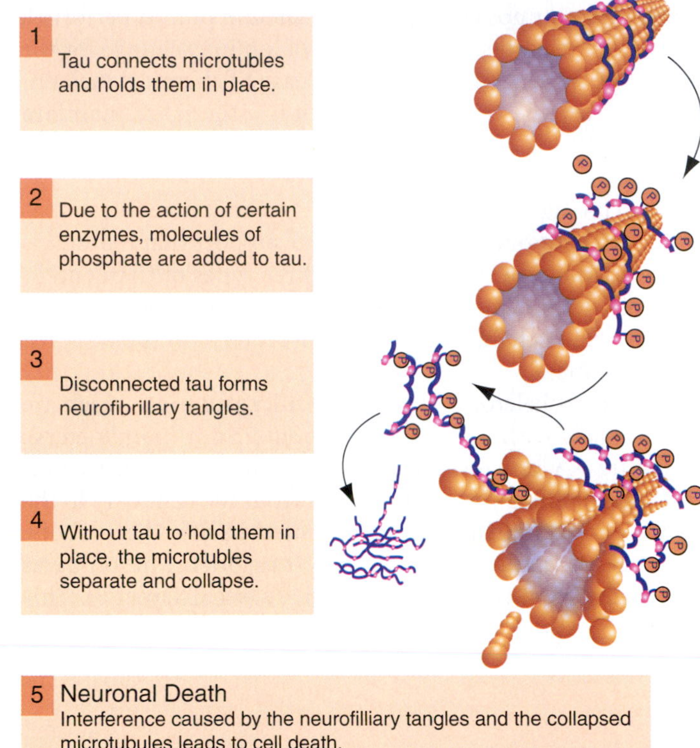

1 Tau connects microtubles and holds them in place.
2 Due to the action of certain enzymes, molecules of phosphate are added to tau.
3 Disconnected tau forms neurofibrillary tangles.
4 Without tau to hold them in place, the microtubles separate and collapse.
5 Neuronal Death
Interference caused by the neurofilliary tangles and the collapsed microtubules leads to cell death.
P

■ **FIGURE 3.4**
Tau Phosphorylation Molecules of phosphate added to the tau protein lead to neurofibrillary tangles and structural collapse.

WHY DOES THIS MATTER?

The Connection Between Neurofibrillary Tangles and Amyloid in Alzheimer's Disease

In addition to neurofibrillary tangles, the brains of patients with Alzheimer's disease show evidence of an abnormal version of a protein known as amyloid. The discovery of a connection between neurofibrillary tangles and amyloid matters because it can lead to the development of new drugs to stop the Alzheimer's process long before behavioral symptoms of memory loss occur.

As we mention in this chapter, one of the characteristics of Alzheimer's disease is the presence of neurofibrillary tangles. These tangles are made from a protein known as tau, which normally plays an essential role in holding together the microtubules that form an important part of the neural cytoskeleton. However, in cases of Alzheimer's disease, the tau proteins detach, and the microtubules separate. This produces a breakdown in cell structure. In particular, the axons of neurons are very dependent on microtubules both for structure and for the transport of important chemicals to and from the cell body. Once the tau proteins detach, they clump together to form neurofibrillary tangles.

Why would the tau proteins begin to detach? It appears that one abnormal type of amyloid, beta amyloid, works together with tau to break apart the microtubules (King et al., 2006). Understanding this very early step in the onset of Alzheimer's disease might lead to treatments that prevent further damage. In mice, using genetic engineering to reduce about half of the tau in the brain was sufficient to prevent many symptoms of Alzheimer's disease without changing the ability of tau to provide structural support (Roberson et al., 2007).

The middle-sized filaments, known simply as **neurofilaments,** are the most common fiber in the neuron. Neurofilaments are usually about 10 nm in diameter, or less than half the size of the microtubules. Their structure is similar to that of hair, and they are quite strong for their size. Neurofilaments run parallel to the length of the axon and provide structural support. The smallest fibers are the **microfilaments,** which range from 3 to 5 nm in diameter. Because most of the microfilaments are located in the branches of the neuron, they may participate in changing the shape and length of these structures during development (Rajnicek, 2006) and in response to learning (see Chapter 12).

The human brain is estimated to have about a hundred billion nerve cells, two million miles of axons, and a million billion synapses, making it the most complex structure, natural or artificial, on earth.

Tim Green, Stephen F. Heinemann, and Jim F. Gusella

The Neural Cell Body The neural cell body, or soma, contains many of the same small structures and carries out many of the same functions as do other cells. In addition, the neural cell body is specialized to participate in the communication function of the neuron. The major features of the neural cell body may be seen in ■ Figure 3.5.

The most prominent structure in the cell body is the **nucleus,** which contains the DNA that directs the cell's functions. The nucleus also contains a substructure, known as the **nucleolus.** The nucleolus builds organelles known as **ribosomes,** which engage in protein synthesis. The ribosomes produce proteins either on their own or in association with the **endoplasmic reticulum,** another small structure, or organelle, located in the cell body. The endoplasmic reticulum may be divided into rough and smooth portions. The rough endoplasmic reticulum has many ribosomes bound to its surface, giving it the bumpy appearance responsible for its name. There are no ribosomes attached to the smooth endoplasmic reticulum. After proteins are constructed by the ribosomes on the rough endoplasmic reticulum, they are moved by the smooth endoplasmic reticulum to the **Golgi apparatus.** This organelle inserts the completed proteins into *vesicles,* or small packages made out of membrane material. **Mitochondria** extract oxygen and pyruvic acid from sugar in the intracellular fluid and construct and release molecules of adenosine triphosphate (ATP). ATP is the major energy source for the neuron. Wherever you see many mitochondria, you can be sure activities requiring a lot of energy are taking place.

Dendrites Most neurons have a large number of branches known as dendrites, from the Greek word for "tree." Along with the cell body, the dendrites serve as locations at which information from other neurons is received. The greater the surface area of dendritic membrane a neuron has, the larger the number of connections or synapses it can form with other neurons. At each synapse on a dendrite, special ion channels serving as receptor sites are embedded in the neural membrane. These receptor sites interact with molecules of neurotransmitter released by adjacent neurons that float across the **synaptic gap,** a fluid-filled space between the transmitting and receiving neurons.

Some dendrites form knobs known as **dendritic spines.** As illustrated in ■ Figure 3.6, spines provide additional locations for synapses to occur. Spines appear to be able to change their shape based on the amount of activity occurring at the synapse, which contributes to the processes of learning and memory. Because of the essential roles that dendrites play in learning and memory, abnormal dendritic spines are an underlying cause of some types of human mental retardation. As shown in ■ Figure 3.7, the dendritic spines of people with retardation are unusually long and thin (Purpura, 1974). Purpura observed that the dendritic spines of children with mental retardation were similar to the undeveloped dendritic spines of human fetuses. This implies that the spines of people with retardation failed to mature normally in response to learning. Aaron Grossman and his colleagues (Grossman, Elisseou, McKinney, & Greenough, 2006) have identified a particular protein, *fragile X mental retardation protein (FMRP),* as being essential to the normal maturation of dendritic spines. Mice lacking the gene encoding FMRP show spine immaturity similar to Purpura's samples.

neurofilament A neural fiber found in the cell cytoskeleton that is responsible for structural support.

microfilament The smallest fiber found in the cell cytoskeleton that may participate in the changing of the length and shape of axons and dendrites.

nucleus The substructure within a cell body that contains the cell's DNA.

nucleolus (new-klee-OH-lus) A substructure within a cell nucleus where ribosomes are produced.

ribosome (RIE-boh-zome) An organelle in the cell body involved with protein synthesis.

endoplasmic reticulum (en-doh-PLAZ-mik reh-TIK-you-lum) An organelle in the cell body that participates in protein synthesis.

Golgi apparatus (GOAL-jee) An organelle in the cell body that packages proteins in vesicles.

mitochondria (my-toh-KON-dree-uh) Organelles that provide energy to the cell by transforming pyruvic acid and oxygen into molecules of adenosine triphosphate (ATP).

synaptic gap The tiny fluid-filled space between neurons forming a synapse.

dendritic spine A knob on the dendrite that provides additional membrane area for the formation of synapses with other neurons.

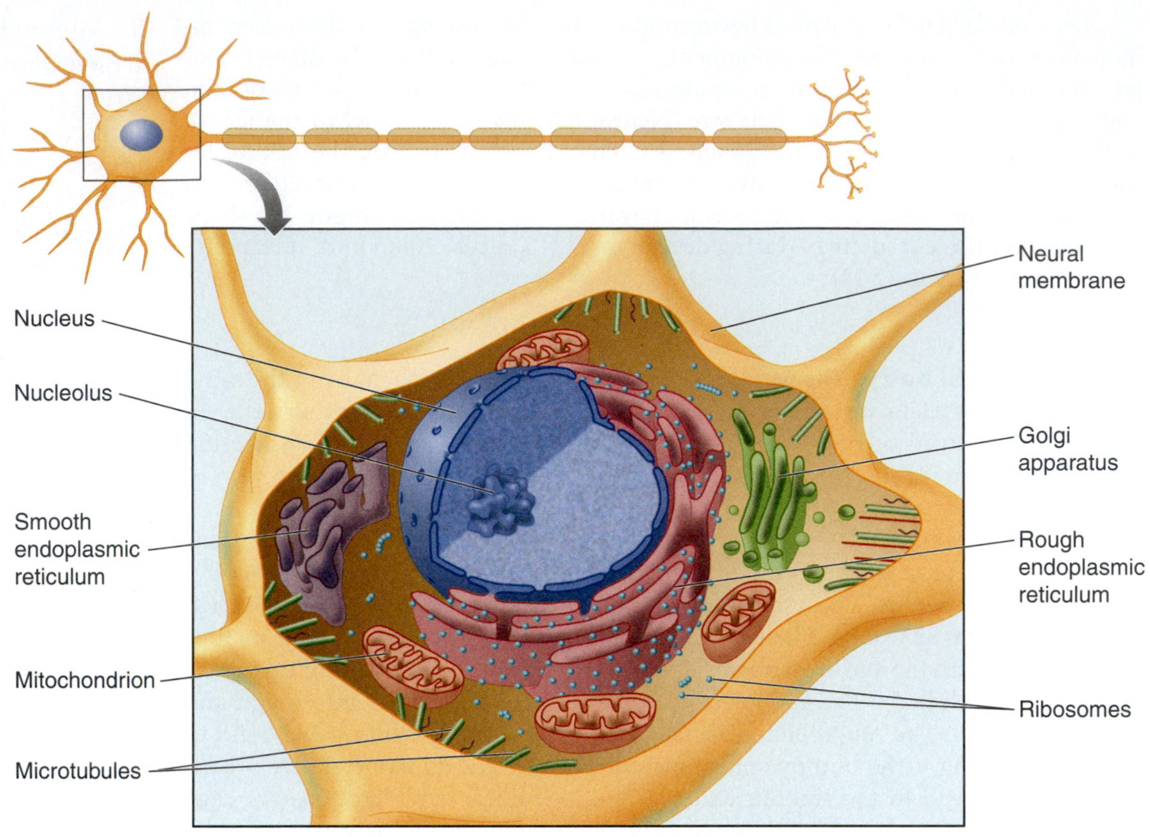

FIGURE 3.5
The Neural Cell Body Neurons share a number of features with other cells. Most have a membrane, a nucleus, a nucleolus, mitochondria, ribosomes, smooth and rough endoplasmic reticuli, and Golgi apparati.

FIGURE 3.6
Axons and Dendrites Action potentials originate in the axon hillock and then travel the length of the axon to the axon terminal. The arrival of action potentials at the axon terminal signals the release of neurotransmitters from the synaptic vesicles. Molecules of neurotransmitter diffuse across the synaptic gap, where they interact with receptors embedded in the dendrite of the adjacent neuron.

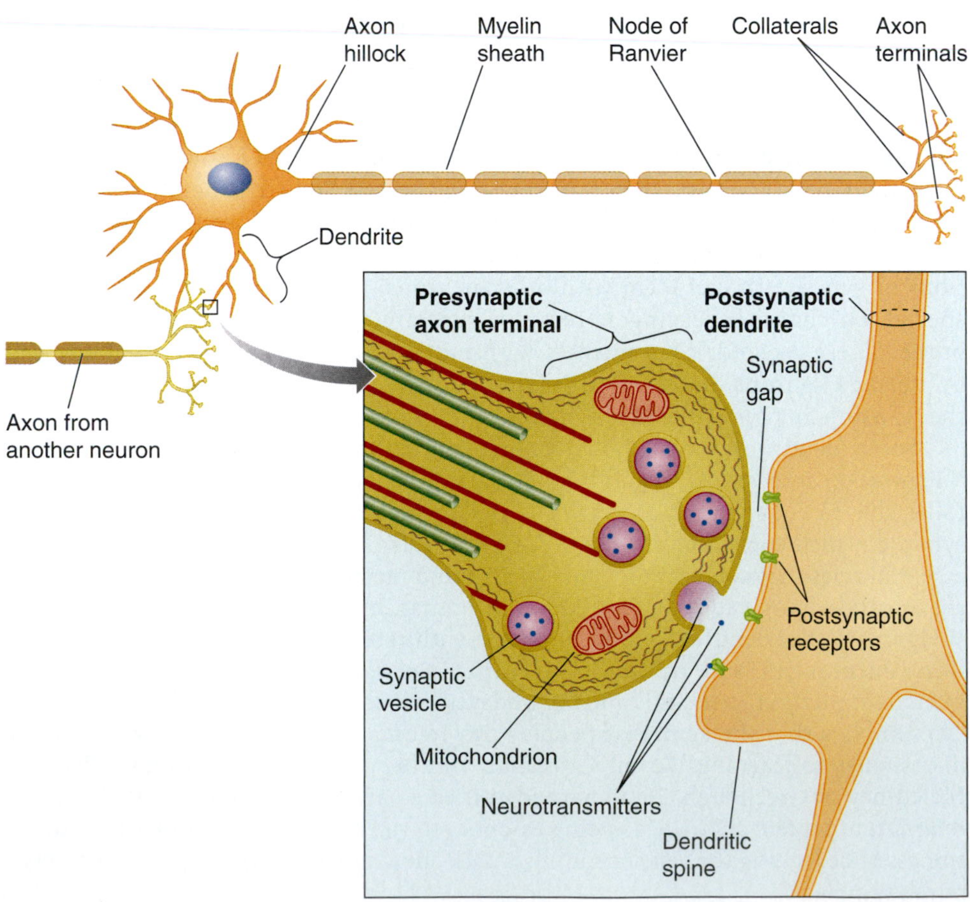

The Axon As shown in Figure 3.6, although a neuron may have large numbers of dendrites, it typically has only one axon. The axon is responsible for carrying neural messages to other neurons. The cone-shaped segment of axon that lies at the junction of the axon and the cell body is known as the **axon hillock.** Action potentials arise in the axon hillock and are then transmitted down the length of the axon.

Axons vary substantially in diameter. In vertebrates, including humans, axon diameters range from less than 1 micrometer (μm, or 10^{-6}, meter) to about 25 micrometers. In invertebrates, such as the squid, axon diameter can be as large as 1 mm. Axon diameter is crucial to the speed of signaling. Larger diameter axons are much faster than smaller diameter axons. Does this mean that the squid thinks faster than we do? Not at all. As we'll see shortly, many vertebrate axons are insulated by **myelin,** a material that allows for rapid signal transmission in spite of smaller axon diameter.

Axons also vary in length. Some neurons have axons that barely extend at all from the cell body and that communicate with adjacent cells. These neurons are referred to as **local circuit neurons.** Other neurons, known as **projection neurons,** have very long axons. Consider for a moment that you have neural cell bodies in your spinal cord with axons that extend as far as your big toe. Depending on your height, these axons are likely to be about three feet long. You might think of the local circuit neurons as being similar to your local telephone calling area, whereas the projection neurons are your long-distance telephone system.

The ends of many axons are divided into branches, known as **collaterals.** As a result, a neuron with only one axon may still communicate with a large number of other cells. At the very end of each axon collateral is a swelling known as the **axon terminal.** The axon terminal contains large numbers of both mitochondria and synaptic vesicles that contain chemical messengers. **Synaptic vesicles** are made from the same double-lipid molecule structure as the cell membrane and are approximately 50 nm in diameter.

Many, but not all, axons in vertebrate nervous systems are covered by myelin. In the adult human, the vast majority of central nervous system neurons and peripheral motor neurons are myelinated. Peripheral sensory nerves may or may not be myelinated, with the smallest diameter fibers less likely to be so (see Chapter 7). Myelin is formed by certain types of glia that wrap themselves or their branches around segments of axon. Myelin does not cover the entire length of an axon. The axon hillock is completely uncovered and between each myelin segment there is a bare space of axon membrane known as a **node of Ranvier.** Nodes of Ranvier occur somewhere between 0.2 mm to 2.0 mm apart down the length of the axon, depending on both the diameter and length of the axon. Large diameter axons have thicker myelin and greater distances between nodes of Ranvier.

There are a number of important advantages to myelin. First of all, as mentioned earlier, myelin allows human axons to be smaller in diameter without sacrificing transmission speed. Space is a precious commodity in the nervous system. The smaller the diameter of our axons, the more neural tissue we can pack into our skulls, and the more information we can process. In addition, myelin reduces the energy requirements of neurons by decreasing the amount of work done by sodium-potassium pumps. Myelin segments wrap so tightly around axons that there is little to no extracellular fluid between the myelin and the axon membrane. As a result, there is no need for ion channels under a myelin sheath. The only places on a myelinated axon that have large numbers of ion channels are the axon hillock and the nodes of Ranvier. In contrast, an unmyelinated axon has ion channels along its entire length. During signaling, therefore, fewer ions move through the ion channels of a myelinated axon membrane than through an unmyelinated axon membrane of the same length. Because the sodium-potassium pumps work to restore ions to their pre-signaling locations, less of this work needs to be done in a myelinated axon.

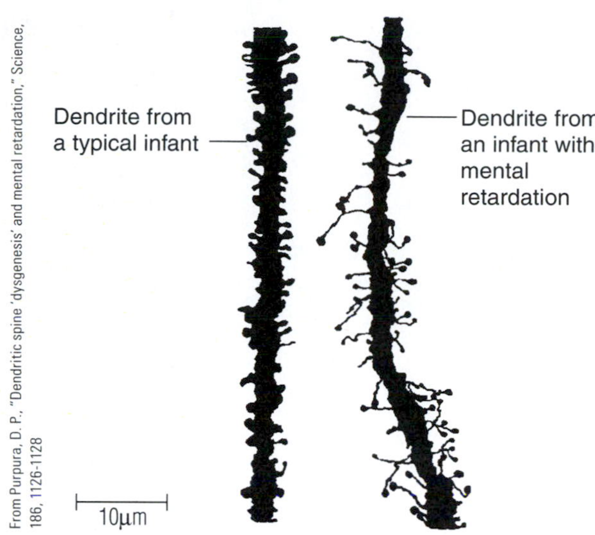

From Purpura, D. P., "Dendritic spine 'dysgenesis' and mental retardation," Science, 186, 1126-1128

FIGURE 3.7 Abnormal Dendrites and Mental Retardation Compared with the dendrites from a typical infant on the left, the dendrites from an infant with mental retardation are abnormally long and thin. Dominick Purpura has observed that the dendrites of children with mental retardation resemble the dendrites of the human fetus. The abnormal dendrites may cause retardation by failing to mature in response to environmental input.

axon hillock The cone-shaped segment of axon located at the junction of the axon and cell body that is specialized for the generation of action potentials.

myelin (MY-lin) The fatty insulating material covering some axons that boosts the speed and efficiency of electrical signaling.

local circuit neuron A neuron that communicates with neurons in its immediate vicinity.

projection neuron A neuron with a very long axon that communicates with neurons in distant areas of the nervous system.

collateral One of the branches near the end of the axon closest to its targets.

axon terminal The swelling at the tip of an axon collateral specialized for the release of neurotransmitter substances.

synaptic vesicle A small structure in the axon terminal that contains neurotransmitters.

node of Ranvier (RAHN-vee-ay) The uncovered section of axon membrane between two adjacent segments of myelin.

Structural Variations in Neurons

There are a number of ways that we can categorize neurons. We have already seen how neurons can be classified as either local circuit or projection neurons based on the length of their axons. As shown in ■ Figure 3.8, another strategy is to classify neurons according to the number of branches they have extending from the neural cell body.

Unipolar neurons have a single branch extending from the cell body, as indicated by the name. These neurons are typical of invertebrate nervous systems. In vertebrates, unipolar cells may be found in the sensory systems and in the autonomic nervous system. For example, some unipolar cells are involved with the somatosenses (touch, temperature, and pain). Just beyond the cell body of a unipolar neuron, the single branch divides in two, with one part extending back toward the central nervous system and the other part extending toward the skin and muscle.

A second structural type is the **bipolar neuron.** These cells have two branches extending from the neural cell body: one axon and one dendrite. Bipolar neurons play important roles in sensory systems, including in the retina of the eye (see Chapter 6).

John Allman and his colleagues (Watson, Jones, & Allman, 2006) are particularly interested in a special type of bipolar cell, known as a Von Economo neuron (VEN), named after one of its discoverers (Von Economo & Koskinas, 1929). Unlike most neuron types, VENs appear to have developed recently in primate evolution. They are found in humans and great apes but not in lesser apes and monkeys (Nimchinsky et al., 1999). Both their numbers and the size of their cell bodies are much larger in humans than in the great apes. These cells occur only in the anterior cingulate cortex (ACC) and in the junction of the frontal lobe and insula area of the temporal lobe. Allman et al. (2005) believe that the VENs are specifically designed to provide fast, intuitive assessments of complex situations.

The most common structural type of neuron in the vertebrate nervous system is the **multipolar neuron.** Multipolar neurons have many branches extending from the cell body. Usually, this means that the cell has one axon and numerous dendrites. Multipolar neurons may be further classified according to shape. Pyramidal cells in the cerebral cortex and the hippocampus have cell bodies that are shaped like pyramids. The Purkinje cells of the cerebellum have dramatic dendritic trees that allow a single cell to form as many as 150,000 synapses.

Functional Variations in Neurons

Another strategy for classifying neurons is to look at the role they play within the nervous system. **Sensory neurons** are specialized to receive information from the outside world. Our senses of vision, hearing, touch, taste, and smell all depend on specialized receptor neurons. These neurons can translate many types of information, such as light or sound waves, into neural signals that the nervous system can process. **Motor neurons** transmit commands from the central nervous system (the brain and spinal cord) directly to muscles and glands. The vast majority of neurons are known as **interneurons.** Interneurons are not specialized for either sensory or motor functions but act as bridges between the sensory and motor systems.

Glia

Glia, the cells in the nervous system that support the activities of neurons, are generally categorized by size. The **macroglia** are the largest varieties of glial cells, and the **microglia** are the smaller varieties. The major features of each type of glial cell are summarized in Table 3.1.

Macroglia There are three primary types of macroglia: astrocytes, oligodendrocytes, and Schwann cells. The **astrocytes** provide a variety of support functions to neurons, whereas the **oligodendrocytes** and **Schwann cells** supply the myelin covering that insulates axon fibers.

unipolar neuron A neuron with one branch that extends a short distance from the cell body then splits into two branches.

bipolar neuron A neuron with two branches: one axon and one dendrite.

multipolar neuron A neuron that has multiple branches, usually one axon and numerous dendrites.

sensory neuron A specialized neuron that translates incoming sensory information into electrical signals.

motor neuron A specialized neuron that communicates with muscles and glands.

interneuron A neuron that serves as a bridge between sensory and motor neurons.

macroglia Large glial cells, including astrocytes, oligodendrocytes, and Schwann cells.

microglia Tiny, mobile glial cells that migrate to areas of damage and digest debris.

astrocyte (AS-troe-site) A large, star shaped glial cell of the central nervous system, responsible for structural support, isolation of the synapse, control of the extracellular chemical environment at the synapse, and possibly communication.

oligodendrocyte (ah-li-goh-DEN-droh-site) A glial cell that forms the myelin on central nervous system axons.

Schwann cell (shwahn) A glial cell that forms the myelin on axons in the peripheral nervous system.

Type	Appearance	Location	Examples of Some Functions
Unipolar neuron	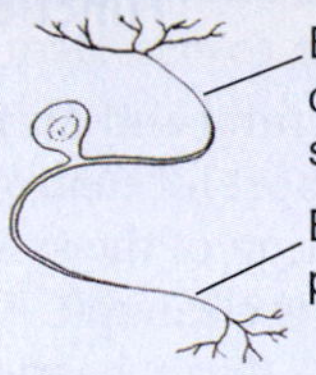 Branch to the central nervous system Branch to the periphery	Near spinal cord, with processes extending to skin, muscle, organs, and glands	Somatosenses: transmits touch, temperature, pain Autonomic system: directs glands and organs
Bipolar neuron	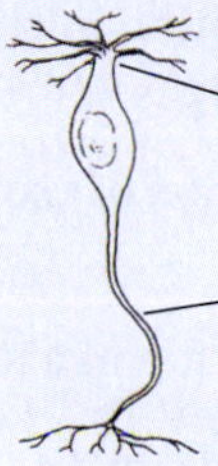 Dendrite Axon	Retina Cochlea Olfactory bulb Tongue	Transmits information in several sensory systems
Multipolar	 Dendrite Axon Von Economo neuron (VEN)	Anterior cingulate cortex (ACC) Insula	Provides fast, intuitive assessments of complex situations
	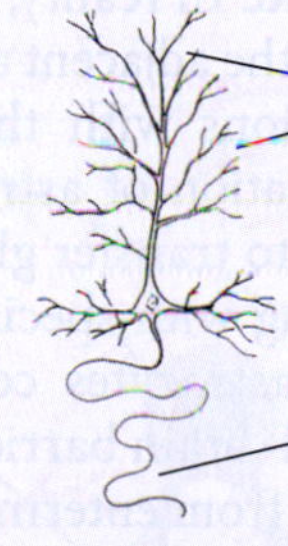 Dendrites Axon Pyramidal cell	Cerebral cortex	
	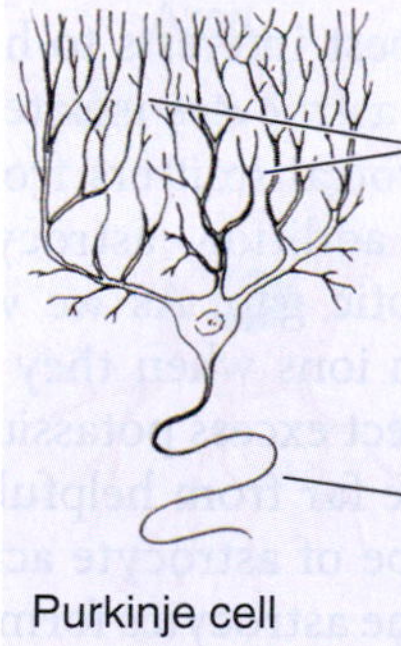 Dendrites Axon Purkinje cell	Cerebellum	
	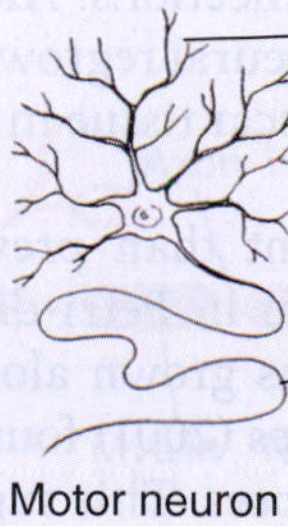 Dendrites Axon Motor neuron	Spinal cord, with axons extending to muscles and glands	Carries commands to muscles and glands

FIGURE 3.8 Structural and Functional Classification of Neurons Most vertebrate unipolar and bipolar neurons are found in sensory systems, where they encode and transmit information from the outside world. Multipolar neurons typically serve as motor neurons, transmitting commands to glands and muscles, or as interneurons, providing bridges between sensory and motor neurons.

It is still open to question whether psychology is a natural science, or whether it can be regarded as a science at all.

Ivan Pavlov

Schwann cell provides a single myelin segment on one peripheral axon. It takes large numbers of Schwann cells to myelinate a peripheral nerve.

We can see the importance of myelin by studying conditions in which it is damaged. The disease multiple sclerosis (MS) involves a progressive demyelination of the nervous system (see Chapter 15). The end result is neural signaling that may not work properly, leading to a range of symptoms from mild (increased fatigue) to more severe (vision and mobility problems) to death.

Oligodendrocytes and Schwann cells differ in their reactions to injury. Schwann cells actually help guide the regrowth of damaged axons, whereas the oligodendrocytes lack this capacity. If axon regrowth were impossible in the peripheral nervous system, we would not bother to reattach severed fingers or limbs. As shown in ■ Figure 3.11, surgeons are even transplanting hands and faces from cadavers to living people, which would be pointless unless nerve growth eventually provided some sensation and motor control (Petit, Minns, Dubernard, Hettiaratchy, & Lee, 2003).

■ **FIGURE 3.11 Regrowth of Peripheral Axons Makes Body Part Transplants Possible** Alba Lucia Cardona of Columbia lost both arms 30 years ago in a laboratory explosion. Spanish doctors recently transplanted two cadaver arms onto Cardona's body, a process that would not make sense without the ability of peripheral nerves to regenerate and reestablish some movement and sensation in the attached body parts. Unfortunately, duplicating this success in the central nervous system remains a challenge for scientists attempting to repair damage to the spinal cord and brain.

Microglia You may not particularly like the idea of having "brain debris," but like any cells, neurons and glia do die. Rather than leave the debris lying around where it might interfere with neural function, microglia serve as the brain's cleanup crew. At rest, the branches of microglia reach out and sample their immediate environments (Nimmerjahn, Kirchhoff, & Helmchen, 2005). Should they detect any one of the many types of molecules related to cell damage, whether from head injury, stroke, or other sources, these tiny cells travel to the location of the injury, where they digest the debris.

Uncontrolled activation of microglia, however, can damage the brain through their release of substances that produce inflammation. Microglia have also been observed to digest healthy cells located next to damaged cells (Kim & Joh, 2006). Consequently, inflammation caused by microglia activation is under investigation as a contributor to neurodegenerative diseases, including Alzheimer's disease, Parkinson's disease, and multiple sclerosis.

INTERIM SUMMARY 3.1

Summary Points

1. The nervous system is made up of two types of cells, neurons and glia. Neurons are responsible for processing information, and glia perform a variety of support functions. **(LO1)**

2. The neural membrane is composed of a two-molecule-thick layer of phospholipids. Embedded within the phospholipid membrane are ion channels and pumps, which are specialized proteins that allow chemicals to pass into and out of the neuron. The neural cytoskeleton provides structural support and the ability to transport needed substances within the neuron. **(LO2)**

3. The cell body contains important organelles that participate in the basic metabolism and protein synthesis of the cell. In addition, the cell body is a site of synapses with other neurons. **(LO3)**

4. Neurons communicate with other cells through special branches known as axons and dendrites. **(LO4)**

5. Neurons may be classified according to the number of branches extending from their cell bodies and their functions. **(LO5)**

6. Macroglia provide a variety of support functions to neurons, including the formation of myelin. Microglia remove debris resulting from damage to neurons. **(LO6)**

Review Questions

1. What are the roles of the dendrites and dendritic spines, and what structural features enable them to carry out these functions?

2. What are the different functions carried out by the macroglia and microglia?

The Generation of the Action Potential

Now that we have a working knowledge of the major structures involved in neural communication, we are ready to talk about how the process actually works. The first step in neural communication is the development of an electrical signal, the action potential, in the axon hillock of the sending, or presynaptic, neuron. When the action potential arrives at the axon terminal, the process switches from electrical to chemical signaling. The presynaptic neuron releases molecules of neurotransmitter from its terminal. The neurotransmitter molecules float across the synaptic gap to the waiting postsynaptic neuron. It is then up to the postsynaptic neuron to decide whether to send the message along. Although we believe that the vast majority of neural signals involve action potentials, recent evidence suggests that messages can be carried the length of an axon using complex chemical reactions instead of action potentials (Fasano et al., 2007). Further research will be necessary to understand the relative significance of these two signaling mechanisms.

Generation of an electrical signal within neurons requires a source of energy. The energy source for electrical signaling is provided by the characteristics of the intracellular and extracellular fluids.

The Ionic Composition of the Intracellular and Extracellular Fluids

In our discussion of the neural membrane, we found that one of the important responsibilities of the membrane is to keep the intracellular and extracellular fluids apart. In addition, the sodium-potassium pumps discussed earlier also work to maintain the differences between these two fluids. It is the difference between these two types of fluid that provides the neuron with a source of energy for electrical signaling.

The intracellular and extracellular fluids share a common ingredient, water, but differ from each other in the relative concentrations of ions they contain. When certain chemicals are dissolved in water, they take the form of ions. For instance, table salt (sodium chloride, or NaCl) dissolves in water, forming separate sodium ions (Na^+) and chloride ions (Cl^-). The ions remain separate rather than rejoining to form salt because their attraction to water is stronger than their attraction to each other. The plus and minus associated with each type of ion indicates its electrical charge. This, in turn, is a function of the ion's relative numbers of protons and electrons. A negatively charged ion has more electrons than protons, whereas a positively charged ion has fewer electrons than protons.

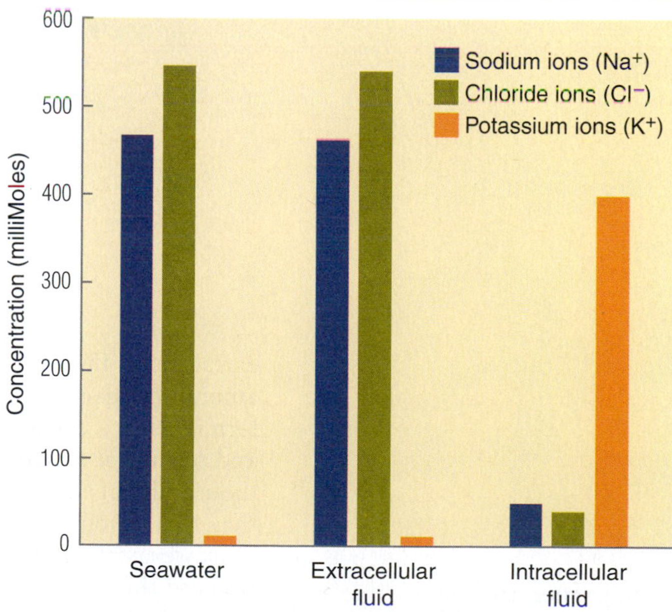

FIGURE 3.12
The Composition of Intracellular and Extracellular Fluids
Extracellular fluid is similar to seawater, with large concentrations of sodium and chloride but small concentrations of potassium. Intracellular fluid has a large concentration of potassium but relatively little sodium and chloride.
Source: Data from Doumin (2004) and Smock (1999).

As shown in Figure 3.12, extracellular fluid is characterized by large concentrations of sodium and chloride ions and a relatively small concentration of potassium (K^+) ions. If you have difficulty remembering which ions go where, keep in mind that extracellular fluid is very similar to seawater. As organisms moved from the seas onto land, they essentially packaged some of the seawater and brought it with them in their bodies. Intracellular fluid is quite different. The intracellular fluid of the resting neuron contains large numbers of potassium ions and relatively few sodium and chloride ions. In addition, there are some large proteins in ion form within the intracellular fluid that are negatively charged.

Because of the distribution of ions and other charged particles, particularly large, negatively charged proteins, the electrical environment inside the neuron is more negative than it is on the outside. How do we know? As shown in Figure 3.13, we can actually record the difference between the two environments by inserting a tiny glass microelectrode through the membrane of the neuron itself. We can use a voltmeter to measure the difference between the microelectrode and a wire placed in the

FIGURE 3.13
Measuring the Resting Potential of Neurons Axons from invertebrates such as the giant squid can be dissected and maintained in a culture dish for study. Because these axons are so large in diameter, electrodes can be inserted into the intracellular fluid. If we compare the recordings from two electrodes, one located in the intracellular fluid of the axon and the other in the extracellular fluid, our recording shows that the inside of the cell is negatively charged relative to the outside. The relatively larger number of negatively charged molecules in the intracellular fluid compared with the extracellular fluid is responsible for this difference.

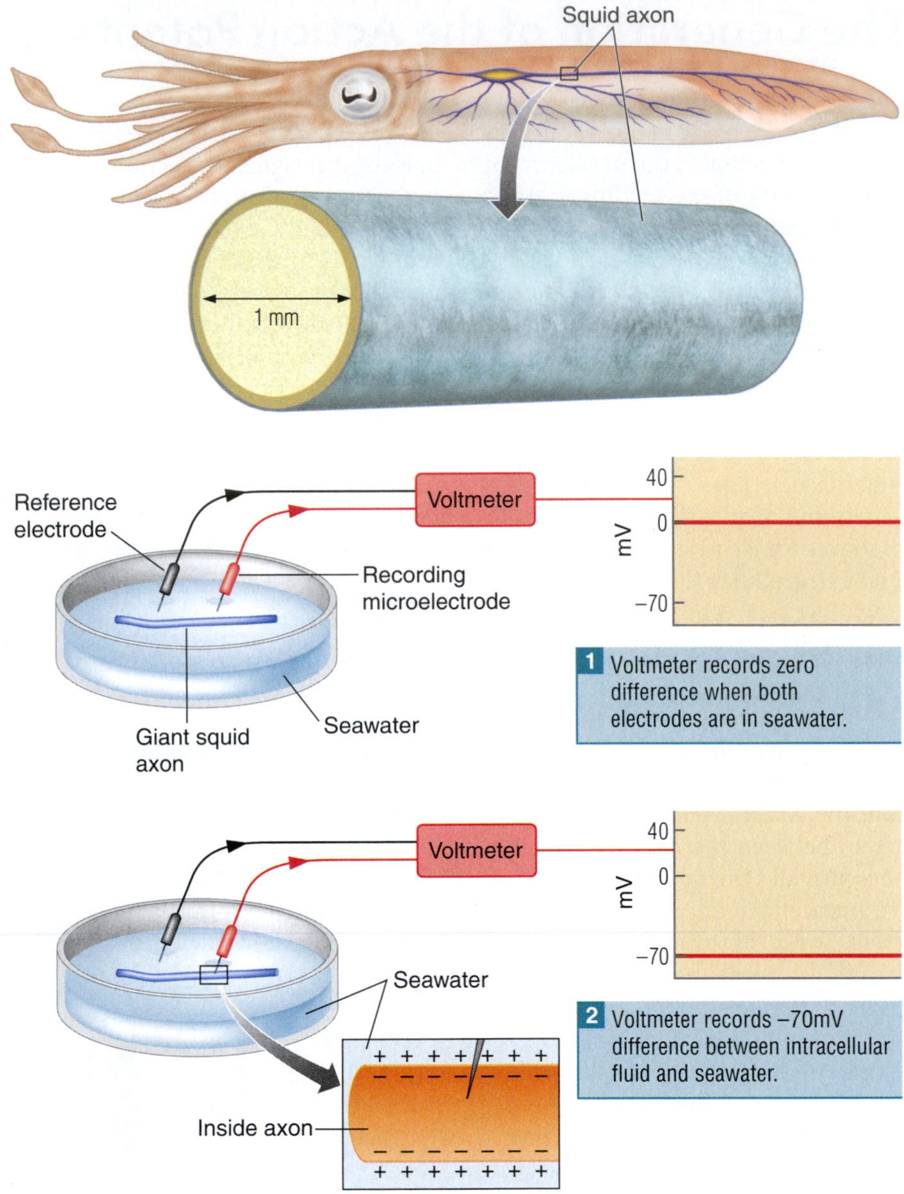

extracellular fluid adjacent to our cell. We use the same process when measuring the amount of charge left in a battery. The difference between the positive and negative terminals in a car battery is 12 volts. In contrast, the difference between the inside and outside of a neuron is approximately 70 millivolts (mV.) A millivolt is one one-thousandth of a volt, so your neurons definitely work on a different scale of electricity than that of your car. It is conventional to assign the outside environment a value of 0; thus, we speak of this 70mV difference across the membrane as negative, or –70mV. Because this difference is measured when the cell is not processing a message, it is known as the **resting potential** of the cell.

resting potential The measurement of the electrical charge across the neural membrane when the cell is not processing information.

diffusion The force that moves molecules from areas of high concentration to areas of low concentration.

concentration gradient An unequal distribution in the concentration of molecules across a cell membrane.

THE MOVEMENT OF IONS

Neural signals, or action potentials, result from the movement of ions. To understand the development of these signals, we need to know what forces cause ions to move.

Diffusion is the tendency for molecules to distribute themselves equally within a medium such as air or water. In other words, like city dwellers seeking the quiet countryside, molecules will move from a crowded location to a less crowded location. In more formal terms, diffusion pressure moves molecules along a **concentration gradient** from areas of high concentration to areas of low concentration. Another important cause of movement of molecules is **electrical force.** As you may already know from playing with magnets, opposite signs attract and like signs repel. Ions work the same way. Table salt forms readily when it dries out because the positively charged sodium is highly attracted to the negatively charged chloride.

With diffusion and electrical force in mind, let's revisit the distribution of ions on either side of the neural membrane in the resting cell. For the purposes of this exercise, assume that the neural membrane allows ions to move freely back and forth (which it doesn't do in the real world). As shown in ■ Figure 3.14, potassium is found in larger concentrations on the inside of the cell than on the outside. Diffusion would move the potassium ions along their concentration gradient from the inside (the area of higher concentration) to the outside (the area of lower concentration). However, diffusion pressure is balanced by electrical force in this case. Potassium is a positively charged ion. As such, it is content to stay in the negative environment on the inside of the cell and reluctant to venture into the relatively positive environment outside the cell. The net distribution of potassium reflects a balance, or *equilibrium*, between diffusion pressure and electrical force. Walther Nernst (1864–1941) received the Nobel Prize in 1920 for developing an equation for computing the equilibrium potential, or the point at which diffusion and electrical force balance one another, for a particular ion.

Chloride is the mirror image of potassium. Chloride, a negatively charged ion, is more concentrated outside the cell than inside it. Therefore, diffusion pressure works to push chloride into the cell. Once again, diffusion is counteracted by electrical force. The negative interior of the cell repels the negatively charged chloride ions, whereas the relatively positive exterior attracts them. Chloride finds its equilibrium.

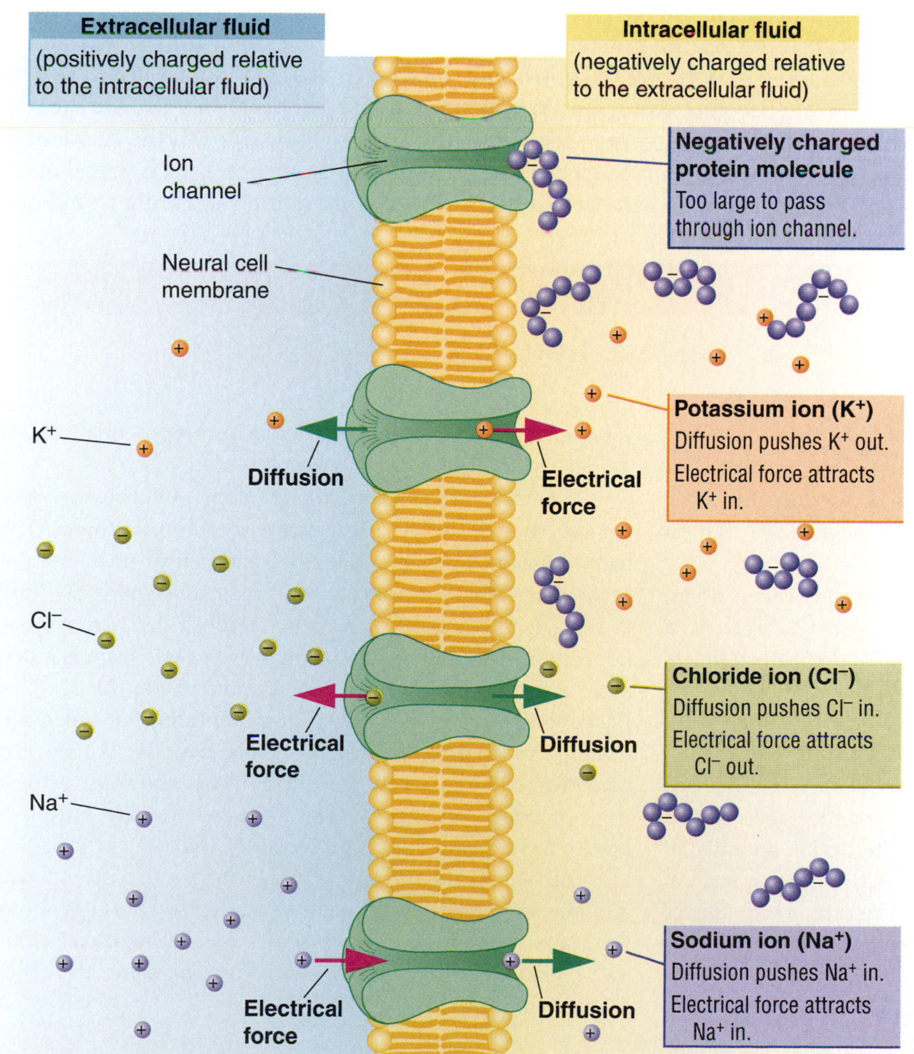

■ **FIGURE 3.14**
Diffusion and Electrical Force In a resting neuron, diffusion and electrical force balance each other to determine an equilibrium for potassium and chloride. In contrast, both diffusion and electrical force act to push sodium into the neuron. The large protein molecules found in the intracellular fluid cannot move through the membrane due to their size. Because of their negative charge, they contribute to the relative negativity of the intracellular fluid.

electrical force The force that moves molecules with like electrical charges apart and molecules with opposite electrical charges together.

I like nonsense; it wakes up the brain cells.
Dr. Suess

Now we come to the interesting case of sodium. Sodium is found in greater concentration on the outside than on the inside of the cell. By now, you know that means that diffusion will work to push sodium into the cell. But unlike the cases of potassium and chloride, electrical force is not working against diffusion but in the same direction. The positive sodium ions should be very attracted to the negative interior of the cell. With both diffusion pressure and electrical force pushing sodium into the cell, how do we account for the fact that most of the sodium is found on the outside? The answer lies in the nature of our very important neural membrane.

So far, we have assumed that the neural membrane allows ions to move freely. In the real world, it does not. Although the membrane contains sodium channels, these are generally closed when the cell is at rest. Some sodium does find its way into the cell. After all, there is enormous pressure from both diffusion and electrical force pushing sodium inside. But most of the sodium that leaks into the cell is removed by the sodium-potassium pumps. The net result is that sodium concentrations within the neuron are maintained at low levels in spite of the actions of diffusion and electrical force.

The Resting Potential

The resting neural membrane allows potassium to cross freely. In other words, we would say that the membrane is permeable to potassium. If the membrane were permeable to potassium and no other ions, the resting potential of the cell would be about –80mV rather than the actual measurement of –70mV. The difference between these figures is the result of some sodium leaking into the cell. Because sodium is positively charged, the interior of the cell moves in a positive direction from –80mV to –70mV. This is an average figure. In reality, the resting potentials of different types of neurons may range between –40mV to –80mV.

Because the resting potential in a neuron is so dependent on the movement of potassium, the importance of controlling the concentration of potassium in the extracellular fluid becomes quite clear. We mentioned earlier that astrocytes have the important task of collecting excess potassium in the vicinity of neurons. If the concentration of potassium increases in the extracellular fluid, the resting potential is wiped out. The neuron would act like a battery that had lost its charge, and no signaling would occur.

WHY DOES THIS MATTER?

Lethal Injection

Lethal injection is now the most common form of capital punishment used in the United States. The methods used to perform lethal injections matter because we are called on as members of a democracy to participate thoughtfully in ethical decisions.

The procedure uses a combination of three drugs, administered intravenously: a barbiturate that induces coma, a muscle paralysis agent, and potassium chloride (Human Rights Watch, 2006). It is the potassium chloride that actually produces death, typically within one minute of administration. As we mentioned in this chapter, the distribution of potassium across the neural membranes (and the membranes of heart cells, too) is essential for electrical signaling. By increasing the concentration of potassium in the extracellular fluid, the resting potential of cells is increased. This renders the cell inactive because sodium channels will not reopen until the cell returns to its normal resting potential. Because neurons enjoy the protection of the astrocytes and the blood–brain barrier, potassium chloride injections actually work first on the heart. Muscle cells work in very similar ways to neurons. Without a resting potential, cardiac muscle cells cannot signal and therefore stop.

The effects of potassium chloride alone would be extremely painful, so it is never given without other anesthesia. The barbiturate provides this pain relief, and it is given before the other drugs and in doses that far exceed those normally used in surgery. These doses would also produce death alone, but not for one half hour or so. The muscle paralysis agent is much more controversial, as it plays no essential role in the death of the condemned prisoner. Instead, it prevents any movements in response to the effects of the potassium chloride. As such, it is administered more for the benefit of those who must witness the procedure, and who might be upset by the prisoner's involuntary movements occurring during the dying process.

Lethal injection remains a highly controversial issue, above and beyond capital punishment itself, due to concerns about the training of prison personnel, the possibility of conscious awareness that cannot be expressed due to paralysis, and other humane concerns.

The Action Potential

So far, our discussion has centered on the resting cell. Our next step is to describe the changes that take place when the cell signals by producing an action potential. We will explore the technique used by Nobel Laureates Alan Hodgkin and Andrew Huxley to identify the ionic basis of action potentials (Hodgkin, 1992; Hodgkin & Huxley, 1952).

To understand the sequence of events responsible for the action potential, we need first to clarify how one is measured. A favorite source of axons for study has been the squid. Because squid can grow up to 10 to 15 feet in length, they have long axons. As invertebrates, squid have axons that are very large in diameter as well. These characteristics make it possible for researchers to insert electrodes into the intracellular fluid of a dissected squid axon. An axon dissected out of a squid will remain active for many hours when placed in a trough containing seawater, which substitutes for the extracellular fluid due to its similar ionic composition. During this time, researchers can stimulate the axon and record its activity. To measure action potentials, we would need to insert a recording electrode into the squid axon, and another into the extracellular fluid (or its experimental equivalent). We should now be able to read a resting potential of approximately –70mV.

Threshold Because there is no natural input to the disembodied squid axon we are studying, we need to employ a stimulating electrode in addition to the recording electrodes. Normally, a neuron reacts either to sensory input or to chemical messages from other neurons. In the squid axon experiment, we duplicate the effects of these natural inputs with a tiny, depolarizing electrical shock. Whether we're discussing politics or electricity, polarization means that we're on opposite ends of a continuum. Conversely, **depolarization** means that we're moving closer together. In response to a depolarizing shock to the squid axon, the interior of the cell will become more similar to the exterior of the cell, that is, it will be relatively less negative than before.

It is a good morning exercise for a research scientist to discard a pet hypothesis every day before breakfast. It keeps him young.

Konrad Lorenz

Shocks that produce a depolarization of less than 5mV to 10mV have no further effects on the axon, which quickly returns to the resting potential. However, if we apply a shock that results in a depolarization of at least 5mV to 10mV, we begin a chain of events that will lead to the production of an action potential. In other words, when our recording reaches about –65mV, we have reached the cell's **threshold** for producing an action potential. Reaching the threshold for an action potential is similar to pulling the trigger of a gun. As you squeeze the trigger, nothing happens until you reach a critical point. At that point, a sequence of events begins that leads to the firing of the gun, and no actions will stop the sequence once it is initiated. The sequence of events that characterizes an action potential is shown in Figure 3.15.

Channels Open and Close During an Action Potential The first consequence of reaching a cell's threshold is the opening of voltage-dependent sodium channels. Once the sodium gates open, sodium is free to move into the cell, and both diffusion and electrical force ensure that it does so rapidly.

The rush of sodium ions into the neuron is reflected in the recording, which rises from a threshold of around –65mV up to a peak of about +40mV. In other words, at the peak of the action potential, the inside of the neuron is now positively charged relative to the extracellular fluid, a complete reversal of the resting state. The peak of the action potential is similar to sodium's equilibrium of about +50mV. In other words, if the membrane allowed sodium to move freely, the inside of the cell would be positive relative to the extracellular fluid.

Voltage-dependent potassium channels are also triggered at threshold, but their response is much slower than the sodium channels. Toward the peak of the action potential, potassium begins to leave the cell, and the recording drops back to resting levels. Why does potassium move out of the cell toward the peak of the action potential? Recall that potassium is positively charged. In the resting cell, potassium is attracted to the negatively charged interior of the cell and relatively repulsed by the positive exterior. At the peak of the action potential, however, the positive potassium

depolarization The movement of an electrical charge within a cell in a more positive direction.
threshold The level of depolarization at which an action potential is initiated.

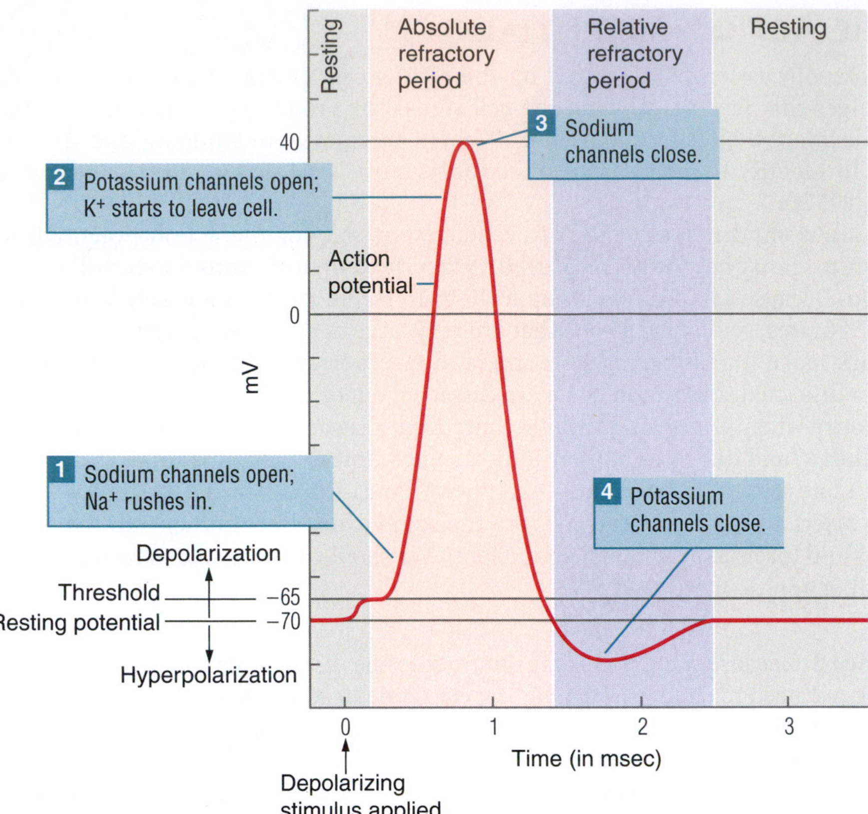

FIGURE 3.15
The Action Potential Once a cell's threshold is reached, an action potential will be generated by a sequential opening and closing of ion channels in the neural membrane. Voltage-dependent sodium and potassium channels are triggered at the threshold. The sodium channels open and close very rapidly, allowing sodium to rush into the cell. As a result, the cell is depolarized. The potassium channels open near the peak of the action potential and close more slowly than the sodium channels. Potassium leaves the now positive intracellular environment, which brings the cell back to its original negative state. Because the sodium channels will not open again until the cell is close to its negative resting state, there is an absolute refractory period in which the cell cannot fire. Due to remaining hyperpolarization during the relative refractory period, a larger than normal stimulus is necessary for the production of an action potential.

ions find themselves in a more positive environment within the neuron. The exterior looks relatively attractive. As a result, potassium moves outside. As these positively charged ions leave the neuron, the interior of the cell becomes negative again, as shown in the downward slope of the recording.

Once the cell returns to the resting level, it actually overshoots its target and becomes even more negative than when at rest. This **hyperpolarization,** in which the cell becomes more negative than it is at rest, is a result of voltage-dependent potassium channels remaining open. Once they close, the cell will return to its normal resting level. Throughout the process, the sodium-potassium pumps are hard at work to return sodium ions to the extracellular fluid.

There are several important differences between the sodium and potassium voltage-dependent channels that are involved with action potentials. First of all, the sodium channels open very rapidly, whereas the potassium channels open slowly. This difference accounts for the rapid rise in our recording of the action potential. Second, the sodium channels remain open only briefly and are then inactivated until the cell reaches its resting potential again. The potassium channels remain open for a longer period of time.

You may want to review the case of *fugu* poisoning presented at the beginning of the chapter. The *fugu* toxin specifically blocks the voltage-dependent sodium channels responsible for the rising phase of the action potential. Without the movement of sodium at this point, there is no signaling.

Refractory Periods The characteristics of the sodium and potassium channels limit the frequency with which the cell can fire. Once the voltage-dependent sodium channels have been activated, they cannot be opened again until the cell has been restored to its resting potential. This interval, in which no stimulus whatsoever can produce another action potential, is known as the **absolute refractory period.** The absolute refractory period begins with the opening of sodium channels and ends as the cell approaches the resting potential. An atom bomb could go off next to this person, and neurons in the absolute refractory period would be unable to respond.

hyperpolarization The movement of the electrical charge within a cell in a more negative direction.

absolute refractory period The period in which an action potential will not occur in a particular location of an axon regardless of input.

While the cell is relatively hyperpolarized following an action potential, it can respond, but only to larger than normal input. We refer to this period as the **relative refractory period.** Because the cell is now quite negative, the sodium channels are ready to open again. However, due to the hyperpolarization caused by the open potassium channels, more depolarization than normal is needed to reach threshold.

The Action Potential Is All-or-None We do not encode information by producing fat or thin or tall or short action potentials. An action potential is either produced or it isn't. Consequently, we speak of action potentials as being all-or-none.

If we can make only one type of signal, how do we respond to different levels of stimulation? The rate of neural firing can vary to reflect stimulus intensity. Large amounts of stimulation produce rapid neural firing, whereas less intense input produces slower rates of firing. Firing rate does have physical limits, however. Because each action potential lasts about 1 msec, the maximum neural firing rate is about 1,000 action potentials per second. In addition to firing rate, the number of active neurons can vary with stimulus intensity. Intense input will recruit action potentials from many neurons, whereas lower levels of stimulation will activate fewer neurons.

The Propagation of the Action Potential

Once a single action potential has been formed at the axon hillock, the next step is **propagation,** by which the signal reproduces itself down the length of an axon. This ability to reproduce the original signal ensures that the signal reaching the end of the axon is as strong as the signal formed at the axon hillock.

Earlier, we measured an action potential by using one recording electrode in the squid axon hillock and another in the extracellular environment. To follow the traveling signal, we now add more electrodes down the length of the axon. As shown in ■ Figure 3.16, we can record action potentials as they pass electrodes down the length of the axon.

As shown in ■ Figure 3.17, the movement of an action potential along an axon is influenced by whether the axon is myelinated. The progress of an action potential in

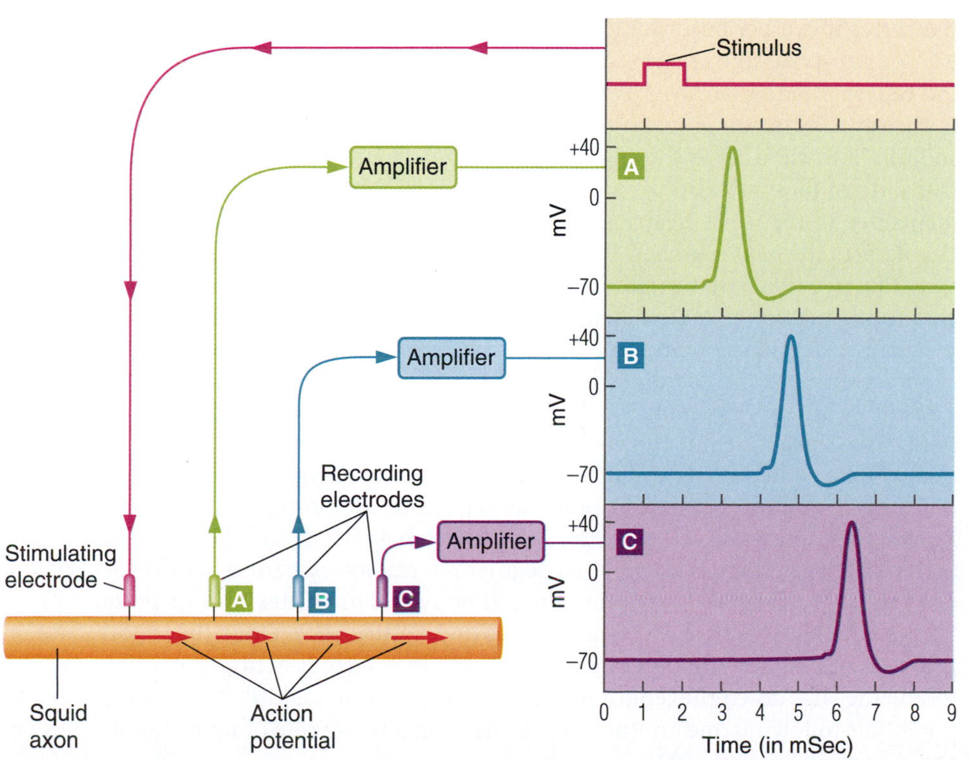

■ **Figure 3.16**
Action Potentials Propagate Down the Length of the Axon
Once formed in the axon hillock, the action potential propagates, or reproduces, along successive segments of the axon membrane until it reaches the axon terminal. With additional recording electrodes, we can observe action potentials being formed at different points along the axon. *Source:* Adapted from Rosenzweig, Leiman, & Breedlove (1999).

relative refractory period The period following an action potential in which larger than normal input will produce a second action potential but in which normal input will be insufficient.

propagation The transmission of a wave through a medium; in neurons, it is the replication of the action potential down the length of the axon.

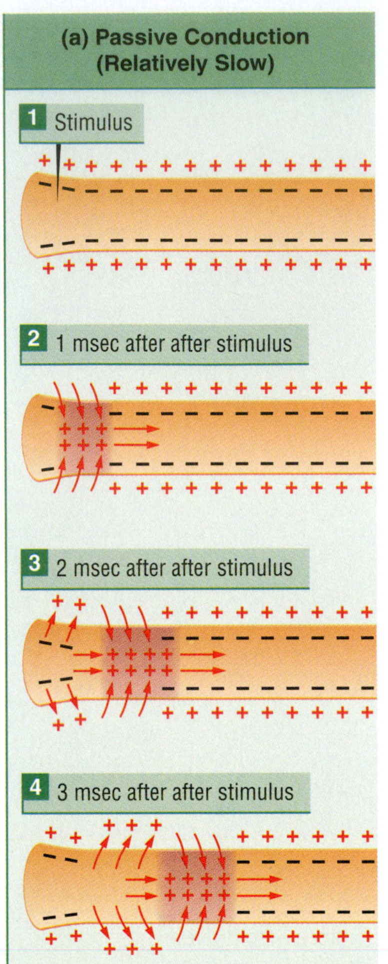

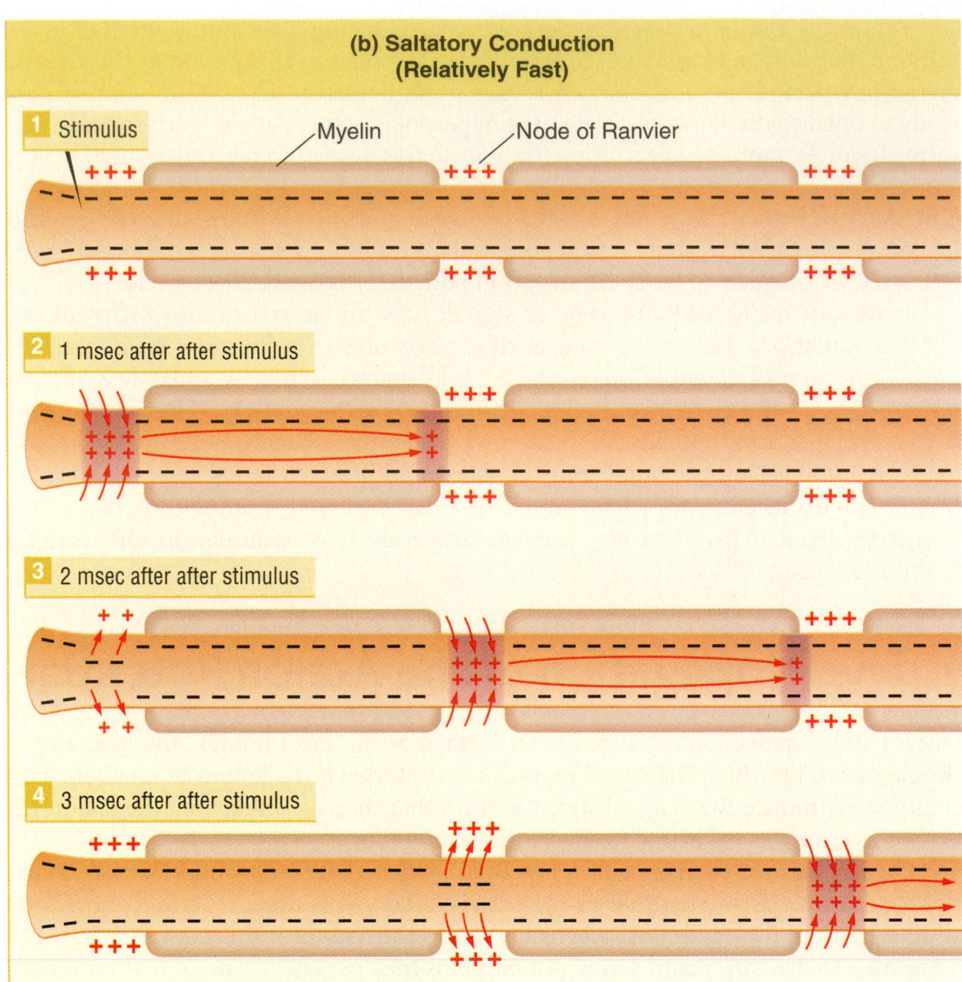

FIGURE 3.17
Propagation in Unmyelinated and Myelinated Axons In the passive conduction in unmyelinated axons (a), the action potential must be replicated at each successive segment. Salutatory conduction in myelinated axons (b) is much faster because action potentials occur only at the nodes of Ranvier.

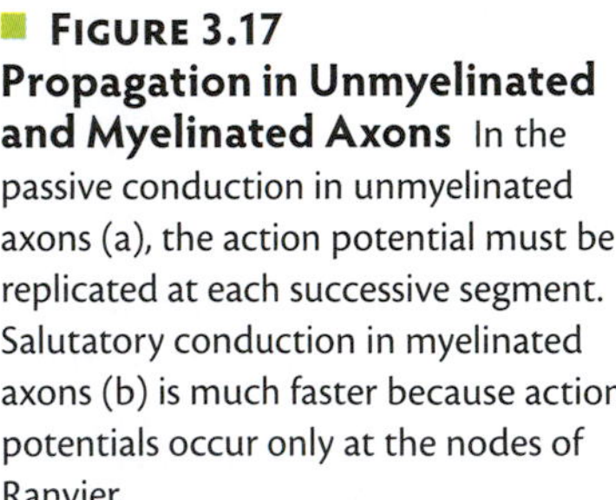

an unmyelinated axon is known as **passive conduction.** When we last saw our unmyelinated squid axon, the generation of an action potential at the axon hillock resulted in the entry of sodium ions into the cell. Now that they are inside, these ions will behave like water in a leaky hose. Some of these sodium ions will leak out of the cell through the sodium-potassium pumps and other ion channels, and others will remain inside the cell membrane, or hose. Where are the remaining sodium ions likely to go? Due to the same diffusion pressure and electrical force that brought them into the cell, the sodium ions will drift to the adjacent axon segment. At the same time, incoming positive sodium ions will also push positive potassium ions ahead into adjacent axon segments due to their like electrical charges. The arrival of these positively charged ions depolarizes the next segment. If this segment reaches threshold, the events leading to an action potential will be reproduced. A recording electrode in this segment will indicate another action potential identical to the one we recorded at the axon hillock.

Can the action potential move backward toward the cell body, too? Technically, if an action potential were produced for the first time in the middle of an axon as a result of an experimental shock, there's no reason why it couldn't go in either or both directions. In reality, however, the prior segment will still be in refractory period and won't be able to fire. Because refractory periods prevent an immediate reoccurrence of an action potential in previous segments, action potentials generally move in one direction, from cell body to axon terminal. At the axon hillock, site of the first action potential, there is no previous segment in refractory period. As a result, current does appear to flow backward into the cell body and dendrites. At this point, nobody knows whether this backward current has any significance. Once the initial segment has regained its resting potential, it can initiate a second action potential that will follow the first down the length of the axon. If an axon couldn't have multiple action potentials following one another in this manner, a firing rate of up to 1,000 times per second would be impossible.

passive conduction The movement of an action potential down the length of an unmyelinated axon.
saltatory conduction The movement of an action potential from node of Ranvier to node of Ranvier, down the length of a myelinated axon.

Now we are ready to consider the propagation of action potentials in myelinated axons. To produce action potentials, we need ion channels. In the myelinated axon, ion channels appear only at the nodes of Ranvier, the bare spaces of axon membrane between adjacent segments of myelin. Under the myelin segment itself, there is no contact between the membrane and extracellular fluid at all. How does myelin produce the faster, more efficient propagation of action potentials? The myelinated axon is like a leaky hose that has been patched. The patches, or myelin, prevent leakage of the sodium ions, at least until they reach a node of Ranvier. Just as water moves faster through the patched hose, so do the sodium ions move faster in the myelinated axon. Once the sodium ions reach a node of Ranvier, they produce another action potential due to the presence of voltage-dependent channels in that area. The nodes are especially rich in these channels. The density of channels at a node of Ranvier is about ten times greater than the density of channels at any comparable location on an unmyelinated axon (Rasband & Schrager, 2000).

Because the signal appears to jump from node to node down the length of the axon, we refer to propagation in the myelinated axon as **saltatory conduction.** *Saltatory* comes from the Latin word for "leaping" or "dancing." The action potential essentially passes through the segments of axon covered by myelin, just as an express train skips all but the most important stops. In contrast, propagation in the unmyelinated axon is like the local train that makes every single stop along its route.

In a typical invertebrate unmyelinated axon, the action potential will be passively conducted at a rate of about 5 meters per second. In contrast, a typical human myelinated fiber can conduct action potentials at about 120 meters per second. Not only are myelinated fibers faster, they are faster in spite of having a smaller diameter. As fast as we are, however, the nervous system does not communicate anywhere near the speed of light, as was once believed. Part of the delay in communication occurs between neurons, at the synapse.

INTERIM SUMMARY 3.2

Summary Table: Major Features of Electrical Signaling

Event	Location	Mechanisms of Action
Resting potential	Inactive segments of axon	• Equilibrium between diffusion and electrical force exists for K^+ and Cl^-. • Na^+ is actively prevented from entering the neuron.
Action potential	Begins at the axon hillock and propagates down the length of the axon	• Depolarization to threshold triggers opening of Na^+ channels. • Entering Na^+ ions make voltage inside neuron more positive. • Opening of K^+ channels near peak of action potential allows K^+ to leave the neuron. • Loss of K^+ returns neuron to the resting potential.
Absolute refractory period	Segments of axon that have just experienced an action potential	• Na^+ channels are unable to open a second time until neuron regains the resting potential.
Relative refractory period	Segments of axon that have just experienced an absolute refractory period	• Return to resting potential resets Na^+ channels. Hyperpolarization due to loss of K^+ ions makes an action potential less likely.
Propagation of action potential	Entire length of axon, beginning at axon hillock	• Drift of Na^+ and K^+ ions to adjacent segments of axon causes segments to reach threshold, triggering replication of the action potential. • Existence of refractory period in the preceding segment prevents backward propagation.

(continued)

INTERIM SUMMARY 3.2 (continued)

Summary Points

1. The intracellular fluid contains large amounts of potassium and smaller amounts of sodium and chloride. The extracellular fluid contains large amounts of sodium and chloride and smaller amounts of potassium. **(LO7)**
2. The resting potential of neurons averages about -70mV. In other words, the interior of the cell is negatively charged relative to the exterior. An action potential is a reversal of this polarity. **(LO7)**
3. Absolute and relative refractory periods, during which further action potentials are either impossible or less likely, result from the nature of the sodium and potassium channels. **(LO7)**
4. Action potentials move down the length of unmyelinated axons by the relatively slow process of passive conduction. Action potentials move much more rapidly down the length of myelinated axons by the process of saltatory conduction. **(LO7)**

Review Questions

1. How do diffusion and electrical force account for the chemical composition of intracellular and extracellular fluids when the neuron is at rest?
2. How do neurons signal stimulus intensity when the action potential is all-or-none?

The Synapse

The birth and propagation of the action potential within the presynaptic neuron makes up the first half of our story of neural communication. The second half begins when the action potential reaches the axon terminal and the message must cross the synaptic gap to the adjacent postsynaptic neuron. Figure 3.18 shows an electron micrograph of many axons forming synapses on a cell body.

The human brain contains about 100 billion neurons, and the average neuron forms something on the order of 1,000 synapses. Remarkably, these numbers suggest that the human brain has more synapses than there are stars in our galaxy (Kandel & Siegelbaum, 1995). In spite of these large numbers, synapses take one of only two forms. At **chemical synapses,** neurons stimulate adjacent cells by sending chemical

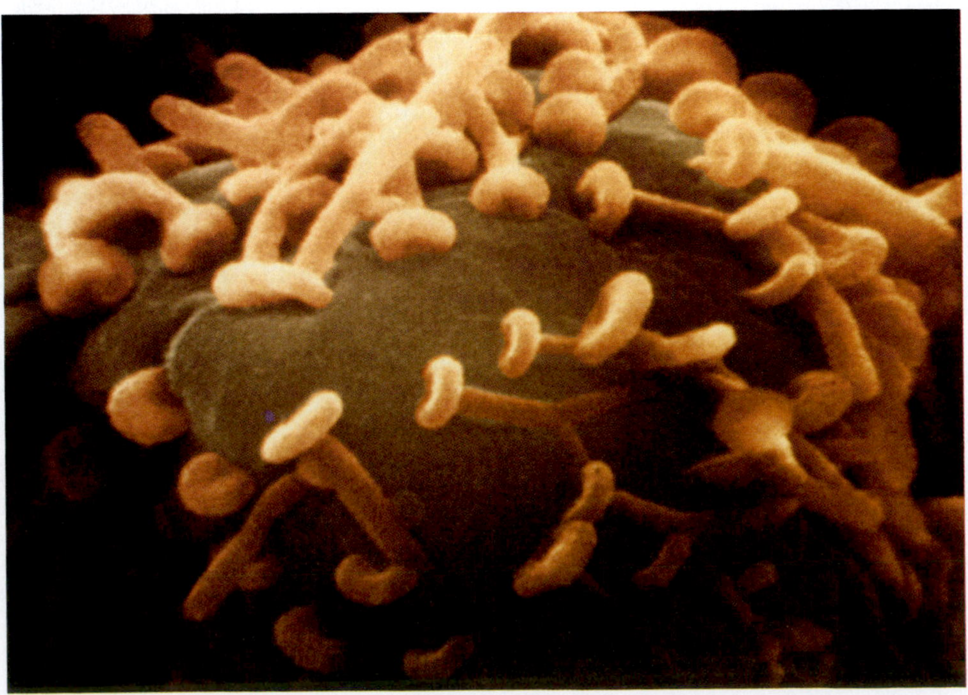

FIGURE 3.18 Neurons Communicate at the Synapse This colored electron micrograph shows the axon terminals from many neurons forming synapses on a cell body.

chemical synapse A type of synapse in which messages are transmitted from one neuron to another by chemical neurotransmitters.

electrical synapse A type of synapse in which a neuron directly affects an adjacent neuron through the movement of ions from one cell to the other.

TABLE 3.2 A Comparison of Electrical and Chemical Synapses

Type of Synapse	Width of Synaptic Gap	Speed of Transmission	Method of Transmission	Type of Message	Types of Cells Involved
Electrical	3.5 nm	Nearly instantaneous	Direct movement of ions from one cell to the other	Excitatory only	Requires large presynaptic neuron to influence small postsynaptic neurons
Chemical	20 nm	Up to several milliseconds	Release of chemical neurotransmitters	Excitatory or inhibitory	Small presynaptic neurons can influence large postsynaptic neurons

messengers, or neurotransmitters, across the synaptic gap. At **electrical synapses,** neurons directly stimulate adjacent cells by sending ions across the gap through channels that actually touch. Because the gap at an electrical synapse is so narrow and the movement of ions is so rapid, the transmission is nearly instantaneous. Table 3.2 provides a comparison of the major features of electrical and chemical synapses.

Electrical Synapses

Electrical synapses between two cells are found not just in animals but in plants as well, which suggests that they are very ancient in terms of evolution. Not only do we retain small numbers of electrical synapses in the human nervous system, but electrical communication also occurs in the heart and liver. An electrical synapse is illustrated in Figure 3.19.

In contrast to chemical synapses, the gap between two neurons in an electrical synapse is quite small. The average gap between the presynaptic and postsynaptic neurons at a chemical synapse is about 20 nm wide, whereas the gap between cells at an electrical synapse is only 3.5 nm wide. Because of this tiny gap, the presynaptic and postsynaptic cells at an electrical synapse are joined by special protein channels that essentially connect the two cells. These channels make it possible for positive current from the presynaptic neuron to flow directly into the postsynaptic neuron.

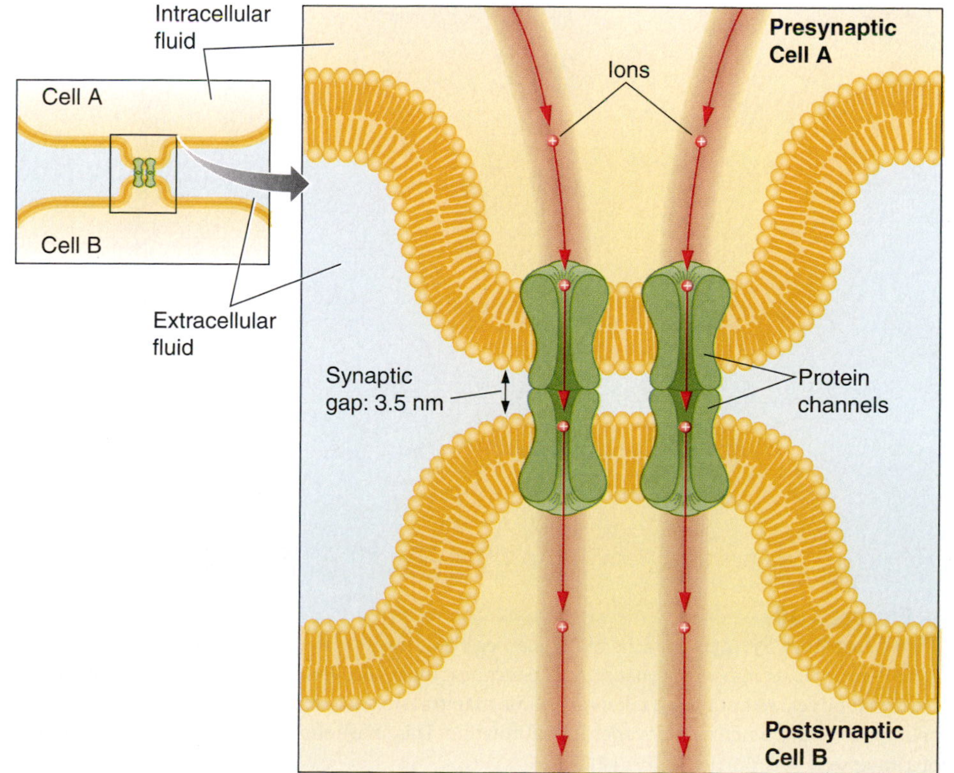

FIGURE 3.19
The Electrical Synapse In electrical synapses, channels connecting the two neurons across a synaptic gap of only 3.5 nm allow for the direct movement of ions from one cell to the other. Electrical synapses have the advantage of nearly instantaneous communication between neurons.

Although electrical synapses make up a very small minority of the synapses in the brains of mammals, they do provide several advantages. One advantage of the electrical synapse is speed. Transmission of a message from one cell to another is nearly instantaneous. In contrast, chemical synapses take anywhere from 0.3 millisecond to several milliseconds to complete the series of steps involved with transmitting the message from one cell to the next. Consequently, electrical synapses are frequently found in circuits responsible for escape behaviors, particularly in invertebrates (Bennett & Zukin, 2004). Electrical synapses also synchronize activity such as the release of hormones in response to activity in the hypothalamus. Abnormalities in the synchrony typically produced by electrical synapses in the thalamus might be responsible for some seizure activity (Landisman et al., 2002).

Although electrical synapses are fast, chemical synapses have the advantage of providing a much greater variety of messages. The only type of message that can be sent at an electrical synapse is an excitatory one. Excitation means that one cell can tell the next cell to produce an action potential. In contrast, chemical synapses allow for both excitatory and inhibitory messages to be sent. In inhibition, the next cell is told *not* to produce an action potential. Another major advantage of chemical synapses over electrical synapses is that a very small presynaptic neuron using chemical messengers can still influence a very large postsynaptic neuron. In the case of the electrical synapse, it takes a very large presynaptic neuron to influence a tiny postsynaptic neuron, simply due to the electrical requirements of this type of transmission.

Chemical Synapses

We can divide our discussion of the signaling at chemical synapses, such as the one shown in Figure 3.20, into two steps. The first step is release of the neurotransmitter chemicals by the presynaptic cell. The second step is the reaction of the postsynaptic cell to the neurotransmitters.

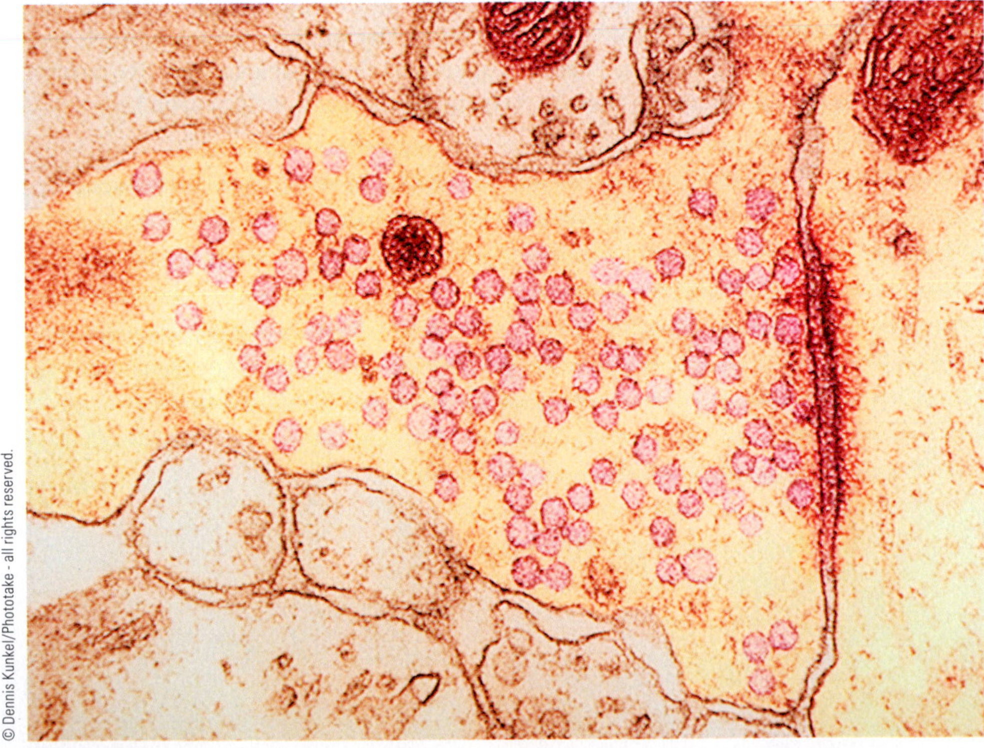

Figure 3.20
The Chemical Synapse In chemical synapses, neurotransmitter substance released by the presynaptic neuron floats across the synaptic gap to receptor molecules embedded in the membrane of the postsynaptic cell. Although this takes more time than transmission at an electrical synapse, it allows neurons to send a much greater variety of information. This image shows an electron microscopic image of a synapse.

Neurotransmitter Release In response to the arrival of an action potential at the terminal, a new type of voltage-dependent channel will open. This time, voltage-dependent calcium (Ca^{2+}) channels will play the major role in the cell's activities. The amount of neurotransmitter released is a direct reflection of the amount of calcium that enters the presynaptic neuron (Heidelberger, Heinemann, Neher, & Matthews, 1994; von Gersdorff & Matthews, 1994). A large influx of calcium triggers a large release of neurotransmitter substance.

Calcium is a positively charged ion (Ca^{2+}) that is more abundant in the extracellular fluid than in the intracellular fluid. Therefore, its situation is very similar to sodium, and it will move under the same circumstances that cause sodium to move. Calcium channels are rather rare along the length of the axon, but there are a large number located in the axon terminal membrane. Calcium channels open in response to the arrival of the depolarizing action potential. Calcium does not move immediately, however, because it is a positively charged ion and the intracellular fluid is positively charged during the action potential. As the action potential recedes in the axon terminal, however, calcium is attracted by the relatively negative interior. Once calcium enters the presynaptic cell, it triggers the release of neurotransmitter substance within about 0.2 msec.

Prior to release, molecules of neurotransmitter are stored in synaptic vesicles. These vesicles are anchored by special proteins near release sites on the presynaptic membrane. The process by which these vesicles release their contents is known as **exocytosis,** illustrated in ■ Figure 3.21. Calcium entering the cell appears to release the vesicles from their protein anchors, which allows them to migrate toward the release sites. At the release site, calcium stimulates the fusion between the membrane of the vesicle and the membrane of the axon terminal, forming a channel through which the neurotransmitter molecules escape.

A long-standing assumption regarding exocytosis is that each released vesicle is fully emptied of neurotransmitter. However, some researchers have suggested the possibility that there are instances of partial release, which they have dubbed "kiss and run" (Harata et al., 2001). In kiss and run, vesicles are only partially emptied of neurotransmitter molecules before closing up again and returning to the interior of the axon terminal. If vesicles did indeed have the ability to kiss and run, the process of neurotransmission would be much faster than if they had to be filled from scratch after each use (Aravanis, Pyle, Harata, & Tsien, 2003). In addition, kiss and run raises the possibility that the vesicles themselves control the amount of neurotransmitter released to some extent. The prevalence and significance of the full-release and kiss-and-run modes remains an active area of research interest (Harata, Aravanis, & Tsien, 2006).

Following exocytosis, the neuron must engage in several housekeeping duties to prepare for the arrival of the next action potential. Calcium pumps must act to return calcium to the extracellular fluid. Otherwise, neurotransmitters would be released constantly rather than in response to the arrival of an action potential. Because the vesicle membrane fuses with the presynaptic membrane, something must be done to prevent a gradual thickening of the membrane that would interfere with neurotransmitter release. The solution to this unwanted thickening is the recycling of the vesicle material. Excess membrane material forms a pit, which is eventually pinched off to form a new vesicle.

Before we leave the presynaptic neuron, we need to consider one of the feedback loops the presynaptic neuron uses to monitor its own activity. Embedded within the presynaptic membrane are special protein structures known as **autoreceptors.** Autoreceptors bind some of the neurotransmitter molecules released by the presynaptic neuron, providing feedback to the presynaptic neuron about its own level of activity. This information may affect the rate of neurotransmitter synthesis and release (Parnas, Segel, Dudel, & Parnas, 2000).

Neurotransmitters Bind to Postsynaptic Receptor Sites The newly released molecules of neurotransmitter substance float across the synaptic gap. On the postsynaptic side of the synapse, we find new types of proteins embedded in the postsynaptic cell membrane, known as **receptor sites.** The receptor sites are characterized by **recognition molecules** that respond only to certain types of neurotransmitter substance. Recognition molecules extend into the extracellular fluid of the synaptic

You certainly can't tell anything from the microscopic structure of the brain whether the person was an idiot or a genius.
Ashley Montagu

Never trust anything that can think for itself, if you can't see where it keeps its brain.
J.K. Rowling

exocytosis (ek-soe-sie-TOE-sis) The process in which vesicles fuse with the membrane of the axon terminal and release neurotransmitter molecules into the synaptic gap.

autoreceptor Receptor site located on the presynaptic neuron that provides information about the cell's own activity levels.

receptor site A special protein structure embedded in neural membrane that responds to chemical messengers.

recognition molecule A molecule within a receptor site that binds to specific chemical messengers.

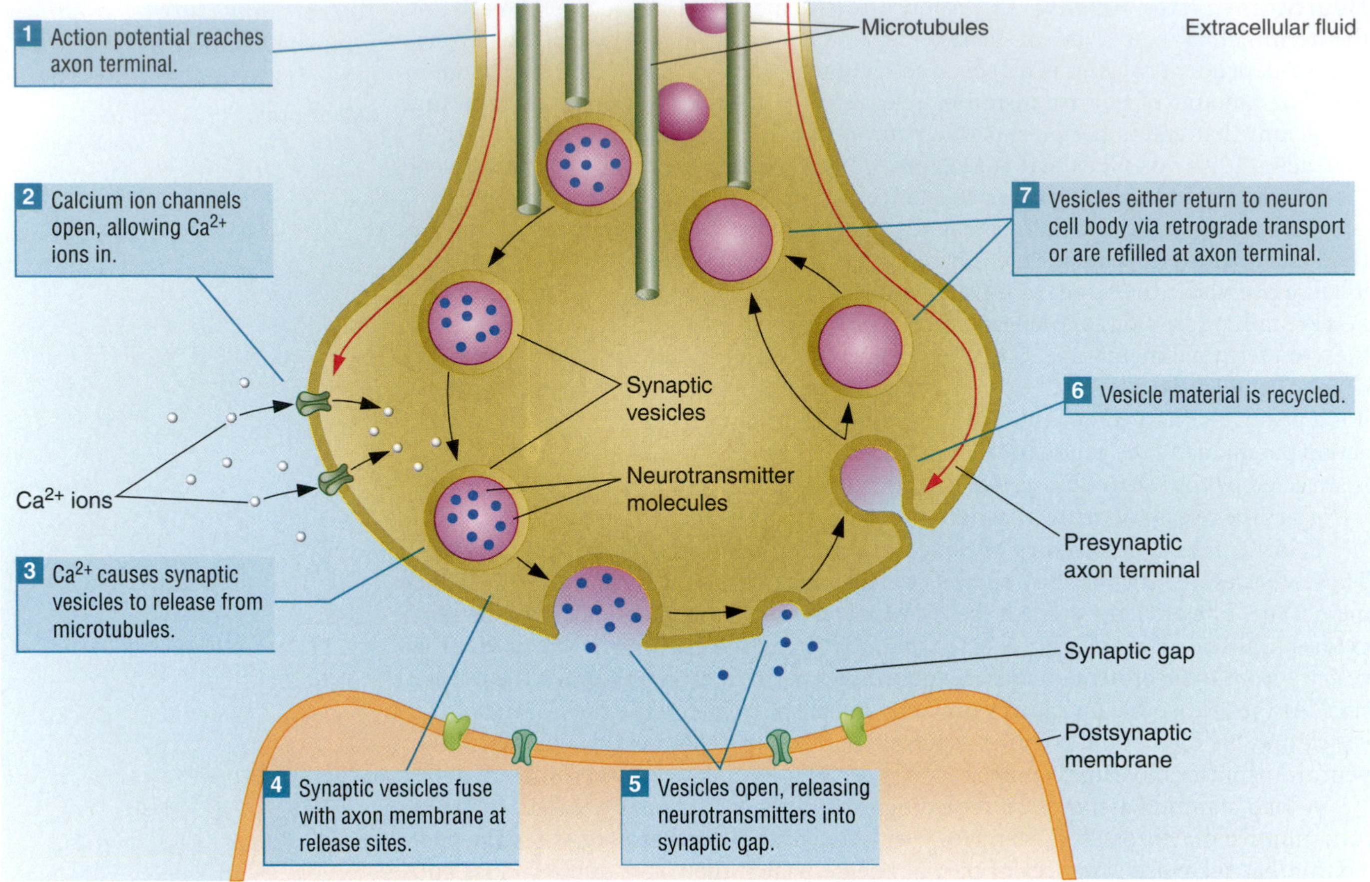
1 Action potential reaches axon terminal.
Microtubules
Extracellular fluid
2 Calcium ion channels open, allowing Ca2+ ions in.
7 Vesicles either return to neuron cell body via retrograde transport or are refilled at axon terminal.
Synaptic vesicles
6 Vesicle material is recycled.
Ca2+ ions
Neurotransmitter molecules
Presynaptic axon terminal
3 Ca2+ causes synaptic vesicles to release from microtubules.
Synaptic gap
Postsynaptic membrane
4 Synaptic vesicles fuse with axon membrane at release sites.
5 Vesicles open, releasing neurotransmitters into synaptic gap.

■ **FIGURE 3.21**
Exocytosis Results in the Release of Neurotransmitters Calcium is a positively charged ion (Ca^{2+}) that is more abundant in the extracellular fluid than in the intracellular fluid. Therefore, its situation is very similar to sodium, and it will move under the same circumstances that cause sodium to move. Calcium channels are rather rare along the length of the axon, but there are a large number located in the axon terminal membrane. Calcium channels open in response to the arrival of the depolarizing action potential. Calcium does not move immediately, however, because it is a positively charged ion and the intracellular fluid is positively charged during the action potential. As the action potential recedes in the axon terminal, however, calcium is attracted by the relatively negative interior. Once calcium enters the presynaptic cell, it triggers the release of neurotransmitter substance within about 0.2 msec.

gap, where they come into contact with molecules of neurotransmitter. The molecules of neurotransmitter function as keys that fit into the locks made by the recognition molecules.

Two major types of receptors are illustrated in ■ Figure 3.22. Once the neurotransmitter molecules have bound to receptor sites, ligand-gated ion channels will open either directly or indirectly. In the direct case, known as an **ionotropic receptor,** the receptor site is located on the channel protein. As soon as the receptor captures molecules of neurotransmitter, the ion channel opens. These one-step receptors are capable of very fast reactions to neurotransmitters. In other cases, however, the receptor site does not have direct control over an ion channel (Birnbaumer, Abramowitz, & Brown, 1990). In these cases, known as **metabotropic receptors,** a recognition site extends into the extracellular fluid, and a special protein called a **G protein** is located on the receptor's intracellular side. When molecules of neurotransmitter bind at the recognition site, the G protein separates from the receptor complex and moves to a different part of the postsynaptic cell. G proteins can open ion channels in the nearby membrane or activate additional chemical messengers within the postsynaptic cell known as **second messengers.** (Neurotransmitters are the first messengers.) Because of the multiple steps involved, the metabotropic receptors respond more slowly, in hundreds of milliseconds to seconds, than the ionotropic receptors, which respond in milliseconds. In addition, the effects of metabotropic activation can last much longer than those produced by the activation of ionotropic receptors.

ionotropic receptor (eye-on-oh-TROE-pik) A receptor protein in the postsynaptic membrane in which the recognition site is located in the same structure as the ion channel.

metabotropic receptor (met-ab-oh-TROE-pik) A protein structure embedded in the postsynaptic membrane containing a recognition site and a G protein. Neurotransmitters binding to these receptors do not directly open ion channels.

G protein A protein found on the intracellular side of a metabotropic receptor that separates in response to the binding of neurotransmitter substance and travels to adjacent areas of the cell to affect ion channels or second messengers.

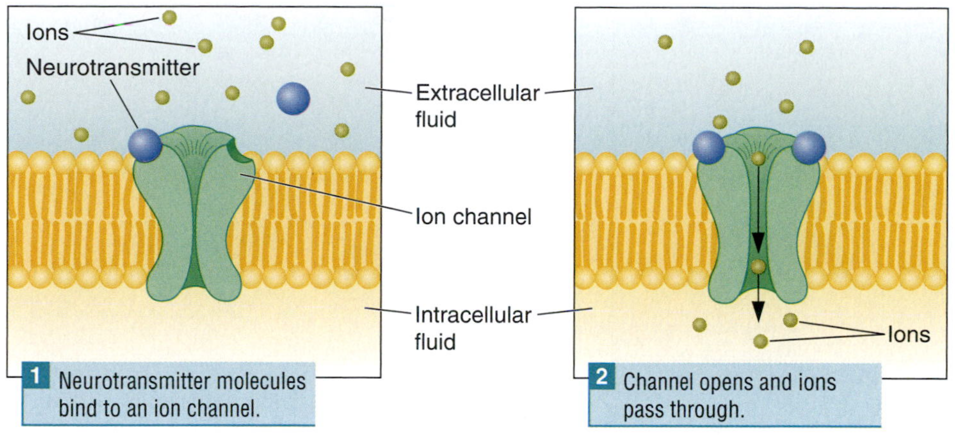
Ions
Neurotransmitter
Extracellular fluid
Ion channel
Intracellular fluid
Ions
1 Neurotransmitter molecules bind to an ion channel.
2 Channel opens and ions pass through.

(a) Ionotropic Receptor

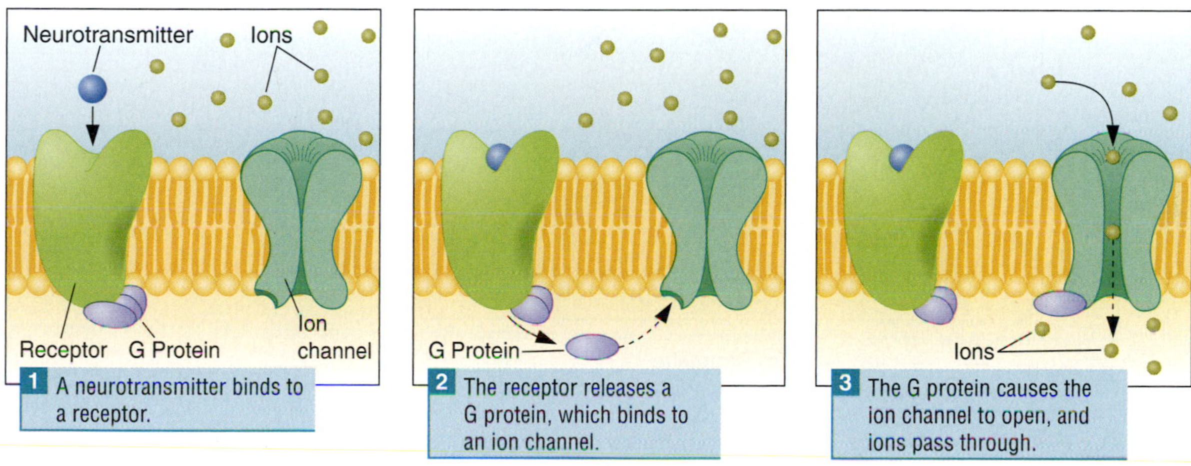
Neurotransmitter
Ions
Receptor
G Protein
Ion channel
1 A neurotransmitter binds to a receptor.
G Protein
2 The receptor releases a G protein, which binds to an ion channel.
Ions
3 The G protein causes the ion channel to open, and ions pass through.

(b) Metabotropic Receptor

■ **FIGURE 3.22 Ionotropic and Metabotropic Receptors** Ionotropic receptors, shown in (a), feature a recognition site for molecules of neurotransmitter located on an ion channel. These one-step receptors provide a very fast response to the presence of neurotransmitters. Metabotropic receptors, shown in (b), require additional steps. Neurotransmitter molecules are recognized by the receptor, which in turn releases internal messengers known as G proteins. G proteins initiate a wide variety of functions within the cell, including opening adjacent ion channels and changing gene expression.

What is the advantage to an organism of evolving a slower, more complicated system? The answer is that the metabotropic receptor provides the possibility of a much greater variety of responses to the release of neurotransmitter. The activation of metabotropic receptors can result not only in the opening of ion channels, but also in a number of additional functions. Different types of metabotropic receptors influence the amount of neurotransmitter released, help maintain the resting potential, and initiate changes in gene expression (Pan et al., 2008). Unlike the ionotropic receptor, which affects a very small, local part of a cell, a metabotropic receptor can have wide-ranging and multiple influences within a cell due to its ability to activate a variety of second messengers.

Termination of the Chemical Signal Before we can make a second telephone call, we need to hang up the phone to end the first call. If we want to send a second message across a synapse, it's necessary to have some way of ending the first message.

As shown in ■ Figure 3.23, neurons have three ways of ending a chemical message. The particular method used depends on the neurotransmitter involved (See Chapter 4). The first method is simple diffusion away from the synapse. Like any other molecule, a neurotransmitter diffuses away from areas of high concentration to areas of low concentration. The astrocytes surrounding the synapse influence the speed of neurotransmitter diffusion away from the synapse. In the second method for ending chemical transmission, neurotransmitter molecules are deactivated in the synapse by enzymes in the synaptic gap. In the third process, **reuptake,** the presynaptic membrane uses its own set of receptors known as **transporters** to recapture molecules of neurotransmitter substance and return them to the interior of the axon terminal. In the terminal, the neurotransmitter can be repackaged

second messenger A chemical within the postsynaptic neuron that is indirectly activated by synaptic activity and interacts with intracellular enzymes or receptors.

reuptake A process for ending the action of neurotransmitters in the synaptic gap in which the presynaptic membrane recaptures the transmitter molecules.

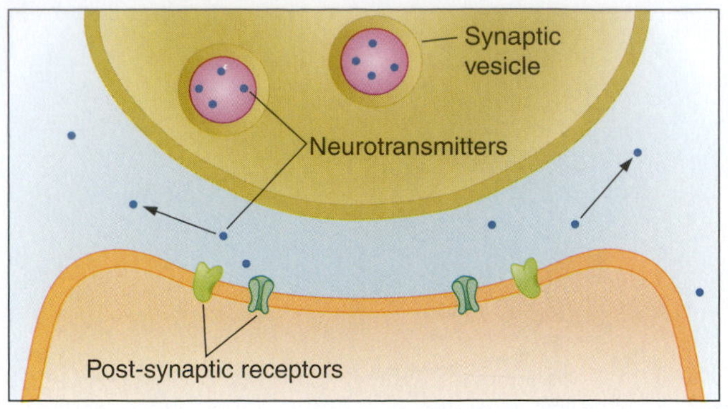

(a) Diffusion

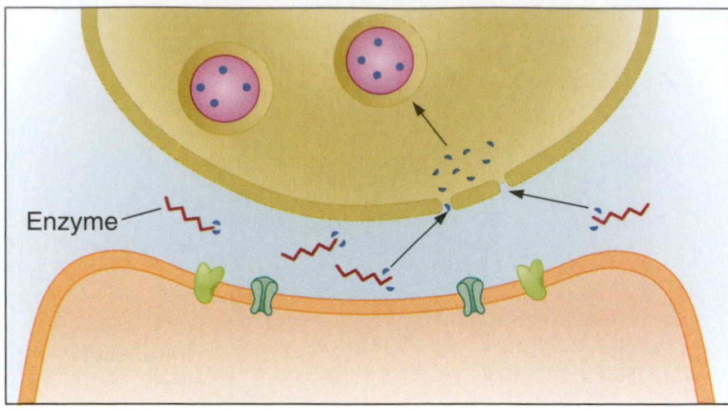

(b) Deactivating Enzymes

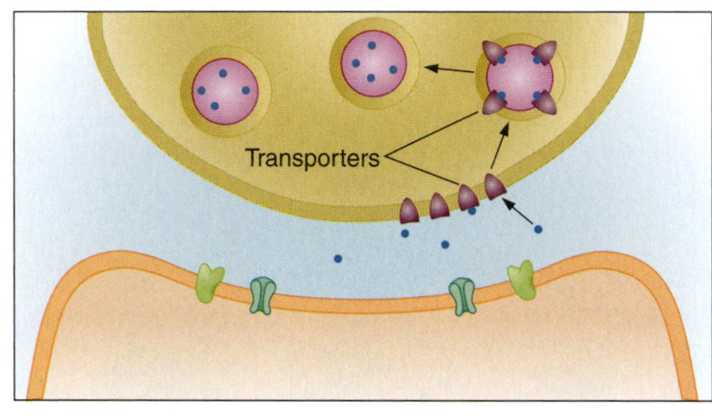

(c) Reuptake

FIGURE 3.23
Methods for Deactivating Neurotransmitters Neurotransmitters released into the synaptic gap must be deactivated before additional signals are sent by the presynaptic neuron. Deactivation may occur through (a) diffusion away from the synapse, (b) through the action of special enzymes, or (c) through reuptake. Deactivating enzymes break the neurotransmitter molecules into their components. The presynaptic neuron collects these components and then synthesizes and packages more neurotransmitter substance. In reuptake, presynaptic transporters recapture released neurotransmitter molecules and repackage them in vesicles.

in vesicles for subsequent release. Unlike the cases in which enzymes deactivate neurotransmitters, reuptake spares the cell the extra step of reconstructing the molecules out of component parts.

Postsynaptic Potentials When molecules of neurotransmitter bind to postsynaptic receptors, they can produce one of two outcomes, illustrated in Figure 3.24.

The first possible outcome is a slight depolarization of the postsynaptic membrane, known as an **excitatory postsynaptic potential,** or **EPSP.** EPSPs generally result from the opening of ligand-gated rather than voltage-dependent sodium channels in the postsynaptic membrane. The inward movement of positive sodium ions produces the slight depolarization of the EPSP. In addition to opening a different type of channel, EPSPs differ from action potentials in other ways. We have described action potentials as being all-or-none. In contrast, EPSPs are known as **graded potentials,** referring to their varying size and shape. Action potentials last about 1 msec, but EPSPs can last up to 5 to 10 msec.

The second possible outcome of the binding of neurotransmitter to a postsynaptic receptor is the production of an **inhibitory postsynaptic potential,** or **IPSP.** The IPSP is a slight hyperpolarization of the postsynaptic membrane, which reduces the likelihood that the postsynaptic cell will produce an action potential. Like the EPSP, the IPSP is a graded potential that can last 5 to 10 msec. IPSPs are usually produced by the opening of ligand-gated channels that allow for the inward movement of chloride (Cl^-) or the outward movement of potassium (K^+). The movement of negatively

transporter A receptor in the presynaptic membrane that recaptures released molecules of neurotransmitter in the process of reuptake.
excitatory postsynaptic potential (EPSP) A small depolarization produced in the postsynaptic cell as a result of input from the presynaptic cell.
graded potential An electrical signal that can vary in size and shape.
inhibitory postsynaptic potential (IPSP) A small hyperpolarization produced in the postsynaptic cell as a result of input from the presynaptic cell.

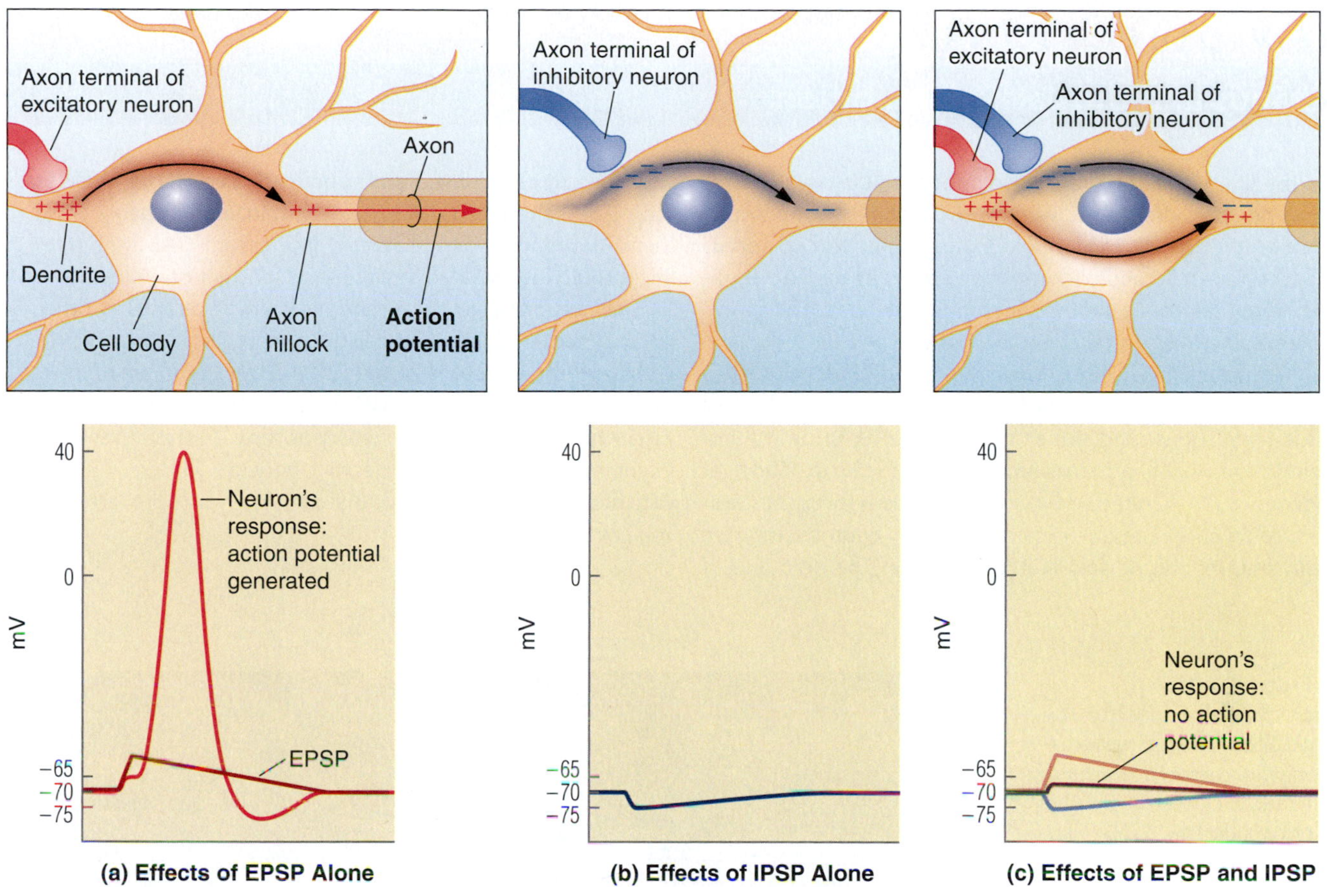

FIGURE 3.24
Neural Integration Combines Excitatory and Inhibitory Input These graphs illustrate the effects of excitatory postsynaptic potentials (EPSPs) and inhibitory postsynaptic potentials (IPSPs) alone and together on the overall response by the postsynaptic neuron. In (a), the EPSP alone depolarizes the postsynaptic cell to threshold and initiates an action potential. In (b), the IPSP alone hyperpolarizes the postsynaptic neuron. In (c), the EPSP and IPSP essentially cancel each other out, and no action potential occurs. *Source:* Data from Kandel (1995).

charged chloride ions into the postsynaptic cell would add to the cell's negative charge. The loss of positively charged potassium cells would also increase a cell's negative charge. A comparison of the characteristics of action potentials, EPSPs, and IPSPs may be found in Table 3.3.

TABLE 3.3 A Comparison of the Characteristics of Action Potentials, EPSPs, and IPSPs

	Action Potential	EPSPs	IPSPs
Role	Signaling within neurons	Signaling between neurons	Signaling between neurons
Duration	1 to 2 msec	5 to 10 msec up to 100 msec	5 to 10 msec up to 100 msec
Size	About 100mV	Up to 20mV	Up to 15mV
Character	All-or-none	Graded depolarization	Graded hyperpolarization
Propagation	Active	Passive	Passive
Channels involved	Voltage-dependent sodium and potassium channels	Ligand-gated sodium channels	Ligand-gated potassium and chloride channels

NEW DIRECTIONS

Tetanus and the Lack of Inhibition

In the United States, there are only about 100 cases of tetanus per year, due to the widespread availability of effective vaccines. Worldwide, over 1 million deaths per year still occur due to tetanus. Tetanus occurs when spores of the bacterium *Clostridium tetani* enter the body through a wound. The spores produce a neurotoxin called tetanospasmin.

Tetanospasmin cannot cross the blood–brain barrier to affect the central nervous system. Instead, the toxin hitches a ride from the wound site to the spinal cord, using the retrograde transport system within axons (Schwab, Suda, & Thoenen, 1979). Once in the central nervous system, the toxin binds to receptor sites for a major inhibitory neurotransmitter, gamma-aminobutyric acid (GABA), and can't be dislodged. If you have any remaining doubts about the need for all of those little IPSPs, the effects of tetanospasmin will probably erase them. Without normal inhibitory input from GABA, muscles begin to go into sudden, involuntary contractions, or spasms. Spasms occur first in the jaw and neck, giving tetanus its other popular name, "lockjaw." As the disease progresses, muscles rip apart and the vertebrae of the spine suffer compression fractures. Figure 3.25 shows a patient in the later stages of the disease, which may lead to respiratory or cardiac arrest. Even with intensive care, 30 to 40 percent of patients will die. Tetanus vaccines are good for about 10 years. When was the last time you got one?

public domain

FIGURE 3.25
Lack of Inhibitory Input Produces Muscle Spasms
Nineteenth century Scottish surgeon Sir Charles Bell, who gave us the Bell-Magendie Law, painted this picture of a soldier dying from tetanus. In late-stage tetanus, so much muscle tension occurs that the unfortunate victim cannot even lie down, but instead maintains this arched position.

Neural Integration The average neuron in the human brain receives input from about 1,000 other neurons. Some of that input will be in the form of EPSPs, some in the form of IPSPs. The task faced by one of these neurons is to decide which input merits the production of an action potential. You may have had the experience of asking friends and family members for help with a moral dilemma. Some of your advisors give you an excitatory "go for it" message, and others give you an inhibitory "don't even think about it" message. After reviewing the input, it is your task, like the neuron's, to consider all of the advice you've received and decide whether to go forward. This decision-making process on the part of the neuron is known as **neural integration.**

neural integration The determination of whether to fire an action potential, based on the summation of inputs to a neuron.

In vertebrates, cells receive their excitatory and inhibitory advice in different locations. The dendrites and their spines are the major locations for excitatory input. In contrast, most of the inhibitory input occurs at synapses on the cell body. Because the dendrites and cell body contain few voltage-dependent channels, they do not typically produce action potentials. Instead, EPSPs from the dendrites and

IPSPs from the cell body spread passively but very rapidly until they reach the axon hillock.

The only time the cell will produce an action potential is when the area of the axon hillock is depolarized to threshold. This may occur as a result of **spatial summation,** in which inputs from all over the cell converge at the axon hillock. The cell adds up all the excitatory inputs and subtracts all the inhibitory inputs. If the end result at the axon hillock is about 5mV in favor of depolarization, the cell will fire. Spatial summation is analogous to adding up all of your friends' votes and following the will of the majority.

Because EPSPs and IPSPs last longer than action potentials, they can build on one another at a very active synapse, leading to **temporal summation.** Although it typically takes a lot of excitatory input to produce an action potential in the postsynaptic cell, temporal summation provides a means for a single, very active synapse to trigger the postsynaptic cell. One particularly persistent (and noisy) friend can definitely influence our decisions.

Neuromodulation

The synapses we have discussed so far involve an axon terminal as the presynaptic element and either a dendrite or a cell body as the postsynaptic element. In addition, we can observe synapses between an axon terminal and another axon fiber. As shown in ■ Figure 3.26, these **axo-axonic synapses** have a modulating effect on the release of neurotransmitter by the target axon. If the presynaptic neuron increases the amount of neurotransmitter released, **presynaptic facilitation** has occurred. If the presynaptic neuron decreases the amount of neurotransmitter released by the target axon, we say that **presynaptic inhibition** has occurred. This type of modulation occurs quite frequently in sensory systems and during some types of learning (see Chapter 12).

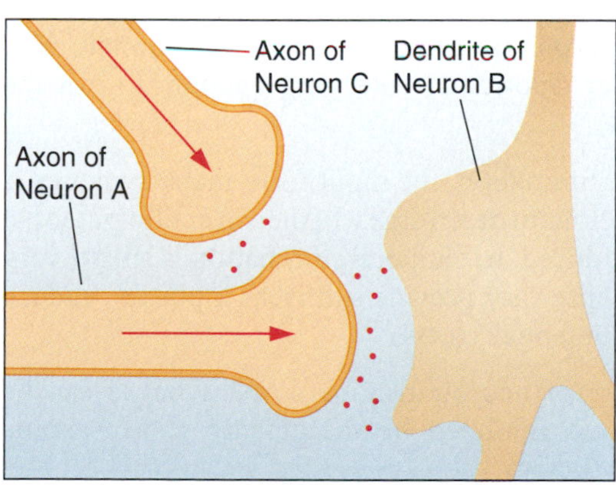

(a) Presynaptic Facilitation

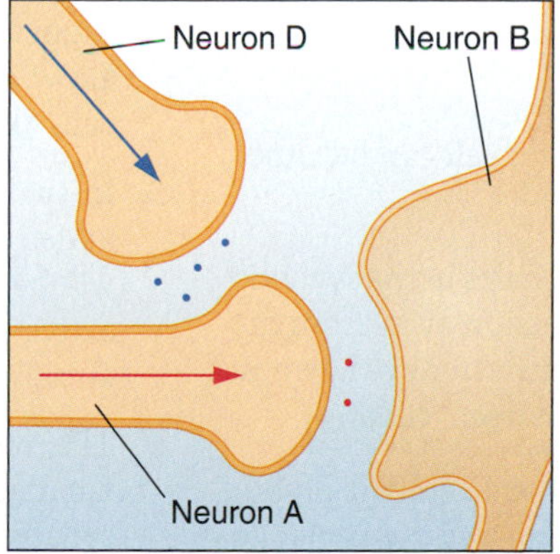

(b) Presynaptic Inhibition

■ **Figure 3.26**
Synapses Between Two Axons Modulate the Amount of Neurotransmitter Released In presynaptic facilitation (a), input from neuron C will increase the amount of neurotransmitter released by neuron A onto neuron B. In presynaptic inhibition (b), input from neuron D will decrease the amount of neurotransmitter released by neuron A onto neuron B.

spatial summation Neural integration in which the combined inputs from many synapses converge on the axon hillock, where an action potential will result if threshold is reached.

temporal summation Neural integration in which excitation from one active synapse is sufficient to initiate the formation of an action potential.

axo-axonic synapse (AX-oh-ax-ON-ik) A synapse in which both the presynaptic and postsynaptic elements are axons.

presynaptic facilitation At a synapse between two axons, the increase of neurotransmitter release by the postsynaptic axon as a result of input from the presynaptic axon.

presynaptic inhibition At a synapse between two axons, the decrease of neurotransmitter release by the postsynaptic axon as a result of input from the presynaptic axon.

INTERIM SUMMARY 3.3

Summary Table: Communication at the Synapse

Event	Location	Mechanism of Action
Exocytosis	Axon terminal	• Ca^{2+} enters the cell. • Vesicles fuse with the axon terminal membrane. • Neurotransmitter is released into the synaptic gap. • Vesicles are returned to the terminal interior and refilled.
Postsynaptic receptors bind neurotransmitter molecules	Postsynaptic membrane	• Receptors bind available neurotransmitter molecules in the gap. • Ion channels are directly opened in ionotropic receptors. • G proteins are released by metabotropic receptors, opening nearby ion channels.
Neurotransmitter deactivation	Synaptic gap	• Neurotransmitter molecules may diffuse away from the synapse, be deactivated by enzymes, or be transported back across the presynaptic membrane.
Postsynaptic potentials	Postsynaptic membrane	• EPSPs result from the opening of ligand-gated Na^+ channels. • IPSPs result from the opening of ligand-gated K^+ or Cl^- channels.
Integration or summation	Axon hillock of postsynaptic cell body	• Drifting positive and negative currents converge at the axon hillock. • If sufficient depolarization occurs at the axon hillock, the postsynaptic cell will generate an action potential.

Summary Points

1. Chemical synapses involve the release of neurotransmitter by the presynaptic cell. Electrical synapses are characterized by very tiny synaptic gaps crossed by ion channels from the presynaptic and postsynaptic neurons. **(LO8)**
2. Receptor proteins on the postsynaptic cell can be either ionotropic or metabotropic. **(LO8)**
3. The action of neurotransmitter molecules in the synaptic gap may be terminated through diffusion away from the gap, by deactivation of the neurotransmitter by enzymes, or by reuptake by the presynaptic neuron. **(LO8)**
4. Postsynaptic potentials are small, local, graded potentials that can last 5 to 10 msec. Excitatory postsynaptic potentials (EPSPs) produce slight depolarizations by opening channels that allow sodium to enter the cell. Inhibitory postsynaptic potentials (IPSPs) produce slight hyperpolarizations by opening channels that allow either chloride to enter or potassium to exit the cell. **(LO9)**
5. In spatial summation, the input from many synapses is added together to determine whether an action potential will be produced. In temporal summation, a single, very active synapse may provide sufficient input to produce an action potential. **(LO9)**
6. The release of neurotransmitters at a synapse can be facilitated or inhibited by the activity at axo-axonic synapses. **(LO10)**

Review Questions

1. Why would presynaptic neurons benefit from having autoreceptors?
2. What are the advantages to presynaptic inhibition and facilitation?

CHAPTER REVIEW

THOUGHT QUESTIONS

1. If you were designing a neural system that had to respond very quickly over long distances, what characteristics would you want your axons to have?
2. If two equally active synapses are located on a distant dendrite and on the cell body, which will have the greatest effect on the axon hillock, and why? What is the likelihood that this cell will produce an action potential?
3. In multiple sclerosis, axons that were meant to be myelinated lose their myelin. In what ways would signaling in these axons be even less effective than in axons designed to be unmyelinated?

KEY TERMS

absolute refractory period (p. 78)
action potential (p. 61)
astrocyte (p. 68)
autoreceptor (p. 85)
axon (p. 61)
axon hillock (p. 67)
axon terminal (p. 67)
bipolar neuron (p. 68)
cell body (p. 61)
cytoskeleton (p. 63)
dendrite (p. 61)
dendritic spine (p. 65)
depolarization (p. 77)
excitatory postsynaptic potential (EPSP) (p. 88)
exocytosis (p. 85)
extracellular fluid (p. 62)
glia (p. 61)
inhibition (p. 84)
inhibitory postsynaptic potential (IPSP) (p. 88)
intracellular fluid (p. 62)
ion (p. 62)
ionotropic receptor (p. 86)
ligand-gated channel (p. 63)
macroglia (p. 68)
metabotropic receptor (p. 86)
microfilament (p. 65)
microglia (p. 68)
microtubule (p. 63)
motor neuron (p. 68)
multipolar neuron (p. 68)
myelin (p. 67)
neurofilament (p. 65)
neuron (p. 61)
neurotransmitter (p. 63)
node of Ranvier (p. 67)
oligodendrocyte (p. 68)
passive conduction (p. 80)
presynaptic facilitation (p. 91)
presynaptic inhibition (p. 91)
relative refractory period (p. 79)
resting potential (p. 74)
reuptake (p. 87)
saltatory conduction (p. 81)
Schwann cell (p. 68)
sensory neuron (p. 68)
sodium-potassium pump (p. 63)
spatial summation (p. 91)
synapse (p. 63)
synaptic gap (p. 65)
synaptic vesicle (p. 67)
temporal summation (p. 91)
threshold (p. 77)
unipolar neuron (p. 68)
voltage-dependent channel (p. 62)

4 Psychopharmacology

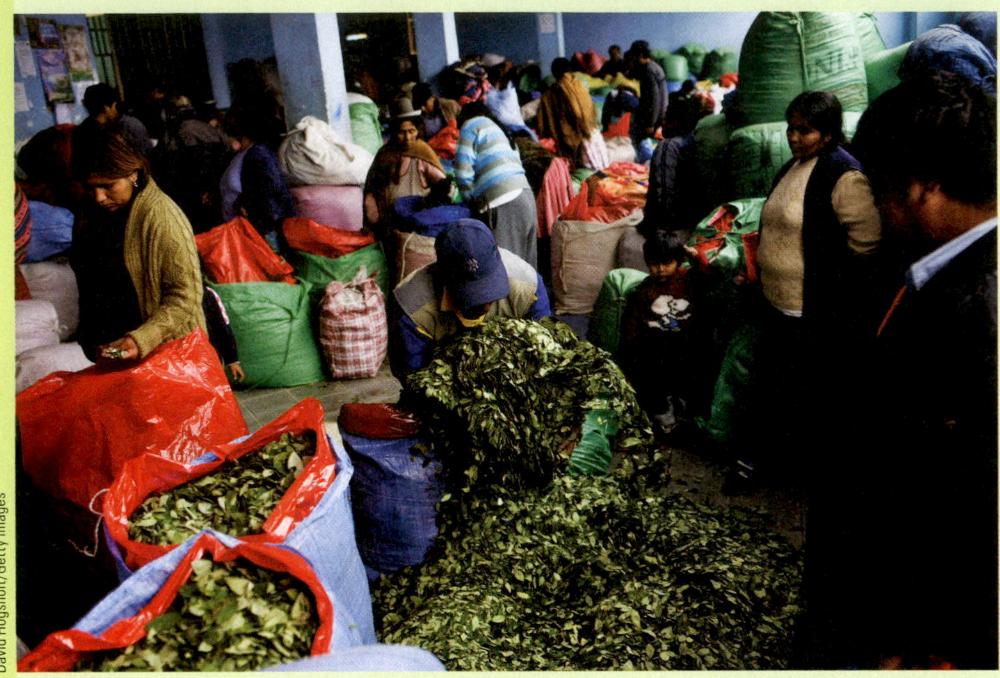

David Hogshoit/Getty Images

▲ **Market Day for Coca Farmers** Cocaine derived from the coca leaf remains one of the most commonly used psychoactive substances world-wide.

Introduction

Over the course of human history, people managed to identify substances that produced psychoactive effects. It's hard to imagine what would lead that first person to cut the outer seed casing of a poppy flower, collect the resulting sap, and ingest or smoke the dried sap to produce a psychoactive result. If nobody had ever done this, we wouldn't know about opium. Ronald Siegel (1989) has suggested that early humans learned to identify drugs by observing the reactions to various plants by their animals. Arabian folklore cited by Siegel describes how goat herders began to use coffee after watching animals that had ingested the beans become friskier.

Most psychoactive substances produce their behavioral effects by interacting with the existing chemistry of the nervous system. In the previous chapter, we traced the generation and propagation of the action potential. Because this electrical signal usually cannot jump across the physical space separating two neurons, neurons turn to chemical messengers to bridge the gap. Our task in this chapter is to review the many types of chemical messengers found in the nervous system and to explore the external substances that affect their functioning. ■

Neurotransmitters, Neuromodulators, and Neurohormones

Chemical messengers, like the serotonin shown in Figure 4.1, fall into three general categories: neurotransmitters, neuromodulators, and neurohormones. **Neurotransmitters** act on neurons in their own immediate vicinity, generally at a synapse. **Neuromodulators** are chemical messengers that act on neurons somewhat farther away by diffusing away from their site of release. **Neurohormones** are capable of producing effects at target cells quite distant from their site of release. Neurohormones often travel in the blood supply to reach their final targets. Regardless of the distance traveled, these chemical messengers will interact only with other cells that have specialized receptor sites to receive them. As we will see later in this chapter, the same chemical can play more than one of these roles.

Identifying Neurotransmitters

Our first step in understanding the biochemistry of the nervous system is to define the characteristics of a neurotransmitter. Because a single chemical can perform a wide variety of functions in a cell, it is challenging to determine when and where it is acting as a neurotransmitter. Newer technologies, such as using antibodies for particular neurotransmitters, make the identification process somewhat easier.

Neurotransmitters are substances released by one cell at a synapse that produce a reaction in a target cell. Beyond this basic definition, neuroscientists generally agree with the following additional criteria:

1. A neurotransmitter must be synthesized within the neuron.
2. In response to the arrival of an action potential, the substance is released in sufficient quantities to produce an effect on the postsynaptic cell.
3. We should be able to duplicate the action of a suspected neurotransmitter experimentally on a postsynaptic cell.
4. Some mechanism exists that ends the interaction between the neurotransmitter and the postsynaptic cell.

Alfred Pasieka/Photo Researchers, Inc.

Figure 4.1
A Close Encounter With Serotonin Polarized light microscopy was used to form this 3-dimensional image of a molecule of serotonin, a neurotransmitter intimately connected to the brain's regulation of mood, appetite, and sleep.

Learning Objectives

After reading this chapter, you should be able to:

LO1 Differentiate among neurotransmitters, neuromodulators, and neurohormones.

LO2 Summarize the major criteria for identifying a substance as a neurotransmitter.

LO3 Identify the major locations, functions, synthesis pathways, receptor characteristics, and process of deactivation for acetylcholine, dopamine, norepinephrine, epinephrine, serotonin, glutamate, GABA, and adenosine triphosphate.

LO4 Identify the major differences among small-molecule, neuropeptide, and gaseous neurotransmitters.

LO5 Provide examples of major neuropeptides.

LO6 Differentiate between agonists and antagonists.

LO7 Provide examples of drugs that produce effects by influencing neurotransmitter production, neurotransmitter storage, neurotransmitter release, receptor activity, reuptake, and enzymatic degradation.

LO8 Review the major principles of drug effects, including the mode of administration, sources of individual differences in reactions to drugs, placebo effects, tolerance, withdrawal, and addiction.

LO9 Identify the major features and modes of action of stimulants, opiates, marijuana, other hallucinogens, alcohol, and St. John's wort.

neurotransmitter A chemical messenger that communicates across a synapse.
neuromodulator A chemical messenger that communicates with target cells more distant than the synapse by diffusing away from the point of release.
neurohormone A chemical messenger that communicates with target cells at great distance, often by traveling through the circulation.

■ **FIGURE 4.2 Major Categories of Neurotransmitters, Neuromodulators, and Neurohormones**

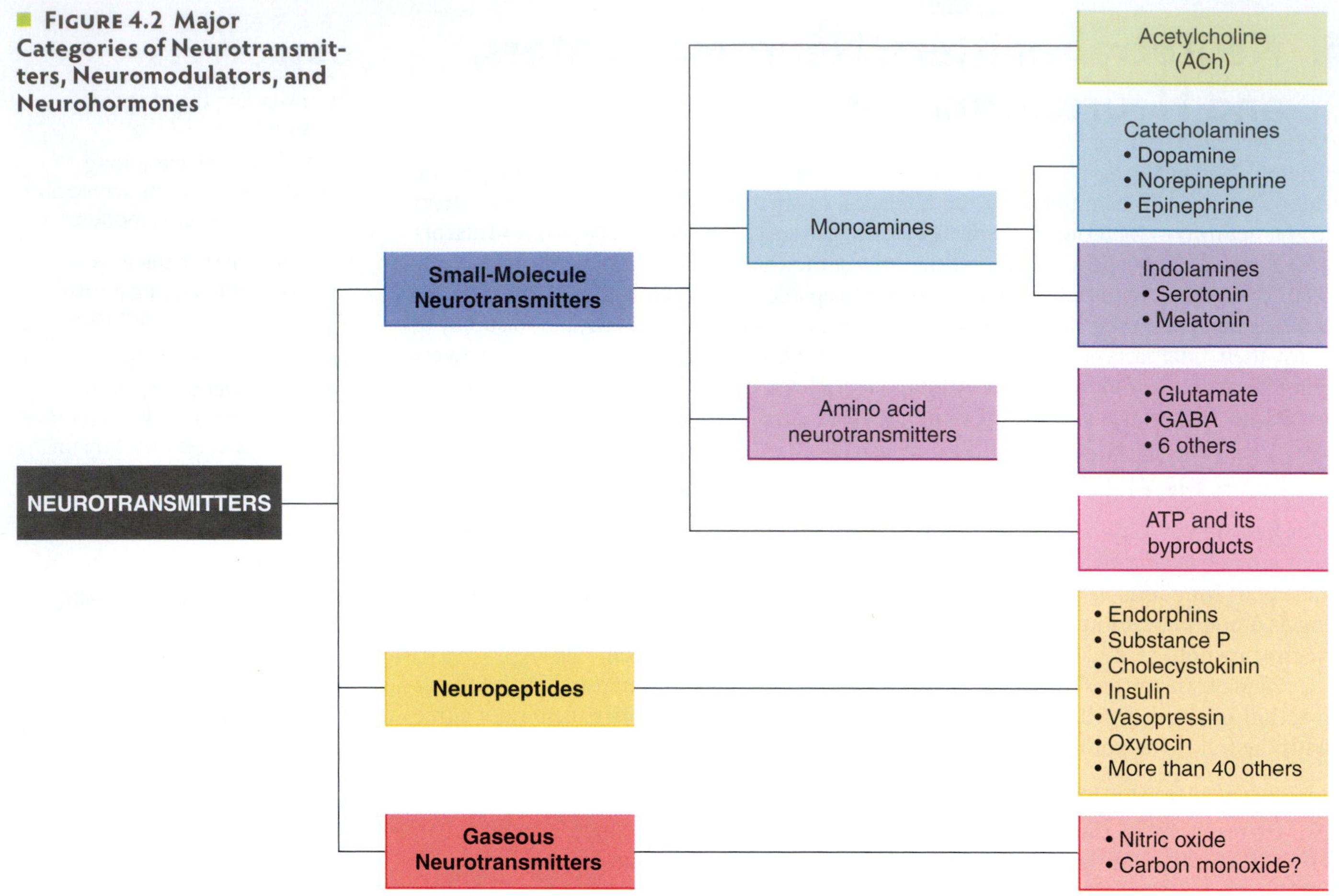

TYPES OF NEUROTRANSMITTERS

Major neurotransmitters fall into two classes, the **small-molecule transmitters** and the **neuropeptides.** The small-molecule transmitters can be further divided into **amino acids** and amines, which are derived from amino acids. Neuropeptides are chains of amino acids. Recently, certain gases have been shown to influence adjacent neurons in ways similar to more classical neurotransmitter substances. ■ Figure 4.2 provides a basic outline for these major classes of neurotransmitters.

Small-molecule transmitters and neuropeptides differ in several important ways that are summarized in Table 4.1. In general, small-molecule transmitters are well suited for responding rapidly as neurotransmitters, whereas neuropeptides are better suited for the slower process of neuromodulation. Small-molecule transmitters are typically synthesized in the axon terminal, whereas neuropeptides are synthesized in the cell body and must be transported the length of the axon. Vesicles containing neuropeptides are used only once, in contrast to the recycling of vesicles possible with small-molecule neurotransmitters. Compared to the release of small-molecule transmitters, the release of neuropeptide vesicles requires higher levels of calcium, which in turn requires a higher rate of action potentials reaching the axon terminal (Fulop & Smith, 2006). Finally, neuropeptides diffuse away from the synapse, whereas the small-molecule transmitters are deactivated by reuptake or enzymes (see Chapter 3).

Early pharmacological pioneer Henry Dale proposed that a single neuron could contain one and only one type of neurotransmitter. Using modern technology, we can see that Dale was only partially correct. Although the existence of two small-molecule transmitters in the same neuron remains controversial (Lapish, Seamans, & Judson Chandler, 2006), most neurons using neuropeptides also contain a small-molecule transmitter (Salio, Lossi, Ferrini, & Merighi, 2006). In these cases, the peptide modulates the effects of the small-molecule transmitter at the synapse.

small-molecule transmitter One of a group of chemical messengers that includes amino acids and amines.

neuropeptide A peptide that acts as a neurotransmitter, a neuromodulator, or a neurohormone.

amino acid An essential component of proteins.

TABLE 4.1 Features of Small-Molecule Transmitters and Neuropeptides

	Small-Molecule Transmitters	Neuropeptides
Synthesis	In axon terminal	In cell body; requires transport
Recycling of Vesicles	Yes	No
Activation	Moderate action potential frequency	High action potential frequency
Deactivation	Reuptake or enzymatic degradation	Diffusion away from the synapse
Function	Fast neurotransmission	Neuromodulation

The Small-Molecule Transmitters A number of small-molecule substances meet all or most of the preceding criteria specified for neurotransmitters and appear to play a vital role in neurotransmission: acetylcholine, five monoamines, several amino acids, and the energy molecule adenosine triphosphate (ATP) and its byproducts.

Neurons that use **acetylcholine (ACh)** as their major neurotransmitter are referred to as *cholinergic neurons.* The cholingeric neuron obtains the building block *choline* from dietary fats. A second building block, *acetyl coenzyme A* (acetyl CoA), results from the metabolic activities of mitochondria, so it is abundantly present in most cells. The enzyme choline acetyltransferase (ChAT) acts on these two building blocks, or precursors, to produce the neurotransmitter acetylcholine. The presence of the enzyme ChAT provides a useful marker for identifying cholinergic neurons because ChAT is found only in neurons that produce ACh.

Cholinergic neurons also manufacture the enzyme **acetylcholinesterase (AChE).** AChE is released into the synaptic gap, where it breaks down any ACh in that location. The choline resulting from the breakdown of ACh can then be recaptured by the presynaptic neuron and resynthesized into more ACh.

ACh is the primary neurotransmitter at the neuromuscular junction, the synapse between a neuron and a muscle fiber (see Chapter 8). ACh is also essential to the operation of the autonomic nervous system. All preganglionic synapses in the autonomic nervous system use ACh as their neurotransmitter. Postganglionic synapses in the parasympathetic division of the autonomic nervous system also use ACh (see Chapter 2).

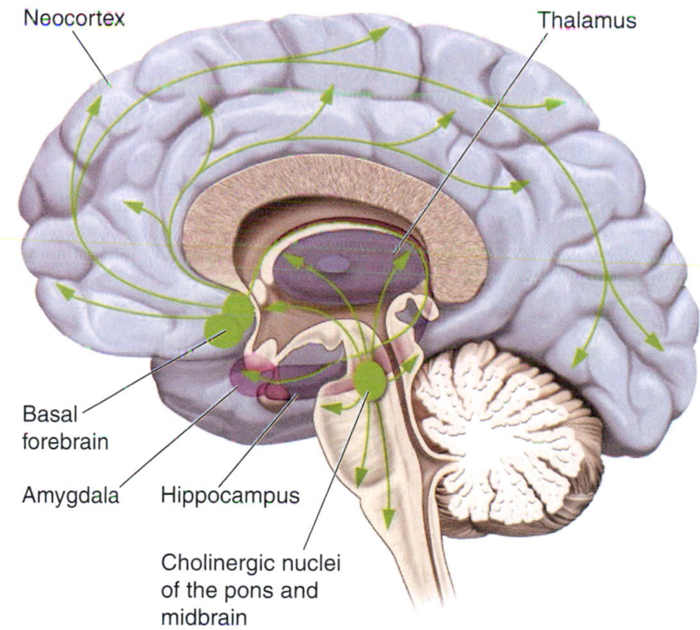

FIGURE 4.3
The Distribution of Cholinergic Systems in the Brain In addition to playing important roles at the neuromuscular junction and in the autonomic nervous system, cholinergic neurons are widely distributed in the brain. Important systems originate in the basal forebrain and brainstem and form projections to the limbic system and neocortex. These systems participate in learning and memory and deteriorate in patients diagnosed with Alzheimer's disease.

In addition to their importance in the peripheral nervous system, cholinergic neurons are widely distributed in the brain. As shown in Figure 4.3, major groups of cholinergic neurons located in the basal forebrain, septum, and brainstem project to the neocortex, hippocampus, and amygdala. As we will see in Chapter 5, these groups of neurons are especially likely to deteriorate as a result of Alzheimer's disease. Not too surprisingly, given the memory loss associated with Alzheimer's disease, these cholinergic neurons appear to participate in learning and memory.

Many subtypes of cholinergic receptors are found in the nervous system (Dani, 2001). Two major subtypes are known as **nicotinic receptors** and **muscarinic receptors.** These receptors take their names from substances other than ACh to which they also react. In other words, a nicotinic receptor responds to both ACh and to nicotine, found in all tobacco products, whereas the muscarinic receptor responds to both ACh and muscarine, a substance derived from the hallucinogenic (and highly poisonous) mushroom *Amanita muscaria.*

acetylcholine (ACh) (ah-see-til-COE-leen) A major small-molecule neurotransmitter used at the neuromuscular junction, in the autonomic nervous system, and in the central nervous system.

acetylcholinesterase (AChE) (ah-seetil-cole-in-ES-ter-aze) An enzyme that breaks down the neurotransmitter acetylcholine.

nicotinic receptor (nick-oh-TIN-ick) A postsynaptic receptor that responds to nicotine and ACh.

muscarinic receptor (muss-kar-IN-ik) A postsynaptic receptor that responds to both ACh and muscarine.

WHY DOES THIS MATTER?

Genes and Addiction to Nicotine

Increasing scientists' understanding of the role of genetics in addiction matters because we could counsel people with a vulnerability to nicotine addiction to avoid using the drug in the first place.

Over 400,000 people die in the United States each year from cigarette smoking, and one out of every five deaths is smoking related (Centers for Disease Control and Prevention, 1993). Yet we all know people who seem to smoke like chimneys without any apparent negative effects on health. Comedian George Burns lived to be 100 years old in spite of his constant smoking of cigars. In fact, Burns' health deteriorated only after he sustained a head injury during a fall in his bathroom. In contrast, others, such as comedian Andy Kaufman, die from lung cancer without having ever smoked. The answer to these discrepancies might lie in our genetic vulnerability to specific forms of cancer. Researchers have identified a gene that is involved with the development of nicotinic receptors that appears to play important roles in lung cancer and addiction to nicotine.

One variant of the gene, found in half of those who have European ancestry, is strongly associated with increased risk of lung cancer. Smokers in general have about a 15 percent chance of developing lung cancer. Smokers with one copy of the gene variant have a 30 percent greater risk than smokers with no copies, and smokers with two copies increase their risk by 80 percent.

Researchers disagree about whether the gene variant can cause lung cancer independently of smoking or simply predispose a person to be a smoker, with the resulting increase in risk for lung cancer (Amos et al., 2008; Hung et al., 2008; Thorgeirsson et al., 2008). Either way, it would be nice to know whether you have genetic variants that predispose you to nicotine addiction and lung cancer, allowing you to make informed choices for yourself and, perhaps more important, for your children.

Nicotinic and muscarinic receptors differ in their mechanisms of action and locations within the nervous system. As we observed in Chapter 3, receptors are either single-step ionotropic or multiple-step metabotropic in structure. Nicotinic receptors are fast ionotropic receptors. In contrast, muscarinic receptors are slower metabotropic receptors. Nicotinic receptors are found at the neuromuscular junction, which is logical given the need for speed in muscular responses. The central nervous system contains both nicotinic and muscarinic receptors, but the muscarinic are more common (Ehlert, Roeske, & Yamamura, 1995). Both types of receptors are also found in the autonomic nervous system.

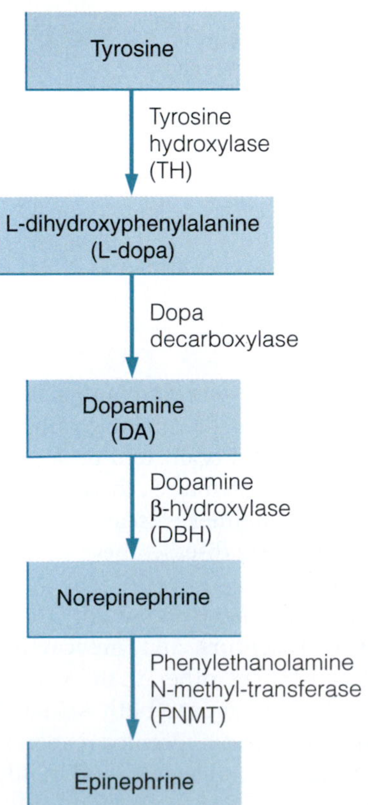

FIGURE 4.4 Catecholamines Share a Common Synthesis Pathway The catecholamines, including dopamine, norepinephrine, and epinephrine, are synthesized from the substrate tyrosine. Tyrosine is converted into L-dopa by the action of tyrosine hydroxylase. L-dopa is converted into dopamine by dopa decarboxylase. The action of dopamine β-hydroxylase on dopamine produces norepinephrine. When norepinephrine reacts with phenylethanolamine N-methyltransferase, epinephrine is produced.

monoamine (mah-noh-uh-MEEN) One of a major group of biogenic amine neurotransmitters, including dopamine, norepinephrine, epinephrine, and serotonin.

catecholamine (cat-uh-KOHL-uh-meen) A member of a group of related biogenic amines that includes dopamine, epinephrine, and norepinephrine.

indoleamine (in-DOLE-uh-meen) One of a subgroup of monoamines, including serotonin and melatonin.

The five **monoamines** are further divided into two subgroups, the **catecholamines** (dopamine, norepinephrine, and epinephrine) and the **indoleamines** (serotonin and melatonin). All of the monoamines are subject to reuptake from the synaptic gap following release. Within the axon terminal, monoamines that are not encased in vesicles are broken down by the action of the enzyme **monoamine oxidase (MAO).**

As shown in Figure 4.4, catecholamine synthesis begins with the amino acid tyrosine. All neurons containing a catecholamine also contain the enzyme tyrosine hydroxylase (TH). When TH acts on tyrosine, the end product is **L-dopa** (L-dihydroxyphenylalanine). The production of **dopamine** requires one step following the synthesis of L-dopa. The enzyme dopa decarboxylase acts on L-dopa to produce dopamine. Dopamine is converted to **norepinephrine** by the action of the enzyme dopamine β-hydroxylase (DBH). This last step takes place within the synaptic vesicles. Finally, the catecholamine **epinephrine** is produced by the reaction between norepinephrine and the enzyme phenylethanolamine N-methyltransferase (PNMT). The synthesis of epinephrine is complicated. PNMT exists in the intracellular

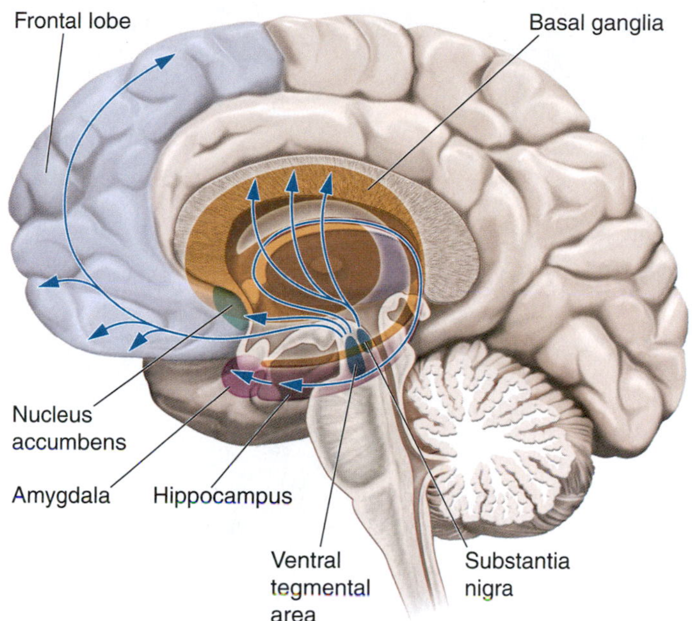

FIGURE 4.5
Dopaminergic Systems in the Brain
Dopaminergic neurons in the midbrain project to the basal ganglia, the limbic system, and the frontal lobes of the cerebral cortex. These systems appear to participate in motor control, reward, and the planning of behavior.

fluid of the axon terminal of neurons that use epinephrine. Once norepinephrine is synthesized within synaptic vesicles, it must be released back into the intracellular fluid, where it is converted by PNMT into epinephrine. The epinephrine is then transported back into vesicles.

Dopamine is widely distributed throughout the brain and is particularly involved with systems mediating movement, reinforcement, and planning. As shown in Figure 4.5, three major dopamine pathways originate in the midbrain. Projections from the substantia nigra of the midbrain to the basal ganglia of the cerebral hemispheres provide an important modulation of motor activity. This pathway appears to be particularly damaged in cases of Parkinson's disease, in which patients have great difficulties initiating movement (see Chapter 8). Another dopaminergic pathway, the mesolimbic system, arises in the ventral tegmentum of the midbrain and projects to various parts of the limbic system, including the hippocampus, the amygdala, and the nucleus accumbens. The mesolimbic system participates in feelings of reward, and it plays an important role in addiction. Finally, another group of dopaminergic neurons in the ventral tegmentum projects to parts of the frontal lobe of the cerebral cortex. These neurons participate in higher-level cognitive functions, including the planning of behavior.

As we saw in the case of ACh receptors, multiple receptor subtypes also exist for dopamine, labeled D_1 through D_5 in order of their discovery. All of these receptors are of the slow metabotropic variety. D_2 receptors (and probably their close relatives, the D_3 and D_4 receptors) serve as both postsynaptic receptors and presynaptic autoreceptors. As we saw in Chapter 3, autoreceptors help the presynaptic neuron monitor its synthesis and release of neurotransmitter substance. The D_2 receptor class has been implicated in both reward and psychotic behavior (Kienast & Heinz, 2006; Seeman et al., 2006).

Epinephrine and norepinephrine were formerly referred to as adrenalin and noradrenalin, respectively. We continue to refer to neurons releasing epinephrine as adrenergic and those releasing norepinephrine as noradrenergic. Epinephrine plays a limited role as a central nervous system neurotransmitter. The "adrenalin rush" we associate with stress actually results from the release of epinephrine from the adrenal glands located above the kidneys in the lower back into the blood supply. Neurons that secrete norepinephrine are found in the pons, medulla, and hypothalamus. Probably the most significant source of norepinephrine is the locus coeruleus of the pons, shown in Figure 4.6. Projections from the locus coeruleus go to the spinal cord and nearly every major part of the brain. The primary result of activity in these circuits is

monoamine oxidase (MAO) (mah-noh-uh-MEEN OX-i-daze) An enzyme that breaks down monoamines.

L-dopa A substance produced during the synthesis of catecholamines that is also administered as a treatment for Parkinson's disease.

dopamine A major monoamine and catecholamine neurotransmitter implicated in motor control, reward, and psychosis.

norepinephrine (nor-ep-in-EF-rin) A major monoamine and catecholamine neurotransmitter.

epinephrine (ep-in-EF-rin) One of the monoamine/catecholamine neurotransmitters; also known as adrenaline.

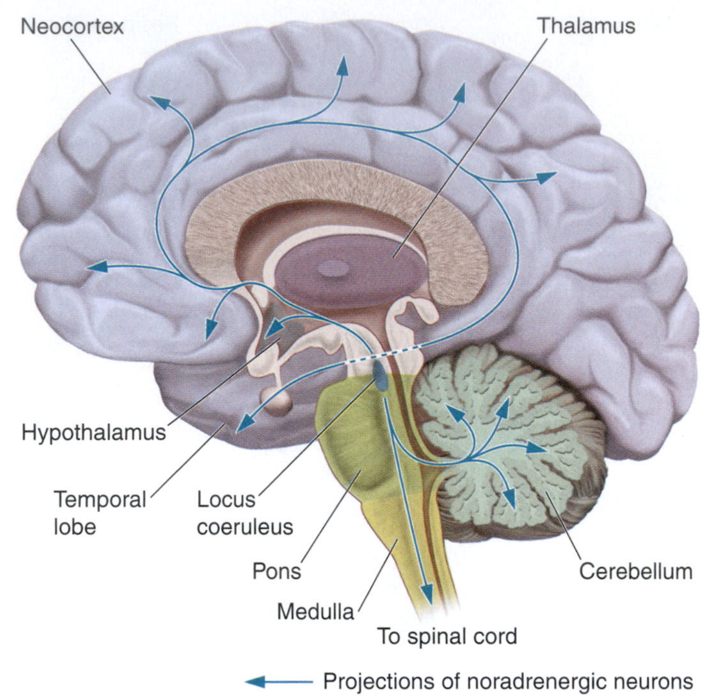

FIGURE 4.6
Noradrenergic Systems in the Brain Neurons using norepinephrine as a neurotransmitter are found in the pons, medulla, and hypothalamus. Projections from these neurons go to nearly every major part of the brain and spinal cord. Their primary role is to produce arousal and vigilance.

to increase arousal and vigilance. In the peripheral nervous system, norepinephrine is found at the postganglionic synapses of the sympathetic nervous system, which is also involved in arousal.

There are at least four receptor types that respond to either norepinephrine or epinephrine. These receptors are found in both the central nervous system and target organs that respond to sympathetic nervous system activity and neurohormones. All of these receptors are metabotropic, which might surprise you given the need for speedy responses associated with the fight-or-flight functions of the sympathetic nervous system.

Indoleamines, including **serotonin** and melatonin, are similar enough in chemical structure to the catecholamines to share the umbrella term of monoamine yet are different enough to warrant their own subheading. The synthesis of serotonin, diagrammed in Figure 4.7, begins with the amino acid tryptophan. Tryptophan is obtained from dietary sources, including grains, meat, and dairy products. Two chemical reactions are required to convert tryptophan into serotonin. The first is the action of the enzyme tryptophan hydroxylase, which converts tryptophan to 5-hydroxytryptophan (5-HTP). Second, the 5-HTP is converted to serotonin by the action of the enzyme 5-HTP decarboxylase.

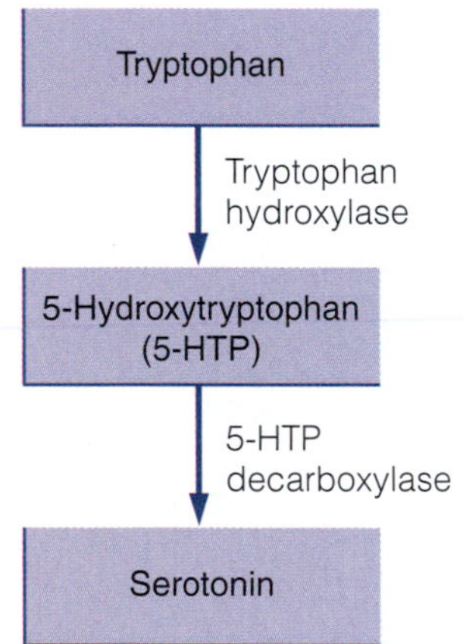

FIGURE 4.7
The Synthesis of Serotonin
Serotonin synthesis begins with dietary tryptophan, which is converted into 5-HTP by the action of tryptophan hydroxylase. 5-HTP is converted into serotonin by the action of 5-HTP decarboxylase.

In spite of their essential roles in behavior and their widespread projections, serotonergic neurons are surprisingly few in number. Estimates suggest there might be as few as 200,000 serotonergic neurons in the human brain (Baker et al., 1991). As shown in Figure 4.8, most of these neurons are located in the raphe nuclei of the brainstem. Their projections travel to the spinal cord, the cerebellum, the limbic system, and the neocortex. Serotonergic activity has been implicated in a variety of behaviors, including sleep, mood, and appetite. At least 15 subtypes of serotonergic receptors have been identified, and most of these function as metabotropic receptors (Leonard, 1992).

After acetylcholine and the monoamines, the next category of small-molecule transmitters is the amino acid neurotransmitters. Although as many as eight amino acids participate as neurotransmitters, two are especially significant: **glutamate** and **gamma-aminobutyric acid (GABA).** Glutamate (also known as glutamic acid) is among the 20 basic amino acids that are used to build other proteins. GABA is not.

Glutamate is the most frequently used excitatory neurotransmitter in the central nervous system (Schwartz, 2000). Glutamate is synthesized from α-ketoglutarate. Once released, glutamate is taken up by both neurons and astrocytes. The synaptic

serotonin (ser-oh-TOH-nin) A major monoamine and indoleamine neurotransmitter believed to participate in the regulation of mood, sleep, and appetite.

glutamate A major excitatory amino acid neurotransmitter.

gamma-aminobutyric acid (GABA) (GAM-uh-ah-meen-oh-bew-TEER-ik) A major inhibitory amino acid neurotransmitter.

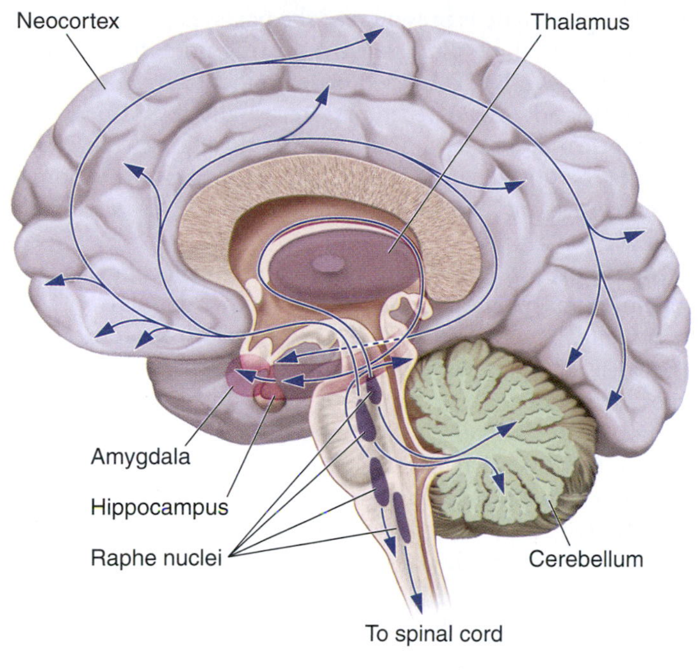

FIGURE 4.8
The Distribution of Serotonergic Pathways in the Brain Most serotonergic neurons are found in the raphe nuclei of the brainstem. Projections from these neurons travel to the spinal cord, cerebellum, limbic system, and neocortex. These systems participate in the control of mood, sleep, and appetite.

area must be cleared of excess glutamate because extended action of glutamate on neurons can be toxic. Some people appear to be oversensitive to the common food additive monosodium glutamate (MSG), which consists of a combination of glutamate and sodium. Adverse reactions include chest pain, headache, nausea, and rapid heartbeat. However, the Food and Drug Administration (FDA) views MSG as a safe food additive for most adults (FDA, 1995; Beyreuther et al., 2007).

Glutamate receptors can be either ionotropic or metabotropic. Three major types of ionotropic glutamate receptors are named after the external substances that also activate them, in the same manner that ACh receptors were named nicotinic or muscarinic. The three glutamate receptors are the N-methyl-D-aspartate (NMDA) receptor, the alpha-amino-3-hydroxy-5-methylisoxazole-4-proprionic acid (AMPA) receptor, and the kainate receptor. Both the AMPA receptor, which is the most common variety, and the kainate receptor operate by controlling a sodium channel. When these receptors bind a molecule of glutamate, a sodium channel opens, and an EPSP is produced.

The NMDA receptor, shown in Figure 4.9, has received a tremendous amount of attention due to its unusual method of action. NMDA receptors are apparently unique in that they are both voltage-dependent and ligand-dependent. In other words, they

FIGURE 4.9
The NMDA Glutamate Receptor The NMDA receptor has two unusual qualities. First, it requires both the binding of glutamate and sufficient depolarization before it responds. At the resting potential, the ion channel is blocked by a molecule of magnesium (Mg^{2+}). Depolarization ejects the Mg^{2+}. If glutamate now binds with the receptor, the channel will open and ions will be allowed to pass. Second, the receptor allows both sodium and calcium ions to enter the neuron.

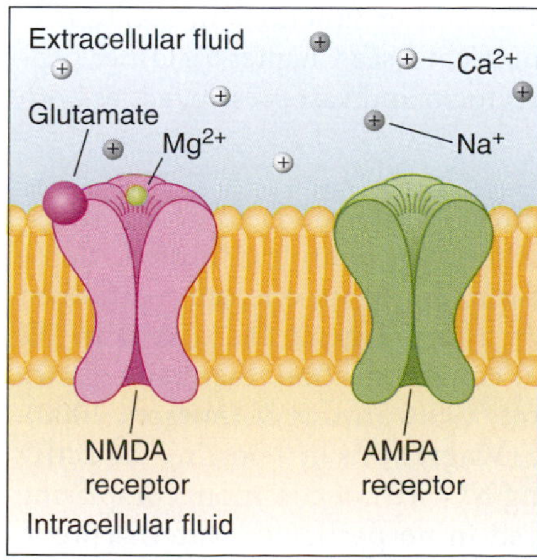

(a) Glutamate Alone

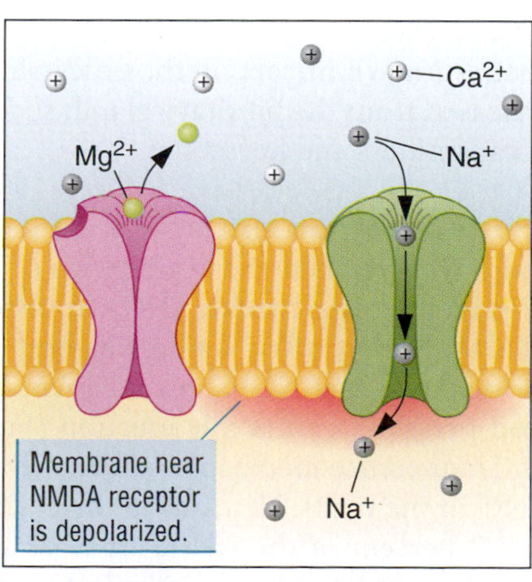

(b) Depolarization Alone

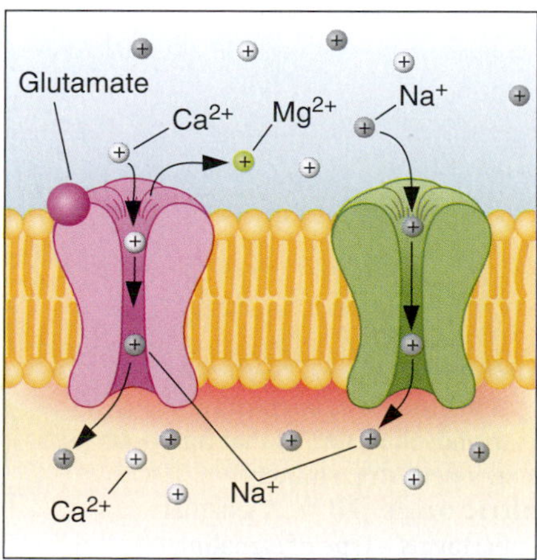

(c) Glutamate and Depolarization

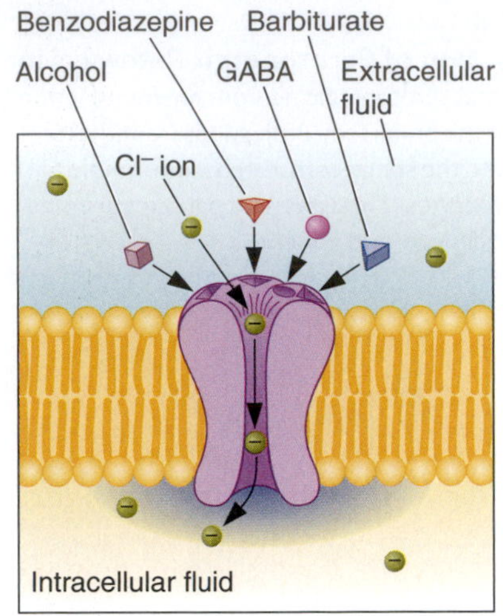

FIGURE 4.10
The $GABA_A$ Receptor Interacts with Several Drugs In addition to binding sites for GABA itself, the $GABA_A$ receptor also contains binding sites that interact with benzodiazepines, barbiturates, and ethanol (alcohol). These drugs depress nervous system activity by increasing the inhibition produced by GABA. Combining any of these drugs can produce a life-threatening level of neural inhibition.

will not open unless glutamate is present *and* the postsynaptic membrane is depolarized at the same time. At the typical negative resting potentials of the postsynaptic neuron, the ion channels of NMDA receptors are blocked by magnesium ions. However, because NMDA and AMPA receptors are usually found near one another on the same postsynaptic membrane, sodium moving through the nearby AMPA receptors will depolarize the postsynaptic cell. When the membrane becomes sufficiently depolarized, the magnesium ions will be ejected from the NMDA receptor, allowing it to open.

NMDA receptors are also unusual in their ability to allow both positively charged sodium and calcium ions to enter the cell, which further depolarizes the cell. In addition, calcium activates enzyme sequences that result in structural and biochemical changes. Because of calcium's ability to trigger lasting changes in neurons, the NMDA receptor is thought to participate in functions such as long-term memory, which we will discuss in Chapter 12. The action of calcium upon entering the cell is also responsible for the toxicity of excess glutamate levels mentioned earlier. As more glutamate stimulates NMDA receptors, more calcium enters neurons. The resulting excess enzyme activity can literally digest and kill the affected neuron. This process might be responsible for much damage following strokes and in a number of brain diseases (Olney, 1994; see Chapter 15).

GABA serves as the major inhibitory neurotransmitter of the central nervous system. GABA is synthesized from glutamate through the action of the enzyme glutamic acid decarboxylase (GAD). There are two types of GABA receptors, referred to as $GABA_A$ and $GABA_B$. $GABA_A$ receptors, shown in Figure 4.10, are ionotropic chloride channels, which allow negatively charged chloride ions to enter the cell. $GABA_B$ receptors are metabotropic potassium channels, which allow positively charged potassium ions to leave the cell. Hyperpolarization occurs whenever negative ions enter the cell or when positive ions leave the cell.

Adenosine triphosphate (ATP) and its byproducts, particularly **adenosine,** also act as neurotransmitters in the central nervous system and in connections between autonomic neurons and the vas deferens, bladder, heart, and gut. ATP frequently coexists in high concentrations in vesicles containing other neurotransmitters, particularly the catecholamines. Adenosine inhibits the release of a wide range of classical neurotransmitters (Dunwiddie, 2001). ATP is involved with the perception of pain, which we will discuss further in Chapter 7.

Neuropeptides There are at least 40 different peptides that act as neurotransmitters, neuromodulators, and neurohormones. Neuropeptides often coexist in the same neuron with a small-molecule neurotransmitter and modify its effect. A single neuron can contain and release several different neuropeptides.

Among the neuropeptides are substance P, which is involved in the perception of pain, and the endogenous morphines (endorphins), substances manufactured in the body that act on the same receptors as opiate drugs. The distribution of receptors for opiates may be seen in Figure 4.11. Peptides involved with digestion, including insulin and cholecystokinin (CCK), have neurotransmitter functions in addition to their better-known impact on the processing of nutrients (see Chapter 9). Other peptides released from the pituitary gland, such as oxytocin and vasopressin, act as both neurotransmitters and hormones.

Gaseous Neurotransmitters Recent developments in the study of neural transmission have stretched the boundaries of our criteria for neurotransmitters. Some gases, including **nitric oxide (NO),** transfer information from one cell to another. Prior to the 1990s, nitric oxide was best known as a precursor for acid rain. We now understand that NO is involved with neural communication, the maintenance of blood pressure, and penile erection (Furchgott, 1999; Snyder & Dawson, 2000). The anti-impotence medication sildenafil citrate (Viagra) acts by boosting the activity of NO in the penis. Neurons in the brain using NO are not common, comprising perhaps 2 percent of the whole, and are scattered in no particular pattern (Bredt, 1992). NO appears to play a particularly important role in regulating communication

adenosine (ah-DEN-oh-seen) A byproduct of adenosine triphosphate (ATP) that functions as a neurotransmitter.
nitric oxide (NO) A gas that performs a type of signaling between neurons.

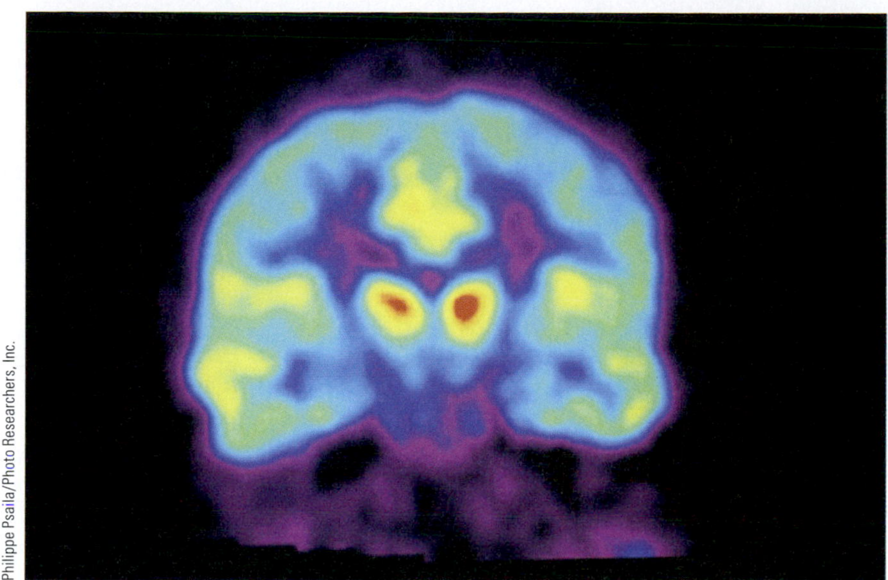

Philippe Psaila/Photo Researchers, Inc.

FIGURE 4.11 Distribution of Opiate Receptors in the Human Brain This PET scan identifies areas of the brain rich in opiate receptors, which appear in red and yellow. These receptors respond both to our naturally occurring endorphins and to externally supplied opiate drugs, including heroin and morphine.

between the thalamus and the cerebral cortex, which in turn influences the amount of sensory input processed by the highest levels of the brain (Alexander, Kurukulasuriya, Mu, & Godwin, 2006).

The mechanism for gaseous transmission is unlike the processes we have discussed so far. Gaseous molecules diffuse through membranes without needing vesicles or a release mechanism. They act on receptors located within cells rather than on receptors embedded in the membrane. It is even possible for gaseous transmitters to travel through one cell and influence its neighbors. Gaseous transmitters break down very quickly without needing the action of enzymes. In addition, gaseous transmitters appear to transfer information from the postsynaptic neuron to the presynaptic neuron, rather than the other way around.

INTERIM SUMMARY 4.1

Summary Table: Characteristics of Selected Neurotransmitters

Neuro-transmitter	Locations	Functions
Acetylcholine (ACh)	• Neuromuscular junction • Preganglionic autonomic synapses • Postganglionic parasympathetic synapses • Basal forebrain projections to hippocampus and amygdala; the septum; the brainstem	• Movement • Autonomic function • Learning and memory
Dopamine	• Substantia nigra and basal ganglia • Ventral tegmentum projections to hippocampus, amygdala, and nucleus accumbens • Ventral tegmentum projections to frontal lobe of the cortex	• Movement • Reinforcement • Planning
Norepinephrine	• Pons (especially locus coeruleus, which projects widely to spinal cord and brain) • Medulla • Hypothalamus • Postganglionic sympathetic synapses	• Arousal and vigilance • Mood

(continued)

INTERIM SUMMARY 4.1 (continued)

Serotonin	Projections originate in the pons, particularly the raphe nucleus, and project widely in the brain and spinal cord	• Sleep • Appetite • Mood
Glutamate	Widely distributed in the central nervous system	• Excitation • Long-term memory
GABA	Widely distributed in the central nervous system	• Inhibition • Mood • Seizure threshold
Adenosine triphosphate (ATP)	• Central nervous system neuromodulator • Autonomic nervous system • Frequently found in axons containing catecholamines	• Pain modulation • Inhibition
Endorphins	• Periaqueductal gray • Hypothalamus • Pituitary gland • Limbic system • Basal ganglia • Spinal cord • Ventral tegmentum	• Pain reduction • Feelings of well-being
Substance P	• Spinal cord	• Pain
Nitric oxide (NO)	• Central and peripheral nervous systems • Smooth muscle	• Relaxes smooth muscle cells in blood vessels • Erection • Possible retrograde signaling

Summary Points

1. Neurotransmitters affect adjacent cells across the synapse. Neuromodulators diffuse away from the synapse to target cells some distance away. Circulating neurohormones reach even more distant target cells. **(LO1)**
2. Neurotransmitters are manufactured within neurons, released in response to the arrival of an action potential, have an observable effect on the postsynaptic cell, and are deactivated following release by reuptake or by the action of enzymes. **(LO2)**
3. Acetylcholine is found at the neuromuscular junction, in the autonomic nervous system, and within the central nervous system. Dopamine is involved with systems controlling movement, reinforcement, and planning. Norepinephrine pathways increase arousal and vigilance. Serotonin participates in the regulation of mood, appetite, and sleep. Glutamate is the most frequently used excitatory neurotransmitter in the central nervous system. GABA generally produces inhibition. ATP and its byproducts appear to act as neurotransmitters. **(LO3)**
4. Small-molecule neurotransmitters include acetylcholine, dopamine, norepinephrine, epinephrine, serotonin, glutamate, GABA, and adenosine. Neuropeptides acting as neurotransmitters include substance P and endorphins, among at least 40 others. **(LO4)**
5. Gaseous neurotransmitters diffuse through membranes and interact with internal receptors to transmit information. Gases can communicate from postsynaptic neurons to presynaptic neurons. **(LO4)**

Review Questions

1. How are neurotransmitters, neuromodulators, and neurohormones similar to and different from one another?
2. What are some of the distinctive features of receptors for ACh, dopamine, glutamate, and GABA?

Drug Actions at the Synapse

Many drugs produce their psychoactive effects through actions at the synapse. Drugs can affect synthesis of neurotransmitters, storage of neurotransmitters within the axon terminal, neurotransmitter release, reuptake or enzyme activity following release, and interactions with either pre- or postsynaptic receptor sites.

Agonists and Antagonists

Drugs can boost or reduce the activity of a neurotransmitter. Drugs that enhance the activity of a neurotransmitter are known as **agonists.** Drugs that reduce the activity of a neurotransmitter are known as **antagonists.** Pharmacologists often limit the use of the terms agonist or antagonist to chemicals that act at receptor sites, but our broader use of the terms in biological psychology includes chemicals that influence neurotransmitter activity in additional ways such as affecting the amount of neurotransmitter that is released.

It is important to avoid equating agonists with postsynaptic or behavioral excitation and antagonists with inhibition. The outcome of the action of an agonist or antagonist depends on the normal effects of the neurotransmitter. If a neurotransmitter generally has an inhibitory effect on the postsynaptic neuron, the action of an agonist would increase the amount of inhibitory input, resulting in reduced postsynaptic activity. The action of an antagonist at this same synapse, interfering with the inhibitory neurotransmitter, would result in greater than normal postsynaptic activity. Consider the case of caffeine. Caffeine, as you are probably well aware, produces behavioral stimulation. As we will see later in the chapter, caffeine is an antagonist for adenosine, which means it reduces adenosine's effects. Because adenosine typically acts as an inhibitor at the synapse, inhibiting an inhibitor leads to behavioral excitation.

Those who have never been brainwashed or addicted to a drug find it hard to understand their fellow men who are driven by such compulsions.

Richard Dawkins

Neurotransmitter Production

Manipulating the synthesis of a neurotransmitter will affect the amount available for release. Substances that promote increased production will act as agonists, whereas substances that interfere with production will act as antagonists.

The simplest way to boost the rate of neurotransmitter synthesis is to provide larger quantities of the basic building blocks, or precursors, for the neurotransmitter. Serotonin levels can be raised by eating high carbohydrate meals, which result in more tryptophan crossing the blood–brain barrier to be synthesized into serotonin (Wurtman et al., 2003).

Drugs can exert antagonistic effects by interfering with the synthesis pathways of neurotransmitters. One example is the drug α-methyl-*p*-tyrosine (AMPT), which interferes with the activity of tyrosine hydroxylase (TH). As we observed earlier in the chapter, TH converts the substrate tyrosine into L-dopa. Consequently, AMPT interferes with the production of dopamine, norepinephrine, and epinephrine.

Neurotransmitter Storage

Certain drugs have an antagonistic effect by interfering with the storage of neurotransmitters in vesicles within the neuron. For example, the drug **reserpine,** used to reduce blood pressure, interferes with the uptake of monoamines into synaptic vesicles. As a result, abnormally small quantities of monoamine neurotransmitters are available for release in response to the arrival of action potentials. Reserpine's interference with the monoamine serotonin often results in profound depression. As many as 15 percent of all patients who used reserpine to lower blood pressure also experienced severe depression (Sachar & Baron, 1979). As a result, reserpine is rarely prescribed today.

Neurotransmitter Release

Drugs often modify the release of neurotransmitters in response to the arrival of an action potential. Some drugs affect release by interacting with presynaptic autoreceptors. Other drugs interact directly with the proteins responsible for exocytosis, which is

agonist Substance that promotes the activity of a neurotransmitter.
antagonist Substance that reduces the action of a neurotransmitter.
reserpine (RES-er-peen) A substance derived from a plant that depletes supplies of monoamines by interfering with the uptake of monoamines into synaptic vesicles; used to treat high blood pressure but often produces depression.

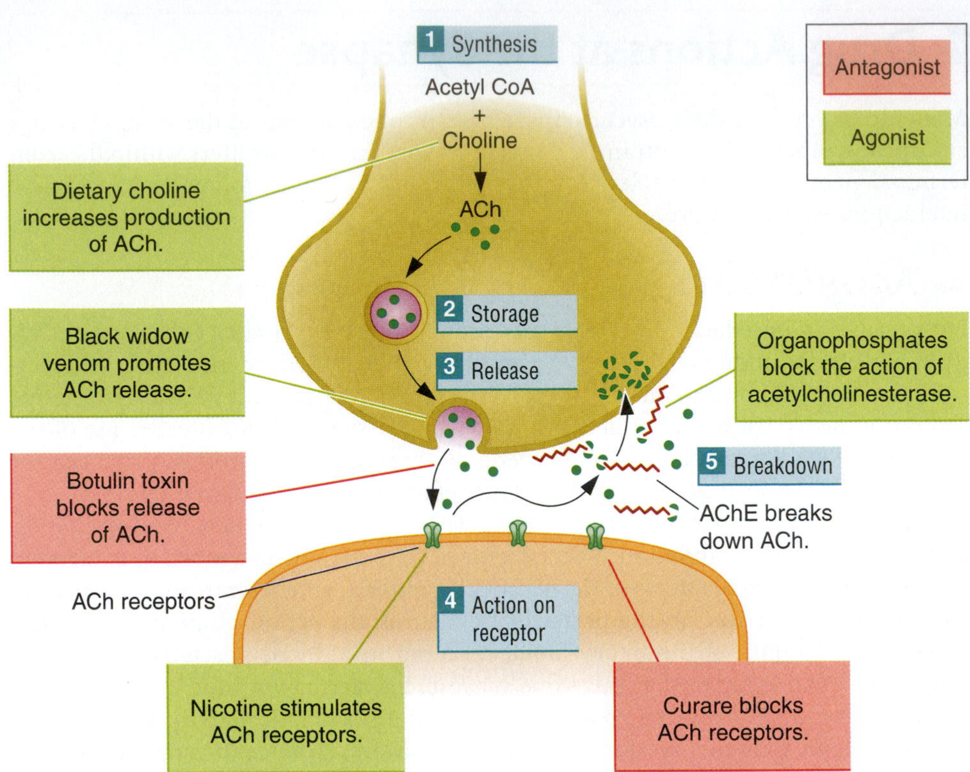

FIGURE 4.12 Drug Interactions at the Cholinergic Synapse Drugs can interact with many ongoing processes at the synapse. Agonists at the cholinergic synapse, which appear in green, include black widow spider venom, nicotine, and dietary choline. Spider venom enhances ACh release, and nicotine activates ACh receptors. Increased intake of dietary choline can increase production of ACh. Antagonists, which appear in red, include botulin toxin, curare, and organophosphates. Botulin toxin blocks the release of ACh, and curare blocks ACh receptors. Organophosphates break down the enzyme AChE, so they technically serve as ACh agonists. Although a reduction in AChE activity might initially boost ACh activity, it eventually has a toxic effect on ACh receptors.

the process responsible for the release of neurotransmitter molecules into the synapse (see Chapter 3). Exocytosis is promoted by agonists but blocked by antagonists.

As shown in ■ Figure 4.12, black widow spider venom is a cholinergic agonist, promoting greater than normal release of ACh at the neuromuscular junction. Greater release of ACh overstimulates muscle fibers, leading to convulsions. In severe cases, the pace of release outstrips the neuron's ability to produce and package ACh, and the neuron essentially runs out of neurotransmitter. As a result, convulsions are followed by muscle paralysis.

Other drugs act as antagonists by preventing neurotransmitter release. Powerful toxins produced by *Clostridium botulinum* bacteria, found in spoiled food, prevent the release of ACh at the neuromuscular junction and at synapses of the autonomic nervous system. The resulting disease, **botulism,** leads rapidly to paralysis and death. Botox® is the trade name for one of the seven botulinum toxins. Botox is used to paralyze muscles to prevent the formation of wrinkles and to treat a variety of medical conditions involving excess muscle tension. Concerns have been raised about the ability of Botox to move from the injection site back to the brain, using retrograde transport in neurons (Antonucci, Rossi, Gianfranceschi, Rossetto, & Caleo, 2008).

Receptor Effects

By far, the greatest number of drug interactions occur at the receptor. In some cases, drugs are similar enough in chemical composition to mimic the action of neurotransmitters at the receptor site. In other cases, drugs can block synaptic activity by occupying a binding site on a receptor without activating the receptor. Finally, many receptors have multiple types of binding sites. Drugs that occupy one or more of these sites can indirectly influence the activity of the receptor. Using the lock-and-key analogy of receptor site activity, both neurotransmitters and agonists at the receptor site act like keys that can open locks. Antagonists act like a poorly made key that fits in the lock but fails to open it. As long as the ineffective key is in the lock, real keys can't be used to open it either.

As we mentioned in our earlier discussion of ACh, the nicotinic and muscarinic receptors received their names due to their ability to respond to both ACh and nicotine or to both ACh and muscarine, respectively. Consequently, both nicotine and muscarine are classified as cholinergic agonists. Other drugs, such as **curare,** act by blocking these receptors. Curare is derived from plant species found in the Amazon

botulism A fatal condition produced by bacteria in spoiled food, in which a toxin produced by the bacteria prevents the release of ACh.

curare (cure-AR-ree) A substance derived from Amazonian plants that causes paralysis by blocking the nicotinic ACh receptor.

region of South America. People in this region have historically used curare to tip their darts for hunting and warfare. In addition, curare is commonly used during surgery, to produce muscle relaxation (Tuba, Maho, & Vizi, 2002). The venom from the cobra, shown in ■ Figure 4.13, acts in much the same way as curare. Because curare and cobra venom occupy the nicotinic receptors located at the neuromuscular junction without breaking down, ACh is unable to stimulate muscle fibers. Inactivation of the muscles of the diaphragm, required for breathing, leads to paralysis and death.

A number of important drugs exert their influence on the $GABA_A$ receptor. As we saw previously in Figure 4.10, this is a complicated receptor with a number of different binding sites. The purpose for these multiple binding sites is not currently understood. Although only one binding site is activated by GABA itself, there are at least five other binding sites on the $GABA_A$ receptor. These additional sites can be activated by the **benzodiazepines,** a class of tranquilizers that includes diazepam (Valium), alcohol, and **barbiturates,** which are used in anesthesia and in the control of seizures. Barbiturates can single-handedly activate the $GABA_A$ receptor without any GABA present at all (Bowery, Enna, & Olson, 2004). Benzodiazepines and alcohol increase the receptor's response to GABA but only when they occupy binding sites at the same time GABA is present. Because GABA has a hyperpolarizing, or inhibitory, effect on postsynaptic neurons, GABA agonists enhance inhibition. The combined action of alcohol, benzodiazepines, or barbiturates at the same $GABA_A$ receptor can produce a life-threatening level of neural inhibition.

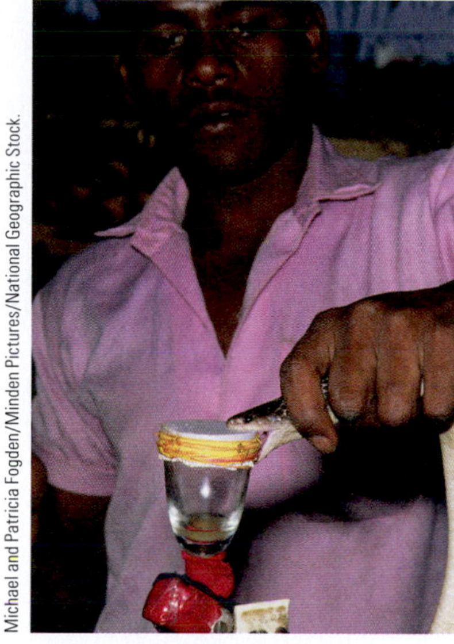

■ **FIGURE 4.13**
Cobra Venom Blocks the Nicotinic ACh Receptor This cobra handler is being careful for a very good reason. Cobra venom blocks nicotinic ACh receptors at the neuromuscular junction, leading to muscle paralysis. Following a bite, the paralysis of muscles such as the diaphragm, which is required for breathing, is frequently followed by death within 6 to 12 hours.

Reuptake Effects and Enzymatic Degradation

Second only to drugs acting at receptor sites in terms of number and importance are drugs that affect the deactivation of neurotransmitters. Some of these drugs influence the reuptake of neurotransmitters, whereas others act on enzymes that break down released neurotransmitters. Drugs that interfere with either reuptake or enzymatic degradation of neurotransmitters are usually powerful agonists. They promote the activity of the neurotransmitter by allowing more of the released substance to stay active in the synapse for a longer period of time.

As shown in Figure ■ 4.14, drugs that inhibit the reuptake of dopamine include cocaine, amphetamine, and methylphenidate (Ritalin). Consequently, each of these

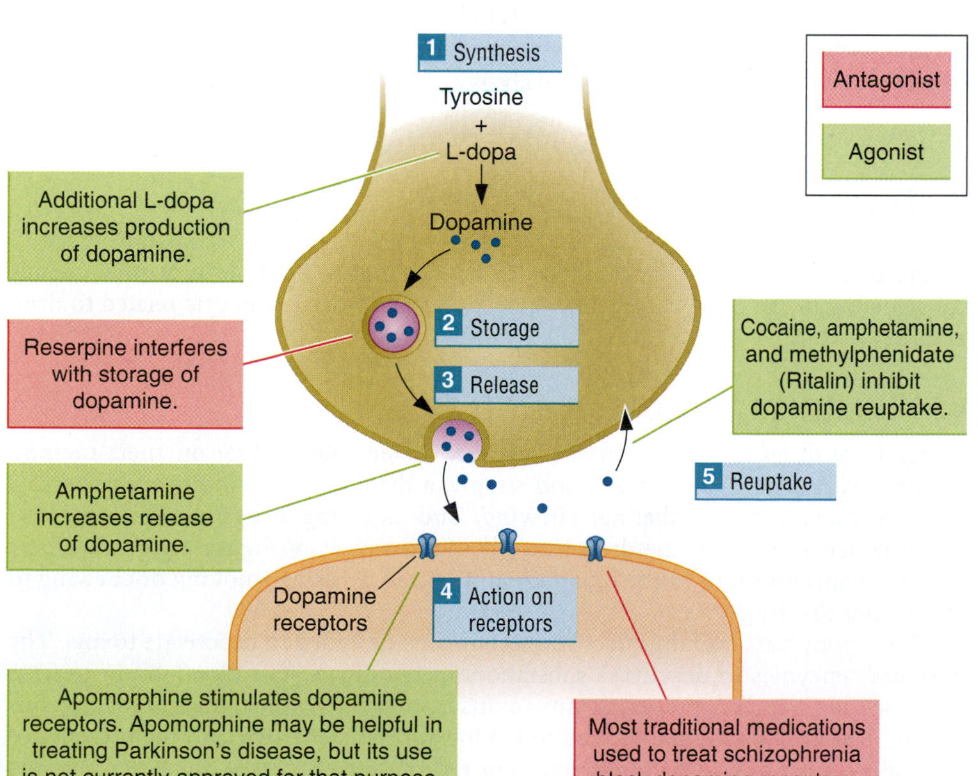

■ **FIGURE 4.14**
Drug Interactions at the Dopaminergic Synapse L-dopa serves as a dopaminergic agonist by promoting increased dopamine synthesis, and amphetamine increases the release of dopamine. Cocaine, amphetamine, and methylphenidate are dopamine reuptake inhibitors. Apomorphine activates dopaminergic receptors. Reserpine exerts an antagonistic effect by interfering with the uptake of monoamines into synaptic vesicles. Some medications used to treat schizophrenia block dopaminergic receptors.

benzodiazepine (ben-zoh-die-AHzi-peen) A major tranquilizer that acts as a GABA agonist.
barbiturate A drug that produces strong sedation by acting as a GABA agonist.

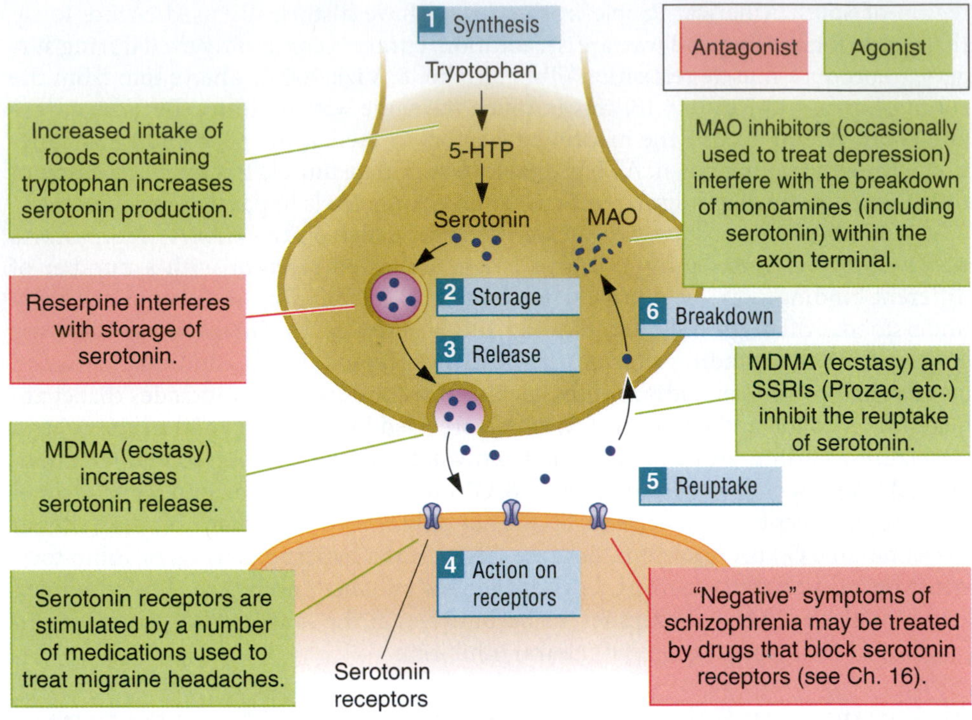

Figure 4.15
Drug Interactions at the Serotonergic Synapse Agonists at the serotonergic synapse include tryptophans, MDMA (ecstasy), many headache remedies, MAO inhibitors, and selective serotonin reuptake inhibitors (SSRIs), including Prozac. Antagonists for serotonin include reserpine and some medications used to treat negative symptoms of schizophrenia. "Negative" symptoms of schizophrenia include social withdrawal and lack of initiative.

drugs is a powerful dopamine agonist. Another important class of **reuptake inhibitors** includes those that act on serotonin. This group includes the antidepressant medication fluoxetine (Prozac), as shown in Figure 4.15. People who suffer from major depressive disorder (see Chapter 16) generally have lower than normal levels of serotonin activity. With slower reuptake, existing serotonin can remain more active in the synapse for a longer period of time, providing some relief from symptoms of depression.

At the cholinergic synapse shown in Figure 4.12, the enzyme acetylcholinesterase (AChE) deactivates ACh. Organophosphates, pesticides originally developed as chemical warfare agents, interfere with the action of AChE. Although the initial effect of drugs that interfere with AChE is to boost ACh activity, too much ACh at the neuromuscular junction eventually has a toxic effect on ACh receptors. The receptors stop responding to ACh, leading to paralysis and, in some cases, death.

Basic Principles of Drug Effects

Before discussing specific types of drugs and their interactions with normal chemical signaling in the nervous system, we need to review basic concepts related to drug effects.

Administration of Drugs

Drugs have different effects on the nervous system, depending on their method of administration. Once in the blood supply, a drug's effects are dependent on its concentration. Eating, inhaling, chewing, and injecting drugs deliver very different concentrations of the drug into the blood supply. Figure 4.16 shows how nicotine concentrations in the blood are influenced by using smoking or chewing to administer the drug.

Your body has several protective mechanisms designed to deactivate toxins. The liver uses enzymes to deactivate substances in the blood. The blood–brain barrier, discussed in Chapter 3, prevents many toxins from entering the tissues of the nervous system. The **area postrema,** located in the lower brainstem, reacts to the presence of circulating toxins by initiating a vomiting reflex. In some cases involving ingested toxins, vomiting clears the stomach and prevents further damage.

reuptake inhibitor Substance that interferes with the transport of released neurotransmitter molecules back into the presynaptic terminal.

area postrema (poh-STREE-muh) A brainstem area, in which the blood–brain barrier is more permeable, that triggers vomiting in response to the detection of circulating toxins.

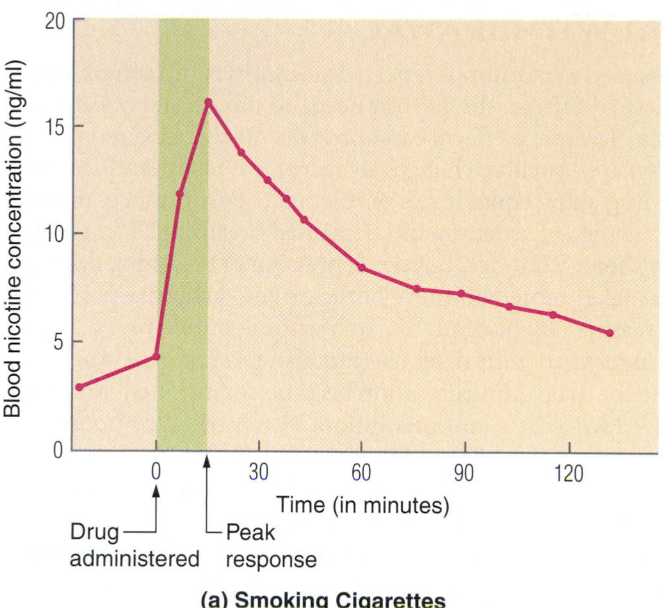

(a) Smoking Cigarettes

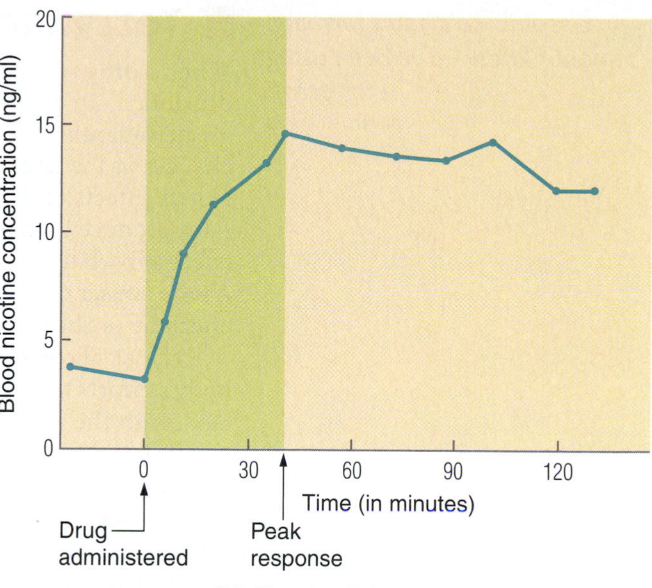

(b) Chewing Tobacco

FIGURE 4.16 Concentration of a Drug in the Blood Supply Depends on the Method of Administration Drug effects are dependent on the concentration of the drug in the blood supply, and some methods of administration produce effective concentrations faster than others. In the case of nicotine, smoking a cigarette produces a much faster increase in blood nicotine concentration than chewing an equivalent dose of tobacco. However, chewing tobacco produces higher sustained concentrations of nicotine than smoking does. *Source:* Adapted from Bennett (1983).

Individual Differences in Response

Drug effects experienced by individuals are influenced by a number of factors, including body weight, gender, and genetics. Larger bodies have more blood than smaller bodies and therefore require larger quantities of a drug to reach an equivalent concentration. Gender effects can be seen in alcohol, which is diluted by the water in muscle tissue. Because a man typically has more muscle than a woman with the same weight, the concentration of alcohol in his blood will be lower than in hers after consuming the same number of drinks. Genetic differences affect a liver enzyme, aldehyde dehydrogenase (ALDH), which participates in the metabolism of alcohol. With low levels of ALDH, alcohol byproducts build up and produce flushing, rapid heartbeat, muscle weakness, and dizziness. Many Asians lack genes for one type of ALDH and therefore experience more unpleasant symptoms associated with drinking (Stoil, 1987–1988). It is not too surprising to find that alcohol consumption is lower among Asians than among members of other ethnicities, although cultural patterns undoubtedly contribute substantially to drinking rates.

Placebo Effects

Drug effects are often influenced by a user's expectations. These indirect outcomes are known as **placebo effects.** (A placebo, from the Latin "I will please," is an inactive substance.) Because placebo effects often show considerable variation among individuals, researchers have not reached a consensus about their importance. Kirsch and Sapirstein (1998) argued that 75 percent of fluoxetine's (Prozac's) ability to improve depressed mood was due to placebo effects, whereas Hrobjartsson and Gotzche (2001) argued that placebo effects could not be demonstrated at all. Convincing demonstrations of placebos occur in response to pain. When a participant expects a placebo to reduce pain, brain imaging demonstrates activation of the endorphin system (Wager et al., 2004; Zubieta et al., 2005). Other strong placebo effects have been observed in the treatment of patients with Parkinson's disease (see Chapter 8; de la Fuente-Fernandez & Stoessl, 2004; Benedetti et al., 2004).

The standard method for controlling placebo effects is the **double-blind experiment.** The first blind refers to the participant. If you agree to participate in such a study, you will not know whether you are receiving the actual drug or the inactive substance (placebo). The second blind refers to the researcher. To prevent biased observations, the researcher will not know which participants are receiving placebo and which are receiving the drugs until after the experiment is concluded. Not all drugs lend themselves to this type of research. For example, efforts to determine the relative benefits of using smoked marijuana for medical purposes (as opposed to traditional pharmaceuticals containing cannabinoids) are handicapped by the obvious difficulty of finding a believable placebo.

placebo effect Perceived benefit from inactive substances or procedures.

double-blind experiment A research design in which neither the participant nor the experimenter knows whether the participant is receiving a drug or a placebo until after the research is concluded.

Cocaine isn't habit forming. I should know—I've been using it for years.
Tallulah Bankhead

Tolerance and Withdrawal

When a drug's effects are lessened as a result of repeated administration, **tolerance** has developed. To obtain the desired effects, the person needs to administer greater and greater quantities of the drug. Tolerance effects can occur due to changes in enzymes, changes at the level of the synapse such as changes in receptor density, and learning. Not all effects of the same drug show equal levels of tolerance. For instance, barbiturates produce both general feelings of sedation and depressed breathing. The sedative effect of barbiturates rapidly shows tolerance, but the depression of breathing does not. As the abuser of barbiturates takes more and more of the drug to achieve the sedative effect, he or she runs an increasing risk of death due to breathing problems.

Classical conditioning associated with drug use can also produce tolerance. The body's efforts to compensate for drug administration become conditioned, or associated, with the stimuli involved with drug administration. This learned component of tolerance might contribute to some cases of drug overdose. Siegel, Hinson, Krank, and McCully (1982) gave rats injections of heroin every day until they began to show signs of tolerance to the drug. At that point, the rats received overdoses of the drug. Half the rats received overdoses in their home cages, and the other half received their overdoses in an unfamiliar environment. Nearly all the rats receiving the overdose in the unfamiliar environment died, whereas only half of the rats receiving the drug in their familiar home cages died. The rats in the unfamiliar environment lacked the learned cues for triggering their bodies' compensations for the drug. Without the ability to compensate, they were quickly overdosed. It is likely that similar factors influence the outcome of drug overdose for human beings. Addicts shooting up in unfamiliar locations may be more prone to overdoses than addicts in a familiar environment (Siegel, Hinson, Krank, & McCully, 1982).

Withdrawal occurs when use of some substances is reduced or discontinued. In general, withdrawal effects are the opposite of the effects caused by the discontinued drug. A person in withdrawal from a sedative will become agitated, whereas a person in withdrawal from a stimulant will become lethargic. It is likely that most characteristics of a withdrawal syndrome reflect the same compensation mechanisms that are responsible for tolerance. As illustrated in ■ Figure 4.17, drug effects

■ **Figure 4.17**
Tolerance and Withdrawal Can Result from Compensation
Repeated administration of a drug often leads to compensating effects, or opponent processes, as the body attempts to maintain homeostasis, or balance. To counteract these effects, the user must take larger quantities of the drug to achieve the same behavioral outcomes (tolerance). When the drug is removed (withdrawal), only the compensating behaviors remain. As a result, withdrawal appears to have the opposite effects of the formerly used drugs.

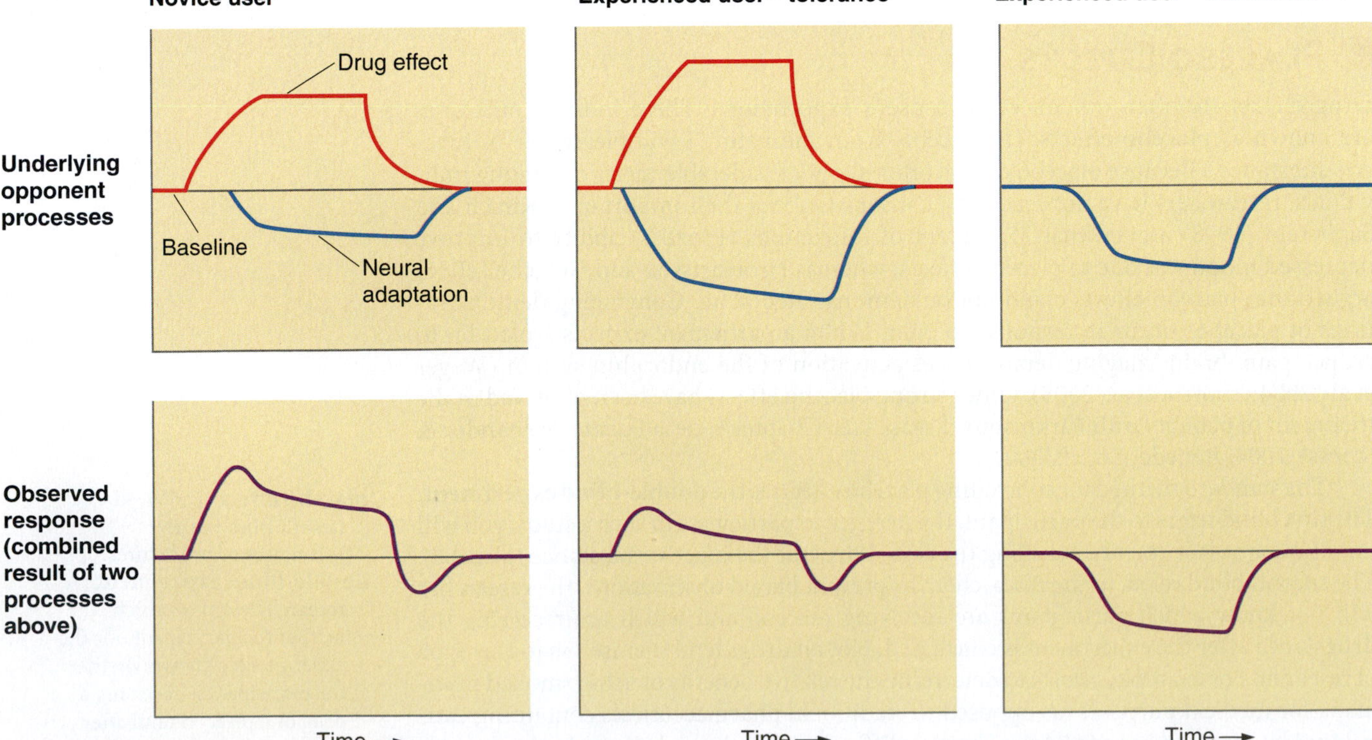

WHY DOES THIS MATTER?

The Hazards of Designer Drugs

Not content with the choices provided by existing psychoactive drugs, people have sought out a wide variety of new designer drugs. Because the name for this group of drugs is so enticing—like designer clothes, it implies chic and expensive but harmless—it is especially important for future psychological and health care professionals to understand the risks posed by these drugs. Designer drugs are synthetic, or lab-produced, versions of illegal drugs such as heroin and amphetamine. The original motivation for producing designer drugs, referred to by chemists as "analogs," was to circumvent drug laws. However, since the passage of the Controlled Substance Analog Act in 1986, all variations of controlled substances are now banned, including variations that have not been invented yet.

Designer drugs are usually easy and cheap to produce and offer the convenience of not having to be smuggled into the country. These factors alone guarantee them an active role in the marketplace. Some designer drugs, including MDMA (ecstasy), seem to provide new effects that are different from those produced by other controlled substances. Unfortunately for the user, these drugs also carry new sets of risks. A case in point is fentanyls, a group of synthetic opiates that produce effects very similar to heroin. A major problem with the fentanyls is their extreme potency. An active dose of a fentanyl is so tiny (about 100 micrograms, with a microgram equaling one millionth of a gram) that overdose is a common occurrence. Fentanyls with the street names "China White" and "Tango and Cash" have been documented in large numbers of fatalities as well as for their ability to produce a movement disorder similar to Parkinson's disease (see Chapter 8).

and compensatory mechanisms generally cancel each other out, leading to fairly stable behavior. When the drug is no longer present, the compensation alone becomes apparent.

Although many abused drugs produce a significant withdrawal syndrome, others do not. Heroin, nicotine, and even caffeine are associated with significant withdrawal symptoms, but cocaine is not (Coffey, Dansky, Carrigan, & Brady, 2000). Symptoms of withdrawal might motivate the addict to administer the drug again, but avoiding withdrawal symptoms is not the sole source of compulsive drug seeking and use.

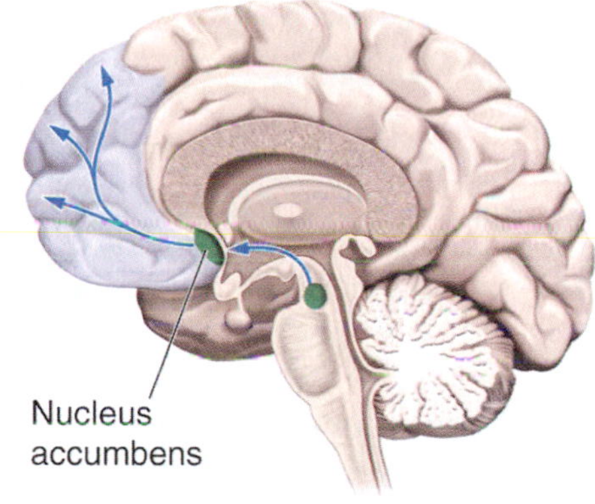

■ **FIGURE 4.18 The Nucleus Accumbens Participates in Reward and Addiction** Stimulation of dopaminergic pathways connected to the nucleus accumbens appears to participate in our general feelings of reward. Interruption of these circuits reduces the self-administration of addictive drugs by animals.

Addiction

The traditional distinction made between physical and psychological dependence has probably outlived its usefulness. Drugs such as cocaine are quite addictive in spite of lacking powerful signs of physical dependence, such as an accompanying withdrawal syndrome. The defining feature of an **addiction** is the compulsive need to use the drug repeatedly.

Causes of Addiction A likely basis for addiction is the ability of a drug to stimulate our natural neural systems of reward, which we experience as feelings of pleasure. These systems reward us for engaging in behaviors that are important either for our personal survival or for the survival of the species. When we eat due to hunger, drink due to thirst, or engage in sexual behavior, the same reward circuits of the brain are activated. Even the possibility of winning money activates the brain's reward circuits (Breiter, Aharon, Kahneman, Dale, & Shizgal, 2001). These behaviors produce activity in dopamine circuits in the brainstem and, quite notably, in the mesolimbic system and in the **nucleus accumbens,** illustrated in ■ Figure 4.18. Addictive drugs produce a variety of behavioral effects, but many share the ability to stimulate more intense and longer-lasting dopamine release than we typically see in response to environmental events (Volkow et al., 2004). Drugs that do not influence either dopamine or the nucleus accumbens are often used habitually, but they do not seem to elicit the cravings and compulsive use associated with addiction. LSD seems to have little if any effect on dopamine circuits at recreational doses. People do not seem to be addicted to LSD, although they might choose to use it regularly.

tolerance The process in which more of a drug is needed to produce the same effect.
withdrawal The symptoms that occur when certain addictive drugs are no longer administered or are administered in smaller quantities.
addiction A compulsive craving for drug effects or other experience.
nucleus accumbens A dopaminergic structure believed to participate in reward and addiction.

Every form of addiction is bad, no matter whether the narcotic be alcohol or morphine or idealism.
Carl Gustav Jung

Considerable research evidence shows that an interruption to the mesolimbic reward system, including the nucleus accumbens, reduces an animal's administration of addictive drugs. Animals can be addicted to drugs through regular injections. Once addicted, the animals will self-administer the drug by pressing a bar to activate an intravenous dose of the drug. Lesions of the nucleus accumbens reduce self-administration (Zito, Vickers, & Robert, 1985). In addition, selective damage to dopaminergic neurons will also reduce self-administration (Bozarth & Wise, 1986). Because damage to dopaminergic neurons and to the nucleus accumbens reduces drug dependency, you might be wondering why these techniques are not used to assist human addicts as well. We do not treat addiction in this manner because damaging these general reward circuits could deprive addicts of all pleasure. It's unlikely that addicts would choose such a course of action.

Dopamine is not only associated with the reward aspects of addiction but also plays a role in attention to stimuli and motivation. Based on imaging studies with addicts, Nora Volkow and her colleagues (2004) speculate that continued drug abuse reduces addicts' responses to normal environmental rewards. At the same time, addicts show a hyperactive response to stimuli associated with drug use such as the sight of drug paraphernalia. In addition, disrupted dopamine activity due to repeated drug abuse results in lower levels of frontal lobe activity, which in turn can account for the poor decision making and lack of inhibition seen in addicts.

Although our interests center on the physical actions of drugs, we should not lose sight of environmental factors that cause and maintain addiction. As the Vietnam War began to wind down, the American health system braced for an anticipated epidemic of heroin addiction among the returning servicemen. Due to the obvious stress of war and the ready availability of heroin in Southeast Asia, many soldiers had used heroin habitually. However, their behavior on returning to the United States took health providers completely by surprise. Fewer than 10 percent of addicted veterans relapsed, in contrast to the 70 percent relapse rate among young civilian addicts (Robins, Helzer, & Davis, 1975).

Treatment of Addiction Once an addiction has been established, it is remarkably difficult to end it. The large number of Hollywood celebrities who experience a revolving door between treatment and relapse appear to be not the exception but the rule.

Leave your drugs in the chemist's pot if you can heal the patient with food.
Hippocrates

A variety of medications have been used to assist addicts, and many more are under development. Methadone is frequently used to wean heroin addicts away from their addiction. Methadone prevents withdrawal symptoms, yet it does not produce

NEW DIRECTIONS

Dopamine Agonists, Parkinson's Disease, and Addictive Behaviors

Further evidence of the importance to addictive behavior of the mesolimbic reward system and the neurotransmitter dopamine comes from the results of using dopamine agonists to treat Parkinson's disease, a disorder that interferes with voluntary movement.

Parkinson's disease results from degeneration in the dopamine-rich neurons of the substantia nigra and the basal ganglia. As these neurons die, less and less dopamine is available for communication in this essential motor system. Consequently, some treatments for the disease involve efforts to boost dopamine activity, and a logical way to do that is to prescribe dopamine agonists, such as L-dopa or levodopa, a naturally occurring amino acid that serves as a building block for dopamine. Other dopamine agonists prescribed for Parkinson's disease activate dopamine receptors.

Unfortunately, dopamine agonists often produce undesirable side effects, including psychotic behavior similar to that seen in schizophrenia (see Chapter 16). In addition, these drugs also promote addiction-like compulsive behaviors, including gambling, excessive sexual behavior, overeating, and overspending (Merims & Giladi, 2008). One patient with Parkinson's disease described by Merims and Giladi responded to treatment with a dopamine agonist by losing nearly a million dollars while gambling over a six-year period. When his medication was changed, he lost the urge to gamble.

the major psychological effects of heroin. Alcoholics are frequently treated with disulfiram, or Antabuse, which interferes with the activity of the enzyme ALDH in metabolizing alcohol. This medication produces a number of unpleasant symptoms when alcohol is consumed. As shown in ■ Figure 4.19, other medications prevent the behavioral effects of a drug altogether, reducing any incentive to administer the drug. Vaccinations against addiction to cocaine, nicotine, methamphetamine, phencyclidine (PCP) and other drugs of abuse are under development (Orson et al., 2007). These vaccinations work by stimulating the immune system, which binds molecules of the problem drug, preventing or delaying its movement from the blood into the brain. Kosten and his colleagues (2002) reported that three injections of a cocaine vaccine produced few side effects and long-term production of antibodies to cocaine in prior users. If this turns out to be a feasible strategy, people at risk for addiction might choose to be immunized. However, vaccinations raise troubling ethical and practical issues. What if a vaccinated addict simply chooses to abuse another substance? What if vaccinations prevent responses to medical treatments such as drugs for pain relief? Further research is necessary to clarify the usefulness of this approach (Orson et al., 2007).

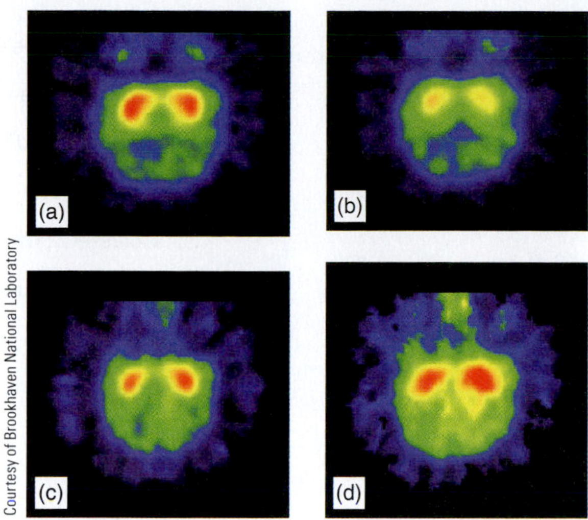

■ **Figure 4.19**
Blocking Cocaine's Effets Cocaine reduces the number of available dopamine receptors. In these images, red indicates areas of high dopamine receptor availability. Images (a) and (c) show normal dopamine activity. (b) After administration of cocaine, formerly red areas are now yellow. (d) After administration of both cocaine and Gamma Vinyl-GABA (GVG), red areas remain red, showing that in the presence of GVG, cocaine does not change dopamine activity.

Interim Summary 4.2

Summary Points

1. Agonists boost the activity of a neurotransmitter, whereas antagonists interfere with the action of a neurotransmitter. Drugs affect behavior by interacting with a variety of processes occurring at the synapse. **(LO5, LO6)**
2. Drugs have very different effects, depending on their mode of administration. Gender, size, and genetics influence individual differences in responses to drugs. **(LO7)**
3. Placebo effects occur when inactive substances appear to produce behavioral and cognitive effects. **(LO7)**
4. Continued use of some drugs can produce tolerance and withdrawal. **(LO7)**
5. Most addictive substances enhance activity in the dopaminergic nucleus accumbens of the brainstem. **(LO7)**

Review Questions

1. What activities at the synapse are affected by drugs?
2. What are the bases for individual responses to drugs?

Effects of Psychoactive Drugs

Psychoactive drugs are usually administered to obtain a particular psychological effect. By definition, these drugs circumvent the protective systems of the blood–brain barrier to gain access to the central nervous system.

Stimulants

Stimulant drugs share the capacity to increase alertness and mobility. As a result, these drugs have been widely embraced among cultures, such as our own, in which productivity and hard work are valued.

Caffeine As a graduate student, I participated in a research project on caffeine. The researchers calmly suggested to me that 20 cups of coffee a day (my reported intake) was "a bit much," and they suggested I cut back to eight or so. What is the nature of the attraction many of us have to caffeine? For most people, **caffeine** increases blood

psychoactive drug A drug that produces changes in mental processes.
caffeine A stimulant drug found in coffee, tea, cola, and chocolate that acts as an antagonist to adenosine.

FIGURE 4.20
Caffeine Content of Common Products *Source:* Adapted from Byer & Shainberg (1995).

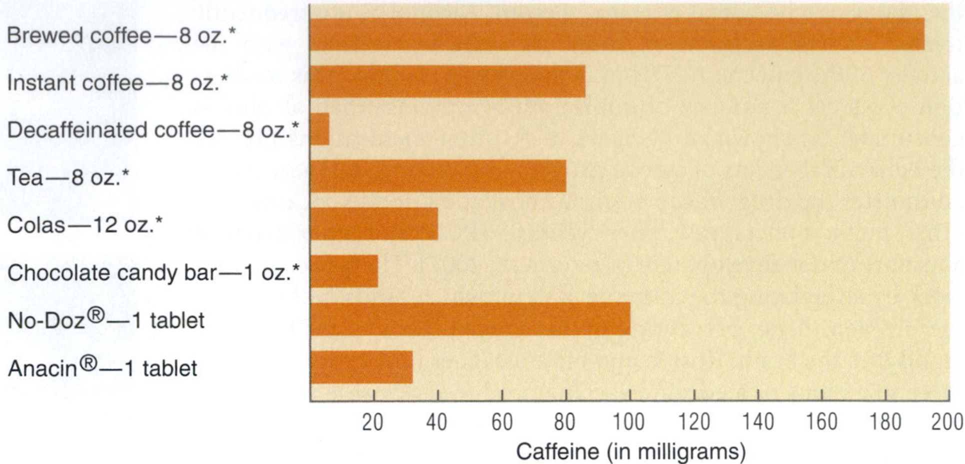

I always keep a bottle of stimulant handy in case I see a snake—which I also keep handy.
W.C. Fields

pressure and heart rate, improves concentration, and wards off sleepiness. As shown in Figure 4.20, the substance is found in tea, coffee, cola drinks, and a number of over-the-counter pain relievers.

Caffeine produces its behavioral effects by acting as an antagonist for adenosine. Caffeine produces excitation by blocking adenosine receptors, reducing the normal inhibitory activity of adenosine. Caffeine's interference with adenosine's inhibition in the hippocampus and neocortex probably accounts for the alertness associated with its use. Interference with normal adenosine activity in the basal ganglia produces improvements in reaction time.

Caffeine is addictive in the sense that it produces a withdrawal syndrome. Because caffeine reduces blood circulation to the brain, withdrawal can produce severe headaches due to suddenly increased blood flow. Not too surprisingly, caffeine withdrawal also produces feelings of fatigue. Some people experience cardiac arrhythmias in response to caffeine. Because caffeine crosses the placenta easily, and the fetus and newborn are relatively unable to metabolize caffeine, it is prudent for pregnant and nursing women to abstain from all sources of caffeine and related compounds (Aldrich, Aranda, & Neims, 1979; Reznick, 1999).

Caffeine use is correlated with lower rates of Parkinson's disease (Ross et al., 2000; Ross & Petrovich, 2001; see also Chapter 8). It is possible that personality or lifestyle factors associated with caffeine use are responsible for this correlation, but evidence for caffeine's ability to protect neurons from Parkinson's-like damage has been reported in animals (Joghataie, Roghani, Negahdar, & Hashemi, 2004). A Parkinson's-like syndrome can be artificially produced by injecting mice with a toxin known as MPTP, which reduces dopamine levels in the basal ganglia. If the MPTP injections are preceded by caffeine, little or no drop in dopamine occurs (Chen et al., 2001). Although such research is far too premature to justify advocating coffee drinking to prevent Parkinson's disease, it is certainly intriguing.

Nicotine After caffeine, the most commonly used stimulant in the United States is **nicotine,** usually delivered in the form of smoking or chewing tobacco. Nicotine increases heart rate and blood pressure, promotes the release of adrenaline into the circulation, reduces fatigue, and heightens cognitive performance. In the peripheral nervous system, nicotine produces muscular relaxation.

In spite of the known negative consequences of smoking, nicotine continues to be a widely used substance, particularly among American youth. One of the most remarkable statistics regarding nicotine is that nearly half of the cigarettes in the United States are consumed by people with diagnosable mental disorders (Lasser et al., 2000). Several explanations might account for these data. People with mental illnesses could be seeking to relieve their symptoms through the use of nicotine (Sacco et al., 2005). More troubling are suggestions that nicotine use actually contributes to the development of mental illnesses, especially depression (Husky, Mazure, Paliwal, & McKee, 2008).

nicotine A stimulant drug that is the major active component found in tobacco.

Nicotine has its primary effect as an agonist at the nicotinic cholinergic receptor. These receptors exist not only at the neuromuscular junction but also at several locations in the brain. Nicotine's action on the cholinergic system arising in the basal forebrain, described earlier, is probably responsible for increased alertness and cognitive performance. In addition to its effects on cholinergic systems, nicotine also stimulates dopaminergic neurons in the nucleus accumbens (Damsma, Day, & Fibiger, 1989; Levin & Rose, 1995). This action on the nucleus accumbens is the likely source of the addictive properties of nicotine. Symptoms of withdrawal include inability to concentrate and restlessness.

Quitting smoking is easy. I have done it thousands of times.
Mark Twain

Cocaine and Amphetamine The behavioral effects of cocaine and amphetamine are quite similar to one another because both drugs are powerful dopamine agonists. These drugs are among the most addictive drugs known. A single recreational dose of cocaine is sufficient to produce addiction in mice (Ungless, Whistler, Malenka, & Bonci, 2001).

In spite of the similarity in behavioral outcomes, the modes of action for these drugs are somewhat different. **Cocaine** acts as a dopamine reuptake inhibitor, whereas amphetamine has a dual action at synapses that use dopamine and norepinephrine. **Amphetamine,** and its widely abused form known as **methamphetamine,** stimulate dopamine and norepinephrine release and inhibit their reuptake. The result of the use of these drugs is higher activity at dopaminergic synapses. At lower doses, these drugs produce alertness, elevated mood, confidence, and a sense of well-being. At higher doses, these drugs can produce symptoms that are similar to schizophrenia (see Chapter 16). Users often experience hallucinations, particularly in the form of tactile sensations such as feeling bugs on the skin. They frequently suffer from paranoid delusions, thinking that others wish to harm them. In some cases, they show repetitive motor behaviors, particularly chewing movements or grinding of the teeth. Methamphetamine users are at least 11 times more likely to experience these psychotic symptoms than nonusers (McKetin, McLaren, Lubman, & Hides, 2006).

Cocaine was originally used by the indigenous people of Peru as a mild stimulant and appetite suppressant. Sigmund Freud recommended cocaine as an antidepressant in his 1885 book, *Über Coca* (*On Coca*). Freud became disenchanted with the drug after he became aware of its potential for addiction. Historically, many popular products contained some form of cocaine, as shown in ■ Figure 4.21. The original formulation of Coca-Cola included extracts of the coca leaf. When cocaine was designated as an illegal substance, Coca-Cola simply substituted caffeine to compensate for the missing stimulant while retaining the remaining extracts of the coca leaf in its highly guarded secret formula.

Amphetamine was originally developed as a treatment for asthma. Inhalers containing amphetamine were sold without prescription throughout the 1940s in spite of the fact that people were opening the inhalers and ingesting the contents. During the past 50 years, amphetamine has been widely used by pilots and military personnel to ward off fatigue. In the 1960s, many Americans received prescriptions for amphetamine as a diet aid because it does suppress appetite. More recently, methamphetamine has emerged as a major drug of abuse, due to its cheap and easy manufacturing process. Long-term use in humans leads to extensive neural damage (Barr et al., 2006), in addition to the more obvious loss of teeth shown in ■ Figure 4.22.

Club Drugs: Ecstasy and GHB **MDMA** (3,4-methylenedioxymethamphetamine, or **ecstasy**) is a currently popular relative of amphetamine among youth. Structurally, MDMA is similar to both methamphetamine and the hallucinogen mescaline. MDMA increases heart rate, blood pressure, and body temperature for a period of about three to six hours. In some cases, dehydration, exhaustion, hypothermia, and convulsions occur (Wills, 1997). MDMA appears to produce increased sociability by stimulating the release of serotonin and the neurohormone oxytocin (Thompson, Callaghan, Hunt, Cornish, & McGregor, 2007).

MDMA is toxic to serotonergic neurons in humans and other animals, as shown in ■ Figure 4.23 (Capela et al., 2007). Using PET scans, researchers have demonstrated that the neurons of people using MDMA are less able to bind serotonin, even after

cocaine A powerful, addictive dopamine agonist derived from the leaves of the coca plant of South America.

amphetamine A highly addictive drug that acts as a potent dopamine agonist.

methamphetamine A variation of amphetamine that is cheaply produced and widely abused in the United States.

ecstasy (MDMA) A close relative of amphetamine that produces its behavioral effects by stimulating the release of serotonin.

Corbis

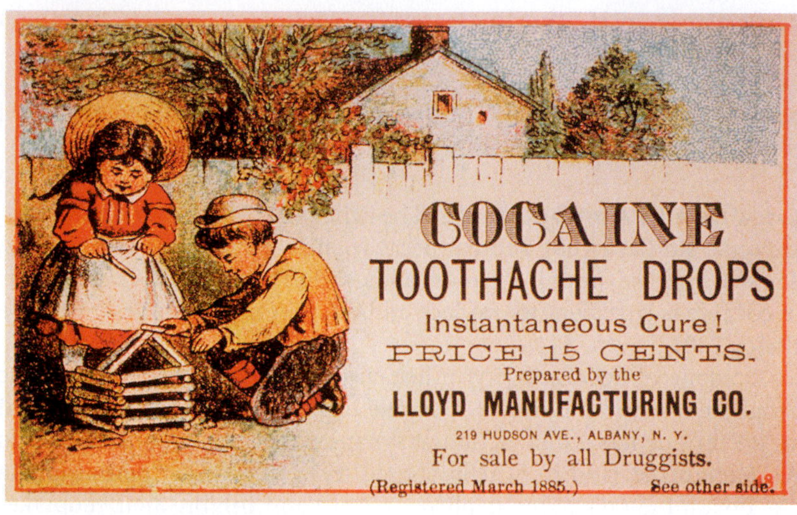

Bettmann/Corbis

■ **FIGURE 4.21**
Cocaine Was an Ingredient in Many Widely Used Products Prior to World War I, many commercial products contained cocaine. Sigmund Freud originally believed that cocaine was an effective antidepressant. The ability of cocaine to produce rapid addiction eventually changed people's minds about the safety of the drug.

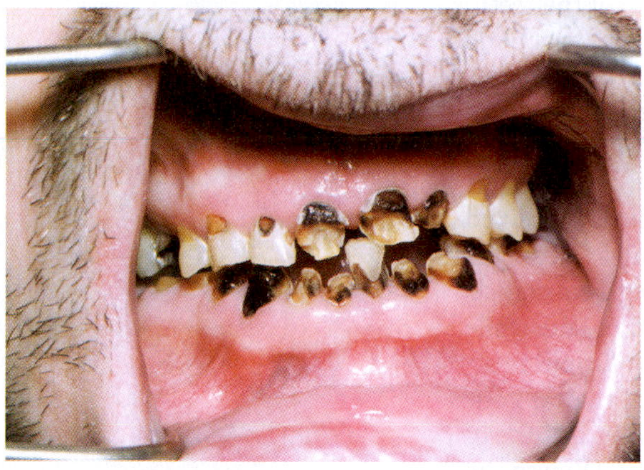

Courtesy of the Minnesota Department of Corrections

■ **FIGURE 4.22**
Methamphetamine Abuse Leads to Multiple Health Consequences Not only does methamphetamine abuse frequently lead to hallucinations and delusions similar to those caused by schizophrenia, but users experience additional health issues, including a characteristic pattern of dental decay known as "meth mouth." This condition results from the mouth dryness and the clenching and grinding of teeth caused by the drug.

lengthy periods of abstinence (McCann et al., 1999). The reduction in sensitivity to serotonin is probably responsible for the depression frequently experienced as a result of MDMA use (Verheyden, Hadfield, Calin, & Curran, 2002; Falck et al., 2008). In addition to producing depression, MDMA use leads to significant memory deficits for at least two years following the last dose (Ward, Hall, & Haslam, 2006). Although some psychodynamic (Freudian) therapists have claimed that MDMA has potential benefits in psychotherapy, particularly for post-traumatic stress disorder (PTSD), research evidence for such benefits is lacking (Parrott, 2007).

Gamma-hydroxybutyrate (GHB) is a liquid sedative rather than a stimulant. However, because it is often taken in conjunction with MDMA, it makes sense to include it in our current discussion. GHB is a naturally occurring substance that is similar in structure to GABA. Use of GHB moved from the bodybuilding community, where it was marketed as a diet aid and muscle builder, to the club scene due to its ability to produce alcohol-like intoxication. GHB is also known as a "date rape" drug due to its sedative action. GHB is responsible for a hazardous withdrawal syndrome similar to that found in chronic alcoholics (Dyer, Roth, & Hyma, 2001). Because of its ability to mimic the inhibitory effects of GABA, it is particularly dangerous when combined with alcohol and other GABA agonists.

OPIATES

Among the natural psychoactive substances found in the sap of the opium poppy (*Papaver somniferum*) are **morphine** and **codeine.** Heroin is synthesized from morphine. An initial step in the production of heroin is illustrated in ■ Figure 4.24. **Opiates** have legitimate medical purposes, including pain management, cough suppression, and the treatment of diarrhea. Before opiates became illegal in the United States around the time of World War I, many medicinal remedies, such as the opium-alcohol mix known as laudanum, were widely used by Americans in all walks of life. Illegal opiate use is

gamma-hydroxybutyrate (GHB) (GAM-uh-hie-drox-ee-BEW-teer-ate) An illegal liquid sedative that appears to affect the thresholds of response for a number of neurotransmitters.

morphine A compound extracted from opium, used to treat pain.

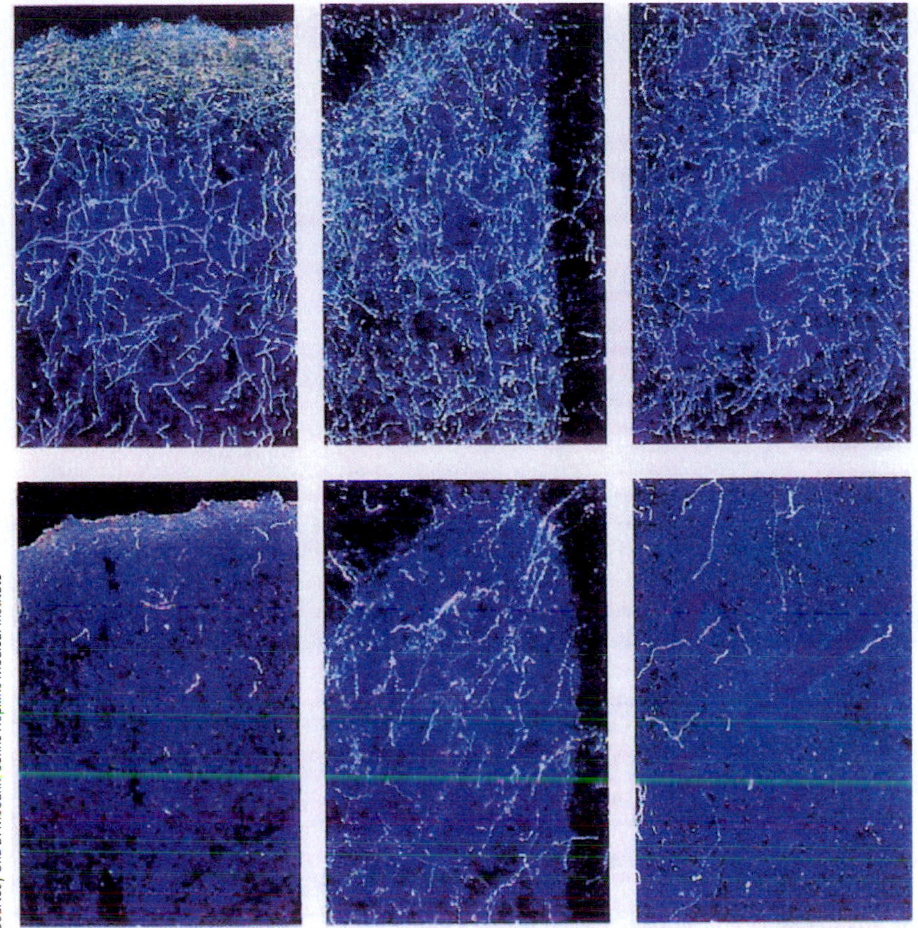

■ **FIGURE 4.23**
MDMA (Ecstasy) Destroys Serotonergic Neurons The images in the top row are taken from a normal monkey. Note the numerous white-stained serotonergic neurons. The images in the bottom row are taken from the same parts of the brain from monkeys who had received MDMA eighteen months previously. Relatively few serotonergic neurons remain.

fairly steady worldwide, with about 8 million users, or 0.14 percent of the population (Regan, 2000; SAMSHA, 2007). Oxycodone hydrochloride (Oxycontin), a relatively new opiate painkiller, has been responsible for a wave of opiate abuse in the United States. Rates of nonprescription Oxycontin use among 12th graders rose 40 percent between 2002 and 2005 (NIDA, 2006).

At low doses, such as those typically used in medicine, opiates produce a sense of euphoria, pain relief, a lack of anxiety, muscle relaxation, and sleep. Higher doses characteristic of abuse produce a tremendous euphoria or rush. The physical mechanism for this response is unclear. With yet higher doses, opiates depress respiration, potentially leading to death.

Pert, Snowman, and Snyder (1974) identified three receptors in the brain that bind with opiates. At about the same time, John Hughes and Hans Kosterlitz (Hughes et al., 1975; Hughes, Kosterlitz, & Smith, 1977) identified neuropeptides produced within the body that activated the opiate receptors in the vas deferens of mice. They named these neuropeptides endogenous morphines, shortened to **endorphins.** Why would we have naturally occurring substances similar to opiates? These endorphins probably help us escape emergency situations in spite of extreme pain. Opiates mimic the effects of our bodies' own endorphins at the opiate receptors (see Chapter 7).

■ **FIGURE 4.24**
Opium Is the Source of Several Psychoactive Substances Opium is obtained from the opium poppy, *Papaver somniferum.* First the seed cases of the poppies are scored using sharp knives. Then the sap that seeps out of the cuts is collected and processed into heroin and other opiates.

codeine An opium derivative used medicinally for cough suppression and pain relief.

opiate An active substance derived from the opium poppy.

endorphin (en-DOR-fin) A naturally occurring neuropeptide that is very closely related to opioids.

MARIJUANA

Cannabis, from the *Cannabis sativa,* or hemp plant, shown in ■ Figure 4.25, is another drug with a long human history. It was included in the pharmacy written by Chinese emperor Shen Neng nearly 5,000 years ago. Marco Polo's writings documented the rituals of the

■ **FIGURE 4.25**
***Cannabis Sativa* Is the Source of Marijuana** In spite of the illegal status of marijuana in the United States, the *Cannabis sativa* plant is widely cultivated.

I've never had a problem with drugs. I've had problems with the police.
Keith Richards

■ **FIGURE 4.26**
Cannabis Can Produce Vivid Visual Hallucinations This painting was based on the verbal descriptions of hallucinations experienced by participants who were given concentrated doses of THC, one of the main psychoactive ingredients in cannabis.

Hashashins, young men in the Middle East who used cannabis to prepare for war. The name of this group is the source of our English word, *assassins.* Cannabis first appeared in Europe when Napoleon's soldiers brought it back to Paris from Egypt. Marijuana, the smoked form of cannabis, came to the United States in the early 1900s. Marijuana experienced a huge increase in use during the 1960s and remains the most commonly used illegal substance in the United States today.

The behavioral effects of cannabis are often so subtle that many people report no changes at all in response to its use. Most individuals experience some excitation and mild euphoria, but others experience depression and social withdrawal. At higher doses, cannabis produces hallucinations, leading to its classification as a hallucinogen. ■ Figure 4.26 illustrates the description of hallucinatory experiences by 14 participants under the influence of cannabis. Marijuana's ability to control nausea has led to a controversy regarding its use as a legal medicine. Although the components of marijuana that suppress nausea are available by prescription in pill form, advocates for medical marijuana argue that the effect of the pills is not as robust as smoking marijuana. As we mentioned earlier, it is virtually impossible to devise the double-blind experiments needed to resolve this issue scientifically.

Cannabis contains over 50 psychoactive compounds, known as cannabinoids. Cannabinoids have been implicated in a wide variety of processes, including pain, appetite, learning, and movement. The most important of these is **tetrahydrocannabinol (THC)**. THC produces some of its behavioral effects by serving as an agonist at receptors for endogenous cannabinoids, substances produced within the body that are very similar to THC in chemical composition. Two types of cannabinoid receptors have been identified, CB1 and CB2, that interact primarily with endogenous cannabinoids, **anandamide** and ***sn*-2 arachidonylglycerol (2-AG),** respectively (Devane et al., 1992; Stella, Schweitzer, & Piomelli, 1997). CB1 receptors are found in the basal ganglia, cerebellum, and neocortex but are especially numerous in the hippocampus and prefrontal cortex. You can see the distribution of cannabinoid receptors in a human brain in ■ Figure 4.27.

The presence of cannabinoid receptors in the hippocampus and prefrontal cortex might explain why THC appears to have negative effects on memory formation (Riedel & Davies, 2005). In addition to directly activating cannabinoid receptors in the hippocampus, THC might also adversely influence hippocampal activity by inhibiting glutamate release (Hampson & Deadwyler, 1999). Because THC has the ability to produce dopamine release at the nucleus accumbens, it has the potential to produce dependency

tetrahydrocannabinol (THC) (tetruh-hie-droh-can-IB-in-ahl) The major ingredient of cannabis.
anandamide (uh-NAN-di-mide)A naturally occurring brain chemical that interacts with cannabinoid receptors.
***sn*-2 arachidonylglycerol (2-AG)** (ES-EN-2 ar-rack-i-don-il-GLIEser-ahl) A possible candidate for a naturally occurring cannabinoid in the nervous system.

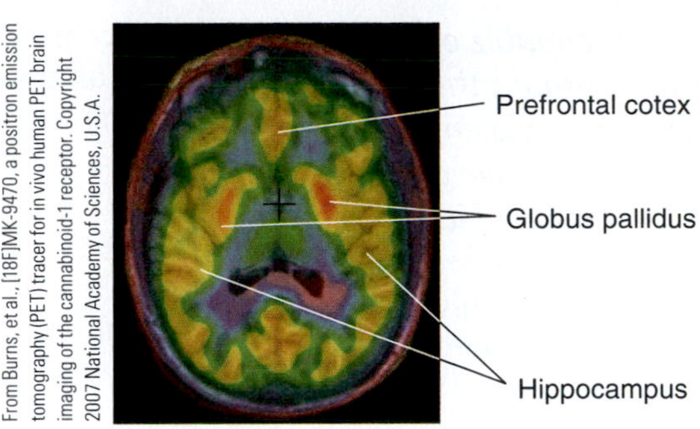

From Burns, et al., [18F]MK-9470, a positron emission tomography (PET) tracer for in vivo human PET brain imaging of the cannabinoid-1 receptor. Copyright 2007 National Academy of Sciences, U.S.A.

FIGURE 4.27
Cannabinoid Receptors in the Human Brain Like our natural opiate receptors that interact with opiate drugs, the brain contains cannabinoid receptors that interact with the major active ingredients found in marijuana. This PET scan shows a high density of cannabinoid receptors (areas of red and yellow) in the prefrontal cortex, the basal ganglia, and the hippocampus. The presence of cannabinoid receptors in the hippocampus and prefrontal cortex is believed to account for marijuana's negative effects on memory.

(Chen, Marmur, Pulles, Paredes, & Gardner, 1993; Merritt, Martin, Walters, Lichtman, & Damaj, 2005). Marijuana uniquely distorts a person's sense of time, distance, and speed. Within 2 hours of smoking, impairment of driving ability is similar to people with a blood alcohol level greater than 0.1, or those who would be legally too drunk to drive (Ramaekers et al., 2006). Marijuana is probably not a good choice for those who have a family history of schizophrenia (see Chapter 16). A 25-year longitudinal study indicated that daily cannabis use nearly doubled the risk of psychotic symptoms in young people under the age of 25 years (Fergusson, Horwood, & Ridder, 2005).

OTHER HALLUCINOGENS

Hallucinogens share the ability to produce hallucinations, or false perceptions. Eastern mystic religions, with their ritualistic use of hallucinogens, were introduced to Europe

WHY DOES THIS MATTER?

Medical Marijuana

The issue of medical marijuana matters because we are being asked as voters to make informed decisions about whether people with serious diseases benefit more from smoked marijuana than from the already available nonsmoked cannabinoid medications.

Marijuana was officially banned in the United States in 1937 with the passage of the Marijuana Tax Act. Given the rarity with which the drug was used at that time, this change had little effect on the behavior of Americans. However, with the drug's increasing popularity beginning in the 1960s, researchers began to pay more attention to its effects. In 1972, a psychiatrist named Tod Mikuriya self-published a book entitled *Marijuana Medical Papers 1839–1972*. The book stimulated a strong interest in the possible medical applications of marijuana.

Proponents of medical marijuana argue that the drug alleviates symptoms of glaucoma, AIDS, and chemotherapy-related weight loss and a variety of neurological and muscular disorders. Marinol, a pill containing a synthetic version of THC, the major psychoactive ingredient in marijuana, has been available by prescription in the United States since the 1970s. Sativex, a mouth spray containing cannabinoids for use by patients with multiple sclerosis, was approved in Canada in 2006 and is undergoing clinical trials in the U.S. However, proponents of medical marijuana argue that these nonsmoked versions have significant drawbacks. For example, the effects of smoking marijuana are quite fast, as opposed to the one-hour delay following ingestion of Marinol. Smoked marijuana contains many cannabinoids, not just THC, so synthetic versions might not produce all of the desirable effects. The psychoactive effects of Marinol are actually reported as more intense than marijuana. Marinol is also much more expensive than marijuana.

Opponents to medical marijuana do not object to the concept that cannabinoids might relieve medical symptoms. Instead, opponents dispute the necessity of using smoked marijuana instead of the nonsmoked prescription alternatives. The United States Food and Drug Administration (FDA) argued that "no sound scientific studies supported medical use of marijuana for treatment in the United States, and no animal or human data supported the safety or efficacy of marijuana for general medical use. There are alternative FDA-approved medications in existence for treatment of many of the proposed uses of smoked marijuana" (U.S. Food and Drug Administration [FDA], 2006, ¶ 2). The United States Supreme Court ruled in 2006 that the federal government could continue to prosecute people for marijuana use, even in states, such as California, with medical marijuana laws. Many physicians are reluctant to recommend smoked marijuana for their patients due to the adverse effects of smoking (Aldington et al., 2008; Tetrault et al., 2007) and marijuana's potential for dependence (Milin, Manion, Dare, & Walker, 2008).

The human mind is capable of excitement without the application of gross and violent stimulants; and he must have a very faint perception of its beauty and dignity who does not know this.
William Wordsworth

as a result of early commerce with India and Asia (La Barre, 1975). Modern analyses of written accounts of "potions" used in witchcraft include a number of hallucinogenic substances. Medieval witches didn't necessarily fly, but some may have believed they could.

Mushrooms Among the most ancient hallucinogens is the *Amanita muscaria* mushroom, which was used for religious purposes across Scandinavia and Siberia. The *Amanita* mushroom is the source of two psychoactive substances, muscimol and ibotenic acid. Muscimol acts as a GABA agonist, whereas ibotenic acid acts as an agonist for glutamate (Regan, 2000). Muscimol's ability to promote the inhibitory action of GABA leads to vivid hallucination. Western-hemisphere mushrooms contain psilocin and psilocybin. Psilocybin acts as a serotonin agonist that produces vivid visual hallucinations and a psychotic state similar to a first episode of schizophrenia (Vollenweider, Vollenweider-Sherpenhuyzen, Bäbler, Vogel, & Hell, 1998).

Mescaline The green peyote cactus (*Lophophora williamsii*) is a source for **mescaline,** which was popularized by Aldous Huxley in his book *The Doors of Perception* (1954). Like many hallucinogens, mescaline appears to act on serotonergic neurons, but the exact mechanism of action is not known.

Phencyclidine (PCP) **Phencyclidine (PCP)** produces a particularly unpleasant set of symptoms. In addition to experiencing vivid hallucinations, users often become aggressive to the point of being physically violent, and muscular tone is either rigid or too flexible. High doses can cause coma or convulsions. PCP acts as an antagonist at the NMDA glutamate receptor. In addition, PCP serves as a dopamine agonist by promoting release (Gorelick & Balster, 1995). Because this drug often leads to a schizophrenia-like psychosis (see Chapter 16), it has been suggested that schizophrenia might involve both dopamine and glutamate activity.

LSD In 1938, the researcher Albert Hoffman reported some unusual sensations after absorbing a compound, **lysergic acid diethylamide (LSD),** through his skin. LSD moved out of the laboratory and into the community after Timothy Leary and other investigators at Harvard University began experimenting with the drug. Hollywood embraced the new drug, and actor Cary Grant and others used LSD in psychotherapy (Regan, 2000). The glamour surrounding LSD didn't last long. It became associated with the infamous killing rampages of Charles Manson and his followers. Timothy Leary was sent to jail, and LSD was classified as a Schedule I drug, having no known medicinal value.

LSD is chemically similar to serotonin and, along with other hallucinogens, appears to act as a serotonergic agonist in the cerebral cortex (Gonzalez-Maeso et al., 2008; Gonzalez-Maeso et al., 2007). However, LSD's ability to produce hallucination remains poorly understood. LSD produces tolerance but not withdrawal (Gresch, Smith, Barrett, & Sanders-Bush, 2005). It does not appear to cause addiction, although users might administer the drug habitually out of preference for the effects. A major but uncommon negative consequence of LSD use is the experience of flashbacks, intrusive and unwanted hallucinations, which can continue long after the person has stopped using the substance (Halpern & Pope, 2003). The occurrence of flashbacks suggests that LSD produces some long-term changes in brain function, but the nature of these changes is not currently understood.

mescaline The active hallucinogenic ingredient found in the peyote cactus.
phencyclidine (PCP) (fen-SIE-klideen) A hallucinogen that acts as an antagonist at the NMDA glutamate receptor
lysergic acid diethylamide (LSD) A hallucinogenic drug that resembles serotonin.

Alcohol

Alcohol is one of the earliest drugs used by humans, dating back into our prehistory. Early humans possibly developed fermented drinks as a safety precaution against the ravages of contaminated water supplies.

At lower doses, alcohol dilates blood vessels, providing a warm, flushed feeling. It reduces anxiety, promotes assertiveness, and reduces behavioral inhibitions, causing people's behavior to be "silly" or "fun." At higher doses, however, assertiveness becomes aggression, and disinhibition can lead to overtly risky behaviors. Motor coordination drops, leading to the alcohol-induced carnage on streets and highways. At very high doses, coma and death can result from suppression of respiration or aspiration of vomit. Alcohol can be quite addictive. A family history of alcoholism is associated with a 300 percent increase in the risk of alcoholism (Schuckit & Smith, 1997).

Alcohol produces its main effects by acting as an agonist at the $GABA_A$ receptor, which normally produces neural inhibition. Alcohol's antianxiety and sedative effects, which are not unlike those caused by the benzodiazepines, probably result from action at this site. Alcohol also stimulates dopaminergic pathways, which might explain the euphoric and addictive qualities of the drug. Alcohol's antagonism at the NMDA glutamate receptor might produce the characteristic memory problems associated with alcohol. Alcohol appears to act on opiate receptors as well. Administration of the opiate antagonist naloxone reduces alcohol consumption (Froelich, Harts, Lumeng, & Li, 1990).

The sway of alcohol over mankind is unquestionably due to its power to stimulate the mystical faculties of human nature.

William James

Alcohol produces rapid tolerance. One source of tolerance is an increase in the production of liver enzymes that eliminate alcohol from the system. Another source of tolerance is changes in receptor number and characteristics, especially at the $GABA_A$ receptor and the NMDA glutamate receptor. These changes produce a dramatic and possibly life-threatening withdrawal syndrome. The person will experience sweating, nausea and vomiting, sleeplessness, and anxiety. In some cases, hallucinations and dangerous seizures occur.

Alcohol has a number of detrimental effects on health. Chronic use of alcohol damages several areas of the brain, including the frontal lobes, which are responsible for many of our higher-order cognitive functions (Harper & Matsumoto, 2005). Alcoholism can lead indirectly to Korsakoff 's syndrome, in which the ability to form new memories is impaired. The lack of dietary thiamine (vitamin B1) common among alcoholics leads to damage to the hippocampus (see Chapter 12). Alcohol can also have devastating effects on the developing fetus, which are explained more fully in Chapter 5. In addition, as little as a half ounce of alcohol per day significantly raises the risk of breast cancer for women with a genetic vulnerability for the disease (Hulka & Moorman, 2002). Countering these health concerns are findings that light to moderate alcohol consumption (about ½ drink per day) is correlated with reduced risk for heart disease (Kloner & Rezkalla, 2007).

St. John's Wort

Dozens of herbal products are currently available in the United States. Few of these substances have undergone the type of testing and evaluation given to prescription drugs prior to approval. Consequently, dangerous chemicals such as ephedrine have only recently been banned.

St. John's wort has been widely used as an antidepressant at least since the Middle Ages. Its active ingredient, hypericin, acts as a serotonin reuptake inhibitor. In addition, hypericin inhibits monoamine oxidase, an enzyme that breaks down all of the monoamines, including serotonin. Controlled research has suggested that St. John's wort is effective in cases of mild depression but not in cases of more severe depression (Shelton et al., 2001). St. John's wort is notable for its frequent adverse interactions with other traditional medicines, including chemotherapy (Dasgupta, 2008).

People who drink to drown their sorrow should be told that sorrow knows how to swim.

Ann Landers

St. John's wort An herb that is frequently used to self-treat mild depression

INTERIM SUMMARY 4.3

Summary Table: Some Commonly Used Drugs and Their Effects

Drug	Behavioral Effects	Mode of Action
Caffeine	Arousal; less need for sleep; reduces headache	Blocks adenosine receptor sites
Nicotine	Alertness; muscular relaxation	Stimulates nicotinic ACh receptors
Cocaine	Euphoria; excitement	Reuptake inhibitor for dopamine
Amphetamine	Alertness; appetite suppression; "rush"	Stimulates release of dopamine and norepinephrine; also a reuptake inhibitor for these neurotransmitters
Ecstasy (MDMA)	Excitement; endurance; increased intimacy	Stimulates release of serotonin
Opiates	Pain reduction; euphoria; relaxation	Stimulate endorphin receptors
Marijuana and other cannabinoids	Hallucination; vivid sensory experience; distortion of time and space; mild euphoria	Stimulates cannabinoid receptors
Hallucinogenic mushrooms	Hallucination	Affects GABA or serotonergic systems
Mescaline	Hallucination	Unknown effects on serotonergic systems
LSD	Hallucination	Unknown effects on serotonergic and noradrenergic systems
Alcohol	Reduced anxiety ; mild euphoria; loss of motor coordination	Stimulates GABA receptors; acts as an antagonist at the NMDA glutamate receptor; stimulates dopaminergic systems
*St. John's wort	Reduction of mild depression	Inhibits MAO and serotonin reuptake

*Effectiveness is not established by controlled studies. Effects based on anecdotal report only.

Summary Points

1. Stimulant drugs increase alertness and mobility. This class includes caffeine, nicotine, cocaine, amphetamine, and ecstasy (MDMA). Opiates produce profound pain relief and, in some forms, a remarkable sense of euphoria. **(LO8)**
2. Many diverse substances produce hallucinations, including marijuana, the *Amanita muscaria* mushroom, psilocybin, mescaline, PCP, and LSD. **(LO8)**
3. Alcohol interacts with the $GABA_A$ receptor, where it boosts the inhibition normally provided by GABA. **(LO8)**
4. St. John's wort is an untested herbal remedy frequently taken for mild depression. **(LO9)**

Review Question

1. What are the possible mechanisms by which drugs produce hallucinations?

CHAPTER REVIEW

THOUGHT QUESTIONS

1. Amino acids, due to their simplicity and ready availability, probably served as the original chemical messengers. What advantages might have led to the evolution of more complex types of neurotransmitter substances?
2. With further advances in our understanding of the human genome, we may be able to identify individuals with higher vulnerability to addiction to particular drugs. What ethical issues would face a society that had this ability? What policies, if any, would you recommend?
3. Which commonly used drug do you think is the safest? The most dangerous? State your reasons.
4. Why are herbal remedies becoming so popular?

KEY TERMS

acetylcholine (ACh) (p. 97)
acetylcholinesterase (AChE) (p. 97)
addiction (p. 111)
adenosine (p. 102)
agonist (p. 105)
amphetamine (p. 115)
antagonist (p. 105)
area postrema (p. 108)
caffeine (p. 113)
catecholamine (p. 99)
cocaine (p. 115)
dopamine (p. 98)
ecstasy (MDMA) (p. 115)
endorphin (p. 117)
epinephrine (p. 98)
gamma-aminobutyric acid (GABA) (p. 100)
gamma-hydroxybutyrate (GHB) (p. 116)
glutamate (p. 100)
indoleamine (p. 98)
lysergic acid diethylamide (LSD) (p. 120)
mescaline (p. 120)
methamphetamine (p. 115)
monoamine (p. 98)
monoamine oxidase (MAO) (p. 98)
muscarinic receptor (p. 97)
neurohormone (p. 95)
neuromodulator (p. 95)
neurotransmitter (p. 95)
nicotine (p. 114)
nicotinic receptor (p. 97)
nitric oxide (NO) (p. 102)
norepinephrine (p. 98)
nucleus accumbens (p. 111)
opiate (p. 116)
phencyclidine (PCP) (p. 120)
placebo effect (p. 109)
psychoactive drug (p. 113)
serotonin (p. 100)
St. John's wort (p. 121)
tetrahydrocannabinol (THC) (p. 118)
tolerance (p. 110)
withdrawal (p. 110)

5 Genetics and the Development of the Human Brain

▲ **Flourescent Fish** Scientists produced colorful "glofish" by adding genes for fluorescence that naturally occur in jellyfish and sea corals to zebrafish embryos.

CHAPTER OUTLINE

Introduction

Although we often think of personality traits as primarily the result of experience, many traits have strong roots in genetics (Kagan, 1994). Kagan noted that when compared with their bolder peers, shy adolescents were more likely to suffer from allergies, to be tall and thin, to have a faster heart rate, and to be pale and blue-eyed. These findings raise ethical dilemmas. We are quite comfortable with discrimination on the basis of psychological characteristics, as when an employer seeks an outgoing personality for a sales position. In contrast, we are staunchly opposed to any discrimination on the basis of physical characteristics. Yet some of the same processes may underlie both our physical appearance and temperament. The contemporary field of behavioral genetics seeks to discover and describe these connections between genes and behavior. ■

Genetics and Behavior

Each of the approximately 100 trillion cells in your body, with the exception of red blood cells and sperm or egg cells, contains two complete copies of the human **genome,** a set of instructions for constructing a human being. Your personal set of genetic instructions is your **genotype,** which interacts with environmental influences to produce your **phenotype,** or your observable characteristics. Your genotype might include a gene for blonde hair and one for brown, whereas your phenotypical hair color is light brown. Your genotype consists of 23 matched pairs of **chromosomes.** One chromosome of each pair was donated by your mother via her egg and the other by your father via his sperm. The chromosomes are made up of molecules of **deoxyribonucleic acid (DNA).** Smaller segments of DNA form individual **genes.** Each gene contains instructions for making a particular type of protein. **Gene expression** occurs when these genetic instructions are converted into a feature of a living cell. Each cell may contain the instructions for an entire human organism, but only a subset of instructions is expressed at any given time and location. Gene expression in a neuron is going to be very different than gene expression in a muscle cell.

Although the vast majority of DNA is found in the chromosomes within the cell nucleus, some DNA is located in mitochondria. All mitochondrial DNA (mDNA) originates from the mother. In addition, mDNA mutates at a fairly regular rate. As a result, mDNA is especially useful to scientists interested in evolution. As shown in ■ Figure 5.1, arguments suggesting that human life first evolved in Africa and migrated to other parts of the world are bolstered by the analysis of mDNA (Wallace, 1997). Mitochondrial DNA is preferred by forensic scientists over other methods of identifying human remains, including the study of DNA and dental records. Using mDNA, researchers were able to positively identify the remains of outlaw Jesse James, using blood samples from two of James's living maternal relatives (Stone, Starrs, & Stoneking, 2001; Hayak et al., 2001).

Different phenotypical traits result from the interactions between alternative versions of a particular gene, known as **alleles.** With two sets of chromosomes, an

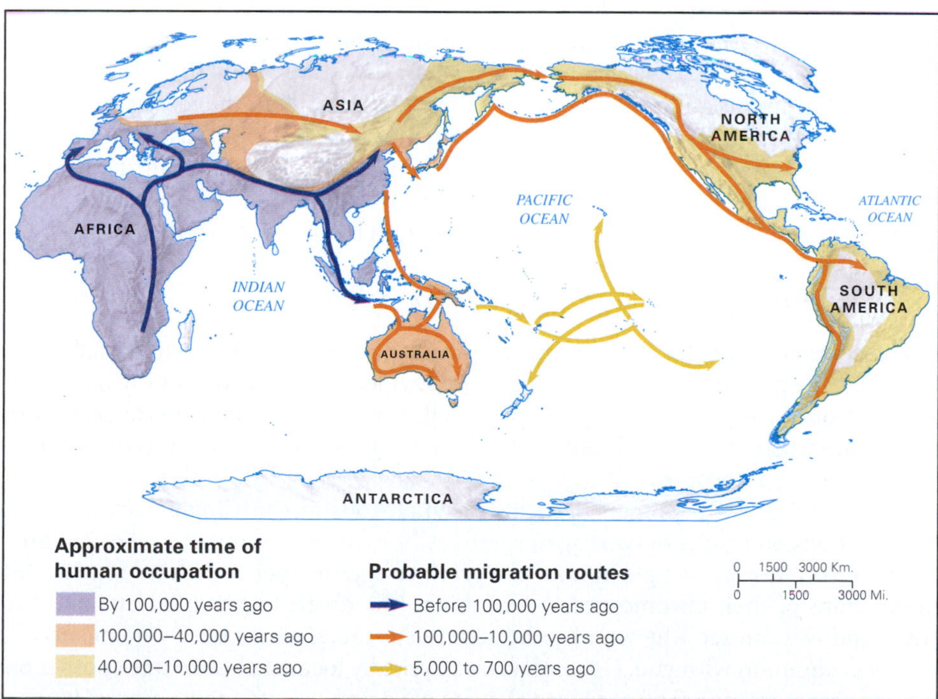

■ **FIGURE 5.1**
Mitochondrial DNA Allows Researchers to Trace Population History Patterns of mitochondrial DNA, which is inherited from the mother only, have led some researchers to suggest that human life originated in Africa and spread outward more than 200,000 years ago.

LEARNING OBJECTIVES

After reading this chapter, you should be able to:

LO1 Describe the core concepts of behavioral genetics.

LO2 Describe sources of genetic diversity; define sex-linked characteristics and the process of X chromosome inactivation.

LO3 Summarize the major conclusions from twin studies regarding the contributions of heredity and environment to human behavior.

LO4 Describe the development of the nervous system from the zygote stage to the formation of the neural tube.

LO5 Summarize the processes of neurogenesis, cell migration, neural differentiation, apoptosis, the growth of axons and dendrites, the formation of synapses, myelination of the nervous system, and the reorganization of synapses.

LO6 Explain the concept of critical periods of development.

LO7 Summarize the major developmental disorders caused by neural tube defects, genetic abnormalities, and environmental toxins.

LO8 Describe the response of the nervous system to damage and explain current research efforts to repair such damage.

LO9 Differentiate between normal aging of the human brain and the effects of dementia due to conditions such as Alzheimer's disease.

genome A complete set of chromosomes.
genotype The genetic composition of an organism.
phenotype The observable appearance of an organism.
chromosome A strand of DNA found within the nucleus of a cell.
deoxyribonucleic acid (DNA) Molecules that compose chromosomes.

Genotype	Phenotype
AA or AO	Type A Blood
BB or BO	Type B Blood
OO	Type O Blood
AB	Type AB Blood

■ **FIGURE 5.2**
Three Alleles Give Rise to Four Types of Blood The genes of Type A and Type B are dominant over Type O, so a person with AO alleles will have Type A blood and a person with BO alleles will have Type B blood. Neither Type A nor Type B is dominant over the other, however, leading to the possibility of Type AB blood.

gene A functional hereditary unit made up of DNA that occupies a fixed location on a chromosome.
gene expression The translation of the genotype into the phenotype of an organism.
allele (uh-LEEL) Alternative version of a particular gene.
homozygous Having two identical alleles for a given gene.
heterozygous Having two different alleles for a given gene.
recessive allele A gene that will produce its characteristic phenotype only when it occurs in a homozygous pair.
dominant allele A gene that produces its phenotype regardless of whether its paired allele is heterozygous or homozygous.
imprinted gene A gene of which only the mother's or the father's copy is expressed, but not both in the normal Mendelian sense.
ribonucleic acid (RNA) A molecule that is similar to DNA that participates in the translation of genetic sequences into proteins.
codon (KOH-don) A sequence of three bases on the DNA molecule that encode one of 20 amino acids.
proteome The set of proteins encoded by the genome.
meiosis Cell division in sexually reproducing organisms that reduces the number of chromosomes in half in the reproductive cells, such as sperm, eggs, and spores.
linkage The characteristic of genes located adjacent to one another to be passed along as a group.
crossing over A process occurring during meiosis in which chromosomes exchange equivalent segments of DNA material.

individual can have, at most, two versions of an allele. However, many more than two versions of an allele can exist within a population. As shown in ■ Figure 5.2, there are three different alleles for blood type (A, B, and O). Because the alleles occur in pairs, with one allele from each parent, they give rise to four blood types: Type A (AA or AO), Type B (BB or BO), Type AB (AB), or Type O (OO).

If a person has two identical alleles at a given site, the individual is considered to be **homozygous** for that gene. If a person has two different alleles, such as a gene for Type A blood and a gene for Type O, he or she will be considered **heterozygous** for that gene. A **recessive allele** will produce its phenotype only when it occurs in a homozygous pair. The gene for Type O blood is recessive, which means that the only way a person can have the Type O phenotype is if he or she receives a gene for Type O from each parent. A **dominant allele** produces a phenotypical trait regardless of whether its pair is homozygous or heterozygous.

There are a few genes that do not follow these rules of dominance. Approximately 1 percent of mammals' genes are **imprinted,** which means that only one allele is expressed. The identity of the expressed gene depends on which parent supplied the allele. In other words, only the father's version is expressed in the case of some genes and only the mother's in others. Imprinted genes have been implicated in a number of genetic disorders, behavioral disorders (including autism and bipolar disorder), and vulnerability to cancer (Falls, Pulford, Wylie, & Jirtle, 1999).

From Genes to Proteins

Genes are constructed from combinations of four biochemicals known as bases or nucleotides: adenine (A), cytosine (C), guanine (G), and thymine (T). As shown in ■ Figure 5.3, sequences of bases in DNA are translated into proteins. A strand of DNA produces a copy of itself on a strand of **ribonucleic acid (RNA).** The bases along the DNA and RNA strands occur in groups of three, known as **codons.** Each codon provides instructions for the production of one of 20 amino acids, which are joined by ribosomes to form a chain. When complete, the chain folds into a shape based on its amino acid sequence and is now officially a protein.

The complexity of human beings does not arise from their number of genes. There are somewhere between 20,000 and 25,000 genes in the human genome (International Human Genome Sequencing Consortium, 2004). It is somewhat humbling to consider that yeast cells have about 6,000 genes; flies have about 13,000; and plants have 26,000. Humans and other creatures differ substantially in the rate of expression of genes in the brain. The rate of human gene expression in the blood and in the liver is basically the same as in the chimpanzee, but human gene activity in the brain is much higher (Pääbo, 2001; Enard et al., 2002). We are also uniquely human due to our **proteome,** the set of proteins encoded and expressed by the genome.

Sources of Genetic Diversity

Egg and sperm cells are formed through the process of **meiosis,** shown in ■ Figure 5.4. In meiosis, the parental chromosome pairs are divided in half, leaving only one chromosome from each pair in an egg or sperm cell. When the egg and sperm cells from the two parents combine, the resulting zygote once again contains the full complement of 23 pairs of chromosomes.

Mathematically, the process of meiosis is analogous to shuffling a deck of cards. A meiotic division results in two egg or sperm cells, each containing one set of 23 chromosomes. As a result, a single human can produce eggs or sperm with 2^{23} (8,388,608) combinations of their chromosomes. Add this to the diversity provided by the other parent, and you can see why your brothers and sisters have some, but by no means all, features in common with you. Genes that are physically located close to one another on the same chromosome are often passed along to offspring as a group in a process known as **linkage.** However, linked genes are not automatically inherited together. In the process of **crossing over,** illustrated in ■ Figure 5.5, chromosomes lining up prior to meiotic division physically cross one another and exchange equivalent sections of genetic material. This results in unique combinations of genes not seen in either parent.

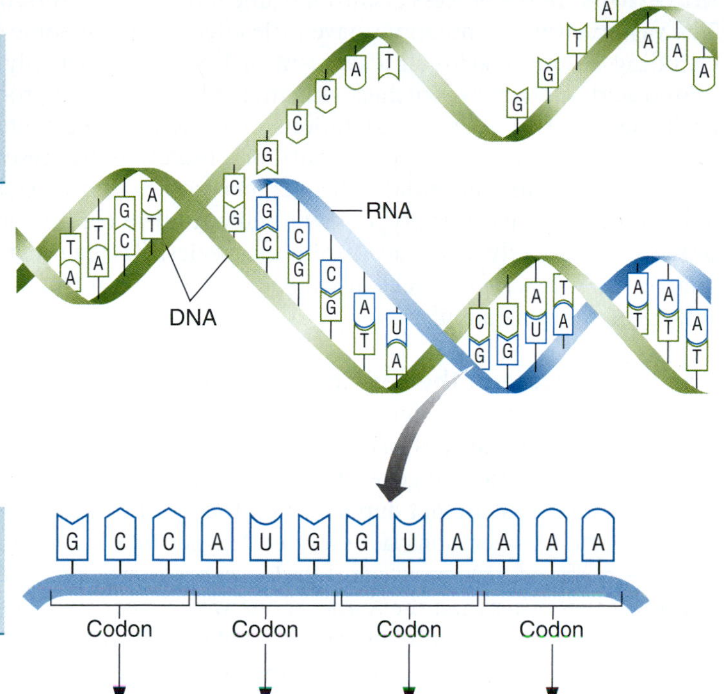

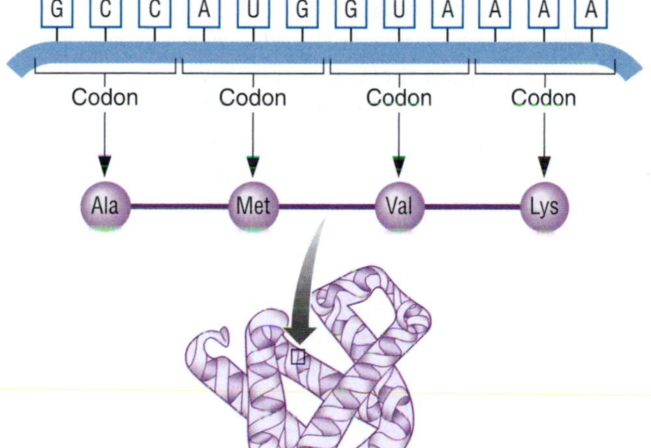

■ **FIGURE 5.3**
The Process of Gene Expression A strand of DNA transcribes itself into a complementary chain of RNA. Each set of three bases (a codon) instructs a ribosome to make a particular amino acid: in this example, alanine (Ala), methionine (Met), valine (Val), and lysine (Lys). The amino acids are linked together to form a protein.

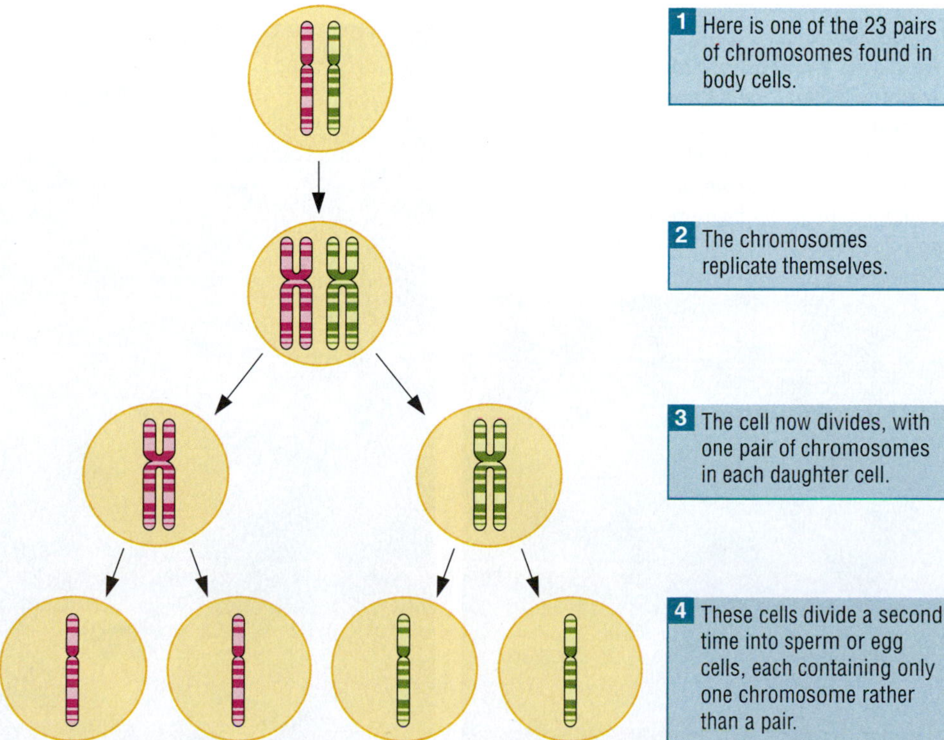

1 Here is one of the 23 pairs of chromosomes found in body cells.
2 The chromosomes replicate themselves.
3 The cell now divides, with one pair of chromosomes in each daughter cell.
4 These cells divide a second time into sperm or egg cells, each containing only one chromosome rather than a pair.

■ **FIGURE 5.4**
Cell Division by Meiosis Sperm and egg cells are produced through meiosis.

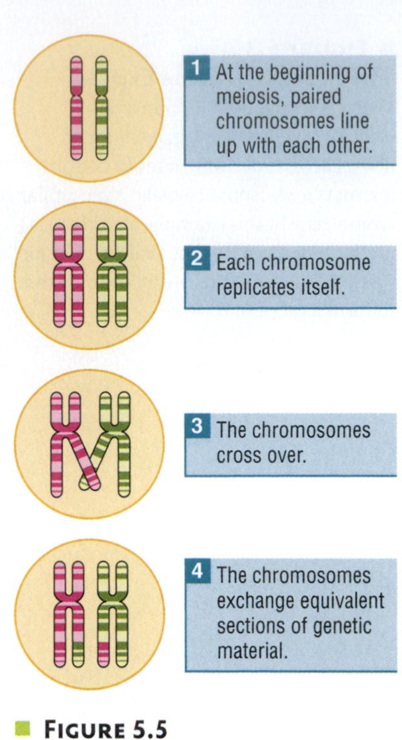

1 At the beginning of meiosis, paired chromosomes line up with each other.
2 Each chromosome replicates itself.
3 The chromosomes cross over.
4 The chromosomes exchange equivalent sections of genetic material.

■ **FIGURE 5.5**
Crossing Over Contributes to Genetic Diversity The process of crossing over, in which two chromosomes exchange equivalent segments of genetic material, adds to diversity by shuffling the parental genes that are inherited together.

Mutations In the process of chromosome replication, errors, or **mutations,** happen. The vast majority of mutations have little effect. There is some overlap in the genetic encoding of amino acids. If a segment of DNA that normally encodes a particular amino acid is somehow switched with another segment that produces the same amino acid, there will be no effect. Mutations may occur in segments of DNA that do not appear to influence phenotypical traits, or a mutation may result in a recessive allele. Inheriting a dominant mutant allele or two copies of a recessive mutant allele will affect an organism's phenotype. If the mutant allele conveys some advantage to the organism, it is likely to spread within the species. On the other hand, a mutant allele may have negative, even fatal consequences for the organism. In the latter case, it may disappear from the population.

The Special Case of the Sex Chromosomes A close-up view of the sex chromosomes may be seen in ■ Figure 5.6. Most of the active genes on the Y chromosome are involved with male fertility (Jegalian & Lahn, 2001), whereas the X chromosome contains a wide variety of genes. **Sex-linked characteristics** result from genes on the X chromosome that are not duplicated on the Y chromosome. For example, recessive genes resulting in hemophilia, described further in ■ Figure 5.7, and genes resulting in some forms of red-green colorblindness, are located on the X chromosome. On chromosomes other than the X and Y, one would need two copies of a recessive gene or only one copy of a dominant gene to produce the trait in the organism. In the case of genes occurring on the X chromosome, however, a single recessive gene influences the phenotype when there is no corresponding gene on the Y chromosome. For this reason, males are far more likely to experience sex-linked disorders than females, who are likely to have a compensating dominant gene on their second X chromosome.

The lack of matching pairs for most genes on the sex chromosomes appears to have led to a phenomenon known as **X chromosome inactivation.** Because many genes on the X chromosome are not duplicated on the Y chromosome, females could produce double the amounts of some proteins compared to males. To compensate for this imbalance in mammals, most of the genes on one X chromosome in each female cell are randomly silenced during development (Jegalian & Lahn, 2001). The actual identity of the silenced X chromosome genes varies from cell to cell, and a very small percentage escape silencing altogether.

■ **FIGURE 5.6**
The X and Y Chromosomes Are Not a Matched Pair The X chromosome (right) resembles most of the other 22 in appearance, but the Y (left) is quite unusual. Not only is it much smaller, with only a few dozen genes compared with the X's 2,000 or so, but it has unusually high amounts of "junk" DNA that doesn't seem to encode anything useful.

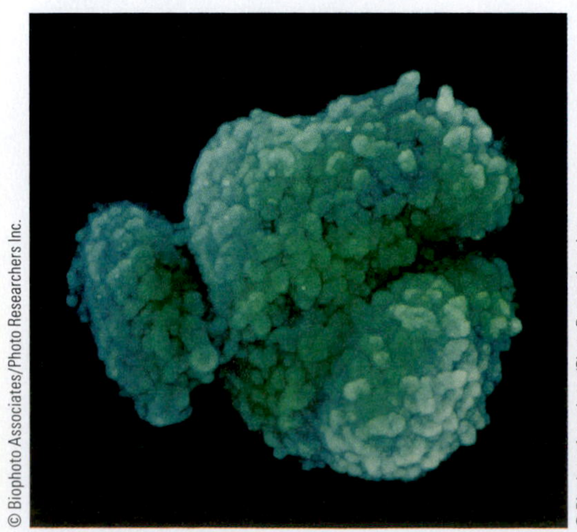

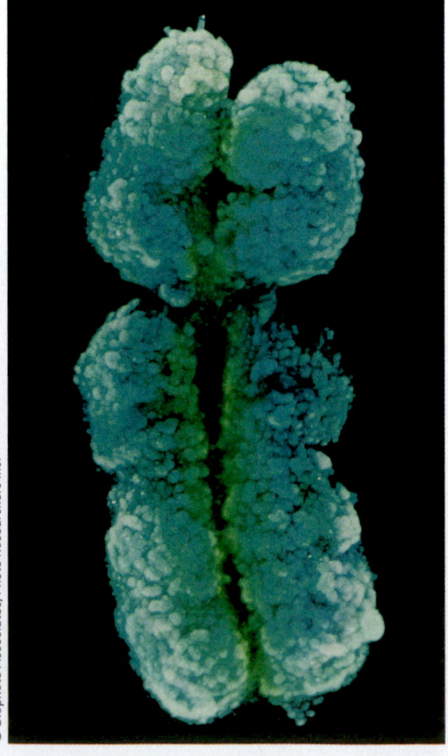

mutation A heritable alteration of genes.

sex-linked characteristics Phenotypical characteristics that result from expression of genes on the X chromosome that are not duplicated on the Y chromosome.

X chromosome inactivation The process by which one X chromosome in each female cell is silenced to equalize the amount of proteins produced by males and females.

single nucleotide polymorphism (SNP) Variation that occurs in a gene when a single base is changed from one version to the next.

An interesting example of this random X chromosome inactivation process is found in the coloring of calico cats, like the one shown in ■ Figure 5.8. Only female cats can be calicos because the genes for orange or black fur are located in the same area of the X chromosome. A male cat could have only orange or only black fur, but not both, because he has only one X chromosome. A female cat with an orange gene on one X and a black gene on the other X will be a calico. In each cell, the fur-color genes on one X chromosome will be silenced. In cells with a silenced orange gene, the fur will be black. In cells with a silenced black gene, the fur will be orange. As a result, the cat will have a random pattern of orange and black fur.

Sven Bocklandt and his colleagues (2006) have suggested that variations in the degree of x-inactivation of mothers may be related to the sexual orientation of sons (see Chapter 10). Typically, as we have noted, X chromosome inactivation occurs in random patterns from cell to cell. In most cases, the number of cells in which the maternal X has been silenced is approximately the same as the number of cells in which the paternal X has been silenced. Variations occur in this process, resulting in some individuals who have the silenced X from one parent in much greater numbers than the X from the other parent, a condition referred to as "extreme skew." Extreme skewing is more common among mothers who had given birth to gay sons (13%) than among mothers of heterosexual sons (4%). Twenty-three percent of mothers with two or more gay sons showed extreme skewing. How X chromosome inactivation patterns in the mother may interact with the sexual orientation of a son remains unknown. In addition, the majority of mothers of gay sons did not show extreme skewing, so this is not a simple solution to the origin of sexual orientation.

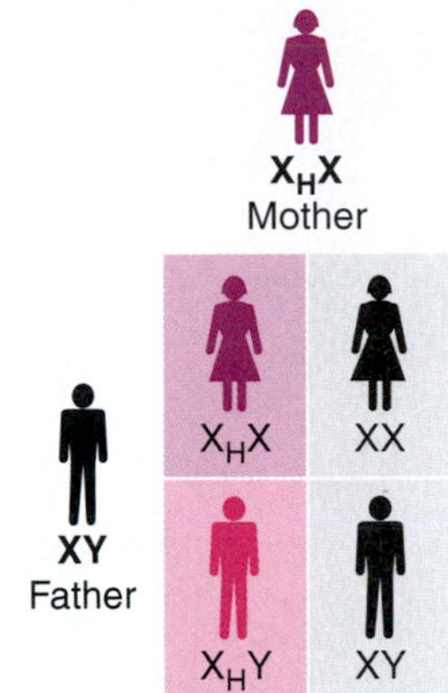

■ **FIGURE 5.7**
Probabilities of Hemophilia
Hemophilia is a sex-linked condition in which blood fails to clot. If a mother carries the hemophilia gene on one of her X chromosomes (X_H) and the father has a typical X chromosome, each daughter will have a 50 percent chance of being typical and a 50 percent chance of being a carrier for the hemophilia gene. The couple's sons have a 50 percent chance of having hemophilia. Without a healthy X to counteract the X carrying the hemophilia gene, sons will have the condition if they inherit the hemophilia gene from their mothers.

Single Nucleotide Polymorphisms (SNPs) Genetics researchers are particularly interested in alleles whose genetic code differs in only one location. These alleles are known as **single nucleotide polymorphisms,** or **SNPs** (pronounced "snips"). A SNP occurs when a sequence of nucleotides making up one allele differs from the sequence of another at just one point, such as AAGGTTA to ATGGTTA. For example, the *APOE* gene on chromosome 19 produces a protein that helps keep cholesterol levels low. There are three alleles for the *APOE* gene, known as E^2, E^3, and E^4. Each *APOE* allele has 299 codons, or sets of three nucleotides. As shown in ■ Figure 5.9, the 112th codon on this string encodes cystine in the E^2 and E^3 alleles but argenine in the E^4 alleles. The 158th codon encodes argenine in E^3 and E^4 but cystine in E^2. These are

WHY DOES THIS MATTER?

A Growing Need for Genetics Counselors

Genetics counseling matters because most people are unprepared to make informed decisions based on the increasingly sophisticated information we are able to provide to individuals about their own genetic makeup. Professionals trained to interpret the results and help guide decision-making can bridge the gap between the science and the consumer.

Along with the tremendous increase in our understanding of the human genome has come an obvious commercial bonanza in the form of genetic testing. Carrier screening for couples will tell them the odds of their producing a child with a particular genetic disorder. Analysis of amniocentesis and other prenatal tests are used by parents to either terminate pregnancy or prepare for the task of raising a child with a disability. Embryos to be used for assisted reproductive technologies are screened for genetic abnormalities and, in some cases, for the desired sex of the child. Adults can be screened for their genetic vulnerability for certain cancers, for Huntington's disease (see Chapter 8), and for Alzheimer's disease.

In many cases, suppliers are offering direct-to-consumer tests, which are not regulated by the United States government. You can even buy a paternity test at your local drug store (Antonucci, 2008). Simply send in a sample, and you get a result back in the mail. Although some corporations offering these tests require a physician's consent, many do not (Williams, 2006). Even when physicians are involved, many lack sufficient training to provide genetic counseling.

As our knowledge and ability to test genetics improve, the public will face more and more sophisticated decisions of great importance to health and well-being. It is unlikely that most of us are prepared to make such decisions in thoughtful, informed ways. Consequently, we can expect a large increase in demand for trained genetics counselors. If you are a psychology major who enjoys both the science and helping aspects of the field, you might consider investigating one of the graduate genetics counseling programs accredited by the American Board of Genetics Counselors (ABGC, 2008).

© DLILLC/Corbis RF

■ **FIGURE 5.8**
X Chromosome Inactivation
Inactivation of most of the genes on one X chromosome takes place randomly in the cells of females. Because the genes for black and orange fur in cats exist at the same location on the X chromosome, a male cat will be either black or orange but not calico. The calico coloring of the female cat results from inactivation of the gene for orange and black fur by different cells.

tiny differences when compared to the volume of DNA in our bodies, yet they have great significance in the development of disease.

The *APOE* SNP predicts a person's risk for **Alzheimer's disease,** a degenerative, ultimately fatal condition marked initially by memory loss, discussed more fully later in this chapter. A person with two E^4 genes has a 91 percent chance of developing Alzheimer's disease, and the average age of onset is 68 years. With one E^4 gene, a person has a 47 percent chance of getting the disease at an average age of 75 years. With no E^4 genes, the risk of Alzheimer's disease is only about 20 percent, and the average age of onset is 84 years (Kamboh, 1995).

The Roles of Heredity and Environment

Psychologists often attempt to identify the relative contributions of genetics and environment to a particular behavior. As noted in Chapter 1, heritability describes how much variation in a trait observed in a population is due to genetic differences. This is a concept that is frequently misunderstood. *Heritability always refers to populations, not to individuals.* Rosa Hoekstra and her colleagues (2007, p. 372) reported that "individual differences in endorsement on autistic traits show substantial heritability (57%)." How are we supposed to interpret these results? This finding does not mean that 57 percent of a single individual's autistic traits (see Chapter 16) are due to genetics and 43 percent are due to his or her environment. Instead, these findings mean that 57 percent of the variation we see in the autistic traits of Dutch teenagers can be accounted for by their genetic differences. This 57 percent figure might not seem too meaningful to you, but it allows us to compare the relative heritability of different traits. For example, adult male height is about 81 percent heritable, and adult body mass index (BMI, see Chapter 9) is about 59 percent heritable (Silventoinen, Magnusson, Tynelius, Kaprio, & Rasmussen, 2008). So we can say that genetic differences between individuals explain more of the variations we see in height than in autistic traits or BMI within a population.

I'm one of those people you hate because of genetics. It's the truth.
Brad Pitt

Heritability cannot be assessed without taking the environment into account, which is another source of confusion. ■ Figure 5.10 shows that if the environment is constant (everybody is treated exactly the same way), the heritability of a trait is likely to be high. For example, if you surveyed IQ in a population of children from the most affluent, well-educated families in a community, your results would be more influenced by heredity than if you sampled a group of children more representative of the diverse home environments in the community. In the affluent sample, many of the environmental influences we believe contribute to high IQ are likely to be present, such as good nutrition and health care, emphasis on education and achievement, and exposure to intellectually stimulating activities. With these environmental variables held at a fairly constant level, the differences you observe among the affluent children are likely to result from their heredity. The same can be said if you observed children from socially deprived circumstances, in which environmental influences related to high IQ were consistently lacking. Once again, the differences you observe in this homogeneous environment are likely to be due to genetic influences. In your sample of children from across the community, the environments vary more widely, thus heritability of IQ in this sample would be lower. Researchers assessing heritability of human traits attempt to do so within a "typical" range of environments, as in the previously cited work on autistic traits (Hoekstra, Bartels, Verweij, & Boomsma, 2007).

Studies comparing identical, or monozygotic, and fraternal, or dizygotic, twins raised together or apart by adoptive parents are particularly useful in sorting out the relative contributions of heredity and environment. Monozygotic (MZ) twins share the same genes, whereas dizygotic (DZ) twins share the same number of genes (about 50%) as ordinary siblings. All twins, however, share a similar environment, both before and after birth, whereas ordinary siblings who are born at different times experience greater variations in their environments.

Alzheimer's disease A degenerative, ultimately fatal condition marked initially by memory loss.

The Minnesota Study of Twins Reared Apart (Bouchard, 1994; Bouchard, Lykken, McGue, Segal, & Tellegen, 1990) is an ongoing, large-scale study of twins. As shown

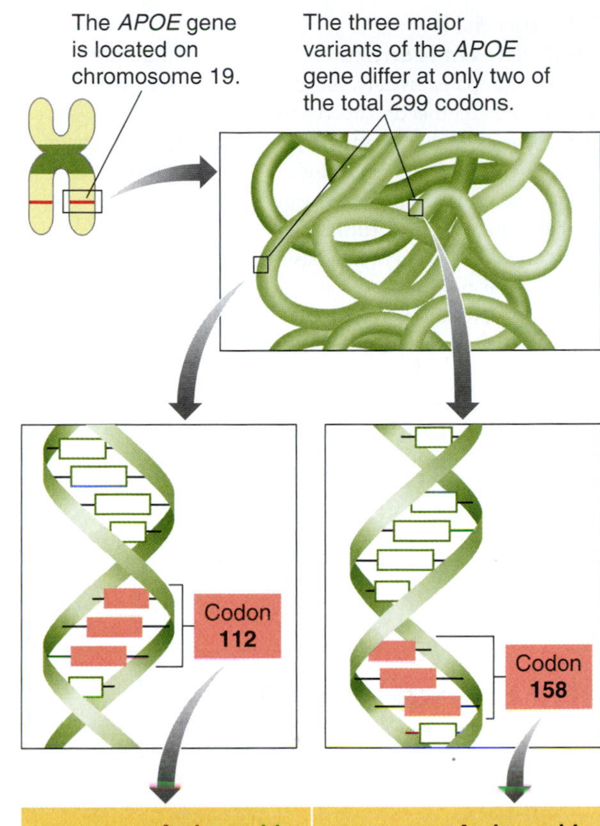

Variant	Amino acid encoded by codon 112	Variant	Amino acid encoded by codon 158
E^2	Cys	E^2	Cys
E^3	Cys	E^3	Arg
E^4	Arg	E^4	Arg

A person with two copies of the *APOE* E^4 variant has a 91 percent chance of developing Alzheimer's; average age at onset is 68 years.

■ **FIGURE 5.9**
SNPs and Disease Single nucleotide polymorphisms (SNPs) occur when a gene sequence differs from other variations by only a single nucleotide. Tiny variations in the *APOE* gene have dramatic consequences for a person's susceptibility to Alzheimer's disease.

in ■ Figure 5.11, the pairs of identical twins in the study were quite similar, regardless of whether they were raised together. Some traits were highly correlated between identical twins, such as the number of ridges in a fingerprint. Other traits showed relatively low correlations, such as nonreligious social attitudes. The critical finding was that identical twins raised either apart or together were very similar, whether the correlation for a particular trait was high or low.

Some of the cases reported by Bouchard and his colleagues were especially striking. Jim Lewis and Jim Springer were identical twins adopted by separate families at 37 days of age and raised without knowledge of each other's existence until the age of 38 years. Both men married first wives named Linda, whom they divorced to marry second wives named Betty. Both had dogs named Toy, and sons named James Alan (although Jim Springer's son's name was spelled James Allan). Both enjoyed woodworking, watching stock-car racing, and drinking Miller Lite beer. Both had had vasectomies, smoked, bit their fingernails, and suffered from migraine headaches.

Does this case convince you that all human variation is genetic? Perhaps it shouldn't. After all, it is entirely possible for unrelated strangers of the same age and sex to find that they have many factors and interests in common. Take for example two women cited in a 2001 Associated Press report. Both women were born on March 13, 1941, and named Patricia Ann Campbell (Myers, 2001). Both had fathers who were bookkeepers named Robert, both studied cosmetology, both painted in oils, and both married military men. Their weddings were eleven days apart and in the year of the press report, both had children ages 21 and 19. They are not at all related to each other.

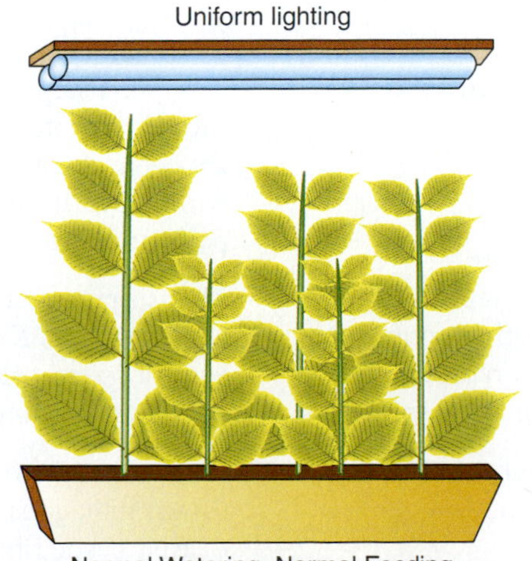

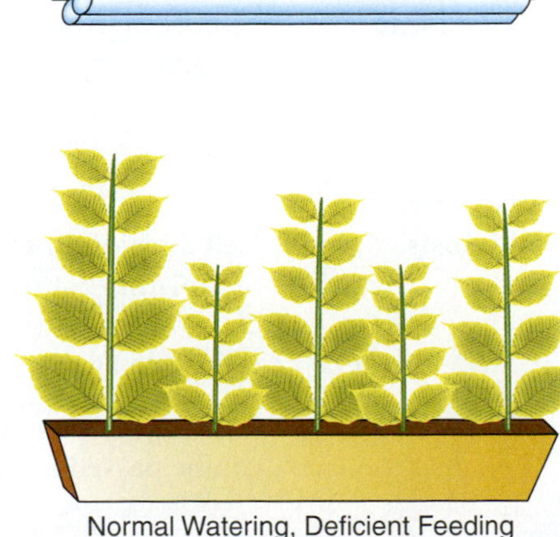

■ **FIGURE 5.10**
Heritability Interacts with Environment To illustrate the pitfalls in the interpretation of genetic data about human traits such as race and IQ, Richard Lewontin provided this example. Two handfuls of corn seeds from a single bag are planted, one in the tray on the left containing nutrient-rich soil and one in the tray on the right containing nutrient-poor soil. Both trays receive the same amount of water and light. Because the plants in a tray are sharing the same environment, the height variability that arises among the plants *within* the tray is the result of 100 percent heritability. However because the plants in the two trays are in two different environments, the height differences *between* the two groups of plants are entirely environmental. In other words, you can have 100 percent heritability within a group, substantial differences in observed traits between groups, and yet have no genetic differences whatsoever between the two groups.

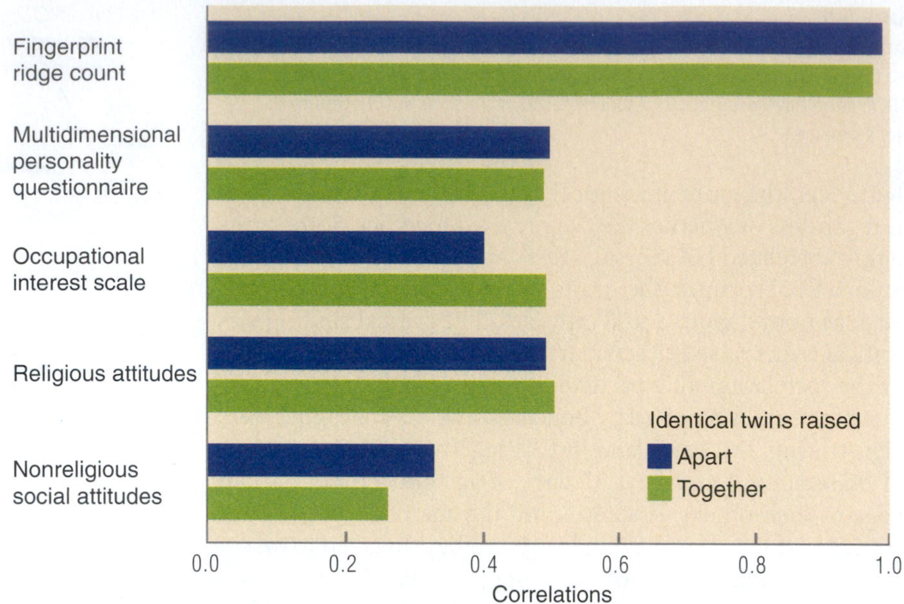

FIGURE 5.11 Similarities in Identical Twins Comparisons between identical twins raised together and apart show that environment appears to play a relatively small role in fingerprint ridge count, responses to a personality questionnaire, and religious attitudes. The groups are more different in measures of occupational interest and nonreligious social attitudes, suggesting a higher degree of environmental influence on these factors.
Source: Adapted from Bouchard, Lykken, McGue, Segal, & Tellegen (1990).

INTERIM SUMMARY 5.1

Summary Table: Important Concepts in Genetics

Concept	Definition	Significance
Genome	The complete set of chromosomes for a species	Identifies the characteristics that define a species. *Example:* The entire human genome.
Genotype	An individual's set of chromosomes	Identifies the genetic basis for individual characteristics. *Example:* Having one allele for blue eyes and a second allele for brown eyes.
Phenotype	The observable characteristics of an individual	Identifies the end result of the interactions between genes and environment. *Example:* Having hazel eyes or being 6 feet tall.
Chromosome	Bodies found within the nuclei of cells that are made up of DNA	Twenty-three pairs of chromosomes make up the entire human genome. *Example:* The X and Y sex chromosomes.
Gene	A functional hereditary unit occupying a fixed location on a chromosome	Genes are responsible for the production of particular proteins. *Example:* Genes for eye color or for the production of dopamine receptors.
Allele	Alternative versions of a particular gene	Trait variations between individuals in a species. *Example:* The A, B, and O alleles for blood type.
Proteome	The set of proteins encoded by the genome	The "next step" in genetic research, the identification of the set of proteins encoded by the genome of a species. *Example:* Analysis might identify proteins associated with vulnerability to diabetes, obesity, stroke, chronic pain, and Parkinson's disease.
Meiosis	Cell division in sexually reproducing organisms that reduces the number of chromosomes to half in reproductive cells such as sperm, eggs, and spores	Meiosis creates a huge number of possible genetic combinations. *Example:* A single human can produce eggs or sperm with 2^{23} (over 8 million) combinations of his or her chromosomes.
Mutation	A change on a gene or chromosome that can be passed to offspring	Results of mutation can be advantageous, neutral, or disadvantageous. *Example:* A mutation causes the disease cystic fibrosis, which causes premature death.

(continued)

INTERIM SUMMARY 4.2 (continued)

SNPs ("snips")	Variations that occur in a gene when a single base is changed from one version to the next	SNPs can be a major source of variation between individuals of a species. *Example: APOE* variants E^2, E^3, and E^4 that affect a person's chances of contracting Alzheimer's disease.

Summary Points

1. The human genome contains two copies of 23 chromosomes, made up of DNA. DNA sequences, or genes, provide instructions for producing proteins. Alternative versions of a gene, or alleles, are dominant or recessive. **(LO1)**
2. Genetic diversity is assured by meiosis, linkage, crossing over, and mutations. **(LO2)**
3. The study of identical and fraternal twins raised together or apart by adoptive parents provides one technique for comparing the relative contributions of genetics and environment. **(LO3)**

Review Questions

1. In what ways are the sex chromosomes different from the other 22 pairs of human chromosomes?
2. How do heredity and environmental factors interact to produce the phenotype of an individual?

Development

Beginning with the merger of a mother's egg and a father's sperm and the complex interactions of the genes they contain, we grow adult human bodies containing approximately 100 trillion cells (Sears, 2005). About 100 billion of those cells will be found in the brain (Scientific American, 1999). Although the process of development does not always proceed smoothly, we still enjoy a remarkable record of accuracy, considering the enormous complexity of the organism we are building.

Growth and Differentiation of the Nervous System

The cell formed by the merger of egg and sperm is known as a **zygote.** From two to eight weeks following conception, shown in ■ Figure 5.12, the developing individual is known as an **embryo.** After the eighth week until birth, the individual is a **fetus.**

A week after conception, the human zygote has already formed three differentiated bands of cells known as **germ layers.** The outer layer is the **ectoderm,** which will develop into the nervous system, skin, and hair. The middle layer is the **mesoderm,** which forms connective tissue, muscles, blood vessels, bone, and the urogenital systems. The final layer is the **endoderm,** which will develop many of the internal organs, including the stomach and intestines.

During the third week following conception, cells in the ectoderm located along the dorsal midline begin to differentiate into a new layer known as the **neural plate.** Remaining cells in the ectoderm will form the skin. Cells differentiate in response to a combination of genes and **inducing factors,** or chemical signals from other cells. In 1924, Hans Spemann and Hilde Mangold demonstrated that the inducing factors responsible for the differentiation of neural tissue from future skin tissue originated in

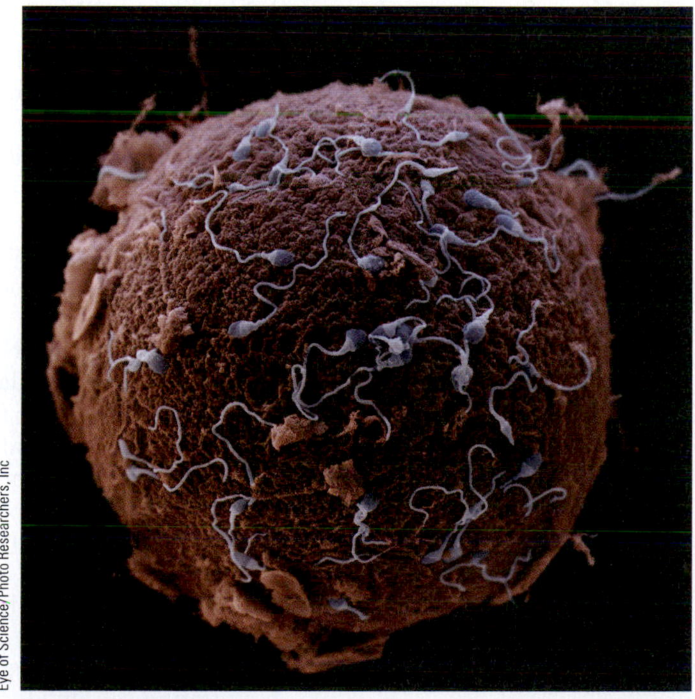

■ **FIGURE 5.12**
Fertilization The first of these sperm to merge successfully with the egg wins in the race to procreate. The resulting zygote will undergo rapid cell division and differentiation.

FIGURE 5.13
The Organizer Experiment
By transplanting cells from the organizer region of one amphibian embryo near the ectoderm of a second host embryo, complete duplicate nervous systems could be formed.

zygote The cell formed by the two merged reproductive cells.
embryo An organism in its early stage of development; in humans, the developing individual is referred to as an embryo between two and eight weeks following conception.
fetus The unborn offspring; used to refer in humans to the developing individual following the embryonic stage until birth.
germ layer One of the first three layers (endoderm, mesoderm, and ectoderm) that differentiate in the developing embryo.
ectoderm One of the initial three germ layers of the embryo, the source of skin and neural tissue.
mesoderm One of the initial three germ layers of the embryo that will form connective tissue such as ligaments, muscles, blood vessels, and the urogenital systems.
endoderm One of the initial three germ layers of the embryo, the source of many internal organs.
neural plate A layer formed by differentiating neural cells within the embryonic ectoderm.
inducing factor A chemical that produces cell differentiation.
neural tube A structure formed by the developing embryonic neural plate that will eventually form the brain and spinal cord, with the interior of the tube forming the ventricle system of the adult brain.
ventricular zone The layer of cells within the lining of the neural tube that give rise to new neural cells.
progenitor cell A stem cell in the ventricular layer that gives rise to either additional progenitor cells or migrating neural cells.
mitosis The process of cell division that produces two identical daughter cells.

an area of the embryo called the organizer region of the mesoderm (Jessell & Sanes, 2000). Spemann and Mangold transplanted cells from the organizer region of one amphibian embryo near the ectoderm layer of a second or host embryo. The transplanted cells followed their own intrinsic pattern and differentiated into mesoderm tissue. However, the transplanted cells signaled the host embryo to form a second complete nervous system, shown in Figure 5.13. More recent research has suggested that without any contact with other embryonic cells, ectodermal cells will form neural tissue (Jessell & Sanes, 2000). Skin will form only when ectoderm cells are exposed to a protein known as bone morphogenetic protein (BMP). Inducing factors released by the organizer region have the capacity to block BMP, resulting in the development of neural tissue.

As the ectodermal cells begin to differentiate, a groove or depression forms along the midline of the neural plate. As shown in Figure 5.14, further cell divisions produce two ridges of tissue on either side of the groove that eventually join to form the **neural tube.** The interior of the neural tube will be retained in the adult brain as the system of ventricles and the central canal of the spinal cord. The surrounding neural tissue will form the brain and spinal cord.

Once the neural tube has been formed, development of the mature nervous system proceeds in a series of six distinct stages: (1) continued birth of neurons and glia; (2) migration of cells to their eventual locations in the nervous system; (3) differentiation of neurons into distinctive types; (4) formation of connections between neurons; (5) death of particular neurons; and (6) rearrangement of neural connections.

The Formation of Neurons and Glia Neurons and glia originate from cells located in the **ventricular zone,** a layer of cells lining the inner surface of the neural tube. These **progenitor** (reproducing) **cells** in the ventricular zone divide by **mitosis,** producing two identical "daughter" cells. Initially, both daughter cells remain and continue to divide in the ventricular zone, which thickens as a result. After about the seventh week following conception, many progenitors in the ventricular zone begin to produce a daughter cell that remains in the zone and a daughter cell that is destined to migrate outward to form a neuron or glial cell (Chan, Lorke, Tiu, & Yew, 2002). As shown in Figure 5.15, progenitor cells producing two additional progenitor cells divide along a cleavage line that lies perpendicular to the surface of the ventricular zone. In contrast, progenitor cells that produce an additional progenitor cell and a migrating cell divide along a cleavage line that is parallel to the ventricular zone surface. The parallel cleavage line means that the daughter cell to the outside will not be attached to the ventricular zone once the division is complete. This cell will be free to migrate. In humans, up to 250,000 new neural cells per minute might be born at the peak of this cell formation process.

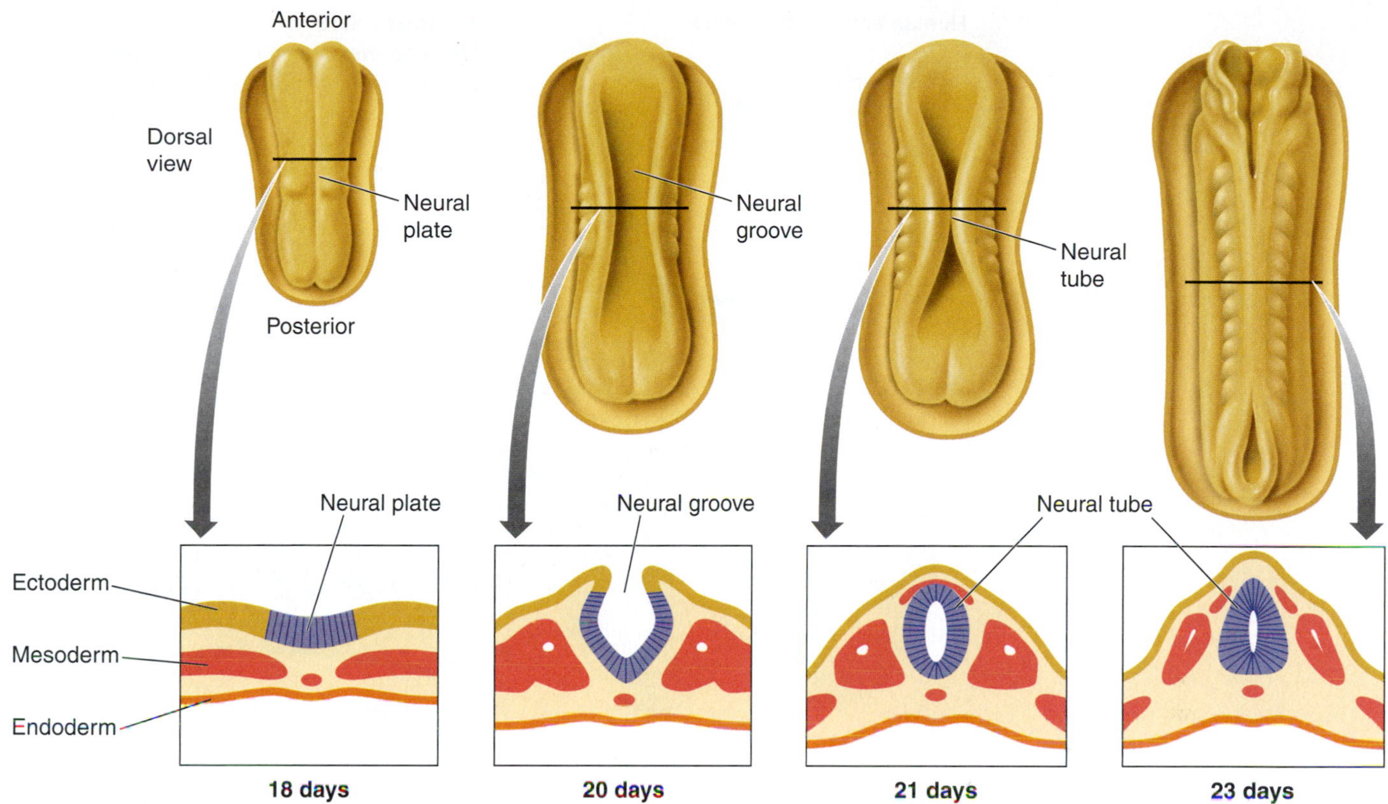

■ **FIGURE 5.14**
The Closing of the Neural Tube Early in development (18 days to 23 days in the human), the developing ectoderm begins to fold and form the neural tube. The tube itself will be retained in the adult brain in the form of the ventricles and central canal of the spinal cord. The surrounding tissue will become the brain and spinal cord.

Cell Migration Migration does not occur in a random manner. Instead, the journey is guided by specialized progenitor cells known as **radial glia,** which grow out from the ventricular layer to the outer margins of the nervous system like the spokes of a wheel (Rakic, 1988). In addition to their critical role in cell migration, they retain the ability to produce additional daughter cells (Weissman, Noctor, Clinton, Honig, & Kriegstein, 2003). About two thirds of the migrating cells wrap around the radial glia and move along them, as shown in ■ Figure 5.16. The remaining third do not follow radial glia but appear to move in a more horizontal direction. Once migration is complete, most radial glia pull back their branches, although some remain in place throughout adulthood.

Migrating cells form the cerebral cortex in an inside-out fashion. Cells destined for the outer cortical layers must somehow travel through the inner layers. In other words, a cell migrating to Layer IV would have to bypass Layers VI and V en route to its final destination. The journey of early migrating cells lasts just a few hours. In contrast, cells migrating to the outermost levels of the cerebral cortex face a journey of up to two weeks. Because of the regularity of migration, researchers are able to determine the timing of certain brain abnormalities with some accuracy and precision. For instance, the disarray found in the hippocampus in some patients with schizophrenia might result from a disruption of migration during the second trimester of pregnancy.

A hen is only an egg's way of making another egg.

Samuel Butler

Differentiation The neural tube is subjected to two separate processes of further differentiation. The first process differentiates the dorsal and ventral halves of the neural tube. The second process differentiates the neural tube along its rostral-caudal axis.

In the dorsal-ventral specialization of the neural tube, neurons in the ventral half develop into motor neurons, and neurons in the dorsal half develop into sensory neurons. The organization of the ventral neural tube into a motor system appears to be under the control of proteins known as *sonic hedgehog* (making one wonder if

radial glia Special glia that radiate from the ventricular layer to the outer edge of the cerebral cortex, serving as a pathway for migrating neurons.

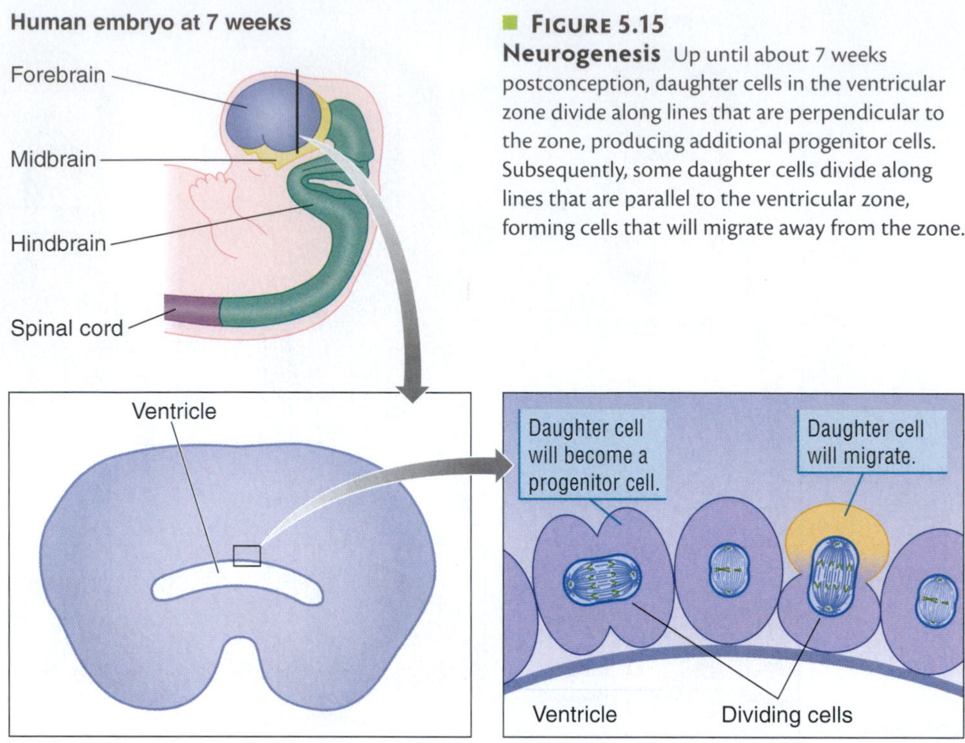

■ **FIGURE 5.15**
Neurogenesis Up until about 7 weeks postconception, daughter cells in the ventricular zone divide along lines that are perpendicular to the zone, producing additional progenitor cells. Subsequently, some daughter cells divide along lines that are parallel to the ventricular zone, forming cells that will migrate away from the zone.

neuroscientists might be filling a little bit too much of their free time with video games). Sonic hedgehog is released by a mesodermic structure known as the **notochord,** which lies just under the neural tube. Eventually, the notochord will develop into the vertebrae surrounding the spinal cord. Differentiation of dorsal neural tube cells into sensory systems occurs in response to BMP, the inducing agent that was also involved with the earlier differentiation of the ectoderm. The ventral sonic hedgehog and dorsal BMP organization extends up through the hindbrain and midbrain. For instance, sonic hedgehog is responsible for the development of the substantia nigra, an important part of the motor system located in the ventral half of the midbrain.

■ **FIGURE 5.16**
Radial Glia Guide the Migration of New Cells About two thirds of the new cells formed in the ventricular layer migrate along radial glia, which are distributed like spokes in a wheel. The remaining third migrate horizontally without apparent need for radial glia.

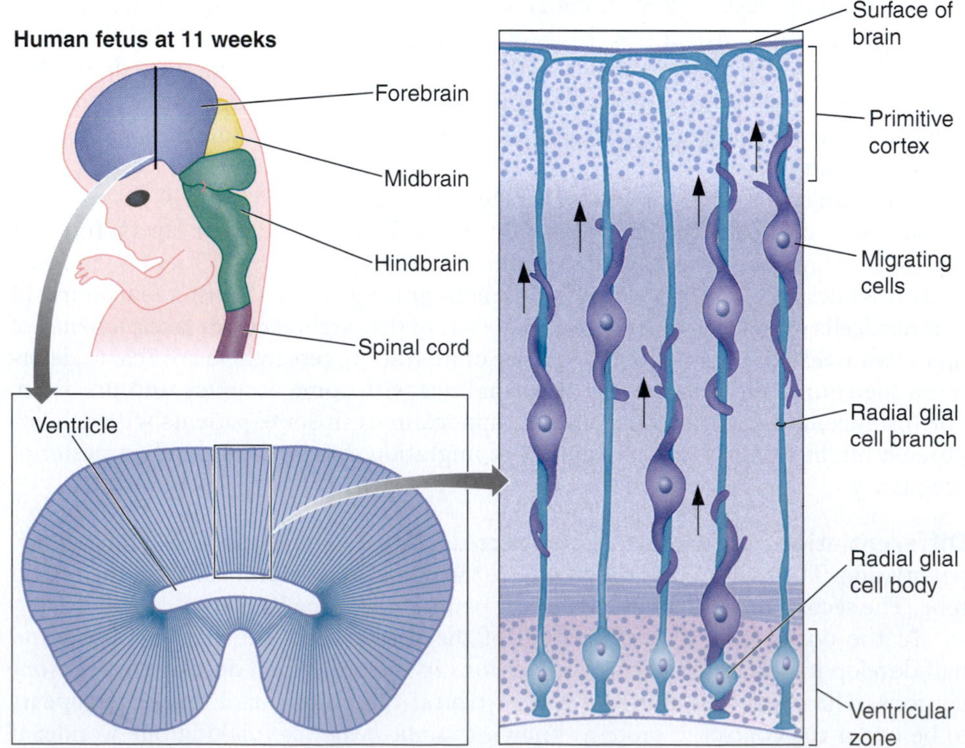

notochord An embryonic mesodermic structure lying under the neural tube that will eventually develop into the spinal vertebrae.

The second differentiation process occurs along the rostral-caudal axis of the neural tube, resulting in the division of the nervous system into the spinal cord, hindbrain, midbrain, and forebrain. The differentiation of the hindbrain appears to be controlled by inducing proteins encoded by *Hox genes*. Different *Hox genes* are expressed in different segments of the hindbrain, resulting in the development of specific cranial nerve nuclei. The midbrain does not show the same segmented organization found in the hindbrain, and *Hox genes* are not expressed this far in the anterior direction. Even less is known about the processes underlying the differentiation of the forebrain, although processes similar to those controlled by *Hox genes* are likely to exist.

As we noted in Chapter 2, areas of the cerebral cortex are characterized by diverse structural features and by different functions such as sensory, motor, or associative processing. The mature organization of the cortex appears to be a combination of internal genetic factors and the external inducing factors we have seen so frequently in our current discussion. Schlagger and O'Leary (1991) transplanted visual cortex into areas normally containing somatosensory cortex in newborn rodents. When tested at a later point in time, the transplanted tissue had taken on the organization that is normal for somatosensory cortex. Apparently, some cortex is capable of being modified according to the type of inputs it receives. In other cases, cortical development occurs independently of input in response to intrinsic genetic factors. Cohen-Tannoudji, Babinet, and Wassef (1994) genetically modified a strain of mice to express a marker gene only within the somatosensory cortex. Marker genes produce a readily identifiable characteristic in cells carrying the gene, either in cell cultures or when transplanted. When tissue from the somatosensory cortex of these mice was transplanted into the cerebellum or nonsomatosensory areas of the cortex of normal mice, it continued to express the marker. In this case, the transplanted tissue responded to internal signals rather than to input from nearby cells.

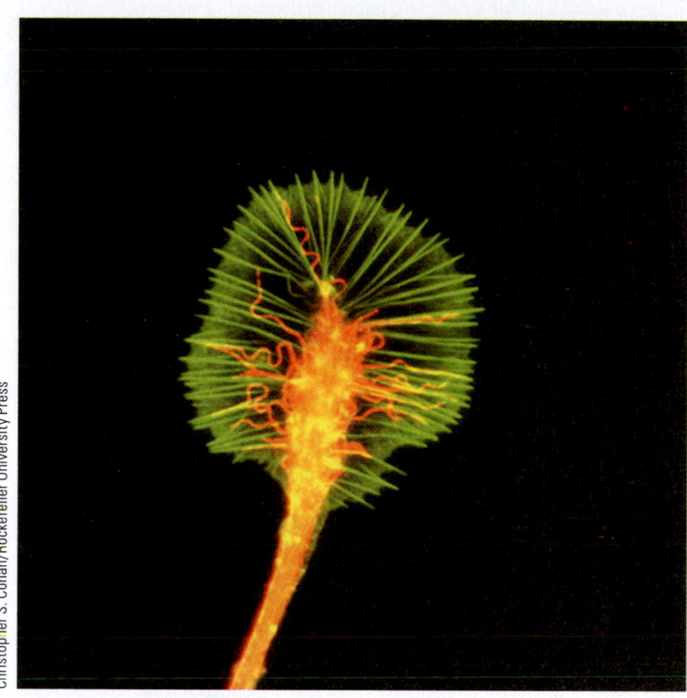
Christopher S. Cohan/Rockefeller University Press

FIGURE 5.17 Growth Cones Guide Axons to Their Targets Growth cones interact with the extracellular environment, guiding the growth of a nerve fiber to the target cell. Filopodia are the fingerlike extensions from the growth cone and lamellipodia appear as webbing or veils between the filapodia.

Growth of Axons and Dendrites Once the neurons are in place, they must form synapses. Growing axons make their journey in a series of steps, with guidance occurring at regular intervals. Later-developing axons can follow the pathways formed by earlier-maturing axons. Axons can sense the structure of the extracellular environment and appear to prefer more adhesive surfaces. So-called "guidepost cells" along the route release chemicals that either attract or repel the growing axon.

Early research by Roger Sperry (1945) demonstrated that axons followed some type of chemical pathway to their target. Today, we know a great deal more about the processes suggested by Sperry. As shown in ■ Figure 5.17, developing axons and dendrites end in **growth cones,** or swellings. The growth cones have both sensory and motor abilities that help the developing branch find the right pathway. Growth cones have three basic structural parts: (1) a main body containing mitochondria, microtubules, and other organelles; (2) **filopodia,** or long, fingerlike extensions from the core; and (3) **lamellipodia,** additional flat, sheetlike extensions from the core, located between the filopodia. The filopodia and lamellipodia are capable of movement, and they have the ability to stick to elements of the extracellular environment, pulling the growing branches along behind them. Microtubules from the main body of the cone move forward as the cone extends, forming a new segment of axon or dendrite.

As shown in ■ Figure 5.18, filopodia can signal the growth cone to move forward, move backward, or turn in a particular direction. The filopodia respond to both attracting and inhibiting chemicals released by guidepost cells along the way. A dramatic example can be observed in the growth of visual axons near the optic chiasm.

growth cone The swelling at the tip of a growing axon or dendrite that helps the branch reach its synaptic target.

filopodia (fill-oh-POE-dee-uh) Long, fingerlike extensions from growth cones of axons and dendrites.

lamellipodia (lah-mel-oh-POH-dee-uh) Flat, sheetlike extensions from the core of growth cones, located between the filopodia.

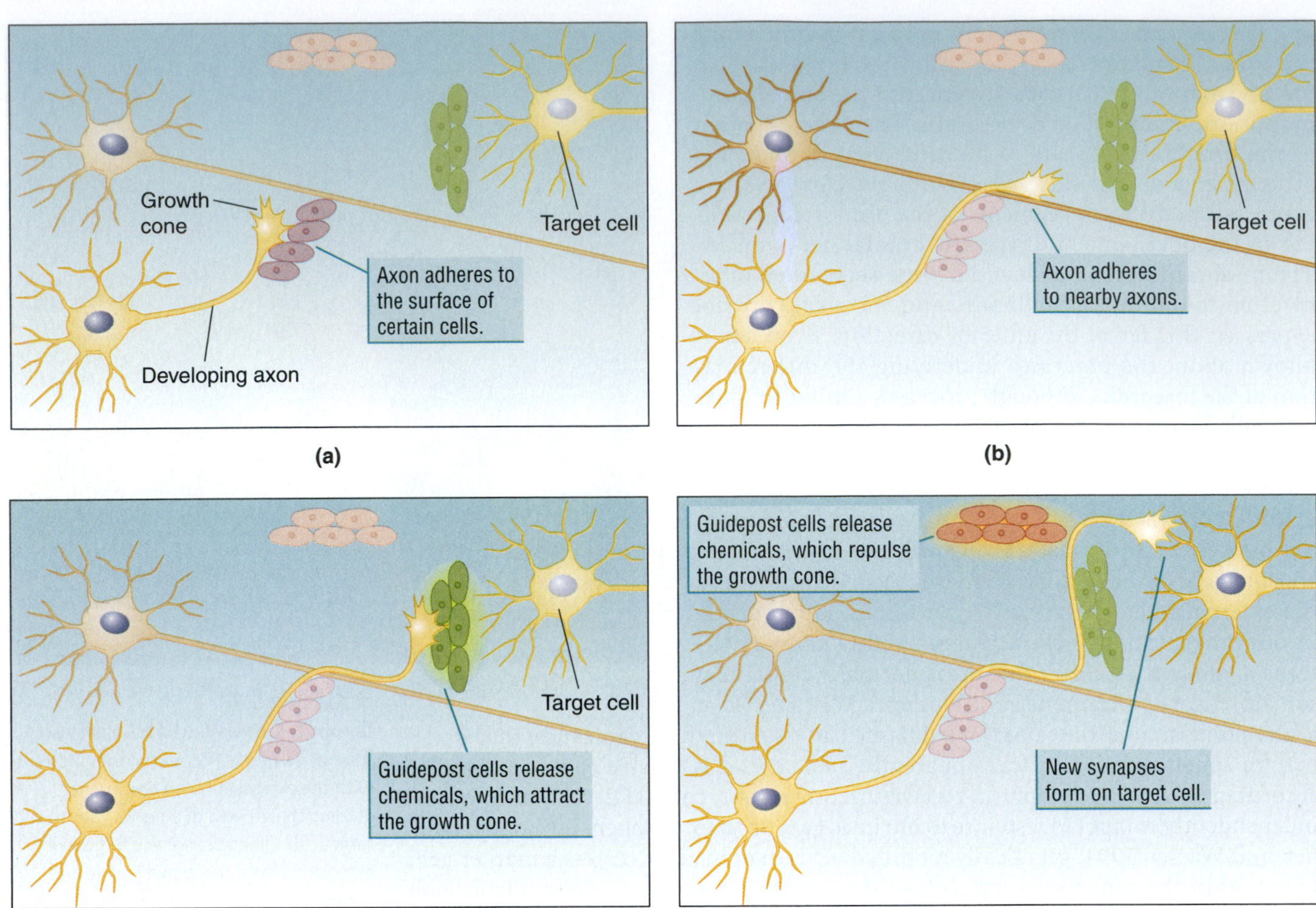
Growth cone
Target cell
Axon adheres to the surface of certain cells.
Developing axon
(a)
Target cell
Axon adheres to nearby axons.
(b)
Target cell
Guidepost cells release chemicals, which attract the growth cone.
(c)
Guidepost cells release chemicals, which repulse the growth cone.
New synapses form on target cell.
(d)

FIGURE 5.18
Growth Cones Respond to a Variety of Cues To reach their eventual targets, growth cones respond to the extracellular environment by (a) sticking to the surfaces of other cells, (b) sticking to other axons traveling in the same direction, (c) growing toward chemical attractants, and (d) being repulsed by chemicals.

In humans, about half of the visual axons cross the midline at the optic chiasm and continue contralaterally, whereas the other half remain on the same side of the midline, proceeding ipsilaterally. Godemont, Wang, and Mason (1994) applied dye to the retina and charted the course of the dyed axons to the optic chiasm. The growing axons appeared to respond to a group of guidepost cells located at the midline of the optic chiasm. The contralateral axons made contact and passed these guidepost cells, whereas the ipsilateral axons appeared to be repelled by these cells.

Axons that are growing in the same direction often stick together in a process known as **fasciculation.** Molecules on the surfaces of the growing axons, known as **cell adhesion molecules (CAMs),** literally cause the axons to stick together as they proceed in the same direction. As the growth cones approach their target, they begin to form either dendrites or axon collaterals (see Chapter 3). Now that the branches are in the correct general area, experience will interact with intrinsic factors to fine-tune the new connections.

Formation of Synapses One question about the development of synapses regards the determination of the type of neurotransmitter that will be used. At the sweat glands, which are relatively easy to study due to their peripheral location, mature sympathetic axons release acetylcholine (ACh) rather than their usual norepinephrine (see Chapter 2). Studies of cultured sympathetic neurons show that a switch from releasing norepinephrine to releasing ACh can be induced by exposure to chemical signals originating in the target cells, or the sweat glands in this case (Jessell & Sanes, 2000). We can conclude that interaction with the target cells influences the type of neurotransmitter released by the presynaptic cell. How this process occurs in the central nervous system, where a single postsynaptic neuron responds to multiple types of neurotransmitter, is currently unknown.

fasciculation (fas-ik-you-LAY-shun) The process by which axons growing in the same direction stick together.

cell adhesion molecule (CAM) A molecule on the surface of a growing axon that promotes fasciculation.

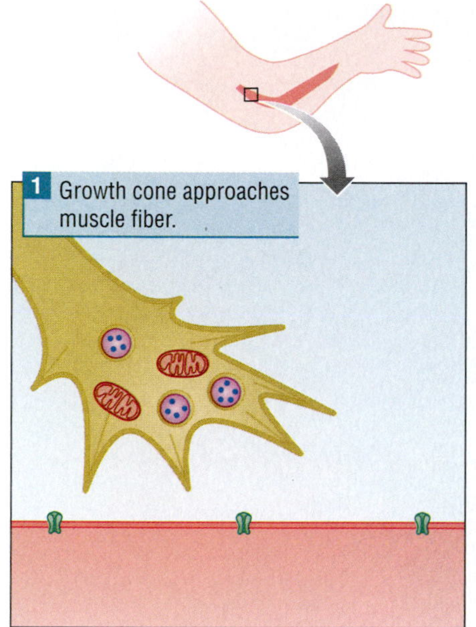

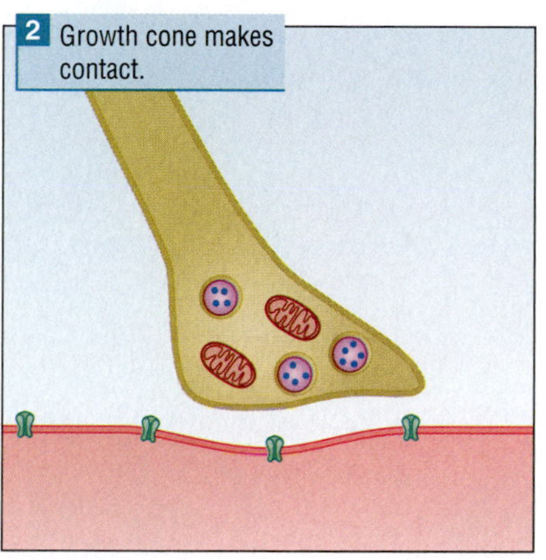

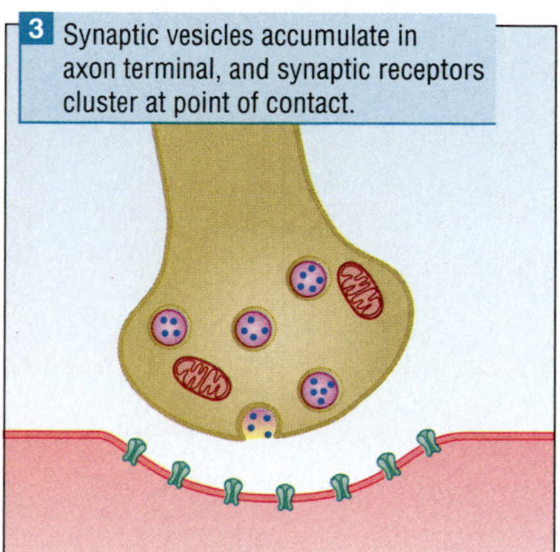

2 Growth cone makes contact.

3 Synaptic vesicles accumulate in axon terminal, and synaptic receptors cluster at point of contact.

■ **FIGURE 5.19**
Steps in the Formation of a Synapse at the Neuromuscular Junction

To complete the process of wiring the nervous system, the incoming axon must identify appropriate postsynaptic cells, and appropriate pre- and postsynaptic structures must develop. The process of synapse formation can be observed easily at the neuromuscular junction, as shown in ■ Figure 5.19. Prior to any contact with a motor axon, the muscle fiber has already formed receptors for acetylcholine (ACh), the neurotransmitter used at the neuromuscular junction. Initially, the receptors are evenly distributed within the membrane of the muscle fiber. Once the synapse is mature, however, the receptors are densely clustered at synaptic sites and rarely found in nonsynaptic motor fiber membrane areas.

A delicate sequence of chemical release by both the presynaptic and postsynaptic structures stimulates movement of the receptors to the synaptic site. Mutant strains of mice lacking essential presynaptic substances fail to develop normal clustering of ACh receptors, typically leading to death (Sanes & Jessell, 2000). Signals from the muscle fiber also affect the development of the motor axon terminal. Relatively less is known about the process of synaptic specialization in the brain and spinal cord, but it is likely that similar processes occur.

Cell Death During the course of development, large numbers of cells die in the process known as **apoptosis,** or programmed cell death. The term *apoptosis* comes from the Greek word for "falling leaves." Apoptosis during development was first described by Viktor Hamburger (1975), who observed that nearly half of the spinal motor neurons produced by chick embryos died before the birds hatched. Cohen, Levi-Montalcini, and Hamburger (1954) were able to isolate a substance they called **nerve growth factor (NGF).** As shown in ■ Figure 5.20, an isolated neuron will sprout significant numbers of branches in response to NGF. Advancing axons absorb NGF released by target cells. Target cells produce limited quantities of NGF, for which advancing axons compete. Neurons that fail to receive adequate amounts of NGF experience apoptosis, whereas neurons that absorb NGF are spared. NGF is now known as one member of a class of chemicals called **neurotrophins.**

Neurotrophins influence the survival of a neuron by interrupting cellular suicide programs that culminate in apoptosis. All cells appear to contain **cell death genes** (Johnson & Deckwerth, 1993). When activated by cell death genes, enzymes known as **caspases** break up DNA and proteins, which quickly leads to cell death. When neurotrophic factors bind to receptors on a neuron, caspase activity is inhibited, and the cell survives. Failure to obtain sufficient stimulation from neurotrophins will result in the expression of the cell death genes and the activation of caspases, and the cell will die.

Cell death serves important functions in the developing nervous system. Too many surviving cells might result in problems. High concentrations of neurotrophins

apoptosis (ay-pop-TOE-sis) Programmed cell death.
nerve growth factor (NGF) The first identified neurotrophin.
neurotrophin (neur-oh-TROE-fin) Substance released by target cells that contributes to the survival of presynaptic neurons.
cell death gene A gene responsible for triggering the activity of caspases, leading to apoptosis.
caspase (KASS-pays) An enzyme within a cell that cuts up DNA and produces cell death.

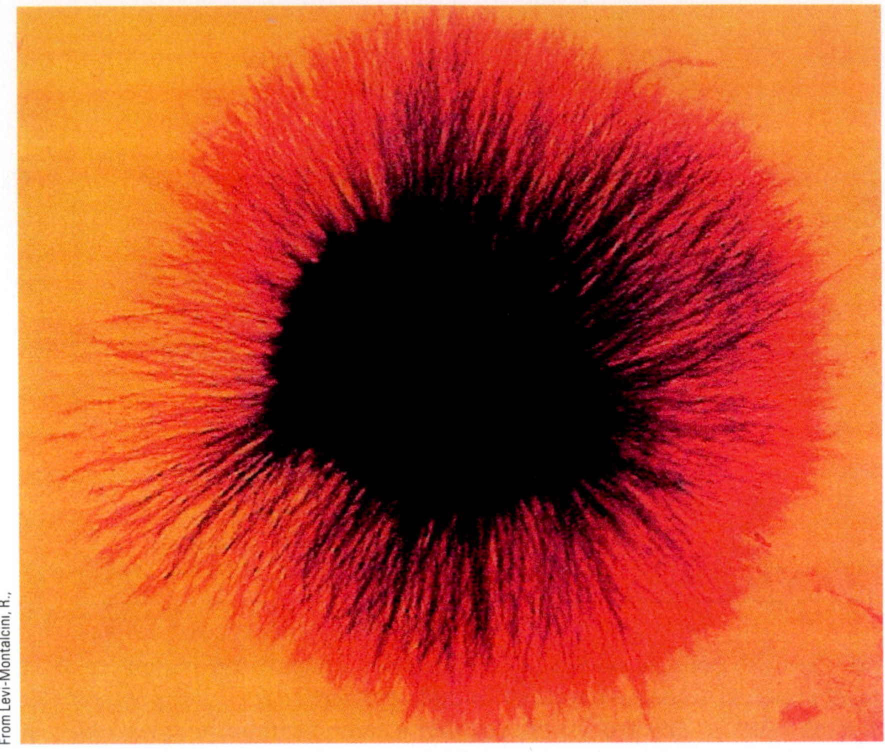

FIGURE 5.20 Growing Axons Compete for Nerve Growth Factor When NGF is added to the solution bathing an isolated neuron, the neuron responds by sending out countless branches.

(hence lower apoptosis rates) are found in cases of autism (Katoh-Semba et al., 2007; Nishimura et al., 2007; Tsai, 2005). Children who were eventually diagnosed with autism had higher levels of neurotrophins in their neonatal blood samples than typically developing children or children with cerebral palsy (Nelson et al., 2001).

Synaptic Pruning Not only do we appear to lose large numbers of neurons during the course of development, but we also seem to lose large numbers of synapses as well. Just as the brain initially overproduces neurons, followed by a refinement in their numbers, we experience a burst of synaptic growth followed by a period of **synaptic pruning,** in which the number of functional synapses is reduced. As shown in Figure 5.21, Huttenlocher (1994) suggested that pruning might eliminate up to 42 percent of all synapses in the human visual cortex after the first year of life.

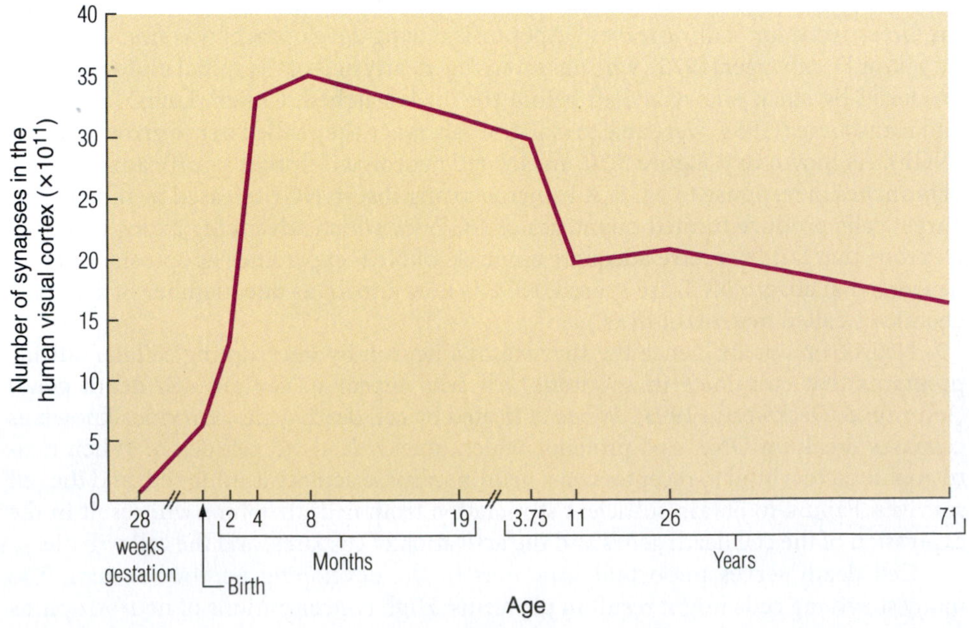

FIGURE 5.21 Synaptic Rearrangement over the Life Span In the human visual cortex, the number of synapses peaks at about the age of one year and decreases until about the age of ten years. The number of synapses remains relatively stable in adulthood. *Source*: Adapted from Huttonlocher (1994).

synaptic pruning The process in which functional synapses are maintained and nonfunctional synapses are lost.

We have seen previously that competition for neurotrophins determines which neurons survive and which die. It is likely that a similar competition determines which synapses are retained. Changeux and Danchin (1976) suggested that only those synapses that participate in functional neural networks are maintained. The nervous system clearly operates according to a "use it or lose it" philosophy.

Myelination Myelination of the developing nervous system follows both a structural and a functional pattern of development. Structurally, myelination occurs in a rostral direction starting in the spinal cord, followed by successive myelination of the hindbrain, midbrain, and forebrain. Within the forebrain, myelination proceeds simultaneously from inferior to superior and from posterior to anterior. Functionally, the sensory parts of the cortex appear to be myelinated at an earlier time than the motor parts of the cortex.

The first human myelin can be observed in cranial and spinal nerves about 24 weeks after conception. Like many animals, human beings experience a burst of myelination around the time of birth, but the process is by no means complete at such an early age. The last area to be myelinated is the prefrontal cortex, which is responsible for some of our most sophisticated cognitive functions. The prefrontal cortex is not completely myelinated until early adulthood (Sowell, Thompson, Holmes, Jernigan, & Toga, 1999). Differences in myelination might account for the fact that young adults in their early twenties were more accurate in judging facial expressions than teens (Baird et al., 1999). The teens showed greater activation in the amygdala, perhaps providing a "gut feeling" about the expressions they viewed, whereas the young adults showed greater activation of their more completely myelinated frontal lobes, producing a more reasoned response.

Man with all his noble qualities . . . still bears in his bodily frame the indelible stamp of his lowly origin.

Charles Darwin

Effect of Experience on Development

By the time a human or other animal is born, much of the wiring of the nervous system is in place. However, throughout the life span, we retain the ability to rearrange our synaptic connections. Without this flexibility, or **plasticity,** it is unlikely that we would be able to learn and store new memories. In some cases, the time frame of plasticity is limited, in which case we refer to the window of time in which change can occur as a **critical period.** In other cases, it appears as though change can occur indefinitely.

This final adjustment to our neural wiring occurs as a result of the strengthening or weakening of existing synapses due to experience. In general, synapses are strengthened when the pre- and postsynaptic neurons are simultaneously active and weakened when their activity is not synchronized. The importance of correlated activity in strengthening synapses was first suggested in the 1940s by Donald Hebb. As a result, synapses strengthened by simultaneous activity are often referred to as **Hebb synapses.**

Experience and the Visual System Figure 5.22 shows the impact of grafting a third eye onto a frog embryo on the eventual organization of the frog's visual centers in the brain. Normally, the frog's right eye connects with the left optic tectum, its equivalent of the human superior colliculus, and the left eye connects with the right optic tectum. The frog's genetic pattern is hardly prepared to manage input from a third eye. Instead, competition between axons originating from an original eye and the grafted eye for the same area of optic tectum results in a pattern of alternating connections from one eye and then the other. The experience of processing information from a third eye produces a rearrangement of the optic tectum.

We see this same type of process at work in the development of the human visual system. As we will see in Chapter 6, input from the retinas of the two eyes remain separate in both the lateral geniculate nucleus (LGN) of the thalamus and in the primary visual cortex of the occipital lobe. Early in development, the cells of the LGN and the primary visual cortex receive input from both eyes. The first

plasticity The ability to change.
critical period A segment of time during development in which a particular experience is influential and after which experience has little or no effect.
Hebb synapse A synapse strengthened by simultaneous activity; named after Donald Hebb.

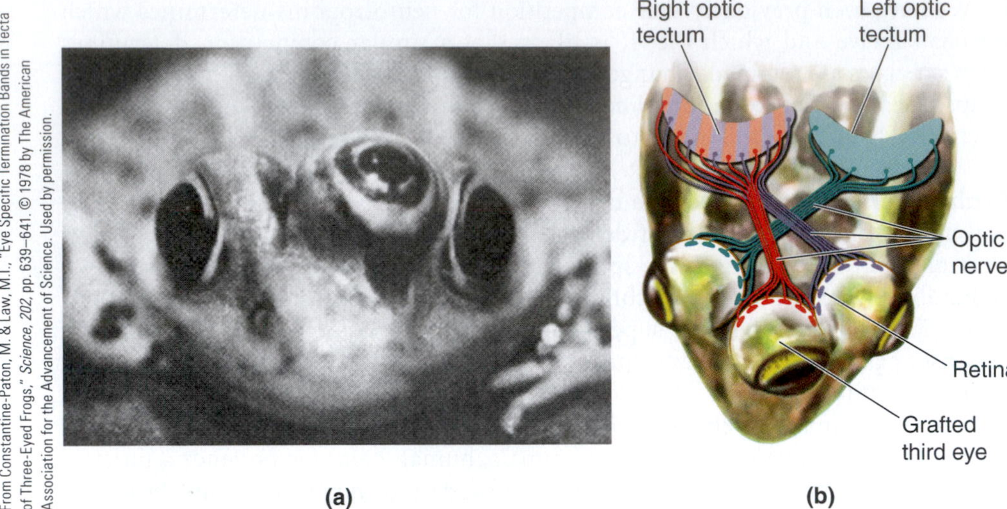

FIGURE 5.22 Input Influences the Development of the Optic Tectum (a) If a third eye is grafted onto a frog embryo, axons from the third eye compete with one of the original eyes for synapses in the frog's optic tectum. (b) As a result of the competition, the axons from each competing eye connect with alternating bands of tectum.

axons to arrive at the LGN originate from the eye on the opposite (contralateral) side of the head. Shortly thereafter, axons from the eye on the same (ipsilateral) side of the head arrive at the LGN. During this initial period of development, input from the two eyes is not segregated in the layers of the LGN, as will be the case in the mature animal.

Segregation, in which LGN cells become selectively activated by input from one eye or the other, appears to proceed according to the process suggested by Hebb. As illustrated in Figure 5.23, input from the two eyes competes for the control of a given LGN cell. The input that is more highly correlated with activity in the LGN cell will be retained, whereas the input from the other eye, which is not as well correlated with activity in the LGN cell, will be weakened. When we say the input from one eye is "correlated" with the output of the LGN cell, this means that the synapse is active at the same time as many others influencing the same LGN cell. Eventually, a given LGN cell will be activated only by input originating in a single eye.

A similar process takes place as the LGN axons arrive in the primary visual cortex, located in the occipital lobe. Initially, LGN axons processing information from the two eyes are not segregated in the visual cortex. Later on, however, the cortex becomes organized in highly defined ocular dominance columns, or areas of cells that respond to only one eye or the other. Once again, simultaneous activity appears to be the critical factor responsible for segregation. In a series of elegant experiments, David Hubel and Torsten Wiesel (1965, 1977) demonstrated how experience with the sensory environment could influence the segregation of inputs into ocular dominance columns in cats and rhesus monkeys. By suturing one eye of newborn kittens and monkeys closed and recording from cells in the visual cortex, Hubel and Wiesel (1965, 1977) were able to chronicle the effects of experience on the organization of ocular dominance columns in the cortex (see Chapter 6).

As shown in Figure 5.24, recordings from a normal cat demonstrated that most cortical cells responded to light falling in either eye. However, Hubel and Wiesel (1977) found other cells that responded to only one eye or the other. In the kitten subjected to monocular deprivation, the right eye was sutured closed for the first three months of life. Then the right eye was opened, and the left eye was sutured closed for the next three months. Subsequent recordings showed that the reversal of open eyes had little impact on the organization of the kitten's visual cortex. Most cells continued to respond only to light falling in the left eye, which had been open during the first three months of life. None of the cells recorded responded to light falling in both eyes. Hubel and Wiesel argued that these data support the existence of a critical period during which the visual cortex can be modified by experience. Although the concept of suturing the eyes of baby animals may be disturbing to you, many children have benefited from the resulting knowledge that corrective surgery for vision must take place as early as possible.

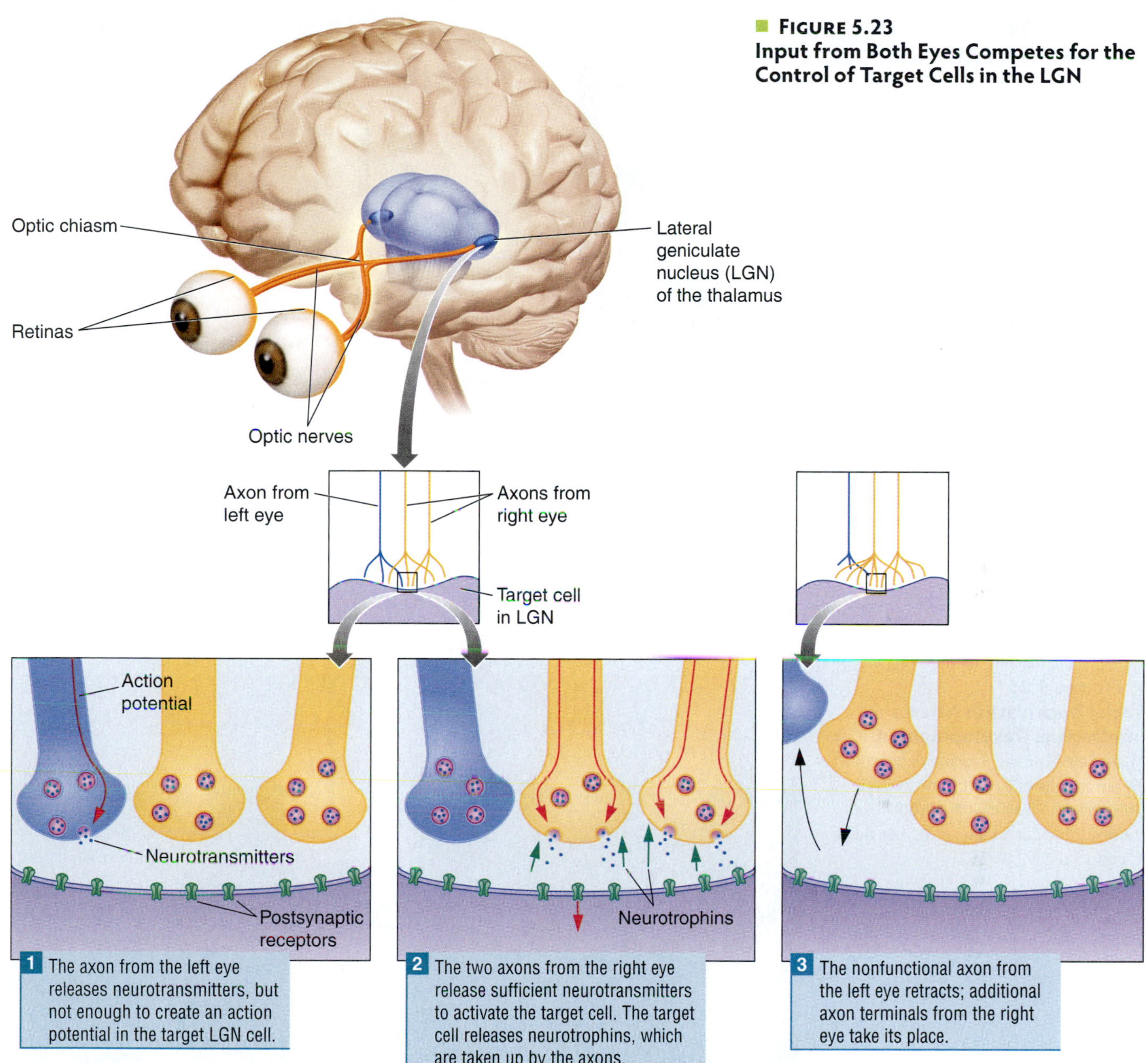
Optic chiasm
Retinas
Optic nerves
Lateral geniculate nucleus (LGN) of the thalamus
Axon from left eye
Axons from right eye
Target cell in LGN
Action potential
Neurotransmitters
Postsynaptic receptors
Neurotrophins
1 The axon from the left eye releases neurotransmitters, but not enough to create an action potential in the target LGN cell.
2 The two axons from the right eye release sufficient neurotransmitters to activate the target cell. The target cell releases neurotrophins, which are taken up by the axons.
3 The nonfunctional axon from the left eye retracts; additional axon terminals from the right eye take its place.

■ **FIGURE 5.23**
Input from Both Eyes Competes for the Control of Target Cells in the LGN

Experience and Social Behavior Certain experiences might be necessary to refine the development of brain areas related to complex social behaviors as well as the sensory systems. Konrad Lorenz (1952) described the phenomenon of **imprinting** in several species of birds. If a newly hatched chick saw Lorenz right away instead of the mother bird, it persisted in treating Lorenz as its mother. As in the visual system, imprinting shows a critical period, a window of time in which experience will modify behavior.

Unfortunate conditions maintained in Romanian orphanages in the 1970s provided insight into the effects of stimulation on human development. The children in these orphanages, such as those shown in ■ Figure 5.25, had very few opportunities to interact with other people or the environment. Elenor Ames (1997) followed the development of Romanian orphans adopted by Canadian parents. Children adopted prior to 6 months of age appear to have recovered from their earlier deprivation. Children adopted later in life improved but did not make as good a recovery as the children adopted earlier. These findings suggest that human intellectual development is also subject to critical periods.

imprinting The process in which baby animals, particularly birds, learn to follow their mother immediately upon seeing her after birth or hatching.

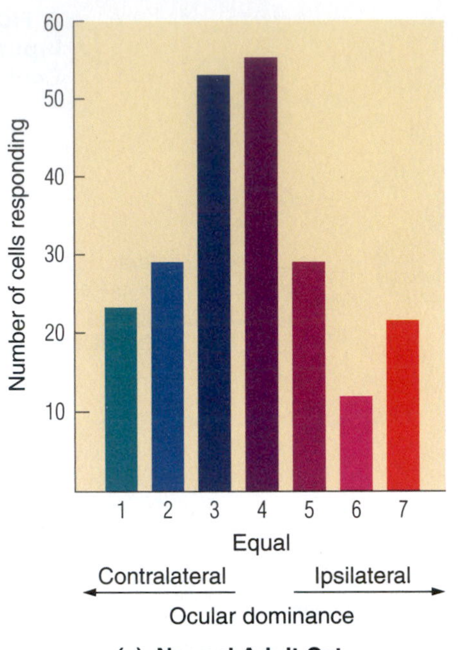

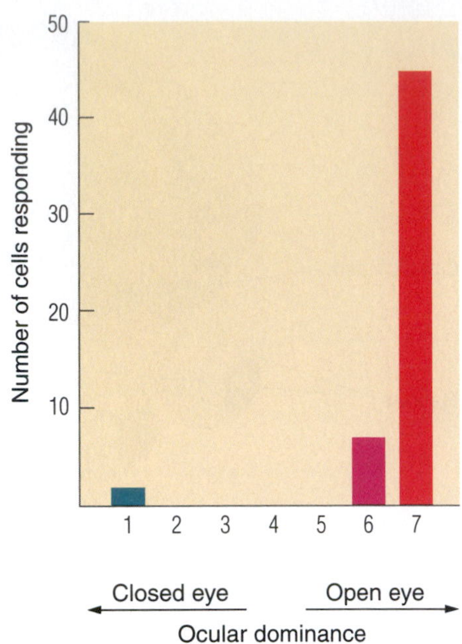

FIGURE 5.24
Early Experience Affects the Organization of Ocular Dominance Columns In a classic series of experiments by Hubel and Wiesel, manipulation of input during the critical period of visual development changed the organization of the primary visual cortex in cats. Cells labeled 1 or 2 respond primarily to input from the contralateral eye, whereas cells labeled 6 or 7 respond primarily to input from the ipsilateral eye. Cells labeled 3, 4, or 5 respond equally to either eye. Normal experience (a) results in a fairly equal distribution of cells responding to each eye. Suturing one eye closed for the first three months of life (b) reduces the number of cortical cells responding to the closed eye or to both eyes. *Source*: Adapted from Hubel & Wiesel (1965).

FIGURE 5.25
Social Deprivation Affects Intellectual Development in Humans Romanian orphans adopted before the age of 6 months recovered from their earlier social deprivation, but those adopted at later ages did not make as good a recovery.

Ending a Critical Period Critical periods for development have endpoints. Lorenz (1952) found that imprinting in baby geese would occur during the first two days of life but not at later ages. Very few people who learn a second language after puberty will be able to pass as native speakers. Several hypotheses have been proposed to account for the closing of critical periods of development. Growth spurts in myelin have been observed in parts of the brain involved with language and spatial relations between the ages of 6 and 13 years (Thompson et al., 2000). The conclusion of this growth period coincides with reduced abilities to learn additional languages. The presence or absence of neurotrophins might also influence the timing of critical periods (Berardi, Pizzorusso, & Maffei, 2000).

Disorders of Brain Development

Given the complexity of cell production, migration, differentiation, and connection, it seems to be a major miracle that most of us end up with a reasonably functional brain. Severe developmental errors usually result in miscarriage, or spontaneous abortion. A small percentage of children will be born with a variety of abnormal conditions due to errors in development.

Neural Tube Defects As we observed earlier, an important part of development is the closing of the neural tube. Two major types of neural tube defects are anencephaly and spina bifida.

Anencephaly, in which significant portions of the brain and skull fail to develop, occurs when the rostral neural tube does not develop properly. The majority of fetuses with anencephaly either die in utero or do not survive for more than a few hours after birth.

In **spina bifida,** the caudal portion of the neural tube fails to close normally. Surgery is typically used within the first 24 hours of life to correct the condition. Nonetheless, most children with spina bifida will experience paralysis of the lower limbs. Although the condition produces a number of physical and psychological challenges, people with spina bifida live well into adulthood with modern treatment. Efforts to repair the spinal damage prior to birth might be useful in many cases (Zambelli et al., 2007).

Although the exact causes of neural tube defects remain unknown, deficiencies of folic acid might be responsible for a large number of cases. Folic acid occurs naturally in dark green leafy vegetables, egg yolks, fruits, and juices. It is also added to fortified breakfast cereals and other products. However, the average American diet does not contain sufficient levels of folic acid to effectively prevent neural tube defects (Spina Bifida Association of America, 2001). Consequently, 42 nations require fortification of products like breakfast cereal with folic acid as a preventive measure. Unfortunately, folic acid fortification might lead to increased risk for colon cancer (Solomons, 2007).

Genetic Disorders A wide variety of genetic errors can occur in development, and it is beyond the scope of our current discussion to provide more than a sample.

Trisomy 21, also known as **Down syndrome,** is characterized by an individual having three, rather than the normal two, copies of chromosome 21. Down syndrome occurs about 1.5 times out of 1,000 births (de Grouchy & Turleau, 1990). The major cause of trisomy 21 is abnormal division, or disjunction, of the mother's twenty-first chromosome during meiosis. Disjunction is related to maternal age, so rates of Down syndrome increase from 1 out of 1,000 births to mothers under 33 years of age to 38 out of 1,000 to mothers over 45 (Trimble & Baird, 1978).

The relationship between the extra twenty-first chromosome and the physical and mental characteristics of Down syndrome is currently unknown. Individuals with Down syndrome usually function in the moderately retarded range of intellect, with IQs between 35 and 50. This level of intellect allows attainment of second-grade academic skills and requires living and working in a supervised setting. Physical features of Down syndrome include a small skull, large tongue, almond-shaped eyes, a flat nasal bridge, and abnormalities of the hands and fingers. Individuals with Down syndrome are also subject to heart deformities, which contribute to shorter life expectancy. As we shall see later in the chapter, Down syndrome is also correlated with a high risk of Alzheimers' disease.

The most common heritable condition is **fragile-X syndrome.** The *FMR-1* gene on the X chromosome usually has between 6 and 50 codon repeats, or consecutive segments of the same codon along a strand of DNA. People with up to 200 repeats are healthy, but having more than 200 repeats leads to the fragile-X condition. The large numbers of repeats allow the chromosome to break physically. About 1 in 1,500 to 2,000 males and 1 in 2,000 to 2,500 females are affected by this condition (Kahkonen et al., 1987). The intellectual consequences of the condition vary from

anencephaly (an-en-SEF-uh-lee) A neural tube defect in which the rostral neural tube does not develop normally, resulting in incomplete formation of the brain and skull.

spina bifida (SPIE-nuh BIFF-i-duh) A neural tube defect in which the caudal part of the tube does not close properly.

Down syndrome An abnormal genetic condition resulting from a genotype with three copies of chromosome 21, responsible for moderate mental retardation and a characteristic physical appearance.

fragile-X syndrome A heritable genetic disorder that produces cognitive and physical abnormalities.

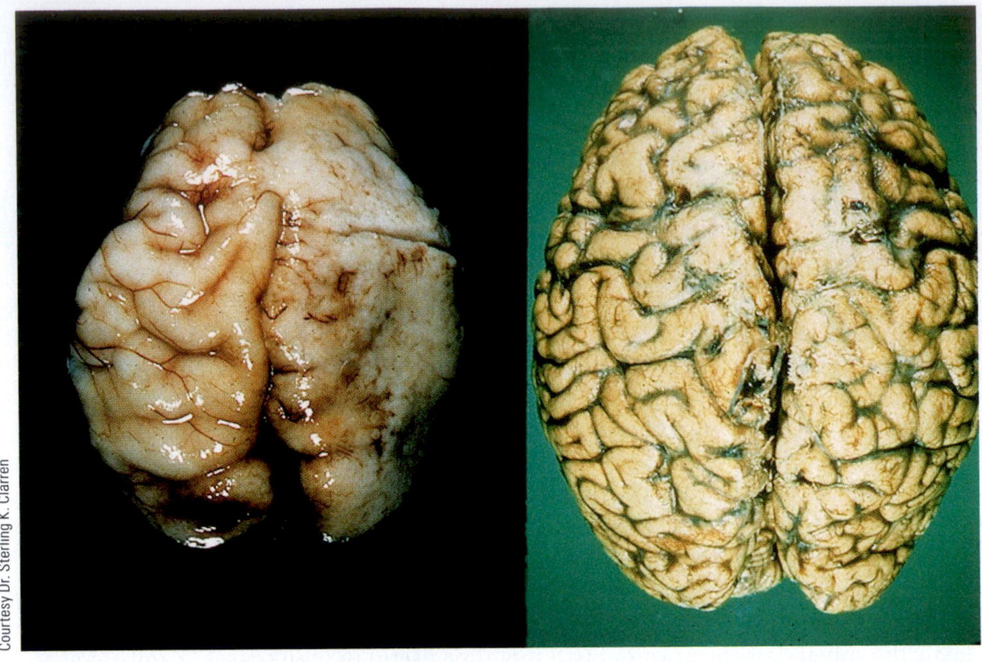
Courtesy Dr. Sterling K. Clarren

FIGURE 5.26 Fetal Alcohol Syndrome Produces Physical and Intellectual Abnormalities One of the most frequent preventable causes of mental retardation and behavioral problems is maternal use of alcohol and other drugs during pregnancy. These brains were taken from two fetuses of the same age. The one on the left had fetal alcohol syndrome, whereas the one on the right developed typically.

typical intelligence to moderate retardation. Physical characteristics include low-set ears and a large forehead and jaw. Males with the syndrome often show unusual social withdrawal, although fewer than 5 percent of fragile-X cases meet the formal criteria for autism (Flint & Yule, 1994).

In other types of genetic abnormalities, the body is either unable to produce important chemicals or overproduces the chemicals. These metabolic disorders account for approximately 3 to 7 percent of severe cases of mental retardation (Moser, Ramey, & Leonard, 1990). The best understood of these metabolic disorders is **phenylketonuria,** or **PKU.** This disorder occurs about once in 10,000 births, although 1 out of every 50 people is a carrier for the disorder (DiLella & Woo, 1987). PKU results from a recessive gene, leading to a lack of liver enzymes needed to convert the amino acid phenylalanine into tyrosine. Consequently, people with PKU produce an abnormal byproduct, phenylpyruvic acid, which damages the brain early in development. Mental retardation can be prevented by avoiding foods containing phenylalanine until a person's mid-20s. These foods include high-protein items such as milk, dairy products, meat, fish, chicken, eggs, beans, and nuts (University of Washington PKU Clinic, 2000).

Environmental Toxins One of the most thoroughly understood environmental causes of mental retardation is maternal alcohol use, leading to **fetal alcohol syndrome.** Currently, there are no known safe levels of alcohol use during pregnancy, and pregnant women are strongly encouraged to abstain completely from alcohol. Children with fetal alcohol syndrome experience growth retardation, skin folds at the corners of the eyes, nose and mouth abnormalities, small head circumference, and reduced IQ (Streissguth et al., 1991). They are more likely to be diagnosed with attention deficits, poor impulse control, and severe behavioral problems. The impact of fetal alcohol syndrome on the brain is illustrated in Figure 5.26.

Alcohol can have direct effects on the developing fetus, and the malnutrition and poor health of the drinking mother might also have indirect effects (Steinhausen, Willms, & Spohr, 1994). In addition, pregnant women who use alcohol are also more likely to be using other drugs. Alcohol, tobacco, marijuana, or cocaine used singly during pregnancy can produce significant reductions in the gray matter of the resulting child, but combinations of two or more of these drugs produce even more dramatic results (Rivkin et al., 2008). These are not short-term

phenylketonuria (PKU) (fee-nil-key-tone-UR-ee-uh) A heritable condition in which the individual does not produce enzymes necessary for the breakdown of phenylalanine; left untreated, the condition produces mental retardation.

fetal alcohol syndrome A set of physical and cognitive characteristics that result from maternal use of alcohol during pregnancy.

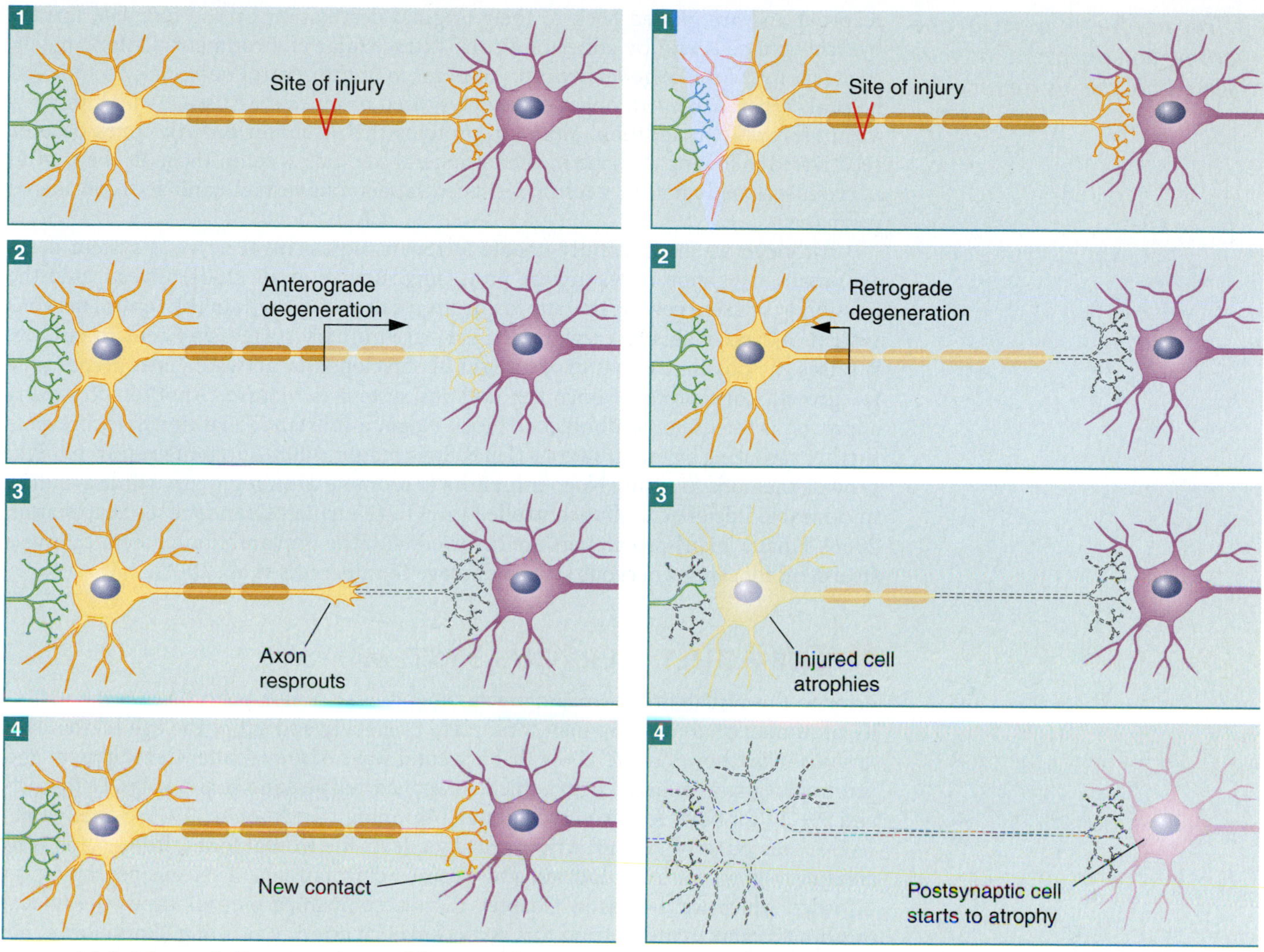

(a) Anterograde Degeneration and Regeneration

(b) Retrograde and Transneuronal Degeneration

FIGURE 5.27
Neuronal Responses to Damage (a) In anterograde degeneration, the segment of axon separated from the cell body by damage will die. On occasion, the axon will resprout and regrow to its former targets. (b) In retrograde degeneration, damage to an axon produces the deterioration of the entire neuron. Cells that normally receive input from the damaged cell also deteriorate in a process known as transneuronal degeneration.

effects, either. Gray matter thickness and head circumference were still reduced in the children exposed prenatally to multiple drugs when they reached 10–13 years of age (ibid., 2008).

Redevelopment in Response to Damage

Any damage to the cell body of a neuron will result in neural death, due to the importance of cell body activities for the basic functioning of the cell. Figure 5.27 illustrates the possible outcomes of damage to an axon. The segment of the axon that is now separated by the damaged area from the cell body will deteriorate in a process known as **anterograde** (forward) **degeneration.** The remaining segment, still attached to the cell body, regrows in some instances and not in others. Typically, damage that is very close to the cell body is more likely to produce **retrograde degeneration,** in which the axon stub and the cell body degenerate and die. The death of a neuron has repercussions among the other neurons with which it was formerly connected. Without input from the now-dead cell, postsynaptic cells deteriorate due to **transneuronal degeneration.**

As we noted in Chapter 3, damaged axons in the peripheral nervous system can regrow successfully, due at least in part to the response of the Schwann cells. Axons

anterograde degeneration The deterioration of the axon segment separated from the cell body by damage to the axon.

retrograde degeneration The deterioration of the cell body and remaining axon stub produced by damage to an axon.

transneuronal degeneration The deterioration of postsynaptic cells in response to loss of input from damaged presynaptic neurons.

True terror is to wake up one morning and discover that your high school class is running the country.
Kurt Vonnegut

resprout and are guided back to their original destination by the template formed by Schwann cells and by adhering to the extracellular environment. Unfortunately, the response of the oligodendrocytes to damage in the central nervous system is less helpful. When damaged, oligodendrocytes often produce scar tissue, which inhibits axon regrowth. In addition, although proteins that occur in growth cones become reactivated following damage in the peripheral nervous system, those in the central nervous system do not. As a result, most central nervous system damage is considered permanent.

Although we are currently unable to repair most central nervous system damage, many new approaches appear promising. Bomze et al. (2001) investigated the possibility of using genetic therapy to encourage axon regrowth in the central nervous system. Although this research is in a very preliminary stage using cells in culture, it raises the possibility that drugs might be developed to activate genes responsible for growth cone proteins once the nervous system is mature. Another promising approach is the use of antibodies to block **Nogo,** a substance that normally prevents further sprouting by mature axons (Hu & Strittmatter, 2008). Ongoing research might provide methods for using Nogo inhibitors to promote axon regrowth, while avoiding undesirable side effects of uncontrolled growth (Fournier, GrandPre, & Strittmatter, 2001). Finally, many researchers are involved with the implantation of stem cells as a treatment for central nervous system damage (Bambakidis et al., 2008).

The Adult Nervous System

Prior to the availability of imaging technologies, researchers believed that the majority of human brain development took place prenatally and up to the age of about 18 months. Now, however, we know that a second wave of gray matter development and pruning begins at puberty, with a thickening of cortex peaking at about age 11 for girls and age 12 for boys, followed by a gradual thinning (Giedd et al., 1999; Sowell et al., 1999). This burst of new growth especially affects the frontal lobes, influencing teen abilities to plan, control impulses, and reason. Schizophrenia, a serious psychological disorder, which we discuss in Chapter 16, is accompanied by four times the typical thinning of gray matter during this second major period of pruning (Rapoport et al., 1999). As we noted previously, myelination of the brain also continues to develop and influence the behavior of teens and young adults.

The human brain is thought to have fully matured by the age of 25, and few changes occur until about the age of 45. At that time, the weight of the brain begins to decrease significantly. These changes typically do not result in dramatic cognitive and behavioral changes in healthy adults. Results from the Baltimore Longitudinal Study of Aging (2000) show that aging produces very mild changes in speed of learning and problem solving, and that the changes occur rather late in life for most people.

I recently had my annual physical examination, which I get once every seven years, and when the nurse weighed me, I was shocked to discover how much stronger the Earth's gravitational pull has become since 1990.
Dave Barry

Individuals vary widely in the extent and speed of cognitive decline they experience. Both genetic and lifestyle factors probably contribute to this variability. People with higher intelligence are less likely to be diagnosed with Alzheimer's disease and other degenerative conditions associated with aging. In addition, intelligent people appear to experience a slower decline even if they do have a degenerative condition (Kemppainen et al., 2008). The reasons for the intelligence factor are hotly disputed. Some researchers point to the larger number of brain cells generally correlated with higher intelligence. A person with more cells can afford to lose some (Tisserand, Bosma, Van Boxtel, & Jolles, 2001). Intelligent people are likely to be more financially secure, increasing their access to better diets, reduction of stress, and better health care. Intelligent people are more likely to remain intellectually active throughout their lives, a factor that might protect the brain. Robert Friedland and his colleagues (Friedland et al., 2001; Lindstrom et al., 2005) questioned participants regarding their leisure activities between the ages of 20 and 60. Participants with **dementia** had watched much more television than the healthy participants, who were more likely to spend their time on active hobbies or reading. Once again, we see that the brain clearly follows the rule of "use it or lose it."

Nogo A substance that normally prevents further sprouting by mature axons.
dementia Deterioration of cognitive abilities resulting from brain disorders.

NEW DIRECTIONS

Can We Stop the Aging Process?

Normal aging might result from cell duplication. Although some body cells do not duplicate, such as neurons, others undergo several hundred duplications in the course of a lifetime. Each duplication, however, has a cost. At each end of a chromosome is a structure known as a *telomere.* The telomere doesn't encode any proteins. Instead, it functions like the blank parts of a videotape that precede and follow a film. These allow you to start the VCR without missing any of the "movie."

Each time a cell is duplicated, part of the telomere is left off the resulting chromosomes. An 81-year-old person has telomeres that are about 60 to 70 percent as long as they were at birth (Slagboom, Droog, & Boomsma, 1994). Shortened telomeres put meaningful genes at risk, and more accidents can happen as aged cells duplicate. Werner's syndrome, a genetic disorder, causes unusually rapid telomere shortening and premature aging.

Aging might also occur due to oxidative stress, in which some of the byproducts of cell metabolism can damage cells. In rodents, oxidative stress can be reduced substantially and longevity increased by reducing daily calorie intake by 30 percent (Heilbronn et al., 2006). To answer the question of whether caloric restriction has the same effect in humans will require further investigation (ibid.), although one generally does not see a large number of very old, overweight people.

Technology often proceeds faster than ethics. If we gain the ability to increase human life spans, what impact will that have on our societies?

Age is an issue of mind over matter. If you don't mind, it doesn't matter.

Mark Twain

Neurogenesis in Adulthood For many years, it was assumed that all **neurogenesis,** or new neuron formation, was complete at birth in mammals. The only exception appeared to be neurons associated with the sense of smell.

The first suggestion that more extensive neurogenesis might occur in mature animals came from Barnea and Nottebohm (1994), who discovered that songbirds produced new neurons when they learned new songs. Elizabeth Gould and her colleagues (Gould, Reeves, Graziano, & Gross, 1999) showed not only that new neurons were being produced by adult rhesus monkeys but also that they migrated to the hippocampus and association areas of the cerebral cortex. Similar findings in the human brain and in mice have been reported by Gage (2000). The new neurons did not migrate to primary visual cortex. As we discovered previously, visual organization appears to possess a critical period that closes in childhood. We would be surprised, therefore, to find new neurons migrating to the visual cortex.

Although the numbers of neurons added to the mature brain are quite small compared with neurogenesis early in development, these new neurons may play a very important role in the modification of the brain in response to experience. Adult neurogenesis might also protect the mature brain from the effects of stress. The use of antidepressant medications appears to increase neurogenesis in the rat hippocampus, possibly contributing to the drugs' efficacy in treating stress-related depression (Malberg, Eisch, Nestler, & Duman, 2000).

Alzheimer's Disease Alzheimer's disease is one of a number of degenerative conditions associated with aging that results in dementia, or the loss of normal cognitive and emotional function.

Behaviorally, the condition usually begins with mild memory loss. As the disease progresses, problem solving, language, and social behavior deteriorate. The patient begins to experience severe symptoms of hallucination and delusional thinking. Eventually, basic life skills begin to deteriorate, and the person needs careful supervision and care. Prior to death, many of these patients are unable to move or speak.

The behavioral symptoms of Alzheimer's disease result from a characteristic pattern of neural degeneration, shown in ■ Figure 5.28. The emergence of abnormal structures known as **neurofibrillary tangles** is one of the hallmark features of the disease. Tangles result from the detachment of the **tau** protein, which normally holds structural microtubules in place (See Chapter 3). Without tau, the microtubules are not able to maintain their structure, and the neuron basically folds in on

neurogenesis The birth of new neural cells.

neurofibrillary tangle An abnormal internal structure of neurons found in cases of Alzheimer's disease.

tau An intracellular protein responsible for maintaining the structure of microtubules; broken down in conditions such as Alzheimer's disease.

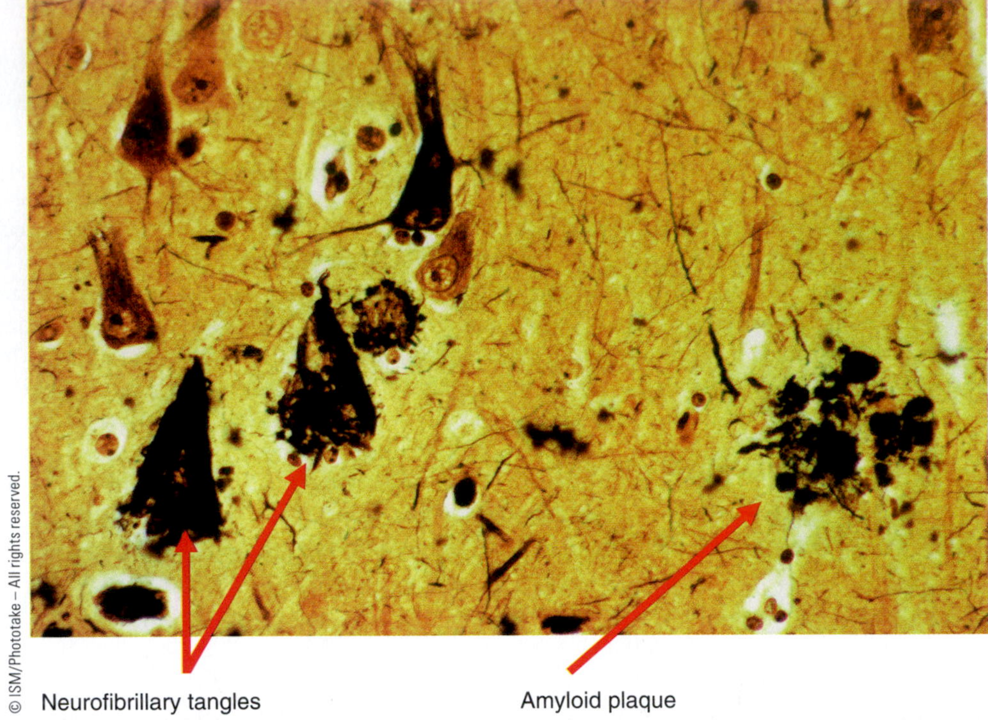

FIGURE 5.28
Alzheimer's Disease Produces Structural Abnormalities in Neurons This image illustrates the abnormal structural effects of Alzheimer's disease on neurons. The cone-shaped elements are neurofibrillary tangles, and the brown clumps are amyloid plaques found in the brain of a patient who died from Alzheimer's disease.

Old age isn't so bad when you consider the alternative.
Maurice Chevalier

itself and collapses. The disruption in tau might result from the action of another protein found in the neurons of patients with Alzheimer's disease called **amyloid.** Amyloid contributes to the detachment of tau and the subsequent disruption of cell structure and function. In addition, amyloid collects in plaques, or abnormal patches, on axons of affected neurons and within blood vessels serving the brain. Individuals with Down syndrome frequently show this characteristic abnormality, leading to interest in a possible role for chromosome 21 in Alzheimer's disease. Amyloid is formed from a larger molecule, the *amyloid precursor protein (APP)*, which occurs in normally functioning cells. The functions of APP are currently unknown. A particular form of amyloid, called an ADDL (for amyloid b-derived diffusible ligands) may be the real culprit behind Alzheimer's disease (Klein, Krafft, & Finch, 2001). Unlike the other types of amyloid studied previously, ADDLs can dissolve and travel within the brain. The locations affected by ADDLs correspond closely with the types of damage observed in patients with Alzheimer's disease. Finally, ADDLs can interfere with learning and memory long before cell death begins to occur.

The damage to the brains of patients with Alzheimer's disease follows a characteristic pattern. One of the first areas to show measurable changes due to the disease is the posterior cingulate cortex (Valla, Berndt, & Gonzalez-Lima, 2001). The memory impairment found at the onset of the disease probably results from deterioration in the hippocampus and adjacent tissue in the temporal lobe. Other cognitive symptoms, such as language and problem-solving deficits, probably arise from damage to the association areas of the cortex. The amygdala and other limbic system structures connected to the hypothalamus are also affected, leading to the emotional changes often observed in patients. As we observed previously, neuron death can lead to deterioration among a cell's postsynaptic connections through the process of transneuronal degeneration. This process spreads deterioration rapidly throughout the brain of the patient with Alzheimer's disease.

Alzheimer's disease typically occurs after the age of 70, but the potential for the disease might be apparent at much younger ages. In a study of nuns who shared the same environmental conditions from late adolescence until old age, researchers found a correlation between a nun's writing ability at 19 years of age and her eventual likelihood of being diagnosed with Alzheimer's disease (Snowdon, 1997). Because

amyloid A protein associated with the degeneration of tissue, such as in patients with Alzheimer's disease and other types of dementia.

writing ability is a reflection of basic intelligence, this study may simply confirm other work suggesting a correlation between intelligence and risk for Alzheimer's disease.

Earlier in the chapter, we mentioned that having the E^4 variant of the *APOE* gene was a genetic risk for late-onset Alzheimer's disease. We do not know why this allele is associated with Alzheimer's disease, but it appears to influence the development of amyloid. Other cases of Alzheimer's disease result from genetic mutations in a gene for substances that normally remove amyloid plaques (Levy-Lahad et al., 1995).

Currently, there are no effective treatments for reversing the course of Alzheimer's disease. Because one of the characteristics of Alzheimer's disease is a decrease in cholinergic activity in the brain, medications that boost acetylcholine levels or activity might be helpful (Barnes et al., 2000). At best, however, current approaches to treatment slow the progression of the condition, but they do not reverse the damage already in place.

WHY DOES THIS MATTER?

Treating Alzheimer's Disease

Finding new methods for treating Alzheimer's disease matters not only for humane reasons but because public health researchers estimate that the number of patients with the condition will grow by no less than 300 percent in the next 50 years (Sloane et al., 2002). Given the expense in caregiver time and financial resources of caring for each patient, efforts to prevent and treat Alzheimer's disease should have a high priority.

In spite of considerable time and effort, scientists still do not have any treatments that stop or reverse the symptoms of Alzheimer's disease. Four medications have been approved for use in Europe and the United States for Alzheimer's disease. Three of these medications act by inhibiting acetylcholinesterase (AChE), the enzyme that breaks down acetylcholine (ACh) in the synaptic gap (see Chapter 4). When AChE is inhibited, the patient with Alzheimer's gets more "bang for the buck" out of each molecule of his or her depleted supply of ACh because the likelihood that a molecule will interact with a receptor is increased. Side effects of AChE inhibitors are consistent with what you already know about the roles of ACh in the autonomic nervous system and at the neuromuscular junction and include nausea and vomiting, muscle cramps, decreased heart rate, decreased appetite, and increased gastric acid.

The fourth medication, memantine, blocks glutamate at the NMDA receptor (see Chapter 4). Many neurodegenerative diseases, including Alzheimer's disease, are accompanied by excitotoxicity, or damage from too much glutamate-induced excitation (Olney, 1994). As you may recall, the NMDA glutamate receptor allows both sodium and calcium into a neuron. The calcium will both stimulate neurotransmitter release and initiate a cascade of enzymes that produce structural change in the cell. Too much calcium, and its associated activities, can be toxic to neurons. Blocking the action of glutamate at the NMDA receptor provides some relief from further damage and improves cognitive function (Areosa & Sherriff, 2003; Bakchine & Loft, 2008). One of the challenges of using glutamate antagonists, which include phencyclidine (PCP or angel dust) as well as memantine, is their tendency to induce psychotic behavior, including hallucination.

Aggressive patients with advanced Alzheimer's disease are frequently medicated with drugs typically used to treat schizophrenia and other psychotic conditions (see Chapter 16). Recently, long-term research suggests that this practice might not be beneficial enough to justify the risks associated with the use of antipsychotic drugs (Ballard et al., 2008).

This leaves us with relatively little we can do for a growing population of patients with Alzheimer's. Hopefully, preventive measures, which might include vaccination or lifestyle changes, will help us avoid the personal and societal costs of growing numbers of patients.

INTERIM SUMMARY 5.2

Summary Table: Milestones in Nervous System Development

Period of Life	Nervous System Development
	• Starting at about 2–3 weeks following conception, billions of neurons are formed.
Prenatal period	• Neurons migrate to their appropriate locations. • Synapses begin forming and are influenced by fetal activity. • Myelination begins at about the 6th month following conception.
Birth	• The brain weighs 300 to 350 grams (about 0.75 lbs). • A period of rapid brain growth begins, extending into adolescence, primarily due to myelination. • Myelination of the auditory and visual systems is completed soon after birth. • Myelination of the corticospinal motor tract is completed by the age of about 18 months.
Childhood	• Experience plays a significant role in the refinement and reorganization of synapses. • Adult brain weight of 1,300 to 1,500 grams (about 2.9–3.3 lbs) is achieved. • At puberty, a second burst of gray matter growth is followed by a period of synaptic pruning.
Adolescence	• Synaptic pruning takes place, largely based on experience. • Synapses continue to develop and reorganize. • Some limited number of new neurons might be formed. • Synapse reorganization continues in some parts of the brain, whereas others experience critical periods of development.
Adulthood	• Myelination of the frontal lobes is completed. • Brain weight decreases after the age of 45, but cognition in healthy adults appears relatively unaffected.

Summary Points

1. Within one week following conception, the human embryo divides into three germ layers. Inducing factors differentiate the ectoderm layer into skin and neural tissue. **(LO5)**
2. New neural cells are produced in the ventricular zone lining the neural tube. After migrating to their eventual location, they differentiate into neurons and glia. **(LO6)**
3. Growth cones respond to the chemical and physical properties of the extracellular environment to reach their destinations. Once axons and dendrites are in place, both pre- and postsynaptic structures influence synaptic development. **(LO6)**
4. Significant numbers of new neurons die during the development process. Synapses follow a similar pattern of overproduction followed by pruning. **(LO6)**
5. Although many parts of the brain retain the ability to change throughout the lifetime, some processes, including vision and language learning, have critical periods in which change and learning occur. **(LO7)**
6. Abnormal development can occur due to neural tube defects, genetic disorders, and exposure to environmental toxins. **(LO8)**
7. Although most central nervous system damage is permanent, promising new treatments, such as the implantation of stem cells, may be available soon. **(LO9)**
8. Healthy aging is associated with some loss of brain weight, but changes in learning speed and problem solving are mild and occur rather late in life. Alzheimer's disease and other pathological conditions produce a steady deterioration of brain function. **(LO10)**

Review Questions

1. What factors are responsible for the early differentiation of cells in the nervous system?
2. How do activity and experience fine-tune the connections of the developing brain?

CHAPTER REVIEW

THOUGHT QUESTIONS

1. Given that there is no known cure for Alzheimer's disease, would you be interested in genetic testing that would identify your *APOE* alleles? Why or why not?
2. How would you respond to the following statement by neuroscientist Simon LeVay: "When we have gained the power to manipulate our own physical and mental traits and those of our offspring, society will have to wrestle with profound questions about what constitutes a normal human being, what kinds of human diversity are desirable or permissible, and who gets to make these decisions on behalf of whom."
3. Based on your knowledge of the timeline of embryonic and fetal brain development, what advice would you give to sexually active women of childbearing age?

KEY TERMS

allele (p. 125)
Alzheimer's disease (p. 130)
amyloid (p. 150)
anterograde degeneration (p. 147)
apoptosis (p. 139)
chromosome (p. 125)
crossing over (p. 126)
deoxyribonucleic acid (DNA) (p. 125)
dominant allele (p. 126)
ectoderm (p. 133)
embryo (p. 133)
endoderm (p. 133)
fetus (p. 133)
gene (p. 125)
gene expression (p. 125)
genotype (p. 125)
growth cone (p. 137)
heterozygous (p. 126)
homozygous (p. 126)
imprinted gene (p. 126)
linkage (p. 126)
meiosis (p. 126)
mesoderm (p. 133)
mitosis (p. 134)
mutation (p. 128)
neural tube (p. 134)
neurofibrillary tangles (p. 149)
neurogenesis (p. 149)
neurotrophin (p. 139)
phenotype (p. 125)
radial glia (p. 135)
recessive allele (p. 126)
retrograde degeneration (p. 147)
ribonucleic acid (RNA) (p. 126)
synaptic pruning (p. 140)
tau (p. 149)
transneuronal degeneration (p. 147)
zygote (p. 133)

6 Vision

CHAPTER OUTLINE

AP/Wide World

▲ **Martina Navrotilova** Every tennis champion has mastered the first rule of tennis: keep your eye on the ball.

Introduction

Primates, including human beings, experience a dramatically colorful world. In contrast, the visual world of dogs features only the blues, yellows, and grays shown in ■ Figure 6.1. Some nocturnal mammal species probably do not see color at all.

What advantages do we enjoy as a result of our ability to see many colors? According to Sumner and Mollon (2000), primates might have developed excellent color vision to find better food such as younger, tastier leaves or fruits. Changizi, Zhang, and Shimojo

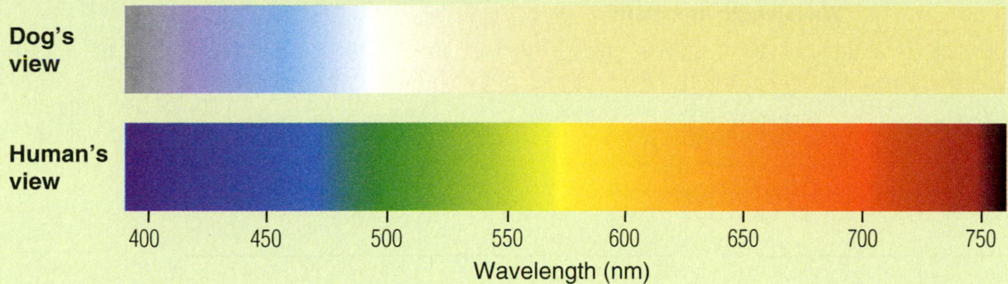

■ **FIGURE 6.1**
The Visual Worlds of Dogs and Humans Dogs have two types of color receptors, whereas humans and other primates have three. Colors that look red to humans would probably look yellow to the dog, and greens would look white or gray.

(2006) believe that primates excel in judging shades of red, which might be helpful in discriminating emotional states (such as a blush) or sexual signals (such as the red rump of the female monkey in estrus). We might even use color to track large numbers of objects such as members of our favorite football team (Halberda & Feigenson, 2006). Normally, humans can pay attention to only three objects at a time, but by using color, we can tell instantly if we have the right mix of drinks in the cooler or how much money is represented by the pot of chips in the center of the poker table.

Whether we're searching for food or scanning the millions of colors displayed by a computer monitor, the process of vision begins with light. In this chapter, we will trace the processing of the light stimulus from its initial detection by the eye through its final interpretation by the cerebral cortex. ■

LEARNING OBJECTIVES

After reading this chapter, you should be able to:

LO1 Describe the major features of visible light as a stimulus.

LO2 Describe the major features of the eye.

LO3 Differentiate between the structure, function, and location of rods and cones and describe their relationships to scotopic and photopic vision.

LO4 Trace the pathways of information from the photoreceptors to the secondary visual cortex.

LO5 Explain the concepts of receptive field, antagonistic center-surround organization, and lateral inhibition.

LO6 Summarize the processes responsible for visual object perception, depth perception, and color vision.

LO7 Describe the effects of aging and visual disorders on human vision.

Characteristics of Light

Visible light, or the energy we can see, is one form of **electromagnetic radiation** produced by the sun. As shown in ■ Figure 6.2, electromagnetic radiation can be described as moving waves of energy. **Wavelength,** or the distance between successive peaks of waves, is decoded by the visual system either as color or as shades of gray. The **amplitude** of light waves refers to the height of each wave, which is translated by the visual system as brightness. Large-amplitude waves are perceived as bright, and low-amplitude waves are perceived as dim.

Electromagnetic radiation can also be described as the movement of tiny, indivisible particles known as photons. **Photons** always travel at the same speed (the so-called speed of light), but they can vary in the amount of energy they possess. It is this variation in energy levels among photons that gives us waves with different wavelengths and amplitudes. You can think of a light wave as describing the movement of large numbers of photons, much as a wave in the ocean describes the movement of large numbers of water molecules.

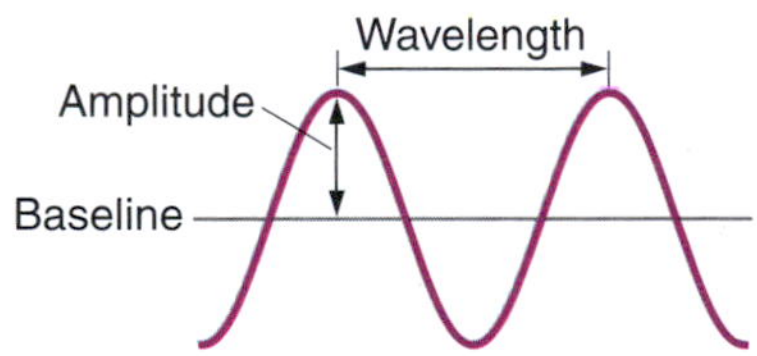

■ **FIGURE 6.2**
Dimensions of Electromagnetic Radiation The amplitude, or height, of light waves is encoded as brightness. Wavelength, or the distance between successive peaks, is encoded as color or shades of gray.

THE ADVANTAGES OF LIGHT AS A STIMULUS

Why is electromagnetic energy, rather than some other feature of the environment, an effective stimulus for a sensory system? Electromagnetic energy, and visible light in particular, has features that make it a valuable source of information. First, electromagnetic energy is abundant in our universe. Second, because electromagnetic energy travels very quickly, there is no substantial delay between an event and an organism's ability to see the event. Finally, electromagnetic energy travels in fairly straight lines, minimizing the distortion of objects. What we see is what we get, literally.

electromagnetic radiation Radiation emitted in the form of energy waves.
wavelength The distance between successive peaks of a wave; determines color in light.
amplitude The height of a wave; in vision, the source of the subjective experience of brightness.
photons Individual, indivisible, very small particles that form waves of electromagnetic energy.

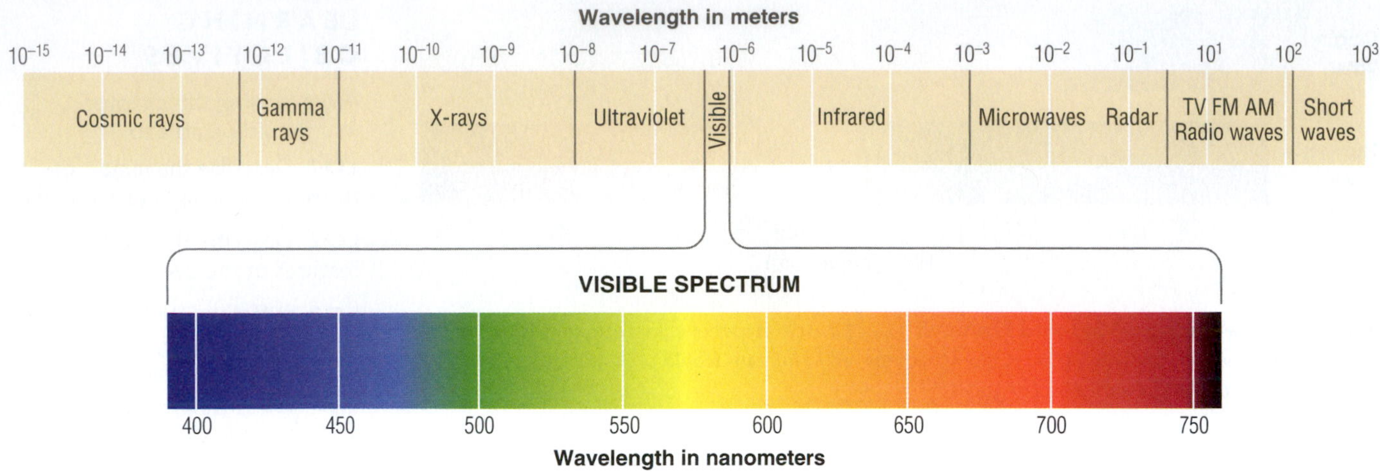

FIGURE 6.3
The Electromagnetic Spectrum Visible light is a small fraction of the electromagnetic spectrum, which is shown as a function of wavelength.

The Electromagnetic Spectrum

The light from the sun contains a mixture of wavelengths and appears white to the human eye. Placing a prism in sunlight will separate the individual wavelengths, which we see as individual colors. Light shining through water droplets is affected the same way, producing the rainbows we enjoy seeing after a rainstorm. Light that is visible to humans occupies a very small part of the electromagnetic spectrum. As you can see in Figure 6.3, the range of electromagnetic energy visible to humans falls between 400 and 700 **nanometers** (nm). A nanometer is 10^{-9} meters, or one billionth of a meter. When we say a light has a wavelength of 400 nanometers, this means that the peaks of the wave are 400 nanometers apart. Shorter wavelengths, approaching 400 nm, are perceived by humans as violet and blue, whereas longer wavelengths, approaching 700 nm, are perceived as red.

Gamma rays, x-rays, ultraviolet rays, infrared rays, microwaves, and radio waves lie outside the range of wavelengths the human eye can detect. These forms of energy have features that make them less desirable stimuli for a sensory system. Shorter wavelengths, such as ultraviolet rays, are typically absorbed by the ozone layer of the Earth's atmosphere, leaving little energy left over for most organisms to sense. Nonetheless, some creatures, including bees, are able to see parts of the ultraviolet spectrum. Longer wavelengths, such as microwaves, tend to penetrate objects rather than reflect back from them, a feature that is valuable in cooking but not in vision.

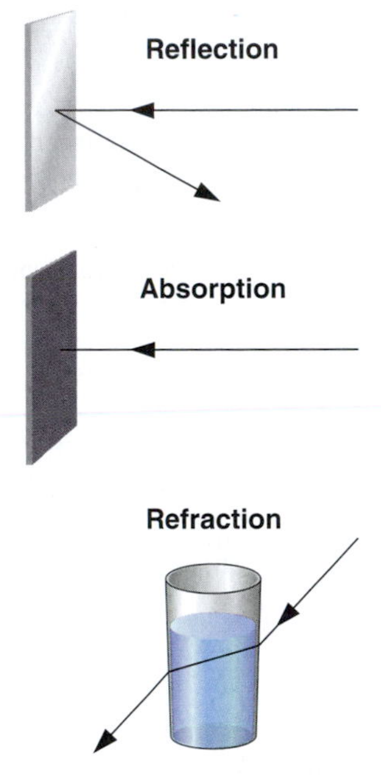

FIGURE 6.4
Light Interacts with the Environment Most of the light we see is reflected, or bent back, from objects. We do not see light that is absorbed by objects, although we can feel the energy as heat. Light is bent, or refracted, as it travels through air or water.

Absorption, Reflection, and Refraction

As shown in Figure 6.4, objects can absorb, reflect, or refract electromagnetic radiation. In some cases, an object's physical characteristics will absorb or retain certain wavelengths. In other cases, light is reflected from the surface of objects, or bent back toward the source. Most of the light energy entering the eye has been reflected from objects in the environment.

Absorption and **reflection** determine the colors we see. The color of an object is not some intrinsic characteristic of the object but, rather, the result of the wavelengths of light that are selectively absorbed and reflected by the object. Instead of saying that my sweater is red, it is more accurate to say that my sweater has physical characteristics that reflect long wavelengths of visible light (perceived as red) and absorb shorter wavelengths. "Light-colored" clothing keeps us cooler because materials perceived as white or light-colored reflect more electromagnetic energy. "Dark" clothing keeps us warmer because these materials absorb more electromagnetic energy. You can easily demonstrate this concept by timing the melting of ice cubes in sunlight when one ice cube is covered by a white piece of cloth and the other by a black piece of cloth.

Air and water **refract,** or change the direction of, traveling waves of light in different ways. Because human eyes developed for use in air, they don't work as well underwater. To see clearly underwater, we need goggles or a face mask to maintain a bubble of air next to the eye. Consequently, even though our bodies are underwater, our eyes remain exposed to light that has been refracted by air, and they function normally. Fish

nanometer (nan-AH-met-er) A unit of measurement equaling 10^{-9} m used to measure wave frequency.
absorption The ability to retain something rather than reflect or transmit it to another location.
reflection The bending back of light toward its source.
refraction The deflection, or changing of direction, of light at a boundary such as that between air and water.

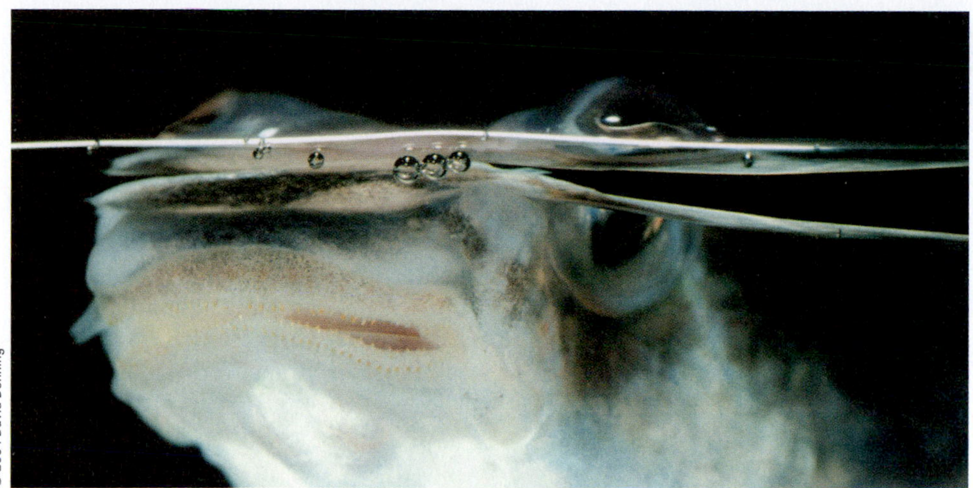

■ **FIGURE 6.5**
A Novel Solution to the Problem of Needing to See in Both Air and Water To catch the water-borne insects that make up its diet and to avoid predators, *Anableps anableps* must see both above and below the water. Normally, eyes that are designed to see in air will provide blurry images underwater. *Anableps* solves the dilemma with its unique eyes, each of which has two pupils—one above and one below the water. Locals refer to *Anableps* as "cuatros ojos," or "four eyes."

eyes are perfectly adapted to a life underwater. To focus light properly as it is refracted by water, the outer surface of the fish eye is rippled, which reduces distortion or blurriness. In addition, the *lens* of the eye, which acts like a magnifying glass, is configured differently for viewing light through air or water. The human lens is shaped like an aspirin tablet, whereas the fish lens is shaped like a sphere. Some organisms, such as diving birds, move in and out of the water, which poses difficulty for either the human or fish eye. The cormorant solves the problem of blurry underwater vision with a special eyelid that closes when the bird dives after a fish. The nearly transparent eyelids act like built-in goggles and maintain the clarity of the bird's vision while underwater. The *Anableps anableps* of Central and South America, shown in ■Figure 6.5, swims with its eyes half in and half out of the water. Each eye has two pupils, one above and one below the water. The upper half of *Anableps*' eye is designed to see light coming through air, whereas the lower half is adapted to light moving through the water. Local people refer to the fish as "cuatro ojos," or "four eyes."

INTERIM SUMMARY 6.1

Summary Table: Features of Light as a Stimulus

Feature	Significance
Wavelength	Distance between peaks of the waves; determines the perceived color of objects.
Amplitude	Height of the wave; determines brightness.
Absorption	Objects that absorb more visible light energy appear dark-colored.
Reflection	Objects that reflect more visible light energy appear light-colored. We perceive the reflected wavelengths as the color of an object.
Refraction	Refraction, as by air and water molecules, changes the direction of light.

Summary Points

1. Human vision responds to the visible light portion of the electromagnetic radiation spectrum. Electromagnetic radiation can be described in terms of waves or as the movement of large numbers of particles known as photons. **(LO1)**
2. Visible light interacts with objects in the environment in ways that make light a useful source of information. Light is plentiful, travels in a fairly straight line, and reflects off many objects. **(LO1)**

Review Questions

1. What are the advantages of being able to see in the visible light spectrum as compared with other portions of the electromagnetic spectrum?
2. What do we mean by absorption, reflection, and refraction of light waves?

The Structures and Functions of the Visual System

Seeing is not always believing.
Martin Luther King, Jr.

We begin our discussion of visual processing at the eye. Animals have different solutions for the exact placement of the eyes in the head. Some have eyes in front like humans and cats, whereas others have eyes on the sides of the head, as do rabbits and horses. As we will see later in this chapter, having eyes in the front of the head provides superior depth perception that is advantageous for hunting (and handy for playing basketball). The eyes-on-the-side placement is usually found in prey species and allows these animals to scan large areas of the environment for predators while feeding.

Protecting the Eye

A number of mechanisms are designed to support and protect the eye. Eyes are located in the bony **orbit** of the skull, which can deflect many blows. In addition, the eye is cushioned by fat. When people are starving, they show a characteristic hollow-eyed look due to the loss of this important fat cushion.

A second line of defense is provided by the eyelids. The eyelids can be opened and closed either voluntarily or involuntarily. Involuntary closure of the eyelids, or a **blink,** both protects the eye from incoming objects and moistens and cleans the front of the eye. Under most circumstances, we blink about once every four to six seconds (Burr, 2005). Surprisingly, we don't see these periods as mini-blackouts. Blinks are correlated with less activity in the prefrontal cortex and other areas believed to participate in consciousness (Bristow et al., 2005). We might not respond to the sudden blackouts produced by a blink because parts of the brain that would normally provide awareness of such an event are also less active.

Tears, another feature of the eyes' protective system, are produced in the lacrimal gland at the outer corner of each eye. The fluid is composed primarily of water and salt but also contains proteins, glucose, and substances that kill bacteria. Tears flush away dust and debris and moisten the eye so that the eyelids don't scratch the surface during blinks. Tears that are shed in response to emotional events contain about 24 percent more protein than tears responding to irritants, such as onions, but the exact purposes of this difference remain unknown (Frey, DeSota-Johnson, Hoffman, & McCall, 1981).

WHY DOES THIS MATTER?

Why Do We Cry?

Understanding our own emotional tears and those of other people matters because crying serves as an important means of nonverbal communication and possibly contributes to stress reduction.

Most mammals have the capability of shedding tears, but usually do so only when in pain. Humans, and possibly elephants and gorillas, seem to be the only species that respond to strong emotions by crying. We have already seen that the composition of emotional tears is quite different from tears shed in response to onions, but what purpose might these emotional tears serve?

One hypothesis suggests that the composition of emotional tears actually helps us rid the body of several proteins that are associated with stress (Frey, DeSota-Johnson, Hoffman, & McCall, 1981). Literally, we should feel better after removing these chemicals during a good cry. A second line of reasoning suggests that crying is a form of communication. Beginning in infancy, we learn to cry to get help. Of course, crying produces both visual and auditory cues. Hearing a baby's wail definitely motivates us to investigate, but most parents can tell you that seeing a child's face covered in tears stimulates stronger emotional responses. By crying as adults, we may be still communicating nonverbally to others, especially when strong emotions make it difficult for us to talk. Actors and actresses work very hard to train themselves to shed tears on cue because this behavior convinces us that we are seeing true grief and sadness.

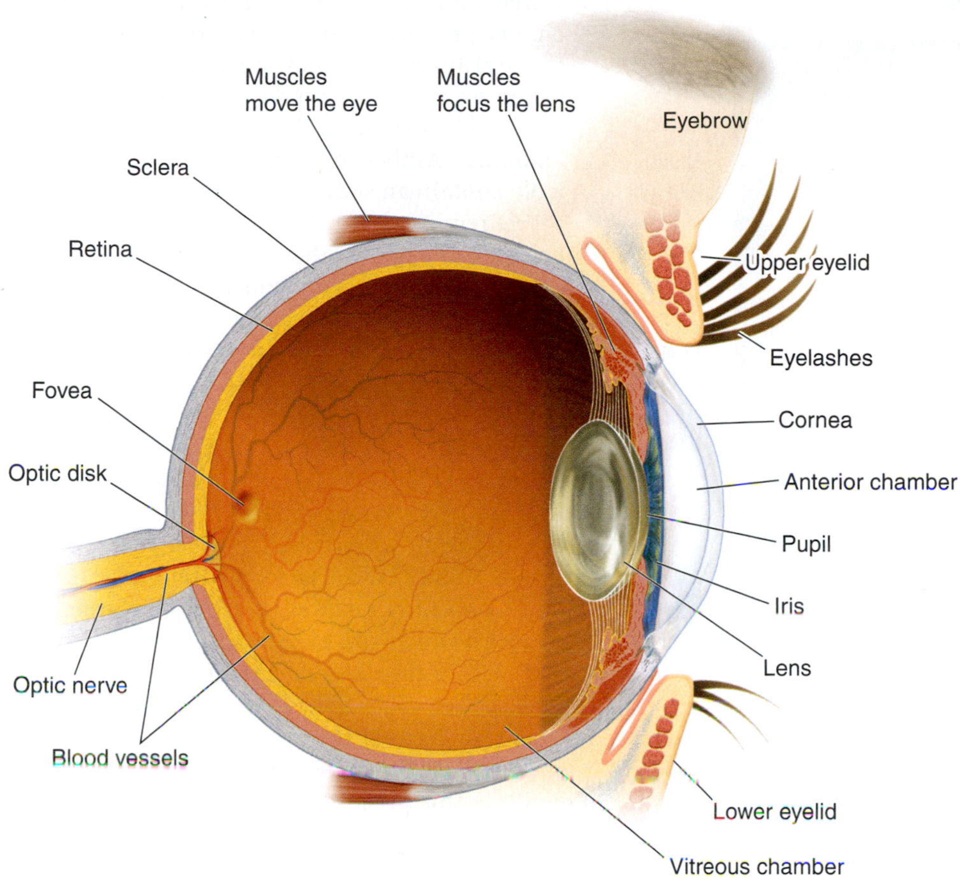

FIGURE 6.6
The Structure of the Eye

THE ANATOMY OF THE EYE

The human eye is roughly a sphere with a diameter of about 24 mm, just under one inch, and individual variations are very small, no more than 1 or 2 mm. Newborns' eyes are about 16–17 mm in diameter (about 6/10 of an inch) and attain nearly their adult size by the age of 3 years. The "white" of the eye, or **sclera,** provides a tough outer covering that helps the fluid-filled eyeball maintain its shape. The major anatomical features of the eye are illustrated in Figure 6.6.

Light entering the eye first passes through the outer layer, or **cornea.** Because the cornea is curved, it begins the process of bending or refracting light rays to form an image in the back of the eye. The cornea is actually a clear, blood vessel–free extension of the sclera. Special proteins on the surface of the cornea discourage the growth of blood vessels (Cursiefen et al., 2006). The lack of a blood supply and the orderly alignment of the cornea's fiber structure make it transparent. As living tissue, the cornea still requires nutrients, but it obtains them from the fluid in the adjacent **anterior chamber** rather than from blood. This fluid is known as the **aqueous humor.** The cornea has the dubious distinction of having a greater density of pain receptors than nearly any other part of the body.

After light travels through the cornea and the aqueous humor of the anterior chamber, it next enters the **pupil.** The pupil is actually an opening formed by the circular muscle of the **iris,** which comes from the Greek word for rainbow. The iris adjusts the opening of the pupil in response to the amount of light present in the environment. Pupil diameter is also affected by your emotional state through the activity of the autonomic nervous system. The color of the iris is influenced primarily by its amount of melanin pigment, which varies from brown to black, in combination with the reflection and absorption of light by other elements in the iris such as its blood supply and connective tissue. The irises of people with blue or gray eyes contain relatively less melanin than the irises of people with brown eyes. Consequently, some

orbit The bony opening in the skull that houses the eyeball.
blink A rapid closing of the eyelids.
sclera (SKLARE-uh) The white outer covering of the eye.
cornea (KOR-nee-uh) The transparent outer layer of the eye.
anterior chamber The area of the eye located directly behind the cornea, containing aqueous humor.
aqueous humor (A-kwee-us) The fluid located in the anterior chamber that nourishes the cornea and lens.
pupil The opening in the front of the eye controlled by the iris.
iris The circular muscle in the front of the eye that controls the opening of the pupil.

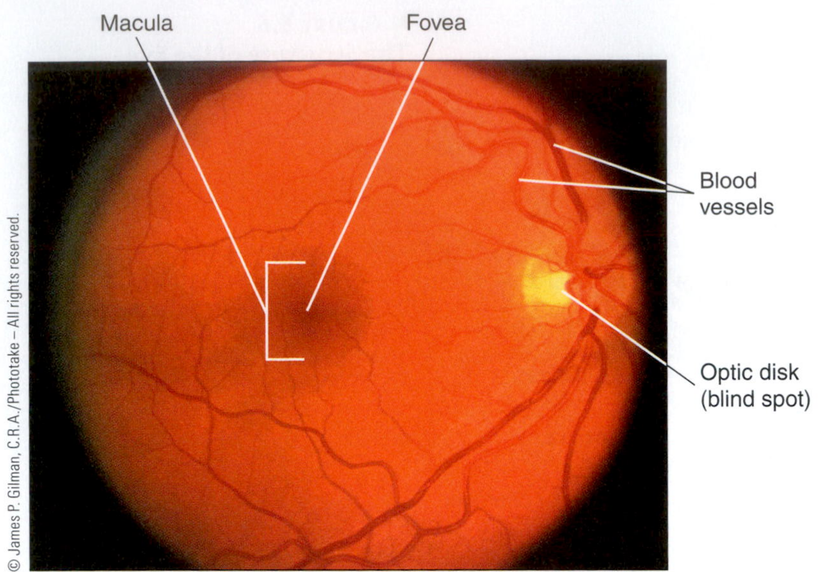

■ **FIGURE 6.7**
Landmarks of the Retina Blood vessels serving the eye and the axons of the **optic nerve** exit the eye in the optic disk. The macula is an area of the retina not covered by blood vessels. Within the macula is a small pit, known as the fovea. Detailed vision is best for images projected onto the macula and fovea.

wavelengths are reflected and scattered from the blue or gray iris in ways that are similar to light in the atmosphere, which is also perceived as blue. Green eyes contain a moderate amount of melanin, and brown or black eyes contain the greatest amounts. "Amber" eyes, brown eyes with a golden look, contain an additional yellowish pigment.

Directly behind the iris is the **lens.** The lens helps focus light on the retina in the back of the eye and functions very much like the lens of a camera. Like the cornea, the lens is transparent due to its fiber organization and lack of blood supply. It, too, depends on the aqueous humor for nutrients. Muscles attached to the lens allow us to adjust our focus as we look at objects near to us or far away. This process is called **accommodation.**

The major interior chamber of the eye, known as the **vitreous chamber,** is filled with a jellylike substance called **vitreous humor.** Unlike the aqueous humor, which circulates and is constantly renewed, the vitreous humor you have today is the same vitreous humor with which you were born. Under certain circumstances, you can see floaters, or debris, in the vitreous humor, especially as you get older.

Finally, light will reach the **retina** at the back of the eye. The image that is projected on the retina is upside down and reversed relative to the actual orientation of the object being viewed. You can duplicate this process by looking at your image in both sides of a shiny spoon. In the convex, or outwardly curving side, you will see your image normally. If you look at the concave side, you will see your image as your retina sees it. The visual system has no difficulty decoding this image to give us a realistic perception of the actual orientation of objects.

The word retina comes from the Latin word for "fisherman's net." As the name implies, the retina is a thin but complex network containing special light-sensing cells known as **photoreceptors.** The photoreceptors are located in the deepest layer of the retina. Before light can reach the photoreceptors, it must pass through the vitreous humor, numerous blood vessels, and a number of neural layers. We don't normally see the blood vessels and neural layers in our eyes due to an interesting feature of our visual system. Our visual system responds to change and tunes out stimuli that remain constant. Because the blood vessels and neural layers are always present, we don't "see" them.

Several landmarks on the retina can be seen in ■ Figure 6.7. The blood vessels serving the eye and the axons forming the optic nerve exit the back of the eye in a place known as the **optic disk.** This area does not contain any photoreceptors at all, which gives each eye a blind spot. Under normal conditions, we don't notice these blind spots, but you can find your own by following the directions in ■ Figure 6.8.

Toward the middle of the retina, we can see a yellowish area about 6 mm in diameter that is lacking large blood vessels. This area is known as the **macula,** from the Latin word for "spot." When we stare directly at an object, the image of that object is projected by the cornea and lens to the center of the macula. As a result, we say that

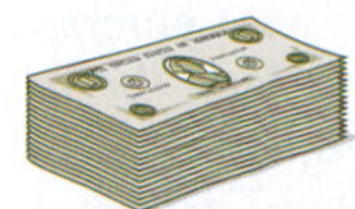

■ **FIGURE 6.8**
Demonstrating the Blind Spot of the Eye There are no photoreceptors in the optic disk, essentially leaving a hole in our vision. Our brain "fills in the hole," so we don't normally see it. Beginning with the book at arm's length, close one eye and focus on the dot. Move the book toward your face until the stack of money "disappears."

lens The clear structure behind the pupil and iris that focuses light on the retina.
accommodation The ability of the lens to change shape to adjust to the distance of the visual stimulus.
vitreous chamber (VIT-ree-us) The large inner cavity of the eyeball.
vitreous humor The jellylike substance contained by the vitreous chamber.
retina The elaborate network of photoreceptors and interneurons at the back of the eye that is responsible for sensing light.
photoreceptor Specialized sensory cell in the retina that responds to light.
optic nerve The fiber pathway formed by the axons of the ganglion cells as they leave the eye.
optic disk The area in the retina where blood vessels and the optic nerve exit the eye.
macula (MACK-you-luh) A 6 mm round area in the retina that is not covered by blood vessels and that is specialized for detailed vision.
central vision The ability to perceive visual stimuli focused on the macula of the retina.

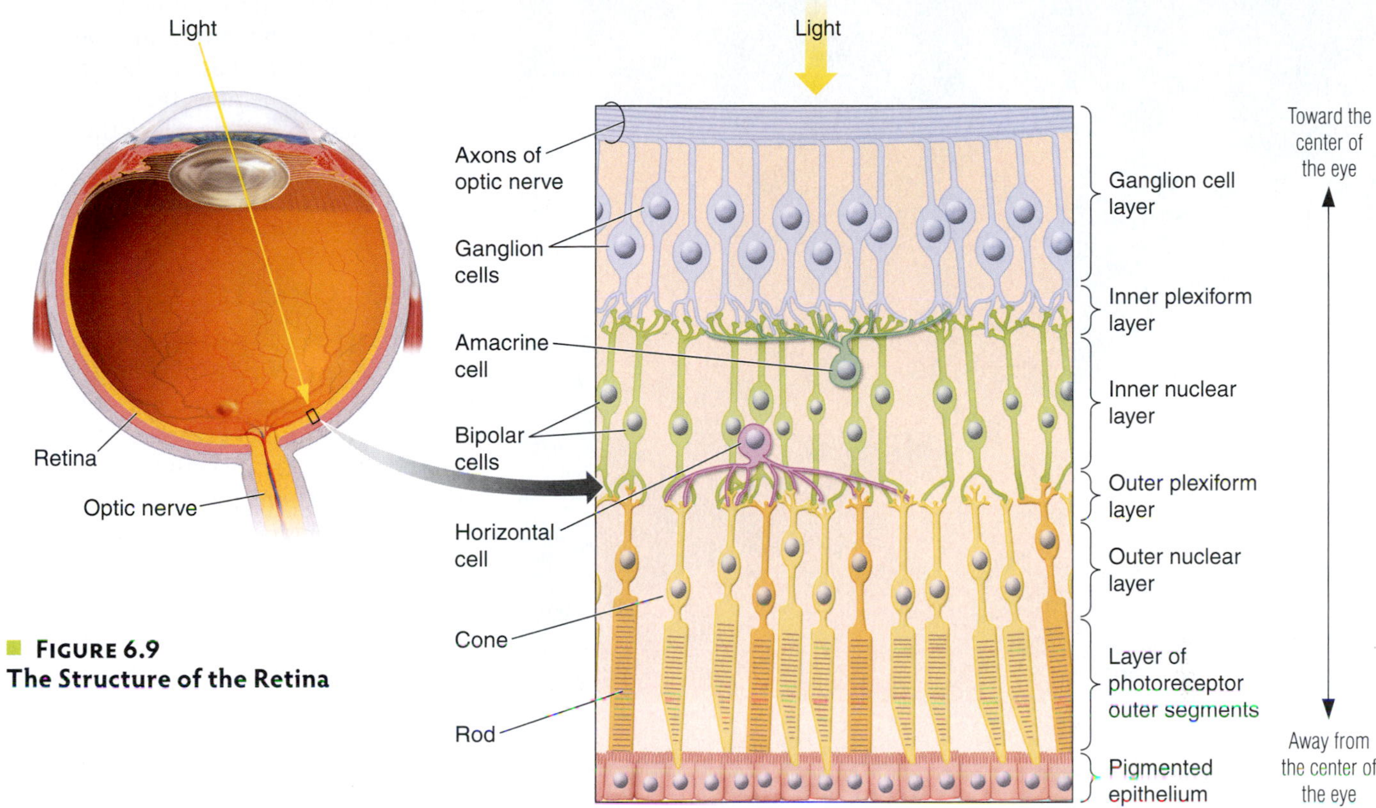

FIGURE 6.9
The Structure of the Retina

the macula is responsible for **central vision** as opposed to **peripheral vision.** Peripheral vision is our ability to see objects that are off to the side while looking straight ahead.

In the very center of the macula, the retina becomes thin and forms a pit. The pit is known as the **fovea,** which is about 1.8 mm in diameter. In humans, the fovea is particularly specialized for detailed vision and contains only one type of photoreceptor, the cones, which permit vision in bright light. Primates, including humans, are the only mammals whose foveas contain only cones. Other mammals, such as cats, have retinal areas that are similar to a fovea, but these contain both cones and the photoreceptors known as rods, which allow vision in dim light.

The retina is embedded in a pigmented layer of cells called the **epithelium.** These cells support the photoreceptors and absorb random light. Because of this absorption of random light, the interior of the eye looks black when seen through the pupil. When a bright light source, such as a camera flash, is pointed directly at the eye, we see the reflection of the true red color of the retina that results from its rich blood supply. The shine we see reflected from the eyes of some animals at night has a different origin. Although it is normally advantageous to reduce reflection in the eye, the epithelium of some nocturnal animals, such as the cat, contains a white compound that acts more like a mirror. By reflecting light through the eye a second time, the odds of perceiving very dim lights at night are improved.

The Layered Organization of the Retina

Although it is only 0.3 mm thick, the retina contains several layers of neurons and their connections, illustrated in Figure 6.9. Three layers of cell bodies are separated by two layers of axons and dendrites.

The retina's first layer is the **ganglion cell layer.** Each ganglion cell has a single axon, and these axons form the optic nerve as it leaves the retina. In the **inner plexiform layer,** the dendrites of ganglion cells form connections with the **amacrine** and **bipolar cells.** The cell bodies of the bipolar, amacrine, and horizontal cells are located in the **inner nuclear layer.** In the **outer plexiform layer,** the bipolar cells form

peripheral vision The ability to perceive visual stimuli that are off to the side while looking straight ahead.

fovea (FOH-vee-uh) A small pit in the macula specialized for detailed vision.

epithelium (ep-i-THEE-lee-um) The pigmented layer of cells supporting the photoreceptors of the retina.

ganglion cell layer The layer of retinal interneurons farthest from the photoreceptors, which contains ganglion cells and gives rise to the optic nerve.

inner plexiform layer The location in the retina containing axons and dendrites that connect the ganglion, bipolar, and amacrine cells.

amacrine cell (AM-uh-krin) A retinal interneuron in the inner nuclear layer that integrates signals across adjacent segments of the retina.

bipolar cell A cell in the inner nuclear layer of the retina that forms part of the straight pathway between the photoreceptors and the ganglion cells.

inner nuclear layer The layer of retinal interneurons containing amacrine, bipolar, and horizontal cells.

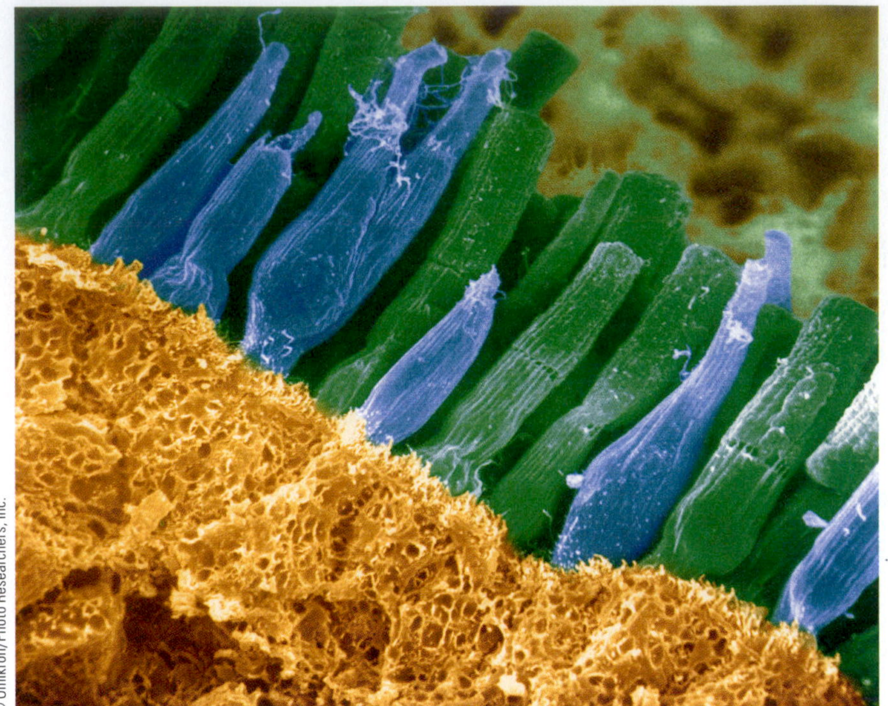

■ **FIGURE 6.10**
Rods and Cones The human eye contains approximately 120 million rods and 6 million cones, named after the shapes of their outer segments.

connections with **horizontal cells** and the photoreceptors. The **outer nuclear area** contains the cell bodies of the photoreceptors. If you remember that "inner" in this case refers to layers toward the center of the eye, whereas "outer" refers to layers away from the center of the eye, these terms become more reasonable.

Photoreceptors

The two types of photoreceptors, **rods** and **cones,** are named according to the shape of their **outer segments,** shown in ■ Figure 6.10. The outer segment is the part of the photoreceptor that absorbs light. The outer segment contains **photopigments,** chemicals that interact with incoming light.

The human eye contains about 120 million rods (Schwartz, 1994). Rods are responsible for **scotopic vision,** or the ability to see in dim light. Rods have a long, cylinder-shaped outer segment containing large numbers of disks, like a large stack of pancakes. These disks contain a photopigment known as **rhodopsin.** The disks of the rods store large amounts of photopigment, which allows the rods to be about 1,000 times more sensitive to light than cones are. Under ideal conditions, the human eye can see a single photon, or the equivalent of the light from a candle flame 30 miles away (Hecht, Shlaer, & Pirenne, 1942). The cost for this extraordinary sensitivity to light is in the clarity and color of the image provided by the rods. Rods do not provide any information about color, and they do not produce sharp images. At night under starlight, our vision is no better than 20/200. An object seen at night from a distance of only 20 feet would have the same clarity as the object viewed from a distance of 200 feet at high noon. It's a good idea to keep that fact in mind while driving at night.

There are only about 6 million cones in the human eye. Cones are responsible for **photopic vision,** or vision in bright light. Photopic vision is sensitive to color and provides images with excellent clarity. The outer segment of cones is shorter and more pointed than that of the rods. Cones store one of three different photopigments in a folded membrane rather than in disks, as the rods do. Because cones work best in bright light, we do not really see color at night. We might know that we're wearing a green sweater, and, in a sense, we may think it looks green as a result of that memory, but we require fairly bright light and the action of our cones to truly see the color. Table 6.1 summarizes the differences between scotopic and photopic vision.

As we move from the fovea to the outer margins of the primate retina, the concentration of rods increases and the number of cones decreases. As a result, the center of the retina is superior for seeing fine detail and color in the presence of bright light, whereas the periphery is superior for detecting very dim light. Because of this uneven distribution of rods and cones across the retina, we see better in dim light when we do not look directly at an object. Prior to the advent of night goggles, soldiers traveling at night were trained to look slightly to the side of a location where they suspected enemy movement, rather than straight at the location. Stargazers know that if you look directly at a dim star, it tends to disappear, but if you shift your vision a little to the side, the star becomes visible once again.

Transduction by Photoreceptors **Transduction** is the process of translating a physical stimulus into electrical signals that can be understood and processed by the nervous system. In vision, photoreceptors transduce light energy into electrical signals that can be sent to the brain for further processing. Because rods and cones transduce light energy in similar ways, we will focus on the process as carried out by rods.

outer plexiform layer The retinal layer containing axons and dendrites forming connections between bipolar cells, horizontal cells, and the photoreceptors.
horizontal cell A retinal interneuron located in the inner nuclear layer that integrates signals from across the surface of the retina.
outer nuclear area The location in the retina containing the cell bodies of the photoreceptors.
rod A photoreceptor that responds to low levels of light but not to color.
cone A photoreceptor that operates in bright conditions and responds differentially to color.
outer segment The portion of a photoreceptor containing photopigments.
photopigment A pigment contained in the photoreceptors of the eye that absorbs light.
scotopic vision (skoh-TOP-ik) The ability to perceive visual stimuli in near darkness due to the activity of rods.
rhodopsin (roh-DOP-sin) The photopigment found in rods.

TABLE 6.1 Scotopic and Photopic Vision

	Scotopic Vision (Dim Light)	Photopic Vision (Bright Light)
Photoreceptor used	**Rods**	**Cones**
Peak wavelength sensitivity	502 nm	420 nm (blue or short-wavelength cones) 530 nm (green or medium-wavelength cones) 560 nm (red or long-wavelength cones)
Ability to distinguish color	None	Color sensitive
Sensitivity to dim light	Excellent	Poor
Acuity	Poor	Excellent
Location of photoreceptors in the retina	Primarily in the periphery	Primarily in the fovea

Rhodopsin, the photopigment found in rods, has two parts, **opsin** and **retinal.** Opsin is a protein chain, whereas retinal is a chemical made from vitamin A. Vitamin A deficiencies can negatively affect your supply of rhodopsin, so eating carrots, which are rich sources of vitamin A, can truly improve your night vision. When retinal is bound with opsin, the resulting molecule of rhodopsin has a tail that bends at carbon atom number 11. Consequently, this is known as the **11-cis** form of the photopigment. When light enters the eye, photons are absorbed by rhodopsin molecules. As shown in ■ Figure 6.11, the absorption of light energy changes the retinal from the 11-cis form to the **all-trans** form. This change in structure causes the rhodopsin molecule to break apart rapidly. To understand what happens next, we need to understand the normal resting state of the photoreceptors.

The Dark Current Photoreceptors operate differently from most neurons. In the generic neuron we discussed in Chapter 3, the membrane potential at rest was approximately −70mV. In contrast, the resting potential of a rod outer segment in complete darkness is about −30mV. In other words, photoreceptors are relatively depolarized (more positive) even when they are resting. Fesenko, Kolesnikov, and Lyubarsky (1985) discovered that rods are constantly depolarized by the inward movement of sodium ions through the outer-segment membrane. This movement of positive ions into the resting photoreceptor is known as the **dark current** because it occurs in the dark.

Sodium channels in neurons are typically kept closed when the cells are at rest. However, Fesenko and his colleagues (1985) showed that sodium channels in rods are kept open by a second messenger, **cyclic guanosine monophosphate (cGMP),** which is constantly produced by the photoreceptor. When rhodopsin molecules break apart after absorbing light energy, enzymes that break down cGMP are released. With less cGMP available, fewer sodium channels remain open, and fewer positive sodium ions enter the cell. The photoreceptor becomes more negative, or hyperpolarized (Baylor, 1987).

When the rod returns to darkness, enzymes stimulate the molecules of retinal and opsin to rejoin as rhodopsin. Rhodopsin takes about 30 minutes to regenerate (Rushton, 1961). This relatively slow regeneration process explains the gradual improvement in vision that takes place when we move from bright sunlight into a darkened theater.

The end result is that photoreceptors are depolarized in the dark and hyperpolarized in the presence of light. Photoreceptors produce graded potentials (signals that vary in size) rather than action potentials. Bright light leads to greater hyperpolarization, whereas dim light leads to less hyperpolarization. Like ordinary neurons, photoreceptors release neurotransmitters (the excitatory neurotransmitter glutamate in this case) when depolarized. Photoreceptors release the largest amounts of glutamate while in the dark. When exposure to light produces hyperpolarization, the photoreceptor responds by releasing less glutamate. This might

photopic vision (foe-TOP-ik) The ability to perceive visual stimuli under bright light conditions due to the activity of cones.

transduction The process of translating a physical stimulus into neural signals.

opsin A protein found in photopigments.

retinal A chemical contained in rhodopsin that interacts with absorbed light.

11-cis The form taken by retinal while it is bound to opsin in the absence of light.

all-trans The form taken by retinal after light is absorbed by the rod outer segment.

dark current The steady depolarization maintained by photoreceptors when no light is present.

cyclic guanosine monophosphate (cGMP) (SIE-klik GWAN-oh-seen moh-noh-FOSS-fate) A second messenger within photoreceptors that is responsible for maintaining the dark current by opening sodium channels.

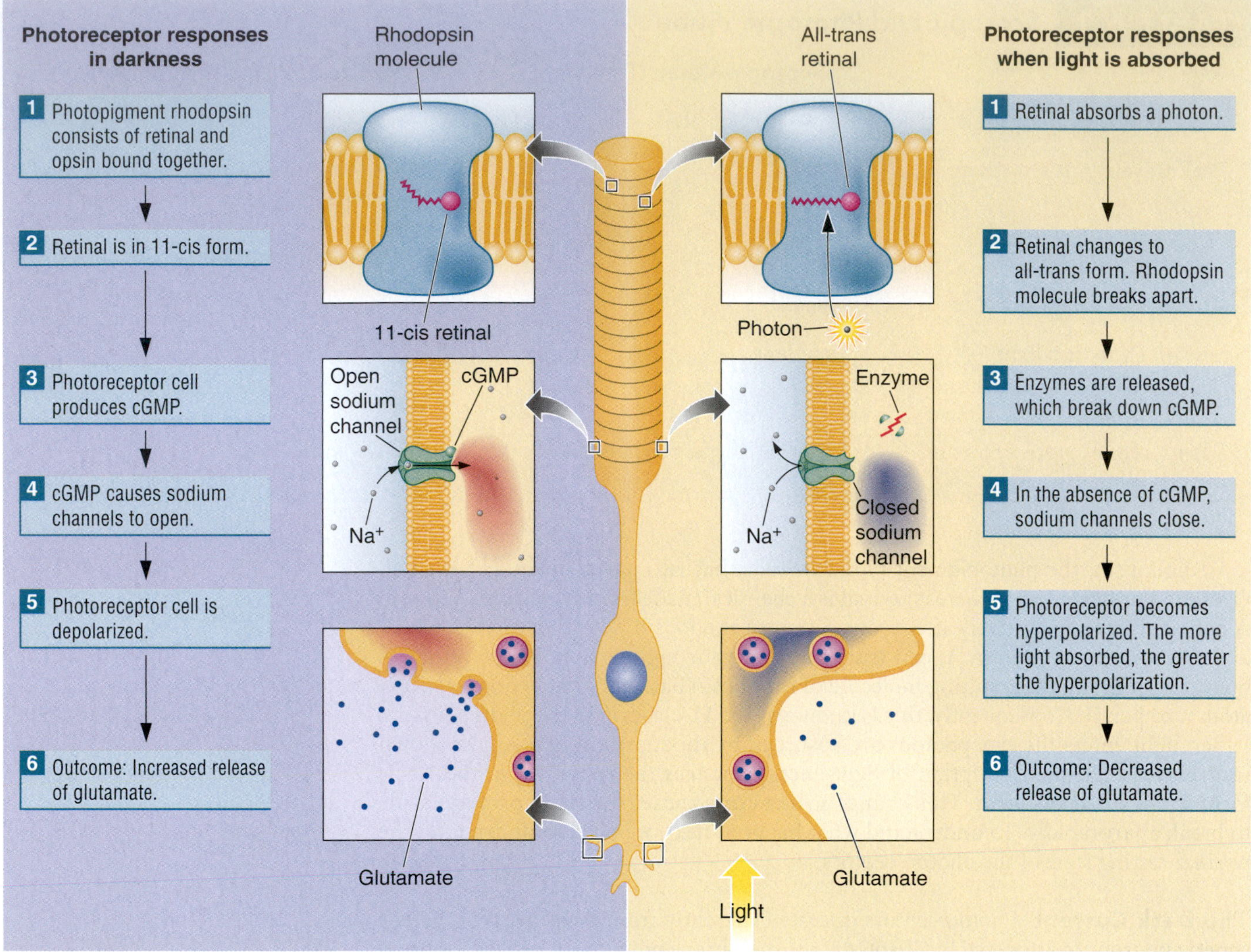

2 Retinal is in 11-cis form.

11-cis retinal

All-trans retinal

1 Retinal absorbs a photon.

FIGURE 6.11
Transduction in the Rod

FIGURE 6.12
The Responses of Rods and Cones to Different Wavelengths The photopigments contained in rods and cones show peak sensitivities to lights of different wavelengths.

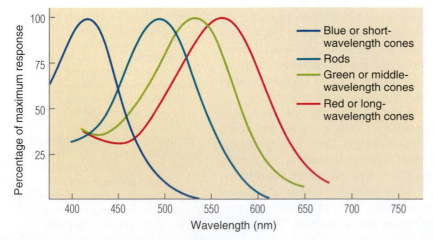

appear counterintuitive to you because stimulation by light is actually turning off the receptors. Rest assured that the cells upstream of the photoreceptors (bipolar and horizontal cells) are fully capable of sorting out this strange input.

DIFFERENCES BETWEEN RODS AND CONES

As you can see in Figure 6.12, rods and cones respond to a wide range of wavelengths, but their photopigments each have different peak sensitivities. There are three classes of cones. The so-called blue or short-wavelength cones, which contain the photopigment cyanolabe, respond maximally to wavelengths of 419 nm (violet). The green, or middle-wavelength cones, containing chlorolabe, have peak responses to 531 nm (green), and the red or long-wavelength cones, containing erythrolabe, peak at 558 nm (yellow; Dartnall, Bowmaker, & Mollon, 1983; Wald & Brown, 1958). The rhodopsin in rods absorbs photons most effectively at wavelengths of 502 nm (a bluish-green).

Rods and cones need different amounts of light to respond. Rhodopsin breaks apart when relatively little light has been absorbed, which explains in part the rods' great sensitivity to low levels of light. The cone photopigments are much more resistant to breaking apart and will do so only in the presence of bright light. This is one of the reasons that cones are active in daylight rather than during the night.

Each of us lives within the universe—the prison—of his own brain. Projecting from it are millions of fragile sensory nerve fibers, in groups uniquely adapted to sample the energetic states of the world around us: heat, light, force, and chemical composition. That is all we ever know of it directly; all else is logical inference.

Vernon Mountcastle

Processing by Retinal Interneurons

The photoreceptors (rods and cones) are the only true receptor cells in the entire visual system. In Figure 6.9, we saw the four other types of cells in the retina that help process information from the photoreceptors. The bipolar and ganglion cells provide a direct pathway for information from the photoreceptors to the brain that is modified by input from the horizontal and amacrine cells. The horizontal and amacrine cells integrate information across the surface of the retina. You can think of the photoreceptor-bipolar-ganglion connections as running perpendicular to the back of the eye, whereas the horizontal and amacrine connections run parallel to the back of the eye.

Horizontal Cells The horizontal cells are located in the inner nuclear layer. They receive input from the photoreceptors and provide output to another type of cell in the inner nuclear layer, the bipolar cell. The major task of horizontal cells is to integrate information from photoreceptors that are close to one another. The spreading structure of the horizontal cell is well suited to this task. Like the photoreceptors, horizontal cells communicate through the formation of graded potentials rather than of action potentials.

Bipolar Cells Bipolar cells, also located in the inner nuclear layer, receive input from photoreceptors and from horizontal cells. In turn, bipolar cells communicate with the amacrine cells in the inner nuclear layer and with ganglion cells. Like the photoreceptors and horizontal cells, bipolar cells produce graded potentials rather than action potentials.

Rather than responding to the total amount of light present, bipolar cells begin the process of identifying contrast, or the relative amount of light falling on one area of the retina as opposed to that falling on another area. Bipolar cells accomplish this task by responding to light falling on photoreceptors located in the bipolar cells' **receptive fields,** a type of organization we will see repeated throughout the visual system as well as in other sensory systems, such as touch. Any single visual interneuron, such as a bipolar cell, receives input from a single set of photoreceptors located in a specific area on the retina. That area is referred to as the interneuron's receptive field (Hartline, 1938). You can think about the retina as a mosaic of receptive fields. If a pinpoint light is directed to the retina, it is possible to identify which interneurons are responding to the light by recording their activity. A light stimulus must fit within a cell's receptive field to influence its activity. The cell is "blind" to light falling outside its receptive field on the retina.

Let's imagine that we are doing a single-cell recording from one bipolar cell to map its receptive field. When we shine a pinpoint of light into our participant's eye, we find that our bipolar cell depolarizes. When we turn the light off, the cell returns to its normal resting status. If we move our light a little bit to the side, then the cell hyperpolarizes. We have discovered that our bipolar cell has three settings: a neutral resting potential in the absence of stimulation, an on response when it depolarizes, and an off response when it hyperpolarizes. The on-response and off-response areas of the receptive field make up a doughnut shape on the retina, illustrated in ■ Figure 6.13. If we shine light in the center of the doughnut, the bipolar cell depolarizes. Shining a light on the doughnut surrounding the center hyperpolarizes the bipolar cell. A light that covers both center and surround creates an excitatory ("on") response in the center and an inhibitory ("off") response in the surround. These effects cancel each other out, and the cell remains neutral. Cells that depolarize when light hits the center of their receptive field are called on-center. Cells that hyperpolarize when light hits the center of their receptive field are called off-center. About half the bipolar cells in the human retina are on-center, and the other half are off-center.

This arrangement of the receptive fields is referred to as an **antagonistic center-surround organization.** The response of a bipolar cell depends on the amount of light

receptive field A location on the retina at which light affects the activity of a particular visual interneuron.

antagonistic center-surround organization A characteristic of visual interneuron receptive fields, in which light illuminating the center has the opposite effect on the cell's activity as light in the surround.

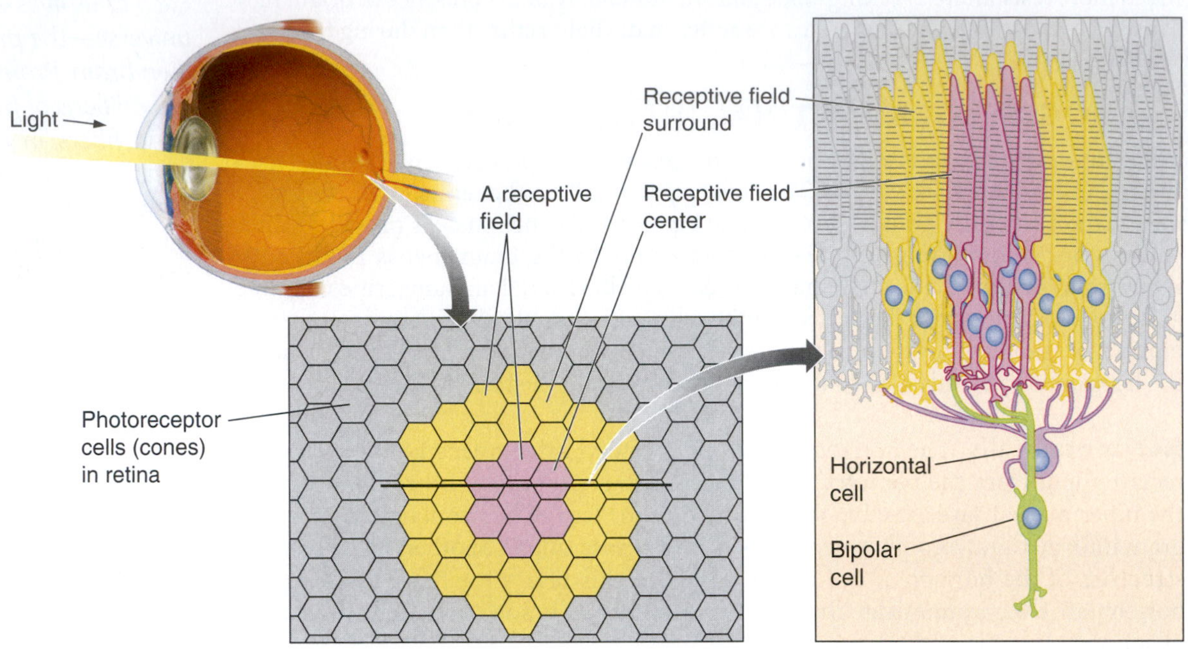

(a) On-Center/Off-Surround Receptive Field of a Bipolar Cell

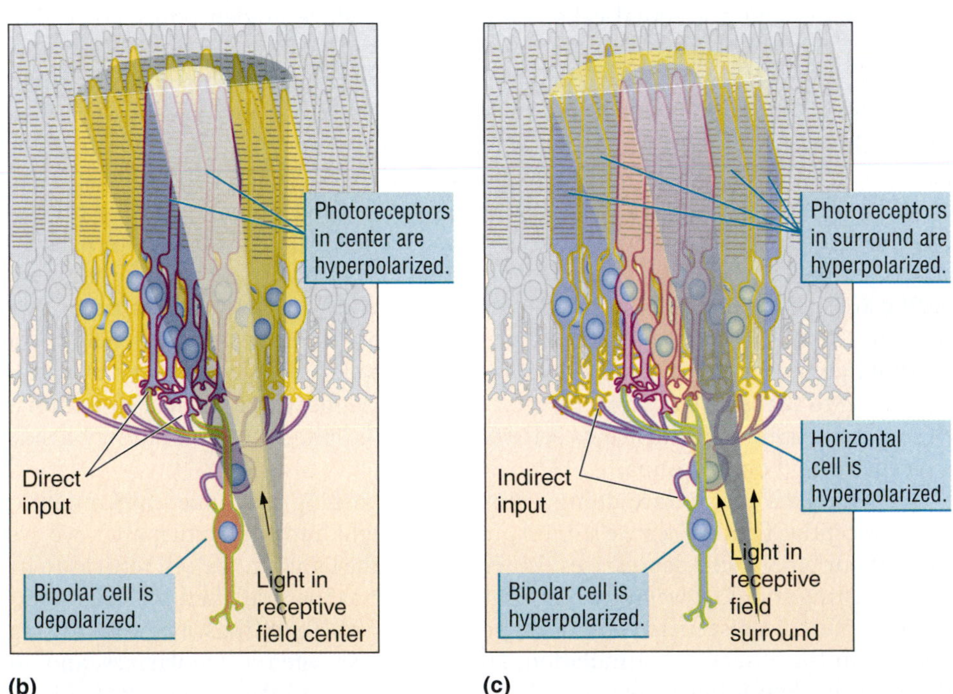

FIGURE 6.13

A Retinal Bipolar Receptive Field In (a), we see that a bipolar cell receives direct input from photoreceptors in the center of its receptive field. The bipolar cell also receives indirect input via horizontal cells connected to photoreceptors in the surround of the receptive field. Light falling on photoreceptors outside the receptive field would have no effect on this particular bipolar cell. Parts (b) and (c) show the response to light of an on-center bipolar cell. In (b), light falls only on the center and depolarizes the bipolar cell. In (c), light falls only on the surround. The bipolar cell hyperpolarizes in response to input from the horizontal cells. The effect of light on the center is always the opposite of the effect of light on the surround. Light falling on both the center and surround would simultaneously produce excitatory and inhibitory influences on the bipolar cell, and its activity would remain unchanged.

falling on its center relative to the amount of light falling on its surround. It is called antagonistic because light falling on the center of the receptive field always has the opposite effect on the cell's activity from light falling on the surround.

Photoreceptors and horizontal cells serving the center (doughnut hole) and surround (the doughnut) compete with each other to activate the bipolar cell in a process

We think too small, like the frog at the bottom of the well. He thinks the sky is only as big as the top of the well. If he surfaced, he would have an entirely different view.
Mao Zedong

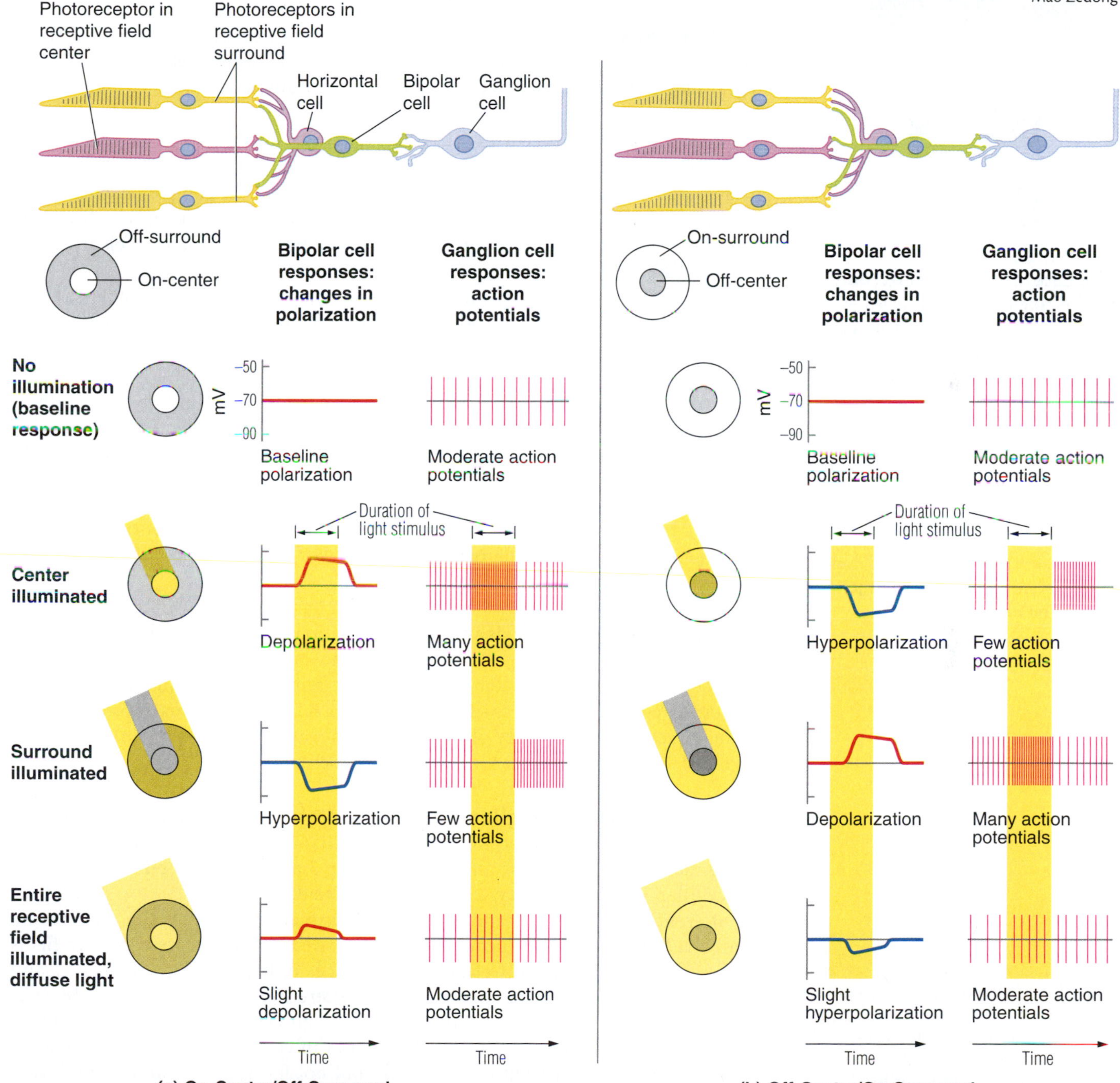

FIGURE 6.14
Receptive Fields of Bipolar and Ganglion Cells The left-hand panel illustrates the responses of an on-center bipolar cell and a ganglion cell with which it communicates to lights of various widths falling in different parts of the receptive field. Light in the center excites the cells, whereas light in the surround inhibits their activity. In the right-hand panel, we see an example of an off-center bipolar cell and one of its associated ganglion cells. Here, the opposite conditions stimulate the cells. Light in the surround excites the cells, whereas light in the center inhibits them.

If only we could pull out our brain and use only our eyes.
Pablo Picasso

known as **lateral inhibition.** *Lateral* means that the process occurs across the surface of the retina. In lateral inhibition, active photoreceptors and horizontal cells limit the activity of neighboring, less active cells. This produces a sharpening, or exaggeration, of the bipolar cells' responses to differences in light falling on adjacent areas. Through lateral inhibition, bipolar cells begin to identify the boundaries of a visual stimulus by making comparisons between light levels falling in adjacent areas of the retina. The message sent by the bipolar cells is "I see an edge or boundary."

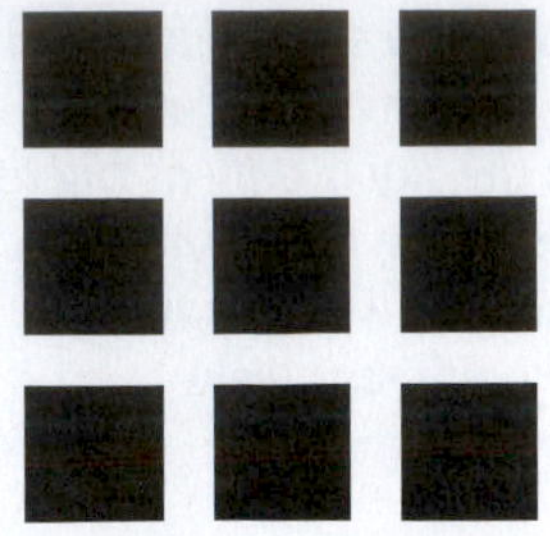

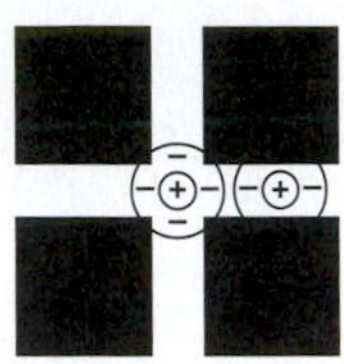

Figure 6.15
The Lateral Inhibition Account of the Hermann Grid When you view the upper image, you will see small gray circles at the intersections that disappear when you look directly at an intersection. In the lower image, we see diagrams of receptive fields superimposed over the grid. Because more of the surround is illuminated at the intersection, the response to the light is reduced, leading to the perception of gray. However, some psychologists prefer explanations for this illusion that involve processing in the visual cortex rather than the retina.

Amacrine Cells Amacrine cells, also located in the inner nuclear layer, form connections with bipolar cells, ganglion cells, and other amacrine cells. In addition to integrating visual messages, amacrine cells process movement.

Ganglion Cells Ganglion cells receive input from bipolar and amacrine cells. Unlike the interneurons and photoreceptors discussed so far, ganglion cells form conventional action potentials. However, ganglion cells are never completely silent. The presence of light simply changes the ganglion cells' spontaneous rate of signaling. The axons of ganglion cells leave the eye and form the optic nerve, which travels to higher levels of the brain.

The human eye has approximately 1 million ganglion cells, yet they must accurately communicate input from about 126 million photoreceptors. The ganglion cells accomplish this editing task through the organization of their receptive fields.

Ganglion Receptive Fields Ganglion receptive fields show the same antagonistic center-surround organization that we observed in the receptive fields of bipolar cells. As shown in Figure 6.14, ganglion cells replicate the information passed to them by the bipolar cells. On-center bipolar cells connect to on-center ganglion cells, whereas off-center bipolar cells connect to off-center ganglion cells. Ganglion cell receptive fields vary in size. Receptive fields vary from 0.01 mm in diameter in the macula to 0.5 mm (50 times larger) in the periphery. Cells with small receptive fields respond best to fine detail.

A classic illusion known as the Hermann grid has traditionally been explained in terms of ganglion receptive fields and lateral inhibition. Small gray circles appear at the intersections of the white stripes. According to the lateral inhibition explanation, the gray circles result from the greater amount of light falling on surrounds at the intersections compared to the stripes, as shown in Figure 6.15. However, many psychologists currently question the accuracy of this explanation, and prefer to explain the illusion in terms of visual processing at the cortical level (Schiller & Carvey, 2005).

The Three Types of Ganglion Cells About 90 percent of human ganglion cells are **P cells** (P stands for parvocellular, or small cells), 5 percent are **M cells** (M stands for magnocellular, or big cells), and the remaining 5 percent are **K cells** (K stands for koniocellular) (Shapley & Perry, 1986; Hendry & Reid, 2000).

Differences among M, P, and K cells are summarized in Table 6.2. M cells are larger than P cells and have thicker, faster axons. M cells have larger receptive fields than P cells. M cells respond to smaller differences in light between the center and surround, whereas P cells require a greater difference. This implies that M cells respond to subtle differences of contrast such as when viewing gray letters on a black background. P cells respond to larger differences in contrast such as when viewing black letters on a white background. M cells, but not P cells, respond to stimuli that are turned on and off rapidly, such as the flicker of a monitor or television screen. A final difference is that P cells respond only to lights of a particular color, whereas M cells respond to light regardless of its color. K cells share most of the characteristics of P cells.

M cells are primarily responsible for providing information about large, low-contrast, moving objects, whereas P cells are responsible for information about smaller, high-contrast, colorful objects. This distinction between magnocellular pathways and parvocellular pathways is preserved up through some of the highest levels of cortical visual processing.

lateral inhibition The process in which active cells limit the activity of neighboring, less active cells.
P cell Retinal ganglion cell that is small and responds to high contrast and color.
M cell Large ganglion cell that responds to all wavelengths regardless of color, subtle differences in contrast, and stimuli that come and go rapidly.
K cells A small percentage of ganglion cells that do not fit the criteria for P or M cells exactly and respond to blue and yellow light.

TABLE 6.2 The Three Types of Ganglion Cells

	M Cells	P Cells	K Cells
Ganglion cells (%)	5 percent	90 percent	5 percent
Apparent purpose	To detect large, low-contrast objects and movement	To provide detailed information about motionless objects, including color	To provide information about color
Response to color	None	Red-green	Blue-yellow
Destination in LGN	Magnocellular layers	Parvocellular layers	Koniocellular layers
Size	Large	Small	Small
Speed	Fast	Slower	Slower
Receptive field size	Large	Small	Small
Sensitivity to contrast	Sensitive to low contrast	Sensitive to high contrast	Sensitive to high contrast
Response to movement	Excellent	Poor	Poor

Optic Nerve Connections

The ganglion cell axons exit the eye through the optic disk, forming an optic nerve leaving each eye. The optic nerves preserve the organization of the retina. In other words, axons from adjacent ganglion cells remain next to one another in the optic nerves.

As shown in ■ Figure 6.16, each human optic nerve divides in half, with the outer half continuing to travel to the same side of the brain (ipsilaterally) while the inner half crosses to the other side of the brain (contralaterally). This partial crossing ensures that information from both eyes regarding the same part of the visual field will be processed in the same places in the brain. If you hold your eyes steady by looking at a focal point, information from the visual field to the left of the focal point will be transmitted to the right hemisphere. Information from the visual field to the right of the focal point will be transmitted to the left hemisphere. In humans, about 50 percent of the fibers from each eye cross to the opposite hemisphere. In rabbits and other animals with eyes placed on the side of the head, 100 percent of the fibers cross the midline to the opposite side. Because each of a rabbit's eyes sees a completely different part of the rabbit's visual field, there is no need for the rabbit to reorganize the input.

The optic nerves cross at the **optic chiasm** (named after its X shape, or chi in Greek). The nerves continue past the optic chiasm as the **optic tracts.** Most of the axons in the optic tract proceed to the thalamus, which in turn projects to the primary visual cortex of the brain. However, a few axons leave the optic tract and synapse in the suprachiasmatic nucleus of the hypothalamus, providing the light information used to regulate daily rhythms (see Chapter 11). About 10 percent of the axons in the optic tract project to the **superior colliculus** in the midbrain.

The Superior Colliculus In many species, including frogs and fish, the superior colliculus is the primary brain structure for processing visual information. Because humans have a cerebral cortex for this purpose, they use the superior colliculus to guide movements of the eyes and head toward newly detected objects in the visual field.

The Lateral Geniculate Nucleus of the Thalamus Most of the remaining 90 percent of optic tract axons form synapses in the **lateral geniculate nucleus (LGN),** located in the dorsal thalamus. As shown in Figure 6.17, the LGN is a layered structure that is bent in the middle. The bend is the source of the name geniculate, which comes

optic chiasm (KEY-azm) The area at the base of the brain where the optic nerves cross to form the optic tracts; the location of a partial decussation of the optic nerves in humans.

optic tracts The fiber pathways between the optic chiasm and destinations in the forebrain and brainstem.

superior colliculus A structure in the tectum of the midbrain that guides movements of the eyes and head toward newly detected objects in the visual field.

lateral geniculate nucleus (LGN) The nucleus within the thalamus that receives input from the optic tracts.

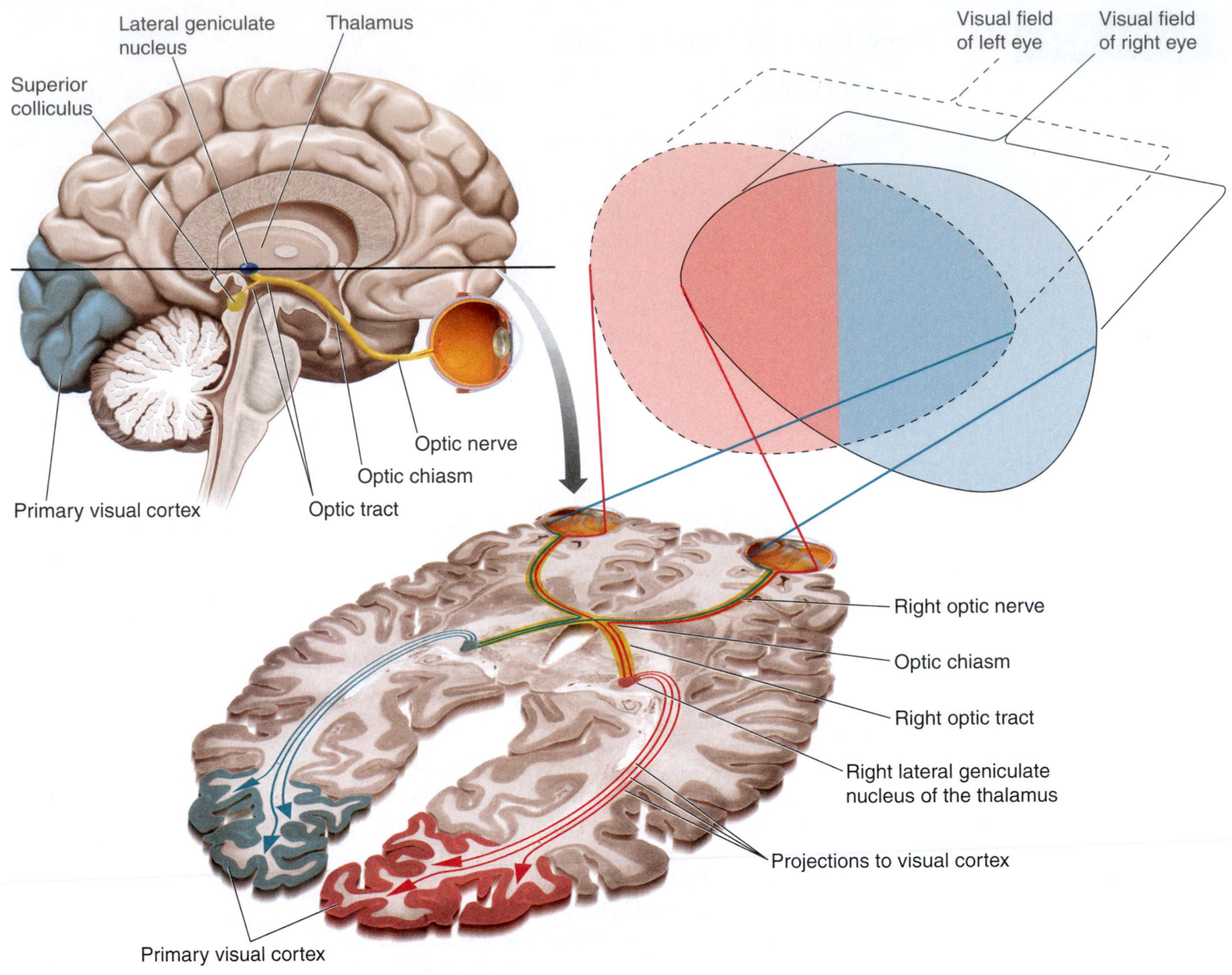

FIGURE 6.16
The Pathways from Eye to Cortex The optic nerves leaving the human eye partially cross at the optic chiasm. As a result, images in the left visual field seen by both eyes go to the right hemisphere, whereas images from the right visual field go to the left hemisphere. From the optic chiasm, most axons in the optic tracts synapse in the lateral geniculate nucleus (LGN) of the thalamus. The LGN sends visual information to the primary visual cortex of the occipital lobe.

from the Latin for "bent knee" (as does the term genuflect, which describes the bending of the knee that Catholics perform prior to entering a pew to worship).

In primates, including humans, the LGN has about the same area as a credit card, but is about three times thicker. The LGN features six distinct stacked layers, numbered from ventral to dorsal. Layers 1 and 2 (the most ventral layers) contain larger neurons than the other four layers. These **magnocellular layers** receive input from the M cells in the retina.. The other four are referred to as **parvocellular layers,** which receive input from the P cells. Between each of the six layers are very small neurons making up the **koniocellular layers,** which receive input from the K cells. The LGN keeps information from the two eyes completely separate. ■ Figure 6.17 shows how alternating layers of the LGN receive input from the ipsilateral and contralateral eyes.

Neurons in the LGN show the same antagonistic center-surround organization of receptive fields that we observed in the retinal bipolar and ganglion cells. In LGN neurons, however, the lateral inhibition between center and surround is much stronger than we observed among retinal cells. This greater inhibition causes cells in the LGN to amplify or boost the contrast between areas of light and dark.

magnocellular layers (mag-noh-CELL-ue-ler) The two ventral layers of the LGN that receive input from M cells in the ganglion layer of the retina.

parvocellular layers (par-voh-CELL-ue-ler) The four dorsal layers of the LGN that receive input from P cells in the ganglion layer of the retina.

koniocellular layers (cone-ee-oh-CELL-ue-ler) Layers of very small neurons between the larger six layers of the lateral geniculate nucleus that receive input from K cells in the ganglion layer of the retina.

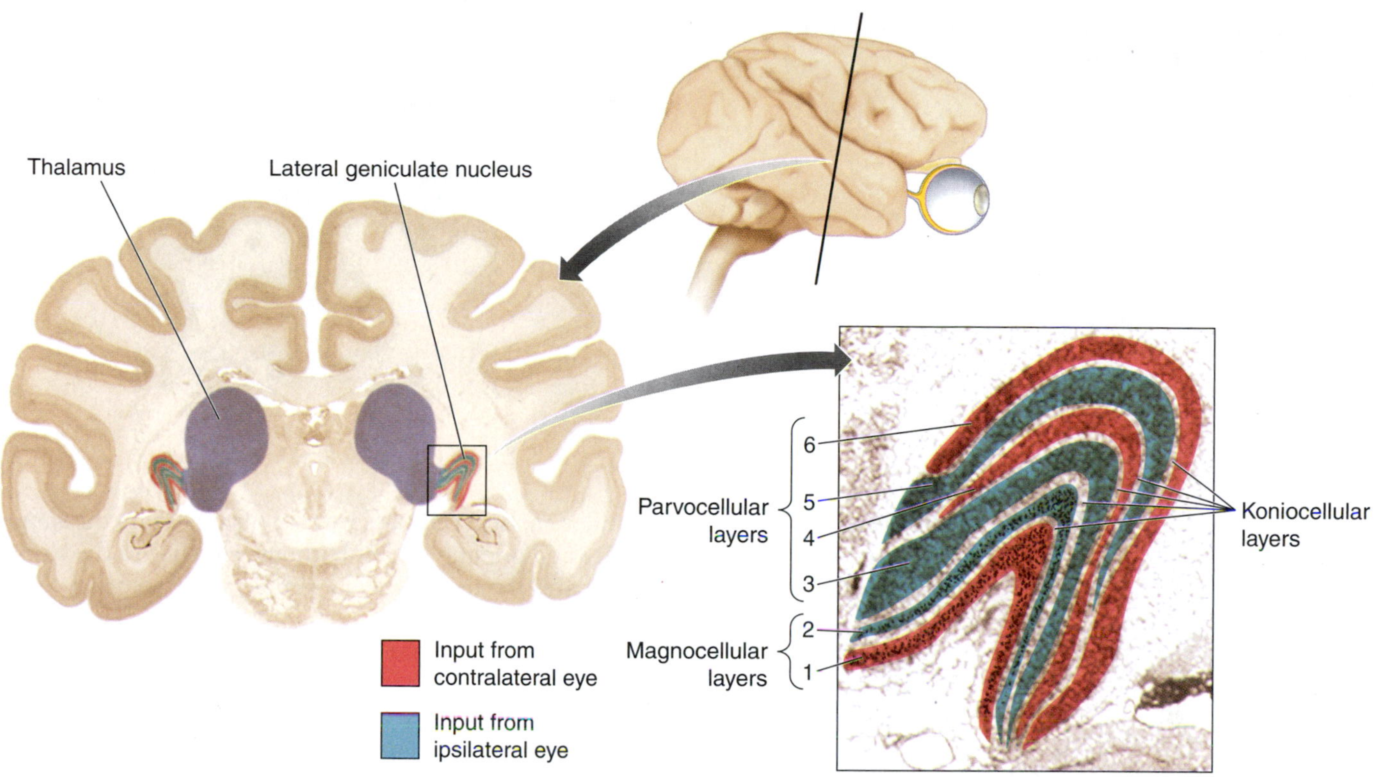

FIGURE 6.17
The Lateral Geniculate Nucleus (LGN) Has a Layered Organization Layers 1 and 2 are the magnocellular layers, which receive input from M cells in the ganglion layer. Layers 3–6 are the parvocellular layers, which receive input from the P cells. Between the six main layers are the koniocellular layers, which receive input from K cells.

Surprisingly, the retina is not the major source of input to the LGN. About 80 percent of the input to the LGN comes from the primary visual cortex, located in the occipital lobe (Sillito, 1995). The function of this input remains unclear. The LGN also receives input from the brainstem reticular formation. This input allows an animal to modify the flow of information to the cortex from the LGN based on its level of arousal and alertness.

The exact role of the LGN in visual processing is not well understood. The LGN might modify input to the cortex based on arousal. The LGN might also organize or sort information prior to sending it to the cortex.

The Striate Cortex

Primary visual cortex is often referred to as **striate cortex,** due to its striped appearance. Striate cortex, located in the occipital lobe, contains approximately 250 million neurons as opposed to the 1 million neurons found in the LGN (Connolly & Van Essen, 1984; Spear, Kim, Ahmad, & Tom, 1996).

The cortex in this area ranges from 1.5 to 2 mm in thickness, or about the height of the letter m on this page. Like other areas of cortex, the striate cortex has six distinct layers, which can be seen in Figure 6.18. Compared with other areas of cortex, striate cortex is relatively thicker in layers II and IV, which receive most of the input from other parts of the brain. Layer IV receives input from the LGN. Striate cortex is thinner in layers III, V, and VI, which contain output neurons that communicate with other parts of the brain.

Cortical Receptive Fields

Although cortical neurons have receptive fields, these fields do not respond to the simple dots of light that activate bipolar and ganglion cells in the retina and cells within the LGN.

Based on a series of meticulous single-cell recording experiments, Hubel and Wiesel (1959) defined **simple cortical cells** as those cells that respond to stimuli shaped like bars or edges that have a particular slant or orientation in a particular location on the retina. These cells probably help us respond to object shape. Simple cortical cell receptive fields maintain an antagonistic center-surround organization, but the shape of the receptive field is more elongated or racetrack-shaped than doughnut-like.

primary visual cortex The location in the occipital lobe for the initial cortical analysis of visual input. Also known as striate cortex.

striate cortex (STRY-ate) Another name for primary visual cortex in the occipital lobe.

simple cortical cell A cell that responds to stimuli in the shape of a bar or edge with a particular slant or orientation in a particular location on the retina.

FIGURE 6.18
The Striate Cortex of the Occipital Lobe Compared with other areas of cortex, primary visual cortex is thicker in layers II and IV, which receive input from other parts of the brain. Layer IV receives input from the lateral geniculate nucleus.

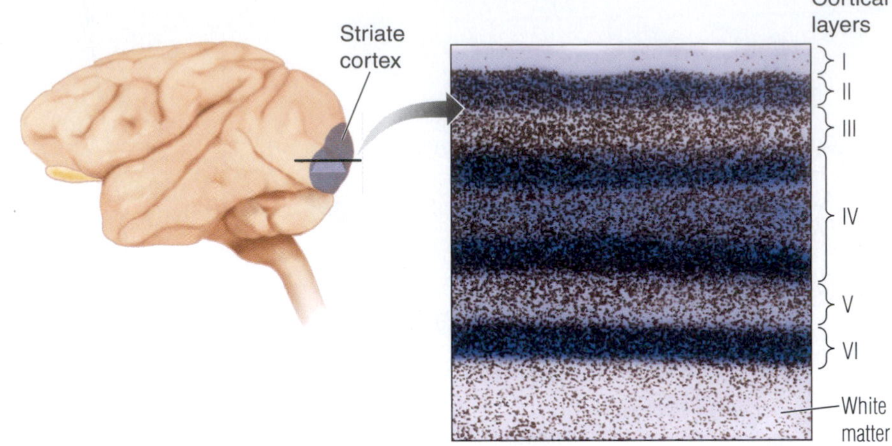

Hubel and Wiesel defined **complex cortical cells** as cortical cells that share the simple cells' preference for stimulus size and orientation but without reference to the stimulus's location. Figure 6.19 compares the responses of a simple and a complex cell to various types of light falling within a receptive field.

Some complex cortical cells respond to lines moving in a particular direction. A cell might respond to a vertical line moving from right to left across the receptive field but not to a line moving left to right. Consequently, complex cortical cells probably participate in the perception of movement (Regan, Beverley, & Cynader, 1979). Fatigue in these directional cells might be responsible for the waterfall illusion (Addams, 1934/1964). If you stare at a waterfall for a minute or two, then look away, the scene being viewed will appear to be moving in an upward direction. This phenomenon occurs due to the temporary fatigue of downward motion detectors.

Cortical Columns If we moved a recording electrode perpendicular to the surface of the cortex, we would find that the neurons are organized in a cortical column. Neurons in cortical columns communicate with one another but do not form many connections with neighboring columns more than half a millimeter away (Mountcastle, 1978).

One type of column found in the striate cortex is known as an **ocular dominance column.** These are columns of cortex perpendicular to the cortical surface that respond to input from either the right eye or the left eye but not to both. These columns take advantage of the strict segregation of input from either eye that we observed in the LGN. The columns are about 1 mm wide and alternate (right eye–left eye–right eye, etc.) across the surface of the visual cortex.

Orientation columns are much thinner than the ocular dominance columns. Each orientation column responds to lines of the same angle. Neighboring columns respond to angles shifted about 10 degrees. Adjacent orientation columns respond to a complete rotation of 180 degrees, 10 degrees at a time. A complete set of these columns, which is about 1 mm wide, is referred to as a **hypercolumn.**

Cytochrome Oxidase Blobs **Cytochrome oxidase blobs** are named after an enzyme, cytochrome oxidase (Hubel & Livingstone, 1987; Livingstone & Hubel, 1984; Wong-Riley, 1989). Areas with high concentrations of cytochrome oxidase appear to process considerable information regarding color.

Cortical Modules We have seen how cortical neurons respond to line orientation, movement, and color. At some point, our visual system puts these separate characteristics back together to form coherent images. Hubel and Wiesel (1962) suggested that the unit responsible for this integration is the **cortical module.** As shown in Figure 6.20, cortical modules include two sets of ocular dominance columns, 16 blobs, and two hypercolumns, each responding to the entire 180 degrees of line orientation. Newer mapping techniques suggest that modules are more accurately viewed as approximations because the boundaries between modules are much less precise than suggested by Hubel and Wiesel (Blasdel, 1992).

complex cortical cell A cortical interneuron that shows a preferred stimulus size and orientation but not location within the visual field.
ocular dominance column A column of cortex perpendicular to the cortical surface that responds to input from either the right or left eye, but not to both.
orientation column A column of primary visual cortex that responds to lines of a single angle.
hypercolumn A complete set of orientation columns.
cytochrome oxidase blob (SIGH-toh-krome OX-i-daze) An area of primary visual cortex rich in the enzyme cytochrome oxidase that responds to color.
cortical module A unit of primary visual cortex containing two sets of ocular dominance columns, 16 blobs, and two hypercolumns.

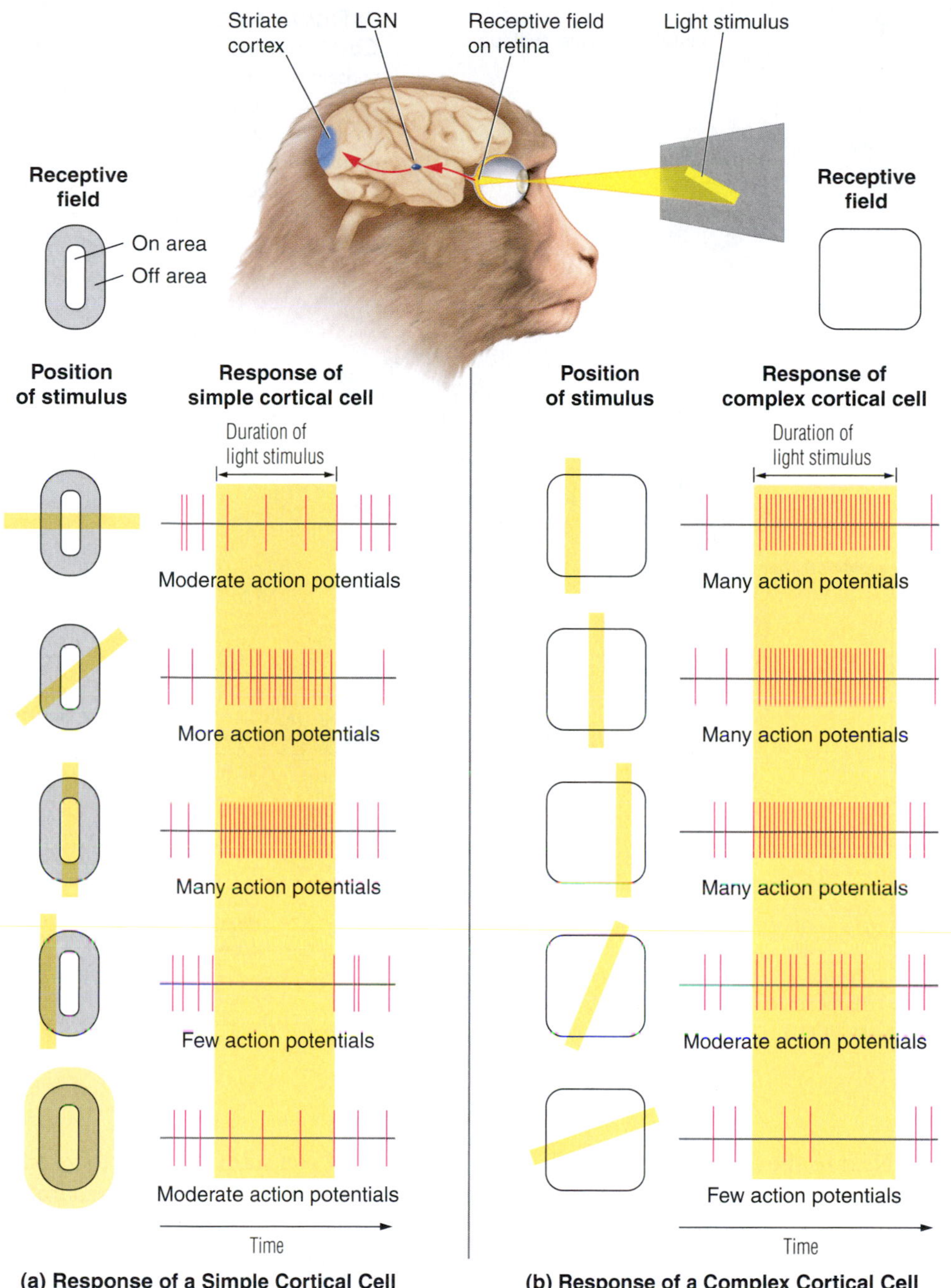

FIGURE 6.19
Cortical Receptive Fields While recording from a simple cortical cell, different patterns of activity result from viewing bars of light with different orientations in a particular location on the retina. Unlike the simple cortical cells, complex cells do not respond to stimuli according to their exact location within the receptive field. However, they share the simple cells' preference for bar orientation and size.

We have about 1,000 modules, and each one makes up a 2 mm × 2 mm area of primary visual cortex. Each module contains the neurons it needs to process the shape, color, and movement of an image falling on a specific part of the retina. You can think of the visual field as a mosaic with 1,000 tiles, each served by a different cortical module. However, different parts of the retina do not get equal amounts of cortical processing space. Although the fovea contains only 0.01 percent of the retina's total area, signals from the fovea are processed by 8 to 10 percent of the striate cortex (Van Essen & Anderson, 1995).

VISUAL ANALYSIS BEYOND THE STRIATE CORTEX

The striate cortex begins, but by no means finishes, the task of processing visual input. At least a dozen additional areas of the human cerebral cortex participate in visual processing. Because these areas are not included in the striate cortex, they are often referred to as extrastriate areas. These areas are also referred to as secondary visual cortex.

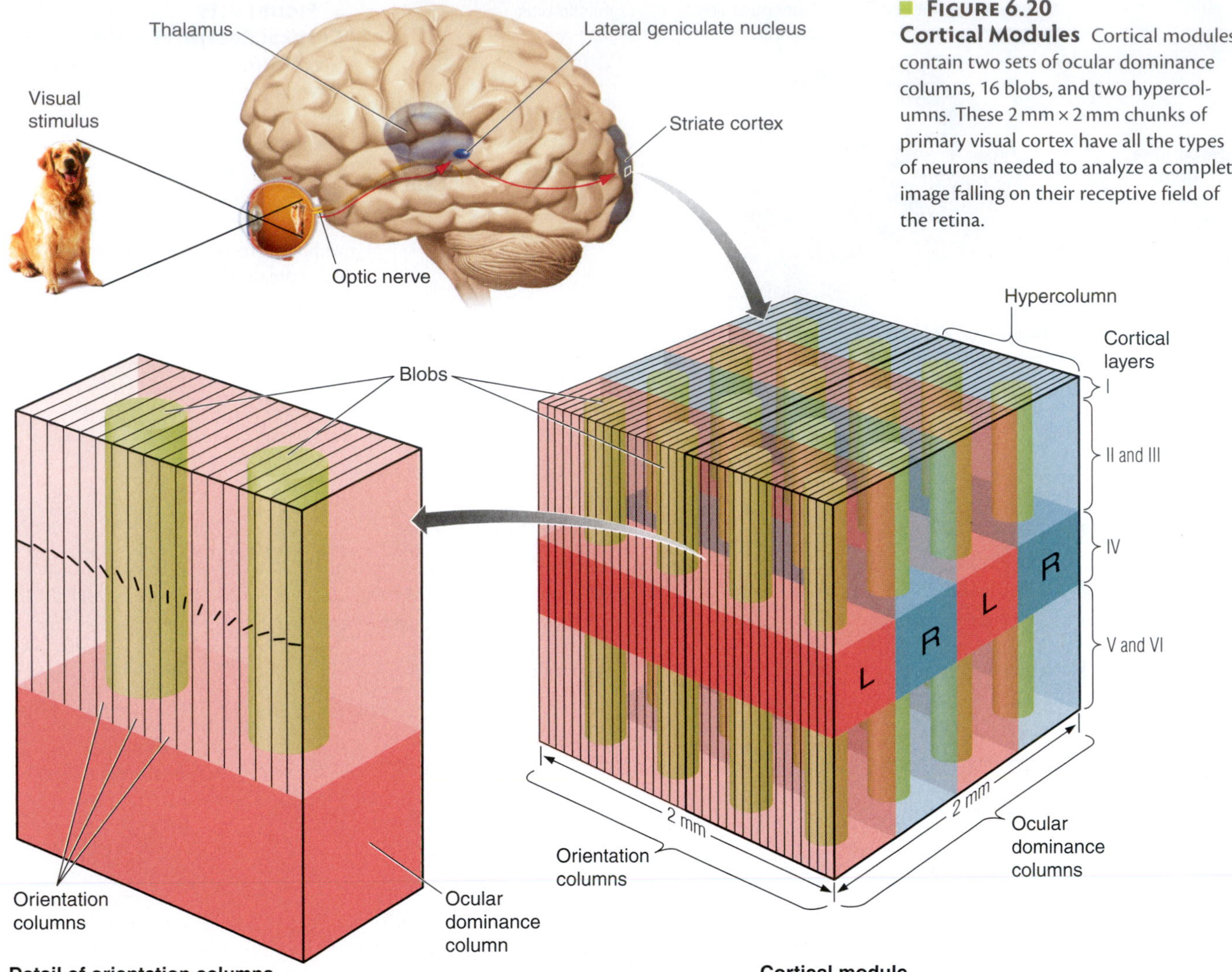

■ **FIGURE 6.20**
Cortical Modules Cortical modules contain two sets of ocular dominance columns, 16 blobs, and two hypercolumns. These 2 mm × 2 mm chunks of primary visual cortex have all the types of neurons needed to analyze a complete image falling on their receptive field of the retina.

dorsal stream A pathway leading from the primary visual cortex in a dorsal direction thought to participate in the perception of movement.

ventral stream A pathway of information from the primary visual cortex to the inferior temporal lobe that is believed to process object recognition.

Area MT An area in the medial temporal lobe believed to participate in motion analysis.

Area MST An area in the medial superior temporal lobe believed to participate in large-scale motion analysis.

Area IT An area in the inferior temporal lobe believed to participate in object recognition.

fusiform face area (FFA) (FUSE-ee-form) An area in the inferior temporal lobe believed to participate in the recognition of familiar faces, especially in the right hemisphere.

Next to the striate cortex is an area known as V2. If you stain V2 for cytochrome oxidase, a pattern of stripes emerges. Alternating thick and thin stripes are separated by interstripe regions. The thick stripes form part of the magnocellular pathway and project to a visual pathway known as the **dorsal stream.** The dorsal stream travels from the primary visual cortex toward the parietal lobe and then proceeds to the medial temporal lobe. The dorsal stream, commonly referred to as the "where" pathway, specializes in the analysis of movement, object locations, and the coordination of eyes and arms in grasping or reaching.

The thin stripes and interstripe regions of V2 project to another visual region known as V4, continuing the parvocellular pathway. Area V4 participates in a second major pathway, the **ventral stream,** which proceeds from the primary visual cortex to the inferior temporal lobe. This second pathway, commonly referred to as the "what" pathway, specializes in object recognition. These pathways, introduced by Ungerleider and Mishkin (1982), are illustrated in ■ Figure 6.21.

The Dorsal Stream **Area MT,** which stands for the medial temporal lobe, appears to play an important role in the processing of motion. Input to Area MT is primarily from the magnocellular pathways. Recall that the cells in this pathway have large receptive fields and often show responses to rapidly changing light conditions and direction of movement. Most of the cells in Area MT respond to movement in a particular direction. Unlike previous motion detectors, however, Area MT cells respond to movement across large regions of the visual field.

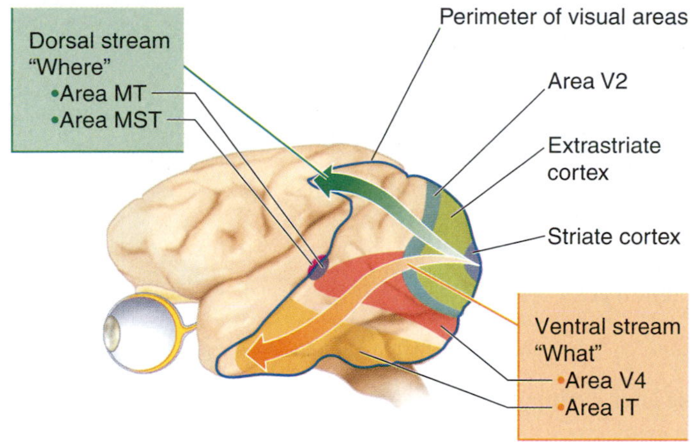

■ **FIGURE 6.21 The Ventral "What" Stream and the Dorsal "Where" Stream** Information leaving the primary visual cortex in the ventral stream forms synapses in Areas V4 and IT. These areas participate in object recognition. Information in the dorsal stream forms synapses in Areas MT and MST, which contribute to our perception of movement. This image shows the locations of these visual processes in the rhesus monkey cortex.

Further processing of motion occurs adjacent to Area MT in **Area MST,** which stands for the medial superior temporal lobe. Tanaka and Saito (1989) found that Area MST neurons respond to stimulus rotation, stimulus expansion, and stimulus contraction. These are very large, global types of movement that do not produce consistent responses in other areas. Area MST helps us use vision to guide our movements.

Melvyn Goodale and his colleagues (Goodale & Humphrey, 2001; Milner & Goodale, 1995; Goodale & Milner, 1992) suggested that the dorsal stream would be more accurately characterized as a "how" stream than as a "where" stream. According to this view, not only does the dorsal stream tell us an object's location, but it also provides information about how to interact with an object. Patients with damage to the dorsal stream can judge the orientation of an object, such as lining up a card with a slot, but are unable to combine orientation and action to push the card through the slot.

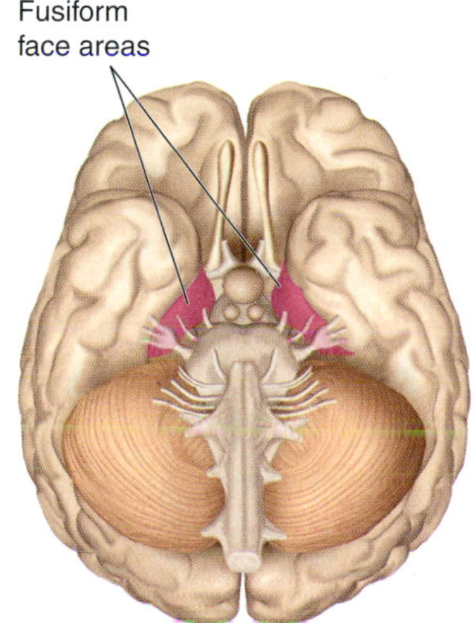

■ **FIGURE 6.22 The Fusiform Face Area (FFA)** The fusiform face area (FFA) is located within the fusiform gyrus of the inferior temporal lobe. This area, especially in the right hemisphere, appears to play a significant role in the identification of faces and members of learned categories, such as species of birds and models of cars.

The Ventral Stream As the information from the primary cortex and Area V2 travels ventrally toward the temporal lobe, we come to Area V4. The cells in this area have large receptive fields and respond to both shape and color. Cells in Area V4 project to the inferior temporal lobe, or **Area IT.** Cells in Area IT respond to many shapes and colors. In humans and monkeys, a small section of Area IT known as the **fusiform face area** (FFA), shown in ■ Figure 6.22, appears to respond most vigorously to faces and to members of learned categories, such as species of birds or models of cars (Gauthier, Skudlarski, Gore, & Anderson, 2000). Monkeys viewing blurred photographs are more likely to report "seeing" faces when their FFAs are stimulated (Afraz, Kiani, & Esteky, 2006).

INTERIM SUMMARY 6.2

Summary Table: Anatomical Features of the Visual System

Feature	Significance
Cornea	Bends light toward the retina
Anterior chamber	Contains fluid for nourishing the cornea and lens
Iris	Muscle that controls the amount of light entering the eye
Pupil	Opening in the iris
Lens	Focuses light onto the retina
Vitreous chamber	Fluid-filled chamber behind the lens

(continued)

INTERIM SUMMARY 6.2 (continued)

Retina	Contains photoreceptors and initial processing neurons
Macula	Responsible for central, as opposed to peripheral, vision
Fovea	Pit in the macula specialized for detailed vision
Optic nerves	Axons from retinal ganglion cells that exit the eye
Lateral geniculate nucleus (LGN)	Area of the thalamus that receives input from the optic nerves
Primary visual cortex	Receives input from the lateral geniculate nucleus; responsible for initial processing of an image
Dorsal stream	Analysis of movement
Ventral stream	Object recognition

Summary Points

1. Before reaching the retina, light travels through the cornea, the anterior chamber, the opening of the pupil controlled by the iris, the lens, and the vitreous chamber. **(LO2)**
2. The retina is a thin layer of visual interneurons and photoreceptors. **(LO2)**
3. The 120 million rods in the human eye are responsible for scotopic (dim light) vision, whereas the 6 million cones are responsible for photopic (bright light) vision. **(LO3)**
4. The human eye's 1 million ganglion cells integrate the input from about 126 million photoreceptors and send the information to the brain via action potentials in the optic nerves. The optic tracts proceed to the lateral geniculate nucleus (LGN) of the thalamus, with smaller branches connecting with the hypothalamus and superior colliculi. **(LO4)**
5. The primary visual cortex (striate cortex) is located in the occipital lobe. It contains simple cortical cells and complex cortical cells that participate in the encoding of shape and movement. Information about movement is processed by the dorsal stream, whereas information about object recognition is processed by the ventral stream. **(LO4)**
6. Processing of visual information from the level of the retina up through the LGN and primary visual cortex is characterized by responses to antagonistic center-surround receptive fields. **(LO5)**

Review Questions

1. What cells and connections make up the layers of the retina?
2. How is the striate cortex organized, from simple cells up through cortical modules?

Visual Perception

Sensation is usually defined as the obtaining of information from the environment and the transmission of that information to the brain. Once the brain receives the information, it begins the process of perception. **Perception** involves the interpretation, or meaningful analysis, of sensory data. At this point, we investigate how the cerebral cortex constructs a visual reality out of the input we have discussed so far.

HIERARCHIES

The model of cortical visual processing proposed by Hubel and Wiesel implies a hierarchical organization in which simple cells contribute input to increasingly complex cells. At each level of processing, more complex responses are generated from simpler responses. The result of such a system would be a "grandmother cell," or a single cell that could combine all previous input to tell you that your grandmother was at the door to pay a visit. This hypothetical neuron, capable of responding to a very specific stimulus and no others, has also been referred to as a **feature detector** (Barlow, 1972).

sensation The process of obtaining information about the environment and transmitting it to the brain for processing.

perception The process of interpreting sensory signals sent to the brain.

feature detector A hypothetical neuron that responds to a single feature of the visual stimulus.

public domain

■ **FIGURE 6.23**
Problems for the Hierarchical Model of Vision Can you figure out what is in the picture? If I tell you that this is a picture of a Dalmatian dog, can you see the picture clearly? This visual experience would be difficult to explain in terms of neurons that act as feature detectors. The stimulus doesn't change when you learn the identity of the object, but the interpretation does.

The feature detector model received considerable support from recordings of single cells in the temporal lobes of eight patients undergoing surgery for epilepsy (Quiroga, Reddy, Kreiman, Koch, & Fried, 2005). One patient had a cell that fired in response to all images that included actress Jennifer Aniston, but not at all to images of other faces, landmarks, or objects. Another patient had a cell that responded to photos of actress Halle Berry, images of Berry in her *Catwoman* costume, caricatures of Berry, and even a letter sequence spelling her name.

People only see what they are prepared to see.

Ralph Waldo Emerson

Although the idea of a strict hierarchical structure culminating in feature detectors is attractive in many ways, it does not fit perfectly with what we know about brain organization. First of all, we would need an immense number of feature detectors to respond to the large numbers of objects and events that we can recognize. This extravagance in the use of cells is out of character for the highly efficient nervous system. Second, the ability of cortical visual neurons to respond equally to changes in more than one stimulus dimension (orientation and movement, for example) is not consistent with a feature detector. A true feature detector should respond only in the presence of its ideal stimulus and never in its absence. Finally, the feature detector model would struggle to explain our response to the apparently random pattern of dots shown in ■ Figure 6.23. Once you know that the image represents a Dalmatian dog, you can instantly pick out the shape of the dog. This requires knowledge and memory of the appearance of Dalmatian dogs. It is unlikely that a single cortical cell acting as a Dalmatian dog feature detector could incorporate such complex inputs from memory.

Spatial Frequencies

Striate cortex may not respond to isolated lines and bars but, rather, to patterns of lines. The simplest patterns of lines are known as **gratings,** as shown in ■ Figure 6.24. A high-frequency grating has many bars in a given distance, whereas a low-frequency grating has relatively few bars. A high-contrast grating has a large amount of difference in intensity between bars, such as very bright white next to black. A low-contrast grating has a more subtle difference in intensity between bars, such as a dark gray next to black. The human visual system could perform a rough mathematical analysis, or **spatial frequency analysis,** of the gratings found in the visual field (De Valois & De Valois, 1980). This is very different from the hierarchical approach, which implies a reality built out of bars and edges.

grating A striped stimulus used to study responses to spatial frequency.

spatial frequency analysis A way of describing visual processing as a basic mathematical analysis of the visual field.

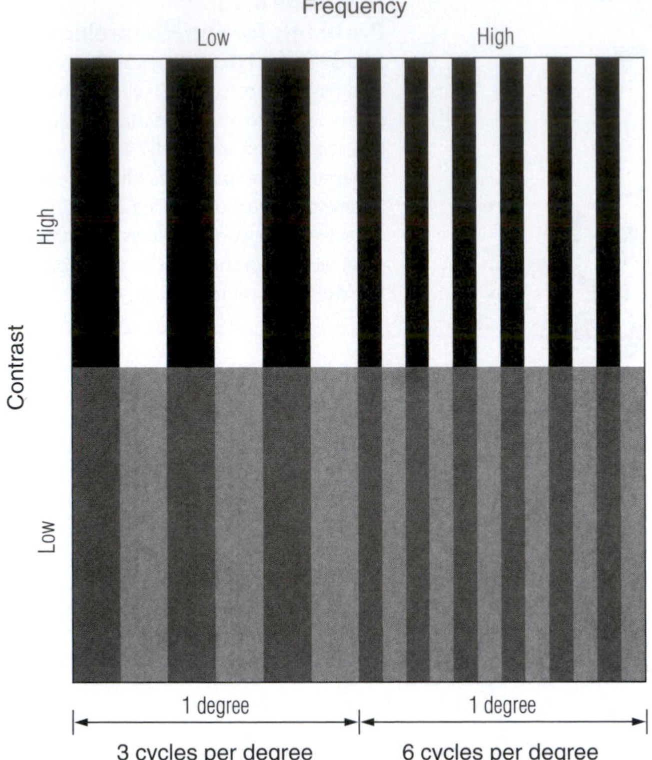

■ **FIGURE 6.24**
Spatial Frequencies It has been suggested that the visual system works by performing a mathematical analysis of spatial frequencies in the visual field. Gratings can be described in terms of frequency (number of bars in a given distance) or contrast (the difference in intensity between adjacent bars).

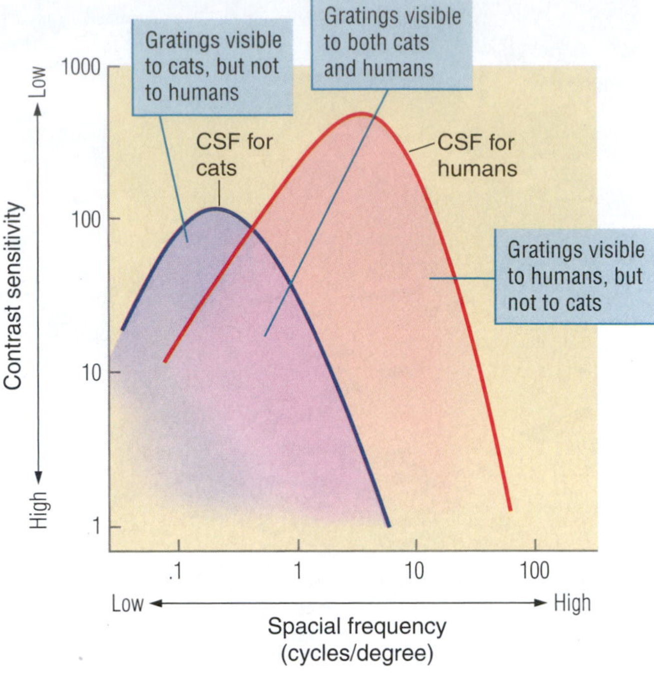

■ **FIGURE 6.25**
A Cat's View of the World A contrast sensitivity function (CSF) measures how much contrast is needed for a grating to look different from a uniformly colored disk as a function of spatial frequency. The resulting functions for cats and humans show significant overlap. However, you can see more fine detail (higher spatial frequencies) than your cat can. The cat can see better at lower spatial frequencies than you can.

Observing responses to gratings can give us a window into the visual world of other species. Thresholds for contrast can be identified over a range of frequencies. In other words, how much contrast is needed in adjacent bars of a grating before they can be distinguished from a uniform gray stimulus? The resulting graph is known as a **contrast sensitivity function,** or **CSF.** We can obtain CSFs from nonhuman species by training them to choose a grating rather than a uniformly colored stimulus to obtain food. When the animal's responses become no more accurate than chance, we can assume that the animal can no longer tell the difference between a grating and a uniformly colored stimulus. This determines the CSF for that animal.

■ Figure 6.25 compares the CSFs of cats and humans. At higher spatial frequencies (lines in the grating get closer together), your vision is better than your cat's. This means that human beings see more fine detail than cats do. On the other hand, kitty has an advantage over you at low spatial frequencies. This means that a low-frequency (large), low-contrast (dark gray vs. black) shadow on the wall will get your cat's attention but not yours. You will think kitty is after ghosts again.

contrast sensitivity function (CSF) The mapping of an individual's thresholds for contrast over a range of frequencies.
retinal disparity The slightly different views of the visual field provided by the two eyes.
binocular cell A cell in the cerebral cortex that responds to input from both eyes.
disparity-selective cell A binocular cortical cell that responds when its preferred features are seen by different parts of the two eyes.
trichromacy theory The theory that suggests human color vision is based on our possessing three different color photopigments.

THE PERCEPTION OF DEPTH

The image projected on the retina is two-dimensional, so the visual system uses a number of cues to provide a sense of depth. Several of these cues are monocular, requiring the use of only one eye. Perspective, in which lines we expect to be parallel, such as the edges of a road, are made to converge or come together at the horizon, is a centuries-old artistic device to give the illusion of depth on a flat surface such as a painting. Texture, shading, and a comparison of the size of familiar objects can also provide a very realistic impression of depth in two dimensions.

The depth cues mentioned so far do not require the use of two eyes. We also have binocular (two-eye) depth cues that are even more effective. When eyes face

■ **FIGURE 6.26**
Stereograms Demonstrate Retinal Disparity We can see three dimensional figures within stereograms because our visual system perceives the slight difference in the views of the visual field provided by the two eyes. Unless you are one of the 5–10 percent of the population that is stereoblind, you should be able to pick out the hidden image in the stereogram, part (a). The hidden image is shown in part (b).

front, as in humans and other predatory species, the two eyes produce overlapping, but slightly different, images of the visual field (as we saw earlier in Figure 6.16). The differences between the images projected onto the retinas of both eyes results in **retinal disparity.** Because retinal disparity increases with the distance of the object from the viewer, we can use the degree of disparity as a strong cue for depth. This phenomenon has been exploited in random-dot stereograms or "magic eye pictures" (Julesz, 1971). Infants as young as 4 months of age can perceive depth in random-dot stereograms (Fox, Aslin, Shea, & Dumais, 1980), as can monkeys, cats, and falcons. If you can't see the stereogram in ■ Figure 6.26, you may be one of the 5–10 percent of the population who are stereoblind.

Binocular cells in the cortex respond most vigorously when both eyes are looking at the same features of a visual stimulus (Hubel & Wiesel, 1962). Binocular cells also respond to degrees of retinal disparity. Some cells fire more when their preferred features appear to be at an identical distance. Others fire more when the preferred features are seen by different parts of the two eyes. These cells are known as **disparity-selective cells.** We coordinate the activity of these cells to judge retinal disparity. In areas of the anterior parietal lobe, information about retinal disparity is combined with judgments of how the shape of an object changes due to movement to construct the final impression of a three-dimensional object (Durand et al., 2007; Georgieva, Todd, Peeters, & Orban, 2008).

Coding Color

As you can see in ■ Figure 6.27, red, green, and blue lights can be mixed to generate all colors, and mixing them together will give you a white light (which can be separated with a prism or by water droplets that produce a rainbow). Consequently, red, green, and blue are considered to be the primary colors of light.

■ **FIGURE 6.27**
Mixing Lights We might be accustomed to thinking of primary colors as red, yellow, and blue, but that works only for paint. In the world of light, red, green, and blue can be mixed to form all other colors. A mixture of all three colors of light looks white.

Trichromacy **Trichromacy theory** suggests that human color vision is based on our having three (tri) different color photopigments. As we saw in Figure 6.12, the three photopigments are maximally responsive to lights of different wavelengths.

Based on a series of color-matching tasks with human participants, Thomas Young proposed his trichromatic theory of color vision in 1807, long before any knowledge was available regarding the types of human photoreceptors. Hermann von Helmholtz (1856–1866) expanded Young's theory by proposing three different color receptors in the retina. Both men are credited with the trichromatic theory, which is typically referred to as the Young-Helmholtz theory of color vision.

Although the trichromatic theory accounts for many of the phenomena related to color vision, it leaves other features unexplained. For instance, if you stare at the yellow, green, and white flag in ■ Figure 6.28 and then focus on the dot in the white

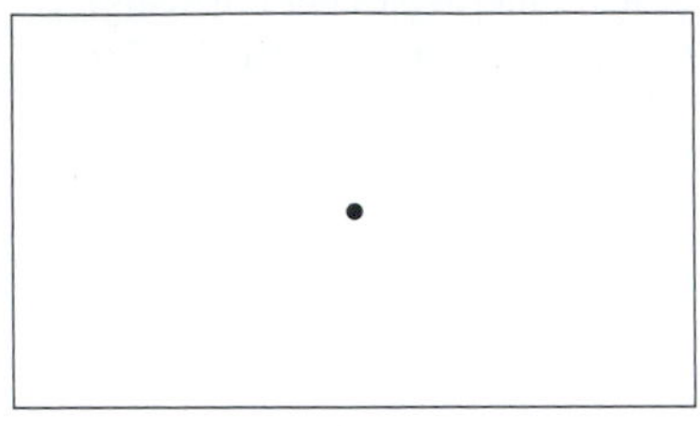

■ **FIGURE 6.28**
Color Afterimages Illustrate Opponency If you stare at the dot in the center of the yellow, green, and white flag for a minute, then shift your gaze to the dot in the white space below, you should see the flag in its traditional red, white, and blue.

space below, you will get an afterimage of the flag in its more traditional red, white, and blue. Clearly, there is more to color vision than trichromacy.

Opponent Processes Ewald Hering observed that mixing blue and yellow lights yielded the sensation of gray and that colorblind individuals seemed to lose the ability to discriminate between green and red rather than having difficulties seeing just one of the colors. These observations could not be explained in terms of the trichromatic theory. In his 1878 work, *On the Theory of Sensibility to Light*, Hering suggested an alternate theory of opponent processes based on three types of receptors: a red–green receptor, a blue–yellow receptor, and a black–white receptor.

Opponent process theory gains support from the organization of color receptive fields in the visual system. P and K ganglion cells have center-surround receptive fields that respond differentially to color. P cells show red–green center-surround organization. In other words, we can locate receptive fields for P cells that have a center that responds maximally to red and a surround that responds to green. Other receptive fields will have centers that respond maximally to green and surrounds that respond to red. The K cells show antagonistic center-surround organizations responding to blue and yellow. However, unlike the P cells, these blue–yellow ganglion cells always have blue centers and yellow surrounds but not the reverse.

You may be wondering how the input from three cone types can result in the opposition of four colors: green versus red and blue versus yellow. As shown in ■ Figure 6.29, the green and red case is straightforward. These ganglion cells are receiving input from cones that respond maximally to red or green. The blue and yellow case is slightly different. These ganglion cells receive input from blue cones, of course, which they compare to a mixture of input from red and green cones, which in the world of light add up to yellow.

Which of the two theories of color vision is correct? It appears that both are correct but that they operate at different stages in the analysis of color. The Young-Helmholtz trichromatic theory provides an accurate framework for the functioning of the three types of cones in the retina. At levels of color analysis beyond the retina, Hering's opponent process theory seems to fit observed phenomena neatly.

Colorblindness Occasional errors occur in the chromosomes that carry the genes that encode the cone photopigments. As a result, individuals with these genes show several kinds of atypical responses to color, known as colorblindness.

Dichromacy (having two cone photopigments) is the most common type of abnormality and results from a missing or abnormal cone pigment. Because genes for the red and green photopigments appear on the X chromosome, this type of dichromacy is sex-linked. Men are about ten times more likely to be colorblind than women (Hurvich, 1981). ■ Figure 6.30 shows us what your author might look like to a dichromat.

There are very rare cases in which the blue photopigment is missing. The gene for the blue photopigment is located on Chromosome 7 (Nathans, 1989), so these cases are not sex-linked and appear equally in males and females. Rarer still are cases of **monochromacy.** This condition occurs when a person has only one type of cone or

opponent process theory A theory of human color vision based on three antagonistic color channels: red-green, blue-yellow, and black-white.

dichromacy Having eyes that contain two different cone photopigments.

monochromacy The ability to see in black and white only.

anomalous trichromacy A condition characterized by having three cone photopigments that respond to slightly different wavelengths than normal.

tetrachromat (teh-truh-KROH-mat) An organism possessing four cone photopigments.

color contrast The fact that colors can look different depending on the surrounding colors.

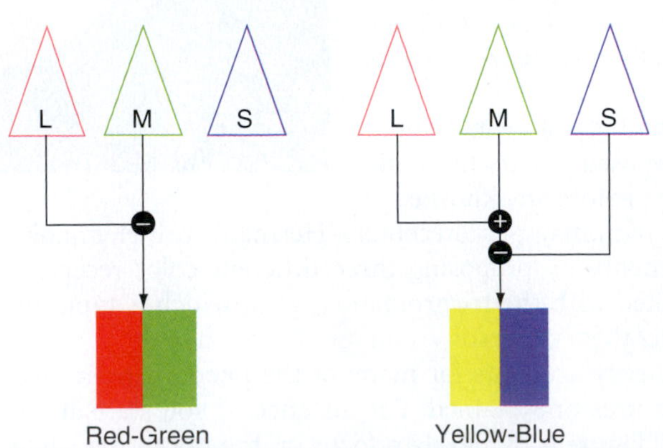

■ **FIGURE 6.29**
Opponency According to Hering's theory we have separate red-green and yellow-blue channels. In the red-green channel, P ganglion cells receive input from cones that are maximally sensitive to red (L for long) and green (M for medium). K ganglion cells compare input from cones maximally sensitive to blue (S for short) with a mixture of input from L and M cones, which in the world of light produces yellow.

■ **FIGURE 6.30 Looking Through the Eyes of a Dichromat** This image shows your author as she appears to trichromats (left) and to dichromats (right) who are missing the medium (green) cone photopigments.

a complete absence of cones. In either case, the person can't see color at all. Monty Roberts, who served as the inspiration for the film *The Horse Whisperer*, credits his unique ability to study animal motion and expression to his monochromacy (Roberts & Scanlan, 1999). Some individuals have three cone pigments, but their peak response occurs at slightly different wavelengths than is typical. This leads to a condition known as **anomalous trichromacy.** These individuals match colors in a slightly different way than most people, but they might not even know that they are unusual. As many as 50 percent of all women may be **tetrachromats,** or people with four different color pigments (Neitz, Kraft, & Neitz, 1998). These individuals match colors in a manner that would be predicted by their having four color pigments rather than three.

■ **FIGURE 6.31 Color Contrast** Color contrast, or the differences in appearance when colors are viewed against different backgrounds, is a likely result of color opponency in the central nervous system. All letters in this image are really the same color.

Color Contrast and Color Constancy Perception does not occur in a vacuum. In the case of **color contrast,** illustrated in ■ Figure 6.31, colors can look very different depending on their context. Because of color contrast, Edwin Land (1959), the inventor of the Polaroid camera, could use red and green filters to give his photographs the appearance of a wide set of colors. Color contrast is primarily an effect of the opponency of color processing in the visual system.

WHY DOES THIS MATTER?

Why Girls Like Pink

Many a contemporary parent, hoping to raise a strong, career-minded daughter, is dismayed by the daughter's consistent preference for that pink top with lilac flowers that Aunt Tilly sent as a birthday present. Does this mean that no matter how hard we try to provide an androgynous environment for our daughters that advertising and socialization will win? Not necessarily. Understanding differences in how males and females see color matters because it helps explain how biological factors work alongside cultural factors to influence children's color choices.

Dichromats, typically male, usually have two genes on their one X chromosome for slightly different versions of the "red" photopigment or two slightly different genes for the "green" photopigment. Consequently, we know that the mothers of dichromats must also have an X chromosome with genes for two red or two green photopigments. Combining the photopigment genes on the mothers' two X chromosomes (genes for two photopigments on one X and one gene for a photopigment on her other X) with the gene for the blue photopigment located on Chromosome 7, we can see that these women should have genes for four different cone photopigments. In other words, they are tetrachromats.

Researchers have estimated that around 50 percent of all women have four cone photopigments instead of the typical three (Neitz, Kraft, & Neitz, 1998). What does the world look like to a person with four cone photopigments rather than the usual three? In some cases, the differences in the two red or two green photopigments are so small that these women would experience the same essential visual reality as a trichromat. However, if the photopigments were less similar, it is possible that these women could see as many as 100 million colors. Perception of colors in the pink, red, and violet wavelengths would be most affected by tetrachromacy.

Psychologists have frequently dismissed female preferences for pink, red, and violet as a result of cultural conditioning. However, the ability of many girls to see richer variations among these colors might provide a better account for these preferences (Jameson, Highnote, & Wasserman, 2001). So liking a pink and purple top does not necessarily mean that your daughter has changed her mind about wanting to be President of the United States.

> *Of different colors equally perfect, that will appear most excellent which is seen near its direct contrary . . . blue near yellow; green near red: because each color is more distinctly seen, when opposed to its contrary, than to any other similar to it.*
>
> Leonardo da Vinci

Color constancy describes the fact that an object's colors do not appear to change even as the light falling on that object changes. Your red sweater looks red at high noon out-of-doors, under indoor lights in the classroom, and on the way to the parking lot in twilight. Some of the color constancy effect is a result of adaptation. In any sensory process, adaptation occurs when prolonged stimulation reduces the response of neurons. In addition to adaptation, Semir Zeki (1983) has identified neurons in Area V4 of the visual cortex that might contribute to color constancy. When a green square was illuminated by white or red lights, the primary visual cortical cells of Zeki's monkeys responded differently. However, Zeki found cells in V4 that responded to green squares regardless of the light used to illuminate the squares. These cells could form the basis of higher-order color constancy.

The Development of the Visual System

Although we can't ask young infants about what they can see, we can still establish the same types of contrast sensitivity functions (CSF) that we found earlier for adults and cats. Infants prefer to look at patterns rather than at uniform screens. We assume that if an infant looks at a grating longer than at a uniform circle, the infant must see a difference between the two. ■ Figure 6.32 compares CSF curves for adults and for infants between the ages of 1 and 3 months. The infant cannot see fine detail at a distance. In addition, the CSF curves show that the infant needs more contrast than an adult does to see. This probably relates to the preference most babies show for large, high-contrast, colorful objects.

As we age, predictable changes occur in our vision. In middle age, the lens accommodates more slowly to changes in focal distance. This condition is known as **presbyopia,** or "old sight." Older adults also have trouble responding quickly to changes in lighting, as

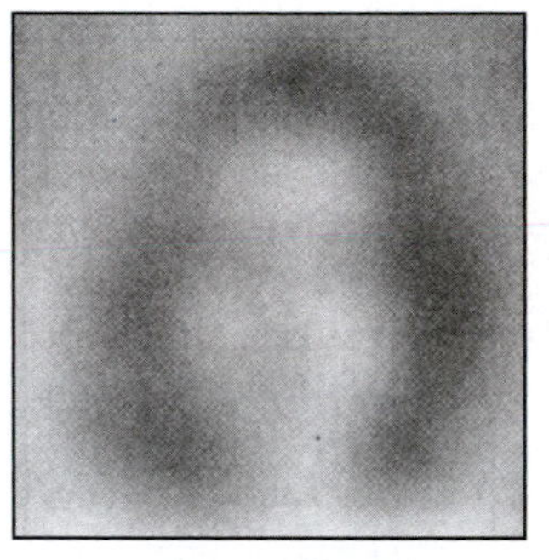

1 month

2 months

3 months

adult

From Ginsberg, A., "Contrast perception in the human infant," 1983. Unpublished manuscript.

■ **FIGURE 6.32**

The Development of Contrast Sensitivity Adults can see everything an infant can see, but the infant cannot see the fine detail at a distance that the adult can see. Using the infant CSF, we can remove the spatial frequencies that the infant can't see. The resulting photographs provide insight into the visual world of young children.

when exiting a dark theater into the sunlight. The lens, which provides most of the focus of light onto the retina, continues to grow throughout the life span. As fibers are continually added to the structure of the lens, it takes on a yellow hue. Although this change in color provides more protection from ultraviolet rays that might otherwise harm the aging retina, the yellow lens will also distort the person's perception of blue and green. Aging is also associated with smaller pupils, probably due to the loss of elasticity in the muscles of the iris. Smaller pupils allow less light into the eye, negatively affecting the quality of vision.

Aging might have a negative effect on the cortical processing of visual information. Schmolesky,Wang, Pu, and Leventhal (2000) investigated the effects of aging on neurons responding to line orientation or motion in the primary visual cortex. In young monkeys, these researchers found that 90 percent of the measured neurons showed an orientation preference, whereas 70 percent showed a preference for a direction of movement. In aged monkeys, only 42 percent of the cells showed an orientation preference, and 25 percent showed a direction of movement preference. The aged neurons seemed to become less selective, firing at just about anything going on in the visual field.

The most pathetic person in the world is someone who has sight, but no vision.

Helen Keller

Disorders of the Visual System

A variety of conditions can interfere with vision, ranging from the very mild and correctable to a complete loss of vision. Vision problems occur due to problems in the eye and retina as well as to central problems in the brain.

Amblyopia

Lazy eye, or **amblyopia,** occurs when one eye cannot focus on objects. If left untreated, the brain will learn to ignore the input from the less functional eye. Binocular depth perception will be permanently lost.

Cataracts

Cataracts, such as the one shown in ■ Figure 6.33, result from clouding of the lens of the eye. Cataracts become more frequent with age. However, some ethnic populations, including Arabs and Sephardic Jews, have a high rate of cataracts at birth. Severe cataracts are usually treated by surgically removing the clouded lens. Following surgery, the person requires extremely strong glasses or the implant of an artificial lens. Removal of a lens can also negatively influence color vision. Following removal of a lens for cataracts, French impressionist painter Claude Monet saw nearly everything as blue.

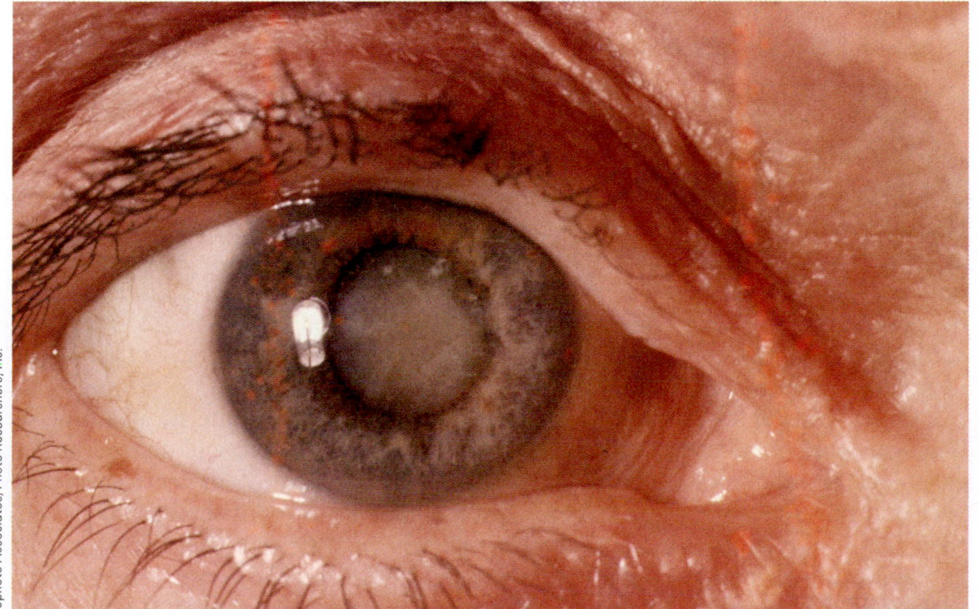

■ **Figure 6.33**
Cataracts Result From Clouding of the Lens Proteins, including the fibers making up the lens of the eye, can lose their structure in response to exposure to a variety of external factors, including heat and ultraviolet radiation. Just as the white of an egg is transformed from clear to opaque when cooked, the proteins in the lens can lose their clarity as well. Airline pilots, who are exposed to high levels of radiation from outer space, experience more frequent cataracts than people with most other occupations.

color constancy The concept that an object's color looks the same regardless of the type of light falling on the object.
presbyopia (prez-bee-OH-pee-uh) The reduced rate and extent of accommodation by the lens that results from aging.
amblyopia (am-blee-OH-pee-uh) A condition also known as lazy eye, in which one eye does not track visual stimuli.
cataract Clouding of the lens.
myopia (my-OH-pee-uh) An abnormal condition in which the eyeball is too long; also known as nearsightedness.

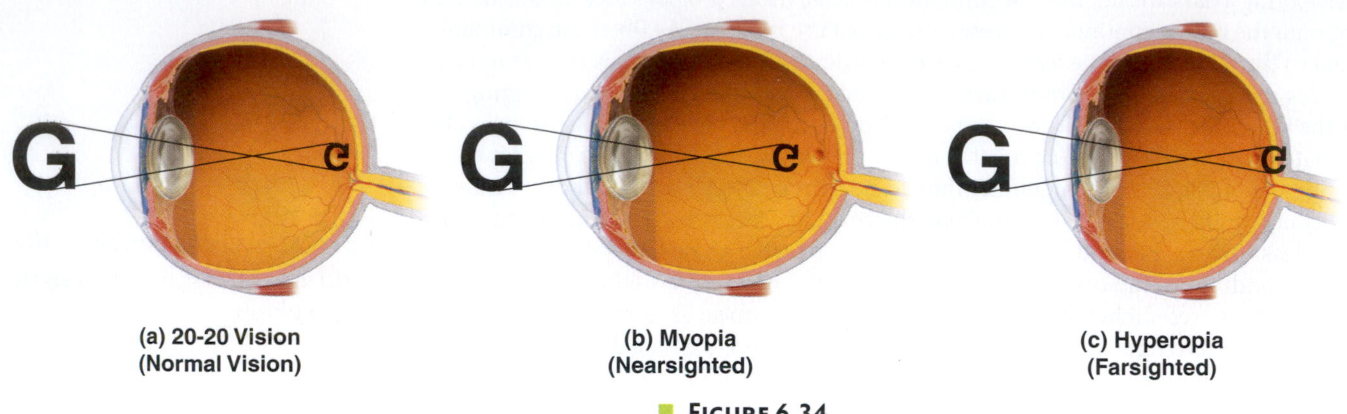

(a) 20-20 Vision (Normal Vision)

(b) Myopia (Nearsighted)

(c) Hyperopia (Farsighted)

FIGURE 6.34
Eyeball Shape Influences the Quality of Vision Eyeballs that are either too long or too short cause vision problems, because the focused image falls either short of the retina or beyond the retina.

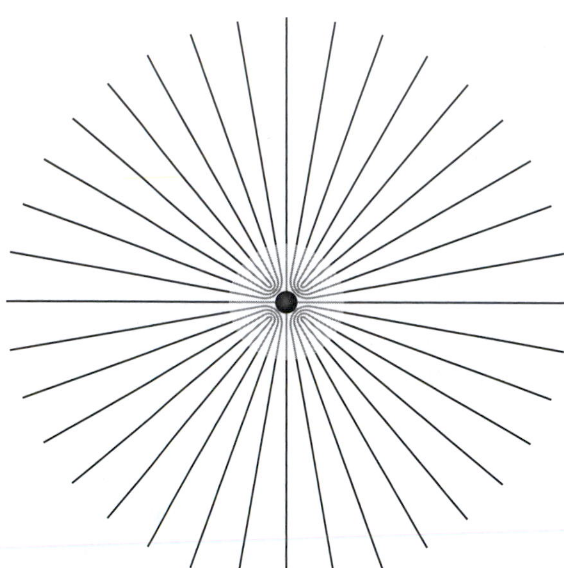

FIGURE 6.35
Astigmatism Unlike myopia and hyperopia, astigmatism does not result from eyeball shape. Instead, the uneven shape of the cornea causes the retinal image to be imperfect. View this image one eye at a time. If some of the spokes appear darker than others, you probably have astigmatism.

VISUAL ACUITY PROBLEMS

Some common visual acuity problems are illustrated in Figure 6.34. If the eyeball is slightly elongated, the image focused by the lens will fall short of the retina. This condition is known as **myopia,** or nearsightedness. The person can see well when looking at close objects, but the ability to see objects in the distance is impaired. If the eyeball is too short, the best image would be focused somewhere behind the retina. This condition is **hyperopia,** or farsightedness. Distance vision will be quite good, but close objects, including letters on the pages of books or newspapers, will be blurry. Laser surgery involves the reshaping of the cornea to correct these visual problems. Unlike myopia and hyperopia, **astigmatism** does not result from eyeball length. Instead, this condition results from unevenness in the shape of the cornea. If some of the spokes in Figure 6.35 look lighter to you than others while you fixate on the dot, you might have astigmatism.

myopia (my-OH-pee-uh) An abnormal condition in which the eyeball is too long; also known as nearsightedness.
hyperopia (hi-per-OH-pee-uh) An acuity problem resulting from a short eyeball; also known as farsightedness.
astigmatism (uh-STIG-muh-tizm) A distortion of vision caused by the shape of the cornea.
scotoma (scoe-TOE-muh) An area in the visual field that can't be seen, usually due to central damage by stroke or other brain injury.
blindsight An abnormal condition in which parts of the visual field are not consciously perceived but can be subconsciously perceived by extrastriate cortex.
visual agnosia (ag-NOSE-ee-uh) A disorder in which a person can see a stimulus but cannot identify what is seen.
prosopagnosia (pro-soh-pag-NOH-see-uh) The inability to recognize known faces.

BLINDNESS

Blindness, or the total loss of vision, can occur as a result of damage at many levels. Damage to the eye or optic nerves could prevent input to normally functioning visual cortical areas. If the cortical systems are still operating properly, treatments that improve input can restore some vision. A 62-year-old man who had been blind since he was 36 years old volunteered to have a tiny camera wired to his brain. This input is sufficient to let him locate objects in a room and read 2-inch-tall letters from a distance of five feet (Dobelle, 2000).

Other individuals are blind due to cortical damage. When the striate cortex is damaged, the patient has a **scotoma,** or region of blindness, that will depend on the exact location and amount of cortical damage. These patients often demonstrate the very odd phenomenon of **blindsight** (Cowey & Stoerig, 1991). Although they claim they cannot see lights that are flashed in the area of their scotoma, these patients can point on command to the source of the light. It is likely that visual input to the extrastriate cortex, which does not result in conscious awareness of light, is responsible for these unusual effects (Silvanto, 2008). These findings suggest that processing by striate cortex is essential for conscious awareness of visual stimuli.

VISUAL AGNOSIAS

Visual agnosias are disorders in which a person can see a stimulus but has difficulty recognizing what is seen. The word *agnosia* comes from the Greek for "without knowledge." Responding to the image of a carrot, one patient said, "I have not the glimmerings of an idea. The bottom point seems solid and the other bits are feathery. It does not seem logical unless it is some sort of brush" (Humphreys & Riddoch, 1987, p. 59). The patient is attending to the major features of the stimulus (pointy end, leafy green part) but can't recognize the object.

In **prosopagnosia,** vision is retained, but the person cannot recognize the faces of people he or she knows (Barton, 2003). Patients with prosopagnosia can tell one face apart from another and can tell the gender of the people from pictures of their faces. In spite of these skills, these patients can't recognize faces as people they know, not even their own image in the mirror. As we mentioned earlier, the fusiform face area (FFA) is probably responsible for facial recognition. Prosopagnosia is usually associated with damage to this area due to stroke or other accidents, although other cases can run in families, indicating a genetic basis (Kennerknecht et al., 2006).

INTERIM SUMMARY 6.3

Summary Table: Examples of Major Visual Disorders

Disorder	Symptoms	Causal Factors	Treatment
Cataracts	Mild blockage of light to complete blindness; distortion of color vision	Clouding of the lens	Surgical removal of the lens
Myopia (nearsightedness)	Difficulty seeing distant objects	Elongation of the eyeball	Corrective lenses, laser surgery
Hyperopia (farsightedness)	Difficulty seeing close objects, reading	Shortening of the eyeball	Corrective lenses
Astigmatism	Difficulty seeing distant objects	Uneven cornea shape	Corrective lenses
Scotoma	Regions of blindness in visual field	Stroke, physical injury to visual cortex	None
Prosopagnosia	Inability to recognize familiar faces	Damage to the fusiform gyrus	None

Summary Points

1. The cortex constructs a visual reality through either hierarchical processing or a basic mathematical analysis of contrast and frequencies. **(LO6)**
2. Depth perception results from monocular and binocular cues. **(LO6)**
3. The trichromacy approach to color perception is based on the fact that we have three types of cone photopigments that respond differentially to lights of different wavelengths. Our visual system also shows a pattern of red–green and blue–yellow opponency. **(LO6)**
4. Infants see less fine detail at a distance than adults do. Older adults experience less visual quality due to presbyopia, slow adaptation to changes in light, yellowing of the lens, smaller pupils, and less selectivity in cortical responses to visual input. **(LO7)**
5. Many conditions can interfere with vision, either at the level of the eye or the level of the brain. **(LO7)**

(continued)

INTERIM SUMMARY 6.2 (continued)

Review Questions

1. How can contrast sensitivity functions (CSF) tell us what an organism can see?
2. What does colorblindness teach us about the nature of color vision?

NEW DIRECTIONS

The Effect of Culture on Perception

Although our emphasis in this chapter has been on the features of the visual system common to all human beings, some interesting cultural differences emerge in the processing of visual images. As noted by Richard Nisbett and his colleagues (Nisbett et al., 2001; Nisbett & Matsuda, 2003), North American thinking tends to be analytical, whereas East Asian thinking is holistic. In other words, North Americans focus their attention on objects and assign them to categories, while East Asians focus on contextual information, relationships, and similarities. These differences in general cognitive strategy appear to extend to the processing of visual information.

Nisbett and his colleagues (Chua, Boland, & Nisbett, 2005) measured the eye movements of American and Chinese participants as they viewed visual scenes in which a main object, like the tiger in Figure 6.36, appears against a complex background.

The Americans focused faster and longer on the main object of the picture, while the Chinese spent equal amounts of time focusing on the object and its context. Although Nisbett and his colleagues attribute these differences to overall cultural factors, such as the varying values placed on individuality and collectivism, we really do not understand the possible cultural or biological influences on this phenomenon. Nonetheless, this research provides a valuable reminder that the world can look very different to people, even if we are using the same basic visual systems.

FIGURE 6.36
American and Asian Participants Show Different Patterns of Visual Scanning When viewing this photo of a tiger, American participants spent more time viewing the tiger than the background, whereas Asian participants spent approximately equal amounts of time viewing the tiger and the background. This image shows tracings from one representative American participant (left) and one representative Asian participant (right).

CHAPTER REVIEW

THOUGHT QUESTIONS

1. If you had to lose either your scotopic or photopic vision, which would you choose to give up and why? What would be the consequences of your choice?
2. If increasing numbers of ultraviolet rays reaching the Earth favor the evolution of a more yellow lens, what effect might this have on the colors we perceive?
3. Currently, very few states regularly test the vision of senior drivers. Based on your knowledge of the changes in vision typical of aging, what types of tests would you recommend? What possible restrictions might you suggest if people fail certain types of tests?

KEY TERMS

amacrine cell (p. 161)
bipolar cell (p. 161)
central vision (p. 161)
color constancy (p. 180)
color contrast (p. 181)
complex cortical cell (p. 172)
cone (p. 162)
cornea (p. 159)
cortical module (p. 172)
cytochrome oxidase blobs (p. 172)
dark current (p. 163)
dorsal stream (p. 174)
fovea (p. 161)
horizontal cell (p. 162)
hypercolumn (p. 172)
iris (p. 159)
lateral geniculate nucleus (LGN) (p. 169)
lateral inhibition (p. 168)
lens (p. 160)
ocular dominance column (p. 172)
opponent process theory (p. 179)
optic chiasm (p. 169)
optic nerve (p. 160)
optic tracts (p. 169)
orientation column (p. 172)
perception (p. 176)
peripheral vision (p. 161)
photopic vision (p. 162)
photopigment (p. 162)
photoreceptor (p. 160)
primary visual cortex (p. 171)
pupil (p. 159)
receptive field (p. 165)
retina (p. 160)
rod (p. 162)
sclera (p. 159)
scotopic vision (p. 162)
sensation (p. 176)
simple cortical cell (p. 171)
superior colliculus (p. 169)
transduction (p. 162)
trichromacy theory (p. 179)
ventral stream (p. 174)

7 Nonvisual Sensation and Perception

AP Images

▲ **Acrobats Depend on the Somatosenses** Feedback from receptors that tell us about the position and movement of our bodies helps these acrobats achieve the balance they need to perform amazing physical feats.

CHAPTER OUTLINE

Introduction

Our sensory systems can be trusted to provide current, accurate information about the environment. It is only when things go wrong that we realize our perceptions are carefully constructed images of reality, not reality itself. Some patients with psychological disorders experience profound perceptual disturbances such as hearing voices that do not exist or having the sense that others are controlling their thoughts and movements. Neuroscientists are beginning to discover patterns of neural activity that are correlated with these distortions of reality.

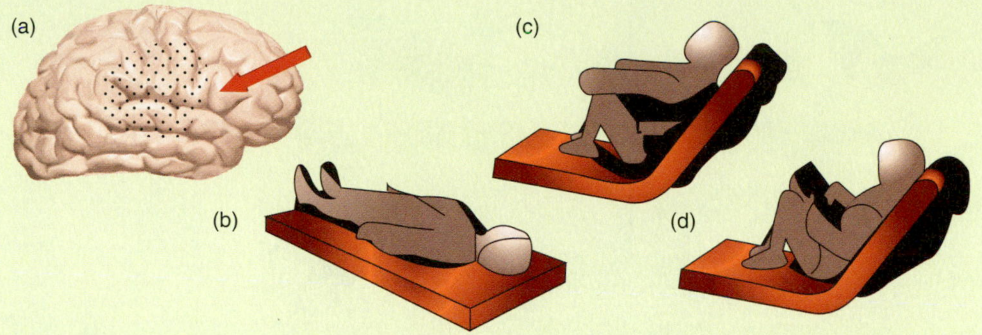

■ **Figure 7.1**

Electrical Stimulation Produces Phantom Person In preparation for epilepsy surgery, electrical stimulation was applied to a patient's brain. (a) The arrow indicates the location of brain stimulation that produced in the patient the sensation of a phantom person hovering behind her. Drawings (b), (c), and (d) indicate the patient's body in brown and the phantom body in black.

Source: After Arzy, S., Seeck, M., Ortigue, S., Spinelli, L., & Blanke, O. (2006). Induction of an illusory shadow person. *Nature*, 443(7109), 287.

In one dramatic example, Olaf Blanke and his colleagues (Arzy, Seeck, Ortigue, Spinelli, & Blanke, 2006) applied electrical stimulation during a presurgical evaluation to the brain of a 22-year-old patient who had epilepsy but no known psychopathology. As shown in ■ Figure 7.1, stimulation applied near the junction of the temporal and parietal lobes produced a strong sensation of another person just behind the patient, who mirrored many of her movements. The patient described the experience by saying, "He is behind me, almost at my body, but I do not feel it." This area of the brain has been implicated previously in misattributions by patients with schizophrenia of their own actions to other people (Farrer, 2004). Although we must be cautious about interpreting data from individuals with disorders such as epilepsy, these observations point to a role for the temporoparietal junction in perceptions regarding the boundaries between self and other. ■

Learning Objectives

After reading this chapter, you should be able to:

LO1 Identify the major features of sound as a stimulus.

LO2 Trace the process of hearing from the outer ear to the brain.

LO3 Describe the processes of perceiving pitch, loudness, and the location of sounds.

LO4 Summarize the major disorders of hearing.

LO5 Describe the structure and function of the vestibular system.

LO6 Trace the processing of touch, thermoreception, and nociception from the receptors to the brain.

LO7 Describe the major features of the olfactory receptors and trace the olfactory pathways from the nose to the brain.

LO8 Summarize the major features of taste receptors and trace the taste pathways leading from the tongue to the brain.

Audition

The best and most beautiful things in the world cannot be seen, nor touched...but are felt in the heart.

Helen Keller

When Helen Keller, who was both blind and deaf, was asked which disability affected her the most, she replied that blindness separates a person from things, whereas deafness separates a person from people. In addition to processing the speech of others, we use the sense of **audition,** or hearing, to identify objects in the environment and to determine where objects are in relation to our bodies.

Ours is a uniquely human auditory world. Just as we can see a broad but limited range of the electromagnetic spectrum, we can also hear a wide but limited range of sound. ■ Figure 7.2 compares the range of sound frequencies that can be sensed by several different species. Your dog begins howling seconds before you hear the ambulance siren, because the dog's hearing is better than yours for these high-pitched sounds. Neither you nor your dog is likely to hear the even higher pitched vocalizations that bats use to locate food and navigate (Griffin, 1959).

Sound as a Physical Stimulus

You may have heard the famous riddle, "If a tree falls in the forest and nobody is around to hear it, does it make a sound?" The psychologist's answer to this riddle is both yes and no. The answer is "yes" if we are asking whether the falling tree produces a physical sound stimulus, but the answer is "no" if we're talking about sound as the perceptual experience of hearing.

audition The sense of hearing.

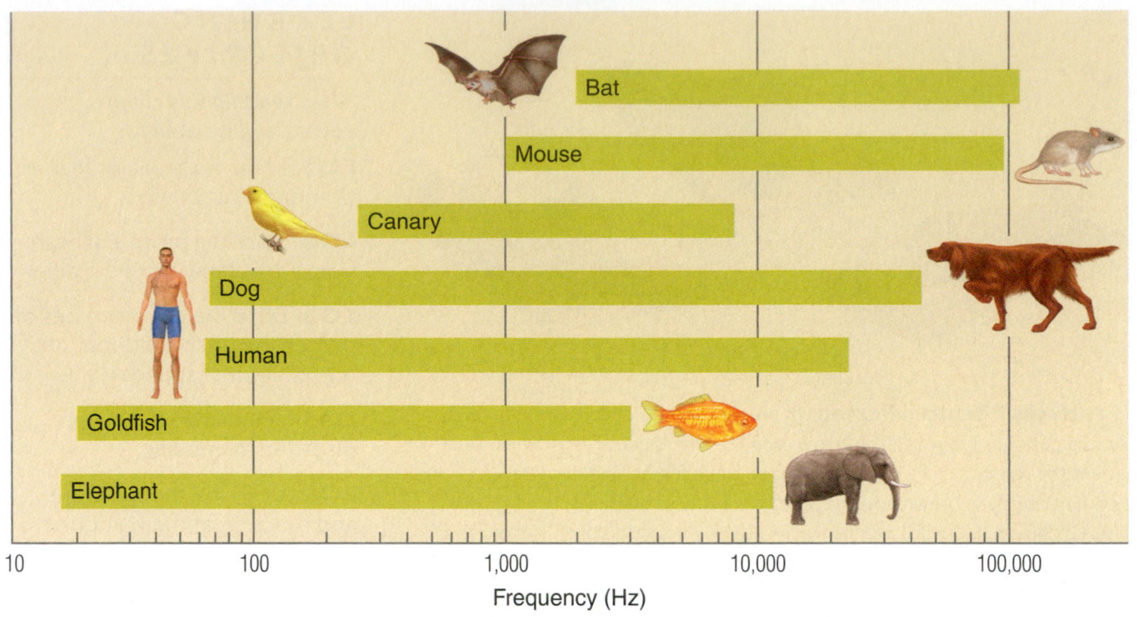

■ **FIGURE 7.2**
The Auditory World Differs Across Species This figure illustrates the range of frequencies that fall within the sensory capacities of several species, including humans.

■ **FIGURE 7.3**
Sound Reflection Is Used in Echolocation The bat is able to navigate through small openings in nylon mesh in total darkness by using echolocation.

Sound as a physical stimulus begins with the movement of an object in space. Movement sets off waves of vibration in the form of miniature collisions between adjacent molecules that produce outwardly-moving bands of high and low pressure, much like ripples in a pond. Because sound waves require this jostling between molecules, sound cannot occur in a vacuum such as outer space. Those explosions we enjoy in *Star Wars* films may be good entertainment, but they are not great science.

For humans, the medium that carries sound is usually air, but we can also sense sounds that travel through liquids and solids. Like light, sound interacts with the environment as it travels from its source to the perceiver. Fabrics absorb sound waves and can be helpful in reducing noise. Sound reflected from surfaces is used by a number of species for echolocation. The bat shown in ■ Figure 7.3 is using echolocation to find its way through a nylon grid in the dark. Although humans are not the best at using echolocation, we can improve with practice.

As shown in Table 7.1, sound energy, like electromagnetic energy, can be described in the form of waves. The height, or **amplitude,** of a wave, indicates the amount of vibration produced by the sound, which in turn is perceived as loudness by the listener. Low-amplitude waves are characteristic of soft sounds, and high-amplitude waves are perceived as loud. The **frequency** of the wave, or the number of cycles per unit of time, indicates wavelength. Wavelength usually corresponds to the perceived pitch of a sound. Long wavelengths are perceived as having low pitch, whereas short wavelengths produce sounds with higher pitch. The simplest type of sound wave is a **pure tone,** which has a single frequency. Most sounds consist of combinations of waves. Waves that do not regularly repeat themselves are perceived as **noise,** as opposed to identifiable tones.

amplitude The height of a periodic curve measured on its vertical axis.
frequency The number of cycles of a periodic wave per unit of time.
pure tone The simplest type of sound, characterized by a single sine wave.
noise Completely random combinations of sound waves.
decibel (dB) A unit used to express a difference in intensity between two sounds, equal to 20 times the common logarithm of the ratio of the two levels.

Intensity Sounds can vary dramatically in terms of intensity from a quiet whisper to the rock band that actually makes your bones vibrate. To manage such a wide range of intensities, a logarithmic scale of sound intensity based on the **decibel** (dB) is used. The threshold for hearing, or the least intense sound that a human can hear, is set at 0 dB. This is roughly equivalent to the sound made by a mosquito flying three meters away from you. As shown in Table 7.2, a whisper produces a sound intensity of 20 dB, whereas an iPod turned up to maximum loudness can reach 120 dB. At 130 dB, we experience pain. This is a useful warning because exposure to sounds at this level of intensity might permanently damage our hearing.

TABLE 7.1 Sounds Vary Along the Dimensions of Amplitude, Frequency, and Complexity

Wave Characteristic	Perception of Characteristic	Examples	
Amplitude (intensity) Amplitude measures the height of the wave. Amplitude	Loudness	High-amplitude waves are perceived as loud sounds.	Low-amplitude waves are perceived as soft sounds.
Frequency (wavelength) Frequency measures the number of wave cycles per unit of time. Frequency	Pitch	Low-frequency waves are perceived as low-pitched sounds.	High-frequency waves are perceived as high-pitched sounds.
Timbre (complexity) Timbre describes the specific combination of a fundamental frequency and harmonic frequencies in a given sound.	The distinct quality or uniqueness of a sound. Allows us to distinguish which instrument produced a note.	Pure tones have a single frequency.	Complex tones are made up of several frequencies.

TABLE 7.2 Intensity Levels of Common Sounds

Source of Sound	Intensity Level
Threshold of hearing (TOH)	0 dB
Rustling leaves	10 dB
Whisper	20 dB
Normal conversation	60 dB
Busy street traffic	70 dB
Vacuum cleaner	80 dB
Water at the foot of Niagara Falls	90 dB
Walkman at maximum level	100 dB
Front rows of rock concert	110 dB
Propeller plane at takeoff	120 dB
Threshold of pain (e.g., machine-gun fire)	130 dB
Military jet at takeoff	140 dB
Instant perforation of eardrum	160 dB

What you see and hear depends a good deal on where you are standing; it also depends on what sort of person you are.

C. S. Lewis

Frequency Frequency refers to the number of cycles per unit of time, or the wavelength, of a sound stimulus. The unit used to measure the frequency of sound is the **hertz (Hz).** A 500 Hz sound completes 500 cycles in one second.

Speech and music are made up of complex combinations of frequencies. A tone's note or pitch is determined by the wave having the lowest frequency, which is referred to as the tone's **fundamental frequency.** Additional waves occurring in the tone are known as **harmonics,** which determine the tone's **timbre,** or quality. The same note played by a clarinet and by a piano will have the same pitch, but differences in timbre will identify which instrument produced the note.

Ultrasound refers to stimuli with frequencies beyond the upper range of human hearing, or about 20,000 Hz. Ultrasound waves are used to clean objects or to produce noninvasive images for medical purposes. **Infrasound** refers to frequencies below the range of human hearing, or less than about 20 Hz. Many animals, including elephants and marine mammals, use infrasound for communication. In humans, however, infrasound stimuli produce dizziness, nausea, uncontrolled bowel movements, and other unpleasant symptoms and are under study as a possible means of nonlethal crowd control (Vinokur, 2004).

hertz (Hz) A unit of sound frequency equal to one cycle per second.

fundamental frequency The wave having the lowest frequency in a complex tone.

harmonic An additional wave produced by a complex tone that is an integer multiple of the tone's fundamental frequency.

timbre The quality of a sound that distinguishes it from other sounds of the same pitch and volume.

ultrasound Sound at frequencies above the range of human hearing, or higher than about 20,000 Hz.

infrasound Sound at frequencies below the range of human hearing, or lower than about 20 Hz.

pinna The visible part of the outer ear.

auditory canal A tube-shaped structure in the outer ear that leads to the tympanic membrane.

tympanic membrane The membrane separating the outer and middle ears.

oval window A membrane that forms the boundary between the middle and inner ears.

ossicles (OSS-i-kuhls) The bones of the middle ear.

malleus (MALL-ee-us) The first of three ossicles in the middle ear.

incus The middle of three ossicles found in the middle ear.

stapes (STAY-pees) The innermost of the three ossicles of the middle ear.

tensor tympani (TEN-sohr tim-PAN-ee) One of two muscles of the middle ear responsible for the acoustic reflex.

stapedius (stuh-PEE-dee-us) One of the muscles responsible for the acoustic reflex.

acoustic reflex The protective restriction of the movement of the tympanic membrane and the ossicles, resulting in a reduction of sound to the inner ear by a factor of 30 dB.

The Structure and Function of the Auditory System

The components that make up the ear are generally divided into three parts: the outer, middle, and inner ear.

The Outer Ear The major structures of the ear are illustrated in ■ Figure 7.4. The outer ear consists of the structures visible outside the body: the **pinna** and the **auditory canal.** The pinna serves to collect and focus sounds, just like a funnel. The pinna also plays an important role in locating the source of sound. Movement of the pinna allows some species to further localize sound or to indicate emotional states, as when a dog puts its ears back while snarling. Sound collected by the pinna is channeled through the auditory canal, a tube-shaped structure about 2.5 cm long and about 7 mm wide.

The Middle Ear The **tympanic membrane,** or eardrum, forms the boundary between the outer ear and middle ear. The boundary between the middle ear and inner ear is formed by another membrane, the **oval window.**

The three **ossicles** bridging the middle ear are the **malleus** (hammer), **incus** (anvil), and **stapes** (stirrup). Each of these tiny bones is about the size of a single letter of print in this text. The purpose of these bones is to transfer sound energy from the outside air to the fluid in the inner ear without losing too much of it. As you may have noticed when swimming, sounds waves originating in air lose much of their energy when they enter the water. If a friend calls out to you while you're under water, the sound is not very clear. The ear faces a similar problem, as sound energy must travel through the air of the outer and middle ears to the fluid of the inner ear.

The middle ear solves this transfer problem in two ways. First, the connections between the ossicles are hinged, which creates a lever action that increases the force of the vibration that the stapes bone delivers to the oval window. Second, force applied to the much smaller oval window produces much more pressure than the same force applied to the large tympanic membrane. With both force and pressure increased at the oval window, the ear can recover about 23 dB of the 30 dB that would otherwise be lost when sound is transferred from the air in the middle ear to the fluid in the inner ear.

The movement of the tympanic membrane and the ossicles is restricted by two small muscles, the **tensor tympani** and the **stapedius.** The tensor tympani is attached to the tympanic membrane, and the stapedius is attached to the stapes. Together, these muscles are responsible for the **acoustic reflex,** in which the contraction of the two muscles reduces the movement of the ossicles. As a result, sound transferred to the inner ear is reduced by up to 30 dB (Evans, 1982). The exact purpose of the acoustic reflex is unknown. It might help protect our ears from loud noises, although it engages too slowly to prevent damage due to gunshots and explosives. Because the reflex

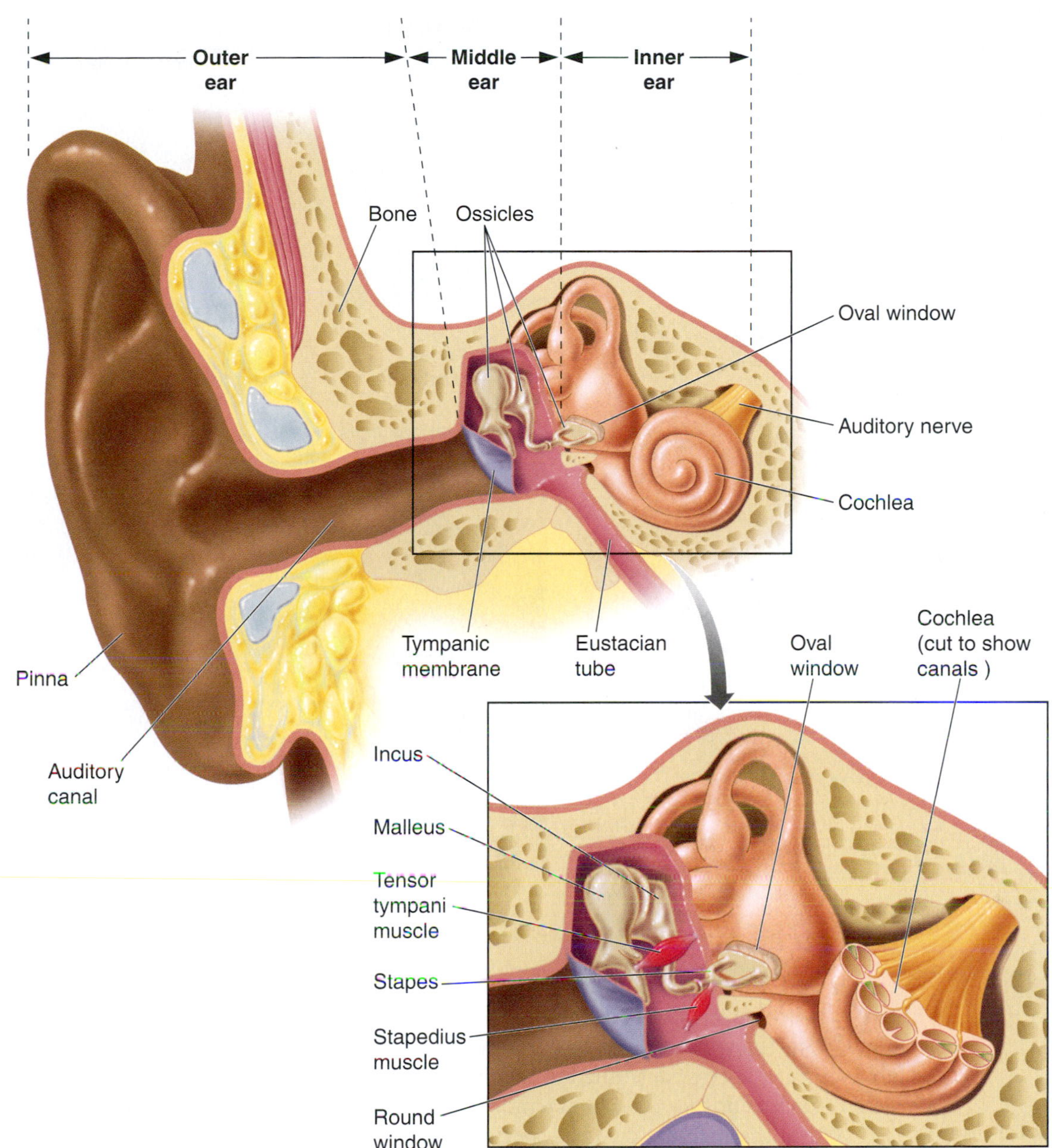

■ **FIGURE 7.4**
The Anatomy of the Ear

reduces perception of low-frequency sounds more than of high-frequency sounds, it might help us discriminate speech against low-frequency background noise.

The Inner Ear The inner ear contains two sets of fluid-filled cavities embedded in the temporal bone of the skull. One set, known as the semicircular canals, is part of the vestibular system, which will be discussed later in this chapter. The other set is known as the **cochlea** ("snail" in Greek). The fluid-filled cochlea contains specialized receptor cells that respond to the vibrations transmitted to the inner ear. The cochlea is about 32 mm long and 2 mm in diameter. When rolled up like a snail shell, the human cochlea is about the size of a pea.

The cochlea is divided into three parallel chambers, illustrated in ■ Figure 7.5. Two of the chambers, the **vestibular canal** and the **tympanic canal,** are connected to each other near the **apex,** which is the part of the cochlea most distant from the oval window. These two chambers contain a fluid known as **perilymph,** which is similar to cerebrospinal fluid (see Chapter 2). The third chamber, the **cochlear duct,** contains a very different type of fluid, known as **endolymph.** The endolymph is rich in potassium and low in sodium. The fluids (and chambers) are separated by two membranes. **Reissner's membrane** separates the vestibular canal and the cochlear duct. The **basilar membrane** separates the tympanic canal and the cochlear duct.

cochlea (KOKE-lee-uh) The fluid-filled structure of the inner ear containing auditory receptors.
vestibular canal (ves-TIB-you-lar) One of the chambers found in the cochlea.
tympanic canal (tim-PAN-ik) One of the chambers found in the cochlea.
apex The part of the cochlea most distant from the oval window.
perilymph (PEAR-ee-limf) Fluid found in the vestibular and tympanic canals of the inner ear.
cochlear duct (KOKE-lee-ar) One of three chambers found in the cochlea.
endolymph (EN-doh-limf) The fluid found in the cochlear duct.

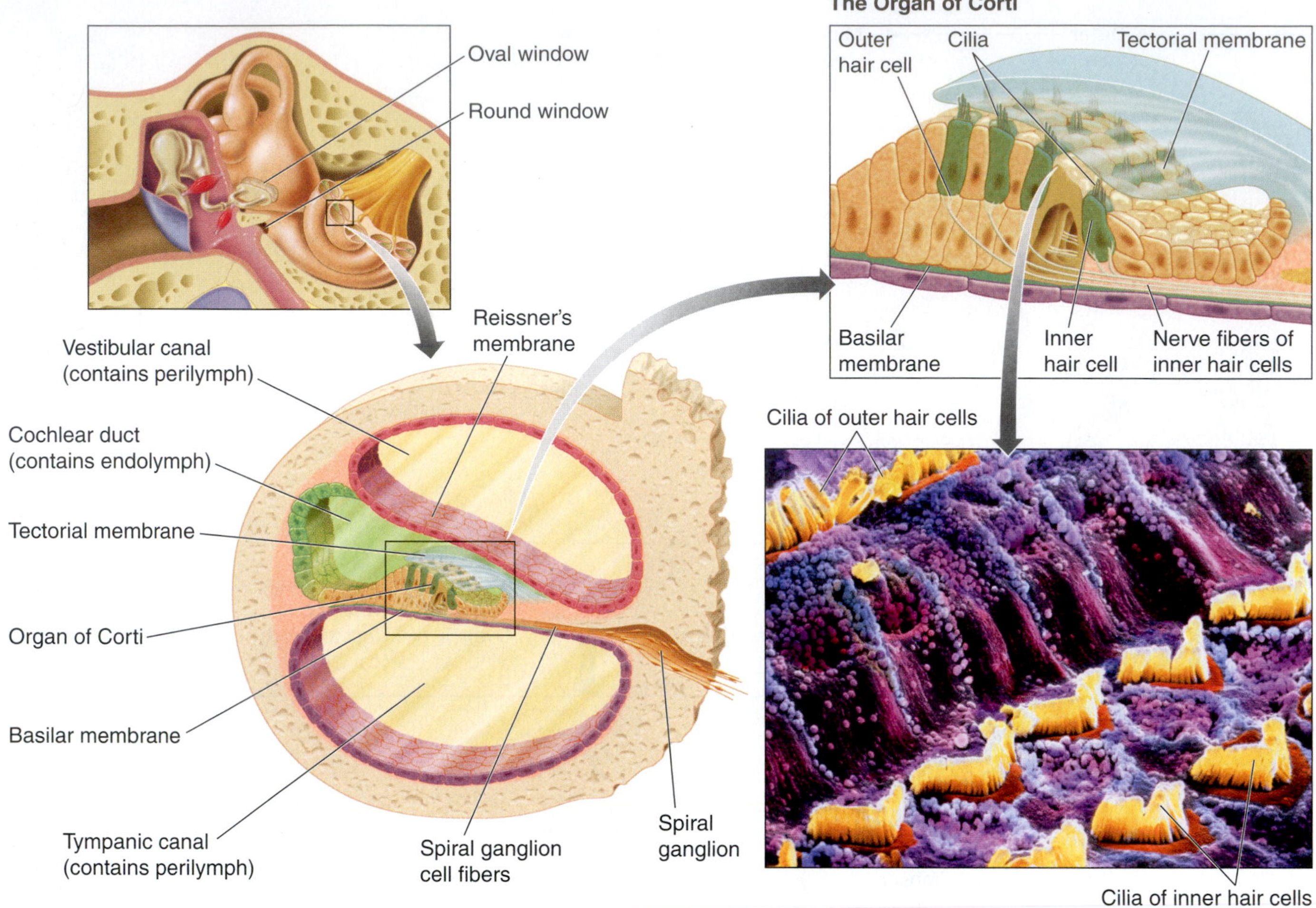

FIGURE 7.5
The Cochlea

At the base of the cochlea, at the boundary between the middle and inner ears, the oval window covers the vestibular canal. The tympanic canal is covered by another membrane, known as the **round window.** Because the vestibular and tympanic canals are connected, pressure applied to the oval window by the stapes travels through the perilymph and pushes the round window out into the middle ear.

Within the cochlear duct is a specialized structure known as the **organ of Corti,** which is responsible for translating vibrations in the inner ear into neural messages. The organ of Corti, consisting of rows of hair cells, rests on the basilar membrane. Over the top of the hair cells, and actually attached to some of them, is the **tectorial (roof) membrane.** The tectorial membrane is attached to the cochlear duct at only one side and can move independently from the basilar membrane.

Several structural features of the basilar membrane are relevant to its response to sound. The membrane is about five times wider at its apex (far end) than at its base (beginning). In addition, the basilar membrane is about 100 times stiffer at its base than at its apex. These structural differences are similar to the range of size and flexibility found in the different strings of a guitar. When vibration produces pressure changes within the cochlea, the basilar membrane responds with a wavelike motion, similar to the motion of a rope or whip that is snapped. It will move less at the stiff, smaller end near the base than at the wide, floppy end at the apex. As shown in Figure 7.6, high-frequency sounds will cause a peak vibration of the basilar membrane near its base, whereas low-frequency sounds will cause a peak vibration closer to its apex.

The movement of the basilar membrane is sensed by the hair cells attached to the organ of Corti. Out of the approximately 15,500 hair cells in each human inner ear, about 3,500 of them are known as **inner hair cells,** which are the actual auditory receptors. The inner hair cells are located near the connection between the tectorial membrane and cochlear duct. The remaining 12,000 hair cells are

Reissner's membrane (RICE-ners) A membrane that separates the vestibular canal and the cochlear duct in the inner ear.

basilar membrane (BASS-i-lar) A structure in the cochlea that separates the tympanic canal and the cochlear duct.

round window A membrane covering the end of the tympanic canal.

organ of Corti A structure within the cochlear duct responsible for translating vibrations in the inner ear into neural messages.

tectorial (roof) membrane (tek-TOHR-ee-uhl) A membrane in the inner ear that covers the top of the hair cells and is actually attached to some of them.

inner hair cell An auditory receptor cell located near the connection between the tectorial membrane and cochlear duct.

1 The ossicles transfer vibrations from the tympanic membrane to the oval window.
2 The movement of the oval window creates waves in the perilymph within the vestibular canal.
3 The waves push the basilar membrane up and down.
4 The waves travel back along the tympanic canal from the apex to the round window.
5 The waves push the round window in and out.
Apex
Vestibular canal
Tympanic canal
Round window
Cochlear duct
(a) Sound Transferred to Basilar Membrane
Oval window
Vestibular canal
Wave in perilymph
Apex
Round window
Tympanic canal
Cochlear duct
(b) Cochlea (unrolled for clarity)
Base of basilar membrane (narrow, thick, and stiff)
Basilar membrane (surrounding structures of cochlear duct removed for clarity)
Peak basilar membrane response to frequency of 1000Hz
Apex of basilar membrane (wide, thin, and flexible)
Location of peak basilar membrane response to frequency of
20,000
4,000
1,000
100
Hertz
(c) Basilar Membrane

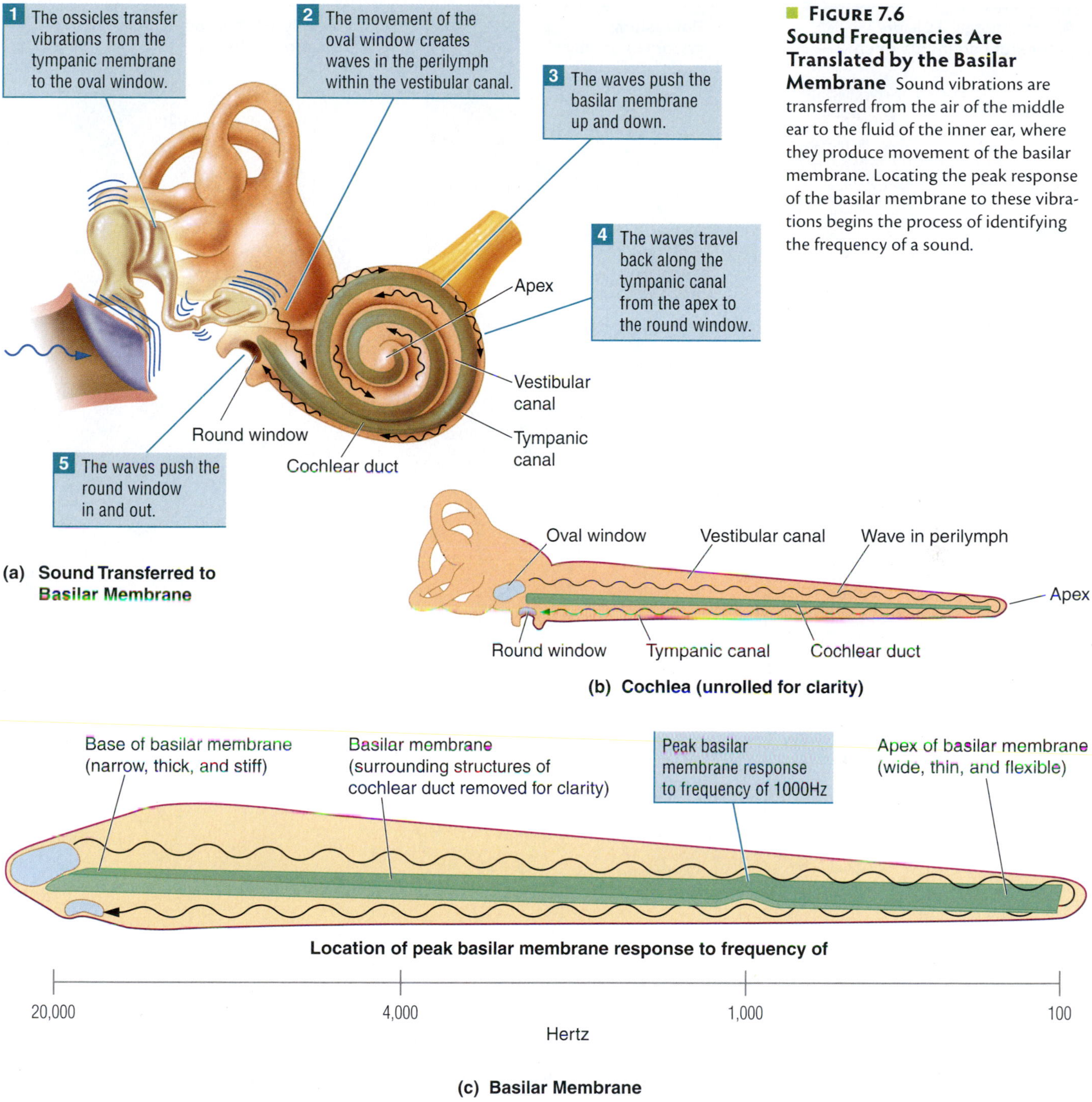

FIGURE 7.6 Sound Frequencies Are Translated by the Basilar Membrane Sound vibrations are transferred from the air of the middle ear to the fluid of the inner ear, where they produce movement of the basilar membrane. Locating the peak response of the basilar membrane to these vibrations begins the process of identifying the frequency of a sound.

known as **outer hair cells,** which appear to amplify sound. Both have hairlike **cilia** extending from their tops, but only the cilia from outer hair cells are attached to the tectorial membrane (Dallos, 1984). Although there are many more outer hair cells in the ear, only 5 percent of the **auditory nerve (cranial nerve VIII)** fibers connect with outer hair cells. The remaining 95 percent of auditory nerve fibers connect with the inner hair cells.

Movement of the cilia back and forth within the endolymph alternately hyperpolarizes and depolarizes the hair cells away from their resting potential of –70mV. The amount of movement needed to produce a response in the hair cells is quite small. If cilia were the size of the Eiffel Tower in Paris, the movement required to produce a response would equate to only 1 cm (about 0.4 inches; Hudspeth, 1983). The depolarization and hyperpolarization of the hair cells result from the opening and closing of mechanically gated potassium channels located in the tips of the cilia, shown in Figure 7.7. When all of the cilia are straight up, as in a completely quiet environment, the channels are

outer hair cell An auditory receptor cell located on the organ of Corti that may serve to amplify sounds.

cilia Microscopic, hairlike projections that extend from a structure.

auditory nerve (cranial nerve VIII) The nerve that makes contact with the hair cells of the cochlea; cranial nerve VIII.

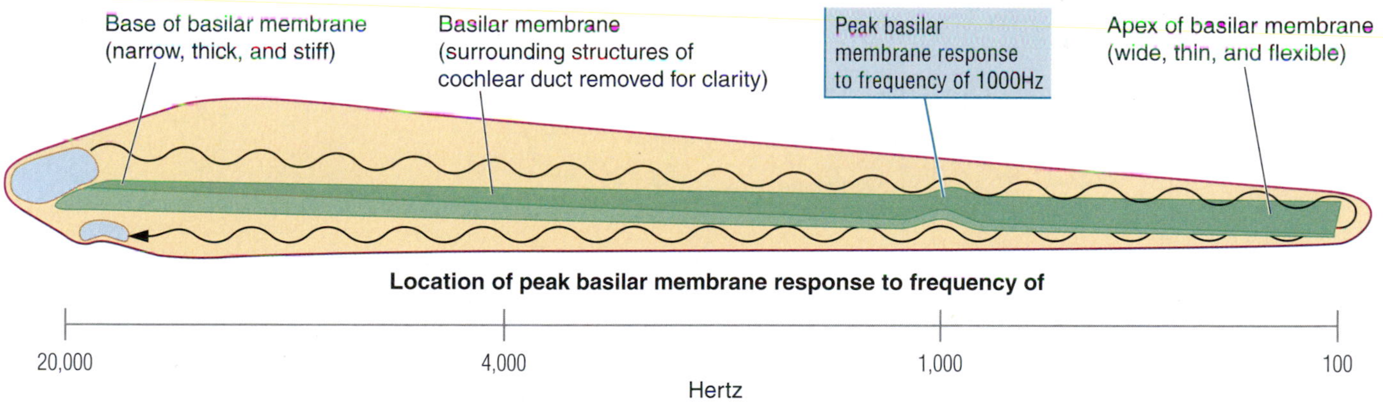

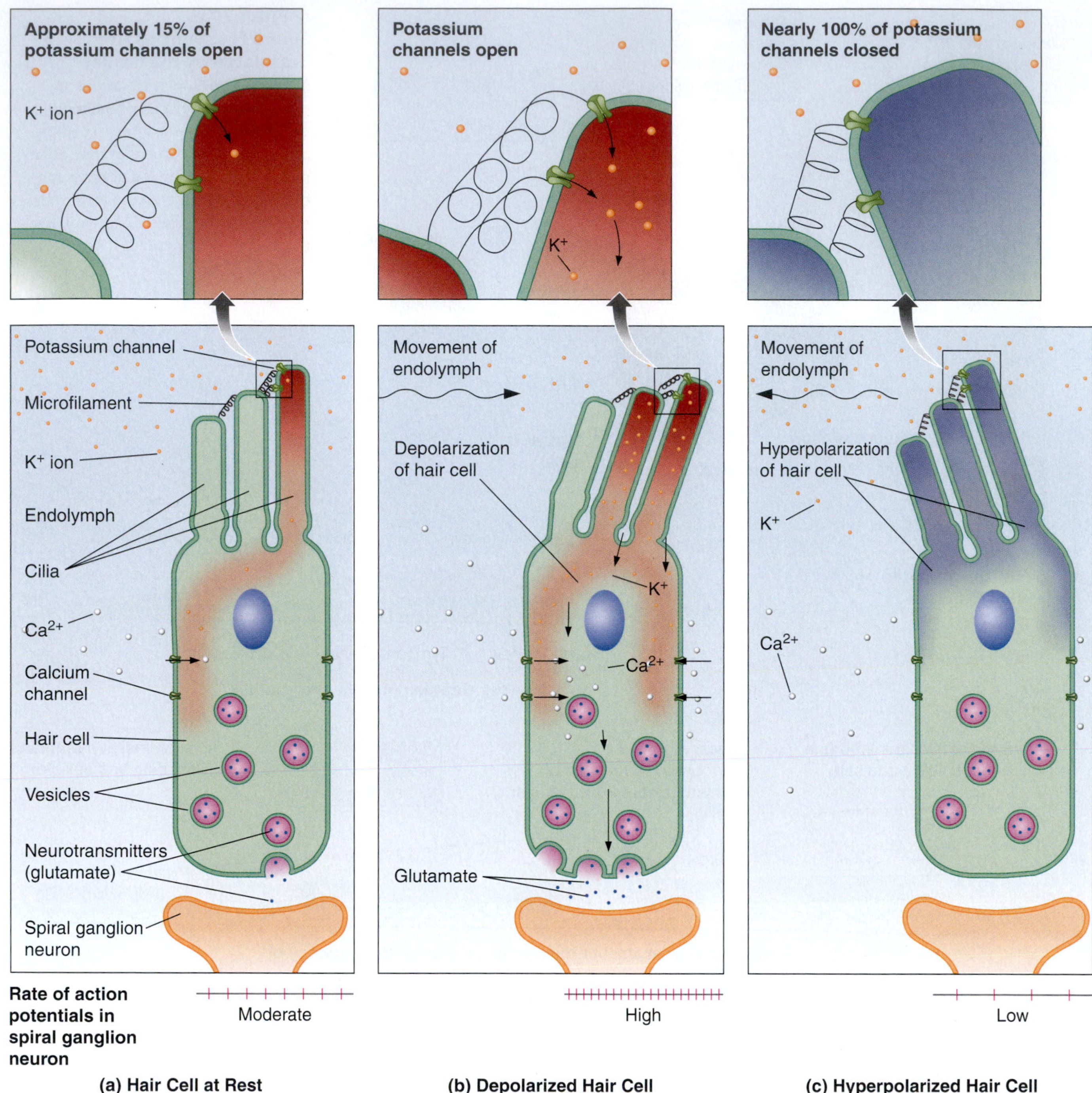

FIGURE 7.7

The Movement of Cilia Regulates Neurotransmitter Release by Hair Cells (a) In the resting hair cell, approximately 15 percent of the potassium (K^+) channels are open. The resulting influx of K^+ slightly depolarizes the cell, leading to the opening of calcium (Ca^{2+}) channels and the release of relatively small amounts of neurotransmitter onto spiral ganglion neurons. Consequently, the spiral ganglion neurons form action potentials at a moderate rate. (b) When the moving endolymph displaces the cilia of the hair cell toward their tallest member, many more K^+ channels open. A greater influx of Ca^{2+} occurs, followed by an increase in the amount of neurotransmitter released by the hair cell and a higher rate of action potentials in the spiral ganglion neurons. (c) When the moving endolymph displaces the cilia of the hair cell toward their shortest member, the K^+ channels close, and the cell hyperpolarizes. Less Ca^{2+} enters the cell, fewer molecules of transmitter are released, and the rate of action potentials in the spiral ganglion neurons is reduced.

partially open. Small amounts of potassium will enter the cell. When the cilia bend one way, tension on the filaments connecting adjacent cilia opens the channels further, and greater amounts of potassium will enter the cell. Bending the cilia in the opposite direction releases the tension on the filaments, closing the channels.

Normally, when potassium channels are opened, potassium leaves the neuron, causing hyperpolarization. However, unlike most extracellular fluid, the endolymph

■ **FIGURE 7.8**
Auditory Pathways from the Cochlea to the Cortex

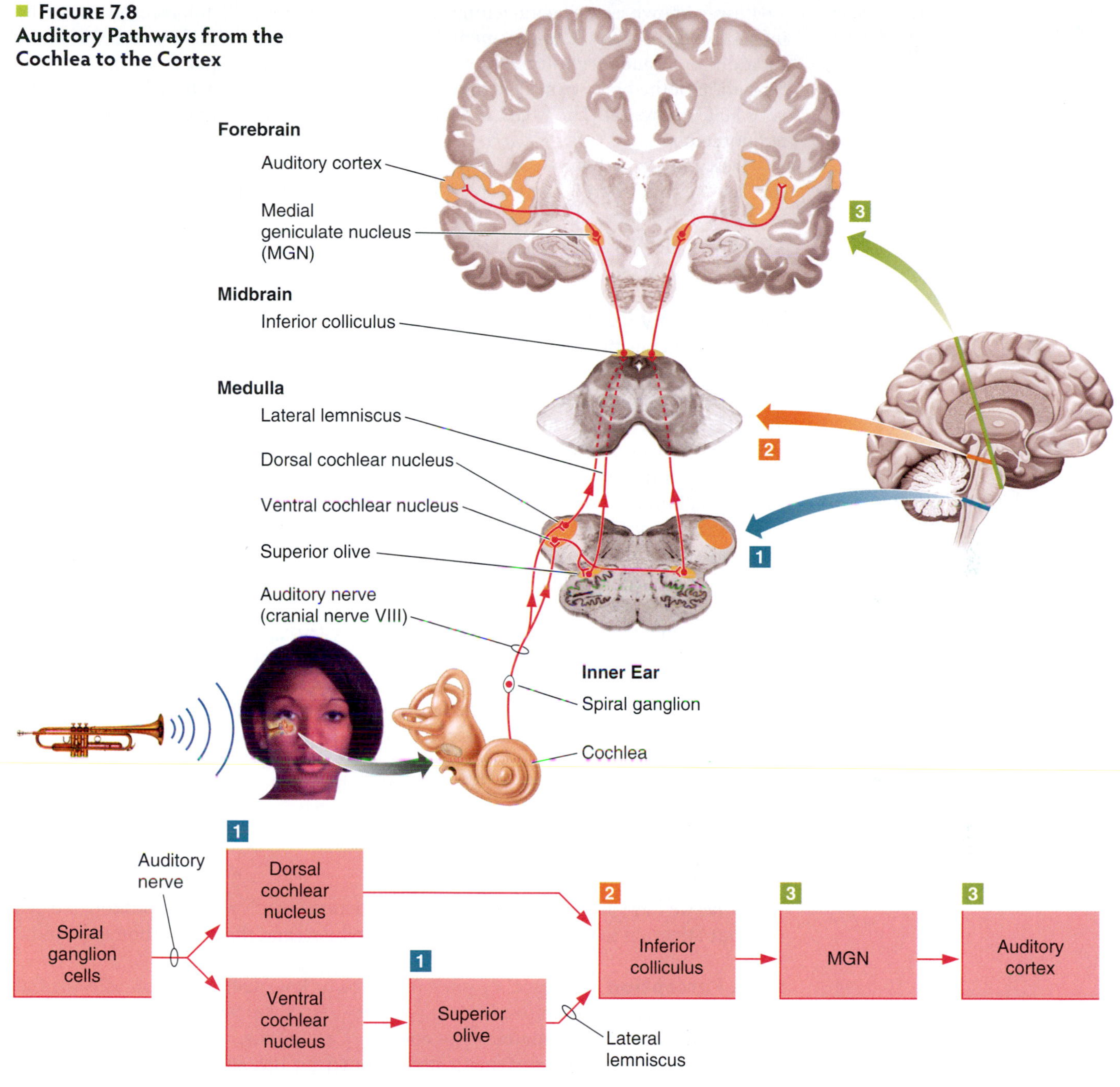

surrounding the hair cells contains a higher concentration of potassium than is found in the intracellular fluid of the hair cells. Consequently, when potassium channels in hair cells open, potassium will move into the relatively negative internal environment of the cell due to both diffusion and electrical force. Potassium's positive charge depolarizes the hair cell, leading to the opening of voltage-dependent calcium channels and neurotransmitter release. Most hair cells use the excitatory neurotransmitter glutamate.

Central Auditory Pathways As shown in ■ Figure 7.8, **spiral ganglion** neurons are bipolar in structure. One set of fibers makes contact with the hair cells. The other set projects to the dorsal and ventral cochlear nuclei of the medulla as part of the auditory nerve (cranial nerve VIII). Input from both cochlear nuclei eventually reaches the inferior colliculi of the midbrain. However, axons from the ventral cochlear nuclei first synapse in the superior olive in the medulla, which in turn forms connections via

spiral ganglion Structure found in the inner ear whose axons form the auditory nerve.

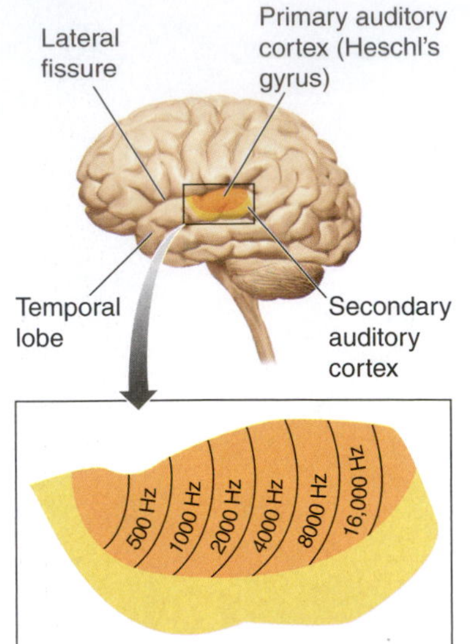

FIGURE 7.9 Tonotopic Organization Is Maintained by the Auditory Cortex Neurons responding to lower frequencies are located in the rostral portions of Heschl's gyrus, and those responding to higher frequencies are located in the more caudal portions.

a pathway known as the lateral lemniscus with the inferior colliculi. Neurons from the inferior colliculi project to the **medial geniculate nucleus (MGN)** of the thalamus. In addition to auditory information, the MGN also receives input from the reticular formation of the brainstem. This input adjusts hearing sensitivity based on the organism's state of arousal. The MGN in turn projects to the auditory cortex located in the temporal lobe.

Descending pathways appear to modify the activity of auditory fibers as they contact the inner hair cells (Dallos, 1981). If the superior olive is electrically stimulated, the inner hair cells become temporarily less sensitive (Brown & Nuttall, 1984). This input might block background noise (Kawase, Delgutte, & Liberman, 1993) or sharpen focus on one source of sound (Guinan, 1996).

The Auditory Cortex **Primary auditory cortex,** also known as **Heschl's gyrus,** is located just below the lateral fissure in the temporal lobe.

As shown in ■ Figure 7.9, primary auditory cortex is organized in columns that respond to single frequencies. Lower frequencies produce a response in columns located rostrally in Heschl's gyrus, whereas higher frequencies produce a response in columns located in the more caudal portions of the gyrus. In some columns, input received by both ears produces a stronger response than input received by a single ear. In other columns, the opposite holds true: input received from a single ear produces a stronger response than input received by both ears. Other neurons within the auditory cortex respond to differences in intensity.

Surrounding Heschl's gyrus are areas known collectively as **secondary auditory cortex.** These areas appear to be activated by more complex types of stimuli such as clicks, general bursts of noise, and sounds with particular frequency patterns. Research with rhesus monkeys has demonstrated that some neurons in the secondary auditory cortex respond best to vocalizations from other monkeys (Rauschecker, Ian, & Hauser, 1995). These neurons are located in the part of the temporal lobe that is analogous to **Wernicke's area** in humans, suggesting that humans also have specialized neurons for the detection of speech sounds. Wernicke's area, which is located near the junction of the temporal and parietal lobes, is involved with the comprehension of language in humans.

AUDITORY PERCEPTION

Now that we have an understanding of the structures involved with audition, we can turn our attention to the perception of pitch, loudness, and the localization of sounds.

Pitch Perception We associate pitch (the high or low quality of a sound) with frequency, although that is an overly simplistic view. Pitch can vary due to factors other than frequency, such as the intensity or context of a stimulus.

Most frequencies are systematically encoded by the auditory system through **tonotopic organization.** Neurons responding to one frequency are located next to neurons responding to similar frequencies. As a result, one cue for assessing the frequency of a sound is the location of active neurons. From the level of the basilar membrane up through the spiral ganglia, the medial geniculate nucleus, and the auditory cortex, different frequencies are processed at different locations. Georg Von Békésy's place theory explains the tonotopic organization of the basilar membrane. According to this theory, the peak of the wave traveling along the length of the basilar membrane is correlated with a sound's frequency. Place theory works well for sounds above 4,000 Hz. Below frequencies of 4,000 Hz, the response of the basilar membrane does not allow for precise localization. In these cases, frequency theory, in which patterns of neural firing match the actual frequency of a sound, provides a better model than place theory for the processing of sound.

Loudness Perception Although the decibel level of a sound wave and its perceived loudness are related, they are not the same thing. Decibels describe the physical qualities of the sound stimulus, whereas loudness is the human perception of that stimulus. The perception of loudness does not change at the same rate as the decibels do.

medial geniculate nucleus Nucleus of the thalamus that receives auditory input.
primary auditory cortex Cortex located just below the lateral fissure in the temporal lobe that provides the initial cortical processing of auditory information.
Heschl's gyrus (HESH-uhlz) Primary auditory cortex.
secondary auditory cortex Areas surrounding Heschl's gyrus in the temporal lobe that process more complex types of stimuli.
Wernicke's area (VARE-nik-eez) The part of the human secondary auditory cortex that specifically decodes speech.
tonotopic organization A system in which different frequencies are processed in different locations.

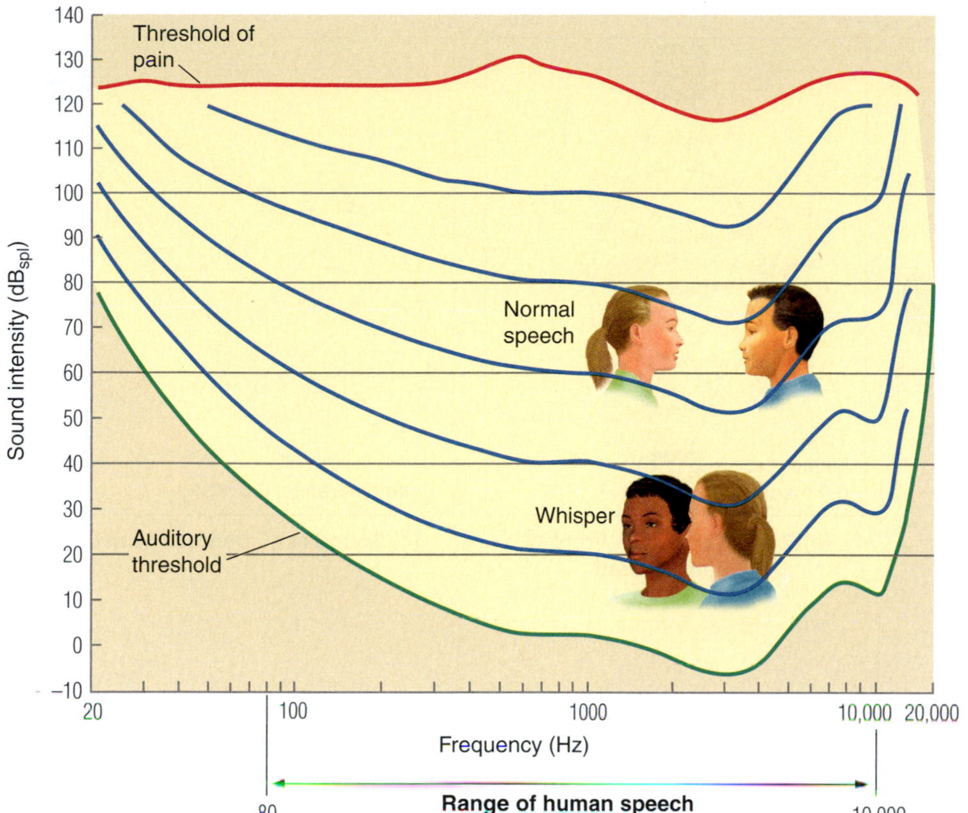

■ **FIGURE 7.10**
Equal Loudness Contours These functions plot the results of allowing participants to adjust the intensity of different tones until they sound equally loud. Low frequencies are usually perceived as quieter than high frequencies at the same level of intensity. We are especially sensitive to frequencies found in speech.

Loudness doubles with each 10 dB increase in stimulus intensity (Stevens, 1960). In other words, a stimulus that is 10 dB greater than another is perceived as only twice as loud.

The ears of men are lesser agents of belief than their eyes.
Herodotus

Our ability to detect loudness varies with the frequency of a sound. By allowing participants to adjust the intensity of different tones until they sound equally loud, we can plot functions known as **equal loudness contours.** As shown in ■ Figure 7.10, low frequencies are usually perceived as quieter than high frequencies at the same level of intensity. At very high intensities of 80 to 100 dB, you can see that all frequencies are perceived as being nearly equally loud.

Auditory neurons can respond to higher sound amplitudes by increasing their rate of response. However, the range of sound amplitudes we can hear is too broad to be completely encoded in this manner. Normally, a single neuron can respond to a range of about 40 dB, whereas at some frequencies, humans can perceive a range of 130 dB. Although a single neuron might have a limited range of 40 dB, a population of neurons with different ranges can provide the coverage we require. In addition, although auditory neurons have a preferred frequency to which they respond, they will in fact respond to similar frequencies if amplitude is high enough. The recruitment of these additional neurons contributes to our perception of loudness.

Localization of Sound Our primary means of localizing sound in the horizontal plane (in front, behind, and to the side) is a comparison of the arrival times of sounds at each ear. As illustrated in ■ Figure 7.11, the differences in arrival time are quite small, between 0 msec for sounds that are either straight ahead or behind you to 0.6 msec for sounds coming from a point perpendicular to your head on either side. Because arrival times from sounds immediately in front or behind you are identical, these sounds are very difficult to localize accurately.

Distinctions between arrival times of sound at each ear are made by neurons in the superior olive. These neurons are known as binaural neurons because they receive input from both ears. Binaural neurons respond most vigorously when input from both ears reaches them simultaneously. If input from the two ears arrives at slightly different times, the cells will respond less vigorously.

equal loudness contours
Functions that result when participants are allowed to adjust the intensity of different tones until they sound equally loud.

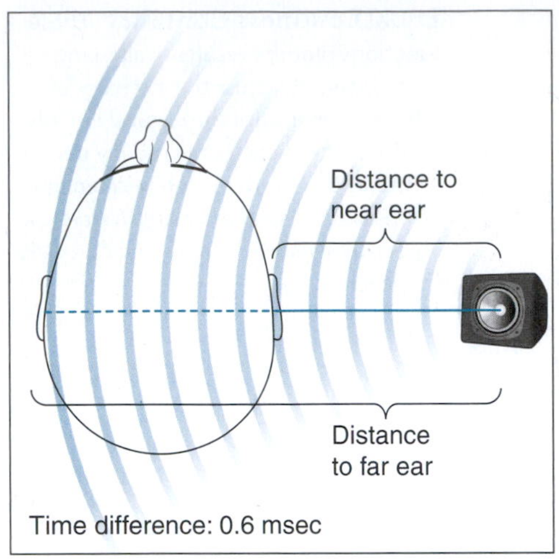

(a) Sound Perpendicular to Head

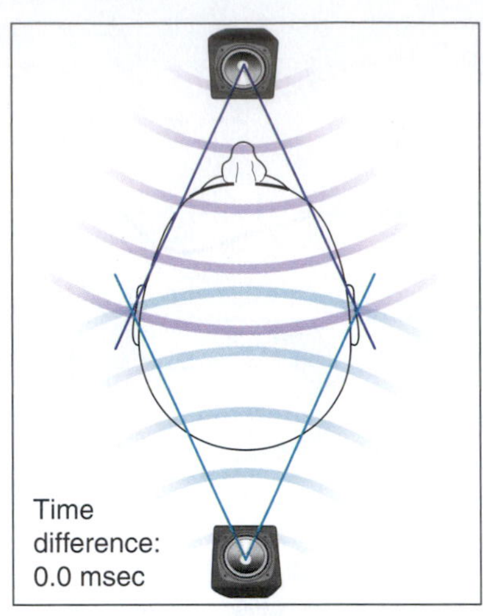

(b) Sound Directly in Front of or Behind Head

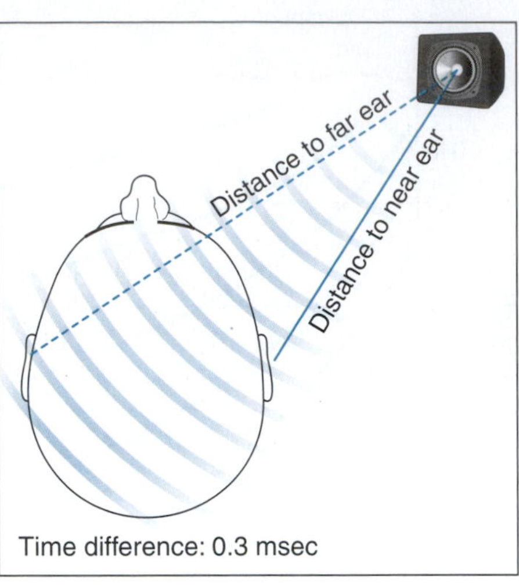

(c) Sound at 45 Degrees from Head

FIGURE 7.11
We Localize Sound by Comparing Arrival Times at Both Ears
(a) There will be a relatively large difference in the time of arrival of sound (0.6 msec) to the right and left ears, and the individual will have no difficulty localizing the source of the sound. (b) There is no difference between the arrival times to the two ears of sounds directly in front or behind the listener, and without additional cues, these sounds will be very difficult to localize accurately. (c) A 0.3 msec difference in arrival times would suggest a sound source of about 45 degrees from the head.

Several unique physiological features allow auditory neurons to produce the rapid responses required for sound localization. Many cells in the auditory system respond and reset more rapidly than other types of neurons, due at least in part to large numbers of potassium channels. Synapses are unusually large, providing the ability to release large amounts of neurotransmitter within a given time. Specialized glutamate receptors, found only in the auditory system, are also built for rapid transmission. Finally, many brainstem auditory neurons have myelin not only on their axons but also on their cell bodies.

In addition to arrival times, we also assess the differences in the intensities of sound reaching each ear. Because the head blocks some sound waves, a sound "shadow" is cast on the ear farthest away from the source of sound, producing a weaker signal to that ear. This system does not work for lower-frequency sounds, which move around the head without producing a noticeable shadow.

The pinna of the ear is essential for localizing sounds in the vertical plane (above or below). When different-shaped false pinnas were attached to human participants, sound localization was impaired. However, with practice wearing their new pinnas, the participants learned to localize sounds correctly (Hofman, Van Riswick, & Van Opstal, 1998). Sound localization also involves vision. While watching a movie, we perceive sound as originating from the actors' lips, in spite of the fact that the speakers producing the sound are typically above and to the sides of the screen. This integration of visual and auditory information occurs in the caudal areas of the auditory cortex, which become more active when monkeys watch a video than when they simply listen to sound (Kayser, Petkov, Augath, & Logothetis, 2007).

What matters deafness of the ear, when the mind hears. The one true deafness, the incurable deafness, is that of the mind.
Victor Hugo

Hearing Disorders

Hearing loss arises from a wide variety of causes and affects nearly 30 million Americans (NIDCD, 2006). A person is considered legally deaf when speech sounds of 82 dB or less cannot be heard. Typical speech occurs at about 60 dB.

Age-related hearing loss results from a variety of factors, including poor circulation to the inner ear or the cumulative effects of a lifetime of exposure to loud noise. After the age of 30, most people cannot hear frequencies above 15,000 Hz. After the age of 50, most people can't hear sounds above 12,000 Hz, and people over 70 have difficulty with sounds over 6,000 Hz. Because speech normally ranges up to 8,000 Hz, many elderly people begin to have difficulty understanding the speech of others. Teens who frequent concerts and clubs are much more likely to report hearing problems (Hanson & Fearn, 1975; Chung et al., 2005; Holgers & Pettersson, 2005). Earbud devices, such as those used by the popular iPod, boost signals 6 to 9 dB and tend to be used for long periods due to their convenience. Experts recommend using such devices for no more than an hour per day at no more than 60 percent of their maximum volume to avoid hearing loss (Garstecki, 2005). Everyday noises from vehicles, machinery, and appliances can also contribute to hearing loss.

Hearing loss resulting from problems in the outer or middle ear is referred to as conduction loss. Conduction loss can result from a buildup of wax in the ear canal, infections of the middle ear, and a disease known as otosclerosis. Most cases of otosclerosis occur when the stapes (stirrup) becomes immobilized by a buildup of abnormal bone at its base. People with conduction loss can be helped by use of a hearing aid, which acts by amplifying sound signals.

Hearing loss also occurs due to damage to the inner ear, the auditory pathways, or the auditory cortex. Medications, such as quinine and antibiotics, damage hair cells in sensitive individuals. Nicotine produces hearing loss by reducing blood supply to the ear (Zelman, 1973). For people with cochlear or brainstem damage, implants can restore the ability to process speech sounds (Møller, 2006). Talk show host Rush Limbaugh underwent an apparently successful cochlear implant procedure in 2001.

INTERIM SUMMARY 7.1

Summary Table: Important Structures Related to Audition

Structure	Location	Function
Pinna	Outer ear	Sound collection
Auditory canal	Outer ear	Resonating tube that conducts sound from the outer to middle ear
Tympanic membrane	Middle ear	Movement begins the process of translation of sound waves to neural signals
Ossicles	Middle ear	Deliver vibration to the oval window of the cochlea
Cochlea	Inner ear	Fluid-filled structure containing auditory receptors
Inner hair cells	Inner ear	Frequency discrimination
Outer hair cells	Inner ear	Amplify responses to sound energy
Spiral ganglion	Inner ear	Source of fibers synapsing with hair cells; forms auditory nerve (cranial nerve VIII) that connects to the medulla
Dorsal cochlear nucleus; ventral cochlear nucleus	Medulla	Receives input from the spiral ganglion
Superior olive	Medulla	Transmits information from the ventral cochlear nucleus to the inferior colliculi; important for sound localization
Inferior colliculi	Midbrain	Sound localization; auditory reflexes
Medial geniculate nucleus of the thalamus	Diencephalon	Transmits sound information from the inferior colliculi to auditory cortex; may modulate output based on organism's level of arousal
Primary auditory cortex	Heschl's gyrus in the temporal lobe	Initial level of processing for auditory input
Secondary auditory cortex	Areas surrounding Heschl's gyrus	Higher-level processing of auditory input; Wernicke's area participates in language comprehension

(continued)

INTERIM SUMMARY 7.1 (continued)

Summary Points

1. Sound begins with the movement of an object in a medium, producing a disturbance that may be described in terms of wavelength and amplitude. **(LO1)**
2. The outer ear contains the pinna and the auditory canal; the middle ear contains the tympanic membrane and ossicles. **(LO2)**
3. The cochlea of the inner ear is responsible for transducing sound waves into neural signals. These signals are carried centrally by the auditory nerve (cranial nerve VIII). Subsequent processing of auditory information occurs in the cochlear nuclei, the superior olive, the inferior colliculi, the medial geniculate nucleus of the thalamus, and auditory cortex. **(LO2)**
4. Auditory perception involves the analysis of pitch, sound intensity, and localization. **(LO3)**
5. Loss of hearing can result from conduction loss, loud noise, and damage to the inner ear, auditory pathways, or brain structures responsible for hearing. **(LO4)**

Review Questions

1. What are the functions of the outer ear and the middle ear?
2. How does the auditory system process pitch and intensity?

The Body Senses

The **somatosensory system** provides us with information about the position and movement of our bodies and about touch, temperature, and pain. Although these senses might not seem as essential as vision or hearing, we are severely disabled by their loss. You might think it would be a blessing to be born without a sense of pain. On the contrary, people like the gentleman in ■ Figure 7.12, who have impaired pain reception, typically die prematurely due to their inability to respond to injury.

Culver Pictures

■ **FIGURE 7.12**
The Human Pincushion Some people, like the man depicted in this photograph, are born without any sensitivity to pain. Although you might assume that this would be an advantage, it really isn't. Most of these individuals die prematurely due to their inability to respond to injury.

THE VESTIBULAR SYSTEM

The **vestibular system** provides information about the position and movements of our heads, which contribute to our sense of balance. When the vestibular system is impaired, perhaps by a bad head cold or by motion sickness, the result is usually an unpleasant period of nausea and dizziness.

Movement Receptors The sensory organs of the vestibular system are found in the inner ear, adjacent to the structures responsible for audition. The vestibular structures may be divided into two types, the **otolith organs** and the **semicircular canals,** shown in ■ Figure 7.13. The otolith organs consist of two separate structures, the **saccule** and the **utricle.**

The otolith organs provide information about the angle of the head relative to the ground, as well as information about **linear acceleration.** We sense linear acceleration when our rate of movement changes, such as when our car pulls away from a stop sign. Both the saccule and utricle contain hair cells similar to those we encountered earlier in our discussion of audition. The hair cells in the saccule are arranged along a vertical membrane, whereas the hair cells in the utricle are arranged along a horizontal membrane. Cilia extend from each hair cell into a gelatinous layer. Covering the gelatinous layer are **otoliths,** which are stones made of calcium carbonate. When the otoliths move due to the acceleration of the head, force is exerted on the hair cells. The hair cells either depolarize or hyperpolarize in response to this force, which in turn affects the firing rates of fibers in the auditory nerve (cranial nerve VIII). Individual hair cells have a preferred direction of head movement to which they respond. As a result of this organization, all possible movements and directions of the head will be encoded by a unique pattern of hair cell responses.

somatosensory system The system that provides information about the body senses, including touch, movement, pain, and temperature.
vestibular system The sensory system that provides information about the position and movement of the head.

FIGURE 7.13
The Vestibular Structures of the Inner Ear
(a) Together, the utricle, saccule, and semicircular canals provide information about the position and movement of the head. (b) The utricle and saccule contain hair cells, whose cilia extend into a gelatinous layer covered by otoliths. (c) Tilting the head exerts force on the cilia of the hair cells, which in turn modify signaling in the auditory nerve (cranial nerve VIII).

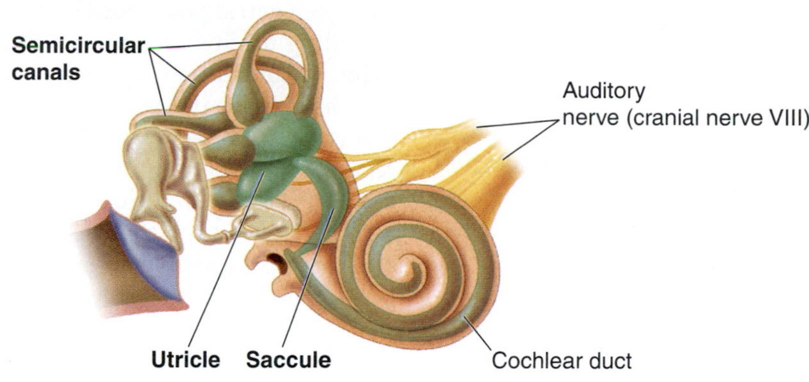

(a) The Vestibular System

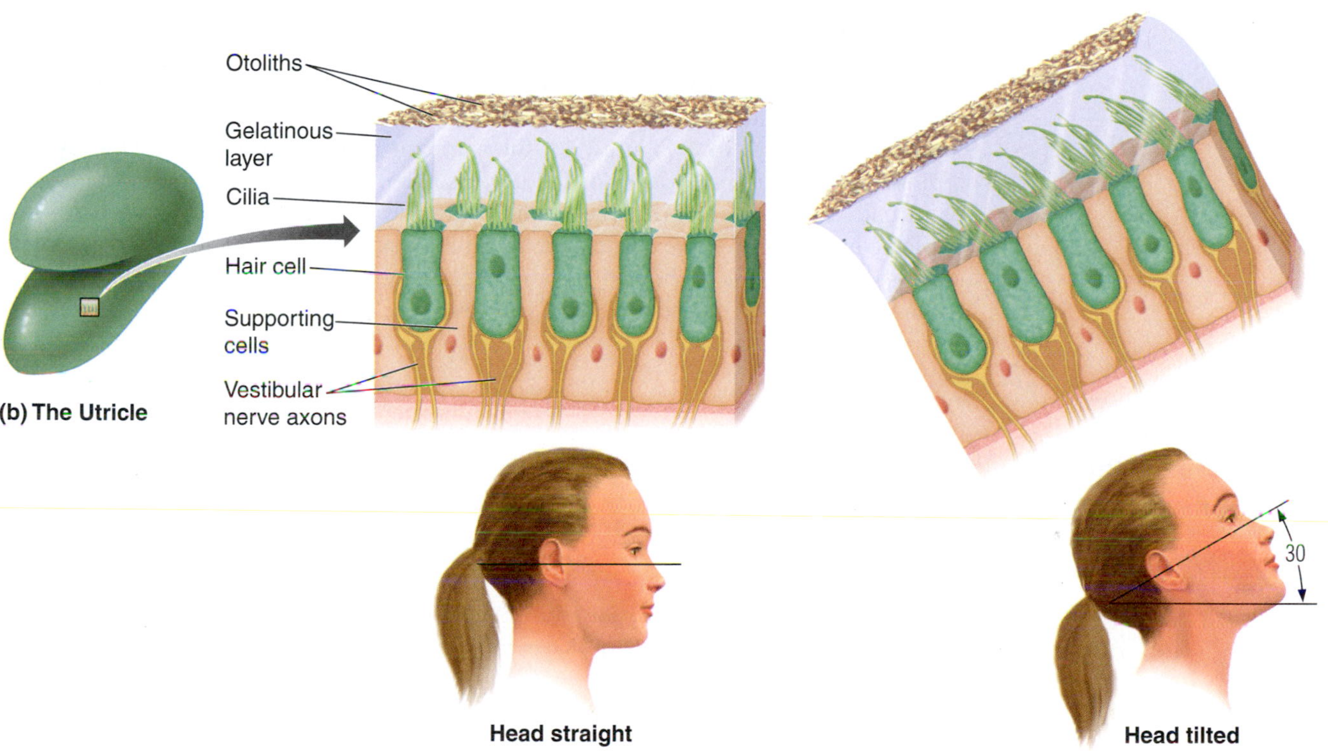

(c) Activation of Hair Cells

The semicircular canals consist of three looping chambers at approximately right angles to one another. These structures respond to rotational movements of the head and contribute to our ability to walk upright (Fitzpatrick, Butler, & Day, 2006). Rotating the head causes the endolymph within the canals to bend hair cells. When extensive movement stops (perhaps at the end of an amusement park ride), the endolymph reverses its course, and you may have the odd fleeting sensation that your head is moving now in the opposite direction.

Central Pathways Axons originating in the otolith organs and semicircular canals form part of the auditory nerve (cranial nerve VIII). These axons synapse in the vestibular nuclei in the pons and medulla and in the cerebellum. The cerebellum also participates in maintaining balance and motor coordination (see Chapter 2). In turn, information from the cerebellum, the visual system, and the somatic systems converge on the vestibular nuclei. This allows us to coordinate information from the vestibular system with other relevant sensory input.

Axons from the vestibular nuclei make connections both in the spinal cord and in higher levels of the brain. Input to the spinal cord motor neurons provides a means to adjust our posture to keep our balance. Vestibular nuclei axons also form connections

otolith organ (OH-toh-lith) A structure in the inner ear vestibular system that provides information about the angle of the head relative to the ground and about linear acceleration.

semicircular canal One of three looping chambers found in the inner ear that provide information regarding the rotation of the head.

saccule (SACK-yool) One of the structures of the otolith organs.

utricle (YOU-tri-kuhl) One of the structures of the otolith organs.

linear acceleration The force perceived when our rate of movement changes.

otolith (OH-toh-lith) A stone made of calcium carbonate that is attached to the hair cells in the otolith organs.

with the **ventral posterior (VP) nucleus** of the thalamus, which receives information regarding touch and pain as well. From the VP nucleus, information is sent to the **primary somatosensory cortex** and primary motor cortex.

Reality is merely an illusion, albeit a very persistent one.
Albert Einstein

Input from the vestibular system is highly integrated with visual processing. It is essential for accurate vision that we maintain a stable view of our surroundings regardless of what our body is doing. Rotations of the head result in reflexive movements of the eyes in the opposite direction. As a result of these reflexes, you maintain a steady view of the world while riding on the most extreme roller coaster. On the other hand, if your vestibular senses and your visual senses give conflicting information to your brain, you may feel nauseated or dizzy.

Touch

Our sense of touch begins with our skin, the largest and heaviest organ of the human body. Our skin provides a boundary separating what is inside from what is outside. It prevents dehydration and protects the body from dirt and bacteria. Human skin comes in two basic varieties, hairy skin and **glabrous,** or hairless, **skin.** Human glabrous skin is found on the lips, palms of the hands, and soles of the feet. When viewed in cross-section, as in ■ Figure 7.14, the skin can be divided into the outer layer of **epidermis** and the inner layer of the **dermis.** The outermost layer of the epidermis is actually constructed of dead cells. Below the dermis, we find **subcutaneous tissue,** which contains connective tissues and fat. Human skin varies dramatically in thickness across different areas of the body, from about half a millimeter on your face to twenty times that thickness on the bottom of your foot.

■ **Figure 7.14**
Mechanoreceptors of the Skin

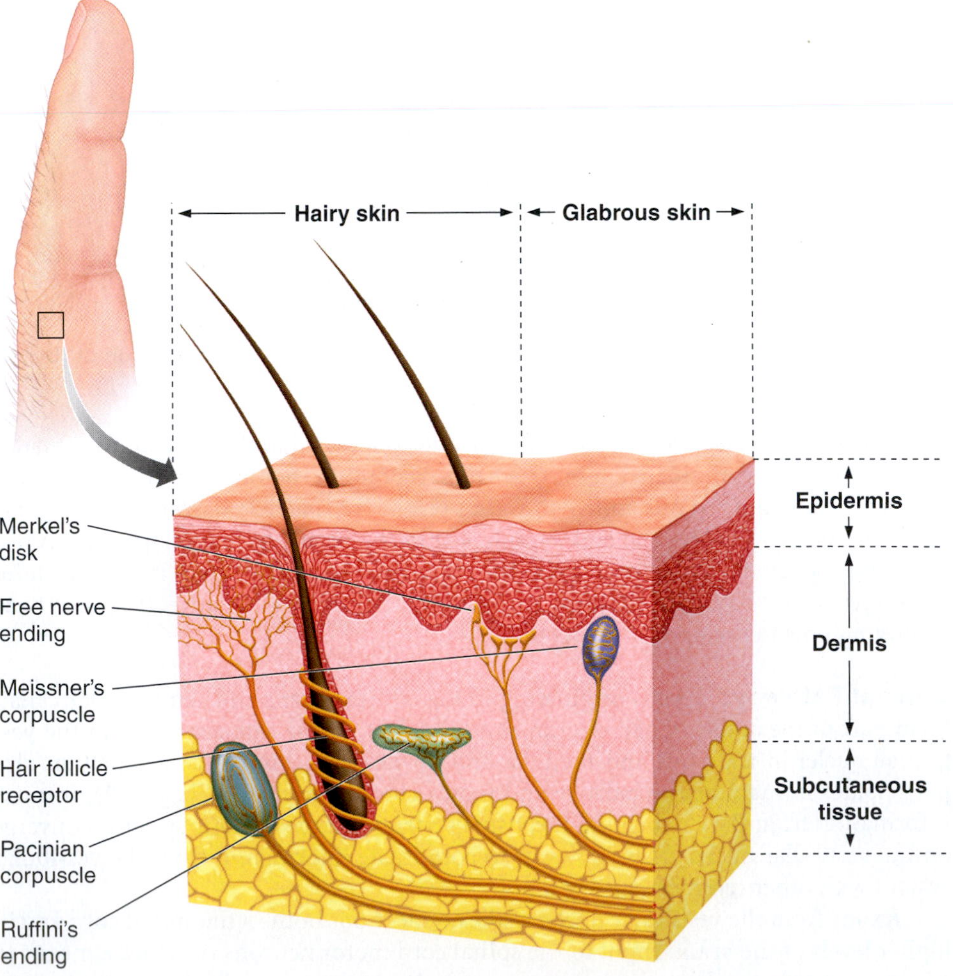

ventral posterior (VP) nucleus The nucleus of the thalamus that receives information regarding pain, touch, and the position and movement of the head.
primary somatosensory cortex Cortex located in the postcentral gyrus of the parietal lobe that is responsible for the initial cortical processing of somatosensory input.
glabrous skin (GLAB-rus) Hairless skin.
epidermis The outermost layer of the skin.
dermis The layer of skin lying below the outermost epidermis.
subcutaneous tissue The layer of tissue lying below the dermis.

TABLE 7.3 Major Features of the Mechanoceptors

Mechanoreceptor	Encapsulated?	Rate of Adaptation	Size of Receptive Field	Quality of Stimulus Sensed
Meissner's corpuscles	Yes	Rapid	Small	Pressure
Pacinian corpuscles	Yes	Rapid	Large	Vibration
Merkel's disks	No	Slow	Small	Pressure
Ruffini's endings	No	Slow	Large	Stretch

Touch Receptors The majority of the receptor cells for touch are referred to as **mechanoreceptors.** This term reflects the response of these receptor cells to physical displacement such as bending or stretching. In addition to their locations in the skin, mechanoreceptors are also found in our blood vessels, joints, and internal organs. Those unpleasant sensations of pressure from a too-full stomach or bladder are provided courtesy of mechanoreceptors in the walls of these organs.

Although mechanoreceptors come in a wide variety of shapes and sizes, they share a number of common features. Within each mechanoreceptor are unmyelinated axon fibers. The membranes of these axons contain sodium ion channels that respond to physical stretching or changes in membrane tension. When the membrane of the axon is stretched, the ion channels open, and sodium enters the cell. If sufficient amounts of sodium enter the cell, an action potential is generated.

Table 7.3 contains a summary of the major features of mechanoreceptors. Mechanoreceptors are categorized according to their structure, size of receptive field, rate of adaptation, and type of information that is processed. Structurally, mechanoreceptors are either encapsulated or not. In **encapsulated receptors,** the axon fibers are surrounded by a fluid-filled capsule formed of connective tissue. The two major types of encapsulated mechanoreceptors are the **Meissner's corpuscles** and the **Pacinian corpuscles.** The Meissner's corpuscles are found at the junction of the epidermis and dermis, whereas the Pacinian corpuscles are located deep in the skin, in the joints, and in the digestive tract. Nonencapsulated receptors include the **Merkel's disks** and **Ruffini's endings.** The Merkel's disks, like the Meissner's corpuscles, are located in the upper areas of the skin, whereas the Ruffini's endings are located at deeper levels. We also find free nerve endings distributed within the skin. As their name implies, these receptors do not have any specialized structure but are simply the unmyelinated nerve endings of sensory neurons. In addition, some receptors wrap themselves around hair follicles and respond to the bending of a hair.

In vision, we spoke of a neuron's receptive field as the area of the retina in which light affects the activity of that neuron. In the case of touch, a receptive field describes the area of skin or other tissue that provides information to a particular receptor. Meissner's corpuscles and Merkel's disks both have very small receptive fields, which means that they can identify the borders of very small stimuli. In contrast, Pacinian corpuscles and Ruffini's endings have very large receptive fields and provide only general information about the borders of stimuli.

Variations in sensitivity from one part of the body to the next result from the density and receptive field size of the mechanoreceptors serving that area. As illustrated in ■ Figure 7.15, sensitivity of various parts of the body can be assessed using a two-point discrimination test. This test measures how close together two stimuli have to be before the person can perceive only a single stimulus. Our fingers and lips are far more sensitive than our backs and the calves of our legs. Not only do fingers and lips have a greater density of mechanoreceptors overall than other areas of the body, but they also contain high concentrations of Merkel's disks and Meissner's corpuscles, with their small receptive fields.

mechanoreceptor A skin receptor that senses touch, pressure, or vibration.

encapsulated receptor A mechanoreceptor in which the axon fibers are surrounded by a fluid-filled capsule formed of connective tissue.

Meissner's corpuscle (MY-snerz KOR-puss-uhl) An encapsulated, fast-adapting mechanoreceptor with small receptive field that responds primarily to pressure.

Pacinian corpuscle (puh-CHIN-ee-uhn) An encapsulated, rapidly adapting mechanoreceptor with large receptive field that provides information about pressure and vibration.

Merkel's disk (MER-kuhls) A nonencapsulated, slow-adapting mechanoreceptor with small receptive field that provides information primarily about pressure.

Ruffini's ending (ruff-EE-nees) A nonencapsulated, slow-adapting mechanoreceptor with large receptive field that provides information regarding stretch.

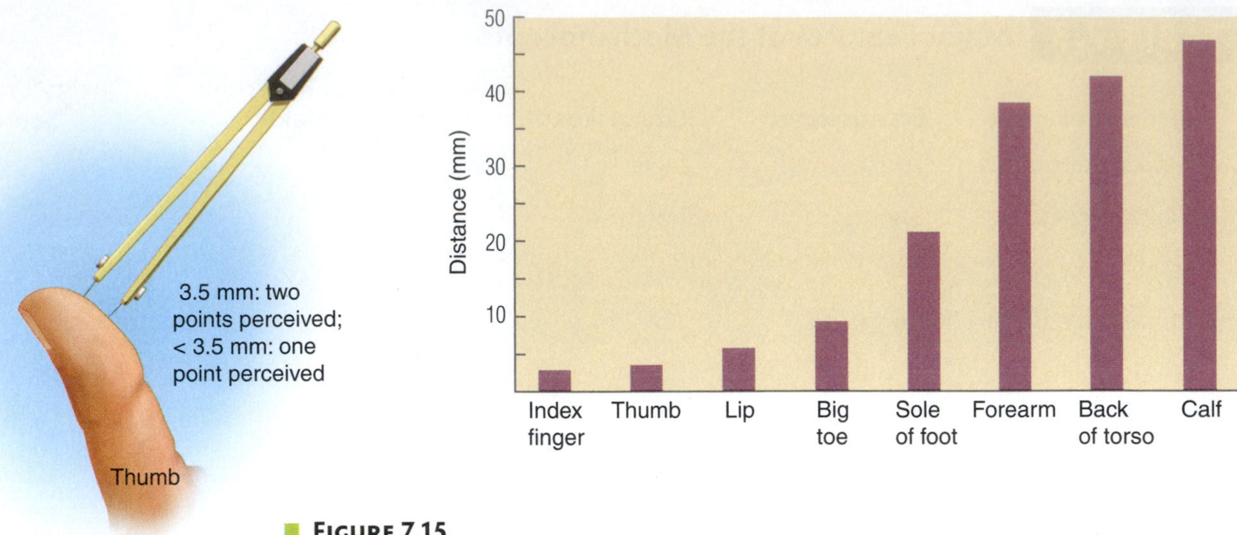

■ **FIGURE 7.15**
Two-Point Discrimination Thresholds The human body is not equally sensitive to touch. If you measure how close two points can be before the subject perceives only one stimulus, you can map the sensitivity of different parts of the body. The calf is much less sensitive than the index finger.

A receptor's rate of adaptation refers to the length of time it will continue to respond to unchanging stimuli. A receptor that adapts rapidly will respond vigorously when stimulation begins or ends but will remain rather inactive while the stimulus is applied continuously. In contrast, a slow-adapting receptor will continue to respond steadily as long as the stimulus is present. We can classify our four major types of mechanoreceptors according to their rate of adaptation. Meissner's corpuscles and Pacinian corpuscles both demonstrate rapid adaptation, whereas Merkel's disks and Ruffini's endings are slow adapting.

A final feature of mechanoreceptors is the type of information processed. The relationship of mechanoreceptor type to the quality of the sensation is neither precise nor perfectly understood. In general, however, mechanoreceptors appear to be somewhat specialized in the type of information they provide. Free nerve endings typically supply information regarding pain and temperature, which we will discuss later in this chapter. Meissner's corpuscles, Merkel's disks, and Pacinian corpuscles all provide information about pressure. However, due to having larger receptive fields, the Pacinian corpuscles do not provide the fine spatial resolution that characterizes the Meissner's corpuscles and Merkel's disks. On the other hand, the Pacinian corpuscles are superior to the others in detecting vibrating stimuli. The Ruffini's endings provide input regarding stretch.

Touch Pathways We begin the journey from the mechanoreceptor in the skin back toward the brain by looking at the nerves that serve the receptors. As shown in ■ Figure 7.16, the sensory fibers of the peripheral nervous system are classified into four categories based on diameter and speed. The largest fibers, called Aα (alpha-alpha), carry information from the muscles and will be discussed in Chapter 8. The smaller three sets of fibers serve the mechanoreceptors. The second-largest set, the Aβ (alpha-beta) class, carries information from the Meissner's corpuscles, Merkel's disks, Pacinian corpuscles, and Ruffini's endings toward the central nervous system. The smallest two groups, the myelinated **Aδ (alpha-delta) fibers** and the unmyelinated **C fibers,** carry information from the free nerve endings regarding pain and temperature. C fibers also alert you to the presence of an itch.

Sensory fibers travel from the skin to join the dorsal roots of the spinal cord. The area of the skin surface served by the dorsal roots of one spinal segment is known as a **dermatome.** As shown in ■ Figure 7.17, a map of all of the dermatomes shows a striped or banded pattern on the body. Dermatomes are easily identified in the disease known as shingles, which is caused by the same virus responsible for chickenpox

Aδ (alpha-delta) fiber A myelinated fiber that carries information about cold and sharp pain to the central nervous system.
C fiber A small, unmyelinated fiber that carries information about temperature, itch, and dull, aching pain to the central nervous system.
dermatome The area of the skin surface served by the dorsal roots of one spinal segment.

Class of Axon	Diameter of Axon	Speed of Transmission	Receptor Types
Aα (Alpha-alpha) fibers	13–20μm	80–120m/sec	Feedback from muscle fibers
Aβ (Alpha-beta) fibers	6–12μm	35–75m/sec	Mechanoreceptors of skin: Meissner's corpuscles Merkel's disks Pacinian corpuscles Ruffini's endings
Aδ (Alpha-delta) fibers	1–5μm	5–30m/sec	Pain, temperature receptors of skin: Free nerve endings
C fibers	0.2–1.5μm	0.5–2m/sec	Pain, temperature and itch receptors of skin: Free nerve endings

Axon
Myelin

FIGURE 7.16
The Four Classes of Sensory Axons Differ in Size and Speed The largest, fastest afferent axons (Aα) serve the muscles and will be discussed in Chapter 8. The second-largest and fastest axons (Aβ) serve the mechanoreceptors. Fast, sharp pain and temperature are carried by the myelinated Aδ fibers, whereas the small, unmyelinated C fibers carry dull, aching pain, temperature, and itch.

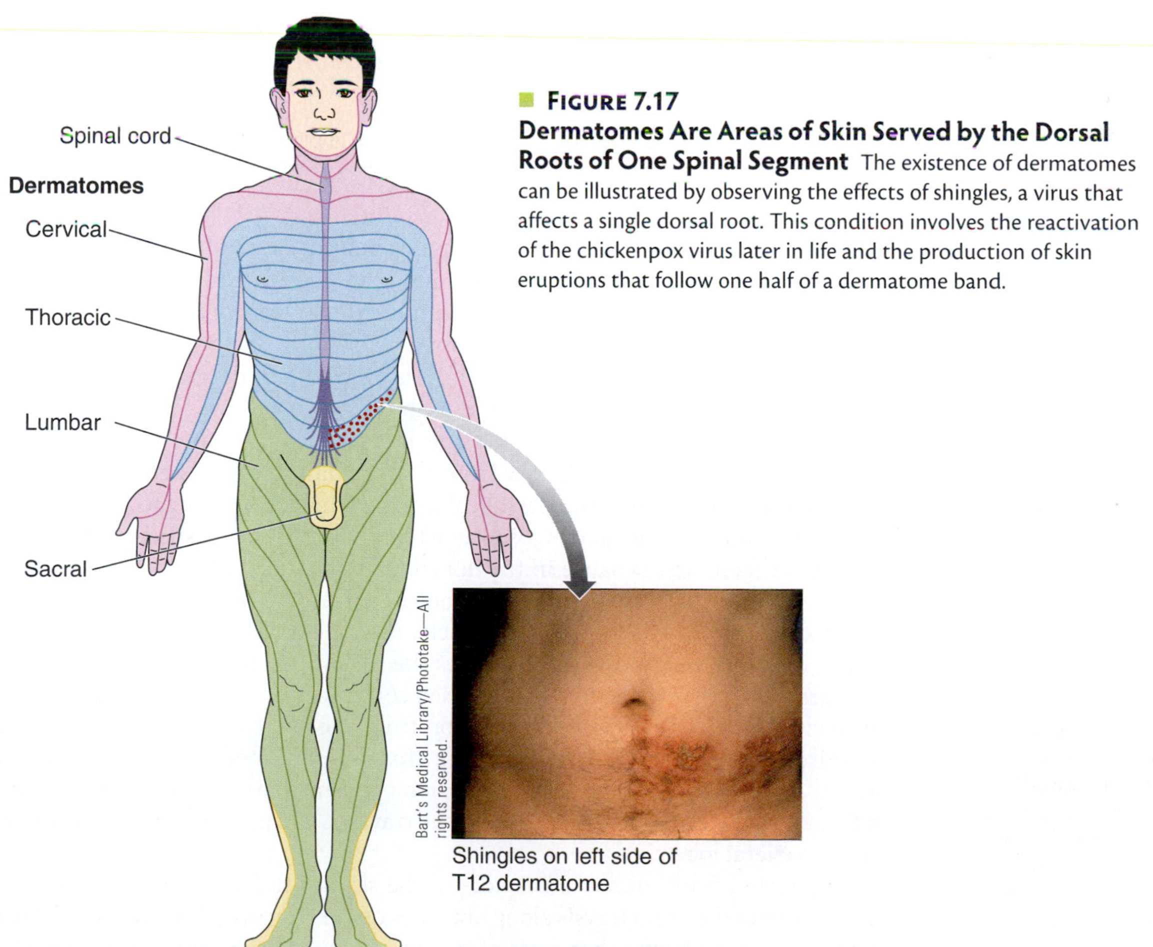

FIGURE 7.17
Dermatomes Are Areas of Skin Served by the Dorsal Roots of One Spinal Segment The existence of dermatomes can be illustrated by observing the effects of shingles, a virus that affects a single dorsal root. This condition involves the reactivation of the chickenpox virus later in life and the production of skin eruptions that follow one half of a dermatome band.

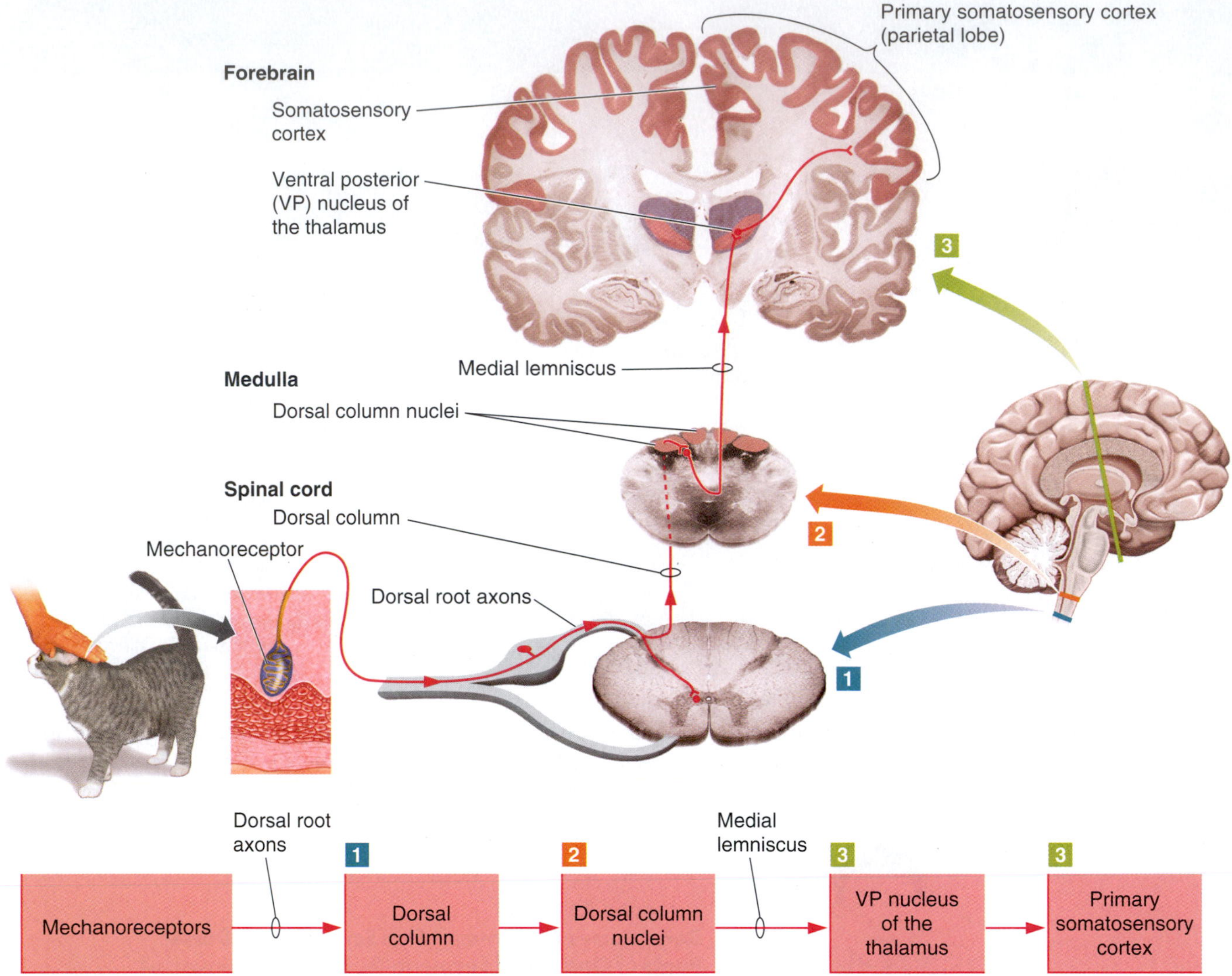

■ **FIGURE 7.18**
Touch Pathways The mechanoreceptors send information to the primary somatosensory cortex in the parietal lobe via the dorsal column–medial lemniscal pathway.

(*herpes zoster*). In some people, the virus awakens decades after the original infection and produces the skin eruptions shown in Figure 7.17. In addition, the virus increases the excitability of the sensory neurons, producing a burning, painful sensation along the dermatome. The reactivated virus appears to confine its mischief to a single dorsal root, leading to symptoms in one half of an individual dermatome. Fortunately, an effective vaccine for shingles is now available.

The pathways leading from the mechanoreceptors to the brain are illustrated in ■ Figure 7.18. When the axons from the mechanoreceptors enter the spinal cord, they follow a route called the dorsal column–medial lemniscal pathway. As suggested by the pathway's name, axons join the white matter of the ipsilateral **dorsal column** and make their first synapse in the dorsal column nuclei of the medulla. The lack of synapses until this point greatly contributes to the speed of this system.

Axons from the dorsal column nuclei form a large band of white matter known as the **medial lemniscus,** which crosses the midline of the medulla. From this point forward, sensory information is processed contralaterally. In other words, the left side of the brain processes touch information from the right side of the body. The medial lemniscus continues to travel rostrally through the medulla, pons, and midbrain before synapsing on the ventral posterior (VP) nucleus of the thalamus, shown in ■ Figure 7.19. Axons from the VP nucleus travel to the primary somatosensory cortex of the parietal lobe.

Sensation from mechanoreceptors in the skin of the face, mouth, tongue, and the dura mater of the brain travels along branches of the **trigeminal nerve (cranial nerve V).** Additional input from other parts of the head are carried by the facial nerve (VII), the

dorsal column The spinal pathway that carries information about touch and position to the medulla.

medial lemniscus (lem-NIS-us) The pathway originating in the dorsal column nuclei and synapsing in the ventral posterior (VP) nucleus of the thalamus that is responsible for carrying information about touch and position.

trigeminal nerve (cranial nerve V) A nerve that carries sensation from mechanoreceptors, temperature receptors, and pain receptors in the skin of the face, mouth, tongue, and the dura mater of the brain.

glossopharyngeal nerve (IX), and the vagus nerve (X). Axons forming these cranial nerves synapse on their respective ipsilateral nuclei in the brainstem, which serve the same purpose as the dorsal column nuclei in the spinal cord. From these cranial nerve nuclei, axons cross the midline and travel to the VP nucleus, which in turn passes the information to the primary somatosensory cortex in the parietal lobe.

You may be wondering what the dorsal column nuclei, cranial nerve nuclei, and the VP nucleus might be doing to the incoming sensory information. These synapses provide opportunities for the cortex to influence the input it receives through descending pathways. In addition, activity in one neuron inhibits its neighbor, leading to a sharpening or enhancement of its signal.

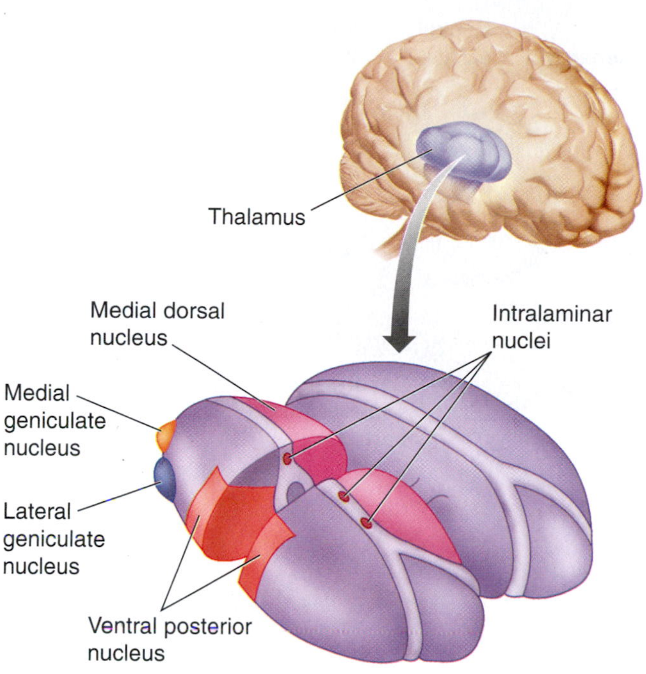

Figure 7.19 Somatosensory Areas of the Thalamus Somatosensory information is processed by the ventral posterior (VP) and intralaminar nuclei of the thalamus.

Somatosensory Cortex Primary somatosensory cortex is found in the postcentral gyrus of the parietal lobe, just caudal to the central sulcus that divides the parietal and frontal lobes. Using single-cell recording, we can demonstrate that areas of the cortex serving the head and neck are located at the lower, ventral part of the postcentral gyrus, whereas areas serving the legs and feet extend over the top of the gyrus onto the medial surface of the parietal lobe. A map of the body's representation in the cortex is known as a *homunculus*, or "little man." A cortical map and an example of a homunculus are shown in Figure 7.20. Areas of the body receive cortical representation according to their need for precise sensory feedback. In humans, the hands and face are given a much larger portion of the cortex than their size would suggest. Rats devote a great deal of space to whiskers, whereas lips seem to have a very high priority in squirrels and rabbits.

Four areas, shown in Figure 7.20a, can be identified within primary somatosensory cortex. These areas may be represented as four separate parallel homunculi running the length of the postcentral gyrus. The axons from the VP nucleus of the thalamus synapse in areas 3a and 3b. These areas in turn project to areas 1 and 2 as well as to secondary somatosensory cortex areas in adjacent sections of the parietal lobe. In typical cortical fashion, communication goes in both directions because areas 1 and 2 project back to areas 3a and 3b.

The four areas appear to process different types of stimuli. Area 3b receives input regarding size, shape, and texture of touched objects. Size and shape information is sent to area 2, and texture information is sent to area 1. Both areas 3b and 1 respond most vigorously to light touch on the skin. Area 3a responds primarily to the movement of joints, tendons, or muscles. Both areas 3a and 2 respond most vigorously to movement but hardly at all to touch.

Secondary somatosensory cortex is located in the posterior parietal lobe. Identifying the types of stimuli responsible for the activation of secondary somatosensory cortex is challenging because this area responds to such a wide variety of input. In addition to its role in sensation, the secondary somatosensory cortex is also involved with complex spatial perception, including the position of the body in three-dimensional space.

Plasticity of Touch The somatosensory cortex appears to rearrange itself in response to changes in the amount of input it receives. In adult monkeys who have had a finger surgically removed, the areas of the somatosensory cortex previously responsive to the missing finger now respond to stimulation of adjacent fingers (Kaas, Nelson, Sur, & Merzenich, 1981). In these cases, the brain is adapting to a reduction in input from a specific part of the body. Increased stimulation from a body part will also result in changes in the mapping of the somatosensory cortex. When monkeys were trained to use specific fingers to discriminate between tactile surfaces to earn a food

secondary somatosensory cortex Areas in the parietal lobe adjacent to primary somatosensory cortex that process a wide variety of complex somatosensory inputs.

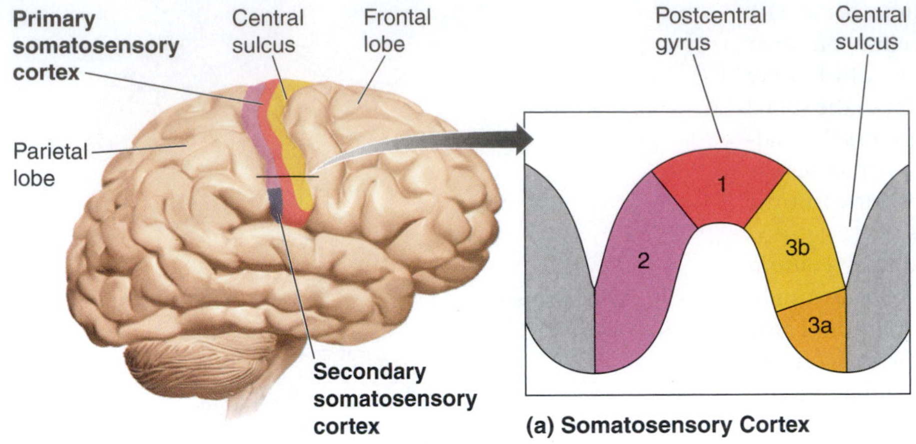

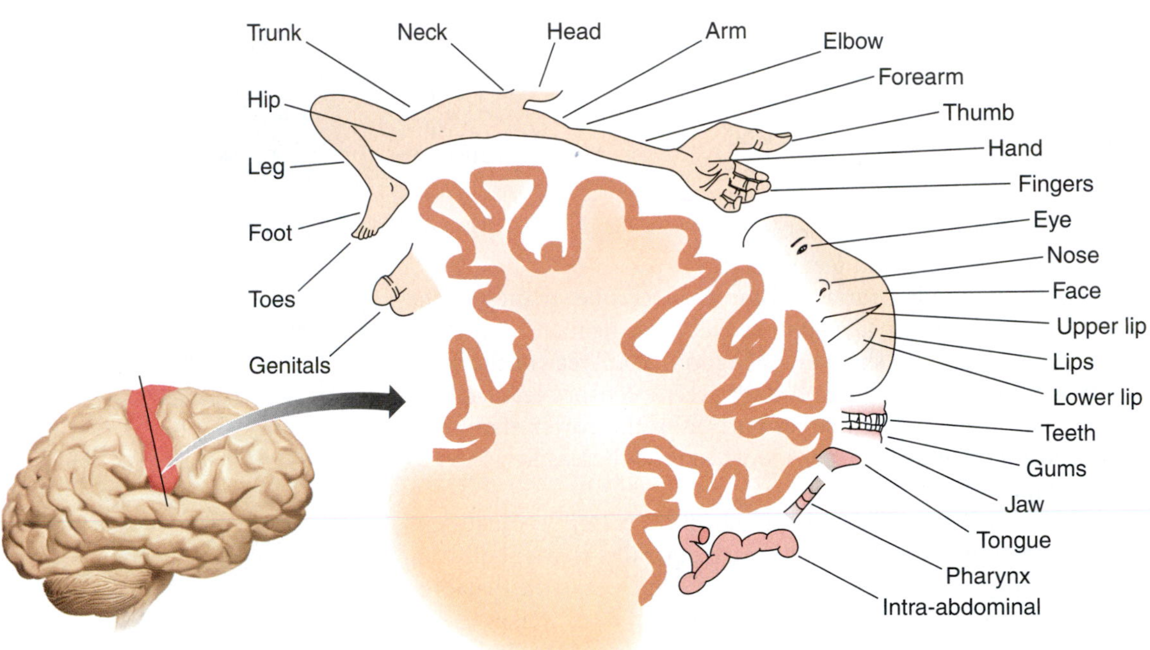

FIGURE 7.20 Somatosensory Cortex (a) The somatosensory cortex can be further divided into areas 1, 2, 3a, and 3b. The areas form extensive communication links with one another but process different aspects of a stimulus. (b) Just as body parts are not equally sensitive, they do not get the same amount of representation in the somatosensory cortex. Relative representation may be mapped as a homunculus.

reward, the area of the somatosensory cortex receiving input from the trained fingertips actually expanded (Merzenich & Jenkins, 1993). This process probably represents a reorganization of synapses.

Plasticity occurs in the human somatosensory cortex as a result of both loss and enhancement of input. Amputation of a limb often causes phantom pain, in which pain is perceived as arising in the missing body part, or referred sensations, in which touching a body part such as the cheek is perceived as touch of the missing limb (Ramachandran, 2005). Imaging demonstrates that the part of somatosensory cortex previously responsive to an amputated arm subsequently responds to touching the face (Ramachandran & Rogers-Ramachandran, 2000). One of Ramachandran's patients was embarrassed to report that he experienced a sensation of orgasm in his missing foot (Ramachandran & Rogers-Ramachandran, 2000). These observations suggest that the brain rapidly reorganizes its representation of the body following amputation.

The increased representation due to training that was observed by Merzenich and Jenkins in monkeys has a parallel in the cortical organization of some musicians. Highly trained string musicians have a larger than normal area of somatosensory cortex representing touch in the fingers (Elbert, Pantev, Weinbruch, Rockstroh, & Taub, 1995; Hashimoto et al., 2004). A similar reorganization of somatosensory cortex occurs when blind individuals learn to read Braille (Pascual-Leone & Torres, 1993). Wilton (2002) showed that young people worldwide are using their thumbs much more than previous generations did to play video games and type messages on cell phones. It is likely that such changes in behavior will also be reflected in the organization of the somatosensory cortex, with greater cortical space assigned to thumbs among those who use these digits more frequently.

Somatosensory Disorders Damage to primary somatosensory cortex produces deficits in both sensation and movement of body parts served by the damaged area (Corkin, Milner, & Rasmussen, 1970). Damage to secondary somatosensory cortex, particularly on the right side of the brain, results in an odd phenomenon known as neglect syndrome. Patients with this syndrome have difficulty perceiving either a part of the body or a part of the visual field. Drawings by a patient with neglect syndrome may be seen in ■ Figure 7.21. Oliver Sacks (1985) described a patient who believed that the hospital staff was playing a horrible joke on him by putting an amputated leg, which was actually his own very firmly attached leg, into his bed. While trying to remove the leg from his bed, the man frequently fell on the floor. Fortunately for Sacks's patient and others with neglect syndrome, the condition generally improves over time.

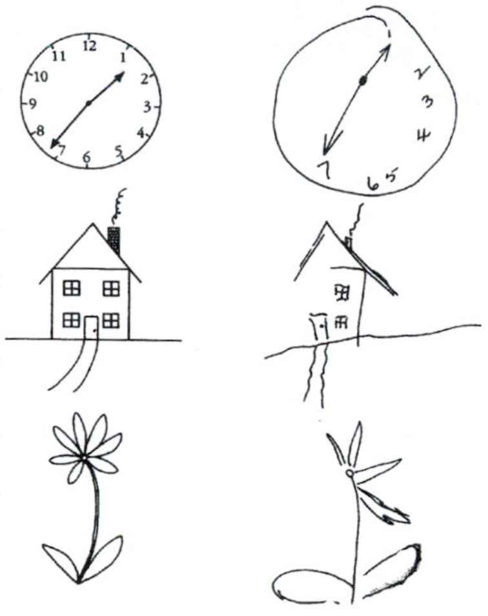

■ **FIGURE 7.21**
Drawings by a Patient with Neglect Syndrome Damage to the secondary somatosensory cortex, particularly on the right hemisphere, results in neglect syndrome. Patients with this syndrome have difficulty perceiving a part of the body or a part of the visual field. Because the patient attempting to copy the model cannot perceive the entire visual field, he or she draws only part of each object.

Temperature

Thermoreceptors are free nerve endings in the skin that respond to surface temperature. Different sets of thermoreceptors respond to warmth or cold, and neither type responds to mechanical stimulation (Duclaux & Kenshalo, 1980). The cell membranes of thermoreceptors contain special proteins that respond to changes in temperature by opening and closing channels (Bautista et al., 2007; Colburn et al., 2007; Dhaka et al., 2007). Thermoreceptors are distributed in irregular patterns across the surface of the skin. Spots that are approximately 1 mm in diameter respond to either hot or cold, but not to both. The skin between the spots is relatively insensitive to temperature.

The surface of your skin is typically about 33°C. As shown in ■ Figure 7.22, **warm fibers** begin to fire at about 30°C and increase their firing rates as temperature increases to about 45°C. At this point, thermoreceptors begin to respond less, and pain receptors begin to respond. **Cold fibers** begin to respond at skin temperatures of about 35°C and increase their response rate until the skin temperature decreases to about 10°C. Below 10°C, firing generally stops, leading to the numbing loss of sensation that occurs at cold temperatures. Some cold receptors appear to fire not only between 10°C and 35°C but also in response to temperatures above 45°C. It's not clear why this paradoxical response occurs. At extreme temperatures, pain receptors are recruited in addition to thermoreceptors. The pain you experience when you hold an ice cube too long results from the activation of special proteins in neurons that sense pain. Mice genetically engineered to lack these proteins appear to be insensitive to pain, even when placed on a very cold surface (Zimmermann et al., 2007).

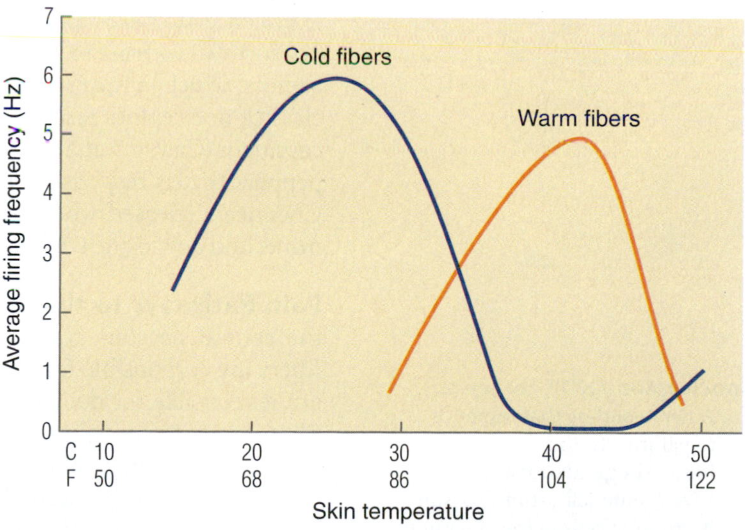

■ **FIGURE 7.22**
Responses by Cold and Warm Fibers Warm fibers begin to fire at about 30°C and increase their rates as temperatures increase to 45°C. Cold fibers begin to respond at about 35°C and increase their response until temperatures reach about 10°C.

Both pain and temperature share a pathway from the skin to the brain. Cold receptors are linked with the faster, myelinated Aδ fibers as well as with the slower, unmyelinated C fibers. Warm receptors are linked with C fibers only. Because pain and temperature share routes from the spinal cord to the brain, we will trace these pathways in greater detail in our discussion of pain.

thermoreceptor A nerve ending in the skin that responds to surface temperature.
warm fiber A nerve ending in the skin that responds to heat.
cold fiber A nerve ending in the skin that responds to cold.

PAIN

No other sensory modality is as dramatically affected by culture, emotion, context, and experience as our sense of pain. The connection between culture and the experience of pain is vividly illustrated by the hook-swinging ritual practiced in India (Kosambi, 1967). This ritual, designed to promote the health of children and crops, involves hanging a male volunteer from steel hooks embedded into the skin and muscles of his back. Instead of suffering excruciating pain, the volunteers appear to be in a state of exaltation.

Pain is inevitable. Suffering is optional.
Dalai Lama

A Purpose for Pain Given the anguish experienced by chronic pain patients, it would seem initially miraculous to be able to do away with this sensory modality altogether. Research on those born without effective pain reception suggests otherwise. Patients who perceive no pain frequently die at young ages, primarily due to degeneration of joints and the spine. We need pain to remind us to stop when we are injured, to assess a situation before proceeding, and to allow the body time to heal. Pain is not a perfect warning system. In many potentially fatal conditions, such as in some types of cancer, pain does not surface until the condition is quite advanced. In other cases, the pain people experience far exceeds the threat to their safety. The pain associated with many headaches, stomachaches, and backaches occurs in the absence of any tissue damage.

Receptors for Pain Free nerve endings that respond to pain are called **nociceptors.** Nociceptors respond to a variety of stimuli associated with tissue damage. Some nociceptors respond most vigorously to mechanical injury such as the damage caused by a sharp object. The pressure of the mechanical stimulus on the nociceptor membrane opens mechanically gated ion channels, leading to the generation of action potentials. Other nociceptors respond to extreme temperature. Some nociceptors appear to respond to both mechanical stimulation and temperature.

A variety of chemicals can also activate nociceptors. The unpleasant soreness we experience after exercising vigorously is produced by a buildup of lactic acid. Lactic acid produces an increase in hydrogen ions in the extracellular fluid. These ions activate nociceptors, which in turn send unpleasant messages of soreness to the brain. An interesting class of nociceptors responds to chemicals known as vanilloids, a group that includes capsaicin (Caterina et al., 1997). Capsaicin is best known as the ingredient found in hot peppers that is responsible for the heat sensations we enjoy while eating spicy foods. Chemicals released when a cell is damaged, such as potassium ions, enzymes, histamine, and adenosine triphosphate (ATP), also stimulate nociceptor activity.

Pain Pathways to the Brain Information from the nociceptors is carried toward the central nervous system by two types of nerve fiber. The faster, myelinated Aδ fibers are responsible for that quick, sharp "ouch." The slower, unmyelinated C fibers are responsible for dull, aching types of pain sensation. Both types of ascending pain fibers appear to use glutamate as their primary neurotransmitter (Li & Tator, 2000; Jin, Nishioka, Wakabayashi, Fujita, & Yonehara, 2006).

As shown in ■ Figure 7.23, pain fibers enter the spinal cord via the dorsal root. Once inside the cord, they synapse in the **substantia gelatinosa,** a group of cells in the outer gray matter of the dorsal horn. In addition to releasing glutamate, these neurons are also capable of releasing **Substance P** in the dorsal horn of the spinal cord. Substance P appears to stimulate changes in the dendrites of the cells in the substantia gelatinosa. These structural changes might account for adaptations to pain based on personal experience (Mantyh et al., 1997).

Fibers originating in the substantia gelatinosa immediately cross the midline of the spinal cord to join the **spinothalamic pathway** that runs the length of the ventral surface of the spinal cord. These fibers travel up through the brainstem and finally synapse within the thalamus. Pain and temperature information from the head and neck is transmitted to the thalamus in a similar manner. This information travels first along the trigeminal nerve, which synapses in the **spinal trigeminal nucleus** of the brainstem. Fibers from the spinal trigeminal nucleus form the **trigeminal lemniscus,** which terminates in the thalamus.

nociceptor (NOH-see-sep-ter) A nerve ending that responds to painful stimuli.

substantia gelatinosa (sub-STAN-shuh jell-a-tun-OH-suh) A group of cells in the outer gray matter of the dorsal horn that receive synapses from pain fibers.

Substance P A neurotransmitter substance associated with the sense of pain that also serves as a stimulus at some nociceptors.

spinothalamic pathway (spy-noh-thuhl-AM-ik) Fibers that carry pain and temperature information from the substantia gelatinosa to the thalamus.

spinal trigeminal nucleus A nucleus in the brainstem that receives pain and temperature information from the head and neck.

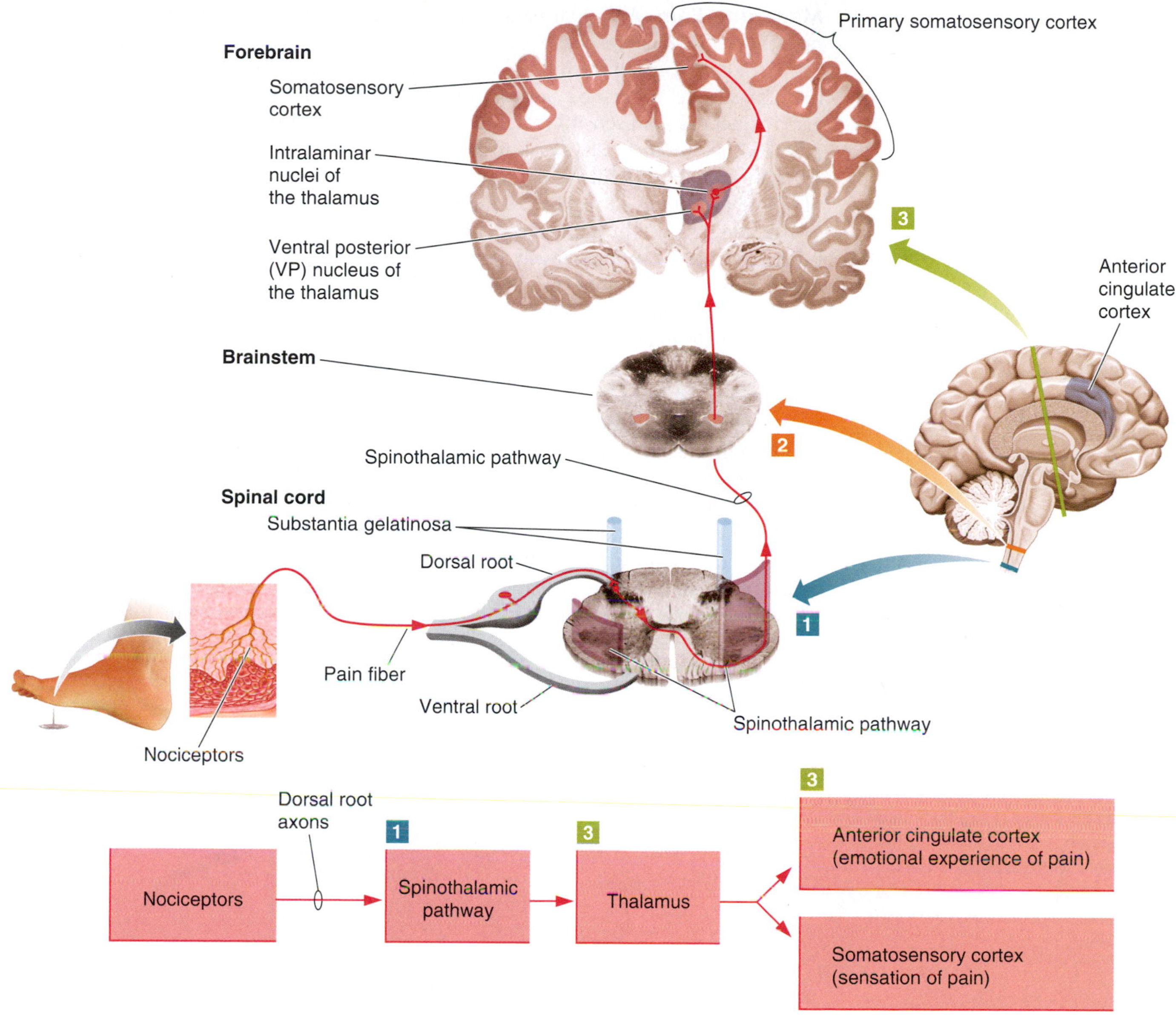

FIGURE 7.23 Ascending Pain Pathways Upon entering the dorsal root, pain fibers form synapses within an area known as the substantia gelatinosa. The messages then travel centrally along spinothalamic pathways.

The spinothalamic and trigeminal lemniscus fibers synapse in one of two locations in the thalamus. Some fibers synapse in the VP nucleus, which also receives information from touch receptors. However, input regarding pain and temperature remains separate in the VP nucleus from input regarding touch. Other fibers connect with the **intralaminar nuclei** of the thalamus, shown in Figures 7.19 and 7.23. Both areas of the thalamus then form connections with the anterior cingulate cortex (ACC) and, to a lesser degree, the somatosensory cortex. The ACC participates in our anticipation and emotional responses to pain. If participants are told to expect a mild amount of pain from placing their hands in hot water, the ACC is less active than when they are told to expect more pain (Rainville, Duncan, Price, Carrier, & Bushnell, 1997). People who chose an immediate but large electric shock over a delayed but smaller shock, demonstrating that they "dreaded" the upcoming shock, showed increased activity in the ACC (Berns et al., 2006).

Surprisingly, pain information also appears to activate circuits normally associated with addiction and reward (Becerra, Breiter, Wise, Gonzalez, & Borsook, 2001; Borsook et al., 2006). When male volunteers were exposed to a painful heat stimulus on their hands, MRI images indicated that activation in reward circuits, including the nucleus accumbens, preceded activation of the classic pain circuits. As discussed in Chapter 4, the nucleus accumbens is essential to addictive behaviors. Reward circuits analyze both positive and aversive stimuli that have an impact on survival.

trigeminal lemniscus (tri JEM ih nuhl lem-NIS-kus) A pathway carrying pain and temperature information from the spinal trigeminal nucleus to the thalamus.

intralaminar nucleus (in-truh-LAM- in-ar) One of many nuclei in the thalamus that receive some pain and temperature input.

Managing Pain Although pain certainly has its purpose, we are also motivated to help those who face the challenges of chronic pain.

Although some of the individual differences in response to pain are due to culture and experience, a person's number of endogenous opioid receptors (see Chapter 4) also influences pain sensitivity (Zubieta et al., 2001). These researchers administered painful injections of saltwater into participants' facial muscles. Participants reported on their pain levels while undergoing PET scanning. Those with the highest amount of opioid activity as shown by the PET scans reported less pain.

If you are distressed by anything external, the pain is not due to the thing itself but to your own estimate of it; and this you have the power to revoke at any moment.
Marcus Aurelius

In some cases, the pain signal can be modified by additional sensory input to the brain. Most of us spontaneously respond to bumping our elbow by rubbing it vigorously. Rubbing your elbow might actually lessen the ability of pain receptors to communicate with the brain. Melzack and Wall (1965) proposed a model known as a gate theory of pain to account for this phenomenon. According to this model, input from touch fibers might compete with input from nociceptors for activation of cells in the substantia gelatinosa. Activation of the touch fibers effectively reduces the amount of pain information that can reach the brain.

In other cases, descending control from the brain has a dramatic influence on our perception of pain. As noted in Chapter 2, many higher-level brain structures form connections with the periaqueductal gray (PAG) of the midbrain, shown in ■ Figure 7.24. Electrical stimulation of the PAG generally produces a significant reduction of pain. In addition, PAG appears to be the location for a large number of opioid receptors, and opiates such as morphine probably achieve pain relief through their actions in the PAG. The convergence of descending control and ascending pain information in the PAG

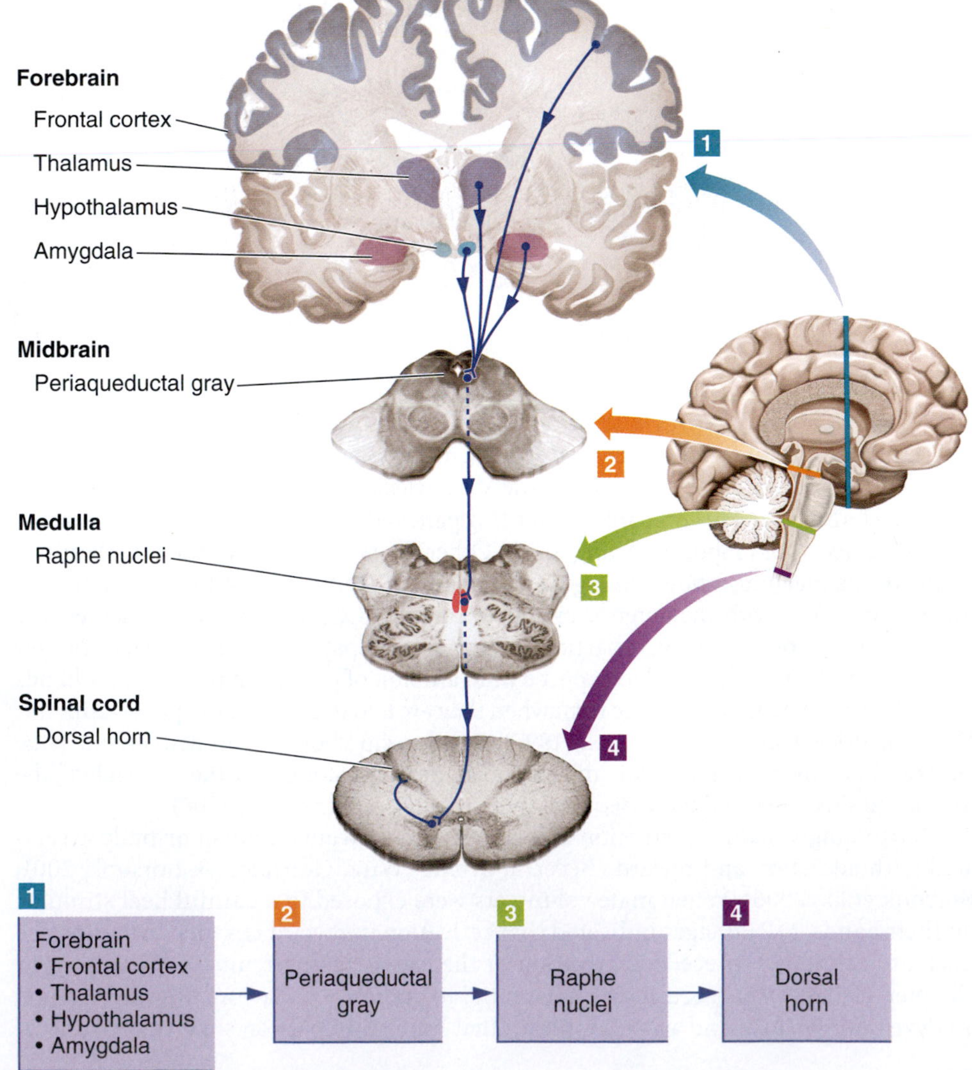

■ **FIGURE 7.24 Descending Messages Influence Pain Information** Many higher-level structures of the brain form connections with the periaqueductal gray (PAG) of the midbrain, a major locus for endogenous opioids. The PAG in turn forms connections with the raphe nuclei in the medulla and neurons in the spinal cord that can modulate incoming pain information.

provides an opportunity for the modification of incoming pain messages by higher-level cognitive processes.

One of the most troubling types of pain is chronic pain, which continues long after injuries have healed and affects nearly 10 percent of the United States population. Typical medications, such as aspirin and opiates, are relatively ineffective for managing this type of pain. Chronic pain is associated with increased activity in prefrontal areas, whereas physical pain like a burn produces more activity in the thalamus (Millecamps et al., 2007). Researchers have suggested that chronic pain is more of a memory problem than a sensory problem, as if the brain has difficulty forgetting about the pain (ibid.).

Photo Richard Hawking

Figure 7.25 Stress Can Minimize Incoming Pain Messages Climber Joe Simpson survived a three-day descent from a 21,000-foot peak in the Andes in spite of a badly broken leg and knee, frostbite, and extreme exposure. Even the subsequent donkey journey to safety must have produced agonizing pain.

Being disabled by pain during an emergency is not in the best interests of survival, so it should come as no surprise that extreme stress often reduces the perception of pain. In a dramatic example, climber Joe Simpson overcame the pain from a badly broken leg and knee, frostbite, and extreme exposure to descend a 21,000-foot peak in the Andes. After seeing Simpson fall off an ice ledge, his climbing partner had given him up for dead. The journey took Simpson, shown in Figure 7.25, three days to complete. Stress might produce analgesia, or pain relief, by promoting the release of endogenous opioids (endorphins) in the brain.

Attitudes toward pain also play a significant role in our perceptions of the experience. Athletes and nonathletes share similar pain thresholds, or levels of stimulation identified as painful. However, these groups are quite different in their tolerance of pain (Sternberg, Bailin, Grant, & Gracely, 1998). In particular, athletes in contact sports such as boxing, rugby, and football appear to tolerate higher levels of pain before identifying a stimulus as painful. A sense of control can reduce the need for pain medication. Patients who are allowed to self-administer morphine for pain actually require less medication than patients who receive injections from hospital staff (Viscusi & Schechter, 2006).

INTERIM SUMMARY 7.2

Summary Table: Somatosensory Pathways

Sensory Modality	Receptor Types	Axon Types	Route to Somatosensory Cortex
Touch	Mechanoreceptors	Aβ fibers	• Fibers enter spinal cord via dorsal root. • Axons join the dorsal column and synapse in the dorsal column nuclei of the medulla. • Axons from the dorsal column nuclei form the medial lemniscus and synapse in the VP nucleus of the thalamus. Cranial neurons V, VII, IX, and X carry touch information from the head to brainstem nuclei, which form connections with the VP nucleus of the thalamus. • The VP nucleus projects to primary somatosensory cortex in the parietal lobe.
Temperature	Thermoreceptors	Cold receptors transmit information via Aδ fibers and C fibers. Warm receptors transmit information via C fibers.	• Routes are identical to pain pathways.

(continued)

INTERIM SUMMARY 7.2 (continued)

Pain	Nociceptors (free nerve endings)	Aδ fibers and C fibers	• Fibers enter spinal cord via dorsal root. • Fibers synapse in substantia gelatinosa. • Pain information travels via the spinothalamic pathway and trigeminal lemniscus to the VP nucleus and intralaminar nuclei of the thalamus. • Information is transmitted to the anterior cingulate cortex and primary somatosensory cortex.
Vestibular system	Hair cells within the saccule, utricle, and semicircular canals	Varied	• Fibers join the auditory nerve (cranial nerve VIII). • Axons synapse in cerebellum and vestibular nuclei. • Vestibular nuclei axons project to the spinal cord motor neurons and to the VP nucleus of the thalamus. • Information travels from the VP nucleus to primary somatosensory and motor cortex.

Summary Points

1. The vestibular system provides information about the position and movement of the head. **(LO5)**
2. Major mechanoreceptors located within the skin include Meissner's corpuscles, Pacinian corpuscles, Merkel's disks, Ruffini's endings, and free nerve endings. **(LO6)**
3. Touch information travels along the dorsal column–medial lemniscal pathway to the dorsal column nuclei of the medulla, to the contralateral ventral posterior nucleus of the thalamus, and to the primary somatosensory cortex of the parietal lobe. **(LO6)**
4. Temperature at the surface of the body is sensed by free nerve endings in the skin called thermoreceptors. Information from thermoreceptors follows the same pathways as information from the pain system. **(LO6)**
5. Pain is sensed by free nerve endings called nociceptors. Ascending pain fibers synapse in the substantia gelatinosa, the thalamus, and the cingulate and somatosensory cortices. Descending information regarding pain is transmitted to the periaqueductal gray (PAG). **(LO6)**

Review Questions

1. How is the primary somatosensory cortex organized? How does experience change the organization of primary somatosensory cortex?
2. What factors modify an individual's perception of a painful stimulus?

The Chemical Senses

Philosopher Immanuel Kant (1798) considered smell to be the "most dispensable" sense. Nonetheless, our chemical senses do provide warning of danger, such as smelling smoke from a fire or the taste of spoiled food. Contrary to Kant's view, people who have lost their sense of smell due to head injury often experience profound depression (Zuscho, 1983; Doty et al., 1997).

Olfaction

olfaction The sense of smell.

Olfaction, the sense of smell, begins with the detection of molecules suspended in the air. In addition to having the capacity to be suspended in air, olfactory stimuli must

WHY DOES THIS MATTER?

Subliminal Smells and Likeability

Researchers have found a relationship between subliminal smells and likeability, which matters because you now know that wearing perfume or aftershave lotion will help make people like you—but only if it is a small enough amount to be unnoticeable.

Although we are accustomed to our dog's happy sniff of recognition, we often discount the importance of our own senses of smell in matters of relationships. However, the truth of the matter is that humans are also influenced by smell and, in particular, very faint smells, when it comes to judging others.

Participants in one study were shown faces with neutral expressions and then asked to rank them on a scale from extremely likeable to extremely unlikeable (Li, Moallem, Paller, & Gottfried, 2007). Just before viewing each face, a participant would sniff a bottle containing different concentrations of one of three types of odorant: lemon (good), sweat (bad), and ethereal (neutral). In case you are not familiar with the ethereal label, this smell is often represented by anisole, a colorless liquid with a mild licorice scent. The concentrations of these three odorants varied from consciously detectible to barely detectable, and the participants were told that a scent would be present on 75 percent of the trials. Most of the participants stated that they were not aware of the barely detectable odors.

People who reported being aware of a scent did not seem to be influenced by the scent when judging the likeability of the faces. However, those who were unaware of the barely detectable odors appeared to use the pleasantness of the smell as a cue for the likeability of the face. The more pleasant the odor, the more likeable they rated the face, but only when the odor was undetectable.

What does this mean for the perfume industry and people who enjoy wearing pleasant scents? We can assume that too much is not a good idea. If we want to make others respond more positively to us by using a scent, a little bit apparently goes a long way.

be soluble in fat because the material surrounding our smell receptors is composed of fatty substances.

Air containing olfactory stimuli is taken in through the nostrils and circulated within the nasal cavities connected to the nostrils. The congestion you experience during a bad cold limits this circulation, reducing your ability to smell.

Individuals vary in their sensitivity to smell. As we age, our sensitivity to smell decreases (Rawson, 2006). Females are generally more sensitive to smell than males (Koelega & Koster, 1974), and smokers are less sensitive to smell than nonsmokers (Ahlstrom, Berglund, Berglund, Engen, & Lindvall, 1987). Our ability to perceive a particular odor is also affected by how long we are exposed to the odor. Smell adapts rapidly, a fact to keep in mind when applying your favorite perfume.

Olfactory Receptors The neural receptors for olfaction are contained in a thin sheet of cells within the nasal cavity known as the **olfactory epithelium,** illustrated in ■ Figure 7.26. Unlike many other types of neurons, olfactory receptor cells regularly die and are replaced in a cycle lasting approximately four to six weeks. In addition to the receptor cells, the olfactory epithelium also contains glia-type support cells that produce mucus. Basal cells in the epithelium give rise to new receptors when needed.

Olfactory receptor cells are bipolar, having two branches extending from the cell body. One branch reaches out to the surface of the epithelium. Cilia, or hairlike structures, extend from the end of this branch into the mucus that covers the epithelium. Molecules dissolved in the mucus bind and interact with these cilia. The binding of an odorant molecule to a receptor site on a cilium begins a process that results in an influx of sodium and calcium into the receptor neuron. If the resulting depolarization is large enough, it will produce action potentials sent along the branch of the receptor neuron that projects toward the olfactory bulb. These fibers collectively form the olfactory nerve (cranial nerve I), which makes its way centrally to the olfactory bulb.

Olfactory receptors must catalog the many thousands of different smells that we are able to discriminate. Buck and Axel (1991) suggest that we use approximately 1,000 types of receptor cells to accomplish this task. An individual receptor cell provides rather general information about an odorant molecule. The task of sorting out the qualities of the odorant is left to higher levels of the brain (Zou, Horowitz,

olfactory epithelium The layer in the nasal cavity containing olfactory receptors.

FIGURE 7.26
Olfactory Information Travels from the Epithelium to the Brain

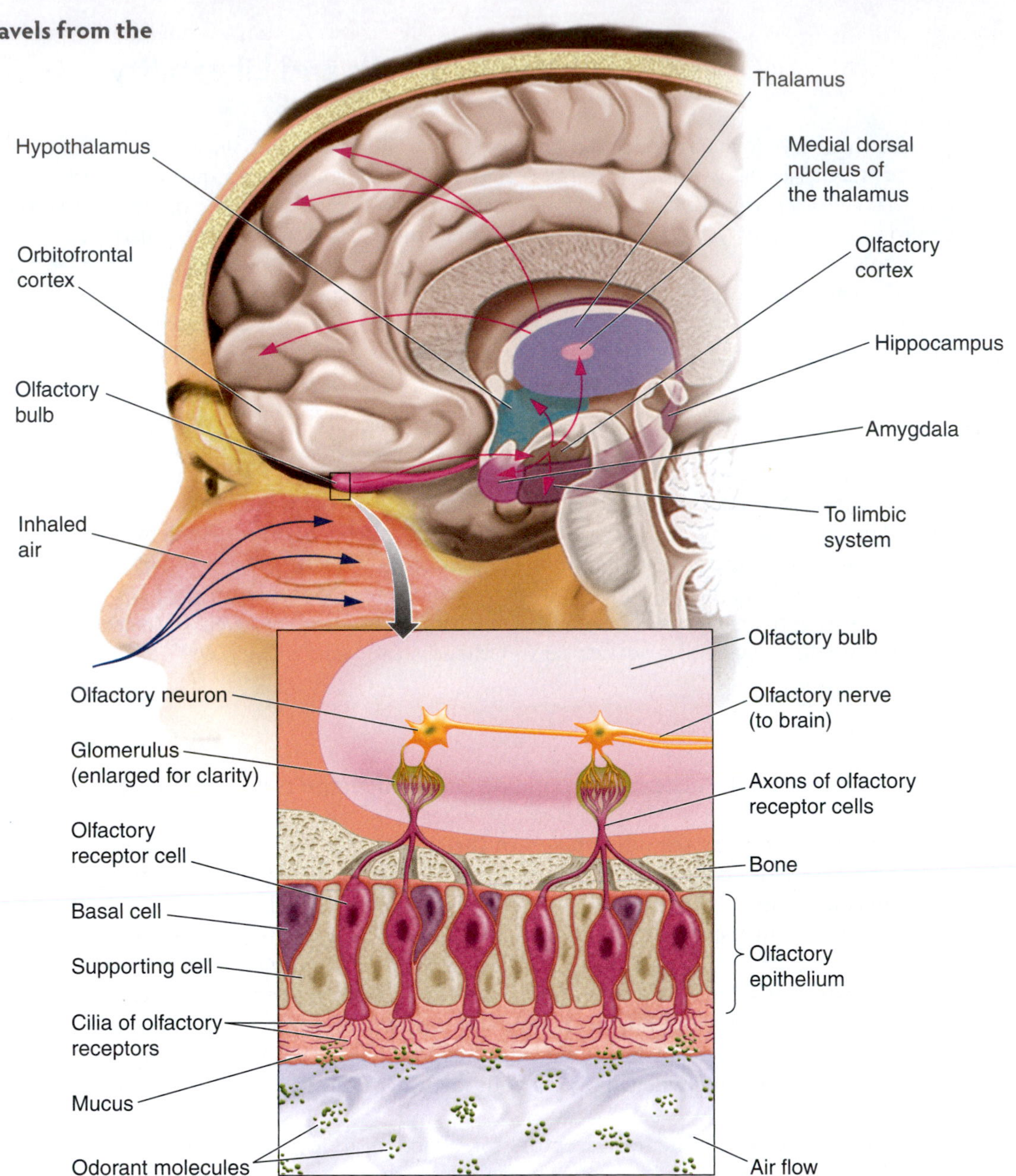

Montmayeur, Snapper, & Buck, 2001). In addition to these general olfactory receptors, mammals have a second group of receptors that do not respond to typical odorants. Instead, these receptors respond to pheromones such as compounds found in urine (Liberles & Buck, 2006).

Although the majority of scientists believe that odorant molecules interact with receptors like keys fitting into locks, others believe that this approach fails to explain many observations about our sense of smell. For example, odorants with very similar shapes often smell quite different, and conversely, odorants with very different shapes can smell quite similar. To explain these discrepancies, some researchers believe that the olfactory system responds to the vibration of odorant molecules rather than to their shapes (Brookes, Hartoutsiou, Horsfield, & Stoneham, 2007).

Olfactory Pathways The axons from the olfactory receptor cells make their way to one of our two olfactory bulbs via the olfactory nerve (cranial nerve I). Receptor axons synapse within olfactory bulb structures known as **glomeruli.** In each glomerulus, approximately 25,000 olfactory receptor axons form synapses on about 100 olfactory neurons. Each glomerulus receives information from only one type out of the 1,000

glomeruli (glow-MER-you-lee) Structures found within the olfactory bulbs.

kinds of receptor cells. In this manner, precise information about the odorant stimulus is transmitted to the olfactory bulbs. It is likely that the bulbs also participate in some initial sorting of odorant categories, but further work is necessary before an odorant can actually be identified. The processing of components making up complex odors remains separate in the olfactory bulb, suggesting that the integration of these components and recognition of odors (the perfume of a rose, for example) occurs at even higher levels of processing in the brain (Lin, Shea, & Katz, 2006).

Axons from the olfactory bulbs form the **olfactory tracts.** As these tracts proceed toward the brain, they are quite vulnerable to damage, particularly from traffic accidents. As the head is jerked back and forth due to impact, the olfactory fibers leaving the nose can be sheared by the nearby edges of the skull bones (think of the nasal "triangle" of the skeleton). People typically respond to the resulting loss of their sense of smell by developing symptoms of depression (Deems et al., 1991) and often resort to flavoring their food with pepper sauce to give it some noticeable flavor.

Olfaction is unique among the major senses in that information travels to the neocortex without synapsing in the thalamus first. Axons from the olfactory tracts synapse in the **olfactory cortex.** The olfactory cortex is located below the anterior portions of the frontal lobe. The olfactory cortex forms connections with the medial dorsal nucleus of the thalamus, which in turn projects to the insula, located at the junction of the frontal and temporal lobes within the lateral fissure, and the orbitofrontal cortex (Sobel et al., 2000). The orbitofrontal cortex might participate in the identification of the pleasant or unpleasant qualities of olfactory stimuli. Connections also occur with many structures of the limbic system, including the amygdala and hypothalamus.

Olfactory information is widely distributed in the brain and is used by systems involved with odor identification, motivation, emotion, and memory. Olfaction is disturbed in a number of types of psychopathology. People with schizophrenia show deficits in olfaction, possibly due to general problems with frontal lobe functioning (see Chapter 16). Their immediate family members also show deficits in olfaction relative to healthy controls, suggesting a genetic basis for differences in olfactory function (Compton et al., 2006). Patients with major depressive disorder, anorexia nervosa, and alcoholism show specific patterns of olfactory deficits, illustrating the complex relationships between olfaction and emotion (Lombion-Pouthier, Vandel, Nezelof, Haffen, & Millot, 2006).

Nothing awakens a reminiscence like an odor.
Victor Hugo

Taste

The most likely original purpose of our sense of taste was to protect us from eating poisonous or spoiled food. Many bitter-tasting substances are actually poisonous, and we are attracted to tastes that boost our chances of survival. Taste is actually a small part of the eating experience. When we eat, we perceive not only the taste of the food but also qualities such as temperature, texture, and consistency (Gibson, 1966). In addition, taste interacts with smell to give us the flavor of a food. You have probably noticed that food just doesn't taste very good when your sense of smell is decreased by a bad cold. If you close your eyes and hold your nose, you are unable to distinguish between a slice of apple and a slice of raw potato.

Taste begins with the dissolving of molecules in the saliva of the mouth. Saliva is similar in chemical composition to saltwater. Substances that do not dissolve in saliva cannot be tasted, although you can still obtain information about the size, texture, and temperature of objects in the mouth.

Most of us are familiar with four major categories of taste: sweet, sour, salty, and bitter. However, you may not have heard of the fifth type of taste, known by the Japanese term **umami,** which, roughly translated, means savory or meaty. Umami taste receptors on the tongue have been identified by Chaudhari, Landlin, and Roper (2000). In addition, some taste receptors respond to free fatty acids, enabling us to detect the fats in food (Gilbertson, Fontenot, Liu, Zhang, & Monroe, 1997).

Taste Receptors Receptors for taste are found not only on the tongue but also in other parts of the mouth. For our present purposes, we'll confine our discussion to the receptors of the tongue, shown in Figure 7.27.

olfactory tract A fiber pathway connecting the olfactory bulbs to the olfactory cortex.

olfactory cortex Cortex in the frontal lobe that responds to the sense of smell.

umami (you-MAH-mee) One of the five basic taste groups, characteristic of tastes found in seaweed and other "meaty or savory" elements of Asian cuisine.

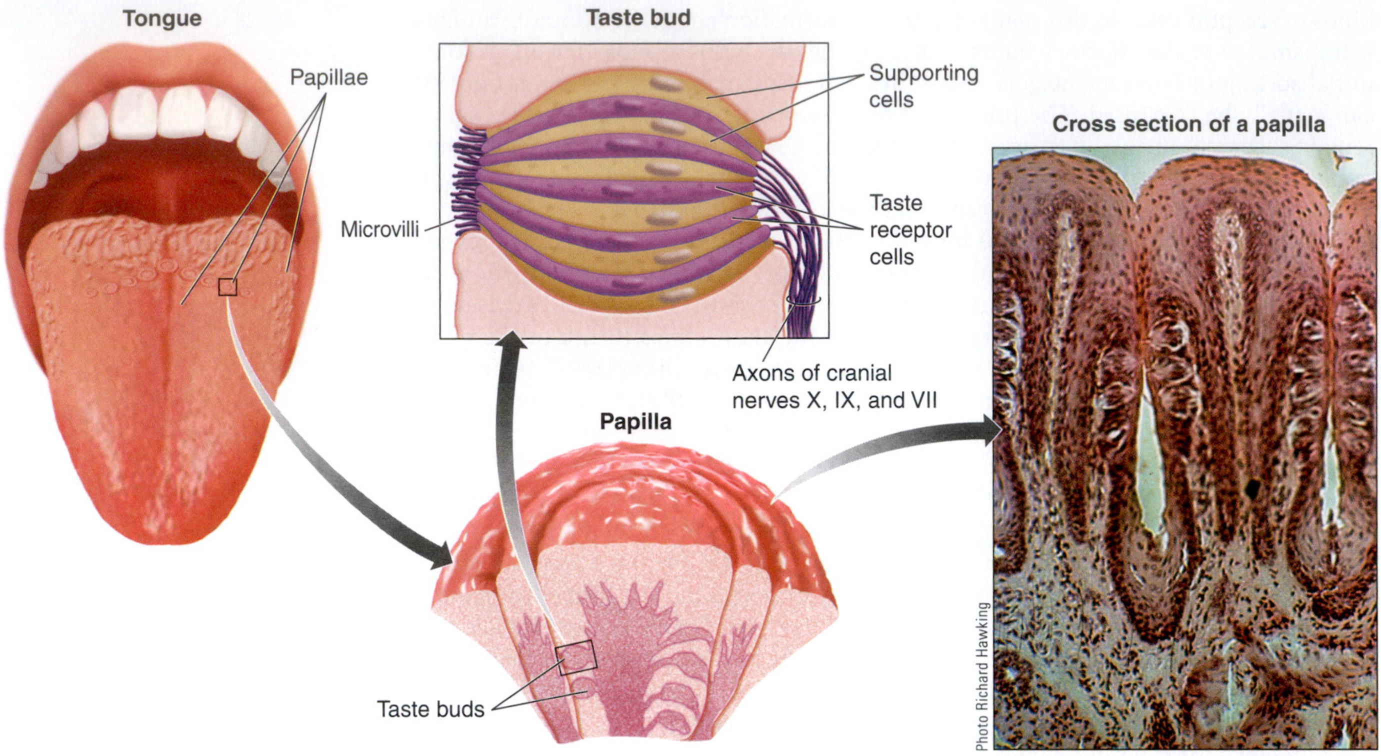

FIGURE 7.27
The Taste Receptors

Each bump on the surface of the tongue, known as a **papilla,** contains somewhere between 1 and 100 taste buds, which are too small to be seen with the naked eye (Bradley, 1979). Some papillae, such as those in the very center of the tongue, contain no taste buds at all. Taste buds live for only about 10 days, after which time they are replaced. Burning your tongue on hot liquid reduces your sense of taste initially, but recovery occurs within a few days. In total, the average person has about 6,000 taste buds, although significant variation can occur from one person to the next (Miller & Reedy, 1990). Linda Bartoshuk (2000) has identified people with unusually high numbers of taste buds, whom she has named "supertasters." Not only do these individuals experience taste with greater intensity, giving them what Bartoshuk refers to as a "neon" sense of taste compared to the "pastels" experienced by others, but they also appear to be more sensitive to oral pain and to the texture of foods.

Nothing would be more tiresome than eating and drinking if God had not made them a pleasure as well as a necessity.
Voltaire

Most taste buds contain somewhere between 50 and 150 taste receptor cells. The taste receptor cells are not technically considered to be neurons, although they do have the capability of forming synapses. Each taste receptor has a number of thin fibers known as **microvilli** that extend into the saliva. Substances interact with the microvilli in different ways. Some molecules, such as sodium, pass through the cell's ion channels. Others bind to ion channels, either blocking them or opening them. Finally, some taste molecules bind to receptors on the taste cell and activate second messenger systems (see Chapter 4). The tongue also contains pain receptors that are sensitive to capsaicin, the main "hot" ingredient in peppers. Mice lacking capsaicin receptors happily consumed water containing capsaicin at levels that were rejected by normal mice (Caterina et al., 2000).

For many years, researchers believed that receptors for different taste qualities were located in different parts of the tongue. You probably have seen little maps showing where each taste was sensed. More recent research demonstrates that this earlier view is incorrect. Receptors for all five taste qualities are found in all areas of the tongue (Huang et al., 2006).

papillae (PAP-i-lie) Bumps on the tongue containing taste buds and taste receptors.
microvilli (my-kroh-VILL-ee) Small fibers extending from taste receptors.

Taste Pathways Pathways linking the taste receptors to the brain are shown in Figure 7.28. Although taste receptors do not have a true axon, they are able to contact and influence taste fibers serving the tongue. These taste fibers form parts of cranial nerves VII, IX, and X. These nerves in turn form synapses with the gustatory nucleus,

WHY DOES THIS MATTER?

The Pros and Cons of Being a Supertaster

Linda Bartoshuk's research on supertasters matters because it helps us understand individual differences in food preferences that have implications for health and weight control.

According to Bartoshuk's research on individual differences in taste sensation, about one quarter of the United States population are supertasters, another quarter are nontasters, and the remaining half fall somewhere between these two extremes. Women are more likely than men to be supertasters, perhaps an echo of their roles in selecting safe food for our hunter-gatherer ancestors. Asians are more likely to be supertasters than Caucasians.

Other than having a very discriminating sense of taste, what other implications are there for supertasters? On the plus side, supertasters tend to find fatty and sugary foods less appealing, resulting in a tendency to weigh less and experience less heart disease than other types of tasters. On the minus side, the supertasters' intense reaction to bitter foods makes them less fond of vegetables. Although a general ability to avoid bitter foods might have survival advantages, since most poisonous plants taste quite bitter, an avoidance of bitter vegetables can also lead to serious health problems.

In a study of 200 older men with colon cancer, Bartoshuk, Marc Basson, and their colleagues (Basson et al., 2005) found that the number of cancerous polyps a man had was directly related to the intensity of his experience of bitter tastes. The more sensitive a man was to bitter tastes, the more likely he was to have cancer, probably due to his avoidance of the foods that generally reduce colon cancer risk.

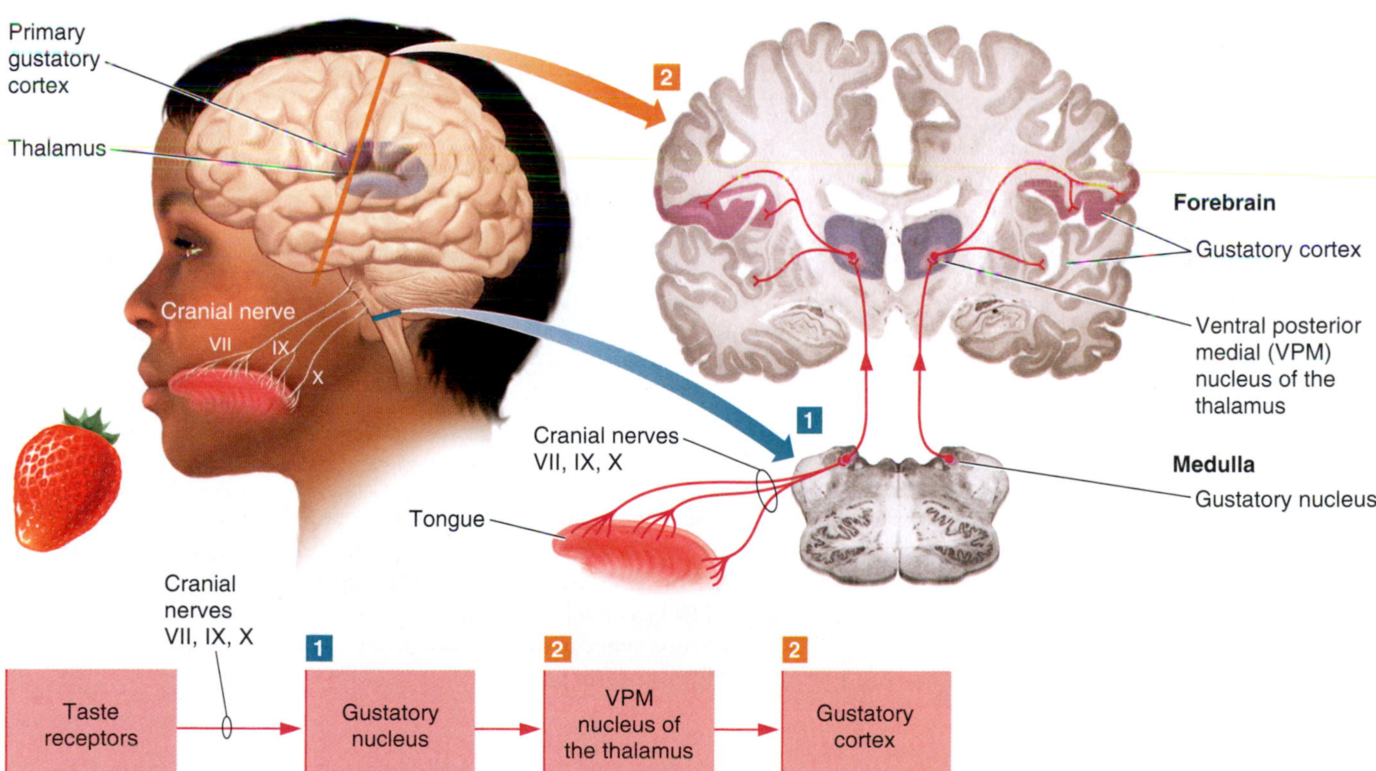

FIGURE 7.28
Taste Pathways to the Brain

which is a part of the solitary nucleus of the medulla. Axons from the gustatory nucleus synapse in the **ventral posterior medial (VPM) nucleus of the thalamus.** Finally, axons from the VPM synapse in the gustatory cortex in the parietal lobe, adjacent to areas of the somatosensory cortex serving the mouth and tongue. The identity of the taste sensation is probably determined at this level. Other fibers make their way to the orbitofrontal cortex. As in the case of olfaction, this input probably encodes the pleasantness, or emotional qualities, of taste.

ventral posterior medial (VPM) nucleus of the thalamus The nucleus of the thalamus that receives information regarding taste.

NEW DIRECTIONS

Yellow Smoky Voices and Sounds Like Briny Pickles

The arts commonly attempt to combine experiences across sensory modalities, whether through music composed to highlight the emotions of a movie scene or dance choreographed to enhance the emotional qualities of a piece of music. Nearly 4 percent of human beings, however, experience synesthesia, a condition in which sensations in one sensory modality spontaneously trigger an associated sensation in another modality (Simner & Hubbard, 2006). The most common variants are color-letter synesthesia (seeing a particular letter as red, for example) or color-days of the week synesthesia (Friday is yellow).

Alexander Luria (1968) made an extensive case study of patient S, who not only experienced marked synesthesia but also used his synesthesia as the basis for a remarkably gifted memory. When S heard a tone of 50 cycles per second at 100 dB, he "saw a brown strip against a dark background that had red, tongue-like edges. The sense of taste he experienced in response to this tone was like that of sweet and sour borscht, a sensation that gripped his entire tongue" (Luria, 1968, p. 23).

As unusual as synesthesia might seem, it appears to have a logical basis in brain activation. A cross-activation hypothesis suggests that synesthesia results when adjacent areas are activated by a single stimulus (Ramachandran & Hubbard, 2001). In the cases of color-letter synesthesia, for example, brain areas that process the identification of letters and color are next to one another in secondary visual cortex. An alternate explanation is that synesthesia might occur when the brain's balance of excitation and inhibition is disturbed (Grossenbacher & Lovelace, 2001). This hypothesis is consistent with the observation of synesthesia as a result of the use of hallucinogenic drugs such as LSD.

INTERIM SUMMARY 7.3

Summary Table: Major Features of the Chemical Sensory Systems

Sensory Modality	Receptor Types	Pathways and Connections
Olfaction	Bipolar cells embedded in the olfactory epithelium	• Axons from the receptors synapse in the glomeruli of the olfactory bulbs. • Axons from the olfactory bulbs form the olfactory tract and synapse in the olfactory cortex. • The olfactory cortex sends information to the thalamus, limbic system, insula, and orbitofrontal cortex.
Taste	Taste buds on the tongue and elsewhere in the mouth	• Fibers serving the taste receptors join cranial nerves VII, IX, and X. • These axons synapse in the gustatory nucleus of the medulla. • Axons from the gustatory nucleus synapse in the ventral posterior medial (VPM) nucleus of the thalamus. • VPM axons synapse in somatosensory cortex and in the orbitofrontal cortex.

Summary Points

1. Olfactory receptors lining the olfactory epithelium of the nasal cavity respond to airborne molecules by sending messages via the olfactory nerve to the olfactory bulb. The olfactory bulb axons project to the olfactory cortex, which forms widely distributed connections with the cerebral cortex and the limbic system. **(LO7)**
2. Interactions between taste receptors and dissolved chemicals activate parts of cranial nerves VII, IX, and X, which synapse with the gustatory nucleus of the medulla. Gustatory nucleus axons synapse in the ventral posterior medial nucleus of the thalamus, which in turn projects to the gustatory cortex and to the orbitofrontal cortex. **(LO8)**

Review Questions

1. What are the major features of olfactory receptors?
2. What are the five major types of taste stimuli?

CHAPTER REVIEW

THOUGHT QUESTIONS

1. If you had to give up one of your senses, which one would it be, and why?
2. Why does the representation of pain information in the central nervous system make it difficult to treat chronic pain with surgery?
3. How might the gradual loss of olfactory and taste sensitivity affect the eating habits of seniors?
4. What steps can you take to reduce environmental causes of hearing loss?

KEY TERMS

amplitude (p. 190)
audition (p. 189)
auditory nerve (cranial nerve VIII) (p. 195)
basilar membrane (p. 193)
C fiber (p. 206)
cochlea (p. 193)
decibel (dB) (p. 190)
dermatome (p. 206)
frequency (p. 190)
glomerulus/glomeruli (p. 218)
hertz (Hz) (p. 192)
mechanoreceptors (p. 205)
medial geniculate nucleus (p. 198)
Meissner's corpuscles (p. 205)
Merkel's disk (p. 205)
nociceptors (p. 212)
olfaction (p. 216)
olfactory cortex (p. 219)
olfactory tracts (p. 219)
ossicles (p. 192)
otolith organs (p. 202)
Pacinian corpuscles (p. 205)
pinna (p. 192)
primary auditory cortex (p. 198)
primary somatosensory cortex (p. 204)
Ruffini's ending (p. 205)
secondary auditory cortex (p. 198)
secondary somatosensory cortex (p. 209)
semicircular canals (p. 202)
somatosensory system (p. 202)
thermoreceptors (p. 211)
tympanic membrane (p. 192)
ventral posterior (VP) nucleus of the thalamus (p. 204)
ventral posterior medial (VPM) nucleus of the thalamus (p. 221)
vestibular system (p. 202)
Wernicke's area (p. 198)

8

Movement

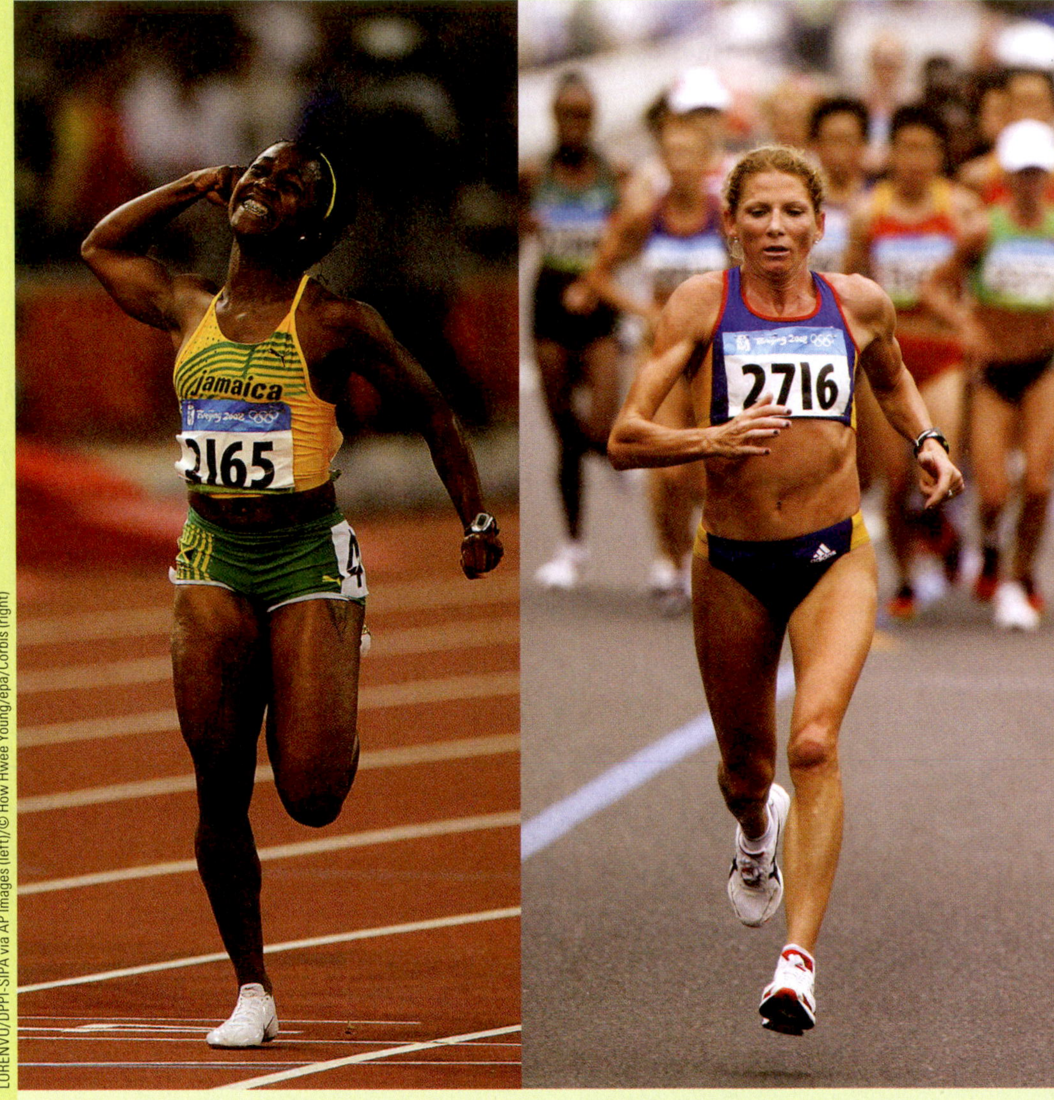

LORENVU/DPPI-SIPA via AP Images (left)/© How Hwee Young/epa/Corbis (right)

▲ **Different Muscles for Different Jobs** The muscle types that make for elite sprinters, like Shelly-Ann Fraser (left), are different from the muscle types of elite marathoners, like Constantina Tomescu (right).

CHAPTER OUTLINE

Introduction

Near midnight on a warm evening at the 2008 Summer Olympics in Beijing, 21-year-old Shelly-Ann Fraser of Jamaica showed that she was the fastest woman in the world at that point in time, clocking 10.78 seconds to win the gold medal in the 100-meter sprint. Earlier the same day, Constantina Tomescu of Romania was the first woman across the finish line of the 26-mile-plus marathon course in a time of 2 hours, 26 minutes, and 44 seconds.

What accounts for the success of these athletes over others? One person might have more mental toughness than the other, or a better training diet, or even better shoes.

However, the answer might rest in the genes that encode the muscle fibers in Fraser's and Tomescu's legs. It is likely that they have the perfect composition of muscle fibers required for their respective events and that their muscles use energy a bit more efficiently than their nearest competitors'. Their abilities would not translate to each other's event. The muscle composition of a sprinter such as Fraser is very different from the muscle composition of a marathoner such as Tomescu. Fraser would be lucky to walk the distance of the marathon, whereas Tomescu would lose the 100 meters before she got out of the starting blocks.

Even if we don't have the natural ability and dedication to reach the pinnacle of athletic performance, our muscles usually do a good job of getting us around and carrying out skilled movements. In this chapter, we will gain a greater understanding of how our nervous system commands are translated into movement.

LEARNING OBJECTIVES

After reading this chapter, you should be able to:

LO1 Describe the three major types of muscle, the major features of the muscle fiber, and the process of muscle fiber contraction.

LO2 Describe the action of flexors and extensors at a joint.

LO3 Summarize the processes responsible for the initiation and control of muscle contractions.

LO4 Identify the structures and processes responsible for providing feedback from muscles to the central nervous system.

LO5 Describe the major types of motor reflexes.

LO6 Trace the lateral and ventromedial spinal motor pathways.

LO7 Identify the roles of the cerebellum, basal ganglia, primary motor cortex, pre-SMA, and supplementary motor cortex in the control of movement.

LO8 Describe the processes responsible for initiating movement and understanding the movement of others.

LO9 Summarize the effects of toxins on the neuromuscular junction and movement.

LO10 Identify the causes, symptoms, and treatments of major disorders of movement.

Muscles

Muscles make up the majority of the human body's tissues and are responsible for the movement of the body and the movement of materials within the body. The human body contains somewhere between 640 and 850 muscles, depending on which anatomist you ask.

Types of Muscle

The muscles of the body, shown in Figure 8.1, can be divided into two types based on their appearance: smooth muscle and striated muscle. **Smooth muscle** is found in the lining of the digestive tract, within the arteries, and in the reproductive system. Smooth muscles move nutrients through the digestive tract, control blood pressure, and mix sperm with seminal fluid, among other tasks. The smooth muscles are controlled by the autonomic nervous system.

Striated muscle, named after its striped appearance, can be further divided into two types, cardiac muscle and skeletal muscle. **Cardiac muscle** produces the pumping action of the heart. The **skeletal muscles** attached to bones produce the majority of body movement. Other skeletal muscles are responsible for moving our eyes and lungs. Our discussion of movement will focus on the skeletal muscles because these are responsible for the majority of our behavior.

Muscle Anatomy and Contraction

Skeletal muscles, illustrated in Figure 8.2, are made up of long, very thin cells referred to as **muscle fibers.** Human muscle fiber cells usually extend the length of the muscle and are up to 30 cm long and from 0.05 to 0.15 mm wide.

The Muscle Fiber The membranes encasing each muscle fiber are similar to the membranes of neurons. Like neural membranes, the muscle fiber membrane contains receptor sites, in this case for the neurotransmitter acetylcholine (ACh). When a molecule of ACh is bound to a receptor site in the muscle fiber membrane, sodium channels open. Sodium rushing into the muscle fiber depolarizes the cell and triggers an action potential. In Chapter 3, we observed that action potentials in neurons travel in only one direction—from the axon hillock down the length of the axon. In contrast, the action potential in a muscle fiber spreads out in two directions on either side of the receptor site. Each action potential produces a single contraction of the muscle fiber, known as a **twitch.**

smooth muscle A type of muscle found in the lining of the digestive tract, within arteries, and in the reproductive system; controlled by the autonomic nervous system.

striated muscle A type of muscle named for its striped appearance; including cardiac and skeletal muscles.

cardiac muscle A type of striated muscle found in the heart.

skeletal muscle A type of striated muscle that is attached to bones and is responsible for the majority of body movements.

muscle fiber An individual muscle cell.

twitch The contraction of a single muscle fiber.

■ **FIGURE 8.1**
The Human Body Has Three Types of Muscle
Muscle types are named after their appearance or location. (a) Smooth muscle is found in the digestive tract, blood vessels, and reproductive system. (b) Striated (striped) muscle gets its name from its striped appearance. There are two types of striated muscle. Cardiac muscle keeps our hearts beating. Skeletal muscles move our bones, eyes, and lungs.

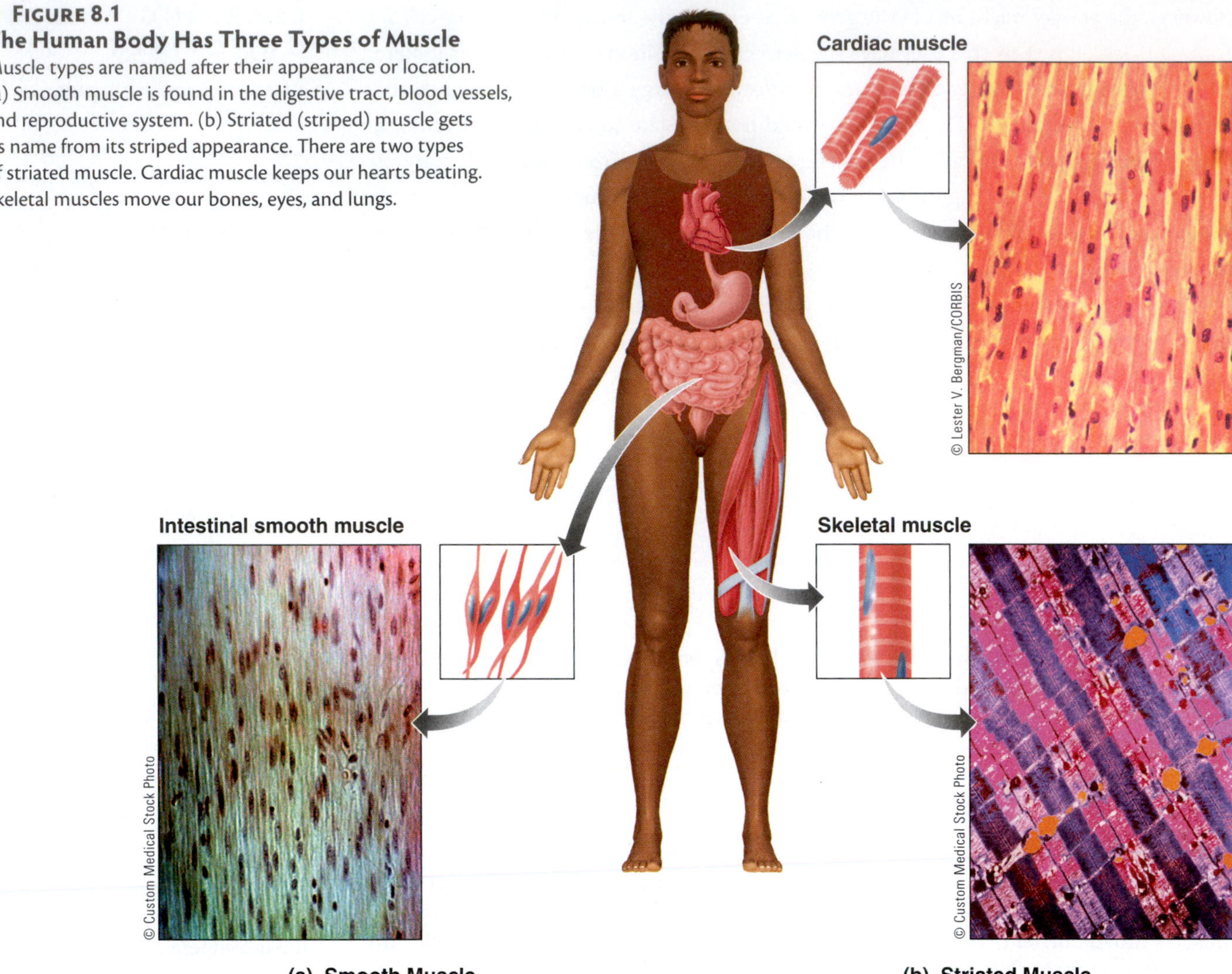

The Structure of Myofibrils The interior of the muscle fiber is made up of long strands of protein called **myofibrils.** The myofibrils run the length of the fiber and are responsible for producing fiber contractions.

Single segments of a myofibril are called **sarcomeres,** which are arranged end to end. The boundary of each sarcomere is known as a **Z line** because the boundary looks like a Z shape under a microscope. Attached to each Z line are a number of thin filaments made up of the protein **actin.** Lying between each pair of thin filaments is a thick filament made up of the protein **myosin.**

Muscle Fiber Contraction Muscle contractions are caused by the movement of the thick myosin filaments along the length of the thin actin filaments. As the filaments slide by each other, the Z lines move closer together, and the sarcomere shortens. As the sarcomeres shorten, the muscle contracts. This process is illustrated in ■ Figure 8.3.

In a resting muscle fiber, actin is covered by the protein **troponin,** which prevents actin from interacting with myosin. The arrival of an action potential at the muscle fiber is the catalyst for a series of events that allows actin and myosin to interact. The action potential triggers the release of calcium from internal organelles within the muscle fiber. Calcium in turn binds with troponin, neutralizing troponin's blocking effect. Freed from troponin, actin binds with myosin.

As a result of the binding, the myosin molecules rotate, causing the thick myosin filaments to slide past the thin actin filaments. In a process requiring energy, the myosin molecules subsequently separate from the actin molecules. As long as calcium and energy are still present in the muscle fiber, the binding and unbinding process

myofibril (my-oh-FIE-brill) A long fiber strand running the length of a muscle fiber that is responsible for contraction.
sarcomere (SAR-coh-mear) A myofibril segment bound on either side by a Z line and spanned by thin filaments.
Z line A boundary line for each sarcomere within a myofibril.
actin A protein that makes up the thin filaments of the myofibril.
myosin (MY-oh-sin) A protein that makes up the thick filaments of the myofibril.
troponin (truh-POE-nin) The protein covering of an actin molecule that prevents the molecule from binding with myosin when a muscle is in the resting state.

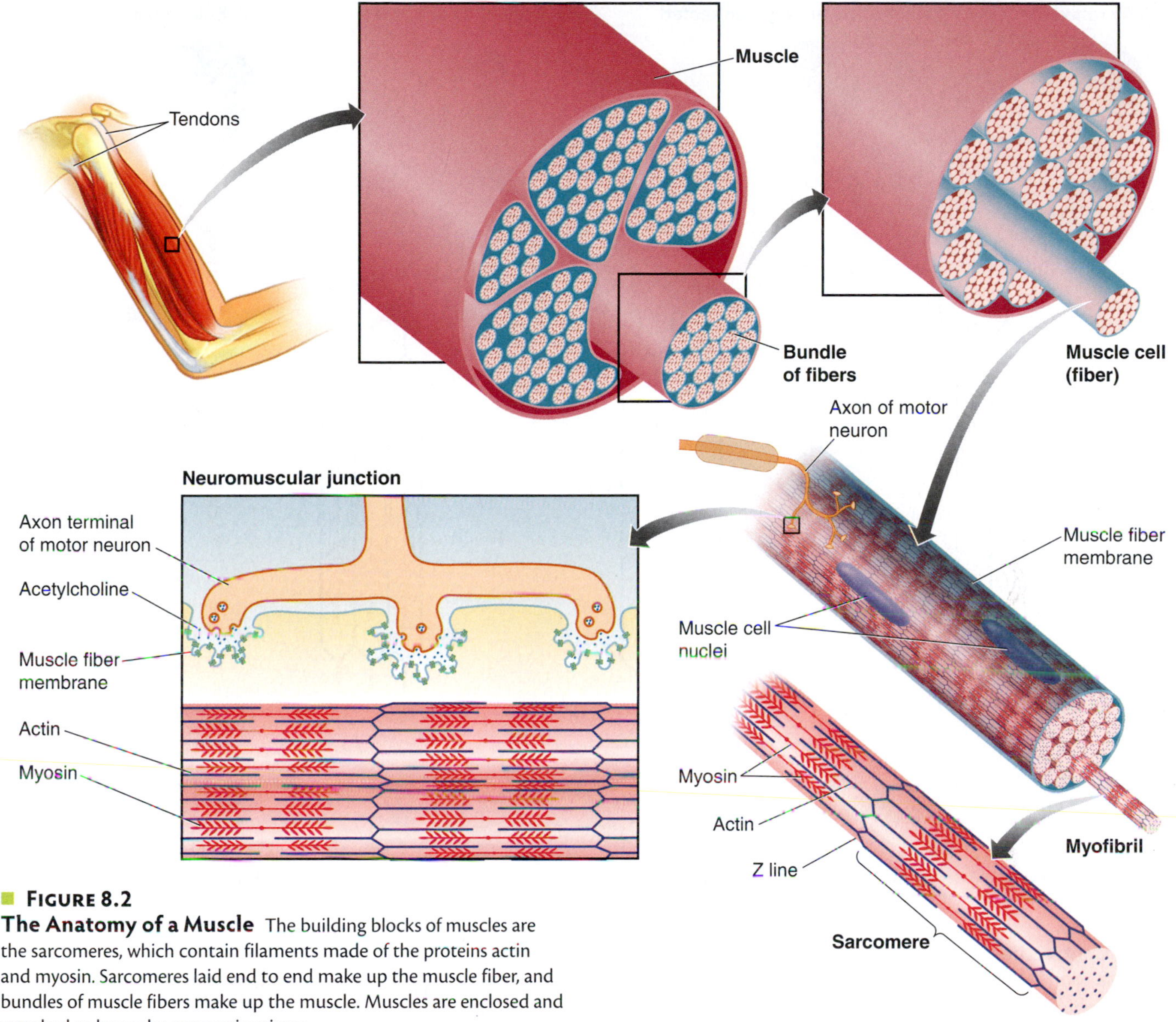

FIGURE 8.2
The Anatomy of a Muscle The building blocks of muscles are the sarcomeres, which contain filaments made of the proteins actin and myosin. Sarcomeres laid end to end make up the muscle fiber, and bundles of muscle fibers make up the muscle. Muscles are enclosed and attached to bones by connective tissue.

repeats itself, and the myosin filaments move step by step along the length of the actin filaments. Consequently, the muscle fiber gradually contracts.

In the absence of further action potentials, the muscle fiber will relax. Calcium is taken up again by the internal organelles, in a process similar to the reuptake of a neurotransmitter by a presynaptic neuron. When no longer bound by calcium, troponin once again blocks the interaction of myosin and actin, and the thin and thick filaments slide apart. The sarcomeres and the muscle fiber return to their resting length. If there is a shortage of energy in the cell, the detachment of myosin molecules from actin molecules can't take place, and the muscle becomes locked in its contracted state. This process accounts for the muscular stiffness, or rigor mortis, that occurs after death.

Fiber Types and Speed In humans, the thick myosin filaments in muscle fibers come in three varieties. Type I fibers are known as **slow-twitch fibers,** and Types IIa and IIb are known as **fast-twitch fibers.** Type IIb fibers can contract up to ten times faster than Type I fibers. The contraction velocity of Type IIa fibers falls somewhere between Type I and Type IIb. Most skeletal muscles contain mixtures of all three types of fibers but in different proportions. The postural muscles of the back, neck, and legs are dominated by slow-twitch fibers. The muscles of the arms and shoulders contain higher proportions of fast-twitch fibers.

slow-twitch fiber A muscle fiber containing Type I myosin filaments and large numbers of mitochondria that contracts slowly using aerobic metabolism; primarily responsible for movement requiring endurance.

fast-twitch fiber A muscle fiber containing Type IIa or Type IIb myosin filaments that contains few mitochondria, uses anaerobic metabolism, and contracts rapidly; primarily responsible for movement requiring explosive strength.

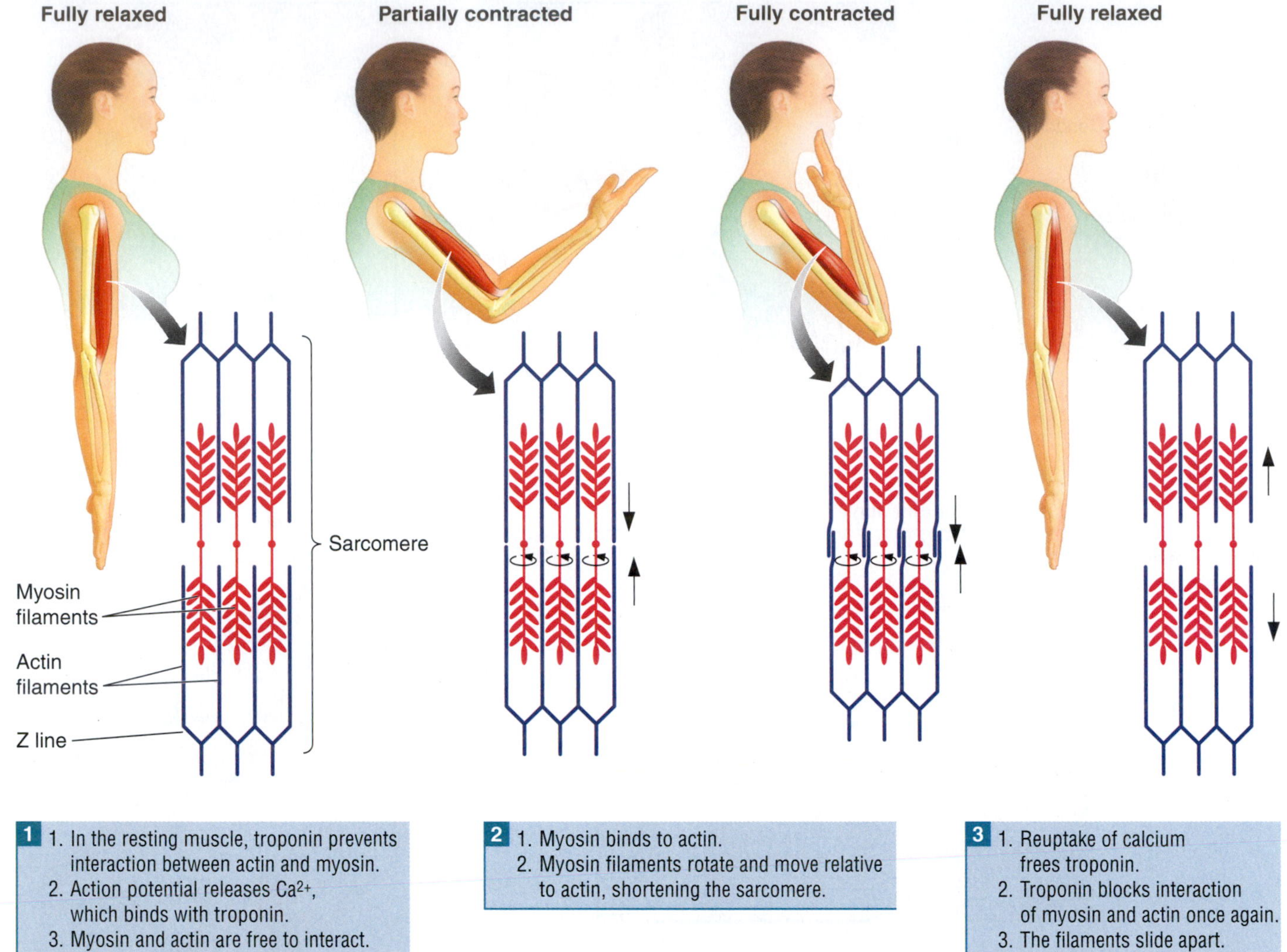

Fully relaxed
Partially contracted
Fully contracted
Fully relaxed
Sarcomere
Myosin filaments
Actin filaments
Z line
1 1. In the resting muscle, troponin prevents interaction between actin and myosin.
2. Action potential releases Ca2+, which binds with troponin.
3. Myosin and actin are free to interact.
2 1. Myosin binds to actin.
2. Myosin filaments rotate and move relative to actin, shortening the sarcomere.
3 1. Reuptake of calcium frees troponin.
2. Troponin blocks interaction of myosin and actin once again.
3. The filaments slide apart.

FIGURE 8.3
Muscle Contraction

WHY DOES THIS MATTER?

Why Do Muscles Get Tired?

Understanding why muscles get tired might lead to the development of new drugs for people with heart disease and other conditions in which muscles weaken. Such drugs would also be attractive to athletes wishing to enhance their performances. We all know what it feels like to have tired muscles. Maybe you were a little too ambitious in your workout, or thought helping your friend move to a new apartment would not be a big deal. More seriously, a person's heart muscle can become fatigued, leading to life-threatening heart disease. As common as these situations are, it was only recently that scientists discovered why our muscles run out of steam.

As we have seen in this chapter, the release and reuptake of calcium within the muscle fiber plays an important role in the fiber's ability to twitch, or contract. Researchers have discovered that after a muscle has contracted repeatedly, the calcium channels in the fibers' internal organelles become leaky (Bellinger et al., 2008). Without the normal ebb and flow of calcium in response to neural input to the fiber, the fiber begins to contract more weakly. In addition, the leaking calcium initiates the activity of enzymes that further damage the muscle. This same group of scientists is experimenting with a drug that will block the calcium leakage, which would help prevent muscle damage and maintain a muscle's ability to contract. Such a drug would be very beneficial to patients with heart disease, but the potential for abuse by athletes is significant.

Fast- and slow-twitch fibers use energy differently. Slow-twitch fibers use oxygen-using, or **aerobic, metabolism,** whereas the fast-twitch fibers use **anaerobic metabolism,** which occurs in the absence of oxygen. Endurance activities, such as distance running, rely primarily on aerobic slow-twitch fibers. Explosive, powerful

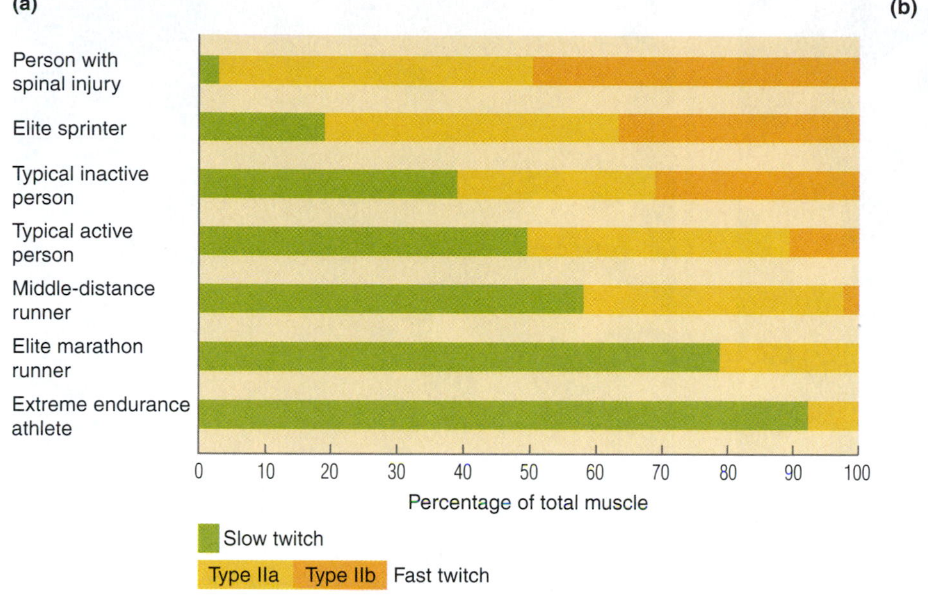

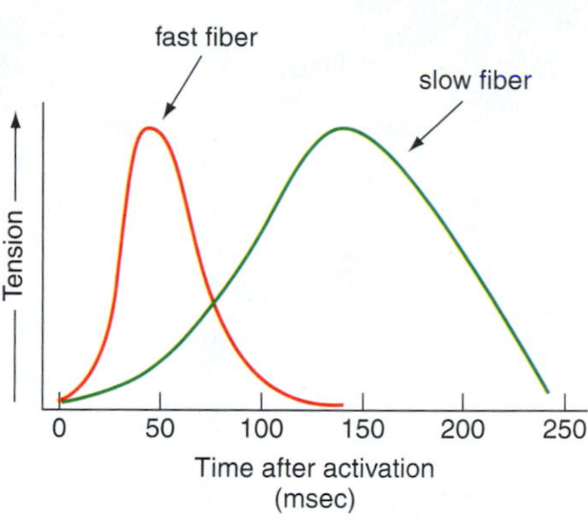

FIGURE 8.4
Human Fiber Types (a) The average adult has approximately equal amounts of fast- and slow-twitch muscles. People who have spinal injury lose most of their slow-twitch fibers. Athletes involved in power events, such as sprinting, usually have a higher proportion of fast-twitch muscles than athletes involved with endurance sports.
(b) Because fast fibers produce muscle tension very quickly, they are useful for explosive movements such as sprinting and weightlifting. The slower fibers can produce equal tension, but require a longer time to do so. Slower fibers are used in endurance activities such as long distance running and swimming.
Source: Data from Anderson, Schjerling, & Saltin (2000).

movements, such as sprinting, jumping, and weightlifting, employ anaerobic fast-twitch fibers. Muscles dominated by fast-twitch fibers appear white (like the white meat of a turkey breast), whereas those containing slow-twitch fibers appear dark or red (like the dark meat of a turkey's legs and thighs). The red color reflects the presence of *myoglobin*, an iron-based muscle protein that stores the oxygen necessary for aerobic metabolism. Diving animals, such as seals and whales, owe part of their ability to remain submerged to the unusually high amounts of myoglobin contained in their muscles.

The average adult human has approximately equal numbers of fast- and slow-twitch fibers in the quadriceps muscle on the front of the thigh. However, people vary widely in the composition of their muscles. Jesper Andersen and his colleagues (Andersen, Schjerling, & Saltin, 2000) have observed some people with as few as 19 percent slow-twitch fibers in the quadriceps and other people with up to 95 percent slow-twitch fibers. This variation is probably the result of a single gene, *ACTN3*, which normally encodes a protein used by fast-twitch fibers (MacArthur & North, 2007). If a person receives two copies of a common mutation of the *ACTN3* gene, he or she will produce none of the fast-twitch protein at all, and would likely excel at long-distance running and other endurance sports. The proportion of fast- and slow-twitch fibers in the quadriceps muscle of people engaged in different levels of activity is shown in Figure 8.4.

There is nothing, I think, more unfortunate than to have soft, chubby, fat-looking children who go to watch their school play basketball every Saturday and regard that as their week's exercise.

John F. Kennedy

THE EFFECTS OF EXERCISE ON MUSCLE

We know that exercise can build muscles. In many cases, muscle enlargement is desirable. However, enlargement of the cardiac muscle often results in life-threatening heart disease. Muscle enlargement occurs in response to muscle fiber damage. When fibers are damaged due to weightlifting or other strenuous activity, more actin and myosin filaments are produced. Lack of activity reverses this process quickly because filament proteins are either broken down faster or synthesized more slowly when muscles are not used (Vandenburgh, Chromiak, Shansky, Del Tatto, & Lemaire, 1999). During space travel, in which lower gravity reduces the activity of major postural muscles, astronauts can lose as much as 20 percent of their muscle mass in as little as two weeks (Andersen et al., 2000).

Under certain circumstances, changes in muscle fiber type do occur. Endurance exercise tends to convert the very fast Type IIb fibers into Type IIa fibers. However, we have little evidence that exercise converts either type of fast-twitch fiber into the slow-twitch Type I fiber or vice versa (Andersen et al., 2000). People who are paralyzed as a result of spinal cord injury experience a dramatic increase in fast-twitch fibers and

aerobic metabolism A chemical processes that requires oxygen.
anaerobic metabolism A chemical process that does not require oxygen.

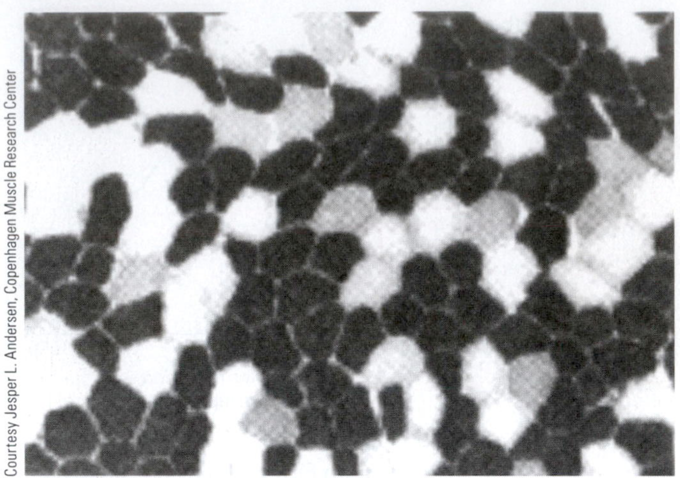

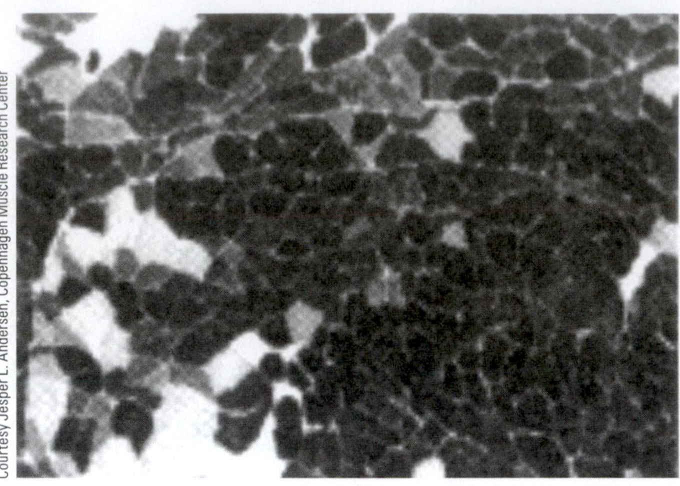

FIGURE 8.5
Aging Affects the Quantity, Shape, and Distribution of Muscle Fibers As we age, we lose muscle fibers, which cannot be regrown. A comparison of the young muscle in the left photo with the aged muscle in the right photo shows other changes. The young muscle has angular-shaped fibers and a checkerboard distribution of fast- (light) and slow- (dark) twitch muscles. The aged muscle shows rounded fibers and clustering of fiber types.

a loss of slow-twitch fibers (see Figure 8.4). Apparently, neural input to the muscle, which is lacking in cases of spinal cord injury, is necessary for the maintenance of slow-twitch fibers.

The Effects of Aging on Muscles

The loss of muscle mass as a result of aging begins as early as age 25 and accelerates through the remainder of the life span. By the age of 50, most people have lost at least 10 percent of the muscle mass they had at age 25, and that figure rises to 50 percent by the age of 80.

Age-related changes can be observed in both the muscles and the neurons that control them. When older adults move a muscle, the firing rates of the associated neurons is lower than the rate seen in younger adults, resulting in slower and weaker muscle responses (Knight & Kamen, 2007). As shown in Figure 8.5, the muscle fibers of young people seen in cross-section are angular, whereas in elderly people, the fibers are rounder. In addition, youthful muscles have a more even distribution of slow- and fast-twitch fibers. In the elderly muscle, the types appear clustered together. Elderly people appear to have a much higher proportion of hybrid muscles, neither slow nor fast, when compared with younger people. Although one cannot stop age-related changes in muscle fibers and neural firing rates, weightlifting can help offset this decline.

Sex Differences in Musculature

Male hormones, or androgens, play a significant role in the development of muscle tissue. Six-year-old boys already have significantly more muscle mass than girls of the same age (Wang et al., 1999). In most cases, the average male is simply going to be stronger than the average female. With more female involvement in organized sports, however, the gap between male and female strength is getting smaller. The difference between top male and female performance times in the mile was about 50 seconds in the 1930s but dropped to about half that difference by the 1990s. Even in weightlifting, traditionally a male domain, female performances are improving. When I tell knowledgeable lifters that at age 16 my daughter did a 463-lb. squat during a strict American Powerlifting Federation competition, they simply assume I don't know anything about weightlifting.

Women face specific challenges in intense physical activity, however. There is some evidence that women's joints and muscles remain more relaxed during movement than men's, which can lead to increased instability and injury (Holloway, 2000). The wider angle women have between their hips and knees due to pelvic width and between their upper to lower arms puts additional stress on their knees and elbows. These structural differences between male and female skeletons can be seen in Figure 8.6. Due to the higher incidence of anterior cruciate ligament (ACL) damage in females, hormones have been suspected of playing a role in joint instability leading to injury. However, female hormones such as estrogen play little, if any, role in the

FIGURE 8.6
Gender Differences in Joint Structure Female skeletons have larger angles at the elbow and knee than male skeletons, putting greater strain on these joints during athletic activity.

WHY DOES THIS MATTER?

Why Women Win the Prize for Strongest Human Muscle

Although it's unlikely that we'll see weightlifting contests in which all of our muscles are tested, human beings do have some remarkably strong ones, including the masseter or jaw muscle, the quadriceps of the thigh, and the gluteus maximus of the buttocks. However, the prize for strongest muscle should be awarded to the one muscle that only women have: the uterus, a relatively small structure weighing about 2½ pounds that is capable of exerting between 100 and 400 newtons of force with each contraction during childbirth. (A newton is the amount of force required to give a one-kilogram object the acceleration of one meter per second.) Understanding the capability of the uterus matters because it gives us a better appreciation for this amazing engine of pregnancy and birth.

The upper portion of the uterus features spiraling smooth muscles, which are continuous with the cervix, the lower portion of the uterus that opens into the vagina. As childbirth progresses, the cervix, which is not muscle at all, thins out and dilates. During a contraction, the muscles of the upper portion shorten, pulling the cervix over the baby's head and expelling the baby.

In addition to having extraordinary strength, the muscle of the uterus is remarkable in other ways. It is not exactly a muscle that you can build up in the gym, yet it does not lose strength from lack of use. In fact, it does quite the opposite. Even when children are born many years apart, the experience of giving birth once generally makes the process of labor about four hours faster with subsequent deliveries (Agboola & Agobe, 1976).

increased risk of joint injury seen in female athletes (Pollard, Braun, & Hamill, 2006; Wentorf, Sudoh, Moses, Arendt, & Carlson, 2006).

The Interaction of Muscles at a Joint

Muscles can do only one thing: contract. The contraction of a single muscle can either straighten or bend a joint, but not both. As a result, a muscle is able to pull a bone in a single direction but is unable to push it back. Relaxing the muscle will not necessarily cause a limb to move back to its original position.

To move a joint in two directions requires two muscles. Muscles are arranged at a joint in **antagonistic pairs,** as shown in ■ Figure 8.7. Muscles that straighten joints are referred to as **extensors,** and muscles that bend joints are known as **flexors.** To bend the knee, the flexor muscles of the thigh must contract while the extensor muscles relax. To straighten the leg, the extensor muscles must contract while the flexors relax. Movement at some joints is more complicated than simple flexion and extension. Additional muscles are needed at joints such as the shoulder, hip, wrist, and ankle to allow for rotation and other complex movements.

The function of muscle is to pull and not to push, except in the case of the genitals and the tongue.

Leonardo da Vinci

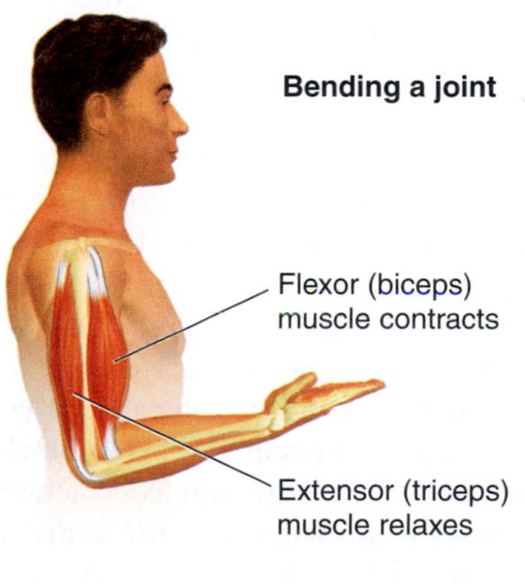

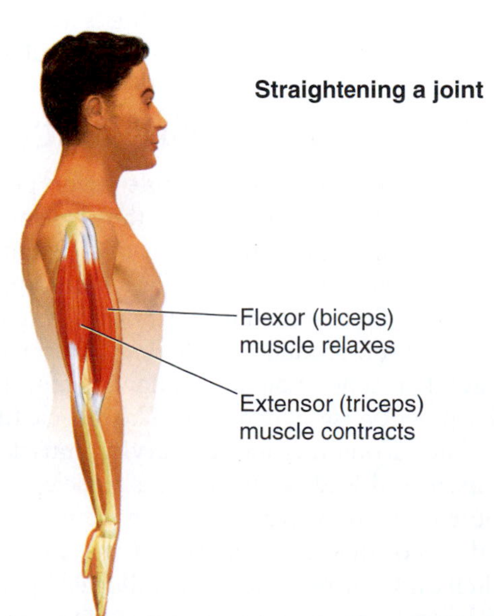

■ **Figure 8.7**
Muscles Form Antagonistic Pairs at Joints Each joint has at least one pair of antagonistic muscles, one flexor and one extensor. Contraction of the biceps muscle flexes (closes) the elbow joint, whereas the triceps muscle extends (opens) the joint. Try flexing and extending your elbow while touching the biceps and triceps muscles. You will be able to feel them working during their respective movements.

antagonistic pair Two opposing muscles, one a flexor and one an extensor, arranged at a joint.
extensor A muscle that acts to straighten a joint.
flexor A muscle that acts to bend a joint.

Neural Control of Muscles

The contraction of skeletal muscles is directly controlled by motor neurons originating in either the spinal cord or in the nuclei of the cranial nerves. Just as skeletal muscles are not evenly distributed throughout the body, motor neurons are not evenly distributed throughout the spinal cord. As shown in ■ Figure 8.8, the ventral horns of the spinal cord, which contain the motor neurons, appear large in segments C (Cervical) 3 through T (Thoracic) 1 and again in L (Lumbar) 1 through S (Sacral) 3. The enlargement of the ventral horns in these areas is due to the large number of motor neurons required to innervate the muscles of the arms and legs, respectively.

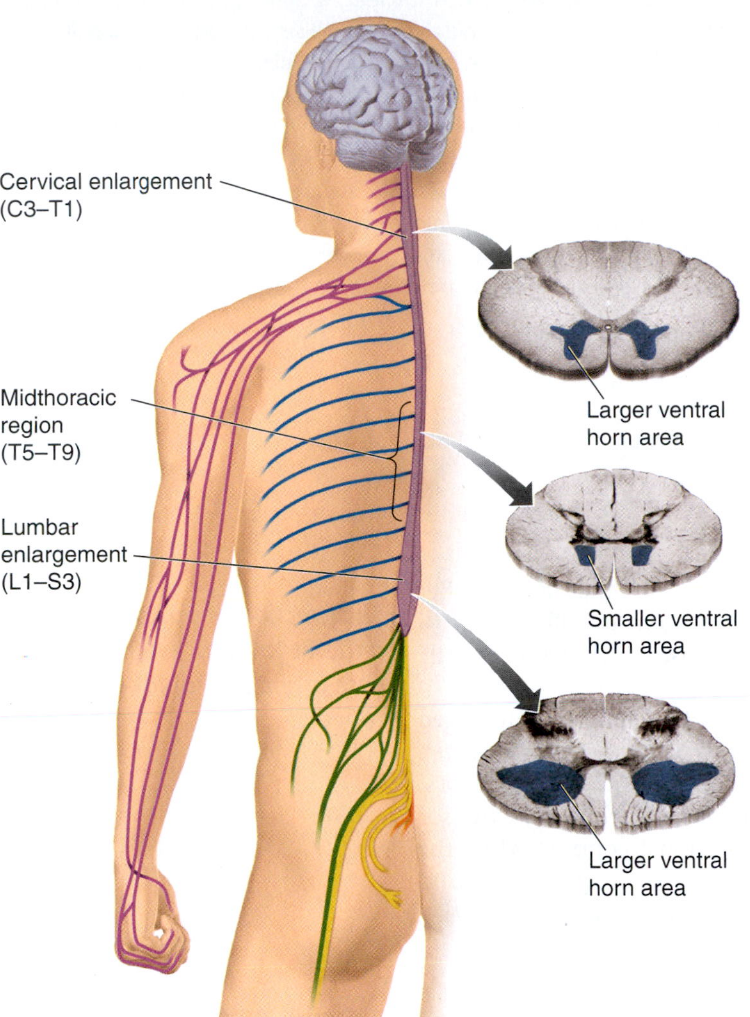

■ **FIGURE 8.8 Distribution of Spinal Motor Neurons** The spinal cord bulges in the segments that serve the arms and legs, due to the large number of alpha motor neurons located in the ventral parts of those segments. In comparison, relatively few alpha motor neurons serve the torso.

Alpha Motor Neurons

The spinal motor neurons directly responsible for contracting muscles are known as **alpha motor neurons.** These are large myelinated neurons capable of rapid signaling. The alpha motor neurons form highly efficient connections with muscle fibers at a location called the **neuromuscular junction.** Because of the efficiency of this connection, a single action potential in the motor neuron terminal is capable of producing an action potential in the muscle fiber, leading to a single contraction, or twitch.

The Motor Unit

A **motor unit** is made up of a single alpha motor neuron and all the muscle fibers it innervates. A single motor unit includes either fast- or slow-twitch fibers but not a mixture of both (Burke, 1978). Motor neurons serving slow-twitch muscles have smaller cell bodies and innervate fewer muscle fibers. Consequently, these units generate relatively little force. In contrast, motor neurons serving the very fast IIb fibers have relatively large cell bodies and large-diameter axons, which are capable of rapid signaling. These motor units generate 100 times the force produced by units made up of slow-twitch fibers (Loeb & Ghez, 2000). Motor units containing Type IIa fibers fall between these extremes.

The Control of Muscle Contractions

As mentioned previously, a single action potential in the alpha motor neuron usually results in a single contraction in the associated muscle fiber. How, then, do we manage to produce muscular movements of different forces and durations?

There are two methods for controlling the force of our movements (Guyton, 1991). The first method is to vary the firing rate of motor neurons. Rapid firing by the motor neuron produces a sustained contraction in the muscle fiber. Contractions last longer than action potentials, allowing temporal summation to occur at the neuromuscular junction (see Chapter 3). The muscle fiber responds with increasing contraction.

The second method for varying muscle responses is known as **recruitment.** As an increased load is placed on a muscle, as when you pick up a heavy object, more motor units are recruited to provide extra tension in the muscle. Recruitment proceeds according to the nature of the motor units (Henneman, 1991). Smaller, slow-twitch units are recruited first, followed by the intermediate Type IIa units, and finally the largest, fastest Type IIb units. The smaller neurons that innervate slow-twitch

alpha motor neuron A spinal motor neuron directly responsible for signaling a muscle fiber to contract.
neuromuscular junction A synapse formed between an alpha motor neuron axon terminal and a muscle fiber.
motor unit The combination of a single alpha motor neuron and all the muscle fibers that it innervates.
recruitment The process of gradually activating more motor units as an increasing load is placed on a muscle.

fibers are more easily excited by synaptic input, which might account for them being recruited first. Recruiting the smaller motor units first ensures that the body uses the smallest amount of force and energy to get a job done.

The Control of Spinal Motor Neurons

The alpha motor neurons do not initiate movement on their own. Instead, these neurons are activated by input from other parts of the motor system. Alpha motor neurons receive input from three types of neurons: neurons from muscle spindles and Golgi tendon organs, neurons of the brainstem and motor cortex, and spinal interneurons.

Feedback from the Muscle Spindle Muscle spindles are specialized sensors that form part of a feedback loop from the muscle fibers to the spinal cord. If an object, a cup of coffee, for example, is placed in your outstretched hand, your hand might initially drop a bit in response to the weight of the cup before returning to its original position. You compensate for the added weight in your hand by increasing contraction in the muscles of your arm. This adjustment requires a precise feedback loop that measures how much your muscles have stretched.

The first element in the feedback loop is the **muscle spindle.** As shown in Figure 8.9, muscle spindles are structures embedded in the muscle that serve as a source of information about muscle length. The spindle gets its name from its shape, which is similar to the spindle on a spinning wheel. Each muscle spindle contains approximately a dozen **intrafusal muscle fibers.** *Fusal* comes from the Latin word for "spindle," so the intrafusal fibers are located "within the spindle." Muscle fibers responsible for contraction, which have been the subject of our discussion up to this point, are **extrafusal muscle fibers,** or the fibers "outside the spindle." Muscle spindles lie parallel to the extrafusal fibers, so that when the muscle stretches, so do its associated spindles. Muscles needed for fine motor movements, such as those in the hand, have more muscle spindles than do muscles used primarily for force, such as those in the torso and legs. Larger numbers of muscle spindles provide the more precise feedback required for fine movements.

Wrapped around the middle section of the spindle are very large, very fast axons known as **Ia sensory fibers.** We observed the Ia (or Aα, Alpha-alpha) fibers in Chapter 7 (see Figure 7.16). These fibers generate action potentials every time the muscle spindle stretches. Within the spinal cord, the Ia fibers synapse on interneurons and on the alpha motor neurons.

Here's how the system works. As the cup in our example is placed in your hand, your arm muscle will stretch due to the added weight. The stretching of your arm muscle will also stretch the muscle spindle. The Ia (or Aα) fibers surrounding the muscle spindle will sense the increased stretch and will excite the alpha motor neurons in the spinal cord. Excitation of the alpha motor neurons will cause the muscle to balance the stretch with further contraction. The cup is now safe.

We have seen that the alpha motor neurons provide input to the extrafusal fibers. The intrafusal fibers have their own set of motor neurons, known as **gamma motor neurons,** also shown in Figure 8.9. Why would the intrafusal fibers need input when they do not contribute to the overall contraction of a muscle? Without the gamma motor neurons, the intrafusal fibers could not provide accurate information about how far the muscle was stretched. When the extrafusal fibers contract, the intrafusal fibers would become limp if they did not also contract. This would cause the Ia sensory fibers to stop signaling, and the brain and spinal cord would not know how long the muscle was. To solve this problem, gamma motor neurons and alpha motor neurons are activated simultaneously by input from the brain. The gamma motor neurons cause a small contraction of the spindle at nearly the same time that the alpha motor neurons contract the extrafusal fibers. In this way, the spindle matches the length of the muscle, and the Ia fibers can provide continuous feedback.

Feedback from Golgi Tendon Organs The muscle spindles do a good job of providing the brain and spinal cord with information about muscle length, or the

muscle spindle A sensory structure that provides feedback regarding muscle stretch.

intrafusal muscle fiber (in-truh-FEW- suhl) One of the fibers that make up a muscle spindle.

extrafusal muscle fiber (ex-truh-FEW-suhl) One of the fibers outside the muscle spindle that is responsible for contracting the muscle.

Ia sensory fiber A large, fast sensory axon that connects a muscle spindle to neurons in the spinal cord.

gamma motor neuron A small spinal neuron that innervates the muscle spindles.

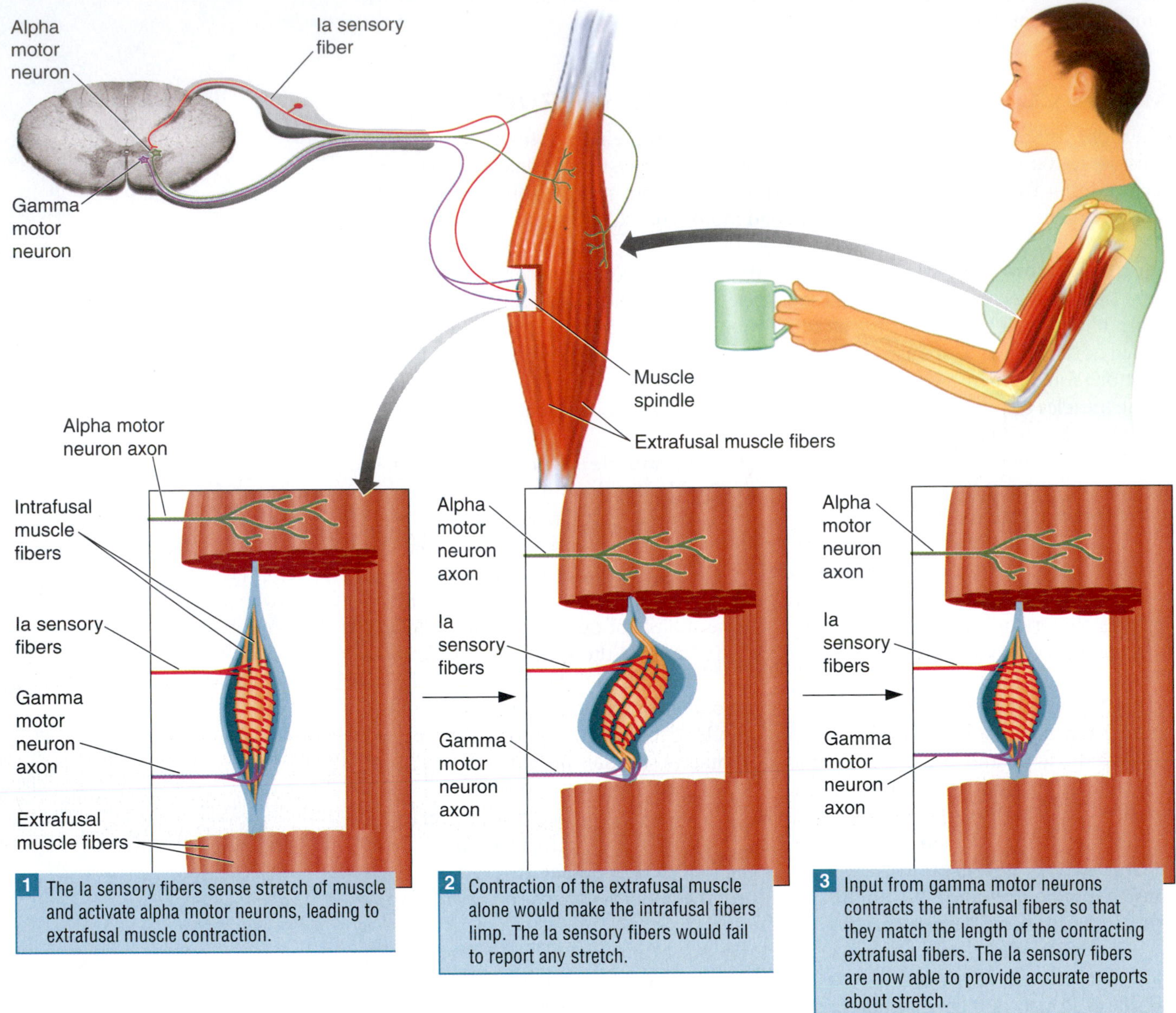
Alpha motor neuron
Ia sensory fiber
Gamma motor neuron
Muscle spindle
Extrafusal muscle fibers
Alpha motor neuron axon
Intrafusal muscle fibers
Ia sensory fibers
Gamma motor neuron axon
Extrafusal muscle fibers
1 The Ia sensory fibers sense stretch of muscle and activate alpha motor neurons, leading to extrafusal muscle contraction.
Alpha motor neuron axon
Ia sensory fibers
Gamma motor neuron axon
2 Contraction of the extrafusal muscle alone would make the intrafusal fibers limp. The Ia sensory fibers would fail to report any stretch.
Alpha motor neuron axon
Ia sensory fibers
Gamma motor neuron axon
3 Input from gamma motor neurons contracts the intrafusal fibers so that they match the length of the contracting extrafusal fibers. The Ia sensory fibers are now able to provide accurate reports about stretch.

FIGURE 8.9
Muscle Spindles Provide Feedback About Muscle Length

degree of stretch. However, we also need feedback regarding the degree of muscle contraction, or force. This information is provided by the **Golgi tendon organs,** which are located at the junction between a muscle and its tendon.

Like the muscle spindles, the Golgi tendon organs are innervated by sensory axons, the **Ib sensory fibers.** Ib fibers are a second type of Alpha-alpha (Aα) fiber, but are smaller than the large, fast Ia fibers that innervate the spindles. The Ib fibers from the Golgi tendon organs enter the spinal cord and form synapses with spinal interneurons. In turn, these interneurons form inhibitory synapses on alpha motor neurons.

To understand how the Golgi tendon organ feedback loop works, we return to the example of holding a coffee cup steady. The Ia fibers from muscle spindles in your fingers and arm sense the stretch needed to hold the cup and activate the alpha motor neurons. The Golgi tendon organs respond to the resulting increase in muscle tension by sending signals to the spinal interneurons via the Ib sensory fibers. In response to this input, the interneurons inhibit the alpha motor neurons, and muscle contraction is reduced. However, the reduced muscle contraction results in less Golgi tendon

Golgi tendon organ (GOAL-jee) A structure located in the tendons of muscles that provides information about muscle contraction.

Ib sensory fiber A small, slower Alpha-alpha (Aα) sensory axon that connects the Golgi tendon organs to neurons in the spinal cord.

organ activity, less input to the spinal interneurons, and less inhibition of the alpha motor neurons. The muscle contracts again. Not only does this system help prevent damage to the muscle fibers from too much contraction, but it also maintains the steady control over muscle tension that we need, particularly for fine motor movements. This process is illustrated in ■ Figure 8.10.

Feedback from Joints In addition to receiving feedback about muscle length and tension, we also receive information about position and movement from mechanoreceptors in the tissues surrounding each joint. These mechanoreceptors, which we discussed in Chapter 7, respond primarily to movement of the joint, and they are relatively quiet when the joint is at rest. Receptors located in the skin near joints also supply information about movement and position (Edin, 2001). Free nerve endings can signal pain resulting from extreme joint positions. It appears that joint receptors are not entirely necessary for judging the location of a joint. People who have undergone full hip or knee replacement surgery lose all of their joint receptors in the procedure, yet they can still describe the position of their joint without looking.

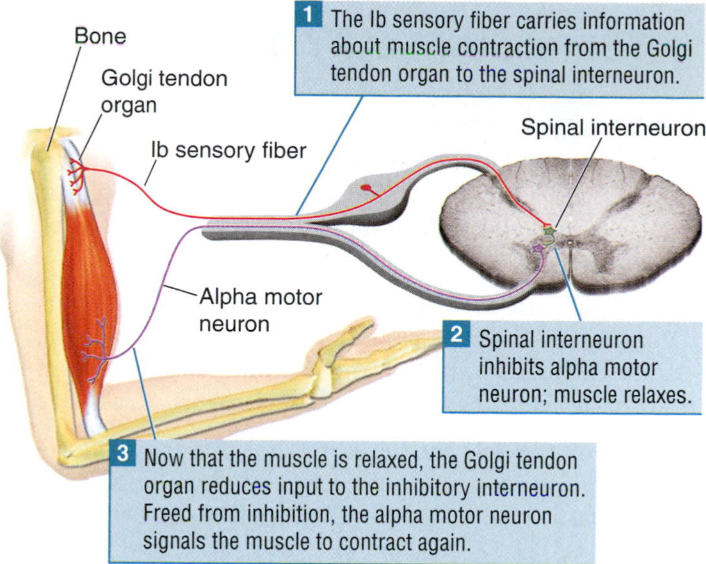
Bone
Golgi tendon organ
Ib sensory fiber
1 The Ib sensory fiber carries information about muscle contraction from the Golgi tendon organ to the spinal interneuron.
Spinal interneuron
Alpha motor neuron
2 Spinal interneuron inhibits alpha motor neuron; muscle relaxes.
3 Now that the muscle is relaxed, the Golgi tendon organ reduces input to the inhibitory interneuron. Freed from inhibition, the alpha motor neuron signals the muscle to contract again.

■ **FIGURE 8.10 Golgi Tendon Organs Provide Feedback About Muscle Contraction**

INTERIM SUMMARY 8.1

Summary Table: The Control of Spinal Motor Neurons

Cell Type	Location	Source of Input to these Cells	Fiber Type	Action Produced
Alpha motor neurons	Ventral horns of the spinal cord, some cranial nerve nuclei	Motor cortex, brainstem, muscle spindles, spinal interneurons		Alpha motor neurons produce action potentials in muscle fibers, leading to contraction.
Muscle spindles	Lie parallel to muscle fibers within a muscle	Respond to stretch of associated muscle fibers	Ia sensory fibers	Muscle spindles synapse with alpha motor neurons and spinal interneurons, allowing muscle contraction to adjust to muscle stretching.
Gamma motor neurons	Ventral horns of the spinal cord, some cranial nerve nuclei	Motor cortex, brainstem		Gamma motor neurons contract the muscle spindle to match spindle length to surrounding muscle fibers.
Golgi tendon organs	Junctions between muscles and tendons	Respond to tension in muscle	Ib sensory fibers	Golgi tendon organs synapse with spinal interneurons, inhibiting activity of alpha motor neurons, reducing contraction.

(continued)

INTERIM SUMMARY 8.1 (continued)

Summary Points

1. Muscles can be divided into three types: smooth muscles, cardiac muscles, and skeletal muscles. Together, the cardiac and skeletal muscles are known as striated muscles. **(LO1)**

2. Skeletal muscles are made up of individual muscle fibers surrounded by a membrane similar to that of a neuron. Muscle fiber contractions result from the movement of myosin filaments relative to actin filaments. **(LO1)**

3. Pairs of muscles, one flexor and one extensor, perform antagonistic functions at each joint. Additional muscles participate in complex rotational movements at a joint. **(LO2)**

4. Alpha motor neurons in the spinal cord or cranial nerve nuclei produce muscle contraction through their activity at the neuromuscular junction. **(LO3)**

5. Muscle spindles provide information about muscle stretch. Gamma motor neurons help the muscle spindle match the length of the muscle, providing continuous feedback. **(LO3)**

6. Golgi tendon organs located in the connective tissue between muscle and bone provide information regarding muscle contraction. Additional joint receptors provide information regarding the movement of joints. **(LO4)**

Review Questions

1. What is the sequence of events within the myofibril that leads to contraction?

2. What is a motor unit, and how do the units differ in terms of size, precision of movement, and muscle fiber type?

Reflex Control of Movement

The spinal cord is responsible for a number of reflex movements designed to protect us from injury, to maintain posture, and to coordinate the movement of our limbs.

Monosynaptic Reflexes

At most physical exams, the physician hits the patient's knee with a small hammer. This demonstration of the patellar tendon or knee-jerk reflex determines whether a basic spinal stretch reflex is in good working order. Some medical conditions, such as diabetes or Parkinson's disease, reduce or eliminate the reflex. Other medical conditions, such as meningitis (see Chapters 2 and 15), often produce exaggerated responses.

The patellar tendon reflex, illustrated in ■ Figure 8.11, is an example of a **monosynaptic reflex,** or a reflex that requires the interaction of only two neurons at a single synapse. Tapping on the tendon that serves the quadriceps muscle of the leg, which is located just below the knee, slightly stretches the muscle. Stretch causes the Ia sensory fibers in the muscle spindles to stimulate the alpha motor neurons that serve the quadriceps. Responding to input from the alpha motor neurons, the quadriceps muscle contracts, and your foot kicks. You probably have noticed that this happens very quickly. It takes a lot longer to read about it than to do it.

Polysynaptic Reflexes

Polysynaptic reflexes involve more than one synapse. One of the simplest polysynaptic reflexes is the **reciprocal inhibition** of one set of muscles when the other member of its antagonistic pair produces a voluntary movement. If we contracted both extensors and flexors at the same joint, it would be a standoff, and movement of the joint would not occur. Through reciprocal inhibition, if the extensor is contracting, the flexor is inhibited, and vice versa. In some circumstances, such as when we stiffen our elbows while catching a ball, the stability provided by simultaneous contraction of antagonistic muscle pairs is actually desirable. Achieving simultaneous contraction rather than reciprocal inhibition requires descending control from the brain, which acts by changing the firing patterns of spinal interneurons.

monosynaptic reflex A spinal reflex, such as the patellar reflex, that requires the action of only one synapse between sensory and motor neurons.

polysynaptic reflex A spinal reflex that requires interaction at more than one synapse.

reciprocal inhibition A polysynaptic reflex that prevents the simultaneous contraction of flexors and extensors serving the same joint.

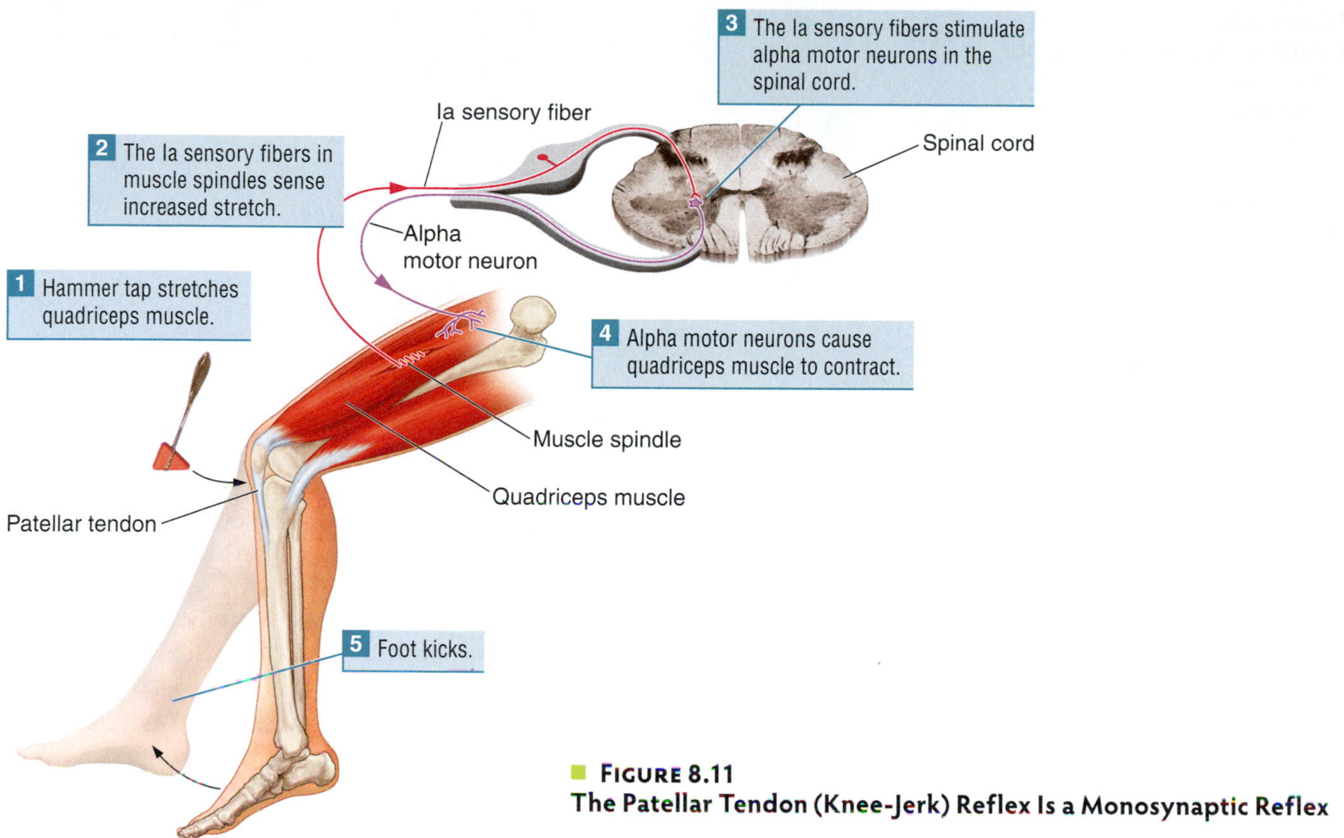
3 The Ia sensory fibers stimulate alpha motor neurons in the spinal cord.
Ia sensory fiber
Spinal cord
2 The Ia sensory fibers in muscle spindles sense increased stretch.
Alpha motor neuron
1 Hammer tap stretches quadriceps muscle.
4 Alpha motor neurons cause quadriceps muscle to contract.
Muscle spindle
Quadriceps muscle
Patellar tendon
5 Foot kicks.

■ **FIGURE 8.11**
The Patellar Tendon (Knee-Jerk) Reflex Is a Monosynaptic Reflex

Another familiar example of a polysynaptic reflex is the **flexion reflex.** We rely on flexion reflexes to protect us from further injury, such as when we jerk our hand away after touching a hot surface on the stove. It's a good thing that the spinal cord, rather than the brain, manages this function. By the time the brain perceived the problem, generated solutions, evaluated solutions, and implemented solutions, your hand would be in bad shape. The flexion reflex begins as sensory neurons transmit information about the painful stimulus to interneurons in the spinal cord. The interneurons excite the alpha motor neurons serving the flexor muscles of the affected limb. At the same time, alpha motor neurons serving the opposing muscle, the extensor, are inhibited. As a result, your hand is successfully pulled back from the heat source.

More complicated polysynaptic reflexes help coordinate the movement of several limbs at once. When we walk, we naturally balance our weight from side to side and swing our arms. These complex movements require many more synapses than the previous simple reflexes. In addition, there is growing evidence that the rhythm of movements such as walking is governed by spontaneously active pacemaker neurons within the spinal cord (Grillner et al., 1998; Gordon & Whelan, 2006).

The difference between the mile and the marathon is the difference between burning your fingers with a match and being slowly roasted over hot coals.

Hal Higdon

Reflexes over the Life Span

The reflexes we have discussed so far are present throughout the human life span. Other types of reflexes are characteristic of young children, but tend to diminish as the nervous system matures. These childhood reflexes are not lost by the nervous system, but they become inhibited or overwritten by other processes. When this normal inhibition of childhood reflexes fails due to brain damage or the use of alcohol and other drugs, the reflexes will reappear.

Among the normal childhood reflexes is the **Babinski sign,** a type of polysynaptic flexion reflex. When you stroke the bottom surface of the foot, infants will spread their toes with the big toe pointing up. The Babinski sign does not appear to confer any particular benefit to the infant. Instead, the reflex probably reflects the immaturity of the infant's motor system. In typical adults, stroking the bottom of the foot causes the toes to curl down, not up. Adults with damage to either the motor cortex or

flexion reflex A polysynaptic spinal reflex that produces withdrawal of a limb from a painful stimulus.

Babinski sign (buh-BIN-skee) A polysynaptic flexion reflex present in infants and in adults with neural damage, in which stroking the foot causes the toes to spread with the big toe pointing upward.

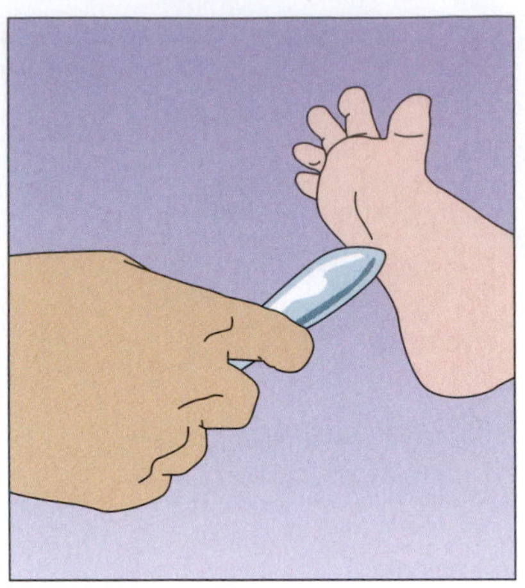

(a) Typical infant version of Babinski sign

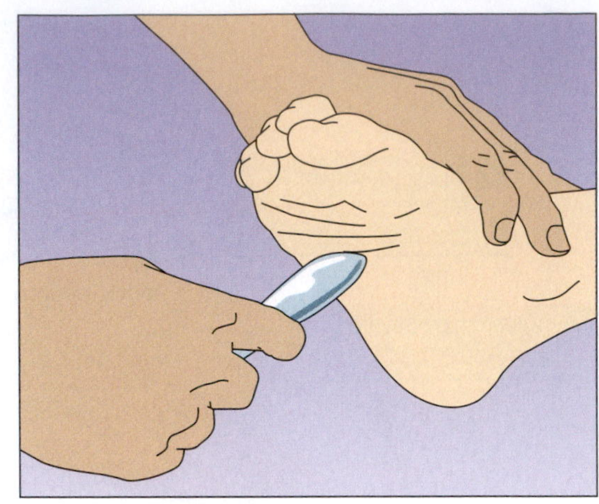

(b) Typical reaction to the stroking of the foot in subjects over two years old

FIGURE 8.12
The Babinski Sign (a) Stroking the bottom of an infant's foot causes the toes to spread and the big toe to point upward, a movement known as the Babinski sign. (b) Stroking the bottom of an adult's foot results in the downward curling of the toes. In adults, the Babinski sign often indicates brain damage.

spinal motor pathways will show the infant's version of the reflex (Gardner, 1968). An illustration comparing the typical adult reaction with the infant's Babinski sign may be seen in Figure 8.12.

Motor Systems of the Brain

It's not how you hold your racket, it's how you hold your mind.
Perry Jones

The alpha motor neurons that contract muscle fibers are at the lowest end of a chain of command for initiating movement. In addition to input from interneurons and stretch receptors, the alpha motor neurons receive direction from neurons located in the cerebellum, basal ganglia, red nucleus, brainstem, and cerebral cortex. As we will see, some of these motor pathways initiate voluntary movement, whereas others are responsible for subconscious, automatic movements.

SPINAL MOTOR PATHWAYS

As shown in Figure 8.13, signals from the brain to the spinal alpha motor neurons travel along two routes. The first route, known as the lateral pathway, is located in the lateral part of the spinal column. This pathway originates primarily in the cerebral cortex and is the pathway through which the brain controls voluntary fine movements of the hands, feet, and outer limbs. You use this pathway to write notes, to drive your car, and to type on your keyboard.

The second route, known as the ventromedial pathway, travels along the ventromedial part of the spinal column. Most of the neurons that supply axons to this pathway are located in the brainstem rather than in the cerebral cortex. As a result, these ventromedial pathways carry commands from the brain for automatic movements in the neck, torso, and portions of the limbs close to the body. You use the ventromedial pathway for behaviors such as maintaining posture and muscle tone and moving the head in response to visual stimuli. The functions of these two pathways are easier to remember if you think of the lateral pathway as a long-distance system serving more distal structures (hands, feet, limbs) and the ventromedial pathway as a relatively local system serving more proximal structures (neck and torso.)

Cell bodies giving rise to the axons of the **lateral pathway** are located either in the primary motor cortex of the frontal lobe or in the red nucleus of the midbrain. The two components of the lateral pathway are the corticospinal tract and the rubrospinal tract. As its name implies, the corticospinal tract originates in the motor cortex of the brain. These fibers are some of the fastest and longest in the central nervous system. The fibers of the rubrospinal tract originate in the red nucleus (*rubro* refers to red). As you may recall from Chapter 2, the red nucleus receives substantial input from the motor cortex and forms connections with alpha motor neurons in the spinal cord. Consequently, the

lateral pathway A large collection of axons that originates in the cerebral cortex, synapses on either the red nucleus or alpha motor neurons, and controls voluntary movements.

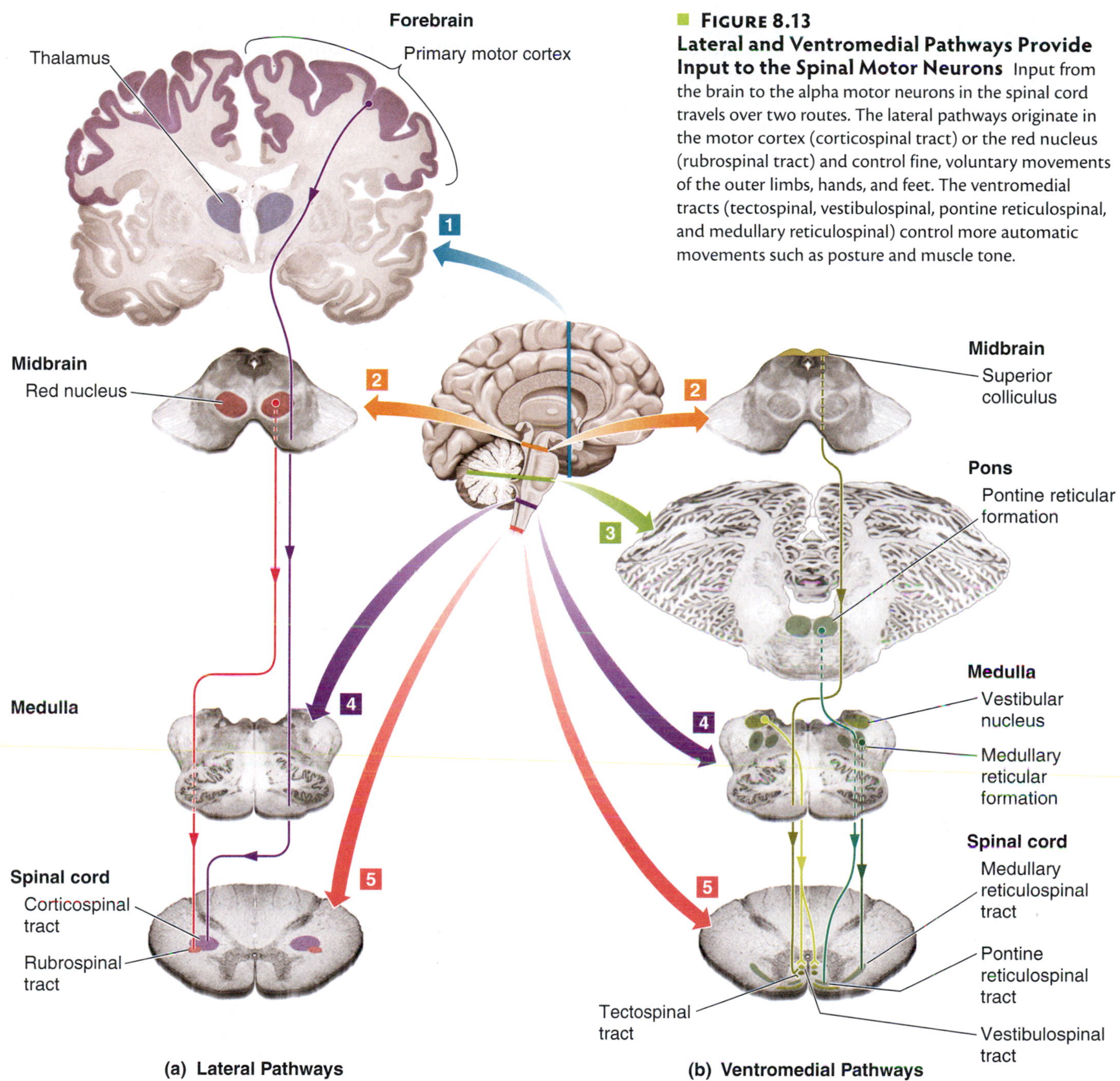

■ **FIGURE 8.13**
Lateral and Ventromedial Pathways Provide Input to the Spinal Motor Neurons Input from the brain to the alpha motor neurons in the spinal cord travels over two routes. The lateral pathways originate in the motor cortex (corticospinal tract) or the red nucleus (rubrospinal tract) and control fine, voluntary movements of the outer limbs, hands, and feet. The ventromedial tracts (tectospinal, vestibulospinal, pontine reticulospinal, and medullary reticulospinal) control more automatic movements such as posture and muscle tone.

motor cortex exerts both direct control (via the corticospinal tract) and indirect control (via the rubrospinal tract) on the alpha motor neurons of the spinal cord.

As these pathways travel from the cortex to the spinal cord, they decussate or cross the midline. The rubrospinal tract decussates immediately, and the corticospinal tract decussates at the junction of the medulla and the spinal cord. Crossing the midline means that the right hemisphere's motor cortex controls the left side of the body, whereas the left hemisphere's motor cortex controls the right side of the body. Although the advantages of this organization remain a mystery, the results are most obvious when a person has damaged either the motor cortex or the descending lateral pathways due to a stroke or other accident. If the damage occurs in the right hemisphere, the left side of the body will be weakened or paralyzed. If the damage occurs in the left hemisphere, the right side of the body will be weakened or paralyzed.

The four **ventromedial pathways** stimulate the alpha motor neurons to help maintain posture and carry out reflexive responses to sensory input such as moving the head and torso in coordination with our eye movements. The ventromedial

ventromedial pathway A spinal motor pathway originating in the brainstem and carrying commands for subconscious, automatic movements of the neck and torso.

pathways also assist in behaviors such as walking, in spite of the fact that these behaviors are largely under cortical control. These pathways originate in various parts of the brainstem, including the vestibular nuclei of the medulla, the superior colliculi of the midbrain, and the reticular formation in the pons and medulla. Once again, you can use the names of these tracts to remember their points of origin. The tectospinal tract originates in the tectum of the midbrain, primarily in the superior and inferior colliculi (see Chapter 2). The vestibulospinal tract originates in the vestibular nuclei of the medulla, and the pontine and medullary reticulospinal tracts originate in the reticular formation at the levels of the pons and medulla, respectively.

The Cerebellum

Additional descending control of the motor system originates in the cerebellum. Although the cerebellum does not appear to initiate movement, it plays a very important role in the sequencing of complex movements. As you ride a bicycle or shoot a basket, your cerebellum is coordinating the contraction and relaxation of muscles at just the right time.

To understand the value of the cerebellum, it's helpful to see what happens when the cerebellum is not working. One common example of poor cerebellar function occurs when a person drinks alcohol. The cerebellum is one of the first structures in the brain to show the effects of alcohol, leading to a lack of balance and coordination. As a result, law enforcement personnel check the function of the cerebellum to assess drunkenness. Most sobriety tests, such as walking a straight line, are essentially the same as the tests a neurologist would use to diagnose lesions in the cerebellum.

How does the cerebellum help us coordinate sequenced movements? It appears that the cerebellum is able to inform the motor cortex about such factors as the direction, force, and timing required to carry out a skilled movement. In many cases, this process requires learning. The cerebellum is constantly comparing the cortex's intended movements with what actually happened. Adjustments as needed are made for future activity. Obviously, this is not a foolproof system. Basketball great Shaquille O'Neal continues to miss free throws in spite of a cerebellum that serves him unusually well in other aspects of playing basketball.

People call me the painter of dancers, but I really wish to capture movement itself.
Edgar Degas

The Basal Ganglia

Moving rostrally toward the cerebral cortex, we come next to the basal ganglia, a collection of large nuclei embedded within the white matter of the cerebral hemispheres. The location of the basal ganglia is illustrated in ■ Figure 8.14. Among their many tasks, only some of which involve motor activity, the basal ganglia participate in the choice and initiation of voluntary movements.

As we saw in Chapter 2, the basal ganglia consist of the caudate nucleus, the putamen, the globus pallidus, and the subthalamic nucleus. Some anatomists include the substantia nigra of the midbrain in their discussion of the basal ganglia, due to the close linkages between these structures. Complex interactive loops connect the basal ganglia with the thalamus and the motor cortex in the frontal lobe. The basal ganglia inhibit the activity of the thalamus. As a result, you might think of the basal ganglia as a gate or filter for intentional activity. Only those voluntary actions that pass the basal ganglia with sufficient strength will be implemented.

As we will see later in the chapter, a number of disorders result from abnormalities in the basal ganglia, including Parkinson's disease and Huntington's disease. These are cases in which motor activity is either lower (Parkinson's) or higher (Huntington's) than normal. In addition to these two primarily motor disorders, the basal ganglia are implicated in a number of psychological disorders, including obsessive-compulsive disorder and attention deficit/hyperactivity disorder (see Chapter 16).

The Motor Cortex

Cortex located in the precentral (before the central sulcus) gyrus has been identified as primary motor cortex, the main source of voluntary motor control. In the gyrus just rostral to primary motor cortex, additional motor areas were identified by Wilder

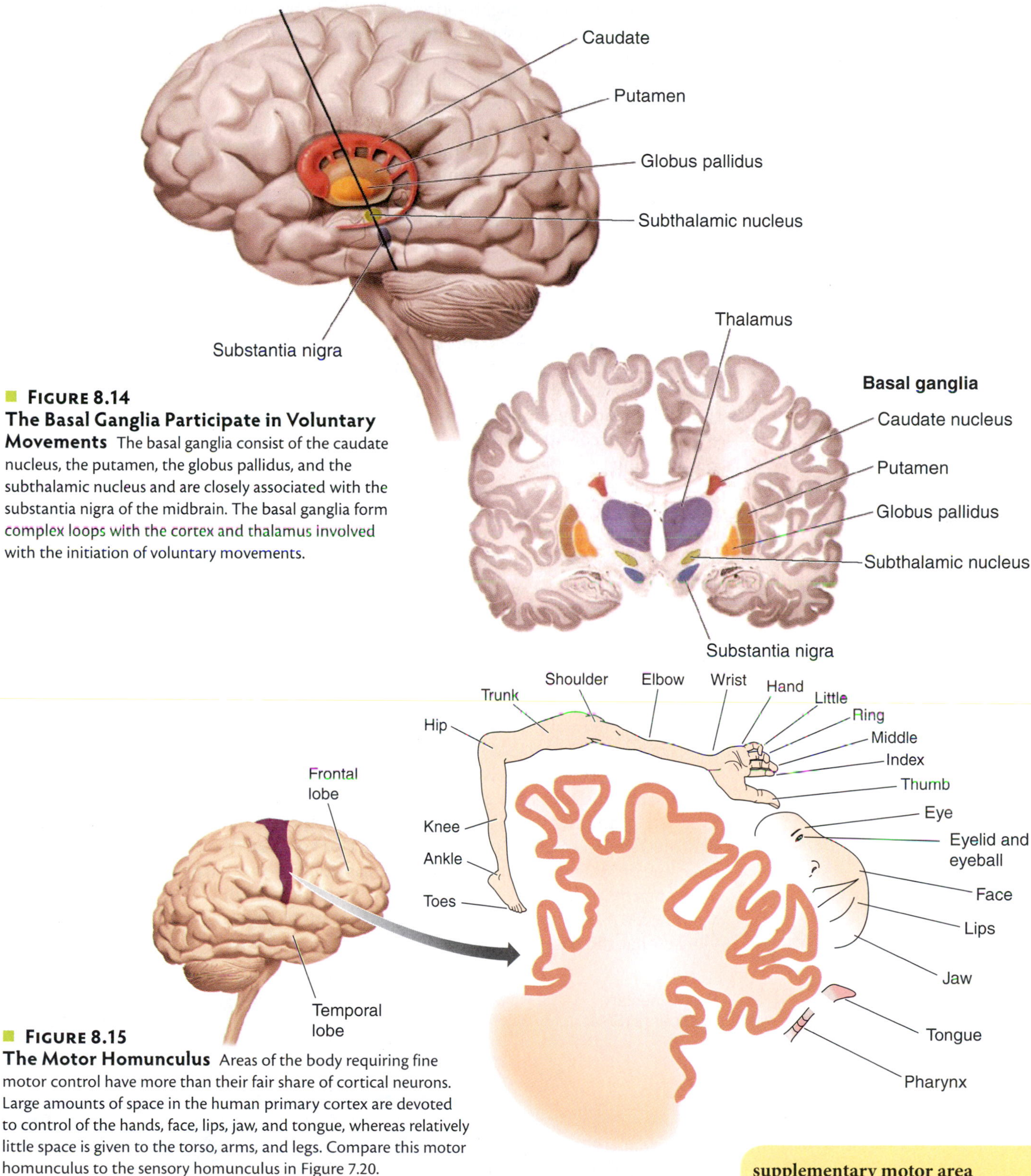

■ **FIGURE 8.14**
The Basal Ganglia Participate in Voluntary Movements The basal ganglia consist of the caudate nucleus, the putamen, the globus pallidus, and the subthalamic nucleus and are closely associated with the substantia nigra of the midbrain. The basal ganglia form complex loops with the cortex and thalamus involved with the initiation of voluntary movements.

■ **FIGURE 8.15**
The Motor Homunculus Areas of the body requiring fine motor control have more than their fair share of cortical neurons. Large amounts of space in the human primary cortex are devoted to control of the hands, face, lips, jaw, and tongue, whereas relatively little space is given to the torso, arms, and legs. Compare this motor homunculus to the sensory homunculus in Figure 7.20.

Penfield (Penfield & Rasmussen, 1950). Penfield named one the **supplementary motor area (SMA)** and the other the premotor area (PMA). The PMA is now usually referred to as the **pre-SMA.**

The Organization of Primary Motor Cortex Using stimulation techniques, we can map the primary motor cortex in the precentral gyrus. You can see an example of a motor cortex map, or homunculus, in ■ Figure 8.15. In Chapter 7, we saw a similar map of the sensory cortex in the parietal lobe.

supplementary motor area (SMA) Motor area located in the gyrus rostral to the precentral gyrus; involved with managing complex sequences of movement.

pre-SMA A motor area located in the gyrus rostral to the precentral gyrus; this area participates in holding a motor plan until it can be implemented; formerly referred to as the premotor area (PMA).

The first thing you might notice is that the homunculus is upside down. Neurons controlling voluntary movement of the head are found in the most ventral portions of the precentral gyrus, whereas neurons controlling the feet are located in the opposite direction. Neurons serving the feet are found where the gyrus has actually curved across the top of the hemisphere into the longitudinal fissure, which separates the two hemispheres.

As we observed in the case of the sensory homunculus (see Figure 7.20), the proportions of the homunculus are quite different from the proportions of our body. Once again, parts of the body that require delicate control are given a larger share of cortical territory. Face, lips, jaw, and tongue are given a great deal of space to manage the fine movements required by speech. Hands also get a disproportionate amount of cortical space, allowing for the many fine movements we need for tool use. In contrast, the torso gets very little space at all, especially considering the actual size of this body part. There isn't much to do with torsos other than maintain posture, bend, lift, and twist.

You start chasing a ball and your brain immediately commands your body to "Run forward! Bend! Scoop up the ball! Peg it to first!" Then your body says "Who, me?"
Joe DiMaggio

The Initiation and Awareness of Movement What happens when we decide to move? You might be thinking that this would be a good time to close your text and take a snack break (which is fine as long as you also decide to come back and reopen the book). Using imaging technology, we now have a better understanding of the neural events associated with the planning and implementation of voluntary motor behaviors.

Imaging technologies such as PET and fMRI have been used to track the initiation of movement in human volunteers (Roland, 1993; Deiber et al., 1999). Participants were asked to carry out movements of the fingers from memory. As shown in ■ Figure 8.16, the first areas to show increased activity were the frontal and parietal lobes. These areas might be viewed as the parts of the brain that actually "think" about the movement and its consequences before the movement is initiated.

Within the frontal lobe, several areas appear to be involved with motor control: the supplementary motor area (SMA), the pre-SMA, and components of the anterior cingulate cortex (ACC). The initiation of complex tasks is accompanied by increased activation in pre-SMA, whereas simpler tasks activate just the SMA (Picard & Strick, 1997). The ACC appears to coordinate an organisms's history of reward with the selection of voluntary movement (Shima & Tanji, 1998).

Activity in the pre-SMA appears to hold a complex plan until it can be implemented. Weinrich and Wise (1982) taught monkeys to move their arms toward a target. The monkeys were given one signal that identified the location of the target, followed by another signal that told the monkey that it was time to respond. Pre-SMA neurons fired in response to the first signal and continued firing until the second signal came on, at which time the monkey initiated the correct arm movement. Pre-SMA activity helps us bridge delays between the planning and initiation of movement.

Pre-SMA and SMA are also the targets of input from the thalamus. We saw previously that the basal ganglia form inhibitory connections with the thalamus. It is at

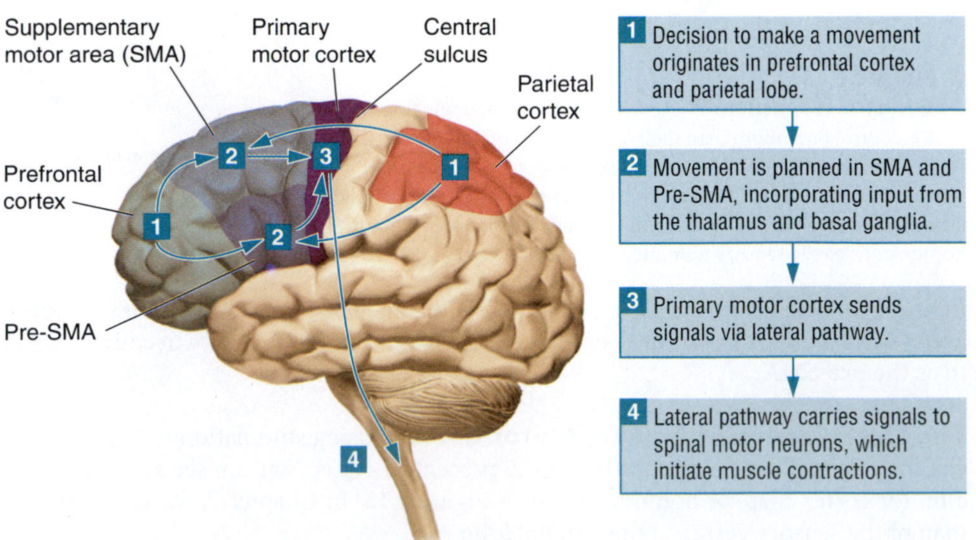
Supplementary motor area (SMA)
Primary motor cortex
Central sulcus
Parietal cortex
Prefrontal cortex
Pre-SMA
1
2
3
4
1 Decision to make a movement originates in prefrontal cortex and parietal lobe.
2 Movement is planned in SMA and Pre-SMA, incorporating input from the thalamus and basal ganglia.
3 Primary motor cortex sends signals via lateral pathway.
4 Lateral pathway carries signals to spinal motor neurons, which initiate muscle contractions.

■ **FIGURE 8.16 The Initiation of Voluntary Movement**

(a) The Monkey and Apparatus

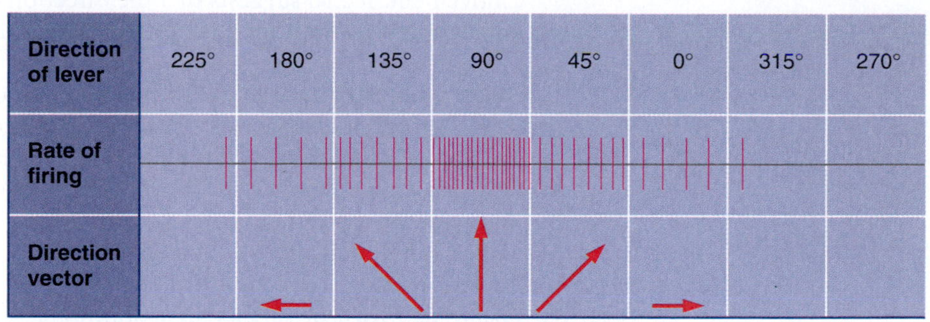

(b) Responses of a Single Cell

Movement direction	Response of Cell 1	Response of Cell 2	Population vector (sum of two responses)
90°			
0°			

(c) Individual Direction Vectors and Population Vectors from Two Neurons

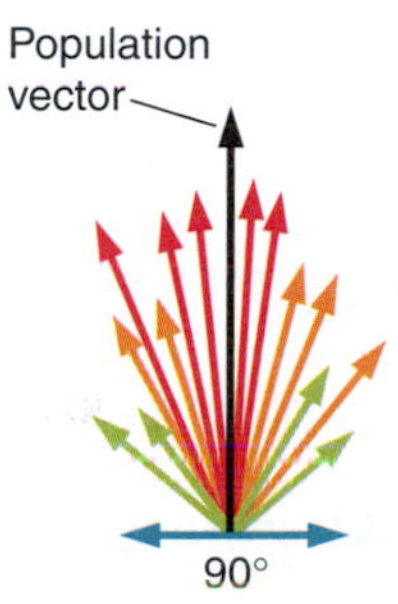

(d) Vector Representing Summed Activity from a Population of Neurons

FIGURE 8.17 The Direction of Movement Is Encoded by Populations of Neurons (a) Monkeys were trained to move a joystick in response to a small light moving around a circle. (b) Although single-cell recordings indicated that neurons responded most vigorously to a preferred direction, they also indicated that cells would respond to directions that varied as much as 45 degrees from the preferred direction. (c) Responses of single cells can be combined into population vectors. (d) The summed response of each population of neurons accurately predicts the direction of the monkey's movement. In other words, the population of cells essentially tallies up individual cell "votes" on the best direction to move.

this point in the sequence that the basal ganglia influence the choice of intentional behaviors. If input from the thalamus to pre-SMA and SMA is not overly inhibited by the basal ganglia, the sequence will continue. If the input from the thalamus is inhibited, the sequence will be abandoned.

Pre-SMA and SMA activation is followed by activation in primary motor cortex. Inputs from pre-SMA, SMA, and the thalamus converge on some very large cells located in Layer V of the primary motor cortex. These cells are referred to as **pyramidal cells** because of their pyramid shape, and the diameter of their cell bodies can be nearly 0.1 mm. These pyramidal cell axons are an important source of input to the brainstem and to spinal motor neurons. Once the motor cortex is activated, information flows down the lateral pathways to the spinal cord, either directly or through the red nucleus of the brainstem. The axons from the lateral pathways then synapse on the alpha motor neurons, which initiate the muscle contractions needed to carry out the descending commands.

The Coding of Movement In the case of vision, single-cell recording techniques can be used to discover the precise type of stimulus to which a particular cell will respond. Similar efforts to identify the responsibilities of single neurons in the primary motor cortex have produced curious results. Even though our movements are generally very precise, individual primary motor cortex neurons seem to be active during a wide range of movements. This finding has led Apostolos Georgopoulos and his colleagues (Georgopoulos, Taira, & Lukashin, 1993) to propose the idea that movement is encoded by populations of motor neurons rather than by single cells.

In Georgopoulos's research, monkeys were observed as they moved an arm in one of eight possible directions. Single cells in the monkey's primary motor cortex responded to a wide range of movement, but they responded most vigorously to a single preferred direction. The best predictor for whether the monkey's arm would move in a particular direction was a population vector, or the sum of the activity of the entire population of neurons in the area being observed. An example of the population vectors computed by Georgopoulos is shown in Figure 8.17. This finding predicts that large numbers of motor cortex cells, rather than a small group, should be active during any type of

pyramidal cell A large, pyramid-shaped neuron found in the output layers (Layers III and V) of the cerebral cortex, including primary motor cortex.

movement. It also suggests that the direction of a movement represents the averaging of all inputs from the entire population of neurons.

The best and fastest way to learn a sport is to watch and imitate a champion.
Jean-Claude Killy

Mirror Neurons Not only do motor neurons code for movement, but they might also help us understand the behavior of others. **Mirror neurons,** which are special motor neurons discovered by Giacomo Rizzolatti and his colleagues (1996), fire whenever an individual carries out an action, such as reaching, or simply watches another individual carry out the same act.

Although the exact functions of mirror neurons remain unknown, they appear to participate in a number of essential processes. Because human mirror neurons have been identified in Broca's area, additional speculation on the role of these neurons in the evolution of language has been proposed (Rizzolatti & Arbib, 1998). Language could have originally developed out of systems of gesture and imitation made possible by mirror neurons. Mirror neurons might also form the basis for imitation, empathy, and theory of mind (TOM), the ability to predict and understand the thoughts of others. Mirror neuron activity might allow us to simulate others' thoughts subconsciously by literally putting ourselves mentally in another person's shoes.

INTERIM SUMMARY 8.2

Summary Table: Central Motor Systems

Structure or Pathway	Location	Principal Connections	Functions
Lateral pathway	Lateral spinal cord	Motor cortex to spinal motor neurons	Voluntary fine movements of hands, feet, and outer limbs
Ventromedial pathways	Ventromedial spinal cord	Brainstem to spinal motor neurons	Maintain posture; carry out reflexive responses to sensory input
Cerebellum	Hindbrain	Spinal motor neurons, forebrain motor systems	Sequencing of complex movements, muscle tone, balance, and coordination
Basal ganglia	Forebrain	Motor cortex, thalamus	Choice and initiation of voluntary movements
Primary motor cortex	Precentral gyrus of the frontal lobe	Other cortical areas, basal ganglia, brainstem, spinal motor neurons	Initiation of voluntary movements
Pre-SMA	Rostral to the primary motor cortex	Thalamus, primary motor cortex	Managing movement strategies
Secondary motor cortex	Rostral to the primary motor cortex	Thalamus, primary motor cortex	Managing movement strategies
Anterior cingulate cortex	Rostral portion of the gyrus dorsal to the corpus callosum	Red nucleus and spinal motor neurons	Selection of voluntary movement based on prior reward

Summary Points

1. Monosynaptic reflexes, such as the stretch reflex, require the interaction of only one sensory and one motor neuron. Polysynaptic reflexes involve more than one synapse. **(LO5)**
2. The lateral pathways connect the primary motor cortex with the spinal motor neurons and are responsible for voluntary movements. The ventromedial pathways originate in the brainstem and are responsible for reflexive movements. **(LO6)**

(continued)

INTERIM SUMMARY 8.2 (continued)

3. The cerebellum is involved with the timing and sequencing of complex movements. The basal ganglia form complex loops with the cortex and the thalamus and serve as a gate or filter for intentional activity. **(LO7)**
4. Cortical areas involved in the control of voluntary movement include the primary motor cortex, the supplementary motor area (SMA), the pre-SMA, and the anterior cingulate cortex (ACC). **(LO7)**
5. The initiation of voluntary movement is correlated with sequential activity in the prefrontal cortex and parietal cortex, followed by activity in pre-SMA and SMA, and finally by activity in the pyramidal cells of the primary motor cortex. These primary motor neurons control movement as a function of cell population activity rather than as a function of single-cell activity. **(LO8)**
6. Special motor neurons known as mirror neurons are active when an individual either performs a movement or sees another individual perform the same movement, forming a basis for the understanding of the behavior of others. **(LO8)**

Review Questions

1. What functions are carried out by reflexive or involuntary processes?
2. What steps lead to the initiation of a voluntary movement?

Disorders of Movement

We can learn a great deal about the neural control of movement by observing what goes wrong when the system is damaged. Because movement disorders obviously cause enormous human suffering, our further understanding might also lead to more effective treatments.

Toxins

A variety of toxic substances interfere with movement by acting on synapses within the motor system. Many of these effects take place at the neuromuscular junction, which uses the neurotransmitter acetylcholine (ACh). Toxins that are cholinergic agonists boost the activity of ACh at the neuromuscular junction, affecting muscle tone. For example, black widow spider venom overstimulates the release of ACh from the alpha motor neuron, causing the muscles to spasm in painful convulsions. In unusually severe cases, the alpha motor neuron runs out of ACh and can no longer signal the muscles to contract, leading to paralysis and possibly death.

Although large doses of cholinergic agonists are capable of producing death, cholinergic antagonists are generally far more dangerous and potent. These substances paralyze muscles, including those required for respiration. We observed the deadly actions of the cholinergic antagonists curare and botulinum toxin in Chapter 4. The venom of the Taiwanese cobra also binds tightly to the nicotinic ACh receptor and is nearly impossible to dislodge, leading rapidly to paralysis and death.

Myasthenia Gravis

Myasthenia gravis results when a person's immune system, for reasons that are not well understood, produces antibodies that bind to the nicotinic ACh receptor (Engel, 1984). Over time, the ACh receptors degenerate and become less efficient, leading to extreme muscle weakness and fatigue. The degeneration usually affects the muscles of the head first, resulting in droopy eyelids and slurred speech. As the degeneration proceeds, the patient might experience difficulty swallowing and breathing.

Myasthenia gravis is typically treated with medications that suppress the immune system. This approach slows the production of the troublesome antibodies. Another approach is to administer medications that inhibit acetylcholinesterase (AChE), the enzyme that deactivates ACh at the synapse. Because the ability of AChE to break down ACh is reduced, more ACh remains active in the synaptic gap. Fortunately, most

mirror neuron A special motor neuron that responds to a particular action, whether that action is performed or simply observed.

myasthenia gravis An autoimmune condition caused by the degeneration of ACh receptors at the neuromuscular junction, resulting in muscle weakness and fatigue.

FIGURE 8.18
Muscle Damage from Duchenne Muscular Dystrophy
Muscular dystrophy results from abnormal or missing dystrophin, a protein that protects muscle fibers from damage that occurs during normal movement. As a result, muscle tissue turns to scar tissue and eventually wastes away. This photograph shows muscle tissue from a patient with the most severe version of muscular dystrophy, Duchenne muscular dystrophy.

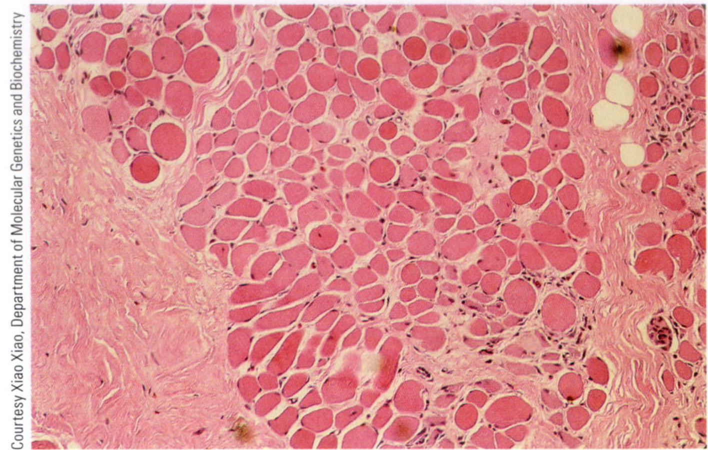

Courtesy Xiao Xiao, Department of Molecular Genetics and Biochemistry

cases of myasthenia gravis have a positive long-term prognosis when these treatment regimens are adhered to carefully.

Muscular Dystrophy

Muscular dystrophy is not a single disease but, rather, a group of inherited diseases characterized by progressive muscle degeneration. These diseases are caused by abnormalities involving the protein dystrophin, which makes up part of the muscle fiber membrane. Dystrophin protects the membrane from injuries due to the force that occurs during normal movement. Muscular dystrophy is a sex-linked disorder, typically affecting males, because the gene responsible for encoding dystrophin is located on the X chromosome (see Chapter 5).

In the most severe type of muscular dystrophy, Duchenne muscular dystrophy, dystrophin is not produced at all. Without the protective action of dystrophin, muscles are damaged during normal activity. Whenever a muscle is damaged, as in weightlifting, the muscle compensates by rebuilding. As a result, children with Duchenne muscular dystrophy initially experience extreme muscle development and often look like bodybuilders by the age of 5 or 6. However, the rebuilding process cannot continue indefinitely. As shown in Figure 8.18, the muscle turns to scar tissue before gradually wasting away. This disorder eventually reduces mobility and results in a shortened life span.

Currently, there are no effective treatments for muscular dystrophy. Among the treatments being currently explored are stem cell implants and gene therapy (Qu-Peterson et al., 2002; Walter et al., 2005, Alter et al., 2006). Limited human trials using a procedure that "edits" faulty genes rather than attempting to replace them has shown significant potential for eventually curing muscular dystrophy (Bertoni, 2008).

Polio

Polio occurs only in human beings and is caused by a contagious virus that specifically targets and destroys spinal alpha motor neurons. The last wild variety case of polio in the United States was reported in 1979, although adverse reactions to vaccinations produced about 10 cases per year until vaccination techniques were changed in 2000 (Alexander et al., 2004). War, poverty, and misinformation about vaccinations continue to delay worldwide eradication of this disease (Centers for Disease Control, 2007). An example of the respirators for polio patients, known as iron lungs, is shown in Figure 8.19.

muscular dystrophy A group of diseases characterized by extreme muscle development followed by muscle wasting, due to abnormalities in the protein dystrophin.
polio A contagious viral disease that attacks the spinal motor neurons, producing paralysis.

Accidental Spinal Cord Damage

The spinal cord can be accidentally damaged when the protective vertebrae surrounding the cord are broken and compress or sever the cord itself. These tragic accidents, such as that suffered by Hollywood actor Christopher Reeve while horseback riding in 1995 and by approximately 8,000 Americans per year in automobile accidents, generally result in permanent paralysis of the muscles served by neurons below the level of damage. If the damage occurs in the cervical, or neck, region of the spinal cord, the person will experience quadriplegia, or the loss of movement in both arms and legs. If the damage occurs in the lumbar region of the lower back, the person will experience paraplegia, the loss of movement in the legs.

Until his death in 2004, Reeve lobbied for additional research funds for spinal cord damage and its treatment. Although effective treatments are still years away, progress is occurring. A "cocktail" containing stem cells derived from the brains of adult mice, growth hormones, and anti-inflammatory drugs helped improve the mobility of rats with spinal injuries (Karimi-Abdolrezaee, Eftekharpour, Wang, Morshead, & Fehlings, 2006). High doses of steroid drugs administered within eight hours of injury are helpful in some cases, although the usefulness of this approach remains controversial (Sayer, Kronvall, & Nilsson, 2006). In 2007, NFL football player Kevin Everett sustained a spinal injury during a game that his physician described as "catastrophic." Everett's doctors used steroids, surgery, and a controversial cooling technique to prevent swelling in his spinal cord (Cappuccino, 2008). Against all odds, Everett eventually regained nearly normal movement. In spite of these promising treatment options, spinal damage should still be considered a permanent injury.

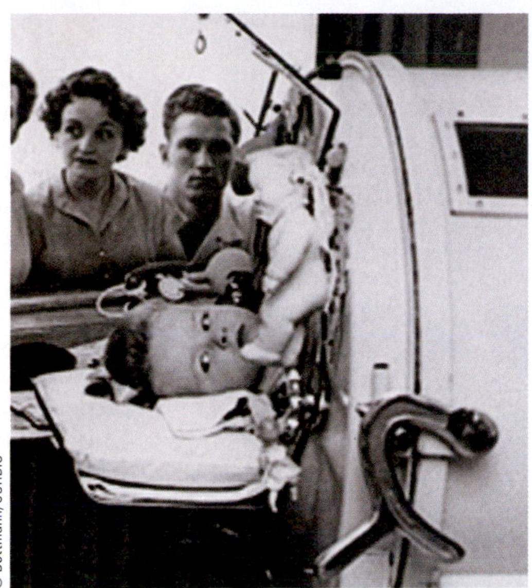

■ **Figure 8.19**
The Effects of Polio Prior to the discovery of effective polio vaccines in the 1950s, iron lung machines were common fixtures in most American hospitals, including this Los Angeles facility. Although about 95 percent of patients with polio do not experience paralysis, about 1 percent are so severely afflicted that they must spend the remainder of their lives in one of these machines.

Amyotrophic Lateral Sclerosis (Lou Gehrig's Disease)

Amyotrophic lateral sclerosis (ALS) is also known as Lou Gehrig's disease, after the outstanding baseball player of the 1930s whose life was ended by the disease. Physicist Stephen Hawking suffers from ALS, as did actor David Niven. ALS results from the degeneration of motor neurons in the spinal cord and brainstem. The muscles served by these motor neurons degenerate when their input ceases.

The causes of ALS are still somewhat mysterious. Ninety percent of cases appear in people with no known family history of the disease, whereas approximately 10 percent of the cases run in families. Daniel Rosen and his colleagues (1993) found that about 15 to 25 percent of patients with familial ALS (FALS) had an abnormal version of a gene known as *SOD-1*. Over 100 mutant variations of *SOD-1* have been identified in patients with FALS (Selverstone, 2005). The mutant forms of *SOD-1* cause damage to motor neurons in multiple ways, including interference with the normal functions of mitochondria (Hervias et al., 2006).

Nikolaos Scarmeas and his colleagues (Scarmeas, Shih, Stern, Ottman, & Rowland, 2002) noted that people who develop ALS are much more likely than the general population to have always been lean and to have participated in college-level varsity athletics. Professional soccer players in Italy were found to have a much higher rate of ALS than members of the general public (Chio, Benzi, Dossena, Mutani, & Mora, 2005). Something related to extremely vigorous physical activity might trigger the disease in susceptible individuals. Obviously, there are thousands of lean university athletes who have never developed ALS, along with many nonathletes who have developed ALS, so the exact basis for this correlation remains unknown. Other cases of ALS might be triggered by viral infections (Berger et al., 2000; Ravits, 2005). Although these correlational data are intriguing, further research is necessary to pinpoint the causes of ALS.

Currently, there are no effective treatments for people with the disease, although recent work is again encouraging. Mice can be genetically engineered to develop human ALS. Joseph Poduslo and his colleagues (Reinholz, Merkle, & Poduslo, 1999) developed an antioxidant enzyme that delayed the progression of ALS in mice. Antioxidants might deactivate harmful free radicals, which result from some chemical reactions in the body. Another promising approach involves drugs that block caspases, the enzymes that mediate apoptosis (suicide) in damaged cells (see Chapter 5). ALS mice treated with a caspase inhibitor survived 22 percent longer than untreated mice (Li et al., 2000).

amyotrophic lateral sclerosis (ALS) (ae-my-oh-TRO-fik LAT-er-uhl scler-OH-sis) A disease in which motor neurons of the spinal cord and brainstem progressively deteriorate, leading to death.

Parkinson's Disease

Parkinson's disease is characterized by a progressive difficulty in all movements, muscular tremors in the resting hand, and frozen facial expressions. These symptoms were first observed and described by the English physician James Parkinson in the early 1800s. Patients with Parkinson's disease experience enormous difficulty initiating voluntary movements, such as standing up from a chair. The disease produces a characteristically stooped posture. Patients' reflexive movements are also impaired, and they fall easily if they lose their balance. Parkinson's disease also affects the peripheral nervous system because the number of noradrenergic terminals in the heart is also reduced by the disease (Goldstein et al., 2000). Parkinson's is often associated with drops in blood pressure, dizziness, and other symptoms of autonomic nervous system disorder (Goldstein, Holmes, Dendi, Bruce, & Li, 2002). Eventually, the condition leads to premature death. Normally, Parkinson's disease affects people after the age of 50 years. Men are twice as likely to develop the disorder, possibly due to some protection women gain from estrogen (Baldereschi et al., 2000; Leranth et al., 2000).

The direct causes of Parkinson's disease are quite clear. This disease occurs when the dopaminergic neurons of the substantia nigra in the brainstem begin to degenerate. As we discussed previously, the substantia nigra forms close connections with the basal ganglia in the cerebral hemispheres. The end result of degeneration in the substantia nigra is a lack of typical dopaminergic activity in the basal ganglia. Because the basal ganglia are intimately involved with the production of voluntary movements, it should come as no surprise that the patients show great difficulties in voluntary movement.

The factors responsible for the degeneration of the substantia nigra remain unknown. Genetics play a role in some cases. Parkinson's disease cases can be divided into early-onset and late-onset categories. At least eight genes have been implicated in the development of the early-onset cases but not in the late-onset cases (Hardy, Cai, Cookson, Gwinn-Hardy, & Singleton, 2006). In the early-onset cases, genes encoding a substance known as alpha synuclein are abnormal (McCann, 2000). As a result, alpha synuclein forms filaments within the neuron that interfere with axonal transport. This process might account for the degeneration of the dopaminergic axons originating in the substantia nigra.

Other cases appear to result from exposure to environmental toxins (Tetrud, Langston, Irwin, & Snow, 1994). Support for this hypothesis comes from an unfortunate accidental experiment involving young heroin addicts who suddenly developed symptoms of Parkinson's disease (Langston, 1985). The addicts had shared a homemade synthetic heroin, which contained a chemical known as MPTP. When MPTP binds with the enzyme monoamine oxidase, which is found in large quantities in the substantia nigra, it forms a very toxic substance known as MPP^+. MPP^+ is attracted to the pigment neuromelanin, which is also found in large quantities in the substantia nigra. You may recall that substantia nigra means "black substance" and that the structure is named in part because of its pigmentation. The affinity between MPP^+ and neuromelanin results in the accumulation of MPP^+ in the substantia nigra, leading to degeneration of the neurons.

Obviously, the vast majority of people with Parkinson's disease have never been exposed to heroin, synthetic or otherwise. However, similar toxins are present in the environment that act like MPTP. People who report having applied insecticides and herbicides on their home gardens or farms are significantly more likely to develop Parkinson's disease than relatives who do not have any direct pesticide exposure (Hancock et al., 2008). Previous reports suggesting that living or working on a farm and consuming well water were related to the development of Parkinson's have not been confirmed by more recent, better controlled investigations (ibid.).

Experiencing head trauma raises a person's risk of developing Parkinson's disease, particularly if the trauma resulted in loss of consciousness or the need for hospitalization (Bower et al., 2003). Individuals with a history of head trauma leading to loss of consciousness were 11 times more likely than controls to develop Parkinson's disease later in life. Professional boxers, such as Muhammad Ali and Jerry Quarry, frequently develop Parkinson's-like symptoms as a result of repeated concussion (see Chapter 15).

Parkinson's disease A degenerative disease characterized by difficulty in moving, muscular tremors, and frozen facial expressions.

One of the strangest findings in the quest to understand Parkinson's disease is the fact that drinking caffeinated coffee reduces the odds of developing the disease (Chade, Kasten, & Tanner, 2006). G. Webster Ross and his colleagues (2000) reported that men who didn't drink any coffee at all were four to five times more likely to develop Parkinson's disease than were the heaviest coffee drinkers, who drank about five cups of coffee per day. Researchers are unsure whether caffeine imparts some protective factor or if people with a sensation-seeking personality, prone to heavy coffee use, are simply less likely to develop the disease (Evans et al., 2006).

The traditional treatment for Parkinson's disease is the medication levodopa, or l-dopa. L-dopa is a precursor in the synthesis of dopamine, so additional l-dopa should help the neurons in the substantia nigra manufacture more of the neurotransmitter. However, l-dopa loses its effectiveness as the numbers of substantia nigra neurons decrease and feedback loops inhibit the further production of dopamine. Because l-dopa affects all dopaminergic systems, not just those originating in the substantia nigra, it also has a variety of undesirable side effects. Increasing overall dopamine activity often results in psychotic behavior, including hallucination and delusional thinking. As we noted in Chapter 4, the increased activity of dopaminergic neurons associated with schizophrenia and with the abuse of dopamine agonists such as amphetamine can produce similar types of psychotic behaviors.

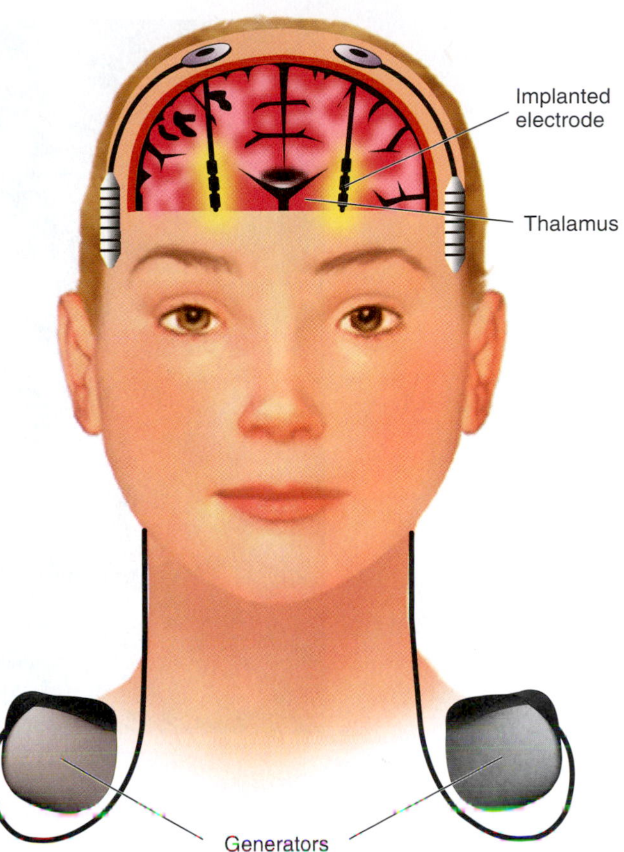

■ **Figure 8.20**
Deep Brain Stimulation Treatment for Parkinson's Disease
To date, thousands of patients with Parkinson's disease have been treated with this electricity-based technique that requires the insertion of two generators under the skin, usually near the collarbone. The generators, each about two inches in diameter, emit tiny electrical pulses that pass along wires, also under the skin, through electrodes implanted in select areas of the brain. Some patients experience a tingling sensation, but typically the stimulation pulses go unnoticed.

Surgery has also been used to treat advanced cases of Parkinson's disease. In a procedure known as a pallidotomy, a part of the globus pallidus of the basal ganglia is destroyed. Seventy-six percent of patients who underwent pallidotomy on both sides of the brain and 64 percent of the patients who underwent pallidotomy on only one side of the brain rated their outcomes as excellent or good in spite of side effects that included speech difficulties (Favre, Burchiel, Taha, & Hammerstad, 2000). Another surgical approach to Parkinson's is the thalamotomy, in which a small area of the thalamus is destroyed. These procedures, when successful, generally reduce unwanted muscle tension and tremor. An alternative to surgery is electrical stimulation, shown in ■ Figure 8.20. Wires are surgically implanted in the thalamus and are connected to two pulse generators each implanted near the patient's collarbone. The generators maintain a steady electrical signal that interferes with signals that lead to tremor. Patients report greater satisfaction from electrical stimulation than from a thalamotomy, but the surgical procedure is much less expensive (Schuurman et al., 2000).

A more controversial approach to Parkinson's treatment is the use of fetal cell implants (Piccini et al., 1999). Results have been mixed, with some patients reporting improved movement while others have experienced uncontrolled movement. The use of donor cells obtained from between six and eight aborted fetuses raises significant ethical issues for this approach. The use of embryonic stem cells (see Chapter 1) to treat Parkinson's disease shares some of the same ethical and procedural problems as the use of fetal cells but continues to show promise (Roy et al., 2006). An example of PET scans from Parkinson's patients before and after fetal cell implant treatment may be seen in ■ Figure 8.21.

Gene therapy might also lead to effective treatments. Jeffrey Kordower and colleagues (2000) used viruses to carry human genes for glial cell line–derived neurotrophic factor (GDNF) into the brains of rhesus monkeys with Parkinson's disease. GDNF has been shown to stimulate the growth of dopaminergic neurons. After treatment, the monkeys' coordination improved, and the dopamine activity in their brains had doubled. Working with rats that had a chemically induced version of Parkinson's disease, researchers reduced symptoms by inserting genes that increased production of l-dopa (Kirik et al., 2002). More work needs to be done before this type of treatment is available for humans, but the outlook is optimistic.

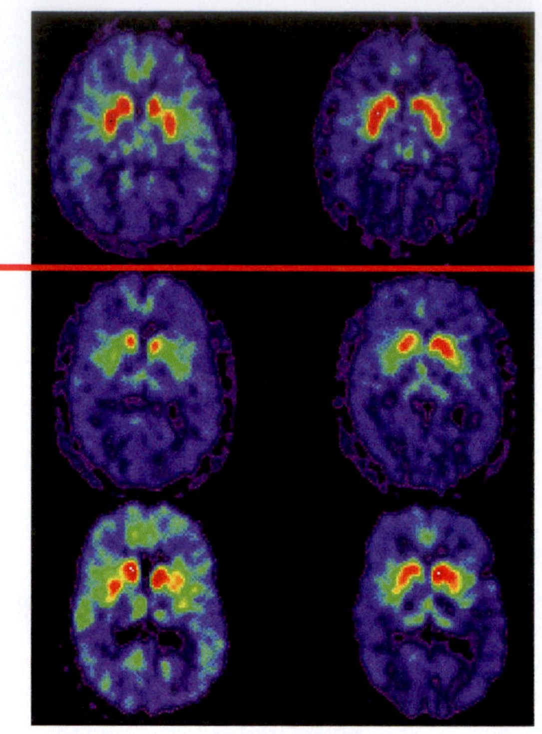

Images provided courtesy of Sanjiv Sam Gambhir, M.D., Ph.D., Stanford University.

FIGURE 8.21 Fetal Cell Implants Are Used to Treat Parkinson's Disease Using a radioactive version of the dopamine precursor l-dopa as a tracer, researchers can evaluate the level of dopamine activity in the brain. These images compare a healthy participant (top) to a patient with Parkinson's disease both before and after treatment with fetal cell implants. Note the increased activity (areas of red and yellow) in the basal ganglia in the "post-transplant" image.

HUNTINGTON'S DISEASE

Huntington's disease strikes in middle age and produces involuntary, jerky movements. As the disease progresses, cognitive symptoms such as depression, hallucination, and delusion occur. Fifteen to twenty years after the onset of symptoms, the patient dies. There is no known cure for this disease, which strikes about one person out of 1,000. The disease was first identified by George Huntington, a doctor on Long Island, in 1872. Eventually, Huntington's original patients were found to be part of one extended family going back to a pair of brothers who came to America from England in 1630. A number of family members were burned as witches in Salem in 1693, probably due to the odd behaviors associated with the disease (Ridley, 1999).

The cause of Huntington's disease is simple and well understood. The *Huntingtin* gene on Chromosome 4, named after George Huntington, encodes the brain protein huntingtin. At the end of the *Huntingtin* gene is a codon, or sequence that encodes an amino acid, that can repeat between 6 and more than 100 times. (see Chapter 5). Most people have between 10 and 15 repeats of this sequence. A person having fewer than 35 repeats will remain healthy, but a person with 39 or more repeats will develop Huntington's disease. Higher numbers of repeats are correlated with an earlier onset of symptoms (Gusella et al., 1996). To make matters worse, this gene is one of the few examples of a dominant gene for a disease. It doesn't help at all to have one normal *Huntingtin* gene. If you have one abnormal gene, you will have the disease. If one of your parents has the disease, then you have a 50 percent chance of developing the disease yourself. In 1993, the *Huntingtin* gene was identified, which made genetic testing possible for those who are at risk for the disease (Gusella & McDonald, 1993).

How does the mutant huntingtin protein produce the symptoms of Huntington's disease? The version of the huntingtin protein produced by the abnormal gene appears to accumulate, particularly in the cells of the basal ganglia. This accumulation of abnormal proteins forms a sticky lump in the cells and triggers cellular suicide (apoptosis). A comparison of the basal ganglia from a healthy person and a Huntington's patient is shown in Figure 8.22.

Currently, there are no effective treatments for Huntington's disease, in spite of the fact that the responsible gene has been recognized for quite a few years. Progress is being made, however. Michael Hayden and his colleagues (Graham et al., 2006) genetically engineered mice to be resistant to certain caspases, enzymes that produce apoptosis. Caspase-resistant mice that had the abnormal *Huntingtin* genes did not develop the disease, but rather retained normal neurological functioning. Although the application of this finding to treating human cases is likely years away, these results represent a substantial breakthrough in our understanding of the disease's progression.

The deterioration associated with Huntington's disease can be postponed by maintaining a high level of activity in a stimulating environment. Anton van Dellen and his colleagues (Spires et al., 2004) compared the progression of Huntington's disease in mice living in standard cages with that of mice living in an enriched environment, which included tunnels, tubes, and a rotation of objects to explore. The mice in the enriched environment showed a slower progression of symptoms than the mice living in standard cages. Mice are certainly not people, however, and much further research is needed before we know whether this is an effective strategy for slowing the human version of the disease.

Huntington's disease A genetic disorder beginning in middle age that results in jerky, involuntary movements and progresses to psychosis and premature death.

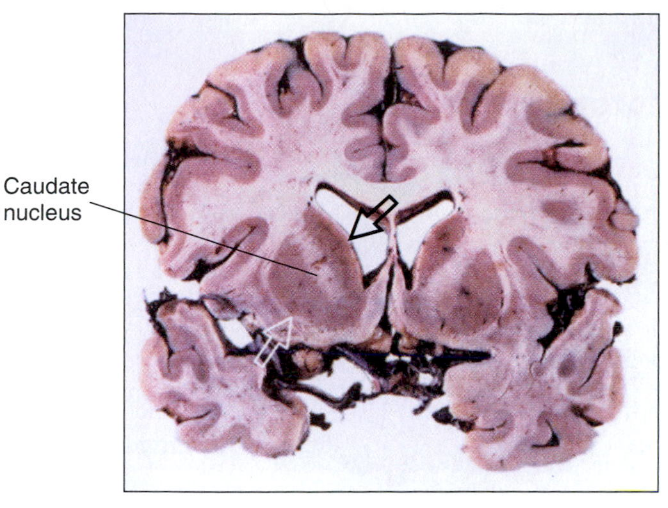

(a)

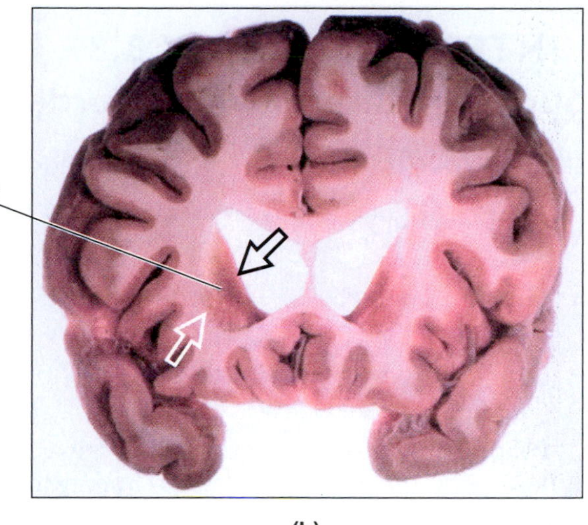

(b)

FIGURE 8.22
Huntington's Disease Causes Degeneration of the Caudate Nucleus of the Basal Ganglia The left image (a) shows a healthy human brain, whereas the right image (b) shows the brain of a person suffering from Huntington's disease. The arrows in both images indicate the boundaries of the caudate nucleus. In the brain of the person with Huntington's disease, the caudate nucleus is quite a bit smaller than normal, and the lateral ventricles have enlarged to take up the extra space.

NEW DIRECTIONS

How Much Stronger and Faster Can We Get?

Athletic records continue to be broken. Since the early 1900s, records for the sprints and jumps in track and field have improved between 10 and 20 percent. Endurance events, such as the marathon, have improved an even more dramatic 30 percent. Can this trend continue?

The answer will probably depend on the extent to which athletes will be willing to modify their bodies to improve performance and how tolerant of these efforts the public and governments will be. The current use of performance-enhancing drugs, such as anabolic steroids, is likely to be eclipsed in the near future by new, genetically based methods. Eric Svensson and his colleagues (1997) used genetic techniques to boost the natural EPO levels in monkeys. EPO is a peptide hormone that stimulates the production of oxygen-carrying red blood cells, making this substance a favorite among cyclists and other endurance athletes. Although tests for synthetic EPO were used effectively at the 2000 Sydney Olympic Games, the type of genetic manipulations performed by Svensson et al. will probably defy detection.

Potential treatments for muscle wasting conditions such as muscular dystrophy are also likely to get the attention of athletes. Genetically altering a single enzyme in mice produced a strain of "mighty mice" with altered metabolisms who could run on a treadmill for six hours straight before stopping (Hakimi et al., 2007). H. Lee Sweeney (2004) describes the methods he and his colleagues used to engineer mice to overproduce insulin growth factor-I (IGF-I). Not only did the mice develop skeletal muscles that were 20–50 percent larger than those of typical mice, but as the engineered mice aged, they retained the regenerative capacities of younger animals. Sweeney also notes that muscle mass could be rapidly increased by chemicals that inhibit myostatin, which normally acts as a brake on muscle growth. Mutations in the myostatin gene produce the remarkable musculature of Belgian Blue cattle, as shown in Figure 8.23.

These methods are not without risk. As we observed in Chapter 1, using a virus to insert a gene resulted in the death of teenager Jesse Gelsinger in 1999. Sweeney's IGF-I is also risky because it can produce cardiac disease and tumor growth if its level in the blood circulation rises beyond a certain point. Muscle growth of 20 to 50 percent would strain bones and connective tissue that are not designed for the increased force, a problem that plagues many steroid-using athletes already. We all know, however, that some athletes are more than willing to sacrifice their long-term health to win today. These techniques could raise both athletic performance and the costs to the participants to new levels.

FIGURE 8.23
Gene Doping The replacement of typical genes with genes that enhance performance, or gene doping, is likely to replace the use of steroids and other drugs to improve athletic performance. One candidate for genetic modification is the gene for myostatin, a protein that limits muscular growth. Belgian Blue cattle have a mutation in the myostatin gene that allows for unusual muscle development.

INTERIM SUMMARY 8.3

Summary Table: Major Disorders of the Motor Systems

Disorder	Symptoms	Causes	Treatments
Myasthenia gravis	Muscle weakness, fatigue	Autoimmune damage to the nicotinic ACh receptor	Medications that inhibit the immune system or AChE.
Muscular dystrophy	Progressive muscle degeneration	Abnormalities in the gene that encodes for the protein dystrophin	None currently approved. Gene replacement and muscle cell replacement under investigation.
Polio	Damage to spinal motor neurons leading to mild to severe muscle paralysis	Virus	Prevented by immunization
Accidental spinal cord damage	Paralysis in muscles served by the spinal cord areas below the point of damage	Compression or laceration of the spinal cord	None currently approved. Stem cell therapy, methods for promoting axon regrowth under investigation.
Amyotrophic lateral sclerosis (ALS)	General weakness, muscle atrophy, cramps, muscle twitching	Possible link to genetic inheritance, possible link to viral infection	None currently approved. Use of medications to slow the progression of the disease under investigation.
Parkinson's disease	Progressive difficulty initiating movement	Possible link to exposure to toxins	Fetal cell implants, electrical stimulation, surgical removal of sections of the basal ganglia or thalamus, medication. Gene therapy and stem cell implants under investigation.
Huntington's disease	Involuntary, jerky movements; depression, hallucinations, delusions	Abnormalities in the gene that encodes for the protein huntingtin	Experimental gene replacement, stem cell implants, and medications under investigation.

Summary Points

1. A number of toxins interfere with movement due to their action at the cholinergic neuromuscular junction. **(LO9)**
2. Myasthenia gravis is an autoimmune disease that produces extreme muscle weakness and fatigue due to the breakdown of ACh receptor sites at the neuromuscular junction. Muscular dystrophy is a collection of diseases that produce extreme muscular development followed by muscular degeneration. Polio is a contagious viral disease that attacks spinal motor neurons, causing some degree of paralysis. Accidental spinal damage results in the loss of voluntary movement produced by nerves below the level of injury. **(LO10)**
3. Amyotrophic lateral sclerosis (ALS) is a degenerative condition resulting from the progressive loss of motor neurons in the spinal cord and brainstem. **(LO10)**
4. Parkinson's disease produces difficulty moving, tremor in resting body parts, frozen facial expressions, and reduced heart innervation. **(LO10)**
5. Huntington's disease is a genetic disorder characterized by involuntary movement and cognitive decline. **(LO10)**

Review Questions

1. What effects do toxins have on the neuromuscular junction, and how does this affect movement?
2. What physical changes underlie the symptoms of Parkinson's disease?

CHAPTER REVIEW

THOUGHT QUESTIONS

1. What advice would you give an elderly person who wanted to maintain or improve muscle strength?
2. Why do you think we evolved three types of muscle fibers?
3. Damage or abnormalities in the prefrontal cortex and basal ganglia might be responsible for some impulsive behavior. Using your knowledge of the initiation of movement, explain why abnormalities in these areas might lead to impulsivity.
4. If you had a parent with Huntington's disease, would you take the genetic screening? What factors would influence your decision?
5. At what levels of the motor system do we treat fine motor activities, such as speech and the movement of our fingers and hand, differently from gross motor activities, such as posture?

KEY TERMS

actin (p. 226)
alpha motor neuron (p. 232)
cardiac muscle (p. 225)
extensor (p. 231)
extrafusal muscle fiber (p. 233)
fast-twitch fiber (p. 227)
flexor (p. 231)
gamma motor neuron (p. 233)
intrafusal muscle fiber (p. 233)
mirror neuron (p. 244)
monosynaptic reflex (p. 236)
motor unit (p. 232)
muscle spindle (p. 233)
myofibril (p. 226)
myosin (p. 226)
polysynaptic reflex (p. 236)
pre-supplementary motor area (pre-SMA) (p. 241)
recruitment (p. 232)
sarcomeres (p. 226)
skeletal muscle (p. 225)
slow-twitch fiber (p. 227)
smooth muscle (p. 225)
striated muscle (p. 225)
supplementary motor area (SMA) (p. 241)
troponin (p. 226)
twitch (p. 225)
Z line (p. 226)

Temperature Regulation, Thirst, and Hunger

CHAPTER OUTLINE

▲ **Motivation** Our bodies are finely tuned to maintain ideal levels of temperature, fluids, and nutrients.

Introduction

Between 1980 and 2002, the number of obese adults in the United States doubled, and the rates of obese children and adolescents tripled (Becker, Burwell, Herzog, Hamburg, & Gilman, 2002; Hamburg, & Gilman, 2002; Ogden, 2006). As shown in ■ Figure 9.1, rates of obesity in the United States range from a low of 18.7 percent of the population of Colorado to a high of 32 percent in Mississippi. Automobile and theater seats are now larger, and the seatbelt extender is a commonly used device in many airplanes. At the same time, most of us know at least one dangerously thin person who suffers from an eating disorder. What factors might account for the simultaneous occurrence of these two extremes within a single culture?

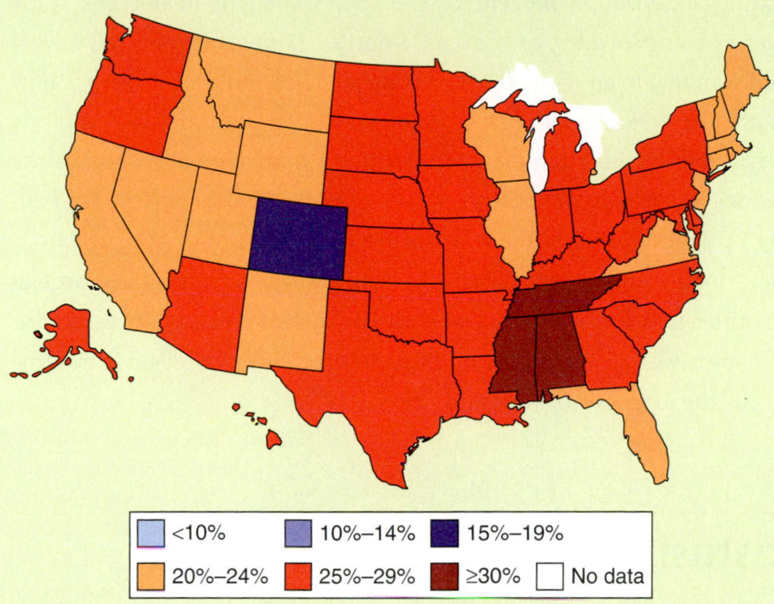

■ **FIGURE 9.1**
The American Obesity Epidemic Rates of obesity vary in the United States from a low of 18.7 percent in Colorado to a high of 32 percent in Mississippi. Approximately 65 percent of American adults are overweight or obese. *Source*: U.S. Department of Health and Human Services, Centers for Disease Control and Prevention (2008).

As we'll see in this chapter, internal systems controlling body temperature, fluid intake, and weight are tightly regulated and are generally successful at maintaining ideal levels. In human beings, however, environmental factors can play significant roles in disrupting or overriding these finely tuned regulatory systems. Anne Becker and her colleagues chronicled the impact of American television on disordered eating in the South Pacific islands of Fiji (Becker, 2004; Becker et al., 2002). Becker reported that dieting was previously unknown in a culture that valued a "robust, well-muscled body" for both sexes, as shown in ■ Figure 9.2. The Fijian language has a term, *going thin*, to express concern about a person's noticeable weight loss. In the United States, we might ask one another, "Have you lost weight? You look great!" Fijians are more likely to say with dismay, "Are you sure you're okay? You look like you're going thin."

■ **FIGURE 9.2**
External Influences Can Change Cultural Ideals of Beauty Anne Becker's research into the eating habits of young Fijian women suggests that the introduction of American television programs led to higher rates of dieting and eating disorders. This Fijian woman meets the pretelevision Fijian ideal of beauty—a robust, well-muscled body.

LEARNING OBJECTIVES

After reading this chapter, you should be able to

LO1 Explain the terms homeostasis, set point, and motivation.

LO2 Describe the mechanisms and behaviors that ectotherms and endotherms use to maintain core temperature.

LO3 Differentiate between osmotic and hypovolemic thirst and identify cues for the initiation and cessation of drinking.

LO4 Describe the regulation of fluids by the central nervous system.

LO5 Describe the process of digestion.

LO6 Describe the brain and hormonal mechanisms responsible for hunger and satiety.

LO7 Summarize the definitions, causes, and treatments for obesity, anorexia nervosa, and bulimia nervosa.

Soon after the arrival of popular American television in 1995, with its frequent images of glamorous ultrathin actresses, 74 percent of the adolescent girls in Becker's study reported themselves as being "too big or too fat." Another 17 percent reported having deliberately induced vomiting in an effort to control weight, whereas Becker reports only 3 percent doing so prior to 1995. Overall, Becker found that Fijian girls today were as likely to be dieting as their American counterparts, representing a fundamental shift since she began her observations in 1988. Because Becker's data are correlational, we cannot conclude that watching TV directly produced the change in eating habits among young Fijians. However, her results strongly suggest that culture, in this case values transmitted through TV, plays a significant role in the development of body dissatisfaction and disordered eating habits. In this chapter, we will explore many other interactions between our internal regulatory systems and the external environment. ■

Homeostasis

Pride costs more than hunger, thirst, or cold.
Thomas Jefferson

Without much conscious awareness or effort on our part, our bodies maintain **homeostasis.** Homeostasis, a term coined by psychologist Walter Cannon (1932), refers to an organism's ability to adjust its physiological processes to maintain a steady internal balance or equilibrium. To achieve homeostasis, regulatory systems actively defend certain values, or **set points,** for variables such as temperature, fluid levels, and weight. The defense of these set points is similar to the thermostat of your home's heating system. If the air temperature drops below the setting, the furnace is turned on. Once the desired temperature is reached, the furnace turns off again.

Deviations from the body's ideal values of temperature, fluid levels, or weight are rapidly assessed by the nervous system. Once deficits are recognized, the nervous system makes appropriate internal adjustments and motivates behavior designed to regain the ideal state. The process of **motivation** both activates and directs behavior. When homeostasis has been compromised, the nervous system first activates behavior by generating tension and discomfort in the form of drive states such as thirst or hunger. Drive states arise in response to physiological needs and disappear again, usually with a sense of relief, when those needs are met. Once the organism is activated by a drive state, it will initiate behavior to solve the specific problem. The action chosen to reestablish homeostasis will not be random. We do not respond to hunger cues by getting a drink of water. Instead, the activity of the nervous system ensures that we will be motivated specifically to seek out food.

As demonstrated by the frequency of obesity and eating disorders, the systems maintaining homeostasis are not foolproof. Regulatory systems can help us identify a problem, but our reaction to this information usually involves a complicated set of psychological and biological processes.

Regulation of Body Temperature

Temperature regulation involves all of the major features of a homeostatic system that we have discussed so far: a precisely defined set point, mechanisms for detecting deviations away from the set point, and, finally, internal and behavioral elements designed to regain the set point.

Animals inhabit niches that vary dramatically in external temperature, from the frozen Arctic to steaming equatorial jungles. Some bacteria exist in the hot volcanic vents in the ocean floor. Extreme temperatures limit life through their impact on the chemical properties of living cells. If temperatures are too low, ice crystals form within cells and damage the cell membrane. In high temperatures, the proteins necessary for carrying out cell functions become unstable. No matter where they live, animals must maintain an internal temperature that is ideal for the normal activity of their bodies' cells.

homeostasis A physiological state of equilibrium or balance.
set point A value that is defended by regulatory systems, such as core temperature or a particular body weight.
motivation The process of activating and directing behavior.

■ **FIGURE 9.3**
Surface-to-Volume Ratios Affect Temperature Regulation (a) The higher an animal's surface-to-volume ratio, the harder it must work to maintain core temperature. The amount of heat loss is a function of the body surface area, and body volume determines the amount of heat generated by metabolic activity. Because smaller animals have larger surface-to-volume ratios, maintaining core temperature is harder for them than for larger animals such as humans. (b) Rats have larger surface-to-volume ratios than humans or elephants. Consequently, rats must work much harder than humans or elephants to maintain core temperature.

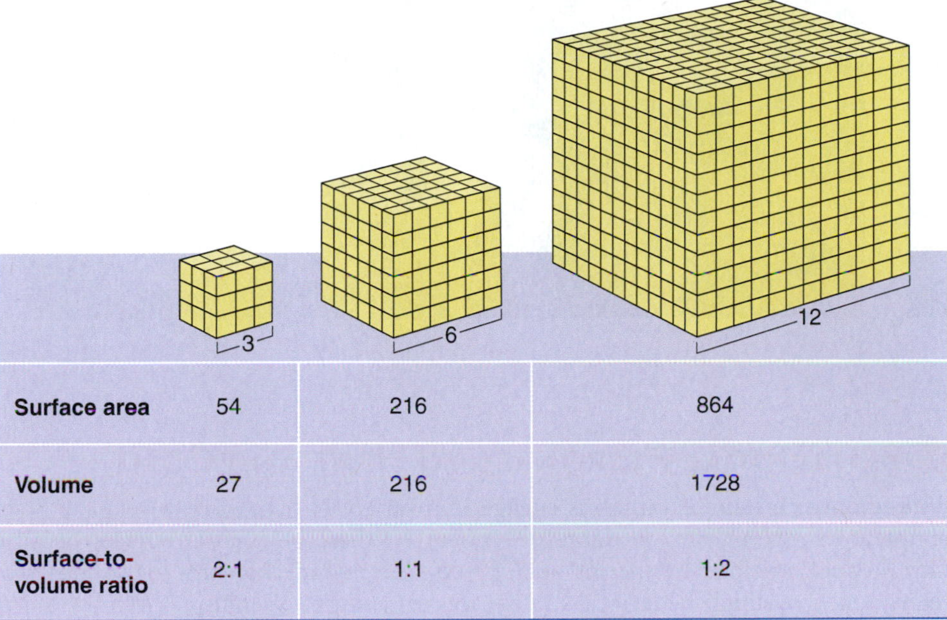

Surface area	54	216	864
Volume	27	216	1728
Surface-to-volume ratio	2:1	1:1	1:2

(a)

Rat—1:6.67

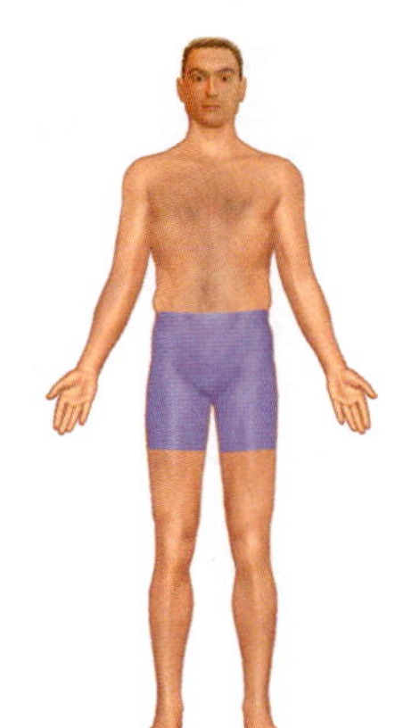

Human—1:35.3

Elephant—1:150

(b)

ADAPTATIONS TO TEMPERATURE

Two solutions have evolved to help animals maintain an optimum body temperature in a varying environment. Mammals and birds are referred to as **endotherms** (*endon* is the Greek word for "within") due to their ability to maintain body temperature through internal metabolic activity. Amphibians, reptiles, and fish are referred to as **ectotherms** (*ektos* is the Greek word for "outside") because they rely on external factors, such as basking in the sunlight or retreating to the shade below a rock, to maintain ideal body temperature. The common terms *warm-blooded* and *cold-blooded* are misleading because the internal temperatures maintained by all animals fall within a few degrees of one another. Endotherms and ectotherms simply use different methods to maintain a standard body temperature.

The maintenance of body temperature is influenced by an animal's surface-to-volume ratio. The larger the overall volume of the body, the more heat is produced by metabolic activity. Heat is lost to the surrounding environment as a function of the animal's surface area. As shown in ■ Figure 9.3, smaller animals have more surface area relative to the overall body volume than larger animals do, so small animals must use much more energy to maintain a constant body temperature.

Within a species, populations of animals evolve features that fit a particular environmental niche. In cold climates, surface area and heat loss are reduced in animals that have compact, stocky bodies and short legs, tails, and ears. To promote heat loss in warm climates, animals have greater surface area in the form of slim bodies and long appendages. Examples of these adaptations among different types of foxes can be seen in ■ Figure 9.4. This trend can be seen among human beings as well, although there are obviously many exceptions.

endotherm An animal that can use internal methods, such as perspiration or shivering, to maintain body temperature.

ectotherm An animal that relies on external methods, such as moving into the sun or shade, for maintaining body temperature.

FIGURE 9.4
Adaptations to Climate Occur Within Species Animals in warm climates disperse heat by having slim bodies and long appendages. Animals in cold climates conserve heat by having compact, stocky bodies and short legs, tails, and ears. These foxes are found in (left) warm, (center) temperate, and (right) Arctic climates.

Behavioral Responses to Heat and Cold

Both endotherms and ectotherms engage in a variety of behaviors to regulate body temperature. Ectotherms are more dependent on these behavioral devices because they do not share the endotherms' ability to use internal mechanisms for temperature regulation. One simple behavioral strategy for regulating temperature is to move to the right type of environment. Both snakes and people stretch out in the sun when they seek additional warmth or move to the shade when they need to cool off.

Body position can be adjusted in response to changes in temperature. If we're very warm, we tend to stretch out our bodies to increase our surface area and lose more heat. When we're very cold, we curl up in an attempt to reduce our exposed surface area. Social animals huddle together more when cold, so sitting too close to a warm, crackling fireplace might not be in the best interests of romance. Animals can change the weight, color, and composition of their fur in response to seasonal changes in temperature. Humans use dark, heavy clothing to absorb and maintain heat, whereas lighter clothing helps reflect and dissipate heat. Further protection from temperature changes is provided by dens, burrows, nests, and other shelters.

Endothermic Responses to Heat and Cold

In addition to behavioral adaptations, endotherms demonstrate a variety of automatic internal responses to deviations from the temperature set point. Humans defend a temperature set point of 98.6°F (37°C). When internal temperature drops below this set point, we shiver. Shivering results from muscle twitches, which can be so intense that teeth chatter together. The muscle activity involved in shivering produces heat, but at the cost of a high expenditure of energy. Blood vessels constrict, keeping most of the blood away from the surface of the skin, where heat loss is greatest. In some cases, blood vessel constriction is too extreme, leading to a condition known as Raynaud's disease. This condition produces sudden spasms in arteries, particularly those in fingers and toes, in response to cold. As shown in ■ Figure 9.5, the affected digit or digits lose feeling and appear white.

If cold conditions persist in spite of shivering, the thyroid gland increases the release of thyroid hormone. Higher levels of thyroid hormone are associated with greater overall metabolic activity, which warms the body. Deficits in thyroid activity are often diagnosed on the basis of the patient's lower-than-normal body temperature (Barnes & Galton, 1976). In human infants and small animals, the sympathetic nervous system responds to cold by stimulating greater metabolic activity in so-called

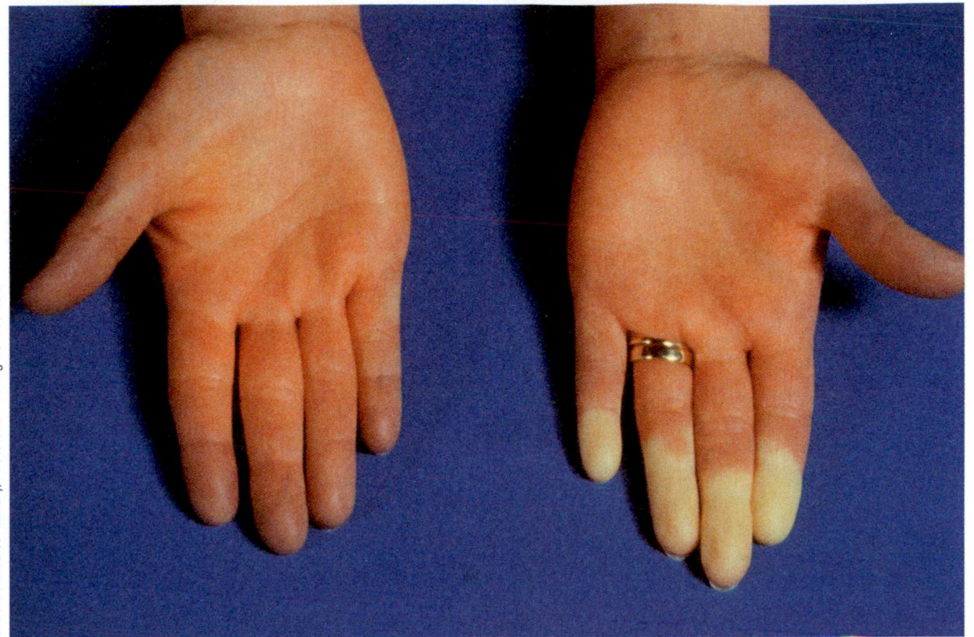

FIGURE 9.5
Raynaud's Disease Produces an Extreme Reaction to Cold Blood vessels normally constrict in response to cold. In Raynaud's disease, this constriction becomes extreme, leading to a lack of circulation in the affected digit. People with Raynaud's disease are cautioned to avoid sudden cold and to use gloves when removing food from their freezers.

brown fat cells. Brown fat cells are located primarily in the torso, close to the vital organs. The fat cells appear brown due to large numbers of mitochondria, the organelles responsible for energy production.

Very warm temperatures produce their own set of responses. Perspiration cools the skin through evaporation. Human beings have around 2.5 million sweat glands and lose an average of a liter (0.22 gallon) of sweat each day under average conditions (Stiefel Laboratories, 2001). Animals, such as dogs, which do not perspire much, pant or lick their fur. Licking the fur produces cooling by evaporation in much the same way that perspiration does. Blood vessels near the surface of the skin dilate in hot environments, allowing more heat loss to the external environment. As a result, people often become very red-faced in warm temperatures.

Happiness is the absence of fever.

Marcel Proust

Deviations in Human Core Temperature

The body's core temperature refers to the temperature maintained for vital organs within the head and torso. Although we can survive drastic changes in the temperature of the body's outer shell, much smaller deviations in our core body temperature can have serious consequences.

Disturbances in the body's ability to maintain the normal core temperature set point can result in the hot flashes experienced by nearly 80 percent of women in the months or years surrounding menopause. Hot flashes last seconds to minutes and are characterized by sweating, flushing, heart palpitations, and a subjective feeling of being very warm. Although the exact mechanism underlying hot flashes is not well understood, it is likely that changes in estrogen associated with menopause are responsible for the malfunction (Stearns et al., 2002). The frequency and severity of hot flashes increase if a woman uses alcohol daily (Sievert, Obermeyer, & Price, 2006).

We all know how miserable a **fever** of only a few degrees feels, and very high fevers (in excess of 41°C /105.8°F) can cause brain damage. Fevers due to illness result when chemical byproducts of bacteria or viruses, known as **pyrogens,** enter the brain, causing the brain to increase the core temperature set point. We'll see exactly how this occurs in the next section on brain mechanisms and temperature. Body temperature will rise gradually until the new set point is reached. Although uncomfortable, fever does have beneficial effects in fighting disease (Kluger, 1991; Roth, 2006). Many disease-causing organisms can tolerate a much narrower temperature range than can the infected animal or person. Raising the host's set point kills many of the invading organisms, assisting the immune system in its task of ridding the body of disease. Among the pathogens that are reduced by fever are the viruses responsible for many

fever A carefully controlled increase in the body's thermal set point that is often helpful in ridding the body of disease-causing organisms.

pyrogen A chemical produced by bacteria or viruses that contributes to the production of a fever.

AP Images

FIGURE 9.6 Heat Stroke Claimed the Life of Minnesota Vikings Football Player Korey Stringer Although the body's temperature regulation system is generally very effective, it can be overwhelmed in conditions of extreme exertion, high temperatures and humidity, inadequate fluid intake, and heavy clothing. A recent rash of tragic fatalities among football players serves as a reminder that heat stroke is not a risk only for people who are elderly or ill.

upper respiratory diseases and the bacteria responsible for gonorrhea and syphilis. Prior to the discovery of antibiotics, patients with syphilis were deliberately infected with malaria to induce fever (Bruetsch, 1949). Because of the potential benefits of fever, current medical practice suggests using medication to reduce a fever only if other health risk factors are present or when discomfort is excessive (World Health Organization, 1993).

A fever represents a carefully monitored increase in the body's temperature set point. In contrast, heat stroke, or **hyperthermia,** occurs when the body's normal compensations (such as sweating and dilating the blood vessels close to the skin) cannot keep core temperature within normal limits. If core temperature rises above 40°C/104°F, a person can become confrontational, faint, and confused. Sweating stops, compounding the problem of overheating. Heat stroke is a life-threatening condition and requires immediate medical assistance (Weinmann, 2003).

Heat stroke often results from engaging in strenuous physical activity or wearing heavy clothing in hot, humid environments, conditions that limit the body's ability to get rid of excess heat. Although not typically the result of illness alone, heat stroke interacts with immune system functioning (Carter, Cheuvront, & Sawka, 2007; Lim & Mackinnon, 2006). People with existing infections are more likely to develop heat stroke during exercise. Special care should be taken by individuals who have existing infections and are engaged in strenuous activities.

A string of heat-stroke deaths among young athletes raised public awareness of this condition. Between 1995 and 2001, sixteen football players died from heat stroke (Bailes, Cantu, & Day, 2002). Minnesota Vikings lineman Korey Stringer, shown in Figure 9.6, lost his life as a result of heat stroke following summer practice in 2001. Stringer's core temperature was 108°F when he finally reached a hospital (CNN.com, 2001). A combination of heavy physical exertion, insufficient fluid intake, nearly 100 degree outside temperatures, humidity, and heavy clothing and pads probably contributed to the deaths of Stringer and other football players. In addition, the players' surface-to-volume ratios probably made it difficult for them to dissipate excess heat effectively. Recall that slender animals with long appendages cope better with heat. At 6'4" and 335 pounds, Stringer was at a tragic disadvantage in coping with his hostile environmental conditions.

Low core temperatures are also life threatening. **Hypothermia** (low core body temperature) has killed many stranded hikers and ocean swimmers. Hypothermia occurs when core body temperature drops below 35°C/95°F. Uncontrolled, intense shivering, slurred speech, pain, and discomfort occur. At core temperatures below 31°C/87.8°F, the pupils dilate, behavior resembles drunkenness, and consciousness is gradually lost (Search and Rescue Society of British Columbia, 1995).

Deliberately producing mild hypothermia has become a common method of reducing brain damage following cardiac arrest or open heart surgery (Nolan et al., 2003). Cooling can be achieved using a special mattress, intravenous fluids, or applications of ice. Although the mechanism by which cooling prevents damage is not completely understood, it is likely that cooling counteracts typical negative reactions to an interruption in the blood supply to the brain, such as the increased activity of free radicals, excitatory neurotransmitters, and calcium (Greer, 2006).

BRAIN MECHANISMS FOR TEMPERATURE REGULATION

Temperature regulation is too important for survival to be left to a single system. Instead, temperature regulation results from the activity of a structural hierarchy, beginning with the spinal cord and extending through the brainstem to the hypothalamus. Sensitivity to temperature change increases from the lower to the higher levels of this hierarchy. Lower levels, such as the spinal cord, do not respond to heat or cold until an animal's core temperature is as much as two to three degrees away from the set point. Patients with spinal cord damage, which prevents temperature regulation of the body by the brainstem and hypothalamus, frequently complain about their inability to manage temperature control of their arms and legs. Higher levels of the hierarchy act as much more precise thermostats. The hypothalamus initiates compensation whenever core temperature deviates as little as 0.01 degree from the ideal set point (Satinoff, 1978).

hyperthermia (heat stroke) A life-threatening condition in which core body temperature increases beyond normal limits in an uncontrolled manner.

hypothermia A potentially fatal core body temperature below 31 degrees C/87.8 degrees F.

The **preoptic area (POA)** of the hypothalamus, shown in ■ Figure 9.7, along with adjacent areas of the anterior hypothalamus and septum, coordinates incoming information from thermoreceptors with structures that trigger appropriate responses to higher core temperatures, such as panting, sweating, and the dilation of blood vessels. The posterior hypothalamus is responsible for initiating responses to cooler core temperatures, such as shivering and blood vessel constriction. In addition to receiving input from skin receptors (see Chapter 7) and the spinal cord, the hypothalamus is sensitive to the body's core temperature as reflected by thermoreceptors within the hypothalamus itself.

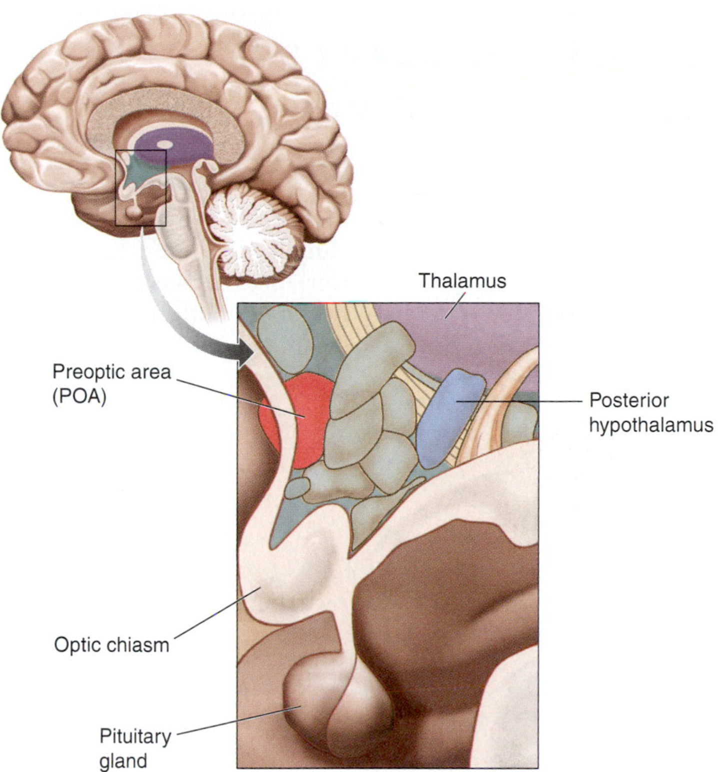

■ **FIGURE 9.7**
The Hypothalamus Controls Temperature Regulation The preoptic area (POA) of the hypothalamus, along with adjacent areas of the anterior hypothalamus and septum, coordinates incoming information from thermoreceptors with structures responsible for appropriate responses to higher core temperatures such as panting, sweating, and the dilation of blood vessels. The posterior hypothalamus is responsible for initiating responses to cooler core temperatures such as shivering and blood vessel constriction.

The POA contains three types of neurons: warm-sensitive, cold-sensitive, and temperature-insensitive (Boulant, 2000). Warm-sensitive neurons increase their firing rates and inhibit cold-sensitive neurons as core temperature increases. As temperature drops, the firing rates of warm-sensitive neurons decrease, reducing their inhibition of the cold-sensitive neurons, which respond by increasing their firing rates. Temperature-insensitive neurons retain a fairly steady rate of responding under all temperature conditions. Temperature set points possibly reflect a comparison of the activity of temperature-sensitive and temperature-insensitive neurons (Hammel, 1965).

A series of clever experiments demonstrated that temperature sensors in the hypothalamus can override input from skin sensors. Rats can be taught to press a bar to obtain a brief puff of cool air (Corbit, 1973; Satinoff, 1964). The rate at which the rats press the bar corresponds to changes in either skin temperature or hypothalamic temperature. Skin temperature mirrors changes in room temperature, whereas hypothalamic temperature can be manipulated by bathing the hypothalamus with warm or cool water applied through a surgically inserted micropipette. When either skin temperature or hypothalamic temperature is raised, the rat will press more frequently to obtain cool puffs of air. However, cooling the hypothalamus alone will reduce or suppress bar pressing even when the room (and hence the skin receptors) remains very warm (Kupfermann, Kandel, & Iverson, 2000).

As mentioned earlier, pyrogens entering the brain act to gradually increase the body's temperature set point, causing fever. Not surprisingly, the pyrogens' target in the brain is located in the hypothalamus. The blood–brain barrier is relatively weak near the POA, which allows pyrogens to exit the blood supply and enter the tissue. Once in the POA, pyrogens stimulate the release of prostaglandin E2, which in turn inhibits the firing rate of warm-sensitive neurons (Mackowiak & Boulant, 1996). Due to the reduced activity of these central thermoreceptors, the body responds by producing and retaining heat, leading to increased heart rate, shivering, and the other unpleasant symptoms of fever.

Temperature Regulation in Infancy

Newborn animals are often relatively helpless when it comes to adapting to temperature, primarily due to age-related metabolism, high surface-to-volume ratios, immature abilities to shiver, and low body fat stores. Human infants possess much more body fat at birth than other primate infants, possibly as a protection from hypothermia (Pawlowski, 1998). If early hunter-gatherers had little if any clothing and slept on the ground, maintaining infant body temperature would be challenging even in the warm African climate. Premature infants must spend time in a warm incubator before leaving the hospital because their ability to regulate temperature is unusually immature (Rutter, 1996). Animals that are born as part of a litter demonstrate social responses to temperature. The infants switch places regularly so that no single animal cools too much on the outside of the group or overheats at its center. They huddle closer together in cooler temperatures and farther apart in warmer ones (Alberts, 1978).

preoptic area (POA) A part of the hypothalamus involved in a number of regulatory functions.

INTERIM SUMMARY 9.1

Summary Table: Strategies Used to Maintain Body Temperature Homeostasis

Temperature	Behavioral Strategies	Internal Strategies
Cold temperatures	• Move to a warmer place or shelter • Huddle with others to conserve heat • Curl up to decrease exposed surface area • Add more clothing, preferably dark colors	• Shivering • Constriction of blood vessels • Increased release of thyroid hormone to increase metabolic rate • Increased metabolism in brown fat stores
Warm temperatures	• Move to cooler, shadier place or shelter • Stretch out • Wear less clothing, preferably light colors	• Perspiration and panting • Dilation of blood vessels

Summary Points

1. When deviations from set points occur, the process of motivation activates and directs behavior designed to remedy the situation. **(LO1)**
2. Endotherms can maintain body temperature through internal activity, whereas ectotherms rely on external factors. **(LO2)**
3. The hypothalamus, brainstem, and spinal cord produce a hierarchy of responses to changes in temperature, with the hypothalamus providing the most precise level of control. **(LO2)**

Review Questions

1. What are the mechanisms used by endotherms to regulate internal temperature?
2. What are the differences between fever and hyperthermia?

Thirst: Regulation of the Body's Fluid

As animals moved out of the ocean environment onto dry land, they devised ways to bring part of their watery environment with them. Maintaining appropriate fluid levels is essential to survival.

The fluids of the body contain many dissolved chemical molecules. Molecules that have been dissolved in a fluid are known as **solutes** and the fluid that contains the solutes is known as a **solution.** If a solute breaks into ions when it is dissolved, it is referred to as an **electrolyte.** You might recognize this term from laboratory blood tests or from the advertising of sports drinks. Some of the important electrolytes involved in healthy body functioning include sodium, calcium, potassium, chloride, magnesium, and bicarbonate. As we will see shortly, sodium is the most important electrolyte for managing the body's fluid levels.

Intracellular and Extracellular Fluids

The body has three major compartments for storing water, illustrated in ■ Figure 9.8. About two thirds of the body's water is contained within cells as the intracellular fluid. The remaining third is found in the extracellular fluid, which is further divided into the blood supply (about 7 percent of the body's water total) and the **interstitial fluid** surrounding the body's cells (about 26 percent of the body's water total). Cerebrospinal fluid makes up a tiny percentage of the extracellular fluid.

As we have seen previously, the composition of the extracellular and intracellular fluids is quite different. Extracellular fluid has higher concentrations of sodium and chloride, and intracellular fluid has higher concentrations of potassium. Even though the identity of the solutes in these two compartments is different, the relative concentration of total solutes is the same. Two solutions with equal concentrations of solutes

solute A chemical dissolved in solution.
solution A fluid containing solutes.
electrolyte A substance that has broken up into ions in solution.
interstitial fluid (in-ter-STI-shul) A type of extracellular fluid surrounding the body's cells.

are referred to as **isotonic.** Intravenous (IV) fluids provided in medical treatment are typically isotonic solutions containing sugars and sodium. In other words, the IV fluid has the same concentration of solutes as normal body fluids, although the exact identity of the solutes might be different. The body can absorb the fluids and solutes without requiring further adjustments to intracellular and extracellular fluid levels.

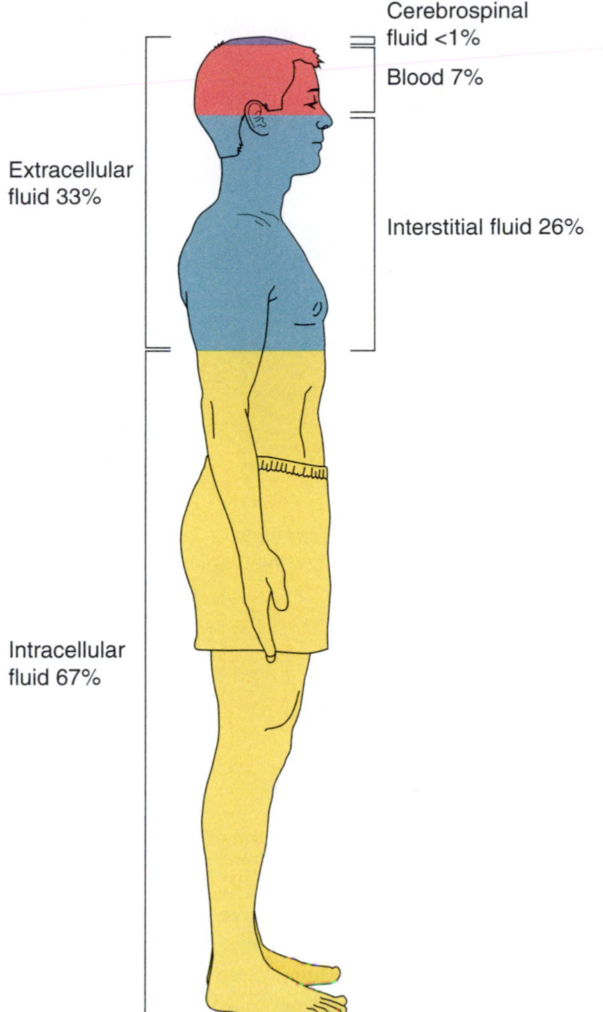

■ **Figure 9.8**
The Body's Fluids Are Held in Three Compartments About two thirds of the body's fluid is stored as intracellular fluid. The remaining third is stored as extracellular fluid, divided between the interstitial fluid surrounding cells (26 percent) and the blood supply (7 percent). The cerebrospinal fluid accounts for less than 1 percent of the body's fluids.

Osmosis Causes Water to Move

The balance found in the isotonic state reduces any movement of fluid into or out of the body's cells due to **osmosis.** Osmosis, illustrated in ■ Figure 9.9, is the force that causes water to move from an area with lower concentration of solutes to an area with higher concentration of solutes. Osmosis is similar to diffusion in that both processes produce the movement of molecules. In diffusion, which we discussed in Chapter 3, solutes tend to spread themselves out equally in a space, moving from areas of high to low concentration. In osmosis, it is the water that moves across a barrier, such as a cell membrane, to equalize concentrations of the solutes on either side.

Solutions that are lower in concentration of solutes than a reference solution are referred to as **hypotonic,** and solutions that are relatively higher in concentration of solutes are referred to as **hypertonic.** Hypotonic and hypertonic solutions have different effects on the body's fluid levels. Emergency treatment of people who nearly drown varies accordingly. In a freshwater near-drowning, the person often breathes in large amounts of fresh water. The extracellular fluid becomes highly hypotonic, or less concentrated than the intracellular fluid. In an effort to regain balance, osmotic pressure will drive water from the less concentrated extracellular fluid into the more concentrated cells, possibly rupturing cell membranes. In a saltwater near-drowning, the extracellular fluid becomes hypertonic, or more concentrated than the intracellular fluid. In this case, osmotic pressure will drive water out of the less concentrated intracellular fluid into the highly concentrated extracellular fluid. Exposed cells will rapidly dehydrate, disrupting their ability to carry out normal functions. In either case, damage is particularly prevalent in the lungs, further contributing to the lack of oxygen that has already occurred due to submersion (Shepherd & Martin, 2002).

The Role of the Kidneys

Given normal access to food and water, people usually consume more water and sodium than they really need to maintain fluid balances. However, livestock in the field are often provided with a salt lick, and athletes or soldiers engaging in high levels of physical activity in hot, humid conditions benefit from salt supplements.

Any excess sodium or water is excreted by the two **kidneys,** located in the lower back. Blood enters the kidneys, where it is filtered through a complex system made up of over a million structures known as nephrons. Impurities and excess water and sodium are removed by the nephrons and sent to the bladder for excretion as urine. The filtered blood returns to the circulation. In cases of kidney failure, patients must undergo regular sessions of kidney dialysis. Machines are used in an effort to duplicate the filtering normally performed by the kidneys.

In addition to urination, we lose water through several other normal body processes. Steaming breath on a cold day demonstrates that some water is lost during simple breathing or respiration. About 1 liter (0.22 gallon) of fluid per day is lost through perspiration. Evaporation through the skin and defecation also reduce the body's water supply. Table 9.1 shows the relative loss of fluids from the body during normal daily activity.

isotonic Having the same concentration of solutes as a reference solution.

osmosis The movement of water to equalize concentration on two sides of a membrane.

hypotonic Having a relatively lower concentration of solutes than a reference solution.

hypertonic Having a relatively higher concentration of solutes than a reference solution.

kidney One of a pair of structures located in the lower back responsible for maintaining fluid balance and for producing urine.

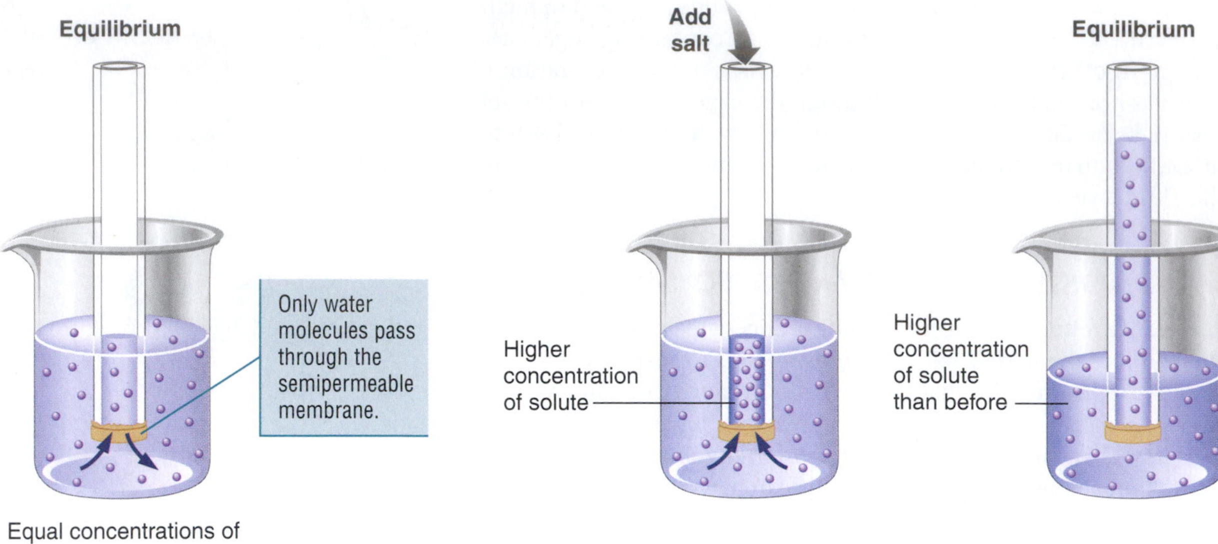

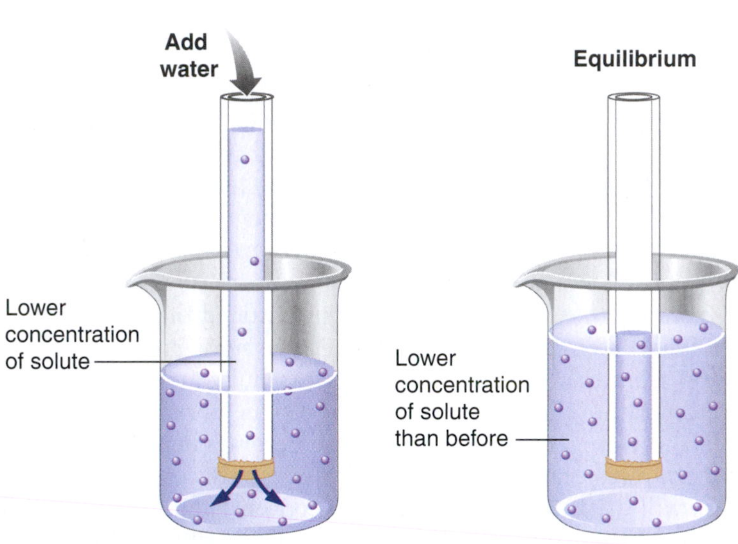

Figure 9.9
Osmosis Causes Water to Move Water will move from an area of higher concentration of solutes to an area of lower concentration of solutes. When salt is added into a tube separated from a container by a membrane, water will enter the tube to equalize the concentration of solutes on both sides of the membrane. When water is added to the tube, water will move into the container.

The Sensation of Thirst

Animals vary in their need to take in water during the day. Some desert-dwelling species never seem to drink at all. Animals that spend a lot of time in the water are nearly always ingesting some. As shown in Table 9.1 humans need an average of about 2.5 liters (0.55 gallons) of water per day. This is roughly equivalent to the eight glasses of water a day that we are commonly advised to consume. No offense to mothers' advice or to corporations marketing bottled water, but there is nothing special about consuming plain water. Any source of fluid will do. As a matter of fact, we take in about half the fluids we need through the foods we eat without drinking any beverages at all, so following the eight-glasses-a-day rule is likely to provide an excess of fluids.

When a drop in the body's water supply is perceived, two processes are initiated. We experience the sensation of thirst, and our bodies begin to conserve whatever water we still have. Walter Cannon (1929) proposed that the sensation of a dry mouth was the critical stimulus responsible for feelings of thirst, which in turn lead to drinking. Cannon's hypothesis is quite wrong. Although the feelings of a dry, dusty mouth and throat certainly stimulate us to take a drink, these feelings are too quickly relieved to be trusted completely as a means of fluid regulation. As anyone with outdoors experience can relate, swirling a mouthful of water from a canteen is usually enough to make the dry-mouth sensation go away. Claude Bernard (1856) provided more direct evidence against the dry-mouth theory. Bernard surgically produced an opening, or fistula, in the esophagus of animals. As long as the fistula remained closed and all

TABLE 9.1 Sources of Typical Daily Fluid Loss and Intake in Humans

Typical Daily Loss		Typical Daily Intake	
Source	**Approximate Daily Quantity**	**Source**	**Approximate Daily Quantity**
Urine	1.4 liters/4.928 cups*	Fluids from beverages	1.2 liters/4.224 cups
Perspiration, evaporation, respiration	0.9 liters/3.168 cups	Fluids contained in food	1.0 liters/3.52 cups
Feces	0.2 liters/0.704 cups	Water	0.3 liters/0.056 cups
TOTAL LOSS	**2.5 liters/8.8 cups**	**TOTAL INTAKE**	**2.5 liters/8.8 cups**

* 1 cup = 8 ounces

water consumed reached the stomach, the animals drank normally. However, when the fistula was open, allowing all of the consumed water to escape without reaching the stomach, Bernard's animals drank continuously. Their mouths were certainly quite wet, but this did not inhibit their drinking in any way.

Kissing is like drinking salted water: you drink and your thirst increases.

Chinese Proverb

Thirst actually occurs as a result of two more sophisticated processes. In the first case, **osmotic thirst** occurs in response to cellular dehydration that results from drops in the intracellular fluid volume. In the second case, **hypovolemic** (low volume) **thirst** occurs in response to drops in blood volume. The double-depletion hypothesis suggests that a combination of these processes contributes to thirst. However, osmotic thirst appears to be the more common mechanism, whereas hypovolemic thirst serves as a less frequently used emergency backup system.

Mechanisms of Osmotic Thirst

You probably have some relevant experience with the most common cause of osmotic thirst: eating salty foods. After you eat and digest a salty meal, your blood becomes more concentrated with sodium. The higher salt content makes the blood hypertonic, or more concentrated, relative to the intracellular fluid. Osmotic pressure will move water out of the cells in an effort to regain the balanced, isotonic state. Receptors sense the lower volume of water in the cells, and you begin to feel very thirsty.

A similar process results in the overdrinking, or polydipsia, that is typical of untreated **diabetes mellitus.** We will discuss diabetes in more detail later in this chapter. People with untreated diabetes are unable to move sugars out of the blood supply, causing the blood to become hypertonic. The cells attempt to compensate by releasing water, and strong sensations of thirst result. The combination of polydipsia and fluids moving from the cells into the blood supply provides an excess of fluids that stimulates urination. Urination further concentrates the blood supply, and the cycle continues. Strong sensations of thirst accompanied by frequent urination are early warning signs of diabetes mellitus.

Cellular dehydration is detected by specialized **osmoreceptors** located in the brain. Verney (1947) coined the term *osmoreceptors* and predicted that these specialized neurons might alter their firing rate when their intracellular fluid levels changed. An area located around the third ventricle, the **organum vasculosum of the lamina terminalis (OVLT),** has been implicated in the detection of cellular dehydration. The OVLT, shown in ■ Figure 9.10, is particularly well situated for a role in detecting blood solute levels because the blood–brain barrier is weak in this area. A series of elegant experiments by Charles Bourque and his colleagues not only established the OVLT as a probable location for osmoreceptors but also provided insight as to how these neurons encode changes in the concentration of their surrounding fluids (Bourque & Oliet, 1997; Nissen, Bourque, & Renaud, 1993). OVLT cells from rats were kept alive in an artificial medium resembling interstitial fluid. If the surrounding fluid was

osmotic thirst Thirst produced by cellular dehydration.

hypovolemic thirst (hi-poe-voe-LEEM-ik) Thirst that results from a decrease in the volume of the extracellular fluid.

diabetes mellitus A disease characterized by insulin deficiency, resulting in hunger, excess sugar in blood and urine, and extreme thirst.

osmoreceptor (oz-moe-ree-SEP–tor) A receptor that detects cellular dehydration.

organum vasculosum of the lamina terminalis (OVLT) (or-GAN-um vas-cue-LOE-sum LAM-in-uh ter-min-AL-is) An area located around the third ventricle in the brain that detects cellular dehydration.

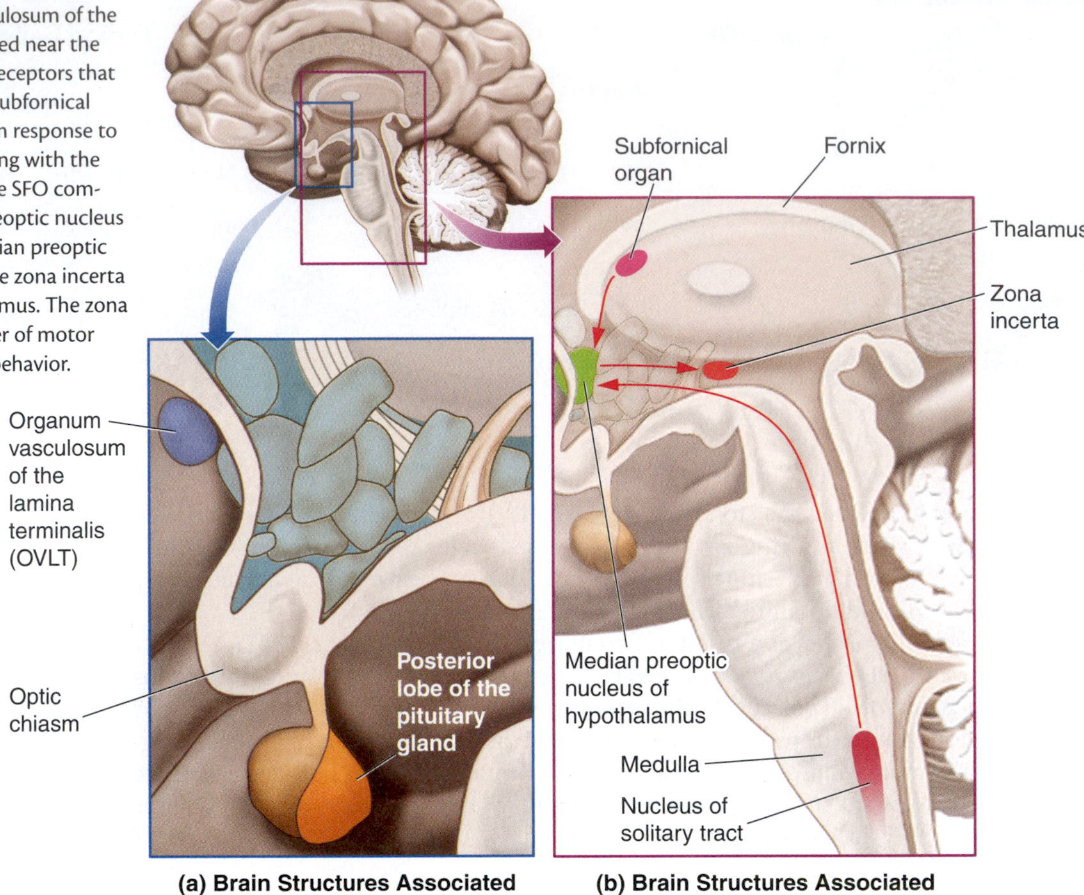

Figure 9.10 Detecting and Resolving Osmotic Thirst (a) The organum vasculosum of the lamina terminalis (OVLT), located near the third ventricle, contains osmoreceptors that detect osmotic thirst. (b) The subfornical organ (SFO) initiates drinking in response to detection of angiotensin II. Along with the nucleus of the solitary tract, the SFO communicates with the median preoptic nucleus of the hypothalamus. The median preoptic nucleus communicates with the zona incerta by way of the lateral hypothalamus. The zona incerta connects with a number of motor areas responsible for drinking behavior.

made hypertonic, leading to loss of fluid from the cells, the OVLT cells increased their firing rates. When the surrounding fluid was made hypotonic, leading to movement of water into the cells, firing rates decreased.

Mechanisms of Hypovolemic Thirst

Hypovolemic thirst results when we experience a drop in the volume of interstitial fluid, blood, or both. The most obvious cause for hypovolemic thirst is the loss of blood due to internal bleeding or a severe injury.

Lower blood volume is sensed by receptors in the heart and kidneys. The wall of the heart muscle contains **baroreceptors** that measure blood pressure. As blood volume decreases, blood pressure decreases as well. The kidneys contain blood-flow receptors that also respond to changes in blood volume. When low blood volume is perceived, thirst is initiated, and the kidneys act to conserve remaining fluids.

Hormones, Sodium, and Thirst

When either cellular dehydration or hypovolemia is sensed, a sequence of hormone actions helps return fluid levels to their set point. As shown in Figure 9.11, both osmoreceptors and baroreceptors stimulate release of **antidiuretic hormone (ADH),** also known as **vasopressin,** by the posterior pituitary gland. Diuretic medications promote water loss through urination, so an antidiuretic promotes water retention.

ADH has two major effects on the kidneys. First, ADH signals the kidneys to reduce urine production. Second, ADH stimulates the kidneys to release the hormone **renin** into the blood supply. Renin is also released in response to activity in the kidneys' blood-flow receptors. Once in the bloodstream, renin triggers the conversion of

baroreceptor A receptor in the heart and kidneys that measures blood pressure.

antidiuretic hormone (ADH) A hormone that promotes retention of fluid by signaling the kidneys to reduce urine production and by stimulating the release of renin. Also known as vasopressin.

vasopressin (VAS-oh-press-in) Another name for antidiuretic hormone (ADH).

renin A substance released by the kidneys that converts angiotensinogen into angiotensin II.

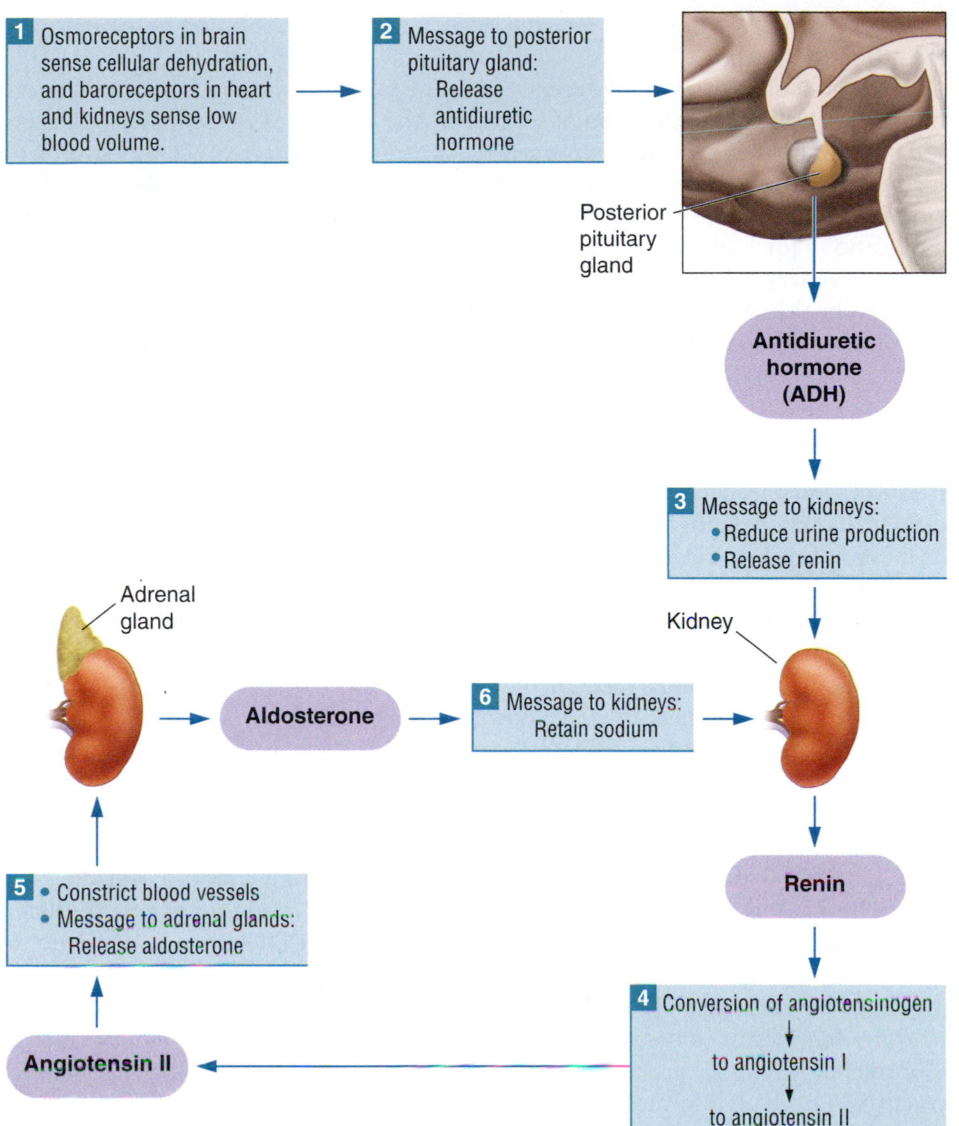
1 Osmoreceptors in brain sense cellular dehydration, and baroreceptors in heart and kidneys sense low blood volume.
2 Message to posterior pituitary gland: Release antidiuretic hormone
Posterior pituitary gland
Antidiuretic hormone (ADH)
3 Message to kidneys: • Reduce urine production • Release renin
Kidney
Renin
4 Conversion of angiotensinogen to angiotensin I to angiotensin II
Angiotensin II
5 • Constrict blood vessels • Message to adrenal glands: Release aldosterone
Adrenal gland
Aldosterone
6 Message to kidneys: Retain sodium

FIGURE 9.11 Antidiuretic Hormone Begins a Sequence of Events Leading to Fluid Conservation

angiotensinogen, a blood protein, into **angiotensin II.** There is an angiotensin I, which is produced as a brief, interim step between the blood proteins and angiotensin II, but angiotensin II is the important, biologically active component. Angiotensin II constricts blood vessels, helping to maintain blood pressure. Angiotensin II also triggers the release of the hormone **aldosterone** from the adrenal glands, located above the kidneys. Aldosterone signals the kidneys to retain sodium rather than excrete it in the urine.

Levels of water and sodium are intricately bound together but are managed by different processes. ADH controls the retention of water, and aldosterone controls the retention of sodium. Sodium is essential to the maintenance of the extracellular fluid. Without sodium solutes, the extracellular fluid would become hypotonic, and too much water would move into the cells. When blood volume is lost, as in a serious injury, treatments designed to increase extracellular sodium levels prevent further loss of water into the cells and stimulate some release of water from cells into the blood supply.

Low blood volume stimulates a specific hunger for sodium. Although it might seem odd that thirst and sodium craving can occur simultaneously (eating salty foods usually makes us more thirsty), this is exactly what happens during hypovolemia. There are a number of ways to induce hypovolemia experimentally without removing a quantity of blood. Injections of formalin (Rescorla & Freberg, 1978) or propylene glycol (Fitzsimons, 1961) can produce both excessive thirst and salt cravings in experimental animals. Once hypovolemia is artificially induced,

angiotensinogen (an-gee-oh ten-SIN-oh-gen) A blood protein converted into angiotensin II by renin.

angiotensin II (an-gee-oh-TEN-sin) A hormone that constricts blood vessels to maintain blood pressure and triggers the release of aldosterone.

aldosterone (al-DOS-ter-one) A hormone that signals the kidneys to retain sodium.

animals will prefer a normally rejected hypertonic sodium solution to regular water (Fitzsimons, 1961).

Normal sodium levels represent a balance between dietary intake and excretion by the kidneys. If excretion of sodium by the kidneys is inadequate, high blood pressure and its associated complications, such as stroke, often occur. Chronically high sodium levels in the blood promote the release of water from cells into the circulation due to osmosis. This higher blood volume increases blood pressure. Most medications for high blood pressure are diuretics because promoting urination is an effective way to reduce blood volume. Lower-than-normal sodium levels are also a risk to health. Vomiting and diarrhea due to illnesses such as the flu can reduce sodium, and therefore blood volume and blood pressure, to dangerously low, life-threatening levels.

The Initiation of Drinking

How does thirst lead to drinking behavior? Angiotensin II appears to stimulate drinking through its action on the **subfornical organ (SFO),** which was illustrated in Figure 9.10. Its location is below (sub) the fornix, near the junction of the two lateral ventricles. Like the OVLT, the SFO is located in an area at which the blood–brain barrier is weak. Much research supports the role of the SFO as a target for angiotensin II in the brain. Kadekaro and his colleagues (1989) surgically disconnected the SFO from other parts of the brain. Even without normal neural input, neurons in the SFO increased their firing rates when angiotensin II was injected into the blood supply. This result strongly supports the idea that the SFO can respond to circulating angiotensin II alone, without neural input from other areas of the brain. Lesions of SFO interfere with angiotensin-induced drinking (Simpson, Epstein, & Camardo, 1978). Electrical stimulation of the SFO produces drinking behavior (Smith, Beninger, & Ferguson, 1995).

The SFO in turn forms connections with the **median preoptic nucleus,** also shown in Figure 9.10. Unlike the OVLT and the SFO, the median preoptic nucleus is not located in an area where the blood–brain barrier is weak. Although the structure does contain receptors for angiotensin II, it cannot respond to angiotensin circulating in the blood. Lind and Johnson (1982) have suggested that angiotensin serves as a neurotransmitter in connections between the SFO and the median preoptic nucleus. The median preoptic nucleus also receives input from the **nucleus of the solitary tract (NST),** which is located in the medulla. The nucleus of the solitary tract in turn receives input from baroreceptors in the circulatory system and osmoreceptors located in the digestive tract. The median preoptic nucleus communicates with the **lateral hypothalamus (LH),** which projects to the **zona incerta** of the midbrain. The zona incerta sends information to a number of motor regions, including the basal ganglia, the red nucleus, and the ventral horn of the spinal cord (Ricardo, 1981). Stimulation of the zona incerta produces drinking behavior, suggesting that this structure is responsible for initiating the motor components of drinking behavior.

subfornical organ (SFO) (sub-FOR-ni-kul) An area of the brain, located near the junction of the two lateral ventricles, that regulates drinking.

median preoptic nucleus An area of the hypothalamus that is involved with drinking behavior.

nucleus of the solitary tract (NST) A structure in the medulla that processes information from baroreceptors, osmoreceptors, glucoreceptors, and taste receptors.

lateral hypothalamus (LH) A part of the hypothalamus that participates in behavioral responses to thirst and in the initiation of feeding behavior.

zona incerta (ZOE-nuh in-SER-ta) An area of the midbrain that participates in the initiation of drinking behavior.

hyponatremia (hi-pon-uh-TREE-mee-uh) A life threatening condition in which sodium concentrations in the extracellular fluid are too low.

Cessation of Drinking

We typically stop drinking long before water levels in either the intracellular or extracellular compartments return to normal. Fluid receptors have been identified in the mouth, throat, and at various levels of the digestive system. Lesions of the septal area of the brain generally produce overdrinking, suggesting that this structure plays a role in the cessation of drinking (Liao & Yeh, 2000). Finding the correct stopping point for fluid consumption is not critical because any excess water can usually be excreted.

Overdrinking under certain conditions, however, results in **hyponatremia,** a condition in which extracellular sodium levels drop 10 percent or more below normal (Vellaichamy, 2001). Untreated hyponatremia results in nausea, vomiting, cramps, and disorientation. If the condition persists, seizures, coma (due to swelling of the brain), and death may follow. A large number of medical problems result in hyponatremia, including congestive heart failure, kidney failure, and some tumors. Recently, the condition has become more common due to the increased popularity of extreme endurance events.

WHY DOES THIS MATTER?

When Too Much Fluid Is Not a Good Thing

Typically, we do not have to worry about drinking too much water because excess water can be removed easily through urination. Under some circumstances, however, the normal regulation of fluid levels fails, often with very serious effects. We have already discussed overdrinking in the context of endurance sports and disease, but there are other situations in which this problem occurs. Understanding how we regulate fluids matters because the consequences of both underdrinking and overdrinking can be fatal.

One of the dangerous effects of MDMA (ecstasy, see Chapter 4) is the drug's ability to increase the secretion of ADH (Wolff et al., 2006). As in the case of endurance athletes with hyponatremia, increased ADH levels inhibit urination and stimulate drinking. Consequently, users of MDMA who have access to water may overdrink, leading to the movement of too much water into brain cells, which in turn can cause coma and, potentially, death (Traub, Hoffman, & Nelson, 2002).

Drinking too much water also resulted in the tragic death of 28-year-old Jennifer Lea Strange, who entered a contest sponsored by a local radio station called "Hold your wee for a Wii" (Associated Press, 2007). Strange drank over two gallons of water without urinating. After returning home, she called in sick to her employer, and was found dead five hours later. The county coroner reported that she had died of water intoxication in her effort to win her three children a Nintendo Wii. The DJs responsible for the contest were fired.

Urination might also fail as a method for preventing a buildup of fluids when people are drinking alcohol. Not only is alcohol a diuretic, which means that it stimulates the production of urine, but it also acts as a general anesthetic, dulling the messages from the bladder that tell us it's time to find a restroom. Consequently, one of the more unpleasant effects of binge drinking is rupture of the bladder caused by overfilling (Dooldeniya et al., 2007). Patients in this unfortunate situation might have symptoms that are mistaken for a urinary tract infection, but a correct diagnosis is critical. One to five percent of patients die from the infections associated with a burst bladder (ibid.).

Under normal circumstances, extracellular fluid levels are negatively correlated with sodium concentrations. When fluid levels are high, sodium concentrations are low, and vice versa. During extreme endurance activities, however, low fluid levels and low sodium concentrations can coexist. During a long race, an athlete might lose unusually high amounts of sodium and water through perspiration, vomiting, and urination. As a result, conflicting messages will be sent to the fluid regulation system. The release of ADH cannot simultaneously increase in response to low fluid levels and decrease in response to low sodium concentrations. Because protecting blood volume enjoys a higher priority in terms of survival, the pituitary will continue to pump out ADH under these circumstances. Water is retained due to ADH's inhibition of urination, even though this further reduces the concentration of sodium (Hiller, 1989). As the extracellular fluid becomes increasingly hypotonic, water moves into the cells, generating a strong sensation of hypovolemic thirst. In response to these sensations, the athlete might drink large amounts of plain water during the race, further compounding the hyponatremia (Noakes, 1993). Hyponatremia can be prevented by making sure the athlete ingests sufficient sodium before and during the race, in the form of either salt tablets or salty drinks and foods.

FIGURE 9.12
Do Sports Drinks Prevent Dehydration? Drinking plain water is not always the best way to maintain fluid levels, particularly when people are physically active in hot and humid conditions. The extra sodium provided by sports drinks might be helpful in maintaining fluids during heavy exercise. Content from one brand of sports drink to another can vary dramatically, and athletes should read labels carefully.

Thirst and Sports Drinks

In 1966, scientists at the University of Florida developed a new beverage that helped the Gator football players retain their energy during games in the high heat and humidity conditions of Gainesville. The beverage was very aptly named Gatorade. Most sports drinks provide more sodium than do water, soft drinks, juice, or other beverages. The extra sodium in sports drinks helps athletes retain fluids and might also prevent hyponatremia. The saltier taste encourages athletes to drink more fluids than they might otherwise be willing to do. Although the average couch potato doesn't need a sports drink while walking around the block, people engaged in higher-intensity activities, like the football player in Figure 9.12, often find such drinks useful.

INTERIM SUMMARY 9.2

Summary Table: Brain Mechanisms for Initiating Drinking

Stimulus	Receptors	Step 1	Step 2	Step 3	Step 4	Step 5
Osmotic thirst	Osmoreceptors	OVLT	OVLT, NST, and SFO communicate with the median preoptic area.	Median preoptic area communicates with the lateral hypothalamus (LH).	LH communicates with the zona incerta.	Zona incerta initiates drinking through connections with the motor systems.
Hypovolemic thirst	Cardiac baroreceptors	Communicate with the NST via the vagus nerve				
	Kidney baroreceptors	Communicate with the SFO by stimulating increased angiotensin II				

Summary Points

1. Drops in intracellular fluid volume produce osmotic thirst, which is detected by osmoreceptors located in the organum vasculosum of the lamina terminalis (OVLT). **(LO3)**
2. Decreases in the volume of the extracellular fluid, such as blood, result in hypovolemic thirst. Baroreceptors located in the heart and kidneys detect drops in blood pressure. **(LO3)**
3. Both osmoreceptors and baroreceptors stimulate the release of antidiuretic hormone (ADH). ADH signals the kidneys to reduce urine production and initiates a sequence leading to increased production of angiotensin II. Angiotensin II constricts blood vessels to maintain blood pressure and triggers the release of aldosterone. Aldosterone signals the kidneys to retain sodium. **(LO4)**
4. Angiotensin II appears to stimulate drinking by its action on the subfornical organ (SFO). Drinking stops in response to receptors located in the mouth, throat, and digestive system. **(LO4)**

Review Questions

1. What are the differences between osmotic thirst and hypovolemic thirst?
2. Once thirst is perceived, what processes lead to drinking behavior?

Hunger: Regulation of the Body's Nutrients

As a child my family's menu consisted of two choices: take it or leave it.
Buddy Hacket

Emotions and learning exert more influence on our eating behaviors than they do on the regulatory behaviors discussed so far. Not only do we eat to obtain the energy and specific nutrients needed by our bodies, but we eat for pleasure as well. Complex cultural and psychological factors can overwhelm the body's natural regulatory mechanisms, leading to eating disorders such as obesity or anorexia nervosa.

The Influence of Culture on Food Choices

Human beings take in a remarkable variety of nutrients. The traditional diet of the Inuit people who live in Arctic regions contains little vegetable matter at all, whereas people following a vegan diet eat only plant material.

Many American foods are based on dairy products, but this is not the case in every culture. Some people no longer produce the enzymes necessary to process fresh milk products after infancy, resulting in lactose intolerance. The use of dairy products correlates with the geographical distribution of lactose intolerance. As shown in ■ Figure 9.13, the highest rates of lactose intolerance occur among Asians, whose

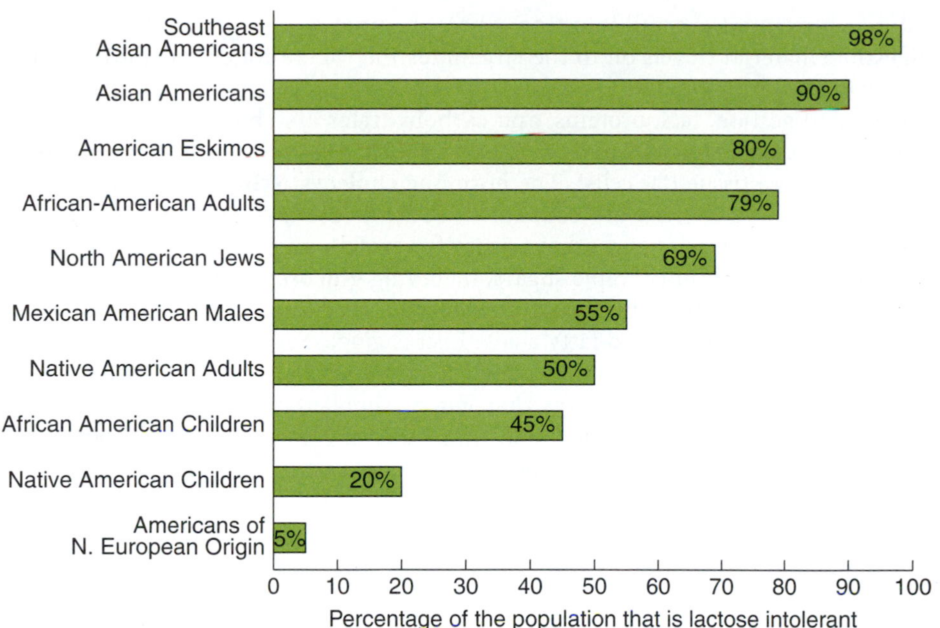

FIGURE 9.13 Lactose Tolerance Correlates with Use of Dairy Products People who became relatively dependent on milk products as a source of protein, such as Scandinavians and other Northern Europeans, are much more likely to be tolerant of lactose. Where the practice of keeping dairy herds was not historically prevalent, such as in Asia, higher numbers of people show lactose intolerance, and dairy products are not popular. *Source*: Adapted from Basu et al (1996).

consumption of dairy products is very low. Lactose intolerance is rare among people from Scandinavia and parts of the Middle East, where reliance on dairy products has been historically high (Rozin & Pelchat, 1988).

Learned food preferences begin at a surprisingly early point in life (Mennella & Beauchamp, 2005). Exposure to flavors through the amniotic fluid or breast milk appears to influence later food choices. When pregnant and nursing women consumed carrot juice rather than plain water, their infants ate much more cereal that was prepared with carrot juice than with water, and they were rated as appearing to enjoy the carrot cereal more (Mennella, Jagnow, & Beauchamp, 2001). This mechanism could promote learning about safe and available foods in very young children.

FIGURE 9.14 The Major Structures of the Digestive Tract

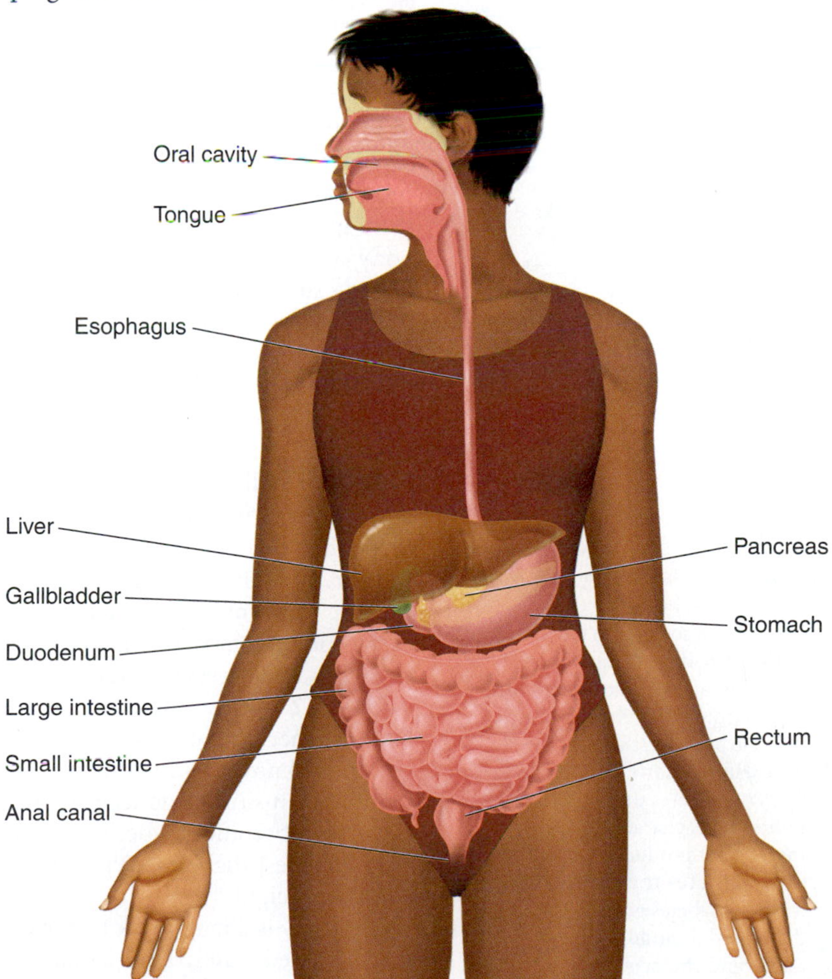

THE PROCESS OF DIGESTION

Foods are broken down into usable chemicals by the digestive tract, shown in Figure 9.14. Digestion begins in the mouth, where saliva is mixed with food. The water and enzymes contained in saliva begin the breakdown of food into a semiliquid state that can then be swallowed. Saliva is automatically secreted when food enters the mouth, courtesy of the autonomic nervous system. However, Pavlov demonstrated conclusively that this process is quickly modifiable through experience. If you see or smell a delicious chocolate cake in the oven, you might experience anticipatory salivation based on your past experience with chocolate cakes.

After food is swallowed, it proceeds through the esophagus to the stomach, where it is mixed with hydrochloric acid and pepsin. These chemicals break down the food particles into even smaller pieces. The partially digested food is released periodically through the duodenum into the small intestine, where the process of digestion is completed. Indigestible material travels on to the large intestine, where water is reabsorbed and feces are formed.

During digestion, fats, proteins, and carbohydrates are absorbed into the blood supply and circulated to waiting tissues. Fats are either used for immediate energy or stored by adipose tissue (fat cells). The hormone **cholecystokinin (CCK)** is released when large quantities of fat are consumed. Proteins are broken down into amino acids and used by muscles and other tissues for growth and protein synthesis. Carbohydrates are broken into simple sugars, including **glucose.** Under normal circumstances, glucose is the exclusive source of energy for the brain, whereas the rest of the body can use both glucose and fatty acids. Excess glucose is stored as fat by adipose tissue or converted by the liver into a complex carbohydrate called **glycogen** for storage. If the body requires more energy than can be supplied by the glucose circulating in the blood, such as during a period of fasting, the liver converts stored glycogen back into readily available glucose. Consequently, we maintain a fairly steady level of blood glucose over time.

Part of the secret of success in life is to eat what you like and let the food fight it out inside.
Mark Twain

If continued fasting depletes stores of glycogen, all body structures except the brain begin to use fatty acids from adipose tissue for energy. Energy can be supplied by ketones, chemicals produced from stored fat by the liver. People following extremely low-carbohydrate diets, such as the Atkins diet, often rely on ketones for energy. In addition, fasting causes muscle tissue to break down, and the liver converts the resulting amino acids into glucose. This is a good reason for moderation in dieting. Even with the loss of two to three pounds per week on a sensible, balanced diet, approximately 25 percent of the weight lost will be from bone and muscle (Nunez et al., 1997).

The Pancreatic Hormones

The body's supply of energy from glucose is regulated in large part by two hormones, **glucagon** and **insulin,** that are manufactured by the pancreas. The pancreas, shown in Figure 9.14, is a large gland located behind the stomach. Glucagon converts stored glycogen back into glucose. Levels of glucagon increase during periods of fasting, as the body taps into its glycogen stores to maintain blood glucose levels. Insulin helps store glucose as glycogen and assists in moving glucose from the blood supply into body cells. As shown in ■ Figure 9.15, levels of insulin normally increase after a meal, helping some glucose circulating in the blood supply to move into cells and the rest to be stored as glycogen. Insulin levels are lowest during long periods of fasting.

Disturbances in the activity of the pancreatic hormones have serious health consequences. **Type 1 diabetes mellitus** is usually diagnosed in childhood or young adulthood and accounts for 5 to 10 percent of all diabetes diagnoses in the United States (National Institute of Diabetes & Digestive & Kidney Diseases [NIDDK], 2002). Type 1 diabetes usually occurs when insulin-producing pancreatic cells are attacked and destroyed by the body's immune system. Without insulin, glucose from food circulates through the bloodstream without being absorbed or stored by the body's tissues. The cells are literally starving while high levels of glucose are excreted in the urine. The excess circulating glucose causes an imbalance of solutes between the intracellular and extracellular compartments, producing enormous thirst. Fatigue, weight loss, excess drinking, and excess urination are classic symptoms of untreated diabetes.

Type 2 diabetes mellitus is diagnosed when individuals produce insulin but their bodies either do not make sufficient amounts of insulin or use insulin efficiently—a condition known as insulin resistance. After a few years of insulin resistance, the amount of insulin produced by the pancreas begins to decline (NIDDK, 2002), and the person becomes diabetic. Symptoms of Type 2 diabetes are the same as in Type 1. Unlike Type 1 diabetes, Type 2 usually can be prevented and treated by maintaining a healthy weight.

Obesity is a major risk factor for Type 2 diabetes. Because obesity rates are rising in the United States, Type 2 diabetes rates are reaching epidemic proportions, affecting over 20 million Americans (Gerberding, 2007). Not only are rates of diabetes

cholecystokinin (CCK) (kole-uh-sis-tuh-KINE-in) A gut hormone released in response to the consumption of fats that also acts as a central nervous system neurotransmitter that signals satiety.

glucose A type of sugar found in foods that is a major source of energy for living organisms.

glycogen (GLIE-kuh-gen) A complex carbohydrate used to store energy in the liver.

glucagon (GLUE-kuh-gone) A pancreatic hormone that converts glycogen into glucose.

insulin A pancreatic hormone that facilitates the movement of sugars from the blood supply into the body's tissues.

type 1 diabetes mellitus The form of diabetes that appears early in life and is characterized by insufficient production of insulin.

type 2 diabetes mellitus The form of diabetes generally diagnosed in middle-aged adults and characterized by resistance to insulin.

expected to double by 2025 (ibid.), but Type 2 diabetes, once rarely diagnosed in people below the age of 40, is affecting more children and youth (Ludwig & Ebbeling, 2001). Although the causes of Type 2 diabetes are varied and not well understood, one possibility appears to be the use of fructose, an inexpensive sweetener frequently used in processed foods (Miller & Adeli, 2008). When consumed in excess, fructose leads to insulin resistance and other pre-diabetic states.

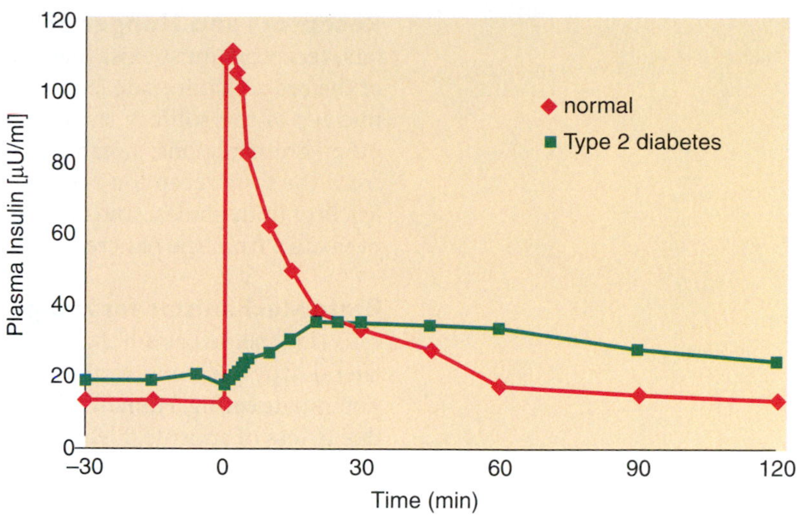

FIGURE 9.15
Insulin Release Is Reduced in Type 2 Diabetes Following a meal (time 0), a healthy person experiences a large spike in insulin levels in the circulation. In contrast, a person with Type 2 diabetes has a much slower and less dramatic release of insulin. Consequently, the person with Type 2 diabetes will not be able to move glucose out of the blood into cells requiring nutrients. The appetite-suppressing action of insulin is also less effective for a person with diabetes.

The Initiation of Eating

We respond to both external and internal cues that make us feel hungry. Among the external cues are factors such as time of day, the delightful sights and smells of favorite foods, or the social setting we are in when food is presented. These external cues often encourage us to eat when our bodies do not need nutrients or to eat more food than we require to meet our energy needs.

Internal hunger cues are generated when our body is genuinely short on nutrients. One internal sign of hunger occurs when our stomachs begin to rumble. In an early study on the role of stomach contractions in hunger, Walter Cannon persuaded his colleague A. L. Washburn to swallow a balloon attached to an air pump (Cannon & Washburn, 1912). The balloon allowed Washburn's stomach contractions to be monitored. Although Washburn's feelings of hunger did correlate with his stomach contractions, hunger appears to be much more complicated. Patients who have had their stomachs removed still experience hunger sensations in the general region where the stomach used to be. We typically initiate eating long before our stomachs begin to growl, so other systems must also be involved in making us feel hungry.

Hunger can occur as a function of blood glucose levels. Glucose levels in the blood are high just following a meal. As glucose levels drop, a person begins to feel hungry again. Glucose levels are intimately tied to insulin levels. Insulin is normally released in response to eating or even to the anticipation of eating. Therefore, we would expect high levels of insulin and glucose to correspond to satiety, whereas low levels of insulin and glucose should correspond with fasting and feeling hungry. Unfortunately for our hypothesis, two observations are inconsistent with this simple approach. First of all, injections of insulin generally produce feelings of hunger instead of satiety (Vijande et al., 1990). Second, patients with diabetes experience substantial hunger in spite of high levels of circulating glucose. An improved glucose hypothesis suggests that it is not the total amount of circulating glucose that determines whether we feel hungry but the availability of that glucose to our cells (Mayer, 1955). In a healthy person, circulating glucose is the same as available glucose, and hunger will occur when blood glucose levels are low. However, in the person with diabetes, circulating glucose is not available to cells due to reduced insulin functioning. As a result, hunger occurs in spite of ample supplies of glucose. An injection of insulin drives circulating blood glucose into cells, reducing the amount of available glucose and producing sensations of hunger.

Another explanation for why we feel hungry is a "lipostatic theory" that suggests that hunger results from low fat supplies (Kennedy, 1953). A person of normal weight generally maintains enough body fat to provide calories for five to six weeks of total starvation. Obesity obviously increases the amount of time an individual can survive without food. A person monitored by Stewart and Fleming (1973) survived a total fast of 382 days, while his weight went from 207 kilograms (455.4 pounds) to 81.6 kilograms (179.5 pounds). It is also likely that we have mechanisms for assessing levels of circulating amino acids. However, assessing these mechanisms experimentally would be difficult to do because depriving a research participant of these essential building blocks for proteins would affect much more than just hunger.

Receptors and Hunger If hunger results from low levels of available glucose and fats, receptors must exist that can assess nutrient levels and communicate with areas of the brain that initiate feeding behavior. **Glucoreceptors** have been identified in the nucleus of the solitary tract (NST) in the brainstem. The NST communicates with other brain regions, notably with the hypothalamus. The NST also receives input from the taste reception system (see Chapter 7). Other receptors in the liver monitor levels of both glucose and fatty acids. Glucoreceptors in the liver influence the release of insulin from the pancreas and communicate with the NST via the vagus nerve.

Brain Mechanisms for Hunger Early research suggested that the lateral hypothalamus (LH) served as a hunger center (Anand & Brobeck, 1951). Rats with lesions in the lateral hypothalamus would starve to death in the presence of food because they would not initiate eating. Human patients with tumors in the LH often lose considerable weight due to loss of appetite. Electrical stimulation of the LH produces immediate feeding.

Subsequent research raised doubts about a simplistic role for the LH as a feeding center. If rats with LH lesions were force-fed, they eventually began to initiate feeding on their own again. The LH probably participates in initiating eating, but other structures that will be described in the next section are also involved.

Hunger is the best sauce in the world.
Cervantes

Neurochemicals and Hunger Feeding behavior is influenced by complex interactions among several neurochemicals. Fat cells produce and secrete a substance known as **leptin,** from *leptos*, the Greek word for "thin" (Zhang et al., 1994). When fat stores are low, levels of circulating leptin will also be low. As shown in ■ Figure 9.16, initial reports that administering additional leptin to obese rodents reduced their weight led many researchers to believe that leptin could be used to treat human obesity. Unfortunately, obese humans already produce large amounts of leptin, but they seem to be resistant to its effects (Friedman & Halaas, 1998). Providing more leptin is unlikely to help obese individuals lose weight.

Leptin communicates with neurons in the **arcuate nucleus** of the hypothalamus, shown in ■ Figure 9.17. When leptin levels are low, cells in the arcuate nucleus use **neuropeptide Y (NPY)** and **agouti-related protein (AgRP)** to communicate with the LH and with the **paraventricular** (around the ventricle) **nucleus (PVN)** of the hypothalamus. Consequently, the parasympathetic division of the autonomic nervous system is activated, and feeding behavior is stimulated.

Experimental evidence supports a role for NPY and AgRP in the initiation of feeding. When NPY is applied directly to the hypothalamus, animals will begin eating

■ **FIGURE 9.16**
Leptin Knockout Rats Become Obese Genetically engineered rats lacking the *obese* gene (*ob*) are unable to produce leptin and are enormously obese, like the rat in the back. When these obese rats are injected with leptin, they lose weight, like the rat in front. Researchers have been disappointed to learn that the same process is unlikely to help obese humans, who are already producing large amounts of leptin but appear to be resistant to its effects.

glucoreceptor (glue-koe-ree-SEP-tor) A receptor that is sensitive to the presence of glucose.
leptin A substance secreted by fat cells that helps the body regulate its fat stores.
arcuate nucleus (AR-cue-ut) A cluster of neurons involved with feeding located within the hypothalamus.
neuropeptide Y (NPY) A peptide neurochemical secreted by the arcuate nucleus of the hypothalamus that initiates eating.
agouti-related protein (AgRP) A small protein secreted by the arcuate nucleus that initiates eating.
paraventricular nucleus (PVN) (pear-ah-ven-TRI-cu-lar) A portion of the hypothalamus involved with the regulation of hunger.

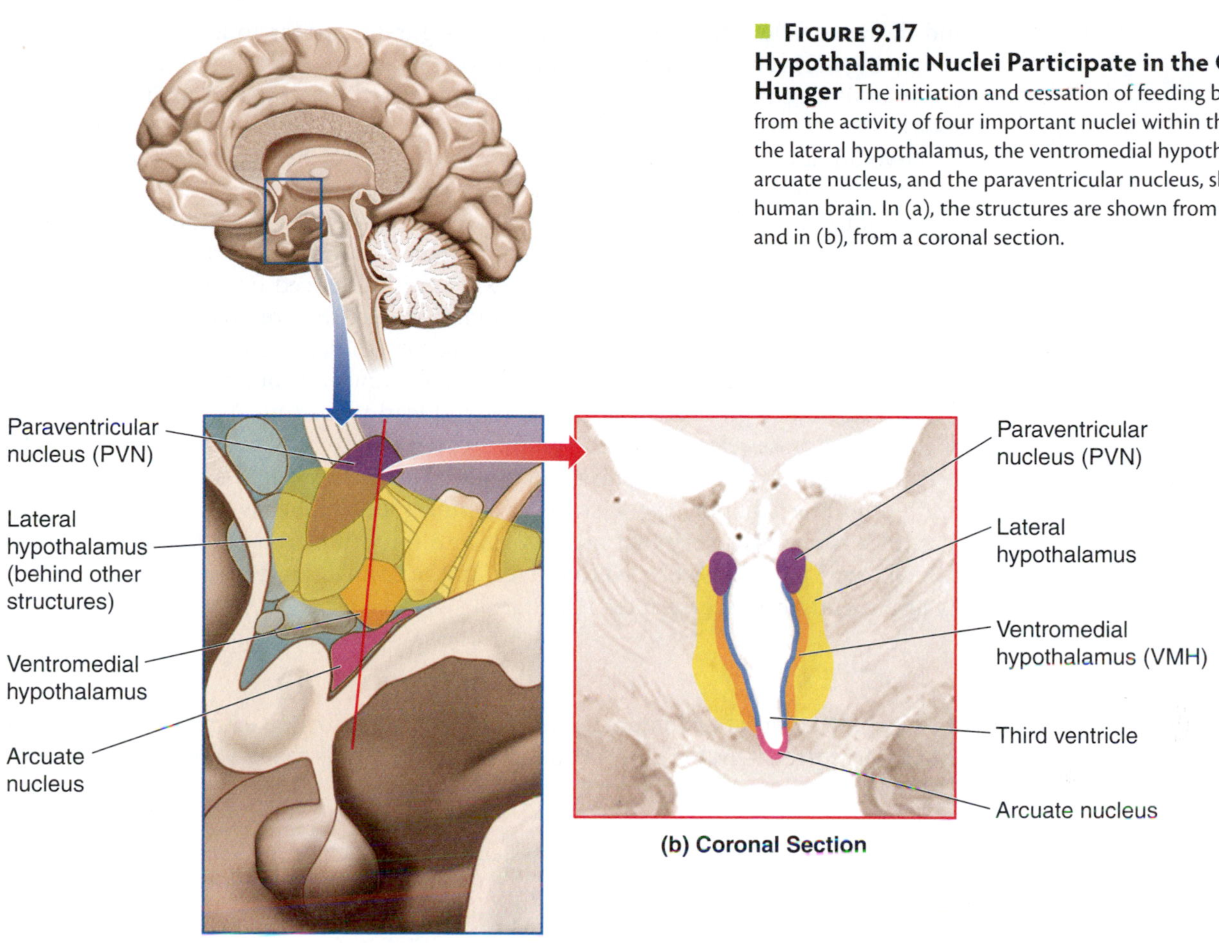

FIGURE 9.17
Hypothalamic Nuclei Participate in the Control of Hunger The initiation and cessation of feeding behavior result from the activity of four important nuclei within the hypothalamus: the lateral hypothalamus, the ventromedial hypothalamus, the arcuate nucleus, and the paraventricular nucleus, shown here in a human brain. In (a), the structures are shown from a sagittal view, and in (b), from a coronal section.

immediately (Stanley, Magdalin, Seirafi, Thomas, & Leibowitz, 1993). If NPY receptors in the hypothalamus are blocked, animals will fail to eat following either food deprivation or NPY infusions (Myers, Wooten, Ames, & Nyce, 1995). AgRP acts as an antagonist at a special receptor site in the lateral hypothalamus known as an MC4 receptor. When MC4 receptors are blocked, feeding is initiated. We will see later how agonists at these same MC4 receptors inhibit feeding.

In addition to activating the parasympathetic nervous system and stimulating eating behavior, the release of NPY and AgRP in the lateral hypothalamus and PVN suppresses the release of two pituitary hormones, **thyroid-stimulating hormone (TSH)** and **adrenocorticotropic hormone (ACTH).** TSH and ACTH both increase metabolic rate, so suppressing them slows the body's use of energy, allowing some of the nutrients taken in during feeding to be used to replenish the fat stores. Parasympathetic activity, feeding behavior, and TSH/ACTH suppression work together to allow an animal to find, eat, and store nutrients. As fat stores return to normal levels, more leptin is released, NPY and AgRP are less active, and the feeding cycle tapers off.

Some neurons within the lateral hypothalamus communicate via yet another important peptide neurotransmitter, **melanin-concentrating hormone (MCH).** These neurons project widely throughout the cerebral cortex and might provide the necessary link between the hypothalamus' identification of hunger and higher-order motivated behaviors that lead to eating and the storage of nutrients. Mice genetically modified to be incapable of producing MCH burned energy faster, ate less, and had less body fat (Shimada, Tritos, Lowell, Flier, & Maratos-Flier, 1998). Unfortunately, these mice are also much more likely to die of starvation than normal mice.

The hormone **ghrelin** is produced primarily by the pancreas and the lining of the stomach, and receptors for ghrelin have been found in the arcuate nucleus and the ventromedial hypothalamus (Inui et al., 2004). Levels of ghrelin are highest during fasting

thyroid-stimulating hormone (TSH) A pituitary hormone that stimulates the growth and function of the thyroid gland, which in turn increases metabolic rate.

adrenocorticotropic hormone (ACTH) (uh-DREE-noh-kore-ti-koh-TROE-pik) A pituitary hormone that stimulates the adrenal glands.

melanin-concentrating hormone (MCH) A hormone that interacts with leptin and plays a role in the regulation of eating.

ghrelin (GRELL-in) A hormone produced in the stomach that stimulates feeding behavior.

and decrease following a meal. Not only does ghrelin appear to act as a short-term circulating hormone that stimulates hunger, but it also appears to affect feeding by acting on brain circuits involved with memory and reward (Olszewski, Schiöth, & Levine, 2008).

Two additional neuropeptides, known as **orexins** or hypocretins, are produced in the lateral hypothalamus (de Lecea et al., 1998; Sakurai et al., 1998). Injection of orexins into the hypothalamus results in increased eating in rats (Sakurai et al., 1998). Levels of both NPY and the orexins are higher following food deprivation (Sahu, Kalra, & Kalra, 1988). Cells releasing orexins are influenced by leptin levels. When leptin levels are high, indicating sufficient fat is stored, the orexin cells are inhibited, and feeding is reduced. When leptin levels are low, indicating fat stores are low, the orexin cells are active, orexins are released, and feeding is stimulated. Orexin cells are also stimulated by ghrelin, which again should lead to feeding. Neurons that release orexins, like those releasing MCH, project widely in the cerebral cortex as well as to regulatory centers in the midbrain and pons. These neurons play a more general role in linking internal homeostatic states to complex feeding behaviors (Sakurai, 2002). In addition, the discovery that orexins play an important role in the sleep disorder narcolepsy (Siegel, 1999) has led to interest in the connection between feeding, activity levels, and sleep (see Chapter 11).

Great eaters and great sleepers are incapable of anything else that is great.
Henry IV of France

Satiety

We use both external and internal cues to decide when to stop eating as well as when to start. Unfortunately, the current obesity epidemic shows that we are quite capable of overriding or ignoring our internal cues.

Assessing Satiety **Satiety,** or fullness, occurs long before sufficient nutrients make their way into cells. Stomach fullness provides an early warning signal to tell us that we have eaten enough. In extreme cases of obesity, some people have a portion of their stomach stapled in hopes of feeling full faster and therefore eating less. The intestines also provide satiety signals. The duodenum, shown previously in Figure 9.14, joins the stomach and the small intestines. When duodenal glucoreceptors sense sugars, eating generally stops quickly. The arrival of food, especially very fatty food, at the duodenum signals the release of the peptide cholecystokinin (CCK). CCK promotes the release of insulin by the pancreas and contracts the gallbladder to release bile to help break down fats. CCK clearly contributes to feelings of satiety (Stacher, 1986), but the exact mechanism for this effect is unclear. CCK also functions in the brain as a neurotransmitter related to satiety. CCK antagonists increase eating, indicating that CCK has an inhibitory effect on feeding behavior (Cooper & Dourish, 1990).

Figure 9.18
Weight Gain in VMH Syndrome
Lesions of the ventromedial hypothalamus result in substantial weight gains. This rat is about three times heavier than a normal rat.

Courtesy Neal Miller, Department of Psychology, Yale University

Brain Mechanisms for Satiety Early research suggested that the **ventromedial hypothalamus (VMH),** shown in Figure 9.17, might serve as a satiety center. Lesions of the VMH in rats produced VMH syndrome, characterized by large weight gains and picky eating habits (Hoebel & Teitelbaum, 1966). If their food is mixed with quinine, which is quite bitter, VMH rats will eat much less than normal control rats (Sclafani, Springer, & Kluge, 1976). A rat with VMH syndrome is shown in Figure 9.18.

As we found in the case of the LH and feeding, it is overly simplistic to view the VMH as a single center for satiety. Lesions of the VMH not only destroy the VMH nucleus itself but also damage important adjacent fiber pathways. Among these pathways are fibers connecting the paraventricular nucleus (PVN) to the nucleus of the solitary tract (NST) in the brainstem. As we learned previously, the NST receives information from glucoreceptors and taste receptors and participates in energy storage. Disruption of this pathway could easily produce abnormal eating patterns. VMH lesions also result in excess insulin production. Chronically low-circulating glucose levels due to excess insulin produce constant hunger and feeding.

Neurochemicals and Satiety When body fat levels are high, higher concentrations of leptin are found in the blood. High levels of circulating leptin interact with a

orexin A peptide neurochemical produced in the lateral hypothalamus that stimulates eating. Also known as hypocretin.
satiety The sensation of being full, cessation of eating.
ventromedial hypothalamus (VMH) An area within the hypothalamus that participates in satiety.

second set of neurons in the arcuate nucleus, distinct from the neurons that respond to low levels of leptin. This second set of neurons is the source of two additional neuropeptides, **alpha melanocyte stimulating hormone** (**αMSH**) and **cocaine- and amphetamine-regulated transcript (CART).** Projections from the arcuate nucleus neurons travel once again to the PVN, LH, and autonomic nervous system control centers in the brainstem and spinal cord. Alpha-MSH and CART cause the pituitary gland to release TSH and ACTH, raising body metabolic rates. Alpha-MSH and CART also activate the sympathetic division of the autonomic nervous system, increasing metabolism and body temperature and inhibiting feeding behavior.

In the lateral hypothalamus, αMSH competes directly with AgRP for activation of the MC4 receptors. Recall that AgRP initiated feeding behavior by blocking these receptors. Alpha-MSH serves as an agonist at the MC4 receptor. When the MC4 receptors are activated by αMSH, feeding is inhibited. When the MC4 receptors are blocked by AgRP, feeding is stimulated. In addition, high levels of circulating leptin discourage feeding by directly inhibiting the synthesis and release of NPY and AgRP (Howlett, 1996). ■ Figure 9.19 summarizes some of the systems we have discussed so far that regulate feeding and satiety. As we'll see in the following section, these systems do not always function perfectly.

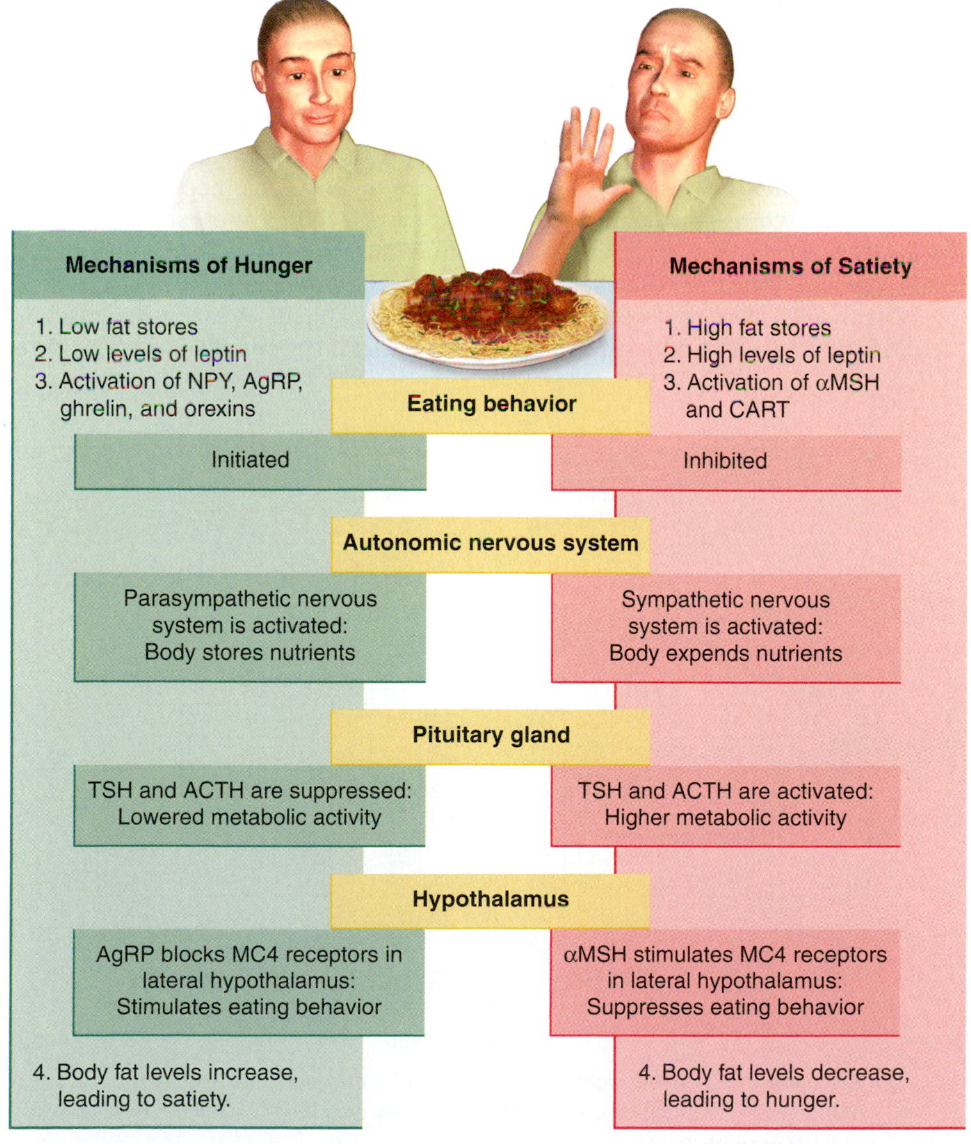
Mechanisms of Hunger
1. Low fat stores
2. Low levels of leptin
3. Activation of NPY, AgRP, ghrelin, and orexins
Mechanisms of Satiety
1. High fat stores
2. High levels of leptin
3. Activation of αMSH and CART
Eating behavior
Initiated
Inhibited
Autonomic nervous system
Parasympathetic nervous system is activated: Body stores nutrients
Sympathetic nervous system is activated: Body expends nutrients
Pituitary gland
TSH and ACTH are suppressed: Lowered metabolic activity
TSH and ACTH are activated: Higher metabolic activity
Hypothalamus
AgRP blocks MC4 receptors in lateral hypothalamus: Stimulates eating behavior
αMSH stimulates MC4 receptors in lateral hypothalamus: Suppresses eating behavior
4. Body fat levels increase, leading to satiety.
4. Body fat levels decrease, leading to hunger.

■ **FIGURE 9.19 Neurochemical Correlates of Hunger and Satiety** Fat stores determine leptin levels, which in turn trigger a cascade of events leading to either hunger or satiety.

alpha melanocyte-stimulating hormone (αMSH) A neurochemical originating in the arcuate nucleus, believed to inhibit feeding behavior.

cocaine- and amphetamine-regulated transcript (CART) A neurochemical, originating in the arcuate nucleus, believed to inhibit feeding behavior.

Obesity and Eating Disorders

Many people seem to have a great deal of difficulty maintaining a healthy body weight. Because our bodies evolved to survive with a limited, difficult-to-obtain food supply, we struggle for balance in modern cultures in which food is amply available (Chakravarthy & Booth, 2004).

Defining Normal Weight

To define the boundaries of an eating disorder, it is helpful to define healthy body weight. Results of animal research strongly suggest that lower body weights are healthier. Mice that underwent caloric restriction experienced greater health and life span than mice allowed to eat freely (Weindruch, Walford, Fligiel, & Guthrie, 1986). The more caloric intake was restricted, the longer the mice lived, with the mice that received only 65 percent of their "normal" food living 67 percent longer than mice that were allowed to eat as much as they wanted. Sohal and Weindruch (1996) have suggested that eating promotes some unknown byproducts that accelerate the aging process at the cellular level. In additional work from Weindruch's lab (Lee, Weindruch, & Prolla, 2000), calorie-deprived mice maintained a more youthful level of gene activity.

One should eat to live, not live to eat.
Benjamin Franklin

Expert opinions regarding a person's optimum weight vary widely. One currently popular system for determining ideal weight is the computation of a **body mass index (BMI).** The BMI is computed by dividing a person's weight in kilograms by the square of his or her height in meters. People with a resulting BMI of between 18.5 and 24.9 appear to live the longest, with the risk of death from all causes, including cancer and heart disease, increasing when a person's BMI reaches 25 or above (Calle, Thun, Petrelli, Rodriguez, & Heath, 1999). A BMI of 25 to 29.9 is defined as overweight. A BMI of 30 to 39.9 is **obese,** and a BMI of 40 or more is morbidly obese. Morbid obesity limits activity and normal physiological functions, and puts a person at high risk for disease and death. You can check your own BMI using ■ Figure 9.20.

BMI is not a perfect system for assessing healthy weight. A major drawback to the BMI system is its blindness to factors of sex, skeletal structure, and musculature.

Height (inches) \ Weight (pounds)	80	90	100	110	120	130	140	150	160	170	180	190	200	210	220	230	240	250
80	9	10	11	12	13	14	15	17	18	19	20	21	22	23	24	25	26	28
78	9	10	12	13	14	15	16	17	19	20	21	22	23	24	25	27	28	29
76	10	11	12	13	15	16	17	18	20	21	22	23	24	26	27	28	29	30
74	10	12	12	14	15	17	18	19	21	22	23	24	26	27	28	30	31	32
72	11	12	14	15	16	18	19	20	22	23	24	26	27	28	30	31	33	34
70	12	13	14	16	17	19	20	22	23	24	26	27	29	30	32	33	35	36
68	12	14	15	17	18	20	21	23	24	26	27	29	30	32	34	35	7	38
66	13	15	16	18	19	21	23	24	26	27	29	31	32	34	36	37	39	40
64	14	15	17	19	21	22	24	26	28	29	31	33	34	36	38	40	41	43
62	15	17	18	20	22	24	26	27	29	31	33	35	37	38	40	42	44	46
60	16	17	20	22	23	25	27	25	31	33	35	37	39	41	43	45	47	49
58	17	19	21	23	25	27	29	31	34	36	38	40	42	44	46	48	50	52
56	18	21	22	25	27	29	31	34	36	38	40	43	45	47	49	52	54	56
54	19	22	24	27	29	31	34	36	39	41	43	46	48	51	53	56	58	60
52	21	23	26	29	31	34	36	39	40	44	47	49	52	55	57	60	62	65
50	23	25	28	31	34	37	39	42	45	48	51	53	56	59	62	65	68	70
48	24	28	31	34	37	40	42	46	49	52	55	58	61	64	67	70	73	76

BMI under 18.5: Underweight
BMI between 18.5–24: Healthy weight
BMI between 25–29: Overweight
BMI between 30–39: Obese
BMI over 40: Severely/morbidly obese

■ **Figure 9.20**
Body Mass Index Provides a Measure of Ideal Weight Body mass index (BMI) is computed by dividing your weight in kilograms by the square of your height in meters. (We have converted the scale to inches and pounds.) BMIs between 18.5 and 24.9 are considered healthy. A person with a BMI of 25 to 29.9 is considered overweight, and a person with a BMI of 30 to 39.9 is obese. BMIs of 40 and above are considered morbidly obese.

body mass index (BMI) A measure comparing height and weight that is used to determine underweight, healthy weight, overweight, and obesity.

obesity The state of being extremely overweight, with a body mass index of 30 to 39.9, or a weight that is 20 percent higher than typical.

By this measure, many of our most fit professional athletes would be considered overweight or obese. The BMI assumes that men and women of the same height should weigh similar amounts, in spite of the typically heavier muscle mass found in males (see Chapter 8). Although BMIs indicating overweight or obesity are correlated with increased risk of death, people with normal BMIs who have higher than normal waist circumference also experience increased risk of death (Koster et al., 2008).

Ideal weight can also be assessed by measuring body fat. One of the most accurate techniques for measuring body fat is the submersion test, illustrated in Figure 9.21, in which the person is submersed in a tank of water. Body fat of 32 percent or more for women and 25 percent or more for men is considered obese. "Average" body fat for men is in the 15 to 18 percent range and about 22 to 25 percent for women. Females should not allow body fat to go below 12 percent, due to the negative impact this has on fertility, but men can sustain body fat of as little as 5 percent. Athletes of both sexes are often lower in body fat than these general minimums, but this is due to their relatively higher muscle mass rather than to any unusually low levels of fat (Prior et al., 2001).

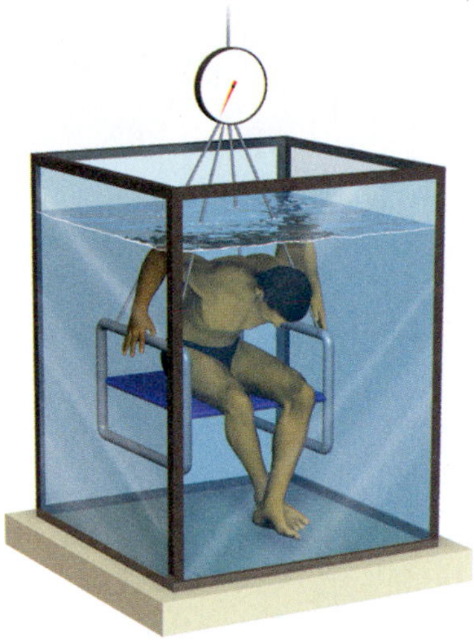

FIGURE 9.21 The Submersion Test of Body Composition The submersion test is considered one of the most accurate measures of body fat. The person's weight outside the tank is compared with the person's weight when completely submerged in water. Bone and muscle are more dense than water, and fat is less dense. Remember that fat floats. A person with a lot of bone and muscle will weigh more than a person with less bone and muscle when submersed. Standard formulas are used to compare the two weights, providing an estimate of body fat percentage.

OBESITY

Human beings use energy very efficiently. When at rest, the average human body uses only about 12 calories (actually kcals) per pound per day. In other words, a person who weighs 150 pounds and spends most of his or her day watching television or sitting in front of the computer needs only about 1,800 calories of food. Considering that the typical fast-food meal of a hamburger, fries, and soda contains about 1,500 calories, it becomes easy to see why people are getting a lot heavier.

A large number of complex, interacting factors in our modern lifestyles contribute to obesity. Social factors, such as the acceptance of large body size, are reflected in the fact that having obese friends increases your risk of obesity by 57 percent, and having an obese spouse increases your risk of obesity by 37 percent (Christakis & Fowler, 2007). Stress alone and a high fat diet alone do not necessarily lead to obesity, but the combination of the two appears to increase the release of NPY, which in turn increases appetite (Kuo et al., 2007).

Genetics appear to play an important role in a person's vulnerability to obesity. A twin study suggests that differences in adult women's body sizes could be predicted by their genes more than 50 percent of the time (Livshits, Kato, Wilson, & Spector, 2007). Even viral infections and bacteria have been implicated in the development

NEW DIRECTIONS

Should Obesity Be Considered a Brain Disorder?

Psychologists and psychiatrists use one of two resources to diagnose disorders, the *Diagnostic and Statistical Manual of Mental Disorders*, 4th edition, Text Revised (DSM IV-TR), published in 2000 by the American Psychiatric Association, or the *International Classification of Disease (ICD)* system. Obesity appears in the ICD, but not in the DSM IV-TR. Discussions surrounding the writing of a fifth edition of the DSM have raised the question of whether obesity should be included.

Arguing for inclusion are addiction experts Nora Volkow and Charles O'Brien (2007, 2008). These researchers do not believe that all people who are obese have a brain disorder. However, they argue for the inclusion of individuals whose "drive to consume food is so overpowering that they cannot control these urges, despite attempts to do so and the devastating consequences" (Volkow & O'Brien, 2008, p. 139). The brain disorder of obesity for Volkow and O'Brien is the "pathological disruption of the neurobiological substrates that underlie the 'urge to eat'" (ibid.). Arguing against the inclusion of obesity in the DSM V is Barbara Bruno (2008). Although Bruno acknowledges that many people are unable to restrict their food intake, she objects to "naming a body size as a psychiatric disorder" (Bruno, 2008, p. 138).

This controversy reminds us of the pros and cons of labeling any disorder. Although people can benefit from recognition of their problem by experts, labeling can also result in negative images and stigma. In addition, labeling obesity as a "brain disorder," words chosen by Volkow and O'Brien, appears to overlook the substantial contributions of learning and the environment to eating.

of obesity. Approximately 20 to 30 percent of obese individuals show signs of having been infected with adenovirus-36, which is responsible for some colds, diarrhea, and pinkeye. In contrast, only 5 percent of people with normal body weight show signs of adenovirus-36 infection (Dhurandhar 2000). When bacteria from obese mice were transplanted into typical mice, the typical mice increased their body fat 47 percent in two weeks (Turnbaugh et al., 2006).

Defending the Obese Weight Once a person becomes overweight or obese, the body conspires to maintain the extra weight. After all, our ancestors faced death by starvation more frequently than problems related to obesity. Obese people not only have greater numbers of fat cells than people of normal weight (65 billion rather than 25 billion), but their fat cells also individually weigh more (one microgram as compared to two-thirds microgram). Dieting reduces the size of the individual fat cells but not their number. Liposuction, the surgical removal of fat, typically does not result in permanent weight loss (Dark, Forger, Stern, & Zucker, 1984; FDA, 2002). Because liposuction reduces the number of fat cells in the body, less leptin is produced, leading to increased appetite. If the person continues to overeat, the surgically removed fat is quickly replaced.

Interventions for Obesity All weight loss diets work by reducing the number of calories consumed. Successful long-term weight loss requires lifestyle changes that are sustainable indefinitely. Popular diets tend to allow too few calories, triggering physiological responses aimed at avoiding starvation. The body lowers its metabolic rate, and the dieter might actually gain weight while eating less than before.

One of the very nicest things about life is the way we must regularly stop whatever it is we are doing and devote our attention to eating.
Luciano Pavarotti

Efforts to use chemicals to control weight have been disappointing. During the 1950s and 1960s, amphetamines were prescribed frequently as diet aids. Amphetamines certainly suppress appetite, but their addictive and psychoactive qualities make them completely unsuited for this purpose. More recently, dexfenfluramine (Redux) was first approved and then removed from the American market due to its significant, life-threatening side effects. The popular but unapproved fenfluramine/phenteramine (Fen/Phen) combination produced similar outcomes. Current medications approved for treating obesity include orlistat, which reduces the absorption of consumed fats, and sibutramine, which is an appetite suppressant similar to amphetamine (Rucker, Padwal, Li, Curioni, & Lau, 2007). Weight loss for those using these drugs is modest, in the range of 5 to 10 pounds in one year, and the benefits of this weight loss may not offset the drugs' side effects for many patients.

Many obese patients become discouraged with diets and medications and turn instead to a variety of surgical interventions, including stomach stapling and gastric bypass procedures. Although the weight loss from such procedures is typically significant, such as the average loss of 90 pounds within three months of gastric bypass (Maggard et al., 2005), these procedures represent major surgery, often result in complications, and should be considered carefully. We are still a long way from having an easy fix for obesity. In the meantime, moderate caloric restriction and increasing exercise still work, if people can be convinced to view these habits as a lifestyle change rather than as a temporary fix.

Anorexia Nervosa

Coexisting with obesity in American society is the disorder **anorexia nervosa.** In anorexia, which means "loss of appetite," individuals maintain 85 percent or less of their normal body weight, while demonstrating a distorted image of their bodies as obese. This is one of the few psychological conditions that can kill; up to 10 percent of patients eventually die from the disorder (American Psychiatric Association, 2000). In addition to extremely low weight, individuals will usually show amenorrhea (cessation of menstruation), dry or yellowed skin, fine downy hair (lanugo) on the face, trunk, and limbs, increased sensitivity to cold, and cardiovascular and gastrointestinal problems. More than 90 percent of anorexia patients are female.

anorexia nervosa An eating disorder characterized by voluntary self-starvation and a grossly distorted body image.
bulimia nervosa An eating disorder characterized by cycles of bingeing and purging.

WHY DOES THIS MATTER?

Does Dieting Work?

Understanding how dieting does and does not work matters if you or people you care about find themselves in the position of needing to lose some weight.

It is a common misconception that *nobody* can ever lose weight successfully. In fact, about 20 percent of dieters who lose 10 percent or more of their body weight manage to maintain the loss for at least one year (Wing & Phelan, 2005). Yes, that does mean that the vast majority of dieters do not succeed in the long term, but like people who are trying to quit smoking, many people do not succeed until they have tried several times.

The National Weight Control Registry tracks dieters who have successfully lost 70 pounds or more and have maintained their loss for at least five years. We can certainly learn from the habits of these successful people. What do these dieters have in common? All engage in about one hour of exercise per day, consume a low-calorie and low-fat diet, eat breakfast regularly, monitor their weight regularly, and eat a consistent diet across weekdays and weekends.

Maintaining weight loss appears to get easier over time. People who have maintained a weight loss for two to five years seldom regain the weight. Although some of this improvement may be due to changes in habits, there is also evidence that eating well and maintaining a healthy weight changes the composition of intestinal bacteria (Ley, Turnbaugh, Klein, & Gordon, 2006). As we observed earlier in this chapter, transplanting bacteria from obese mice to typical mice resulted in a big weight gain (Turnbaugh et al., 2006). Perhaps by dieting, people are able to re-establish bacteria that help keep them at a healthy weight.

Bulimia Nervosa

Bulimia nervosa involves a cyclical pattern of binge eating followed by purging through vomiting or use of laxatives. The extent of bingeing varies widely among patients, but the average binge session contains approximately 1,500 calories of food (Rosen, Leitenberg, Fisher, & Khazam, 1986). Bulimia is far more common than anorexia, occurring in 3 percent as opposed to 0.5 to 1 percent of the American population (American Psychiatric Association, 2000). However, some patients with anorexia are also bulimic at times. Bulimia results in fatigue, headaches, puffy cheeks (due to enlarged salivary glands), and loss of dental enamel through repeated vomiting of stomach acid.

Causes of Anorexia and Bulimia

There are obvious environmental factors associated with eating disorders, including exposure to excessively thin and glamorous models and actresses, as shown in ■ Figure 9.22. In the introduction to this chapter, we observed how exposure to American television in the islands of Fiji appears to have contributed to increased rates of dieting and disordered eating. In 1965, models were thinner than the average American woman, but only by 8 percent. Today, models are 23 percent thinner than the average American woman. In response to the deaths of several models from starvation and concerns about the messages being sent to young women, several European countries have banned fashion models whose BMI is less than 18.5. (The average fashion model has a BMI of 16.5.)

The evidence for biological factors leading to eating disorders, however, is more difficult to interpret. Hsu, Chesler, and Santhouse (1990) reported evidence for a genetic predisposition to eating disorders based on the study of monozygotic and dizygotic twins. Families with members diagnosed with anorexia nervosa are also likely to have high rates of major

■ **Figure 9.22**
Anorexia and Fashion Models The average runway model has a BMI of 16.5. American fashion designers have complained that the 18.5 standard set by some European countries would require a 6'0" model to "balloon" to 136 pounds. In contrast, a 6'0" model with a BMI of 16.5 weighs only 121 pounds.

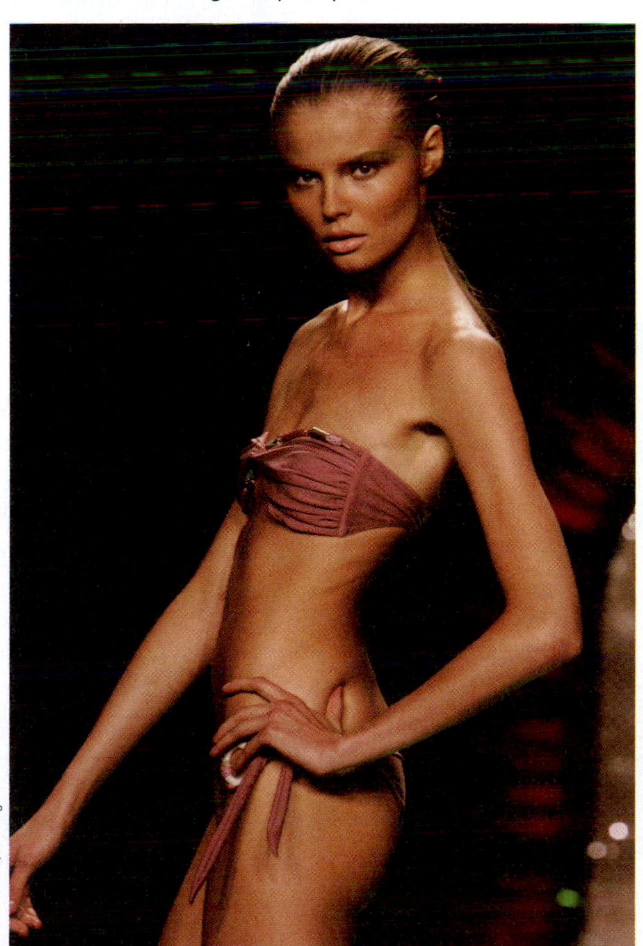

Diane Bondareff/AP Images

depressive disorder (Wade, Bulik, Neale, & Kendler, 2000). It is likely that the general personality characteristics that produce a vulnerability to the development of eating disorders, not the disorders themselves, are inherited.

Once established, eating disorders appear to be maintained at least in part by biological factors. Elevated CART levels have been observed in patients with anorexia nervosa, even after the patients reached normal weight during treatment (Stanley et al., 2003). You might recall that CART raises metabolic rates and inhibits feeding. CART might also reduce the rewarding aspects of eating through its actions in the nucleus accumbens, which is part of the reward circuit implicated in addiction (Jean et al., 2007). CART's action in the nucleus accumbens is mediated by the activity of serotonin. Serotonin abnormalities have been implicated in both eating disorders and major depressive disorder, which might account for the higher risk for these disorders within the same families (Wade et al., 2000).

The binge-and-purge cycling of bulimia might involve processes similar to addiction (Hoebel, Patten, Colantuoni, & Rada, 2000). When food-deprived rats were given access to sugar water, they binged, or consumed large quantities. Bingeing rats, but not control rats, subsequently responded to the opiate antagonist naloxone with anxiety, agitation, and chattering teeth. These symptoms are identical to the responses of rats addicted to morphine when given naloxone. People who fast and then binge on sweets might be setting up a similar addictive process that would make it difficult for them to stop bingeing. This model provides a possible explanation for the higher incidence of substance abuse among family members of patients with bulimia nervosa (Lilenfeld, Ringham, Kalarchian, & Marcus, 2008).

Treatments for Eating Disorders

No medication to date has proved effective in alleviating anorexia (Berkman et al., 2006). Antidepressants, particularly selective serotonin reuptake inhibitors (SSRIs; see Chapters 4 and 16), are frequently useful in the management of bulimia, although cognitive-behavioral therapy is more effective than medication alone (Berkman et al., 2006). The first priority when treating anorexia is keeping the patient alive, which usually requires a period of hospitalization and careful monitoring of food intake. Addressing the distorted body image that characterizes eating disorders is also an essential aspect of treatment.

INTERIM SUMMARY 9.3

Summary Points

1. During the process of digestion, carbohydrates, proteins, and fats are broken down into components, which are either used immediately or stored for later use. **(LO5)**
2. Glucoreceptors in the lateral hypothalamus (LH) participate in the identification of hunger and the initiation of feeding behavior. Feeding behavior is also stimulated by a number of chemicals, including neuropeptide Y, AgRP, orexins, ghrelin, and MCH. **(LO6)**
3. The ventromedial hypothalamus, paraventricular nucleus, and the nucleus of the solitary tract appear to participate in satiety. High levels of leptin stimulate the release of αMSH and CART, which inhibit feeding. **(LO6)**
4. Sensible diets and moderate exercise result in weight loss. Chemical and surgical interventions are popular, but there are no easy fixes available for treating obesity. **(LO7)**
5. Complex cultural and physical processes contribute to the development and course of anorexia nervosa and bulimia nervosa. **(LO7)**

Review Questions

1. In what ways can the environment shape our eating habits?
2. How do leptin levels influence appetite and weight control?

CHAPTER REVIEW

THOUGHT QUESTIONS

1. What adaptations might you expect to see in the body shapes of animals during an extended period of global warming?
2. If you were stranded in a hot place without a source of water, what automatic mechanisms might be activated to conserve your body's fluids? What behavioral solutions might you employ to conserve fluids?
3. What factors have contributed to the enormous increase in obesity in America during the past two decades?
4. Which potential chemical intervention for obesity do you believe to be the most promising? Why?

KEY TERMS

agouti-related protein (AgRP) (p. 274)
alpha melanocyte stimulating hormone (αMSH) (p. 277)
anorexia nervosa (p. 280)
arcuate nucleus (p. 274)
antidiuretic hormone (ADH) (p. 266)
baroreceptor (p. 266)
bulimia nervosa (p. 281)
cocaine- and amphetamine-regulated transcript (CART) (p. 277)
glucoreceptor (p. 274)
ghrelin (p. 275)
homeostasis (p. 256)
hypovolemic thirst (p. 265)
lateral hypothalamus (LH) (p. 268)
leptin (p. 274)
median preoptic nucleus (p. 268)
melanin-concentrating hormone (MCH) (p. 275)
motivation (p. 256)
neuropeptide Y (NPY) (p. 274)
nucleus of the solitary tract (NST) (p. 268)
obesity (p. 278)
orexin (p. 276)
organum vasculosum of the lamina terminalis (OVLT) (p. 265)
osmoreceptor (p. 265)
osmosis (p. 263)
osmotic thirst (p. 265)
paraventricular nucleus (PVN) (p. 274)
preoptic area (POA) (p. 261)
satiety (p. 276)
set point (p. 256)
solute (p. 262)
subfornical organ (SFO) (p. 268)
vasopressin (p. 266)
ventromedial hypothalamus (VMH) (p. 276)
zona incerta (p. 268)

10

Sexual Behavior

CHAPTER OUTLINE

Taxi/Getty Images

▲ **Human Sexuality** Human sexual behavior combines a complex array of biological and learned variables.

Introduction

Male and female behavior is often very different, and we frequently ask how much of a role biology and socialization play in the differences we see. Children begin to prefer sex-typed toys between the ages of 12 and 18 months. At these same ages, children are unable to match sex-typed toys (vehicles and dolls) with male or female faces or voices, suggesting that they have not yet been socialized to think of toys as "male" or "female" (Serbin, Poulin-Dubois, Colburne, Sen, & Eichstedt, 2001). Socialization is even less likely to play a role in the toy choices of monkeys. Young male monkeys spend more time with wheeled toys and balls, whereas young female monkeys prefer dolls, plush animals, and pots (Alexander & Hines,

FIGURE 10.1 David Reimer and the Nature and Nurture of Sex David Reimer was raised as a girl (left) following an accident during his circumcision but ultimately chose to live as a man (above).

2002; Hassett, Siebert, & Wallen, 2008). These results suggest that at least part of the preference we see in toy selection in boys and girls may originate in biology.

Further insight into the nature and nurture of human sexuality comes from the disastrous case of Bruce Reimer. During a routine circumcision in 1965, Bruce's penis was damaged so badly that experts, including John Money, thought he should be raised as a girl. Bruce's genitals were surgically altered, and he began life as Brenda. Several years later, Money (1972) reported that "Brenda" was developing into a perfectly normal female. Independent follow-ups of the case provided a much different view (Colapinto, 2001; Diamond & Sigmundson, 1997). Bruce/Brenda remembers suspecting he was a boy as early as the second grade, when he dreamed of growing up to be a man. By age 14, even after two years of female hormone therapy, Bruce/Brenda refused to continue living as a girl. His parents informed him of his medical history, and he chose immediate male hormone therapy and surgery. Bruce, renamed David, lived as a man, married, and adopted his wife's children. Tragically, David Reimer, who appears in Figure 10.1, took his own life in May 2004.

David Reimer's story suggests that our biological sex may influence our ultimate sense of being a man or a woman more strongly than how we are raised. In this chapter, we will explore the subtle interactions between our genetic sex, our sexual anatomy, our gender identity, and sex-typed behavior.

LEARNING OBJECTIVES

After reading this chapter, you should be able to:

LO1 Describe the normal genetic inheritances of males and females as well as variations that can occur.

LO2 Explain the normal development of male and female gonads, internal organs, external genitalia, and secondary sex characteristics.

LO3 Describe androgen insensitivity syndrome, congenital adrenal hyperplasia, and 5-alpha-reductase deficiency.

LO4 Summarize the physical processes associated with puberty, fertility, menstruation, and contraception.

LO5 Describe the relationships between sex hormones and competition, sexual frequency, and cognitive behavior.

LO6 Summarize research findings on the biological contributions to sexual orientation.

LO7 Summarize the research on biological factors correlated with attraction.

LO8 Describe the biological factors associated with romantic love, sexual desire, and parenting.

Sexual Development

In 355 B.C., Aristotle argued that the sex of a child was the result of the temperature of semen at the time of conception. Hot semen resulted in males, and cool semen resulted in females. Today, we understand that an individual's genetic sex begins with sex chromosomes inherited from two parents. Mothers provide an **X chromosome** to all their offspring; fathers determine the offspring's sex by providing either another X

X chromosome One of two types of sex chromosomes; individuals with two X chromosomes will usually develop into females.

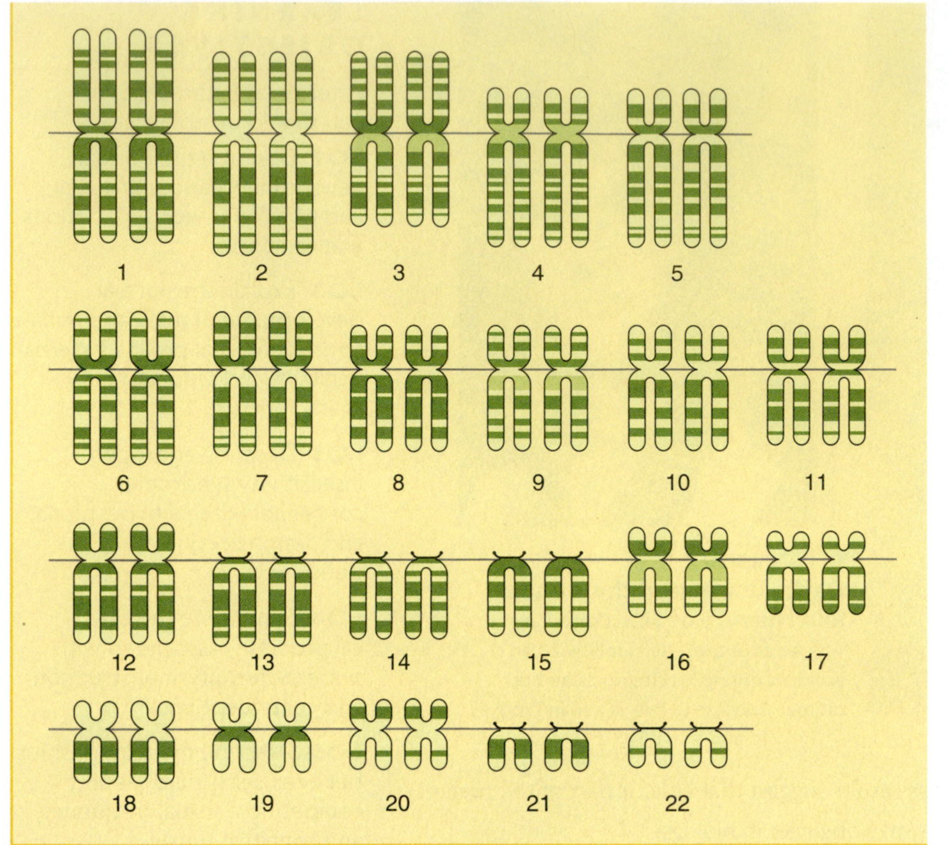

Typical human females and males have 22 chromosome pairs in common.

+

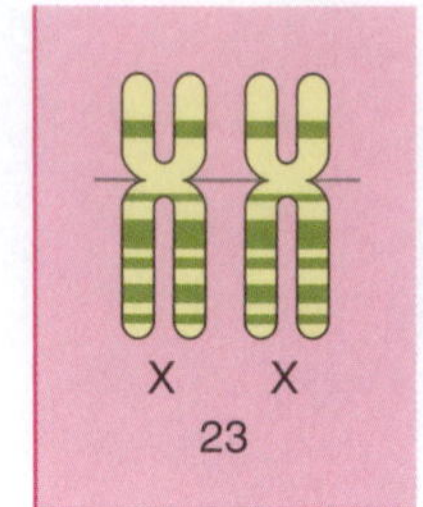

Typical female

OR

+

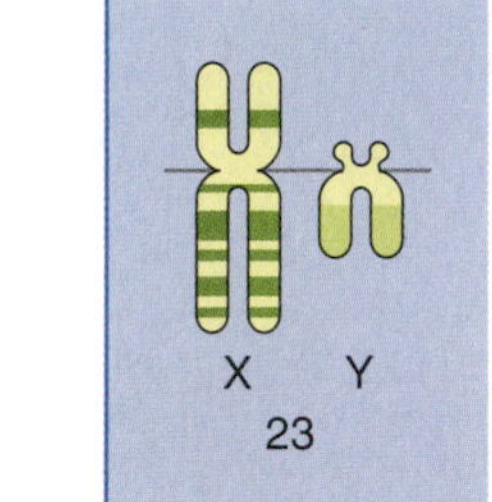

Typical male

The 23rd pair, the sex chromosomes, differentiates between females and males.

Figure 10.2
The Human Genome Twenty-three pairs of chromosomes are found in the nuclei of all human body cells except red blood cells (which have no DNA) and sperm and egg cells (which contain only one copy from each pair of chromosomes).

(producing a female) or a **Y chromosome** (producing a male). The initial receipt of an XX or an XY genotype begins a cascade of hormonal, structural, and behavioral events. These pivotal sex chromosomes, along with the other 22 pairs of human chromosomes, are illustrated in Figure 10.2.

Maleness and femaleness are often viewed inaccurately as distinct and separate categories. In fact, the fetus is initially undifferentiated in regard to sex. Without exposure to male hormones, all babies would be born with outwardly female physical appearance and female behavior.

Sex Chromosome Abnormalities

In the vast majority of cases, the transmission of the sex chromosomes to a child is uneventful. However, in a minority of cases, variations occur. These genetic variations provide insight into the impact of each stage of the developmental process on the sexuality of the mature individual.

We have no record of a viable organism that has a single Y chromosome. However, when a child receives only a single X chromosome (XO) instead of the usual pair (XX or XY), the result is **Turner syndrome,** a condition first described by American endocrinologist Henry Turner in 1938. Turner syndrome occurs in about 1 out of 2,500 live births (National Institutes of Health [NIH], 2004). From Turner syndrome, we have learned that a single X chromosome carries sufficient genetic material to produce an individual who is quite normal in many ways. However, the lack of a second sex chromosome does have an impact on fertility, growth, and hormone production and is associated with higher risk of diabetes, osteoporosis, and cardiovascular disease (Hjerrild, Mortensen, & Gravholt, 2008).

Individuals with Turner syndrome have normal female external genitalia, but the ovaries develop abnormally. Currently unidentified regions on the X chromosome are responsible for the development of the ovaries, and having a single X appears to interfere in this

Y chromosome One of two types of sex chromosomes; individuals with a Y chromosome will usually develop into males.

Turner syndrome A condition caused by an XO genotype, characterized by frequent abnormalities of the ovaries and infertility.

Wellcome Images

■ **FIGURE 10.3**
Turner Syndrome Individuals with Turner syndrome have normal female external appearance and genitalia but are usually infertile due to abnormally developing ovaries. This condition is also associated with short stature, skin folds in the neck, and difficulty with spatial relations tasks.

process (Schlessinger et al., 2002). In most cases, the ovaries do not produce either ova or normal levels of female hormones, leading to infertility. When the X chromosome is missing in some but not all cells, or only portions of the second X are missing, women may be fertile. As shown in ■ Figure 10.3, some women with Turner syndrome are relatively short, reaching an average height of 4'8", and they may have increased skin folds at the neck (National Institutes of Health [NIH], 2004). Intelligence is normal, but specific deficits in spatial relationships and memory can occur (National Institute of Child Health and Human Development [NICHHD], 2000). Human growth hormone, female hormone replacement therapy, and assisted reproductive technologies are used to address the issues of height, hormone production, and fertility.

Klinefelter syndrome, first identified by Harry Klinefelter in 1942, is one of the most common genetic abnormalities related to the sex chromosomes, occurring in 1.79 out of 1,000 male births (Morris, Alberman, Scott, & Jacobs, 2007). Klinefelter syndrome features an XXY genotype. These individuals are male, but they usually experience reduced fertility and require hormone treatment at puberty to promote the development of secondary male sex characteristics (facial hair, deeper voice, development of external genitalia) and to inhibit female characteristics such as breast development (Nielsen, Pelsen, & Sørensen, 1988). Other symptoms associated with having an extra X chromosome are due to interference with the process of x-inactivation, in which one X chromosome in each female cell is randomly silenced (See Chapter 5).

Like Turner syndrome, Klinefelter syndrome is associated with normal intelligence that may be marked by mild cognitive difficulties and social awkwardness (Sørensen, 1987). In the case of Klinefelter syndrome, the cognitive difficulties usually take the form of delayed and reduced verbal skills. Left-handedness is more common among males with Klinefelter syndrome than in the general male population. These findings suggest that Klinefelter syndrome might affect brain lateralization or the localization of specific functions such as language in one hemisphere or the other (Ross et al., 2008).

Klinefelter syndrome A condition in males caused by an XXY genotype, characterized by frequent problems with fertility, secondary sex characteristics, and verbal skills.

The existence of individuals with an XYY genotype was first reported by Sandberg, Koepf, Ishiara, and Hauschka (1961). This variation occurs in about 1 out of 1,000 male births. The physical and behavioral correlates of the condition are typically subtle and generally do not prompt the parents to seek a postnatal genetic analysis (Abramsky & Chapple, 1997). The boys appear to be physically within typical limits, although they tend to be somewhat taller and leaner, suffer from acne, and have a higher risk for minor physical abnormalities of the eye, elbow, and chest. Average IQ scores are slightly below the average of males with normal XY genotypes (Linden, Bender, & Robinson, 1996). Men with the XYY genotype are fertile, but they are slightly more likely than typical men to produce sperm with sex chromosome abnormalities (Rives et al., 2003).

The relationship between the XYY genotype and a higher likelihood of antisocial behavior has been the subject of considerable debate. An initial report suggested that XYY individuals were overrepresented in prisons (Casey, Segall, Street, & Blank, 1966). The popular press immediately embraced the hypothesis that an extra Y chromosome would produce a violent "super male." Serial murderer Richard Speck, convicted for the killings of eight student nurses in Chicago in 1966, falsely claimed to have the XYY genotype in an effort to obtain lenient sentencing (Gould, 1981). Gotz, Johnstone, and Ratcliffe (1999) followed the progress of seventeen men identified as having the XYY genotype at birth. These men did show a significantly higher rate of antisocial and criminal behavior than control participants. However, the majority of the criminal behavior of the XYY men involved property crimes rather than violent crimes (Milunsky, 2004). Further analysis suggested that criminal and antisocial behavior was more closely associated with lower intelligence than with an atypical genotype.

In Chapter 5 we discussed Down syndrome, a genetic abnormality characterized by having three copies of Chromosome 21 instead of the normal pair. In comparison to genetic abnormalities like Down syndrome, abnormalities due to a third sex chromosome appear to have relatively mild effects (Bender, Linden, & Harmon, 2001). In conclusions drawn from a study of more than 13,000 newborns over a 13-year period, Nielsen and Wohlert (1991) found that none of the children with three sex chromosomes were mentally retarded and that all were in regular public school. There were no increases in criminal activity, mental disorders, or physical disorders relative to the population with typical sex chromosomes. However, significant abnormalities do characterize cases involving more than three sex chromosomes.

Three Stages of Prenatal Development

Male and female structural development involves three distinct processes: the development of **gonads,** of internal organs, and of **external genitalia.** In the vast majority of cases, all three processes occur congruently to produce an unambiguous male or female. In a rare condition known as **intersex,** elements of both male and female development occur in the same fetus.

The Development of the Gonads Up until the sixth week after conception, both male and female fetuses have identical primordial gonads that have the capacity to develop into either **ovaries,** the female gonads, or **testes,** the male gonads.

At about six weeks after conception, a gene on the short arm of the Y chromosome, known as the **sex-determining region of the Y chromosome,** or ***SRY,*** is expressed in male embryos (Berta et al., 1990; Jäger, Anvret, Hall, & Scherer, 1990). **Testis-determining factor,** the protein encoded by the *SRY* gene, switches on additional genes that cause the primordial gonads to develop into testes. In female embryos, which lack the *SRY* gene and its ability to produce testis-determining factor, alternate genes guide the development of the primordial gonad into ovaries (Sinclair et al., 1990). Chromosomally male mice genetically modified to lack the *SRY* gene develop ovaries, whereas female mice in which the *SRY* gene has been inserted develop testes (Goodfellow & Lovell-Badge, 1993).

Differentiation of the Internal Organs The differentiation of the internal organs, shown in ■ Figure 10.4, follows the development of the gonads. Until about the third

gonads (GO-nads) The internal organs, ovaries in females and testes in males, that produce reproductive cells (eggs and sperm) and secrete sex hormones.

external genitalia The external sexual organs, including the penis and scrotum in males and the labia, clitoris, and lower third of the vagina in females.

intersex A condition in which elements of both male and female development occur in the same fetus.

ovaries Female gonads; the source of ova and sex hormones.

testes Male gonads; source of sperm and sex hormones.

sex-determining region of the Y chromosome (*SRY*) A gene located on the short arm of the Y chromosome that encodes for testis-determining factor.

testis-determining factor A protein encoded by the *SRY* gene on the Y chromosome that turns the primordial gonads into testes.

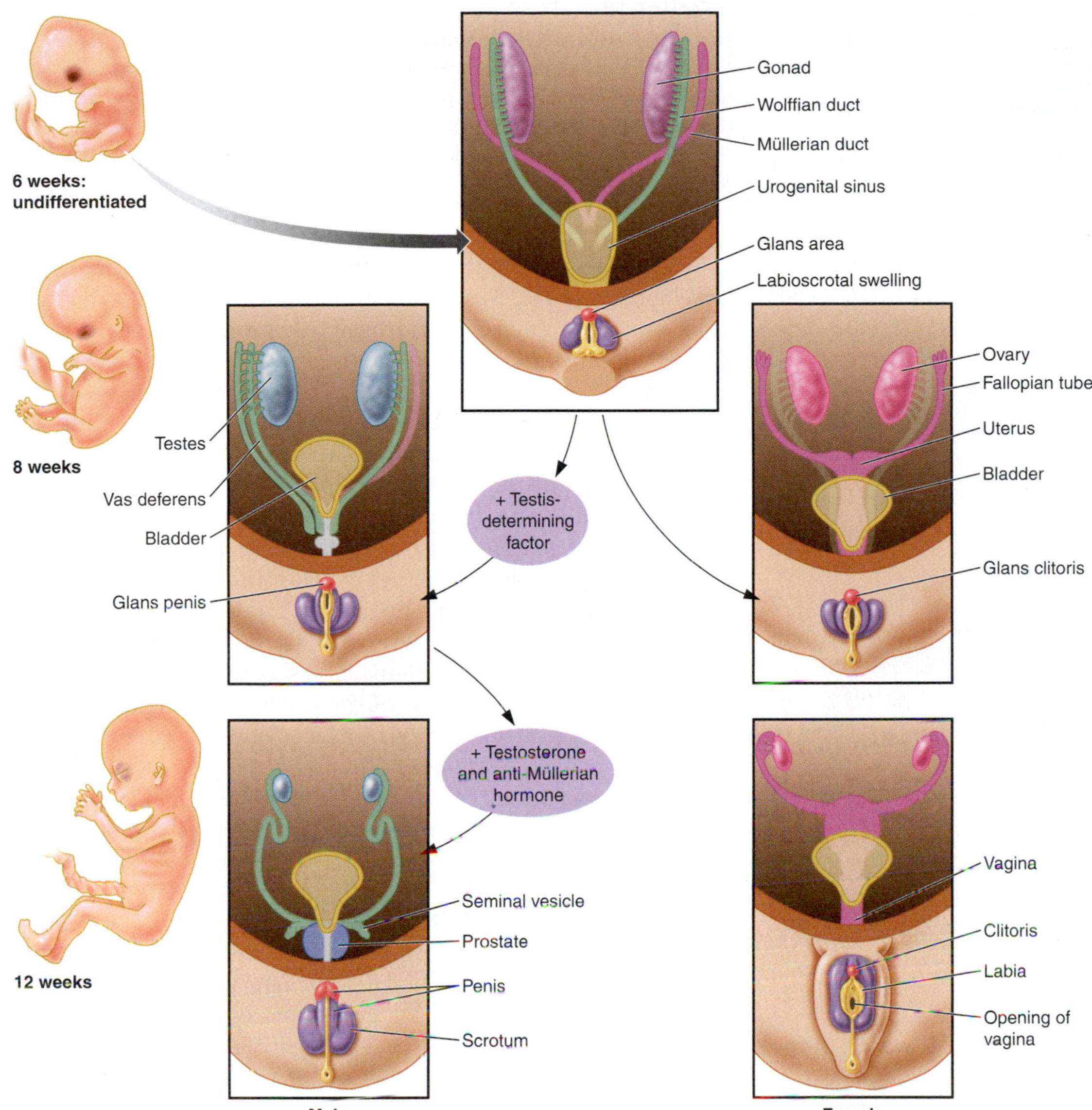

FIGURE 10.4
Differentiation of Gonads and External Genitals During the first six weeks after conception, the primordial gonads are undifferentiated. Subsequently, testis-determining factor encoded by the SRY gene on the Y chromosome will begin to turn the undifferentiated gonads into testes in males. The testes begin to release androgens, causing the external genitalia to develop into a penis and scrotum. Alternate genes guide the development of female gonads into ovaries. In the absence of androgens, the female external genitalia develop into clitoris, labia, and vagina.

month of development in humans, both male and female fetuses possess a male **Wolffian system** and a female **Müllerian system.** Advantages for this apparent duplication are not currently understood. In males, the Wolffian system will develop into the seminal vesicles, the vas deferens, and the prostate. In females, the Müllerian system will develop into the uterus, the upper portion of the vagina, and the fallopian tubes.

During the third month, the male's relatively new testes begin to secrete two hormones, **testosterone** and **anti-Müllerian hormone.** Testosterone, one of several types of male hormone or **androgen,** promotes the development of the Wolffian system. Anti-Müllerian hormone initiates the degeneration of the Müllerian system. In the female fetus, no additional hormones are needed for development. Unlike the testes, the ovaries are not active during fetal development. In the absence of any androgens or anti-Müllerian hormone, the Müllerian system will develop in the typical female direction. Nonfunctional remnants of the Wolffian system remain throughout a woman's life.

Wolffian system (WOLF-ee-un) The internal system that develops into seminal vesicles, vas deferens, and the prostate gland in males.

Müllerian system (muhl-LAIR-ee-an) The internal system that develops into a uterus, fallopian tubes, and the upper two thirds of the vagina in the absence of anti-Müllerian hormone.

testosterone An androgen produced primarily in the testes.

anti-Müllerian hormone A hormone secreted by fetal testes that causes the degeneration of the Müllerian system.

androgen A steroid hormone that develops and maintains typically masculine characteristics.

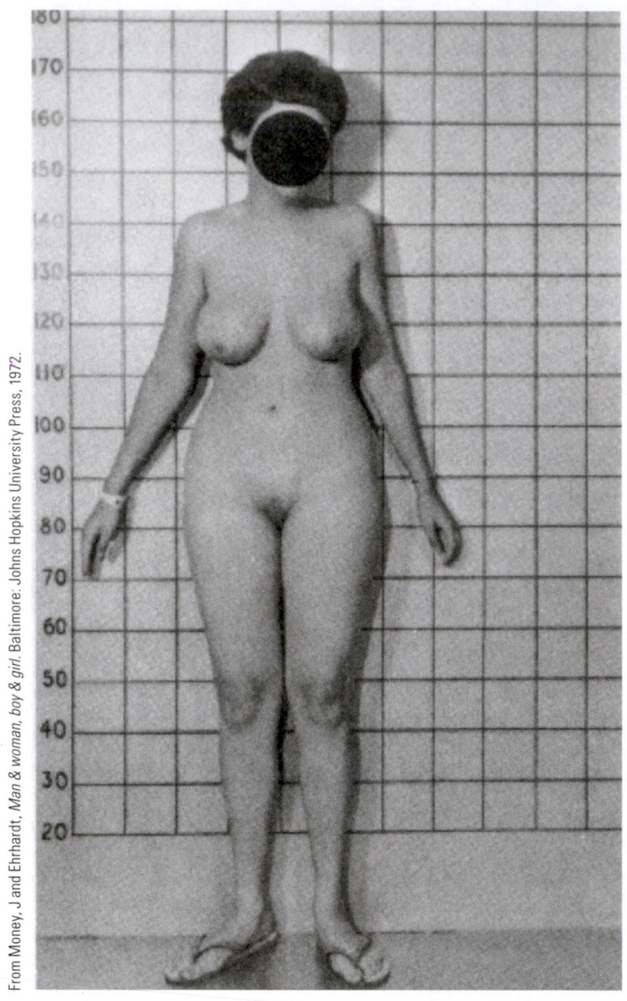

From Money, J and Ehrhardt, *Man & woman, boy & girl*. Baltimore: Johns Hopkins University Press, 1972.

FIGURE 10.5
Androgen Insensitivity Syndrome Androgen insensitivity syndrome (AIS) produces female appearance in spite of an XY genotype. Individuals with AIS lack normal androgen receptors, preventing the Wolffian system from maturing. However, anti-Müllerian hormone still works, so neither the male nor female internal organs develop. The individual will have a shallow vagina, with no uterus, fallopian tubes, and ovaries. External appearance and gender identity remain female.

Androgen insensitivity syndrome (AIS) disrupts the normal development of the Wolffian system in males. In AIS, a defective gene produces abnormal androgen receptors (Gottlieb, Pinsky, Beitel, & Trifiro, 1999). As a result, the fetus's tissues are blind to the presence of androgens. Fetuses with AIS have an XY genotype and normal testes. The testes release androgens and anti-Müllerian hormone in a normal manner, but the lack of functional androgen receptors prevents the development of the Wolffian system. However, anti-Müllerian hormone still works normally, so the female Müllerian system also fails to develop. Because the Müllerian system is responsible for the upper two thirds of the vagina, the result is a shallow vagina and no ovaries, fallopian tubes, or uterus. Although adult individuals with AIS are infertile, their external appearance is quite typically female, as shown in Figure 10.5.

AIS provides a clear view of the difference between chromosomal sex and **gender identity,** our sense of being male or female. Individuals with AIS are genetic males but typically have female appearance and strong female gender identities. Many marry and engage in normal female sexual behavior (Morris, 1953). AIS might be an advantage for women in sports. Although AIS occurs in 1 out of 60,000 male births, it is estimated that 1 out of every 500 women competing at international levels of sport have AIS (Doig, Lloyd-Smith, Prior, & Sinclair, 1997). However, most international sports organizations have eliminated genetic testing.

Development of the External Genitalia The development of the external genitalia, illustrated in Figure 10.4, follows the differentiation of the gonads during the sixth week after conception. The male external genitalia include the penis and scrotum. The female external genitalia include the labia, clitoris, and outer part of the vagina.

No hormonal activity is required in order to develop female external genitalia. However, hormonal stimulation is essential for the development of male external genitalia. A particular androgen, **5-alpha-dihydrotestosterone,** must be recognized by receptor sites for the male external genitalia to develop normally. A reaction between testosterone from the testes and the enzyme 5-alpha-reductase produces 5-alpha-dihydrotestosterone. We will see later in the chapter that the absence of 5-alpha-dihydrotestosterone leads the immature genitalia to develop in the female pattern.

If genetic females are exposed prenatally to excess androgens, their external genitalia become masculinized. **Congenital adrenal hyperplasia (CAH)** is a recessive heritable condition in which the fetus's adrenal glands release elevated levels of androgens. Males with CAH show few observable effects because male fetuses are already typically exposed to high levels of circulating androgens. Females with CAH are exposed to about half the amount of androgens of a typical male and are born with ambiguous external genitalia, as shown in Figure 10.6. The clitoris is enlarged, the labia look similar to a scrotum, and in some cases, there is no vaginal opening. Behavior can also be affected because females with CAH more frequently describe themselves as tomboys, engage in more male-interest play, and are more likely than other women to engage in bisexual and lesbian behavior (Hines, Brook, & Conway, 2004; Meyer-Bahlburg, Dolezal, Baker, & New, 2008; Money, Schwartz, & Lewis, 1984). However, it is important to remember that the majority of women with CAH are heterosexual, and that the majority of bisexual and lesbian women do not have CAH or other, similar conditions.

androgen insensitivity syndrome (AIS) A condition in which a genetic male fetus lacks androgen receptors, which leads to the development of female external genitalia and typically female gender identity and sexual behavior.

gender identity The sense of being male or female, independent of genetic sex or physical appearance.

5-alpha-dihydrotestosterone (die-high-droh-tes-TOS-ter-ohne) An androgen secreted by the testes that masculinizes the external genitalia.

congenital adrenal hyperplasia (CAH) (ah-DREE-nuhl hie-per-PLAY-see-uh) A condition in which a fetus is exposed to higher-than-normal androgens, resulting in masculinization of external genitalia and some cognitive behaviors in affected females.

Development at Puberty

The prenatal development of gonads, internal organs, and external genitalia is only part of the sexual development story. At puberty, additional hormonal events lead to maturation of the genitals and the development of **secondary sex characteristics.** Secondary sex characteristics include facial hair and a deeper voice for males and wider hips and breast development for females.

As shown in Figure 10.7, the average age of puberty has dropped dramatically over the past century and a half, from about 16 to about 12 years of age (Frisch, 1983; Herman-Giddings et al., 1997). Possible explanations for this drop in age at puberty include increased rates of obesity (see Chapter 9). Accumulation of enough body fat to support reproduction might serve as a signal for puberty. When body fat is abnormally low, as in anorexia nervosa, puberty is delayed. Exposure to compounds similar to female hormones in meat and dairy products, shampoo, plastics, and insecticides might also trigger earlier puberty. All edible tissues from animals contain a type of **estrogen,** or female hormone, called **estradiol,** so we can assume that humans have always experienced some level of exposure to outside sources of sex hormones. However, many nations, including the United States, also permit the use of sex hormones to promote growth in cattle production. Consumption of treated meat can increase exposure to estrogens by nearly 40 percent (Aksglaede, Juul, Leffers, Skakkebaek, & Andersson, 2006). Phthalates, compounds frequently found in plastics and cosmetics, have been found to advance puberty in rats (Ge et al., 2007). Phthalates are released into air and fluid from plastic and cosmetic products and are found in measurable levels in most of the world's human population (Sathyanarayana et al., 2008). Because children are especially sensitive to small amounts of hormone, increased exposure from external sources is cause for concern (Aksglaede et al., 2006).

At the onset of puberty, **gonadotropin-releasing hormone (GnRH)** is released by the hypothalamus. This hormone initiates the release of two gonadotropic hormones by the anterior pituitary gland, **follicle-stimulating hormone (FSH)** and **luteinizing hormone (LH).** Both males and females release these same hormones, but with different effects. In response to stimulation by FSH and LH, the testes begin to produce additional testosterone, and the ovaries produce estradiol. The testes also

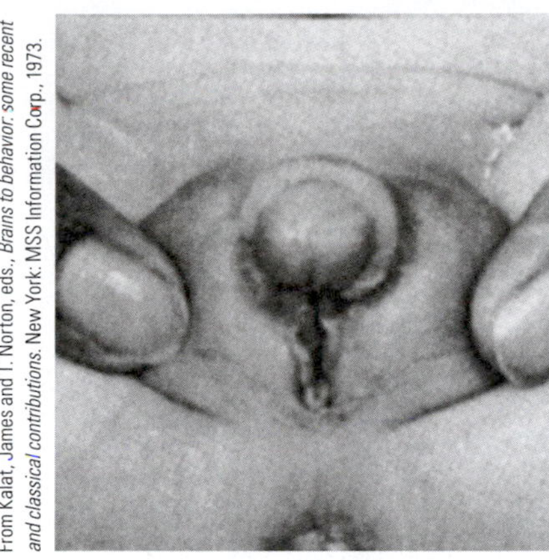

From Kalat, James and T. Norton, eds., *Brains to behavior: some recent and classical contributions.* New York: MSS Information Corp., 1973.

Figure 10.6
Congenital Adrenal Hyperplasia (CAH) Masculinizes Genetic Females Ambiguous external genitalia can result when females are exposed prenatally to high levels of androgens. Males exposed to excess androgens mature at early ages but are otherwise normal.

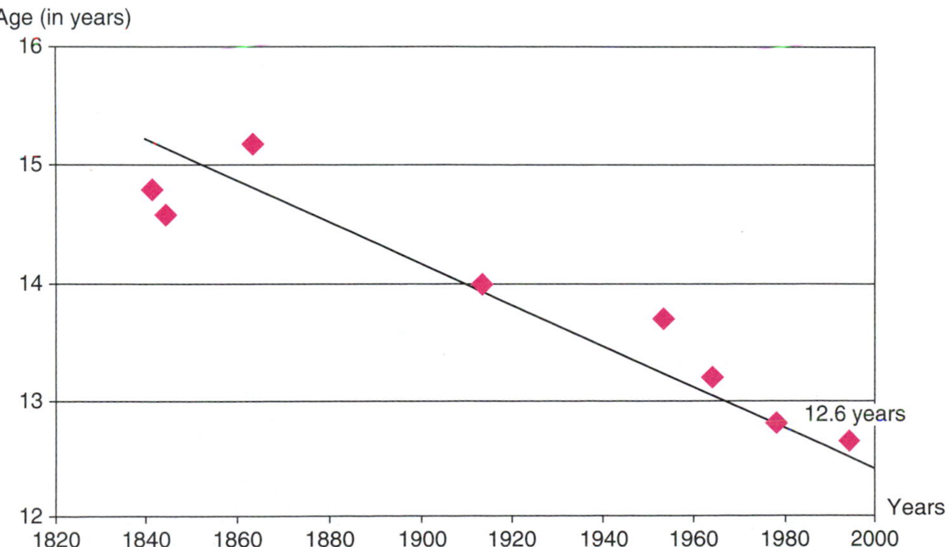

Figure 10.7
Female Age at Puberty Since 1840, the average age of puberty has dropped from nearly 16 years to around 12 years (Ducros, 1978). Among the possible explanations for this drop are increased rates of obesity and exposure to estrogen-like chemicals from foods, plastics, and insecticides.

secondary sex characteristics Characteristics related to sex that appear at puberty, including deepening voice and facial hair growth in males and widening hips and breast development in females.

estrogen A steroid hormone that develops and maintains typically female characteristics.

estradiol (es-trah-DIE-ahl) An estrogen hormone synthesized primarily in the ovaries.

gonadotropin-releasing hormone (GnRH) (go-nad-oh-TROPE-in) A hormone released by the hypothalamus that stimulates the release of luteinizing hormone (LH) and follicle-stimulating hormone (FSH) by the anterior pituitary gland.

follicle-stimulating hormone (FSH) A hormone released by the anterior pituitary that stimulates the development of eggs in the ovaries and sperm in the testes.

luteinizing hormone (LH) (LOO-tin-eye-zing) A hormone released by the anterior pituitary that signals the male testes to produce testosterone and that regulates the menstrual cycle in females.

From Peterson, R. E., J. Imperato-McGinley, T. Gautier and E. Sturla, "Male pseudohermaphroditism due to steriod 5-alpha reductase deficiency," American Journal of Medicine, 62, 174, Figs. 3 and 7.

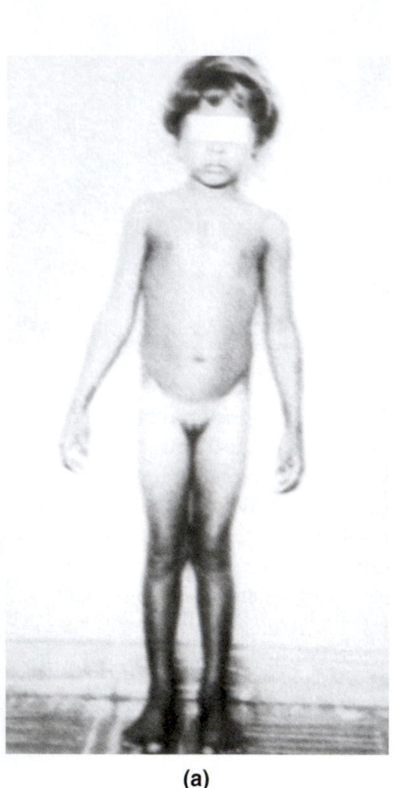

(a)

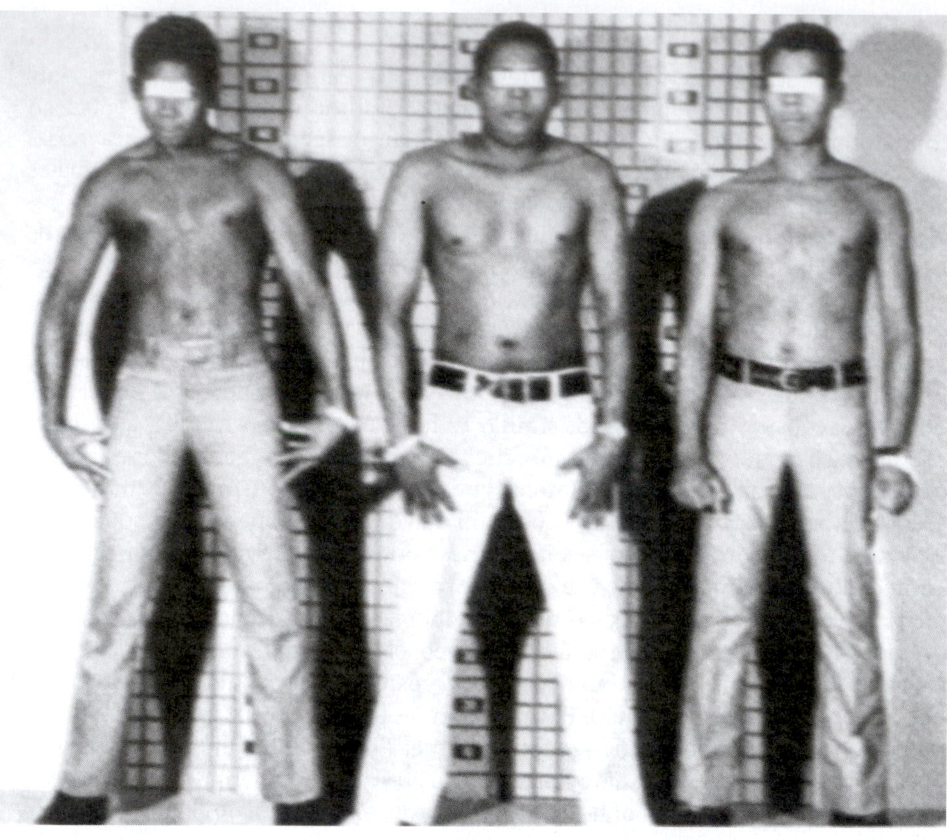

(b)

FIGURE 10.8 5-Alpha-Reductase Deficiency Changes External Appearance at Puberty (a) Individuals born with 5-alpha-reductase deficiency are born with ambiguous external genitalia and are usually raised as girls. This child is 8 years old. (b) At puberty, unconverted testosterone, which is unaffected by the syndrome, produces male secondary sex characteristics. The male on the right is the normal brother of the male on the left, and the males on the left and in the center have 5-alpha-reductase deficiency.

produce small amounts of estrogens, including estradiol, and the ovaries produce small amounts of androgens, including testosterone.

In males, this burst of additional androgens stimulates muscular development, maturity of the external genitalia, facial hair, and enlargement of the larynx, which leads to a deeper voice. In conjunction with LH and FSH, testosterone begins to regulate the production of sperm. Testosterone also affects a male's hairline and can result in baldness later in adulthood. In females, estradiol produces breast growth, maturity of the external genitalia, maturity of the uterus, and changes in fat distribution and quantity. In both sexes, estradiol slows down skeletal growth. Individuals who experience early sexual maturation stop growing at earlier ages.

We have previously reviewed atypical cases in which the first two organizing steps, involving the development of gonads and internal sex organs, were adversely affected. A very rare condition known as **5-alpha-reductase deficiency** affects the last step, the maturation of the external genitalia. This condition, first observed in an extended family group living in the Dominican Republic, affects a male's ability to produce the enzyme 5-alpha-reductase. This enzyme converts testosterone into 5-alpha-dihydrotestosterone. As we saw previously, 5-alpha-dihydrotestosterone is responsible for the masculinization of the external genitalia in the fetus. Without sufficient 5-alpha-reductase, these individuals are born with ambiguous external genitalia and are typically raised as females. Development of male internal sexual structures is not affected by this condition because this process is governed by unconverted testosterone, which is normal in these cases. At puberty, increased levels of testosterone activate the development of secondary sex characteristics in a typical manner. In a surprising turn of events, about 60 percent of the children raised as girls develop normal male external genitalia and take on a male gender role (Cohen-Kettenis, 2005; Imperato-McGinley, Guerrero, Gautier, & Peterson, 1974; Imperato-McGinley, Peterson, Gautier, & Sturla, 1979). In the Dominican Republic, these children are referred to as the "guevedoces," or "eggs (testes) at 12." The transition from young female to teen male is illustrated in Figure 10.8.

5-alpha-reductase deficiency A rare condition in which a child is born with ambiguous genitalia but develops male secondary sex characteristics at puberty.

INTERIM SUMMARY 10.1

Summary Table: Steps in Sexual Development

Chromosomes (determined at conception)	Gonads (6–8 weeks postconception)	Internal Structures (9–12 weeks postconception)	External Structures (6–12 weeks postconception)	Puberty (8–16 years)
XX	At **6 weeks,** primordial gonads are developed but are undifferentiated in male or female structures.	• Müllerian system develops in the absence of androgens and anti-Müllerian hormone. • Primitive, non-functional Wolffian system is retained.	In the absence of androgens such as testosterone, female external structures (labia, clitoris, outer vagina) develop.	• Gonadotropin-releasing hormone (GnRH) stimulates the release of LH and FSH by the pituitary. • LH and FSH signal the ovaries to begin releasing estradiol.
XY	At **6 weeks,** primordial gonads are developed but are undifferentiated in male or female structures. At **8 weeks,** testes-determining factor encoded by the *SRY* gene on the Y chromosome stimulates the development of primordial gonads, leading to testes.	• Testosterone stimulates development of the Wolffian system. • Anti-Müllerian hormone stimulates the deterioration of the Müllerian system.	5-alpha-reductase converts testosterone to 5-alpha-dihydrotestosterone, which in turn masculinizes the external structures into penis and scrotum.	• Gonadotropin-releasing hormone (GnRH) stimulates the release of LH and FSH by the pituitary. • LH and FSH stimulate the release of additional testosterone by the testes.

Summary Points

1. Sexual development begins with chromosomes. A person with two X chromosomes typically will be female, whereas a person with an X and a Y typically will be male. Variations in the number of sex chromosomes may lead to Turner syndrome (XO), Kleinfelter syndrome (XXY), the XYY male, among other conditions. **(LO1)**
2. Testis-determining factor turns the primordial gonads into testes. In the absence of testis-determining factor, ovaries will develop. Prenatal androgens promote the development of male internal organs and masculinize the external genitalia. Anti-Müllerian hormone prevents the development of female organs. **(LO2)**
3. At puberty, follicle-stimulating hormone (FSH) and luteinizing hormone (LH) promote the release of testosterone by the testes and estradiol by the ovaries, leading to the development of secondary sex characteristics. **(LO2)**
4. Variations in the development of internal organs, external genitalia, and secondary sex characteristics occur in androgen insensitivity syndrome, congenital adrenal hyperplasia, and 5-alpha-reductase deficiency. **(LO2)**

Review Questions

1. What processes must occur in order to develop male and female gonads, internal organs, and external genitalia?
2. What abnormalities can occur in sexual development?

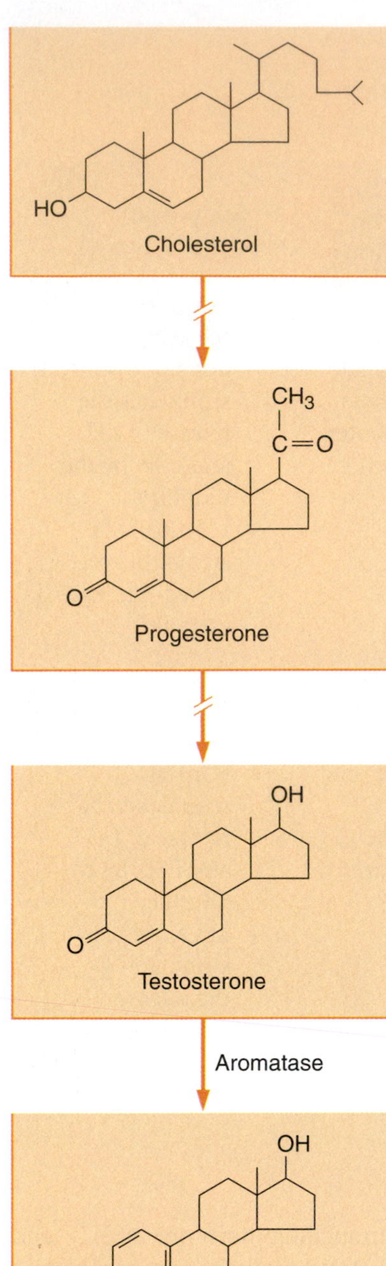

■ **Figure 10.9**
The Synthesis of Human Sex Hormones Sex hormones are steroids derived from cholesterol. There are several chemical reactions, indicated by the broken arrows, that take place in the development of progesterone from cholesterol and testosterone from progesterone. However, there is only one step, aromatization, that is necessary to turn testosterone into estradiol.

follicle (FALL-i-kul) One of several clusters of cells in the ovary each of which contains an egg cell.
ovum A female reproductive cell, or egg.

Hormones and Sexual Behavior

Sex hormones play both organizational and activating roles in sexual development. In prenatal and early postnatal development, sex hormones organize circuits in the brain that differ according to sex. These circuits are then activated by the sex hormones at the onset of puberty.

Sex hormones are classified as steroids, chemicals that are synthesized from cholesterol in the gonads and in lesser amounts, in the adrenal glands. The chemical structure of cholesterol and the synthesis of the major sex hormones are illustrated in ■ Figure 10.9. Males and females both produce androgens and estrogens, but in different amounts. Females produce about 10 percent of the amount of androgens produced by males.

Regulation of Sex Hormones by the Hypothalamus and Pituitary Gland

The hypothalamus exerts control over the release of sex hormones through its secretion of gonadotropin-releasing hormone (GnRH). Light sensed by the retina increases GnRH secretion through its action on melatonin, a neurohormone implicated in the regulation of sleep and produced by the nearby pineal gland (see Chapter 11). Melatonin normally inhibits the release of GnRH, and light in turn inhibits melatonin, which is secreted primarily at night. Light, therefore, increases GnRH release by reducing the inhibition normally produced by melatonin.

In nonhuman species, this response of the hypothalamus to light provides means for producing offspring at the right time of year. Fertility can be timed according to the lengthening or shortening of daylight hours. Human beings show this same competition between GnRH and melatonin release, but the exact impact on sexual behavior is unknown. Like other mammals, human beings do show some evidence of seasonality in birth rates. In countries such as Sweden, where there are strong contrasts between seasons in length of day, fertility is highest during the summer, leading to a spring-season baby boomlet (Rojansky, Brzezinski, & Schenker, 1992). However, most popular media reports of increased birth rates nine months following disasters, such as earthquakes, football strikes, the New York City blackout of 1965, and other confining situations, are not supported by statistical analysis (Udry, 1970).

GnRH secreted by the hypothalamus travels to the anterior pituitary gland, shown in ■ Figure 10.10. In response to GnRH, the anterior pituitary releases the gonadotropins, luteinizing hormone (LH) and follicle-stimulating hormone (FSH). As we saw previously, the initial release of these hormones is associated with the onset of puberty. From puberty on, the gonadotropins continue to play a major role in fertility. In males, LH signals the testes to produce testosterone. Both testosterone and FSH are required for the maturation of sperm. In females, LH and FSH control the menstrual cycle.

The Menstrual Cycle and Female Fertility

As shown in ■ Figure 10.11, the menstrual cycle represents a very stable and predictable fluctuation in events controlled by LH and FSH. On the first day of menstruation, the anterior pituitary gland increases secretion of FSH. When this hormone circulates to the ovaries, they respond by developing **follicles,** small clusters of cells that each contain an egg cell, or **ovum.** One follicle begins to develop more rapidly than the others, and it releases estrogens that inhibit the growth of competing follicles. If more than one follicle matures, and the ova are fertilized, fraternal (nonidentical) twins will develop. Commonly prescribed fertility drugs stimulate the development of follicles and ova and subsequently promote multiple births (Imaizumi, 2003). Estrogens from the follicle also provide feedback to the hypothalamus and pituitary gland, which respond by sharply increasing release of LH. Increased LH levels initiate the release

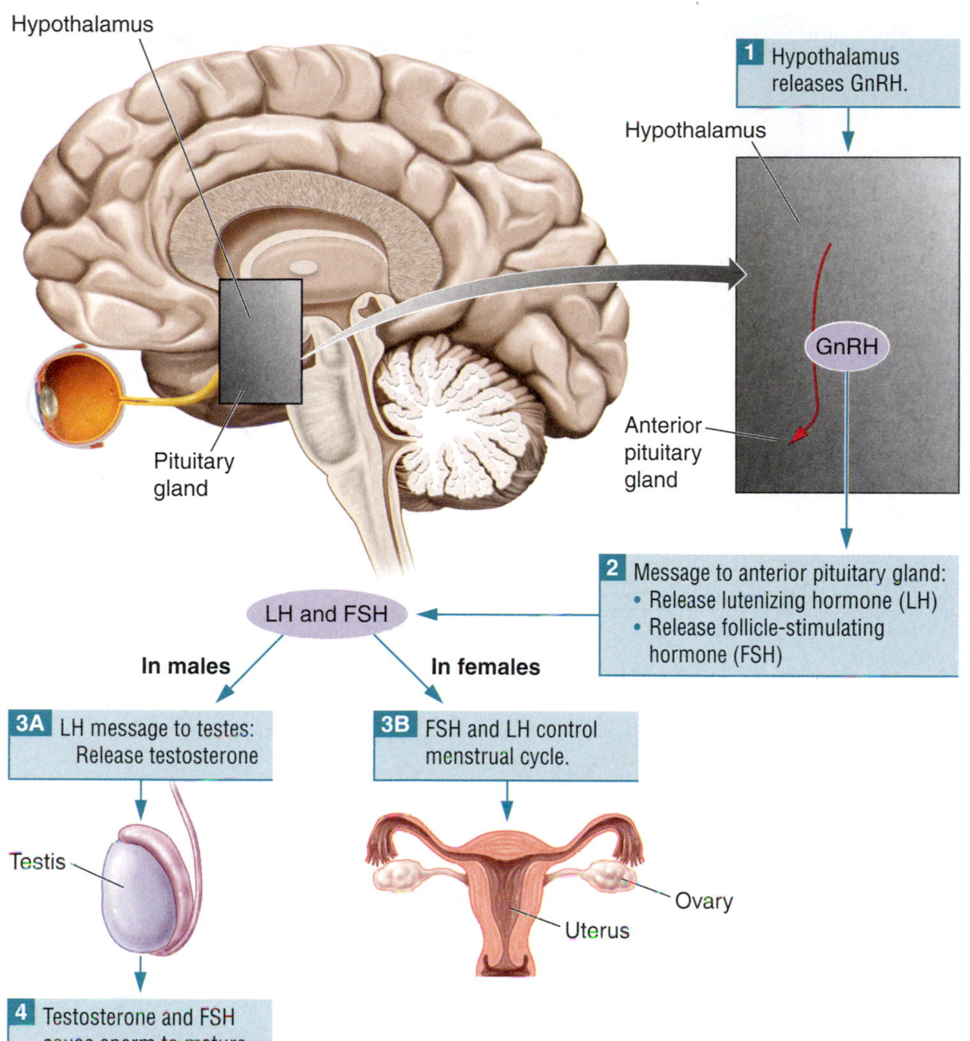
Hypothalamus
1 Hypothalamus releases GnRH.
Hypothalamus
GnRH
Pituitary gland
Anterior pituitary gland
2 Message to anterior pituitary gland:
• Release lutenizing hormone (LH)
• Release follicle-stimulating hormone (FSH)
LH and FSH
In males
In females
3A LH message to testes: Release testosterone
3B FSH and LH control menstrual cycle.
Testis
Ovary
Uterus
4 Testosterone and FSH cause sperm to mature.

■ **Figure 10.10 Hypothalamic Control of the Pituitary Gland** By secreting GnRH, the hypothalamus stimulates the release of luteinizing hormone (LH) and follicle-stimulating hormone (FSH) by the anterior pituitary gland. In males, LH signals the testes to produce testosterone. Both testosterone and FSH are necessary for producing mature sperm. In females, LH and FSH control the menstrual cycle.

of the ovum, or **ovulation,** about two weeks after the first day of the last menstruation. Estradiol released by the ovaries signals the uterus to thicken in anticipation of a fertilized embryo.

After the release of the ovum, the ruptured follicle is now called the **corpus luteum,** which means "yellow body." The corpus luteum releases estradiol and a new hormone, **progesterone.** Progesterone promotes pregnancy (gestation) by preventing the development of additional follicles and by further developing the lining of the uterus. If fertilization does not take place, the corpus luteum stops producing estradiol and progesterone. When levels of these hormones drop, the uterine lining cannot be maintained, menstruation will start, and the entire cycle will repeat.

Correlations Between Mood, Menstruation, and Childbirth Approximately 5 to 8 percent of women experience **premenstrual syndrome** in response to shifts in the hormones that regulate the menstrual cycle (Yonkers, O'Brien, & Eriksson, 2008). Premenstrual syndrome is characterized by physical symptoms of bloating and breast enlargement and tenderness as well as psychological symptoms of depression and irritability. Severe cases of premenstrual mood changes are diagnosed as **premenstrual dysphoric disorder (PMDD).** Women with PMDD experience more depression, changes in appetite (consuming more calories total and more calories from fat), and impaired cognitive performance than women who do not suffer from this disorder (Reed, Levin, & Evans, 2008). These symptoms are consistent with a hypothesis linking serotonin dysfunction with PMDD, leading to the current treatment of medication with SSRIs (ibid.)

ovulation The process of releasing a mature egg from the ovary.

corpus luteum (KOR-pus LOO-tee-um) A yellow mass of cells in the ovary formed by a ruptured follicle that has released an egg.

progesterone (pro-JES-ter-ohne) A hormone produced in the corpus luteum that prevents the development of additional follicles and promotes the growth of the uterine lining.

premenstrual syndrome A condition in which some women experience physical and psychological symptoms immediately prior to the onset of menstruation.

premenstural dysphoric disorder (PMDD) A condition in which premenstrual mood changes are unusually severe.

FIGURE 10.11
The Human Menstrual Cycle The menstrual cycle is tightly regulated by the release of GnRH from the hypothalamus, LH and FSH by the anterior pituitary gland, and estrogens and progesterone from the follicles and corpus luteum.

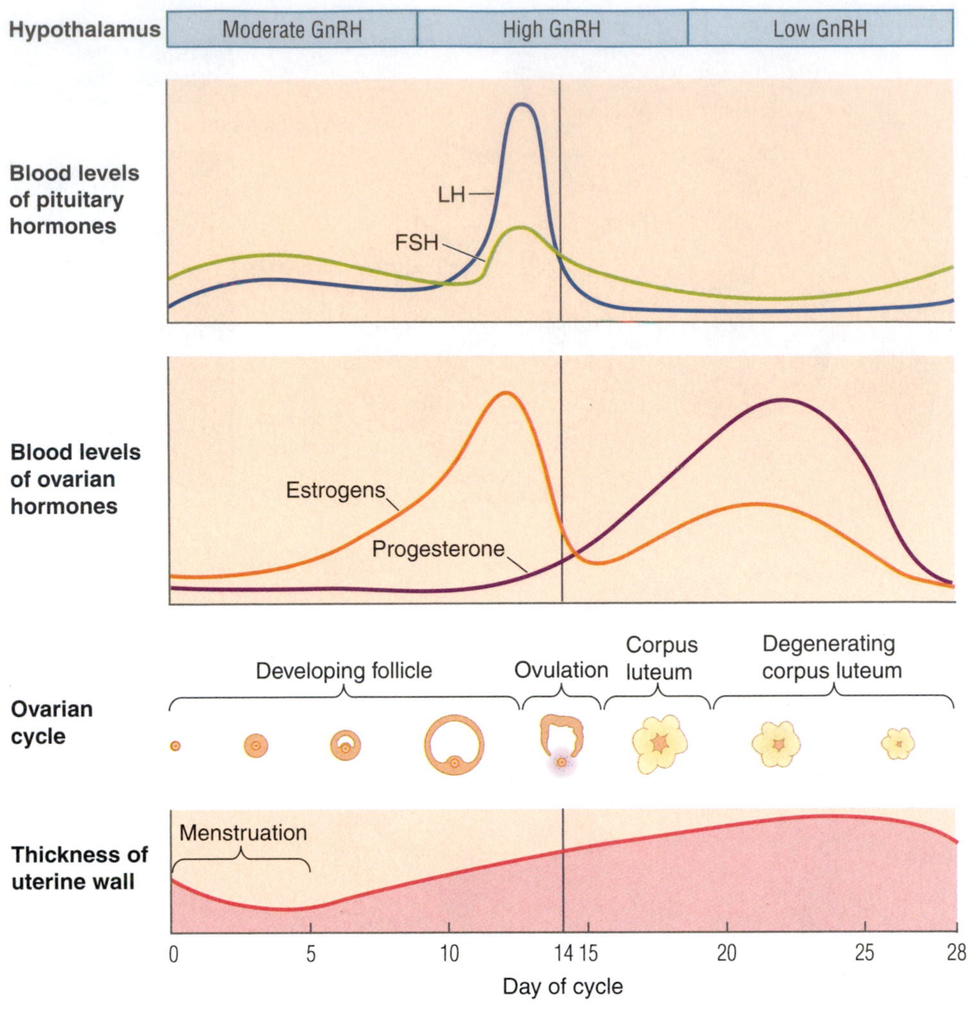

Some men spend a lifetime in an attempt to comprehend the complexities of women. Others pre-occupy themselves with somewhat simpler tasks, such as understanding the theory of relativity!
Albert Einstein

Within one year of the delivery of a baby, approximately 10 to 15 percent of women experience **postpartum depression** as hormones shift from the pregnant state back to normal monthly cycles (Centers for Disease Control [CDC], 2008). Postpartum depression appears to be quite mild in the vast majority of cases. Terp and Mortensen (1998) evaluated psychiatric admissions for women who had given birth in the previous 91 days and compared these rates with admissions data for women who had not given birth in this period. They noted that the risk of psychiatric admission was only slightly increased for the women who had recently given birth. Mothers at highest risk for postpartum depression are young (younger than 20 years of age), unmarried, less educated, and of lower socioeconomic status. A history of being physically abused or using tobacco during the last three months of pregnancy also increases risk (Centers for Disease Control [CDC], 2008).

Female Contraception Women who are exclusively breast-feeding their infants (no water, juice, solid foods, or formula) and are not menstruating have less than a 1 to 6 percent chance of becoming pregnant (Gray et al., 1990; Li & Qiu, 2007). Breast-feeding suppresses GnRH, which in turn interferes with the pulse of LH associated with follicle growth and ovulation (McNeilly, 2001, see Figure 10.11)

Oral contraceptives (birth control pills) work by providing hormones that interfere with normal ovulation. There are two types of commonly used oral contraceptives, the combination pill and the progestin-only pill. The combination pill contains two synthetic hormones, an estrogen and progestin (a hormone similar to progesterone). This pill prevents the maturation of follicles and ovulation. The progestin-only pill prevents the thinning of cervical mucus that typically accompanies ovulation. Subsequently, the passage of sperm into the uterus and fallopian tubes

postpartum depression A condition in which mothers who have recently given birth experience feelings of depression due to their rapidly changing hormonal environment.

becomes less likely. Both pills also act to prevent fertilized eggs from implanting in the lining of the uterus.

All oral contraceptives reduce a woman's testosterone levels. As a result, some women using oral contraceptives experience less acne, a condition that is correlated with testosterone levels (Frangos, Alavian, & Kimball, 2008, Thiboudot & Chen, 2003). As we will see later in this chapter, a woman's sexual interest is influenced by her testosterone levels, and a small number of women using oral contraceptives report reduced sexual drive (Dei, Verni, Bigozzi, & Bruni, 1997). However, a review of 30 years of the medical literature in this area revealed no consistent effects of oral contraceptives on female sexual interest (Schaffir, 2006).

Women can choose methods that have more long-term effects on fertility. In the Norplant method, six matchstick-sized tubes are implanted in a woman's upper arm under local anesthesia. The tubes release a progestin over a period of six months. Medroxyprogesterone acetate (MPA or Depo-Provera contraceptive injection) is administered by injection at three-month intervals (U.S. Food and Drug Administration, 1993). MPA is similar in chemical structure to progesterone and acts to suppress ovulation. In 2004, the U.S. Food and Drug Administration issued a warning about bone density loss associated with long-term use of Depo-Provera (U.S. Food and Drug Administration, 2004).

Emergency contraception is administered within 72 hours of intercourse. The "morning after" pill actually consists of a series of typical birth control pills taken at specified time intervals. The high hormone levels resulting from this procedure interfere with the implantation of an embryo in the uterine lining (Ling, Robichaud, Zayid, Wrixon, & MacLeod, 1979; Ling et al., 1983). Copper-bearing intrauterine wires are also used for emergency contraception purposes (Trussell, Ellertson, Stewart, Raymond, & Shochet, 2004). Mifepristone, also known as RU-486 or the abortion pill, interrupts pregnancies up to nine weeks following conception by blocking the action of progesterone (Fiala & Gemzel-Danielsson, 2006). Recall that progesterone is required to maintain the lining of the uterus. In the absence of progesterone, the uterus lining will shed, along with the implanted embryo, and the pregnancy will be terminated.

The concept of monthly menstruation as a natural part of the female experience has been questioned by Elsimar Coutinho (1999), the Brazilian physician who developed Depo-Provera. According to Coutinho, the number of lifetime menstrual cycles for the average woman has increased from 100 a century ago to over 400 today. Due to frequent pregnancies, reduced amounts of food, later puberty, and lengthy lactation, our female ancestors menstruated less frequently. We know that the risk of many reproductive cancers is reduced with each pregnancy. However, Coutinho argues that it is not the pregnancy that provides the protective benefit but the lack of ovulation, menstruation, and high estrogen levels associated with the menstrual cycle. The use of uninterrupted cycles of birth control pills to reduce the frequency of menstruation has become an accepted medical practice (Edelman et al., 2005; Kwiecien, Edelman, Nichols, & Jensen, 2003).

Sex Hormones and Female Behavior

In the females of species that undergo **estrus,** a period of hours or days in which the female is receptive to males, hormones play an important role in determining the timing and frequency of sexual behavior. Estrus coincides with ovulation in many species, making the likelihood of fertilization quite high. During nonestrus periods, a female will not only reject sexual overtures from males, but she is also likely to respond aggressively to his advances. Only humans and Old World primates experience menstrual cycles, and their sexual activity is quite different from species that have seasonal mating patterns or estrus (Rushton et al., 2001).

My girlfriend always laughs during sex—no matter what she's reading.

Steve Jobs

Sexual Interest in Human Females The sexual activity of human females, who do not display estrus, is under little if any control of the hormones involved with ovulation. Human females show receptivity throughout the menstrual cycle, although some women report feeling slightly more interest in sex around the time of ovulation

estrus (ES-truss) A regularly occurring period of sexual desire and fertility in some mammals.

WHY DOES THIS MATTER?

The Controversy Over Gender Differences in Cognitive Abilities

Although few dispute findings that indicate that men have a slight advantage in spatial skills and women have a slight advantage in verbal skills, the sources and implications of those differences are the subjects of hot debate. Understanding the differences between men and women in cognition matters because we do not accept discrimination on the basis of gender but find it difficult to know when and where discrimination is occurring.

Steven Pinker and Elizabeth Spelke, both of Harvard University, debated the origin of gender differences in cognition in the aftermath of the firing of Harvard University president Lawrence Summers ("The science of gender and science: Pinker vs. Spelke, a debate," 2005). Summers had made public remarks asking whether the underrepresentation of women on faculties of mathematics and science departments might originate to some degree in ability.

Pinker's argument emphasized that although bias and socialization do occur, Summers' question has scientific merit. In other words, intrinsic differences between male and female cognition might contribute to the observed, real-world discrepancies in male and female representation on science and math faculties. Pinker argued that elite university faculties represent the extremes of abilities, and slight differences between groups are statistically magnified at the extreme ends of a normal distribution. For example, we can agree that men as a group are somewhat taller than women; the average American man is 5'10" and the average American woman is 5'4". However, sex differences in height become more extreme as we move away from averages and look at progressively taller people. The ratio of males to females having a height of 5'10" is 30:1, but the ratio of males to females having a height of 6 feet is 2000:1. Very slight differences in average aptitudes for math and science between men and women would also be magnified at the highest levels of performance.

Spelke rejected the idea that men and women differ in aptitude for mathematics and science. Because boys and girls generally perform equally in elementary school math concepts and differences emerge only at later stages in education, she argued, discrimination and social forces are responsible for the smaller pool of qualified women for science and math faculty hiring. Biased socialization early in life by parents, teachers, and counselors tends to redirect talented women into non-math and science academic pathways. Other talented women are passed over due to discrimination, as evidenced by research showing that faculty evaluated an identical résumé more negatively when it was attributed to a female than when it was attributed to a male. The existing discrepancy in math and science faculties might convince girls that these fields are "male."

Regardless of our opinions about gender differences in cognition, we must remind ourselves that conclusions based on group differences should never be applied to individuals. There are many talented women in math and science, and many men have excellent verbal skills. After all, Shakespeare was a male.

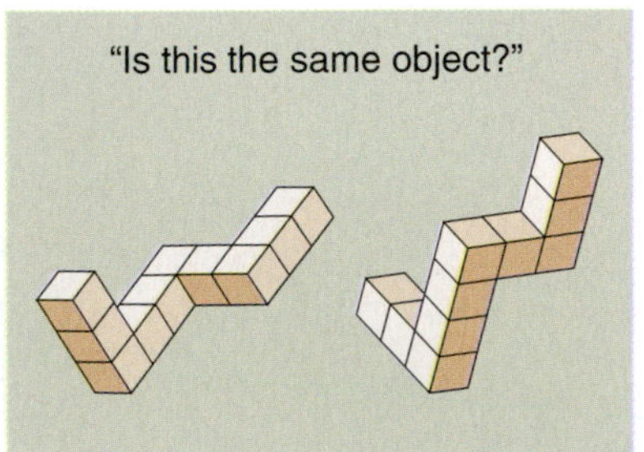

Figure Rotation

■ **FIGURE 10.12**
Sex Influences Cognition Women generally have a slight advantage in verbal tasks such as naming objects that have the same color and listing words that begin with a particular letter. Men have a slight advantage in spatial tasks, such as this figure rotation task. When asked whether the two shapes are the same, males respond somewhat faster than females.

(Slob, Bax, Hop, Rowland, & van der Werff ten Bosch, 1996). Menopause and the surgical removal of the ovaries both exert a dramatic influence on a woman's hormone levels yet have little effect on her sexual interest and activity (Galyer, Conaglen, Hare, & Conaglen, 1999).

A woman's testosterone levels have the greatest impact on her sexual activity. A woman's ovaries produce testosterone as well as estrogens. Women who receive standard estrogen replacement therapy following the surgical removal of their ovaries still report less satisfaction with their sex lives than before surgery (Kingsberg et al., 2007; Shifren et al., 2000). The estrogen therapy alone did not prevent negative changes in sexual interest. After the women were given testosterone through a skin patch, they reported having sex more frequently and enjoying it more. In addition, they scored higher on questionnaires of psychological well-being. Because women derive about half of their testosterone from the adrenal glands, adrenal disease can also have negative impacts on sexual behavior (Mazer, 2002).

Estrogens and Cognition Markus Hausmann and his colleagues (2000) studied the influence of women's hormone levels on the performance of spatial tasks. On tests of mental figure rotations, like the sample shown in ■ Figure 10.12, women received their best scores when testosterone levels were high and their worst scores when estrogen levels were high. In contrast to performance on spatial tasks, verbal fluency and manual dexterity in women appear to be correlated with higher levels of estrogens (Kimura & Hampson, 1994). These hormonal effects are consistent with the observation that males have a slight advantage in spatial tasks, whereas females have a slight advantage in verbal tasks (see Chapter 13).

Estrogens have a protective effect on memory in general, and verbal memory in particular, in postmenopausal women (Sherwin & Henry, 2008). Estrogen replacement therapy (ERT), particularly in the few years immediately following menopause, is helpful in preventing later cognitive decline. Unfortunately, ERT increases risks for cardiovascular disease and cancer.

A woman especially, if she has the misfortune of knowing anything, should conceal it as well as she can.

Jane Austen

Sex Hormones and Male Behavior

In addition to their important organizational roles in the development of male sexual structures and characteristics, androgens activate male behavior as well. Androgens influence male competitiveness, sexual frequency, and cognition.

Androgens and Competition Among male collegiate athletes, testosterone levels appear to increase in anticipation of a competition. Following a competition, testosterone has been shown to increase further in the winners and decrease in the losers (Booth, Shelley, Mazur, Tharp, & Kittok, 1989). Simply observing a competition influences testosterone levels. Men cheering for the successful Brazilian soccer team at the 1994 World Cup competition experienced increases in testosterone, whereas men supporting the losing Italian team experienced a decrease (Bernhardt, Dabbs, Fielden, & Lutter, 1998).

Androgens and Sexual Interest Male sexual frequency varies significantly from culture to culture, reminding us that hormones are just a part of the story. Subjective sexual well-being depends on a number of factors, including relative equality between the sexes, mental and physical health, and the importance of sex to the individual (Laumann et al., 2006).

As long as a young human male's testosterone level falls within normal limits, it does not provide a strong predictor of his sexual frequency (Gray et al. 2005). However, the sexual frequency of older men is more closely correlated with their testosterone levels (ibid.). When testosterone is dramatically reduced below normal levels at any age, significant changes in male sexual behavior occur. MPA, or Depo-Provera, is used not only as a contraceptive method for women, but in larger and more frequent doses, as a form of chemical castration for male sex offenders (Berlin, 1997). MPA reduces circulating testosterone levels in men to pre-puberty levels, generally eliminating any sexual activity (Kravitz et al., 1995; Meyer, Cole, & Emory, 1992).

Men in stable, long-term marriages have lower testosterone levels than single men or men who are within a few years of divorce (Mazur & Michalek, 1998). These findings raise two possibilities. The first explanation is that being partnered reduces testosterone, perhaps due to lower levels of competition with other men for mates. The second explanation suggests that men with lower levels of testosterone are more successful in maintaining stable relationships. Evidence for this second explanation was provided by a longitudinal study in which partnering and unpartnering did not impact men's testosterone levels (van Anders & Watson, 2006). A subsequent study found that men in a monogamous, committed relationship had lower testosterone levels than single men, and men who were involved in multiple committed relationships had the highest testosterone of all (van Anders, Hamilton, & Watson, 2007). Women in multiple committed relationships had higher testosterone than other women, emphasizing again that testosterone plays an important part in sexual interest for both males and females.

Androgens and Cognitive Behavior Men are commonly believed to have slight advantages over women in tasks involving spatial relations, such as map reading, maze learning, and the mental rotation of objects (Kimura, 1992). This male advantage in spatial relations appears early in childhood (Liben & Golbeck, 1980). Further evidence suggesting that this advantage is based on testosterone comes from research showing improved performance on spatial tasks by older men receiving testosterone supplements (Janowsky, Oviatt, & Orwell, 1994). Surprisingly, men who received

AP Photo/Bob Edme

FIGURE 10.13
Elite Athletes Attempt to Boost Performance Through Steroids
After numerous denials, track and field superstar Marion Jones finally admitted to having used steroids. Consequently, she was stripped of all medals she had won from 2000 on, and she was sentenced to six months of jail for perjury.

testosterone supplements also improved their scores on verbal fluency tests by a factor of 20 percent (O'Connor, Archer, & Wu, 2000). We observed previously that estrogens, not testosterone, had a beneficial effect on the verbal fluency of women.

Male Contraceptives Currently, the only methods of contraception available to men are condoms, withdrawal, and vasectomies. A number of additional options designed to prevent male fertility are under investigation. Among the approaches currently being explored are birth control pills for men containing progestin (also a key ingredient in birth control pills for women), an "Intra Vas" device that physically blocks the movement of sperm, and pills that reduce a man's vitamin A levels and, consequently, his fertility (Aaltonen et al., 2007). Work in this area has been slowed by perceptions on the part of the pharmaceutical industry that little market exists for male contraceptive alternatives, especially those that are associated with side effects. However, others argue that men want additional "control" and wish to participate more in reproductive decisions (Harper, 2008).

Anabolic Steroids

Anabolic steroids, synthetic versions of testosterone that build tissue, have legitimate medical uses in cases of malnutrition and other tissue loss. These chemicals have a long history, however, in efforts to enhance physical performance and virility. Ancient Greeks are reported to have consumed animal testicles to gain strength and vitality, and testicle extracts were widely available in Western medicine beginning in the nineteenth century (Kuhn, 2002).

Over the past 50 years, anabolic steroids have become a staple in the world of sports due to their ability to promote muscle growth. In spite of efforts to curtail the use of steroids in sports, new designer drugs are constantly developed to circumvent existing tests. According to a survey of over 50,000 college students, individuals using anabolic steroids for performance-enhancing as opposed to medical reasons were a small (about 1 percent) group of primarily intercollegiate athletes (McCabe, Brower, West, Nelson, & Wechsler, 2007). Both male and female athletes use anabolic steroids to enhance performance. Steroid use ended the career of track and field superstar Marion Jones, shown in Figure 10.13.

What do these substances do that makes them attractive to athletes? Steroids build strength and muscle mass and improve recovery time following muscle damage from weightlifting and other workouts (see Chapter 8). Steroids also produce significant side effects such as acne, enlargement of the clitoris or penis, a lower voice, unusual hair loss or growth, psychological disturbances, and enlarged breasts in males. Disturbances in sodium levels caused by anabolic steroid use can lead to high blood pressure and kidney disease.

Sex Differences in the Nervous System

While acknowledging the importance of social factors in gender differences, researchers have also observed differences in the brains and nervous systems of males and females. Observations of the effects of fetal hormones on structural development and sexual behavior led to the study of the organizing function of hormones on the brain. Exposure to androgens masculinizes the brain as well as the internal and external sexual structures. What exactly do we mean by "masculinizing" a brain or nervous system? First, we must identify features that are **sexually dimorphic,** which means to display structural differences between the sexes. Second, just as we observed in the

anabolic steroid (an-uh-BALL-ik STAIR-oid) A male steroid supplement with a variety of medical applications that is also frequently abused by athletes and bodybuilders.
sexually dimorphic Displaying structural differences between the sexes.

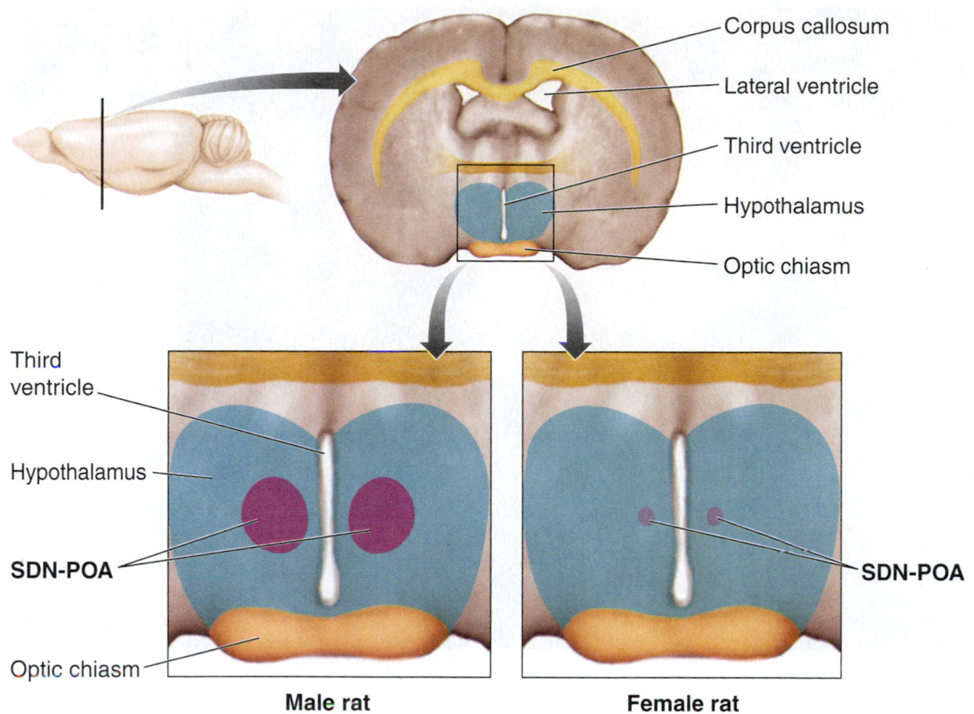

FIGURE 10.14 The SDN-POA of the Hypothalamus Is Sexually Dimorphic The SDN-POA, which is believed to be involved with sexual behavior, is much larger in male rats than in female rats. This difference probably results from the male rats' exposure to androgens shortly after birth.

masculinization of external genitalia, masculinizing the brain would result in sexually dimorphic features that take on the male pattern.

A number of sexually dimorphic structures have been identified. As shown in Figure 10.14, the **sexually dimorphic nucleus of the preoptic area (SDN-POA),** located in the hypothalamus, is much larger in male rats than in female rats (Gorski, Gordon, Shryne, & Southam, 1978). The development of the SDN-POA reflects the early organizing effects of hormone exposure. In rats, a critical window exists within a few days of birth in which exposure to androgens masculinizes the brain. At birth, the SDN-POA of rats is approximately the same size in males and females. Normally, the SDN-POA of the male begins to grow rapidly during the newborn period. If a newborn male rat is castrated, its SDN-POA is much smaller than normal. If a newborn female rat is injected with testosterone, its SDN-POA will be much larger than normal. Castration or injection of older animals does not change the size of the SDN-POA, indicating that this structure responds to early hormonal organization (Gorski, 1980). The precise function of the SDN-POA is not currently well understood, although lesions in this area of the hypothalamus generally reduce male sexual behavior (De Jonge et al., 1989).

Human beings do not have an SDN-POA, but they may have an equivalent. Four clusters of neurons in the preoptic area of the human hypothalamus are known as the **interstitial nuclei of the anterior hypothalamus,** or INAH. INAH-2 and INAH-3 are about twice as large in males as in females (Allen, Hines, Shryne, & Gorski, 1989). Byne et al. (2000) have argued that INAH-3 might be the human analog to the rodent SDN-POA. The exact function of these nuclei is not currently understood, although it is likely that these areas participate in sexual behavior. As we will see later, there may be a correlation between the size of these nuclei and a male's sexual orientation.

Additional structural differences between male and female brains have been discovered in the hypothalamus, thalamus, and in white matter (Breedlove, 1992; Hsu et al., 2008). Although it is likely that some of these differences, such as those in the hypothalamus, are related to sexual behavior, the significance of many of these differences remains unclear. Male and female patterns of performance on cognitive and emotional tasks might be related to some of these observed structural differences.

Sexual dimorphism has also been observed in the spinal cords of mammals. Male rats have more motor neurons in a structure known as the **spinal nucleus of the bulbocavernosus (SNB)** than do female rats. The male rat's motor neurons innervate

sexually dimorphic nucleus of the POA (SDN-POA) A nucleus in the preoptic area of the hypothalamus that is larger in male rats than in female rats.

interstitial nuclei of the anterior hypothalamus (INAH) (in-ter-STISH-uhl) A collection of four small nuclei in the anterior hypothalamus, two of which (INAH-2 and INAH-3) appear to be sexually dimorphic. The size of INAH-3 might be associated with male sexual orientation.

spinal nucleus of the bulbocavernosus (SNB) (bul-boe-kav-er-NO-sus) Motor neurons in the spinal cord that innervate the male rat's bulbocavernosus muscles in the penis.

Courtesy Dr. Stephen Glickman

■ **FIGURE 10.15 Spotted Hyenas Are Exposed to High Levels of Prenatal Androgens** The placenta of the spotted hyena does not prevent the exposure of female pups to high levels of androgens. As a result, the female pups show masculinized external appearance and highly aggressive behavior. The females, such as the one shown in this photo, urinate and give birth through their enlarged clitoris.

the bulbocavernosus muscles of the rat's penis. These muscles, or their equivalent, are missing in adult female rats. Prior to the rats' critical period of masculinization at birth, males and females both possess these muscles and about the same number of SNB cells (Rand & Breedlove, 1987). However, during the critical period, the low levels of androgens in female rats cause the muscles and most of the SNB neurons to die.

I have the heart of a man, not a woman, and I am not afraid of anything.
Elizabeth I

The exact mechanism by which androgens masculinize the brain appears to operate differently in different types of animals. In rodents and some other animals, the chemical process of **aromatization,** in which testosterone is transformed into estradiol, produces masculinization (Feder & Whalen, 1965). Genetic female rats are protected from the masculinizing effects of their mother's circulating estradiol by a substance known as **alpha fetoprotein** (Gorski, 1980). In many other animals, the mother's estradiol is blocked by the placenta. The placenta of the spotted hyena (*Crocuta crocuta*) does not have this capacity. As a result, female hyenas possess physical and behavioral characteristics that are usually considered masculine (Glickman et al., 1992). As you can see in ■ Figure 10.15, the female hyena has a clitoris that is about the same size as the male's penis, and she urinates and gives birth through the clitoris as well. Like the males of many species, the female hyenas behave quite aggressively and maintain a strict dominance hierarchy.

For a number of years, aromatization was believed to be responsible for the masculinization of the human brain. However, we have already seen one situation that does not fit this model. People with AIS, who have male genetic sex but inactive androgen receptors, are still overwhelmingly feminine in their behavior. During fetal development, normal male levels of testosterone would enter their brains. If aromatization of testosterone to estradiol masculinized the human brain, we would expect these individuals to show more typical male brain structure and behavior, but this does not occur (Zuloaga, Puts, Jordan, & Breedlove, 2008). In addition, males with inactive aromatase enzyme have typical male brain structure and behavior (ibid.). Consequently, we can conclude that masculinization of the human brain is not as dependent on aromatization as in rodents and some other mammals. In addition, androgens appear to play a direct role in the masculinization of the human brain that is not dependent on aromatization into estradiol.

aromatization (uh-roe-muh-ti-ZAE-shun) A chemical reaction resulting in an aromatic compound, characterized by a six-carbon ring; for example, the enzyme aromatase transforms testosterone into estradiol.

alpha fetoprotein (fee-toe-PRO-teen) A substance circulated by rats that deactivates estradiol and prevents maternal estradiol from masculinizing female pups.

A number of situations may result in the masculinization of the human female brain. We have already observed that prenatal exposure to circulating androgens in cases of CAH can have this effect. Higher levels of maternal testosterone have been correlated with daughters' more masculine play behavior, such as their choice of toys that are typically preferred by boys (Hines, Golombok, Rust, Johnston, & Golding, 2002). Prenatal exposure to many other substances, including barbiturates and the pesticide DDT, also masculinizes the brains of females (Kelly & Jessell, 1995).

Sexual Orientation

Sexual orientation refers to a stable pattern of attraction to members of a particular sex. Sexual orientation is not synonymous with sexual behavior. Many people engage in same-sex behavior and fantasy while maintaining a strong heterosexual orientation. Stoller and Herdt (1985) described a tribal culture in which all adolescent males are expected to engage in same-sex behavior until they are married to women. In spite of this prior sexual experience, the sexual orientation of these males as adults was overwhelmingly heterosexual. Approximately 3 to 4 percent of males and 1 to 2 percent of females in the American population describe themselves as exclusively homosexual, and about 1 percent describe themselves as bisexual (Smith, 1998).

Hormones, Sexual Behavior, and Sexual Orientation

There is evidence from literature on both animal and human that early exposure to androgens influences adult sexual behavior. As noted previously, male rats have a larger SDN-POA than female rats. Exposure to testosterone during a critical period accounts for this sexual dimorphism. If male rats do not receive exposure to testosterone during this critical period, their SDN-POA remains small, and their adult sexual behavior is unusual. Low-testosterone rats are less likely to engage in sexual behavior with females and more likely to engage in sexual behavior with males than are rats with normal testosterone levels (Matuszczyk, Fernandez-Guasti, & Larsen, 1988). In addition, exposure to testosterone during the critical period increases the size of SDN-POA in female rats and increases the likelihood that they will engage in sexual activity with females as adults. We have already seen that abnormal conditions such as CAH, which involves prenatal exposure to androgens, can increase the likelihood that women will engage in bisexual or lesbian behavior as adults. However, the majority of CAH women are heterosexual. Also, the majority of lesbian and bisexual women do not have a history of CAH or similar conditions.

The heterosexuality or homosexuality of many individuals is not an all-or-none proposition.

Alfred Kinsey

The development of structures that are not involved in sexual behavior often reflects the influence of prenatal hormone exposure. In humans, the high levels of prenatal androgens typical of males have an impact on the development of the inner ear. The inner ear itself produces tiny sounds, known as otoacoustic emissions, as it processes sound into neural impulses. These emissions are stronger in women than in men. Dennis McFadden and Edward Pasanen (1999) measured the otoacoustic emissions of lesbian, bisexual, and heterosexual women. The strength of the emissions in lesbian and bisexual women fell between the normal levels for heterosexual women and for men. McFadden and Pasanen suggested that exposure to prenatal androgens may have influenced both the ear structure and sexual orientation of the lesbian and bisexual women.

Another possible indicator of prenatal exposure to androgens, and the resulting influence on sexual orientation, is the so-called 2D:4D ratio (D stands for digit). Among heterosexual women, the ring (4D) and index (2D) fingers are typically about the same length. In men, the index finger is usually noticeably shorter than the ring finger. Lesbians tended to show the more masculine pattern of finger length, suggesting that they might have experienced prenatal exposure to androgens (Kraemer et al., 2006). Researchers do not find a systematic pattern of finger length among gay men as opposed to heterosexual men, however.

What could cause the differences in prenatal hormonal environments associated with homosexuality? One interesting clue comes from the observation that birth order matters for homosexual men. Men who have older brothers are slightly more likely to be gay than men who have no siblings, younger siblings only, or older sisters

(Blanchard, 1997; Cantor, Blanchard, Paterson, & Bogaert, 2002). The protein products of three genes located on the Y chromosome are believed to provoke the mother's immune response, which should become greater with each successive pregnancy with a male fetus. A strong immune response from the mother might affect the masculinization of the fetus's brain while not affecting the gonads or genitals.

Although the connections between sounds generated by your inner ear, the relative length of your fingers, the number and sex of your siblings, and your sex life may seem hopelessly vague, this research provides some insight into the impact of prenatal androgens on adult sexual orientation.

Brain Structure and Sexual Orientation

As we have seen previously, several brain structures are sexually dimorphic, especially INAH-3 in the hypothalamus. Building on these observations, Simon LeVay asked whether INAH-3 might be different in heterosexual and homosexual men. He found that INAH-3 was two to three times larger in heterosexual men than in homosexual men (LeVay, 1991). The size of INAH-3 among LeVay's homosexual subjects was not significantly different from the size observed in female subjects. ■ Figure 10.16 shows the location of INAH-3, as well as heterosexual and homosexual examples from LeVay's research.

LeVay was cautious in interpreting these results. First of all, because INAH-3 is too small to observe in living participants with current imaging technologies, LeVay studied autopsied brains. This obviously prevented him from obtaining a detailed history of his subjects' sexual behavior. The homosexual men's medical records documented their sexual behavior, as this was relevant to their diagnosis of AIDS, but those of the presumed heterosexual men did not. The study could not be extended to women, because their medical records also lacked any information regarding sexual orientation. In addition, LeVay raised the possibility that the AIDS condition, which affected his homosexual participants, could have caused shrinkage of INAH-3. However,

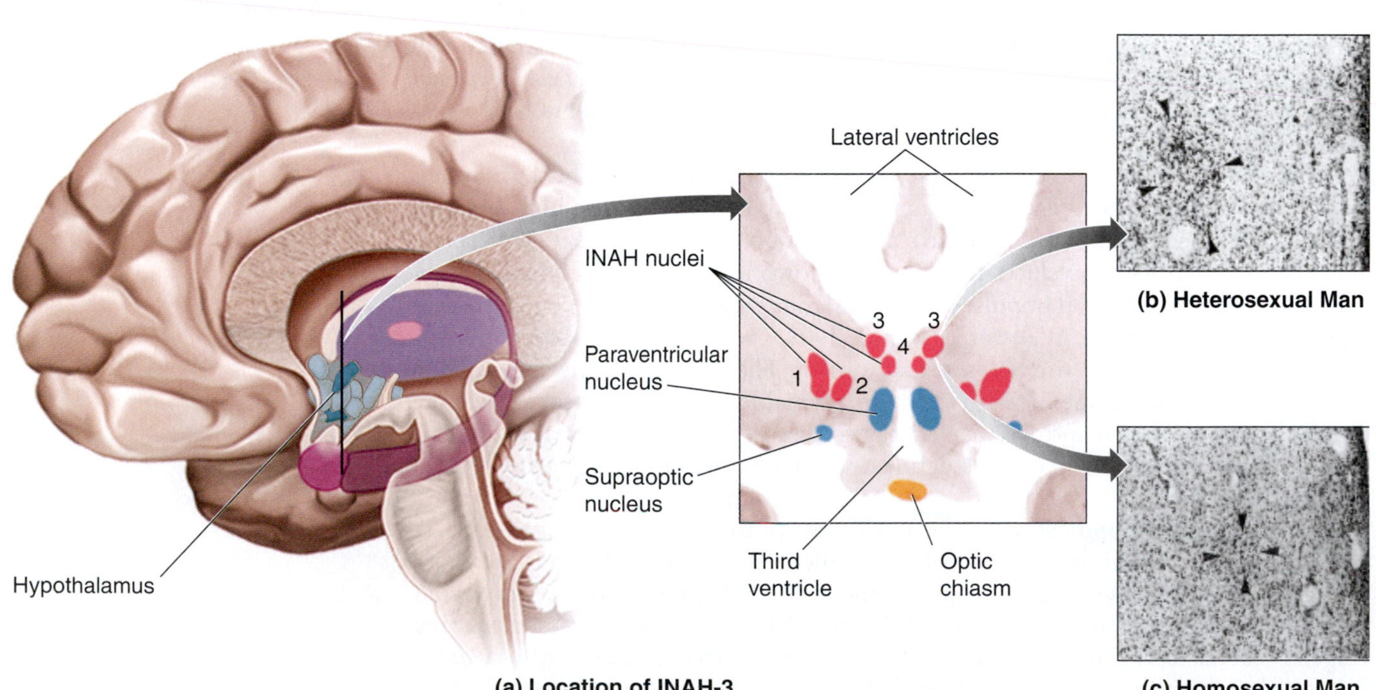

■ **Figure 10.16**
INAH-3 Size Correlates with Sexual Orientation Simon LeVay reported that INAH-3 is smaller among women and homosexual men than among heterosexual men. (a) This image shows the location of INAH-3. The micrograph in (b) is taken from a heterosexual man, whereas the micrograph in (c) is taken from a man who was homosexual.

he didn't give this argument much credibility because INAH-3 in the heterosexual subjects with AIDS followed the heterosexual male pattern. Finally, critics have suggested that engaging in different types of sexual behavior might influence the size of INAH-3. LeVay again discounted this interpretation and suggested that the differences he observed were more logically the result of prenatal factors.

Because this type of research is quite difficult to conduct with human participants, other researchers have investigated the correlation of brain structure and sexual behavior in animals. Among domestic sheep, 6 to 8 percent of rams (males) mate exclusively with other males. Kay Larkin and her colleagues (Larkin, Resko, Stormshak, Stellflug, & Roselli, 2002) studied the sheep equivalent of SDN-POA in rams who engaged in same-sex behavior, in rams that mated with ewes (females), and in ewes. SDN-POA in rams that engaged in same-sex behavior was about the same size as in ewes and differed from SDN-POA in rams that mated with ewes. These results provide a parallel to LeVay's findings in INAH-3, which is a likely human equivalent of SDN-POA.

The anterior commissure, a small band of fibers connecting the two cerebral hemispheres, is also among the structures known to be sexually dimorphic in humans. Laura Allen and Roger Gorski (1992) reported that the size of the anterior commissure varies reliably between homosexual and heterosexual males. Unlike the hypothalamus, the anterior commissure has no direct role in sexual behavior. The observed differences in this structure might simply be an additional marker like the otoacoustic emissions for an unusual fetal hormone environment.

Genes and Sexual Orientation

Genetics appear to influence sexual orientation, although the exact mechanisms are not well understood and are likely to be quite complex. It is currently unknown whether genetics can have direct effects on sexual orientation or indirect effects on prenatal androgen environments. The chances of a homosexual male twin having a homosexual brother are 20 to 25 percent for fraternal twins and about 50 percent for identical twins (Kirk, Bailey, & Martin, 2000). Compared with mothers with heterosexual sons, mothers of homosexual sons showed more extreme skewing, in which one X chromosome is much more likely to be inactivated than the other (Bocklandt, Horvath, Vilain, & Hamer, 2006, see Chapter 5).

INTERIM SUMMARY 10.2

Summary Points

1. FSH and LH regulate the female menstrual cycle. Hormonal birth control methods prevent pregnancy by interfering with aspects of this cycle. **(LO4)**
2. Levels of androgens and estrogens are related to competition, sexual frequency, and cognition. **(LO5)**
3. The prenatal masculinization of the brain in rodents appears to result from testosterone that is aromatized into estradiol in the brains of males. Human masculinization relies less on aromatization than on the direct effect of androgens. **(LO6)**
4. Several structures in the brain and nervous system appear to be sexually dimorphic, or different in males and females. **(LO6)**
5. Research on finger length and otoacoustic emissions suggest that prenatal exposure to hormones may influence sexual orientation. Genetics appear to have some role in the development of sexual orientation. **(LO6)**

Review Questions

1. What does it mean to masculinize the brain?
2. What evidence exists for a biological basis of sexual orientation?

Attraction

Attraction is usually the territory of poets and artists, not neuroscientists. Although this might not be the most romantic approach to attraction that you have ever read, it will provide insight into why you swoon over Jessica Alba or Christian Bale. Viewing beautiful people appears to be quite rewarding. Young heterosexual men were observed with fMRI while looking at the faces of average men, average women, beautiful men, and beautiful women (Aharon et al., 2001). Viewing the faces of the beautiful women activated areas of the brain involved in pleasure and reward, including the nucleus accumbens, which participates in addictive behavior (see Chapter 4). The men were also given the opportunity to press a lever to see pictures of beautiful women. The participants were willing to press the lever 6,000 times in an interval of 40 minutes, analogous to the amount of work rats are willing to do to obtain cocaine.

Cultures often have their own definition of physical beauty, but this may not be the complete source of our opinions. A preference for beauty is evident at a very early age, before the media and other cultural factors have had a chance to influence perceptions. Judith Langlois and her colleagues (Langlois, Roggman, & Rieser-Danner, 1990) found that three- and six-month-old infants spend more time staring at faces adults had judged to be attractive than at faces judged to be unattractive.

The Importance of Symmetry

What would these very young infants find so attractive? One possible factor is body symmetry, or the degree of similarity of one side of the face or body to the other. Although some parts of our bodies are notably asymmetrical, such as the location of our heart toward the left side of our chest, most of our features are relatively symmetrical. Highly symmetrical bodies are generally healthier, and some researchers believe that we are programmed to select healthy mates. As a result, we view symmetry as attractive and beautiful. Symmetrical people have more opportunities for sexual activity (Thornhill & Gangestad, 1994). According to these researchers, symmetrical men became sexually active at earlier ages than less symmetrical men. Both symmetrical males and symmetrical females had larger numbers of previous sex partners. Unfortunately, symmetrical men were less attentive to their partners and much more likely to cheat on them. As the saying goes, beauty is only skin deep.

If every one were cast in the same mould, there would be no such thing as beauty.
Charles Darwin

The Beauty of Fertility and a Good Immune System

Beyond symmetry, we make distinctions in preferred features for males and females. According to Victor Johnston (2000), the preferred female face is youthful, with a delicate jaw, full lips, and wide-set eyes. The preference for these features could reflect a natural attraction to younger females, who are most likely to be fertile. You can see the result of Johnston's analysis in ■ Figure 10.17.

Women's responses to male features are not consistent. Some features are preferred in a short-term relationship (sexual desire) that are not preferred in long-term relationships (romantic love) (Diamond, 2004; Gonzaga, Turner, Keltner, Campos, & Altemus, 2006). Women seem to find masculine men, with their square jaws and other testosterone-related facial features, more attractive as "one night stands" than their less macho counterparts. Evolutionary psychologists suggest that this attraction to masculine men results from the ability of women to recognize good genes. Testosterone is very hard on the immune system (Gaillard & Spinedi, 1998), so a man with features indicating high testosterone levels could not survive without an excellent immune system. In turn, this means that a woman's children would inherit an excellent immune system from such a father.

Balancing this attraction is women's association of negative characteristics with masculine features. Women believe that men with very masculine faces would be more dominant, less faithful, worse fathers, and have colder personalities than their more feminine looking counterparts (Boothroyd, Jones, Burt, & Perrett, 2007). Simply

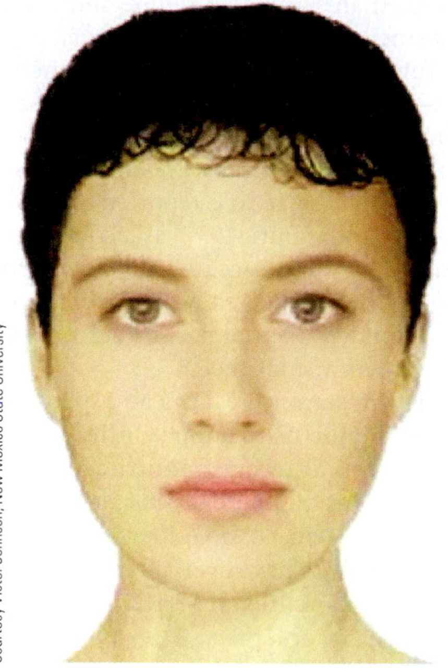
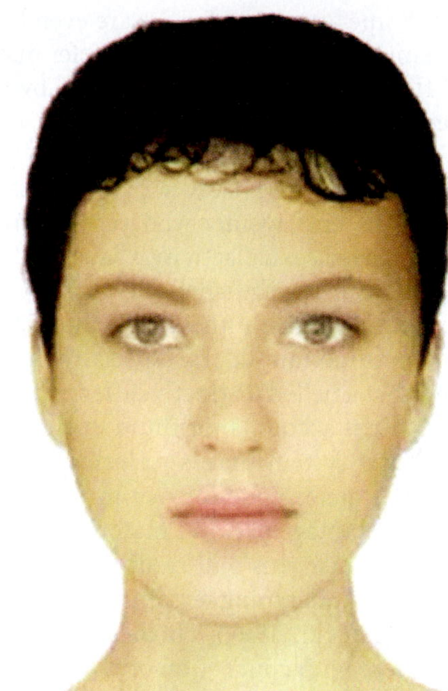

Courtesy Victor Johnson, New Mexico State University

■ **FIGURE 10.17 Beautiful Female Faces Are Symmetrical and Youthful** Using a computer program that digitally averages faces, Victor Johnston produced a composite face, shown on the left. Then he magnified the features that distinguished the face from a male and produced the beautiful hyperfemale on the right, characterized by wide-set eyes, narrow nose, full lips, and delicate jaw. Johnston argued that men are attracted to such faces because they signify youth and fertility.

looking at photographs of men's faces, women were able to anticipate how a man would score on the infant interest questionnaire, a measure of how involved a father a man is likely to be (Penton-voak et al., 2007; Roney, Hanson, Durante, & Maestripieri, 2006). Consequently, women might prefer less masculine-looking men for long-term partnerships because these men are assumed to be less likely to be unfaithful and more willing to invest in parenting. These findings are consistent with observations discussed earlier in the chapter that men with lower testosterone are more likely to be in long-term relationships.

Men pay more attention to women's figures than women pay to men's physiques (Symons, 1995). A woman's figure is far more reflective of her reproductive fitness than a man's, so behavioral geneticists argue that it merits more attention. Devendra Singh has suggested that men prefer women whose waist measurements are approximately 70 percent of their hip measurements (Singh, 1993). Between 1940 and 1990, *Playboy* centerfolds and winners of the Miss America contest became 11 to 16 pounds lighter, but their waist–hip ratio stayed very close to 0.7. The concept of a "magic" waist-hip ratio has been challenged by Tovée, Reinhardt, Emery, and Cornelissen (1998). These researchers found that men consistently preferred women with a body mass index (BMI; see Chapter 9) of 20, regardless of waist–hip ratio.

The kind of man who thinks that helping with the dishes is beneath him will also think that helping with the baby is beneath him, and then he certainly is not going to be a very successful father.

Eleanor Roosevelt

WHY DOES THIS MATTER?

Assortative Mating

Understanding the reasons for being attracted to other people matters, especially if our past choices of partners didn't work out very well. If we recognize some of the subconscious reasons we might find another person attractive, we can make better decisions in the future.

People engage in positive "assortative mating," in which they tend to be attracted to people who resemble them physically. In one typical investigation of this "matching hypothesis," college students who resembled each other were more likely to still be in a relationship nine months later (White, 1980). However, more recent data suggest that the happiest married couples are those in which the wife is rated as significantly more attractive than her husband (McNulty, Neff, & Karney, 2008). The least happy couples were those in which the man was rated as more attractive than his wife.

Although we would like to think that we select a life partner on the basis of compatibility of values, personality, interests, and character, we can't escape these physical attraction factors running in the background. By understanding them and recognizing that they play an important role in attraction, we may be able to make more satisfying choices.

After about 20 years of marriage, I'm finally starting to scratch the surface of that one (what women want). And I think the answer lies somewhere between conversation and chocolate.
Mel Gibson

Some attraction factors are even less obvious than symmetry, figure, and jaw size. We might be programmed to prefer mates that smell a particular way. However, the use of floral and other pleasant scents by the perfume industry, not to mention the large deodorant industry, might be on the wrong track. Real sex appeal is probably based on sweat. Norma McCoy and Lisa Pitino (2002) investigated the effects of underarm secretions of fertile, sexually active, heterosexual females. Compared with women wearing placebo scents, women who were wearing the underarm secretions reported significantly increased sexual activity. Claus Wederkind and Sandra Füri (1997) asked female participants to rate the smell of t-shirts worn by men over two consecutive nights according to sexiness, pleasantness, and intensity of smell. The women showed distinct preferences for certain odors, especially those that reminded them of past or current lovers and that smelled distinctly different from their fathers and brothers.

What accounts for these smell preferences? We seem to react to an aspect of the immune system that is reflected in body odor. **Major histocompatibility complex (MHC) genes** code for our immune system's ability to recognize intruders. It is to your advantage to find a mate whose MHC profile is as different as possible from your own because this will result in the best immune system possible for your children. Couples undergoing fertility treatment are more likely to have overlapping MHC profiles (Ho et al., 1994). This finding suggests that similar parental MHC profiles might interfere with conception or the viability of an embryo or fetus.

Romantic Love, Sexual Desire, and Parenting

Particularly for adolescents and young adults, very few aspects of life reach the importance and confusion associated with romantic love, long-term relationships, and establishing families. Although these processes often overlap, they represent distinct emotional and biological states. Romantic love and the bonding of parent and child both involve the establishment and maintenance of long-term relationships, whereas sexual desire promotes mating and reproduction. It is possible to experience sexual desire without romantic love, just as it is possible to experience romantic love without sexual desire (Diamond, 2004).

Romantic love produces characteristic patterns of activity in the human brain. While undergoing fMRI, participants were shown photographs of people they described as either friends or true loves (Bartels & Zeki, 2000). As shown in ■ Figure 10.18, when participants viewed lovers, increased activity was observed in areas of the brain often associated with reward. Other areas became less active when participants viewed photographs of lovers. These areas are associated with negative emotions and social judgment. Consequently, "love" is not only rewarding, but it makes us less judgmental of the lover.

The bonding that is associated with both romantic love and parenting is influenced by two closely related, yet sexually dimorphic pituitary hormones, **oxytocin** and vasopressin (also known as antidiuretic hormone or ADH; see Chapter 9). In addition to their effects elsewhere in the body, these hormones are active in the brain. In humans, vasopressin is expressed more by males and oxytocin by females (Ishunina & Swaab, 1999; van Londen et al., 1997). For both sexes, oxytocin appears to enhance bonding. Reduced levels of oxytocin in people with autism might account for the reduced sociability associated with this condition and might also explain why males with autism vastly outnumber females (Marazziti & Dell'osso, 2008).

Oxytocin is released by the pituitary gland into the circulation during orgasm for both sexes and during childbirth and breastfeeding in women. Women's oxytocin levels increase in response to a simple hug from their partners (Light, Grewen, & Amico, 2005). Oxytocin's influence on both bonding and sex, especially in women, might explain reports that women are more likely than men to equate sexual desire with feelings of romantic love (Diamond, 2004). In contrast, as we have seen previously in this chapter, sexual desire is primarily associated with testosterone in both men and women.

Although it might seem unromantic, evolutionary psychologists maintain that an overriding goal of sexual behavior is the production of offspring who will survive to

major histocompatibility complex (MHC) gene A gene that encodes our immune system's ability to recognize intruders; might account for female human preferences for male odors.

oxytocin (ok-see-TOE-sin) A hormone, released by the posterior pituitary gland, that stimulates uterine contractions, releases milk, and participates in social bonding, including romantic love and parenting behavior.

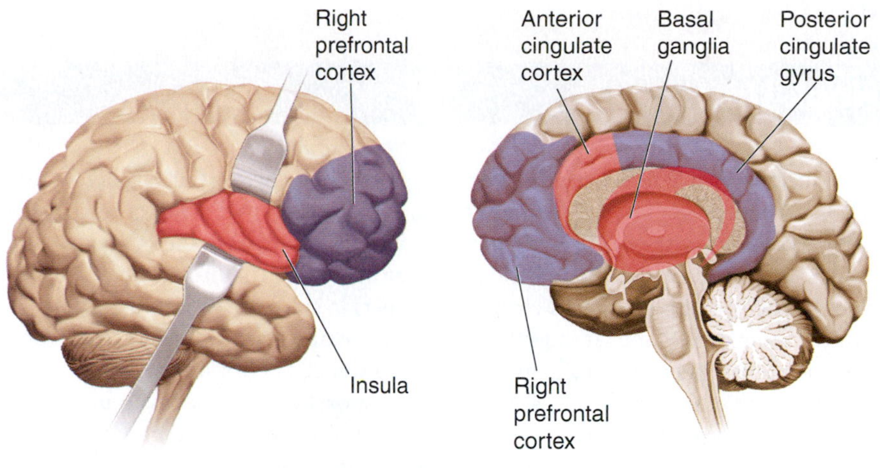

FIGURE 10.18
Brain Activity and Love Bartels and Zeki (2000) compared people's responses to photos of friends and photos of lovers. When viewing lovers, areas of the brain associated with reward and the activity of oxytocin and vasopressin showed increased activity. Areas of the brain that are associated with negative emotion, social judgment, and assessing other people's intentions and emotions were less active when viewing a loved one. Love appears to be a push–pull mechanism in which bonding activates the reward system, and social distance is reduced by silencing social judgment (Bartels & Zeki, 2004).

reproduce. According to this view, males and females, particularly among mammals, are subjected to different types of reproductive pressures. These pressures act to shape different sexual behaviors in males and females. In general, because the cost of reproduction for males consists of some sperm and a few minutes of a male's time, the most efficient reproductive strategy for males is to impregnate as many females as possible. Males should therefore behave in less selective and more promiscuous ways. In terms of reproductive success, few men can compete with Genghis Khan (1162–1227). Approximately 16 million men living today, or about 0.5 percent of the world's population, are closely related to this Mongol emperor (Zerjal et al., 2003). The reproductive pressures on males to be promiscuous are offset by the advantages fathers provide by helping to raise offspring. To the extent that a father's exclusive presence provides a higher survival rate, we would expect more monogamous behavior from males.

For females, the costs of reproduction are quite high. Not only must she maintain a lengthy pregnancy, but the female also typically bears most of the responsibility for offspring until they are mature. As a result, we would expect females to be highly selective because the number of possible offspring is sharply limited by the amount of time required to raise each to maturity. Females need to choose healthy mates to increase the chances that offspring will survive. Monogamy would help the mother retain the protection and other benefits offered by a father. Unfortunately, these characteristics do not always coexist in the same man. High testosterone males with "healthy" immune system genes are also the least likely to be monogamous. No wonder that even 77-year-old Sigmund Freud asked his diary, "What do women want?"

Mammals, including humans, show a variety of mating behaviors. Only 3 percent of mammals practice **monogamy,** in which a pair mates nearly exclusively with each other over time. About 12 percent of primate species, including humans, are most typically monogamous. Most humans practice serial monogamy, by which a person has more than one mate over a lifetime but only one mate at any given time.

To what extent are mating patterns and reproductive strategies biological in origin? For obvious ethical reasons, research on human beings in this area is difficult if not impossible to do. However, one clue comes from the study of the vole, a rather large rodent found in North America. Voles are useful in this context because they show very different mating patterns among similar species. The prairie vole (*Microtus ochrogaster*) is exclusively monogamous, and males participate substantially in the raising of young. The very similar montane vole (*Microtus montanus*) is quite promiscuous, and the males do not interact with the offspring at all. Montane vole mothers are not very nurturant, either, and abandon their pups at a very early age.

The educability of a young person as a rule comes to an end when sexual desire breaks out in its final strength.
Sigmund Freud

The key to these differences in vole behavior appears to be two hormones we met previously, oxytocin and vasopressin. Young, Wang, and Insel (1998) found that the receptor locations for oxytocin and vasopressin were different in prairie and montane voles. The difference in the effects of these two hormones on the brain accounts for the

monogamy The custom of having one mate at a time or for life.

NEW DIRECTIONS

Men, Women, and the Hook-Up

We are still far too close in time to the invention of oral contraceptives and the legalization of abortion in the 1960s and 1970s to fully understand the implications of these changes for human reproductive strategies. If we accept the idea that male and female sexual behavior has been shaped by differing reproductive strategies, what might we expect to see when technology makes it possible to separate sexual behavior from reproduction and the long-term commitment parenting represents to human beings? One new cultural norm made possible by modern contraception is the "friend with benefits" or the "hook-up," a common aspect of campus life in which people come together to have sex without any expectations for an emotional bond or shared activities such as having dinner or seeing a movie.

Sex without bonding assumes that sexual desire and romantic love are easily separable. Some researchers and clinicians have suggested that this separation is easier for males than for females (Diamond, 2004; Grossman, 2007). Although both men and women release oxytocin during orgasm, oxytocin appears to have a greater influence on feelings of romantic love in women than in men. Men's higher levels of testosterone are likely to raise the salience of sexual desire instead. As a result, women in particular might find themselves beginning to bond to their sexual partners in spite of previous intentions to keep things simple. A male partner's unwillingness to change the rules might become a source of great unhappiness.

Another aspect of oxytocin that leads to bonding is that its release can be classically conditioned. In other words, with each successive sexual interaction with a person, that individual becomes a stronger conditioned stimulus for oxytocin release (Witt, Carter, Lederhendler, & Kirkpatrick, 1997). Consequently, we would expect sexual activity to encourage bonding.

Human relationships are nothing if not complicated. What makes one person happy is likely to be very much the opposite for another. Hopefully, through further exploration of the biological and experiential correlates of behavior, we will gain enough understanding to help people make choices that will lead them to happiness and well-being.

different mating and parenting behaviors exhibited by the voles. Vasopressin appears to increase the paternal behaviors of male prairie voles, and oxytocin increases the maternal behaviors of female prairie voles (Wang, Ferris, & De Vries, 1994).

Although much research must be done before we can generalize from voles to humans, researchers are beginning to move in this direction (Bartz & Hollander, 2006). A woman's oxytocin levels during pregnancy and following childbirth predicted maternal bonding behaviors, including gazing, affectionate touching of her infant, vocalizations, and positive mood (Feldman, Weller, Zagoory-Sharon, & Levine, 2007). In a circular fashion, the oxytocin levels of young adults who were not currently in romantic relationships were correlated with their reports of bonding to their parents (Gordon et al., 2008). So far, we have not seen efforts to correlate human male vasopressin to monogamy or parenting.

Sexual Dysfunction and Treatment

All women do have a different sense of sexuality, or sense of fun, or sense of like what's sexy or cool or tough.
Angelina Jolie

Sex therapists Masters and Johnson (1970) estimated that as many as half of all American couples experienced some type of sexual problem. Many of these difficulties are psychological in origin. However, in some other cases, the causes (and cures) are biological. A pharmacological discovery has made treatment of impotence, or **erectile dysfunction,** possible for many men. Erectile dysfunction occurs when a man is unable to achieve an erection sufficient for satisfactory sexual activity. Approximately 30 million men in the United States experience some degree of erectile dysfunction, including about half the men between the ages of 40 and 70 years.

Erections occur as a result of either direct stimulation or cognitive factors. Parasympathetic neurons in the sacral spinal cord respond to both mechanoreceptors in the genitals (direct stimulation) and descending input from the brain (cognitive factors). These parasympathetic neurons release acetylcholine and nitric oxide (NO) into the spongy erectile tissues of the penis, which subsequently fill with blood. Sildenafil citrate (Viagra) promotes erection by enhancing the effects of NO on the erectile tissues (Pfizer, 2002). Research is ongoing regarding possible applications of erectile dysfunction medications to female sexual dysfunctions, but results to date have been disappointing.

erectile dysfunction The inability to get and maintain an erection long enough for satisfactory sexual activity.

INTERIM SUMMARY 10.3

Summary Table: Hormones Associated with Parenting Behavior

Hormone	Effects Observed in Humans	Effects Observed in Animals
Oxytocin	• Released during orgasm • Released during nursing; produces calming, pleasant effect • Promotes uterine contractions during childbirth • Predicts maternal bonding behaviors • Predicts bonding to parents among young adults not currently in romantic relationships	Increases parenting behavior in female prairie voles
Vasopressin	Regulates body fluid levels	Increases parenting behavior in male prairie voles

Summary Points

1. We may be preprogrammed to prefer certain physical characteristics in mates. **(LO7)**
2. Mating and parenting patterns are influenced by biological factors, including the activity of oxytocin and vasopressin. **(LO8)**

Review Questions

1. What physical features appear to be most attractive to males and to females, and how are these related to fertility and health?
2. What are the possible contributions of hormones to parenting behavior?

CHAPTER REVIEW

THOUGHT QUESTIONS

1. If you were a physician who had just delivered a child with ambiguous external genitalia, how would you advise the child's parents?
2. What advice would you give a young athlete about using anabolic steroids as performance enhancement?
3. Why do you think males would evolve a system in which their testosterone levels would fluctuate with winning and losing in competitive situations?

KEY TERMS

androgen (p. 289)
estradiol (p. 291)
estrogen (p. 291)
external genitalia (p. 288)
follicle-stimulating hormone (FSH) (p. 291)
gonads (p. 288)
gonadotropin-releasing hormone (GnRH) (p. 291)
interstitial nuclei of the anterior hypothalamus (INAH) (p. 301)
luteinizing hormone (LH) (p. 291)
monogamy (p. 309)
Müllerian system (p. 289)
ovaries (p. 288)
oxytocin (p. 308)
progesterone (p. 295)
secondary sex characteristics (p. 291)
testes (p. 288)
testosterone (p. 289)
Wolffian system (p. 289)
X chromosome (p. 285)
Y chromosome (p. 286)

11

Sleep and Waking

CHAPTER OUTLINE

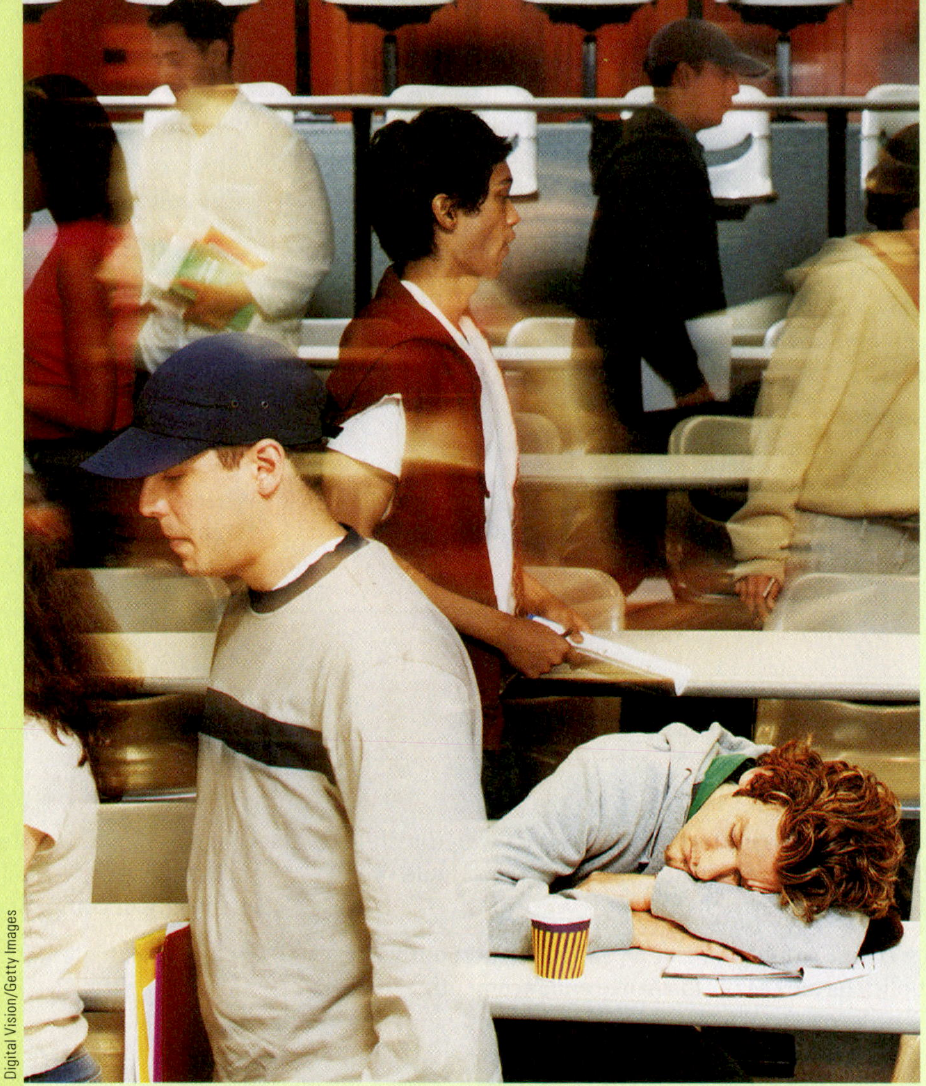

Digital Vision/Getty Images

▲ **The Need for Sleep** Human beings usually sleep between seven and nine hours per day, whenever and wherever they can.

Introduction

If you think studying for final exams is bad, consider these instances of sleep deprivation. In 1959, disc jockey Peter Tripp stayed awake for more than eight days as a publicity stunt. Six years later, a high school student named Randy Gardner stayed awake for almost 11 days in an effort to make it into the *Guinness Book of World Records.* In 2007, Tony Wright, shown in ■ Figure 11.1, went 266 hours without sleep in order to beat Gardner's record. Wright's saga was chronicled online in his blog and by the BBC. Incidentally, *Guinness* no longer maintains a sleep deprivation category due to health concerns.

Although we can obviously survive extreme levels of sleep deprivation, the results of sleepiness can be serious indeed. Sleepiness contributed to the Three Mile Island nuclear

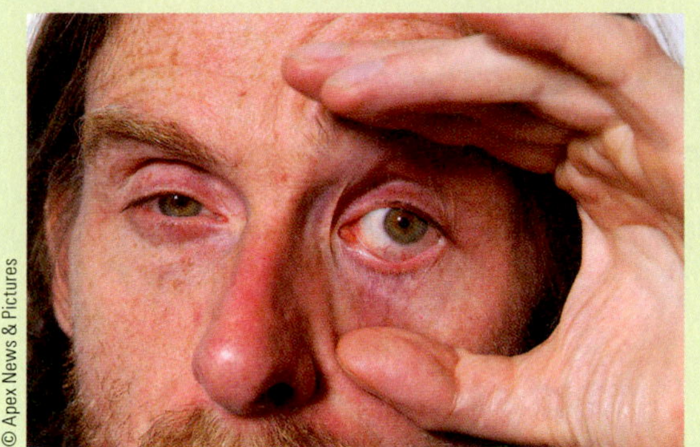

■ **FIGURE 11.1**
A New Sleep Deprivation Record Is Set The most recent record-breaking attempt for sleep deprivation was Tony Wright's 11 days, 2 hours, 4 minutes, and 8 seconds. Tony's efforts were chronicled by the BBC, and thousands of people watched him via webcam.

meltdown in 1979, the Challenger space shuttle explosion in 1986, and the grounding of the oil tanker *Exxon Valdez* in 1989 (Coren, 1996a). Sleep deprivation has also been implicated in the 1984 chemical leak at a factory in Bhopal, India, that resulted in the deaths of 3,800 people (Kurzman, 1987).

There is evidence of a growing epidemic of sleep deprivation among American adults and teens. As shown in ■ Figure 11.2, American adults average only 6 hours 55 minutes of sleep per night (National Sleep Foundation, 2008). Many people try to make up for sleep lost during the week by sleeping more during the weekends. This strategy probably does not work well because we seem to be unable to make up entirely for lost sleep (Van Dongen, Maislin, Mullington, & Dinges, 2003). Understanding the natural cycles of sleep and waking described in this chapter won't add hours to a busy day, but at least you'll know why you respond predictably to these daily rhythms. ■

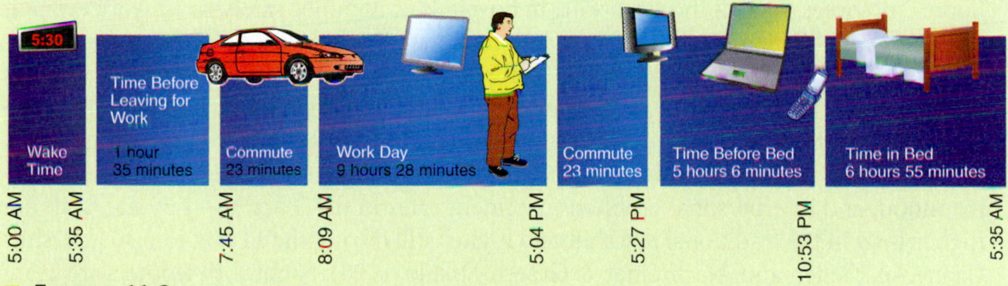

■ **FIGURE 11.2**
A Day in the Life of a Typical American Worker Americans are believed to be somewhat sleep deprived because the average adult spends only 6 hours and 55 minutes in bed, which includes time needed to initiate sleep. Although people try to make up for lost sleep on weekends by sleeping longer, this is not a very effective solution. *Source:* Data from 2008 Omnibus Sleep in America Poll, National Sleep Foundation.

LEARNING OBJECTIVES

After reading this chapter, you should be able to:

LO1 Define circadian and ultradian rhythms and describe the contributions of circadian rhythms to jet lag, adaptation to shift work, and seasonal affective disorder.

LO2 Explain the processes responsible for maintaining circadian rhythms.

LO3 Identify the major features of the waking state, non-rapid-eye-movement (NREM) sleep, and rapid-eye-movement (REM) sleep.

LO4 Describe changes in sleep over the life span.

LO5 Describe the characteristics and major theories of dreaming.

LO6 Summarize the theories regarding the functions of sleep.

LO7 Identify the brain mechanisms responsible for wakefulness, NREM, and REM.

LO8 Summarize the contributions of biochemical factors to sleep.

LO9 Identify and describe the major types of sleep disorders.

Circadian Rhythms

Seasonal migrations, mating seasons, and the human menstrual cycle are just a few examples of behaviors that occur at regular intervals in response to internal, biological clocks. Our focus in this chapter is on the rhythms associated with sleep and wakefulness. Together, the interplay of sleep and waking cycles follow **circadian,** or daily, **rhythms.** The term *circadian* comes from the Latin words for "about a day."

To establish and maintain these rhythms, internal biological clocks interact with stimuli known as **zeitgebers.** (*Zeit* means "time" in German; *geber* means "to give"; hence these are "time givers.") Light is the most important zeitgeber for human beings. In the absence of natural light, human **free-running circadian rhythms** last approximately

circadian rhythm (sir-CAY-dee-ahn) A repeating cycle of about 24 hours.
zeitgeber (ZITE-gay-ber) An external cue for setting biological rhythms.
free-running circadian rhythm A rhythm that is not synchronized to environmental time cues.

24.2 hours to 24.9 hours (Czeisler & Gooley, 2007; Sack, Brandes, Kendall, & Lewy, 2000). Exposure to sunlight each day helps reset, or **entrain,** the internal biological clock to the 24-hour cycle of the earth's rotation. Totally blind people and sailors on submarines experience free-running cycles that are longer than 24 hours, often resulting in severe sleep disruptions (Skene, Lockley, & Arendt, 1999; Kelly et al., 1999). In addition to light, other zeitgebers include physical activity, feeding, body temperature, and sleep-related hormones discussed later in this chapter (Van Someren & Riemersma-Van Der Lek, 2007).

Variations in Sleep Patterns

Individual sleep patterns result from different versions of the genes responsible for our internal clocks (Dijk & Lockley, 2002; Gottlieb, O'Connor, & Wilk, 2007). People who are most alert and productive in the morning have been referred to as "larks," whereas night people have been referred to as "night owls" (Akerstedt & Froberg, 1976). Many people fall somewhere between these two extremes.

Regardless of normal lifetime sleep patterns, nearly everyone acts like an owl during adolescence (Carskadon, Acebo, & Jenni, 2004; Crowley, Acebo, & Carskadon, 2007; Taylor, Jenni, Acebo, & Carskadon, 2005). Melatonin, one of the neurochemicals involved in the regulation of sleep patterns, drops dramatically at the onset of puberty, possibly contributing to age-related changes in sleep habits (Molina-Carballo et al., 2007; Yun, Bazar, & Lee, 2004). Following adolescence, many temporary owls will revert to their previous state, possibly due to the maturation of neural systems that regulate sleep. Regardless of the origins of adolescent owl behavior, accommodations can be useful. Shifting from a 7:15 A.M. start time to an 8:40 A.M. start time improved both attendance and student grades at Minnesota high schools (Wahlstrom, 2003).

A ruffled mind makes a restless pillow.
Charlotte Brontë

Shift Work, Jet Lag, and Daylight Saving Time

Some employees, such as those working in hospitals or in public safety, must work evening or night shifts. When work demands and circadian rhythms do not match, the consequences can be challenging and possibly dangerous. Between 40 and 80 percent of workers on the 11 P.M. to 7:30 A.M. night shift experience disturbed sleep and a cluster of symptoms referred to as *shift maladaptation syndrome* (Wagner, 1996). These workers obtain 1.5 hours less total sleep than workers on other shifts, leading to frequent health, personality, mood, and interpersonal problems. Accident rates in the 3 P.M. to 11:30 P.M. shift are higher than in the traditional day shift and higher still during the 11 P.M. to 7:30 A.M. shift (Hänecke, Tiedemann, Nachreiner, & Grzech-Sukalo, 1998). Night shift workers are more likely than other workers to develop breast cancer (Davis & Mirick, 2006; Kolstad, 2008). Shift workers are not only a risk to themselves, but their errors also jeopardize the public. Hospital workers, such as nurses, are much more likely to make significant errors during evening or night shifts than during day shifts (Narumi et al., 1999).

Conflicts between internal clocks and external zeitgebers also result in the unsettling experience of **jet lag.** After crossing time zones, people often experience fatigue, irritability, and sleepiness. The travel itself is not to blame, because north–south travel of equal distance does not produce the symptoms of jet lag (Herxheimer & Waterhouse, 2003). Chronic jet lag might have more serious consequences. Airline flight attendants who crossed time zones at least once a week for four or more years had reduced reaction times and made 9 percent more mistakes on memory tasks than local crews who did not cross time zones (Cho, Ennaceur, Cole, & Suh, 2000).

Because the human free-running cycle is more than 24 hours long, people adjust more readily when travel or changes in shift work require us to stay up later and sleep later. In other words, it is easier to adjust to a phase-delay of our cycle (setting the clock to a later point) than to a phase-advance (setting the clock to an earlier point). As shown in Figure 11.3, a New Yorker traveling to Los Angeles goes to bed three hours later but then has the opportunity to sleep later. Most of us don't find that too difficult. In contrast, a Los Angeles resident traveling to New York goes to bed three hours early and awakens in what feels like the middle of the night.

Daylight saving time offers another opportunity to observe our responses to phase shifts. Created to help save energy during World War I, daylight saving time requires

entrainment The resetting of internal biological clocks to the 24-hour cycle of the earth's rotation.
jet lag Fatigue, irritability, and sleepiness resulting from travel across time zones.

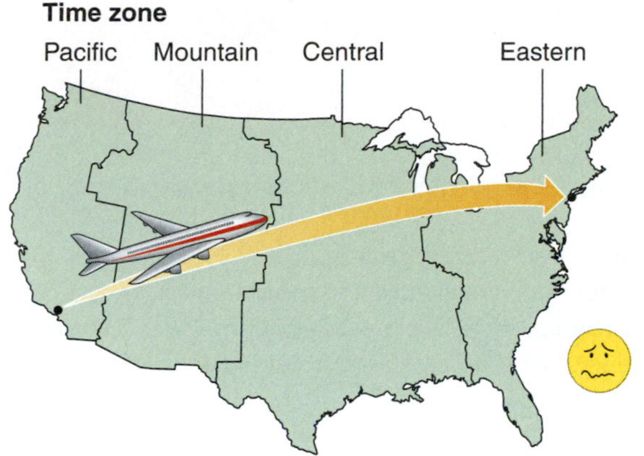

Time zone
Pacific
Mountain
Central
Eastern

Time zone
Pacific
Mountain
Central
Eastern

An Angelino traveling to New York may . . .
go to bed at 10:00 P.M. . . .
and get up at 6:00 A.M.
But it *feels* like . . .
going to bed at 7:00 P.M. . . .
and getting up at 3:00 A.M.
Eastward Travel

A New Yorker traveling to Los Angeles may . . .
go to bed at 10:00 P.M. . . .
and get up at 6:00 A.M.
But it *feels* like . . .
going to bed at 1:00 A.M. . . .
and getting up at 9:00 A.M.

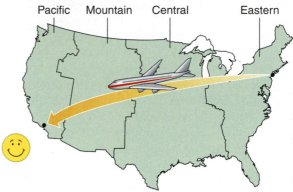

■ **FIGURE 11.3 Jet Lag Is Worse When Traveling East** Traveling eastward is more disruptive than traveling westward. The Los Angeles resident arriving in New York feels like he or she is going to bed three hours earlier than usual (7 P.M. Los Angeles time) and waking up in the middle of the night (3 A.M. Los Angeles time). The New Yorker traveling to Los Angeles has to stay up a little later (1 A.M. New York time) but then can sleep later to compensate (9 A.M. New York time). Most people find the latter scenario much easier.

the setting of clocks forward one hour in spring (a phase advance) and back one hour in fall (a phase delay). The fall shift is equivalent to westward travel and produces relatively little disruption. In contrast, the spring shift produces symptoms similar to jet lag for a day or two. Coren (1996b) correlated Canadian traffic accident data with daylight saving time shifts. The phase-delay shift in fall resulted in a 7 percent decrease in traffic accidents on the following Monday. In the phase-advance shift in spring, Coren observed a comparable 7 percent increase in traffic accidents.

INTERNAL CLOCKS

The body's internal master clock is the **suprachiasmatic nucleus (SCN)** in the hypothalamus, shown in ■ Figure 11.4 (Moore & Eichler, 1972; Stephan & Zucker, 1972). The term *suprachiasmatic* comes from the structure's location above (*supra*) the optic chiasm. Axons of special retinal ganglion cells, known as non-image-forming (NIF) cells, leave the optic nerve and project to the SCN, forming the **retinohypothalamic pathway** (Hendrickson, Wagoner, & Cowan, 1972). Unlike other retinal ganglion cells (see Chapter 6), the NIF cells do not process information about visual images. The NIF cells contain a photopigment, known as **melanopsin,** that is related to, but different from, the other photopigments involved in vision (Brown & Robinson, 2004; Guler et al., 2008).

The SCN is active only during the day, as shown in ■ Figure 11.5 (Schwartz & Gainer, 1977; Schwartz, Reppert, Eagan, & Moore-Ede, 1983). This is true regardless of whether a species is diurnal (awake during the day), like monkeys, or nocturnal (awake at night), like rats. The SCN helps animals distinguish between day and night, but other structures dictate whether an animal is nocturnal or diurnal in its behavior.

The SCN is not dependent on input from other structures to maintain its rhythms. Isolated SCN tissue cultures continued to show rhythmic fluctuations in activity consistent with the source animal's previous day–night cycle (Ding et al., 1994). Transplants of SCN tissue also support its role as a master internal clock (Ralph, Foster, Davis, & Menaker, 1990). It is possible to breed hamsters with short free-running cycles of about 20 hours, in comparison with the normal hamster cycle of about 24 hours. When SCN tissue from a short-period hamster is transplanted into a normal hamster, the normal hamster shows the short free-running cycle. When

suprachiasmatic nucleus (SCN) (sue-prah-kie-as-MA-tik) An area of the hypothalamus located above the optic chiasm; responsible for maintaining circadian rhythms.

retinohypothalamic pathway (REH-tin-oh-HI-poh-thuh-la-mik) A pathway leading from the retina of the eye to the hypothalamus; provides light information necessary for the maintenance of circadian rhythms.

melanopsin A photopigment used by non-image-forming (NIF) retinal cells.

WHY DOES THIS MATTER?

Daytime Sleepiness

College students often neglect sleep to study and socialize. Sixty percent of students reported staying awake for an entire night at least once since coming to college (Thacher, 2008). Engaging in this behavior more frequently was associated with lower GPAs, later regular bedtimes, a preference for evening activities over morning activities, and a tendency to demonstrate symptoms of depression.

Skipping sleep matters because it can produce excessive daytime sleepiness. A frequently used measurement for daytime sleepiness is the Epworth Sleepiness Scale (Johns, 1991). Take a few minutes to see if you, too, are at risk of excess daytime sleepiness.

TABLE 11.1 Epworth Sleepiness Scale

In contrast to just feeling tired, how likely are you to doze off or fall asleep in the following situations? (Even if you have not done some of these things recently, try to work out how they would have affected you.) Use the following scale to choose the most appropriate number for each situation.

0 = Would never doze
1 = Slight chance of dozing
2 = Moderate chance of dozing
3 = High chance of dozing

Situation	Chance of Dozing
Sitting and reading	___
Watching TV	___
Sitting inactive in a public place (i.e., theater)	___
As a car passenger for an hour without a break	___
Lying down to rest in the afternoon	___
Sitting and talking to someone	___
Sitting quietly after lunch without alcohol	___
In a car, while stopping for a few minutes in traffic	___
Total score	___

A score of greater than 10 is a definite cause for concern because it indicates significant excessive daytime sleepiness.

SCN tissue from a normal hamster is transplanted into a short-period hamster, the hamster shows normal 24-hour cycles. In both cases, the behavior of the transplant recipient matches the behavior of the donor.

The SCN acts as a master clock that coordinates the activities of other internal, peripheral clocks that exist in most body cells. Cells from the SCN, liver, lung, and muscle of rats were observed following six-hour phase shifts in the rats' light-dark schedules (Yamazaki et al., 2000). The SCN adjusted to the new time after only one or two cycles of light and dark, but peripheral clocks in the other tissues were much slower to respond. Lung and muscle tissue required 6 cycles to adjust to the new time, and the liver required more than 16 cycles. The effects of phase shifts on muscles, lungs, and other tissues appear to last long after the initial discomfort is gone.

The rhythms of the SCN are heavily influenced by the presence of light. In contrast, the peripheral clocks are more easily influenced by daily feeding cycles (Mendoza, 2007). Abrupt changes in feeding patterns, such as feeding nocturnal mice

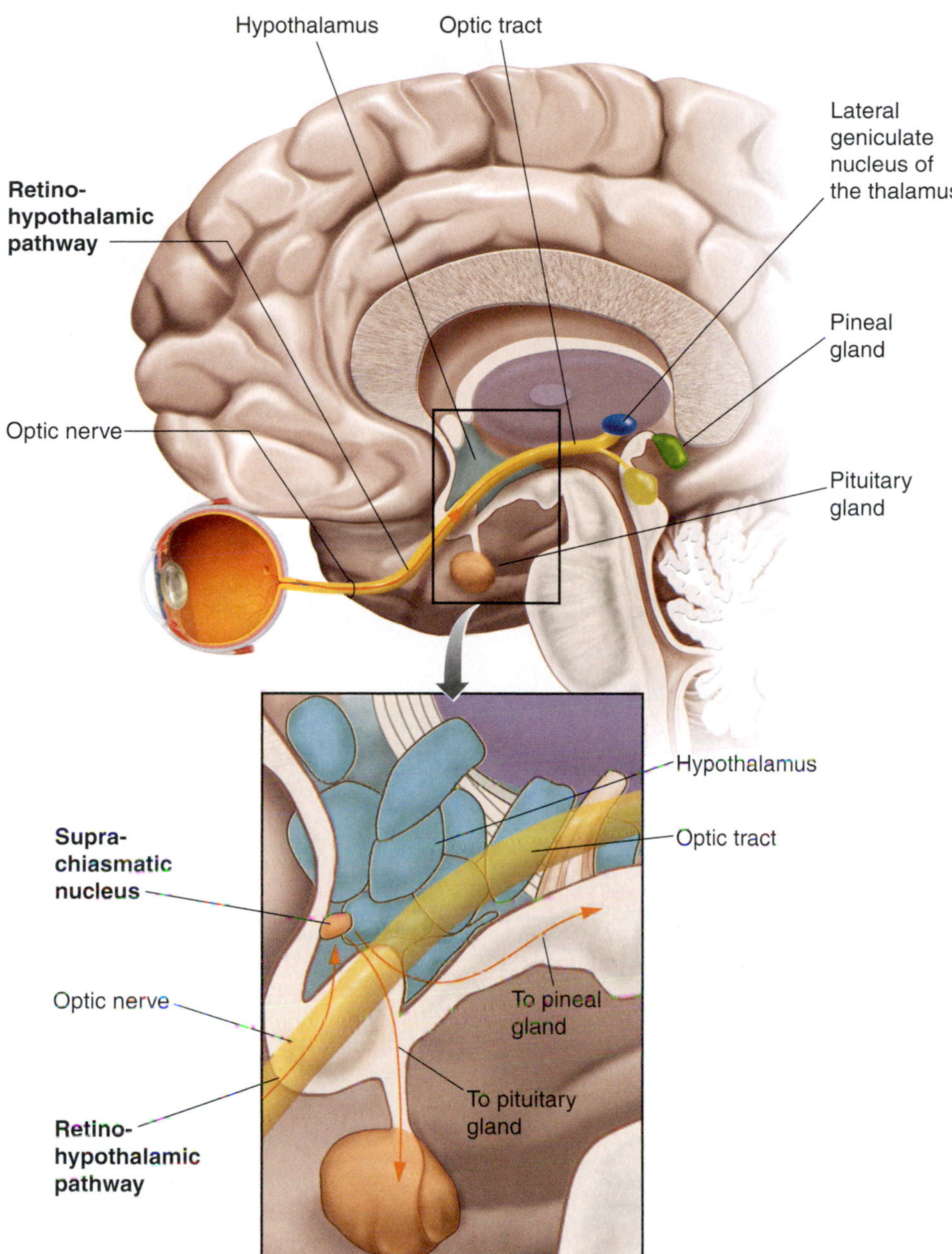

FIGURE 11.4
The Suprachiasmatic Nucleus
The SCN is well situated to serve as the body's master internal clock. Its proximity to the optic nerves provides necessary information regarding environmental light. Its links to other parts of the hypothalamus and to the pituitary and pineal glands allow the SCN to influence rhythmic behaviors by controlling the release of hormones.

during the day only, can reset the animals' circadian rhythms by influencing these peripheral clocks (Hirota & Fukada, 2004). Many travelers attempt to compensate for jet lag by immediately adjusting their mealtimes to their current time zone.

The Cellular Basis of Circadian Rhythms

How can a structure like the SCN tell time? The answer lies in the oscillation of protein production and degradation within a cell, illustrated in Figure 11.6. The ebbing and flowing of special proteins require approximately 24 hours. Research with fruit flies (*Drosophila melanogaster*) has allowed researchers to identify three separate genes and their protein products that are involved with cellular circadian rhythms. These genes and their proteins are *per* (for *period*; Konopka & Benzer, 1971), *tim* (for *timeless*; Sehgal, Price, Man, & Young, 1994), and *Clock* (*circadian locomotor output cycles kaput*, Vitaterna et al., 1994). Together, per and tim proteins inhibit the Clock protein, whereas the Clock protein promotes the production of more per and tim proteins. Consequently, as levels of per and tim proteins increase, inhibition of the Clock protein ensures that no further per and tim proteins will be produced. As levels of per and tim proteins drop over time, the

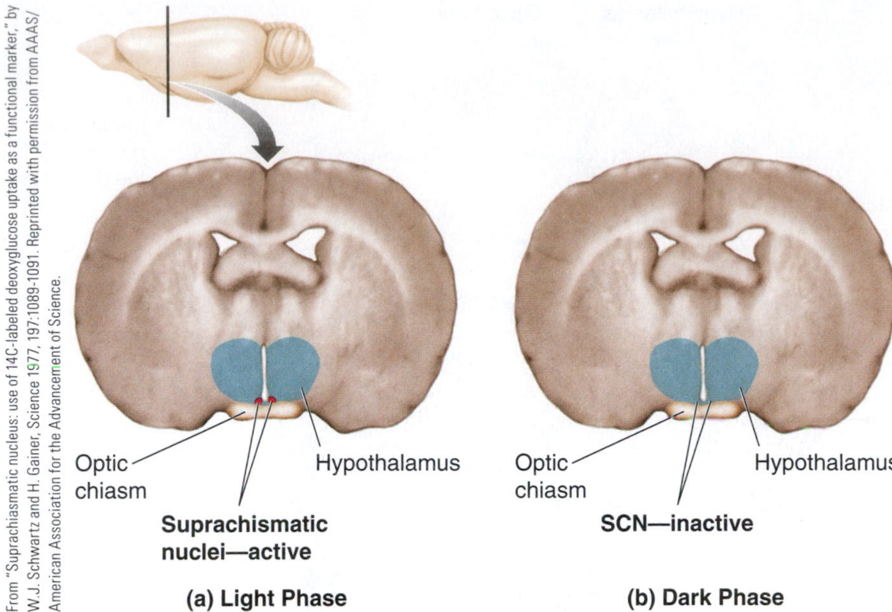
Optic chiasm
Hypothalamus
Suprachismatic nuclei—active
(a) Light Phase
Optic chiasm
Hypothalamus
SCN—inactive
(b) Dark Phase
From "Suprachiasmatic nucleus: use of 14C-labeled deoxyglucose uptake as a functional marker," by W.J. Schwartz and H. Gainer, Science 1977, 197:1089-1091. Reprinted with permission from AAAS/ American Association for the Advancement of Science.

FIGURE 11.5 The SCN Is Active During the Day In the image on the left (a), the SCN (colored red) is active during the rat's light phase. These areas are not active in the image on the right (b), which represents the rat's dark phase. The SCN perceives the difference between day and night but does not dictate whether an animal is nocturnal or diurnal in its behavior. *Source:* Schwartz et al. (1979).

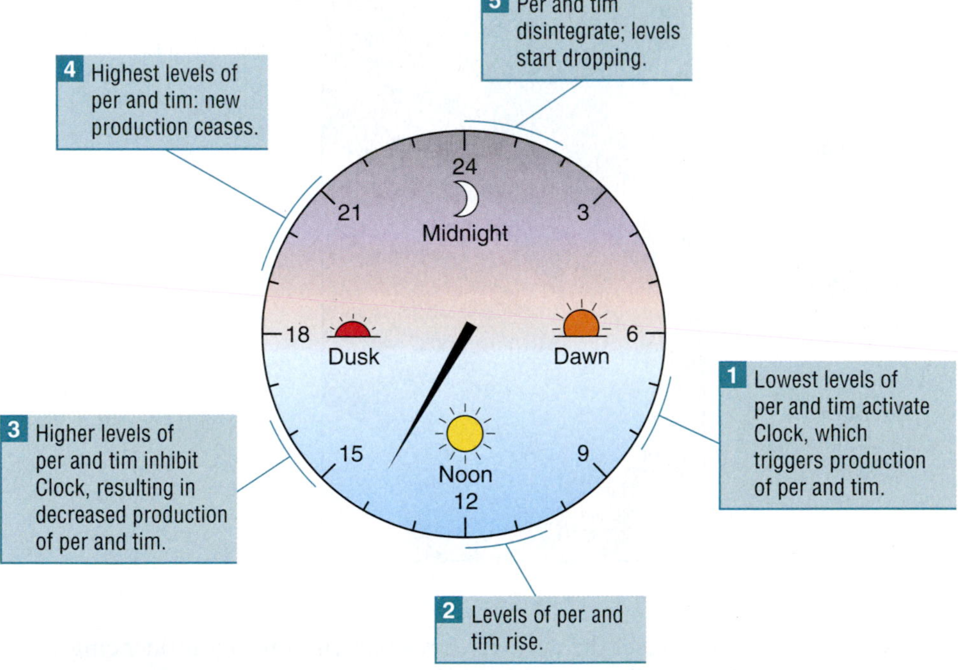
5 Per and tim disintegrate; levels start dropping.
4 Highest levels of per and tim: new production ceases.
24
Midnight
21
3
18
Dusk
Dawn
6
15
Noon
12
9
1 Lowest levels of per and tim activate Clock, which triggers production of per and tim.
3 Higher levels of per and tim inhibit Clock, resulting in decreased production of per and tim.
2 Levels of per and tim rise.

FIGURE 11.6 Cycles of Protein Production and Degradation Form the Basis of the Cellular Clock in Fruit Flies

reduced inhibition of the Clock protein results in increased production of more per and tim proteins. Neural activity reflects the oscillation of the levels of these internal proteins, providing a mechanism for communicating rhythms to other cells. Similar genetic processes occur in mice and other mammals, including humans (Paquet, Rey, & Naef, 2008).

Biochemistry and Circadian Rhythms

The SCN both regulates and responds to the hormone **melatonin,** an indoleamine secreted by the pineal gland. Lesions of the SCN abolish the circadian release of melatonin. Melatonin levels are very low during the day, begin to rise in the hours before sleep, and usually peak at about 4 A.M., a time when nearly everybody finds it very difficult to stay awake (Aeschbach et al., 2003). Totally blind individuals experience a melatonin peak at a different time each day, often leading to sleep difficulties. People with pineal gland tumors or other medical conditions affecting melatonin report sleep

melatonin An indoleamine secreted by the pineal gland that participates in the regulation of circadian rhythms.

NEW DIRECTIONS

Light Pollution

Discovery of inexpensive, artificial light sources about 100 years ago has changed the light environment for many of the earth's inhabitants. By 2001, 62 percent of the world's population, including 99 percent of the population of Europe and the United States, became exposed regularly to night light greater than nights with a full moon (Cinzano, Falchi, & Elvidge, 2001). Less than one hour of exposure to artificial lighting, especially the new forms featuring short-wave or blue light (including fluorescent lights), can produce as much as a 50 percent reduction in circulating melatonin levels (Pauley, 2004). As you have learned in this chapter, melatonin provides one of the key signals for the maintenance of circadian rhythms.

Should we be worried? Changes in melatonin release have been implicated in coronary heart disease, oxidative stress, decreased immune function, and cancer in humans and animals (Navara & Nelson, 2007). In particular, breast cancer appears linked to exposure to artificial light (Schernhammer & Schulmeister, 2004). Night shift workers have higher rates of breast cancer than workers on other shifts. This effect probably arises from melatonin's contributions to immune system function and its ability to suppress estrogen synthesis (Dopfel, Schulmeister, & Schernhammer, 2007). Given that we can hardly escape the constant night lighting of our environment, what steps can we take to minimize its potential for negative health consequences? Efforts to move back to more reddish (long wave) standard light bulbs, which have less impact on melatonin, from the popular energy-saving compact fluorescent lights, which emit more blue (short wave) light, is unlikely due to concerns about global warming and energy costs. Fortunately, ongoing research points to other correlations between low melatonin levels and lifestyle factors that are, in fact, under our control. High body mass index (BMI; see Chapter 9) and smoking are also linked to low melatonin levels (Schernhammer, Kroenke, Dowsett, Folkerd, & Hankinson, 2006), suggesting that maintaining a healthy weight and avoiding smoking could be helpful in offsetting some negative effects of artificial lighting.

problems (Haimov & Lavie, 1996). Melatonin release is suppressed by light (Lewy, Wehr, Goodwin, Newsome, & Markey, 1980). Although bright lights are more likely to suppress melatonin, dimmer lights typical of indoor lighting also have the ability to suppress production and release (Duffy & Wright, 2005).

Melatonin supplements have been reported to improve cases of jet lag, shift maladaptation syndrome, and other sleep disorders (Hardeland et al., 2008). Treatment with melatonin can be helpful in cases in which visual impairments interfere with normal sleep patterns (Sack, Brandes, Kendall, & Lewy, 2000; Skene et al., 1999). Individuals with autism spectrum disorder (see Chapter 16) have low levels of melatonin (Melke et al., 2007) and occasionally use melatonin supplements to help regulate sleep patterns (Jan & O'Donnell, 1996). Adverse reactions to melatonin are rare, but we should recognize that melatonin use remains an alternative medical approach lacking thorough testing.

Levels of the hormone **cortisol** also fluctuate with patterns of waking and sleeping. As shown in ■ Figure 11.7, cortisol levels are normally high early in the morning and lower at night. Higher levels of cortisol are associated with higher blood pressure, higher heart rate, and the mobilization of the body's energy stores. In addition to normal daily fluctuations, cortisol is also released during times of stress (see Chapter 14). Consequently, stress-induced high cortisol levels during the night are correlated with poor sleep quality (van Cauter, Leproult, & Plat, 2000). Cortisol might also contribute to the experience of jet lag (Cho et al., 2000). Flight crews who cross more than eight time zones have one third more cortisol in their saliva when compared with ground crews. The stress of crossing time zones could stimulate cortisol release.

Seasonal Affective Disorder

During the winter months at higher latitudes (areas closer to the poles of the Earth), the reduction in daylight hours can interfere with circadian rhythms. Consequently, some people will experience a type of depression known as **seasonal affective disorder (SAD).** Rates of SAD vary from 1.4 percent in Florida to 9.7 percent in New Hampshire (Modell et al., 2005). The exact mechanisms behind SAD are not very clear. Serotonin levels typically drop in the fall and winter, and people vulnerable to SAD might experience a greater than normal decrease, leading to symptoms of depression (See Chapter 16;

cortisol A hormone released by the adrenal glands that promotes arousal.

seasonal affective disorder (SAD) A type of depression that results from insufficient amounts of daylight during the winter months.

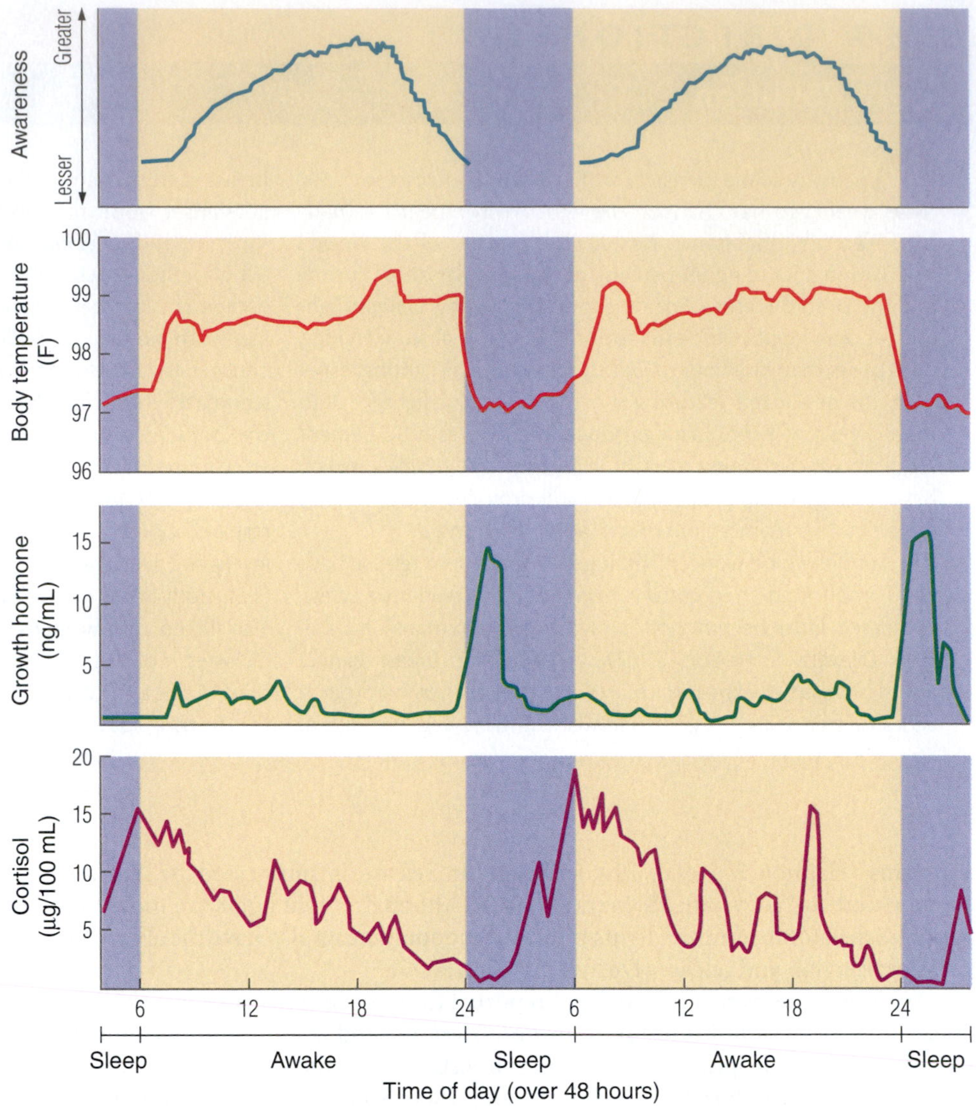

FIGURE 11.7 Body Temperature and Hormone Secretions Follow Circadian Rhythms Over the course of two days, we can see that body temperature and alertness are positively correlated. Growth hormone is released primarily during Stages 3 and 4 of NREM, whereas cortisol levels are highest first thing in the morning and decrease during the day *Source:* Adapted from Coleman (1986).

Jepson, Ernst, & Kelly, 1999). SAD might also be influenced by disruptions in melatonin release caused by uneven patterns of daily light (Levitan, 2007).

SAD is treated by exposure to bright lights, with or without melatonin and antidepressants. Although the light used in therapy (2,500 lux) is much stronger than what is normally experienced indoors (100 lux), it is more like the light on an overcast day than the light at the beach on an August afternoon (10,000 lux). Light therapy administered at dawn corrects cases in which people stay up too late, whereas light therapy in the evening helps people who are sleepy too early (Lewy, 2007).

Not all populations living at high latitudes experience SAD frequently. Magnusson, Axelsson, Karlsson, and Oskarsson (2000) reported that Icelanders experience no more frequent or severe symptoms of depression during winter than during summer. The Icelanders might enjoy protective genetic influences. Compared to Canadians living at the same latitudes, Icelanders experience lower rates of SAD (Axelsson, Stefánsson, Magnússon, Sigvaldason, & Karlsson, 2002).

Stages of Wakefulness and Sleep

We can place wakefulness and sleep along a continuum of brain activity using electroencephalogram (EEG) recordings. As we observed in Chapter 1, the EEG provides a general measure of overall brain activity. **Desynchronous** brain activity arises from the relatively independent action of many neurons and is correlated with alertness. **Synchronous** activity occurs when neurons are firing more in unison and characterizes deep stages of sleep. Consider the contrast between a typical afternoon of activity at the community

desynchronous Having different periods and phases; in EEG, represents high levels of brain activity.

synchronous Having identical periods and phases; in EEG, represents relatively low levels of brain activity.

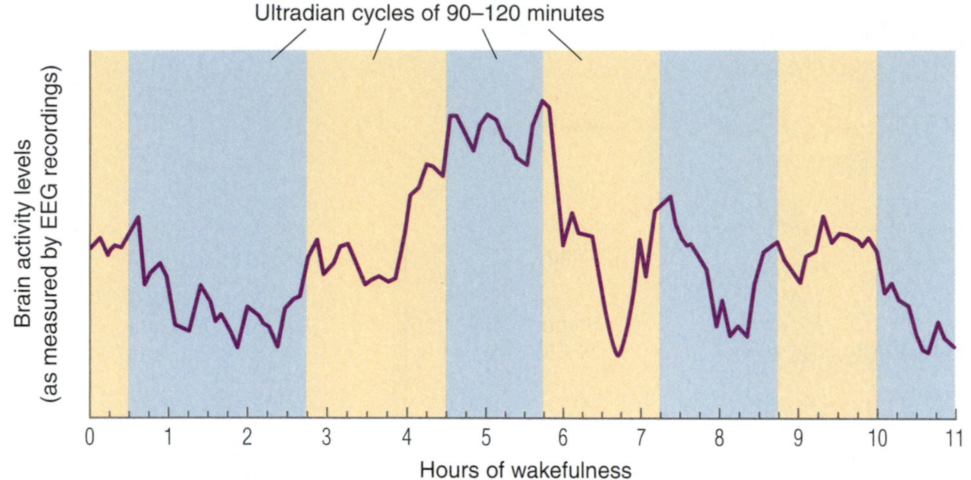

FIGURE 11.8 Ultradian Rhythms Characterize Wakefulness in Humans Not only do our REM cycles appear approximately every 90 to 120 minutes during sleep, but brain activity levels also ebb and flow in 90- to 120-minute intervals during wakefulness. *Source:* Adapted from Kaiser & Sterman (1994).

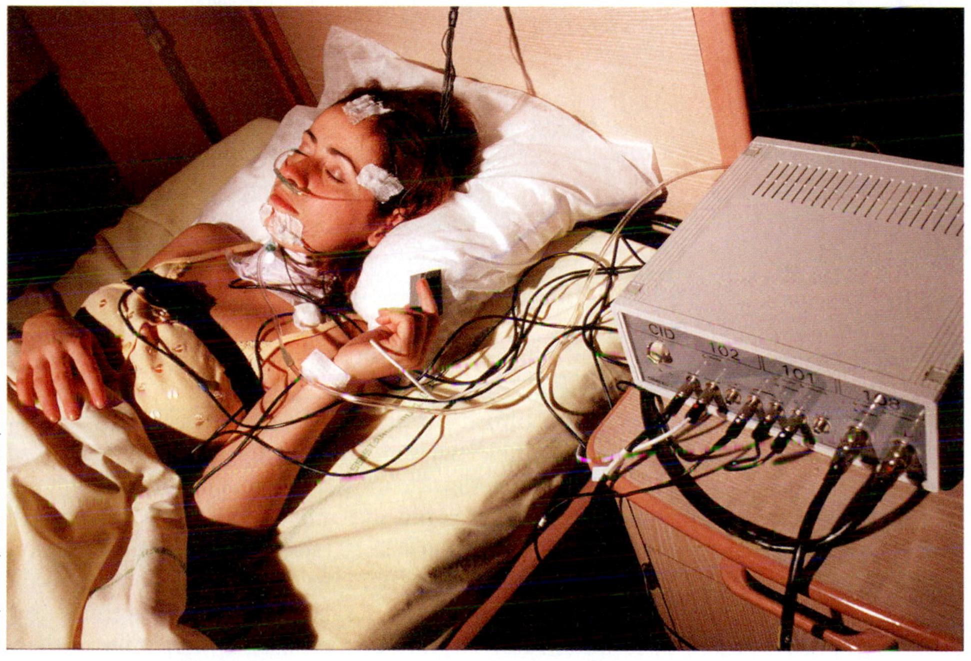

GARO/PHANIE/Photo Researchers, Inc.

FIGURE 11.9 Sleep Research Involves Multiple Measurements Participants in sleep experiments are wired with scalp electrodes for EEG, electrodes around the eyes to measure eye movement, and electrodes on their major postural muscles. As if that weren't enough, they are being observed and probably filmed through a two-way mirror by researchers.

swimming pool (desynchronous) and the actions of a team of synchronized swimmers (synchronous). More diverse activities are taking place in the desynchronous case.

Wakefulness

During wakefulness, EEG recordings alternate between **beta wave** and **alpha wave** patterns of brain activity (see Figure 11.8). Beta activity is characterized by highly desynchronized, rapid (15 to 20 cycles per second), irregular, low-amplitude waves. During beta activity, a person will be actively thinking and very alert. Alpha waves are slightly slower, larger, and more regular than beta waves, with a frequency of 9 to 12 cycles per second. A person showing alpha activity is awake but quite relaxed. Alpha and beta activity alternate throughout periods of wakefulness. As shown in Figure 11.8, periods of high and low alertness during wakefulness follow **ultradian cycles** of 90 to 120 minutes in humans (Lavie & Kripke, 1981). People naturally experience fluctuations in their ability to concentrate during a long lecture, regardless of how fascinating the speaker and material might be.

beta wave A brain waveform having 15 to 20 cycles per second, associated with high levels of alertness during wakefulness.

alpha wave A brain waveform having 9 to12 cycles per second, associated with less alertness and more relaxation than beta activity during wakefulness.

ultradian cycle (ul-truh-DEE-an) A cycle that occurs several times in a single day.

Brain Activity During Sleep

Recording the activity of sleeping people is not easy. As shown in Figure 11.9, volunteers must sleep with scalp electrodes for EEG recordings, electrodes near their eyes to measure eye movement, and additional electrodes to measure heart rate and muscular

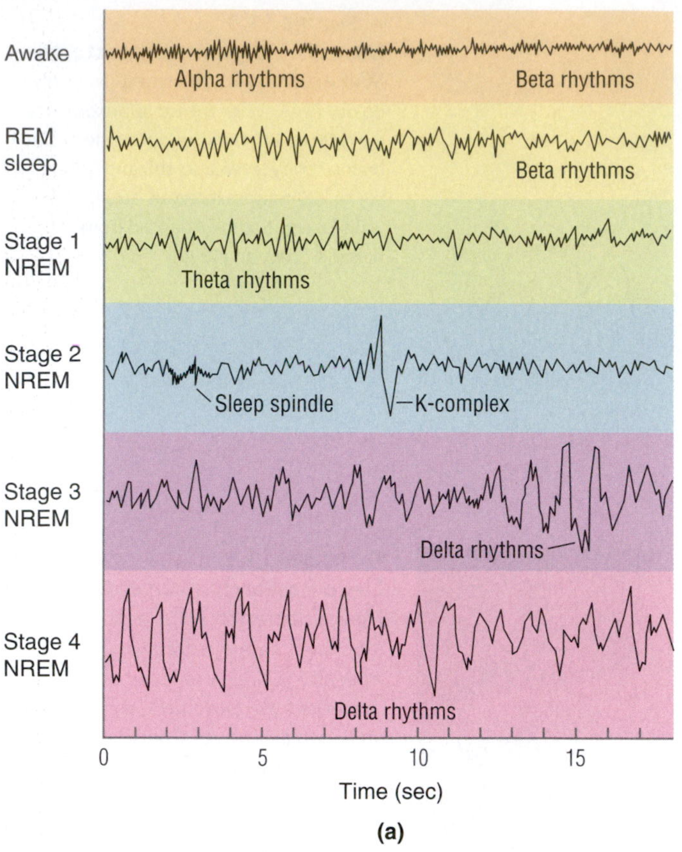

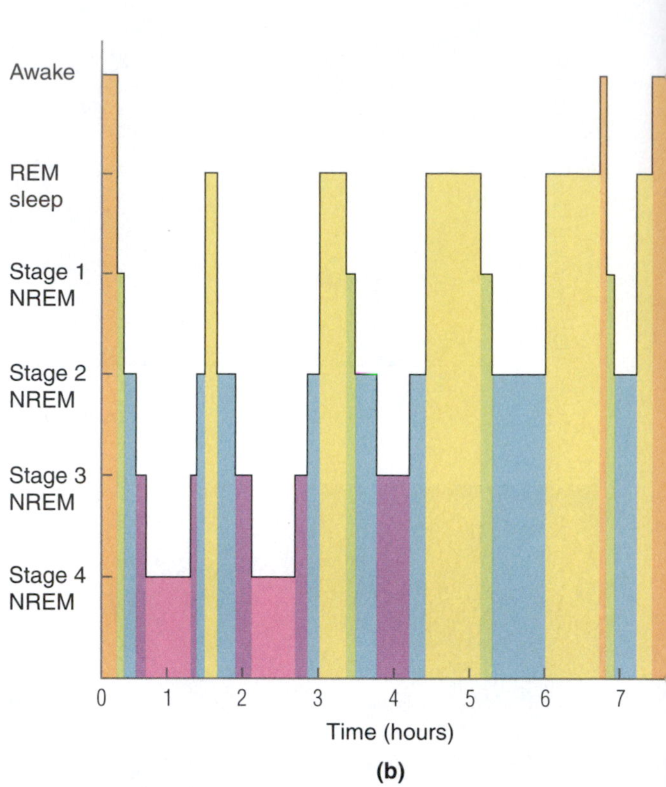

FIGURE 11.10
Human Sleep Cycles (a) This image illustrates EEG patterns characteristic of wakefulness, REM, and the four stages of NREM. (b) EEG recordings show the cycling of sleep stages over an eight-hour period. The first four hours contain most of the Stage 3 and Stage 4 NREM, and the second four hours contain most of the REM sleep. *Source:* Part (a) adapted from Horne (1998); part (b) adapted from Cartwright (1978).

tension. They are being observed and filmed through a two-way mirror. Fortunately, most sleep research has been done in university settings with student volunteers, and apparently, students can manage to sleep under the most trying conditions.

Sleep consists of alternating periods of **rapid-eye-movement (REM) sleep** and **non-REM (NREM) sleep.** As shown in Figure 11.10, sleep begins when a person enters Stage 1 of NREM. In Stage 1, the EEG is difficult to distinguish from the waking EEG of a drowsy person. Some **theta wave** (4 to 7 cycles per second) activity now occurs, and heart rate and muscle tension begin to decrease. This early stage of sleep is disturbed occasionally by a muscle jerk, usually in an arm or leg, referred to as **myoclonia.** This experience is often accompanied by a brief visual image, such as stumbling on the stairs or on a curb. Although myoclonia interrupts sleep, no harm is being done to the sleeper.

After 10 to 15 minutes, Stage 1 gives way to Stage 2 NREM, which accounts for about 50 percent of the night's entire sleep. Further reductions in heart rate and muscle tension occur. The EEG begins to show **sleep spindles,** short bursts of 12 to 14 cycle-per-second waves lasting about half a second that are generated by interactions between the thalamus and the cortex. Although spindles are prominent in Stage 2, they do occur in other stages of NREM. The **K-complex** is a brief burst of brain activity that is seen only in Stage 2. Although K-complexes occur spontaneously, they are also seen in response to unexpected stimuli, such as loud noises. Spindles and K-complexes might reflect the brain's efforts to keep us asleep while continuing to monitor the external environment. We usually sleep through familiar stimuli, such as the hum of an air conditioner, but wake in response to unexpected stimuli such as the sound of a door opening.

After about 15 minutes in Stage 2, we enter Stage 3 and Stage 4 NREM sleep. During these stages, body temperature, breathing, blood pressure, and heart rate are at very low levels due to the activity of the parasympathetic nervous system. Both Stage 3 and Stage 4 feature **delta wave** activity, which is the largest, slowest (1 to 4 cycles per second), most synchronized waveform of the sleeping state. Stages 3 and 4 differ from

rapid-eye-movement (REM) sleep A period of sleep characterized by desynchronous brain activity, muscle paralysis, eye movement, and storylike dream behavior.

non-REM sleep (NREM) A period of sleep characterized by slow, synchronous brain activity, reductions in heart rate, and muscle relaxation.

theta wave A brain waveform having 4 to 7 cycles per second found primarily in lighter stages of NREM sleep.

myoclonia (my-oh-CLOH-nee-uh) A muscle jerk occurring in early stages of sleep.

sleep spindle A short burst of 12 to 14 cycle-per-second waves observed during NREM sleep.

each other in that a greater proportion of Stage 4 (about half) consists of delta waves. Awakening from Stage 4 is difficult and disorienting. You might have received a telephone call about an hour after going to sleep, when you are likely to be in Stage 4. If you hear the telephone at all, it might take several seconds to locate the phone and wake up enough to have a decent conversation.

After approximately 90 minutes of NREM, a first period of REM sleep occurs. This stage is also referred to as *paradoxical* sleep, reflecting its combination of brain activity resembling wakefulness with the external appearance of deep sleep. Vivid dreaming, which we will discuss later in more detail, generally occurs during this stage. The transition between Stage 4 and REM is rather abrupt, but it usually involves brief passages through Stage 3 and Stage 2 sleep. Subsequent periods of REM sleep continue the ultradian cycles observed during wakefulness, occurring at approximately 90-minute intervals. In eight hours of sleep, the average person typically experiences five periods of REM.

During REM, the EEG shows activity very similar to beta activity observed during wakefulness, with occasional periods of theta activity as well (Gelisse & Crespel, 2008). The eyes make the periodic back-and-forth movements that give this stage its name. The sympathetic nervous system becomes very active. Heart rate, blood pressure, and breathing become rapid or irregular. Males experience erections, and females experience increased blood flow in the vicinity of the vagina (Hirshkowitz & Moore, 1996). At the same time, major postural muscles are completely inactive, effectively paralyzing the sleeper. Some smaller muscles, such as those in the fingers, retain the capacity to jerk or twitch during REM sleep. Cats' paws frequently twitch during a REM episode, leading to speculation that they are chasing mice in their dreams.

The cycling between NREM and REM sleep in humans follows a characteristic pattern over eight hours of sleep, as illustrated in Figure 11.10. The first four hours are characterized by longer periods of NREM and brief periods of REM. Stages 3 and 4 are especially dominant. REM dominates hours 5 through 8, and NREM remains in the lighter stages. Stages 3 and 4 are usually infrequent or absent altogether during the last four hours of sleep. We usually spend the last half hour or so of the night's sleep in REM and often wake up with the awareness that we have just been dreaming.

Fatigue is the best pillow.
Benjamin Franklin

Sleep Throughout the Life Span

Nightly sleep patterns change as a function of age, as shown in ■ Figure 11.11. Not only does the overall amount of sleep change, but the composition of sleep is altered as well. Newborn infants spend as much as 14 to 16 hours per day in sleep. About half of the newborn's sleeping time is spent in REM sleep, in comparison with approximately 20 percent in adolescence and adulthood (McCarley, 2007). Babies born prematurely show even greater percentages of REM sleep than other infants. The more prematurely the child is born, the greater percentage of his or her sleep time is spent in REM. Babies born during the seventh month of pregnancy spend up to 80 percent of their sleeping time in REM. REM sleep can be recorded for the first time in the fetus at about this same point in development (Inoue et al., 1986).

By the age of one year, the child's sleep time has been reduced to 13 hours, which includes one to two hours of napping that will continue until about the age of three. Between the ages of 1 and 5 years, most children sleep approximately 8.7 hours (Acebo et al., 2005). The amount of delta wave (Stages 3 and 4 NREM) activity is highest between the ages of 3 and 6 years. At puberty, there is a further slight decrease in REM and a substantial decrease in Stages 3 and 4 sleep (Dahl, 1996). Teens often feel the need for increased amounts of sleep, possibly nine to ten hours per night, but they do not often have the opportunity to sleep this much (Carskadon et al., 1980).

NREM sleep declines further as people approach midlife. Time spent in Stages 3 and 4 of NREM declines from 20 percent of the night in men under 25 years of age to less than 5 percent of the night for men over 35 (van Cauter, Leproult, & Plat, 2000). Around the age of 50, total sleep time begins to decrease by about 27 minutes per decade

K-complex A brief burst of brain activity occurring during Stage 2 slow-wave sleep.

delta wave A brain waveform having 1 to 4 cycles per second that occurs during Stages 3 and 4 of NREM sleep.

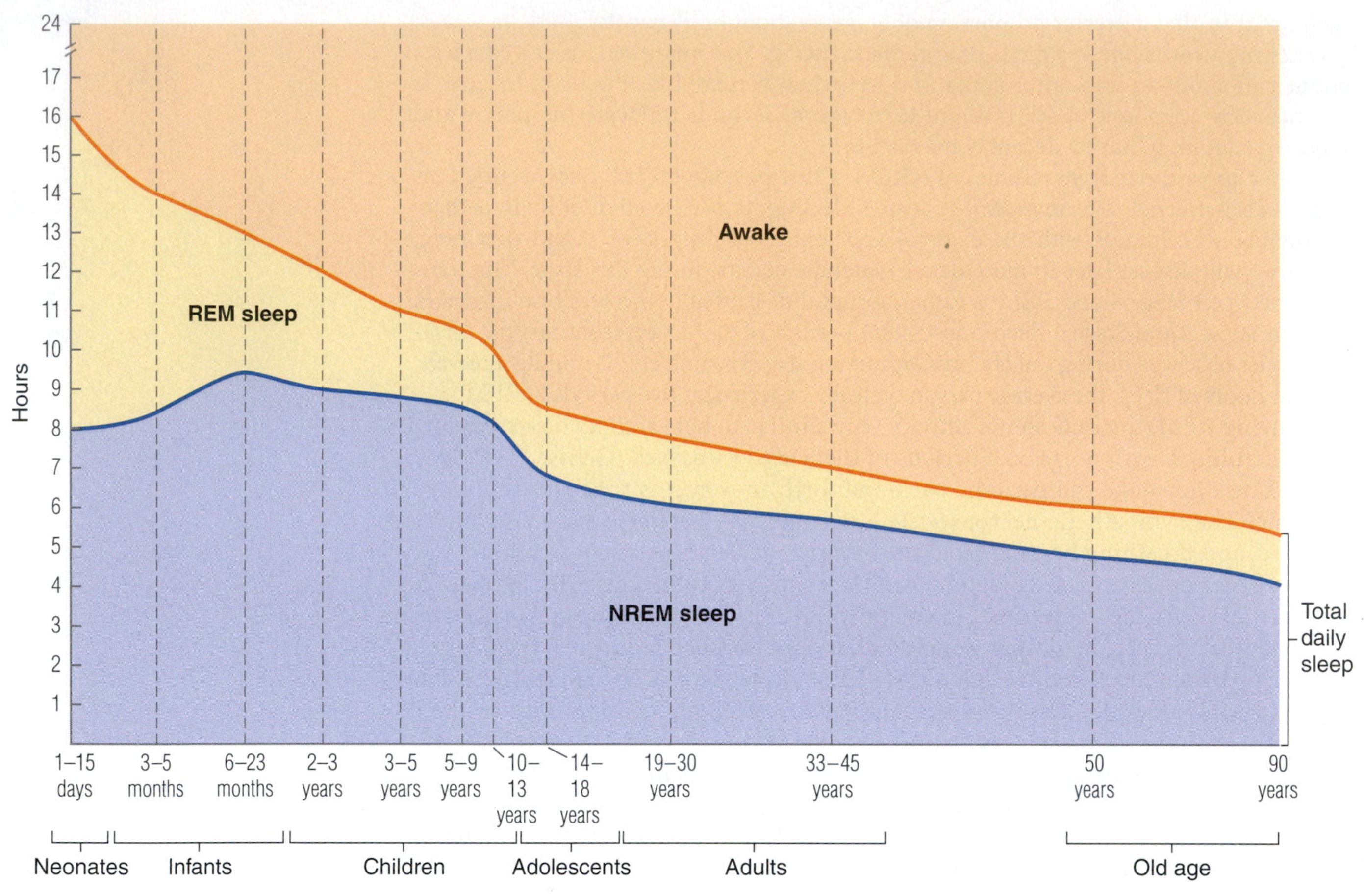

FIGURE 11.11
Sleep Patterns over the Lifespan
Young children spend more time sleeping, and their sleep contains a disproportionately higher amount of REM. As we age, we experience a decrease in the total amount of sleep and in the amount of Stages 3 and 4 NREM. *Source:* Adapted from Roffwarg, Muzio, & Dement (1962).

into a person's eighties. Increased awakening accompanies a reduction in sleep spindles with age (Crowley, Trinder, Kim, Carrington, & Colrain, 2002). Drops in sex hormones associated with aging might be at least partly responsible for some of the age-related changes observed in sleeping patterns. Women approaching menopause frequently experience disruptions in sleep (Hollander et al., 2001). Kruijver and Swaab (2002) identified receptors for estrogen and progesterone in the human SCN, suggesting that sex hormones have a very direct role in the regulation of biorhythms. Although some age-related changes in sleep quality and quantity appear inevitable, healthy, mentally active seniors usually enjoy a better quality of sleep (Driscoll et al., 2008).

Dreaming During REM and NREM

Until the 1950s, the study of dreams was hampered by the inability of research participants to remember dreams very well upon awakening. The discovery that dreams are usually associated with REM sleep allowed researchers to awaken volunteers and assess the dream experience (Dement & Kleitman, 1957).

Dream as if you'll live forever, live as if you'll die today.
James Dean

Dreaming behavior occurs during both REM sleep and NREM. However, dreams are more likely to be reported by volunteers awakened during REM sleep than during NREM. REM dreams are lengthy, complicated, vivid, and storylike, providing us with the sense of firsthand experience with the events taking place. In contrast, NREM dreams are short episodes characterized by logical single images and a relative lack of emotion.

Psychologists have found that most dreams appear to be rather ordinary. Calvin Hall (1951) reviewed the content of thousands of dreams collected from volunteers and found that most dreams occur in familiar places and involve routine activities. We participate as characters in our dreams only about 15 percent of the time, and imaginary strangers are more likely to appear in our dreams than familiar people.

Allen Hobson and Robert McCarley (1977) proposed an activation-synthesis theory of dreaming, in which they argue that the content of dreams reflects ongoing

TABLE 11.2 A Comparison of Night Terrors and Nightmares

	Night Terrors	Nightmares
Time of night	Within four hours of bedtime	Late in sleep cycle
State on waking	Disoriented, confused	Upset, scared
Response to caregivers	Unaware of presence, not consolable	Comforted
Memory of events	None unless fully awakened	Vivid recall of dream
Return to sleep	Usually rapid unless fully awakened	Often delayed by fear
Sleep stage during which event occurs	Partial arousal from deep NREM sleep	REM sleep

neural activity. When sleeping volunteers were sprinkled with water, they subsequently reported dreams of rain and other water-related themes. Dreams of being unable to move in a dangerous situation accurately mirror the muscle paralysis present during the REM state. Common dreams of flying or falling could be caused by the unusual activation of the vestibular system during REM sleep (Hunt, 1989). Dreams with sexual content are consistent with the physical sexual arousal that occurs during REM sleep.

Francis Crick and Graeme Mitchison (1983) proposed a computerized neural network model that sees dreaming as a way for the brain to forget irrelevant and unnecessary information. Jonathan Winson (1985) rejected both the Hobson-McCarley and Crick-Mitchison hypotheses in favor of a more evolutionary approach. In Winson's model, animals evolved the ability to integrate sensory experience with stored memories during REM sleep rather than while awake. Dreaming, in this view, is just a window into the brain's processing of the day's events. In another evolutionary approach, the threat simulation hypothesis, dreaming is viewed as a way to simulate escape from threatening situations (Revonsuo, 2000). In other words, animals gain a survival advantage if they can "practice" dealing with threatening situations in their dreams. The advantages of dreaming could combine some or all of these proposed elements, and further research is needed to clarify the issue.

In dreams, we enter a world that's entirely our own.
Albus Dumbledore (J.K. Rowling)

Although we often put our children to bed saying, "sweet dreams," it appears that about 70 percent of our dreams have negative emotional content (Hall & Van de Castle, 1966). Among the dreams most frequently reported by college students are those of being chased, falling, flying, appearing naked, being unable to find a restroom, being frozen with fright, and taking exams for which one is unprepared (Schredl, Ciric, Götz, & Wittmann, 2004). Men report more aggression in their dreams than do women (Schredl et al., 2004). Viewing upsetting entertainment or reports of natural disaster increases the likelihood of negative dreams. In the weeks following the 1989 earthquake in San Francisco, 40 percent of students in San Francisco universities reported dreaming about earthquakes, compared with 5 percent of students in Arizona (Wood, Bootzin, Kihlstrom, & Schacter, 1992).

When the content of a REM dream is especially upsetting, we refer to the experience as a **nightmare.** Nightmares first appear when children are between 3 and 6 years of age and tend to decrease in frequency as puberty approaches. Although adults experience nightmares, they are typically not as disturbed by them as children generally are. However, recurrent, disturbing nightmares occur in a number of psychological disorders such as post-traumatic stress disorder (PTSD; see Chapter 16). People troubled by nightmares can benefit from training in **lucid dreaming,** in which the dreamer is aware that he or she is dreaming and uses this awareness to control or direct the content of the dream (Spoormaker & van den Bout, 2006).

Nightmares are often mistaken for **night terrors,** but they are very different phenomena. Nightmares are dreams that occur during REM, whereas night terrors occur during NREM, particularly during the first three hours of sleep. Table 11.2 outlines some of the major differences between these two sleep events. Somewhere between 1 and 4 percent of children will experience a night terror, usually between

nightmare A REM dream with frightening content.

lucid dreaming Thoughtful dreaming; the dreamer is aware that he or she is dreaming and can manipulate the experience.

night terror An NREM episode in which the individual is partially aroused, disoriented, frightened, and inconsolable.

the ages of 4 and 12 years (Pagel, 2000). Most episodes begin with an abrupt scream, followed by sweating and an accelerated heartbeat. The sleeper sits upright in bed and stares forward but is not responsive. If awakened, the person shows the disorientation and confusion typically demonstrated when a sleeper is disturbed during very deep NREM. Mental imagery during night terrors is rare and, if present, tends to be of the single-image variety characteristic of NREM dreams. Individuals often report feelings of pressure on the chest, which children interpret as a monster or bear sitting on them. There is usually no memory of the night terror the next day. A genetic predisposition appears to contribute to night terrors; 80 percent of people with this condition report a family history for the behavior (American Psychiatric Association, 2000). In addition, boys tend to experience night terrors more frequently than do girls. Fortunately, most children eventually outgrow their night terrors, although not fast enough for their weary family members. Adults who experience night terrors are more likely to have been diagnosed with some type of psychopathology, commonly anxiety or personality disorders (American Psychiatric Association, 2000).

INTERIM SUMMARY 11.1

Summary Table: Stages of Waking and Sleep

Stage of Waking or Sleep		Brain Activity Recorded by EEG	Related Phenomena
Wakefulness		Alpha/beta	• Alternation of periods of alertness (beta waves) with periods of relaxation (alpha waves) • Logical thought • Continuous voluntary movement • Highly responsive to external stimuli
Non-rapid-eye-movement (NREM) sleep	1	Some theta	• Logical thought • Periodic involuntary movement • Continued responsiveness to external stimuli • Reduced heart rate and muscle tension
	2	Larger proportion of theta	• Reductions in responsiveness to external stimuli • Further reductions in heart rate and muscle tension • Sleep spindles appear • K-complexes appear
	3	Some delta	• Further reductions in heart rate and muscle tension
	4	Larger proportion of delta	• Profound reductions in heart rate and muscle tension • Very low responsiveness to external stimuli
Rapid-eye-movement (REM) sleep		Similar to beta, some theta	• PGO spikes correspond to eye movements • Paralysis of major muscle groups in the limbs and torso • Irregular autonomic activity • Sexual arousal • Vivid dreaming

Summary Points

1. Daily or circadian rhythms respond to both internal signals and external zeitgebers. Ultradian rhythms occur several times within a single day. **(LO1)**
2. The body's master internal clock is the suprachiasmatic nucleus (SCN), which receives information about light via the retinohypothalamic pathway and influences clocks in other tisuses. **(LO2)**
3. Physiological measures, including the electroencephalogram (EEG), show distinctions between the stages of waking, rapid-eye-movement sleep (REM), and non-rapid-eye-movement sleep (NREM). **(LO3)**
4. The amount of overall sleep, as well as the relative proportions of REM sleep and NREM, change over the life span. **(LO4)**

(continued)

INTERIM SUMMARY 11.1 (continued)

5. Dreams occurring during REM are lengthy, complicated, vivid, and storylike, whereas NREM dreams are short episodes characterized by logical single images and a relative lack of emotion. **(LO5)**

Review Questions

1. How do shift work, jet lag, and daylight saving time affect our normal circadian rhythms?
2. What is the basis for the rhythms observed in the SCN?

The Functions of Sleep

Dreaming permits each and every one of us to be quietly and safely insane every night of our lives.

William Dement

You would think that any activity that takes up a third of your life would have a very clear and easily identified purpose. This is not the case with sleep.

Most animals show activity levels that follow circadian rhythms with at least one period of time in which they are relatively quiet and less responsive to external stimuli. Even the humble fruit fly takes a seven-hour rest each day (Shaw, Cirelli, Greenspan, & Giulio Tononi, 2000). However, "sleep" seems to take many forms across different species, and it is unlikely that sleep serves a single purpose for all animals (Siegel, 2008). Functions requiring sleep in one species can be managed during wakefulness in another. We do know that lack of sleep in humans can have negative effects. In a rare genetic condition known as fatal familial insomnia (FFI), middle-aged people gradually lose the ability to sleep and eventually die (Liberski, 2008).

Sleep Keeps Us Safe

Sleep prevents some animals from being active during parts of the day when they are least safe from predation. Being inactive, however, is not a safe thing to do unless you are in a secure location. Allison and Cicchetti (1976) were able to predict a species' sleep habits quite accurately on the basis of the animals' risk of predation and their access to shelter. For instance, the horse is a heavily preyed upon animal in the wild, and it generally lives out in the open. Consequently, wild horses sleep as little as one to two hours per day. Rabbits are also frequent prey, but because they have burrows in which to hide, they sleep much more than the horse. Predators, such as the lions in Figure 11.12, tend to sleep whenever and wherever they desire for lengthy periods of time. A sample of different species and their average sleep times is shown in Figure 11.13.

© Stephen Frink/CORBIS

FIGURE 11.12 Safety Predicts a Species' Sleep Habits Like most large predators, lions don't have to worry too much about when and where to sleep.

Sleep Restores Our Bodies

Sleep, particularly NREM, helps us restore our bodies and conserve energy. Sleep deprivation results in a number of negative physical consequences, including reduced immune system function (Zager, Andersen, Ruiz, Antunes, & Tufik, 2007), inability to heal (Murphy et al., 2007), and the inhibition of adult neurogenesis in the hippocampus (Mueller et al., 2008).

Small animals, which tend to have higher metabolic rates, generally sleep more than larger animals, whose metabolic rates are lower. Human forebrain metabolic activity is greatly reduced during NREM sleep compared to wakefulness, contributing to an efficient use of energy (Siegel, 2008). Metabolism rates are positively correlated with the production of free radicals, which can be harmful to many tissues. During NREM sleep, lower body temperatures and rates of metabolism might provide an ideal environment for repairing the damage produced by free radicals during wakefulness (Siegel, 2005).

Most **growth hormone (GH)** is released during Stage 3 and Stage 4 NREM (see Figure 11.7). In childhood, GH is primarily responsible for physical growth,

growth hormone (GH) A hormone released during Stages 3 and 4 of slow-wave sleep that promotes growth, increases in bone and muscle mass, and immune system function.

Figure 11.13 Predation, Shelter, and Sleep Patterns We can predict the amount of time an animal will sleep on the basis of its risk of predation and whether it has a den, burrow, or other safe place to sleep. Animals that are frequently preyed upon and that also sleep in the open, such as horses, sleep very little. Prey species with burrows sleep a lot, which keeps them out of danger. Predators tend to sleep well no matter what.

but throughout life, it contributes to building muscle and bone mass and maintaining immune system function. The release of growth hormone during NREM peaks around the onset of puberty and begins to drop by age 21 (Savine & Sonksen, 2000). Both growth hormone levels and healing of injuries are reduced by sleep deprivation (Murphy et al., 2007). Supplementation with GH increases lean muscle mass and bone mass in elderly participants (Brill et al., 2002).

Sleep Helps Us Remember

The relationship between sleep and memory is complex and controversial. Originally, many psychologists believed that the positive role of sleep in memory formation resulted from a lack of interference. In other words, you were more likely to remember things you learned right before sleep because sleep limited the amount of new data entering the system. Today, researchers believe that sleep plays a more active role in the consolidation of memories. Staying up all night resulted in poor memory retention for a visual task, and two additional nights of sleep did not compensate for the initial deprivation (Stickgold, James, & Hobson, 2000). Memories for word pairs were stronger following a period of NREM than following a period of wakefulness (Gais & Born, 2004). Other research has indicated that REM sleep improves the retention of highly emotional material (Wagner et al., 2001; Wagner et al., 2002). Memories for procedures, such as how to solve a puzzle or ride a bicycle, are enhanced following Stage 2 NREM sleep (Smith & MacNeill, 1994; Smith & Fazekas, 1997).

It is a common experience that a problem difficult at night is resolved in the morning after the committee of sleep has worked on it.
John Steinbeck

Sleep-related changes in memory might be different from the changes that occur when we learn something while awake (Stickgold & Walker, 2007). Wakeful learning might be a simple matter of strengthening connections, whereas sleep-related memory processes might involve the reorganization of existing memory systems to accommodate new information. The day's memories can be reactivated during NREM and then strengthened for wakeful recall during REM (Ribeiro & Nicolelis, 2004). Further research is needed to provide a clearer picture of the relationship between sleep and memory. Nonetheless, it is safe to say that students who wish to retain the material they have studied would benefit from a good night's sleep.

Benefits of NREM Sleep

NREM sleep appears to be particularly involved with the restorative functions of sleep. Individuals who are deprived of NREM sleep will rebound, or attempt to make up for this deprivation during their next opportunity to sleep. Volunteers can be selectively deprived of Stages 3 and 4 NREM by awakening them when their EEGs begin to show the characteristic delta waves. After a night of deprivation, volunteers typically complain of muscle and joint pain (Moldofsky & Scarisbrick, 1976). It is possible that some of the muscle and joint aches and pains experienced by seniors might arise from age-related reductions in Stages 3 and 4 sleep.

Increased physical demands during the day correlate with a need for increased amounts of sleep the following night, reinforcing the role of NREM in the restoration of the body. Runners competing in ultramarathons (races that are twice the length of a marathon) add a surprisingly modest 20 to 30 minutes to their sleep the following night. Most of this increase is in the form of NREM. When highly trained athletes skip a day of exercise, they experience a substitution of about 15 to 20 minutes of REM sleep for NREM (Hague, Gilbert, Burgess, Ferguson, & Dawson, 2003).

FIGURE 11.14
The Echidna and REM Sleep
Researchers once believed that the echidna (*Tachyglossus aculeatus*), an egg-laying relative of the platypus native to Australia and New Guinea, did not show true REM sleep. More recent reports indicate that the echidna and platypus, like other mammals and birds, do experience REM sleep.

Benefits of REM Sleep

Identifying a function for REM sleep is challenging. Only birds and mammals show true REM sleep. Researchers once believed that the echidna, shown in Figure 11.14, and its relative the platypus did not show true REM, but more recent reports indicate that even these primitive, egg-laying mammals are capable of REM (McCarley, 2007).

One consistent observation for both humans and animals is that REM sleep increases after learning has taken place, possibly due to the participation of sleep in the consolidation of memory mentioned earlier. On the other hand, individuals in whom REM sleep is regularly suppressed due to brain injury (Lavie, 1998) or medication retain an ability to learn. In one case, an Israeli soldier who suffered a brain wound that prevented either REM sleep or dreaming, was still able to learn new information (Dement & Vaughan, 1999). Individuals taking SSRI medications (see Chapters 4 and 16) experience less REM sleep, yet are still able to learn (Pace-Schott et al., 2001). REM sleep is clearly not the only mechanism for consolidating new information in memory.

Changes in REM sleep over the lifespan suggest that REM sleep plays a role in brain development. The large proportion of REM sleep observed in the fetus and in young children correlates with periods of time in which the brain is undergoing great change (see Chapter 5). As we mature, the brain continues to change, although far less dramatically. As a result, the adult's need for REM sleep is reduced.

Although adults need less REM sleep than children do, and some individuals seem to do quite well without REM sleep at all, REM deprivation does produce changes in behavior. Dement (1960) awakened volunteers each time they entered REM sleep. As deprivation progressed, the deprived volunteers tried more and more frequently to enter REM sleep. After several days of deprivation, participants showed

WHY DOES THIS MATTER?

Sleep and Obesity

Two current public health trends, increases in obesity and decreases in sleep, might be interacting with one another or simply representing unrelated, parallel processes. Identifying any interactions between the two trends matters because we need to provide the public with the best health advice possible.

An early clue that sleep deprivation and obesity might be linked came from a study of healthy, male volunteers who slept only four hours per day for six days (Spiegel, Leproult, & Van Cauter, 1999). The volunteers' impaired glucose and insulin responses following the sixth day of sleep deprivation were comparable to those seen in people in the early stages of Type 2 diabetes mellitus (see Chapter 9). In another study, healthy male volunteers slept four hours per night on two consecutive nights, resulting in appetite changes equivalent to eating an extra 350 to 500 calories per day (Spiegel, Tasali, Penev, & Van Cauter, 2004). Eating 500 extra calories per day would add up to a 50-pound gain over the course of one year. Further research in animals has established a direct role for clock gene function in the types of appetite changes observed in these human volunteers (Laposky, Bass, Kohsaka, & Turek, 2008; Turek et al., 2005). Consequently, it becomes more plausible that the current trends of obesity and sleep deprivation are not independent and coincidental, but that sleep deprivation is a likely contributor to our current obesity epidemic.

a phenomenon known as **REM rebound.** When allowed to sleep normally, they spent an unusually large amount of their sleep time in REM. The fact that we try to make up for lost REM sleep suggests that REM sleep does have a necessary function in the adult brain.

REM deprivation appears to have many of the same effects as overall loss of sleep, such as irritability and difficulty concentrating. On the other hand, it appears we can have too much of a good thing. As we will see in Chapter 16, people with major depressive disorder enter REM sleep at earlier points in the sleep cycle and spend a greater proportion of their sleep time in REM. Many antidepressant medications suppress and delay REM sleep. Further research is needed to reconcile these data and develop a better understanding of the various roles and purposes of REM sleep.

Brain Mechanisms of Wakefulness and Sleep

There is weariness even in too much sleep.
Homer

For many years, sleep was viewed as an absence of activity. Nothing could be further from the truth. Both wakefulness and sleep are active processes that are carefully choreographed by the brain. These states are not simply the results of activity in "waking" or "sleep" centers but, rather, involve reciprocal circuits of excitation and inhibition. For example, wakefulness not only results from excitation in some parts of the brain but also requires the inhibition of sleep.

The Control of Wakefulness

Staying awake requires the cooperation of a complex network of structures located in the brainstem and basal forebrain. No one structure is uniquely responsible for wakefulness, and several wakefulness structures participate in REM sleep as well. Key structures involved in sleep and wakefulness are illustrated in ■ Figure 11.15.

Two pathways originating in the reticular formation of the medulla are essential to wakefulness. One pathway proceeds from the medulla to the posterior hypothalamus and on to the basal forebrain. The other pathway projects to a group of cells, known as the **cholinergic mesopontine nuclei,** located at the junction of the pons and midbrain. These neurons project to the thalamus, which in turn influences the activity of the cerebral cortex. The thalamus also receives input from the midbrain reticular formation.

In addition to these two pathways, the locus coeruleus of the pons also participates in wakefulness through its rich connections to the thalamus, hippocampus, and cortex (see Chapter 2). The locus coeruleus provides a good example of how a single structure participates in diverse states of awareness. The locus coeruleus is most active when people are vigilant and alert, but is relatively less active when a person is relaxed. The locus coeruleus is quieter still during NREM sleep, and is totally silent during REM.

The anterior raphe nuclei also play important roles in managing sleep–waking cycles. These serotonergic nuclei communicate with the preoptic area and suprachiasmatic nucleus of the anterior hypothalamus as well as with the cortex and are active during wakefulness. Like the locus coeruleus, the raphe nuclei are less active during NREM than during wakefulness and are silent during REM.

The Initiation and Control of NREM Sleep

Once wakefulness has been initiated, it is maintained by ongoing activity in wakefulness pathways as well as by incoming stimulation from the outside world. How then do we make a transition from wakefulness to NREM sleep?

One key to the initiation of sleep appears to be found in the preoptic area of the hypothalamus, which forms inhibitory feedback loops to the wakefulness pathways. These hypothalamic circuits appear to manage homeostatic control of wakefulness, sometimes referred to as **sleep debt.** In other words, these circuits keep track of the

REM rebound The increased amount of REM sleep following a period of REM deprivation.

cholinergic mesopontine nuclei A group of cells located at the border of the pons and midbrain that use ACh as their major neurotransmitter and participate in the maintenance of wakefulness. "Meso" refers to mesencephalon, or midbrain, and "pontine" refers to the pons.

sleep debt The homeostatic control of sleep, in which sleep promotion is related to the preceding duration and intensity of wakefulness.

duration and intensity of wakefulness and actually promote sleep after a certain period of time has passed. Continued activation of the preoptic area by input from the serotonergic raphe nuclei will eventually lead to inhibition of the circuits promoting wakefulness, allowing sleep to occur (Gallopin et al., 2000). These preoptic cells are often referred to as NREM-on cells because electrical stimulation of these cells produces immediate NREM sleep, and lesions result in insomnia. NREM-on cells are most active during NREM and relatively inactive during wakefulness and REM.

Unless some pathology is present, such as the narcolepsy described later in this chapter, the first segment of sleep is always NREM. Without input from the wakefulness circuits, neurons in the thalamus begin to synchronize the activity of cortical neurons, eventually leading to the slow, large waves observed in the deeper stages of NREM sleep. As this synchronization progresses, the cortex becomes progressively less "tuned" to the outside world, and wakefulness becomes more difficult to achieve.

As NREM begins, activity in the locus coeruleus and the raphe nuclei, as well as their release of norephinephrine and serotonin, respectively, gradually declines, preparing the brain for its first episode of REM sleep. During REM, these areas are virtually silent.

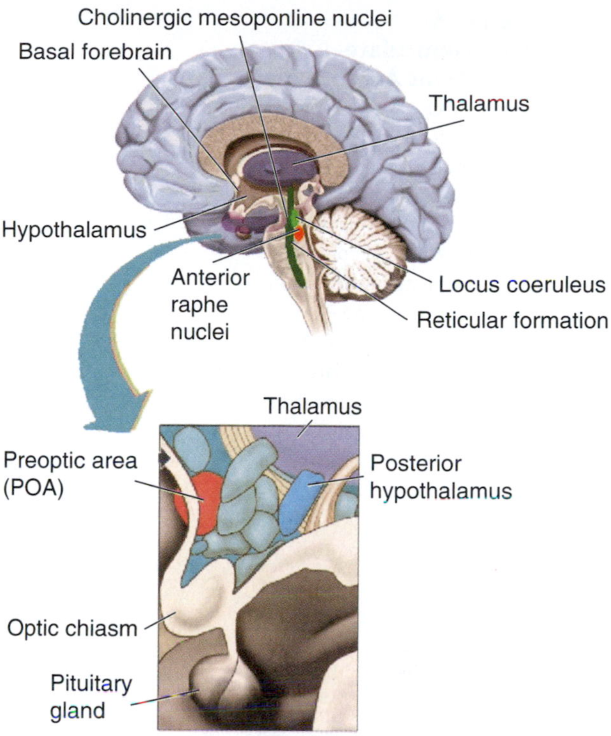

FIGURE 11.15
Key Structures Involved With Wakefulness, NREM, and REM

The Initiation and Control of REM Sleep

Some of the same areas of the brain are active during both wakefulness and REM sleep. Our interest is in pinpointing those areas that are uniquely activated during REM alone. REM-on areas are active during REM but not during wakefulness, and REM-off areas are active during wakefulness but not during REM.

Most of the key REM-on areas are located in the pons (McCarley, 2007). In particular, parts of the rostral pontine reticular formation near the border of the midbrain seem particularly important because lesions of this area selectively abolish REM sleep (Steriade & McCarley, 2005). This area is inactive during wakefulness and NREM sleep but is very active during REM. Critical REM-off components are the locus coeruleus and the raphe nuclei. As these structures reduce their activity during NREM, they disinhibit the activity of the rostral pontine reticular formation, allowing REM to occur (McCarley, 2007). After REM has occurred for about 30 minutes in human beings, the locus coeruleus and raphe nuclei reactivate, inhibiting the rostral pontine reticular formation and ending REM. Either wakefulness or another cycle of NREM will follow.

Areas of the pons are responsible for several distinctive features of REM sleep, including the eye movements that give this stage its name and muscular paralysis. The purpose of rapid eye movements is unknown. The movements result from activity in the pontine reticular formation that stimulates the superior colliculi of the midbrain, which in turn stimulate a different part of the pontine reticular formation, resulting in the characteristic eye movements. Each eye movement is accompanied by a characteristic waveform known as a **PGO spike,** illustrated in Figure 11.16. These waveforms also originate in the pontine reticular formation (P) and travel to the lateral geniculate nucleus of the thalamus (G; the visual center of the thalamus) and the occipital cortex (O). The muscular paralysis accompanying REM results from inhibitory messages traveling from the pontine reticular formation to the medulla and, from there, to the motor systems of the spinal cord. Although the primary motor cortex of the brain is quite active during REM, the only muscles that are able to respond fully during REM are the eye muscles, muscles of the middle ear, and those involved with breathing.

As shown in Figure 11.17, imaging studies of REM sleep indicate little activity in either the primary visual cortex of the occipital lobe (after all, the eyes are closed) or the frontal lobe (Maquet, 1999). However, there is significant activity in secondary visual cortex. The inactivity of the frontal lobe, which participates in waking

PGO spike An electrical waveform observed during REM sleep, originating in the pons and traveling to the thalamus and occipital cortex. Each PGO wave is associated with an eye movement.

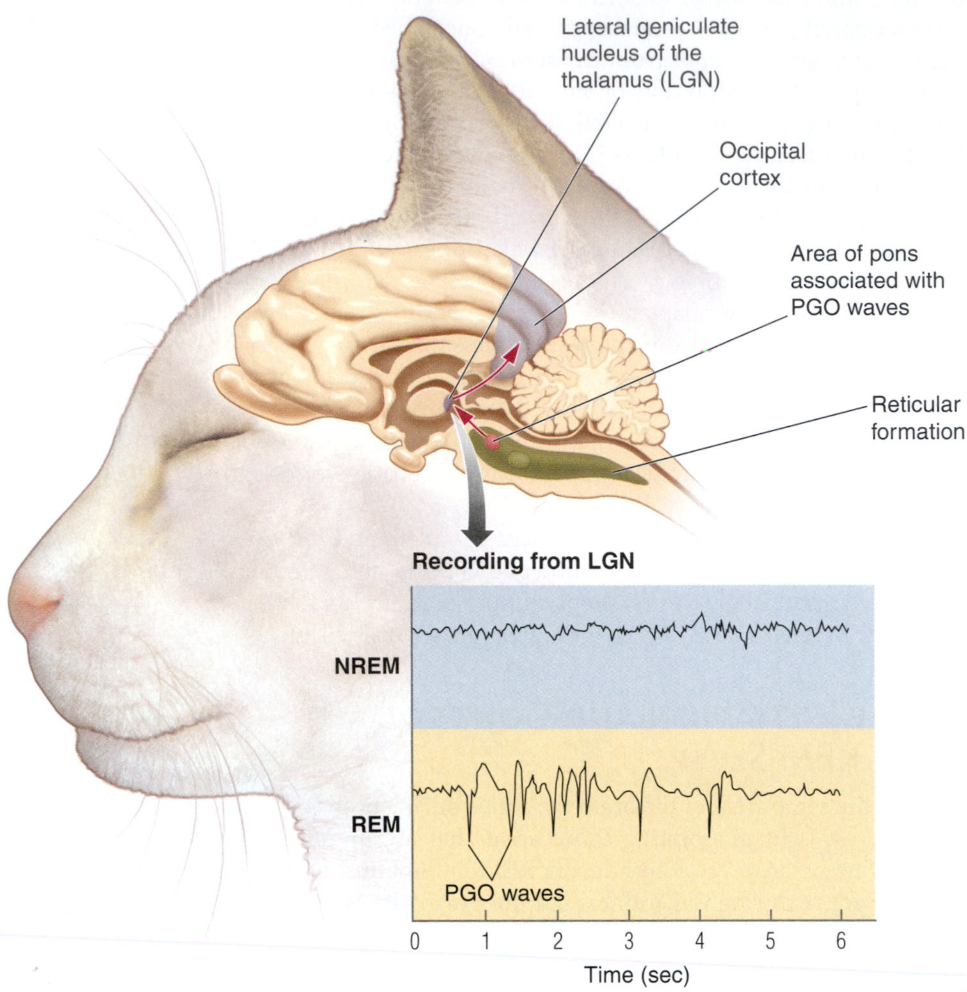

■ **FIGURE 11.16 PGO (Pons-Geniculate-Occipital) Waves Accompany REM Sleep** PGO waves can be recorded in the lateral geniculate nucleus of the thalamus in sleeping cats. The upper recording shows the relative lack of activity in this part of the brain during NREM, in contrast to the dramatic spiking in the lower recording that occurs during REM. Both the occipital cortex—the O in PGO—and the lateral geniculate—the G—are involved with vision. The significance of these waves and their associated eye movements during REM sleep is still a mystery.

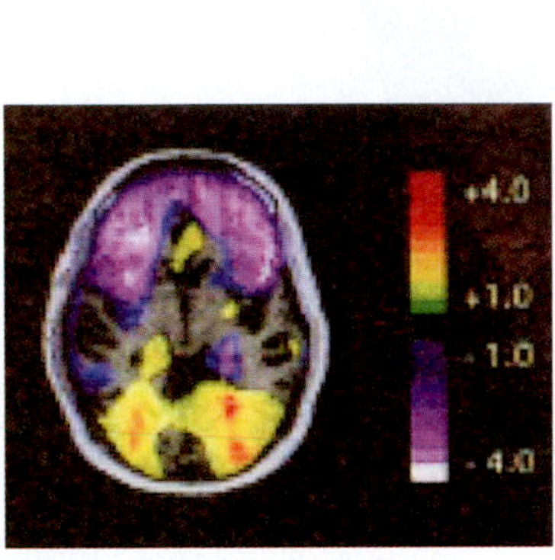

Courtesy A. R. Braun, National Institute of Deafness, NIH, Bethesda

■ **FIGURE 11.17 Comparing Patterns of Brain Activity** PET scans can be used to compare brain activity during two states, such as activity during REM versus activity during wakefulness. Taking one PET scan of a brain during REM and another of a waking brain, a researcher compared their activity pixel by pixel and plotted the results on a composite image. The scale to the right of the image allows us to apply colors to represent the differences observed during the two states. Areas that are more active during REM sleep than during wakefulness will be colored red or yellow (+1 to +4), areas that are about equally active during REM and wakefulness will not be colored (0), and areas that are less active during REM than during wakefulness will be colored blue or purple (−1 to −4). We can see that the secondary visual cortex, located toward the bottom of the image, is more active during REM than wakefulness (yellow) and the frontal lobes, located toward the top of the image, are less active during REM than wakefulness (purple).

judgments, might account for the often bizarre, illogical, and socially inappropriate content of our dreams. The hippocampus, in contrast, is quite active, possibly due to the suspected role in memory consolidation for REM sleep. The amygdala and anterior cingulate cortex are also quite active, perhaps leading to the rapidly changing, emotional quality of dreaming.

The Biochemistry of Wakefulness and Sleep

We have already seen how melatonin helps synchronize our sleep–waking cycles to the 24-hour rotation of the earth. As you can see in Table 11.3, a wide array of additional neurochemicals participates in the maintenance of our sleep–waking cycles.

Acetylcholine (ACh) release by the pons and basal forebrain is associated with both wakefulness and REM sleep (Vazquez & Baghdoyan, 2001). The loss of cholinergic neurons in Alzheimer's disease might account for the lack of attention and sleep problems that accompany that condition. Cholinergic agonists, such as nicotine, produce a high level of mental alertness.

TABLE 11.3 The Role of Neurochemicals in the Control of Wakefulness, NREM, and REM

Neurochemical	Locations at Which Neurochemical Is Active	Relation of Activity to Sleep and Waking	Effect of Agonists for Neurochemical	Effect of Antagonists for Neurochemical
Acetylcholine	• Pons • Basal forebrain	• High during wakefulness and REM • Low during NREM	• Increased arousal • Increased REM sleep	• Decreased arousal • Decreased REM sleep
Histamine	• Thalamus • Hypothalamus	• High during wakefulness • Low during NREM and REM		• Increased drowsiness and sleep
Norepinephrine	Locus coeruleus	• High during wakefulness • Low during NREM • No activity during REM	• Increased arousal • Decreased REM	• Increased REM sleep
Serotonin	Raphe nuclei	• High during wakefulness • Low during NREM • No activity during REM	• Increased sleep time • Decreased REM	• Increased REM sleep • Increased arousal
Adenosine	Widely distributed areas in the brain	• Accumulates in the brain during wakefulness; probably helps induce sleep	• Possibly promotes sleep	• Inhibits sleep

Some neurons in the thalamus and hypothalamus use histamine as their major neurotransmitter. These neurons project widely throughout the forebrain, and their activity is associated with alertness. Histamine activity is high during wakefulness but relatively low during NREM and REM sleep. Traditional antihistamines (histamine antagonists) used for suppressing cold and allergy symptoms are known to produce drowsiness. Modern antihistamines do not cross the blood–brain barrier, thereby avoiding the production of drowsiness.

As we have seen previously, serotonin and norepinephrine levels are highest during wakefulness, drop off during NREM sleep, and are very low during REM sleep. People with major depressive disorder (see Chapter 16) initiate REM too early and too frequently during the night, possibly due to reduced serotonin activity. Antidepressant drugs boost serotonin activity and often suppress REM. Drugs that stimulate the release of norepinephrine, such as amphetamine, delay sleepiness (Siegel & Rogawski, 1988).

Caffeine keeps us awake by blocking receptors for adenosine, an ATP byproduct that has an inhibitory effect on many brain systems (see Chapter 4). When adenosine is inhibited, alertness is maintained. When artificially applied, it induces sleep (Radulovacki, 1985). Adenosine accumulates throughout the day, and if sleep is postponed, concentrations continue to rise until sleep occurs (Porkka-Heiskanen, 1999). Adenosine specifically inhibits neurons releasing neurochemicals associated with wakefulness, including acetylcholine, serotonin, and norepinephrine. During the night's sleep, adenosine levels once again drop, allowing wakefulness to occur again in the morning.

INTERIM SUMMARY 11.2

Summary Table: Brain Mechanisms of Sleep and Arousal

	Wakefulness	NREM	REM
Reticular formation:			
Midbrain	Active	Inactive	Inactive
Pons	Inactive	Inactive	Active
Medulla	Active	Inactive	Inactive
Basal forebrain	Active	Inactive	Inactive
Locus coeruleus	Active	Less Active	Inactive
Raphe nuclei	Active	Less Active	Inactive
Preoptic area of the hypothalamus	Less Active	Active	Inactive

Summary Points

1. Sleep might keep us safe from predation, preserve energy, and restore our bodies. **(LO6)**
2. NREM provides opportunities to rest and repair the body, and REM sleep promotes brain development. Both components of sleep appear to enhance memory formation. **(LO6)**
3. Activity in the basal forebrain, parts of the reticular formation, the raphe nuclei, and the locus coeruleus are associated with wakefulness and vigilance. NREM becomes possible when the wakefulness circuits are inhibited and activity in the raphe nuclei and locus coeruleus drops, whereas the different aspects of REM sleep are controlled by parts of the reticular formation located in the pons. **(LO7)**
4. Neurochemicals associated with the regulation of sleep and wakefulness include serotonin, norepinephrine, histamine, acetylcholine, and adenosine. **(LO8)**

Review Questions

1. What do studies of REM and NREM deprivation contribute to our understanding of the functions of these sleep components?
2. In what ways should sleep be considered an active, as opposed to a passive, process?

Sleep Disorders

The *Diagnostic and Statistical Manual of Mental Disorders* (DSM IV-TR; American Psychiatric Association, 2000) distinguishes between two major classes of sleep disorder, the **dyssomnias** and the **parasomnias.** Dyssomnias involve difficulties in the initiation, maintenance, timing, and quality of sleep. Parasomnias occur when unusual behaviors disturb ongoing sleep.

Dyssomnias

The most common sleep disorder is **insomnia,** in which a person has difficulty initiating or maintaining enough sleep to feel rested. Individual needs for sleep vary widely. In one case of "healthy insomnia," an elderly female participant slept only one hour per night without any apparent detrimental effects (Meddis, Pearson, & Langford, 1973).

Onset insomnia occurs when a person is unable to go to sleep. Sleep can be delayed by multiple factors, including stress, anxiety, and use of stimulant drugs. **Maintenance insomnia** occurs when sleep is frequently interrupted or early waking occurs. Frequent

dyssomnia (dis-SOM-nee-ah) A sleep disorder that involves difficulty initiating or maintaining sleep.
parasomnia (pear-uh-SOM-nee-ah) A sleep disorder that involves the intrusion of unusual behaviors into sleep.
insomnia The inability to sleep a normal amount of time.

waking can result from stress, substance use, or psychopathology. As we'll see in Chapter 16, major depression often results in frequent waking. Drinking alcohol will put a person to sleep quickly, but early-morning wakefulness often occurs as the alcohol effects wear off.

In any case of insomnia, diagnosis should be left to sleep experts. Occasionally, people overestimate the extent of their sleeplessness. Some people even dream that they are awake, a condition often referred to as *pseudoinsomnia* (Borkovec, Grayson, O'Brien, & Weerts, 1979). For minor cases of insomnia, behavioral adjustments are usually helpful. Keeping to a regular sleeping schedule, avoiding stimulants, and writing down "to do" lists prior to sleep may be all that's needed. If insomnia is associated with psychopathology, it should resolve along with the disorder during treatment.

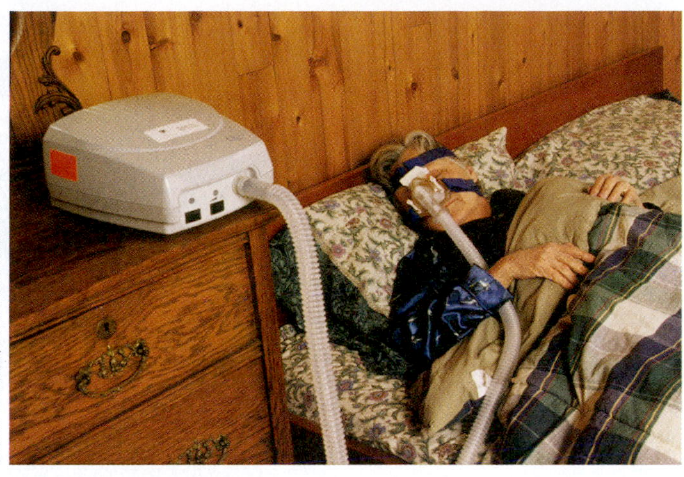

FIGURE 11.18
A Treatment for Sleep Apnea
For those who suffer from sleep apnea, the continuous positive airway pressure (CPAP) mask can provide significant relief. The continuous delivery of air keeps the person's airways clear and prevents episodes of not breathing.

Medications prescribed for insomnia include benzodiazepines and other sedatives. Sedatives speed up the onset of sleep by about 15 minutes and lengthen the night's sleep by perhaps a half hour (Buscemi et al., 2007). This small increase might not warrant the risk of dependence and other possible side effects of these medications. However, long-term sleep loss has its own risks. If behavioral treatment is ineffective, medications may be the only remaining option.

Another type of dyssomnia is **sleep apnea,** in which a person stops breathing during sleep. It is not uncommon for people to stop breathing during sleep for very short periods, and breathing during REM sleep can be quite irregular. In sleep apnea, breathing ceases for as long as a minute or two, resulting in reduced oxygen levels in the blood. The person awakens gasping for air, as if he or she had been underwater. Although sleep returns relatively quickly, sleep apnea affects the quality of sleep enough to cause symptoms of sleep loss the next day.

Sleep apnea often occurs in obese individuals who snore, indicating that airway obstructions might be the root of the problem. Losing weight or surgically correcting any obstructions in the airway can be helpful. In other cases, abnormalities occur in brainstem neurons responsible for the maintenance of breathing during sleep. Using machines such as the one shown in ■ Figure 11.18 to regulate airflow during sleep is an inconvenient but relatively effective solution.

Probably the most dramatic of the dyssomnias is **narcolepsy.** Narcolepsy consists of "sleep attacks," in which aspects of REM sleep intrude into wakefulness (Dahl, Holttum, & Trubnick, 1994). These sleep attacks usually last from 10 to 20 minutes, although they can continue for as long as an hour. In a sleep attack, people with narcolepsy enter REM sleep immediately and awaken feeling refreshed. Sleepiness soon returns, however, with attacks occurring approximately every two to three hours. Narcolepsy might have affected Harriet Tubman, one of the leaders of the Underground Railroad around the time of the American Civil War. Tubman, shown in ■ Figure 11.19 (far left), had many close calls while aiding escaped slaves. The emotion of the escape might have triggered sleep attacks, which came at the most inconvenient times.

In addition to sleep attacks, other aspects of REM sleep can intrude into the wakefulness of patients with narcolepsy. **Cataplexy** is a condition in which the muscle paralysis that is normally associated with REM sleep occurs when the person is completely awake. Cataplexy does not cause a loss of consciousness. The muscle paralysis can be fairly minor, affecting part of the face, for instance, or large-scale enough to cause the person to collapse in a heap on the floor. Cataplexy is nearly always preceded by a strong emotional reaction or stress. Unfortunately, having sex is a common emotional trigger for the disorder.

Many patients with narcolepsy also experience **sleep paralysis,** or muscle paralysis that either precedes actual sleep or lingers once the person has awakened. In some patients, REM dreaming phenomena intrude into wakefulness in the form of **hypnogogic hallucinations** (preceding sleep) or **hypnopompic hallucinations** (upon awakening). The imagery in these hallucinations is similar to REM dreaming, but the person remains awake.

onset insomnia Insomnia in which the individual has difficulty getting to sleep at bedtime.

maintenance insomnia Insomnia in which the individual cannot stay asleep during the night.

sleep apnea A sleep disorder in which the person temporarily stops breathing, then awakens gasping for air.

narcolepsy (nar-koh-LEP-see) A sleep disorder characterized by the intrusion of REM sleep, and occasionally REM paralysis, into the waking state.

cataplexy (CAT-a-plex-y) A feature of narcolepsy in which REM muscle paralysis intrudes into the waking state.

sleep paralysis A feature of narcolepsy in which REM muscle paralysis occurs preceding or following actual sleep.

hypnogogic hallucination (HIP-noh- GOG-ik) A REM-type dream that intrudes into the waking state prior to the onset of sleep.

hypnopompic hallucination (HIP-noh-POMP-ik) A REM-type dream that intrudes into the waking state upon awakening.

Figure 11.19
Narcolepsy Didn't Stop Harriet Tubman In spite of her suspected narcolepsy, Harriet Tubman (1820–1913) helped hundreds of slaves escape through the Underground Railroad during the Civil War era. Tubman appears on the left in this photo with some of the former slaves whom she helped. Unfortunately, narcoleptic attacks are often brought on by stress. Tubman had a number of close escapes when she experienced sleep attacks while being pursued by Confederate troops and irate slave owners.

Narcolepsy results from disruptions in the synthesis of orexins (also known as hypocretins) or in their receptors. As we saw in Chapter 9, orexins also play a major role in appetite (Siegel, 1999, 2004). In general, orexins appear to monitor the internal and external states of the animal and adjust the wakefulness required for survival (Ohno & Sakurai, 2008). Orexins are typically found in the cerebrospinal fluid of people without narcolepsy but are absent or greatly reduced in patients with the disorder. In addition, cells in the hypothalamus that normally secrete orexins are missing or damaged in the brains of patients with narcolepsy (Thannickal et al., 2000). Narcolepsy can be treated successfully with stimulant medications such as modafinil (Wise, Arand, Auger, Brooks, & Watson, 2007).

Every closed eye is not sleeping, and every open eye is not seeing.
Bill Cosby

Parasomnias

Whereas the dyssomnias involve problems in the initiation and maintenance of normal sleep behavior, parasomnias are interruptions that occur during sleep. We have already reviewed two of the parasomnias: nightmares and night terrors. Based on twin and family analyses, parasomnias appear to share a common genetic background (Hublin, Kaprio, Partinen, & Koskenvu, 2001). People with at least one parasomnia typically have family members with either the same parasomnia or another one.

In **sudden infant death syndrome (SIDS),** a basically healthy baby, usually between two and four months of age, dies while asleep. Sleeping position appears to play a major role in many cases of SIDS. At ages two to four months, babies are not very skilled at turning over. Between 1992 and 2003, SIDS rates in the United States dropped 50 percent after the American Academy of Pediatrics recommended putting infants to sleep on their backs instead of on their stomachs, as shown in Figure 11.20 (National Institute of Child Health and Human Development, [NICHHD] 2008; Malloy & Freeman, 2004).

No single factor appears to account for all cases of SIDS (Filiano & Kinney, 1994). In their triple-risk model of SIDS, Filiano and Kinney argue that SIDS involves a vulnerable infant in a critical period of development exposed to an external stressor. Among the vulnerabilities of infants are race, gender, and abnormalities in the serotonergic systems of the medulla (Paterson et al., 2006). African American babies are twice as likely to die from SIDS as white babies, and Native American infants are three times as likely to die from SIDS as white babies (NICHHD, 2002). Boys are at higher risk than girls (NICHHD, 2002). In addition to sleeping position, exposure

sudden infant death syndrome (SIDS) A syndrome in which an otherwise healthy infant stops breathing and dies during sleep.

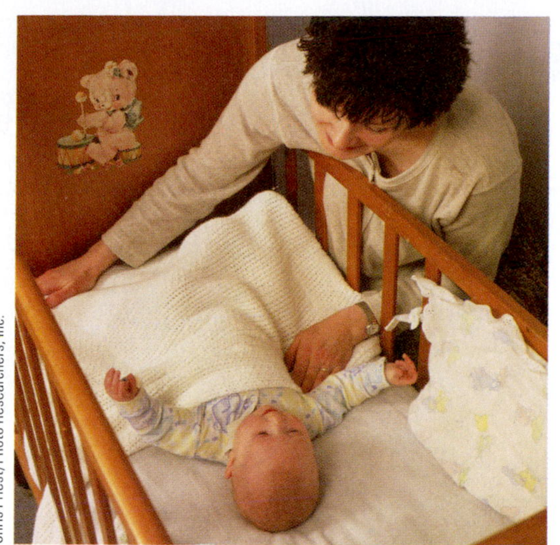

Chris Priest/Photo Researchers, Inc.

FIGURE 11.20
Sleeping Position Helps Prevent SIDS SIDS rates in the United States dropped 50 percent between 1992 and 2003 after the American Academy of Pediatrics (AAP) issued new recommendations for infant sleeping position. Unlike previous recommendations to put infants to sleep on their stomachs, the new AAP recommendations included putting babies to sleep on their backs with a blanket tucked in no higher than the chest. No pillows, stuffed animals, quilts, or other soft objects should be near the baby's face.

to cigarette smoke (Klonoff-Cohen, Edelstein, & Lefkowitz, 1995) and sharing a bed with parents (Paterson et al., 2006) might act as external stressors.

Another parasomnia, sleep talking, typically occurs in lighter stages of sleep of both REM and NREM. Sleep talking is most common in young people, and diminishes with age. The talking person is often responsive to external stimuli. My college roommate and I were both frequent sleep talkers, and we would politely take our turns speaking. Eventually, the fact that my roommate's conversation had nothing to do with my own would wake me up. There is no support for the myth that people speak only the truth during sleep. Most of the time, the speaker's words don't seem to make much sense at all.

Somnambulism, or sleepwalking, is much more common in children than in adults; most sleepwalkers are between the ages of 4 and 12 years (Kryger, Roth, & Dement, 1994). At least 15 percent of children have one episode of sleepwalking, and 5 percent of children sleepwalk at least one time per week. During an episode, the child walks anywhere from a few seconds to 30 minutes. Body movements are typically uncoordinated and aimless rather than purposeful. As a result, sleepwalking can lead to physical injury from falling down stairs and similar accidents. Sleepwalking is probably a deep NREM phenomenon because episodes occur during the first three hours of sleep, awakened individuals show considerable disorientation, and the paralysis accompanying REM makes walking during this stage unlikely. Like other parasomnias, sleepwalking appears to run in families, and episodes can be triggered by sleep deprivation, use of alcohol or other medications, stress, or fever (Pressman, 2007).

There ain't no way to find out why a snorer can't hear himself snore.

Mark Twain

In cataplexy, we observed the intrusion of REM paralysis into the waking state. In **REM behavior disorder,** we see the absence of normal REM paralysis when it is supposed to occur. Instead of being paralyzed while dreaming, people with REM behavior disorder act out their dreams, occasionally destroying furniture and injuring their sleeping partners and themselves. Schenck, Bundlie, Ettinger, and Mahowald (1986) describe a case study of a man who dreamed of playing football. During this episode, the man knocked everything off his dresser, hit his head against the wall, and hit his knee on the dresser. REM behavior disorder appears to be an inherited problem in most cases, but it can also result from brain damage, particularly in the pons (Culebras & Moore, 1989). As we discussed previously, structures within the pons are responsible for inhibiting motor movement during REM. When these areas are lesioned in cats, the cats behave as if they were acting out their dreams (Jouvet, 1972). REM behavior disorder might also accompany neurodegenerative diseases, especially Parkinson's disease (Gugger & Wagner, 2007). REM behavior disorder is usually treated with sedative medications, such as the benzodiazepines, or with melatonin (Gugger & Wagner, 2007).

Restless leg syndrome (RLS) occurs when one of a person's limbs, usually a leg, experiences a sensation of tingling and moves at regular intervals of 15, 30, or 45 seconds. In the National Sleep Foundation (2000) Omnibus Sleep in America Poll, about 15 percent of the respondents reported symptoms of RLS. RLS occurs frequently in children and adults with attention deficit/hyperactivity disorder (Wagner, Walters, & Fisher, 2004; Dement, 2000). Other medical conditions, such as kidney disease, pregnancy, and anemia, might be at fault (Hening, Allen, Tenzer, & Winkelman, 2007). Treatment generally consists of massage, the application of heat or cold, avoidance of caffeine, and, if necessary, medication.

somnambulism (som-NAM-bu-liz-um) Sleepwalking.

REM behavior disorder A sleep disorder in which the normal REM paralysis is absent.

restless leg syndrome (RLS) A sleep disorder in which a limb, usually a leg, moves at regular intervals during sleep.

INTERIM SUMMARY 11.3

Summary Table: Sleep Disorders

Type of Disorder	Name of Disorder	Major Features	Treatment (if any)
Dyssomnias (Problems in initiating and maintaining normal sleep)	Insomnia	Difficulty initiating or maintaining sleep	• Avoidance of stimulants • Regular sleeping schedules • Treatment of underlying psychopathology (if present) • Medication
	Sleep apnea	Failure to maintain normal breathing patterns during sleep	• Weight loss • Surgical correction of airways • Mechanical regulation of airflow during sleep
	Sudden infant death syndrome (SIDS)	Unexplained death of otherwise healthy infant during sleep	• Avoiding smoking in household with infants • Avoiding putting infant to sleep on stomach or with blankets or stuffed animals
	Narcolepsy	Inappropriate intrusions of sleep phenomena into normal waking	• Medication • Stress management
Parasomnias (Interruptions of sleep)	Sleep talking	Speech during early stages of NREM and REM	• None • Appears to diminish with age
	Somnambulism	Sleepwalking	• None • Appears to diminish with age
	REM behavior disorder	Lack of normal muscle paralysis during REM sleep	• Medication
	Restless leg syndrome (RLS)	Regular movements of limbs during sleep	• Correction of any underlying medical conditions • Massage • Application of heat or cold • Medication

Summary Points

1. Sleep disorders are categorized as dyssomnias or parasomnias. **(LO9)**
2. Among the dyssomnias are insomnia, sleep apnea, and narcolepsy. Parasomnias include nightmares, night terrors, sleep talking, sleepwalking (somnambulism), REM behavior disorder, and restless leg syndrome (RLS). **(LO9)**

Review Question

1. What treatments are available for dyssomnias and parasomnias?

CHAPTER REVIEW

THOUGHT QUESTIONS

1. A recent survey asked participants to rate their "highs," or experiences that made them feel especially wonderful. For middle-aged respondents, one of the top five highs was eight hours of uninterrupted sleep. Why do you think this item was reported as a high by people in this age group?
2. Describe the likely effects that being blind would have on your daily sleep–waking cycles. What advice would you give a blind person to improve the quality of his or her sleep?
3. Using the information you learned in this chapter, explain the relationship between low serotonin and the sleep disturbances characteristic of depression.

KEY TERMS

alpha wave (p. 321)
beta wave (p. 321)
cataplexy (p. 335)
circadian rythym (p. 313)
cortisol (p. 319)
delta wave (p. 322)
desynchronous (p. 320)
dyssomnia (p. 334)
insomnia (p. 334)
melatonin (p. 318)
narcolepsy (p. 335)
non-REM sleep (NREM) (p. 322)
parasomnia (p. 334)
PGO spike (p. 331)
rapid-eye-movement (REM) sleep (p. 322)
suprachiasmatic nucleus (SCN) (p. 315)
synchronous (p. 320)
theta wave (p. 322)
ultradian cycle (p. 321)
zeitgeber (p. 313)

12 Learning and Memory

© Blend Images/Alamy

▲ **Human Beings Are Master Learners** The ability to learn provides a powerful tool for adapting to new environments.

CHAPTER OUTLINE

Introduction

At some point in their academic careers, most students long for a perfect memory; however, perfect recall might not be as good as it sounds. Russian physician Alexander Luria (1968) wrote a case study of his patient known as "S." We met S in Chapter 7 during our discussion of synesthesia, the experience of a sensation in multiple sensory modalities. As a result of his synesthesia, S's memory was extraordinary. In one instance, Luria presented S with a sheet of paper with 48 numbers in four columns. After studying the sheet for a few minutes, S recalled the numbers perfectly. Luria could ask S to recall the numbers in any order—across rows, diagonally, down columns. S retained this information months later. As helpful as this skill might appear to students, S's extraordinary memory definitely had its drawbacks. Although he could remember vast numbers of facts, he was unable to organize his knowledge using concepts, categories, and generalizations. His memory skills actually prevented S from truly thinking about what he knew. S's dilemma reinforces the commonsense notion that you should be careful what you wish for—a perfect memory might not be so wonderful after all. ■

Learning

The behavior of organisms can be separated into three major categories: reflexes, instincts, and learned behaviors. **Reflexes** are involuntary responses to stimuli. These behaviors are produced by prewired neural connections or reflex arcs. Reflexes have the advantage of producing rapid, reliable responses, but their inflexibility can be a disadvantage when the environment changes.

Like reflexes, **instincts** are automatic, but their resulting behaviors are more complex. Most instinctive behaviors involve mating or parenting behavior (Tinbergen, 1951). In the courtship display of the male peacock, shown in ■ Figure 12.1, the identification of an appropriate female partner initiates a chain of predictable, stereotyped behaviors. Although somewhat modifiable by experience, instinctive behaviors are consistent enough to be referred to as fixed action patterns.

Learning, or a relatively permanent change in behavior (or the capacity for behavior) due to experience, provides organisms with the most flexible means for responding to the environment. Human beings occupy nearly every niche on the planet, from blazing equatorial environments to the frigid Arctic. Much of this adaptability stems from the remarkable human capacity for learned behavior. Our definition of learning specifies that only those behavioral changes that result from experience will be considered learned. This specification excludes changes in behavior that occur due to maturation or growth. The requirement that learning be "relatively permanent" excludes brief or unstable changes in behavior. Fatigue, boredom, illness, and mood all influence behavior, but in a temporary and transitory manner. Exactly how permanent memories really are is open to debate, as we will see later in this chapter.

LEARNING OBJECTIVES

After reading this chapter, you should be able to:

LO1 Distinguish between learned, reflexive, and instinctive behaviors.

LO2 Describe the synaptic changes that coincide with habituation, sensitization, and classical conditioning in *Aplysia californica*.

LO3 Explain the roles of the amygdala, the cerebellum, and the cerebral cortex in the classical conditioning of vertebrates.

LO4 Distinguish between the major categories of memory.

LO5 Describe the roles of the brain structures associated with learning and memory.

LO6 Explain the process of long-term potentiation (LTP) and the relationship of this process to learning and memory.

LO7 Identify major biochemical factors involved in the formation of long-term memory.

LO8 Explain repression, post-traumatic stress disorder, flashbulb memories, and the effects of normal aging on memory.

Types of Learning

Learning occurs in one of two ways. **Associative learning** occurs when an organism forms a connection between two features of its environment. Classical conditioning, which allows organisms to learn about signals that predict important events, falls into this category. **Nonassociative learning,** including the processes of habituation and

■ **Figure 12.1**
Peacock Courtship Displays Are Instinctive Once the appropriate environmental cues are perceived, an available female in this case, the male peacock instinctively engages in a courtship display. Once initiated, instinctive behaviors proceed in a predictable, stereotyped manner.

reflex An involuntary response to a stimulus.
instinct A stereotyped pattern of behavior elicited by particular environmental stimuli.
learning A relatively permanent change in behavior or the capacity for behavior due to experience.
associative learning A type of learning that involves the formation of a connection between two elements or events.
nonassociative learning A type of learning that involves a change in the magnitude of responses to stimuli rather than the formation of connections between elements or events.

sensitization, involves changes in the magnitude of responses to stimuli rather than the formation of connections between specific elements or events.

Habituation and Sensitization **Habituation** occurs when an organism reduces its response to unchanging, harmless stimuli. You might notice the sound of your air conditioner or furnace turning on or off, yet you really don't hear the machine while it's running. **Sensitization** occurs when repeated exposure to a strong stimulus increases response to other environmental stimuli. For example, following major disasters such as earthquakes, people often experience exaggerated responses to movement, light, and noise. Increasing our overall level of responsiveness as a result of detecting one type of harmful stimulus makes us able to react more quickly to other sources of potential harm, even if the precise stimulus that signals danger changes.

Learning without thinking is useless. Thinking without learning is dangerous.
Confucius

Classical Conditioning In **classical conditioning,** organisms learn that stimuli act as signals that predict the occurrence of other important events. Credit for discovering and articulating the basic phenomena of classical conditioning goes to the famous Russian physiologist Ivan Pavlov (1927). Pavlov distinguished between conditioned and unconditioned stimuli and responses. The term *conditioned* refers to the presence of learning, whereas *unconditioned* refers to factors that are innate or unlearned. Therefore, a **conditioned stimulus (CS)** refers to an environmental event whose significance is learned, whereas an **unconditioned stimulus (UCS)** has innate meaning to the organism. In many of Pavlov's classic experiments, a ticking metronome served as a conditioned stimulus, and food was used as the unconditioned stimulus. Dogs lack innate responses to ticking metronomes, but they generally are born knowing what to do with food.

Conditioned responses (CR) are those behaviors that must be learned, whereas **unconditioned responses (UCR)** appear without prior experience with a stimulus. Salivating in response to the presence of food in the mouth is unconditioned because the dog does this without prior experience with food. Salivating in response to a ticking metronome is a conditioned response because the dog does this only as a result of experience. The development of conditioned responses constitutes the change in behavior that tells us learning has occurred. Once learning has taken place, the organism not only responds to the unconditioned stimulus but now responds to stimuli that reliably predict its arrival. This ability to anticipate future events and prepare responses provides significant advantages to an organism in the struggle for survival.

habituation A type of learning in which the response to a repeated, harmless stimulus becomes progressively weaker.
sensitization A type of learning in which the experience of one stimulus heightens response to subsequent stimuli.
classical conditioning A type of associative learning in which a neutral stimulus acquires the ability to signal the occurrence of a second, biologically significant event.
conditioned stimulus (CS) In classical conditioning, an initially neutral event that takes on the ability to signal other biologically significant events.
unconditioned stimulus (UCS) In classical conditioning, an event that elicits a response without prior experience.
conditioned response (CR) In classical conditioning, a learned reaction to the conditioned stimulus.
unconditioned response (UCR) In classical conditioning, a spontaneous unlearned reaction to a stimulus without prior experience.
Aplysia californica (uh-PLEE-zhuh cal-i-FOR-ni-kuh) An invertebrate sea slug frequently used as a subject of experiments on learning and memory.
gill-withdrawal reflex In *Aplysia*, a protective reflex in which the gill is retracted in response to touch.

Using Invertebrates to Study Learning

Invertebrates are not only capable of learning, but their large-celled, simple, and, hence, easily observed nervous systems also make them ideal subjects. Some invertebrate learning research is bizarre, such as G. A. Horridge's (1962) demonstration that headless cockroaches can learn classically conditioned responses. More typically, researchers have relied on the sea slug, ***Aplysia californica,*** shown in Figure 12.2.

To understand learning processes in *Aplysia*, it is helpful to know a bit about its anatomy. On the dorsal surface of the animal, you can locate the gill, which the animal uses to breathe. The gill can be covered by a structure known as the mantle shelf. At one end of the mantle shelf is the siphon, a tube through which the animal releases waste and seawater. Touching the animal's siphon reliably produces a protective response known as the **gill-withdrawal reflex,** in which the gill is retracted. The gill-withdrawal reflex will eventually habituate. In other words, when the siphon is touched repeatedly, the gill-withdrawal reflex will gradually diminish.

Habituation in *Aplysia* Beginning in the 1960s, Eric Kandel and his colleagues began to trace the neural pathways responsible for the habituation of the *Aplysia* gill-withdrawal reflex. As shown in Figure 12.3, simple invertebrates such as *Aplysia* have neural nets as opposed to brains. Within these neural nets, ganglia, or collections of cell bodies, serve as major processing centers. The siphon is served by 24 touch receptors whose cell bodies are located in the animal's abdominal ganglion. In

Visual&Written SL/Alamy

■ **FIGURE 12.2**
Aplysia californica The sea slug, *Aplysia californica,* has been a useful subject in the search for the underlying neural mechanisms of habituation, sensitization, and classical conditioning.

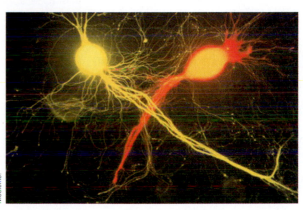

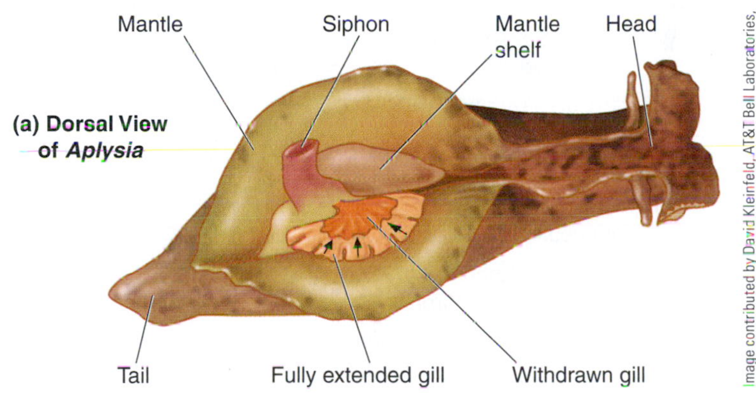

Image contributed by David Kleinfeld, AT&T Bell Laboratories, and Brian Salzberg, University of Pennsylvania School of Medicine.

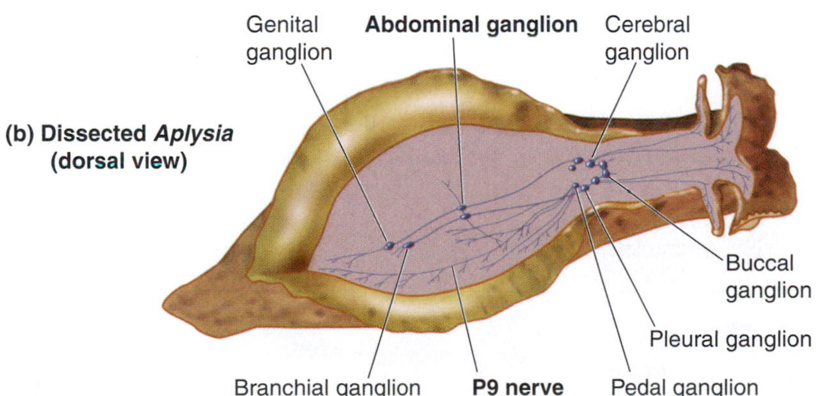

■ **FIGURE 12.3**
The Dissection of *Aplysia* Simple neural networks make *Aplysia* an ideal candidate for the study of learning. (a) This view of *Aplysia* shows the major anatomical features involved with learned responses. (b) Many learned responses in *Aplysia* involve neurons in the animal's abdominal ganglion. P9 is the largest nerve serving the tail. (c) The large size and distinctiveness of *Aplysia* neurons make them ideal for electrical recording.

the *Aplysia* abdominal ganglion, the touch receptors form synapses with a number of excitatory and inhibitory interneurons as well as with the six motor neurons serving the gill.

Kandel and his colleagues considered several possible hypotheses that might account for habituation within this simple network. With repeated stimulation, the sensory neurons serving the siphon might become less responsive. This possibility was discarded after recordings from the sensory neurons demonstrated steady, ongoing activity in response to touch, even after the gill-withdrawal reflex had become very weak. Another possibility was a reduction in the gill muscle's ability to react in response to input from the motor neurons. This explanation was ruled out when electrical stimulation of the motor neurons reliably produced muscle contraction, even after habituation had occurred.

This leaves a final alternative. Repeated touching of the siphon might produce changes at synapses between the sensory neurons of the siphon and motor neurons that serve the gill muscles. Kandel successfully demonstrated that repeated touching of the siphon reduced the size of excitatory postsynaptic potentials (see Chapter 3) in both the interneurons and the motor neurons. As shown in ■ Figure 12.4, a smaller amount of input to the motor neurons resulted in diminished activity between the motor neurons and gill muscles, which in turn produced a weak withdrawal reflex.

Kandel further demonstrated that the reduced activity at the synapse between the sensory and motor neurons in habituation was a direct result of the release of less neurotransmitter (Castelucci, Carew, & Kandel, 1978). The repeated stimulation depletes the amount of available neurotransmitter in the presynaptic sensory neuron, producing short-term habituation lasting from minutes to several hours (Zhao & Klein, 2002).

■ **Figure 12.4**
Habituation and Sensitization in *Aplysia*

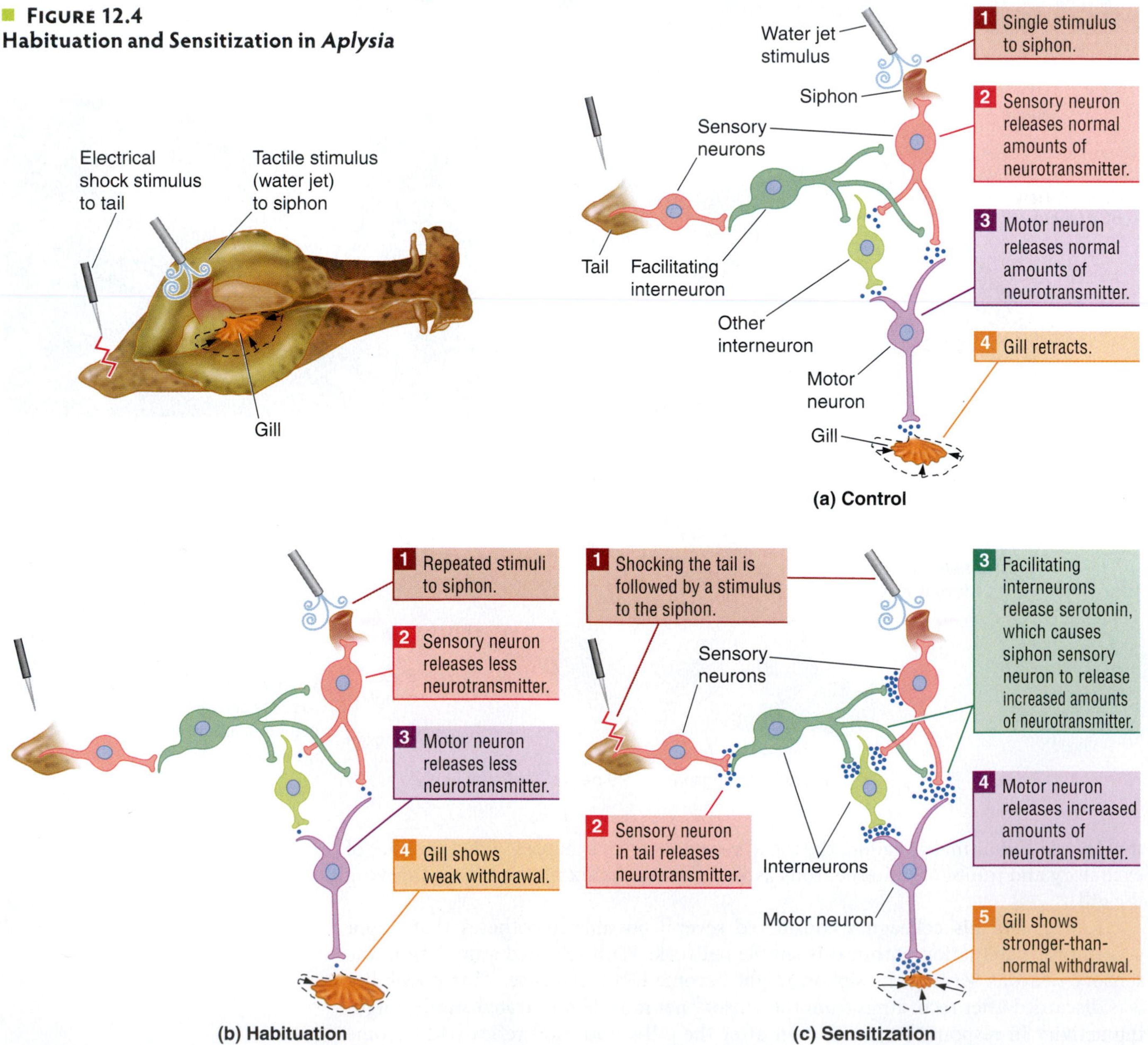
Electrical shock stimulus to tail
Tactile stimulus (water jet) to siphon
Gill
Water jet stimulus
Siphon
Sensory neurons
Tail
Facilitating interneuron
Other interneuron
Motor neuron
Gill
1 Single stimulus to siphon.
2 Sensory neuron releases normal amounts of neurotransmitter.
3 Motor neuron releases normal amounts of neurotransmitter.
4 Gill retracts.
(a) Control
1 Repeated stimuli to siphon.
2 Sensory neuron releases less neurotransmitter.
3 Motor neuron releases less neurotransmitter.
4 Gill shows weak withdrawal.
(b) Habituation
1 Shocking the tail is followed by a stimulus to the siphon.
Sensory neurons
2 Sensory neuron in tail releases neurotransmitter.
Interneurons
Motor neuron
3 Facilitating interneurons release serotonin, which causes siphon sensory neuron to release increased amounts of neurotransmitter.
4 Motor neuron releases increased amounts of neurotransmitter.
5 Gill shows stronger-than-normal withdrawal.
(c) Sensitization

Some people will never learn anything, for this reason, because they understand everything too soon.

Alexander Pope

Habituation, even in *Aplysia*, can last up to three weeks (Carew & Kandel, 1973). Three weeks of memory might not seem like much to a college student, but for a simple organism such as *Aplysia*, this might be equivalent to a doctoral degree. Depletion of available neurotransmitter is unlikely to be the cause of this longer-lasting habituation. Instead, long-term habituation probably depends on postsynaptic processes involving the NMDA glutamate receptor (Glanzman, 2006; Roberts & Glanzman, 2003). As we discussed in Chapter 4, the NMDA glutamate receptor has special qualities that allow it to participate in the structural changes that accompany learning. Chemicals that block glutamate receptors effectively prevent the development of long-term habituation (Ezzeddine & Glanzman, 2003).

Sensitization in *Aplysia* Habituation in *Aplysia* occurs in a single pathway connecting sensory input from the siphon to neurons controlling the movement of the gill. In sensitization, however, a stimulus gains the ability to influence more than one neural pathway. After *Aplysia* is sensitized by the administration of an electric shock to the head or tail, touching the siphon results in an enhanced gill-withdrawal response.

A diagram of the basic connections responsible for sensitization is shown in Figure 12.4. Shocking the animal's tail stimulates sensory neurons, which form excitatory synapses with a group of interneurons. These interneurons, in turn, form synapses with the sensory neurons serving the siphon. The synapses between the interneurons and sensory neurons are axo-axonic in form. In other words, the axon from the interneuron forms a facilitating synapse at the axon terminal of the sensory neuron (see Chapter 3). The interneurons release serotonin at these axo-axonic synapses (Brunelli, Castellucci, & Kandel, 1976). When receptors on the sensory axon terminal bind molecules of serotonin, a metabotropic process (see Chapter 4) closes potassium channels. With the closing of the potassium channels, action potentials reaching the sensory axon terminal last longer than they would in a typical response to a siphon touch. (Recall from Chapter 3 that the opening of potassium channels is responsible for the repolarization of the cell during an action potential. Delaying repolarization extends the duration of the action potential.)

Longer action potentials produce a greater influx of calcium into the sensory neuron, which in turn results in the release of larger amounts of neurotransmitter by the sensory axon terminal. The increased release of neurotransmitter produces a stronger response by the motor neurons and the gill muscles, leading to the stronger gill-withdrawal reflex that we observe in sensitization.

Adjustments at the synaptic level account for the immediate changes we see in habituation and sensitization. Undoubtedly, longer-lasting changes in behavior require some structural modifications to the neurons as well. As a result of repeated exposure to habituation or sensitization, changes occur in the number of presynaptic terminals of sensory neurons (Bailey & Chen, 1983). As illustrated in ■ Figure 12.5, the animals that had undergone sensitization training showed the highest numbers of terminals, 2,800, compared with 1,300 for the control animals and only 800 in the animals that had undergone habituation training. In sensitized animals, the dendrites of the motor neurons were also modified to accommodate the increased number of presynaptic elements. These structural changes appear to involve actin, a protein that makes up the microfilaments of the cytoskeleton (see Chapter 3; Colicos, Collins, Sailor, & Goda, 2001; Cingolani & Goda, 2008).

Although our discussion so far has focused on presynaptic changes in sensitization (Byrne & Kandel, 1996), this type of learning involves postsynaptic changes as well (Glanzman, 2006). Sensitization involves an increase in the numbers of another type of glutamate receptor, the AMPA receptor (see Chapter 4). It also appears that the coordination of pre- and postsynaptic changes occurs through retrograde signals from the postsynaptic motor cell back to the presynaptic sensory cell or interneuron (Glanzman, 2006).

Learn from yesterday, live for today, hope for tomorrow.

Albert Einstein

Classical Conditioning in *Aplysia* In addition to their ability to display nonassociative learning, *Aplysia* are also capable of demonstrating associative learning

Figure 12.5
Structural Changes in Synapses Result from Learning Bailey and Chen (1983) counted the number of axon terminals found on sensory neurons following sensitization and habituation. Habituation reduced the number of terminals, whereas sensitization increased the number of terminals. In animals undergoing sensitization, the motor neuron dendrites also showed signs of modification.

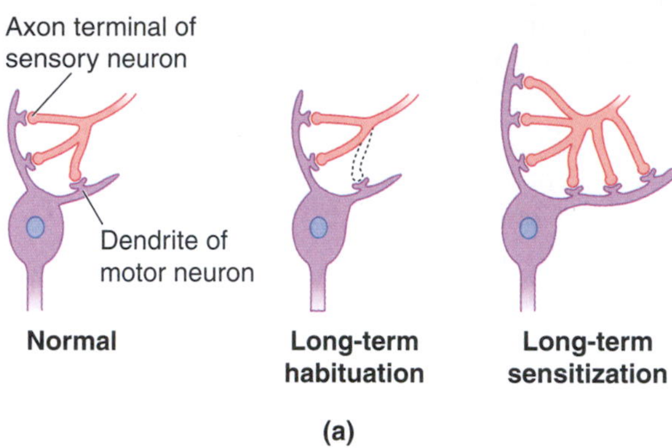

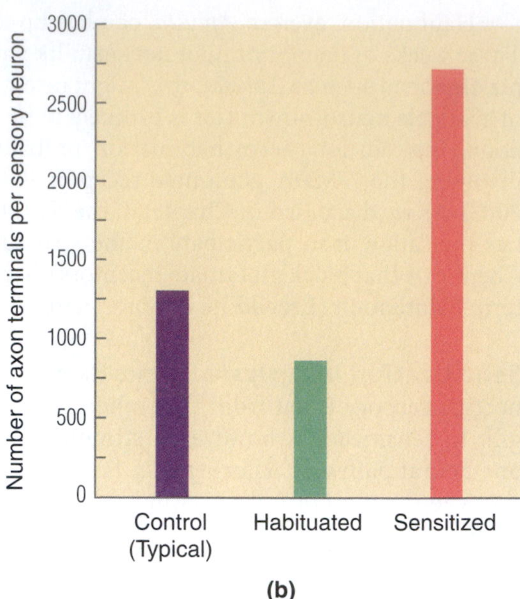

in the form of classical conditioning. In a typical experiment, a slight touch of the mantle shelf serves as the conditioned stimulus (CS^+), and an electrical shock to the tail serves as the unconditioned stimulus (UCS). To provide a control stimulus that is not paired with shock, the siphon (CS^-) of the *Aplysia* is occasionally touched, but not frequently enough to produce habituation.

Prior to training, touching the mantle shelf produces little if any movement of the gill. After several pairings of the mantle shelf touch (CS^+) and the electrical shock to the tail (UCS), the mantle shelf touch is applied alone to see whether any learning has occurred. Typically, the mantle shelf by itself will now elicit a stronger gill-withdrawal reflex (CR). In contrast, no changes are observed in the animal's response to the siphon touch (CS^-), which has never been paired with shock (UCS). The change in the ability of the CS^+ to elicit strong gill-withdrawal reflexes meets our definition of classical conditioning.

Anyone who stops learning is old, whether at twenty or eighty.
Henry Ford

Let's take a closer look at the mechanisms responsible for this type of learning, illustrated in Figure 12.6. As we observed in sensitization, change in the gill-withdrawal reflex parallels change in the amount of neurotransmitter released by the sensory neurons onto the motor neurons serving the gill muscles. The mantle shelf touch (CS^+) produces action potentials in the sensory neuron. When these action potentials reach the axon terminal, calcium (Ca^{2+}) enters the cell and determines the amount of neurotransmitter to be released onto the motor neuron controlling the gill-withdrawal reflex. The shock to the tail (UCS) results in the release of serotonin by an interneuron onto the sensory axon serving the mantle in the same manner that we observed in our discussion of sensitization. Once again, potassium channels close, increasing the amount of neurotransmitter that is released by the sensory neuron onto the motor neuron. Most important, we can see how the conditioned and unconditioned stimuli interact to boost the amount of neurotransmitter released by the sensory neuron. Whenever large concentrations of Ca^{2+} are present, the processes leading to potassium channel closing are enhanced (Abrams, Yovell, Onyike, Cohen, & Jarrad, 1998). The arrival of the signal from the CS^+ at the sensory axon terminal triggers the increase in Ca^{2+} necessary to enhance the effects of the serotonin released by the interneuron in response to the UCS. As in the cases of habituation and sensitization, postsynaptic mechanisms leading to structural change also contribute to classical conditioning (Antonov, Antonova, Kandel, & Hawkins, 2003; Antonov, Ha, Antonova, Moroz, & Hawkins, 2007).

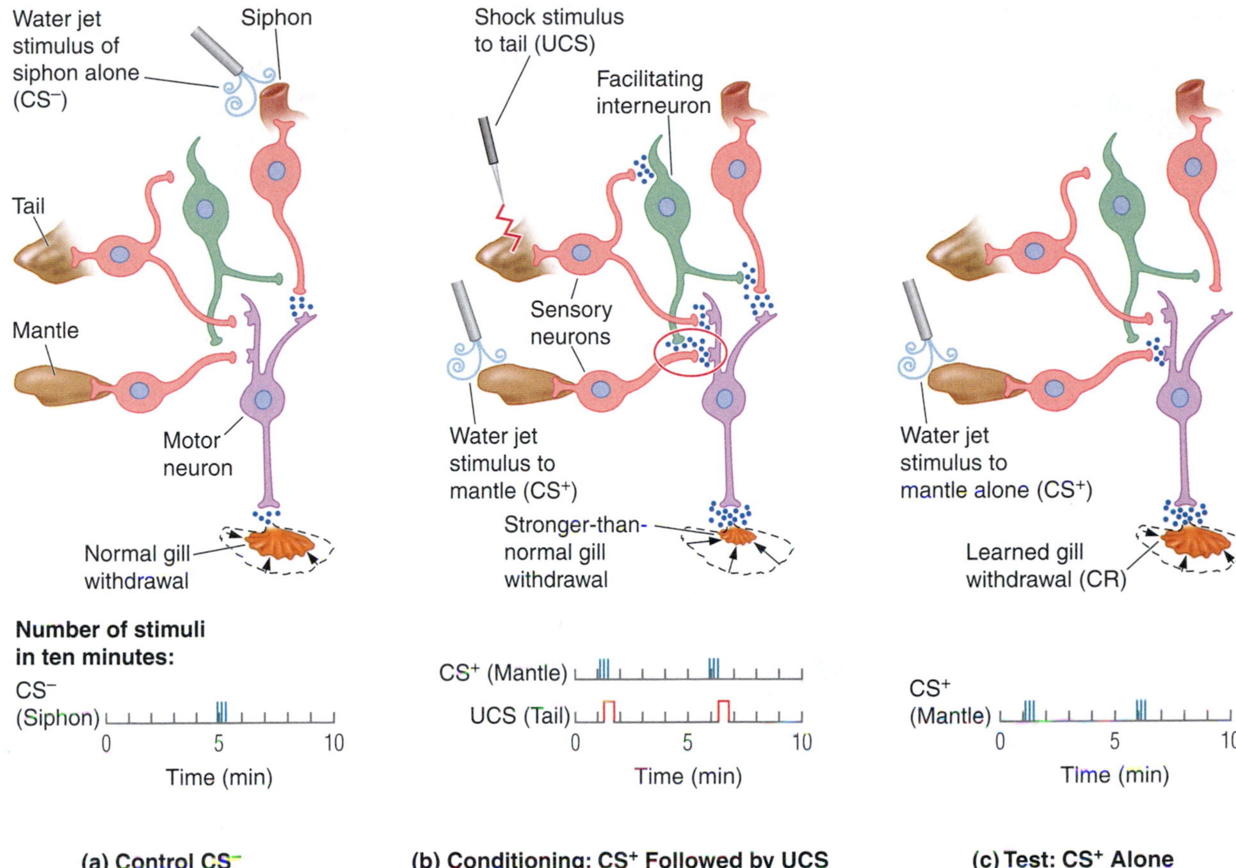

FIGURE 12.6
Classical Conditioning in *Aplysia* (a) Touching the siphon (CS^-) is not paired with shock and serves as a control. (b) Touching the mantle (CS^+) is always followed by shock to the tail (UCS). (c) After several pairings of touching the mantle (CS^+) followed by shock (UCS), touching the mantle alone now triggers gill withdrawal (CR). In the circled area in (b), the mantle shelf sensory neurons are sequentially activated, first by touching the mantle shelf and then by input from interneurons serving the tail. This sequence produces increased presynaptic facilitation, leading to the recording of greater postsynaptic potentials in the motor neuron than those recorded prior to training.

WHY DOES THIS MATTER?

The Cost of Learning

If a headless cockroach can perform classically conditioned responses (Horridge, 1962), we understand that you do not need a human brain to learn. What is perhaps more difficult to understand is why so many animals use learning so sparingly. If learning is such an advantage, why haven't more species evolved complex learned behaviors? The answer appears to be that there is no free lunch—learning is an expensive, life-shortening process for an organism. Understanding this insight matters because it gives us a greater appreciation of the sacrifices the human species has made to use learning as its primary survival strategy.

The cost of learning was demonstrated in an experiment in which fruit flies learned to associate one flavor of jelly (orange or pineapple) with the bitter taste of quinine (Burger, Kolss, Pont, & Kawecki, 2008). Bitter tastes usually indicate toxins. The first generation of flies took many hours to learn this association, but when the researchers collected the eggs of the "smarter" flies and trained these offspring, 15 generations later, the result was flies that could learn the rules in less than an hour. This sounds great, until you get to the part where the "quick-learning" flies died 15 percent faster than flies that were not selected for learning.

The strengthening of synapses and the genetic and biochemical changes associated with learning take a toll on an organism. For this reason, species will evolve more learning capacity only when the costs of learning are outweighed by the survival benefits (finding more food, etc.).

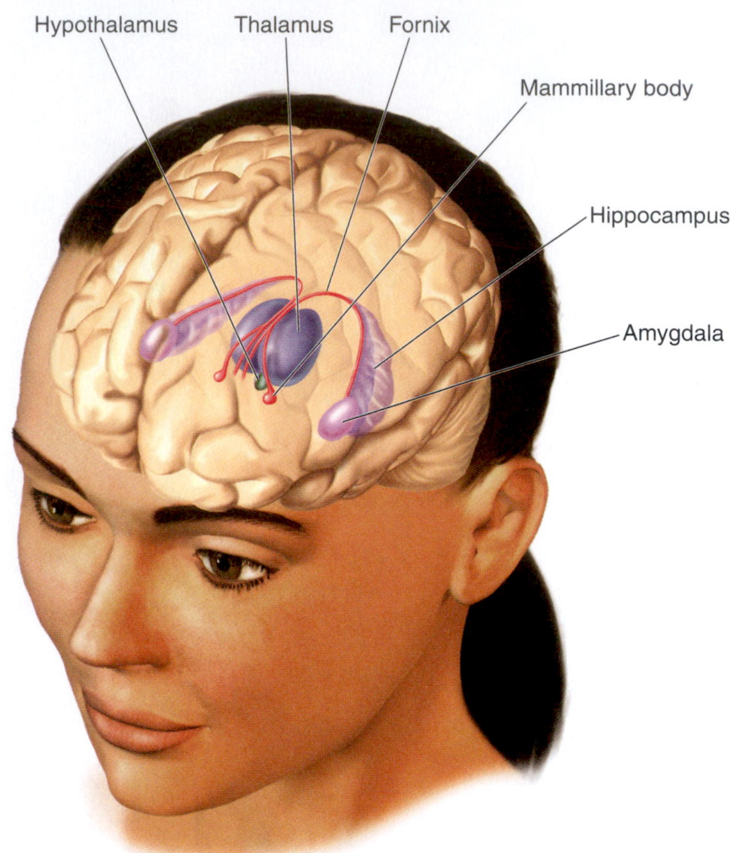

FIGURE 12.7
The Amygdala and Its Associated Structures

CLASSICAL CONDITIONING IN VERTEBRATES

To identify the neural basis of classical conditioning in vertebrates, researchers have investigated a number of different situations, including fear responses in rats and eyeblink conditioning in rabbits. Compared to investigations of invertebrate learning, which prominently feature presynaptic changes, the emphasis in vertebrate conditioning is on postsynaptic processes such as protein synthesis in the postsynaptic cells.

Classical Conditioning of Fear Many emotional responses to environmental stimuli are learned by the process of classical conditioning, such as the jitters students feel before a big exam or a child's fear of dogs following a dog bite. The amygdala, shown with its associated structures in Figure 12.7, plays an important role in the classical conditioning of emotional responses (Wilensky, Schafe, Kristensen, & LeDoux, 2006). Lesion studies, recording studies, and research involving the administration of NMDA antagonists all point to the importance of the amygdala in this type of learning (LeDoux, 1994; Quirk, Repa, & LeDoux, 1995; Gewirtz & Davis, 1997; Fanselow & LeDoux, 1999).

In a typical investigation of classically conditioned fear in rats, a stimulus such as a tone (CS) is followed by electrical shock to the feet (UCS). The conditioned response (CR) is a reduction in behaviors that are incompatible with fear, such as feeding. Following the pairing of a shock with a tone, the tone by itself will begin to serve as a danger signal that evokes fear and inhibits feeding. Information about the tone (CS) and the shock (UCS) converges in the amygdala (Wilensky et al., 2006). When the same cells are receiving input about both the CS and UCS within a short period of time, the resulting high influx of calcium triggers a cascade of events, similar to those observed in *Aplysia,* that result in protein synthesis and more sensitivity to subsequent CS input. Consequently, when the CS is presented alone, the newly conditioned circuits within the amygdala respond more strongly than before and are capable of generating the fear response.

Classical Conditioning of the Eyeblink Additional insight into the mechanisms of classical conditioning in vertebrates comes from investigations into conditioned eyeblinks in the rabbit by Richard Thompson and his colleagues (Christian & Thompson, 2003; Lee & Thompson, 2006; Thompson, Thompson, Kim, Krupa, & Shinkman, 1998). In this preparation, a tone (CS) is followed by a puff of air directed at the rabbit's eye (UCS), which causes movement of the rabbit's **nictitating membrane** (UCR), an additional inner eyelid found in some birds, fish, and mammals, but not in humans. After several pairings of the tone and puff, the tone alone will elicit the movement of the nictitating membrane (CR). Considerable evidence points to a role for the cerebellum in this type of classical conditioning (Woodruff-Pak & Disterhoft, 2008).

Thompson and his colleagues focused on a particular structure in the cerebellum known as the **interpositus nucleus.** Recordings from cells in the interpositus nucleus initially show little response to the tone CS. However, as learning proceeds, a steady increase in this structure's response occurs (Thompson, 1986). Further evidence for the importance of the interpositus nucleus in classical conditioning was demonstrated through a series of reversible lesion experiments, illustrated in

nictitating membrane An additional, moveable inner eyelid found in some birds, fish, and mammals but not in humans.
interpositus nucleus A cerebellar nucleus thought to be essential to classical conditioning in vertebrates.

Figure 12.8. Inactivating the interpositus nucleus by cooling it effectively prevents classical conditioning. When the cooling wears off, rabbits begin to learn the conditioned response as if they had had no prior experience at all.

No man has a good enough memory to make a successful liar.

Abraham Lincoln

When we lesion a structure, it is possible that behavior will change due to the loss of that structure. On the other hand, the changed behavior we observe might be due to a lack of information traveling via fibers that are also affected by the lesion. The red nucleus is a brainstem structure involved in motor control that receives substantial input from the cerebellum and is directly responsible for performance of the eyeblink response (Robleto & Thompson, 2008). If the interpositus nucleus has only an indirect effect on learning via its connections with other structures, inactivation of the red nucleus should also prevent learning. In fact, inactivation of the red nucleus by cooling prevents the nictitating-membrane response. However, when the red nucleus recovers, the animals produce strong conditioned responses (Krupa, Thompson, & Thompson, 1993). Learning did occur, although performance was suppressed when the red nucleus was inactivated. It appears, then, that the interpositus nucleus is primarily responsible for the formation of the classically conditioned response of the nictitating membrane in rabbits.

Evidence from human studies also points to a role for the cerebellum in classical conditioning. Human participants do not have nictitating membranes, of course, but they can learn to blink in response to stimuli paired with a puff of air directed at the eye. Using PET scans, Logan and Grafton (1995) observed changes in the cerebellar activity of their human participants during classical conditioning. Individuals with cerebellar damage have a difficult time learning the conditioned eyeblink

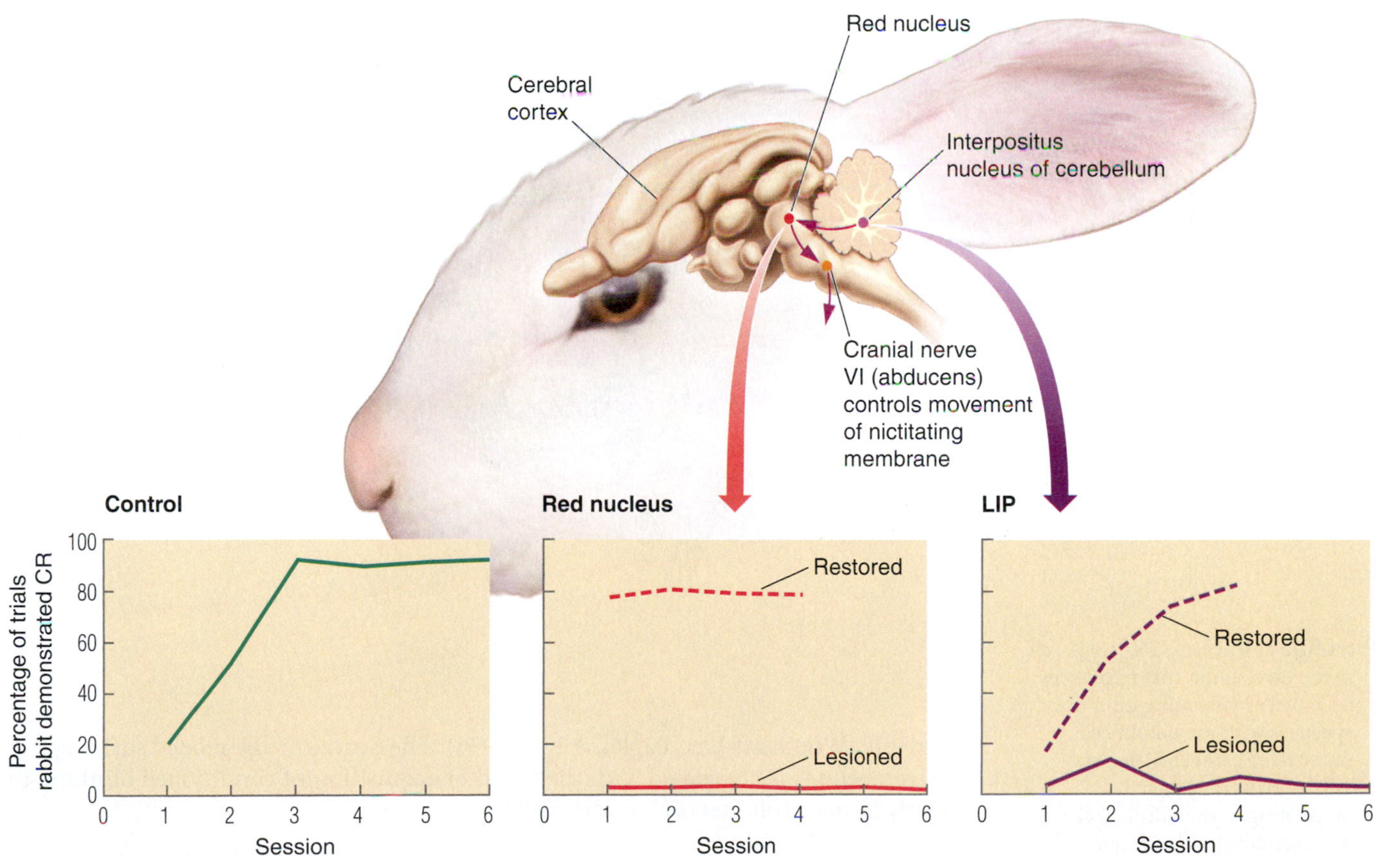

FIGURE 12.8
The Role of the Interpositus Nucleus in Classical Conditioning Temporarily disabling the red nucleus by cooling prevents conditioned responding by rabbits trained in a conditioned eyeblink paradigm. However, the response resumes immediately when the red nucleus recovers. In contrast, temporarily disabling the interpositus nucleus by cooling appears to prevent learning because these animals demonstrate the same subsequent learning curve as controls. *Source:* Adapted from Krupa, Thompson, & Thompson, 1993.

■ **FIGURE 12.9 Connections Within the Cerebellum** The Purkinje cell network might provide a mechanism for learning.

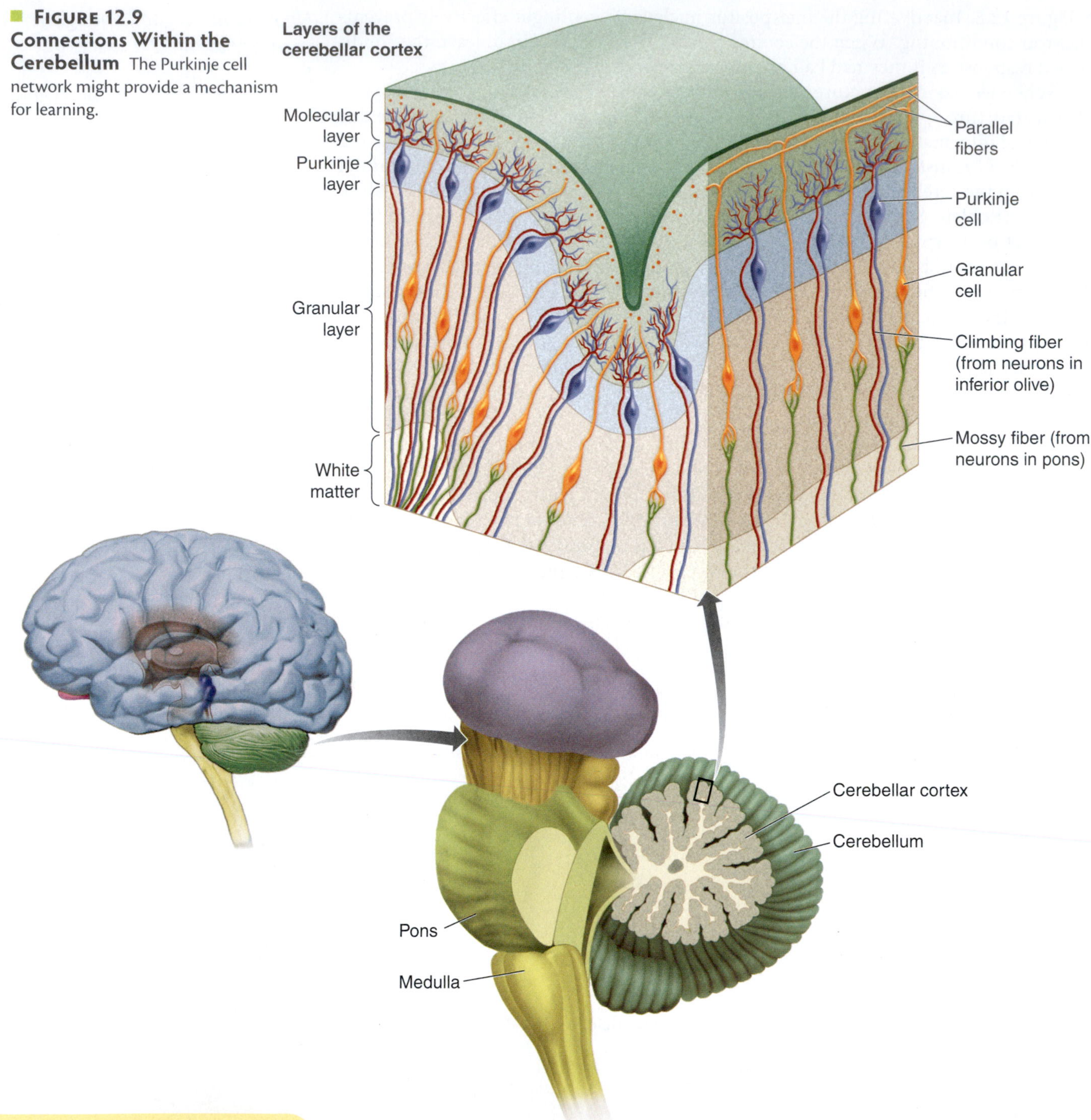

Purkinje cell (per-KIN-jee) A cell in the cerebellum that influences its activity by forming inhibitory synapses with the output cells in the deep cerebellar nuclei.
climbing fiber A fiber originating in the inferior olive of the brainstem that forms synapses on the large Purkinje cells of the cerebellar cortex.
parallel fiber A fiber originating in the granule cells of the cerebellum that synapses on the Purkinje cells.
granule cell A cell within the cerebellum that is the source of parallel fibers.

response (Woodruff-Pak, Papka, & Ivry, 1996). The degree of age-related shrinkage of the cerebellum is correlated with the speed of acquisition of conditioned blinking in elderly human volunteers (Woodruff-Pak et al., 2001).

Cerebellar Circuits and Classical Conditioning The rather unusual anatomy of the cerebellum, shown in ■ Figure 12.9, seems ideally designed to carry out classical conditioning. In the cerebellar cortex, large **Purkinje cells** receive inputs known as **climbing fibers** from neurons located in the inferior olive in the medulla. In addition, the Purkinje cells receive input from **parallel fibers.** These fibers originate in an adjacent layer of cerebellar cells known as **granule cells.** Cerebellar granule cells make up possibly half the neurons in the entire brain. These granule cells in turn receive input

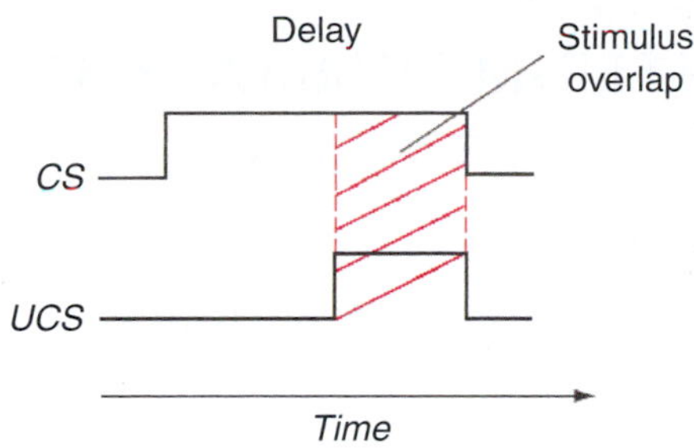

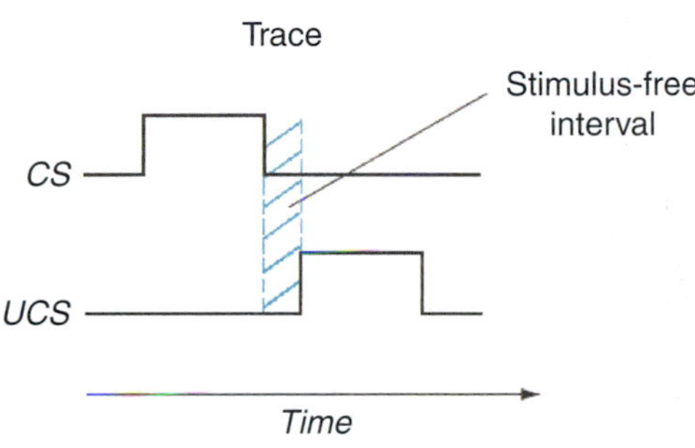

FIGURE 12.10
Delay Versus Trace Conditioning In delay conditioning, an example of nondeclarative or implicit learning, the onset of the UCS overlaps with the CS. In contrast, the CS and UCS do not overlap in trace conditioning, which is considered to be an example of declarative or explicit learning.

from **mossy fibers,** which originate from neurons in the pons. Integrating input from the parallel and climbing fibers, the Purkinje cells form inhibitory synapses on the output cells of the cerebellum, located in the **deep cerebellar nuclei.** As the result of this network, the Purkinje cells are perfectly situated to influence the output of the cerebellum.

James Albus (1971) suggested learning will occur if the climbing-fiber and parallel-fiber synapses onto a Purkinje cell are activated at the same time. Masao Ito (1984) provided support for Albus's predictions. Ito recorded EPSPs in the Purkinje cells in response to electrical stimulation of the parallel fibers. Subsequently, both climbing and parallel fibers were simultaneously stimulated. The paired stimulation produced a reduction in Purkinje cell EPSPs that lasted up to one hour. The reduced activity in the Purkinje cells is known as **long-term depression,** or LTD.

Further research showed that the reduction in EPSPs was due to a reduced responsiveness by the Purkinje cell to glutamate released by the parallel fibers. Activity in the climbing and parallel fibers produces three simultaneous events within the postsynaptic Purkinje cell. Calcium (Ca^{2+}) and sodium (Na^{+}) flow into the cell. At the same time, a second (or postsynaptic chemical) messenger known as **protein kinase C** is activated. Together, these three events produce a decrease in the number of available glutamate receptors found in the Purkinje cell membrane. As a result of having fewer receptors to activate, subsequent input produced LTD in the form of reduced EPSPs. Although it might seem difficult to see a connection between learning and LTD, which is a reduction in activity, LTD involving the inferior olive-climbing fiber system is recognized as essential for learning the eyeblink CR (Christian & Thompson, 2003; Woodruff-Pak & Disterhoft, 2008).

Trace Conditioning and Extinction The type of classical conditioning we have discussed so far in *Aplysia,* rabbits, and humans was described by Pavlov as **delay conditioning.** As shown in ■ Figure 12.10, the CS in traditional delay conditioning overlaps the UCS somewhat, with no stimulus-free interval between the CS and UCS. In **trace conditioning,** a stimulus-free interval occurs, and bridging the interval requires more than just cerebellar activity alone.

The first clue that delay and trace conditioning were managed by different learning processes arose from research with mutant mice, whose abnormal cerebellums interfered with their delay conditioning but not their trace conditioning (Kishimoto et al., 2002; Kishimoto, Hirono et al., 2001; Kishimoto, Kawahara et al., 2001). Next, human patients with cerebellar lesions showed greater impairment in delay than in trace conditioning (Gerwig et al., 2008; Gerwig et al., 2006).

Subsequent research has demonstrated that bridging the time gap between the CS and UCS in trace conditioning requires the participation of forebrain areas, including areas of sensory cortex, the hippocampus, and the prefrontal cortex (Woodruff-Pak & Disterhoft, 2008). Instead of a direct projection of information about the CS to the cerebellum via nuclei in the pons, trace conditioning requires the forebrain structures to hold the CS information during the stimulus-free interval, after which the information is transmitted to the pons and cerebellum.

Why is this difference in conditioning paradigms important? As we will see later in this chapter, we can distinguish between declarative or conscious memory processes (also known as explicit learning) and nondeclarative or unconscious memory processes (also known as implicit learning). Trace conditioning in humans appears to require conscious, declarative processes (Clark, Manns, & Squire, 2001). Consequently, trace conditioning provides an excellent model for the study of declarative memories in many species.

mossy fiber (cerebellum) A fiber connecting a neuron in the pons to the granule cells of the cerebellum.

deep cerebellar nuclei Structures that contain the major output cells of the cerebellum; recipients of input from the cerebellar Purkinje cells.

long-term depression (LTD) A type of synaptic plasticity in which postsynaptic potentials in target cells are reduced.

protein kinase C A second messenger found in the Purkinje cells of the cerebellum.

delay conditioning A type of classical conditioning in which CS onset precedes and overlaps UCS onset.

trace conditioning A type of classical conditioning in which the CS and UCS do not overlap in time.

INTERIM SUMMARY 12.1

Summary Table: Types of Learning

Type of Learning	Description	Possible Underlying Mechanisms in Invertebrates	Possible Underlying Mechanisms in Vertebrates
Habituation	A reduction in response to a repeated stimulus	Persistent changes in activity at the synapse between sensory neurons and either interneurons or motor neurons; postsynaptic structural changes in longer-lasting learning	Currently unknown
Sensitization	A type of learning in which experiencing one stimulus heightens the response to subsequent stimuli	Enhancement of activity at axo-axonic synapses between interneurons and sensory neurons; postsynaptic structural changes in longer-lasting learning	Currently unknown
Classical conditioning	A type of associative learning in which a neutral stimulus acquires the ability to signal the occurrence of a second, biologically significant event	Convergence of input from both the conditioned stimulus (CS) and the unconditioned stimulus (UCS) increases the amount of neurotransmitter released by the sensory neuron and stimulates postsynaptic changes in glutamate receptors.	Participation of the amygdala in classically conditioned fear responses in rats. Participation of circuits in the cerebellum, including the interpositus nucleus, in the conditioning of skeletal reflexes such as the eyeblink. Participation of forebrain structures in trace conditioning.

Summary Points

1. Reflexes, instinctive behaviors, and learning fall along a continuum of flexibility. Reflexes produce rigid patterns of response, whereas the flexibility of learned behaviors is well suited to rapidly changing environments. Major types of learning include habituation, sensitization, and classical conditioning. **(LO1)**
2. Research using *Aplysia* suggests that learning results from both pre- and postsynaptic changes. **(LO2)**
3. Classical conditioning in vertebrates involves the amygdala (emotional learning) and the cerebellum (skeletal reflexes). In addition to the cerebellum, trace conditioning requires activity in the forebrain. **(LO3)**

Review Question

1. What cellular changes are associated with habituation, sensitization, and classical conditioning in invertebrates?

Memory

Although memory commonly refers to the storage and retrieval of information, there is no absolute boundary between the processes of learning and those of memory. Learning and memory are best viewed as occurring along a continuum of time.

Types of Memory

information processing models theories of memory that seek to explain the management of information by the brain, from detection to storage to retrieval.

Information processing models of memory assume that information flows through a series of stages on its way to permanent storage in memory, as shown in ■ Figure 12.11 (Atkinson & Shiffrin, 1968, 1971). Not only do these models provide a helpful framework for thinking about memory, but they also predict the participation of different brain structures in each stage of processing.

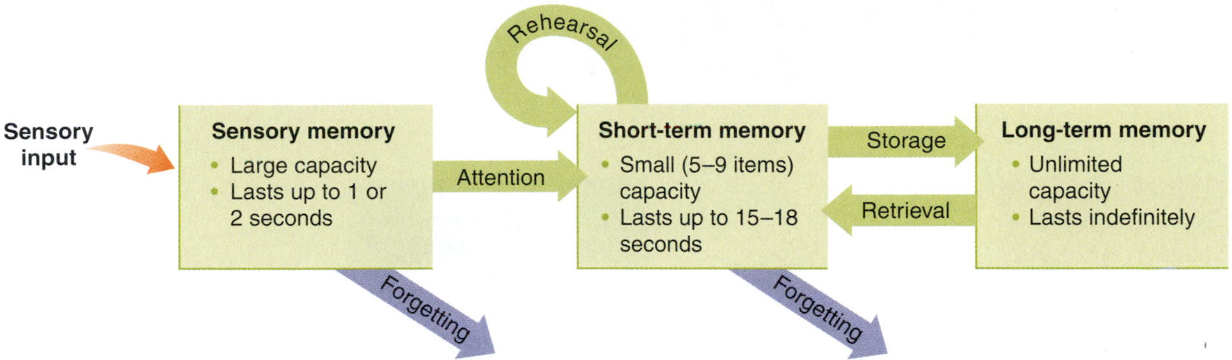

FIGURE 12.11 The Atkinson-Shiffrin Model of Memory According to the information processing model proposed by Atkinson and Shiffrin, information is processed in a sequence of steps. The sensory memory holds large quantities of information for several seconds. Short-term memory holds limited quantities of information for limited periods of time. Long-term memory can hold unlimited amounts of information for unlimited periods of time. Information that does not move to the next stage for processing will be permanently lost.

According to the Atkinson-Shiffrin model, any information sensed by an organism initially enters the **sensory memory.** This first memory stage can hold a large amount of data for a very brief period of time, on the order of a few seconds. From this initial set of data, we select information for further processing and move it to the next stage of memory, the **short-term memory,** or "working" memory. This stage contains all the data that we are currently thinking about. Short-term memory has a very limited capacity, somewhere between five and nine unrelated items (Miller, 1956). When we try to add additional items, previous information is often lost. If somebody asks you the time while you're trying to remember the telephone number whispered by your attractive classmate, disaster can result. In addition to having a limited capacity, short-term memory is also notable for its temporary nature. Classic research by Peterson and Peterson (1959) showed that material in short-term memory was lost rapidly, in 15 to 18 seconds, but others believe that loss occurs in as little as 2 seconds (Sebrechts, Marsh, & Seamon, 1989). Information in short-term memory is sorted into temporary storage areas or buffers for auditory, visual, or combined types of information, which are managed by a "central executive" process (Baddeley, 2000; Baddeley & Hitch, 1974).

The final destination for information in the Atkinson-Shiffrin model is **long-term memory,** shown in ■ Figure 12.12. Unlike short-term memory, long-term memory seems to have few, if any, limitations on capacity or duration. Elderly people still recall childhood memories of events that occurred many years in the past and retain the ability to learn and remember facts read in the morning newspaper, in spite of the large quantity of information already stored from a lifetime of experience.

Long-term memories are divided into three categories: *semantic, episodic,* and *procedural* memories (Tulving, 1972, 1985, 1987, 1995). **Semantic memory** contains basic knowledge of facts and language. Using your semantic memory, you can answer questions such as "Who was the first president of the United States?" or "What is a bagel?" **Episodic memory** relates to your own personal experience. You use your episodic memory to remember the *episodes* of your life—what you ate for breakfast or the time you chose your first puppy. **Procedural memory** stores information about motor skills and procedures such as riding a bicycle, using a software program, or cooking your favorite meal. Semantic and episodic memories are grouped together as **declarative memories.** These types of memories are declarative in the sense that they can easily be described in words, or "declared." In contrast, procedural memories are often quite difficult to describe verbally but are easy to demonstrate or perform (Squire, 1987). Writing an essay about how to ride a bicycle for someone who has never even seen a bicycle is much harder than showing the person how to ride. Declarative and procedural memories differ in one other important way. Declarative memories are typically recalled consciously or explicitly, whereas procedural memories are usually recalled unconsciously or implicitly. Learning a skill, such as driving a car, requires quite a bit of attention and conscious effort. Once mastered, however, a skill such as driving can become quite automatic. In addition to procedural memories, classical conditioning, habituation, and sensitization are also considered examples of nondeclarative or implicit processes. As we observed previously, however, trace conditioning (a type of classical conditioning) shares many similarities with declarative memory.

sensory memory An initial stage in memory formation in which large amounts of data can be held for very short periods.

short-term memory An intermediate memory store in which limited amounts of data can be held for a limited amount of time; without further processing, such information is permanently lost.

long-term memory A memory store in which apparently unlimited amounts of data can be held for an unlimited amount of time.

semantic memory A type of declarative, explicit memory for facts and verbal information.

episodic memory A type of declarative, explicit memory for personal experience.

procedural memory A type of implicit memory for performing learned skills and tasks.

declarative memory An explicit memory for semantic and episodic information that can easily be verbalized, or "declared."

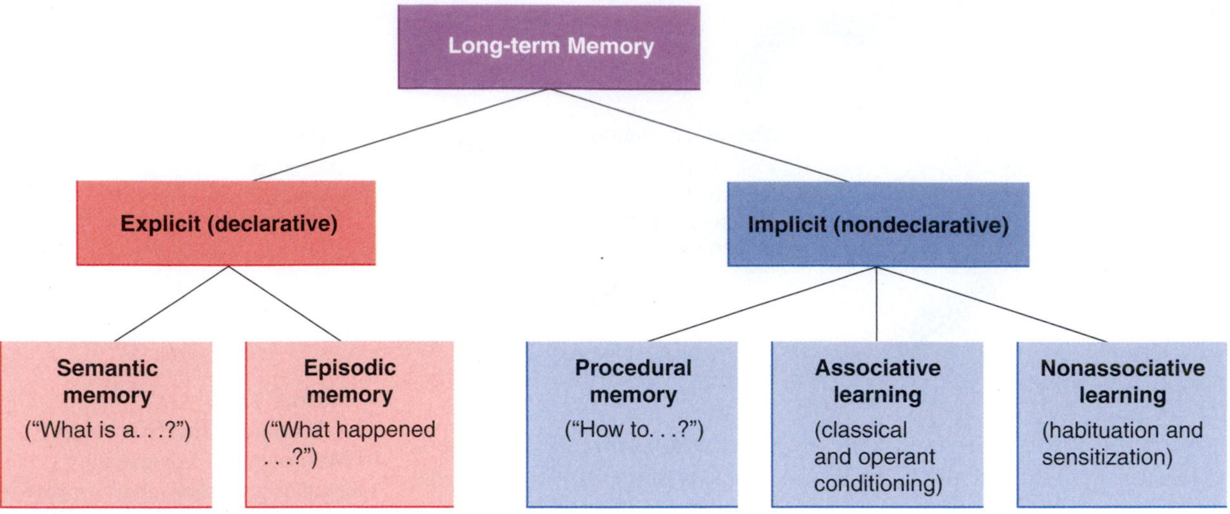

FIGURE 12.12
Types of Long-Term Memory

The distinction between explicit and implicit memories can be demonstrated in patients suffering from a type of memory loss known as **anterograde amnesia.** In cases of anterograde amnesia, patients have good recall for events that occurred prior to the time of their brain damage, but they seem unable to remember anything they experience following their brain damage. However, the inability of these patients to remember the present, such as the name of the current president of the United States, is not due to a complete memory failure. Squire (1987) demonstrated that patients with anterograde amnesia were able to learn to solve the Tower of Hanoi puzzle, in which a stack of rings must be moved from one peg to another one at a time without placing a larger ring on top of a smaller ring. When asked about the puzzle, most patients could not recall seeing it before, and they certainly had no confidence that they could solve it. When given the opportunity, however, the patients solved the puzzle skillfully. In other words, their brain damage did not prevent them from forming implicit memories of how to solve the puzzle, although it did prevent them from explicitly remembering that they knew how to solve it. Where exactly are these memory functions located? To answer this question, psychologists have engaged in an extended search for the **engram,** or the physical representation of memory in the brain.

Brain Mechanisms in Memory

The search for the elusive engram involved both animal experimentation and human case studies. Although we still do not have the final answer on where our memories are stored, significant progress has been made in our understanding.

Early Efforts to Locate Memory Functions Karl Lashley (1929) was one of the earliest psychologists to tackle the problem of locating the engram. Lashley reasoned that the engram might be located in the association cortex, areas of cortex that are not locked into a specific sensory or motor function.

To test his hypothesis, Lashley performed a series of lesions on rats both before and after they were trained to run through mazes to find food. Rats that received cortical lesions prior to any training were slow to learn their way through the maze. Rats that received cortical lesions following their training seemed to have forgotten many of their previously learned behaviors. Lashley's next task was to investigate the influence of the size and location of his lesions on the rats' maze performance. Surprisingly, Lashley reported that the location of his lesions didn't seem to matter much. Instead, the deficit in the rats' performance seemed due to the size of the lesion. As shown in Figure 12.13, larger lesions appeared to produce poorer performance, regardless of where the lesion was made. Lashley mistakenly concluded that all parts of the cortex make an equal contribution to learning and memory, a concept he referred to as equipotentiality. In other words, Lashley believed that the engram is distributed

anterograde amnesia (an-TARE-oh-grade) Memory loss for information processed following damage to the brain.
engram A physical memory trace in the brain.

■ **FIGURE 12.13**
Karl Lashley Observed the Results of Brain Lesions on Maze-Learning Performance (a) Lashley trained rats to run a maze and then performed brain lesions on them. (b) As larger amounts of cortex were damaged, errors in running the maze increased.
Source: Adapted from Lashley, 1929.

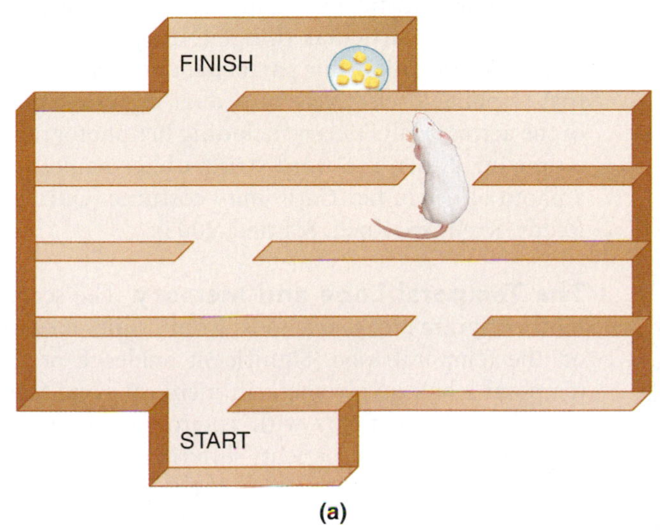

(a)

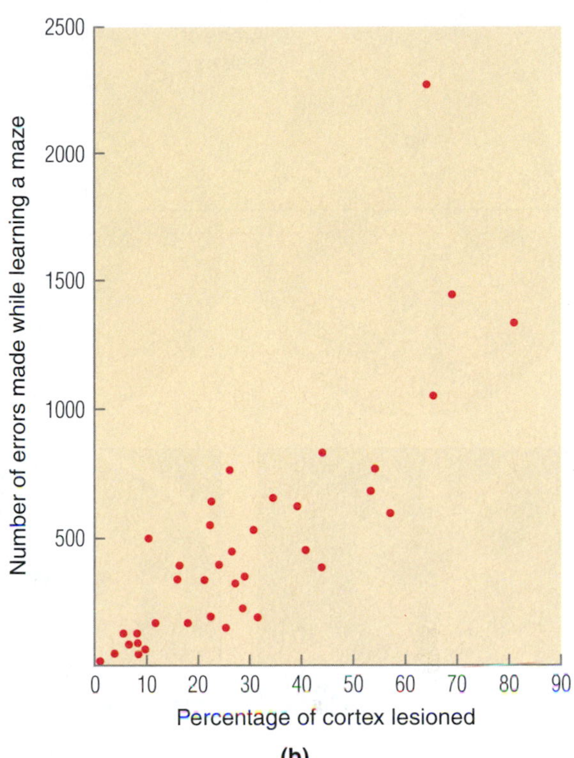

(b)

evenly across the cortex, such that no single area is more responsible for learning and memory than any other. He also believed that the parts of the cortex are basically interchangeable. As a result, the more cortex you have, the better your memory will be, a concept Lashley referred to as mass action.

Why is Lashley's conclusion believed to be a mistake? First, as we will see shortly, more recent data suggest that all parts of the cortex are *not* equally likely to participate in memory. Lashley's lesions were huge. It is likely that lesions of this size would affect multiple aspects of maze-learning behavior. This makes the identification of parts of the brain responsible for a specific function a difficult, if not impossible, task. Second, maze learning is a complex task involving a number of sensory and motor processes. If a lesion affected a rat's sense of smell, for instance, it is likely that the rat could compensate by using its visual or tactile memories. Retained functions would allow the rat to perform similarly, regardless of the particular modality affected by a lesion, leading to the appearance of equipotentiality. We should not conclude, however, that Lashley's work was all in vain. Lashley's major contribution was his suggestion that memories are in fact distributed across the cortex rather than stored in one specific location. This conclusion stimulated further efforts to identify areas of the brain responsible for storing memory.

Further evidence that memories are localized in the brain was contributed by neurosurgeon Wilder Penfield (1958), who investigated the cortical mapping of more than 1,000 patients undergoing surgery for seizure disorders. In about 8 percent of his patients, Penfield found that stimulation of the temporal lobe produced an experiential response in the patient. In response to stimulation, one of Penfield's patients said "street corner." When Penfield asked him to elaborate, the patient went on to say, "South Bend, Indiana, corner of Jacob and Washington" (Penfield, 1958, p. 25). It is possible that Penfield was simply observing a side effect of seizure disorder rather than some universal principle of memory storage in the brain. All of Penfield's patients suffered from seizure disorder and only a small minority reported experiential responses to stimulation, limiting our ability to generalize from these findings to all typical participants. However, Penfield's work did focus the interests of other researchers on a possible role for the temporal lobe in the formation and retention of long-term memories.

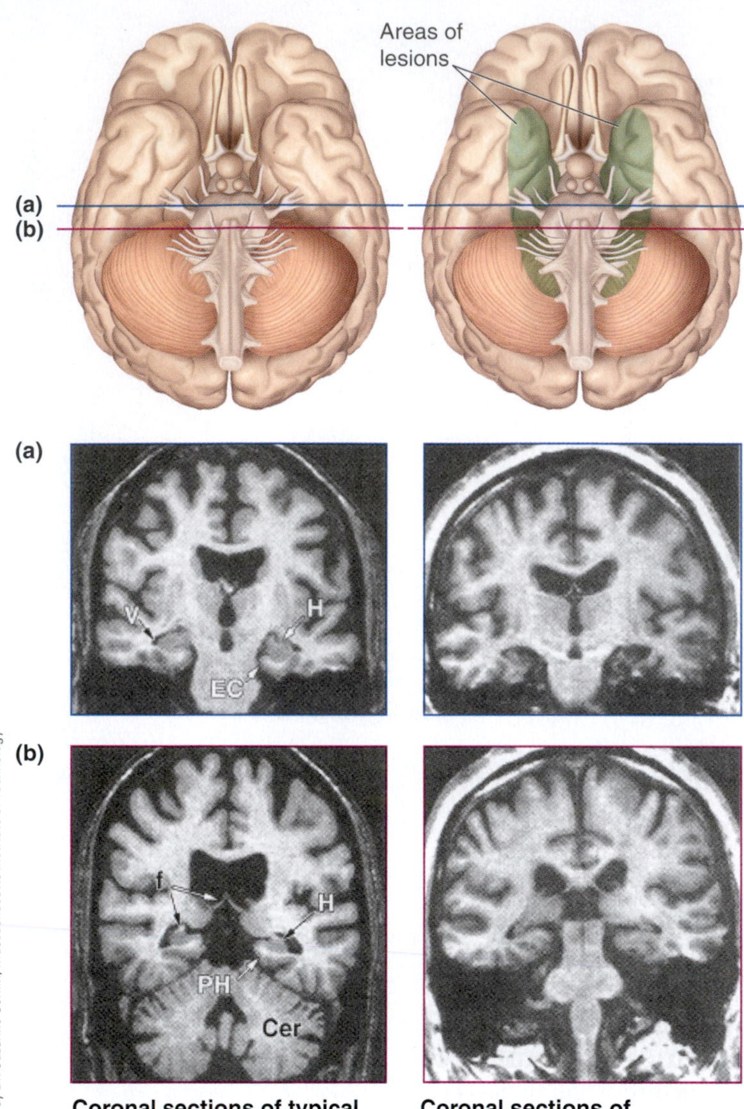

FIGURE 12.14
Surgical Removal of Temporal Lobe Tissue in Patient H. M.
To control life-threatening seizures, patient H. M. underwent surgery that removed the hippocampus, amygdala, and part of the association cortex from both temporal lobes. These MRI scans compare a typical control participant with patient H. M. You can see that H. M. has some hippocampus (H) but no entorhinal cortex (EC). In this image, (V) refers to the lateral ventricle, (f) refers to the fornix, (PH) refers to the parahippocampal cortex, and (Cer) refers to the cerebellum.

Other investigators have presented evidence for very specific, localized memory storage, using single-cell recordings. Activity of single neurons in patients undergoing surgery for epilepsy corresponded to the type of information being processed (Ojemann, Schoenfield-McNeill, & Corina, 2002). Instead of generic memory neurons, Ojemann states that neurons "show statistically significant relationships to memory for a particular thing" (Neary, 2002). In a similar investigation, one participant had a single cell that responded selectively to several representations of the actress Halle Berry, including her photograph, a drawing of her, the word string of her name, and a photo of her in her *Catwoman* costume (Quiroga, Reddy, Kreiman, Koch, & Fried, 2005).

The Temporal Lobe and Memory The search for the engram received a boost from studies focused on the temporal lobe. Significant evidence of the temporal lobe's involvement in memory came from case studies of patients with anterograde amnesia. As mentioned earlier, patients suffering from anterograde amnesia appear to retain their newly acquired procedural, implicit memories while experiencing a dramatic deficit in their ability to form new explicit memories. One of the most thoroughly studied cases of anterograde amnesia is a man known in the literature only as patient H. M. As a result of a childhood bicycle accident in which he suffered brain damage, H. M. experienced severe seizures that required extensive surgery when he was 27. As shown in ■ Figure 12.14, the hippocampus, amygdala, and part of the association cortex of the temporal lobe were removed from both his right and left hemispheres (Corkin, Amaral, Gonzalez, Johnson, & Hyman, 1997). Had the surgery affected only one hemisphere, H. M.'s behavioral changes would have been far less dramatic.

The good news for H. M. was that his seizure disorder was much improved and his personality, vocabulary, and above-average IQ appeared unchanged. He remembered most of the information he had acquired prior to surgery, but his anterograde amnesia was profound. He seemed completely unable to transfer any new information about people, places, events, and numbers from short-term memory to long-term memory. Brenda Milner (1966), an associate of Wilder Penfield, made an extensive study of patient H. M.'s memory deficits and found that H. M.'s surgery did not affect all types of memory equally. H. M.'s short-term memory allowed him to engage in normal conversation as long as there were no big gaps between statements. Much to Milner's surprise, H. M. performed as well as typical control participants on procedural memory tasks. In one of Milner's tasks, illustrated in ■ Figure 12.15, H. M. was required to draw the shape of a star while looking at a sample star and his own hand in a mirror. H. M. mastered the task and performed as well as typical controls (Milner, 1965). If asked, however, he would deny ever having performed the task.

The case of H. M. provides further support for the differentiation of explicit and implicit memories as well as for the stage approach to memory articulated by the Atkinson-Shiffrin model. Damage to the medial temporal lobes, such as in the case of H. M., affects explicit but not implicit memories. H. M.'s damage does not affect long-term memories that have already been stored, but it does affect the transfer of new information from short-term to long-term memory. It is unlikely that the

■ **FIGURE 12.15**
The Mirror-Drawing Task Brenda Milner was surprised to observe that patient H. M. retained the ability to learn the mirror-drawing task at about the same rate as typical control participants. This suggested to Milner that H. M.'s memory deficits were declarative rather than procedural.
Source: Milner, 1965.

(a) Mirror-tracing Task

Day 1

Errors per trial

30 20 10 0

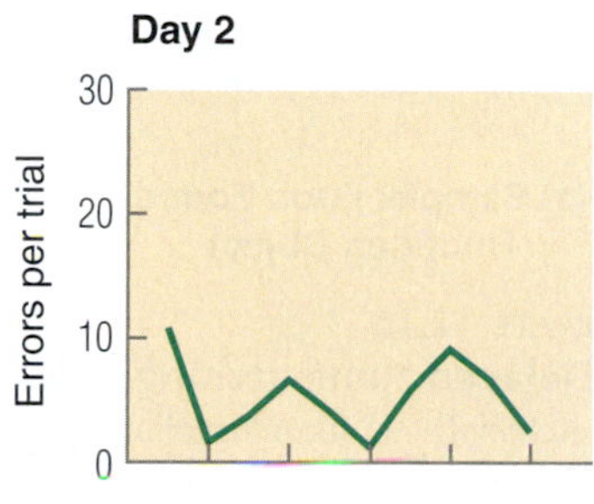

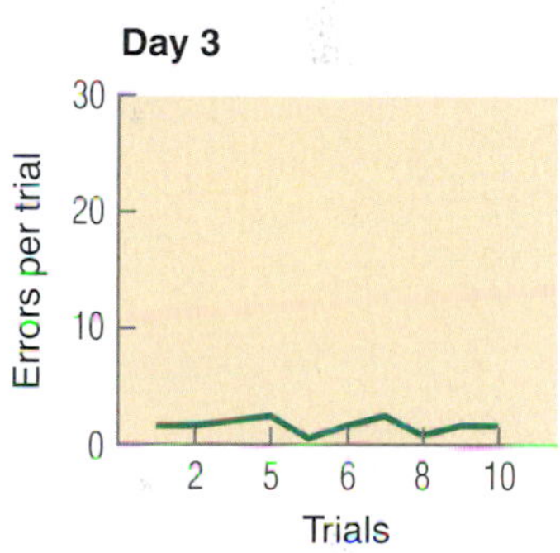

(b) Performance of H. M.

hippocampus itself is a storage location for the elusive engram. The fact that patients such as H. M. still retain fairly stable memories dating from their presurgical lives suggests that the actual representations of these memories do not reside in the medial temporal lobe itself. Nor is the medial temporal lobe necessarily essential for the retrieval of stored memories.

Expanding on information from case studies such as H. M., groups led by Mortimer Mishkin (Mishkin & Appenzeller, 1987) and Larry Squire (1987) looked at the results of temporal lobe lesions on the memory performance of rhesus monkeys. Both groups used a memory task known as the **delayed nonmatching to sample (DNMS) task.** In this task, illustrated in ■ Figure 12.16, the monkey is presented with a single object that covers a food reward. After some period of time (the delay), the monkey is then presented with two objects. One of the objects is the one the animal saw prior to the delay. The other is new. The monkey's task is to select the new object from the pair. The delays varied from a few seconds to several minutes. Solving the problem after a delay of minutes requires the use of long-term memory.

Both the Mishkin and Squire groups found that monkeys with medial temporal lobe lesions in both hemispheres performed poorly on the DNMS task, especially as the delay period increased. Experienced control monkeys could select the correct stimulus about 90 percent of the time. Performance by the lesioned monkeys after 8 to 10 seconds was nearly identical to the performance of control monkeys, supporting the view that the lesions did not compromise short-term memory. After a delay of 2 to 10 minutes, however, the lesioned monkeys performed correctly less than 60 percent of the time. Like patient H. M., these monkeys appeared to have difficulty forming new long-term memories.

delayed nonmatching to sample (DNMS) task A standard test of memory in which the subject must identify the novel member of a stimulus pair following a delay.

(a) Sample: Food Found Under an Object

(b) Test: Choose the Object That Is New (Nonmatching)

(c) Food Found Under the Nonmatching Object

FIGURE 12.16
The Delayed Nonmatching to Sample (DNMS) Task To find food successfully, monkeys must select the nonmatching (new) stimulus following a delay. Monkeys with medial temporal lobe damage appear to have difficulty forming new memories and subsequently perform poorly on the task.

Structures typically damaged by medial temporal lobe lesions include the amygdala, the hippocampus, and the surrounding areas of cortex known as the **parahippocampal cortex** and the **rhinal cortex.** In addition, the pathways connecting these structures to one another, as well as to other parts of the brain, are also damaged. The amygdala appears to play a role in processing emotional memories, but damage to the amygdala alone does not produce anterograde amnesia. As a result, attention has focused on the hippocampus and the surrounding parahippocampal and rhinal cortices as structures involved in the formation of long-term memories.

parahippocampal cortex (pear-uh-hip-oh-KAM-puhl) An area of cortex just ventral to the hippocampus.
rhinal cortex (RIE-nuhl) An area of cortex ventral to the hippocampus.
entorhinal cortex (en-toh-RINE-uhl) A subdivision of the rhinal cortex, which lies ventral to the hippocampus.
perirhinal cortex (pear-ee-RINE-uhl) A substructure of the rhinal cortex.
fornix A pathway carrying information from the hippocampus to the hypothalamus.
Ammon's horn One of two major layers of neurons found in the hippocampus.
dentate gyrus One of two major layers of neurons found in the hippocampus.
perforant pathway A pathway made up of axons originating in the rhinal cortex that form synapses in the dentate gyrus of the hippocampus.
mossy fiber (hippocampus) An axon from the dentate gyrus that synapses on cells found in CA3 of Ammon's horn.
Schaffer collateral pathway A pathway connecting CA3 to CA1 in Ammon's horn of the hippocampus.

Long-Term Potentiation (LTP) Beginning in the 1970s, researchers began to investigate neural mechanisms in the hippocampus that appear to provide a basis for learning and memory (Bliss and Lømo, 1973). To understand these mechanisms, we must first explore the major anatomical features of the hippocampus and surrounding structures, shown in Figure 12.17. The hippocampus consists of a gentle arc just medial to the lateral ventricle in each hemisphere. Ventral to the hippocampus are the parahippocampal cortex and the rhinal cortex, which in turn is made up of the **entorhinal** and **perirhinal cortices.** Input from the association areas of the cortex enters the parahippocampal and rhinal cortices, which in turn transmit the information to the hippocampus. Output from the area generally travels along the **fornix,** a pathway that terminates in the hypothalamus. A closer look at the hippocampus shows us that it is a folded structure with two main layers of neurons. One layer is known as **Ammon's horn,** and the other layer is known as the **dentate gyrus.** Ammon's horn is further divided into four sections, named CA1 to CA4. (CA stands for the Latin term for Ammon's horn, *cornu Ammonis.*)

The pathways connecting the hippocampus to the rest of the brain, as well as the connections formed within the hippocampus itself, are also central to our understanding of the functions of this structure. Input from the rhinal cortex travels along the **perforant pathway,** whose axons form synapses on the cells of the dentate gyrus. Axons from the dentate gyrus, also known as **mossy fibers,** synapse on cells found in CA3 (the third division of Ammon's horn). Axons from CA3 form two branches. One branch, the **Schaffer collateral pathway,** synapses with the cells of CA1. The other branch exits the hippocampus as the fornix.

As demonstrated by Bliss and Lømo (1973), the application of a rapid series of electrical shocks to one of these pathways increases the postsynaptic potentials recorded in their target hippocampal cells. In other words, experience makes these synapses more efficient. By a rapid series of shocks, we mean that somewhere between 50 and 100 stimuli are applied at a rate of 100 stimuli per second, a rate that is found among

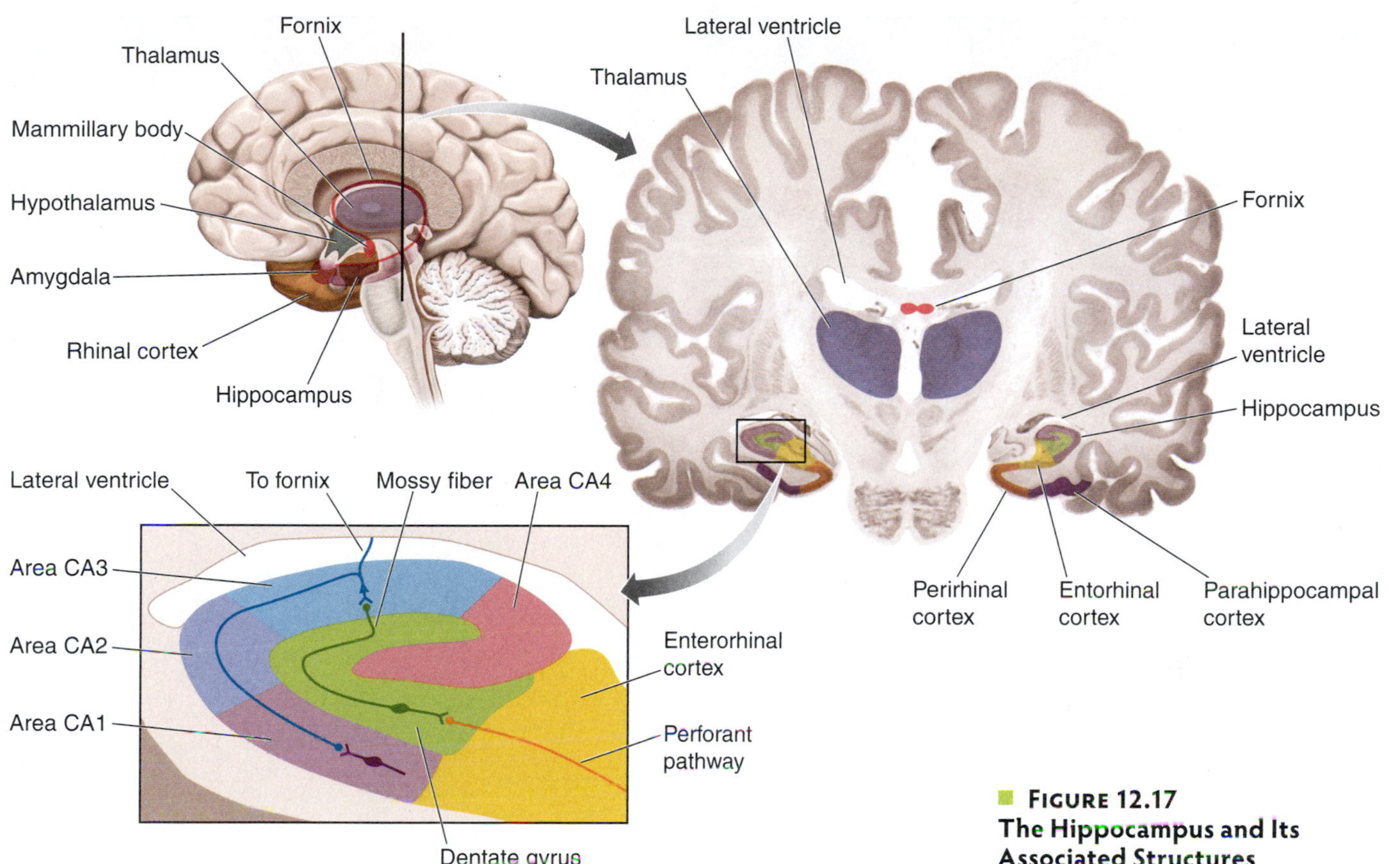

FIGURE 12.17 The Hippocampus and Its Associated Structures

naturally firing axons. When stimuli are presented at a rate of 2 per second or less, synaptic change fails to occur. The change in responsiveness in the target cells after the rapid series of shocks is known as **long-term potentiation,** or **LTP.** LTP can be demonstrated in living animals as well as in isolated slices of hippocampus and other brain tissues. In the living animal, LTP might last indefinitely. In the brain slice, LTP will last a period of several hours.

Several factors point to LTP as an important memory device. First, the fact that LTP lasts a long time is important because we believe that some memories last throughout life. Second, it takes only seconds of input to produce LTP. In many cases, we are able to remember very brief exposures to stimuli. In addition, LTP occurs in ways predicted by the cellular learning model proposed by Canadian psychologist Donald Hebb in 1949. Hebb stated:

> When an axon of cell A is near enough to excite a cell B and repeatedly or persistently takes part in firing it, some growth process or metabolic change takes place in one or both cells such that A's efficacy, as one of the cells firing B, is increased. (p. 62)

Both the Hebbian synapse and LTP require relatively simultaneous firing, or **associativity,** in the pre- and postsynaptic neurons. In addition, only those synapses that are simultaneously active appear to be strengthened. LTP also requires **cooperativity,** which means that several synapses onto the target postsynaptic neuron must be simultaneously active. NMDA glutamate receptors, illustrated in ■ Figure 12.18, are particularly well-suited to facilitate both associativity and cooperativity. For glutamate from a presynaptic neuron to influence postsynaptic NMDA receptors, both neurons must be simultaneously active (associativity). The channel of the NMDA receptor is normally blocked by a molecule of magnesium (Mg^{2+}). Depolarization of the postsynaptic cell acts to expel the Mg^{2+} from the channel. This depolarization typically requires the activity of other synapses onto the same postsynaptic neuron (cooperativity). When a molecule of glutamate is bound to the now

long-term potentiation (LTP) A type of synaptic plasticity in which the application of a rapid series of electrical shocks to an input pathway increases the postsynaptic potentials recorded in target neurons.

associativity A condition believed necessary for learning in which the pre- and postsynaptic neurons are nearly simultaneously active.

cooperativity A condition for the formation of LTP in which several synapses onto the target postsynaptic neuron must be simultaneously active.

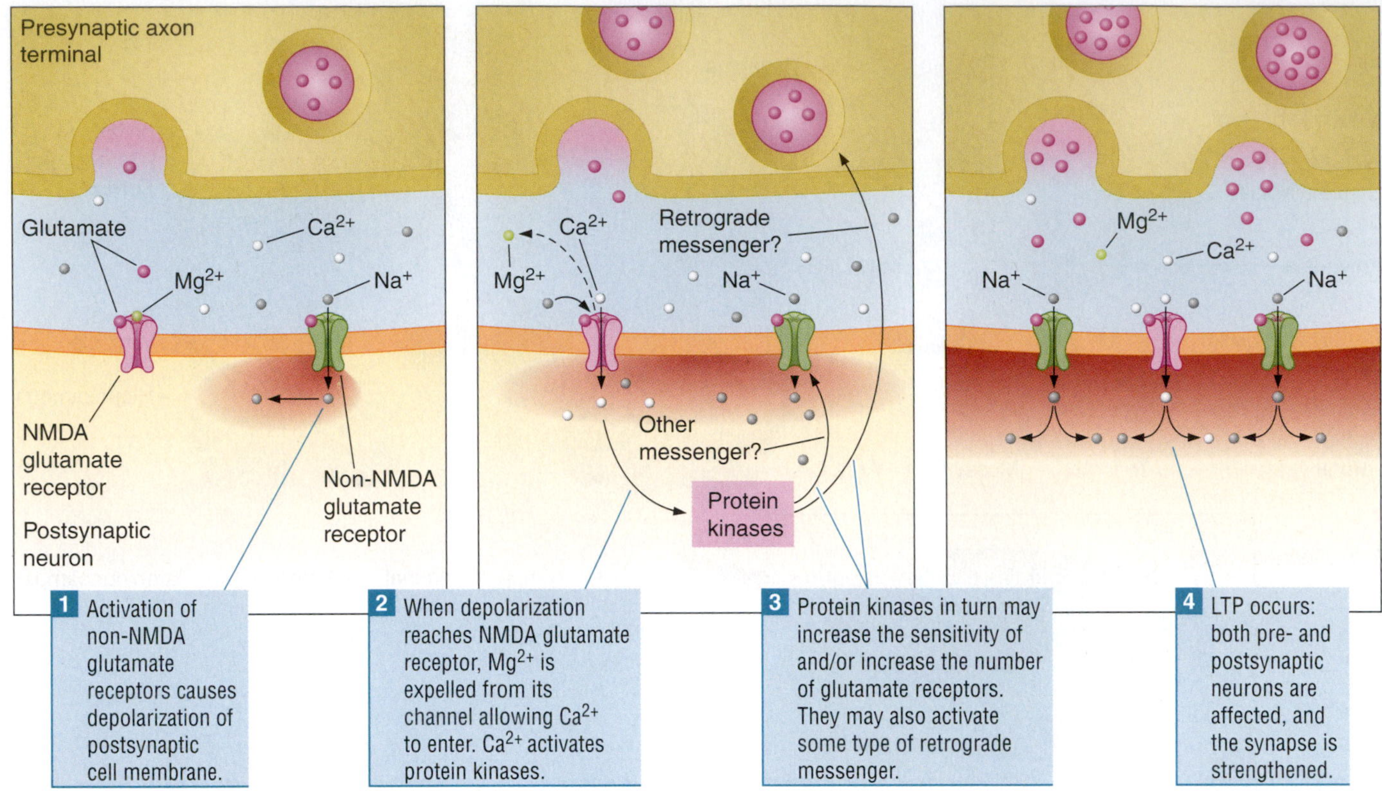
Presynaptic axon terminal
Glutamate
Ca2+
Mg2+
Na+
NMDA glutamate receptor
Non-NMDA glutamate receptor
Postsynaptic neuron
Retrograde messenger?
Other messenger?
Protein kinases
1 Activation of non-NMDA glutamate receptors causes depolarization of postsynaptic cell membrane.
2 When depolarization reaches NMDA glutamate receptor, Mg2+ is expelled from its channel allowing Ca2+ to enter. Ca2+ activates protein kinases.
3 Protein kinases in turn may increase the sensitivity of and/or increase the number of glutamate receptors. They may also activate some type of retrograde messenger.
4 LTP occurs: both pre- and postsynaptic neurons are affected, and the synapse is strengthened.

FIGURE 12.18
LTP and the NMDA Receptor

unblocked receptor, both sodium (Na^+) and calcium (Ca^{2+}) enter the cell. The entrance of Ca^{2+} stimulates several second messengers within the cell, which initiate the structural changes necessary to strengthen the synapse.

LTP appears to be a general process of learning that "can be implemented by a variety of receptors and signaling systems" (Cooke & Bliss, 2006, p. 1,660). Presynaptic processes appear to be important to LTP in some locations, whereas postsynaptic processes predominate at others. Some synapses showing LTP involve the neurotransmitter glutamate, whereas others do not. Although LTP was originally observed in the hippocampus and remains important for the understanding of the role of the hippocampus in memory, the phenomenon has also been demonstrated throughout the central nervous system, from the cerebral cortex to the spinal cord (Cooke & Bliss, 2006).

LTP and Spatial Memory Studies of spatial memory, or an organism's ability to map a location, provide further evidence linking LTP to memory. O'Keefe and Dostrovsky (1971) demonstrated that mice might use different patterns of activation in the hippocampus to represent their location in space. By using single-cell recordings, researchers have been able to conclude that hippocampal spatial maps are formed within minutes of entering a new environment. These maps remain stable for months. All of this should sound somewhat familiar to you by now—rapid formation and stability over time are features of both long-term memories and LTP.

Several research approaches have been used to investigate links between LTP and spatial memory. Genetic mutations can be produced in the chemical pathways responsible for LTP. Joe Tsien and his colleagues (Tsien, Huerta, & Tonegawa, 1996) reported that knocking out the gene that encodes a component of the NMDA receptor found in the cells of CA1 has a negative impact on LTP in the Schaffer collateral pathway. LTP is also negatively affected when genetic mutations affect the second messengers in CA1 cells (Mayford et al., 1996). Does this inability to produce normal LTP affect spatial memory? The answer to this question is yes, but not in the way you might have guessed. Animals with impaired LTP can still form spatial maps. However, impaired LTP prevents the animals from forming stable, well-defined maps. When a mouse

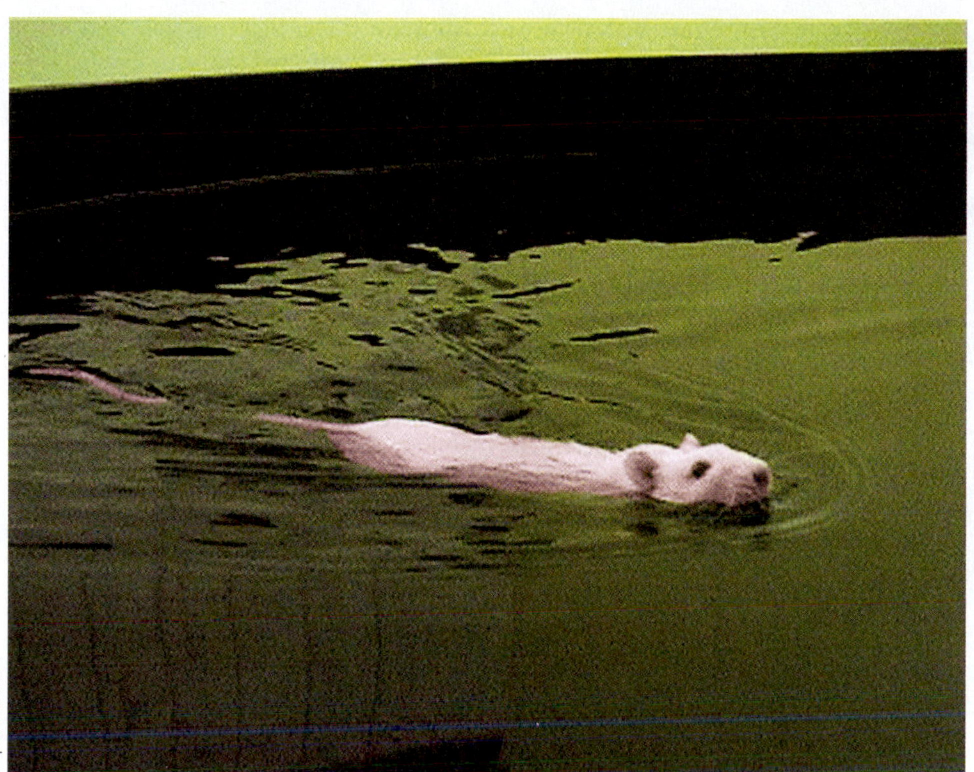

■ **FIGURE 12.19 The Morris Water Maze Requires Spatial Memory** Rats are excellent swimmers, as evidenced by their abilities to board ships anchored in European harbors to travel to the New World. However, they cannot swim indefinitely. To solve the Morris Water Maze, the rat must recall the location of a submerged platform.

with impaired LTP returns to a familiar place, it forms a new map instead of reactivating a previous one. In many ways, the mouse acts a lot like patient H. M., who is unable to learn the route to his postsurgery home.

Spatial learning in rodents can also be impaired by the application of NMDA receptor antagonists (W. C. Abraham & Mason, 1988; Morris, Anderson, Lynch, & Baudry, 1986). When these chemicals are applied to the hippocampus in rats, the rats are unable to learn the location of an underwater platform in the Morris water-maze shown in ■ Figure 12.19. At the same time, these drugs prevent the development of LTP in the hippocampus of these rats. However, the drugs do not have any effect on performance or LTP if they are applied after spatial learning has occurred (Morris et al., 1986).

WHY DOES THIS MATTER?

Can We Make Ourselves Smarter?

As we seek solutions to the memory deficits associated with trauma, healthy aging, and dementia, we might discover ways to improve our abilities to learn and remember. These results matter, not only because we could enhance human performance but also because such changes would raise significant ethical concerns.

An understanding of the biochemistry of learning provides several potential targets for change. "Smart" mice result from genetically engineering a gene that encodes a specific subtype of the NMDA glutamate receptor known as NR2B (Cao et al., 2007; Tang et al., 1999). These mice perform better in a number of memory tasks, including classically conditioned fear, recognition of novel versus familiar objects, t-maze performance, and Morris water maze performance. The genetically enhanced mice also demonstrate stronger LTP in the hippocampus. Another approach leading to "smart" mice was the genetically engineered deletion in the brain of an enzyme known as cyclin-dependent kinase 5 (Cdk5), which normally participates in apoptosis during development (Cheung, Gong, & Ip, 2008; Hawasli et al., 2007). Once again, the genetically engineered mice performed better in tasks such as the Morris water maze.

Although it seems unlikely that we would be willing to engage in this type of genetic manipulation with human beings, it might be possible that improved understanding of the biochemistry of learning and memory will lead to drugs that enhance cognitive performance. Such discoveries might be wonderful for patients with dementia, but use by healthy, young students would require careful ethical consideration.

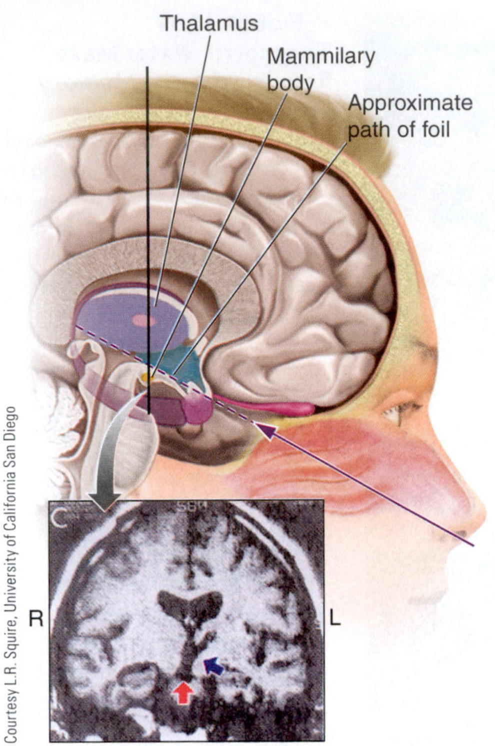

FIGURE 12.20 Damage to the Diencephalon in Patient N. A. The purple arrow in the illustration (above) traces the pathway of a fencing foil into the left hemisphere of patient N. A.'s brain. In the MRI image (below) the red and purple arrows indicate areas damaged by the foil. (Note that the mammillary body indicated in the illustration can no longer be seen in the MRI, as it was obliterated by the accident. Normally, it would appear near the tip of the red arrow.)

The Diencephalon and Memory The hippocampus and other areas of the temporal lobe are tightly connected to the thalamus. Disruption to these structures or to their connections appears to result in amnesia (Gold & Squire, 2006).

Case studies of patients with diencephalic lesions support the role of this area in memory. Patient N. A. suffered brain damage as a result of a freak accident in which he was stabbed through the nostril with a fencing foil (a long thin metal blade) held by one of his roommates. As shown in Figure 12.20, N. A. suffered a lesion in his left dorsomedial thalamus (Squire, Amaral, Zola-Morgan, & Kritchevsky, 1989). Patient N. A. experienced significant anterograde amnesia as well as some retrograde amnesia, affecting memories from several years prior to his accident (Squire & Moore, 1979). In many ways, the memory loss experienced by N. A. was quite similar to that of H. M. His intelligence and short-term memory were preserved, but he had difficulties forming new declarative (explicit) memories.

Chronic alcoholics who develop **Korsakoff's syndrome** experience anterograde amnesia similar to that of patients H. M. and N. A. Alcoholism often results in a deficiency of thiamine, also known as vitamin B_1. Thiamine is important to nervous system functioning because it participates in the synthesis of the neurotransmitter acetylcholine. Untreated thiamine deficiencies lead to damage in the dorsomedial thalamus and mammillary bodies of the diencephalon (Mair, Warrington, & Wieskrantz, 1979). In addition to their anterograde amnesia, patients with Korsakoff's syndrome usually experience severe retrograde amnesia, possibly due to lesions in the cerebellum, brainstem, and cortex as well as in the diencephalon. Animal research confirms observations made in these human case studies. Monkeys with lesions of the anterior and dorsomedial nuclei of the thalamus and of the mammillary bodies have great difficulty with the DNMS task (Parker, Eacott, & Gaffan, 1997).

Semantic Memory and the Cerebral Cortex There appears to be considerable evidence that semantic knowledge, or our basic knowledge of facts and language, is widely distributed in the cortex. Different areas of association cortex are activated during semantic memory tasks based on the particular characteristics of the concept being processed. As shown in Figure 12.21, Alex Martin and his colleagues (Martin, Wiggs, Ungerleider, & Haxby, 1996) used PET scans to identify brain areas that participants activated while naming either animals or tools. While naming animals but not tools, participants activated their left medial occipital lobes, which are involved in processing visual input. While naming tools but not animals, the participants activated the left premotor area and the left middle temporal gyrus. These latter areas are associated with concepts related to tool use, such as hand movements and the production of action words. The distribution of semantic knowledge is also supported by case studies of patients with damage to their association cortex. McCarthy and Warrington (1990) describe a patient who had substantial difficulty describing living things but who retained a perfect capacity for describing inanimate objects such as wheelbarrows.

Creditors have better memories than debtors.
Benjamin Franklin

Retrieving these distributed memories requires a coordinated effort (Damasio, 1989). Antonio Damasio suggests that this type of coordination might occur in a "convergence zone," or a particular location responsible for assembling separate aspects of a memory into a whole. Among the likely candidates for a convergence zone for semantic memories are areas along the left lateral inferior frontal gyrus (Hagoort, 2005; Hagoort, Hald, Bastiaansen, & Petersson, 2004). These areas became more active when rules of language or world knowledge were violated than when correct language usage or factual information were presented to participants (Hagoort et al., 2004).

Korsakoff's syndrome (KORE-suh-koffs) Anterograde amnesia resulting from thiamine deficiency, typically found in chronic alcoholics.

Episodic Memory and the Cerebral Cortex A number of former students have told me that they remember my teaching them that "rats can't barf." Not only did

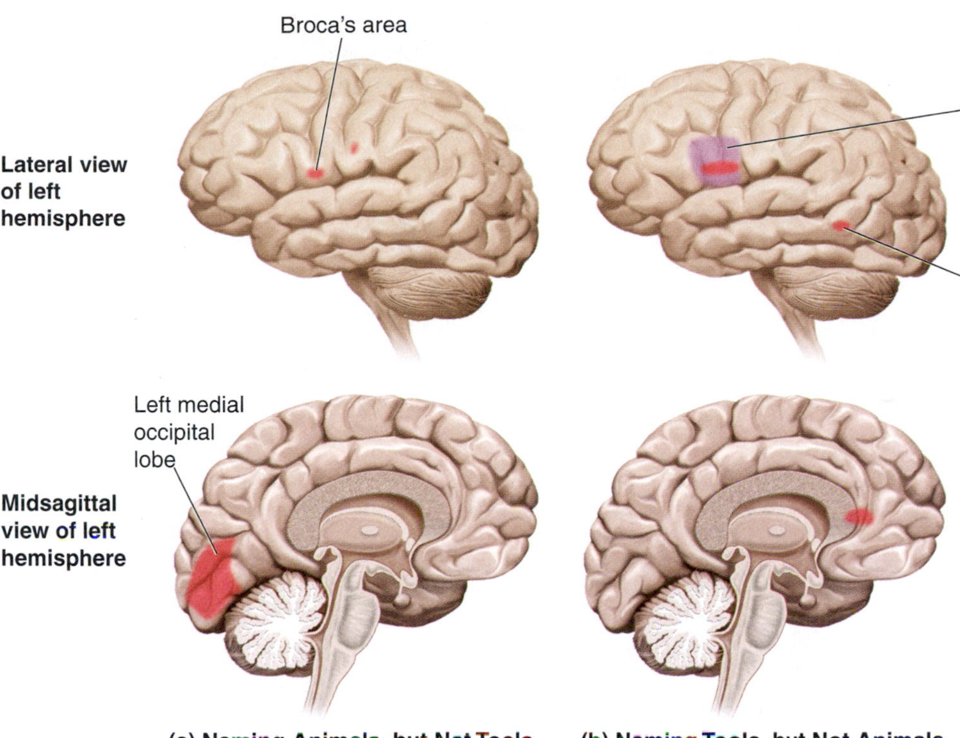

FIGURE 12.21 Semantic Memories Are Widely Distributed Participants were scanned while silently naming animals or tools. Areas that became active in both conditions cancel each other out and are not highlighted. (a) Silently naming animals, but not tools, activated the left medial occipital lobe. (b) Naming tools, but not animals, activated the left premotor area and left middle temporal gyrus, areas associated with concepts and hand movements related to tool use. *Source:* Adapted from Martin et al., 1996.

these students expand their semantic memories (accurately, by the way) with a fact about rats, but they formed episodic memories about when, where, and from whom they learned the fact.

Tulving's concept of an independent episodic memory store for our personal experiences is supported by case studies with patients with cortical damage. Patients who experience damage to the prefrontal areas of the cortex often experience a memory deficit known as **source amnesia.** These patients retain their semantic memories but are unable to remember how and when they learned a bit of information. Patient K. C. damaged his left frontal-parietal cortex and right parietal-occipital cortex as the result of a traffic accident (Tulving, 1989). In addition, this patient also experienced shrinkage of the hippocampus and the parahippocampal cortex (Rosenbaum et al., 2000). K. C. retains his general semantic knowledge, as evidenced by his knowledge of the rules of chess. However, he can't remember many facts from his past, such as how and when he learned to play chess.

Let us then suppose the Mind to be, as we say, white Paper, void of all Characters, without any Ideas; How comes it to be furnished? ...To this I answer, in one word, from Experience...

John Locke

Episodic memories are essential to our sense of self, leading to the intriguing notion that we might be able to locate a sense of "self" in the brain. Imaging studies indicate that the anterior prefrontal cortex and the posterior cingulate cortex participate in the retrieval of personal, episodic memories (Abraham, von Cramon, & Schubotz, 2008; Gilbert et al., 2006). As illustrated in Figure 12.22, Fink et al. (1996) viewed brain activity while participants listened to their own autobiographical stories or to autobiographical stories written by other people. When listening to their own autobiographical material, participants showed greater activation in the right frontal and temporal lobes than they did when they listened to the stories of other people's lives.

We might use our episodic memories to distinguish between fantasy and reality. When participants were asked whether it would be possible to have a conversation with a real or fantasy person (George Bush or Cinderella), brain areas associated with declarative memories in general, such as the hippocampus and other medial temporal lobe structures, were activated (Abraham et al., 2008). However, other areas appear to be differentially active. When considering reality, structures associated with episodic memory, such as the prefrontal cortex and posterior cingulate cortex, were active. These results imply that we consult our personal experience to determine reality.

source amnesia Memory loss for the circumstances in which a particular fact or skill was learned.

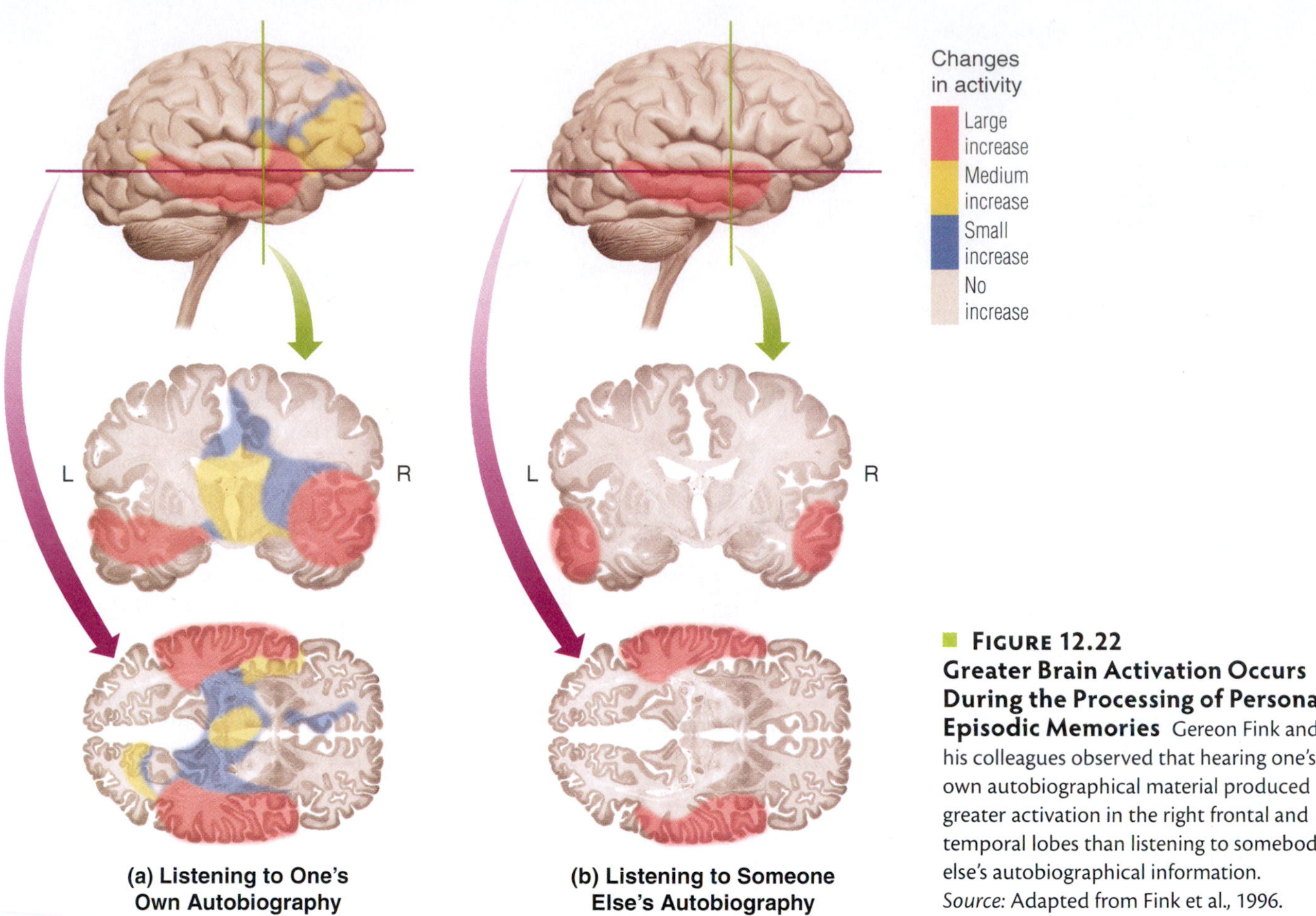

Figure 12.22 Greater Brain Activation Occurs During the Processing of Personal Episodic Memories Gereon Fink and his colleagues observed that hearing one's own autobiographical material produced greater activation in the right frontal and temporal lobes than listening to somebody else's autobiographical information.
Source: Adapted from Fink et al., 1996.

In contrast, when considering fantasy, areas associated with semantic processing, such as the left inferior frontal gyrus (IFG) showed greater activity (ibid.). Recall that the IFG showed greater activation when semantic rules of language and world knowledge were violated (Hagoort et al., 2004), which of course they are when imagining a conversation with Cinderella. Disturbances in this distinction might form the basis for the delusions, or false beliefs, that characterize some psychological disorders (see Chapter 16).

Short-Term Memory and the Brain According to the Atkinson-Shiffrin model, new information coming into the memory system, as well as information being recalled from long-term storage, is held for relatively brief periods of time in short-term memory. Baddeley (1974, 2000) further divided short-term memory, or working memory, into four components: a central executive, the phonological loop, the visuospatial scratchpad, and an episodic buffer. Is it possible to locate these processes in the brain?

The dorsolateral prefrontal cortex (DLPFC) and the anterior cingulate cortex (ACC) are believed to provide the neural basis for the central executive (Kaneda & Osaka, 2008). These areas provide important attentional aspects of short-term memory. Human patients with prefrontal cortex lesions have significant difficulty with the Wisconsin card-sorting test (Barceló & Knight, 2002). The cards used in this test can be sorted according to several dimensions such as symbol, color, number, and shape. Patients with prefrontal lesions can learn a sorting rule—for example, "put all the cards with the same-colored objects together"—but they can't seem to adjust when the rule changes. They persevere with a previous rule (such as sorting by color) when they are prompted to switch to sorting by shape. The patients experience specific deficits in their ability to shift attention to the new sorting dimension.

■ **FIGURE 12.23**
Object Permanence The short-term memory abilities of a young child can be assessed by hiding a toy while the child is watching. After a delay, the child is allowed to search for the toy. Prior to the age of 7 or 8 months, most children are unable to use their memories of watching the toy being hidden to help them successfully locate it. Immaturity of the prefrontal cortex might account for these results.

Further evidence supporting a role for the prefrontal cortex in short-term memory comes from research on the development of memory. The short-term memories of young monkeys and of human infants can be assessed by an object permanence test, illustrated in ■ Figure 12.23, in which a toy is hidden in one of two locations (with the subject watching). After a delay, the infant or young monkey can search for the toy. Human infants are unable to find the hidden toy until they are about 7 or 8 months old (Diamond & Goldman-Rakic, 1989). Prior to this age, the child will look for the toy in the location at which it was last found, whether or not this is the location at which the child most recently watched the toy being hidden. Diamond and Goldman-Rakic (1989) compared the performances of adult monkeys with prefrontal cortical lesions to those of adult monkeys with inferior parietal lesions on the object permanence task. The monkeys with the inferior parietal lesions performed normally on the task. However, the monkeys with the prefrontal lesions performed similarly to immature human infants. These data suggest that a certain level of maturity in the prefrontal cortex is necessary for short-term memory.

Evidence for an executive role for the anterior cingulate cortex (ACC) in short-term memory comes from comparisons of people with large or small short-term memory capacities for verbal information. People with large capacities show more activation of the ACC than people with smaller capacities (Osaka et al., 2003). The differing capacities were also associated with different memory strategies. People with smaller capacities used rehearsal, or simple repetition, to maintain information in short-term memory, whereas people with larger capacities were more likely to use semantic strategies, such as imagery and making stories (Osaka et al., 2003; Turley-Ames & Whitfield, 2003). These observations support a role for the ACC in the processing of verbal information in short-term memory.

The Striatum and Procedural Memory The striatum, including the basal ganglia and nucleus accumbens, are involved with the formation of procedural memories (Barnes, Kubota, Hu, Jin, & Graybiel, 2005). As we saw in Chapter 2, the basal ganglia are part of our motor system, so it would seem logical that these structures would be involved in the learning and memory of motor patterns. The nucleus accumbens contributes an evaluation of emotion and reward to the learning of procedures (Arnsten, Ramos, Birnbaum, & Taylor, 2005).

During trial-and-error learning, such as finding food in a maze, the striatum not only encourages exploration but also participates in "exploitation," or the evaluation of changes leading to greater accuracy and reward (Barnes et al., 2005). In one study, rats learned to run to one arm of a t-maze to obtain chocolate. They subsequently

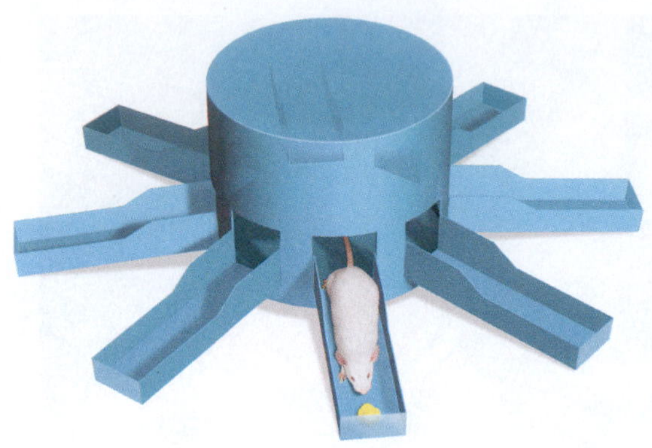

■ **FIGURE 12.24**
The Radial Arm Maze The radial arm maze can be modified to investigate declarative and procedural memories. The rat's task is to locate food as quickly as possible, which requires it to form representations of which arms have contained food and which arms have already been visited.

experienced extinction, during which chocolate was no longer available, followed by reacquisition, or a second period of training with the chocolate reward. At the outset of training (exploration), the striatum neurons were active throughout the run. As training progressed and the rats' performances became faster and more accurate (exploitation), firing in the striatum was observed only near the beginning and end of a run. During extinction, the exploration pattern of firing reemerged, and the exploitation pattern returned during reacquisition. These results suggest that the striatum assists in the learning of procedures by evaluating the outcomes of behavior.

The role of the striatum in procedural, but not declarative, memories was demonstrated by observing the effects of lesions on rats trained in one of two different maze tasks (Packard, Hirsh, & White, 1989). In one task, the rats learned which arms of a radial maze, such as the one shown in ■ Figure 12.24, contained food. This task is assumed to be a test of declarative memory because the rat must use its explicit episodic memories about arms that have been visited to perform successfully. The second task involves a maze in which food is located in arms that are lit by small lights. The rat does not need to remember much about the maze but must learn to associate light with the availability of food. Consequently, this light maze serves as an implicit procedural memory task. Different brain lesions affect performance in the two types of mazes. Lesions to structures associated with the hippocampus impaired performance on the declarative task (the standard maze), but performance on the procedural task (the light maze) remained normal. However, rats with lesions in the basal ganglia performed poorly on the procedural task but experienced little difficulty with the declarative task.

cyclic AMP (cAMP) A second messenger that participates in processes such as changes that occur as a result of learning and the responses of photoreceptors to light.

protein kinase A (PKA) An enzyme capable of modifying proteins responsible for structural change in the axon terminal.

cAMP-PKA-MAPK-CREB pathway The sequence leading to long-term changes in behavior and protein synthesis.

mitogen-activated protein (MAP) kinase A second messenger that responds to extracellular stimuli by initiating intracellular processes such as gene expression and apoptosis.

CREB-1 A protein that activates genes that might be responsible for structural changes associated with long-term memory.

CREB-2 A protein that normally inhibits the transcription of genes associated with structural changes in long-term memory.

ubiquitin carboxyterminal hydrolase (you-BIK-wi-tin car-box-ee-TER-min-uhl HIE-droh-laze) An enzyme that allows PKA to be rather continuously active, possibly contributing to long-term memory.

Biochemical Factors in Long-Term Memory

To start our discussion of biochemical processes in learning, we return to *Aplysia* and the implicit learning process of sensitization. As we observed previously, a single sensitization training session is enough to produce changes in behavior lasting several minutes. This change can result from the action of serotonin at the axo-axonic synapse between an interneuron and a sensory neuron. As illustrated in ■ Figure 12.25, the binding of serotonin by the sensory neuron activates an enzyme, adenylyl cyclase, which in turn converts adenosine triphosphate (ATP) into the second messenger, **cyclic AMP (cAMP).** Subsequently, cAMP activates **protein kinase A (PKA).** PKA has three major effects: (1) PKA decreases the potassium (K^+) current, which prolongs the action potential. As a result of the prolonged action potential, more calcium (Ca^{2+}) enters the axon terminal; (2) PKA also signals the movement of more vesicles into the release zone; and (3) PKA opens more Ca^{2+} channels. These processes result in the enhanced release of glutamate by the sensory neuron.

Sensitization trials that are repeated and spaced out over time produce behavioral changes lasting several weeks. The sequence leading to long-term changes in behavior and protein synthesis is known as the **cAMP-PKA-MAPK-CREB pathway,** shown in ■ Figure 12.26. These processes take up where the short-term modification left off, with the activation of PKA. When PKA is recurrently activated, as it is in repeated sensitization training, it activates another second messenger, **mitogen-activated protein (MAP) kinase.** PKA and MAP kinase are transported back from the axon terminal to the neural cell body, where together they activate a genetic switch in the cell nucleus. The switch is a protein known as **CREB-1** (for cAMP response element binding protein). Simultaneously, the two kinases (MAP and CREB-1) block the inhibitory actions of **CREB-2,** a factor that normally prevents the transcription of certain genes.

Activating CREB-1 and inhibiting CREB-2 causes two important genes to be expressed. The first gene activates another enzyme, **ubiquitin carboxyterminal hydrolase.** This enzyme allows PKA to be nearly continuously active. As a result, neurotransmitter release continues to be elevated long after training has ceased. The

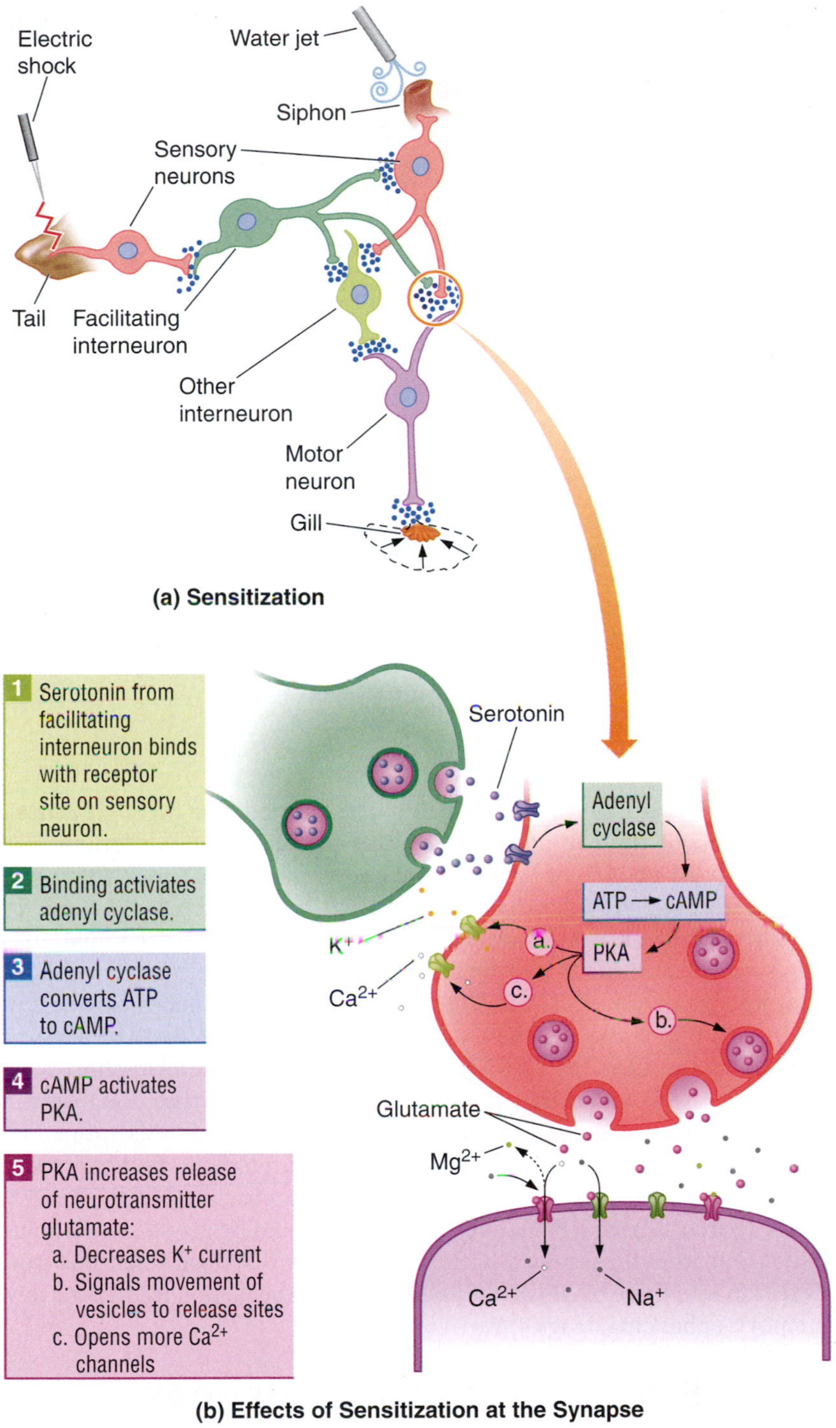

FIGURE 12.25 Biochemical Correlates of Sensitization in *Aplysia*

second activated gene encodes a protein, **C/EBP.** C/EBP in turn activates other genes that stimulate the growth of new synaptic terminals on the sensory neuron. As we observed previously, *Aplysia* given repeated sensitization training show approximately twice the number of sensory neuron synaptic terminals as do control animals. These biochemical and structural changes stimulated by the cAMP-PKA-MAPK-CREB pathway probably account for the long-term presynaptic changes observed following repeated sensitization training. Similar processes might underlie all long-term memory formation. The cAMP-PKA pathway also appears to be important to changes associated with learning and memory in the brains of mammals (Arnsten et al., 2005).

C/EBP A substance activated by CREB-1 that in turn activates genes related to synaptic growth.

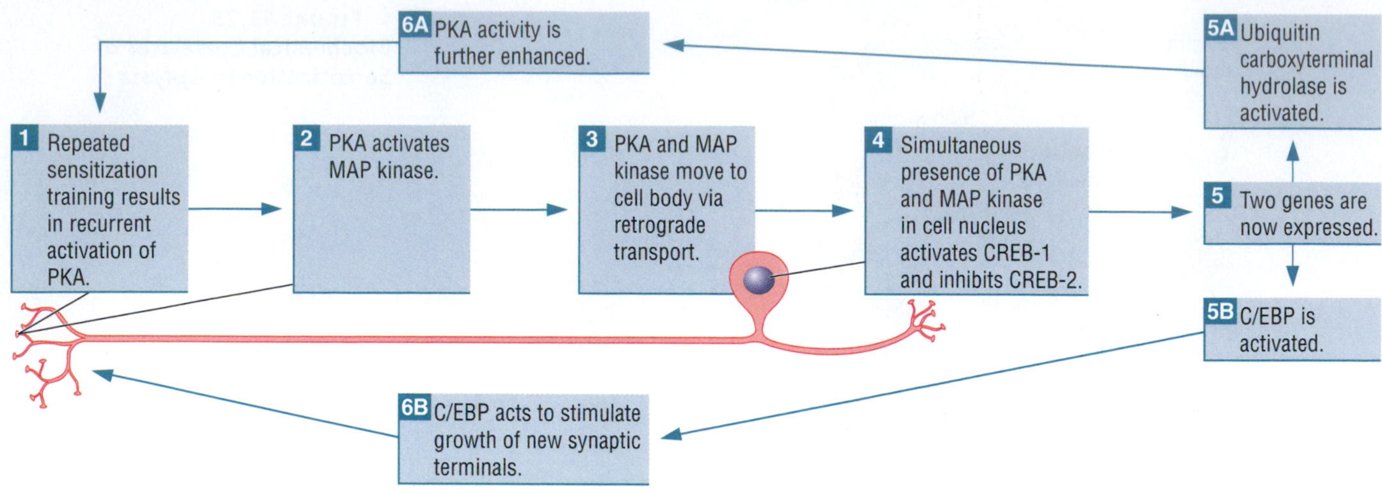

Figure 12.26
The cAMP-PKA-MAPK-CREB Pathway Leads to Long-Term Changes in Behavior
Repeated sensitization training in *Aplysia* produces behavioral changes lasting several weeks. When PKA is recurrently activated by repeated sensitization trials, a sequence of biochemical events is initiated that leads to maintenance of PKA activity and structural changes in the sensory neurons. These processes might account for long-term behavioral change.

Biochemical pathways of learning can be modified through genetic manipulation. The fruit fly, *Drosophila*, is capable of classical conditioning. Fruit flies will learn to avoid odors that have been paired with electric shock (Jellies, 1981). Different genetic variants of *Drosophila* were identified as having serious deficits in learning the odor-shock association. Researchers have named these impaired flies (and the genes responsible for their impairment) *radish, turnip, dunce, rutabaga, amnesiac,* and, less creatively, *PKA-R1* (Dudai, 1989). Particular genes can be turned on and off by heating or cooling the fly (Drain et al., 1991). When the action of PKA was blocked in the flies, the flies were unable to learn and form short-term memories. Yin et al. (1994) found that too much CREB-2 blocks flies' long-term memory but not short-term memory. Conversely, extra CREB-1 produces immediate long-term memory under conditions that normally would produce only short-term retention. Mice have been genetically modified to produce a variant of CREB that is constantly active (Barco, Alarcon, & Kandel, 2002). LTP could be produced with weaker stimuli in neurons from the genetically altered mice compared with neurons from wild mice. Research into these biochemical pathways could very soon lead to the development of memory-enhancing drugs.

Those who cannot remember the past are condemned to repeat it.
George Santayana

The Effects of Stress on Memory

The experience of trauma is widely believed to influence memory. Freud believed that traumatic memories can become so inaccessible that they are essentially lost or repressed. In contrast, memories of trauma in posttraumatic stress disorder (PTSD) are often unusually vivid and intrusive (see Chapter 16). Flashbulb memories for traumatic events seem to be recalled with unique precision. Few of us will ever forget the first news we heard of the terrorist attacks on the World Trade Center or images like the one shown in ■ Figure 12.27. How can we reconcile these experiences, in which stress appears to interfere with memory in some instances and to enhance memories in others?

To answer this question, David Diamond and his colleagues (2007) returned to a framework originally proposed over 100 years ago by Yerkes and Dodson (1908), which later became known as the Yerkes-Dodson Law. According to the Yerkes-Dodson Law, illustrated in ■ Figure 12.28, stress effects on memory interact with the complexity of a task. If the task is simple, such as asking a mouse to

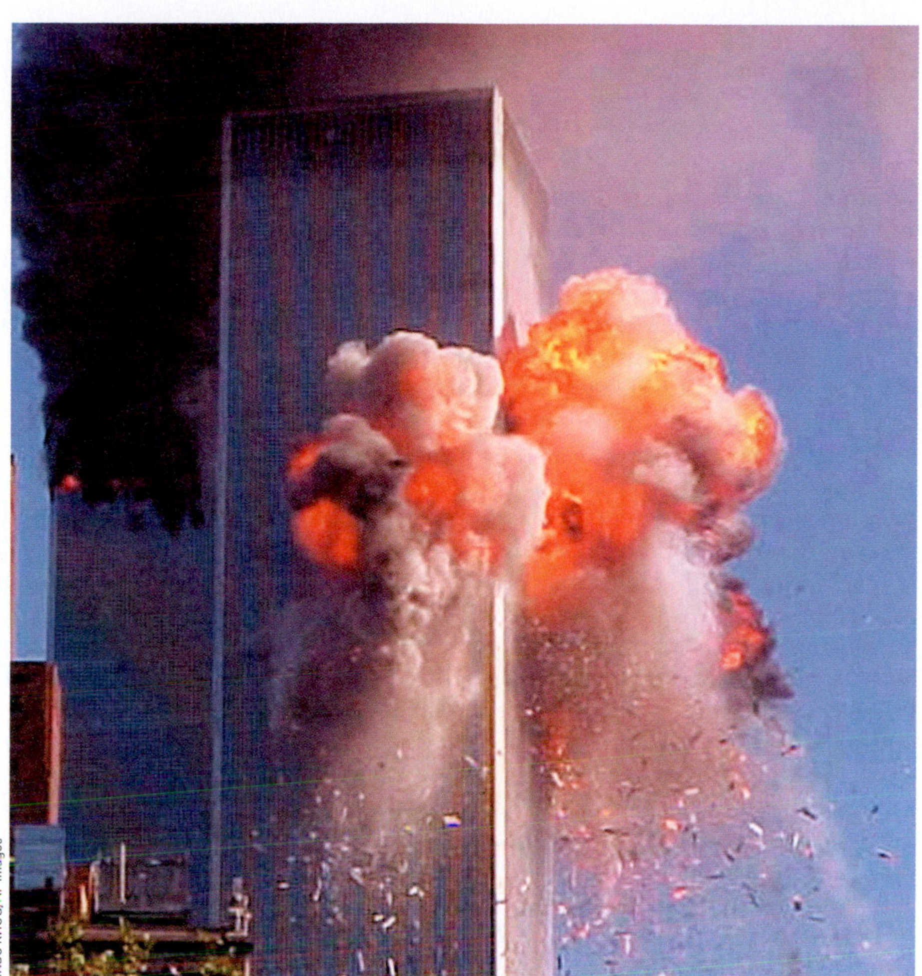

FIGURE 12.27 Flashbulb Memories Seem More Vivid and Complete Few of us will ever forget the images of the terrorist attacks on the World Trade Center. It is possible that moderate levels of stress produce unusually clear memories, whereas more extreme stress begins to interfere with accurate memory encoding.

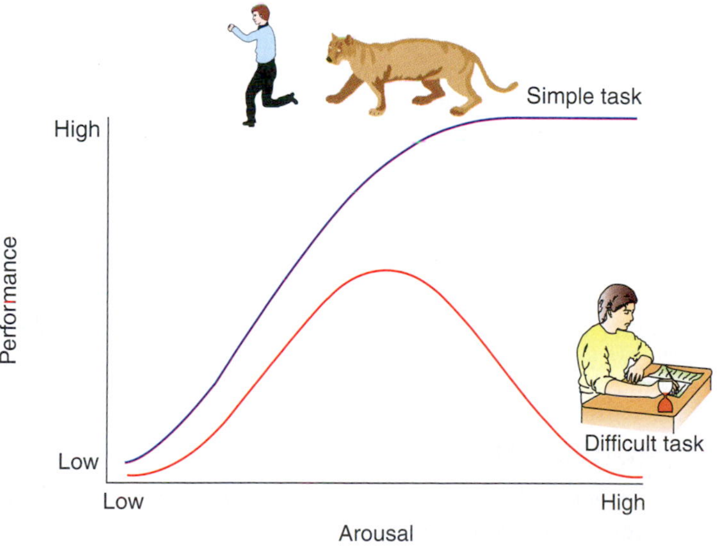

FIGURE 12.28 The Yerkes-Dodson Law Describes the Relationship Between Arousal and Performance The Yerkes-Dodson Law predicts that the complexity of a task interacts with an organism's arousal level to determine the quality of performance. For simple tasks, greater arousal leads to a relatively linear improvement in performance. For difficult tasks, moderate amounts of arousal lead to optimum performance, whereas high arousal leads to weaker performance.

avoid shock (the stressor) by choosing a light or dark escape box, performance of the task will improve in a linear fashion with increasing stress (stronger shocks). When tasks are more complicated, such as asking the mouse to choose between two escape boxes with equal levels of illumination, performance is no longer linear. Instead, performance increases as stress increases to a certain point and then decreases with

The difference between false memories and true ones is the same as for jewels: it is always the false ones that look the most real, the most brilliant.
Salvador Dali

stronger stress. According to Diamond et al. (2007), these interactions between stress levels and task are critical to understanding repression, posttraumatic memories, and flashbulb memories.

Although many researchers have argued that stress uniformly impairs the formation of memory (repression) by inhibiting the hippocampus, this approach is not consistent with substantial research showing that LTP in the hippocampus is actually enhanced by emotions (Seidenbecher, Balschun, & Reymann, 1995). The key to this discrepancy is timing. Diamond et al. (2007) argue that the onset of stress initially enhances memory formation, as in the case of traumatic and flashbulb memories. This initial phase of seconds or minutes, however, is followed by a refractory period of hours or even days, during which the ability to form new memories is impaired. What would be the advantages of this period of relatively impaired memory formation? First, continued stimulation of the hippocampus due to stress could be toxic to hippocampal neurons (Hoschl & Hajek, 2001). Second, emotional events often have survival implications, and a refractory period might serve to protect memories for these important events from the interference produced by new learning or the modifications observed by Loftus (2005).

Activity of the hippocampus during stressful events is accompanied by parallel, independent LTP in the amygdala. Like LTP in the hippocampus, LTP in the amygdala is enhanced immediately following the onset of stress but later experiences a refractory period. The independence of these two processes can be illustrated by a case study cited by Diamond et al. (2007) in which a man nearly buried alive in sand was constantly fearful during the day and troubled by nightmares of death but could not remember the stressful event itself. In this case, the amygdala successfully processed the emotional component of the stressful event, but the hippocampus (damaged by lack of oxygen) was unable to encode the declarative details of the event.

In addition to its impact on the hippocampus and amygdala, stress affects the functions normally carried out by the prefrontal cortex, including coping skills, decision making, planning, and multitasking. The prefrontal cortex functions best when levels of dopamine and norepinephrine are moderate as opposed to very low or very high. The inverted U-shaped relationship between performance of complex tasks, stress, and the accompanying release of dopamine and norepinephrine in the prefrontal cortex is consistent with the Yerkes-Dodson Law (Diamond et al., 2007).

Further understanding of these processes might help us prevent and treat traumatic and false memories. As we will see in Chapter 14, chemicals known as glucocorticoids, including cortisol, are released during stress and increase the activity of the amygdala (LeDoux, 1993; McGaugh, 1992). Higher levels of cortisol are correlated with the reporting of more false memories (Payne et al., 2007). Propanolol, which blocks the effects of glucocorticoids in the brain, might prevent the formation of traumatic memories when administered immediately following a traumatic event (Miller, 2004; Pitman et al., 2002). By manipulating certain enzymes in animals, researchers are making progress in their ability to "erase" some long-term memories, raising the possibility of new approaches to the treatment of PTSD (Shema, Sacktor, & Dudai, 2007; Cao et al., 2008).

Aging and Memory

Some aspects of learning and memory undergo age-related changes, even in healthy older adults. For example, eyeblink conditioning, which we discussed earlier in this chapter, is more difficult and takes longer in older participants (Flaten & Friborg, 2005). However, most measures of cognitive ability in healthy older adults remain stable. This stability might arise from modifications in brain activity that compensate for age-related declines in brain function (Beason-Held, Kraut, & Resnick, 2008). As people age, decreased blood flow is observed in many parts of the brain essential to memory and cognition, especially in the frontal and temporal lobes. However, the aging brain also shows areas of increased activation. Beason-Held et al. (2008) suggest that these areas of increased activity represent a reorganization of the brain

Memory, of all the powers of the mind, is the most delicate and frail.
Ben Jonson

that allows cognitive performance to remain stable in spite of age-related deficits in brain function.

Comparisons of healthy young adults, healthy older adults, patients with Alzheimer's disease (see Chapter 5), and those at high risk for Alzheimer's disease provide further insight into the nature of aging effects on cognition (Sperling, 2007). Comparisons of young and older adults demonstrated no differences in hippocampal activation during the encoding of face-name pairs that were subsequently recalled successfully. However, young participants show reduced activation of the parietal lobe and the posterior cingulate cortex during successful encoding. High-performing older participants showed similar areas of deactivation, while lower-performing older participants did not. These lower-performing participants might be experiencing very early stages of dementia. Participants at risk for Alzheimer's disease, either because of their genetic vulnerability or evidence of mild cognitive impairment, actually demonstrate increased hippocampal activity during encoding compared to healthy older participants. This increased activity might provide another example of the brain's effort to compensate for decline observed by Beason-Held et al. (2008). Eventually, this compensation fails as dementia progresses, and activity in the hippocampus is reduced below that seen in healthy older controls (Sperling, 2007).

NEW DIRECTIONS

Can We Prevent Age-Related Memory Loss?

The idea of experiencing age-related memory problems holds little appeal. Is it possible to prevent or minimize such loss?

Schaie (1994) conducted a 35-year-long longitudinal study of more than 5,000 participants and identified several factors that are correlated with maintaining good cognitive function in old age. Attainment of above-average education, engaging in complex, non-routine professions, and earning high income appear to protect against cognitive decline. Obviously, these factors are highly correlated with one another and would likely protect against many other health problems throughout the life span as well. Schaie's data also emphasize the importance of strong social relationships. People who maintain close family ties retain more cognitive function in their senior years. Schaie also reports that "being married to a spouse with high cognitive status" is also good for your brain (p. 310). We must be cautious when interpreting Schaie's data. These lifestyle factors are typical of people with above-average intelligence. People who are intelligent experience a more gradual decline in cognitive abilities during aging, even when they are diagnosed with a degenerative condition such as Alzheimer's disease (Whalley et al., 2000).

With the large Baby Boom generation entering its senior years, concerns about maintaining cognitive health have spawned a whole new industry of "brain-improving" activities. Nintendo is offering "Brain Age," and Cognifit's "Drive Fit" program is marketed to seniors concerned about diminishing driving skills. Sudoku and crossword puzzles have gained in popularity. Whether any of these "brain exercises" really work remains to be examined in carefully controlled empirical research.

INTERIM SUMMARY 12.2

Summary Table: Brain Structures and Their Roles in Memory

Structure	Possible Role in Memory	Results of Damage
Temporal lobe (including the hippocampus and surrounding structures)	• Transfer of information from short-term to long-term memory • Management of declarative (explicit) memories	• Anterograde amnesia • Existing long-term memories are retained • Ability to form new procedural (implicit) memories is retained • Difficulty with formation of new long-term memories required to solve the DNMS task (monkeys) • Difficulty with the spatial learning tasks (rodents) • Possible difficulties forming accurate memories of traumatic events (flashbacks or repression)
Diencephalon (including the thalamus and mammillary bodies)	• Transfer of information from short-term to long-term memory • Similar to temporal lobe because these areas are highly interconnected	• Anterograde amnesia • Some retrograde amnesia • Difficulty with DNMS task (monkeys)
Association cortex	• Semantic memory • Encoding long-term memory • Retrieval of long-term memory	• Naming difficulties such as being able to name animals but not tools
Prefrontal cortex	• Episodic memory • Short-term memory	• Source amnesia • Difficulty shifting attention • Immature object permanence (monkeys)
Basal ganglia	• Procedural (implicit) memory	• Failure to learn new procedures and skills

Summary Points

1. Memory can be conceptualized as a series of stages, including sensory memory, short-term memory, and long-term memory. Long-term memory is further divided into declarative (explicit) and nondeclarative (implicit) memories. **(LO4)**
2. Patients with damage to the medial temporal lobes experience anterograde amnesia, the inability to form new declarative memories. **(LO5)**
3. Long-term potentiation (LTP), first observed in the hippocampus, might provide a basis for the changes necessary for forming long-term memories. **(LO6)**
4. Diencephalic structures also play a role in declarative memory formation. **(LO5)**
5. Semantic and episodic memories appear to be widely distributed in the neocortex, yet tightly interconnected. The prefrontal cortex appears to play a significant role in short-term memory. Procedural memories are mediated by the striatum. **(LO5)**
6. The biochemical changes accompanying long-term memory involve the cAMP-PKA-MAPK-CREB pathway. **(LO7)**
7. Unusual memory phenomena, including repression, flashbacks associated with posttraumatic stress disorder, and flashbulb memories, might result from the effects of different levels of stress on the amygdala, hippocampus, and prefrontal cortex. **(LO8)**
8. In healthy aging, patterns of brain activity during memory processing might compensate for age-related changes to maintain cognitive function. **(LO8)**

Review Questions

1. How did the work of Lashley, Penfield, and Milner contribute to our understanding of memory?
2. What memory changes are associated with normal, healthy aging?

CHAPTER REVIEW

THOUGHT QUESTIONS

1. If researchers succeed in identifying chemicals that will enhance people's ability to learn and remember, what impact might that have on human society?
2. Most of us have had the experience of watching an event with a group of people, only to discover that our memory of the event is quite different from the memories formed by the other observers. What processes might be responsible for the individual nature of such memories?
3. Researchers in biological psychology have concentrated on simpler forms of learning such as habituation, sensitization, and classical conditioning. How could researchers begin to tackle more complex types of learning such as operant conditioning?
4. Recent research suggests that neurogenesis in adulthood can erase prior memories. What implications does this research have for the use of neural stem cells to treat central nervous system damage?

KEY TERMS

anterograde amnesia (p. 354)
classical conditioning (p. 342)
conditioned response (CR) (p. 342)
conditioned stimulus (CS) (p. 342)
declarative memory (p. 353)
engram (p. 354)
episodic memory (p. 353)
explicit memory (p. 354)
instinct (p. 341)
habituation (p. 342)
implicit memory (p. 354)
learning (p. 341)
long-term memory (p. 353)
long-term potentiation (LTP) (p. 359)
procedural memory (p. 353)
reflex (p. 341)
semantic memory (p. 353)
sensitization (p. 342)
sensory memory (p. 353)
short-term memory (p. 353)
unconditioned response (UCR) (p. 342)
unconditioned stimulus (UCS) (p. 342)

13 Lateralization, Language, and Intelligence

AP Images

▲ **American Sign Language** Insight into the brain's processing of language is provided by the study of people using American Sign Language (ASL), a language of sight and movement instead of sound.

CHAPTER OUTLINE

Introduction

Savant behaviors are exceptional skills and talents found in people whose intellectual functioning otherwise falls within the range of mental retardation. Dustin Hoffman's character in the film *Rain Man* was able to count the number of pennies in a jar instantly but was unable to make change for a dollar. Such cases, however, are not restricted to Hollywood. Leslie Lemke, a patient who is blind and mentally retarded, heard Tchaikovsky's Piano Concerto No.1 played one time on television. Several hours later, Lemke sat down at the piano, which he had never studied, and played the entire concerto without error (Treffert & Wallace, 2002). Such a task would be beyond the abilities of most talented, highly-trained, professional musicians. How can we account for such remarkable abilities in people whose general level of functioning is otherwise quite low?

Although the origin of savant behaviors remains a mystery, current speculation centers on possible damage to the left hemisphere, leading to compensating activity in the right hemisphere. The exceptional talents demonstrated by savants usually occur in modalities that we associate with right-hemisphere function such as art, music, mathematics, and spatial skills.

Bruce Miller and his colleagues (1998) used single photon emission computed tomography (SPECT) to compare the brain activity of a nine-year-old boy with autism to that of elderly patients with frontotemporal dementia (FTD). The elderly patients were developing new, savant-like artistic skills as their conditions progressed, whereas the youngster appeared to have been an artistic savant from the day he was able to grasp a crayon. An example of Miller and colleagues' SPECT images and art produced by a patient with FTD are shown in ■ Figure 13.1. The SPECT imaging showed that the elderly patients with FTD and the boy with autism had very similar deficits in the left hemisphere.

All of us may have the necessary circuitry to be savants, but our left-hemisphere dominance can overshadow these abilities. Repeated transcranial magnetic stimulation (rTMS), which temporarily changes the activity of underlying cortex, was applied to healthy participants in the same left-hemisphere regions that were damaged in the participants studied by Miller et al. (1998). Following stimulation, some participants experienced savant-like abilities that lasted a few hours (Snyder, Bahramali, Hawker, & Mitchell, 2006, Treffert & Wallace, 2002).

Why would human beings harbor extraordinary abilities without typically being able to use them? Although scientists continue to explore savant behavior, it is likely that these abilities reflect the activity of isolated subroutines that are rarely seen in the end products of human intelligence. In this chapter, we will see how human intelligence is multifaceted and that our abilities to learn, communicate, and problem solve require the recruitment and cooperation of multiple specialized structures and patterns of activity in the brain.

LEARNING OBJECTIVES

After reading this chapter, you should be able to:

LO1 Describe savant behavior and identify the behavioral results of hemispherectomy and the split-brain operation.

LO2 Describe the major theories that account for the development of lateralization.

LO3 Describe the correlations between lateralization, handedness, and behavior.

LO4 Describe theories pertaining to the origins of language.

LO5 Summarize the controversies surrounding the use of language by nonhuman animals.

LO6 Summarize the major findings regarding brain representation for multiple languages and for American Sign Language.

LO7 Describe the features of aphasia, agraphia, dyslexia, and stuttering.

LO8 Differentiate between theories of a single factor versus multiple factors in intelligence.

LO9 Discuss the influences of heredity and brain structure on intelligence.

■ **FIGURE 13.1**
Patients with Frontotemporal Dementia (FTD) Can Develop Savant-like Behavior
In (a), a SPECT image of a patient with FTD shows relatively little activity in the left frontal and temporal lobes (seen on the left side of the image), whereas activity in comparable parts of the right hemisphere is enhanced. (b) This painting was produced by a 64-year-old woman with FTD who had not shown artistic talent prior to the onset of her disease.

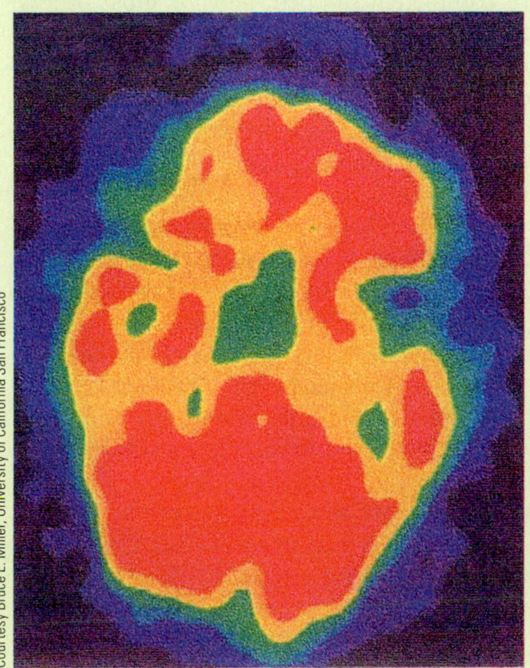

(a)

(b)

Courtesy Bruce L. Miller, University of California San Francisco

Lateralization of Function

Organisms are not perfectly symmetrical. Most of us know that we need to try on both shoes before we purchase them because our feet are slightly different in size. This asymmetry extends to our brains as well. The right and left hemispheres are not just typically different in size; substantial evidence suggests that they differ in function as well. The localization of a function in one hemisphere or the other is known as **lateralization.** In Chapter 2, we saw that much was learned about localization of cognitive function from the behavior of Phineas Gage following his bizarre accident. So too, much of what we know about brain lateralization comes from studies of epilepsy patients who have undergone surgery to reduce life-threatening seizures that could not be controlled with medication.

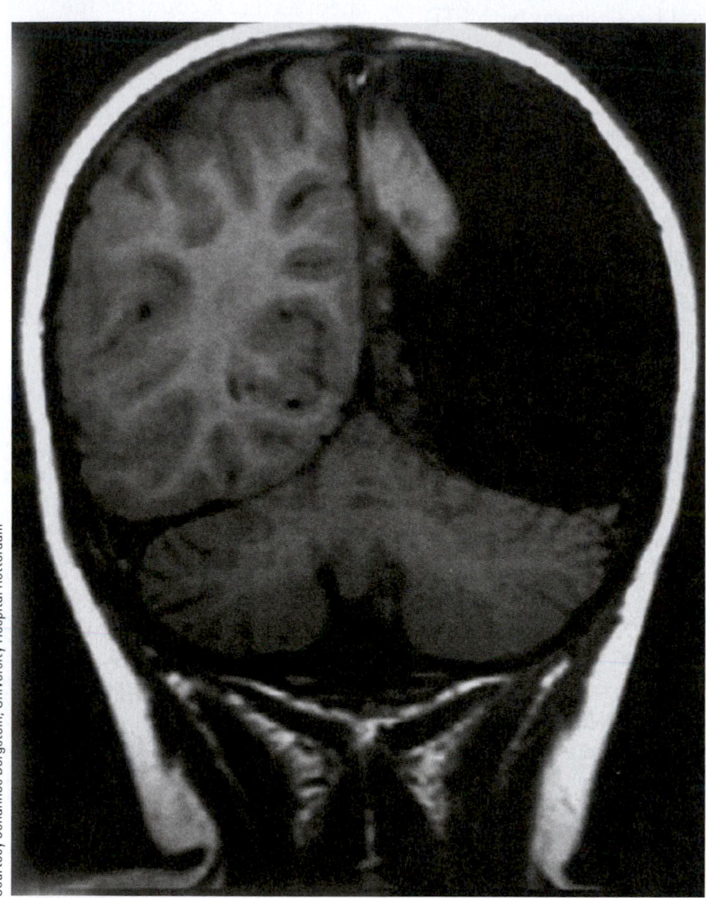

Courtesy Johannes Borgstein, University Hospital Rotterdam

FIGURE 13.2 Young Children with Rasmussen's Syndrome Are Frequent Candidates for Hemispherectomy Although her entire right hemisphere was removed at age three, this seven-year-old child retains her bilingual ability and has only slight motor problems in her left arm and leg. She leads an otherwise completely normal life.

Hemispherectomy

Rasmussen's syndrome is a rare brain disorder that produces seizures in only one hemisphere of the brain. It usually affects children after the age of five years, and its causes are currently unknown. The seizures produced by Rasmussen's syndrome, unlike those in many other disorders, do not respond to medication or to more commonly performed surgeries, including the split brain procedure we discuss in a later section. The most effective treatment for Rasmussen's is a hemispherectomy, or the complete removal of one entire hemisphere. The cortex of the frontal, parietal, temporal, and occipital lobes is removed, leaving the underlying white matter, basal ganglia, thalamus, and ventricles. Following surgery, the remaining cavity eventually fills with cerebrospinal fluid. The seven-year-old child whose brain is shown in Figure 13.2 underwent a hemispherectomy for Rasmussen's syndrome at age three years.

What results might we expect from such a radical treatment? For about 75 to 80 percent of the patients, seizures are completely stopped, and for most others, seizure activity is greatly reduced. But what is the cost to the patient? In Chapter 2, we learned that each of the two cerebral hemispheres has special roles in behaviors such as movement and language. What impact might a hemispherectomy have on these behaviors? Rather than being completely paralyzed on one half of the body as we might expect, most children move with a slight limp and perhaps an ankle brace. Language development is also surprisingly normal, although the removal of the left hemisphere impacts language to a greater extent than removal of the right hemisphere (Curtiss, de Bode, & Mathern, 2001). How is overall intelligence affected by the loss of half the cerebral cortex? Once again, the results are surprising (Vining et al., 1997). The procedure is associated with a 10-point increase on intelligence tests, probably due to a reduced need for the sedative medications typically used to control seizures (see Chapter 15). In one case, a boy who underwent the procedure on his left hemisphere at age five eventually developed superior intelligence and language abilities, allowing him to complete graduate studies (Smith & Sugar, 1975).

The success of the hemispherectomy is related to the young age of the patients and would likely have more severe and detrimental effects in adults (see Chapter 5). The fact that we are capable of living with one hemisphere certainly does not imply that we don't need or use all parts of our brains. Instead, the two hemispheres appear to provide unique and distinct contributions to our highest levels of human cognitive functions.

savant behavior Extraordinary skills and talents found in those whose overall level of intellectual functioning usually falls in the mentally retarded range.

lateralization The localization of a function in one hemisphere or the other.

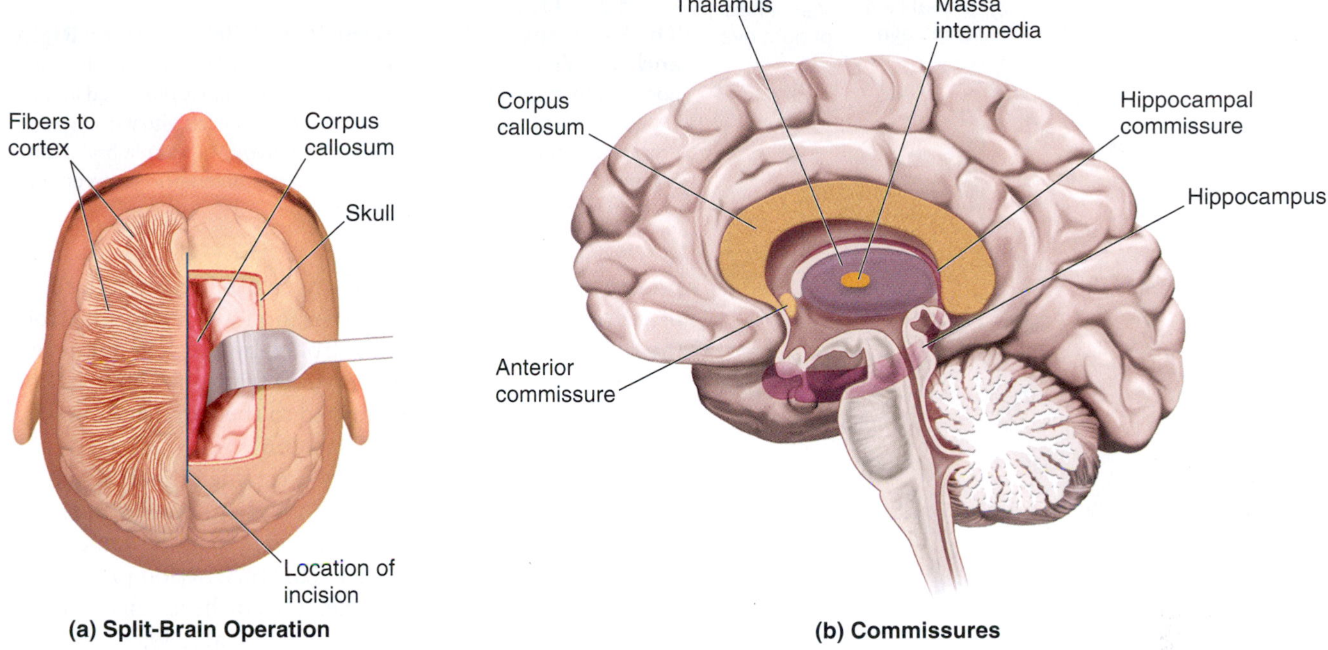

FIGURE 13.3
The Split-Brain Operation (a) During the split-brain operation, the cortex is retracted, providing access to the corpus callosum, which is then severed. (b) Four commissures connect the two cerebral hemispheres: the corpus callosum, the anterior commissure, the massa intermedia, and the hippocampal commissure. Joseph Bogen's classic split-brain procedure involved severing all four.

THE SPLIT BRAIN

The **split-brain operation,** in which pathways connecting the right and left cerebral hemispheres are severed, has been used to reduce life-threatening seizures that cannot be controlled with medication. Figure 13.3 illustrates the pathways, or commissures, that link the two hemispheres. The largest of these is the corpus callosum. The anterior commissure links the two temporal lobes, and the **hippocampal commissure** links the right and left hippocampi. In animals and some humans, the **massa intermedia** forms a bridge between the right and left medial thalamus.

Although split-brain surgeries date back to the 1930s, the most thoroughly studied cases were performed in the 1960s by Joseph Bogen. Bogen severed all four commissures in 16 patients who had been suffering uncontrollable seizures (Bogen, Schultz, & Vogel, 1988). By separating the two hemispheres, as shown in Figure 13.3, a seizure originating in one half of the brain is restricted to that half. Seizures result from abnormal electrical events, which in turn lead to observable clinical events such as convulsions (see Chapter 15). When the propagation of abnormal electrical activity is restricted to a single hemisphere, electrical disturbances might not reach the thresholds required to produce observable clinical symptoms, such as convulsions. Split-brain procedures reduce both the severity and overall frequency of seizures. Forty-one percent of the patients in one sample were completely free of seizures following surgery, and another 45 percent had seizures less than half as frequently as before surgery (Sorenson et al., 1997).

Surprisingly, Bogen's patients experienced no changes in personality, intelligence, or speech (Gazzaniga, 1970; Sperry, 1974). However, the surgery can result in some odd behaviors. Sperry (1964; as cited in Ornstein, 1977, p. 53) described patients after split-brain operations as people "with two separate minds," and occasionally, those minds disagreed with each other. One patient would pull his pants down with one hand while the other hand pulled the pants back up. Normally, these so-called "alien hand syndrome" effects decrease with time.

Roger Sperry, Michael Gazzaniga, and their colleagues explored the unique behavioral outcomes of this surgery. These investigations took advantage of the fact that the

split-brain operation A treatment for seizure disorder in which the commissures linking the two cerebral hemispheres are severed.
hippocampal commissure A pathway linking the right and left hippocampal structures.
massa intermedia (MASS-uh in-ter-MEE-dee-uh) The connection between the right and left thalamic nuclei.

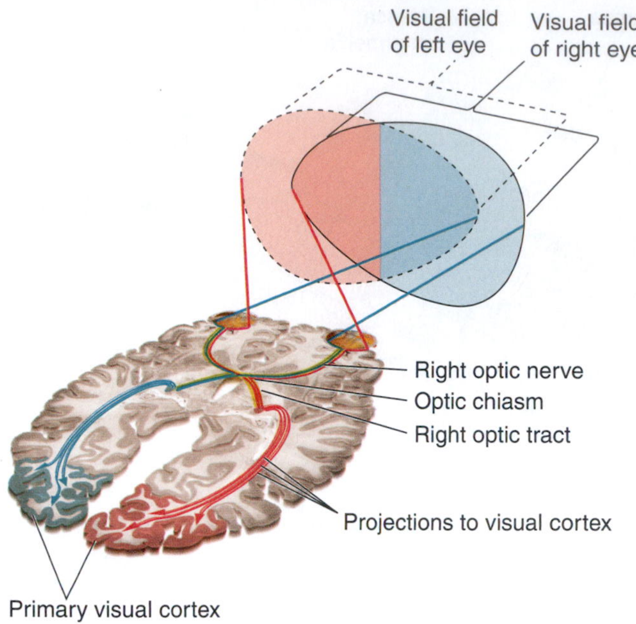

FIGURE 13.4
The Relationship Between the Visual Fields and the Right and Left Visual Cortices Assuming that the eyes and head are stationary, information from the right visual field (blue) is processed in the left visual cortex. Conversely, information from the left visual field (red) is processed in the right visual cortex. In the patient with a split brain, this organization allows researchers to demonstrate differences between the properties of the right and left hemispheres.

processing of certain types of information is lateralized. For instance, we know that both sensation and motor control in the left half of the body are controlled by the right hemisphere of the brain. Similarly, information from the right half of a person's visual field is transmitted to the left visual cortex, as shown in Figure 13.4 (see Chapter 6).

In one typical experiment by Gazzaniga (1967), illustrated in Figure 13.5, participants who had previously undergone split-brain operations were instructed to focus on a dot located in the center of the visual field. This instruction prevents the participants from moving either eyes or head, ensuring that each hemisphere "sees" only half the visual field. To the left of the dot appeared the word *HE*, and to the right of the dot was the word *ART*. When Gazzaniga asked which word was presented, the participants responded by saying "art." Because information from the right visual field crosses to the left hemisphere, the participants were relating the stimulus seen by the left hemisphere. Because language is primarily a left-hemisphere function in most people, the left hemisphere responded to Gazzaniga's question with the stimulus it had seen.

FIGURE 13.5
Differences in Language Capacities Between the Two Hemispheres When the participant in a split-brain study was asked what she saw, she replied "art," the word seen by the verbal left hemisphere. When asked to point with the left hand to the word she saw, she pointed to HE, the word seen by the right hemisphere. The left hand is controlled by the right hemisphere.

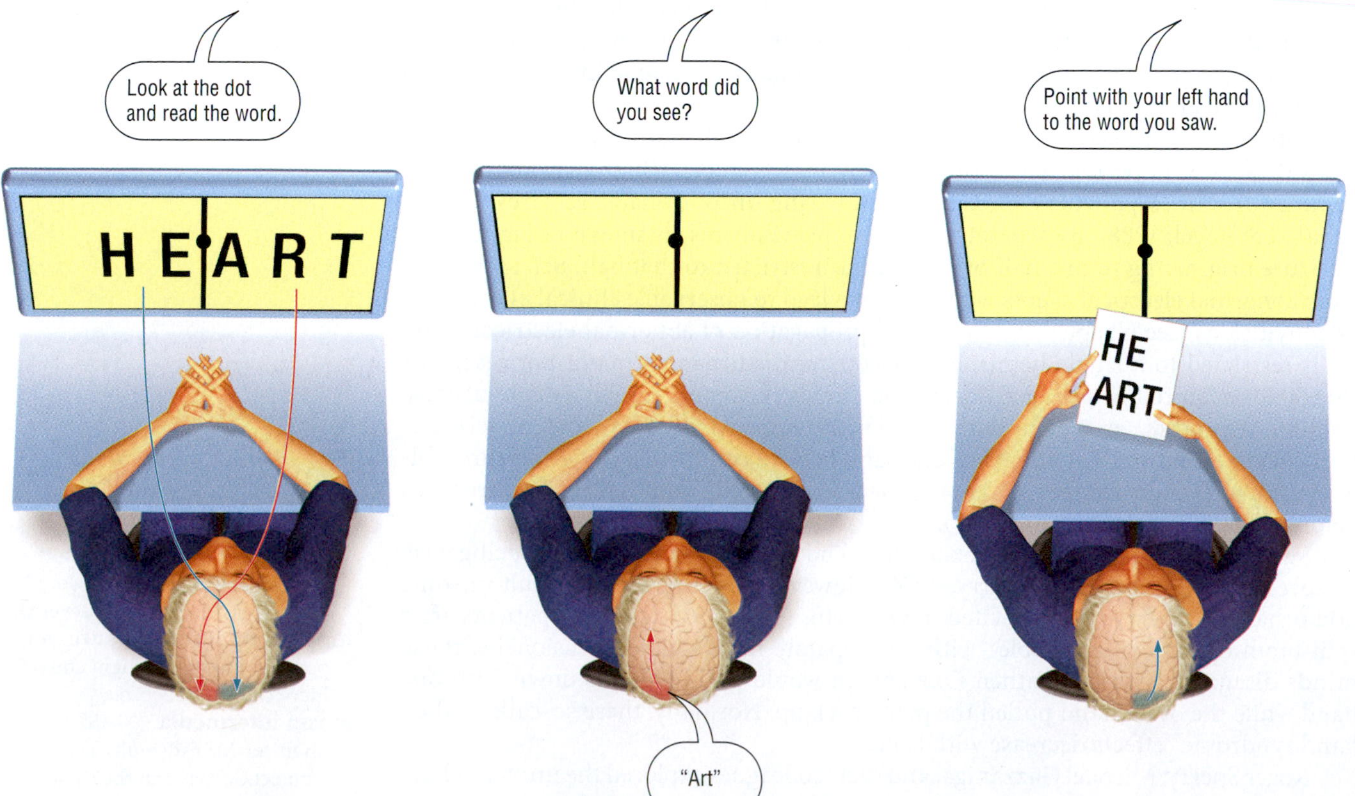

Numbers, letters, and short words can be processed by the right hemisphere as long as a nonverbal response is required. When Gazzaniga's participants were asked to point with their left hands to the word that had been seen, the participants pointed to the word *HE*. Because the left hand is controlled by the right hemisphere, in this case the right hemisphere is "telling" what it had seen. The word *HE* appeared in the left visual field, and the information was transmitted to the right hemisphere.

In further research, pictures of objects were flashed on either the right or left side of a screen (Gazzaniga, 1983). When an image of a spoon was presented in the left visual field (processed by the right hemisphere), the participants were able successfully to identify a spoon from a set of similar objects using the left hand. At the same time, when questioned verbally, the participants were unable to say what they had just seen. The participants believed that they were guessing when they selected the spoon and were very surprised that they had picked out the correct object without "knowing" what they saw. If the word *stand* is presented to the right hemisphere, participants stand up. When asked by the experimenter to explain the action, a participant might reply that he or she needed to get up and stretch. The verbal left hemisphere, observing the action of standing but being unaware of the command, attempts to provide a reasonable explanation for the behavior. These observations led Gazzaniga (1988) to describe the left hemisphere as an "interpreter" that tries to make sense out of our actions.

In addition to differences in the localization of language, the two hemispheres appear to differ in the processing of other types of information. Logical, sequential information is processed more effectively by the left hemisphere, whereas emotional, intuitive information is processed by the right hemisphere. The processing of spatial relations, as in thinking about a three-dimensional figure, is superior in the right hemisphere. Although all of the participants studied by Sperry and Gazzaniga were right-handed, their ability to draw or copy a three-dimensional figure was superior when using the left hand, which is controlled by the right hemisphere.

We should interpret the behavior of patients after split-brain surgery with caution. Not only have these patients undergone extensive, invasive surgery, but the epilepsy that required surgery in the first place could have affected brain function and organization. Fortunately, there is an alternative method for investigating lateralization in healthy, typical individuals. In the Wada test, named after its inventor, Juhn Wada, the anesthetic sodium amytal is applied to one cerebral hemisphere through a catheter inserted in the groin area and advanced into one of the carotid arteries in the neck. As a result of this procedure, illustrated in ■ Figure 13.6, one cerebral hemisphere is literally put to sleep. If the patient has language localized to the anesthetized hemisphere, speech and most comprehension will be absent. Although the Wada test is considered to be the gold standard of presurgery lateralization evaluation techniques, newer and less invasive technologies, particularly fMRI, are being explored as alternatives (Abou-Khalil, 2007).

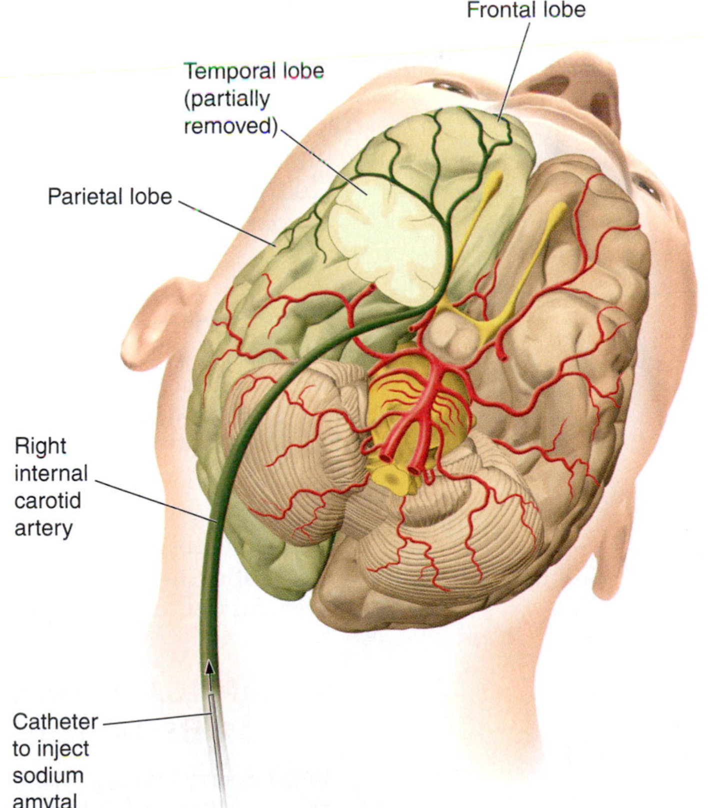

■ **FIGURE 13.6**
The Wada Test By anesthetizing one hemisphere with an injection of sodium amytal, researchers can determine which hemisphere processes language. If the hemisphere that manages language is the one anesthetized, the patient will be unable to speak or comprehend.

The Development of Lateralization

Lateralization is not exclusive to human beings. Preferences for one hand (or paw) are generally accepted as indications of functional asymmetry in the brain. Paw preferences during reaching for food have been observed in mice, rats, cats, and dogs (Sun & Walsh, 2006). Chimpanzees and other great apes show structural asymmetries in their brains that are similar to those in humans (Cantalupo & Hopkins, 2001; Gannon, Holloway, Broadfield, & Braun, 1998).

What advantages might lateralization provide? Rogers (2000) suggested that lateralization allows organisms to multitask, or to split their attention between different aspects of the environment. Chicks incubated in the dark do not lateralize some of their visually guided responses, and therefore, they can serve as a control group for normally lateralized chicks incubated in the light. Compared with the dark-incubated, nonlateralized chicks, the light-incubated, normally lateralized chicks were more efficient in managing the dual tasks of identifying potential predators while feeding. Lateralization also helped the chicks discriminate between grain and pebbles (Rogers, Andrew, & Johnston, 2007). These abilities would confer obvious advantages to the chicks' survival.

What produces lateralization in humans? Geschwind and Galaburda (1987) suggested that prenatal androgens play key roles in the lateralization of language and visuospatial skills. This hypothesis predicts gender differences in lateralization, given the much higher exposure of males to prenatal androgens. One example of gender differences in lateralization is the higher proportion of males who are left-handed (Mathews et al., 2004). Handedness, as we will see later in this chapter, is correlated with lateralization.

A logical test of the role of androgens in lateralization is to observe individuals exposed to abnormally high levels of prenatal androgens. As we discussed in Chapter 10, some individuals experience high levels of prenatal androgens due to congenital adrenal hyperplasia (CAH). No significant differences in handedness or language laterality were found between females with CAH and their unaffected relatives, but males with CAH were slightly more likely to be left-handed than their unaffected relatives (Mathews et al., 2004). According to Mathews et al. (2004, p. 820), their data provided "weak but inconsistent support for a role for androgens in the development of hand preferences in humans, and little or no support for hormonal influences on language lateralization."

Inkwells on Left Advocated for Left-Handed Pupils

(Article headline), New York Times, 1951

If prenatal androgens do not play as strong a role in lateralization as we previously believed, what other factors might be involved? Stephan, Fink, and Marshall (2007) argue that structural and functional lateralization originates in differences in the connectivity found in the two hemispheres. For example, genes known to participate in the development of axons and dendrites are expressed differently in the right and left hemispheres between three and five months following conception (Sun et al., 2005). The differential expression of these genes might result in very different wiring patterns in the two hemispheres, leading to the structural and functional differences we observe later in life (Stephan, Fink, & Marshall, 2007).

Environmental factors have been implicated in the development of lateralization. A study of 180,000 Swedish male military recruits suggested that routine ultrasounds conducted during their mothers' pregnancies resulted in higher numbers of left-handers (Kieler, Cnattingius, Haglund, Palmgren, &Axelsson, 2001). Three follow-up studies confirmed these initial results (Salvesen, 2002). Although no studies support any relationship between prenatal ultrasound and later neurological problems in children, further research into this phenomenon seems warranted (Salvesen, 2007).

Implications of Hemispheric Asymmetry for Behavior

Roger Sperry (1982, p. 1225) observed, "The left-right dichotomy in cognitive mode is an idea with which it is very easy to run wild." What are the implications of lateralization in the typical intact brain?

One common assertion about hemisphere lateralization is the concept of a dominant hemisphere (Bakan, 1971; Zenhausen, 1978). People who are "left-brain dominant" are described as logical, verbal, and analytic. "Right-brained" people are supposed to be artistic and intuitive. Anecdotal data, such as the large number of left-handed statesmen, musicians, artists, and athletes, compared with a much smaller number of left-handed writers, contribute to popular beliefs about hemisphere dominance. However, experimental support for this notion is weak. Springer and Deutsch (1998) report no strong correlations between hemisphere dominance and occupational choice or artistic talent.

Handedness, Language, and Hemisphere Lateralization The most significant correlation regarding hemisphere lateralization is the association between handedness and the localization of language. Handedness is surprisingly difficult to establish, but a common standard is the use of a preferred hand for writing (McManus, 1999). Using that standard, approximately equal use of both hands is quite rare, accounting for about 1 percent of the population (Corballis, Hattie, & Fletcher, 2008). Of the 90 percent of the population who are primarily right-handed, about 95 percent localize language primarily to the left hemisphere. Most of the remaining 5 percent localize language to the right, although there are a very small number of right-handed individuals who use both hemispheres for language. Among the 10 percent of people who are primarily left-handed, about 70 percent localize language to the left hemisphere, 15 percent localize language to the right hemisphere, and the remaining 15 percent use both hemispheres fairly equally for language (Corballis, 2003; Rasmussen & Milner, 1977).

There are painters who transform the sun to a yellow spot, but there are others who with the help of their art and their intelligence, transform a yellow spot into sun.

Pablo Picasso

Dichotic Listening Much of the work by Sperry and Gazzaniga on the effects of split-brain surgeries focused on the processing of information by the visual cortex. However, listening tasks also provide insight into lateralization. Although information from one ear is processed by both cerebral hemispheres, it is processed more rapidly by the contralateral auditory cortex. In other words, information presented to the left ear is processed more rapidly by the right hemisphere, whereas information provided to the right ear is processed more rapidly by the left hemisphere.

To investigate the lateralization of auditory processing, Doreen Kimura used **dichotic listening** tasks, in which different sounds are presented simultaneously to the left and right ears (see Figure 13.7). If words reaching the two ears are different, most right-handers show a right-ear advantage, repeating the word they heard in the

WHY DOES THIS MATTER?

Why Do We Have a Preferred Hand?

Understanding the origins of human hand preferences matters because we might gain insight into the structural asymmetries and lateralization that also made language possible.

Some researchers argue that a major genetic mutation occurred in humans about 100,000 years ago, leading to the more extreme lateralization of both language and handedness (Berlim, Mattevi, Belmonte-de-Abreu, & Crow, 2003; Corballis, 1997; McManus, 1985). However, why 90 percent of humans show such a strong preference for using the right hand remains unclear. Although individual members of other species show hand preferences, distributions of right-handers and left-handers within most nonhuman species seem to be about 50:50 (Sun & Walsh, 2006). Chimpanzees show evidence of genetically determined handedness, but the ratio of right-handed to left-handed individuals is about 2:1 as opposed to the 9:1 ratio seen in humans (Lonsdorf & Hopkins, 2005).

Although human handedness is largely under genetic control, different circumstances might favor left-handers and right-handers. Left-handed athletes appear to enjoy an advantage in many sports, including fencing, tennis, and baseball. Whether this is the result of neurological advantages (Azemar, 1993) or simply a strategic advantage due to unfamiliarity (Aggleton & Wood, 1990; Wood & Aggleton, 1989) remains the subject of debate. Faurie and Raymond (2004) investigated handedness in a number of human foraging societies. The percentage of left-handers was strongly correlated with the homicide rate of each society. Among the most violent of these, the Yanomamo of the Amazon basin, 22.6 percent of the population is left-handed. Among the extremely peaceful Dioula-speaking people of Burkina Faso in western Africa, only 3.4 percent of the population is left-handed. As with left-handedness in sports, left-handedness might be more adaptive in violent groups due to its strategic advantages in hand-to-hand combat.

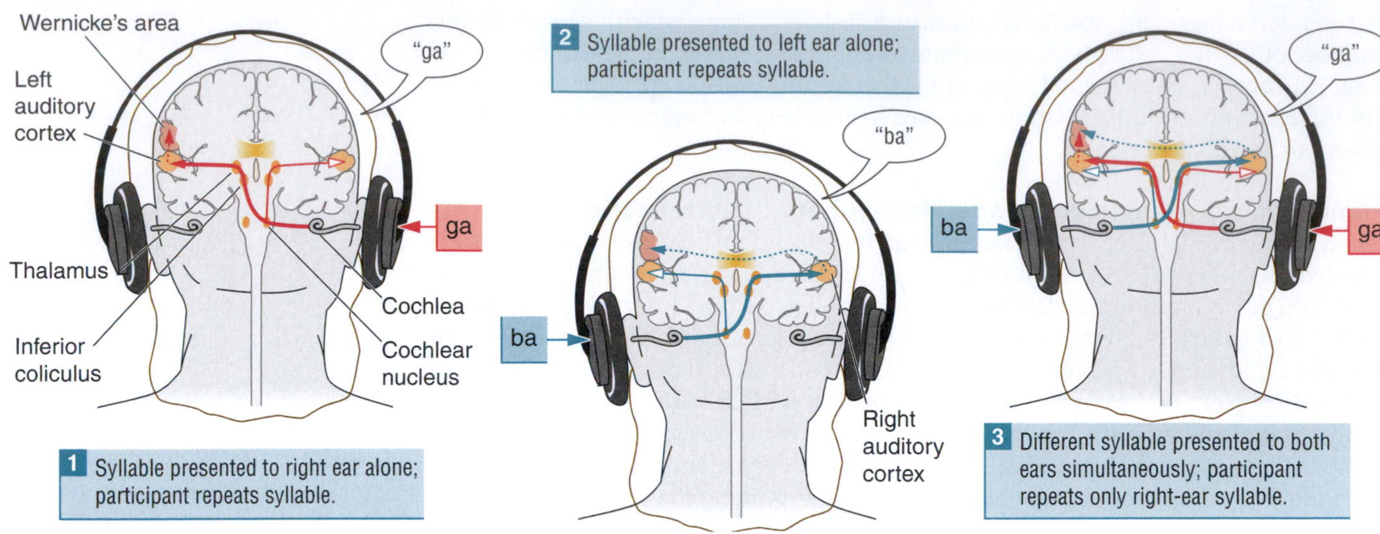

FIGURE 13.7
Dichotic Listening Is Related to Hemisphere Lateralization for Language When conflicting information is provided to the two ears, the person who has language lateralized to the left hemisphere will show a preference for the word heard by the right ear. The information presented to the right ear will reach Wernicke's area in the left hemisphere faster than information presented to the left ear.

right ear (Kimura, 1973).This result suggests that language for these individuals is lateralized to the left hemisphere. As we will see in the next section, right-handers show a left-ear advantage, or right-hemisphere advantage, for emotional information.

If you talk to a man in a language he understands, that goes to his head. If you talk to him in his language, that goes to his heart.
Nelson Mandela

The Lateralization of Prosody and Musical Abilities **Prosody** refers to use of intonation and stress in spoken language to convey emotional tone and meaning. Evidence for right-hemisphere participation in the production and perception of prosody comes from analyses of dichotic listening tasks, imaging studies, and patients with right-hemisphere strokes (see Chapter 15). Just as participants in dichotic listening tasks showed a right-ear advantage for identifying spoken words (Kimura, 1973), they also show a left-ear advantage for determining the emotional tone of a verbal stimulus (Bryden, 1988). Studies using fMRI confirm that the right hemisphere participates in the evaluation of emotional tone in language (Wildgruber, Ackermann, Kreifelts, & Ethofer, 2006; Wildgruber et al., 2005). However, the situation is not simple. These researchers also note that the orbitofrontal cortex of both hemispheres contributes to the explicit, or conscious, evaluation of emotional tone in spoken language. Charbonneau, Scherzer, Aspirot, and Cohen (2003) compared 22 patients with right- or left-hemisphere damage with healthy controls. Participants were asked to discriminate, imitate, and produce emotions of fear, sadness, and anger in facial expressions and in vocal expressions (prosody). The patients with left-hemisphere damage performed as well as the control group in most cases, whereas the patients with right-hemisphere damage showed deficits in processing both facial expressions and prosody.

Researchers have also tried to evaluate the lateralization of musical abilities. Following a stroke that damaged his left hemisphere, composer Maurice Ravel retained his ability to judge pitch and to recognize a piece of music he heard. However, Ravel was unable to play the piano, recognize written music, or compose music. Ravel's outcomes show us that some musical abilities are lateralized to the right hemisphere but that a simple "language-on-the-left, music-on-the-right" model of hemispheric functioning is incorrect. The extent to which music is lateralized is still debatable. Some imaging studies suggest that music and language share overlapping brain resources (Brown, Martinez, & Parsons, 2006). Other investigators using repeated transcranial magnetic stimulation (rTMS) have demonstrated a clear lateralization of music processing to the right hemisphere (Sparing et al., 2007).

The brains of musicians with perfect pitch, or the ability to name a musical note that they hear, appear to be structurally different from those of nonmusicians or from

dichotic listening A task in which different sounds are presented simultaneously to the right and left ears.
prosody The use of pitch and intonation in language to convey emotional tone and meaning.

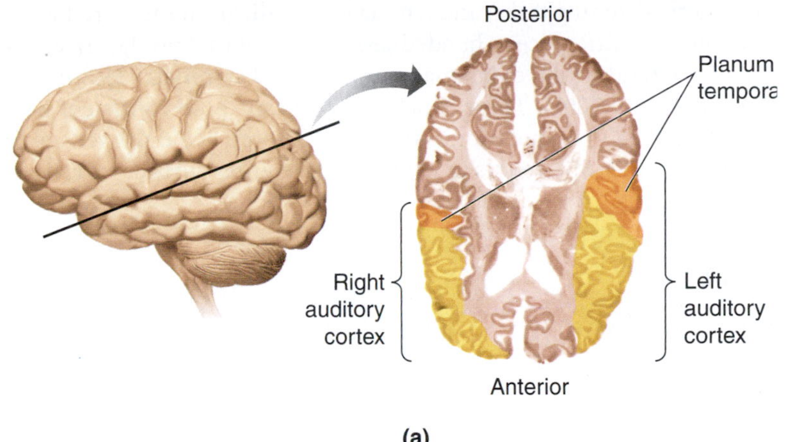

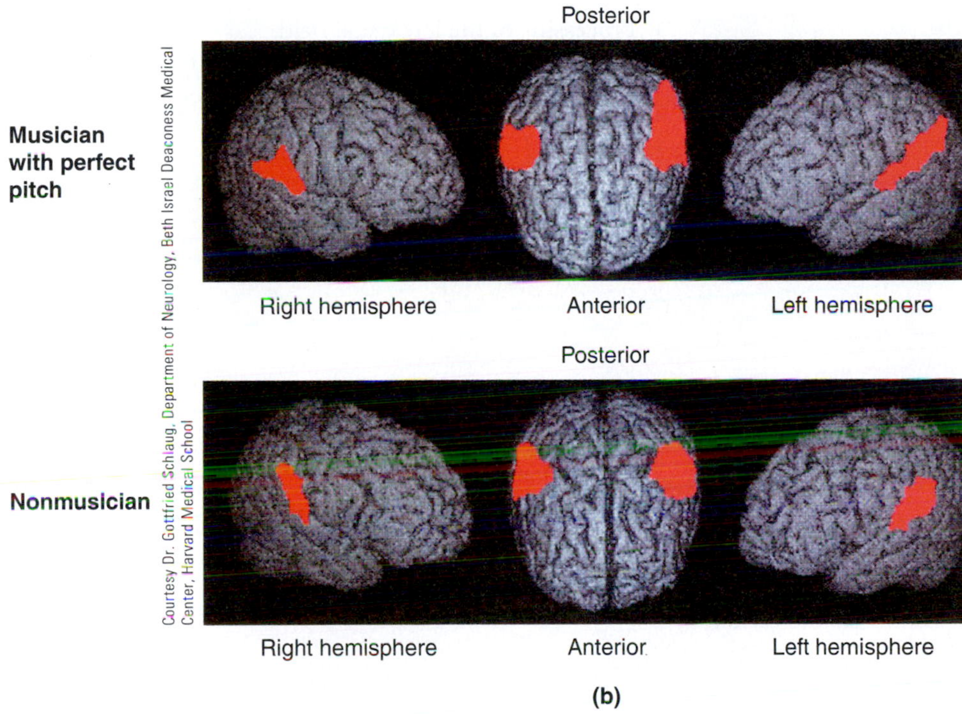

FIGURE 13.8
The Planum Temporale
(a) In most individuals, the left planum temporale is larger in the left than in the right hemisphere. (b) Gottfried Schlaug and his colleagues have found that this asymmetry is even more pronounced in musicians with perfect pitch, as compared with nonmusical participants and musicians who do not have perfect pitch.

those of musicians without perfect pitch (Schlaug, Jancke, Huang, & Steinmetz, 1995). The **planum temporale,** shown in Figure 13.8, is usually somewhat larger in the left hemisphere than in the right in most people. However, the difference between the left and right planum temporale was about twice as large in the musicians with perfect pitch as in the control participants. These results suggest that perfect pitch is mediated by the left hemisphere.

Gender Differences in Lateralization Gender differences in lateralization have been proposed to explain observations of gender differences in language. Halpern (1992) noted that girls begin speaking at younger ages and have larger vocabularies and better reading scores than boys. Three to seven times as many boys as girls are diagnosed with language disabilities (Liederman, Kantrowitz, & Flannery, 2005).

Such discrepancies could result from different degrees of functional asymmetry in the brains of males and females. Some researchers argued that female brains are more functionally symmetrical than male brains (Harris, 1980). For instance, males performing a visuospatial task showed activity in the right hemisphere, whereas females performing the task showed activity in both hemispheres (Johnson, McKenzie, & Hamm, 2002). However, a recent meta-analysis of over 1,000 studies of gender differences in handedness, the asymmetry of the planum temporale, language performance

planum temporale (PLAN-um tem-poor-AL) An area located posterior to the primary auditory cortex in the temporal lobes.

in dichotic listening tasks, and language lateralization measured with fMRI concluded that a gender difference in handedness exists, but that no significant gender differences occur in lateralization of language or structural symmetry (Sommer, Aleman, Somers, Boks, & Kahn, 2008). These conclusions appear more consistent with the lack of support discussed previously for a strong role of prenatal androgens in lateralization. The basis for gender differences in handedness requires further investigation.

INTERIM SUMMARY 13.1

Summary Table: Localization of Function in the Cerebral Hemispheres

Typically Greater Representation in the Left Hemisphere	Typically Greater Representation in the Right Hemisphere
Motor control of the right side of the body	Motor control of the left side of the body
• Processing of the right visual field • Right-ear advantage in dichotic listening tasks	• Processing of the left visual field • Left-ear advantage in dichotic listening tasks
• Language • Mathematics	• Prosody • Music
Logical processing	• Intuition • Spatial relations
	Art

Summary Points

1. Research involving patients who had undergone surgery to treat life-threatening seizures led to an understanding that some functions are not symmetrically organized in the brain. **(LO1)**
2. Lateralization results from genetic influences, but understanding the exact processes responsible for its development requires further research. Lateralization appears to involve differential gene expression in the two hemispheres, differences in connectivity, and environmental influences. **(LO2)**
3. Handedness, language, dichotic listening, the processing of music and prosody, and savant behavior correlate with patterns of lateralization. **(LO3)**

Review Question

1. What are the possible advantages of lateralization of functions in the cerebral hemispheres?

Language

Language has been defined as a system of communicating with others using sounds, symbols, and words to express a meaning, idea, or thought. Jean Aitchison (1983) outlined ten criteria for language, shown in Table 13.1. As we will see in a later section, some animal communication systems demonstrate several of the criteria, although it is possible that only human language meets all ten.

The Origins of Language

No human culture on earth exists without language. Because of this universality, linguists Noam Chomsky (1957) and Steven Pinker (1994) argue that human beings possess the innate ability to learn language. Chomsky believes that language arose indirectly as a result of other adaptations, whereas Pinker views language as the direct result of natural selection. In either case, the enormous survival advantages of language to human culture and cooperation would ensure its retention in the population.

TABLE 13.1 Aitchison's Ten Criteria for Language

Feature	Definition	Example
1. Vocal-auditory canal	Use of vocalization to communicate	Speech and birdsong but not American Sign Language (ASL) or bee dances
2. Arbitrariness	No connection between symbol and what it signifies	Using the word *dog* to refer to the animal
3. Semanticity	Use of symbols to refer to objects and actions	*Chair* can be used to refer to all chairs
4. Cultural transmission	Handed down from generation to generation	We learn language from our families
5. Spontaneous usage	No training or force is necessary to make individuals communicate	Children exposed to language will use language freely
6. Turn-taking	Communication follows social rules	Birds will respond to another bird's song
7. Duality	Use of different sounds and orders of sounds to communicate	*C, A,* and *T* are meaningless until they are combined
8. Displacement	Ability to communicate about objects and events that are distant in time and place	Bee dances direct other bees to distant sources of food
9. Structure-dependence	Use of grammar, or structured "chunks"	Understanding that the "man in the hat" means the same as "he"
10. Creativity	Ability to create novel utterances	Humans and possibly signing apes can say things they have never heard before

Learning spoken language seems to proceed differently than other types of learning. No specific instruction is needed, as it is with related skills for reading and writing. The fact that language learning does not always correlate with intelligence provides evidence for an independent "language module" in the brain. Some individuals with normal intelligence experience great difficulty learning language (Tallal, Ross, & Curtiss, 1989). In contrast, children with Williams syndrome typically score in the moderately mentally retarded range on intelligence tests, but they are fluent speakers who develop very large vocabularies (Bellugi, Wang, & Jernigan, 1994).

When ideas fail, words come in very handy.

Johann Wolfgang von Goethe

Researchers are getting closer to identifying the genes responsible for some aspects of language. One gene reliably associated with speech and language disorders is the forkhead box *P2* gene *(FOXP2),* located on Chromosome 7 (Spiteri et al., 2007). Members of several generations of a particular family, called the KE family, show a mutation in the *FOXP2* gene accompanied by low-normal intelligence and severe difficulties in the production of language (Lai, Fisher, Hurst, Vargha-Khadem, & Monaco, 2001). A number of structural abnormalities have been identified in the KE family, particularly in the caudate nucleus of the basal ganglia (Watkins et al., 2002). The caudate nucleus was smaller in affected family members than in unaffected family members and in typical control participants. During brain development, *FOXP2* targets the basal ganglia and the inferior frontal lobes (Spiteri et al., 2007). These researchers also report that *FOXP2* is expressed differently in these areas of the human brain than in the chimpanzee brain.

The timing of important mutations in the *FOXP2* gene has been used to locate language development in human evolution. Some researchers believe that a critical

FIGURE 13.9
Click Languages May Be Among the Earliest Human Languages
Click languages include sounds made by clicking the tongue. Groups using click languages have been found to be genetically distinct, leading to conclusions that these languages are quite ancient.

mutation required for modern language use occurred only about 100,000 years ago (Corballis, 2004). However, evidence that Neanderthals, the closest extinct relatives of modern humans, also possessed the critical *FOXP2* mutation places modern language ability further back in history to 300,000 to 400,000 years ago (Krause et al., 2007).

Some aspects of language might have developed even earlier, and as we will see in a later section, language behavior might also occur in other animals. Elaborate tool use and cooperation would be difficult to accomplish without some rudimentary form of language. Therefore, we can look for evidence of tool use and cooperation among early hominids as a possible indicator for language ability (see Chapter 2). In addition, skull structure indicating hemispheric asymmetry has been suggested as a possible sign of language development. Using these measures, we can see that early hominid *Homo habilis*, which existed approximately two million years ago, is a possible candidate for language use. *H. habilis* used stone tools and appeared to hunt cooperatively. *Homo erectus*, dating from 1.5 million to 300,000 years ago, is an even more likely candidate for language use. *H. erectus* was capable of more sophisticated tool use and showed evidence of controlling fire. Modern *Homo sapiens* appeared as early as 200,000 years ago. Because we are the same species as these early *Homo sapiens*, we assume they must have been capable of language.

How might the earliest languages have sounded? Click languages, used by African groups ranging from Tanzania to the San of South Africa, might represent the earliest form of human language. As shown in ■ Figure 13.9, click languages use clicks made by the tongue to symbolize words. Studies of genetic relatedness among African groups using click languages show that the groups are highly distinct from one another (Knight et al., 2001). In spite of their common use of click languages, these groups have not had shared ancestors for between 15,000 and 35,000 years. This suggests that the origin of click languages occurred in a time before human beings settled down to begin agriculture (Tishkoff et al., 2007).

NEW DIRECTIONS

Lateralization, Language, and Schizophrenia

Schizophrenia, which we will discuss in detail in Chapter 16, affects about 1 percent of the world's population and represents one of the most serious and disabling psychological disorders. Patients with schizophrenia demonstrate distortions of logical reasoning, perception, movement, and emotion that challenge their abilities to live independent, fulfilling lives. In spite of significant efforts to identify the causes of this disorder, no definitive answers have been discovered. However, recent work on lateralization in patients with schizophrenia has provided clues to the disorder's development.

Many symptoms of schizophrenia are related to the interpretation and organization of language (Berlim et al., 2003). For example, many patients experience auditory hallucinations of voices, which might represent a disturbance in the ability to detect the difference between the "voice" of a person's inner thoughts and real perceptions. Language distortions might have their roots in the finding that many patients with schizophrenia either show no hemispheric asymmetry or a mirror asymmetry in which language is primarily lateralized to the right hemisphere (Petty, 1999; Sommer, Ramsey, Kahn, Aleman, & Bouma, 2001). In addition, patients with schizophrenia are more likely to have a mixed or ambiguous handedness (Crow, 1997).

Because of these intersections between schizophrenia, lateralization, handedness, and language, Timothy Crow and his colleagues (Berlim et al., 2003; Crow, 1997; Crow, Paez, & Chance, 2007) have proposed that schizophrenia arose along with a major genetic change in the human species that resulted in lateralization and language over 100,000 years ago. This linkage between genes involved with both lateralization and schizophrenia might account for the disorder's continued existence in spite of the reductions it produces in reproductive success. Women with schizophrenia are 30 percent less likely to reproduce than healthy women, and men with schizophrenia are 70 percent less like to reproduce than healthy men (Berlim et al., 2003). Without a linkage to some positive attribute, any genetic condition with such a detrimental effect on reproduction should disappear rapidly from a population.

Other recent work has begun to identify specific genes involved with lateralization, handedness, and schizophrenia (Francks et al., 2007; Sun & Walsh, 2006). A further understanding of these genes and their expression during development should lead to more effective prevention and treatments for schizophrenia.

Are Nonhuman Animals Capable of Real Language?

Thanks to words, we have been able to rise above the brutes; and thanks to language we have often sunk to the level of demons.

Aldous Huxley

If we accept the notion that human language occurs as a result of some innate, genetically determined language-learning mechanism, it is also logical to think that such a system might have evolved according to Darwinian concepts, and that creatures other than humans might possess some language capabilities.

Many animals communicate with one another, often in complex ways. Communication, however, is not the same as language (Dronkers, Pinker, & Damasio, 2000). Some animals have a fairly inflexible group of calls used for functions such as signaling danger and identifying territories. Others use signals that communicate magnitude, as in the case of bee dances that indicate the location of food. Finally, animals communicate through sequences of behavior, as in the case of birdsong. These animal behaviors, although clearly used for communication, do not match the flexibility and creativity of human language as described by Aitchison (1983; see Table 13.1).

If we are to find an animal precursor to human language capability, the most logical place to start is with our nearest relatives, the great apes. In three species of great ape, Brodmann's area 44 (part of Broca's area) showed asymmetry between the left and right hemispheres similar to that typically seen in humans (Cantalupo & Hopkins, 2001). Although this doesn't prove that apes have the necessary brain structures for language production, it does suggest that human brain development for language is not completely unique. Other researchers point to the existence of mirror neurons in nonhuman primates as a possible precursor for human language (see Chapter 8). Mirror neurons are activated both when an animal performs an action and when it observes another animal perform an action (Rizzolatti, Fadiga, Gallese, & Fogassi, 1996). Mirror neurons might have provided a mechanism allowing early humans to first gain an understanding of gestures, followed by language. The presence of mirror neurons in Broca's area in both apes and humans suggests a basis for the evolution of language (Corballis, 2004).

Researchers have attempted to teach human-like languages to apes. In 1931, Winthrop N. Kellogg and his wife adopted a baby chimpanzee named Gua, but their attempts to teach him human speech were unsuccessful. Efforts to teach apes sign language have been more promising. Allen and Beatrice Gardner (1969) taught 132 different signs to a chimp named Washoe. The Gardners' work was followed by Francine Patterson (1978), who trained a gorilla named Koko to use signs. Sue Savage-Rumbaugh and her colleagues (Savage-Rumbaugh, Shanker, & Taylor, 1998) have successfully taught a pygmy chimpanzee named Kanzi to associate geometric symbols with words. Even before his own training began, Kanzi appeared to have learned 10 symbols simply by observing his mother's training sessions. Kanzi also seems to be able to understand some human speech. When given 660 verbal requests, Kanzi behaved correctly 72 percent of the time. Savage-Rumbaugh is shown working with another one of her pupils in ■ Figure 13.10.

Whether these animal behaviors constitute real language is the subject of debate. Herbert Terrace (1979) concluded that signing is just advanced imitation that lacks several major features of human language. Whereas human children build vocabularies spontaneously if they are exposed to language (Aitchison's criteria for cultural transmission and spontaneous usage), ape language must be taught laboriously. Word order (Aitchison's structure dependence) does not seem to matter too much to apes, although it has an essential role in human language. Terrace also questioned the objectivity of some observers. When Washoe signed "waterbird" while observing a swan, the Gardners concluded that she was making a new, creative observation. Washoe might simply have noticed a "bird" sitting on the "water" and made the corresponding signs. On the other hand, evidence of spontaneous signing has been observed among a group of trained chimps, who ask one another to chase, tickle, hug, or groom (Fouts & Bodamer, 1987).

Language is, in effect, the vehicle for concepts and ideas that belong to everyone, and it reinforces individual thinking with a vast system of collective concepts.

Jean Piaget

Apes are not the only animals suspected of having language capabilities. Irene Pepperberg (1990) makes a strong case for her African grey parrots based on the birds' ability to communicate in ways that meet many of the criteria for language, such as

FIGURE 13.10 Chimpanzees Can Learn Language-like Behaviors Sue Savage-Rumbaugh of Georgia State University taught Panbanisha, a bonobo, to use a keyboard to produce grammatical sentences. Although apes can be taught to use symbols, linguists disagree over the issue of whether such behavior truly constitutes language.

arbitrariness and semanticity. Others argue for language abilities for dolphins and whales (Caldwell & Caldwell, 1976; Lilly, 1967) and dogs (Bloom, 2004). Whether we believe in animal language or not, we are left with an enormous respect for both the complexity and intelligence of animal behavior and the remarkable sophistication of human language.

MULTILINGUALISM

I speak two languages, Body and English.
Mae West

Multilingualism refers to proficiency in more than one language. More than half of the world's population is **bilingual,** or proficient in two languages (Snow, 1993).

Research into the effects of strokes and other types of brain damage in multilingual patients provides some fascinating insights into the way the brain manages multiple languages. Several variables contribute to the extent of language deficits following a stroke. The fluency or ease of use that the patient achieved in each language, the order in which languages were learned (simultaneous vs. sequential), and how recently a language has been used are all factors that contribute to the patient's outcome. Typically, researchers find that languages learned early in life and languages in which the patient is highly fluent are retained better after brain damage than languages learned later in life or with less fluency. If the patient is equally fluent in two languages, both are affected at about the same level. Holding fluency constant, a language learned at a younger age is retained better than one learned at an older age (Neville et al., 1998). These findings suggest that multiple languages use some of the same areas of the brain but that the degree of overlap is not 100 percent.

Imaging research using healthy participants confirms the observations of patients with known brain damage. Kim, Relkin, Lee, and Hirsch (1998) report that participants who learn multiple languages at early ages do not show much spatial separation between areas of the frontal and temporal cortex that respond to each language. However, "late" language learners show greater spatial separation between areas that process each language in frontal regions, including Broca's area. Perani et al. (1998) argue that proficiency, not necessarily age of acquisition, influences the cortical representation of language. If a speaker is equally proficient in two languages regardless of age of learning, the cortical representations for the languages will overlap to a greater extent than they do in a person who is much more proficient in one language than in another. Even when proficiency is held constant, we still might be able to detect a neural bilingual signature, or a difference in activity, that indicates that the speaker uses more than one language. Participants who were highly proficient, early learners

bilingual Proficient in two languages.

of English as a second language activated the same brain structures as monolingual English speakers, but showed greater activation of a portion of Broca's area (Kovelman, Baker, & Petitto, 2008).

If multiple languages have overlapping representations in the brain, how does the speaker keep them separated? This question has led to a search for the hypothetical "language switch." Hernandez, Martinez, and Kohnert (2000) used fMRI to investigate bilingual participants' reactions to picture-naming tasks. In a single-language task, participants were asked to name objects in one language only. In a mixed-language task, the participants were required to name objects in one of their languages or the other on different trials. During the mixed-language condition, reaction time was slower, and activation of the dorsolateral prefrontal cortex increased when compared with the single-language condition. The language switch might simply be a function of general executive attentional systems of the brain, managed in part by the dorsolateral prefrontal cortex, which is an area of cortex anterior and superior to Broca's area.

American Sign Language

American Sign Language (ASL) raises additional questions about the processing of language. ASL is a language not of sounds but of sight and movement. As such, ASL provides an interesting contrast between language functions, generally lateralized to the left hemisphere, and spatial functions, generally lateralized to the right hemisphere.

Antonio Damasio and his colleagues (Damasio, Bellugi, Damasio, Poizner, & Gilder, 1986) documented the case of a young ASL interpreter who had her right temporal lobe removed to control her seizures. During a Wada test prior to surgery, anesthetizing the left hemisphere produced a number of deficits in both spoken English and ASL signing. Subsequent surgery on the patient's right temporal lobe did not impair her ability to sign. In spite of the spatial nature of ASL, this case suggests that a language is still a language and that the left hemisphere is the likely place for that language to be processed. Damasio's clinical observations have been confirmed by fMRI studies. The same areas of the brain are activated during language tasks regardless of whether the person uses spoken English or ASL (Neville et al., 1998).

In an interesting twist, people who use ASL differ more from non-ASL users in their processing of human movement than in their processing of language (Corina et al., 2007). Hearing participants showed the same patterns of brain activity while watching a person drink from a cup, stretch, or use ASL, indicating the use of a single process for evaluating human movement. In contrast, deaf signers used different patterns of activity to distinguish between the linguistic movements of ASL and nonlinguistic movements.

Communication Disorders and Brain Mechanisms for Language

Earlier in the chapter, we saw how language perception was affected by the split-brain operation. Further clues to the localization of language function have been obtained from case studies of individuals who lose some aspects of language due to strokes or other types of brain damage.

Paul Broca and Patient Tan

You may recall reading in Chapter 2 about Broca's area, an area of cortex typically located in the left inferior frontal region adjacent to motor cortex that is believed to play a role in speech production. This area was named after Parisian physician Paul Broca, who made some of the earliest observations of the localization of language in the brain. In 1861, Broca began to study a 51-year-old man named Leborgne, who had been

American Sign Language (ASL) A language of signs, produced by the hands and arms, that is used by people with hearing impairments.

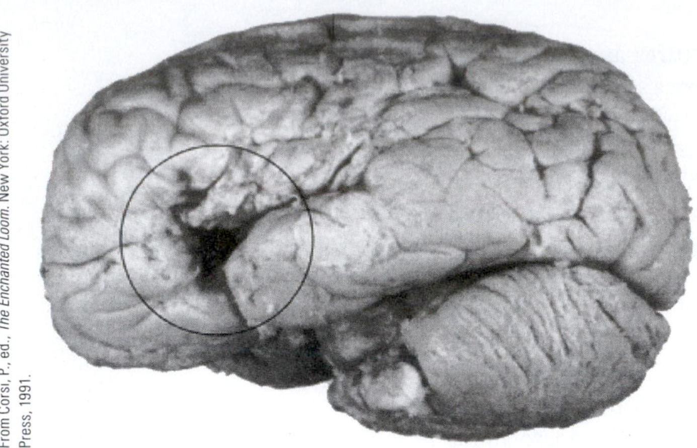

■ **Figure 13.11**
Patient Tan's Brain When Tan died, Paul Broca performed an autopsy and discovered severe damage of the left inferior frontal cortex, just anterior to the primary motor cortex. This area, which now bears Broca's name, is involved with the production of speech.

institutionalized for more than 20 years. Leborgne came to be referred to as "Tan" because when questioned, "tan" was one of a very few syllables he could produce. He apparently understood much of what was said to him, and he retained his ability to answer numerical questions by raising an appropriate number of fingers on his left hand (Herrnstein & Boring, 1965). Leborgne died shortly after Broca's examination of him, and Broca performed an autopsy on his patient's brain, shown in ■ Figure 13.11. Broca found significant damage to the patient's left inferior frontal region, which is believed to play a role in speech production. This area is now referred to as Broca's area in his honor.

Aphasias

An **aphasia** is defined as a total or partial loss of the ability to either produce or comprehend spoken language. Tan's aphasia resulted from brain damage caused by syphilis, but most modern aphasia results from strokes or head injuries. Careful observations of both language symptoms and areas of damage provide important insights into the localization of language. Modern researchers enjoy an advantage that Paul Broca would surely envy: with modern imaging technologies, it is not necessary to wait until the patient dies to determine which areas of the brain are damaged, and damage can be assessed much more accurately. Recently, Tan's preserved brain was imaged using high-resolution MRI (Dronkers, Plaisant, Iba-Zizen, & Cabanis, 2007). Tan's lesions extended more deeply into the brain than Broca had suspected, and the areas described by Broca differ somewhat from our current delineation of Broca's area.

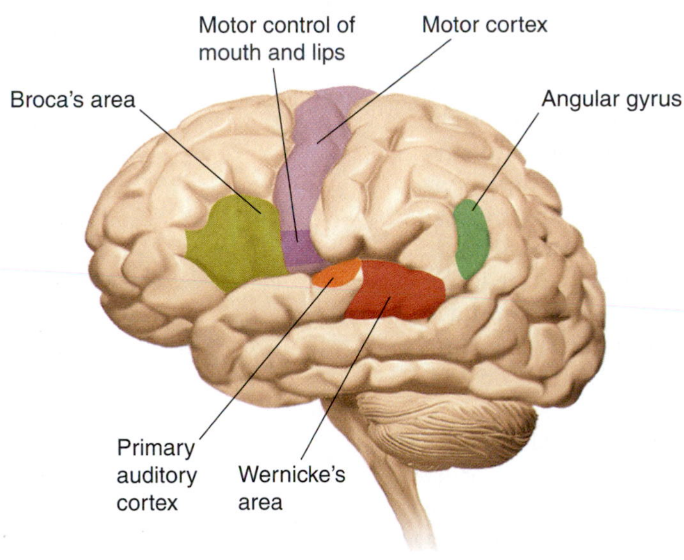

■ **Figure 13.12**
The Major Brain Structures Participating in Language

Broca's Aphasia Today, the symptoms of Broca's patient Tan are known as **Broca's aphasia,** or production aphasia. Damage in these cases affects Broca's area in the frontal lobe, along with associated subcortical regions. The locations of the major brain structures involved in language, including Broca's area, are illustrated in ■ Figure 13.12.

The primary symptom of Broca's aphasia is difficulty in producing speech. Speech is very slow and requires significant effort, and errors occur in the pronunciation of some speech sounds. Although the speech produced generally makes sense, many expected modifying words and word endings are omitted, giving a telegraphic quality to the speech. Adjectives, words such as *both* or *all*, and word endings such as *-s* or *-ed* are often lacking. Broca's aphasia patients also typically show **anomia,** a difficulty retrieving the correct words for the ideas they wish to express, and are unable to repeat complex sentences. In some cases, patients retain the ability to curse, as with Tan's *"Sacre nom de Dieu!"* ("In the name of God!"), which he uttered in frustration when unable to make himself understood with gestures.

Howard Gardner (1976) conducted an interview with a 39-year-old male patient with Broca's aphasia:

> "Why are you in the hospital, Mr. Ford?"
>
> Ford looked at me a bit strangely, as if to say, Isn't it patently obvious? He pointed to his paralyzed arm and said, "Arm no good," then to his mouth and said, "Speech . . . can't say . . . talk, you see." (p. 61)

Although the primary deficit in Broca's aphasia is the ability to speak clearly, comprehension is affected as well. Patients with Broca's aphasia struggle with the

aphasia (uh-FAY-zhuh) A condition involving the loss of the ability to speak or to understand language.
Broca's aphasia A condition marked by the production of slow, laborious speech accompanied by good comprehension, poor repetition, and poor naming.
anomia (uh-NO-mee-uh) A condition characterized by difficulties in finding the words needed to express thought.

meanings of sentences that depend on the same modifying words and endings that they often omit from their own speech. For example, Broca's patients would be unable to comprehend the sentence, "The boy that the girl is chasing is tall" (Dronkers, Pinker, & Damasio, 2000, p. 1177). Comprehension of this sentence depends on a person's ability to process "that" and "is chasing" accurately. Otherwise, a person might depend on word order only, and make incorrect assumptions about who is tall and who is chasing whom.

There is additional evidence that Broca's aphasia is more than a simple motor deficit affecting the production of speech. Broca's patients can still sing songs they know well. Their writing is generally about as good as their speech and shows many of the same errors and omissions. If the damage to Broca's area affected motor control of the vocal apparatus only, one would expect that patients' written communication would not show the same deficits as their speech.

Broca's area might participate in the maintenance of verbal short-term memory through rehearsal. Patients with Broca's aphasia are unable to identify grammatical errors when the salient elements are widely spaced in a sentence. For instance, Nina Dronkers and her colleagues (2000, p. 1179) point out that people with Broca's aphasia have no difficulty identifying the following sentence as ungrammatical: "John was finally kissed Louise." The verbal elements required to make the judgment appear near each other in the sentence (passive verb *was kissed* followed by object *Louise*). In contrast, the patients are unable to identify the following sentence as ungrammatical: "The woman is outside, isn't it?" The elements that don't agree grammatically, "woman" and "it," are separated by a "gap" in the sentence. Using PET scans, Dronkers and her colleagues showed that Broca's area is activated whenever participants must comprehend a sentence with a long gap between related elements of a sentence as opposed to sentences containing a shorter gap. The inability to bridge verbal gaps is consistent with the patterns of impairment in the production and comprehension of speech experienced by patients with Broca's aphasia.

He can compress the most words into the smallest ideas of any man I ever met.

Abraham Lincoln

Wernicke's Aphasia Shortly after Paul Broca presented his revolutionary work on patient Tan, Carl Wernicke published his observations on another type of language deficit (Wernicke, 1874). In honor of his contributions, this syndrome is now referred to as **Wernicke's aphasia,** and the affected area of the brain is known as **Wernicke's area** (see Figure 13.12). Wernicke's area is located on the superior surface of the temporal lobe, adjacent to structures involved with audition (see Chapter 7) and with memory (see Chapter 12).

The symptoms of Wernicke's aphasia are quite different from those of Broca's aphasia. In Broca's aphasia, speech is slow and laborious but generally meaningful. In Wernicke's aphasia, speech is rapid and fluent but virtually meaningless. Patients with Wernicke's aphasia seem totally unaware that they are not making sense, whereas patients with Broca's aphasia are typically frustrated by their inability to communicate.

Howard Gardner interviewed a patient, Mr. Gorgan, who had been diagnosed with Wernicke's aphasia (1976):

> "Thank you, Mr. Gorgan. I want to ask a few—"
>
> "Oh sure, go ahead, any old think you want. If I could I would. Oh, I'm taking the word the wrong way to say, all of the barbers here whenever they stop you it's going around and around, if you known what I mean, that is typing and tying for repucer, repuceration, well we were trying the best that we could while another time it was with the beds over the same thing . . ." (p. 68)

If you don't pay attention to the content, the speech of patients with Wernicke's aphasia sounds rather normal, if slightly fast. Grammar is generally correct, but there appears to be a complete lack of meaning. Substitutions of sounds (*think* for *thing* and *repuceration* for *recuperation* in Gardner's excerpt) are common. Neologisms, or made-up words, are also frequent. Mr. Gorgan tells Dr. Gardner (1976, p. 68), "I have to run around, look it over, trebbin and all that sort of stuff." Mr. Gorgan alone seems to know what "trebbin" might mean.

Wernicke's aphasia (VER-nik-eez) A condition in which speech is fluent, but comprehension, repetition, and naming are quite poor.

Wernicke's area An area of cortex adjacent to primary auditory cortex in the left hemisphere believed to be responsible for decoding speech sounds.

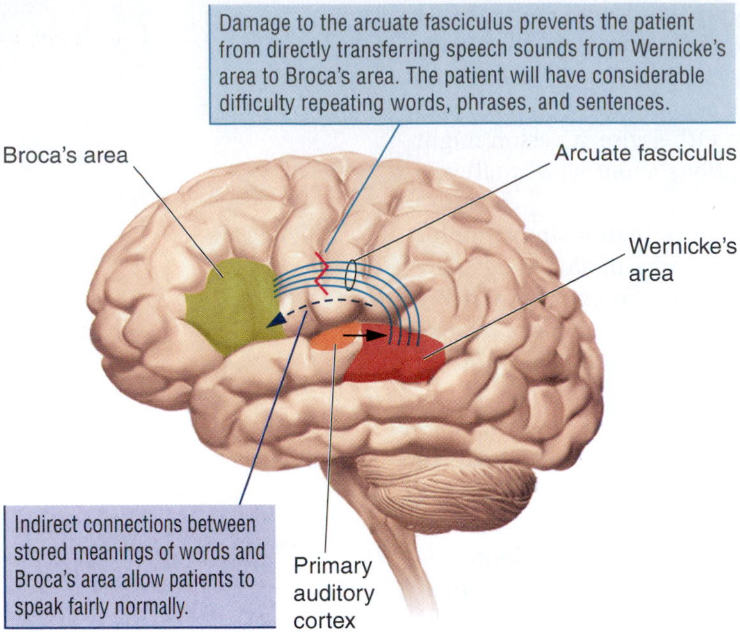

Damage to the arcuate fasciculus prevents the patient from directly transferring speech sounds from Wernicke's area to Broca's area. The patient will have considerable difficulty repeating words, phrases, and sentences.

Broca's area

Arcuate fasciculus

Wernicke's area

Indirect connections between stored meanings of words and Broca's area allow patients to speak fairly normally.

Primary auditory cortex

■ **FIGURE 13.13**
A Hypothetical Model of Conduction Aphasia Damage to the arcuate fasciculus and the adjacent cortex results in conduction aphasia. These patients retain most of their abilities to produce and comprehend speech but have significant difficulties repeating sentences they hear.

The major deficit in Wernicke's aphasia is comprehension, usually for both the written and spoken word. These patients can neither repeat nor understand words or sentences that they hear. They are completely locked into a world without linguistic connection to other people, yet they do not seem overly aware of their circumstances nor are they in any apparent distress.

Conduction Aphasia Wernicke correctly speculated that Broca's area and Wernicke's area must be intimately connected. A band of fibers known as the **arcuate fasciculus** connects the two areas. Furthermore, Wernicke believed that any compromise of this connection would produce a different type of aphasia from that seen in patients with either Broca's or Wernicke's aphasia. Once again, Wernicke was correct. Damage to the arcuate fasciculus and adjacent cortex, shown in ■ Figure 13.13, results in **conduction aphasia.**

In patients with conduction aphasia, speech remains fluent, and comprehension is fairly good. These patients are less impaired in language function than patients with either Wernicke's or Broca's aphasia. The nature of their aphasia becomes most obvious when they are asked to repeat a sentence, a task they find nearly impossible to do. They also struggle with a task known as "confrontation naming," in which they must verbally produce the names of pictures and objects. Finally, they seem to have difficulty assembling speech sounds into words, as shown by their frequent sound substitutions. It is common for these patients to say something like "treen" instead of "train." These symptoms probably result from impairments in the patients' ability to transfer information about speech sounds directly from Wernicke's area to Broca's area due to damage to the arcuate fasciculus.

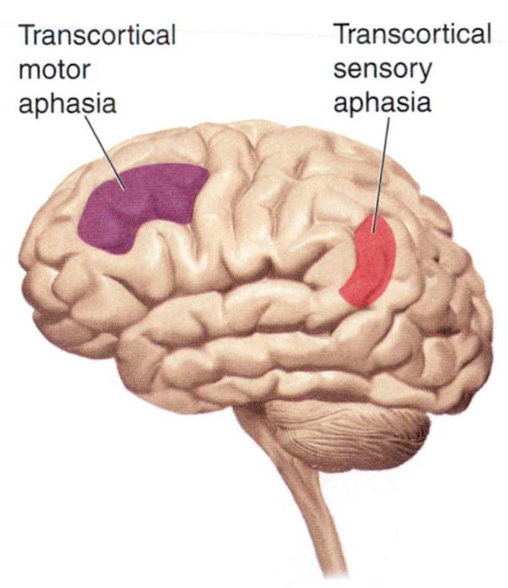

■ **FIGURE 13.14**
Structures Involved in Transcortical Aphasias

Global Aphasia In **global aphasia,** patients lose essentially all language functions. This condition combines all of the deficits of Broca's, Wernicke's, and conduction aphasia. Abilities to speak, comprehend, read, and write are impaired to some extent, depending on the amount of damage the patient has experienced. Most patients are still able to curse, count, say the days of the week, and sing familiar songs. Comprehension is typically limited to a very small set of words.

The amount of cortex damaged in global aphasia is substantial. Both Broca's and Wernicke's areas, as well as much of the cortex and white matter between them, are affected. Most cases of global aphasia are caused by damage to the middle cerebral artery, which serves the language centers of the left hemisphere (see Chapter 2).

Transcortical Aphasias The **transcortical aphasias** result from damage to connections and cortical areas associated with the major language centers. You might think of the transcortical aphasias as isolating the main language areas from other parts of the brain. Patients with transcortical aphasias share some features with patients with either Broca's or Wernicke's aphasia. However, they retain the ability to repeat words that is lacking in these other aphasias. In most cases of **transcortical motor aphasia,** damage occurs in the dorsolateral prefrontal cortex. In other cases, damage is found in the supplementary motor area (SMA), located adjacent to primary motor cortex in the frontal lobe (see Chapter 8). Damage to the cortex at the intersection of the temporal, parietal, and occipital lobes results in the condition of **transcortical sensory aphasia.** These areas are shown in ■ Figure 13.14.

As in cases of Broca's aphasia, patients with transcortical motor aphasia do not speak fluently. Unlike patients with Broca's aphasia, however, these patients are

arcuate fasciculus (AR-kew-ate fuh-SIK-you-luss) A pathway connecting Broca's area and Wernicke's area.

conduction aphasia A condition characterized by fluent speech and good comprehension but poor repetition and naming, believed to result from damage to the arcuate fasciculus and underlying structures.

capable of accurate repetition of complex sentences. The damaged areas are probably responsible for the initiation of speech (supplementary motor area) and the ongoing executive control of speech (dorsolateral prefrontal cortex). Earlier, we discussed a role for the dorsolateral prefrontal area in language switching among bilingual speakers. Additional insight into the normal function of the dorsolateral prefrontal cortex in language comes from PET scans. This area shows activation when participants are asked to produce verbs related to particular nouns, such as *drive* in response to *car* (Dronkers et al., 2001). Participants with transcortical motor aphasia fail at this task, although they can accurately use the same words in normal conversation. As a result, we can think of transcortical motor aphasia as affecting some of the higher cognitive and attentional functions related to language production.

In transcortical sensory aphasia, the connections between the language centers and the parts of the brain responsible for word meaning are disrupted. Patients retain fluent, grammatical speech, but their comprehension is impaired. They experience great difficulty in naming tasks, but their repetition performance is excellent. They can even repeat words from unfamiliar foreign languages. As a result, we can conclude that these deficits affect the patients' ability to understand the meaning of words, although basic processing at the levels of speech sounds and grammar are spared.

Don't you see the whole aim of Newspeak is to narrow the range of thought? In the end we shall make thought crime literally impossible, because there will be no words in which to express it.

George Orwell

Language Models Based on his clinical observations of patients with various aphasias, Carl Wernicke developed a classic model to explain and predict the effects of damage to various areas on language performance. Norman Geschwind (1972) further developed the model, which now bears the names of both men. The Wernicke-Geschwind model emphasized the connections between various speech- and language-processing areas in the brain. According to the model, Broca's area was responsible for speech production, whereas Wernicke's area was responsible for speech comprehension. The arcuate fasciculus was believed to be a one-way pathway connecting Wernicke's area to Broca's area. Although Wernicke's and Broca's areas were believed to communicate with association cortex, they were viewed as having the primary responsibility for decoding, or extracting the meaning from, verbal information.

Although the Wernicke-Geschwind model succeeded in predicting most of the symptoms associated with the various types of aphasia, it is not completely consistent with the wealth of data from modern imaging investigations of language in healthy participants. First, researchers now believe that information travels in two directions, not just one, between Broca's area and Wernicke's area via the arcuate fasciculus. Second, much larger areas of cortex appear to be involved in the processing of language. These areas include sizable chunks of the frontal, temporal, and parietal lobes as well as of the cingulate cortex, **insular cortex** (in the lateral fissure), and the basal ganglia.

A more current model, illustrated in ■ Figure 13.15, proposes three interacting language components (Dronkers, Pinker, & Damasio, 2000). The first is a language implementation system, made up of Broca's area, Wernicke's area, parts of the insular cortex, and the basal ganglia. This system decodes incoming verbal information and produces appropriate verbal responses. Surrounding this implementation system is a mediational system made up of association cortex in the temporal, parietal, and frontal lobes. This system manages communication between the implementation system and the final component, a conceptual system. This third and final system, which is responsible for managing semantic knowledge, is located in higher-level association cortex areas.

Disorders of Reading and Writing

Reading and writing developed relatively recently in human history, probably at some point in the past 5,000 to 6,000 years. Unlike spoken language, people do not learn reading and writing simply through exposure. Once learned, however, these functions also appear to be localized in the brain.

global aphasia A condition in which all language functions are lost, including both language production and comprehension.

transcortical aphasia A language disorder resulting from damage to the connections and cortical areas associated with the major language centers.

transcortical motor aphasia A condition in which language is not fluent, but the ability to repeat is retained.

transcortical sensory aphasia A condition in which comprehension is poor, but the ability to repeat is retained.

insular cortex An area of cortex found with the lateral fissure separating the frontal and temporal lobes.

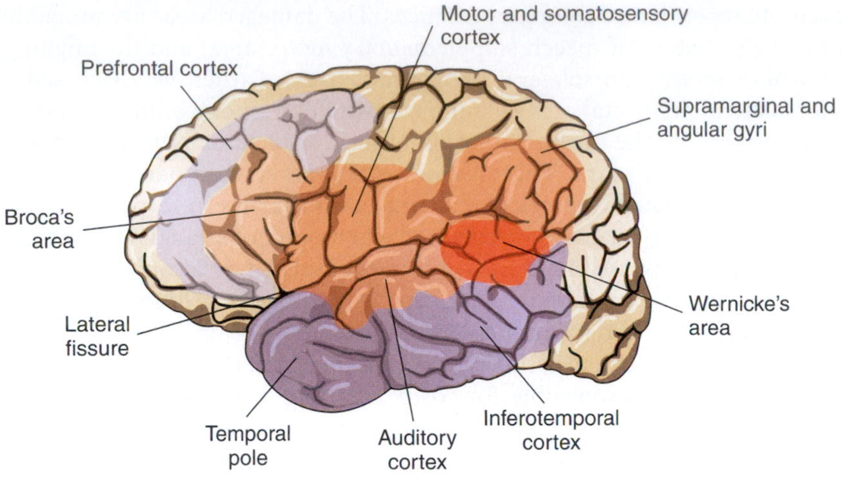

■ **FIGURE 13.15 Language Involves Large Areas of Cortex** Language functions can be divided into three systems. An implementation system, here in shades of orange, decodes language and produces appropriate verbal responses. In addition to the structures shown here, the implementation system includes the basal ganglia and the insular cortex, which lies at the margin of the frontal and temporal lobes within the lateral fissure. A mediational system, shown here in shades of blue, includes areas of association cortex. The mediational system forms a bridge between the implementation system and the third language system, a conceptual system that includes higher-order association areas more widely distributed across the cortex. *Source:* Adapted from Dronkers, Pinker, and Damasio, 2000.

Alexia and Agraphia Deficits can occur in either reading **(alexia)** or writing **(agraphia)** or in both. For most people, reading and writing are localized in the same hemisphere as speech. Reading and writing are typically impaired in most cases of aphasia.

Patients with alexia, or pure word blindness, speak and understand normally but are unable to read or to point to words and letters on command (Geschwind, 1970). Patients retain the ability to recognize words that are spelled out loud to them. Alexia is correlated with damage to two related areas of the brain, the left occipital cortex and the corpus callosum. Damage to the left occipital cortex appears to affect patients' ability to perceive visually both words and word-like shapes (Petersen, Fox, Snyder, & Raichle, 1990). Damage to the corpus callosum prevents transfer of information from the intact right hemisphere visual cortex to the left hemisphere language areas.

One type of agraphia, or the inability to write, results from damage to the motor areas responsible for making skilled movements. Other types of agraphia affect spelling. Patients with **phonological agraphia** are unable to sound out new words or nonsense words. They are able to write familiar words, however, probably through visual imagery. Phonological agraphia occurs in response to damage in the left posterior superior temporal gyrus (near Wernicke's area; Kim, Chu, Lee, Kim, & Park, 2002). Patients with **orthographic agraphia** can spell only phonetically. As a result, they experience great difficulty with words that are not particularly phonetic, such as *rough* or *through.* The exact brain areas involved with orthographic agraphia are unknown, but the condition is frequently observed in patients with dementia (Glosser, Grugan, & Friedman, 1999; Tainturier, Moreaud, David, Leek, & Pellat, 2001).

Dyslexia **Dyslexia** refers to an unexpected difficulty in reading fluently in spite of normal intelligence and exposure to normal teaching methods and is the most common form of learning disability (Shaywitz, Morris, & Shaywitz, 2008). The first patient with dyslexia appearing in the medical literature, Percy F., was described by his physician as "quick at games, and in no way inferior to others of his age. His great difficulty has been ... his inability to learn to read" (Shaywitz, 1996, p. 98). Estimates for the prevalence of dyslexia range from about 10 to 30 percent of the population. Earlier reports of sex differences in dyslexia (e.g., Tallal, 1991) might have exaggerated the differences between boys and girls. Boys are still somewhat more likely to have dyslexia but are more likely than girls to be referred for remedial services due to their more frequent disruptive behaviors (Shaywitz et al., 2008). Famous individuals who probably had dyslexia include Walt Disney, Winston Churchill, and Albert Einstein.

Dyslexia is strongly influenced by genetics. A parent with dyslexia has a 23 to 65 percent chance of producing a child with dyslexia, and 40 percent of the siblings of a child with dyslexia will also have the disorder (Gilger, Hanebuth, Smith, & Pennington, 1996). The genetics of dyslexia are complex, as shown by the greater

phonological agraphia The inability to write by sounding out words.

orthographic agraphia A condition in which a person can spell phonetically but experiences difficulty spelling words that are spelled irregularly, such as *rough.*

dyslexia A condition characterized by difficulty learning to read in spite of normal intelligence and exposure to standard instruction.

phonological awareness The ability to discriminate between rapidly presented speech sounds.

angular gyrus A region of the parietal lobe believed to participate in language and cognition.

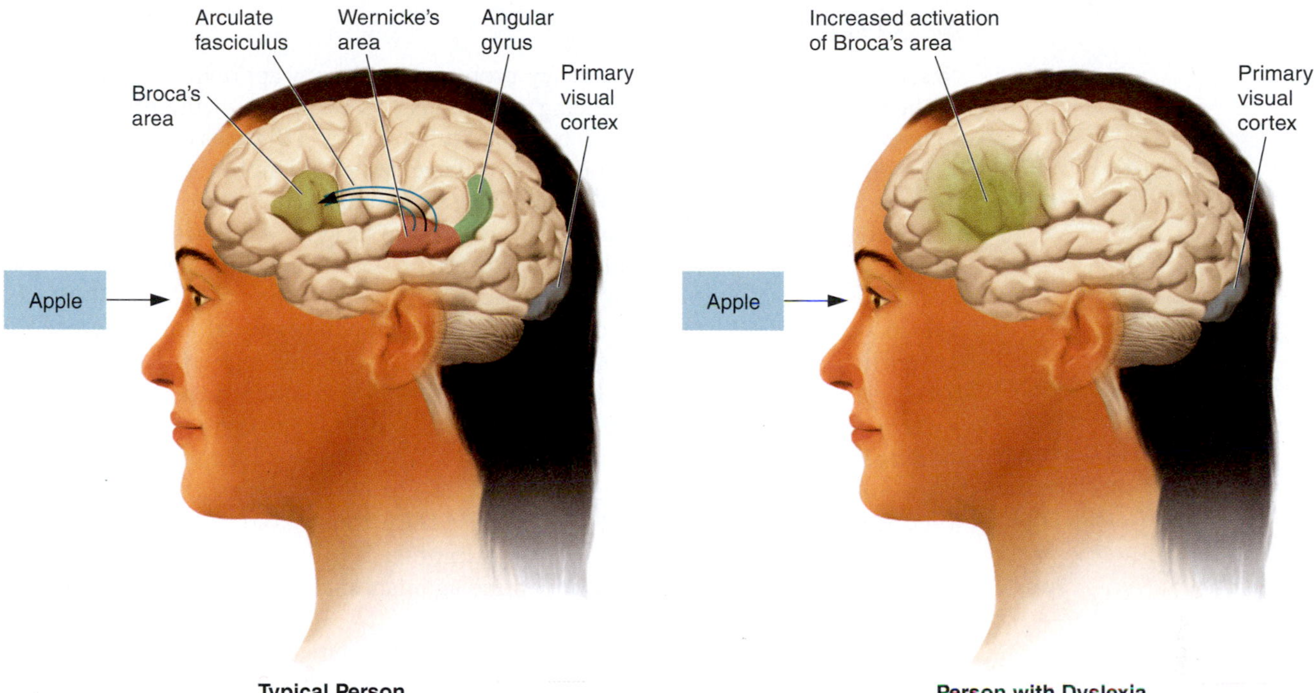

FIGURE 13.16
Dyslexia Affects Brain Activation During Reading Compared with typical readers, people with dyslexia show little activation of the angular gyrus and Wernicke's area and increased activation of Broca's area while reading.

heritability of dyslexia among individuals with higher IQs (Olson et al., 1999). However, in spite of the heavy genetic influences on dyslexia, children with this condition benefit substantially from remedial treatment begun prior to the third grade (Shaywitz et al., 2008).

Anatomical features of dyslexia include differences in hemispheric symmetry. The left planum temporale is usually larger in people whose language functions are located in the left hemisphere. Most researchers report less difference between the right and left planum temporale in participants with dyslexia (Beaton, 1997; Galaburda, Sherman, Rosen, Aboitiz, & Geschwind, 1985). People with dyslexia are slightly more likely to be left-handed or ambidextrous than people without dyslexia (Eglinton & Annett, 1994).

Most cases of dyslexia involve poor **phonological awareness,** or the ability to discriminate verbal information at the level of speech sounds, or phonemes, as evidenced by their difficulties with words that rhyme. During a rhyming task, control participants activated Broca's area, Wernicke's area, and the insular cortex (Frith & Frith, 1996). Participants with dyslexia, however, activated Broca's area alone. Dyslexia is also associated with difficulties in processing rapidly presented stimuli. Individuals with dyslexia seem to process speech sounds (Merzenich et al, 1996) and visual information more slowly than typical control participants (Dronkers et al., 2001). In addition, some individuals with dyslexia experience spatial problems, leading to reversals of letters such as *b* and *d*.

Overactivation of anterior language areas, including Broca's area, coupled with a lack of activation of posterior language areas, including Wernicke's area and the **angular gyrus,** occurs during reading by participants with dyslexia (Shaywitz et al., 1998). As shown in ■ Figure 13.16, typical readers pass information from the visual cortex along the angular gyrus to Wernicke's area, with only slight activation of Broca's area. In readers with dyslexia, the posterior language areas are hardly used at all. Instead, there is a much greater activation in the anterior language areas. Greater understanding of the processes underlying dyslexia has the potential to lead to more effective remedial strategies.

stutter To abnormally repeat or prolong speech sounds when speaking.

Stuttering

Nearly all children experience fluency problems. However, approximately 1 percent of the population **stutters,** producing repetitions (*wa wa want*) or the prolonging of sounds (*n-ah-ah-ah-ow*). Children begin to stutter between the ages of two and seven years, with a peak onset at about five years of age. Males are more than three times as likely as females to stutter (American Psychiatric Association, 2000).

Stuttering appears to be primarily genetic in origin (Andrews, Morris-Yates, Howie, & Martin, 1991). Adults who stutter process some language in the right hemisphere (De Nil, 1999; Van Borsel, Achten, Santens, Lahorte, & Voet, 2003). As a result, both hemispheres try to control the vocal apparatus simultaneously, leading to conflict. This conflict is resolved to some extent when the stuttering person sings because singing activates right-hemisphere areas that are not otherwise involved in speech (Jeffries, Fritz, & Braun, 2003). Imaging studies also suggest that abnormal activity in the basal ganglia and midbrain motor structures might be responsible for stuttering (Brown, Ingham, Ingham, Laird, & Fox, 2005; Giraud et al., 2008; Watkins, Smith, Davis, & Howell, 2008). Because these motor systems use dopamine as their major neurotransmitter, stuttering is improved by dopamine antagonists, such as haloperidol, and worsened by dopamine agonists such as l-dopa (levodopa; Watkins et al., 2008).

To judge well, to comprehend well, to reason well. These are the essential activities of intelligence.
A. Binet, T. Simon

Current treatments for stuttering center on reducing the rate at which speech is produced and on the stress usually associated with the disorder. Other therapy programs involve the use of software programs that teach people to use special breathing techniques, soft voice onsets, and the prolongation of syllables (Giraud et al., 2008). Giraud and her colleagues also noted that these therapies normalized the abnormal basal ganglia and midbrain activity observed during stuttering.

INTERIM SUMMARY 13.2

Summary Table: The Major Aphasias

Type of Aphasia	Location of Damage	Ability to Produce Speech	Ability to Comprehend Meaning of Spoken Words	Does Person Exhibit Paraphasia (Sound Substitutions)?	Ability to Repeat Spoken Words Accurately	Ability to Name Objects
Broca's aphasia	Broca's area	Not fluent	Good	Not common	Poor	Poor
Wernicke's aphasia	Wernicke's area	Fluent	Poor	Common	Poor	Poor
Conduction aphasia	Arcuate fasciculus	Fluent	Good	Common	Poor	Poor
Global aphasia	Broca's area, Wernicke's area, and the arcuate fasciculus	Not fluent	Poor	Variable	Poor	Poor
Transcortical motor aphasia	Supplementary motor area, cortex adjacent to Broca's area	Not fluent	Good	Common	Good	Poor
Transcortical sensory aphasia	Cortex at the junction of temporal, parietal, and occipital lobes	Fluent	Poor	Common	Good	Poor

(continued)

INTERIM SUMMARY 13.2 (continued)

Summary Points

1. The evolution of language might have occurred as early humans formed cooperative societies and shared tool-making skills. **(LO4)**
2. Nonhuman animals clearly communicate, but controversy remains as to whether nonhuman animals truly possess the ability to use language. **(LO5)**
3. In spite of the spatial nature of ASL, research evidence suggests that it is processed by the left hemisphere like other languages. **(LO6)**
4. The clinical study of aphasias, alexias, and agraphias has helped identify the major areas of the brain involved with the comprehension and production of language. **(LO7)**
5. Dyslexia and stuttering are developmental disorders in which an otherwise intelligent person experiences difficulty learning to read (dyslexia) or to articulate clearly (stuttering) when exposed to standard experience and instruction. **(LO7)**

Review Questions

1. How does the brain manage more than one language?
2. What does ASL teach us about the localization of language in the brain?

Intelligence

Sternberg and Salter (1982, p. 3) have defined **intelligence** as our ability to engage in "goal-directed adaptive behavior." In other words, intelligence reflects our ability to learn and solve problems.

Assessing Intelligence

Interest in assessing intelligence arose from compulsory education laws passed during the nineteenth and early twentieth centuries. In 1904, Alfred Binet was charged by the French government with devising an objective means to identify the potential of schoolchildren. Binet and his colleague, Théodore Simon, assumed that relatively bright children behaved cognitively like older children, whereas less intelligent children would behave like younger children. They devised items that they believed would indicate a child's "mental age" or "intelligence quotient" (IQ). Stanford professor Lewis Terman (1916) adapted Binet's test for use in the United States and named his revised version the Stanford-Binet.

The IQ tests used today, such as the Wechsler Adult Intelligence Scale-Revised (WAIS-R) or the Stanford-Binet, are structured in such a way that the results fall along a statistically normal curve. The average IQ score is 100, with a standard deviation of 15. Normal distributions follow a "68-95-99.7" rule. In other words, 68 percent of the population falls within one standard deviation of the mean, or in the case of IQ, between 85 and 115. Only 5 percent of the population will have IQs that are more than two standard deviations away from the mean (below 70 or above 130), and only 0.3 percent will be more than three standard deviations from the mean (below 55 or above 145). The table for Interim Summary 13.3 provides a breakdown of the approximate percentage of the population found within different ranges of IQ scores.

General or Specific Abilities

Psychologists are unable to agree on whether intelligence comprises a single underlying ability or some combination of separate abilities. Charles Spearman proposed

WHY DOES THIS MATTER?

Enhancing Intellect

What if we were able to make people smarter? Although such a concept might appear far-fetched, we already may be in the middle of such an experiment. Worldwide, IQ has increased at a rate of about three IQ points per decade over the past 100 years (Dickens & Flynn, 2001). Among the proposed explanations for this increase include better nutrition (Colom, Lluis-Font, & Andrés-Pueyo, 2005), smaller families, greater parental involvement with children's intellectual development, more experience with testing, and increased cultural complexity.

Although most of us see few ethical dilemmas regarding the enhancement of cognitive performance in cases of medical conditions or psychological disorders, enhancing the intellectual performance of healthy, typical individuals is trickier. Once again, this is not just a hypothetical scenario. Up to 16 percent of students on some college campuses use methylphenidate (Ritalin) to improve academic performance without having been diagnosed with attention deficit/hyperactivity disorder (AD/HD) (Farah et al., 2004).

As we learn more about the function of the brain, including its features correlated with intelligent behavior, we will inevitably encounter ethical dilemmas that are reminiscent of those faced by elite athletes and performance-enhancing drugs. Can a drug-free individual compete? Will enhancements be distributed in an equitable way? Some of the answers may be found in our existing efforts to better ourselves, whether we seek out tutoring or attempt to follow a healthy diet (Farah et al., 2004).

a **general intelligence (g) factor.** In Spearman's view, all intelligent behavior arises from a single trait. Other psychologists are not so sure. Savant behaviors illustrate how certain abilities can be separated from others. Children with Williams syndrome, mentioned earlier in the chapter, generally score in the range of mental retardation on intelligence tests, yet their verbal skills are quite good. Some athletes have exceptional physical skills but struggle to read. Howard Gardner (1983) interprets these and similar findings to mean that we have multiple, independent types of intelligence.

It is likely that both approaches are true to some extent. We seem to have separate abilities for different types of behavior. However, enough of these abilities are typically correlated within individuals to provide some support for Spearman's idea of a general intelligence factor.

Intelligence and Genetics

How much of our intelligence is determined by our genes? Estimates of the heritability of intelligence range from 60 percent (Snyderman & Rothman, 1987) to about 80 percent (Jensen, 1998). This means that scientists expect that anywhere from 60 to 80 percent of the variation in intelligence among humans can be attributed to genetic factors. It absolutely does *not* mean that 60 to 80 percent of an individual's intelligence is determined by his or her genes with the environment determining the remainder (see Chapter 5).

Most research attempting to segment genetic and environmental influences on intelligence has used comparisons between identical (monozygotic) and fraternal (dizygotic) twins (see Chapters 1 and 5). Thompson et al. (2001) used MRI to create three-dimensional maps of human gray matter. Cortical thickness and volume of gray matter are highly correlated with a measure of cognitive ability (Narr et al., 2007, Thompson et al., 2001). As shown in ■ Figure 13.17, monozygotic twins display a .95 correlation in the volume of gray matter (a 1.0 correlation would mean the twins had identical gray matter). The volume of gray matter in monozygotic twins was especially similar in the frontal lobe and language areas. Comparisons to dizygotic twins suggest that genes influence gray matter volume, which in turn is associated with cognitive ability.

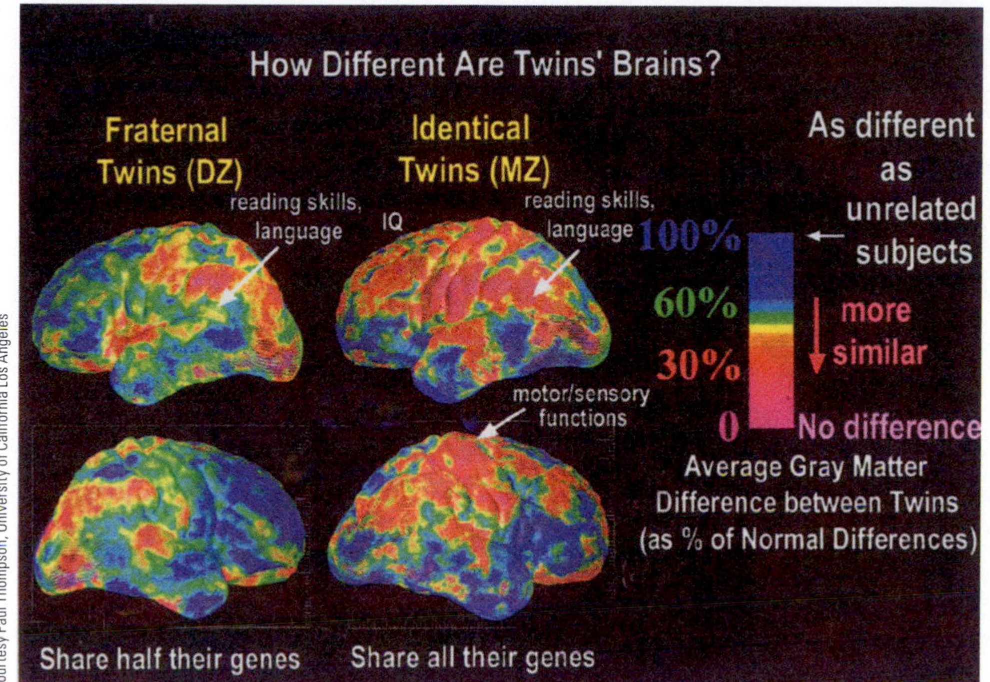

Courtesy Paul Thompson, University of California Los Angeles

FIGURE 13.17
Mass of Gray Matter Correlates with Intelligence and Heredity
Paul Thompson and his colleagues used MRI to measure the gray matter of dizygotic (fraternal) and monozygotic (identical) twins. These researchers concluded that the amount of gray matter in the brains of the identical twins was nearly the same, especially in the frontal lobe and language areas. Their findings suggest a strong association between genetics, brain structure, and some measures of cognitive function.

Although many genes have been identified as responsible for mental retardation, genes associated specifically with high intelligence have been far more elusive. It is likely that a large number of genes are involved in intelligence, each having a relatively small effect. For example, Robert Plomin and his colleagues (Plomin et al., 2004) report a 1.5-point difference in IQ resulting from a single gene.

Genetics and environment typically combine in complex ways to influence intelligence, as illustrated by studies of the effects of breastfeeding on IQ. As a group, children who are breastfed have higher IQs than those who are not, and this result persists into adulthood (Caspi et al., 2007). However, the gain produced by breastfeeding interacts with genetics. Individuals with one form of a gene involved with the metabolism of fatty acids show no IQ benefit from breastfeeding, whereas those with another form of the gene gain as much as seven IQ points when breastfed compared to those with the same genotype who are not breastfed (Caspi et al., 2007).

There are no great limits to growth because there are no limits of human intelligence, imagination, and wonder.
Ronald Reagan

Biological Correlates of Intelligence

How might the brains of highly intelligent people be different from those of more average people? Gray matter volume and cortical thickness in prefrontal and temporal association areas of the brain are highly correlated with intellectual ability (Narr et al., 2007). To less extent, intellect is associated with white matter volume as well.

Dahlia Zaidel (2001) examined slides made from Albert Einstein's brain after he died in 1955 at the age of 76. Zaidel noted that the neurons in Einstein's left hippocampus were much larger than neurons in the right hippocampus. She found this structural asymmetry to be quite different from the brains of ten control participants with normal intelligence. Zaidel admits that it is not known whether this structural difference is at all related to Einstein's genius, but the participation of the hippocampus in memory makes Zaidel's observations quite intriguing. Sandra Witelson and her colleagues (Witelson, Kigar, & Harvey, 1999) found another apparent abnormality in Einstein's brain. Einstein's inferior parietal lobe, an area believed to be related to mathematical and abstract reasoning, was about 15 percent larger than comparable areas in the brains of control participants.

INTERIM SUMMARY 13.3

Summary Table: Distribution of IQ Scores

IQ Score	Population with This Score (%)	Characteristics
130 or above	2	Gifted (academics should be easily mastered)
115–129	14	Above average (above-average academic performance)
85–114	68	Average (average academic performance)
70–84	14	Below average (average to poor academic performance)
50–69	1.7	Mild mental retardation (can learn academic skills up to sixth grade)
35–49	0.2	Moderate mental retardation (can learn academic skills up to second grade)
20–34	0.08	Severe mental retardation (can learn to talk and to perform supervised work)
Below 20	less than 0.02	Profound mental retardation (requires constant supervision)

Summary Points

1. Psychologists do not agree on whether intelligence is a single entity or a combination of multiple abilities. **(LO9)**
2. Estimates of the heritability of intelligence vary widely, from 60 percent to 80 percent. **(LO10)**
3. A possible correlate of intelligence is the amount of gray matter in the brain, particularly in the frontal lobe and language areas. **(LO10)**

Review Question

1. Which structural features in the brain might be correlated with intelligence?

CHAPTER REVIEW

THOUGHT QUESTIONS

1. Some linguists believe that we will go from having thousands of languages worldwide to fewer than a dozen within 100 years. What might be the implications of such a rapid change?
2. What might be the advantages to an animal of localizing functions to one hemisphere of the brain as opposed to distributing the functions over both hemispheres?
3. If being nonright-handed is associated with higher rates of learning disability and immune disease, why do you think nonright-handedness is maintained in the population?
4. We identify people with math and verbal difficulties as being learning disabled. Why don't we also have terms such as musically disabled or athletically disabled?

KEY TERMS

alexia (p. 394)
agraphia (p. 394)
Broca's aphasia (p. 390)
conduction aphasia (p. 392)
dyslexia (p. 394)
general intelligence (g) factor (p. 398)
global aphasia (p. 392)
intelligence (p. 396)
lateralization (p. 376)
orthographic agraphia (p. 394)
phonological agraphia (p. 394)
phonological awareness (p. 395)
prosody (p. 382)
savant behavior (p. 374)
split-brain operation (p. 377)
stutter (p. 396)
transcortical aphasia (p. 392)
transcortical motor aphasia (p. 392)
transcortical sensory aphasia (p. 392)
Wernicke's aphasia (p. 391)

14

Emotion, Reward, Aggression, and Stress

BananaStock/Fotosearch

▲ **The Face of Emotion** Humans in every culture express their emotions primarily through their faces.

CHAPTER OUTLINE

Introduction

One of the most troubling aspects of human behavior is our propensity for harming others of our own kind. Contemporary estimates suggest that 1,000 people a day are killed in local wars around the world (Miller, 2003). Be reassured that we have made some progress. In ancient societies, as many as one quarter of all men were killed in warfare (LeBlanc, 2003). Even with 50 million people killed in World War II alone, modern humans have not approached that 25 percent mark.

Is human violence part of our biological nature, or do we learn to be violent? Consider the ongoing debate regarding violence in video games. After playing a violent game (*Wolfenstein 3D*) or a nonviolent game (*Myst*), college students had the opportunity to punish an opponent with a noise blast of varying intensity (Anderson & Dill, 2000). Those who had played the violent game administered longer noise blasts than those who had played the nonviolent game. At least in the short term, playing a violent game appeared to increase an aggressive behavior. Others argue that the issue is far more complex. Girls, but not boys, played more aggressively with toys after either playing or watching someone else play a violent video game (Cooper & Mackie, 1986). This puzzle is representative of the complex issues surrounding the emotional life of human beings. Are emotions innate or learned? Are emotions enhanced or reduced through expression or observation? Painstaking research is starting to provide insights into these questions.

LEARNING OBJECTIVES

After reading this chapter, you should be able to:

LO1 Describe the major features and purposes of emotion.

LO2 Summarize the contributions of biology and learning to emotional expression.

LO3 Compare and contrast the James-Lange, Cannon-Bard, and Schachter-Singer theories of emotion, and summarize contemporary theories of emotion.

LO4 Identify the nervous system structures involved in emotion.

LO5 Identify areas of the brain involved with feelings of reward and pleasure.

LO6 Explain the possible roles of genetics, brain damage, and biochemistry in aggression.

LO7 Describe the major physical and psychological responses to stress.

Emotion

Whether we're feeling sad, scared, or euphoric, an **emotion** has two major components: a physical sensation, such as a rapid heartbeat, and a conscious, subjective experience or feeling, such as feeling scared. Emotions typically demonstrate **valence,** or a generally positive or negative quality.

The Evolution of Emotion

Charles Darwin (1872) made a careful study of the facial expressions produced by humans and other primates and concluded that emotional expression must have evolved. Because evolution implies beneficial change, we might ask how emotions improved our ancestors' chances of survival. One possible advantage of emotions is their contribution to general arousal. When the brain perceives a situation requiring action, emotions provide the arousal needed to trigger a response. As discussed in Chapter 12, Robert Yerkes and Donald Dodson (1908) observed that arousal interacts with the complexity of a task to predict performance (see Chapter 12, Figure 12.28). For simple tasks, such as outrunning a predator, greater arousal tends to lead to superior performance. For more complex tasks, however, we see deficits in performance when arousal levels are too high. Many of us have had the experience of performing badly on a difficult exam because we are too stressed or anxious.

In addition to contributing to general arousal, emotions manage our approach and withdrawal behaviors relative to particular environmental stimuli (Davidson & Irwin, 1999). The positive emotions associated with eating contribute to our seeking food when we are hungry, and the negative emotions elicited by observing a large snake or rotting food lead to avoidance, providing obvious advantages for survival.

In addition to contributing to general arousal and approach/avoidance behaviors, emotions also enhance survival by helping us communicate. **Nonverbal communication,** consisting of facial expression and body language, provides an important source of social information. For example, body expressions of fear, illustrated in ■ Figure 14.1, communicate important information in an immediate, arousing, and contagious manner (de Gelder, Snyder, Greve, Gerard, & Hadjikhani, 2004).

Expression and Recognition of Emotion

Human adults usually express and interpret emotions accurately. In one experiment, observers accurately judged whether or not a teacher liked an off-camera student after watching only 10 seconds of a videotaped interaction (Babad, Bernieri, & Rosenthal, 1991). We might believe that we can hide our feelings, but the subtleties of emotional expression often give us away.

Controlling Facial Expression Although we use our whole bodies to express emotion, humans pay the most attention to the face, in particular to the eyes

emotion A combination of physical sensations and the conscious experience of a feeling.

valence A positive (attractive) or negative (aversive) reaction to an object or event.

nonverbal communication The use of facial expressions, gestures, and body language to communicate ideas and feelings.

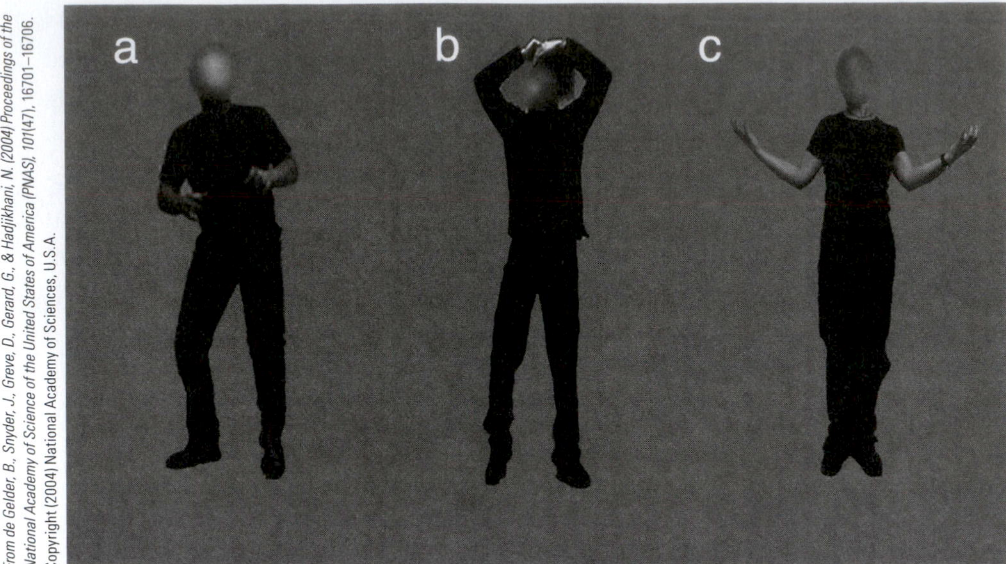

FIGURE 14.1 Emotional Expression Helps Us Communicate Viewing full-body expressions of fear (a), compared to neutral (b) and happy (c) postures, produced strong, immediate activity in brain areas associated with the processing of fearful stimuli and the preparation of responses such as flight. Fearful postures, therefore, are likely to have had significant survival benefits to humans because the need to flee could be communicated rapidly to others without verbal explanation.

(Adolphs, 2007). Early in development, human infants prefer gazing at faces rather than at other types of visual stimuli.

Movement of the human face is controlled by two cranial nerves, the facial nerve (cranial nerve VII) and the trigeminal nerve (cranial nerve V). The facial nerve controls the superficial muscles attached to the skin, which are primarily responsible for facial expressions. The trigeminal nerve controls the deeper facial muscles attached to the bones of the head that are responsible for chewing food and speaking.

The facial nerve has five major branches, with each branch serving a different portion of the face. As shown in Figure 14.2, the facial nerves originate in the two **facial nuclei** located on either side of the midline in the pons. These nuclei do not communicate directly with each other. As we will see later in the chapter, this organization makes it possible for emotional expression to vary in intensity from one half

FIGURE 14.2 Innervation of the Facial Muscles

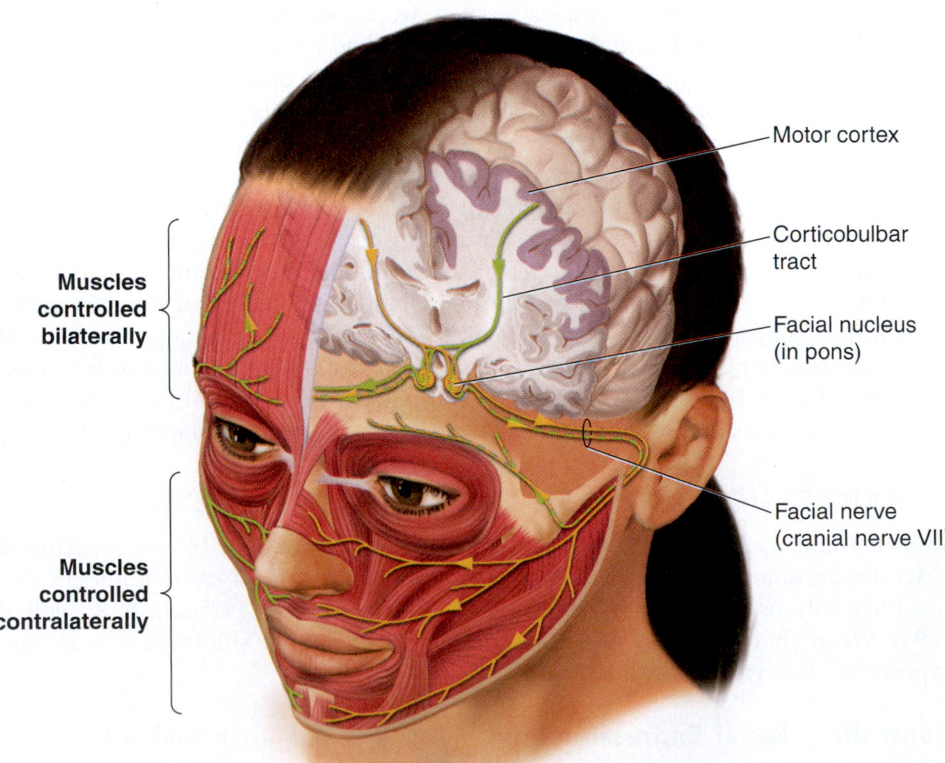

facial nucleus One of two cranial nerve nuclei, located at the level of the pons, that control the facial nerves.

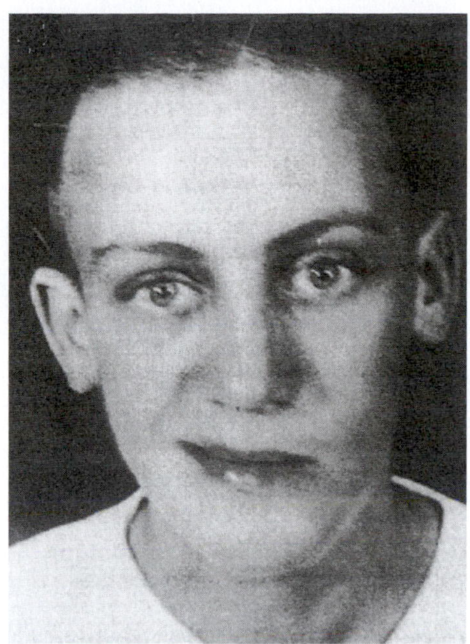
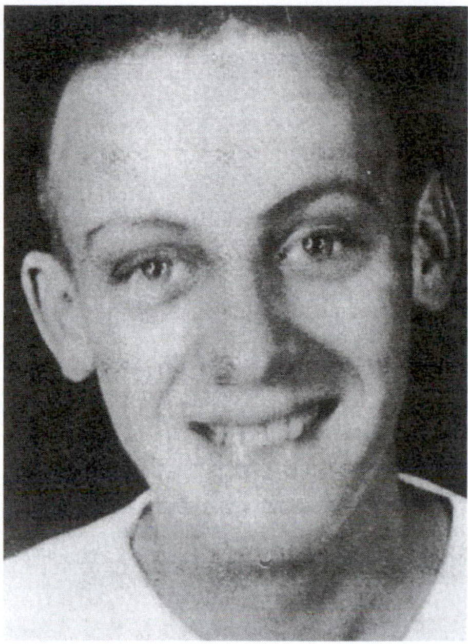

■ **FIGURE 14.3**
Voluntary and Spontaneous Expressions Are Managed by Different Areas of the Brain
This man has a tumor in his right primary motor cortex that prevents him from voluntarily smiling on the left side of his face when asked to do so, as shown in the photo on the left. In contrast, he is able to smile spontaneously in response to a genuine, involuntary emotion, as shown in the photo on the right. These observations suggest that voluntary and spontaneous emotional expressions are mediated by different areas of the brain.

of the face to the other. The facial nuclei receive input from the primary motor cortex located in the precentral gyrus of the frontal lobe as well as from several subcortical motor areas.

The upper third of the face is controlled differently than the lower two thirds (Koff, Borod, & Strauss, 1985; Rinn, 1984). The upper third of the face receives input from both the ipsilateral and contralateral facial nerves, whereas the lower two thirds of the face are controlled primarily by the contralateral facial nerve. When a person suffers damage to the motor cortex of one hemisphere, there is relatively little impact on the muscle tone of the upper face, which continues to receive ipsilateral input from the healthy hemisphere. However, the contralateral lower face will be paralyzed and will appear to sag.

The computer can't tell you the emotional story. It can give you the exact mathematical design, but what's missing is the eyebrows.

Frank Zappa

Two major pathways control facial expression (Morecraft, Louie, Herrick, & Stilwell-Morecraft, 2001). One involves input from the motor cortex and is primarily responsible for voluntary expression. The second is a subcortical system that is primarily responsible for spontaneous expression. We all know that the smiles we make for our driver's license pictures look different from the spontaneous smiles a photographer catches in a candid photo. People with damage to the primary motor cortex, such as the young man shown in ■ Figure 14.3, are unable to smile on command on the side of the mouth contralateral to their damage. However, when they hear a good joke, they can show some spontaneous smiling on the otherwise paralyzed side of the face. This condition is known as volitional (voluntary) facial paresis (paralysis) because the ability to express voluntary emotion is impaired. In contrast, people with Parkinson's disease, which involves subcortical motor structures including the substantia nigra and basal ganglia (see Chapters 2 and 8), lose the ability to smile spontaneously while retaining the ability to smile on command. This condition is referred to as emotional facial paresis because the ability to express spontaneous emotions is impaired.

Biological Influences on Emotional Expression Darwin assumed that emotional expression had a strong biological basis. Supporting that view, some major emotional expressions appear to be universal across human cultures (Keltner & Ekman, 2000). These expressions include anger, sadness, happiness, fear, disgust, surprise, contempt, and embarrassment. Most people, regardless of culture, have little difficulty identifying the major emotional expressions shown in ■ Figure 14.4.

Several other lines of reasoning support Darwin's view. Children's capacities for emotional expression and recognition develop according to a fairly regular timeline, with relatively little influence by experience. Infants who are blind from birth show

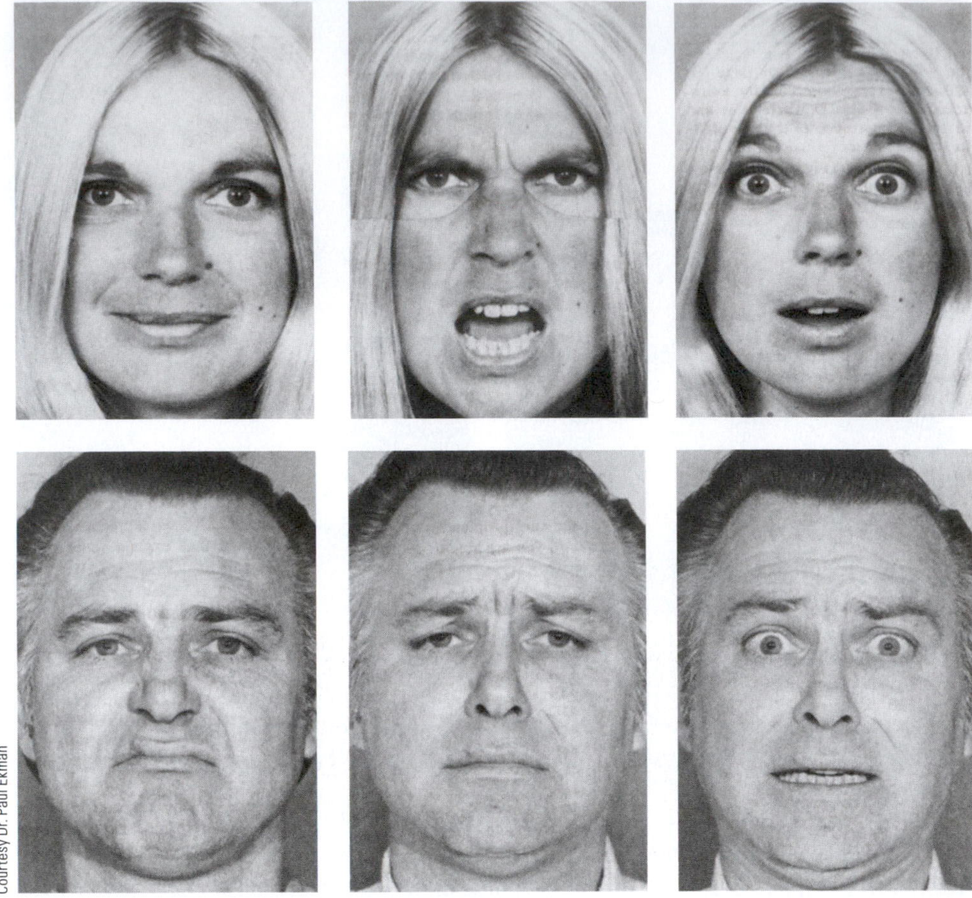

FIGURE 14.4 Major Facial Expressions Are Easily Recognized Around the World These photos represent the possibly universal expressions of happiness, anger, surprise, disgust, sadness, and fear.

a progression in the development of social smiling that is similar to that of sighted infants, in spite of being unable to learn by observing others (Freedman, 1964). Monozygotic (identical) twins are more similar than dizygotic (fraternal) twins in the age at which they begin to show fear of strangers (Freedman, 1974). As shown in Figure 14.5, children raised in several diverse cultures showed similar age-related emotional responses to being separated from their mothers (Kagan, Kearsley, & Zelazo, 1978). Consistent timelines for the development of emotional expression and recognition also characterize nonhuman primate development. Rhesus monkeys raised in isolation still showed fear of pictures of other monkeys engaged in threatening behaviors. The development of their fear response was about the same as that of monkeys raised in normal social circumstances (Sackett, 1966).

Environmental Influences on Emotion Although our basic emotional responses seem largely innate, the influences of culture and learning modify emotional expression. For example, medical doctors undergo training to withhold emotions, such as disgust, that would be inappropriate to express to patients.

The presence of other people often influences the intensity of emotional expression. People make more intense facial expressions in response to odors when in a group as opposed to when they are alone (Jancke & Kaufmann, 1994). Japanese students watching an emotional film alone were more expressive than when they watched with unfamiliar peers. In contrast, the emotional expression of American students did not vary significantly depending on whether they viewed the film alone or in a group (Ekman, Friesen, & Ellsworth, 1972).

The picture emerging is one of innate, genetically determined emotional responses that immediately come under the influence of social and environmental feedback. Blind babies exhibit social smiles at about the same age as sighted infants (around the age of three months), but by adulthood, differences in emotional expression have emerged. Congenitally blind adults show the same numbers and

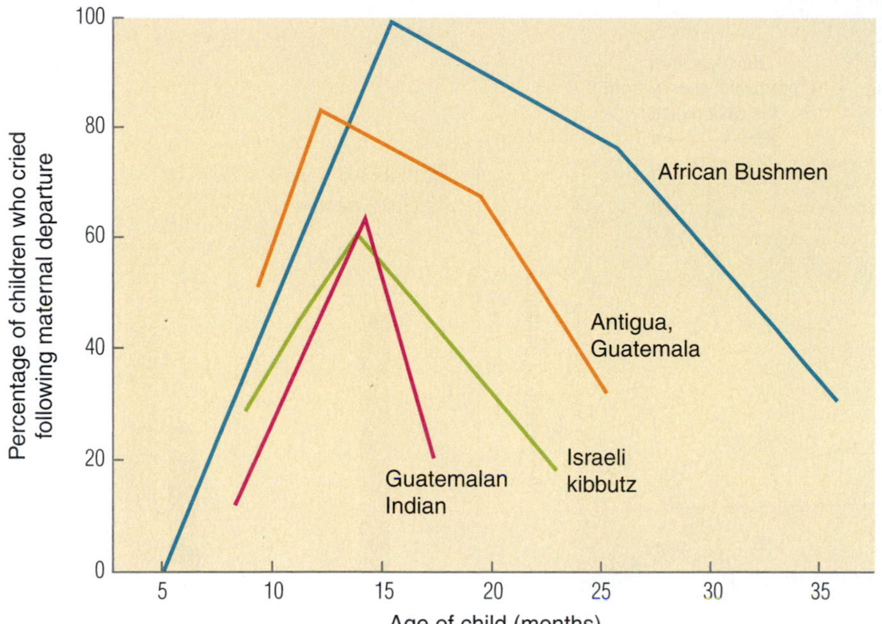

■ **FIGURE 14.5**
Infants' Separation Protests Occur at the Same Times Regardless of Culture Children in diverse cultures show the greatest emotional reactions to separation from their mothers at approximately the same stage in development, suggesting that this emotional behavior has a biological origin.

types of facial expressions as sighted adults. However, observers have more difficulty interpreting their expressions, with the interesting exception of happiness, perhaps the ultimate universal emotion (Galati, Scherer, & Ricci-Bitti, 1997).

The emotions aren't always immediately subject to reason, but they are always immediately subject to action.
William James

Individual Differences in Emotion Individuals are quite different from one another in their overall levels of emotional reactivity. Jerome Kagan (1997) found that newborn infants showed consistent levels of reactivity to an unpleasant odor. Infants who are highly reactive to environmental stimuli are at greater risk for anxiety and mood disorders later in life. Extremely low-reactive infants have a greater tendency toward antisocial behavior. A study of psychopaths incarcerated for murder indicated that these men responded much less than control participants to slides of pleasant, neutral, and unpleasant situations (Herpertz et al., 2001). Individuals also vary in their overall emotional style, or positive or negative emotional tendencies (Davidson & Irwin, 1999).

One source of these individual differences appears to be the amygdala, which plays a crucial role in the interpretation of emotional stimuli. Individuals with major depressive disorder (see Chapter 16) show higher levels of activity in the amygdala than participants without any mood disorder (Abercrombie et al., 1998; Drevets et al., 2002; Drevets et al., 1992). When participants are shown photographs designed to elicit negative or neutral moods, those with higher amygdala activity in response to viewing negative photos also reported more negative mood (Irwin et al., 2004).

Can We Spot a Liar? In spite of our usually reliable ability to recognize emotions, we often find ourselves victimized by liars. Paul Ekman (1996) suggests that deliberate lying is difficult because it requires a great deal of short-term memory (see Chapter 12). As a result, people who are deliberately lying slip in predictable ways. The normally articulate person stumbles verbally, adding "um"s and "uh"s as he or she struggles to assemble a plausible lie. People who are lying tend to stiffen the head and upper body. They nod their heads less frequently and do not use hand gestures as much as when they're telling the truth. Inappropriate smiling and laughing can result from the nervousness caused by lying. In contrast to the stiffer upper body, the feet begin swinging. In the United States, lack of eye contact is interpreted as a sign of dishonesty, but in many other cultures, eye contact is viewed as an impolite expression of dominance.

Let's not forget that the little emotions are the great captains of our lives and we obey them without realizing it.
Vincent Van Gogh

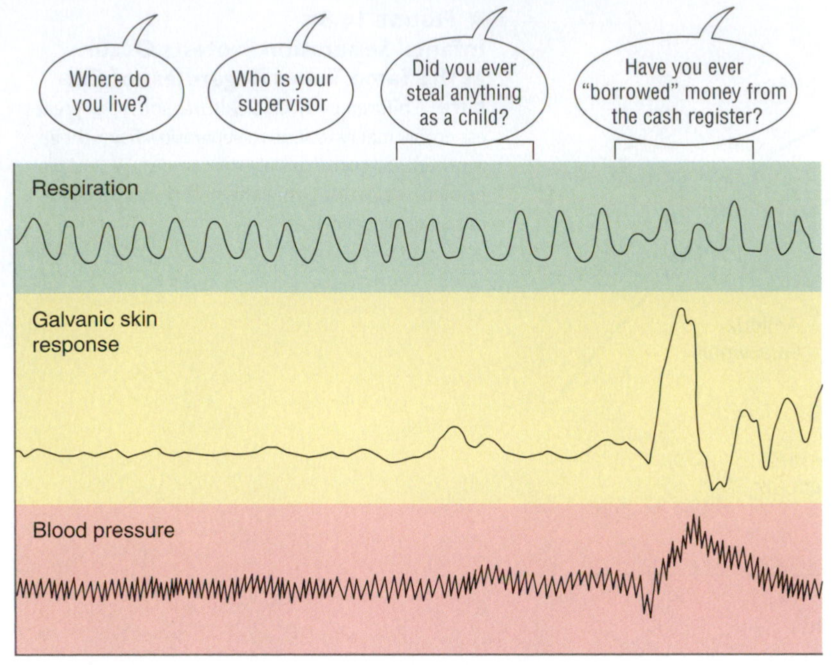

(a) Sample Questions and Responses

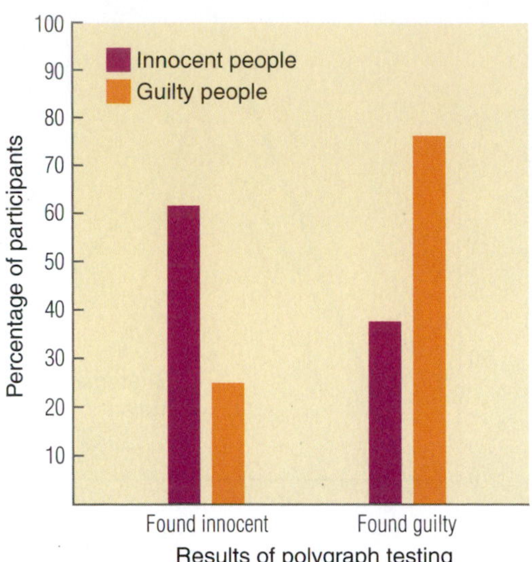

(b) Inaccuracies of Polygraph Testing

Figure 14.6
Polygraph Testing (a) Autonomic measures including respiration, galvanic skin response (an arousal measure using the electrical conductance of the skin), and blood pressure are taken during a series of neutral and emotional questions. (b) In Kleinmuntz and Szucko's experiment using polygraph tests, a panel of "experts" concluded that more than a third of the innocent participants were guilty, whereas a quarter of the guilty were judged to be innocent. *Source:* Adapted from Kleinmuntz & Szucko, 1984.

Polygraph, or lie-detector, tests are widely used by both law enforcement and employers, in spite of their unreliability (Holden, 1986). In one study, illustrated in Figure 14.6, a panel of experts evaluated polygraph data and declared a third of the innocent people to be guilty, whereas a quarter of the guilty were deemed to be innocent (Kleinmuntz & Szucko, 1984). Polygraph data reflect arousal, and an innocent person might be aroused out of fear of being accused. The general lack of arousal often found in antisocial people, along with their failure to see lying as morally wrong, allows many to appear innocent. Because of these inaccuracies, polygraph results are typically not admitted to courtrooms in the United States.

New technologies might soon provide more accurate means of assessing honesty. Functional MRIs may be used in the future to detect changes in brain activation during lying (Spence, Kaylor-Hughes, Farrow, & Wilkinson, 2008; Holden, 2001). In a process known as "brain fingerprinting," EEG recordings are used to determine recognition of crime scene evidence (Farwell, 2002). Although still very much in an experimental stage, the Iowa Supreme Court admitted brain fingerprinting as evidence in a murder case decided in 2003. The timing of responses might indicate truthfulness, with faster responding associated with telling the truth and slower responses indicating a lie (Gregg, 2007). Although we obviously desire the most accurate means of assessing honesty in legal proceedings, these technologies raise significant privacy and other ethical concerns ("Neuroethics needed," 2006).

Theories of Emotion

In our original definition, we noted two components of emotion: a physiological experience and a conscious, subjective experience or feeling. Three classic theories have attempted to characterize the relationships between these components.

polygraph A lie-detector test based on measures of autonomic arousal.

■ **FIGURE 14.7**
The Capilano Canyon Bridge
Dutton and Aron (1974) found that men walking across this bridge were much more likely to be attracted to the female interviewer than men walking on a much safer bridge upstream. Apparently, it was difficult for the men to distinguish between the emotions of fear and sexual arousal.

The James-Lange Theory Both William James (1890) and Danish physiologist Carl Lange (1885/1912) independently developed similar theories. Consequently, the **James-Lange theory** bears the names of both men. This theory suggests that a sequence of events results in an emotional experience. An awareness of our physical state leads to the identification of a subjective feeling. The theory assumes that physical states related to each type of feeling (sadness and happiness, for instance) are highly distinct from one another and that we are capable of correctly labeling these distinct physical states as separate feelings. As James explained, "we feel sorry because we cry, angry because we strike, afraid because we tremble" (1890, p. 1066).

An interesting test of the James-Lange theory involved the behavior of young single men who visited Capilano Canyon in British Columbia (Dutton & Aron, 1974). Capilano Canyon is spanned by a 450-foot-long bridge with low handrails, suspended about 230 feet above rocks and rapids. An attractive female researcher interviewed one half of the participants in the middle of the bridge, shown in ■ Figure 14.7, and the other half on a solid wooden bridge upstream that was not nearly so frightening. Men crossing the swaying bridge made up stories during their interview that were much more sexual in content than men crossing the "safe" bridge. In addition, the men on the swaying bridge were four times as likely to telephone the female researcher later on. Because men were not randomly assigned to bridges, it is possible that more adventurous men were both more likely to use the swaying bridge and to be bolder in pursuing the attractive female. However, the usual interpretation of this experiment is that we do not do a very good job of discriminating between fear and sexual arousal. This might account for the popularity of taking dates to horror films and amusement parks with impossibly high roller coasters, but it also suggests that we are not as accurate in identifying our physical states as required by the James-Lange theory.

Keep your fears to yourself, but share your courage with others.
Robert Louis Stevenson

A variation of the James-Lange theory is the suggestion that our facial expressions affect the way we feel (Izard, 1972, 1977). Intentionally making facial movements can stimulate physical responses that are quite similar to spontaneous emotional expression (Levenson, Ekman, & Friesen, 1990). When participants were instructed to move their faces in a particular way (raise your eyebrows, etc.) without seeing their own faces or knowing they were modeling a particular emotion, they reported feeling the emotions they portrayed. These results have some useful practical implications. If people are feeling depressed or angry, engaging in activities that elicit smiling or laughing might help lift their moods. William James (1890, p. 1066), who battled depression throughout his adult life, gave the following advice: "To feel cheerful, sit

James-Lange theory A theory of emotion in which a person's physical state provides cues for the identification of an emotional state.

Focus New Zealand Photo Library/© Reuters/CORBIS

Figure 14.8
Expressing an Emotion Heightens Feelings The New Zealand All Blacks, a rugby team, prepare for competition by borrowing moves from the Maori *haka*. By displaying fierce facial expressions and body movements, both warriors and rugby players get in the mood for battle.

up cheerfully, look around cheerfully, and act as if cheerfulness were already there." A dramatic use of emotional expression to induce a particular state is the Maori *haka*, shown in Figure 14.8. Traditional Maori warriors preparing for battle engaged in stereotyped grimaces, vocalizations, and battle moves. A contemporary rugby team, the New Zealand All Blacks, uses hakas to prepare for games. Not only does this aid in their mental and physical preparation for the game ("psyching up"), but it no doubt intimidates the opposing team as well.

Imitating the facial expressions of others might contribute to **empathy,** the ability to understand another person's feelings. The early back-and-forth imitation of facial expressions that adults do with infants possibly signifies the beginning of this important capacity. The writer Edgar Allan Poe was apparently aware of the role of mimicry in judging the feelings of others:

> When I wish to find out how wise or how stupid or how good or how wicked is anyone, or what are his thoughts at the moment, I fashion the expression of my face, as accurately as possible, in accordance with the expression of his, and then wait to see what thoughts or sentiments arise in my mind or heart, as if to match or correspond with the expression. (From "The Purloined Letter," 1845, as quoted in Levenson et al., 1990.)

Levenson and Ruef (1992) confirmed Poe's observations by showing that people are most accurate in assessing the emotions of another person when their own emotions match those of the person they are observing.

The idea that the expression of an emotion increases its intensity might seem counterintuitive to you. Our commonsense notion is that having a good cry should make us feel better. People frequently believe that holding anger inside will somehow make it worse. Many of these ideas originate with the concept of **catharsis,** or "purging." The idea of catharsis dates back to Aristotle and has been promoted by psychoanalyst Sigmund Freud and ethologist Konrad Lorenz, among others. According to catharsis theory, emotions are viewed as filling a reservoir. When the reservoir is full, the emotions will "overflow," emptying the person of that emotion. Catharsis theorists recommend that people "let it all hang out" by expressing their emotions (Kennedy-Moore & Watson, 1999). Obviously, the research we reviewed in this

empathy The ability to relate to the feelings of another person.
catharsis The relief of tension through the expression of emotion.

WHY DOES THIS MATTER?

Anger Management

For much of our human history, anger has promoted survival by arousing us to action in times of threat or danger. However, controlling anger matters because it can be a very expensive emotion in terms of energy expenditure and the potential harm we might do. What are the best ways to manage this powerful emotion?

Psychologists studying anger management suggest a number of strategies. Simply relaxing by using deep breathing techniques can be helpful in diffusing tension. Cognitive restructuring, or the use of logic to reconsider provoking situations, is often helpful. Honking your horn and making obscene gestures will not solve traffic jams, whereas recognizing that traffic jams are a typical part of modern city living reduces irritation. When anger occurs in interpersonal situations, efforts to empathize with the other person, acknowledging his or her point of view, can be very helpful. An angry confrontation usually takes more than one person, and it is difficult to be angry with somebody who is doing his or her best to see things your way. If you are at fault in a situation, avoid making excuses. Once again, it is very difficult to stay angry with someone who says, "I'm very sorry. I made a mistake." Some situations that produce justifiable anger, such as working for a biased supervisor, are best resolved by changing your environment, perhaps by looking for a better job or asking for a transfer to another department. Finally, people who can find the humor in the frequently ridiculous nature of human anger, such as getting upset over a parking place, typically have fewer problems with anger management. Note that none of these recommended strategies involve catharsis, or acting out your anger.

We cannot get rid of anger completely, nor should we want to do so, but practicing some of these techniques should help us avoid many of its negative outcomes.

section indicates otherwise. Expressing an emotion is more likely to enhance than reduce your feelings (Bushman, 2002; Tavris, 1989).

The Cannon-Bard Theory The James-Lange theory was extensively criticized by Walter Cannon (1927), who proposed his own theory, later modified by Philip Bard (1934). The end product is known as the **Cannon-Bard theory**. Whereas the James-Lange theory proposes a sequence of events, from physical response to subjective feeling, the Cannon-Bard theory proposes that both the subjective and physical responses occur simultaneously and independently.

Holding on to anger is like grasping a hot coal with the intent of throwing it at someone else; you are the one who gets burned.

Gautama Buddha

How are these theories different? Let's assume that you are innocently reading your textbook when a bear walks in the door of your room. According to the James-Lange theory, the sight of the bear would immediately set off physical responses that the brain would then interpret as fear. In the Cannon-Bard theory, the sight of the bear would immediately and simultaneously trigger an independent, subjective feeling of fear and the physiological fight-or-flight response. According to the Cannon-Bard theory, the central nervous system has the ability to produce an emotion directly, without needing feedback from the peripheral nervous system.

The Schachter-Singer Theory Like the James-Lange theory, the **Schachter-Singer theory** (Schachter & Singer, 1962; Sinclair, Hoffman, Mark, Martin, & Pickering, 1994) assumes that emotions result from a sequence of events. However, unlike the James-Lange theory, the Schachter-Singer theory does not require a specific set of physical responses for each emotion. Instead, a stimulus first produces general arousal. Once aroused, we make a conscious, cognitive appraisal of our circumstances, which allows us to identify our subjective feelings. Arousal might lead to several interpretations, based on the way a person assesses his or her situation. Fans of two basketball teams watching the same game respond to the final score with very different emotions. Returning to our example of the bear entering your room, Schachter and Singer would predict that the sight of the bear would initiate general arousal. To identify the source of your arousal, you would assess your situation, attribute your arousal to the presence of a bear in your room, and identify your subjective feelings as fear.

Cannon-Bard theory A theory of emotion in which the simultaneous activation of physical responses and the recognition of subjective feelings occur independently.

Schachter-Singer theory A theory of emotion in which general arousal leads to cognitive assessment of the context, which in turn leads to the identification of an emotional state.

One direct test of the Schachter-Singer theory involved injecting participants with epinephrine (adrenalin), which produces symptoms of physical arousal (Schachter & Singer, 1962). Participants were told that they were getting an injection of a vitamin and that their vision would be tested as soon as another person arrived to participate in the experiment. The other person was actually an actor employed by the researchers. In half of the trials, the actor behaved in a happy, silly manner, whereas in the other half, he acted angry and stomped out of the room. Participants who had received epinephrine and were exposed to the happy actor rated themselves as feeling happy, whereas participants exposed to the angry actor felt angry. Importantly, when the participants were accurately informed beforehand that they were getting a drug that would produce physiological arousal, the behavior of the actor did not influence their assessment of their emotions.

The Schachter-Singer theory accounts for many of the previously mentioned observations, including the results of the swaying-bridge study. Once aroused by being on the bridge, the male participants assessed their circumstances and attributed their feelings to sexual arousal. A weakness of the Schachter-Singer theory is the assumption that physiological states are not uniquely associated with specific emotions. Many emotional states appear to be associated with distinct patterns of physiological arousal (Levenson et al., 1990).

■ Figure 14.9 shows a comparison of the James-Lange, Cannon-Bard, and Schachter-Singer theories. Each of these classic theories offers important insights into our experience of emotion, yet none definitively resolves our question regarding the relationship of physical and subjective experiences.

Contemporary Theories of Emotion Contemporary theorists note that physical responses associated with an emotion may range from quite specific to quite ambiguous (Cacioppo, Berntson, & Klein, 1992). For example, the physical sensations associated with disgust may be more precise than the physical sensations associated with pride. Emotional stimuli can produce overlapping physical responses such as anger or fear. The initial specificity of the physical response leads to different pathways and cognitive responses. A highly specific physical response leads to unambiguous recognition by the cerebral cortex in the manner proposed by James and Lange. At the other extreme, the least differentiated physical signals will produce general arousal, which will require significant cognitive processing and

■ **FIGURE 14.9**
Three Theories of Emotion

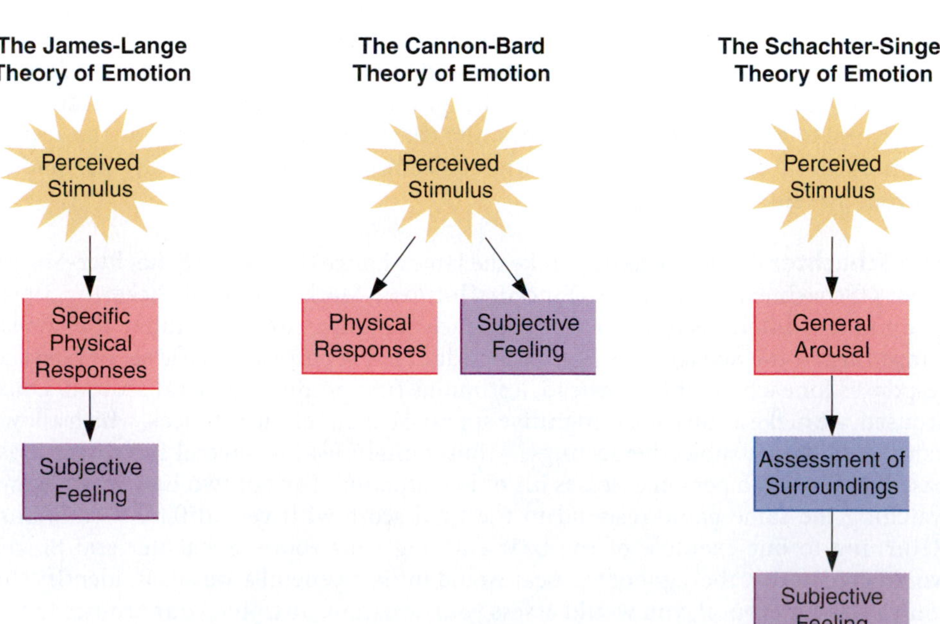

evaluation in a manner consistent with the Schachter-Singer theory. This model correctly predicts that emotional responses may range from immediate to delayed, based on the amount of cognitive processing that is required (Cacioppo, Berntson, Larsen, Poehlmann, & Ito, 2000).

Clinical observations of people whose emotions are impacted by neurological damage provide the basis for yet another view of emotion (Bechara, Damasio, & Damasio, 2000; Damasio, 1994). According to this approach, a stimulus is processed by the sensory cortex if it is immediately present, or by the hippocampus if the stimulus is remembered. Next, these areas activate structures involved with emotion such as the brainstem, hypothalamus, and amygdala. Consequently, messages are sent to the autonomic nervous system and to higher levels of the brain. The somatosensory cortex encodes this entire pattern of experience as a **somatic marker.** The ventromedial prefrontal cortex, in turn, forms associations between somatic markers and facts about the situations that elicited them. On future occasions, should those same circumstances reappear, the brain would then reactivate the appropriate somatic marker. Somatic markers provide a way for the brain to map features of the external world in terms of the changes they stimulate in the body, coloring situations as positive or negative. Patients with damage to the frontal lobes can easily describe graphic images of sex and violence that they are shown, but they are unable to tap into the somatic markers that would provide them with normal emotional responses to these stimuli (Bechara et al., 2000).

Biological Correlates of Emotion

Emotional states are accompanied by complex, interacting physical responses that usually combine activation of the autonomic nervous system, the amygdala, the cingulate cortex, and the cerebral cortex.

I don't need to manufacture trauma in my life to be creative. I have a big enough reservoir of sadness or emotional trauma to last me.

Sting

The Autonomic Nervous System The autonomic nervous system (ANS), which controls many activities of our organs and glands, participates in the general arousal associated with emotional states. The sympathetic division of the ANS is responsible for our fight-or-flight response, whereas the parasympathetic division participates in resting activities such as the digestion of food and the repair of body tissues. The ANS answers primarily to the hypothalamus, either directly or by way of the nucleus of the solitary tract, a structure located in the medulla that receives input from the hypothalamus and participates in the control of the autonomic nervous system.

Some measures of autonomic function, such as heart rate, finger temperature, skin conductance, and muscle activity, appear to produce different patterns during different emotional states (Levenson et al., 1990). However, the degree and reliability of such differences remains in dispute. Cacioppo, Berntson, Larsen, Poehlmann, and Ito (2000) reviewed research conducted from the 1950s until the present and found that attempts to link autonomic measures with specific emotions were largely inconclusive. General differences, such as the correlation of autonomic measures and positive or negative emotions, are clear. Autonomic responses associated with negative emotions generally appear to be stronger than those associated with positive emotions. However, determining differences in autonomic correlates between two positive states (such as happiness and hope) or between two negative states (such as anger and fear) is far more difficult.

The Amygdala Heinrich Klüver and Paul Bucy (1939) removed both temporal lobes in rhesus monkeys. Following recovery, the previously difficult-to-handle rhesus monkeys were much tamer, and their emotions were far less intense. They seemed oblivious to normally fear-producing stimuli. They approached snakes repeatedly, even after being attacked, and allowed themselves to be picked up and stroked (something you definitely don't want to try with a normal adult rhesus). Their nonemotional behavior changed as well. They now explored objects by placing them in their mouths, and their sexual behavior became much more frequent and inappropriate. They were

somatic marker An association formed between stimuli and resulting patterns of physical activation.

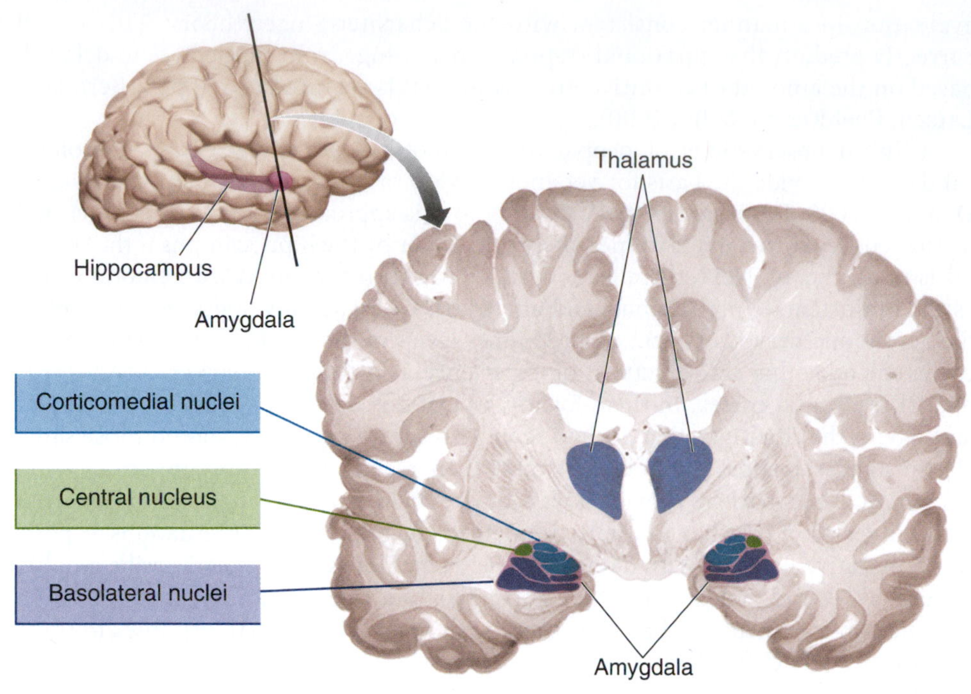

FIGURE 14.10
The Anatomy of the Amygdala
The amygdala, which is located at the anterior tip of each temporal lobe just below the cortex on the medial side, is a complex collection of nuclei that can be divided into three clusters: the basolateral nuclei, the corticomedial nuclei, and the central nucleus.

overly reactive to visual stimuli yet failed to recognize familiar objects. This set of symptoms, whether observed in monkeys or in humans, collectively became known as **Klüver-Bucy syndrome.**

What accounts for the emotional changes seen in Klüver and Bucy's monkeys? The evidence points to the amygdala. Because of the complexity of the amygdala, it is overly simplistic to describe it as a unitary structure with a single function. As shown in Figure 14.10, it is composed of three clusters of nuclei. Different parts of the amygdala participate in a wide variety of processes, including emotion, reward, motivation, learning, memory, and attention (Murray, 2007). We discussed the contributions of the amygdala to learning and memory in Chapter 12.

The amygdala receives information from many areas of the neocortex, especially sensory cortex, from the cingulate cortex and from the hippocampus. In turn, the amygdala projects widely to numerous areas of the brain, including the frontal and temporal lobes of the cortex, the olfactory bulb and cortex, the basal ganglia, the hypothalamus, and the nucleus accumbens.

Extending the findings of Klüver and Bucy, experimental data from studies in which the amygdala is lesioned support a role for this structure in both the identification and expression of emotion. Bilateral damage to the amygdala usually produces reduced emotionality. Fear, anxiety, and aggression appear to be particularly reduced. Following selective lesions in both amygdalas, rhesus monkeys are more likely to engage in social interactions with unfamiliar monkeys, which is normally a very dangerous thing to do in the strictly enforced social hierarchy that characterizes rhesus groups (Emery et al., 2001). Intact monkeys will show great reluctance to reach across a fake snake to retrieve a food reward, but monkeys with lesioned amygdalas show little or no reaction to a fake snake (Izquierdo, Suda, & Murray, 2005; Murray, 2007; Murray & Izquierdo, 2007).

Studies of human participants with amygdala damage parallel these animal results. Patient S. M., whose amygdalas were destroyed by a condition known as Urbach-Wiethe disease, was asked to draw pictures that represented the primary emotions. S.M.'s drawings (Figure 14.11), show that she was able to represent all emotions but fear effectively. She complained to the researchers that "she did not know what an afraid face would look like and therefore could not draw the expression" (Adolphs, Tranel, Damasio, & Damasio, 1995, p. 5887; Adolphs, Tranel, & Damasio, 1998).When shown a series of faces in photographs, she was able to

Klüver-Bucy syndrome (KLOO-ver BYEW-see) A collection of symptoms, including tameness, extreme sexual behavior, and oral exploration, that results from damage to the temporal lobes, and the amygdala in particular.

recognize the emotions of happiness, sadness, and disgust portrayed in the photographs. However, she had selective difficulty identifying anger and fear correctly. S.M.'s impaired abilities to process fear appear to result from her failure to look at the eye region of the faces she was asked to evaluate (Adolphs, 2007). Fear in another's face can be distinguished most effectively from other emotions by observing the eyes. When explicitly instructed to pay attention to the eyes of faces, Patient S.M. was able to evaluate fear normally. Individuals with autism also seem to have serious difficulties identifying the emotions of other people, particularly fear (see Chapter 16). Not only do individuals with autism fail to make eye contact with others beginning at early ages, but one of the consistent physical correlates of autism is abnormality of the amygdala (Amaral, Schumann, & Nordahl, 2008). These findings suggest that the amygdala participates in the active exploration of the social environment as well as in the interpretation of the results of that exploration (Adolphs, 2007).

Joseph LeDoux has outlined a "fear circuit" involving the amygdala to account for some of these behavioral observations in animals and humans (LeDoux, 2000). A pathway connecting the amygdala with the thalamus, which receives significant input from most sensory systems en route to the cortex, provides a rapid, crude evaluation of the emotional significance of a stimulus. This system probably accounts for our quick, automatic focus of attention on a particular source of danger, such as a snake found on a hiking trail.

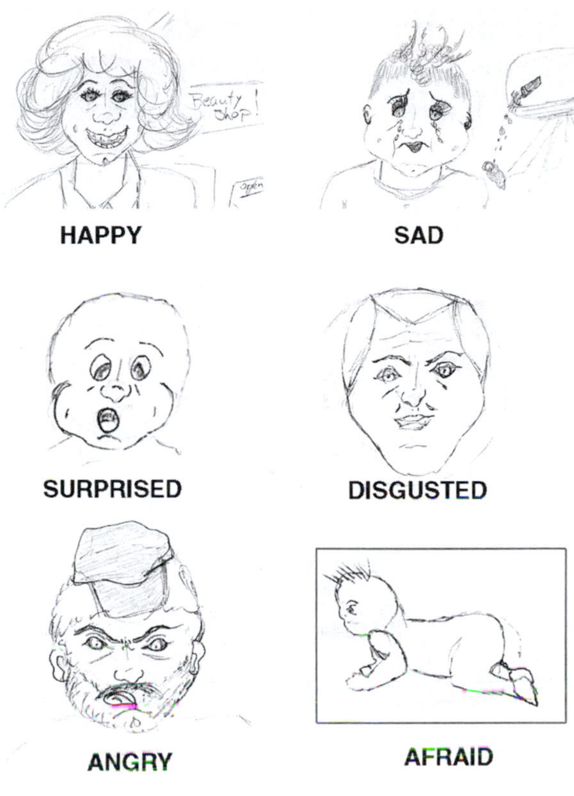

FIGURE 14.11
Damage to the Amygdala Affects the Processing of Fear
Patient S.M. experienced damage to both amygdalas as a result of a rare condition known as Urbach-Wiethe disease. When asked to draw pictures that represented the primary emotions, S.M. did well with all emotions except "afraid."(Adolphs et al., 1995).

As we observed in Chapter 12, the amygdala plays a critical role in the classical conditioning of fear (Wilensky, Schafe, Kristensen, & LeDoux, 2006). Damage to the amygdala interrupts previously learned fear responses and prevents further learning about new sources of danger. The relative independence of the circuit linking the thalamus and amygdala in the classical conditioning of fear can be demonstrated when sensory areas of the cerebral cortex are destroyed. Even without normal cortical input, the thalamus-amygdala circuit allows rats to learn to fear a signal associated with electric shock (LeDoux, Ruggiero, Forest, Stornetta, & Reis, 1987).

Further evidence for the amygdala's role in the processing of negative emotions includes its large number of benzodiazepine receptors (Niehoff & Kuhar, 1983). Benzodiazepines (such as Valium) are major tranquilizers used to reduce anxiety, and their ability to do so might result from their actions in the amygdala. Imaging studies of the human amygdala also support its importance in processing negative emotional valence. Participants show greater activation of the amygdala when viewing facial expressions of fear as opposed to facial expressions of happiness (Davis & Whalen, 2001; Morris et al., 1996).

Although we have emphasized the role of the amygdala in fear and other negative emotional states, evidence for its participation in reward and positive emotional states also exists (Murray, 2007). Healthy control participants preferred abstract images that were associated with the high probability of food rewards, but participants with surgical damage to both amygdalas did not (Johnsrude, Owen, White, Zhao, & Bohbot, 2000). In a related experiment, participants viewing unfamiliar faces were given additional information about the face that was positive ("Emily helps the homeless"), negative ("Bob is a deadbeat dad"), or neutral ("Eric likes carrots") (Somerville, Wig, Whalen, & Kelley, 2006). Activity in the amygdala was associated with the emotional faces, regardless of whether the valence was positive or negative, but not with the neutral faces, even though the participants could not consciously report any information associated with the faces. These findings, along with those of LeDoux regarding the role of the amygdala in fear, suggest that circuits involving the amygdala might connect biologically relevant stimuli with a positive or negative valence, and that this association probably occurs without conscious awareness.

NEW DIRECTIONS

Recognition of Facial Expression and Psychopathology

Correct identification of another person's facial expressions of emotion is critical to competent social functioning. Many types of psychological disorder, which we discuss in Chapter 16, involve problems in navigating the social environment. Underlying some of these social deficits are specific inabilities to read facial expressions of emotion. We have already seen how Patient S.M., who has damaged amygdalas, fails to direct her attention to the eyes of a face to be assessed. Consequently, she was unable to correctly identify facial expressions of fear, which are highly dependent on the appearance of the eyes. Autism, which is also characterized by severe social deficits, is also associated with poor eye contact and interpretation of facial expressions of emotion (Schultz, 2005).

People with schizophrenia typically show deficits not only in their own emotional behavior, but in their ability to react appropriately to the behavior of others. These patients are particularly likely to misinterpret all emotional stimuli, including facial expressions, as threatening, leading to delusions of persecution and paranoia (Phillips, Drevets, Rauch, & Lane, 2003). Individuals with social phobia (Birbaumer et al., 1998) and major depressive disorder (Sheline et al., 2001) show exaggerated responses in the amygdala to facial stimuli, suggesting that they are seeing threat where none exists. In contrast, individuals with psychopathy, who lack feelings of empathy and guilt, appear to be unusually underresponsive to expressions of fear, possibly due to lower activity in the amygdala, hippocampus, and other temporal lobe structures associated with emotion (Kiehl et al., 2001).

Many psychological disorders share overlapping features. A further understanding of the specific deficits in the recognition of emotional expression characterizing each disorder should not only allow us to make better diagnoses but should also lead to more precise treatments.

The Cingulate Cortex The cingulate cortex is a relatively ancient structure in terms of evolution as compared to the remainder of the cerebral cortex. This structure appears to serve as a major gateway between the amygdala, other limbic structures, and the frontal lobes of the cerebral cortex. The anterior cingulate cortex (ACC) is the target of a number of pathways communicating information about physical pain. The emotional quality of pain probably results from its processing at this level of the brain. In addition to physical pain, the ACC may also participate in the processing of social pain, as in the negative feelings associated with being socially excluded by others. Brain activity was observed in participants who believed that they were being excluded from a game by others (Eisenberger, Lieberman, & Williams, 2003). These feelings of exclusion activated the same areas of the cingulate cortex that are normally active when we feel physical pain.

As we will see in subsequent sections on reward and aggression, the ACC cooperates with the orbitofrontal cortex in processing reward and decision-making (Rushworth, Behrens, Rudebeck, & Walton, 2007) and in the inhibition of aggression (Siever, 2008).

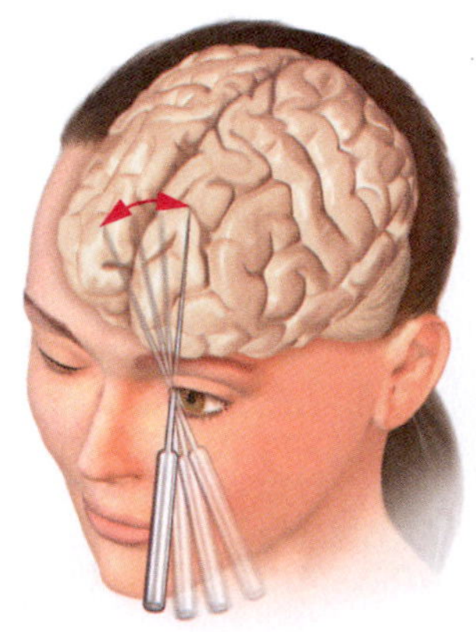

FIGURE 14.12 Frontal Lobotomy Between 1939 and 1951, about 18,000 Americans underwent frontal lobotomies for problems ranging from schizophrenia to depression to anxiety. Parts of the frontal lobes were surgically separated from the rest of the brain in what has been referred to as "ice pick surgery."

The Cerebral Cortex When humans experience cortical damage, particularly in the frontal lobes, emotional disturbance often results. In Chapter 2, we discussed the case of Phineas Gage, the railroad worker whose frontal lobe was damaged in an accident. Although frontal lobe damage does not seem to affect intelligence, patients have difficulty making and following through on plans. Frontal lobe damage is also associated with a reduction in emotional feelings, especially those of fear and anxiety (Rolls, 2004).

Elliot Valenstein (1986) traced the history of medical efforts to influence emotional behavior through frontal lobe surgery. In 1935, John Fulton and Carlyle Jacobsen removed the frontal lobes from two chimpanzees and reported that the chimpanzees became much calmer. Egaz Moniz believed that Fulton and Jacobsen's technique would be beneficial for human patients suffering from a number of mental disorders. He advocated the use of the frontal lobotomy, or the surgical separation of the frontal lobes from the rest of the brain. Between 1939 and 1951, approximately 18,000 Americans were treated with frontal lobotomies for problems ranging from schizophrenia to depression to anxiety. Walter Freeman popularized one version of the procedure, illustrated in Figure 14.12. In what was described as "ice pick surgery," a sharp instrument was inserted above the eye and then wiggled back and forth, severing the connections between the frontal lobe and the anterior cingulate cortex, in particular. In some cases, the procedure did reduce patients' anxiety. However, subsequent side effects, including seizures, lack of inhibition, impulsivity, or lack of initiative, often emerged. Frontal lobotomies were largely discontinued after the discovery of effective antipsychotic medications after World War II (see Chapter 16).

In addition to the specific roles of the frontal lobes in emotion, which we will discuss further in later sections on reward and aggression, we can distinguish between the contributions of the two cerebral hemispheres to emotion (see Chapter 13). In most people, left hemisphere activity is correlated with positive emotions, whereas right hemisphere activity is correlated with negative emotions. Participants viewing positive emotional stimuli showed increased activation in the left hemisphere prefrontal cortex, whereas viewing negative stimuli was correlated with increased activation of the right hemisphere prefrontal cortex (Davidson & Irwin, 1999). Patients who suffer damage exclusively to the left hemisphere are often quite depressed, especially if their damage is located in the left frontal lobe (Gainotti, 1972; Robinson, Kubos, Starr, Rao, & Price, 1984; Sackeim et al., 1982). Patients with right-hemisphere damage, however, are often surprisingly cheerful. These clinical observations are supported by results from the Wada test, also described in Chapter 13, in which one cerebral hemisphere at a time is anesthetized. Anesthetizing the left hemisphere generally results in a lingering feeling of depression, whereas anesthetizing the right hemisphere is associated with apparent happiness (Lee et al., 2004).

As we saw in the discussion of lateralization in Chapter 13, for many people, the right hemisphere plays a greater role than the left in processing emotion (see Chapter 13). Stimuli can be constructed in which half the face demonstrates one facial expression while the other half displays a second, different expression. If the person looks at a focal point in the center of the image, the visual information to the left of the focal point will be processed by the right hemisphere, and the visual information to the right of the focal point will be processed by the left hemisphere. In a patient who had undergone the split-brain operation (also described in Chapter 13), the assessment of facial expression by the right hemisphere was superior to judgment by the left hemisphere (Stone, Nisenson, Eliassen, & Gazzaniga, 1996). In normal, healthy right-handed participants, the right hemisphere processes emotional facial expressions faster and more accurately than the left hemisphere (Bryden, 1982). You can see the effects of this hemisphere difference for yourself by evaluating the faces in Figure 14.13.

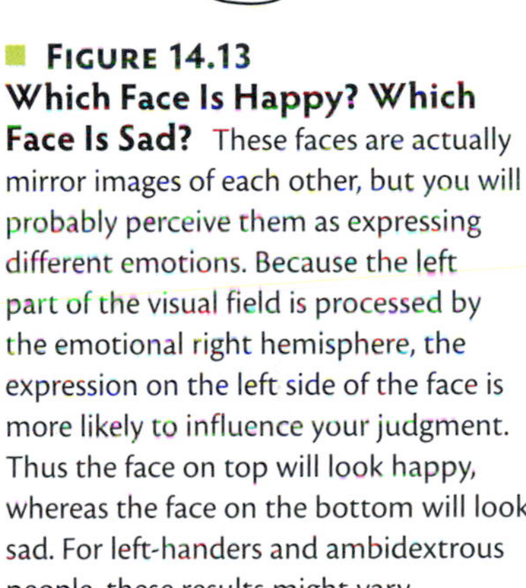

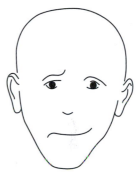

FIGURE 14.13 Which Face Is Happy? Which Face Is Sad? These faces are actually mirror images of each other, but you will probably perceive them as expressing different emotions. Because the left part of the visual field is processed by the emotional right hemisphere, the expression on the left side of the face is more likely to influence your judgment. Thus the face on top will look happy, whereas the face on the bottom will look sad. For left-handers and ambidextrous people, these results might vary.
Source: McGee & Skinner, 1987.

Dichotic listening tasks, in which different information is presented to each ear, are also used to assess the functioning of the two hemispheres. Information presented to the left ear is processed more rapidly by the right hemisphere, whereas information presented to the right ear is processed more rapidly by the left hemisphere. Ley and Bryden (1982) presented sentences with different emotional tones to each ear of their research participants. Participants did a better job recognizing the meaning of sentences when asked to pay attention to input from their right ears. In contrast, participants were more successful at identifying the emotional tone of the sentence when attending to their left ears. These findings are consistent with the concept that the meaningfulness of language is localized in the left hemisphere (right ear advantage) and emotional aspects of language are processed in the right hemisphere (left ear advantage).

Another clue to a difference between the hemispheres in emotional processing is the asymmetry of facial expression. As we mentioned earlier, the right and left facial nerves are relatively independent. This allows higher levels of control, including the cerebral cortex, to influence the intensity of emotions expressed on the right and left halves of the face. In general, the left side of the face (primarily controlled by the right hemisphere) is more expressive than the right side (primarily controlled by the left hemisphere). This is especially true of the lower two thirds of the face, which receives input from the contralateral hemisphere only.

Facial asymmetry can be observed by manipulating photos of faces, in a technique you can easily duplicate with most photo software. Divide the photo in half, and combine each half with a mirror image of itself. In this way, you can construct one composite face made of two right halves and one made of two left halves. As

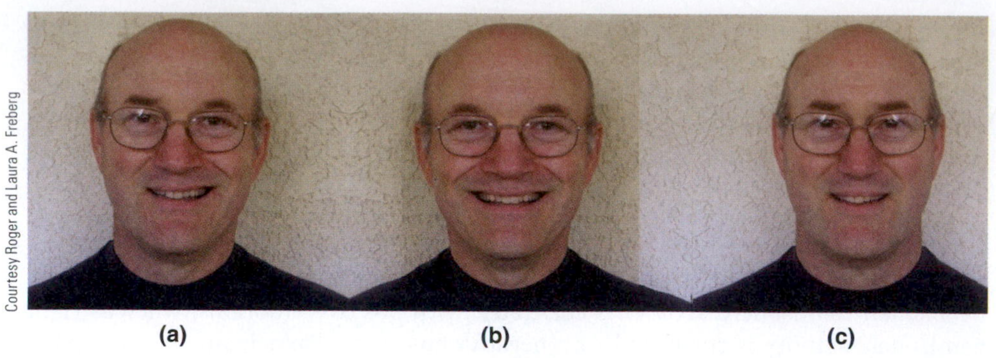

Figure 14.14 Facial Expressions Are Not Symmetrical For most people, the left lower half of the face, controlled by the emotional right hemisphere, is more expressive than the right lower half of the face. The author's husband, Roger, agreed to demonstrate this phenomenon. Image (a) is a photo of Roger. Image (b) is a composite of the two left sides of his face, which clearly show more emotion than (c) the composite of his two right sides.

Sackheim, Gur, and Saucy (1978) demonstrated, the results of this procedure will give you very different intensities of emotional expression (Figure 14.14). When placed beside the original image, the composite made of two left halves of the face is usually judged as the most expressive while the composite of the two right halves of the face is considered the least expressive.

Patterns of Activation and Emotion It is overly simplistic to look for specific areas of the brain that are activated during a particular type of emotional experience. We do not have "happy centers" and "sadness centers" in the brain. Widespread areas of the brain appear to be associated with each specific emotion, and areas associated with different emotions show considerable overlap. Antonio Damasio and his colleagues (Damasio et al., 2000) observed PET scans of 41 participants as they experienced anger, sadness, fear, and happiness. To generate the emotional response, participants were instructed to recall a specific event from their past associated with each emotion. While recalling the event, the participants were asked to attempt to re-create feelings. The results indicated that complex patterns of activity involving multiple regions of the brain characterized each emotion. Although the patterns for the four emotions were distinct from one another, single brain regions might participate in more than one of the emotional states.

INTERIM SUMMARY 14.1

Summary Table: Brain Damage with Emotional Consequences

Area Damaged	Emotional Consequences
Amygdala	Difficulty perceiving negative emotions, particularly fear, expressed by others
Frontal lobe	Reduced fear and anxiety
Left cerebral hemisphere	Depression
Right cerebral hemisphere	Cheerful mood

Summary Points

1. Emotions promote survival by enhancing arousal, organizing approach and avoidance behaviors, and providing a means of communication. **(LO1)**
2. Facial expression is mediated by the facial nerve (cranial nerve VII). Voluntary expressions are controlled by the cerebral cortex, whereas spontaneous expressions are controlled by subcortical structures. **(LO2)**
3. Some basic emotional expressions appear to be universal, but environmental factors and learning influence the intensity and context for emotional expression. **(LO2)**
4. Three classic theories of emotion attempt to organize the relationships between physical reactions and subjective feelings. The James-Lange theory suggests

(continued)

INTERIM SUMMARY 14.1 (continued)

that autonomic responses are used as cues for the recognition of emotional states. The Cannon-Bard theory suggests that both physical reactions and subjective feelings occur simultaneously. The Schachter-Singer theory suggests that the physical reactions contribute to a general arousal, which leads to an assessment of subjective feelings based on context. Contemporary theories of emotion emphasize the complex interactions of physical and emotional states and the existence of learned somatic markers. **(LO3)**

5. The autonomic nervous system, amygdala, cingulate cortex, and cerebral cortices play important roles in emotion. **(LO4)**

Review Questions

1. What behaviors suggest that a person might be lying?
2. How do the three classic theories of emotion differ in their explanations of emotional behavior?

Pleasure and Reward

James Olds and Peter Milner (1954) discovered some of the first evidence that particular locations in the brain are involved with the positive emotions of pleasure and reward. They surgically implanted a wire electrode in the brain of a rat and allowed the animal to wander around a box. Whenever the rat entered a specified corner of the box, electricity was passed through the electrode. Fairly soon, the rat became reluctant to leave that corner of the box. Olds and Milner then added a lever that the rat could press to stimulate its own brain through the electrode, a procedure known as **electrical self-stimulation of the brain,** or **ESB.** The power of ESB to reward behavior is dramatic. Not only will rats learn bar-pressing behavior rapidly when ESB is used as a reward, but they also show very high rates of responding. Routtenberg and Lindy (1965) allowed rats access to two levers for one hour per day. Pressing one lever resulted in food and pressing the other resulted in rewarding ESB. Even though the rats had no access to food outside of this one-hour period per day, they chose ESB over food. Many starved to death as a result.

Rats are obviously unable to explain why the sensations produced by ESB are so compelling. However, electrode implants have also been used with human participants. Robert Heath (1963) reported his observations of two patients with implanted electrodes. One patient frequently activated an electrode located in the septal area, shown in ■ Figure 14.15. He reported that stimulation of the site produced pleasurable sexual feelings, similar to those leading up to an orgasm. He pushed the button for this site frequently in hopes of achieving orgasm, but his efforts were unsuccessful. Heath's second patient also reported pleasant, sexual feelings from septal area stimulation. In addition, this patient frequently stimulated the medial thalamus, in spite of his report that this produced a feeling of irritation. Stimulation of this site gave the patient the feeling that he was about to remember something important. Heath's research reminds us that sites producing emotions other than pleasure also participate in the brain's reward system.

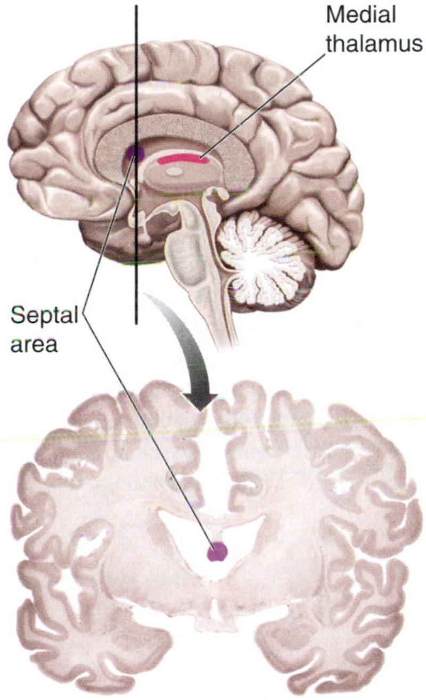

■ **FIGURE 14.15 The Septal Area and Medial Thalamus** Robert Heath (1963) reported that his human participants experienced pleasant sexual feelings when their septal areas were electrically stimulated. When the medial thalamus was stimulated, Heath's patient reported feeling irritated.

THE MESOLIMBIC SYSTEM

Electrical stimulation of the **medial forebrain bundle (MFB)** produces some of the most powerful reinforcement effects (Olds & Olds, 1963). The MFB, shown in ■ Figure 14.16, connects the substantia nigra and ventral tegmental area of the midbrain with forebrain structures, including the lateral hypothalamus and the nucleus accumbens. This system is referred to as the mesolimbic system (see Chapter 2).

Most neurons in the mesolimbic system use dopamine as their primary neurotransmitter. As we observed in Chapter 4, many addictive substances act as dopamine agonists, particularly in the nucleus accumbens. As shown in ■ Figure 14.17, when a rat obtains ESB in the ventral tegmentum, higher quantities of dopamine are released in the nucleus accumbens (Phillips et al., 1992). Drugs that block dopamine activity in the nucleus accumbens reduce the rewarding effects of ESB. Stellar,

electrical self-stimulation of the brain (ESB) A behavior engaged in willingly by research subjects that leads to electrical stimulation of certain parts of the brain.

medial forebrain bundle (MFB) A fiber pathway that is a major site for electrical self-stimulation. The MFB connects the substantia nigra and ventral tegmental area with higher forebrain structures, including the hypothalamus and nucleus accumbens.

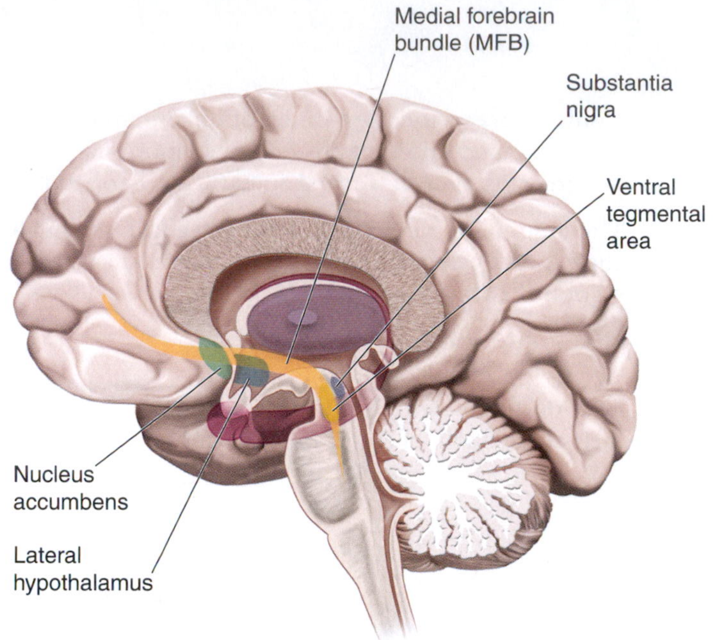

■ **FIGURE 14.16 Connections of the Medial Forebrain Bundle** The medial forebrain bundle (MFB) produces strong self-stimulation effects. The MFB forms widely distributed connections between the brainstem and limbic system. Many of the neurons in this network use the neurotransmitter dopamine and function as a reward circuit in the brain.

Kelley, and Corbett (1983) trained rats to run down the arm of a maze to obtain ESB. Following the injection of a dopamine antagonist, higher levels of stimulation were required to maintain the rats' running behavior.

Activity in the mesolimbic system, and the nucleus accumbens in particular, underlies many types of reward. According to Comings and Blum (2000), eating and sexual behaviors constitute "natural" situations for the activation of reward circuits in the brain. The same circuits, however, can also be activated by "unnatural" situations, including the use of addictive drugs and compulsive eating, compulsive sex, or gambling. Observing rats bar-pressing to the point of exhaustion or starvation to stimulate this circuit helps us capture the essence of compulsive and addictive behavior.

Reward, Decision-Making, and the Cortex

To survive, animals must make accurate approach or avoidance decisions. The mesolimbic system begins the process of responding to rewarding stimuli. Areas receiving input from the mesolimbic system, including the cingulate cortex and the prefrontal cortex, provide further evaluation of the circumstances leading to reward. Does the value of the reward offset the amount of effort required to obtain it? The anterior cingulate cortex (ACC) plays an important role in these types of cost-benefit decisions (Rushworth, 2008; Rushworth et al., 2007). Rats in a t-maze typically will choose a larger reward over a smaller one, even when they must climb over a barrier to obtain the larger reward (Salamone, Cousins, & Bucher, 1994) but will fail to do so following lesions of the ACC. Is the reward likely to be immediate or delayed? Lesions of the orbitofrontal cortex (OFC) reverse the rats' normal preference for larger, delayed rewards over smaller, immediate rewards (Rudebeck, Walton, Smyth, Bannerman, & Rushworth, 2006).

Humans with damage to these cortical systems involved in evaluating reward can make remarkably poor decisions, showing very little regard for the likely consequences of their behaviors. Patient EVR experienced damage to his orbitofrontal cortex during surgery for a tumor. Although he was previously considered a role model in his

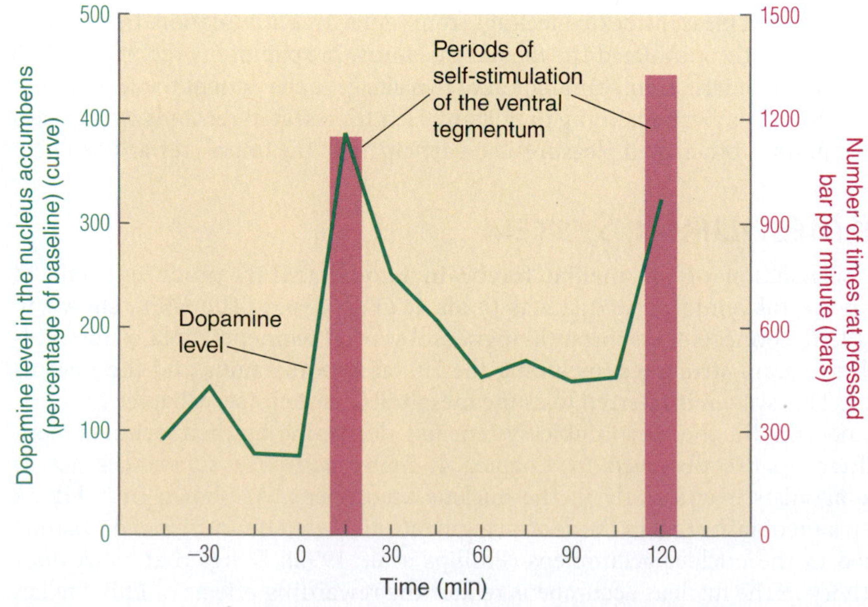

■ **FIGURE 14.17 Dopamine Release in the Nucleus Accumbens Correlates with ESB** Using microdialysis, Phillips et al. (1992) demonstrated that rewarding electrical stimulation in the ventral tegmentum was associated with nearly 400 percent increases in the release of dopamine in the nucleus accumbens. *Source:* Adapted from Phillips et al., 1992.

community, EVR's decision-making skills changed radically following his surgery. He lost his job, went bankrupt, divorced his wife, and married a prostitute (Eslinger & Damasio, 1985).

Anyone can become angry, that is easy. But to be angry with the right person, to the right degree, at the right time, for the right purpose, and in the right way, that is not easy.

Aristotle

Aggression and Violence

We will use the term **aggression** to refer to the intentional initiation of hostile or destructive acts toward another individual. Predatory aggression is premeditated, or planned in advance, goal-directed, and relatively unemotional. In contrast, impulsive aggression occurs immediately in response to some provocative stimulus that produces anger or fear (Siever, 2008). Different patterns of brain activity appear to be involved in these different types of aggression (Mobbs, Lau, Jones, & Frith, 2007).

While recognizing the significant contributions of learning and other environmental influences to aggression, we can identify many biological correlates of violent behavior. Violent behavior will occur when subcortical structures, in particular the amygdala, respond strongly to provocative stimuli without sufficient inhibition from the prefrontal cortex and anterior cingulate cortex (Siever, 2008). In other words, aggressive behavior will not occur as long as aggressive "drives" originating in subcortical areas experience "top-down" control by frontal cortical areas. When this top-down inhibition is insufficient, violence will result.

Genetics and Aggression

To what extent is human aggression rooted in our genetic heritage? Aggression is certainly a trait that can be selectively bred in animals, as evidenced by the breeding of fighting bulls in Spain or pit bulls for dogfighting. Mice (Lagerspetz & Lagerspetz, 1983) and fruit flies (Diereck & Greenspan, 2006) can also be bred selectively for aggressiveness, allowing researchers to begin identifying particular genes that might be involved. Human twin studies indicate significant genetic influences on aggressiveness (Rushton, Fulker, Neale, Nias, & Eysenck, 1986). The heritability of impulsive aggression is particularly high, between 44 and 72 percent (Coccaro, Bergeman, Kavoussi, & Seroczynski, 1997; Seroczynski, Bergeman, & Coccaro, 1999).

Most within-species aggression is confined to the establishment of dominance, and it is unusual for one animal to kill another. Typically, the "loser" need only withdraw to end the aggressive engagement. The only species in which groups of males systematically hunt and kill members of their own species are chimpanzees and humans (Wrangham & Peterson, 1996; Wright, 1994). Within-species aggression might have been incorporated into our genetic heritage as individuals competed with one another for food, territory, and mates. If more aggressive individuals survived, their offspring would inherit these aggressive tendencies.

Whatever the genetic contributions to human aggression may be, societies vary widely in their rates of violence. Worldwide, the average homicide rate, excluding wars, is 10 per 100,000 people (United Nations Office on Drugs and Crime, 2001). Table 14.1 provides homicide rates for selected cities between 1998 and 2000. According to these data, Athens, Greece, had a homicide rate of 0.55 homicides per 100,000 people, compared with a rate of 41.12 in Pretoria, South Africa. Wide variations occur even within the same culture, as evidenced by the New York rate of 8.77 as opposed to the rate in Washington, D.C., of 45.79. If human beings possess a genetic inclination to violence, clearly culture and learning modify the way such an inclination is expressed.

We all boil at different degrees.

Ralph Waldo Emerson

Brain Structures and Aggression

Aggression is correlated with patterns of activity in several brain structures, including the hypothalamus, the amygdala, the anterior cingulate cortex, and the prefrontal cortex.

aggression The intentional initiation of a hostile or destructive act.

TABLE 14.1 Homicide Rates in Selected Cities (1998–2000)

If human beings have a genetic predisposition to violence, culture certainly has the capacity to modify the behavior. Homicide rates per 100,000 people are nearly 40 times higher in Washington, D.C., than in Tokyo, Japan.

City	Homicides Reported	Homicides per 100,000 City Residents (Average per Year)
London, England	538	2.38
Paris, France	181	2.85
Athens, Greece	53	0.55
Moscow, Russia[2]	3,863	18.20
Berne, Switzerland	9	2.35
Canberra, Australia	5	0.54
Ottawa, Canada	23	0.98
Tokyo, Japan	440	1.22
Pretoria, South Africa[1]	1,512	41.12
New York, NY (USA)	1,977	8.77
Washington, D.C. (USA)	733	45.79

[1] 1995–1997
[2] 1997–1999

Early physiologists discovered that removal of the cerebral cortices produced violent rage on the part of previously docile cats and dogs. Because the animals' violence was provoked by ordinary circumstances, such as a pat on the head, it was referred to as **sham rage.** Further research suggested that the role of the cortices, in this case, was to inhibit the action of the hypothalamus and other subcortical structures. When the hypothalamus in cats is electrically stimulated, many of the behaviors seen in cases of sham rage are duplicated (Hess, 1928). The cat will arch its back, spit, and hiss. Its ears will lie flat and its tail will puff out. When the stimulation stops, all rage also stops, and the cat often curls up and goes to sleep. John Flynn (1967) duplicated the rage attack of Hess's cats with stimulation to the medial hypothalamus. With electrodes implanted in the cats' lateral hypothalamus, however, Flynn was able to elicit hunting behavior. Flynn's cats would attack and kill rats in their cages when the lateral hypothalamus was stimulated. Although such studies are ethically improbable in humans, abnormalities of hypothalamic function have been observed in antisocial, violent people (Raine et al., 2004).

Previously in this chapter, we observed the role of the amygdala in mediating fear. It appears that the amygdala, primarily through its connections with the hypothalamus, plays a role in aggression as well. If the amygdala processes a situation as fearful and threatening, a person might respond aggressively. After all, the fight-or-flight response to the perception of a threat does include the fighting option. Many instances of impulsive aggression appear to be defensive, and unusually violent people might be more likely to perceive threat in situations when others do not, causing them to overreact (Siever, 2008). Karl Pribram and his colleagues (Rosvold, Mirsky, & Pribram, 1954) observed a reduction in aggression when the amygdalas of male rhesus monkeys were removed. In a very small number of human patients, lesions of the amygdala reduced violence associated with temporal lobe seizures (Mark & Ervin, 1970).

sham rage A violent reaction to normally innocuous stimuli following removal of the cerebral cortices.

Together, the anterior cingulate cortex and the orbitofrontal cortex, illustrated in ■ Figure 14.18, inhibit aggressive behavior (Siever, 2008). As we observed previously, these areas participate in decision-making by evaluating the anticipated consequences, both positive and negative, of behaviors. Emerging evidence suggests that antisocial behavior leading to violence is associated with abnormalities in the orbitofrontal cortex (see Chapter 16). Individuals with damage to the orbitofrontal cortex were more likely to use physical intimidation and verbal threats in confrontations (Grafman et al., 1996). However, once again we see the importance of distinguishing between impulsive and premeditated, predatory aggression. Impulsive murderers show reduced frontal activation, whereas premeditating murderers do not (Raine et al., 1998).

■ **FIGURE 14.18**
The Orbitofrontal Cortex

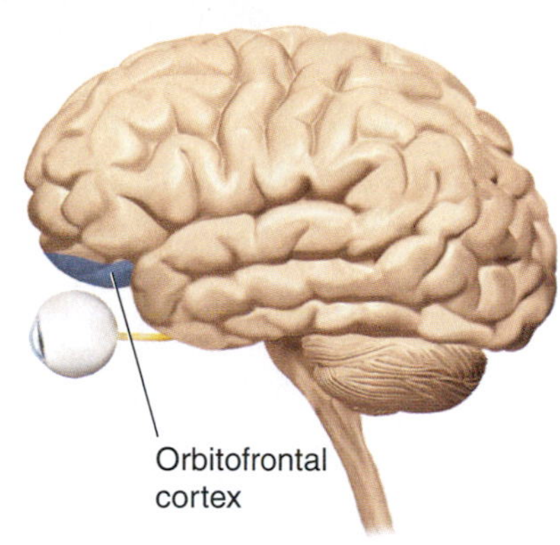

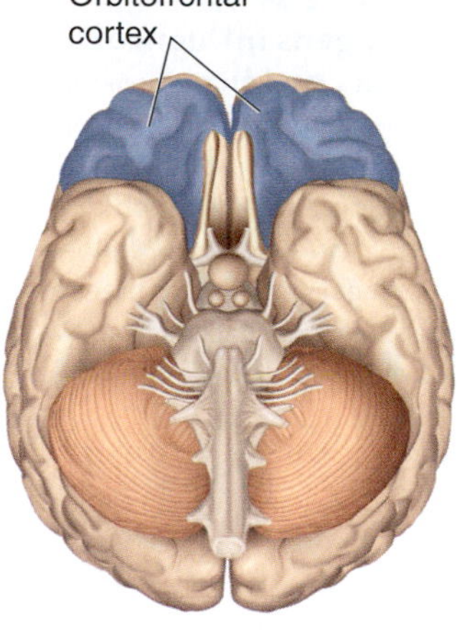

Biochemistry and Aggression

Drug use, particularly alcohol use, interacts with human aggression. Prison studies and police reports show that alcohol use is involved in 65 percent of murders, 88 percent of knife attacks, 65 percent of spousal abuse incidents, and 55 percent of physical child abuse incidents (Steele & Josephs, 1990). Alcohol is also associated with the majority of suicides. Alcohol contributes to violence by reducing the inhibition of aggression normally managed by the cingulate and frontal cortices.

Testosterone might influence aggression by increasing reactivity to threatening stimuli. Women who were given testosterone showed stronger subcortical reactions to images of angry faces (Hermans, Ramsey, & van Honk, 2008). Once again, if subcortical reactions are strong enough to overwhelm cortical inhibition, aggression is the likely outcome. Animal research has shown strong correlations between testosterone levels and aggressive behavior. As shown in ■ Figure 14.19, castration of mice reduced

WHY DOES THIS MATTER?

Brain Damage and the Criminal Justice System

The insanity defense, or finding a person "not guilty by reason of insanity," implies that some people have more control over their behavior than others. Understanding the role of biology in criminal behavior matters because decisions about a person's responsibility for his or her actions directly influence outcomes of incarceration or treatment. In particular, our approach to juvenile crime is likely to be affected by brain research. Parts of the brain responsible for our most sophisticated decision-making are not mature until a person's mid-20s (Mobbs et al., 2007).

In 2005, these issues came very close to home in my little community of San Luis Obispo, California (population 45,000). Eighty-seven-year-old Jerry O'Malley was brutally murdered by a 13-year-old who bludgeoned O'Malley's head with his skateboard, carefully locked up his mobile home to cover up the crime, and stole his car for a joyride (Gumbel, 2005). During the boy's trial, Joseph Wu, director of the Brain Imaging Center at the University of California, Irvine, testified that the young murderer had "abnormally reduced activity in parts of his brain that govern a person's judgment" (Sneed, 2006, p. B1). The murderer told the police, "I knew it was wrong; I just did it," but this statement was excluded for consideration by the judge (Griffy, 2006, p. B1).

How do we deal with such cases? How should we consider the findings of "abnormally reduced activity in parts of the brain that govern a person's judgment?" Is this a matter of incarceration to prevent further harm by this person or a case requiring treatment for a medical condition?

Although a greater understanding of brain correlates and violent behavior should be useful in understanding criminal behavior, we are reminded that not all criminals show evidence of brain damage, and not everyone with brain damage engages in criminal behavior (Mobbs et al., 2007). If you're wondering what became of our 13-year-old murderer, he was sentenced to a state juvenile corrections facility, from which he will automatically be freed at age 25 (Parrilla, 2006).

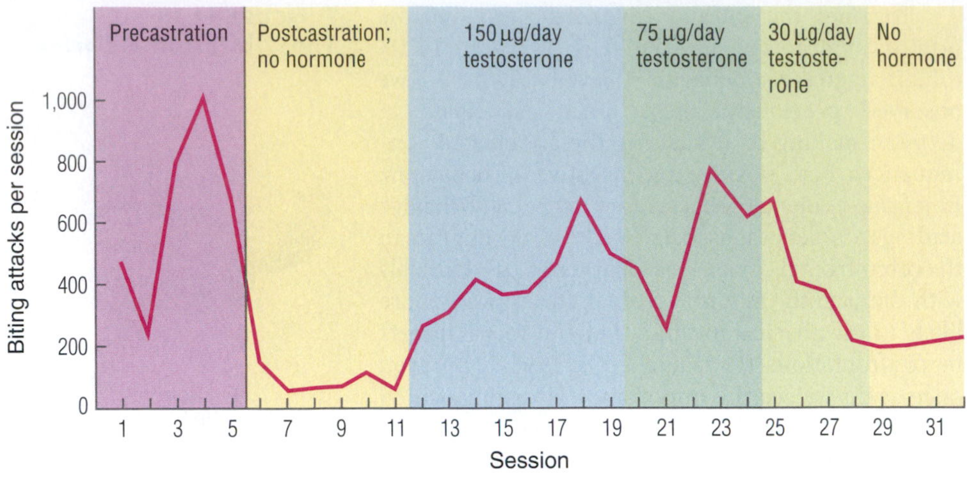

FIGURE 14.19 Androgens Influence Biting Attacks by Mice Male mice demonstrate a significant drop in the number of biting attacks following castration. Administration of testosterone to castrated males reestablished biting behavior close to precastration levels. *Source:* Adapted from Wagner, Beuving, & Hutchinson, 1980.

the incidence of biting attacks to nearly zero. However, administering testosterone to the castrated mice quickly reestablished normal male levels of biting behavior (Wagner, Beuving, & Hutchinson, 1980).

Prenatal exposure to testosterone is correlated with higher aggressiveness in humans. Reinisch, Ziemba-Davis, and Sanders (1991) observed children whose mothers had been given testosterone in an effort to prevent miscarriage. As shown in Figure 14.20, both boys and girls exposed prenatally to extra testosterone showed higher average physical aggression scores than their unexposed siblings of the same sex. As we discussed in Chapter 10, the ratio between a person's index and ring fingers (2D:4D) reflects prenatal androgen exposure. Men with greater 2D:4D ratios, indicating higher prenatal androgen exposure, were more likely to be physically aggressive (Bailey & Hurd, 2005).

There are strings in the human heart that had better not be vibrated.
Charles Dickens

Levels of adult testosterone are not particularly well correlated with human aggression. However, Dabbs and Morris (1990) reported that testosterone levels that are on the high end of the typical range in teen and adult males were positively correlated with delinquency, drug abuse, and aggression. When levels are unusually high, due to factors such as the use of anabolic steroids, more aggression can be the result. Yates, Perry, and Murray (1992) reported that male weightlifters who used steroids were more hostile and aggressive than weightlifters who did not use steroids. Because these are correlational data, we don't know if steroid use causes greater aggression in this case or if aggressive athletes are more likely to choose to use steroids.

Higher testosterone levels among aggressive males might be the result of living in highly competitive, threatening environments rather than serving as the root cause of aggressive behavior. As we observed in Chapter 10, testosterone levels respond to competition. Athletes playing in front of the home crowd against bitter rivals showed the greatest increases in testosterone, leading to the suggestion that territoriality might influence testosterone levels in human males (Wolfson & Neave, 2002).

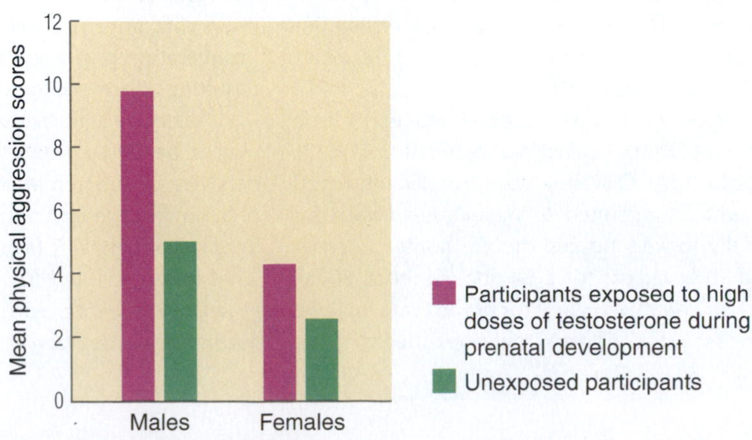

FIGURE 14.20 Prenatal Testosterone Contributes to Aggression Males and females exposed prenatally to high levels of testosterone exhibited higher levels of physical aggression than their unexposed same-sex siblings. *Source:* Adapted from Reinisch, Ziemba-Davis, & Sanders, 1991.

Like testosterone, serotonin levels fluctuate with life circumstances and can predict aggression. Decreased serotonin levels in the amygdala were associated with increases in aggressive behavior in male rats (Toot, Dunphry, & Ely, 2001). Raleigh, Brammer, McGuire, Pollack, and Yuwiler (1992) measured the serotonin levels of male rhesus monkeys, who form very precise social hierarchies. Monkeys at the bottom of the hierarchy had the lowest serotonin levels, whereas those at the top had high serotonin levels. Lower-ranking rhesus monkeys attempting to increase their status initiate more aggression than dominant monkeys.

Serotonin facilitates the activity of the prefrontal cortical regions, including the cingulate cortex and the orbitofrontal cortex. Consequently, higher levels of serotonin should predict greater inhibition of the aggressive drive produced in subcortical regions. Individuals with histories of violent suicide attempts or impulsive violence show evidence of decreased serotonin activity (Siever, 2008). As we will see in Chapter 16, low serotonin levels in humans are also associated with feelings of depression, often described as aggression toward the self. Why low serotonin might promote aggression toward others in some cases, toward the self in other cases, and towards both the self and others, as in murder-suicides, remains unclear.

Stress

Stress is defined as an unpleasant and disruptive state resulting from the perception of danger or threat. The term **stressor** is often used to identify a source of stress. The critical term in our definition is *perception*. The experience of stress is highly variable and idiosyncratic from one person to the next. What matters is that the person perceives him- or herself to be in some kind of dangerous or threatening situation. Regardless of the nature of a stressor, once danger has been perceived and identified, a predictable series of reactions is set into motion.

Hans Selye and the General Adaptation Syndrome

Modern research into stress began with observations by Walter Cannon (1929). Cannon was able to demonstrate that a variety of stressors, including extreme cold, lack of oxygen, and emotional experiences, have the capability of stimulating the sympathetic division of the autonomic nervous system (see Chapter 2). In response, the body prepares for what Cannon termed "fight or flight." Heart rate, blood pressure, and respiration all increase. Functions that are not essential during emergencies, such as digesting food, are inhibited. Stored energy is released, and blood vessels at the surface of the skin contract to drive blood from the surface (preventing excessive bleeding due to injury) and toward the skeletal muscles (preparing for exertion).

Hans Selye extended Cannon's findings during a career that spanned 40 years (1936–1976). Selye investigated the effects of various stressors on the amount of time rats were able to swim in a tank until they sank to the bottom, when they were rescued. Selye's stressors included cold water, cutting off the rats' whiskers, restraint, electric shock, and surgery. Regardless of the stressor used, Selye (1946) observed a consistent reaction, which he labeled the **General Adaptation Syndrome (GAS).**

The GAS consisted of three stages, diagrammed in Figure 14.21. When the stressor is first perceived and identified, an **alarm reaction** is initiated. This is the same state that Cannon described as the fight-or-flight response. If you have had a close call on the highway, you know how this feels. Your heart beats rapidly, you're breathing quickly, your palms are sweaty, and you are highly alert. So far, the system is working well because this is the type of emergency the system was designed to manage.

If the stressful situation continues past this initial alarm stage, we enter into the **resistance stage.** This stage is less physiologically dramatic than the alarm reaction, but our bodies expend considerable energy coping with stress while also attempting to maintain our normal activities. During this stage, judgment and resistance to disease can deteriorate. If stress continues further, we enter the final **exhaustion stage,** in which strength and energy are at very low levels.

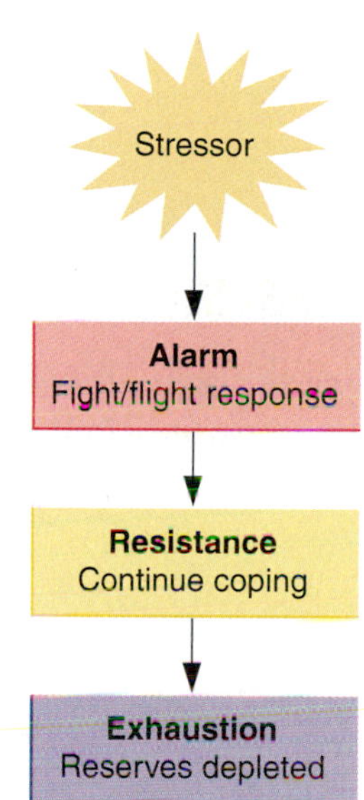

Figure 14.21
Stages of Selye's General Adaptation Syndrome

stress An unpleasant and disruptive state resulting from the perception of danger or threat.
stressor A source of stress.
General Adaptation Syndrome (GAS) A three-stage model for describing the body's response to stress developed by Hans Selye.
alarm reaction The first stage of Selye's General Adaptation Syndrome, characterized by activation of the sympathetic nervous system and mental alertness.
resistance stage The second stage in Selye's General Adaptation Syndrome, characterized by the person's efforts to maintain normal activities while coping with stress.
exhaustion stage The final stage of Selye's General Adaptation Syndrome, characterized by extremely low reserves of strength and energy.

Exhaustion can lead to disorders such as depression (see Chapter 16). In rare cases, such as the stress of forced death marches in time of war, exhaustion can lead to death. In 1942, Walter Cannon described the case of a young, apparently healthy African woman who apparently died of stress after learning that a fruit she had just eaten was spiritually forbidden. Cannon (1942/1957) referred to the case as a "voodoo" death. Robert Sapolsky (2001) studied the effects of chronic stress on baboons in Kenya. Normally, low-status male baboons avoid interacting with high-status males. One year, in response to fears about losing crops to the baboons, the local farmers caged many of the animals. While caged, the low-status males were unable to escape the high-status males, and many low-status males died as a result. They did not die, as you may have guessed, due to wounds from battle. Instead, they died from stress-related conditions such as ulcers and cardiovascular disease.

Physical and Psychological Responses to Stress

Adopting the right attitude can convert a negative stress into a positive one.
Hans Selye

To manage emergencies successfully, physical, cognitive, and behavioral responses must be coordinated. Assume, for the sake of example, that a human ancestor is facing a hungry lion. Physically, the sympathetic division of the autonomic nervous system is preparing our ancestor either to escape or to fight. In a parallel process, the cognitive system becomes highly aroused and vigilant as the hypothalamus instructs the adrenal glands, via the pituitary gland, to release the stimulating hormone cortisol. Behaviorally, we would expect that our ancestor would try to escape the stressor rather than fight.

We can trace the pathways that mediate these physical, cognitive, and behavioral responses. At the outset, the sensory systems detect the threatening stimulus (the lion). Connections with higher cortical processing centers identify the object as a lion and access memories of lion behaviors (including their eating habits). At the same time, sensory information enters the amygdala, which plays an important role in fear (see Figure 14.10). The amygdala sends information to the hypothalamus via a pathway known as the **stria terminalis,** which forms additional connections with neurons in the **bed nucleus of the stria terminalis.** These neurons activate three key areas involved with the stress response, known collectively as the hypothalamic-pituitary-adrenal (HPA) axis, illustrated in ■ Figure 14.22. Incoming messages from the amygdala reach the paraventricular nucleus (PVN) of the hypothalamus, which in turn makes connections with the locus coeruleus, the spinal cord, and the pituitary gland (Tausk, Elenkov, & Moynihan, 2008). The PVN releases **corticotrophin-releasing hormone (CRH)** and vasopressin (ADH, see Chapter 9), which act as chemical messengers between the hypothalamus and the anterior pituitary gland. In response to CRH and vasopressin, the pituitary gland releases another hormone, adrenocorticotropic hormone, or ACTH. ACTH diffused from the pituitary into the bloodstream will eventually reach the adrenal glands, where it stimulates the release of cortisol. CRH and ACTH are released in pulses, each of which accounts for approximately a 15-minute period of cortisol release. Cortisol remains in the bloodstream for about three hours before breaking down.

The amygdala is not the only structure regulating the HPA axis. The hippocampus is also involved in this process. Whereas the amygdala stimulates the release of CRH by the hypothalamus, the hippocampus acts to inhibit CRH release. The hippocampus contains receptors for glucocorticoids, including cortisol. The hippocampus, therefore, acts as part of a feedback loop. If cortisol levels reaching the hippocampus are too high, CRH release by the hypothalamus will be reduced, leading to less release of ACTH and cortisol.

When cortisol reaches the brain via the bloodstream, it has the ability to bind with many types of neurons. Cortisol increases the amount of calcium entering neurons (Kerr, Campbell, Thibault, & Langfield, 1992), leading to an increase in the amount of neurotransmitter released by each affected neuron (see Chapter 3). This should produce the arousal and vigilance needed by our friend facing the hungry lion. Unfortunately, too much calcium can be toxic to neurons. When rats were given daily

stria terminalis (STREE-uh ter-min-AL-us)A pathway carrying information from the amygdala to the hypothalamus.

bed nucleus of the stria terminalis A group of neurons that receive input from the amygdala and activate the HPA axis.

corticotrophin-releasing hormone (CRH) (kore-ti-koh-TROE-fin) A hormone released by the hypothalamus that signals the release of ACTH by the anterior pituitary gland.

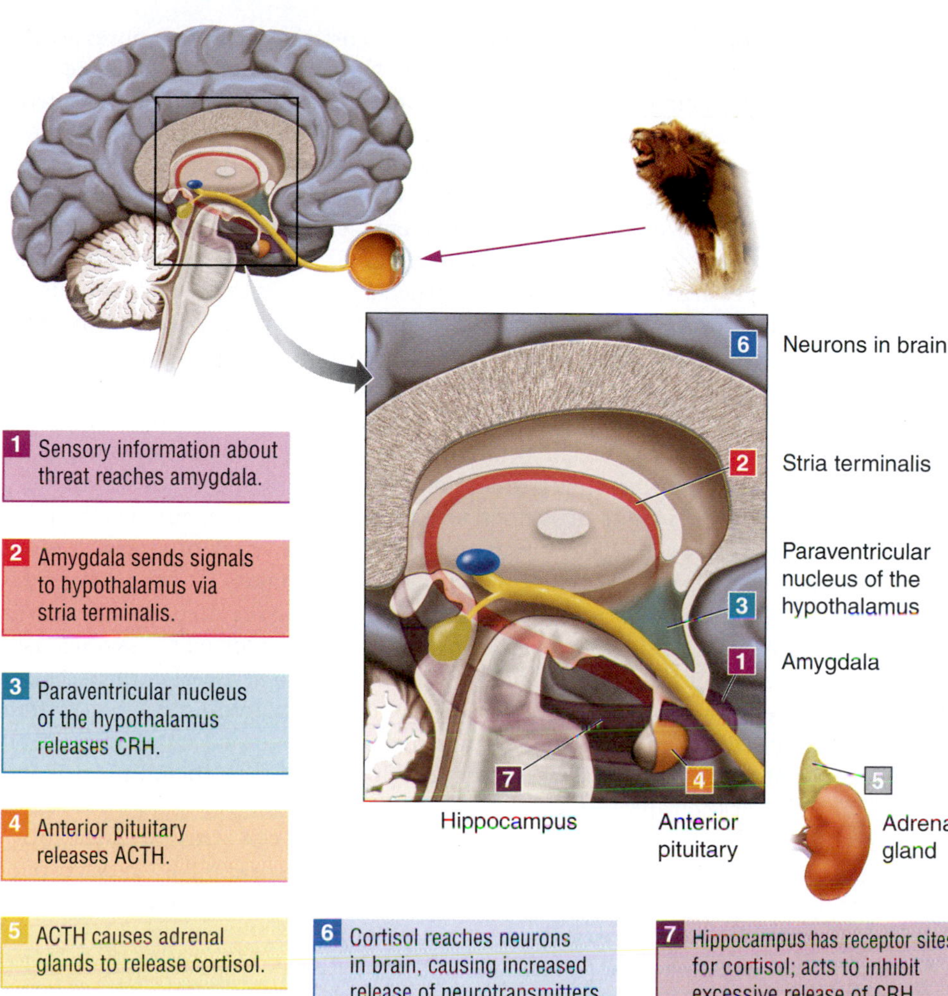

Neurons in brain
Stria terminalis
Paraventricular nucleus of the hypothalamus
Amygdala
Hippocampus
Anterior pituitary
Adrenal gland
1 Sensory information about threat reaches amygdala.
2 Amygdala sends signals to hypothalamus via stria terminalis.
3 Paraventricular nucleus of the hypothalamus releases CRH.
4 Anterior pituitary releases ACTH.
5 ACTH causes adrenal glands to release cortisol.
6 Cortisol reaches neurons in brain, causing increased release of neurotransmitters.
7 Hippocampus has receptor sites for cortisol; acts to inhibit excessive release of CRH.

FIGURE 14.22
The Hypothalamic-Pituitary-Adrenal (HPA) Axis Mediates the Stress Response

injections of the rat cortisol equivalent, corticosterone, dendrites on neurons with corticosterone receptors began to retract, and the neurons themselves began to die within a few weeks (Stein-Behrens, Mattson, Chang, Yeh, & Sapolsky, 1994). If the rats were stressed daily in lieu of receiving the injections, the same results occurred. Sapolsky's stressed baboons, mentioned earlier, experienced neural death particularly in the hippocampus. Some human participants diagnosed with posttraumatic stress disorder (see Chapter 16) have also been found to have smaller-than-average hippocampi. Perhaps consistently high levels of cortisol overwhelm the hippocampal feedback loop that would normally lower cortisol levels. This would make the individuals even more vulnerable to the negative outcomes of chronic stress.

Stress, the Immune System, and Health

When faced with an emergency, our stress response system prioritizes body functions. Functions that are not necessary for handling the immediate emergency are taken offline. Unfortunately for those suffering chronic stress, one of those expendable systems is the **immune system,** the body's frontline defense against infection and cancer. As a result, stress can lead to greater frequency and severity of illnesses.

The immune system produces two types of white blood cells, or **lymphocytes,** that protect us from invaders. The B lymphocytes, produced in bone marrow, release antibodies that destroy foreign substances of a type that the body has previously encountered. Routine immunizations activate B lymphocytes by providing them the opportunity to form antibodies against a variety of disease-causing organisms. T lymphocytes, produced by the thymus gland, directly attack cancer cells and other foreign substances. In addition, the T lymphocytes interact with the B lymphocytes by either boosting or suppressing their activity.

immune system The system used by the body to defend against bacteria, viruses, and other foreign substances.

lymphocyte (LIMF-oh-site) A white blood cell; an important feature of the immune system.

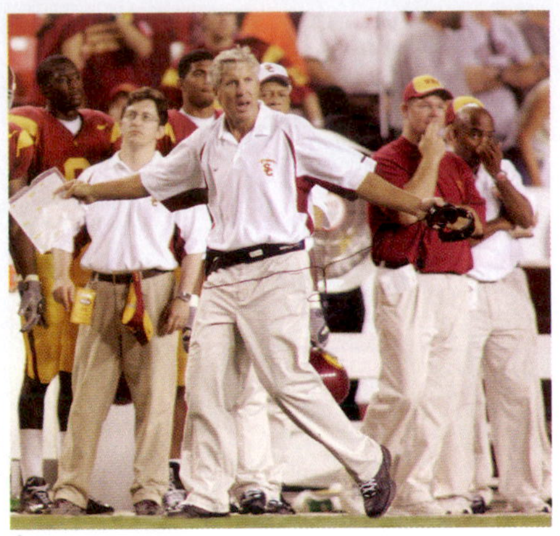
Photo By Grant Halverson/Getty Images

■ **FIGURE 14.23**
The Role of Stress in Heart Disease Is Uncertain Although some researchers suggest that highly competitive people, such as football coach Pete Carroll, might be more vulnerable to heart disease, recent research has suggested that a person's level of hostility presents a greater risk.

The action of stress hormones such as cortisol directly suppresses the activity of lymphocytes (Panesar, 2008). Numerous studies indicate that people experiencing chronic stress are more vulnerable to disease. A meta-analysis of 293 studies with a total of nearly 20,000 participants demonstrated that chronic stressors affecting people's social roles (e.g., death of a loved one, divorce) produce the greatest suppression of the immune system (Segerstrom & Miller, 2004). Not surprisingly to students, exam weeks weaken students' immune responses (Jemmott & Magloire, 1988). Flare-ups of both oral and genital herpes are most likely to occur when a person is experiencing unusual stress (Tausk et al., 2008; Cohen & Herbert, 1996). Both cancer and the progression of HIV infection to AIDS are influenced by stress (Reiche, Morimoto, & Nunes, 2005; Cousins, 1989; Reed, Kemeny, Taylor, Wang, & Visscher, 1994). Unfortunately, knowledge of these relationships can place an even greater burden on sick people, who now believe that their illness wouldn't be so bad if they were somehow better at managing stress.

The extent of stress in our lives does not necessarily predict our health. John Macleod and his colleagues (2002) compared self-reported levels of stress in more than 5,000 men with measures of their medical conditions taken 20 years later. Surprisingly, hospital records of heart disease were lowest among the men who described their stress as being at the highest levels. Factors other than perceived stress obviously influenced the health of these men. One of these factors is a sense of control. Nursing home residents who participate in decisions about their activities live longer than those who do not (Rodin, 1986). The highly stressed men studied by Macleod et al. might have benefited from a number of compensatory strategies, including a strong sense of control over their lives.

Much has also been written about the relationship between stress and heart disease. In particular, men exhibiting the highly competitive, workaholic "Type A" personality, as opposed to the more mellow and relaxed "Type B," were originally believed to be at higher risk for heart disease due to stress (Friedman & Rosenman, 1959, 1974). If Friedman and Rosenman are correct, highly competitive people such as University of Southern California football coach Pete Carroll, shown in ■ Figure 14.23, would be well advised to look after their cardiovascular health carefully. Upon further study, however, it is not the competitive drive that seems to predict heart problems but rather a pattern of hostility found among some Type A's. People most at risk for heart disease are frequently suspicious, angry, and resentful of others (Smith, 1992; Nabi et al., 2008). Although the exact mechanism linking hostility to heart disease remains unknown, hostility, anger, and depression are associated with increased levels of immune system proteins that appear to contribute to heart disease (Boyle, Jackson, & Suarez, 2007).

INTERIM SUMMARY 14.2

Summary Table: Structural and Biochemical Correlates of Increased and Decreased Aggression

	Increased Aggression	Decreased Aggression
Structural correlates	Removal of cerebral cortex	Damage to the amygdala
	Electrical stimulation of the hypothalamus	
	Damage to the orbitofrontal cortex	
Biochemical correlates	Alcohol use	
	High levels of testosterone	Low levels of testosterone (castrated males)
	Low levels of serotonin	

(continued)

Summary Points

1. Electrical self-stimulation research suggests that some structures of the brain participate in a reward or pleasure circuit. **(LO5)**
2. Aggression is influenced by genetics, although aggressive behavior can be modified through culture and learning. **(LO6)**
3. The hypothalamus, amygdala, cingulate cortex, and orbitofrontal cortex are involved with aggression. **(LO6)**
4. Alcohol, high testosterone levels, and low serotonin levels correlate with aggression. **(LO6)**
5. Selye described a three-stage General Adaptation Syndrome (GAS) that occurs in response to stress. The organism will experience alarm, resistance, and exhaustion as long as the source of stress continues to be present. **(LO7)**
6. Stress hormones suppress immune system activity, leading to higher rates of illness among people experiencing chronic stress. **(LO7)**

Review Questions

1. What does the analysis of ESB tell us about the brain's processing of reward?
2. What are the effects of chronic stress on the immune system and on general health?

CHAPTER REVIEW

THOUGHT QUESTIONS

1. How would you assess the ability of catharsis theories to explain people's reactions to violent video games?
2. Which of the theories of emotion presented in this chapter makes the most sense to you, and why?
3. If we discover that brain damage is responsible for most violent criminal acts, what changes, if any, would you propose in the criminal justice and prison systems?
4. Paul Ekman suggests that we aren't very good at detecting liars because "we often want to be misled, we collude in the lie unwittingly because we have a stake in not knowing the truth" (1996, p. 814). In what circumstances do you want to catch a liar? To what circumstances might Ekman be referring in this statement?
5. How might emotional expressiveness be different among those who do not localize language to the left hemisphere (see Chapter 13)?

KEY TERMS

aggression (p. 421)
alarm reaction (p. 425)
Cannon-Bard theory (p. 411)
catharsis (p. 410)
electrical self-stimulation of the brain (ESB) (p. 419)
emotion (p. 403)
empathy (p. 410)
exhaustion stage (p. 425)
General Adaptation Syndrome (GAS) (p. 425)
immune system (p. 427)
James-Lange theory (p. 409)
medial forebrain bundle (MFB) (p. 419)
resistance stage (p. 425)
Schachter-Singer theory (p. 411)
stress (p. 425)
stressor (p. 425)

15 Neurological Disorders

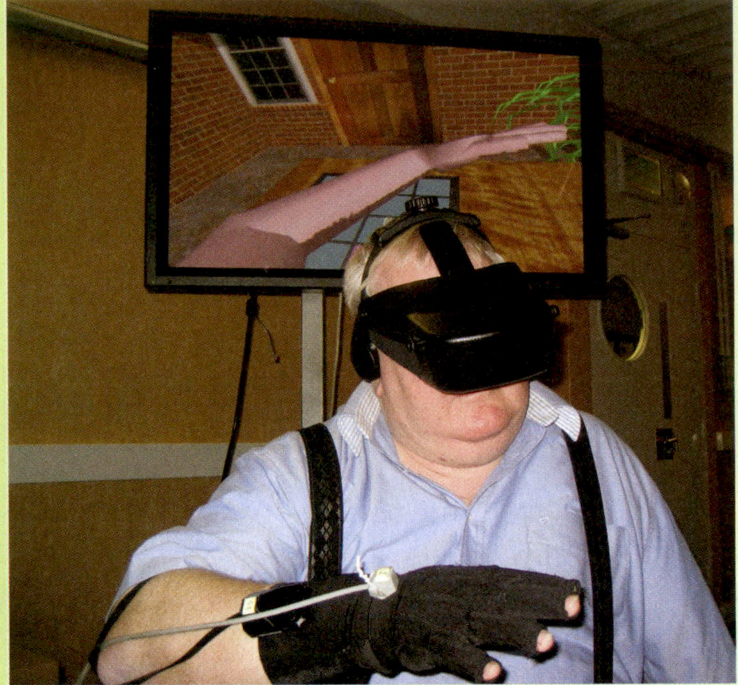

Courtesy of Dr Steve Pettifer, Dr Craig Murray and Mr Toby Howard/ The University of Manchester

▲ **Virtual Reality** Rehabilitation patients with a variety of neurological problems are benefiting from the immersion and realism provided by modern virtual reality technologies.

CHAPTER OUTLINE

Introduction

People generally associate athletic injuries to the brain and nervous system with contact sports such as boxing, American football, rugby, and ice hockey. However, research suggests a troubling pattern seen in soccer players. Both amateur and professional soccer players performed significantly more poorly than swimmers and track-and-field athletes on tests requiring attention, memory, and planning abilities (Matser, Kessels, Jordan, Lezak, & Troost, 1998; Matser, Kessels, Lezak, Jordan, & Troost, 1999). Sortland and Tysvaer (1989), using computerized tomography (CT), found cerebral atrophy in one third of the former members of the Norwegian national football (soccer) team participating in their study.

Athletes playing soccer can sustain head injuries by colliding with one another, with the goalposts, or with the ground. However, the most likely source of injury is the practice of "heading" the ball, a maneuver illustrated in ■ Figure 15.1. Matser et al. (1998) reported that the greatest cognitive deficits occurred among players who headed the ball frequently. Even with correct technique, elite players reported headaches following heading (Tysvaer & Storli, 1989). Although data specifically relating brain injury to the practice of heading is still considered inconclusive, concerns persist. The National Soccer Coaches Association of America (NSCAA) recommends avoiding heading drills for children ages 10 and under (Hoyt, 2002). Some safety advocates are even suggesting that soccer players begin to wear helmets, although this seems to be a very unpopular option.

You might be upset to learn that participating in a very common activity such as soccer carries a risk of head injury. However, as you read this chapter and the next, which

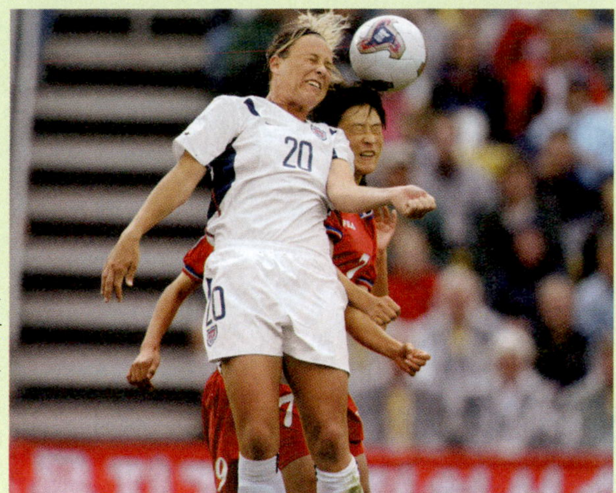

© Thomas E. Witte/NewSport/CORBIS

FIGURE 15.1 Soccer Headers Can Be Risky Heading the ball is a frequently used technique in soccer, adding to the excitement of the game. The use of proper heading technique is likely to be quite safe. However, concerns have been raised regarding the long-term effects of repeated heading on cognition.

covers psychological disorders, I would caution you to guard against "first-year medical student's disease." This is the tendency of students to start believing that they suffer from all of the conditions described in the text. Although it is statistically possible that a student might have one or more of the conditions described here, it's wise to remember that most of these situations are extremely rare. Brain worms do exist, but your chances of having one are slim to none. ■

LEARNING OBJECTIVES

After reading this chapter, you should be able to

LO1 Describe the major features of stroke.

LO2 Distinguish among open head injuries, concussions, and chronic traumatic brain injuries (CTBIs).

LO3 Identify the major types of brain tumors and seizures.

LO4 Describe multiple sclerosis.

LO5 Give examples of brain infections caused by parasites, bacteria, viruses, and fungi.

LO6 Describe the symptoms and causes of AIDS dementia complex (ADC) and the transmissible spongiform encephalopathies (TSEs).

LO7 Identify the events leading to a migraine headache.

LO8 Summarize the major steps involved with neurological assessment.

LO9 Describe the basic principles that predict recovery from brain damage.

LO10 Identify the major types of therapy used for treating brain damage.

Brain Damage

Despite the significant protection that the skull bones, the cerebrospinal fluid, and the blood–brain barrier provide to the brain, damage can occur due to interruptions in the blood supply and from blows to the head. The growth of tumors and the abnormal electrical activity of seizures can also interrupt normal brain functioning.

STROKE

The cells of the nervous system are unable to rely on stored supplies of oxygen, which is delivered to the brain by a rich network of blood vessels, as shown in ■ Figure 15.2. The circulation of blood to neural tissue can be interrupted by ruptures and blockages of the blood vessels serving the brain.

A **stroke** occurs when the brain's blood supply is interrupted by either bleeding or by the sudden blockage of a blood vessel (Cotran, Kumar, Fausto, Robbins, & Abbas, 2005). Risk factors for stroke include age, hypertension, smoking, diabetes, high cholesterol, obesity, and the use of alcohol, cocaine, amphetamines, heroin, and other drugs (American Heart Association, 2008). Risk is also increased when arteries are narrowed gradually by conditions such as arteriosclerosis, or hardening of the arteries.

Cerebral hemorrhage, or bleeding in the brain, generally results from hypertension (high blood pressure) or structural defects in the arteries serving the brain (Donnan, Fisher, Macleod, & Davis, 2008). Some hemorrhages occur due to the rupture of **aneurysms,** balloon-like bulges in the walls of arteries. Others result from blood diseases such as leukemia or exposure to toxic chemicals. Cerebral hemorrhages are frequently fatal due to the brain damage they produce by interfering with the blood supply to neurons and by flooding areas of the brain with salty blood that dehydrates and kills nearby neurons.

Blockages of blood vessels result in **ischemia,** or low oxygen levels. Cases of ischemia account for about 80 percent of all strokes (Donnan, Fisher, Macleod, & Davis, 2008). Ischemia often results in the death of neural tissue, an area known as

stroke A type of brain damage caused by an interruption of the blood supply to the brain.

cerebral hemorrhage A condition caused by bleeding in the brain.

aneurysm (ANN-yur-izm) A balloonlike bulge in the wall of an artery.

ischemia (iss-KEE-mee-uh) A condition in which inadequate blood flow results in insufficient quantities of oxygen being delivered to tissue.

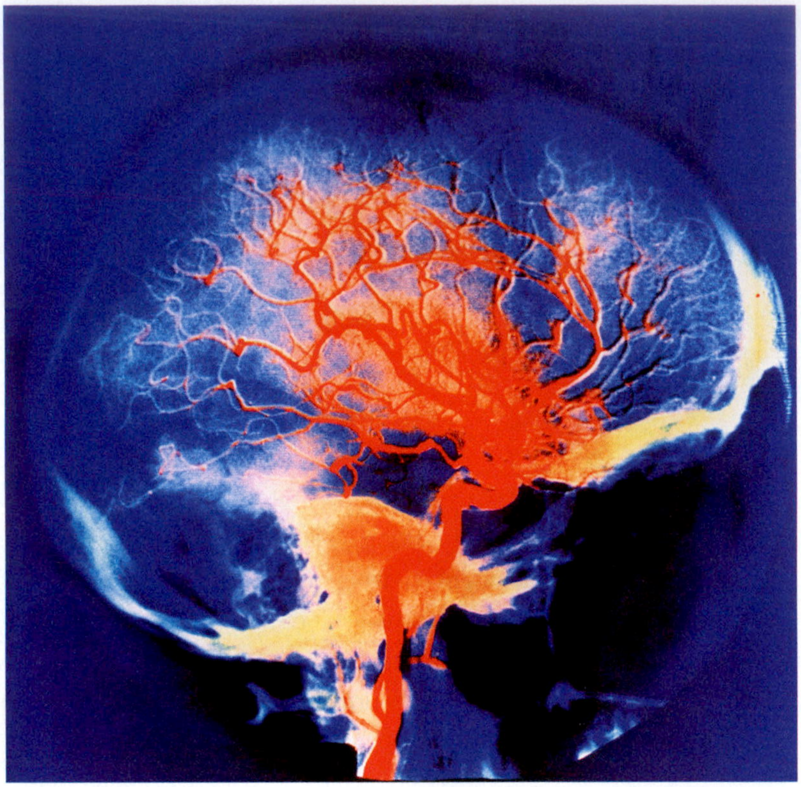

FIGURE 15.2
The Brain's Blood Supply Due to the brain's enormous need for oxygen, it is supplied by a rich network of blood vessels. Interruptions to this supply produce rapid changes in brain function and, potentially, infarct and death.

infarct An area of dead neural tissue.
transient ischemic attack (TIA) A brief (24-hour-or-less) episode of stroke symptoms that does not cause permanent damage.
thrombosis (throm-BOH-sis) A blockage that doesn't move from its point of origin in a blood vessel.
embolism A blood vessel blockage that originated elsewhere and traveled to its current location.
penumbra The area of tissue surrounding an infarct.
traumatic brain injury (TBI) physical damage to the brain.
open head injury A head injury in which the brain is penetrated, as in a gunshot wound.
concussion A head injury that results from a blow to the head without penetration of the brain or from a blow to another part of the body that results in force transmitted to the brain.
coup (KOO) An area of brain damage at the site of the blow to the head.
countercoup (KOWN-ter-koo) An area of brain damage that occurs on the opposite side of the head from the original site of the blow, or coup.
subdural hematoma (sub-DUR-uhl hee-muh-TOH-muh) A mass of clotted blood (like a bruise) that forms between the dura mater and arachnoid following a head injury.
postconcussion syndrome (PCS) A set of symptoms that follow concussion for a period of days to years, including headache, cognitive deficits, and emotional changes.

an **infarct,** like the one shown in ■ Figure 15.3. Infarcts can cause changes in consciousness, sensation, or the ability to move, depending on their size and location. **Transient ischemic attacks (TIAs)** produce brief episodes (24 hours or less) of these stroke symptoms. Although these brief attacks do not cause permanent damage, they are strong predictors of subsequent stroke (Donnan et al., 2008).

Material causing the blockage of a blood vessel can be classified as either a thrombosis or an embolism. A **thrombosis** is a plug of blood or other material that blocks a blood vessel without moving from its point of origin. If a plug passes into smaller and smaller blood vessels until it forms a blockage, we refer to the condition as an **embolism.** Blockages in small blood vessels are far less damaging than blockage of large arteries serving the brain. Nonetheless, multiple small strokes can produce significant damage.

Until the 1980s, it was generally assumed that most of the damage related to ischemia resulted from interruptions to the supplies of oxygen that reach neurons and glia served by the affected blood vessels (Zivin & Choi, 1991). However, autopsy results of patients who died following ischemia showed that only certain cells appeared to be damaged. In particular, cells in the middle layers of the cortex and in the hippocampus appeared to be the most vulnerable. If cell death occurred only because of a lack of oxygen, the damage should have been more widespread. Therefore, other processes must be involved in brain damage caused by ischemia.

In 1969, John Olney coined the term *excitotoxicity* to describe the ability of excess glutamate to kill neurons (see Chapter 4). Olney's hypothesis received further support from reports that glutaminergic antagonists had a protective effect on cells undergoing oxygen deprivation (Simon, Swan, Griffiths, & Meldrum, 1984). Rothman (1984) demonstrated that the presence of high concentrations of magnesium prevented cell death in cultures of rat hippocampal cells. Recall that magnesium blocks one type of glutamate receptor, the NMDA receptor (see Chapter 4). As a result, we now generally believe that cell death following many strokes is largely caused by excess glutamate activity triggered by disruptions in the delivery of oxygen.

Excess glutamate entering a neuron initiates a cascade of events leading to cell death. In response to unusual amounts of glutamate, abnormal calcium activity in the cell stimulates four "executioner" enzymes that damage the cell's energy stores, membranes, cytostructure, and DNA (Besancon, Guo, Lok, Tymianski, & Lo, 2008). Although efforts to minimize damage due to stroke by intervening in this glutamate-initiated cascade have been disappointing to date (Besancon et al., 2008), research in this area continues. In the meantime, other methods including surgery, reducing the formation of new thromboses and emboli, and reducing blood pressure remain standard medical practices for stroke (Donnan et al., 2008). Although some cells die immediately following a stroke, prompt medical attention can save many other neurons and glia in the ischemic **penumbra,** the area immediately surrounding an infarct (Donnan et al., 2008).

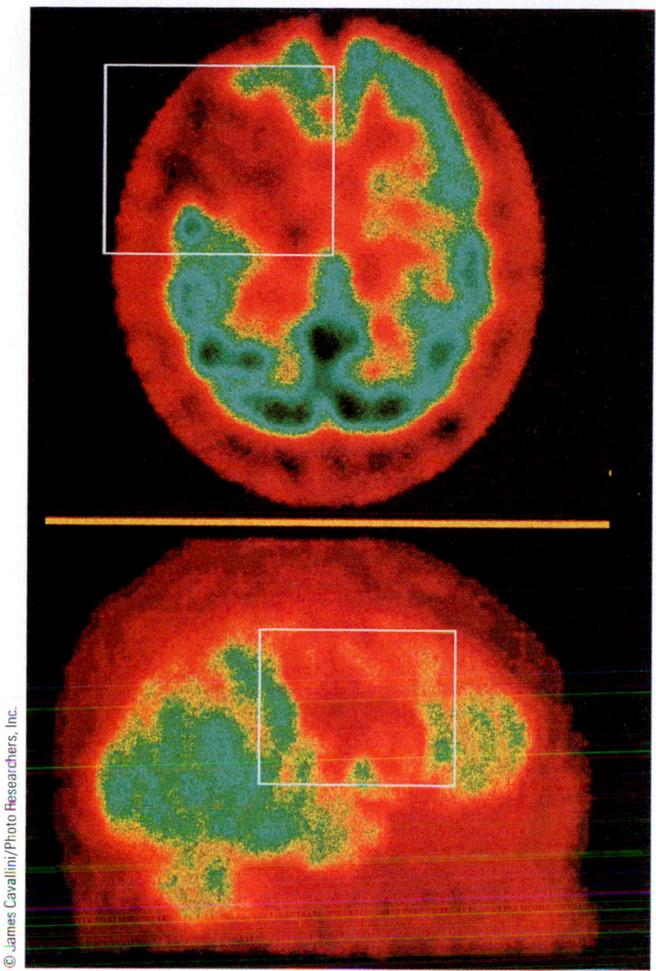

FIGURE 15.3
Brain Infarct When an area of the brain is deprived of oxygen for a sufficient amount of time, cells begin to die. The area of dead tissue is referred to as an infarct. In this image, the patient suffered a fatal infarct in the right frontal lobe.

HEAD INJURIES

Traumatic brain injuries (TBI) are the result of physical damage to the brain. Leading causes of TBI in the United States include traffic accidents, gunshot wounds, and falls (Adekoya, Thurman, White, & Webb, 2002).

Traumatic brain injuries can be divided into two categories. **Open head injuries** involve penetration of the skull, whereas **concussions,** or closed head injuries, do not. Open head injuries usually occur as a result of gunshot wounds or of fractures of the skull in which fragments of bone enter the brain. The severity of the consequences is highly dependent on the areas of the brain that are affected. Injuries that involve damage to ventricles, both hemispheres, or multiple lobes of the brain are most likely to result in death (Martins, Siqueira, Santos, Zanon-Collange, & Moraes, 2003).

Concussions occur in response to a blow to the head or to another part of the body resulting in "impulsive" force transmitted to the brain (Aubry et al., 2002). They can range from mild (no or very brief periods of unconsciousness) to severe (coma). Behavioral, physical, and cognitive consequences often last for months and can be permanent (Lima, Simão Filho, Abib Sde, & de Figueiredo, 2008).

Concussions produce damage in several ways, as illustrated in Figure 15.4. At the site of a blow, known as the **coup,** the brain might be damaged by compression of the skull against the neural tissue. The force of the blow pushes the brain against the side of the skull opposite the coup, producing a second area of damage known as the **countercoup.** A severe coup or countercoup might be accompanied by bleeding, or **subdural** (under the dura mater) **hematoma.** White matter damage can also occur, due to twisting of the brain within the skull in response to the blow. Pressure exerted on the brain by the swelling of injured tissues produces additional damage or interruptions in normal functioning.

Behavioral and cognitive consequences of concussion vary widely. Cortical functions normally taking place at the location of the coup and countercoup are affected adversely. **Postconcussion syndrome (PCS)** occurs in some, but not all, cases of concussion. Cognitive outcomes of PCS include lack of concentration, reduction in processing speed, and deficits in other higher-order cognitive functions such as attention and memory (Sterr, Herron, Hayward, & Montaldi, 2006). Physical symptoms, such as headache, and emotional symptoms, such as depression or irritability, might also occur. The persistence of PCS is correlated with damage in a number of brain structures, including both white matter (corpus callosum and fornix) and gray matter (upper brainstem, base of frontal lobes, medial temporal lobes) (Bigler, 2008).

In years past, concussions without bleeding and with very brief or no loss of consciousness were believed to be no cause for concern. However, with improved imaging, permanent damage from these mild cases can be observed (Levin et al., 1987). Repeated mild head injuries, such as those affecting many athletes, appear to

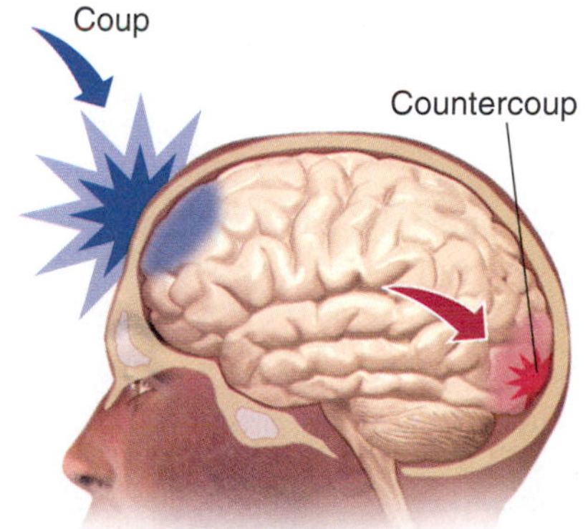

FIGURE 15.4
Coup and Countercoup In concussions, the coup, shown here in blue, is an injury that occurs at the site of the blow. When the blow pushes the brain in the opposite direction, a second area of injury occurs, known as the countercoup, shown here in red.

FIGURE 15.5
Boxers Risk Repeated Head Injuries Boxer Jerry Quarry, shown on the left fighting Muhammad Ali, developed chronic traumatic brain injury (CTBI) as a result of repeated concussions. CTBI causes slurred speech, memory impairment, lack of coordination, personality changes, and a Parkinson-like syndrome.

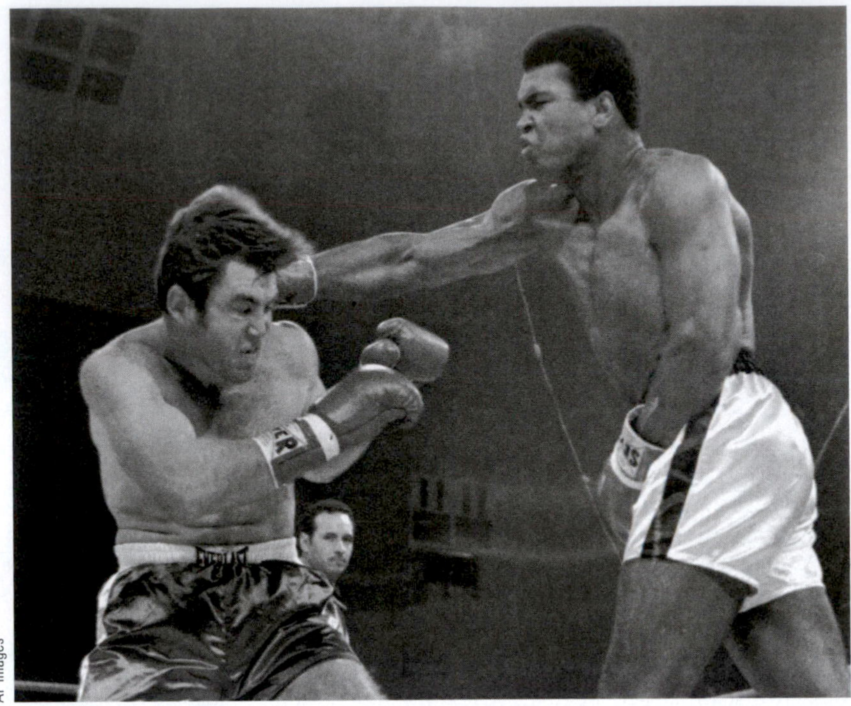

AP Images

Sure there have been injuries and deaths in boxing, but none of them serious.
Alan Minter, professional boxer and Olympic medalist

be especially damaging (Guskiewicz et al., 2003). Professional boxers are subjected to repeated blows to the head over the course of their careers, possibly resulting in **dementia pugilistica,** or boxer's syndrome (Martland, 1928). Dementia pugilistica is a type of **chronic traumatic brain injury (CTBI).** Typically, CTBI is associated with slurred speech, memory impairment, personality changes, lack of coordination, and a Parkinson-like syndrome (see Chapter 8). Autopsy results of CTBI and Alzheimer's disease (see Chapter 5) show similar patterns of degeneration (Jordan, 1998). Many boxers, including Jerry Quarry, shown in Figure 15.5, have experienced symptoms typical of these repeated injuries.

Not all boxers, even those with lengthy careers, are afflicted with CTBI (Jordan, 2000). George Foreman is one notable example of a boxer who escaped this disorder. Boxers who carry the E^4 variant of the *APOE* gene, which has been implicated in some cases of Alzheimer's disease (see Chapter 5), might be more likely to develop CTBI (Jordan et al., 1997). Boxers who had the E^4 variant and had participated in more than 12 professional bouts had greater neurological damage than those who did not carry the E^4 variant. All boxers in the sample who were considered severely impaired possessed the E^4 variant. The presence of the E^4 variant might make a person more vulnerable to the negative effects of brain injury. In one sample, 57 percent of patients with the E^4 variant experienced a negative outcome (death, vegetative state, severe disability) as a result of brain injury, compared with 27 percent of the patients without the allele (Teasdale, Nicoll, Murray, & Fiddes, 1997).

dementia pugilistica (duh-MEN-shuh pew-juh-LISS-ti-kuh) A severe form of chronic traumatic brain injury (CTBI) often experienced by boxers.
chronic traumatic brain injury (CTBI) A type of brain damage caused by repeated concussions.
tumor An independent growth of tissue that lacks purpose.
malignant tumor A type of abnormal cell growth that, lacking boundaries, invades the surrounding tissue and is very likely to recur following surgical removal.
metastasis (met-uh-STAY-siss) The migration of cancerous cells from one part of the body to another.

BRAIN TUMORS

After the uterus, the brain is the organ most likely to give rise to **tumors,** which are independent growths of new tissue that lack purpose. Tumors usually do not grow from mature neurons because these cells do not replicate. Instead, the vast majority of brain tumors arise from glial cells and from the cells of the meninges. Small numbers of tumors originate in the cells lining the ventricles. Some tumors are classified as **malignant tumors** because they lack distinct boundaries and are very likely to recur following surgical removal. In the process known as **metastasis,** malignant tumors shed cells, which travel to other sites of the body and start new tumors. Many tumors in the brain result from cells shed by metastasizing tumors in other parts of the body, such the lungs, breast, or colon. Tumors that originate in the brain rarely metastasize, but when they do so, the shed cells travel through the cerebrospinal fluid to other parts of

WHY DOES THIS MATTER?

Athletes and Post-Concussive Syndrome: When Is It Safe to Play?

Concussions are a frequent consequence of an active life, particularly in contact sports, and coaches and trainers are often faced with decisions about letting a player rejoin a game. Knowing the signs and consequences of concussion matters because repeated head injuries can lead to very serious outcomes.

To help sports personnel make these very important decisions, the American Academy of Neurology has provided a grading system coupled with recommendations for returning to play (Kushner, 2001). According to this system, an athlete with a Grade 1 concussion (no loss of consciousness, concussion symptoms lasting less than 15 minutes) may return to play after 15 minutes without any symptoms. Following a Grade 2 concussion (no loss of consciousness, concussion symptoms lasting more than 15 minutes), the athlete should have one week without any symptoms prior to returning to play. Loss of consciousness for any duration comprises a Grade 3 concussion. If the loss of consciousness lasted seconds, the athlete may return to play after one week without symptoms. If the loss of consciousness lasted minutes or more, two weeks without symptoms must pass before the athlete returns to play.

In recognition of the increased risk posed by repeated concussion, the American Academy of Neurology specifies longer symptom-free periods following a second concussion. However, the Colorado Medical Society and other authors recommend termination of a season following a second Grade 3 concussion or after a third concussion of any type (Kushner, 2001).

Unfortunately, the goals of coaching staff may not always coincide with the athletes' best interests, and injured athletes might hide symptoms to maintain the ability to play. Hopefully, the serious long-term consequences of repeated concussion will lead to a commonsense decision about when to rejoin the game.

the nervous system, as opposed to traveling through the bloodstream to other organs. Other tumors are classified as **benign tumors** because they are contained within their own membrane, are unlikely to recur following removal, and do not metastasize. This does not imply that benign tumors do no harm. As we will see shortly, any unusual mass that occurs in the brain can disrupt normal function. If the benign tumor is not located where it can be surgically removed, it can be as life threatening as the malignant variety.

Symptoms of Tumors Nearly all tumors, once they have attained sufficient size, produce general symptoms due to increased pressure within the skull. These symptoms include headache, vomiting, double vision, reduced heart rate, reduced alertness, and seizures (Chandana, Movva, Arora, & Singh, 2008). Specific disruptions related to the location of the tumor can also occur. For instance, a tumor of the occipital lobe would affect vision. Tumors in the frontal lobe produce changes in emotionality and the ability to plan behavior.

Types of Tumors Tumors are identified according to the tissue from which they arise. **Gliomas** develop in glial cells and account for approximately 45 percent of brain tumors. Gliomas often arise in astrocytes, oligodendrocytes, or mixtures of the two types of cells. **Meningiomas,** such as the one shown in ■ Figure 15.6, are tumors that arise within the tissues of the meninges (see Chapter 2). These tumors are typically benign. Because meningiomas compete with the brain for space, the pressure they exert can produce the headache, vomiting, double vision, and other symptoms of tumors discussed previously. Meningiomas are usually easy to remove surgically because they lie on the surface of the brain instead of invading the tissue within the brain.

The World Health Organization (WHO) issued a classification system for describing central nervous system tumors, ranging from Grade I (least serious) to Grade IV (most serious) (Brat et al., 2008). Grade I tumors are benign, slow-growing, and respond well to surgery. Grade II tumors are malignant, have a higher likelihood of recurrence following surgery, but grow relatively slowly. Grade III tumors are malignant and require more aggressive therapies than Grade II tumors, and Grade IV tumors can

benign tumor An abnormal cell growth that develops within its own membrane and is unlikely to recur following surgery to remove it.

glioma (glee-OH-muh) A tumor that develops from glial cells.

meningioma (meh-nin-jee-OH-muh) A tumor arising from the tissue of the meninges.

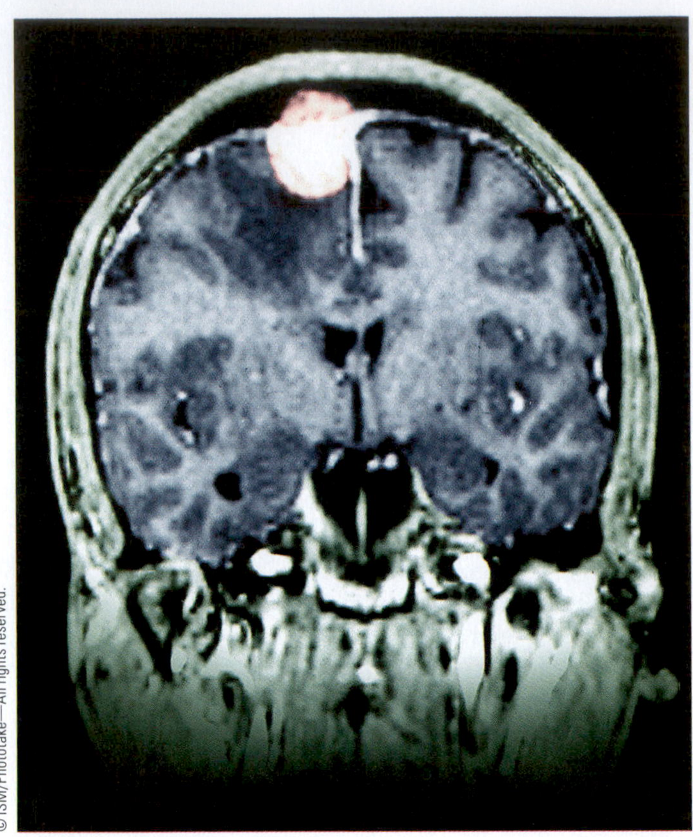

Figure 15.6
A Meningioma Meningiomas, such as the one shown in the light area of this image, are tumors that arise in the meninges surrounding the brain. Although typically benign, meningiomas can still disrupt brain functioning by the pressure they exert on adjacent tissues.

be rapidly fatal. Survival rates following diagnosis can vary from decades to months, depending on the type of tumor.

Treatment for Tumors The most common approach to brain tumors is surgical removal. In addition to surgery, or in cases in which surgery is very risky or impossible, radiation of the tumor is used. Chemotherapy, in which chemicals that destroy tumor cells are applied via the bloodstream, has proven quite challenging for use with brain tumors because most chemotherapy agents do not cross the blood–brain barrier (see Chapter 4). Newer agents are being developed that either interfere with the blood–brain barrier or bypass it completely (Blakeley, 2008; Levin, 2002). Researchers have also implanted dissolving, chemotherapy-releasing wafers during surgery to remove tumors (Massachusetts General Hospital/Harvard Medical School, 2002). Another recent approach is the use of thalidomide to "starve" tumors by reducing the growth of blood vessels supplying them (Fine et al., 2007). Thalidomide became infamous during the 1950s and 1960s because when taken by pregnant women, it produces serious birth defects, such as undeveloped limbs. However, it is proving useful as a treatment of tumors in conjunction with surgery and chemotherapy. In animal models, anticancer genes inserted into stem cells, which are then delivered to a tumor, have produced encouraging results (Aboody, Najbauer, & Danks, 2008).

Seizures and Epilepsy

Seizures are uncontrolled electrical disturbances in the brain that are correlated with changes in consciousness. Seizures often occur as a result of brain injury, infection, or withdrawal from drugs, but other seizures appear without an obvious cause. When patients experience repetitive, unprovoked seizures, they are diagnosed with **epilepsy** (Hauser & Beghi, 2008). To diagnose a seizure disorder reliably, electroencephalography (EEGs) and imaging (CT, PET, or MRI) are used to look for abnormalities in brain activity. However, not all individuals with a seizure disorder will demonstrate abnormal scans, nor do all people with abnormal scans experience seizures.

Patients who experience seizures when exposed to flashing lights of specific intensities and frequencies have a condition known as photosensitive epilepsy. This condition is most common in children and adolescents and rarely occurs later than a person's twenties. Many video games emit just the right type of photostimulation to trigger seizures in sensitive individuals. Precautions include sitting away from televisions and computer monitors, using glare protection, and taking frequent breaks (Epilepsy Foundation, 2002).

Some seizures appear to occur when the brain's balance between excitation and inhibition is disturbed. As we observed in Chapter 4, gamma-aminobutyric acid (GABA) is one of the primary inhibitory neurotransmitters in the brain. Changes in GABA activity can either produce or prevent seizures (Jacob, Moss, & Jurd, 2008). Drugs that inhibit GABA activity produce seizures (Butuzova & Kitchigina, 2008). Withdrawal from drugs that interact with GABA receptors, such as alcohol, also produces severe seizures (Ritvo & Park, 2007; Rogawski, 2005). Many medications used to control seizures enhance the action of GABA (Meldrum & Rogawski, 2007).

seizure An uncontrolled electrical disturbance in the brain.
epilepsy (EP-i-lep-see) A disorder characterized by repeated seizure activity in the brain.
partial seizure A seizure that has a clear area of origin, or focus.
generalized seizure A seizure that affects the brain symmetrically without a clear point of origin.

Types of Seizures Seizures vary widely in terms of their causes, duration, and symptoms. Classification systems help physicians match treatment to the type of seizure (International League Against Epilepsy [ILAE], 2008). We can make an initial distinction between **partial seizures** and **generalized seizures.** Partial seizures originate in an identifiable part of the brain (the focus or focal area) and then spread outward. Generalized seizures do not appear to have a focus or clear point of origin and affect both sides of the brain symmetrically. Some partial seizures are preceded by an **aura,** or premonition of the impending seizure. In some cases, the aura involves sensory distortions, whereas in others, it is simply the sense that a seizure will occur soon. Generalized seizures typically are not accompanied by an aura.

Partial seizures are further divided into simple and complex seizures. **Simple partial seizures** cause movements or sensations appropriate to the location of the starting point, or focus, of the seizure activity. These seizures are not accompanied by changes in consciousness. An example of a simple partial seizure affecting the motor cortex is the **Jacksonian seizure,** named after John Hughlings Jackson, a nineteenth-century observer of seizure disorders. In Jacksonian seizures, motor disturbance moves from one part of the body to the next in what is called the **Jacksonian march,** reflecting the representation of each body part in the motor cortex. For instance, if twitching began in a single finger, it might spread to adjacent fingers, the hand, the arm, and so on.

Complex partial seizures normally begin in the temporal lobes and are associated with alterations in consciousness. During the seizure, the patient is likely to be very confused and will often have no memory of the seizure. In some cases, the person has the sense that he or she is reexperiencing a past event. In others, there is a sense that his or her environment is oddly unknown or foreign.

During partial seizures, neurons within the seizure focus show a characteristic electrical response pattern known as the **paroxysmal depolarizing shift (PDS),** which can be observed in an electroencephalogram (EEG) recording of the patient's brain activity (Westbrook, 2000). The PDS begins with a large, abrupt depolarization of affected neurons that triggers a train of action potentials and is followed by a period of hyperpolarization. This excitatory activity overwhelms the GABA-mediated inhibitory system, leading to high-frequency discharges of action potentials (Westbrook, 2000).

Generalized seizures symmetrically affect both sides of the brain and do not appear to have a focus, or clear point of origin. Generalized seizures appear to result from the activation of circuits connecting the thalamus with the cortex. The differences between the spread of abnormal activation in partial and generalized seizures are illustrated in ■ Figure 15.7.

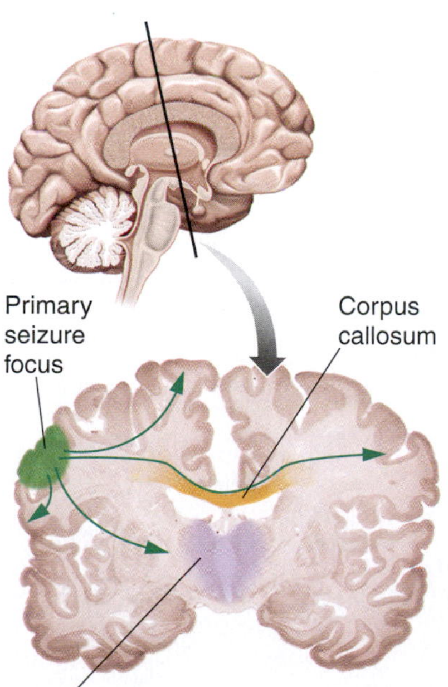

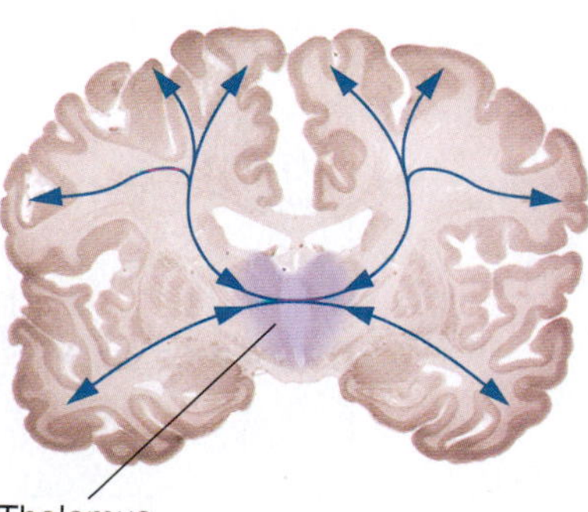

■ **FIGURE 15.7**
Pathways for the Spread of Partial and Generalized Seizures (a) Partial seizures originate in a focus and spread to cortical and subcortical structures.
(b) Generalized seizures do not originate in a focus. Once they begin, generalized seizures spread through the brain symmetrically via connections between the thalamus and cortex.

aura A subjective sensory or motor sensation that signals the onset of a seizure or migraine.

simple partial seizure A seizure with symptoms that relate to the functions of the focal area.

Jacksonian seizure A type of simple partial seizure originating in the motor cortex.

Jacksonian march During some simple partial seizures, the progression of convulsions or twitches from body part to body part related to the organization of the primary motor cortex.

complex partial seizure A type of partial seizure originating in the temporal lobes.

paroxysmal depolarizing shift (PDS) A characteristic electrical pattern that occurs in neurons within a focus during a partial seizure.

grand mal seizure A generalized seizure that results in violent convulsions; also known as a tonic-clonic seizure.

petit mal seizure A mild type of generalized seizure in which the patient experiences a brief period of unconsciousness.

The two major categories of generalized seizure are the **grand mal** and **petit mal seizures.** In French, *grand* means "large," *petit* means "small," and *mal* means "pain." Grand mal seizures are also referred to as tonic-clonic seizures, due to the alternating phases of activity the person experiences. These violent seizures begin with a 10-second **tonic phase** characterized by loss of consciousness, cessation of breathing, and intense muscular contraction. The tonic phase gives way to a **clonic phase,** which lasts about one minute. In this phase, the body experiences violent, rhythmic contractions that often result in broken bones or other physical injuries. Urination and defecation can occur. Due to accompanying autonomic excitation, the person will sweat and salivate profusely. Cycling of tonic and clonic phases is followed by a period of **coma**, lasting about five minutes. The muscles relax, breathing resumes normally, but the person remains unconscious. Following the coma, the person may awaken or transition into sleep. An image of an EEG recording of a grand mal seizure can be seen in ■ Figure 15.8.

The aim of medicine is to prevent disease and prolong life, the ideal of medicine is to eliminate the need of a physician.
William J. Mayo

Petit mal seizures are much less violent than grand mal seizures. For about 10 seconds, the person loses consciousness, and motor movements are limited to blinking, head turns, and eye movements. These seizures are sometimes referred to as "absence seizures" because the person is unaware of his or her surroundings during the seizure. If the person happens to be standing or sitting, he or she does not fall over, in contrast to the complete loss of body control seen in a grand mal seizure. Petit mal seizures are accompanied by a highly characteristic EEG pattern known as a "3/sec spike and wave," which is also illustrated in Figure 15.8.

Treatment for Epilepsy Medications used to treat epilepsy are known as antiepileptic drugs, or AEDs. Many AEDs act as GABA agonists, although others target sodium and calcium channels (see Chapter 3). If medications are not effective, surgery might be indicated (see Chapter 13). Children ages 12 and younger whose seizures do not respond to medication often benefit from following a ketogenic diet, which is heavy in fats and low in carbohydrates, similar to the popular Atkins diet. As a result of this type of diet, the brain uses fat byproducts instead of glucose for fuel. For reasons that are not fully understood, following a ketogenic diet appears to reduce the frequency of seizures (Epilepsy Foundation, 2002).

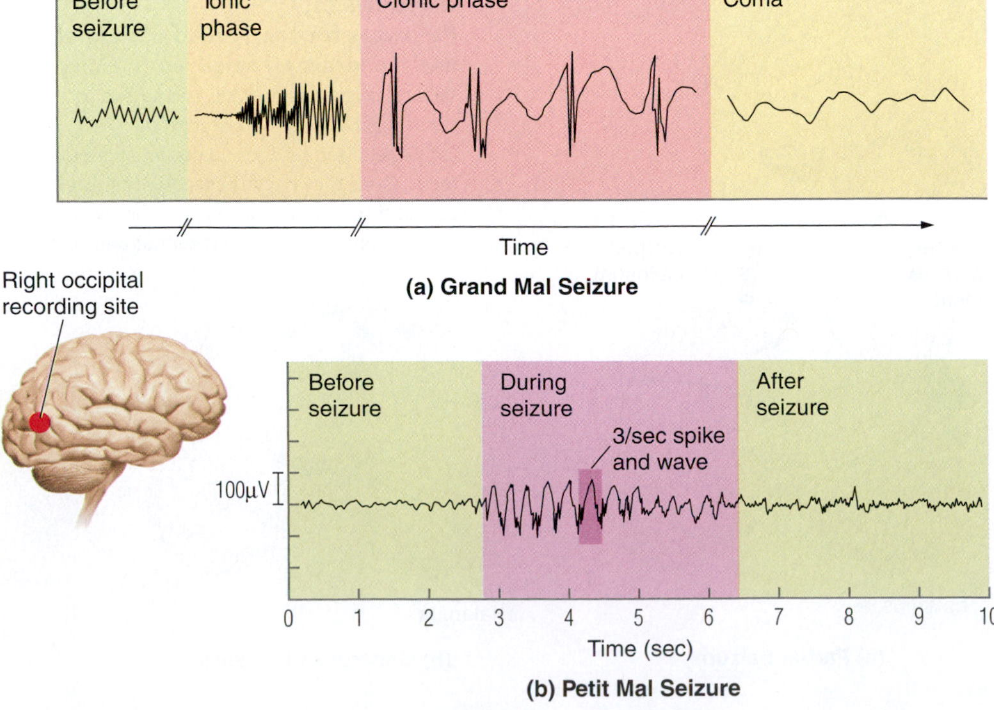

■ **FIGURE 15.8**
EEG Recordings During Generalized Seizures In the upper image, we see recordings made during the stages of a grand mal, or tonic-clonic, seizure. The lower image shows recordings made during a petit mal seizure. These recordings illustrate the characteristic "3/sec spike and wave" pattern that generally accompanies this type of seizure.

tonic phase The initial stage of a grand mal seizure, in which the patient experiences a loss of consciousness, cessation of breathing, and muscular contraction.
clonic phase The second phase of a grand mal seizure, characterized by violent, repetitious muscle contractions.
coma A deep, prolonged period of unconsciousness from which the person cannot be awakened.

INTERIM SUMMARY 15.1

Summary Table: Characteristics of Partial and General Seizures

Type of Seizure	Subtype	Does Seizure Have a Focal Point?	Are Hemispheres Affected Symmetrically?	Major Features of This Type of Seizure
Partial seizures	Simple partial	Yes	No	Movements or sensations appropriate to the location of the focus; example: Jacksonian march
	Complex partial	Yes	No	Begin in temporal lobes; cause cognitive disturbances
Generalized seizures	Grand mal (tonic-clonic)	No	Yes	Tonic phase (loss of consciousness, muscular contraction, cessation of breathing) followed by clonic phase (violent muscular contractions), then coma
	Petit mal	No	Yes	Loss of consciousness; movements restricted to blinking, head turns, and eye movements

Summary Points

1. Strokes are caused by bleeding or the interruption of the supply of oxygen to the brain, leading to excess glutamate activity and localized neural death, or infarct. **(LO1)**
2. Head injuries are classified as open, in which the brain is penetrated, or closed, in which the brain is not penetrated. **(LO2)**
3. Although neurons usually do not form tumors, tumors can arise in the glial cells and meninges of the brain. **(LO3)**
4. Seizures are caused by a number of different conditions and are classified as partial or generalized. **(LO3)**

Review Questions

1. On what basis are some researchers concerned about the mild head injuries that occur in some sports?
2. What are the major causes of seizures?

Multiple Sclerosis

Multiple sclerosis (MS) is an autoimmune condition, in which the immune system attacks the central nervous system. Specifically, MS damages oligodendrocytes (see Chapter 3), leading to the sclerosis, or scarring, that gives the disorder its name and to the demyelination of axons (Zeis & Schaeren-Wiemers, 2008). Typical damage due to MS is shown in ■ Figure 15.9. In some areas, demyelination can lead to damage to the axons themselves. MS typically appears for the first time in young adults and affects nearly twice as many women as men (Alonso & Hernán, 2008).

Because MS can affect white matter in different locations, a variety of cognitive, sensory, and movement problems can occur. Symptoms often include fatigue, muscle weakness, sensory changes, problems with balance, and depression. Pain or tingling sensations in the legs are a common complaint. MS can take several forms in terms of time course and severity. Some patients experience a steady decline in function. Others experience a relapsing–remitting form of the disorder, in which attacks are followed by periods of health. Still others experience a steady decline with superimposed attacks or a transition from relapsing–remitting to a more progressive decline.

Although the autoimmune nature of MS appears quite certain, the exact mechanism responsible for triggering the autoimmune response remains unclear. MS results

multiple sclerosis (MS) An autoimmune disorder that targets the central nervous system, resulting in demyelination and damage to axons.

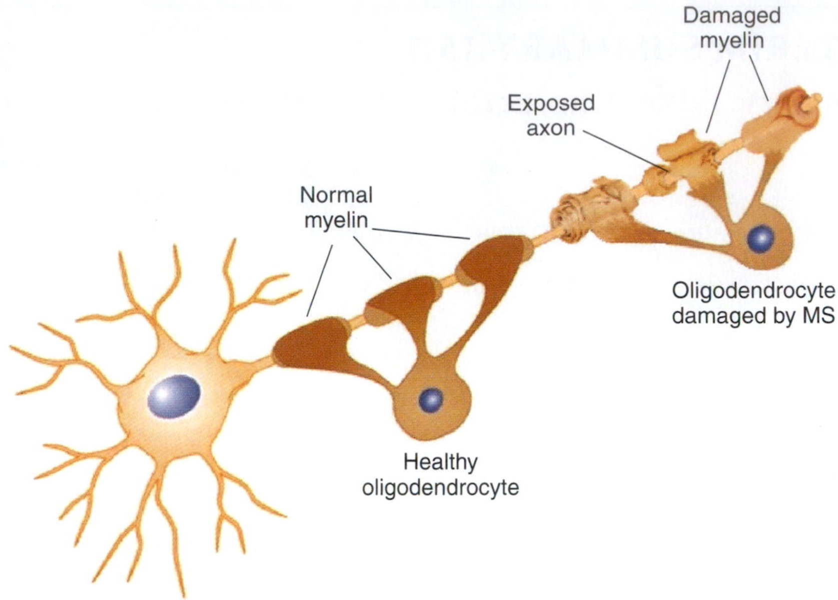

■ **FIGURE 15.9**
Multiple Sclerosis Damages Myelin
In cases of multiple sclerosis, the body's immune system attacks the oligodendrocytes myelinating axons of some central nervous system neurons. Consequently, electrical signals are not transmitted efficiently, leading to a variety of cognitive, sensory, and motor deficits.

from complex interactions between environmental factors and modest heritability (Oksenberg, Baranzini, Sawcer, & Hauser, 2008). Among the environmental factors contributing to MS are exposure to various viruses, including the Epstein-Barr virus responsible for mononucleosis (Levin et al., 2005), and lack of vitamin D due to less exposure to the sun (Islam, Gauderman, Cozen, & Mack, 2007). MS is far less common among people living near the equator than at higher latitudes (Alonso & Hernán, 2008).

Although no cure has been found for MS, a number of medications reduce the severity of attacks and slow the progression of the disease. The relapsing–remitting version of MS is currently most responsive to medical treatment, whereas the progressive forms do not respond as well to existing therapies.

Brain Infections

Certain types of infections manage to circumvent the formidable protection surrounding the brain and nervous system. The psychological consequences of such invasions are dramatic, and most of these disorders are life threatening.

PARASITES

A variety of parasitic infections can affect the central nervous system, but the most common of these is **neurocysticercosis.** This condition results from infection with the pork tapeworm, *Taenia solium,* through the ingestion of *T. solium eggs* in contaminated pork products or in fecal material from infected pigs or humans (Kossoff, 2001). The *T. solium* eggs hatch in the stomach, and the larvae penetrate the intestine and enter the bloodstream. The larvae lodge in soft tissue, notably the skin, muscle, eye, and brain. When this occurs, fluid-filled cysts, approximately 1 to 2 cm in diameter, form around the larvae. The infected person will not experience any symptoms until the encysted worm dies, which can take as long as five years (Kossoff, 2001). Prior to the death of the worm, the body's immune system generally does not recognize or attack it unless the infection involves very large numbers of the parasite. However, when the worm dies, the immune system does act, and inflammation will occur around the cyst. At this time, the most frequent symptom is the sudden onset of partial seizures. A severe case of neurocysticercosis is illustrated in ■ Figure 15.10.

neurocysticercosis (ner-oh-siss-tih-ser-KOH-sis) A condition characterized by brain cysts resulting from parasitic infection by the pork tapeworm, *T. solium.*

Treatment generally consists of medication for seizure control. If the cysts still harbor a live worm, treatment with antiworm (antihelminthic) medications can be useful (Jung, Cárdenas, Sciutto, & Fleury, 2008). If cysts cause uncontrollable seizures,

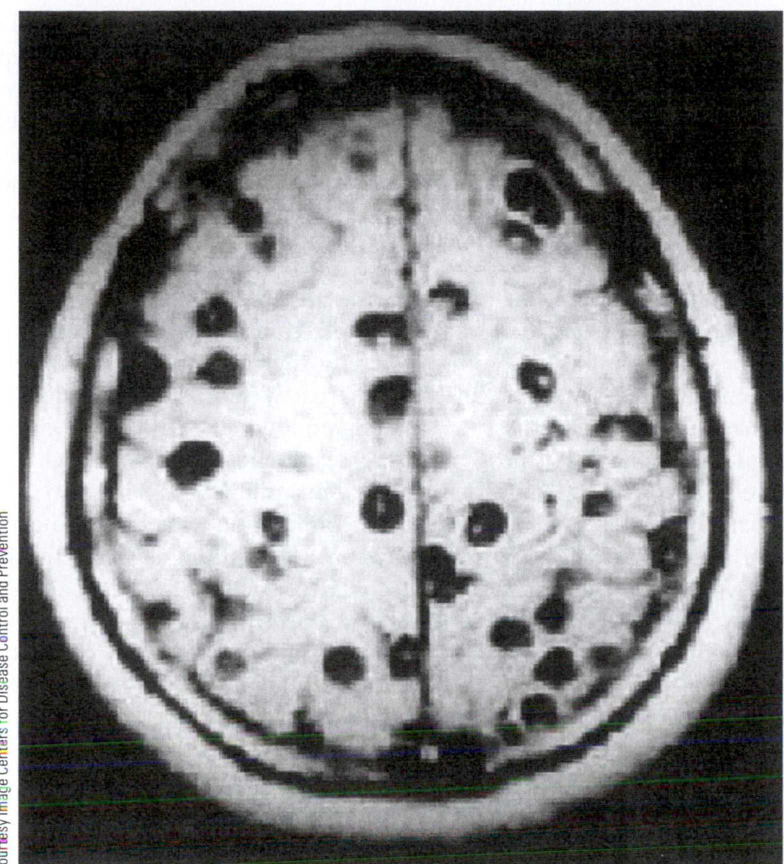

Courtesy Image Centers for Disease Control and Prevention

FIGURE 15.10
Complicated Neurocysticercosis Involves Multiple Infections in the Brain Simple neurocysticercosis usually involves a single cyst and is typical of cases that occur in areas of the world in which the condition is not well established. In the case depicted here, multiple cysts have occurred. These complicated cases usually occur in areas in which the condition is common.

surgery can be performed to remove them. Some progress has been made in preventing the infection, through community education and the development of vaccines for pigs (García et al., 2007).

Bacterial, Viral, and Fungal Infections

Infections of the brain produce a condition known as **encephalitis,** from the Greek *enkephalos* for "brain," and *–itis* for "inflammation." When the infection causes inflammation of the meninges covering the nervous system, the disease is referred to as meningitis (see Chapter 2). Many kinds of bacteria, viruses, and fungi are capable of producing encephalitis and meningitis, and all have serious implications.

Encephalitis Encephalitis is an inflammation of the brain caused by viral infection. In some cases, symptoms are mild. In other cases, encephalitis can lead to convulsions, delirium, coma, and death. Some patients experience permanent impairments to memory, speech, muscle coordination, hearing, and vision.

Two modes of infection produce encephalitis. Primary encephalitis occurs when a virus directly invades the central nervous system. This type of encephalitis frequently occurs as a result of infection with mosquito-borne viruses such as **West Nile virus.** Secondary encephalitis occurs following viral infection of other parts of the body.

There are several variants of primary encephalitis in the United States, including the fairly common but not particularly deadly St. Louis encephalitis and the rare but deadly Eastern equine encephalitis. Probably the most famous type of encephalitis is caused by West Nile virus, which first appeared in the United States in 1999. Like many similar viruses, West Nile virus is transmitted to humans through mosquitoes that have fed on infected birds. Researchers tracking the disease in humans were surprised by both the rate of increase in the number of cases and the speed at which the disease spread geographically. However, it appears that rates of infection in the United States have leveled off (Snapinn et al., 2007).

encephalitis (en-sef-uhl-EYE-tis) A condition characterized by inflammation of the brain.

West Nile virus An encephalitis-causing virus that is carried by birds and transmitted to humans via mosquitoes.

Herpes simplex, the class of viruses responsible for cold sores and genital herpes, produces one of the most serious and likely fatal versions of secondary encephalitis. If a person has a weakened immune system, the herpes virus is able to reactivate and travel to the brain (Whitley, 2006). The damage caused by the virus in encephalitis is similar to that seen in Alzheimer's disease, leading some researchers to suspect a connection between prior herpes infection and subsequent dementia (Zambrano et al., 2008).

Meningitis Inflammation of the meninges, the membranes covering and protecting the brain and nervous system, can result from infection by bacteria, viruses, or fungi. Meningitis produces flulike symptoms, including high temperature, vomiting, diarrhea, and joint and muscle pains. However, meningitis can be distinguished from the flu by the presence of neck stiffness (the inability to touch the chin to the chest), aversion to bright lights, and drowsiness. In some cases, particularly in young children, the rapidly developing fever caused by meningitis often stimulates seizures.

When a lot of remedies are suggested for a disease, that means it can't be cured.
Anton Chekhov

Bacterial meningitis can occur alone or in conjunction with septicemia, or blood poisoning. Bacterial meningitis is caused by several common classes of bacteria. In most people, the body's immune system keeps these bacteria in check, and carrying them actually contributes to the person's natural protection against developing this form of meningitis. Prolonged close contact, coughing, sneezing, and intimate kissing can spread the bacteria. However, the bacteria do not live very long outside the body, so they are not a threat in swimming pools, buildings, and the water supply. Although rare, these infections are considered a medical emergency, with fatality rates between 10 and 20 percent (Meningitis Trust, 2002). Those who recover might still suffer from deafness or brain injury.

Viral meningitis is the most common form of meningitis, but it is generally considered the least dangerous type. Symptoms are similar to those of the bacterial forms of the disease. Many types of viruses can cause meningitis, but the most common are the coxsackie viruses and enteroviruses. Viral meningitis does not respond to antibiotics or to other medications. Headaches, fatigue, and depression can last for weeks or even months.

Some fungi have the ability to produce fungal meningitis. However, these cases are exceedingly rare. Normally, they occur only when a person's immune system has been seriously impaired. Patients with AIDS and those taking medications that suppress the immune system (organ transplant patients or cancer patients) are especially at risk. These cases are slow to develop, hard to diagnose, and difficult to treat.

Meningitis has been shown to be a risk for first-year college students living in dormitories. Both the Centers for Disease Control and the American Academy of Pediatrics recommend that college students learn about the disease and consider vaccination. Between 100 and 125 college students per year become ill with the disease, with 5 to 15 dying from it (Meningitis Foundation of America, 2002).

AIDS Dementia Complex **Acquired immune deficiency syndrome (AIDS)** is a set of symptoms and infections resulting from the damage to the human immune system caused by the **human immunodeficiency virus (HIV). AIDS dementia complex (ADC)** is a collection of neurological symptoms that result either directly from the actions of the HIV virus itself or from other opportunistic infections that can overwhelm the impaired immune system of the HIV patient. The initial symptoms of ADC are relatively mild and can easily be mistaken for depression (see Chapter 16). The patient might complain of difficulty concentrating, forgetfulness, decreased work productivity, low sex drive, social withdrawal, and general apathy. In more advanced cases, serious motor and cognitive problems begin to emerge. Imbalance, clumsiness, and weakness are followed by memory loss and language impairment. In children with HIV, ADC expresses itself primarily in a failure to reach normal developmental milestones. In children, HIV appears to affect the central nervous system from the outset of infection, whereas in adults, ADC usually occurs much later in the course of the disease.

acquired immune deficiency syndrome (AIDS) A disease of the human immune system caused by the human immunodeficiency virus (HIV) that renders the subject highly vulnerable to life-threatening conditions.

human immunodeficiency virus (HIV) The virus responsible for AIDS.

AIDS dementia complex (ADC) A collection of neurological symptoms that result either directly from the actions of the HIV virus itself or from other opportunistic infections overlooked by the impaired immune system of the HIV patient.

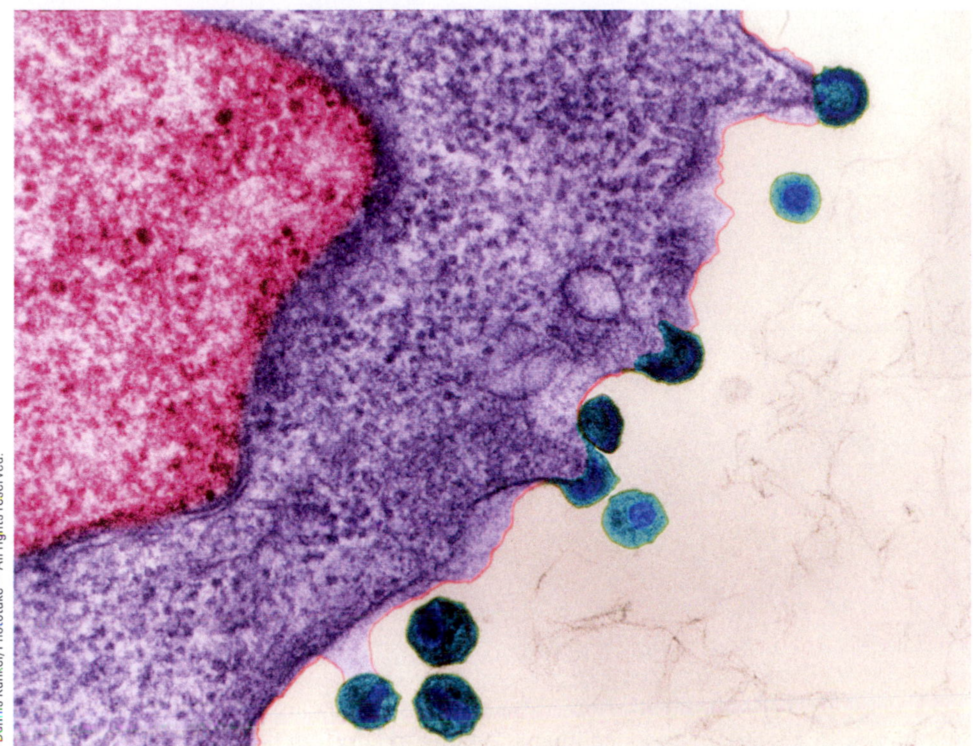

Figure 15.11 HIV Viral Particles Bud from an Infected Cell In cases of AIDS dementia complex, many cells containing the HIV virus can be observed. In the image shown here, the particles budding from an infected cell burst, leading to further spreading of the virus within the brain.

I tell you, it's funny because the only time I think about HIV is when I have to take my medicine twice a day.

Magic Johnson

The action of the HIV virus on neural cell death appears to be indirect. HIV directly invades macrophages (cells that are part of the immune system), microglia, astrocytes, and the vascular endothelial cells that line the blood vessels serving the brain. HIV does not, however, invade neurons themselves (Bowers, 1996). The infected cells release chemical messengers known as cytokines, which then damage neighboring neurons by inducing apoptosis, or programmed cell death (see Chapter 5). Additional damage occurs when a substance found in the external envelope of the HIV virus binds to NMDA receptors. Consequently, too much calcium enters the neuron, triggering neural death. As shown in Figure 15.11, viral particles form buds on infected cells, which frequently burst and continue the spread of the virus.

Treatment for ADC consists of efforts to postpone the inevitable damage. Standard antiretroviral medications used for HIV infection have significantly reduced the prevalence of ADC (Price & Spudich, 2008).

Transmissible Spongiform Encephalopathies (TSEs)

Among the most dramatic neurological disorders are the **transmissible spongiform encephalopathies (TSEs),** a group that includes **bovine spongiform encephalopathy (BSE),** or so-called mad-cow disease. The symptoms common to this group of diseases are devastating: psychological disturbances, including paranoia, anxiety, and depression in humans and skittishness in herd animals; progressive loss of cognitive function; motor disturbances; and finally death. The brains of animals and people who died from TSEs show a spongelike appearance due to clustered cell death, which is the source of the word *spongiform* in the name of the disorders. Figure 15.12 illustrates the spongiform appearance of the brain of a cow infected with mad-cow disease.

The TSE Mystery Our current understanding of TSEs began in eighteenth-century England. At that time, a disease known as **scrapie** was first identified among sheep and goats. The disease got its name from the fact that afflicted animals, such as the sheep

transmissible spongiform encephalopathy (TSE) (SPONGE-ee-form en-seh-full-AW-path-ee) A disease that can be transferred from one animal to another and that produces a fatal, degenerative condition characterized by dementia and motor disturbance.

bovine spongiform encephalopathy (BSE) A form of TSE that primarily affects cattle; mad-cow disease.

scrapie A TSE disease that infects sheep and goats.

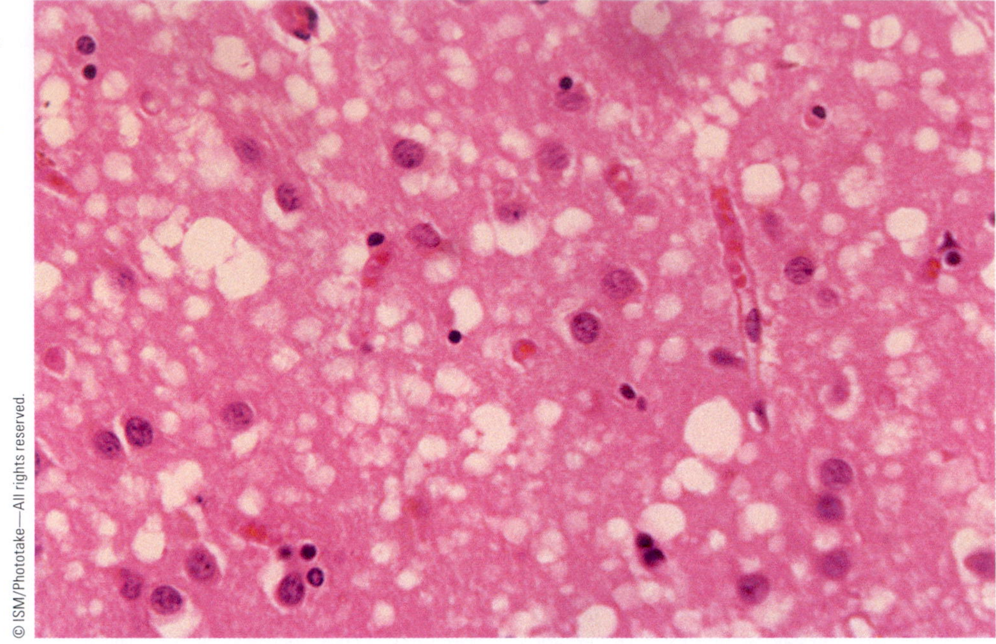

■ **FIGURE 15.12**
Bovine Spongiform Encephalopathy ("Mad-Cow" Disease) This image shows the characteristic damage to the brain that gives the TSEs the name *spongiform*.

in ■ Figure 15.13, often developed intense itching in addition to other TSE symptoms, leading them to scratch repeatedly by scraping against something (Prusiner, 1995). Scrapie was not considered a threat because it appeared unable to infect humans who consumed meat from infected animals.

H. G. Creutzfeldt (1920) and A. Jakob (1921) published the first descriptions of patients with a human form of TSE. The condition described by these physicians became known as **Creutzfeldt-Jakob disease (CJD).** CJD is quite rare, with only 0.5–1 case per million worldwide (UK Creutzfeldt-Jakob Disease Surveillance Unit, 2002). The causality of CJD was mixed, with some cases running in families and others resulting from spontaneous genetic mutation. A very small number of cases of CJD result from the transplanting of tissues or use of contaminated neurosurgical instruments. These cases demonstrated that the causal factors involved in infectious CJD are not destroyed by current medical sterilization techniques.

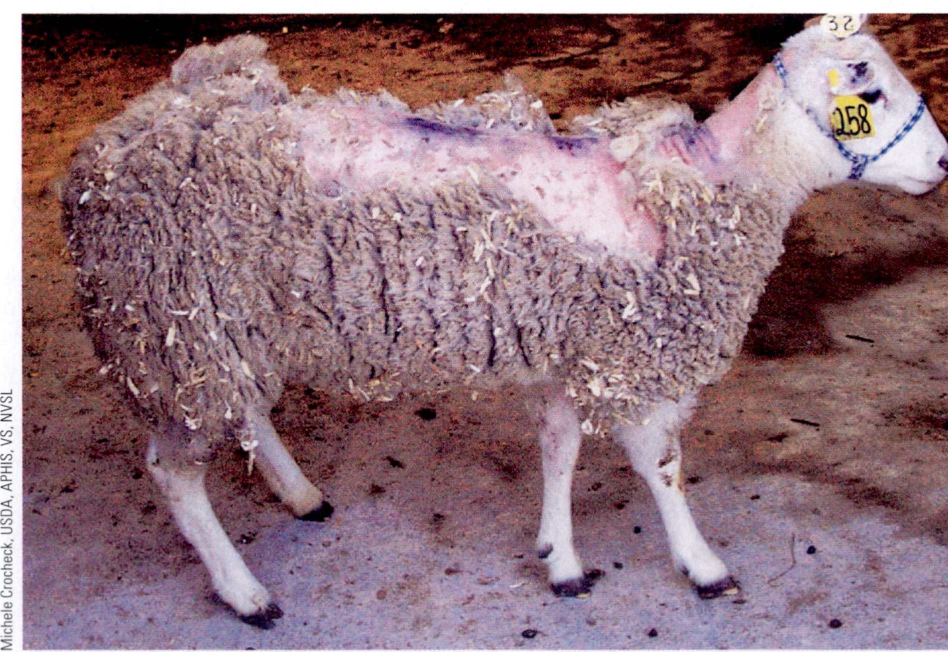

■ **FIGURE 15.13**
A Sheep with Scrapie Scrapie, a TSE affecting sheep and goats, was first observed 300 years ago in England. The condition was named after the fact that afflicted sheep scraped themselves against other objects, removing much of their wool.

Creutzfeldt-Jakob disease (CJD) (KROITS-felt YAH-kobe) A human TSE that results in a progressively degenerative condition characterized by movement and cognitive disorder.

Another piece of the TSE puzzle fell into place during the 1950s, when scholars investigated a neurodegenerative disease known as **kuru,** which was identified among the Fore people of New Guinea. Kuru, shown in ■ Figure 15.14, produced symptoms that were very similar to CJD. Kuru initially appeared to be a genetic condition, but it was eventually traced to the Fore's practice of cannibalism of relatives that was part of their burial ritual (Gadjusek & Zigas, 1957). Following legislation outlawing cannibalism, kuru gradually disappeared.

Proof that kuru was transmissible came from research in which brain tissue from patients who died from the disease was injected into the brains of chimpanzees (Gadjusek, Gibbs, & Alpers, 1966). The infected chimpanzees developed symptoms of kuru, and their brains were found to contain the characteristic spongy tissue associated with a TSE. Monkeys injected with tissue from people who had died of Creutzfeldt-Jakob disease also developed a TSE (Gadjusek, 1973).

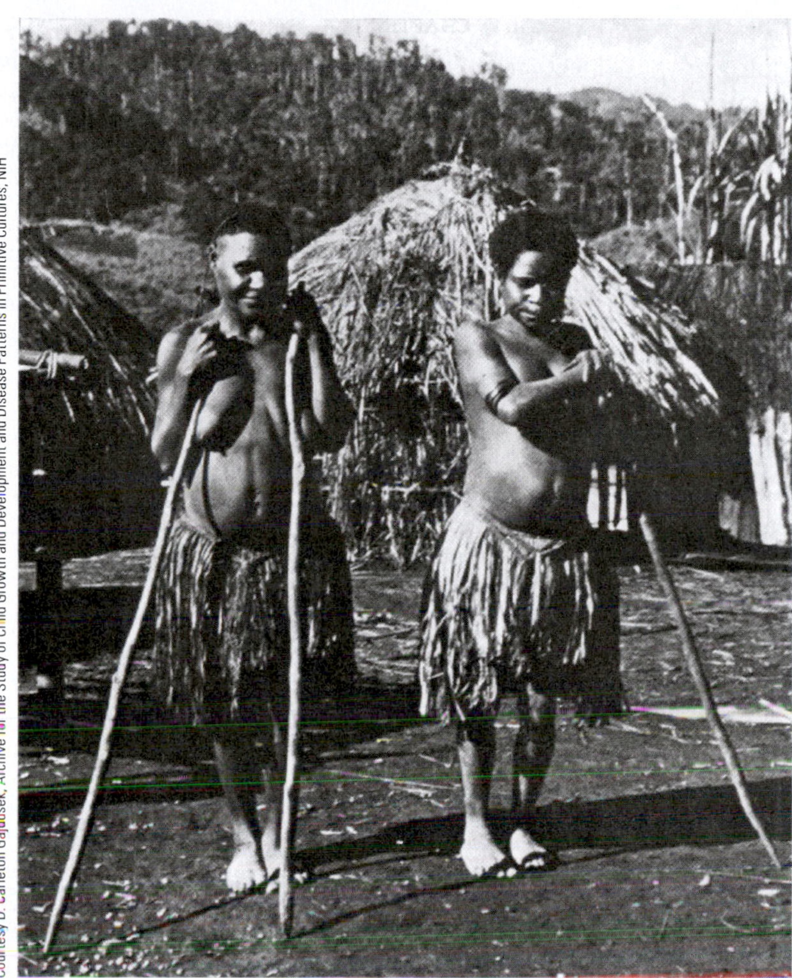

Courtesy D. Carleton Gajdusek, Archive for the Study of Child Growth and Development and Disease Patterns in Primitive Cultures, NIH

■ **FIGURE 15.14**
Kuru Occurred Among the Fore of New Guinea This photograph of two Fore women with kuru was among Gadjusek's original field study photos taken in 1960. Both women required the use of a stick to stand, and they died within six months.

Prions and TSEs Initially, both kuru and CJD were believed to be the result of a very slow-acting virus. However, the infectious agent involved in TSEs acted in ways that were distinct from the behavior of any known viruses. The incubation period was unusually long, and there was no sign of the inflammation typically found in viral infections. The infectious agent seemed remarkably able to withstand hospital sterilization techniques. Stanley Prusiner (1982) proposed that TSEs were caused by a new type of infectious agent, a single protein, which he named a **prion.**

The prion protein can exist in two forms, depending on how it's folded (Prusiner, 1995). The normal version became known as PrP^{c} (prion protein cellular), whereas the abnormal version involved in scrapie became known as PrP^{sc} (prion protein scrapie).

Prusiner (1995) argued that the abnormal version of the protein, PrP^{sc}, is the cause of TSEs. If the abnormal protein somehow manages to get into the brain, it appears to convert normal PrP^{c} proteins into the abnormal form, as shown in ■ Figure 15.15. In cell cultures, the PrP^{sc} filled neurons, eventually causing them to explode. The abnormal prions were then released to convert proteins in adjacent cells.

Prusiner has also attempted to explain the species barrier often observed in TSEs. As noted previously, scrapie in sheep was not viewed as a threat to humans because countries with high scrapie rates do not show corresponding high human TSE levels. One suggestion is that the more similar the abnormal sequence of PrP is to the normal sequence, the more likely transmission can occur. Sheep scrapie can spread to cows because sheep and bovine PrP are different at only seven locations. In contrast, human and bovine PrP are different at 30 locations. However, similarities in some portions of the PrP protein are more crucial to crossing the species barrier than others.

BSE and New Variant Creutzfeldt-Jakob Disease (vCJD) In 1985, an outbreak of BSE (mad-cow disease) occurred, beginning in Great Britain. The BSE epidemic resulted from changes in procedures for producing animal feed. Ground meat and bone meal were included as a protein source in animal feed, allowing infected tissue to be included. Once steps were taken to resolve these feeding practices, the BSE epidemic began to abate, as shown in ■ Figure 15.16.

kuru (KER-oo) A human TSE identified among the Fore of New Guinea, related to their practice of cannibalism.

prion (PREE-on) A protein particle that lacks nucleic acid and is believed to be responsible for TSEs.

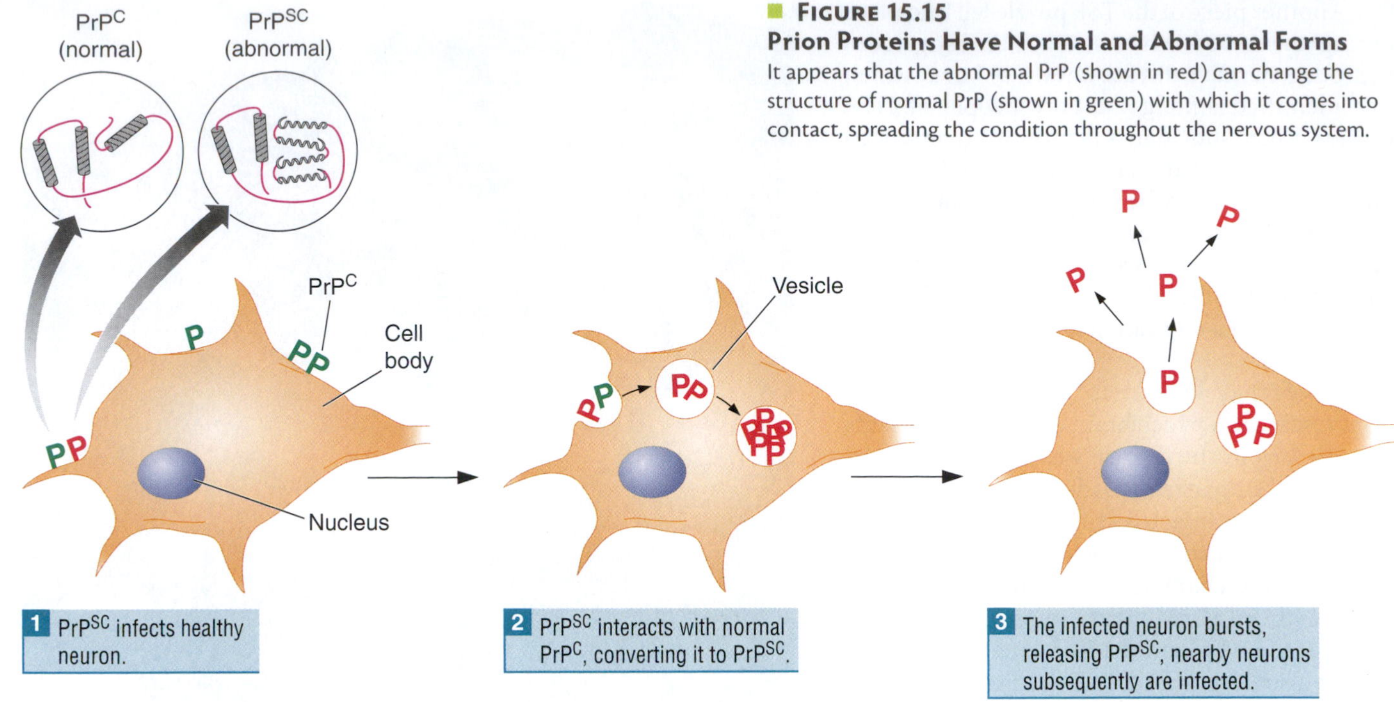

FIGURE 15.15
Prion Proteins Have Normal and Abnormal Forms It appears that the abnormal PrP (shown in red) can change the structure of normal PrP (shown in green) with which it comes into contact, spreading the condition throughout the nervous system.

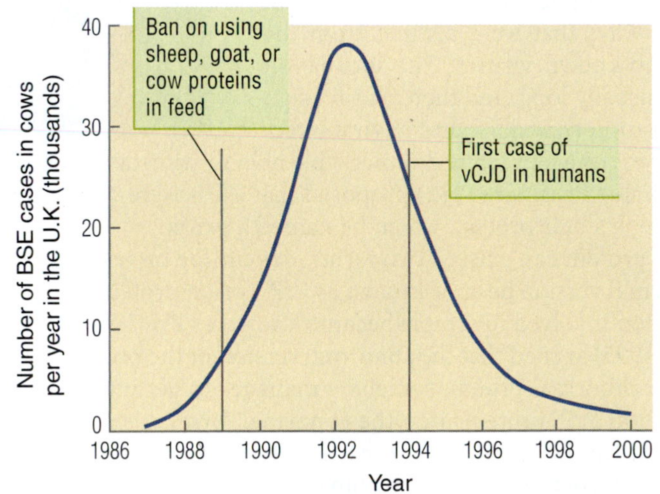

FIGURE 15.16
Time Course of the BSE Epidemic in the United Kingdom Steps that have been taken against the BSE epidemic in the United Kingdom are working. The use of sheep, goats, or cattle in animal feed has been banned, and cattle exports to other countries ceased. These data reflect the long incubation periods of TSEs. The benefits of the new feeding practices did not show until several years had passed. In addition, the first related case of vCJD was diagnosed several years after the disease in cattle had been identified and addressed. *Source*: Adapted from BSE Web site at the University of Illinois, Urbana-Champaign.

The infectious agent responsible for BSE in cows caused a corresponding outbreak of **new variant Creutzfeldt-Jakob disease (vCJD)** in humans (Bruce et al., 1997; Hill et al., 1997). The new variant CJD cases differed from classic CJD on a number of dimensions. Patients with vCJD were an average of 28 years old at diagnosis, whereas classic CJD patients were an average of 63 years old (USDA, 2002). A comparison of age at death for the two versions of CJD is shown in Figure 15.17. Brain pathologies were similar, but vCJD showed greater concentration of prion protein plaques (USDA, 2002).

Efforts to contain BSE include bans on the use of mammal proteins in animal feed and limitations on cattle exports from infected countries. Because the infectious agents do not exist in muscle, steak is probably still safe. However, hamburgers, sausages, and other products that contain nervous system tissues should be avoided (Centers for Disease Control [CDC], 2007). Hopefully, these precautions will make vCJD, like kuru before it, a thing of the past.

new variant Creutzfeldt-Jakob disease (vCJD) A human TSE resembling classic CJD that results from consumption of beef products contaminated by BSE.

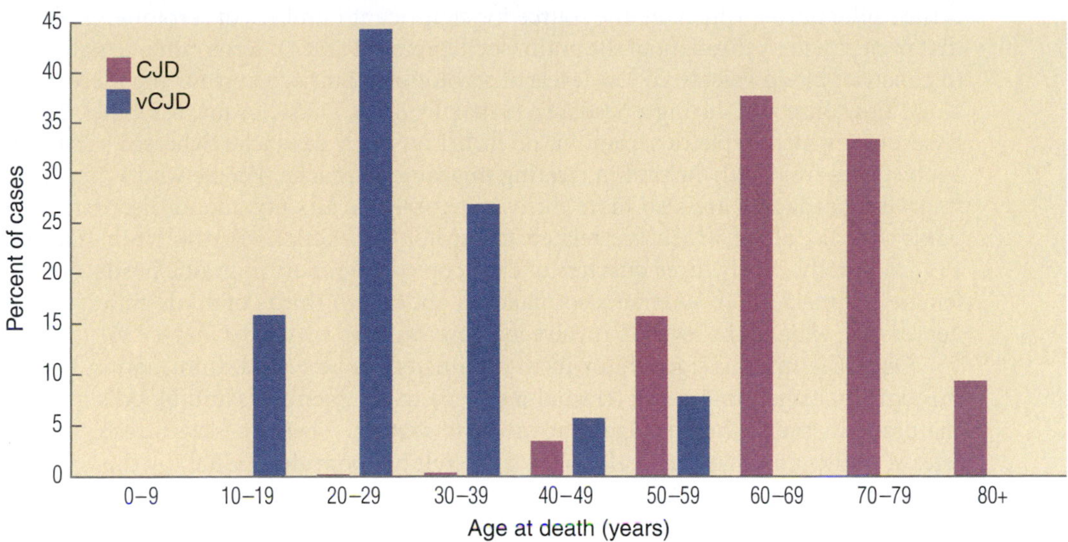

FIGURE 15.17 Classic Creutzfeldt-Jakob Disease Shows a Different Age Prevalence than New Variant Creutzfeldt-Jakob Disease Among the differences between CJD and vCJD, which is believed to result from consumption of BSE-contaminated tissues, are the ages at death. Classic CJD has an average age of onset of 68 years, with death occurring shortly thereafter, as opposed to 28 years for vCJD. *Source:* Ghani et al., 1998.

Migraine

Migraine, which affects as many as 28 percent of the population, produces symptoms of excruciating head pain, nausea, and vomiting for a period of 4 to 72 hours (Stovner, Zwart, Hagen, Terwindt, & Pascual, 2006). For some patients, these symptoms are preceded by an aura, which may take a form similar to that shown in Figure 15.18. For many years, it was assumed that headache pain originated in the blood vessels of the head. This idea was put forward by Sir Thomas Willis in the seventeenth century (Larkin, 1997a). Willis proposed the so-called vascular theory of headache, which suggested that increased blood flow to the brain acted to distend the blood vessels. The distended blood vessels would, in turn, exert pressure on tissues surrounding the brain, producing a sensation of pain.

More contemporary researchers have hypothesized that a "migraine generator" might be located in the brainstem (Weiller et al., 1995). One candidate for a generator

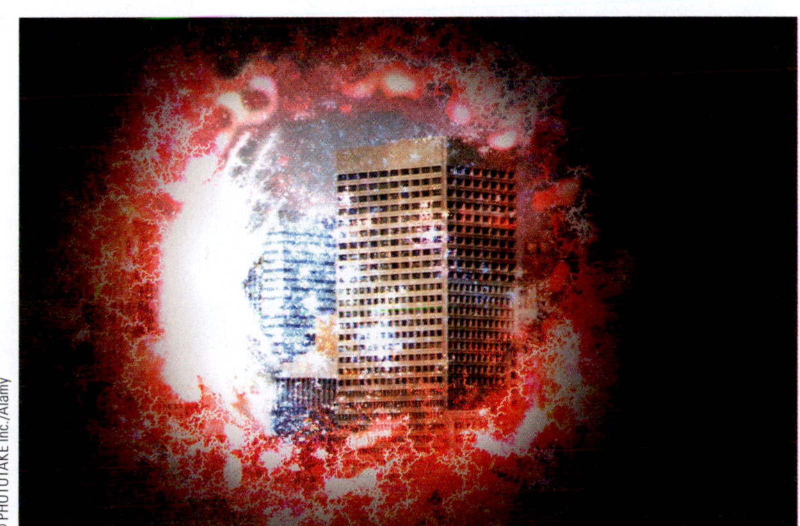

FIGURE 15.18 Migraine Aura Many patients with migraine experience an aura, or period of sensory distortion, prior to a headache. This image is an artist's rendition of a commonly described visual aura.

migraine A genetically related condition, usually featuring a severe form of headache, nausea, and sensory distortions.

trigeminovascular system (trie-jem-in-oh-VASS-kew-lar) The network formed by the trigeminal nerves, meninges, and blood vessels believed to participate in migraine headache.

calcitonin gene-related peptide (CGRP) (kal-si-TOE-nin) A peptide neurotransmitter released by the trigeminal nerve that might participate in the production of migraine headaches.

triptan One of a new class of highly specific serotonin agonists used to treat migraine headache.

is the raphe nuclei, which are the source for significant numbers of serotonergic fibers that project widely throughout the brain (see Chapters 2 and 4). Serotonin normally acts to constrict blood vessels, so low levels of serotonin might account for the increase in blood flow observed during a headache (Sakai, Dobson, Diksic, Aubé, & Hamel, 2008). Reserpine, which depletes serotonin, often brings on a headache, whereas serotonin agonists are frequently helpful in treating migraine headache. People who suffer from migraine headaches are also more likely to experience anxiety, mood disorders, and panic attacks, all of which are related to serotonin functions in the brain (Larkin, 1997b). Finally, nearly three quarters of the people who report migraine headaches are female (Hamel, 2007). Women also make up about two thirds of adult patients with depression, which is believed to involve low serotonin activity (see Chapter 16).

Once the migraine generator in the brainstem is activated, information travels through the trigeminal nerve (cranial nerve V) to the meninges and blood supply of the brain in the so-called **trigeminovascular system.** These messages result in the release of the glutamate and **calcitonin gene-related peptide (CGRP)** by the trigeminal nerve (Xiao, Richter, & Hurley, 2008). The release of these neurotransmitters reactivates the trigeminal nerves and produces dilation of the blood vessels, leading to pain. The critical point here is that increased blood flow is a reaction to events in the brainstem that lead to a headache, not a cause of headache as proposed by Willis.

In most cases, migraine headaches are treated with medications. The newest of these are the **triptans,** which are highly selective serotonin agonists. Triptans prevent the release of CGRP and the subsequent chain of events that leads to a migraine (Xiao et al., 2008). Behavioral adjustments can decrease the frequency of migraines, too. Exposure to light, certain foods, lack of sleep, hormonal irregularities, anxiety, and stress can lead to more frequent headaches.

INTERIM SUMMARY 15.2

Summary Table: Infections with Neurological Consequences

Type of Infection	Causes	Symptoms	Treatments
Neurocysticercosis	Pork tapeworm, *Taenia solium*	• Sudden-onset partial seizures • Nausea, vomiting, headaches • Confusion, inattention, poor balance	• Antihelminthic (anti-worm) medication • Medication for seizure control • Surgery to remove encysted worms
Encephalitis	Viruses	• Brain inflammation • Symptoms vary from mild to very severe, including death	• No treatments currently available • Preventive measures such as mosquito eradication
Meningitis	Viruses, bacteria, or fungi	• Flulike symptoms • Neck stiffness • Aversion to bright light • Drowsiness	• Antibiotics for bacterial infections only
AIDS dementia complex	HIV virus	• Depressive symptoms • Motor disturbance • Cognitive disturbance	• Antiretroviral medications to slow progress of infection
Transmissible spongiform encephalopathies (TSEs)	Possibly prions or slow-acting viruses	• Paranoia, anxiety, depression • Dementia • Motor disturbances • Death	• No treatments currently available • Avoidance of contamination from medical procedures or infected food

(continued)

INTERIM SUMMARY 15.2 (continued)

Summary Points

1. Multiple sclerosis is an autoimmune disorder in which the oligodendrocytes forming myelin in the central nervous system are damaged. (LO4)
2. A number of serious infections by parasites, bacteria, viruses, and fungi can affect the brain. (LO5)
3. Transmissible spongiform encephalopathies (TSEs) are fatal, degenerative conditions characterized by paranoia, depression, dementia, and motor disturbance. (LO6)
4. TSEs appear to be transmitted through abnormal prions, which are proteins that seem able to transform normal proteins into disease-causing prions. (LO6)
5. Migraine, once believed to be the result of a vascular disorder, might arise due to neural events in a brainstem "migraine generator" that involves the neurotransmitter serotonin. (LO7)

Review Questions

1. What are the major types of parasites, bacteria, viruses, and fungi that can infect the brain and meninges?
2. What evidence suggests that TSEs are caused by prions rather than by more conventional agents such as viruses?

Assessment of Neurological Disorders

Although a complete description of techniques used to assess neurological disorders is well beyond the scope of this text, it is helpful to have some familiarity with these practices. If a neurological disorder is suspected, careful observation and questioning are used to pinpoint areas for further examination through imaging and other technologies.

The examiner generally begins the assessment process by obtaining the patient's health history, including past medical problems, health habits, medications taken, and family medical history. Next, details about the current complaint are collected. For instance, if the patient is complaining about pain, the examiner would ask further questions related to the onset, duration, location, quality (sharp or dull), and perceived pathways of the pain. While questioning the patient, the observer takes note of his or her state of awareness (alertness or drowsiness), mood, quality of speech, and cognitive abilities, including short-term and long-term memory.

The physical examination of a patient with a suspected neurological disorder will proceed according to the nature of the patient's complaint. Many suspected problems originating in the cranial nerves (see Chapter 2) are assessed through specific tests of sensory systems, including vision, hearing, taste, and smell. Problems related to the cerebellum are typically identified through assessments of balance, coordination, fine motor movements, and gait (walking movements). For patients complaining of muscular weakness or paralysis, systematic analysis should allow the problem to be localized to the muscles themselves, to the peripheral nerves, to the spinal cord, or to the white or gray matter of the brain. Tests of the strength of specific muscles can provide clues to the location of an injury. Many patients with neurological damage experience disturbances in their ability to sense touch, pain, temperature, vibration, and joint position. Tests of these modalities involve comparisons between the same location on the right and left sides of the body. A relative lack of sensation on one side of the body can help localize the damaged part of the nervous system.

Superficial touch sensitivity can be assessed by lightly stroking an area with cotton or with a fingertip. To test superficial pain sensitivity, both sharp and smooth objects (such as a sterile needle and the edge of a tongue depressor) are pressed against the skin in a random pattern. If this test does not elicit a response, additional tests of temperature and deep pressure are indicated. Squeezing a major muscle, such as the biceps muscle of the arm, provides information about the patient's ability to sense deep pressure. A tuning fork is set at a low frequency and placed on bony areas, such as shoulders, elbows, and toe joints, to assess the ability to sense vibration. A patient's sense of joint position is investigated by moving one of the patient's digits, such as a toe, up or down and then asking the patient to describe the direction of movement. A two-point discrimination test involves moving the points of two sharp objects closer together until the patient perceives only a single stimulus (see Chapter 7). With the person's eyes closed, familiar objects, such as keys, paper clips, or coins, are placed in the hand, and the person is asked to identify the object. Alternatively, a number or letter can be drawn on the person's hand or other body part with a blunt marking pen.

As we observed in Chapter 8, several spinal reflexes can be used to assess proper motor function. In addition to the classic patellar (knee-jerk) reflex, neurologists assess reflexes in the abdomen, arm, ankle, and foot to ascertain the level of suspected motor damage. Stroking a quadrant of the abdomen should produce a slight movement of the umbilicus (otherwise known as the belly button) in the direction of the touch. In male patients, stroking the inner thigh proximally to distally should elicit an upward movement of the scrotum and testicle on the stroked side. Exaggerated reflexive movements accompanied by too much muscle tone generally indicate higher levels of motor damage, whereas absent or weak reflexive movements accompanied by flaccidity (poor muscle tone) usually indicate damage at the spinal level. When a patient is unresponsive due to brain injury, neurologists generally use the Glasgow Coma Scale to describe the patient's level of functioning. Scores range from a high of 15, indicating a person who is responsive to stimuli, to a low of 3 for a completely unresponsive person. A score of 7 indicates a coma.

In addition to these primarily medical assessment procedures, neuropsychologists use batteries of tests, such as the Halstead-Reitan battery, to assess the impact of central nervous system damage on cognitive abilities (Boll, 1981). The Halstead-Reitan battery includes tests of intellect, sensation, motor function, attention, and psychological disorder.

WHY DOES THIS MATTER?

What Is a Neuropsychologist?

We hope that you and your friends and loved ones will never need treatment for any of the conditions in this chapter, but if that happens, you might find yourself faced with a bewildering array of professionals. Understanding the roles of these professionals matters because each brings a different perspective and training to patient care. On a happier note, if you are enjoying your biological psychology course, pursuing a career in neuropsychology might be an excellent fit for your interests and abilities.

Neuropsychologists are trained in clinical psychology with a special emphasis on the correlations between brain and behavior. In particular, the neuropsychologist participates in the assessment and treatment of cognitive deficits resulting from most of the conditions discussed in this chapter, including head injury, stroke, and epilepsy. In addition, neuropsychologists also manage cases of psychological disorder from a biological perspective. Neuropsychologists usually obtain doctoral degrees (Ph.D. or Psy.D.) in psychology before pursuing specialized internships.

The role of the neuropsychologist overlaps somewhat with two medical specialties, neurology and psychiatry. Other than the general differences between M.D.s and Ph.D.s, such as the ability of M.D.s to prescribe medication, the differences among the roles of the neuropsychologist, neurologist, and psychiatrist are somewhat arbitrary. By definition, neurologists, who obtain an M.D., or Doctor of Medicine, degree treat problems associated with the nervous system, which again, includes the conditions discussed in this chapter. They tend to do so at a physical level, leaving the emotional, behavioral, and cognitive outcomes of damage to either psychiatrists (also M.D.s) or neuropsychologists. All three types of professionals are typically employed in similar medical and rehabilitation settings.

Given the current time demands on medical doctors under managed care systems, the neuropsychologist is also described as the professional who does the most talking to the patient, in both the assessment and treatment processes. If that has appeal to you from either the patient or career perspective, this is a profession you might want to investigate further.

Recovery from Damage

In the chapter on brain lateralization (Chapter 13), we observed the results of a dramatic surgery known as hemispherectomy, in which an entire cerebral hemisphere is removed to treat life-threatening seizures. It is commonly believed that the success of this operation is based on the plasticity, or ability to reorganize, that is characteristic of the developing but immature brain (see Chapter 5). The observation that young brains reorganize more effectively than adult brains was first articulated by Margaret Kennard (1936, 1942). Consequently, the notion that how well a brain can reorganize itself after damage is a function of the developmental stage is now known as the Kennard Principle. In addition to the success of hemispherectomy procedures, the Kennard Principle is supported by animal research that indicates a significant potential for reorganization in the immature brain. Goldman-Rakic and Rakic (1984) removed an entire occipital lobe from a rhesus monkey in utero. ■ Figure 15.19 illustrates the dramatic structural reorganization that occurred in the monkey's brain as a result of the lesion.

Time is the great physician.
Benjamin Disraeli

Subsequent research, however, has led to modifications of the Kennard Principle. The principle appears to apply to language functions but not necessarily for all cognitive functions. In an examination of 50 patients who had sustained either prenatal or early postnatal right- or left-hemisphere damage, Woods and Teuber (1973) found that language was typically spared in individuals with left-hemisphere damage. These patients compensated for their left hemisphere damage by redeveloping right-hemisphere locations for language. Consequently, their visuospatial skills were less than predicted by their overall intelligence. In contrast, the patients with early right-hemisphere damage did not show any advantages over young adults who sustained right-hemisphere damage. Early damage to the right hemisphere did not produce a compensatory shift of spatial processing to the left hemisphere.

One possible explanation for this discrepancy between the results of damage in the two hemispheres is a crowding process proposed by Teuber and Rudel (1962). In this view, the brain compensates for early damage by reorganizing any available space. Language functions, typically found in the left hemisphere, mature early, as suggested by the considerable language abilities of two-year-olds. In contrast, right-hemisphere functions generally mature later. Therefore, if the left hemisphere is damaged, its functions can migrate to the still-undeveloped right hemisphere. However, if the right hemisphere is damaged, its functions have nowhere to go. This hypothesis predicts that the effects of damage in young children might not be immediately apparent. As the child matures and new skills must be learned, the effects of early damage can emerge for the first time. Banich, Levine, Kim, and Huttenlocker (1990) provided support for the crowding hypothesis in their analysis of the timing of brain damage on subsequent intellectual performance. One group of children (the congenital group) in this study experienced damage before or during birth, whereas the other group (the acquired group) sustained damage at an average age of 3.25 years. In contrast to the Kennard Principle, the children with the earliest lesions did not make the best recovery. Although the congenital group acquired basic language and social skills, they appeared to experience progressive declines in intellectual functioning after the age of six years. In contrast, the children in the acquired group did not show this age-related decline.

■ **Figure 15.19**
Reorganization Occurs Following Brain Damage The left occipital lobe was surgically removed from the brain of this monkey 83 days after conception. The resulting reorganization can be seen in the differences between the right and left inferior parietal lobule. The boundaries of this gyrus are the intraparietal sulcus (labeled IP in the image) and the lunate sulcus (labeled L). The right-hemisphere inferior parietal lobule is normal. The left-hemisphere inferior parietal lobule appears to be nearly twice normal size, extending nearly to the back of the brain.

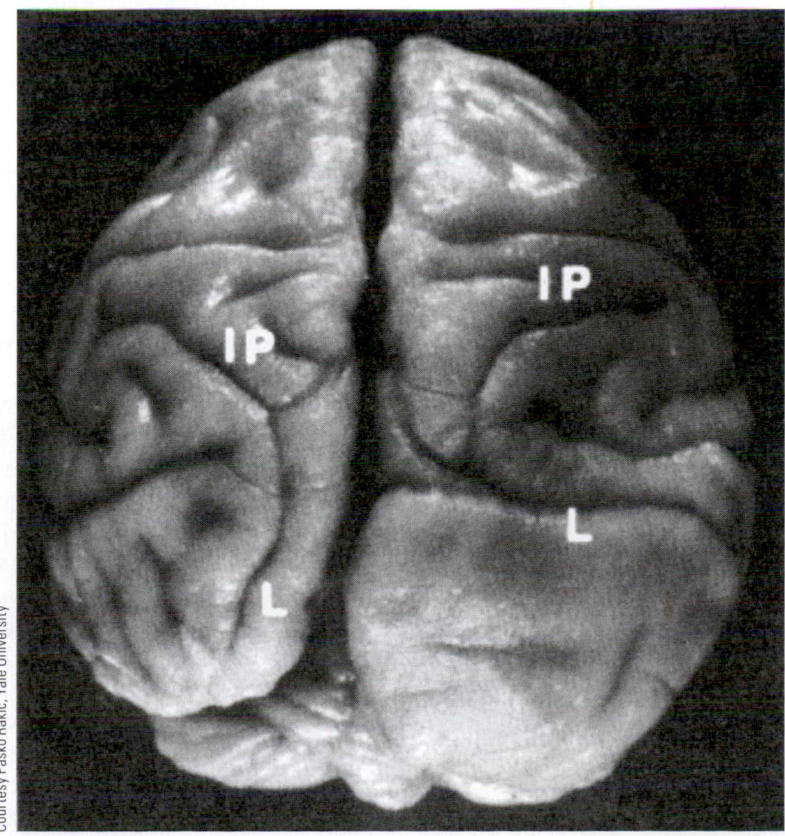

Courtesy Pasko Rakic, Yale University

My disability has not been a severe handicap. Theoretical physics is a good subject for handicapped people because it is all in the mind.
Stephen Hawking

Subsequent research using longitudinal data, in addition to the cross-sectional method used by Banich et al. (1990), has confirmed differences in recovery patterns between children experiencing early and late lesions. Duval, Dumont, Braun, and Montour-Proulx (2002) separated children who had experienced brain damage either before or after the age of seven years into groups. The children with earlier damage did not improve in verbal or procedural intelligence scores, whereas the older children did show improvement. However, as predicted by Banich et al. (1990), the longitudinal methods used by Duval et al. (2002) did not demonstrate an actual decline in intellectual functioning by the group with early damage. Instead, this group simply did not show advantages in recovery.

We do not need to abandon the Kennard Principle completely on the basis of these data. Banich and her colleagues (1990) do point out that the patterns of recovery in the acquired group were nonetheless different from those observed in adults. In our discussion of language in Chapter 13, we noted that damage to Broca's area resulted in deficits in speech production, whereas damage to Wernicke's area resulted in deficits in speech comprehension. The children in Banich et al.'s acquired group did not show such definite correlations between the location of damage and specific cognitive deficits. This finding suggests that children's brains are still somewhat more plastic than the brains of adults.

Recovery of language functions following brain injury appears to be more extensive than recovery of other cognitive processes such as memory. The general consensus seems to be that the majority of any recovery occurs very quickly, within the first three months in the case of stroke (Kreisel, Hennerici, & Bäzner, 2007) and in the first year or two following TBI (Sbordone, Liter, & Pettler-Jennings, 1995). However, patients with TBI interviewed by Sbordone et al. were continuing to make progress at the 10-year mark. These data suggest that efforts to improve functioning should not be abandoned after any specific amount of time after an injury.

Therapy for Brain Damage

Brain injuries from any cause can have debilitating consequences for patients and their families. Fortunately, a variety of therapeutic techniques are available to improve the patients' outcomes and educate and support patients' families.

Rehabilitation

Rehabilitation literally means "to restore to good health." The considerable diversity among types of neurological disorders and their respective symptoms makes a general approach to rehabilitation difficult. However, three factors that typically must be addressed include changes in cognitive abilities related to the disorder, emotional changes due to or in response to the disorder, and physical correlates, such as pain (O'Hara, 1988).

A simple method for improving physical function following brain injury is constraint therapy, in which a good limb is restrained, forcing use of the impaired limb, in combination with rehabilitation exercises (Gauthier et al., 2008). Cognitive function can be improved through reorganization of a function by repetitive training—the so-called mental muscle approach. Just as the function of a muscle might be improved by exercising it, the repetition of a cognitive skill can be used to improve performance. Musso et al. (1999) observed four patients with Wernicke's aphasia, which results in deficits in language comprehension (see Chapter 13). These researchers administered repetitive practice with the Token Test, which tests a participant's ability to comprehend increasingly complex commands (De Renzi & Vignolo, 1962; Spreen & Benton, 1969). Not only did the four patients in this study show improvements in comprehension with practice, but PET scans provided evidence of reorganization in brain areas that normally do not participate in verbal comprehension.

To array a man's will against his sickness is the supreme art of medicine.
Henry Ward Beecher

rehabilitation A therapeutic process designed to restore function after illness or injury.

The "mental muscle" approach focuses on training a general capacity such as attention or language. Alternatively, patients can be trained to carry out specific tasks that

NEW DIRECTIONS

Using Virtual Reality (VR) for Rehabilitation Following Brain Injury

As you saw in the photo at the beginning of this chapter, virtual reality technology allows users to immerse themselves in a realistic artificial environment. Although still far from the holodeck environments portrayed in the *Star Trek* series, today's virtual reality systems are becoming ever more realistic. Among the many possible applications of this technology is its use in rehabilitation following brain injury.

Instead of receiving enrichment, patients recovering from brain damage often experience brain impoverishment because they are unable to provide themselves with the stimulation that could help regain some of their lost function. Tinson (1989) observed that hospitalized patients recovering from stroke spent 30 to 40 percent of their time "disengaged," with only 30 to 60 minutes per day of formal therapy. Through virtual reality simulation, patients can experience moving through a building or up stairs or be exposed to whatever sensory stimulation might be most useful to address their specific deficits (Broeren et al., 2008; Deutsch & Mirelman, 2007). Imaging studies indicate that VR activates the same brain areas as a real interaction with the environment (Rose, Attree, Brooks, & Johnson, 1998). As this technology is refined, we can expect to see improvements in the treatment of patients with brain injuries.

require these cognitive skills. The general approach focuses on brain reorganization, whereas the specific-task approach assumes that patients can learn to use alternate, undamaged strategies for solving specific problems. For example, let's assume that a patient is experiencing difficulties with maintaining attention, a very common symptom of brain damage. Following the mental muscle approach, patients might engage in a variety of repetitive tasks that require attention, such as pressing a buzzer every time they see the number 3. In the specific-skills approach, therapists might select a practical task in which attention is essential, such as driving a car, and specifically train the patient to remaster that task. A meta-analysis that compared repetition strategies with specific-training strategies suggests that the specific-skills approach was more effective than the mental muscle approach (Park & Ingles, 2001).

Pharmacological Therapies

A wide variety of pharmacological approaches to brain damage have been summarized by Steven Cramer (2008). Medications that affect acetylcholine, serotonin, dopamine, and norepinephrine are promising but require further research. Other approaches include the inhibition of chemicals, such as Nogo-A, that normally inhibit axon regrowth. The application of growth factors (see Chapter 5) has been helpful in animal models, but the inability of most of these proteins to cross the blood–brain barrier complicates the use of this therapy in human patients.

Wherever the art of medicine is loved, there is also a love of humanity.

Hippocrates

Damage from strokes without hemorrhage can be minimized if clot-busting drugs are administered promptly. One clot-buster that appears helpful for stroke treatment is found in the saliva of vampire bats (Liberatore et al., 2003). Obviously, the bat needs to keep the victim's blood from clotting.

Neural Tissue Transplants

As we observed in our discussion of Parkinson's disease in Chapter 8, fetal cell transplants in the brain have been used to improve motor function (Lindvall et al., 1992). It is possible that tissue transplants will eventually be helpful in restoring cognitive function in cases of brain damage due to stroke and TBI (Cramer, 2008). Sinden, Hodges, and Gray (1995) describe animal models in which cell grafts improve cognitive functioning following brain damage that is analogous to Alzheimer's disease and ischemia. Clinical trials of cell implants with human stroke patients have also been encouraging (Kondziolka et al., 2003; Meltzer et al., 2001).

The future might bring further progress in the use of transplanted cells to restore lost function. During the Super Bowl television broadcast in 2000, many viewers were amazed and shocked to see actor Christopher Reeve walk across a stage to receive an award, as shown in Figure 15.20. It was widely known that Reeve suffered a cervical

Fallon

■ **FIGURE 15.20**
New Therapies for Spinal Cord Damage Raise Hopes A controversial advertisement broadcast during the 2000 Super Bowl featured a computer-animated image of actor Christopher Reeve walking. Reeve hoped to raise interest in investing in spinal cord repair research, but others argued that the advertisement raised unrealistic hopes.

spinal cord injury during an equestrian competition in 1995 and that he was paralyzed from the neck down. With the help of computer animation, however, Reeve was shown walking again to publicize his advocacy for more funding for spinal damage research.

How close are we today to realizing Reeve's dream of victims of spinal cord injury walking again? Stem cell transplants have been successful in restoring movement in animals with spinal damage (see Chapter 5). A more complete understanding of the cellular and biochemical processes accompanying injury should enable us to treat newly injured patients more effectively. It would be hard to imagine a more rewarding use of our understanding of neuroscience than restoring nervous system functions to people who have lost them due to damage or disease.

INTERIM SUMMARY 15.3

Summary Points

1. Neurological assessments combine examinations of a patient's sensory and motor capabilities with observations of cognitive function. Neuropsychological assessments focus on the cognitive outcomes of central nervous system damage. **(LO8)**
2. The Kennard Principle states that recovery from brain damage is a function of developmental stage, but conflicting data exist. **(LO9)**
3. Rehabilitation in brain injury takes a multidisciplinary approach, addressing cognitive, emotional, and physical issues. **(LO10)**
4. New understanding of the cellular mechanisms that accompany brain damage can lead to more effective medications to treat and prevent damage. **(LO10)**
5. Tissue transplants have been used successfully in many animal studies to restore lost nervous system functions, and clinical trials with human participants are currently under way. **(LO10)**

Review Questions

1. What evidence supports the Kennard Principle? What evidence conflicts with it?
2. What are the relative advantages of the "mental muscle" and specific-skills training approaches to rehabilitation?

CHAPTER REVIEW

THOUGHT QUESTIONS

1. What are the pros and cons of the use of protective headgear for soccer players and professional boxers?
2. Would you recommend genetic counseling for athletes who play contact sports that involve high rates of head injury? Why or why not?
3. Do you think government precautions regarding BSE and vCJD have been adequate, or would you suggest further steps be taken?

KEY TERMS

AIDS dementia complex (ADC) (p. 442)
bovine spongiform encephalopathy (BSE) (p. 443)
cerebral hemorrhage (p. 431)
chronic traumatic brain injury (CTBI) (p. 434)
clonic phase (p. 438)
complex partial seizure (p. 437)
concussion (p. 433)
countercoup (p. 433)
coup (p. 433)
Creutzfeldt-Jakob disease (CJD) (p. 444)
encephalitis (p. 441)
epilepsy (p. 436)
generalized seizure (p. 436)
grand mal seizure (also known as tonic-clonic seizure) (p. 437)
ischemia (p. 431)
migraine (p. 447)
multiple sclerosis (p. 439)
neurocysticercosis (p. 440)
new variant Creutzfeldt-Jakob disease (vCJD) (p. 446)
open head injury (p. 433)
partial seizure (p. 436)
petit mal seizure (p. 437)
prion (p. 445)
rehabilitation (p. 452)
seizure (p. 436)
simple partial seizure (p. 437)
stroke (p. 431)
tonic phase (p. 438)
transmissible spongiform encephalopathy (TSE) (p. 443)
tumor (p. 434)

16 Psychological Disorders

CHAPTER OUTLINE

The Image Bank/Getty Images

▲ **Psychological Disorders Can Set Us Apart** One of the many challenges for people with a psychological disorder is the sense of being alone. Fortunately, our greater understanding of these disorders is leading to more effective treatments.

Introduction

Our understanding of psychological disorders has not been the most enlightened aspect of human history. With the exception of bright spots of knowledge in ancient Egypt and Greece, people have typically accounted for abnormal behavior with supernatural explanations. Medieval Europe experienced mass instances of "dance mania," in which individuals would move in unusual, uncontrollable ways that looked to observers like an odd dance. Their superstitious neighbors assumed that they were possessed and offered the "cure" of being burned at the stake. We now suspect that some "dancers" suffered from Sydenham's chorea, which is a rare consequence of strep infections. As medical knowledge progressed, we gained a greater understanding of the underlying biological causes of disorders. However, even in the 1940s and 1950s, parents were blamed for causing disorders such as schizophrenia and autism through bad child-rearing practices. Today, we combine our understanding of the roles of both biology and experience to explain and treat **psychological disorders.**

In this chapter we will be discussing various disorders described in the fourth edition of the American Psychiatric Association's *Diagnostic and Statistical Manual of Mental Disorders*, or DSM-IV (American Psychiatric Association [APA], 2000). Approximately 26.2 percent of Americans over the age of 18 meet DSM criteria for a psychological disorder in any given year, with anxiety disorders and mood disorders being the most frequent (Kessler, Chiu, Demler, & Walters, 2005). Worldwide, numbers of people with psychological disorders are higher than in the United States because poverty, war, and other environmental factors contribute to increased prevalence (Kessler et al., 2007).

LEARNING OBJECTIVES

After reading this chapter, you should be able to:

LO1 Describe the major symptoms of schizophrenia.

LO2 Summarize the possible causes and treatments of schizophrenia.

LO3 Compare and contrast the main features of major depressive disorder and bipolar disorder.

LO4 Summarize the possible causes and treatments of major depressive disorder and bipolar disorder.

LO5 Identify the main features of obsessive-compulsive disorder, panic disorder, and posttraumatic stress disorder.

LO6 Summarize the diagnostic criteria, possible causal factors, and treatments for autism.

LO7 Summarize the symptoms, possible causal factors, and treatments for attention deficit/hyperactivity disorder.

LO8 Identify the main features of antisocial personality disorder.

Schizophrenia

When people think of psychological disorders, **schizophrenia** comes readily to mind. The film, *A Beautiful Mind*, portrayed the experiences of Nobel Prize–winning mathematician and schizophrenia patient John Nash, shown in Figure 16.1. The word *schizophrenia* is Greek for "split mind," but this should not be confused with a condition characterized by multiple personalities, currently referred to as dissociative disorder. Instead, the split in schizophrenia represents a discrepancy between emotion and thought. Schizophrenia dramatically disrupts many of the basic capacities that are central to human experience—perception, reason, emotion, movement, and social engagement. DSM-IV criteria for schizophrenia specify the presence of **hallucinations** (false perceptions), **delusions** (unrealistic thoughts), disturbances of mood, and disorganized thinking (APA, 2000).

Symptoms of schizophrenia can be divided into categories of positive and negative symptoms. **Positive symptoms** of schizophrenia are behaviors that are not expected to occur normally, such as hallucinations and delusions. Instances of these behaviors are frequently referred to as "psychotic episodes." **Negative symptoms,** such as social withdrawal and mood disturbance, occur when normal and expected behaviors are missing. Healthy people are typically socially active and have moods that are appropriate to their situations, so the social withdrawal and disruptions in mood seen in schizophrenia represent the absence of normal behavior. Although the distinction between positive and negative symptoms may appear arbitrary, these symptoms appear to differ in their underlying causes and responses to treatment.

In 1911, Eugen Bleuler, who coined the term *schizophrenia*, argued that the condition actually represented a group of diseases rather than a single entity (Bleuler & Bleuler, 1986). As shown in Figure 16.2, a 15-year follow-up of people diagnosed with schizophrenia showed a variety of different outcomes over time (Wiersma, Nienhuis, Slooff, & Giel, 1998). About 12 percent recovered after a single psychotic episode and never

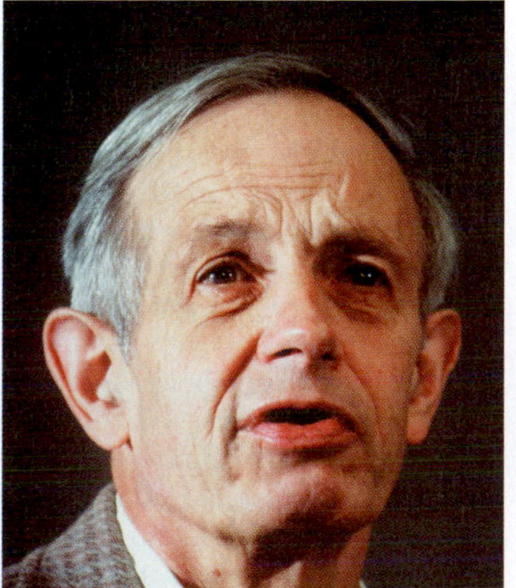

FIGURE 16.1
John Nash Efforts by Nobel Prize–winning mathematician John Nash to overcome his symptoms of schizophrenia were portrayed in the 2001 film *A Beautiful Mind*.

psychological disorder An unusual pattern of thinking, feeling, and behaving that is harmful to the self or to others.
schizophrenia A group of disorders characterized by hallucination, delusion, cognitive impairment, mood disturbance, and social withdrawal.
hallucination A false or distorted perception of objects or events.
delusion A false belief or opinion that is strongly held in spite of conclusive, contradictory evidence.
positive symptom An abnormal behavior, such as hallucination and delusion, that does not occur in healthy individuals but occurs in people with schizophrenia.
negative symptom A normal and expected behavior that is absent due to schizophrenia.

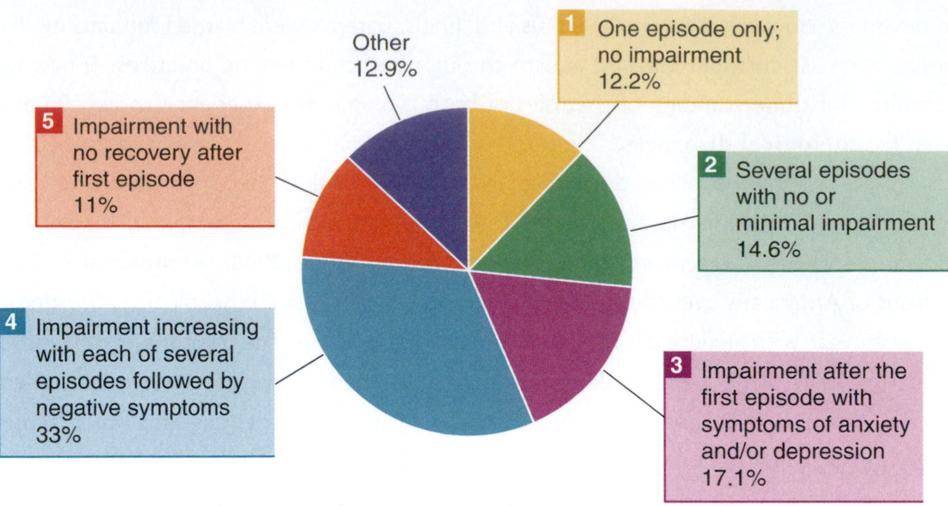

FIGURE 16.2 Outcomes of Schizophrenia Takes Various Forms In a 15-year follow-up of patients diagnosed with schizophrenia, a number of patterns of outcomes emerged. This heterogeneity of outcomes supports the view of schizophrenia as a cluster of disorders rather than a single entity. *Source:* Adapted from Wiersma, Nienhuis, Slooff, & Giel (1998).

had another. Another 30 percent or so experienced periodic psychotic episodes interspersed with times of relatively normal health. About one third experienced repeated and increasingly severe psychotic episodes. Another 11 percent experienced a single psychotic episode with no subsequent recovery. The variety of outcomes supports Bleuler's view of schizophrenia as a cluster of conditions as opposed to a single entity.

Schizophrenia strikes people of all nationalities at about the same rate—0.5 to 1 percent of the population (Shaner, Miller, & Mintz, 2004). Over 2.5 million Americans have been diagnosed with schizophrenia (McGuire, 2000). Most cases of schizophrenia are diagnosed for the first time in individuals between the ages of 18 and 25 years of age, although a sizable minority of cases appear for the first time after age 40 (Howard et al., 2000). Men and women are equally likely to develop schizophrenia (Robins & Regier, 1991).

Insanity in individuals is something rare, but in groups, parties, nations and epochs it is the rule.
Friedrich Nietzsche

GENETICS OF SCHIZOPHRENIA

Substantial evidence exists for a genetic predisposition for schizophrenia. As we observed in Chapter 1, one method for establishing a genetic contribution for a disorder is to observe the **concordance rate,** or incidence of the disorder within groups of closely related people, particularly twins. In schizophrenia, the concordance rate is about 50 percent in identical twins and about 17 percent in fraternal twins (Gottesman, 1991). As shown in Figure 16.3, the odds that a person will develop schizophrenia increase as more closely related family members are diagnosed with the disorder. Results of adoption studies also support a large role for genetics in schizophrenia (Kety, Rosenthal, Wender, & Schulsinger, 1968). Genes are not the entire story, however, as shown by the case of the Genain sisters, identical quadruplets diagnosed with schizophrenia (DeLisi et al., 1984; Mirsky et al., 1984). Although all four sisters had schizophrenia, their outcomes differed substantially. One sister graduated from a two-year business college, married, and had two children, while her sisters' social functioning was described as "grossly inadequate."

The hunt to identify the genes responsible for schizophrenia is an active area of research. A large number of genes might function abnormally in the brains of people with schizophrenia (Owen, Craddock, & Jablensky, 2007; Mirnics, Middleton, Marquez, Lewis, & Levitt, 2000). Susceptibility genes for schizophrenia overlap with those implicated in bipolar disorder, a type of mood disorder we discuss in a later section (Owen, Craddock, & Jablensky, 2007). In one case of identical triplets, two were diagnosed with schizophrenia, whereas the third was diagnosed with bipolar disorder (McGuffin, Reveley, & Holland, 1982).

A majority of individuals with schizophrenia, as well as about 45 percent of their healthy family members, share an abnormality of eye movement that might serve as a useful genetic marker, or indicator of a genetic predisposition, to schizophrenia

concordance rate The statistical probability that one individual will share a trait with another individual, typically a twin or other related person.
saccade (suh-KAHD) The rapid eye movement that occurs when an individual is visually tracking a moving stimulus.

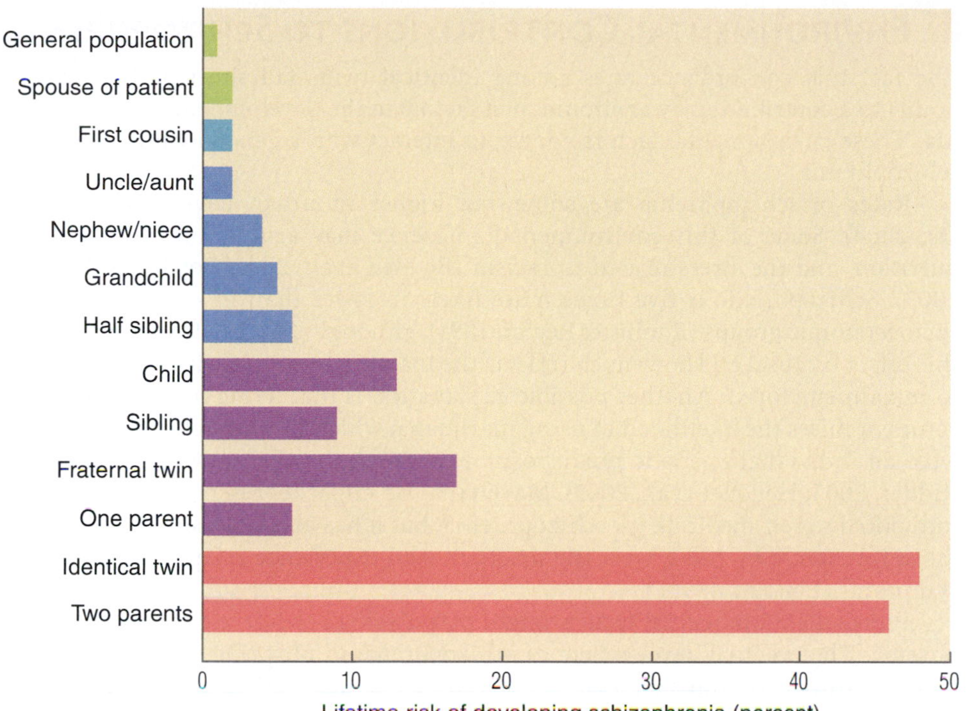

■ **FIGURE 16.3**
The Influence of Genetics on Schizophrenia A person's odds of being diagnosed with schizophrenia increase when closely related family members have the disorder. The fact that the odds of your being diagnosed with schizophrenia increase if you marry a person with schizophrenia might reflect the tendency of people to be attracted to others who share some of their traits. *Source:* Adapted from Gottesman (1991).

(Ettinger et al., 2004; Holzman, Levy, & Proctor, 1976). When we track a moving object, such as a ball's trajectory during a game of tennis, our eyes make characteristic smooth-pursuit movements. For other tasks, such as reading, our eyes jump from one fixation point to the next in jerky movements known as **saccades.** As shown in ■ Figure 16.4, patients with schizophrenia and some of their family members show intrusions of saccades during smooth-pursuit tasks. These abnormal eye movements might represent deficits in executive cognitive functions, normally carried out by the frontal lobes, and in goal-related behavior in particular (Reuter & Kathmann, 2004).

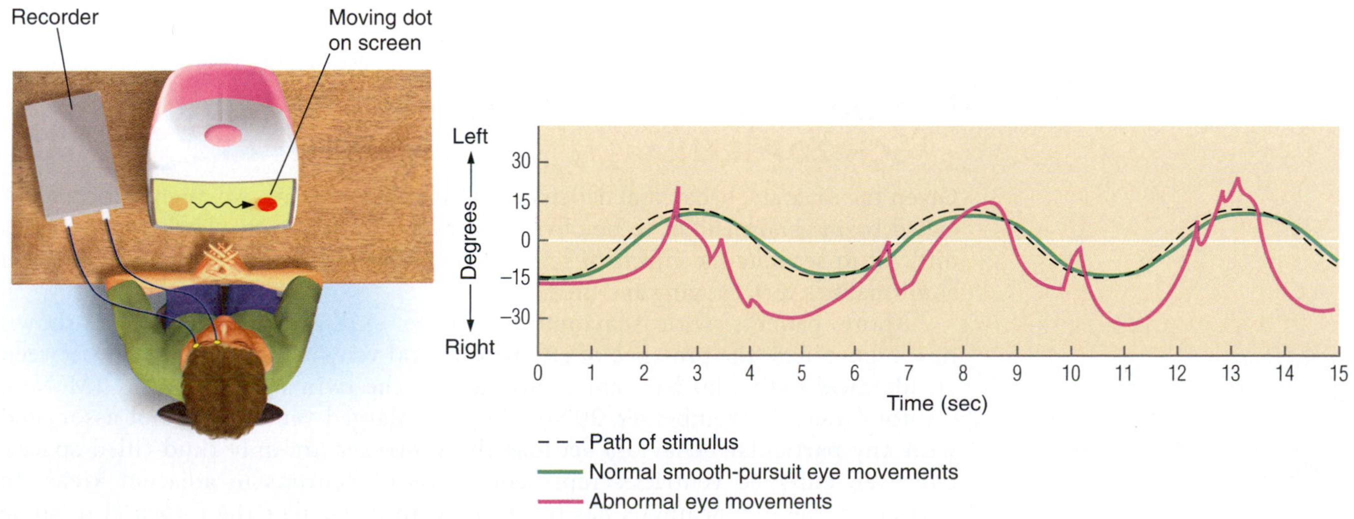

■ **FIGURE 16.4**
A Possible Genetic Marker for Schizophrenia Both patients with schizophrenia and many of their close family members show abnormal visual tracking, in which saccades intrude on smooth-pursuit movements. Although this behavior helps us evaluate the genetic basis of schizophrenia, we do not know its exact underlying cause.

Environmental Contributions to Schizophrenia

The fact that concordance rates among identical twins fall short of 100 percent points to a contribution by environmental factors in the development of schizophrenia. These environmental factors appear to interact with a genetic vulnerability for schizophrenia.

Rates of schizophrenia are somewhat higher in urban environments (Van Os, 2004). Some of this environmental influence may arise from poverty, poor nutrition, and the stress related to racism (Boydell et al., 2001; Boydell & Murray, 2003). Schizophrenia is five times more likely in lower than in middle or higher socioeconomic groups (Robins & Regier, 1991), although it is not clear how much of this effect is causal and how much reflects the inability of people with schizophrenia to remain employed. Another possible explanation is that living in an urban environment raises the likelihood of using marijuana, which in turn appears to interact with an individual's genetic predisposition to psychosis (Fergusson, Horwood, & Ridder, 2005; Henquet et al., 2005). Marijuana use might represent the efforts of an individual to self-medicate for schizophrenia, but it has also been shown to be used more frequently by those with the disorder who experience relapses of psychotic symptoms (Linszen, 1994).

Prenatal environmental factors might play a role in the development of schizophrenia. The eventual development of schizophrenia in offspring is correlated with mothers' difficulties during pregnancy (bleeding and diabetes), abnormal fetal development (low birth weight and small head circumference), and birth complications (emergency caesarean section, lack of oxygen) (Cannon, Jones, & Murray, 2002). Either the experience of a difficult birth triggers schizophrenia or infants vulnerable to schizophrenia possess characteristics that predispose them to difficult prenatal and birth processes.

A mother's exposure to famine or viral infection during her pregnancy can contribute to the development of schizophrenia in her offspring (Brown, 2006; Kyle & Pichard, 2006; Penner & Brown, 2007). People born between January and April (in the northern hemisphere) are slightly more likely than people born in other seasons to be diagnosed with schizophrenia (Davies, Welham, Chant, Torrey, & McGrath, 2003; Hultman et al., 1999). One explanation might be that during the winter flu season, their pregnant mothers were exposed to viruses, especially in colder climates (Cannon, Kendell, Susser, & Jones, 2003). Additional evidence of a role for viral infection in schizophrenia is the observation that people recently diagnosed with schizophrenia have higher levels of viral enzymes in their brains and cerebrospinal fluid (CSF) than healthy controls (Yolken, Karlsson, Yee, Johnston-Wilson, & Torrey, 2000).

Brain Structure and Function in Schizophrenia

Given the dramatic behavioral deficits found in schizophrenia, we might expect associated brain abnormalities to be obvious and easy to document. Unfortunately, it is difficult to separate the effects of schizophrenia from other possible causes of brain abnormalities such as aging and medication.

Many patients with schizophrenia have enlarged ventricles. As shown in ■ Figure 16.5, the presence of enlarged lateral ventricles distinguishes between an identical twin who has schizophrenia and the twin who is healthy (McNeil, Cantor-Graae, & Weinberger, 2000). Having enlarged ventricles is not associated with any particular behaviors because the ventricles are only fluid-filled spaces. However, enlarged ventricles represent a loss of neurons in adjacent areas. In particular, the hippocampus has been found to be smaller than normal in some individuals with schizophrenia (Morgan et al., 2007; Lawrie, Whalley, Job, & Johnstone, 2003; Schulze et al., 2003). In addition, the hippocampus shows an unusual disorganization in some cases of schizophrenia (Kovelman & Scheibel, 1984). As shown in ■ Figure 16.6, the cells of the hippocampus are normally lined

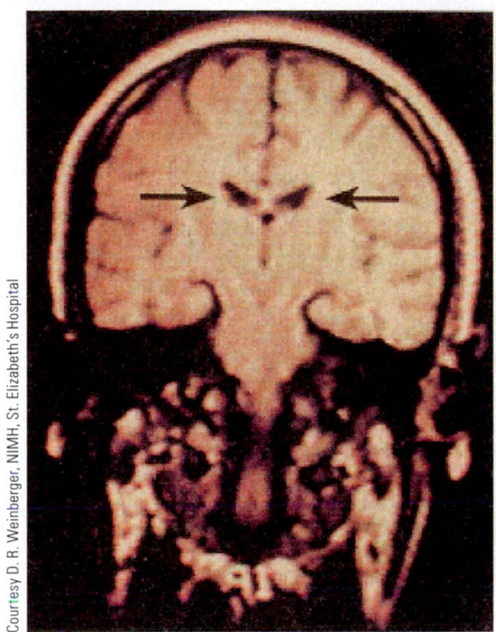
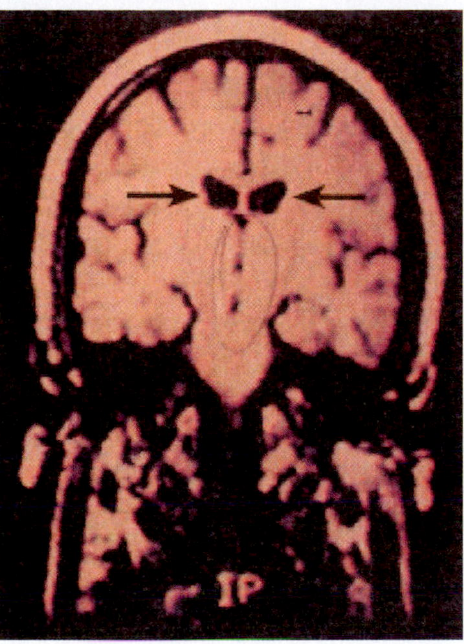

Courtesy D. R. Weinberger, NIMH, St. Elizabeth's Hospital

FIGURE 16.5
Schizophrenia Is Associated with Enlarged Ventricles MRI images of the brains of a pair of identical twins show the discrepancy between normal ventricles and the enlargement of ventricles found in some people who have schizophrenia. The twin on the left is healthy; the twin on the right suffers from schizophrenia.

FIGURE 16.6
Cell Arrangements in the Hippocampus Appear to Be Disorganized in Cases of Schizophrenia The hippocampal cells of a healthy person (left) are lined up neatly. The cell organization of a person with schizophrenia (right) appears to be much more chaotic. It is likely that these two individuals would experience the world in very different ways. We do not know at what point in development such changes take place.

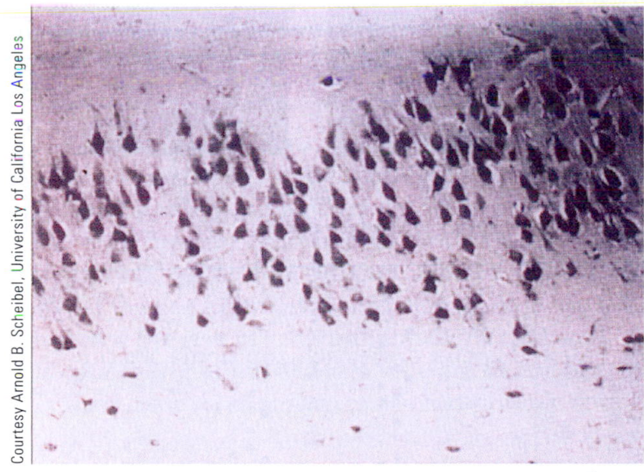
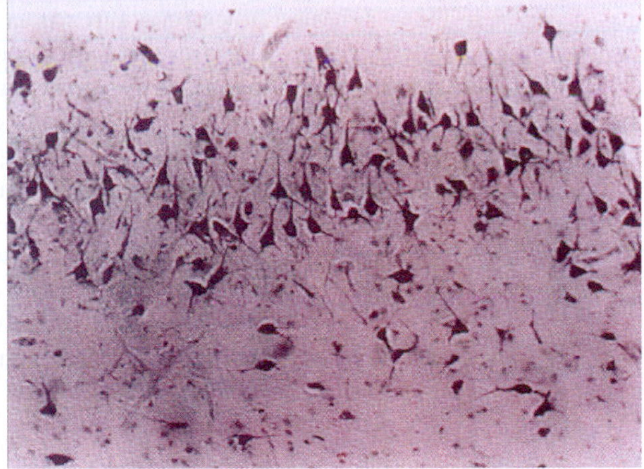

Courtesy Arnold B. Scheibel, University of California Los Angeles

up rather neatly in rows. In the hippocampus of some patients with schizophrenia, the cells are in relative disarray. Given the importance of the hippocampus in memory and cognition, this lack of organization might account for some of the deficits in reasoning and thought found in schizophrenia.

Lower activity in the frontal lobes, or hypofrontality, is associated with some of the negative symptoms of schizophrenia, such as mood disturbance and social withdrawal (Andreasen, Rezai, Alliger, Swayze, Flaum, et al., 1992). As shown in Figure 16.7, measures of glucose metabolism indicate that people with schizophrenia show lower levels of frontal lobe activity than healthy controls both during rest and during difficult cognitive tasks (Weinberger, Aloia, Goldberg, & Berman, 1994). Differences in frontal lobe activity can be used to distinguish between an identical twin with schizophrenia and the healthy member of the pair (Berman, Torrey, Daniel, & Weinberger, 1992).

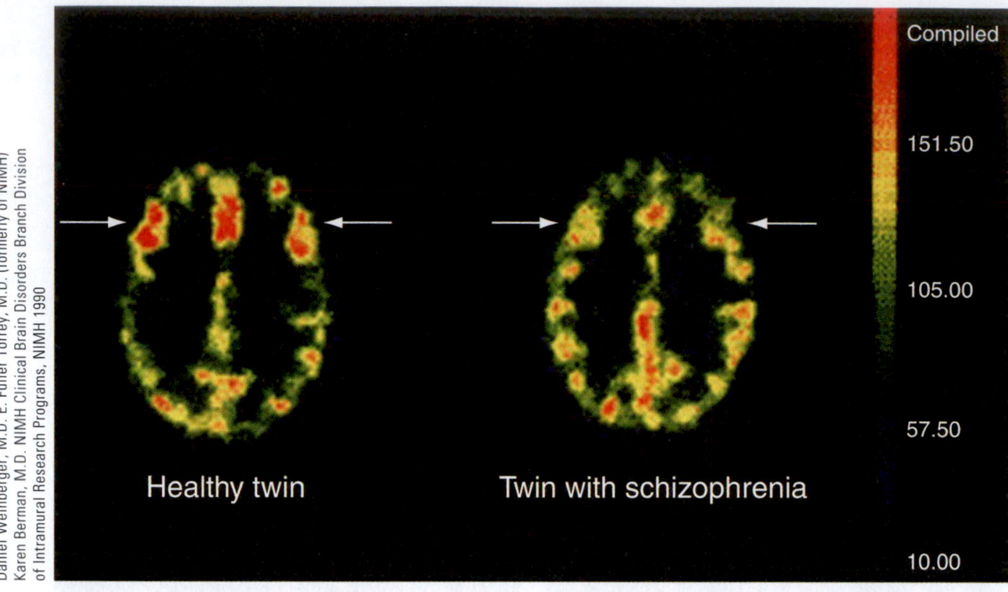

FIGURE 16.7
Hypofrontality Frontal lobe activity (toward the top of the page) appears to be reduced in people with schizophrenia when compared with their healthy identical twins engaged in the same tasks. Active regions of the brain appear red or yellow, and inactive areas are green, blue, violet, and black.

Brains of people with schizophrenia are more symmetrical in structure and function than brains of healthy individuals, and people with schizophrenia are more likely to have ambiguous handedness (Crow, 1997). Based on these observations, Berlim, Mattevi, Belmonte-de-Abreu, and Crow (2003) have suggested that schizophrenia arose in conjunction with cerebral lateralization and the development of language (see Chapter 13). Schizophrenia, according to this view, could be considered as an occasional failure of normal brain lateralization.

One of the puzzles surrounding schizophrenia has been its typical onset in late adolescence and early adulthood. If susceptibility genes interact with environmental factors, especially those that are prenatal, why does it take so long for observable symptoms to develop? One possible solution lies in observations of brain development during the teen years (see Chapter 5). Teens typically experience a burst of cortical gray matter growth at puberty followed by a period of gray matter loss extending into their early twenties. Healthy teens experience relatively little loss of gray matter, whereas teens diagnosed with schizophrenia experience a loss that has been likened to a "forest fire" (Thompson et al., 2001). Discovering the causes for this increased loss will require further research. Comparisons of gray matter in typical teens and teens diagnosed with schizophrenia are shown in Figure 16.8.

Biochemistry of Schizophrenia

The dopamine hypothesis of schizophrenia has been an influential model for many years. This model rests on observations of psychosis resulting from higher levels of dopamine activity along with the efficacy of dopamine antagonists in treating schizophrenia. As noted in Chapter 4, amphetamine, cocaine, and l-dopa (used to treat Parkinson's disease) are potent dopamine agonists. Over time, these drugs often produce behaviors similar to the positive symptoms of schizophrenia, including hallucinations and paranoid delusions (Goetz, Leurgans, Pappert, Raman, & Stemer, 2001). It is very difficult to make a clinical distinction between a person with schizophrenia and a person who has chronically abused stimulant drugs such as amphetamine or cocaine (Brady, Lydiard, Malcolm, & Ballenger, 1991). The dopamine antagonists used to treat schizophrenia, also known as **typical antipsychotic medications,** act primarily by blocking the D_2 dopamine receptor (see Chapter 4) and reduce psychotic symptoms that result from either schizophrenia or stimulant abuse.

typical antipsychotic medication A dopamine antagonist that is used to treat schizophrenia or psychosis resulting from the use of dopamine agonists, such as cocaine and amphetamine.

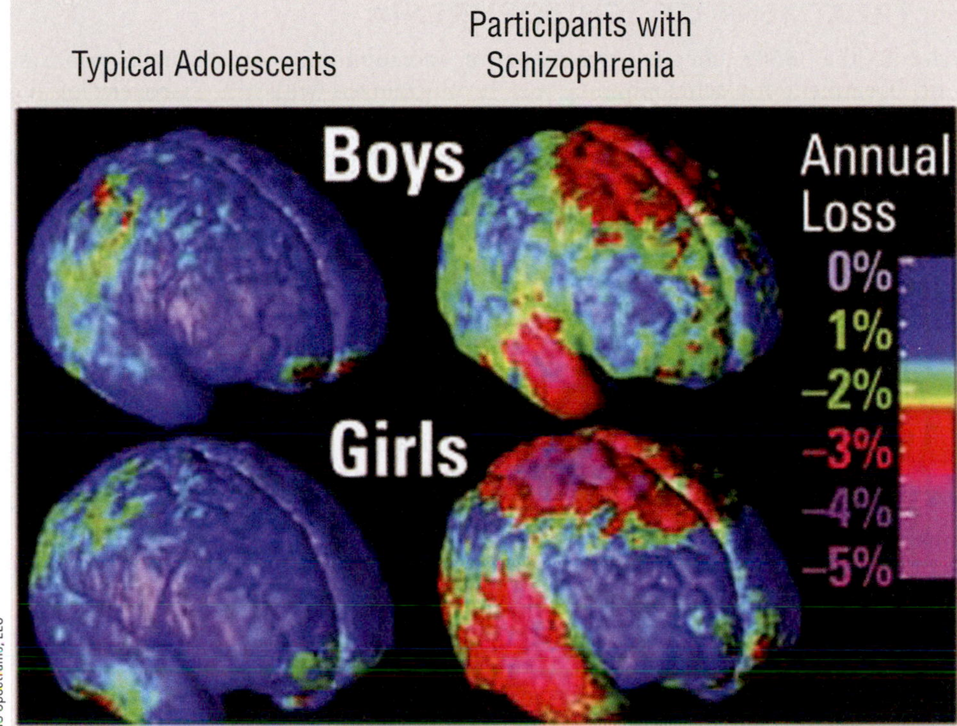

CNS Spectrums, LLC

■ **FIGURE 16.8**
Schizophrenia Is Associated with Larger Losses of Gray Matter in Adolescence
Teens typically experience a burst of cortical gray matter growth at puberty followed by a wave of gray matter thinning that extends into their early twenties. Compared with their healthy peers, teens diagnosed with schizophrenia lose far more gray matter. *Source*: Thompson et al. (2001).

Psychosis may result from conditions associated with high levels of dopamine activity.
- Disorder: Schizophrenia
- Drugs: Levodopa (l-dopa)
  Methamphetamine
  Cocaine

Normal levels of dopamine activity

Motor disturbances and relief from psychotic symptoms may result from conditions associated with low levels of dopamine activity.
- Disorder: Parkinson's disease
- Drugs: Dopamine antagonists (phenothiazines)

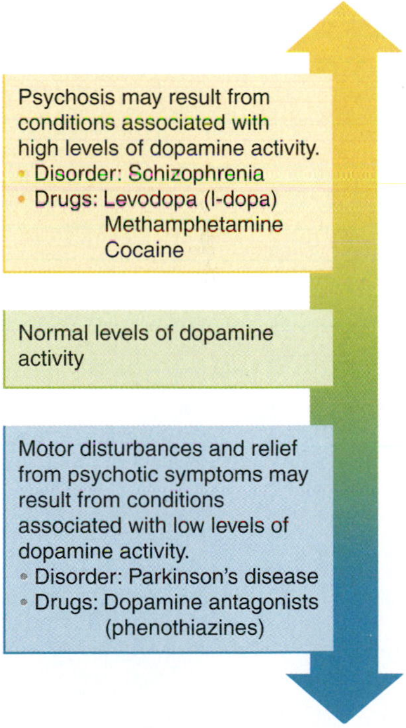

■ **FIGURE 16.9**
Correlations Between Dopamine Activity Levels and Behavior

To summarize evidence for the dopamine hypothesis, illustrated in ■ Figure 16.9, increases in dopamine activity are associated with psychosis, and decreases in dopamine activity are associated with a reduction in psychosis. However, the dopamine hypothesis is probably too simplistic. About one quarter of all patients with schizophrenia fail to respond favorably to treatment with dopamine antagonists such as the **phenothiazines** (Kane & Freeman, 1994). In addition, **atypical antipsychotic medications** provide relief from schizophrenia by acting on neurotransmitters other than dopamine. For example, the atypical antipsychotic clozapine has a greater effect on serotonin systems than on dopamine systems (Syvalahti, 1994).

If the dopamine hypothesis cannot account for all schizophrenia phenomena, what other neurochemicals might be involved? A disturbance in glutamate systems might provide the large-scale effects that would account for the wide range of positive symptoms in schizophrenia. Patients with schizophrenia show evidence of reduced numbers of glutamate receptors in their brains (Konradi & Heckers, 2003). Glutamate and dopamine systems often interact in the brain, and increasing dopamine or decreasing glutamate should result in similar behavioral outcomes. If psychotic symptoms are associated with higher dopamine sensitivity, they might also be related to reductions in glutamate activity. Glutamate's important roles in the normal functioning of the hippocampus and frontal lobes, areas of the brain where abnormalities occur in schizophrenia, also make it an attractive candidate as an underlying mechanism for the disorder. The drug phencyclidine (PCP or "angel dust") provides a useful model for this process (Jentsch & Roth, 1999; Moghaddam & Adams, 1998). PCP is capable of producing several schizophrenia-like symptoms, including auditory hallucinations. PCP not only stimulates dopamine release but also blocks the NMDA glutamate receptor. Psychosis due to PCP use responds favorably to treatment with dopamine antagonists (Jentsch et al., 1997).

phenothiazine (feen-oh-THIE-uh-zeen) One of a major group of dopamine antagonists used in the treatment of psychosis.

atypical antipsychotic medication One of several newer medications used to treat schizophrenia that are not dopamine antagonists.

Treatment of Schizophrenia

Prior to the 1950s, effective treatment for schizophrenia was virtually nonexistent. Treatment for schizophrenia was revolutionized with the discovery of the typical antipsychotics in the 1950s. The first of these to be used were the phenothiazines, including **chlorpromazine** (Thorazine). French surgeon Henri Laborit was so impressed by the calming effects of phenothiazines on his surgical patients that he encouraged his colleagues in psychiatry to experiment with the drugs for treating psychosis. Subsequent research led to the discovery that phenothiazines were effective in treating the symptoms of schizophrenia. Typical antipsychotics primarily benefit patients with schizophrenia by reducing positive symptoms. Negative symptoms, such as social withdrawal and emotional disturbances, do not appear to respond much to these medications (Carpenter, Conley, Buchanan, Breier, & Tamminga, 1995). However, the discovery of the typical antipsychotics allowed many patients, who previously required institutionalization, to resume relatively normal lives. As shown in ■ Figure 16.10, the introduction of typical antipsychotics in the 1950s coincided with a dramatic reduction in the number of mental patients who were institutionalized.

Formerly, when religion was strong and science weak, men mistook magic for medicine; now when science is strong and religion weak, men mistake medicine for magic.
Thomas Szasz

Unfortunately, the typical antipsychotics are not specific in their choice of target. They block dopamine receptors in multiple systems, including those controlling movement. **Tardive dyskinesia** is a common and troubling side effect of these drugs. (*Tardive* refers to "slow," and *dyskinesia* means "difficulty moving.") As shown in ■ Figure 16.11, patients with tardive dyskinesia experience tremors and involuntary movements, especially in the face and tongue. Even when medication is discontinued, movement difficulties often persist permanently. The exact causes of tardive dyskinesia remain elusive. Hypersensitivity to dopamine, disturbances of balances between dopamine and acetylcholine, interference with GABA-dependent inhibition in pathways linking the substantia nigra to the basal ganglia, and excitotoxicity (see Chapter 15) have all been suggested as possible mechanisms (Kulkarni & Naidu, 2003).

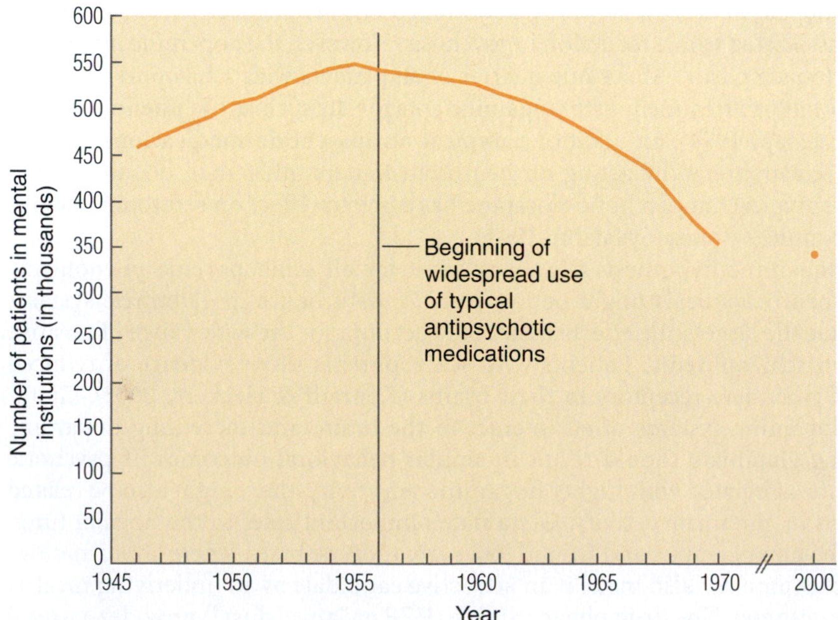

■ **Figure 16.10**
The Introduction of Typical Antipsychotic Medications Reduced the Number of Institutionalized Patients The introduction of typical antipsychotic medications in the 1950s coincided with a rapid reduction in the number of people living in mental institutions.
Source: Adapted from Julien (1995)

chlorpromazine (klor-PROE-muh-zeen) A commonly prescribed dopamine antagonist, also known as Thorazine.

tardive dyskinesia (TAR-div diss-kin-EE-zhuh) A chronic disorder, characterized by involuntary, jerky movements, that occurs as the result of long-term treatment with antipsychotic medications.

Because of the serious side effects associated with typical antipsychotics, along with the lack of response in some patients, more than half of all patients today are treated with newer atypical antipsychotic medications such as olanzapine, clozapine, and rispiridone (Meltzer, 2000). As mentioned earlier, clozapine has a stronger effect on serotonin receptors than on dopamine receptors. An advantage of these newer medications is a reduction in negative symptoms, as well as in positive symptoms, in some patients (Rivas-Vazquez, Blais, Rey, & Rivas-Vazquez, 2000). However, these newer medications are not necessarily safer than the typical antipsychotics. They produce weight gain and diabetes in many patients and still carry the risk of producing tardive dyskinesia (Haddad & Dursun, 2008; Henderson, 2008). Side effects of medication can be avoided in most cases with careful monitoring, but many patients receive poor medication management, indicated by doses above the recommended range and failure to adjust doses based on observed behaviors (Young, Sullivan, Burnam, & Brook, 1998).

In cases in which hallucinations are not responsive to medication, magnetic stimulation of the brain can reduce instances of auditory hallucination for up to 15 weeks (Hoffman et al., 2003). Repeated transcranial magnetic stimulation (rTMS) involves the application of pulses of magnetism through an instrument placed near the scalp (see Chapter 1). As shown in ■ Figure 16.12, application of low-frequency (1 Hz, or one cycle per second) rTMS has been shown to change cortical activity in treated regions.

In addition to medication, psychosocial rehabilitation can be helpful in cases of schizophrenia. Much to the embarrassment of Western medical practitioners, the World Health Organization (WHO) published research suggesting that patients with schizophrenia in developing countries, such as Nigeria, India, and Columbia, were recovering more frequently than patients in wealthier countries, such as the United States and European nations (Sartorius et al., 1986). Improved outcomes occur when patients are given work and social skills training, education about schizophrenia and the importance of medication, affordable housing linked to services, and information about symptom management. Unfortunately, only about 10 percent of patients with schizophrenia in the United States receive any treatment other than medication (McGuire, 2000).

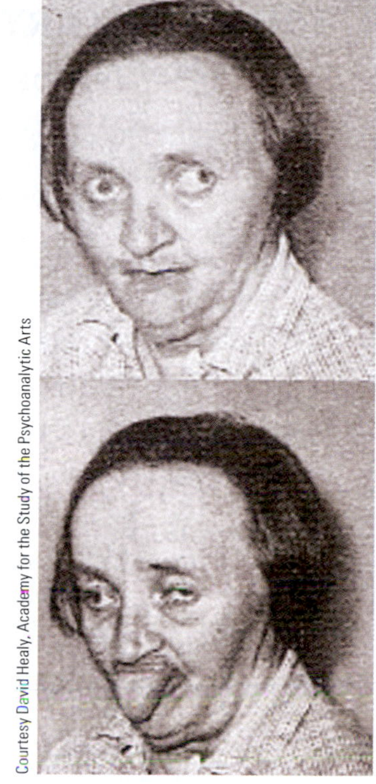

Courtesy David Healy, Academy for the Study of the Psychoanalytic Arts

■ **FIGURE 16.11**
Tardive Dyskinesia Can Occur as a Side Effect of Treatment with Typical Antipsychotic Medications Traditional antipsychotics can produce tardive dyskinesia, characterized by intrusive, involuntary movements and tremors. Use of newer atypical antipsychotics can also lead to tardive dyskinesia but seem to do so less frequently.

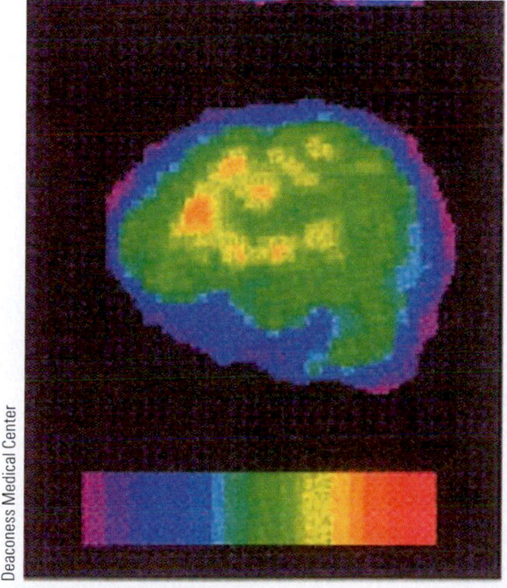

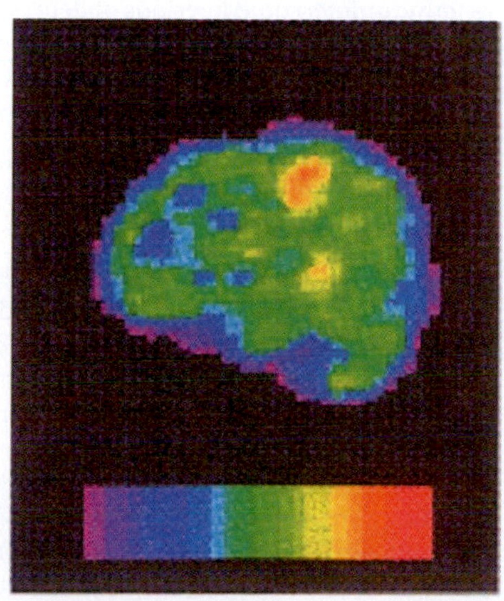

Courtesy Dr. Alvaro Pascual-Leone, Lab for Magnetic Brain Stimulation, Beth Israel Deaconess Medical Center

■ **FIGURE 16.12**
Repeated Transcranial Magnetic Stimulation Reduces Auditory Hallucinations Low-frequency repeated transcranial magnetic stimulation (rTMS) can reduce activity in underlying cortical regions. The image on the left represents pretreatment brain activity in a patient with auditory hallucinations and the image on the right was taken post treatment. Cortical activity is clearly lowered following treatment.

INTERIM SUMMARY 16.1

Summary Table: Comparison of Positive and Negative Symptoms of Schizophrenia

Type of Symptom	Examples	Possible Causes	Responds to Medication?
Positive	• Hallucinations • Delusions • Disorganized speech • Disorganized behavior	• Hippocampal disarray • Possible dopamine and/or glutamate disturbances	Yes
Negative	• Mood disturbance • Social withdrawal	• Brain damage • Enlarged ventricles • Hypofrontality	Better response to atypical than to typical antipsychotics

Summary Points

1. Schizophrenia is a disorder characterized by the presence of hallucinations, delusions, disorganized thinking, social withdrawal, and mood disturbances. **(LO1)**
2. A genetic vulnerability to schizophrenia appears to interact with a variety of environmental factors, including birth complications, prenatal exposure to viruses, marijuana use, and stress, to produce symptoms of the disorder. **(LO2)**
3. Schizophrenia is usually treated with medication, although psychosocial rehabilitation is also quite useful. **(LO2)**

Review Question

1. What are the advantages and disadvantages of the use of medications to treat schizophrenia?

Mood Disorders

The DSM-IV recognizes two types of mood disorder: **major depressive disorder (MDD)** and **bipolar disorder**. In major depressive disorder, individuals experience lengthy, uninterrupted periods of depressed mood and loss of pleasure in their normal activities. In bipolar disorder, the individual alternates between periods of unrealistically elevated mood (mania) and periods of profound depression. Although both variants share the experience of severe depression, these are two separate disorders with unique underlying causes.

Major Depressive Disorder (MDD)

The DSM-IV defines major depressive episodes as periods of pervasive sadness that last for at least 2 weeks (APA, 2000). In addition, people with major depressive disorder often withdraw from activities they previously found rewarding, including hobbies and sex. Major depressive disorder also affects eating habits, energy levels, sleep, and cognition. People report difficulty concentrating and often experience thoughts of hopelessness, guilt, worthlessness, and suicide.

Major depressive disorder has been referred to as "the common cold of psychopathology," reflecting the high frequency of its occurrence compared to other types of psychological disorder. MDD affects approximately 16.2 percent of Americans at some point in their lifetimes (Kessler et al., 2003). Depression recurs in about 35 percent of cases and is chronic and unremitting in about 15 percent of cases (Eaton et al., 2008). Most patients with recurring forms of depression experience five or six lifetime episodes (Birmaher et al., 1996).

Prior to adolescence, rates of MDD for boys and girls are approximately equal. However, rates for boys and girls begin to diverge between ages 13 and 15 (Hankin et al., 1998; Nolen-Hoeksema & Girgus, 1994). As shown in Figure 16.13, adult women are

major depressive disorder (MDD) A disorder in which intense feelings of sadness, hopelessness, and worthlessness persist a minimum of two weeks.

bipolar disorder A mood disorder characterized by alternating cycles of mania and depression.

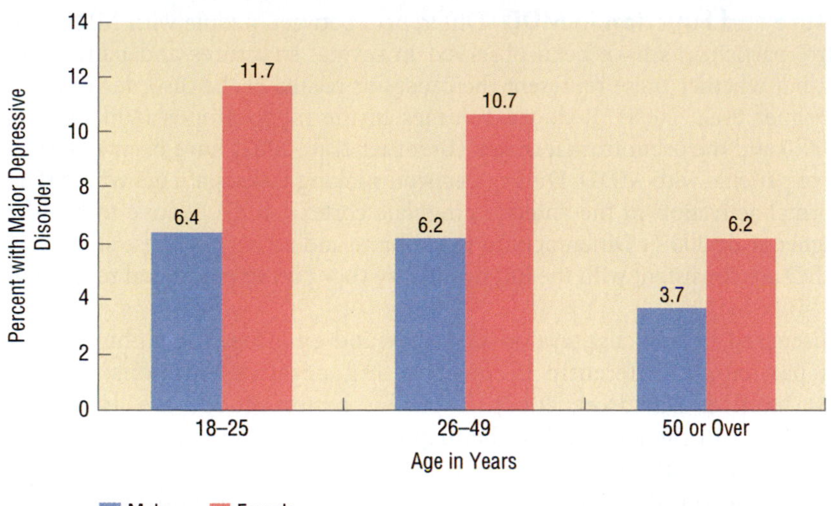

FIGURE 16.13
Sex Differences in Rates of Depression
Women are more likely than men to be diagnosed with depression. During 2006, nearly twice as many women as men were diagnosed with major depressive disorder.

nearly twice as likely as men to be diagnosed with MDD (Culbertson, 1997; Broquet, 1999; Kessler et al., 2003). This discrepancy between rates of depression in men and women has been observed independent of demographic factors such as race and ethnicity, social class, and country of residence (Strickland, 1992), suggesting a biological basis. A number of mood disturbances appear to be either caused or made worse by changes in female hormones, including premenstrual syndrome (PMS), premenstrual dysphoric disorder (PMDD), postpartum depression, and mood disturbances experienced by women undergoing menopause (see Chapter 10; Rapkin, Mikacich, Moatakef-Imani, & Rasgon, 2002). Many of the same medications used for MDD appear to be effective for these conditions (Steiner et al., 2003).

Sit all day in a moping posture, sigh, and reply to everything with a dismal voice, and melancholy lingers.

William James

Genetics of Depression Genes appear to play a moderate role in the development of MDD. Based on analyses of twins, the heritability of depression appears to be around 33 percent (Kendler, Gatz, Gardner, & Pedersen, 2006; Wurtman, 2005). Adoption studies also support a role for genes in the development of depression (Shih, Belmonte, & Zandi, 2004; Wender et al., 1986). A number of genes have been implicated in depression, including those involved with serotonin reuptake (Wurtman, 2005) and the clock genes that regulate circadian rhythms (McClung, 2007; see Chapter 11).

Assessing the heritability of MDD is complicated by the strong interactions observed between genetic predispositions and environmental factors in this disorder. Variations in the serotonin transporter gene, which comes in both long and short forms, do not by themselves predict the development of MDD. However, among individuals who experience stressful life events, those with one or two copies of the short form of the gene were much more likely to develop depression than those with two copies of the long form (Caspi et al., 2003). In the absence of stressful life events, having a short copy is not sufficient to cause depression.

Environmental Factors and Depression As with schizophrenia, prenatal events might contribute to a vulnerability to mood disorder. Mothers who were in their third trimester of pregnancy during a famine known as the "Dutch Hunger Winter" of 1944–1945 not only gave birth to more offspring with schizophrenia, but were also more likely to give birth to individuals who subsequently required hospitalization for major mood disorders (Brown, van Os, Driessens, Hoek, & Susser, 2000).

Stress often serves as a trigger for depressive episodes (see Chapter 14). Stader and Hokanson (1998) asked participants to list daily stressors, such as having an argument with a friend. These self-reports were then correlated with the participants' moods. Depressive episodes were often preceded by significant stressors. Stress might lead to depression by leading to a larger and prolonged release of cortisol (see Chapter 14), particularly in people with short versions of the serotonin transporter gene discussed previously (Gotlib, Joormann, Minor, & Hallmayer, 2008). As we will see in a later section, cortisol regulation appears to be impaired in some people with MDD.

Brain Structure and Function in MDD Differences between people with MDD and healthy control participants have been observed in several structures and patterns of brain activity, but whether these represent the causes or results of the disorder remains unknown (Wagner et al., 2008). Reduced volumes in the hippocampus (Videbech & Ravnkilde, 2004) and the orbitofrontal cortex (Bremner et al., 2002) have been observed in the brains of patients with MDD. During decision-making tasks, patients with MDD showed abnormal activation in the anterior cingulate cortex (ACC) relative to healthy controls (Wagner et al., 2008). Differences in the volume and activity of these structures in cases of MDD are consistent with the important role they play in emotional regulation (see Chapter 14).

As we discussed in our chapters on laterality and emotion, the right and left hemispheres participate differently in positive and negative emotions (Davidson, 1998; Maxwell & Davidson, 2007). Typically, happy moods are associated with greater activity in the left cerebral hemisphere. Depression is correlated with reduced activity in the left frontal lobe and increased activity in the right frontal lobe (Schaffer, Davidson, & Saron, 1983). Damage to the left frontal lobe from a stroke or another pathological condition typically produces a profound depression in the patient, whereas damage to the right frontal lobe appears to have less impact on mood (Shimoda & Robinson, 1999).

Correlations between sleep patterns and depressed mood reflect a larger disturbance in circadian rhythms (Wehr, Sack, Rosenthal, Duncan, & Gillin, 1983). As we discovered in Chapter 11, some people experience a type of depression called seasonal affective disorder (SAD), in which seasonal variations in light interfere with circadian rhythms. Both sleeping more than normal (more than nine hours) and sleeping less than normal (less than seven hours) are symptoms of depression. As shown in ■ Figure 16.14, some people who are depressed enter their first cycle of REM sleep after approximately 45 minutes of sleep rather than

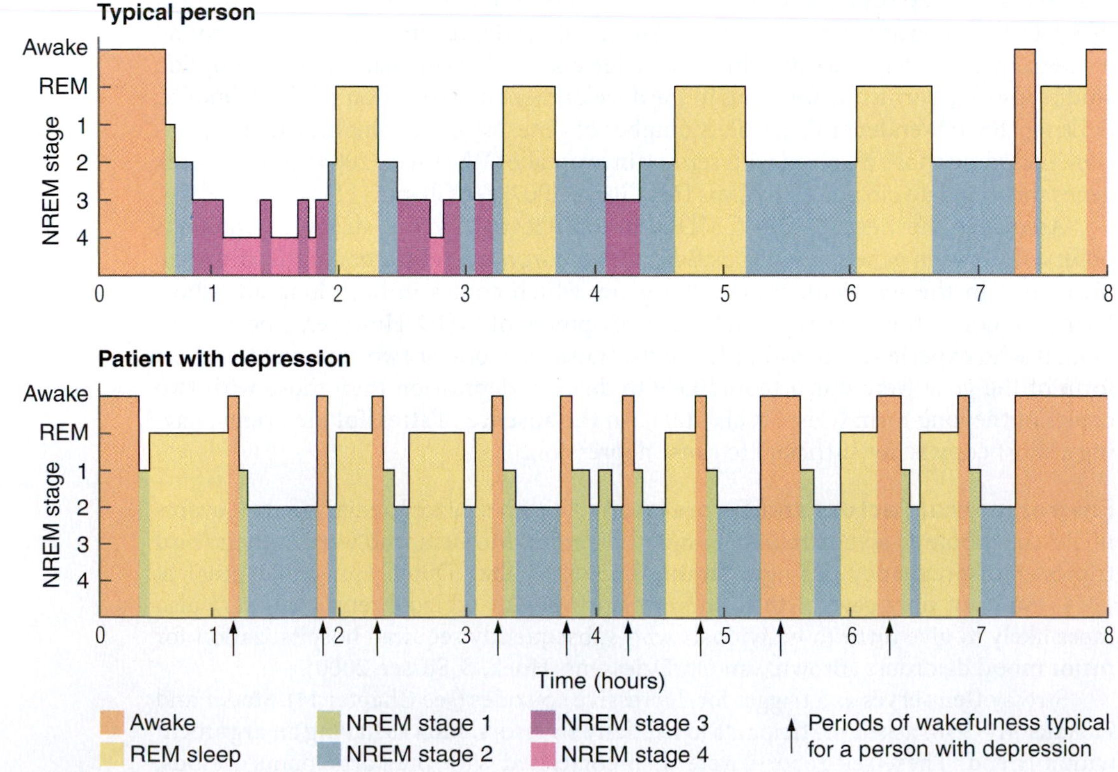

■ **FIGURE 16.14**
Depression Is Associated with Abnormal Patterns of Sleep Compared with data from a nondepressed person, shown in the top row, the depressed person falls asleep much faster, enters REM for the first time much faster, and spends no time in Stages 3 and 4 NREM. The arrows indicate the typical frequent waking experienced by people with depression.
Source: Adapted from Gillin & Borbely (1985).

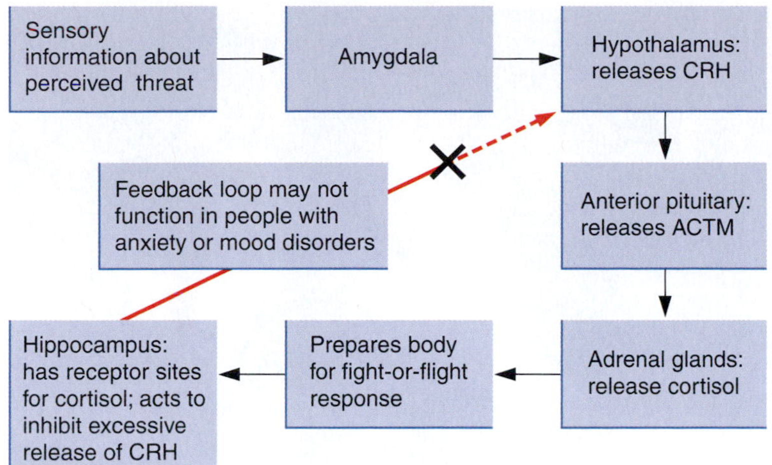

FIGURE 16.15
The Hypothalamic-Pituitary-Adrenal (HPA) Axis Plays an Important Role in Stress and Depression When the amygdala responds to a perceived threat, it activates the HPA system, which in turn secretes cortisol. Cortisol initiates physical changes in the body to prepare for fight-or-flight responses. When the hippocampus identifies circulating cortisol, it inhibits the HPA system. This feedback loop normally keeps cortisol release under control, but it might not be functioning correctly when a person suffers from anxiety or mood disorders.

the normal 90 minutes. Stages 3 and 4 of NREM sleep are reduced, and the lighter Stages 1 and 2 are more prominent. Because it is much easier to awaken during REM or during NREM Stages 1 and 2, frequent waking during the night is a common complaint associated with depression. Further evidence for a relationship between sleep and depression comes from the effects of selective REM deprivation on mood. When people are awakened each time they enter REM sleep, they report a significant reduction in depression (Vogel, Vogel, McAbee, & Thurmond, 1980). In addition, most antidepressants reduce REM to some extent (Pace-Schott et al., 2001; see Chapter 11).

Observations of sleep irregularities suggest that depression results from a phase advance in circadian sleep-waking cycles (Wirz-Justice, 2006). As we discussed in Chapter 11, a phase advance occurs when a person attempts to sleep earlier than normal, as in eastward travel or moving the clock an hour ahead in the spring for daylight savings. A variation of this hypothesis suggests that depression results from irregular circadian rhythms, as opposed to an orderly shift forward (Koenigsberg et al., 2004).

Biochemistry of Depression Several lines of research support abnormalities in monoamine activity, and serotonin activity in particular, as a basis for depression. As we observed in Chapter 4, the drug reserpine interferes with the storage of monoamines in vesicles, reducing the amount of these neurotransmitters available for release. Although reserpine has been used for centuries in Indian folk medicine to treat heart disease, it is rarely used today due to its ability to produce profound depression (Webster & Koch, 1996). **Selective serotonin reuptake inhibitors (SSRIs)**, frequently used to treat depression, act to increase the availability of serotonin at the synapse. People who commit suicide have lower concentrations of serotonin and its byproducts in the brain (Asberg, 1986) and in cerebrospinal fluid (Linnoila & Virkkunen, 1992). People who used violent methods, such as guns, to commit suicide were found to have lower concentrations of serotonin in the prefrontal cortex than did those who used less violent means, such as taking pills (Oquendo et al., 2003).

A monoamine hypothesis of depression is also consistent with the circadian hypotheses discussed previously because monoamines play essential roles in the regulation of sleep and waking cycles (see Chapter 11). Consequently, we might expect to see other chemicals associated with circadian rhythms show irregularities in MDD. Cortisol is one of several glucocorticoids released by the adrenal glands in response to both circadian rhythms and stress-related activity in the so-called hypothalamic-pituitary-adrenal (HPA) axis, shown in Figure 16.15. Because cortisol levels increase in response to stress, this system could provide a link between stressful life events, circadian disruption, and the development of depression. Circadian cortisol release, normally highest early in the morning, shows a phase advance in patients with MDD compared to healthy controls (Koenigsberg et al., 2004). In other words, peak release of

selective serotonin reuptake inhibitor (SSRI) A type of medication, used to treat major depressive disorder and related conditions, that interferes with the reuptake of serotonin at the synapse.

Figure 16.16 Electroconvulsive Shock Therapy (ECT) A patient is shown being prepared for treatment with ECT for serious depression. The patient is given muscle relaxants and anesthesia before shocks are applied through electrodes to induce seizures. The treatments are given over a course of several weeks.

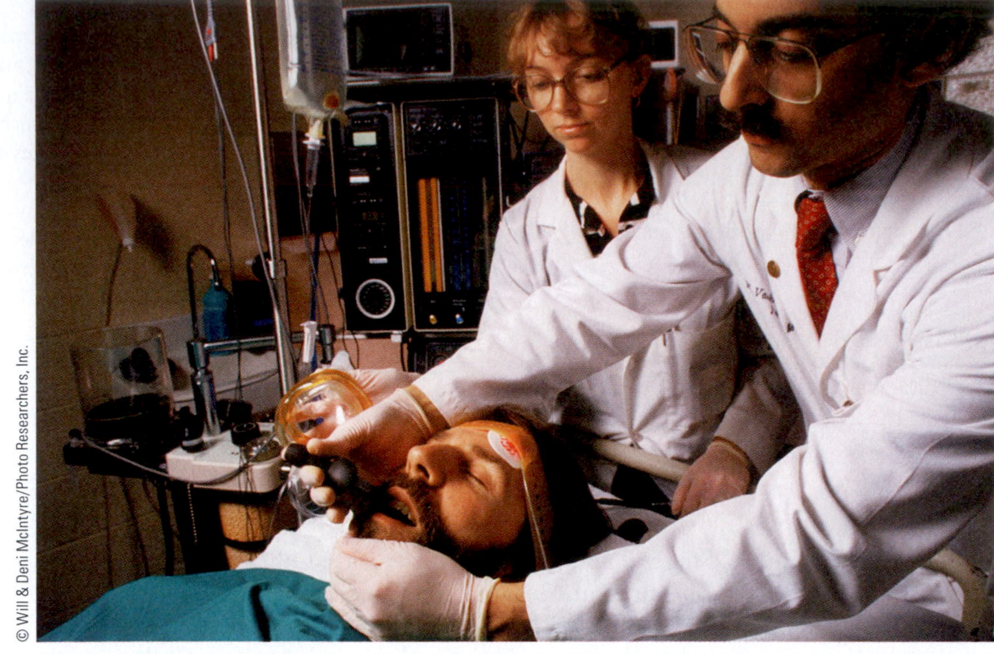

cortisol occurs earlier in the cycle, lending further support to the connection between irregular circadian rhythms and depression.

Abnormalities in glucocorticoid metabolism can be tested directly by using the dexamethasone suppression test (DST). When dexamethasone is injected into healthy participants, cortisol secretion is suppressed. When the test is administered to adults diagnosed with depression, about 75 percent fail to show the expected levels of cortisol suppression (Aihara et al., 2007). Following successful treatment with medication, these patients respond normally to the DST.

Treatment of Depression Treatment for major depressive disorder takes a number of pathways. The most common route is the prescription of some type of antidepressant medication, particularly an SSRI. Effective antidepressant medications appear to share the ability to stimulate neurogenesis in the hippocampus (Perera et al., 2007). In animal studies, drugs that block neurogenesis also prevent the therapeutic effects of antidepressants (ibid.).

Only about 30–35 percent of patients with MDD treated with SSRIs meet criteria for complete remission, leading to the need to find alternate or complementary therapies (Trivedi et al., 2006). Blumenthal et al. (1999) reported that a brisk 30-minute walk or jog three times a week produced the same relief from major depression as typical treatment with antidepressant medications. Research assessing the impact of exercise in conjunction with more traditional therapies is currently underway (Trivedi et al., 2006). Cognitive-behavioral therapy, combining behavioral, cognitive, and self-control therapies, appears to be about as effective as antidepressant therapy alone. A combination of antidepressant and cognitive-behavioral therapy typically produces the best long-term outcomes for patients with depression (Broquet, 1999).

Electroconvulsive shock therapy (ECT), shown in ■ Figure 16.16, can produce significant relief for depressed patients who do not respond to medication (UK ECT Group, 2003). In ECT, the patient is anesthetized and given a muscle relaxant while seizures are induced by electricity applied through electrodes on the head. Six to twelve treatments are given, typically at a rate of three per week. Although the exact mode of action for ECT remains unknown, the procedure does appear to affect responsiveness to dopamine and norepinephrine. In addition, like antidepressant medications, ECT appears to stimulate neurogenesis in the hippocampus (Perera et al., 2007). Largely due to the way ECT was depicted in Ken Kesey's novel, *One Flew Over the Cuckoo's Nest*, and the movie of the same title, many people have a highly negative view of the procedure. Some patients undergoing the procedure have experienced associated memory problems, but the procedure is generally considered

electroconvulsive shock therapy (ECT) A treatment of mood disorders in which convulsions are produced by the passage of an electric current through the brain.

as safe as minor surgery under general anesthesia (American Psychiatric Association [APA], 2003). There is no evidence that the procedure produces permanent brain damage (Weiner, 1984).

Work is the best antidote to sorrow my dear Watson.
Arthur Conan Doyle

Bipolar Disorder

Bipolar disorder is characterized by alternating cycles of depression and mania. **Mania** consists of "a distinct period of abnormally and persistently elevated, expansive, and/or irritable mood, lasting at least one week (or any duration if hospitalization is necessary)" (APA, 2000, p. 357). Further symptoms include inflated self-esteem, decreased need for sleep, higher-than-normal verbal output, flight of ideas, distractibility, increased goal-directed activity, and excessive involvement in pleasure-seeking activities. In the depressive cycle of bipolar disorder, the symptoms are the same as those found in major depressive disorder (APA, 2000).

Bipolar disorder is much less common than major depressive disorder. Between 0.4 and 1.2 percent of the population are thought to experience bipolar disorder, as compared with the estimated 10 to 20 percent experiencing major depressive disorder (Lewinsohn, Klein, & Seeley, 1995). Unlike major depressive disorder, males and females are equally likely to be diagnosed with bipolar disorder. Prior to puberty, bipolar diagnoses are very rare, but prevalence approaches adult rates during adolescence (American Academy of Child and Adolescent Psychiatry [AACAP], 1997; Geller & Luby, 1997).

Bipolar disorder has been linked to enhanced creativity. Kay Jamison (1993) argues that artists are at greater risk for bipolar disorder than other people, and she includes the poet William Blake, composers Handel and Mahler, and visual artists Michelangelo and van Gogh on her list of people whose behavior might fit the profile of bipolar disorder. Many noted actors and actresses, including Carrie Fisher (*Star Wars*) and Vivien Leigh (*Gone With the Wind*), have been formally diagnosed with bipolar disorder. A controlled study comparing patients with bipolar disorder, patients with MDD, and healthy controls participating in creative or noncreative disciplines lends some support to these observations. The patients with bipolar disorder scored similarly on tests of creativity to the healthy controls in creative disciplines and higher than either those with MDD or controls in noncreative disciplines (Santosa et al., 2007).

Causes of Bipolar Disorder Genes appear to play a more significant role in bipolar disorder than in major depressive disorder. Concordance rates among identical twins are often reported to be as high as 85 percent, in contrast to the 30–40 percent usually observed in major depressive disorder (Kieseppä, Partonen, Haukka, Kaprio, & Lönnqvist, 2004). Adoption studies also support a powerful role of genetics in the development of bipolar disorder (Taylor, Faraone, & Tsuang, 2002).

It is assumed that multiple genes are responsible for bipolar disorder. Researchers are especially interested in cases in which schizophrenia and bipolar disorder affect members of the same families (Hattori et al., 2003). These conditions involve a number of similar symptoms, possibly caused by the same genes. In spite of the differences between major depressive disorder and bipolar disorder, these disorders also share some common genes. Among families of patients with major depressive disorder, bipolar disorder is 3 to 4 times more common than among families without any psychopathology (Dubovsky & Buzan, 1999).

There is no greater pain than to remember a happy time when one is in misery.
Dante

Among the many possible environmental factors that interact with susceptibility genes for bipolar disorder is diet. Dietary omega-3 fatty acids, generally found in fish, might provide some protection from bipolar disorder (Noaghiul & Hibbeln, 2003). As shown in Figure 16.17, prevalence rates for bipolar disorder are highest in countries where fish is rarely consumed (such as Germany) and lowest in countries where fish is an important diet staple (such as Iceland). However, attempts to improve symptoms in patients with bipolar disorder or MDD with omega-3 supplementation have produced mixed results (Stahl, Begg, Weisinger, & Sinclair, 2008).

mania An emotional state characterized by abnormally elevated, expansive, or irritable mood.

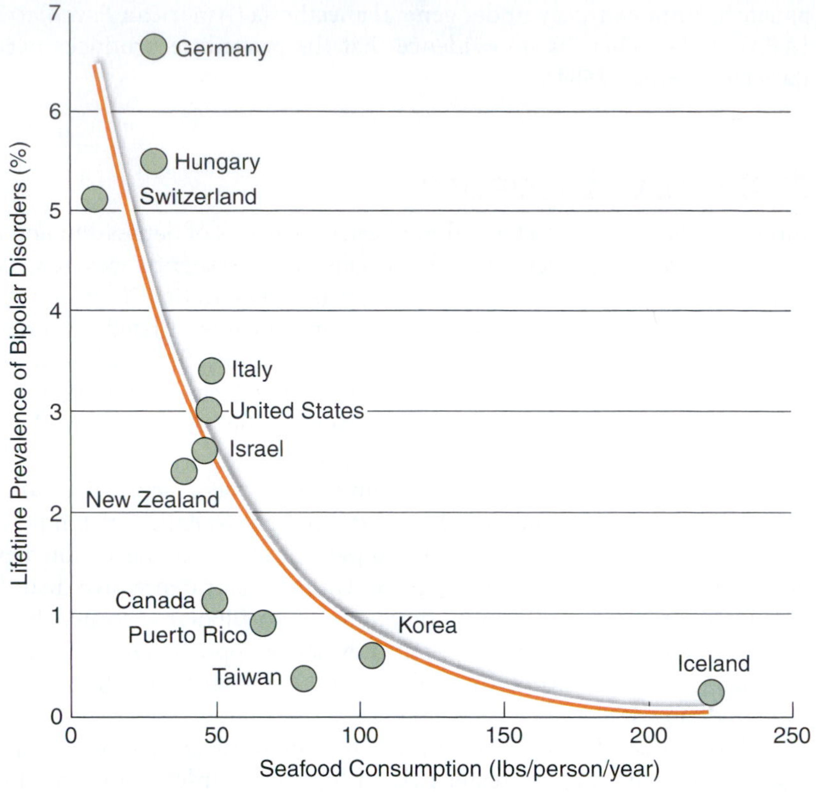

■ **FIGURE 16.17**
Diet May Influence the Prevalence of Bipolar Disorder Nations with heavy seafood consumption, such as Iceland, have lower rates of bipolar disorder than nations where seafood consumption is less typical, such as Switzerland and Hungary. Omega-3 fatty acids have been suggested as a possible protective factor, but further research is needed to confirm a causal relationship. *Source:* Noaghiul & Hibbeln (2003)

Brain Structure and Function in Bipolar Disorder Little is currently known about brain mechanisms responsible for bipolar disorder. As was the case in schizophrenia, subtle reductions in hippocampal volume in patients with bipolar disorder have been observed (Bearden et al., 2008). Elevated activity in the basal ganglia is associated with bipolar disorder (Caligiuri et al., 2003). Enlargements of the amygdala might also be correlated with bipolar disorder (Brambilla et al., 2003). However, we do not know whether these abnormalities precede the onset of bipolar symptoms or result from the illness or treatment for the illness.

Biochemistry and Treatment of Bipolar Disorder As in the case of MDD, there is a strong argument for monoamine abnormalities in bipolar disorder. Both conditions involve disruptions of sleep, which is tightly regulated by monoamine activity. Bipolar disorder is not only characterized by a decreased need for sleep, but sleep deprivation can trigger a manic episode (Kasper & Wehr, 1992). In addition to decreased serotonin activity, patients with bipolar disorder show enhanced levels of norepinephrine activity (Vawter, Freed, & Kleinman, 2000).

A major clue in the effort to unravel the biochemical causes of bipolar disorder is the effectiveness of **lithium** as a treatment. Lithium, a simple metal that is commonly found in the natural environment, levels out the mood fluctuations of bipolar disorder. In addition, lithium appears to promote neurogenesis in the hippocampus of bipolar patients (Bearden et al., 2008). If we understand the action of lithium, we should be able to infer which biochemical processes form the basis of bipolar disorder. Although lithium does not raise or lower overall serotonin levels, it does appear to influence the activity of related second messengers and enzymes (Jope, 1999). In addition, lithium decreases norepinephrine activity by enhancing reuptake. High levels of norepinephrine might produce manic episodes, so reducing norepinephrine levels should stabilize mood. The toxicity and unpleasant side effects of lithium often lead patients to abandon the drug. Fortunately, other medications are available for treating bipolar disorder, including SSRIs, benzodiazepines (e.g.,Valium), antipsychotics, and anticonvulsant mood stabilizers.

lithium (LITH-ee-um) A simple salt that appears to stabilize serotonin and norepinephrine levels in cases of bipolar disorder.

INTERIM SUMMARY 16.2

Summary Points

1. Major depressive disorder is characterized by a constant state of depressed mood and loss of pleasure in normally enjoyable activities, whereas bipolar disorder involves dramatic shifts from manic states to periods of profound depression. **(LO3)**
2. Genes appear to play a role in both major depressive disorder and bipolar disorder, but the genetic influence on bipolar disorder appears to be the stronger. **(LO4)**
3. Monoamine imbalances contribute to both major depressive disorder and bipolar disorder. **(LO4)**
4. Major depressive disorder is treated with medication, cognitive-behavioral therapy, or ECT. Increased aerobic activity is also quite helpful. Bipolar disorder is treated primarily with medication. **(LO4)**

Review Question

1. What are the major similarities and differences between major depressive disorder and bipolar disorder?

Anxiety Disorders

As many as 30 percent of all Americans experience one or more anxiety disorders during their lifetimes (Kessler, Chiu, Demler, & Walters, 2005). Anxiety disorders take many forms, but all share the core element of anxiety, a strong negative emotion arising from the anticipation of danger (Barlow, 1988). Under normal circumstances, a reasonable amount of anxiety is a good thing. Without sufficient anxiety, we might spend far too much money with our credit cards or engage in risky sexual practices. When anxiety becomes overwhelming and unrealistic, however, we cross the line into disordered behavior.

Anxiety (or dread) itself needs no description; everyone has personally experienced this sensation or to speak more correctly this affective condition, at some time or other.

Sigmund Freud

Twin and adoption studies support a genetic predisposition for anxiety disorders in general (Andrews, Steward, Allen, & Henderson, 1990). However, the specific type of anxiety disorder will vary among family members. In other words, a vulnerability to anxiety disorder appears to be inherited, but related people will not necessarily experience the same type of anxiety disorder (DiLalla, Kagan, & Reznick, 1994). Families in which anxiety disorders are common are also more likely to have members with major depressive disorder because these disorders appear to share an underlying genetic basis (Weissman, Warner, Wickramaratne, Moreau, & Olfson, 1997).

We have seen previously how pathways connecting the brainstem, the amygdala and related limbic structures, and the decision-making areas of the frontal lobes are involved with generating fear in the face of danger. Disordered levels of anxiety also involve abnormalities in the HPA axis, which we discussed earlier in the context of depression.

A number of neurotransmitters participate in the management of anxiety, including serotonin, norepinephrine, and GABA (Taylor, Fricker, Devi, & Gomes, 2005; Barlow & Durand, 1995). GABA agonists reduce both the subjective experience of anxiety and the activity of the locus coeruleus, a major source of norepinephrine in the brain (Kalueff & Nutt, 2007). Alcohol and benzodiazepines probably achieve their antianxiety results by enhancing the inhibitory effects of GABA at the synapse, as illustrated in ■ Figure 16.18. Benzodiazepine receptors are particularly common in areas of the brain that participate in the assessment of potential danger, including the hippocampus, the amygdala, and the cerebral cortex. Without appropriate levels of GABA-induced inhibition, a person might overreact to perceived threats in the environment.

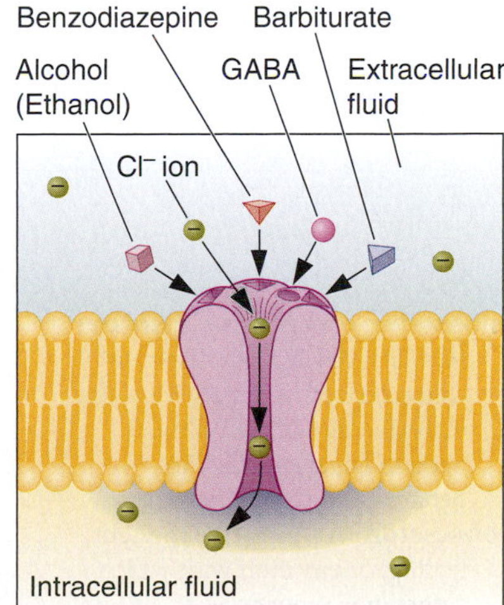

■ **FIGURE 16.18**
The $GABA_A$ Receptor Because alcohol and benzodiazepines enhance the inhibitory effects of GABA, both have similar antianxiety effects.

Treatment for anxiety disorders typically combines medication with cognitive-behavioral therapy to help the person learn to manage reactions to anxiety-producing stimuli. The most commonly prescribed medications include SSRIs, buspirone (a serotonin agonist), tricyclic antidepressants, and benzodiazepines (American Psychiatric

Association [APA], 2006; Velosa & Riddle, 2000). An improved understanding of the biochemical basis of the fear circuits involved in anxiety might lead to more effective medications (Garakani, Mathew, & Charney, 2006).

Of the various types of anxiety disorders, we will focus our discussion on obsessive-compulsive disorder, panic disorder, and posttraumatic stress disorder because these raise especially interesting and representative biological questions.

Obsessive-Compulsive Disorder

Individuals with **obsessive-compulsive disorder (OCD)** are haunted by repetitive, intrusive thoughts (**obsessions**), the need to carry out repetitive behaviors (**compulsions**) such as hand washing or counting objects, or both. The person realizes that the obsessions and compulsions are unrealistic and excessive but is unable to inhibit these thoughts and behaviors. The obsessions and compulsions can be so frequent and disruptive that normal activities are impaired. Approximately 2–3 percent of the American public experiences OCD (APA, 2000).

Typical obsessions include thoughts of germs and disease, fear for the safety of the self or others, symmetry, and religious or moral concerns. Common compulsions include washing, checking, touching, counting, and arranging. Compulsions appear to be efforts to ward off the anxiety produced by the obsessions. For example, people obsessed with germs and disease often compulsively wash their hands hundreds of times per day. OCD often features exaggerations of normal behaviors, including the use of ritual to deal with stress, territoriality, and grooming (Rapoport, 1989). The checking behavior of patients with OCD, in which a person might check door and window locks repeatedly, might be an extreme version of the normal pre-sleep routines of our hunter-gatherer ancestors. The idea that OCD represents exaggerations of natural behavior is supported by observations of similar problems in other species. Dogs occasionally develop an exaggerated grooming version of OCD, in which they repeatedly lick and chew their front paws to the point of causing extensive tissue damage. This behavior can be managed with the same medications used to treat OCD in humans (Seksel & Lindeman, 2001).

Insanity is doing the same thing over and over again and expecting different results.
Albert Einstein

Evidence for a genetic basis for OCD is indicated by the substantial concordance rates (63–87 percent) found in monozygotic twins (Menzies et al., 2008). However, as was the case with depression, it is likely that significant gene–environment interactions occur in OCD (Grisham, Anderson, & Sachdev, 2008). Symptoms of OCD can arise following head trauma, encephalitis, and seizure disorder. Birth complications and streptococcal infections have also been implicated in the development of OCD in young children (Swedo et al., 1997).

OCD is associated with abnormalities in circuits connecting the thalamus, basal ganglia, and orbitofrontal cortex (Saxena, 2003; Szeszko et al., 2004), although other circuits might also participate (Menzies et al., 2008). Imaging studies indicate that the basal ganglia are abnormally active in cases of OCD (Guehl et al., 2008). Medications that successfully reduce the symptoms of OCD also reduce the activity of these structures. In a study of brain activity, patients with OCD and their healthy family members demonstrated underactivity in the orbitofrontal cortex relative to healthy controls without a family history of OCD (Chamberlain et al., 2008). This was especially true during a task that required the participant to adjust to changing rules, suggesting that lower activity in the orbitofrontal cortex might be responsible for some of the rigid, ritualistic behavior observed in OCD.

OCD is typically treated with antidepressant medications and SSRIs in particular (Soomro, Altman, Rajagopal, & Oakley-Browne, 2008). The most severe cases of OCD occur in patients with the lowest serotonin levels (Piacentini & Graae, 1997), making serotonin function a logical target for treatment. Medication is not the only effective treatment available to reduce OCD symptoms. Not only is behavioral therapy effective in some cases of OCD, but it also produces some of the same changes in the basal ganglia as are observed during treatment with medication (Baxter et al., 1992). ■ Figure 16.19 shows PET scans of patients with OCD both before and after drug treatment or behavioral treatment. The results of both types of treatment appear similar. Other patients

obsessive-compulsive disorder (OCD) An anxiety disorder characterized by repetitive, intrusive thoughts and the need to engage in certain behaviors to control anxiety.

obsession An intrusive thought, feeling, or emotion with which a person is preoccupied; characteristic of obsessive-compulsive disorder.

compulsion An irresistible, repeated, impulse to perform an action; characteristic of obsessive-compulsive disorder.

experience relief from severe OCD symptoms through the use of deep brain stimulation of the basal ganglia (Guehl et al., 2008).

Panic Disorder

In a **panic attack**, a person experiences "intense fear or discomfort" accompanied by strong sympathetic arousal leading to heart palpitations, sweating, trembling, and shortness of breath (APA, 2000, p. 432). Once again, we see an anxiety disorder that represents an exaggeration of normal behavior, in this case, the fight-or-flight response (see Chapter 14). **Panic disorder** is diagnosed when repeated panic attacks are followed by at least one month of worrying about having another attack. Single panic attacks are relatively common, with one quarter to one third of college students reporting experiencing one attack in the previous year (Asmundson & Norton, 1993). Panic disorder is much less common than single panic attacks, affecting between 2 and 3 percent of the population (Kessler et al., 2007). About half of all patients with panic disorder also suffer from depression or a second type of anxiety disorder (Kearney, Albano, Eisen, Allan, & Barlow, 1997).

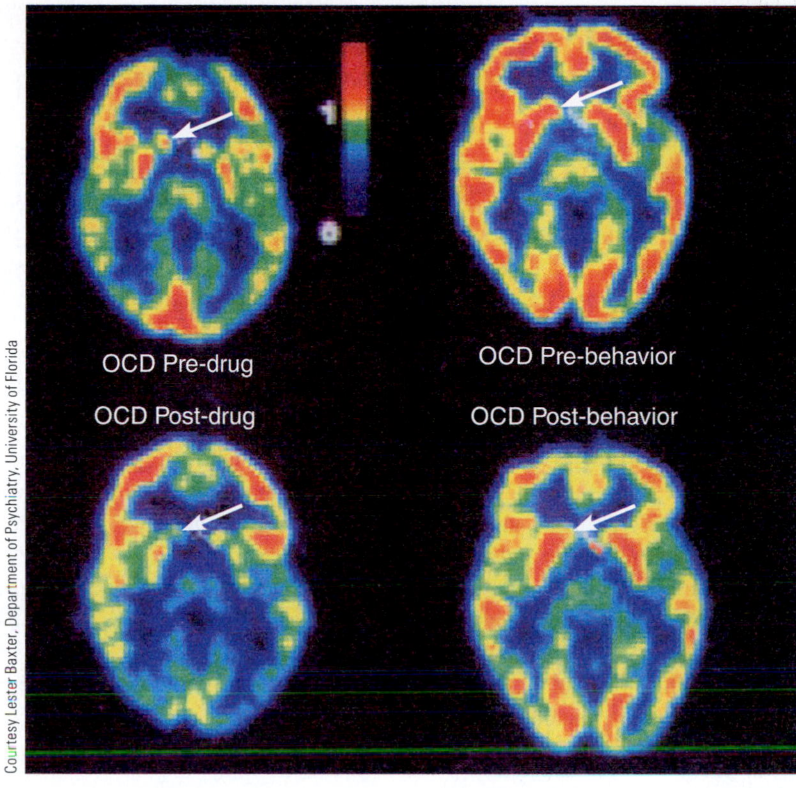

Figure 16.19 OCD and Behavioral Treatment Lewis Baxter and his colleagues (1992) compared PET scans of patients with OCD both before and after either drug treatment or behavioral treatment. In particular, both types of treatment reduced activity in the caudate nucleus, indicated by the arrow.

Panic attacks can be artificially generated in patients suffering from panic disorder by administering sodium lactate (Papp et al., 1993). The sodium lactate appears to provoke panic through its action on the hypothalamus and adjacent areas, which in turn mobilize the sympathetic nervous system for fight or flight (Johnson, Truitt, Fitz, Lowry, & Shekhar, 2008). Imaging research suggests that a circuit including the hippocampus, orbitofrontal cortex, and cingulate cortex also participates in the panic response (Bystritsky et al., 2001). Treatment for panic disorder generally consists of either antidepressant medication, cognitive-behavioral therapy, or a combination of the two (van Apeldoorn et al., 2008).

Posttraumatic Stress Disorder

Posttraumatic stress disorder (PTSD) is the current term for a condition that was known previously as "shell shock" or "battle fatigue." Combat experience is a common trigger for PTSD, but exposure to natural disasters, accidents, assaults, and abuse can also result in the disorder. In PTSD, people exposed to trauma experience recurrent dreams about the traumatic event, unusually vivid and intrusive memories (flashbacks) of the incident, avoidance of stimuli associated with the trauma, hyperarousal, high levels of vigilance, and impairment in daily functioning (APA, 2000).

PTSD usually affects between 3 and 4 percent of American adults in a given year (Kessler et al., 2007), although more than 12 percent of lower Manhattan residents developed the disorder as a consequence of the terrorist attacks of 9/11 (DiGrande et al., 2008). Twice as many women as men develop PTSD. Children appear more vulnerable than adults, with 25 percent of children as opposed to 15 percent of their parents developing PTSD following automobile accidents in which they suffer injuries (de Vries et al., 1999). Combat continues to be one of the most common experiences related to the development of PTSD. About 16 percent of soldiers who have served in Iraq show symptoms of PTSD (Hoge, Terhakopian, Castro, Messer, & Engel, 2007).

Hypotheses regarding the brain mechanisms underlying PTSD have focused on the hippocampus. Imaging studies show that the hippocampus is smaller in patients with PTSD than in healthy controls (Bossini et al., 2008; Bremner et al., 1995). Whether this is a predisposing factor or a result of PTSD remains unclear. Having a small hippocampus might make a person exposed to trauma more vulnerable to the development of PTSD. On the other hand, stress-related elevations of circulating glucocorticoids,

panic attack The experience of intense feelings of impending doom and the need to escape accompanied by strong sympathetic arousal, including heart palpitations, sweating, trembling, and shortness of breath.

panic disorder A condition characterized by repeated panic attacks and worries about having panic attacks.

posttraumatic stress disorder (PTSD) An anxiety disorder arising in response to an extremely stressful event, characterized by intrusive memories, recurrent dreams, avoidance of stimuli associated with the stressful event, and heightened arousal.

WHY DOES THIS MATTER?

Understanding Self-Injury

Most of us go to great lengths to avoid injury. We drive carefully, look both ways before crossing the street, and wear our bike helmets. Consequently, it may come as a surprise that relatively large numbers of people, especially adolescents, engage in self-injury, or the deliberate destruction of body tissue without suicidal intent (Klonsky & Muehlenkamp, 2007). Awareness of self-injury matters because it is often a silent phenomenon, and individuals engaged in this behavior need understanding and effective treatments.

Four percent of adults have a history of self-injury, and 1 percent have self-inflicted a serious injury. Rates in youth are much higher, with 46 percent of ninth and tenth graders reporting a self-injury in the previous year (Lloyd-Richardson, Perrine, Dierker, & Kelley, 2007). The most common type of self-injury is skin-cutting, accounting for 70 percent of cases, followed by banging, hitting, and burning (Klonsky & Muehlenkamp, 2007).

The psychological disorders that predispose individuals to self-injury include several we discuss in this chapter, such as depression and anxiety. In addition, self-injury can accompany eating disorders (see Chapter 9), a history of sexual abuse, substance abuse, and borderline personality disorder, which is characterized by unstable moods and relationships. Given this wide range of associated disorders, finding underlying biological triggers for self-injury is challenging. The most common reason given for self-injury is the need to alleviate anger, anxiety, and frustration (Klonsky & Muehlenkamp, 2007). Following self-injury, individuals report feelings of relief or calm. One possible explanation for the relief experienced following self-injury is the release of endorphins in response to tissue damage (Klonsky, 2007). As we discussed in Chapter 4, endorphins are naturally occurring opiate neurotransmitters that reduce pain and produce feelings of well being, as in "runners' high." Because the emotional states that lead to self-injury are becoming better understood from biological perspectives, future research should be able to inform more effective treatments.

including cortisol, could reduce hippocampal size (Sapolsky, Krey, & McEwen, 1985). After comparing monozygotic and dizygotic twins, Gilbertson et al. (2002) found that hippocampal volume was similar in monozygotic twins, even if one of the twins had experienced trauma and the other had not. However, in another study comparing monozygotic twins, one of whom had combat-related PTSD and the other with no combat experience, only the combat-exposed twin showed smaller hippocampal volume (Kasai et al., 2008). Further research is needed to clarify these discrepancies.

Animal research suggests that stress produces a decrease in benzodiazepine receptor binding in the frontal cortex (Fukumitsu, Tsuchida, Ogi, Uchiyama, & Mori, 2002). Similar reductions in benzodiazepine activity have been observed in the brains of veterans with combat-related PTSD (Geuze et al., 2008; Bremner et al., 2000). Because benzodiazepines, such as Valium, have a tranquilizing effect, reductions in benzodiazepine activity could produce high levels of vigilance characteristic of PTSD.

Treatment for PTSD typically consists of cognitive-behavioral therapy with or without antianxiety or antidepressant medication. Newer therapies might prevent PTSD from developing at all (see Chapter 12). Propranolol, which blocks the effects of glucocorticoids in the brain, might prevent PTSD when administered immediately following a traumatic event (Pitman & Delahanty, 2005; Pitman et al., 2002).

Autism

The word *autism* literally means "within oneself." According to the DSM-IV, **autism** is characterized by deficits in three behavioral domains: communication, social relatedness, and normal range of interests (APA, 2000). Autism is frequently described as a spectrum of disorders because the severity of the observed deficits and the course of the disorder can vary widely from individual to individual. A few children make relatively normal adjustments, but 30–60 percent will be mentally retarded (Amaral, Schumann, & Nordahl, 2008). As we observed in Chapter 13, a small number of individuals with autism exhibit savant behaviors, or particular behaviors that are far superior to the person's overall level of functioning. Most children with autism show evidence of the disorder within the first 18 months of life, whereas 25–40 percent develop normally

autism (AW-tizm) A severe lifetime disorder characterized by impairments in social interaction, range of interests, and communication.

until about the age of 18–24 months, when they begin to regress (Werner & Dawson, 2005). It is possible that these two time courses represent different sets of causal factors, although the behavioral outcomes are indistinguishable.

Recent estimates suggest that about 6.7 people out of 1,000 have autism spectrum disorders (Centers for Disease Control [CDC], 2007), but rates appear to be rising (Merrick, Kandel, & Morad, 2004). Rates of autism in California increased 273 percent between 1987 and 1998 (Shute, 2000). It is unclear whether this rate increase reflects a genuine rise in the incidence of the disorder or a relaxation of diagnostic criteria (Barbaresi, Katusic, Colligan, Weaver, & Jacobsen, 2005). Boys with autism outnumber girls by at least 3 to 1 and possibly by as much as 5 to 1 (Centers for Disease Control [CDC], 2007).

Causes of Autism

There is strong evidence from family and twin studies that autism is influenced by genetics (Le Couteur et al., 1996). Studies of identical twins suggest that the concordance rate for autism is at least 90 percent and possibly even more (Yang & Gill, 2007). Genes that seem most likely to participate in autism are involved with the regulation of brain development (Yang & Gill, 2007). Given the diverse and complex systems of behavior affected by autism, such as sociability and language, it should come as no surprise to learn that no single gene has been shown to contribute to a person's susceptibility to autism. Instead, general tendencies managed by large pools of genes are likely to be involved. For example, people with autism are much more likely to have relatives who are engineers and scientists, whose thinking is highly systematic, than relatives who are artists and poets, whose thinking can be characterized as more emotional and empathic (Baron-Cohen & Belmonte, 2005).

Genetic predispositions for autism likely interact with multiple environmental factors (Happe, Ronald, & Plomin, 2006). Among the environmental factors of concern is exposure to mercury. Although the trace amounts of mercury found in childhood vaccines between 1989 and 2002 has been shown to play no part in the development of autism (Schechter & Grether, 2008), county-by-county rates of autism in Texas and California correlate with industrial mercury emissions (Palmer, 2005). Mercury is just one of a number of dietary and other environmental factors that suppress maternal thyroid levels. In animal models, suppression of maternal thyroid for as little as three days results in changes in the brain architecture of offspring that is similar to that found in autism (Román, 2007).

Brain Structure and Function in Autism

A leading theory of autism suggests that brain development is abnormally accelerated through early childhood, producing first brain enlargement, then a period of deceleration (Amaral et al., 2008). Consistent with this view is the finding that infants eventually diagnosed with autism have much higher levels of circulating neurotrophins than healthy infants within a few days of birth (Nelson et al., 2001). High levels of neurotrophins may lead to less apoptosis and larger brain size (see Chapter 5). This different developmental pathway appears to occur in children with a pattern of early symptom onset, but not in those with normal development followed by regression (Webb et al., 2007).

An alternate view of brain anatomy in autism suggests that minicolumns, representing the smallest units of processing in the brain, are smaller in individuals with autism than in healthy controls (Casanova et al., 2006). The additional finding that the brains of three distinguished scientists without deficits in language and sociability showed minicolumn structure similar to that found in patients with autism suggests that minicolumn dimensions might account for the extreme focus of interests found in autism and possibly savant behavior (Casanova, Switala, Trippe, & Fitzgerald, 2007).

Other brain structures associated with autism include the cerebellum and amygdala. Findings regarding the cerebellum are mixed. Earlier studies using autopsy suggested that the cerebellum was reduced in volume in cases of autism (Bauman, 1996), whereas more contemporary imaging studies show the cerebellum to be enlarged relative to controls (Amaral et al., 2008). Further research is needed to resolve this discrepancy. The amygdala, like total brain volume, appears to follow an abnormal pattern of development, first becoming enlarged relative to age-controls, then remaining the same size as the age-controls catch up (Schumann et al., 2004). Children showing the greatest early enlargement of the amygdala also showed the highest levels of anxiety (Juranek et al., 2006) and the worst social and language skills (Munson et al., 2006).

Dysfunctions in mirror neuron function (see Chapter 8) might account for a number of deficits in autism because mirror neuron function has been implicated in empathy, imitation, and language (Iacoboni & Dapretto, 2006; Iacoboni & Mazziotta, 2007). Deficits in mirror neuron function during imitation and identification of facial expressions have been observed even in high-functioning children with autism relative to healthy controls (Dapretto et al., 2006). Treatments based on improving imitation abilities in children with autism seem promising (Iacoboni & Mazziotta, 2007; Ingersoll, Lewis, & Kroman, 2007).

Biochemistry and Treatment of Autism

Serotonin, GABA, and glutamate abnormalities are associated with autism (Pardo & Eberhart, 2007). In addition to their typical roles in neural communication (see Chapter 4), these neurotransmitters also play an important part in neural migration and positioning during development (see Chapter 5). However, efforts to improve behavior in children with autism using medications have been disappointing (Buitelaar, 2003).

Based on reports that people with autism show evidence of excess peptides from gluten (found in wheat) and casein (found in dairy products), many families have chosen to exclude these food sources from the diets of autistic children. However, existing controlled studies do not provide strong support for this practice (Millward, Ferriter, Calver, & Connell-Jones, 2008). Autism is usually treated with intensive, early-childhood learning experiences provided during most of the child's waking hours (Newsom, 1998). For the small minority of high-functioning children who already have some spontaneous language ability, this aggressive intervention can produce nearly normal functioning (Smith & Lovaas, 1998).

Attention Deficit/Hyperactivity Disorder

Attention deficit/hyperactivity disorder (ADHD) has been diagnosed in 7–8 percent of American schoolchildren (Centers for Disease Control [CDC], 2005) and continues to affect approximately 4 percent of adults (Kessler et al., 2007). Symptoms of ADHD include inattentiveness, impulsivity, and hyperactivity (APA, 2000).

Accurate diagnosis of ADHD is challenging because many of the criteria for the disorder seem to involve very normal behaviors. For instance, the criteria include "often avoids, dislikes, or is reluctant to engage in tasks that require sustained mental effort (such as schoolwork or homework)" (APA, 2000, p. 92). The criteria do specify that these behaviors must be "maladaptive" and "inconsistent with developmental level." Nonetheless, it's easy to see how normal child behavior might be mistaken for ADHD. Angold, Erkanli, Egger, and Costello (2000) found that more than half of the children in a large sample who were prescribed stimulant medications for ADHD did not meet even relaxed diagnostic criteria for the disorder.

attention deficit/hyperactivity disorder (ADHD) A disorder first diagnosed in childhood, characterized by inattention, hyperactivity, or both.

methylphenidate (Ritalin) (meth-ill-FEN-i-date) A close relative of amphetamine that is prescribed to treat attention deficit/hyperactivity disorder.

dextroamphetamine (Dexedrine or Dextrostat) (decks-troh-am-FET-uh-meen) A dopamine agonist used to treat some cases of attention deficit/hyperactivity disorder.

Genetics of ADHD

Twin studies and adoption studies support a significant role for genetics in ADHD (Barkley, 1996). The heritability of ADHD has been estimated to be 80 percent or possibly higher (Tannock, 1998; Faraone & Biederman, 1998). The mechanism for this genetic influence is currently unknown, and it is very likely that multiple genes are involved. Dopaminergic systems are a logical place for researchers to look. Brain structures consistently implicated in ADHD, such as the basal ganglia and prefrontal cortex, are rich in dopaminergic neurons. Traditional medications used for ADHD, which include **methylphenidate (Ritalin)**, **dextroamphetamine (Dexedrine** or **Dextrostat)**, and mixed amphetamine salts (**Adderall**), are known dopamine agonists. Research has therefore focused on genes associated with dopamine, including dopamine transporter genes (Gill, Daly, Heron, Hawi, & Fitzgerald, 1997) and dopamine receptor genes (Ebstein et al., 1996).

Although genetic influences on ADHD are substantial, environmental factors alone or in conjunction with susceptibility genes contribute to the prevalence of the disorder. Among environmental risk factors for ADHD are lead contamination, low birth weight, and prenatal exposure to tobacco, alcohol, and other drugs (Banerjee, Middleton, & Faraone, 2007).

Brain Structure and Function in ADHD

Brain structures implicated in ADHD include the prefrontal cortex, the basal ganglia, and the circuits that connect these two areas. The fact that people with known frontal lobe damage behave in ways that are similar to those with ADHD led to interest in the frontal lobes as a possible area responsible for ADHD symptoms. Specifically, both groups have problems with organization, impulsivity, emotional behavior, and sustained attention. However, there is no evidence of brain damage in individuals with ADHD. Instead, the frontal lobes, and the prefrontal areas in particular, seem to mature more slowly in children with ADHD compared to healthy controls (Shaw et al., 2007). Peak cortical thickness, a measure of brain maturation, occurred in healthy controls around age 7.5 years but not until age 10.5 years in the children with ADHD.

A number of researchers have reported smaller volume of the caudate nucleus, a part of the basal ganglia, associated with ADHD (Castellanos et al., 1994; Filipek et al., 1997; Mataro et al., 1997; Swanson, Castellanos, Murias, LaHoste, & Kennedy, 1998). However, this difference between individuals with and without ADHD disappears by the age of 16 years (Krain & Castellanos, 2006), lending further support to the view of ADHD as a problem of maturation.

Although all cases of ADHD appear to involve the prefrontal areas and basal ganglia, subtypes of ADHD might be differentially affected by problems in these two areas. ADHD with hyperactivity might represent a central problem with the basal ganglia, whereas inattentive ADHD without hyperactivity is more likely to result from problems in the prefrontal cortex (Diamond, 2007).

Biochemistry and Treatment of ADHD

The use of stimulant medication to treat ADHD resulted from an accidental discovery. In 1937, Charles Bradley used the stimulant Benzedrine, a type of dextroamphetamine, to treat the headaches of children referred to him for learning and behavior problems. The stimulant didn't help the children with their headaches, but it did produce a noticeable improvement in their learning. The children referred to Benzedrine as a "math pill" because they found it easier to do their math while using the medication.

Today, children with a diagnosis of ADHD are treated primarily with medication, either alone or in combination with behavioral therapy. The use of medication for ADHD in the United States, which is five times greater than in any other nation, has been the subject of considerable criticism. Nonetheless, medication has a substantial benefit for the majority of children with ADHD (Barkley, 1995; Swanson, McBurnett, Christian, & Wigal, 1995). A large treatment outcome study found that a combination of individually tailored doses of medication in conjunction with behavioral therapy was the most effective treatment approach (Hoza, Waschbusch, Pelham, Molina, & Milich, 2000).

The most commonly prescribed drugs for ADHD are the closely related stimulants methylphenidate (Ritalin), dextroamphetamine, and amphetamine salts (Adderall). These drugs act as dopamine and norepinephrine reuptake inhibitors, and dextroamphetamine and Adderall increase the release of these neurotransmitters as well. Although most patients tolerate these medications well, serious side effects, including growth suppression, weight loss, and sleep disturbance can occur. For patients who do not respond to stimulants, or who experience unacceptable levels of side effects, nonstimulant drugs such as atomoxetine, a norepinephrine reuptake inhibitor, might be helpful (Prasad & Steer, 2008).

Adderall A combination of amphetamine salts prescribed to treat attention deficit/hyperactivity disorder.

WHY DOES THIS MATTER?

Are There "Steroids" for the Mind?

Sports is not the only arena in which competitive professionals have turned to drugs to enhance their performance. Whereas athletes use steroids to enhance their physical abilities, scientists are turning to drugs used to treat ADHD, including methylphenidate (Ritalin), to enhance their mental abilities. Awareness of the use of prescription drugs for cognitive enhancement matters because this practice appears to be very common, and as with the use of steroids for physical enhancement, it raises interesting questions of ethics and health.

In January 2008, the prestigious journal, *Nature*, which has a readership composed primarily of highly educated scientists and engineers, ran an informal survey on the use of prescription drugs for cognitive enhancement and received over 1,400 responses (Maher, 2008). Twenty percent of the respondents admitted to having used modafinil (used to treat narcolepsy), methylphenidate (used to treat ADHD), or propranolol (which we discussed as a possible preventive for PTSD), obtained without a prescription, for the purpose of cognitive enhancement. Sixty-five percent of respondents said they knew a colleague who used one or more of these drugs. Of the three drugs, methylphenidate (Ritalin) was used most often. Most respondents reported using the drugs for the specific purpose of improving concentration and their ability to focus on a particular task.

The ethics associated with the use of drugs for cognitive enhancement are reminiscent of the use of performance-enhancing steroids by athletes. A slim majority (54–45 percent) of the *Nature* respondents believed that students should not be permitted to use such drugs for the purpose of enhancing their performance on college entrance exams and other standardized testing. However, a third believed they would feel pressured to give their children such drugs if other children at school had access to them. As more treatments become available for improving concentration and memory, it is likely that more healthy individuals will want to experience their benefits as well. As with steroid use, it is up to societies to decide what kinds of enhancements are acceptable.

Antisocial Personality Disorder

Antisocial behavior, or the deliberate harming of others, continues to plague human societies at great cost. Many of those who exhibit such behavior meet the DSM-IV criteria for **antisocial personality disorder (APD)**, which is characterized by "a pervasive pattern of disregard for and violation of the rights of others" (APA, 2000, p. 706). Approximately 3 percent of men and 1 percent of women meet the criteria for APD (ibid.).

Although APD and **psychopathy** are often used interchangeably, this practice has led to significant confusion. The DSM-IV definition of APD is based more on a criminal lifestyle and antisocial behavior, whereas psychopathy refers more to personality characteristics than to any specific behaviors (Ogloff, 2006). Psychopaths typically lack guilt, empathy, and normal emotional responses while callously using others to achieve their personal goals (Hare, 1993). Not all criminals are psychopaths, nor are all psychopaths criminals. Between 50 and 80 percent of prison inmates could be diagnosed with APD, but only 15 percent appear to be psychopaths (ibid.). Many psychopaths manage to avoid the criminal system altogether. Widom (1978, p. 72) was able to attract a large number of noncriminal, antisocial participants by placing a newspaper ad calling for "charming, aggressive, carefree people who are impulsively irresponsible but are good at handling people and at looking after number one."

antisocial personality disorder (APD) A personality disorder diagnosed in adults, characterized by a failure to conform to social and legal codes of behavior and the violation of the rights of others.

psychopathy A condition characterized by an abnormal lack of remorse and empathy, often leading to the exploitation of others to meet personal goals.

Genetics of Antisocial Personality Disorder

The confusion over the classification of people engaged in antisocial behavior complicates the search for susceptibility genes. In addition, as was the case with depression, antisocial personality disorder shows complex interactions between genes and environment. Criminal behavior definitely seems to run in families (Moffitt, 2005). However, determining whether genetics or learning is responsible for this finding requires careful analysis.

In one study, the extent of child maltreatment, a known risk factor for later antisocial behavior, interacted with a single gene, *MAOA* (Caspi et al., 2002). Variations in the *MAOA* gene had been implicated in aggression in studies with animals. However, variations in the *MAOA* gene do not by themselves predict human antisocial behavior (Moffitt, 2005). It was only when gene–environment interactions were examined that the variations in the *MAOA* gene had significant effects. Eighty-five percent of the boys with the low-activity version of the *MAOA* gene who experienced severe maltreatment later engaged in some forms of antisocial behavior. In contrast, males with the higher activity version of the *MAOA* gene were not likely to engage in antisocial behavior, even when exposed to severe maltreatment.

Using assessments that target the emotional aspects of psychopathy, as opposed to observations of antisocial behavior, twin studies have indicated substantial heritability (.46 to .67) for psychopathic traits such as fearless dominance, impulsive antisociality, and callousness (Blair, Peschardt, Budhani, Mitchell, & Pine, 2006). These results suggest relatively little environmental influence on the core characteristics of psychopathy. Although child maltreatment appears to interact with genetic predispositions in producing criminal behavior, it is unlikely to produce the emotional "flattening" that characterizes the psychopath (Blair et al., 2006).

Brain Structure and Function in Antisocial Personality Disorder

In our discussion of aggression in Chapter 14, we proposed a model in which limbic activation provides aggressive drive that is normally held in check by inhibitory influences provided by the orbitofrontal cortex and anterior cingulate cortex. According to this view, aggressive violence will result from limbic overstimulation, insufficient frontal inhibition, or both. Not too surprisingly, abnormalities in these structures and their functions have been implicated in antisocial behavior.

Kiehl et al. (2001) reported that criminal psychopaths showed less activity in several limbic structures than noncriminal controls when exposed to stimuli that normally elicit an emotional response, such as the word *torture*. Blair et al. (2002) reported that criminal psychopaths were especially impaired in identifying fear in a person's voice. These impairments in the expression and interpretation of emotion, mediated by circuits involving the amygdala, could interfere with some of the normal controls that prevent us from hurting one another.

Crime isn't a disease. It's a symptom.

Raymond Chandler

Anderson, Bechara, Damasio, Tranel, and Damasio (1999) reported that antisocial behavior appears to be related to damage to the orbitofrontal cortex, illustrated in Figure 16.20. They described two adult participants who had been raised in stable, middle-class homes but had experienced damage to the orbitofrontal cortex before the age of 16 months. As adults, these individuals engaged in stealing, lying, aggressive behavior, poor parenting, and an inability to understand the consequences of their behavior. Davidson, Putnam, and Larson (2000) identified frequent orbitofrontal dysfunctions in murderers, people with aggressive impulsive personality disorder, and

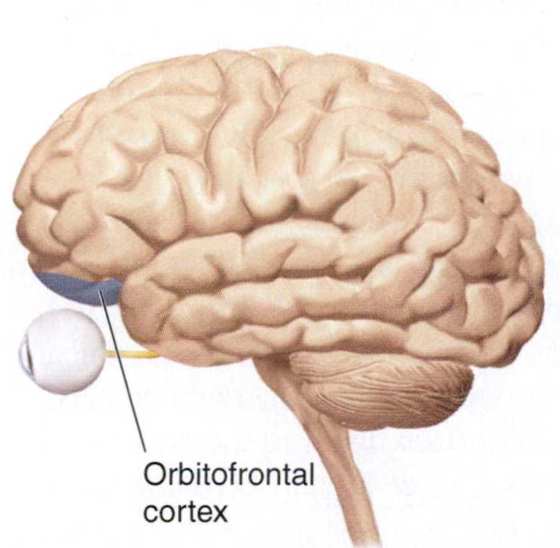

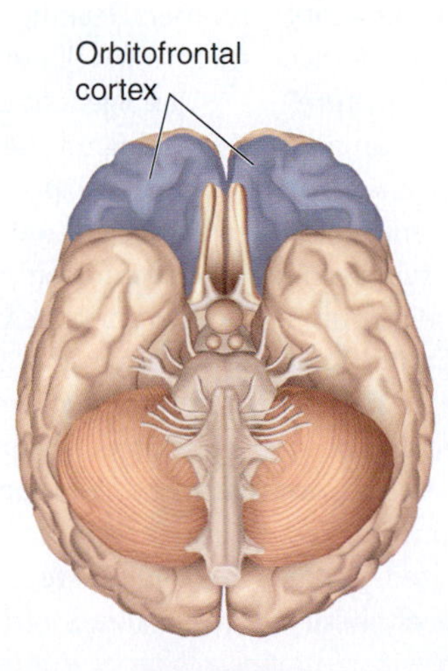

Figure 16.20
The Orbitofrontal Cortex

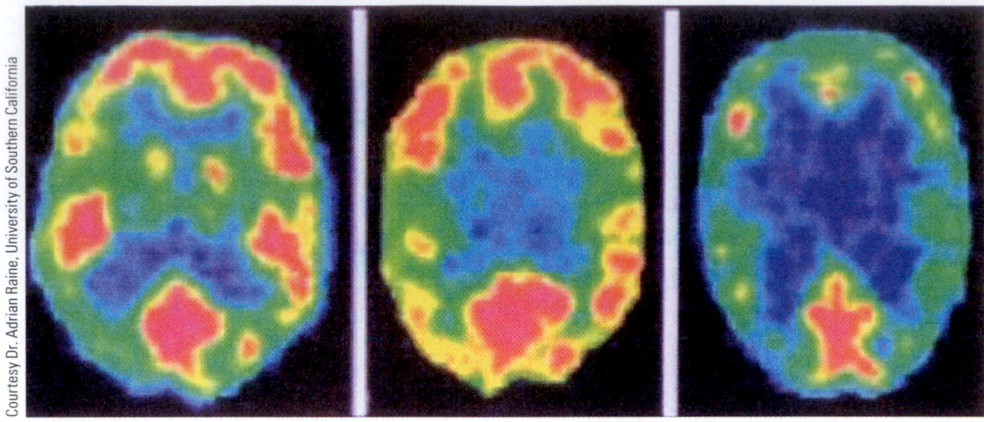

FIGURE 16.21
Brain Activity Among Murderers
Adrian Raine and his colleagues (1998) compared PET scans of normal control participants (left), murderers who had a history of abuse and neglect (middle), and murderers who had not experienced deprivation, abuse, or neglect (right). The brain activity of the abused murderers looks quite similar to that of the normal participants. In contrast, the brain activity of the unabused murderers is unusually low, especially in the frontal lobes.

Courtesy Dr. Adrian Raine, University of Southern California

people diagnosed with antisocial personality disorder. Kip Kinkel, who was accused of murdering his parents and two students in a subsequent school shooting in 1998, was found to have lesions in his orbitofrontal cortex.

Researchers have investigated the interactions of nature and nurture in brain activity related to antisocial behavior. In addition to comparing PET scans of the brains of nonviolent offenders and murderers, Raine, Stoddard, Bihrle, and Buchsbaum (1998) assessed such environmental factors as neglect, poverty, and physical and sexual abuse. As shown in Figure 16.21, the brain activity of the murderers who had experienced abuse and neglect did not appear different from the brain activity of the normal controls. However, the unabused murderers show a dramatically reduced level of brain activity, particularly in the frontal lobes of the brain. As in our previous discussion of heritability of antisocial traits, these results might reflect differences between psychopaths and non-psychopathic offenders.

I never wonder to see men wicked, but I often wonder to see them not ashamed.
Jonathan Swift

Treatment of Antisocial Personality Disorder

Once again, the heterogeneous nature of criminal behavior makes an evaluation of outcomes challenging. We can distinguish between reactive aggression, in which an

NEW DIRECTIONS

Epigenetics and Psychopathology

Throughout this textbook, and particularly in this chapter, we have attempted to identify the contributions of genetics and environment to biology and behavior. Unfortunately, such discussions often imply an either–or mentality rather than capturing the sophisticated mutual influence that science writer Matt Ridley describes as "nature *via* nurture" (Ridley, 2003). Knowledge of the genes correlated with an outcome is important, but so is an understanding of epigenesis, or the switching on and off of a particular gene. Most epigenesis occurs early in development, but researchers are suggesting that epigenesis continues throughout life and often in response to environmental influences (Rutter, Moffitt, & Caspi, 2006; Szyf, McGowan, & Meaney, 2008).

Factors such as diet, stress, and maternal care have been shown to affect epigenesis. Even more startling is the possibility that these later-in-life effects can still be transmitted to future generations. Several labs have demonstrated that a mother mouse's diet can affect the fur color and risk of obesity of her children and grandchildren (Cropley, Suter, Beckman, & Martin, 2006; Waterland, Travisano, Tabiliani, Rached, & Mirza, 2008). Epigenesis was influenced in rat pups neglected by their mothers, leading to stress responses that differed from pups that were well nurtured by their mothers (Weaver et al., 2004).

If epigenesis can produce different stress responses in rats, depending on the quality of the mothering they receive, what of humans exposed to abuse, neglect, and stress? A history of early neglect and abuse appeared to have affected epigenesis in the hippocampus of suicide victims, in comparison to control participants who had died in accidents (Szyf et al., 2008). Exploration of a role for epigenetic effects is well underway in research on anxiety, depression, antisocial disorders, and schizophrenia (Rutter et al., 2006). The reciprocal relationships between genes and the environment are many and complex, but researchers are making important discoveries that will further illuminate our understanding of human behavior, both typical and disordered.

individual responds aggressively, impulsively, and emotionally to a perceived threat, from instrumental aggression, in which a person uses aggression to meet his or her goals in a calculating, unemotional fashion. Instrumental aggression appears to have more in common with predation among animals, although unlike humans, animals rarely engage in this type of behavior within their own species (see Chapter 14). The psychopath often engages in both types of aggression but is more likely than other antisocial individuals to engage in instrumental aggression.

Existing treatment programs for violent offenders are frequently based on learning models that emphasize anger control, social skills, and moral reasoning (Goldstein, Glick, & Gibbs, 1998). These models appear modestly effective in reducing antisocial behaviors among children and youth, but they do not appear to have much effect on individuals with psychopathy (Hornsveld, Nijman, Hollin, & Kraaimaat, 2008). Psychopathy requires additional training in "character formation" (Salmon, 2004). However, many nations view criminal psychopathy as untreatable and rely on incarceration to protect the public.

INTERIM SUMMARY 16.3

Summary Points

1. Anxiety disorders share a core element of unrealistic and counterproductive anxiety. **(LO5)**
2. Autism is heavily influenced by genetics and is correlated with abnormal development in the limbic system and cerebellum. Early, intense behavioral intervention is the typical treatment for autism. **(LO6)**
3. Attention deficit/hyperactivity disorder (ADHD) is characterized by short attention span and high levels of motor activity. Abnormalities in frontal lobe and basal ganglia function might contribute to ADHD. ADHD is typically treated with stimulant medication. **(LO7)**
4. Antisocial behavior is carried out by a heterogeneous population, some of whom are more influenced by environmental factors and others whose behavior reflects psychopathy. **(LO8)**

Review Questions

1. How does activity in the HPA axis contribute to both depression and anxiety?
2. What controversies surround the use of medication to treat ADHD?

CHAPTER REVIEW

THOUGHT QUESTIONS

1. How do the concordance rates for criminality differ from the rates we see in schizophrenia, mood disorders, and autism? What do these rates tell us about the contribution of genes and the environment to the development of these disorders?
2. What parallels do you see between major depressive disorder and the anxiety disorders in terms of genetics, brain structure and function, and biochemistry?
3. How do the research findings regarding brain structure and function in schizophrenia relate to the observed symptoms?
4. Which of the disorders discussed in this chapter are influenced by gender? Why do you think this is the case?

KEY TERMS

antisocial personality disorder (APD) (p. 480)
attention deficit/hyperactivity disorder (ADHD) (p. 478)
autism (p. 476)
bipolar disorder (p. 466)
concordance rate (p. 458)
delusion (p. 457)
hallucination (p. 457)
major depressive disorder (p. 466)
mania (p. 471)
negative symptom (p. 457)
obsessive-compulsive disorder (OCD) (p. 474)
panic attack (p. 475)
panic disorder (p. 475)
positive symptom (p. 457)
posttraumatic stress disorder (PTSD) (p. 475)
psychological disorder (p. 457)
psychopathy (p. 480)
schizophrenia (p. 457)

References

Aaltonen, P., Amory, J. K., Anderson, R. A., Behre, H. M., Bialy, G., Blithe, D., et al. (2007). 10th Summit Meeting consensus: recommendations for regulatory approval for hormonal male contraception. *Journal of Andrology, 28*(3), 362–363.

Abercrombie, H. C., Schaefer, S. M., Larson, C. L., Oakes, T. R., Lindgren, K. A., Holden, J. E., et al. (1998). Metabolic rate in the right amygdala predicts negative affect in depressed patients. *Neuroreport, 9*(14), 3301–3307.

Abi-Dargham, A., Rodenhiser, J., Printz, D., Zea-Ponce, Y., Gil, R., Kegeles, L. S., et al. (2000). Increased baseline occupancy of [D.sub.2] receptors by dopamine in schizophrenia. *Proceedings of the National Academy of Sciences of the United States of America, 97,* 8104.

Aboody, K. S., Najbauer, J., & Danks, M. K. (2008). Stem and progenitor cell-mediated tumor selective gene therapy. *Gene Therapy, 15*(10), 739–752.

Abou-Khalil, B. (2007). An update on determination of language dominance in screening for epilepsy surgery: The Wada test and newer noninvasive alternatives. *Epilepsia, 48*(3), 442–455.

Abraham, A., von Cramon, D. Y., & Schubotz, R. I. (2008). Meeting George Bush versus meeting Cinderella: The neural response when telling apart what is real from what is fictional in the context of our reality. *Journal of Cognitive Neuroscience, 20*(6), 965–976.

Abraham, W. C., & Mason, S. E. (1988). Effects of the NMDA receptor/channel antagonists CPP and MK801 on hippocampal field potentials and long-term potentiation in anesthetized rats. *Brain Research, 462*(1), 40–46.

Abrams, T. W., Yovell, Y., Onyike, C. U., Cohen, J. E., & Jarrad, H. E. (1998). Analysis of sequence-dependent interactions between transient calcium and transmitter stimuli in activating adenylyl cyclase in *Aplysia:* Possible contribution to CS–US sequence requirement during conditioning. *Learning and Memory, 4,* 496–509.

Abramsky, L., & Chapple, J. (1997). 47, XXY (Klinefelter syndrome) and 47, XYY: Estimated rates of and indication for postnatal diagnosis with implications for prenatal counseling. *Prenatal Diagnosis, 17,* 363–368.

Abramson, N. S. (Coordinator). (1986). Randomized clinical study of thiopental loading in comatose survivors of cardiac arrest. Brain Resuscitation Clinical Trial I Study Group. *New England Journal of Medicine, 314,* 397–403.

Acebo, C., Sadeh, A., Seifer, R., Tzischinsky, O., Hafer, A., & Carskadon, M. A. (2005). Sleep/wake patterns derived from activity monitoring and maternal report for healthy 1- to 5-year-old children. *Sleep, 28*(12), 1568–1577.

Addams, R. (1964). An account of a peculiar optical phaenomenon. In W. Dember (Ed.), *Visual perception: The nineteenth century* (pp. 81–83). New York: Wiley. (Original work published 1934)

Adekoya, N., Thurman, D. J., White, D. D., & Webb, K. W. (2002). Surveillance for traumatic brain injury deaths: United States, 1989–1998. *MMWR Surveillance Summaries: Morbidity and mortality weekly report, 51*(10), 1–14.

Adolphs, R. (2007). Looking at other people: Mechanisms for social perception revealed in subjects with focal amygdala damage. *Novartis Foundation Symposium, 278,* 146–159; discussion 160–144, 216–121.

Adolphs, R., Tranel, D., & Damasio, A. R. (1998). The human amygdala in social judgment. *Nature, 393,* 470–474.

Adolphs, R., Tranel, D., Damasio, H., & Damasio, A. R. (1995). Fear and the human amygdala. *Journal of Neuroscience, 15*(9), 5879–5891.

Adzick, N. S., Sutton, L. N., Crombleholme, T. M., & Flake, A. W. (1998). Successful fetal surgery for spina bifida. *Lancet, 352,* 1675–1676.

Aeschbach, D., Sher, L., Postolache, T. T., Matthews, J. R., Jackson, M. A., & Wehr, T. A. (2003). A longer biological night in long sleepers than in short sleepers. *The Journal of Clinical Endocrinology & Metabolism, 88*(1), 26–30.

Afraz, S.-R., Kiani, R., & Esteky, H. (2006). Microstimulation of inferotemporal cortex influences face categorization. *Nature, 442*(7103), 692–695.

Agboola, A., & Agobe, J. T. (1976). A reappraisal of the duration of labor. *Obstetrics and Gynecology, 48*(6), 724–726.

Aggleton, J. P., & Wood, C. J. (1990). Is there a left-handed advantage in 'ballistic' sports? *International Journal of Sport Psychology, 21*(1), 46–57.

Aharon, I., Etcoff, N., Ariely, D., Chabris, C. F., O'Connor, E., & Breiter, H. C. (2001). Beautiful faces have variable reward value: fMRI and behavioral evidence. *Neuron, 32,* 537–551.

Ahlstrom, R., Berglund, R., Berglund, U., Engen, T., & Lindvall, T. (1987). A comparison of odor perception in smokers, nonsmokers, and passive smokers. *American Journal of Otolaryngology, 8,* 1–6.

Aihara, M., Ida, I., Yuuki, N., Oshima, A., Kumano, H., Takahashi, K., et al. (2007). HPA axis dysfunction in unmedicated major depressive disorder and its normalization by pharmacotherapy correlates with alteration of neural activity in prefrontal cortex and limbic/paralimbic regions. *Psychiatry Research, 155*(3), 245–256.

Aitchison, J. (1983). *The articulate mammal: An introduction to psycholinguistics.* London: Hutchinson.

Akerstedt, T., & Froberg, J. (1976). Interindividual differences in circadian pattern of catecholamine excretion, body temperature, performance, and subjective arousal. *Biological Psychology, 4,* 277–292.

Aksglaede, L., Juul, A., Leffers, H., Skakkebaek, N. E., & Andersson, A.-M. (2006). The sensitivity of the child to sex steroids: Possible impact of exogenous estrogens. *Human Reproduction Update, 12*(4), 341–349.

Alberts, J. R. (1978). Huddling by rat pups: Multisensory control of contact behavior. *Journal of Comparative and Physiological Psychology, 92,* 220–230.

Albus, J. S. (1971). A theory of cerebellar function. *Math. Biosci., 10,* 25–61.

Aldington, S., Harwood, M., Cox, B., Weatherall, M., Beckert, L., Hansell, A., et al. (2008). Cannabis use and risk of lung cancer: A case-control study. *European Respiratory Journal, 31*(2), 280–286.

Aldrich, A., Aranda, J. V., & Neims, A. H. (1979). Caffeine metabolism in the newborn. *Clinical Pharmacology and Therapeutics, 25,* 447–453.

Aldrich, M. (1993). The neurobiology of narcolepsy-cataplexy. *Progress in Neurobiology, 41,* 533–541.

Alexander, G. M., & Hines, M. (2002). Sex differences in response to children's toys in nonhuman primates *(Cercopithecus aethiops sabaeus). Evolution and Human Behavior, 23,* 467–479.

Alexander, G. M., Carden, W. B., Mu, J., Kurukulasuriya, N. C., McCool, B. A., Nordskog, B. K., et al. (2006). The native T-type calcium current in relay neurons of the primate thalamus. *Neuroscience, 141*(1), 453–461.

Alexander, G. M., Kurukulasuriya, N. C., Mu, J., & Godwin, D. W. (2006). Cortical feedback to the thalamus is selectively enhanced by nitric oxide. *Neuroscience, 142*(1), 223–234.

Alexander, L. N., Seward, J. F., Santibanez, T. A., Pallansch, M. A., Kew, O. M., Prevots, D. R., et al. (2004). Vaccine policy changes and epidemiology of poliomyelitis in the United States. *The Journal of the American Medical Association (JAMA), 292*(14), 1696–1701.

Allen, L. S., & Gorski, R. A. (1992). Sexual orientation and the size of the anterior commissure in the human brain. *Proceedings of the National Academy of Sciences of the United States of America, 89,* 7191–7202.

Allen, L. S., Hines, M., Shryne, J. E., & Gorski, R. A. (1989). Two sexually dimorphic cell groups in the human brain. *Journal of Neuroscience, 9,* 497–506.

Allison, T., & Cicchetti, D. (1976). Sleep in mammals: Ecological and constitutional correlates. *Science, 194,* 732–734.

Allman, J. M., Watson, K. K., Tetreault, N. A., & Hakeem, A. Y. (2005). Intuition and autism: A possible role for von Economo neurons. *Trends in Cognitive Science, 9*(8), 367–373.

Alonso, A., & Hernán, M. A. (2008). Temporal trends in the incidence of multiple sclerosis: A systematic review. *Neurology, 71*(2), 129–135.

Alter, J., Lou, F., Rabinowitz, A., Yin, H., Rosenfeld, J., Wilton, S. D., et al. (2006). Systemic delivery of morpholino oligonucleotide restores dystrophin expression bodywide and improves dystrophic pathology. *Nature Medicine, 12*(2), 175–177.

Amaral, D. G., Schumann, C. M., & Nordahl, C. W. (2008). Neuroanatomy of autism. *Trends in Neurosciences, 31*(3), 137–145.

American Academy of Child and Adolescent Psychiatry. (1997). AACAP official action: Practice parameters for the assessment and treatment of children and adolescents with bipolar disorder. *Journal of the American Academy of Child and Adolescent Psychiatry, 36*, 138–157.

American Board of Genetics Counseling (ABGC). (2008). Genetic counseling programs—US. Retrieved April 5, 2008, from http://www.abgc.net/english/view.asp?x=1643

American Heart Association. (2008). Stroke risk factors. Retrieved July 8, 2008, from http://www.americanheart.org/presenter.jhtml?identifier=4716.

American Heritage Dictionary of the English Language. (2000). Boston: Houghton Mifflin.

American Psychiatric Association (APA). (2000). *Diagnostic and statistical manual of mental disorders* (4th ed., text rev.). Washington, DC: Author.

American Psychiatric Association (APA). (2003). *Electroconvulsive therapy (ECT).* Retrieved May 26, 2003, from the American Psychiatric Association Web site: http://www.psych.org/public_info/ect~1.cfm.

American Psychiatric Association (APA). (2006). *Practice guidelines for the treatment of psychiatric disorders: Compendium 2006.* Washington (DC): American Psychiatric Publishing.

American Psychological Association (APA). (1992, December 1). *Ethical principles of psychologists and code of conduct.* Retrieved June 9, 2002, from the American Psychological Association Web site: http://www.apa.org/ethics/code.html.

Ames, E. (1997). *The development of Romanian orphanage children adopted to Canada.* Human Resources Development. Burnaby, British Columbia, Canada: Simon Fraser University.

Amos, C. I., Wu, X., Broderick, P., Gorlov, I. P., Gu, J., Eisen, T., et al. (2008). Genome-wide association scan of tag SNPs identifies a susceptibility locus for lung cancer at 15q25.1. *Nature Genetics, 40*(5), 616–622.

Anand, B., & Brobeck, J. R. (1951). Hypothalamic control of food intake in rats and cats. *Yale Journal of Biology and Medicine, 24*, 123–140.

Andersen, J. L., Schjerling, P., & Saltin, B. (2000). Muscle, genes and athletic performance. *Scientific American, 283*, 48–55.

Anderson, C. A., & Dill, K. E. (2000). Video games and aggressive thoughts, feelings, and behavior in the laboratory and in life. *Journal of Personality and Social Psychology, 78*, 772–790.

Anderson, J. R., & Gallup, G. G., Jr. (1999). Self-recognition in nonhuman primates: Past and future challenges. In M. Haug & R. E. Whalen (Eds.), *Animal models of human emotion and cognition* (pp. 175–194). Washington, D.C.: American Psychological Association.

Anderson, S. W., Bechara, A., Damasio, H., Tranel, D., & Damasio, A. R. (1999). Impairment of social and moral behavior related to early damage in human prefrontal cortex. *Nature Neuroscience, 2*, 1032–1037.

Andreasen, N. C., Rezai, K., Alliger, R., Swayze, V. W., II, Flaum, M., et al. (1992). Hypofrontality in neuroleptic-naive patients and in patients with chronic schizophrenia: Assessment with xenon 133 single-photon emission computed tomography and the Tower of London. *Archives of General Psychiatry, 49*, 943–958.

Andrews, G., Morris-Yates, A., Howie, P., & Martin, N. G. (1991). Genetic factors in stuttering confirmed. *Archives of General Psychiatry, 48*, 1034–1035.

Andrews, G., Steward, G., Allen, B., & Henderson, A. S. (1990). The genetics of six neurotic disorders: A twin study. *Journal of Affective Disorders, 19*, 23–29.

Angold, A., Erkanli, A., Egger, H. L., & Costello, E. J. (2000). Stimulant treatment for children: A community perspective. *Journal of the American Academy of Child and Adolescent Psychiatry, 39*, 975–984.

Annett, M. (1985). *Left, right, hand, and brain: The right shift theory.* London: Erlbaum.

Annett, M., & Manning, M. (1990). Reading and a balanced polymorphism for laterality and ability. *Journal of Child Psychology and Psychiatry, 31*, 511–529.

Antonov, I., Antonova, I., Kandel, E. R., & Hawkins, R. D. (2003). Activity-dependent presynaptic facilitation and Hebbian LTP are both required and interact during classical conditioning in Aplysia. *Neuron, 37*(1), 135–147.

Antonov, I., Ha, T., Antonova, I., Moroz, L. L., & Hawkins, R. D. (2007). Role of nitric oxide in classical conditioning of siphon withdrawal in *Aplysia. Journal of Neuroscience, 27*(41), 10993–11002.

Antonucci, F., Rossi, C., Gianfranceschi, L., Rossetto, O., & Caleo, M. (2008). Long-distance retrograde effects of botulinum neurotoxin A. *Journal of Neuroscience, 28*(14), 3689–3696.

Antonucci, M. (2008). Identigene offers off-the-shelf DNA paternity test. Retrieved April 5, 2008, from http://www.mercurynews.com/business/ci_8807435.

Aravanis, A. M., Pyle, J. L., Harata, N. C., & Tsien, R. W. (2003). Imaging single synaptic vesicles undergoing repeated fusion events: kissing, running, and kissing again. *Neuropharmacology, 45*(6), 797–813.

Areosa, S. A., & Sherriff, F. (2003). Memantine for dementia. *Cochrane Database of Systematic Reviews, 3*, CD003154.

Arnold, S. E., Hyman, B. T., Flory, J., Damasio, A. R., & Van Hoesen, G. W. (1991). The topographical and neuroanatomical distribution of neurofibrillary tangles and neuritic plaques in the cerebral cortex of patients with Alzheimer's disease. *Cerebral Cortex, 1*, 103–116. (Figure 5. 35)

Arnsten, A. F. T., Ramos, B. P., Birnbaum, S. G., & Taylor, J. R. (2005). Protein kinase A as a therapeutic target for memory disorders: Rationale and challenges. *Trends in Molecular Medicine, 11*(3), 121–128.

Aronson, S. M. (2007). Galen and the causes of disease. *Medicine and Health, Rhode Island, 90*(12), 375.

Arzy, S., Seeck, M., Ortigue, S., Spinelli, L., & Blanke, O. (2006). Induction of an illusory shadow person. *Nature, 443*(7109), 287.

Asberg, M. (1986). Biochemical aspects of suicide. *Clinical Neuropharmacology, 9*(Suppl. 4), 374–376.

Ashley-Koch, A., Menold, M., Joyner, K., Mason, S., Poole, C., Donnelly, S., et al. (2000). Examination of epigenetic factors and gene-gene interactions influencing genetic susceptibility at chromosomes 7 and 15 for autistic disorder. *American Journal of Human Genetics, 67*, Abstract Nr. 177.

Asmundson, G. J. G., & Norton, G. R. (1993). Anxiety sensitivity and its relationship to spontaneous and cued panic attacks in college students. *Behavior Research and Therapy, 31*, 199–201.

Associated Press. (2007). 3 DJs fired after deadly water-drinking contest. Retrieved April 18, 2008, from http://www.msnbc.msn.com/id/16660273/.

Aston-Jones, G., Rajkowski, J., Kubiak, P., & Alexinsky, T. (1994). Locus coeruleus neurons in monkeys are selectively activated by attended cues in a vigilance task. *Journal of Neuroscience, 14*, 4467–4480.

Atkinson, R. C., & Shiffrin, R. M. (1968). Human memory: A proposed system and its control processes. In K. W. Spence & J. T. Spence (Eds.), *The psychology of learning and motivation: Vol. 2. Advances in research and theory* (pp. 89–195). New York: Academic Press.

Atkinson, R. C., & Shiffrin, R. M. (1971). The control of short-term memory. *Scientific American, 225*, 82–90.

Aubry, M., Cantu, R., Dvorak, J., Graf-Baumann, T., Johnston, K., Kelly, J., et al. (2002). Summary and agreement statement of the First International Conference on Concussion in Sport, Vienna 2001. Recommendations for the improvement of safety and health of athletes who may suffer concussive injuries. *British Journal of Sports Medicine, 36*(1), 6–10.

Axelsson, J., Stefánsson, J. G., Magnússon, A., Sigvaldason, H., & Karlsson, M. M. (2002). Seasonal affective disorders: Relevance of Icelandic and Icelandic-Canadian evidence to etiologic hypotheses. *Canadian Journal of Psychiatry, 47*(2), 153–158.

Azemar, G. (1993). Les gauchers en escrime: Donees statistique et interpretation. *Escrime Inte!Unexpected End of Formularnational, 7*, 15–19.

Baas, P. W., & Qiang, L. (2005). Neuronal microtubules: When the MAP is the roadblock. *Trends in Cell Biology, 15*(4), 183–187.

Babad, E., Bernieri, F., & Rosenthal, R. (1991). Students as judges of teachers' verbal and nonverbal behavior. *American Educational Research Journal, 28*, 211–234.

Bachoud-Lévi, A., Bourdet, C., Brugieres, P., Nguyen, J. P., Grandmougin, T., Haddad, B., et al. (2000). Safety and tolerability assessment of intrastriatal neural allografts in five patients with Huntington's disease. *Experimental Neurology, 161*, 194–202.

Baddeley, A. D. (2000). The episodic buffer: A new component of working memory? *Trends in Cognitive Sciences, 4*, 417–423.

Baddeley, A. D., & Hitch, G. J. (1974). Working memory. In G. Bower (Ed.), *The psychology of learning and motivation* (Vol. 8, pp. 47–89). New York: Academic Press.

Bailes, J. E., Cantu, R. C., & Day, A. L. (2002). The neurosurgeon in sport: Awareness of the risks of heatstroke and dietary supplements. *Neurosurgery, 51*, 286–288.

Bailey, A. A., & Hurd, P. L. (2005). Finger length ratio (2D:4D) correlates with physical aggression in men but not in women. *Biological Psychology, 68*(3), 215–222.

Bailey, C. H., & Chen, M. C. (1983). Morphological basis of longterm habituation and sensitization in *Aplysia. Science, 220*, 91–93.

Bailey, J. M., & Pillard, R. C. (1991). A genetic study of male sexual orientation. *Archives of General Psychiatry, 48*, 1089–1096.

Baird, A. A., Gruber, S. A., Fein, D. A., Maas, L. C., Steingard, R. J., Renshaw, P. F., et al. (1999). Functional magnetic resonance imaging of facial affect recognition in children and adolescents. *Journal of the American Academy of Child and Adolescent Psychiatry, 38*(2), 195–199.

Baird, D. T., Dewar, M., & Glasier, A. (1992). Mifepristone (RU 486) compared with high-dose estrogen and progestogen for emergency postcoital contraception. *New England Journal of Medicine, 327*, 1041–1044.

Bakan, P. (1971, August). The eyes have it. *Psychology Today*, 64–69.

Bakchine, S., & Loft, H. (2008). Memantine treatment in patients with mild to moderate Alzheimer's disease: Results of a randomised, double-blind, placebo-controlled 6-month study. *Journal of Alzheimer's Disease, 13*(1), 97–107.

Baker, K. G., Halliday, G. M., Hornung, J. P., Geffen, L. B., Cotton, R. G., & Törk, I. (1991). Distribution, morphology and number of monoamine-synthesizing and substance P-containing neurons in the human dorsal raphe nucleus. *Neuroscience, 42*(3), 757–775.

Baldereschi, M., Di Carlo, A., Rocca, W. A., Vanni, P., Maggi, S., Perissinotto, E., Grigoletto, F., Amaducci, L., & Inzitari, D. (2000). Parkinson's disease and parkinsonism in a longitudinal study: Twofold higher incidence in men. *Neurology, 55,* 1358–1363.

Ballard, C., Lana, M. M., Theodoulou, M., Douglas, S., McShane, R., Jacoby, R., et al. (2008). A randomised, blinded, placebo-controlled trial in dementia patients continuing or stopping neuroleptics (The DART-AD Trial). *PLos Medicine, 5*(4), e76.

Baltimore Longitudinal Study of Aging. (2000, March 12). *Welcome to the BLSA.* Retrieved May 1, 2001, from the Baltimore Longitudinal Study of Aging Web site: http://www.grc.nia.nih.gov/branches/blsa/blsanew.htm.

Baltimore, D. (2001). Our genome unveiled. *Nature, 409,* 814–816.

Bambakidis, N. C., Butler, J., Horn, E. M., Wang, X., Preul, M. C., Theodore, N., et al. (2008). Stem cell biology and its therapeutic applications in the setting of spinal cord injury. *Neurosurgery Focus, 24*(3–4), E20.

Banerjee, T. D., Middleton, F., & Faraone, S. V. (2007). Environmental risk factors for attention-deficit hyperactivity disorder. *Acta Paediatrica, 96*(9), 1269–1274.

Banich, M. T., Levine, S. C., Kim, H., & Huttenlocker, P. (1990). The effects of developmental factors on IQ in hemiplegic children. *Neuropsychologia, 28,* 35–47.

Barbaresi, W. J., Katusic, S. K., Colligan, R. C., Weaver, A. L., & Jacobsen, S. J. (2005). The incidence of autism in Olmsted County, Minnesota, 1976–1997: Results from a population-based study. *Archives of Pediatric and Adolescent Medicine, 159,* 37–44.

Barceló, F., & Knight, R. T. (2002). Both random and perseverative errors underlie WCST deficits in prefrontal patients. *Neuropsychologia, 40,* 349–356.

Barco, A., Alarcon, J. M., & Kandel, E. R. (2002). Expression of constitutively active CREB protein facilitates the late phase of long-term potentiation by enhancing synaptic capture. *Cell, 108,* 689–703.

Bard, P. (1934). Emotion: I. The neurohumoral basis of emotional reactions. In C. Murchison (Ed.), *Handbook of general experimental psychology* (pp. 264–311). Worcester, MA: Clark University Press.

Barkley, R. (1995). *Taking charge of ADHD: The complete, authoritative guide for parents.* New York: Guilford Press.

Barkley, R. (1996). Attention-deficit/hyperactivity disorder. In E. Mash & R. A. Barkley (Eds.), *Child psychopathology* (pp. 63–112). New York: Guilford Press.

Barkley, R. (1997). *ADHD and the nature of self-control.* New York: Guilford Press.

Barlow, D. (1988). *Anxiety and its disorders: The nature and treatment of anxiety and panic.* New York: Guilford Press.

Barlow, D. H., & Durand, V. M. (1995). *Abnormal psychology: An integrative approach.* Pacific Grove, CA: Brooks/Cole.

Barlow, H. B. (1972). Single units and sensation: A neuron doctrine for perceptual psychology? *Perception, 1,* 371–395.

Barnea, A., & Nottebohm, F. (1994). Seasonal recruitment of hippocampal neurons in adult free-ranging black-capped chickadees. *Proceedings of the National Academy of Sciences of the United States of America, 91,* 11217–11221.

Barnes, B. O., & Galton, L. (1976). *Hypothyroidism: The unsuspected illness.* New York: Crowell.

Barnes, C. A., Meltzer, J., Houston, F., Orr, G., McGann, K., & Wenk, G. L. (2000). Chronic treatment of old rats with donepezil or galantamine: Effects on memory, hippocampal plasticity and nicotinic receptors. *Neuroscience, 99,* 17–23.

Barnes, T. D., Kubota, Y., Hu, D., Jin, D. Z., & Graybiel, A. M. (2005). Activity of striatal neurons reflects dynamic encoding and recoding of procedural memories. *Nature, 437*(7062), 1158–1161.

Baron-Cohen, S., & Belmonte, M. K. (2005). Autism: A window onto the development of the social and the analytic brain. *Annual Review of Neuroscience, 28,* 109–126.

Barr, A. M., Panenka, W. J., Macewan, G. W., Thornton, A. E., Lang, D. J., Honer, W. G., et al. (2006). The need for speed: An update on methamphetamine addiction. *Journal of Psychiatry and Neuroscience, 31*(5), 301–313.

Barrett, S., Landa, R., Beck, J. C., Braun, T. A., Casavant, T. L., Childress, D., et al. (1999). An autosomal genomic screen for autism: Collaborative linkage study of autism. *American Journal of Medical Genetics, 88,* 609–615.

Bartels, A., & Zeki, S. (2000). The neural basis of romantic love. *Neuroreport, 11,* 3829–3834.

Bartels, A., & Zeki, S. (2004). The neural correlates of maternal and romantic love. *NeuroImage, 21,* 1155–1166.

Barton, J. J. (2003). Disorders of face perception and recognition. *Neurologic Clinics, 21*(2), 521–548.

Bartoshuk, L. M. (2000). Comparing sensory experiences across individuals: Recent psychophysical advances illuminate genetic variation in taste perception. *Chemical Senses, 25,* 447–460.

Bartz, J. A., & Hollander, E. (2006). The neuroscience of affiliation: Forging links between basic and clinical research on neuropeptides and social behavior. *Hormones and Behavior, 50*(4), 518–528.

Basile, A. S., Bonci, A., Uhl, G., & Vorel, S. R. (2002). Reinforcement and relapse: New insights into the mechanisms underlying drug abuse (Program No. 213.) Retrieved December 2, 2002, from Society for Neuroscience, *2002 Abstract Viewer/Itinerary Planner* Web site: http://sfn.scholarone.com/itin2002/index.html.

Basson, M. D., Bartoshuk, L. M., Dichello, S. Z., Panzini, L., Weiffenbach, J. M., & Duffy, V. B. (2005). Association between 6-n-propylthiouracil (PROP) bitterness and colonic neoplasms. *Digestive Diseases and Sciences, 50*(3), 483–489.

Basu, A., Alzaid, A., Dinneen, S., Caumo, A., Cobelli, C., & Rizza, R. A. (1996). Effects of a change in the pattern of insulin delivery on carbohydrate tolerance in diabetic and nondiabetic humans in the presence of differing degrees of insulin resistance. *The Journal of Clinical Investigation, 97*(10), 2351–2361.

Bauman, M. (1996). Neuroanatomic observations of the brain in pervasive developmental disorders. *Journal of Autism and Developmental Disorders, 26,* 199–203.

Bautista, D. M., Siemens, J., Glazer, J. M., Tsuruda, P. R., Basbaum, A. I., Stucky, C. L., et al. (2007). The menthol receptor TRPM8 is the principal detector of environmental cold. *Nature, 448*(7150), 204–208.

Baxter, L. R., Jr., Schwartz, J. M., Bergman, K. S., Szuba, M. P., Guze, B. H., Mazziotta, J. C., et al. (1992). Caudate glucose metabolic rate changes with both drug and behavior therapy for obsessive-compulsive disorder. *Archives of General Psychiatry, 49,* 681–689.

Baylor, D. (1987). Photoreceptor signals and vision. *Investigative Ophthalmology and Visual Science, 28,* 34–49.

Bearden, C. E., Thompson, P. M., Dutton, R. A., Frey, B. N., Peluso, M. A., Nicoletti, M., et al. (2008). Three-dimensional mapping of hippocampal anatomy in unmedicated and lithium-treated patients with bipolar disorder. *Neuropsychopharmacology, 33*(6), 1229–1238.

Beason-Held, L. L., Kraut, M. A., & Resnick, S. M. (2008). I. Longitudinal changes in aging brain function. *Neurobiology of Aging, 29*(4), 483–496.

Becerra, L., Breiter, H. C., Wise, R., Gonzalez, R. G., & Borsook, D. (2001). Reward circuitry activation by noxious thermal stimuli. *Neuron, 32,* 927–946.

Bechara, A., Damasio, H., & Damasio, A. R. (2000). Emotion, decision making and the orbitofrontal cortex. *Cerebral Cortex, 10*(3), 295–307.

Becker, A. E. (2004). Television, disordered eating, and young women in Fiji: Negotiating body image and identity during rapid social change. *Culture, Medicine, and Psychiatry, 28*(4), 533–559.

Becker, A. E., Burwell, R. A., Herzog, D. B., Hamburg, P., & Gilman, S. E. (2002). Eating behaviours and attitudes following prolonged exposure to television among ethnic Fijian adolescent girls. *British Journal of Psychiatry, 180,* 509–514.

Bellinger, A. M., Reiken, S., Dura, M., Murphy, P. W., Deng, S.-X., Landry, D. W., et al. (2008). Remodeling of ryanodine receptor complex causes "leaky" channels: A molecular mechanism for decreased exercise capacity. *Proceedings of the National Academy of Sciences of the United States of America, 105,* 2198–2202.

Belliveau, J. W., Kennedy, D. N., Jr., McKinstry, R. C., Buchbinder, B. R., Weisskopf, R. M., Cohen, M. S., et al. (1991). Functional mapping of the human visual cortex by magnetic resonance imaging. *Science, 254,* 716–719.

Bellugi, U., Wang, P. P., & Jernigan, T. L. (1994). Williams syndrome: An unusual neuropsychological profile. In S. H. Broman & J. Grafman (Eds.), *Atypical cognitive deficits in developmental disorders: Implications for brain function* (pp. 23–56). Hillsdale, NJ: Erlbaum.

Bender, B. G., Linden, M. G., & Harmon, R. J. (2001). Life adaptation in 35 adults with sex chromosome abnormalities. *Genetics in Medicine, 3*(3), 187–191.

Benedetti, F., Colloca, L., Torre, E., Lanotte, M., Melcarne, A., Pesare, M., et al. (2004). Placebo-responsive Parkinson patients show decreased activity in single neuron of subthalamic nucleus. *Nature Neuroscience, 7,* 587–588.

Bennett, M. V., & Zukin, R. S. (2004). Electrical coupling and neuronal synchronization in the Mammalian brain. *Neuron, 41*(4), 495–511.

Bennett, W. (1983). The nicotine fix. *Rhode Island Medical Journal, 66,* 455–458.

Berardi, N., Pizzorusso, T., & Maffei, L. (2000). Critical periods during sensory development. *Current Opinion in Neurobiology, 10,* 138–145.

Berger, M. M., Kopp, N., Vital, C., Redl, B., Aymard, M., & Lina, B. (2000): Detection and cellular localization of enterovirus RNA sequences in spinal cord of patients with ALS. *Neurology, 54,* 20–25.

Berkman, N. D., Bulik, C. M., Brownley, K. A., Lohr, K. N., Sedway, J. A., Rooks, A., et al. (2006). Management of eating disorders. *Evidence Report/Technology Assessment, 135,* 1–166.

Berlim, M. T., Mattevi, B. S., Belmonte-de-Abreu, P., & Crow, T. J. (2003). The etiology of schizophrenia and the origin of language: Overview of a theory. *Comprehensive Psychiatry, 44*(1), 7–14.

Berlin, F. S. (1997). "Chemical castration" for sex offenders. *New England Journal of Medicine, 336*(14), 1030.

Berman, K. F., Torrey, E. F., Daniel, D. G., & Weinberger, D. R. (1992). Regional cerebral blood flow in monozygotic twins discordant and concordant for schizophrenia. *Archives of General Psychiatry, 49,* 927–934.

Bernard, C. (1856). *Leçons de physiologie expérimentale appliqué à la medicine faites au College de France* (Vol. 2). Paris: Balliere.

Bernhardt, P. C., Dabbs, J. M., Jr., Fielden, J. A., & Lutter, C. D. (1998). Testosterone changes during vicarious experiences of winning and losing among fans at sporting events. *Physiology and Behavior, 65,* 59–62.

Berns, G. S., Chappelow, J., Cekic, M., Zink, C. F., Pagnoni, G., & Martin-Skurski, M. E. (2006). Neurobiological substrates of dread. *Science, 312*(5774), 754–758.

Bernstein, L. J., Beig, S., Siegenthaler, A. L., & Grady, C. L. (2002). The effect of encoding strategy on the neural correlates of memory for faces. *Neuropsychologia, 40,* 86–98.

Berta, P., Hawkins, J. R., Sinclair, A. H., Taylor, A., Griffiths, B. L., Goodfellow, P. N., & Fellous, M. (1990). Genetic evidence equating SRY and the testis-determining factor. *Nature, 348,* 448–450.

Bertoni, C. (2008). Clinical approaches in the treatment of Duchenne muscular dystrophy (DMD) using oligonucleotides. *Frontiers in Bioscience, 13,* 517–727.

Besancon, E., Guo, S., Lok, J., Tymianski, M., & Lo, E. H. (2008). Beyond NMDA and AMPA glutamate receptors: Emerging mechanisms for ionic imbalance and cell death in stroke. *Trends in Pharmacological Sciences, 29*(5), 268–275.

Betarbet, R., Sherer, T. B., MacKenzie, G., Garcia-Osuna, M., Panov, A. V., & Greenamyre, J. T. (2000). Chronic systemic pesticide exposure reproduces features of Parkinson's disease. *Nature Neuroscience, 3,* 1301–1306.

Beyreuther, K., Biesalski, H. K., Fernstrom, J. D., Grimm, P., Hammes, W. P., Heinemann, U., et al. (2007). Consensus meeting: monosodium glutamate - an update. *European Journal of Clinical Nutrition, 61*(3), 304–313.

Bigler, E. D. (2008). Neuropsychology and clinical neuroscience of persistent post-concussive syndrome. *Journal of the International Neuropsychology Society, 14*(1), 1–22.

Birbaumer, N., Grodd, W., Diedrich, O., Klose, U., Erb, M., Lotze, M., et al. (1998). fMRI reveals amygdala activation to human faces in social phobics. *Neuroreport, 9*(6), 1223–1226.

Birmaher, B., Ryan, N. D., Williamson, D. E., Brent, D. A., Kaufman, J., Dahl, R. E., Perel, J., & Nelson, B. (1996). Childhood and adolescent depression: A review of the past 10 years (Part I). *Journal of the American Academy of Child and Adolescent Psychiatry, 35,* 1427–1439.

Birnbaum, K. (1914). *Die Psychopathischen Verbrecher.* Leipzig, Germany: Thieme.

Birnbaumer, L., Abramowitz, J., & Brown, A. M. (1990). Receptoreffector coupling by G proteins. *Biochimica et Biophysica Acta, 1031,* 163–224.

Blair, R. J., Mitchell, D. G., Richell, R. A., Kelly, S., Leonard, A., Newman, C., & Scott, S. K. (2002). Turning a deaf ear to fear: Impaired recognition of vocal affect in psychopathic individuals. *Journal of Abnormal Psychology, 111,* 682–686.

Blair, R. J., Peschardt, K. S., Budhani, S., Mitchell, D. G., & Pine, D. S. (2006). The development of psychopathy. *Journal of Child Psychology and Psychiatry, 47*(3–4), 262–276.

Blakeley, J. (2008). Drug delivery to brain tumors. *Current Neurology and Neuroscience Reports, 8*(3), 235–241.

Blakeslee, S. (1999, December 28). New theories help explain mysteries of autism. *The New York Times* [Late edition—Final], Sec. F, p. 1.

Blanchard, R. (1997). Birth order and sibling sex ratio in homosexual versus hetersexual males and females. *Annual Review of Sex Research, 8,* 27–67.

Blasdel, G. G. (1992). Orientation selectivity, preference, and continuity in monkey striate cortex. *Journal of Neuroscience, 12,* 3139–3161.

Bleuler, M., & Bleuler, R. (1986). Dementia praecox oder die Gruppe der Schizofreinin: Eugen Bleuler. *British Journal of Psychiatry, 149,* 661–662.

Bliss, T. V. P., & Lømo, T. (1973). Long-lasting potentiation of synaptic transmission in the dentate gyrus of the anesthetized rabbit following stimulation of the perforant path. *Journal of Physiology, 232,* 331–356.

Blood, A. J., Zatorre, R. J., Bermudez, P., & Evans, A. C. (1999). Emotional responses to pleasant and unpleasant music correlate with activity in paralimbic brain regions. *Nature Neuroscience, 2,* 382–387.

Bloom, P. (2004). Can a dog learn a word? *Science, 304,* 1605–1606.

Blumenthal, J. A., Babyak, M. A., Moore, K. A., Craighead, W. E., Herman, S., Khatri, P., et al. (1999). Effects of exercise training on older patients with major depression. *Archives of Internal Medicine, 159,* 2349–2356.

Bock, R. (1993). *Understanding Klinefelter syndrome: A guide for XXY males and their families.* Retrieved February 18, 2003, from the National Institute of Child Health and Human Development Web site: http://www.nichd.nih.gov/publications/pubs/klinefelter.htm-xwhat.

Bocklandt, S., Horvath, S., Vilain, E., & Hamer, D. H. (2006). Extreme skewing of X chromosome inactivation in mothers of homosexual men. *Human Genetics, 118*(6), 691–694.

Bocklandt, S., Horvath, S., Vilain, E., & Hamer, D. H. (2006). Extreme skewing of X chromosome inactivation in mothers of homosexual men. *Human Genetics, 118*(6), 691–694.

Bogen, J. E., Schultz, D. H., & Vogel, P. J. (1988). Completeness of callosotomy shown by magnetic resonance imaging in the long term. *Archives of Neurology, 45,* 1203–1205.

Boger, D. L., Sato, H., Lerner, A. E., Hedrick, M. P., Fecik, R. A., Miyauchi, H., Wilkie, et al. (2000). Exceptionally potent inhibitors of fatty acid amide hydrolase: The enzyme responsible for degradation of endogenous oleamide and anandamide. *Proceedings of the National Academy of Sciences of the United States of America, 97,* 5044–5049.

Boll, T. J. (1981). The Halstead-Reitan Neuropsychological Battery. In S. B. Filskov & T. J. Boll (Eds.), *Handbook of clinical neuropsychology* (pp. 577–607). New York: Wiley Interscience.

Bomze, H. M., Bulsara, K. R., Iskandar, B. J., Caroni, P., & Skene, J. H. P. (2001). Spinal axon regeneration evoked by replacing two growth cone proteins in adult neurons. *Nature Neuroscience, 4,* 38–43.

Booth, A., Shelley, G., Mazur, A., Tharp, G., & Kittok, R. (1989). Testosterone, and winning and losing in human competition. *Hormones and Behavior, 23,* 556–571.

Boothroyd, L. G., Jones, B. C., Burt, D. M., & Perrett, D. I. (2007). Partner characteristics associated with masculinity, health and maturity in male faces. *Personality and Individual Differences, 43*(5), 1161–1173.

Borkovec, T. D., Grayson, J. B., O'Brien, G. T., & Weerts, T. C. (1979). Relaxation treatment of pseudoinsomnia and idiopathic insomnia: An electroencephalographic evaluation. *Journal of Applied Behavior Analysis, 12,* 37–54.

Borkovec, T. M., & Hu, S. (1990). The effect of worry on cardiovascular response to phobic imagery. *Behavior Research and Therapy, 28,* 69–73.

Borsook, D., Becerra, L., Carlezon, W. A., Jr., Shaw, M., Renshaw, P., Elman, I., et al. (2006). Reward-aversion circuitry in analgesia and pain: Implications for psychiatric disorders. *European Journal of Pain, 11*(1), 7–20.

Borsook, D., Becerra, L., Fishman, S., Edwards, A., Jennings, C. L., Stojanovic, M., et al. (1998). Acute plasticity in the human somatosensory cortex following amputation. *Neuroreport, 9,* 1013–1017.

Boscarino, J. A., & Chang, J. (1999). Electrocardiogram abnormalities among men with stress-related psychiatric disorders: Implications for coronary heart disease and clinical research. *Annals of Behavioral Medicine, 21,* 227–234.

Bossini, L., Tavanti, M., Calossi, S., Lombardelli, A., Polizzotto, N. R., Galli, R., et al. (2008). Magnetic resonance imaging volumes of the hippocampus in drug-naïve patients with post-traumatic stress disorder without comorbidity conditions. *Journal of Psychiatric Research, 42*(9), 752–762.

Bouchard, T., Jr. (1994). Genes, environment, and personality. *Science, 264,* 1700–1701.

Bouchard, T., Jr., Lykken, D. T., McGue, M., Segal, N. L., & Tellegen, A. (1990). Sources of human psychological differences: The Minnesota Study of Twins Reared Apart. *Science, 250,* 223–228.

Boulant, J. A. (2000). Role of the preoptic-anterior hypothalamus in thermoregulation and fever. *Clinical Infectious Diseases, 31,* S57–61.

Bourque, C. W., & Oliet, S. H. R. (1997). Osmoreceptors in the central nervous system. *Annual Review of Physiology, 59,* 601–619.

Bower, J. H., Maraganore, D. M., Peterson, B. J., McDonnell, S. K., Ahlskog, J. E., & Rocca, W. A. (2003). Head trauma preceding PD: A case-control study. *Neurology, 60*(10), 1610–1615.

Bowers, M. (1996, December). *AIDS dementia complex.* Retrieved May 30, 2002, from the San Francisco AIDS Foundation Web site: http://www.sfaf.org/treatment/beta/b31/b31adc.html.

Bowersox, S., Kaitin, K. I., & Dement, W. C. (1985). EEG spindle activity as a function of age: Relationship to sleep continuity. *Brain Research, 63,* 526–539.

Bowery, N., Enna, S. J., & Olsen, R. W. (2004). Six decades of GABA. *Biochemical Pharmacology, 68*(8), 1477–1478.

Boydell, J., & Murray, R. (2003). Urbanization, migration and risk of schizophrenia. In R. M. Murray, P. B. Jones, E. Susser, J. van Os, & M. Cannon (Eds.), *The epidemiology of schizophrenia* (pp. 49–67). Cambridge, UK: Cambridge University Press.

Boydell, J., van Os, J., McKenzie, K., Allardyce, J., Goel, R., McCreadie, R. G., et al. (2001). Incidence of schizophrenia in ethnic minorities in London: Ecological study into interactions with environment. *British Medical Journal, 323,* 1336–1338.

Boyle, S. H., Jackson, W. G., & Suarez, E. C. (2007). Hostility, anger, and depression predict increases in C3 over a 10-year period. *Brain, Behavior, and Immunity, 21*(6), 816–823.

Bozarth, M. A., & Wise, R. A. (1986). Involvement of the ventral tegmental dopamine system in opioid and psychomotor stimulant reinforcement. *NIDA Research Monograph, 67,* 190–196.

Bradley, R. (1979). Effects of aging on the sense of taste: Anatomical considerations. In S. S. Han & D. H. Coons (Eds.), *Special senses in aging: A current biological assessment* (pp. 3–8). Ann Arbor: University of Michigan, Institute of Gerontology.

Brady, K. T., Lydiard, R. B., Malcolm, R., & Ballenger, J. C. (1991). Cocaine-induced psychosis. *Journal of Clinical Psychiatry, 52,* 509–512.

Brain Injury Association of America. (2003). *What is brain injury?* Retrieved July 11, 2004, from the Brain Injury Association of America Web site: http://www.biausa.org/Pages/home.html.

Brambilla, P., Harenski, K., Nicoletti, M., Sassi, R. B., Mallinger, A. G., Frank, E., et al. (2003). MRI investigation of temporal lobe structures in bipolar patients. *Journal of Psychiatric Research, 37,* 287–295.

Brandt, R. (2001). Cytoskeletal mechanisms of neuronal degeneration. *Cell and Tissue Research, 305,* 255–265.

Brat, D. J., Parisi, J. E., Kleinschmidt-DeMasters, B. K., Yachnis, A. T., Montine, T. J., Boyer, P. J., et al. (2008). Surgical neuropathology update: A review of changes introduced by the WHO classification of tumours of the central nervous system, 4th edition. *Archives of Pathology and Laboratory Medicine, 132*(6), 993–1007.

Braun, A. R., Balkin, T. J., Wesensten, N. J., Gwadry, F., Carson, R. E., Varga, M., et al. (1998). Dissociated pattern of activity in visual cortices and their projections during human rapid eye movement sleep. *Science, 279,* 91–95.

Breasted, J. H. (1930). *Edwin Smith Papyrus.* Chicago: University of Chicago Press.

Bredt, D. S., & Snyder, S. H. (1992). Nitric oxide, a novel neuronal messenger. *Neuron, 8,* 3–11.

Breedlove, S. M. (1992). Sexual differentiation of the brain and behavior. In J. Becker, S. M. Breedlove & D. Crews (Eds.), *Behavioral endocrinology* (pp. 39–70). Cambridge, MA: MIT Press.

Breiter, H. C., Aharon, I., Kahneman, D., Dale, A., & Shizgal, P. (2001). Functional imaging of neural responses to expectancy and experience of monetary gains and losses. *Neuron, 30,* 619–639.

Bremer, J. (1959). *Asexualization.* New York: Macmillan.

Bremner, J. D., Innis, R. B., Southwick, S. M., Staib, L., Zoghbi, S., & Charney, D. D. (2000). Decreased benzodiazepine receptor binding in prefrontal cortex in combat-related posttraumatic stress disorder. *American Journal of Psychiatry, 157,* 1120–1126.

Bremner, J. D., Randall, P., Scott, T. M., Bronen, R. A., Seibyl, J. P., Southwick, S. M., et al. (1995). MRI-based measurement of hippocampal volume in patients with combat-related posttraumatic stress disorder. *American Journal of Psychiatry, 152,* 973–981.

Bremner, J. D., Vythilingam, M., Vermetten, E., Nazeer, A., Adil, J., Khan, S., et al. (2002). Reduced volume of orbitofrontal cortex in major depression. *Biological Psychiatry, 51*(4), 273–279.

Brill, K. T., Weltman, A. L., Gentili, A., Patrie, J. T., Fryburg, D. A., Hanks, J. B., et al. (2002). Single and combined effects of growth hormone and testosterone administration on measures of body composition, physical performance, mood, sexual function, bone turnover, and muscle gene expression in healthy older men. *Journal of Clinical Endocrinology and Metabolism, 87,* 5649–5657.

Bristow, D., Frith, C., & Rees, G. (2005). Two distinct neural effects of blinking on human visual processing. *Neuroimage, 27*(1), 136–145.

British Lung Foundation. (2002). *A smoking gun? Impact of cannabis smoking on respiratory health.* Retrieved November 14, 2002, from the British Lung Foundation Web site: http://www.lunguk.org/news/a_smoking_gun.pdf.4.

Broca, P. (1878). Anatomie comparée de circonvolutions cérébrales. Le grand lobe limbique et la scissure limbique dans la série des mammiféres.[Comparative anatomy of the cerebral convolutions. The limbic lobe and the limbic fissure in mammals.] *Review d'Anthropologie, 1,* 385–498.

Brodmann, K. (1909/1994). *Localisation in the cerebral cortex by Korbinian Brodmann* (L. J. Garey, Trans.). London: Smith-Gordon.

Broeder, C. E., Quindry, J., Brittingham, K., Panton, L., Thomson, J., Appakondu, S., et al. (2000). The andro project: Physiological and hormonal influences of androstenedione supplementation in men 35 to 65 years old participating in a high-intensity resistance training program. *Archives of Internal Medicine, 160,* 3093–3104.

Broeren, J., Bjorkdahl, A., Claesson, L., Goude, D., Lundgren-Nilsson, A., Samuelsson, H., et al. (2008). Virtual rehabilitation after stroke. *Studies in Health Technology and Informatics, 136,* 77–82.

Brookes, J. C., Hartoutsiou, F., Horsfield, A. P., & Stoneham, A. M. (2007). Could humans recognize odor by phonon assisted tunneling? *Physical Review Letters, 98*(3), 038101.

Brooks, D. C. (1968). Localization and characteristics of the cortical waves associated with eye movement in the cat. *Experimental Neurology, 22,* 603–613.

Broquet, K. (1999). Status of treatment of depression. *Southern Medical Journal, 92*(9), 848–858.

Brown, A. S. (2006). Prenatal infection as a risk factor for schizophrenia. *Schizophrenia Bulletin, 32*(2), 200–202.

Brown, A. S., van Os, J., Driessens, C., Hoek, H. W., & Susser, E. S. (2000). Further evidence of relation between prenatal famine and major affective disorder. *American Journal of Psychiatry, 157,* 190–195.

Brown, C. M., & Nuttall, A. L. (1984). Efferent control of cochlear inner hair cell responses in the guinea pig. *Journal of Physiology, 354,* 625–656.

Brown, J. D. (1991). Staying fit and staying well: Physical fitness as a moderator of life stress. *Journal of Personality and Social Psychology, 60,* 555–561.

Brown, R. L., & Robinson, P. R. (2004). Melanopsin--Shedding light on the elusive circadian photopigment. *Chronobiology International, 21*(2), 189–204.

Brown, S., Ingham, R. J., Ingham, J. C., Laird, A. R., & Fox, P. T. (2005). Stuttered and fluent speech production: An ALE meta-analysis of functional neuroimaging studies. *Human Brain Mapping, 25*(1), 105–117.

Brown, S., Martinez, M. J., & Parsons, L. M. (2006). Music and language side by side in the brain: A PET study of the generation of melodies and sentences. *European Journal of Neuroscience, 23*(10), 2791–2803.

Bruce, M. E., Will, R. G., Ironside, J. W., McConnell, I., Drummond, D., Suttie, A., et al. (1997). Transmissions to mice indicate that "new variant" CJD is caused by the BSE agent. *Nature, 389,* 498–501.

Bruck, K. (1961). Temperature regulation in the newborn infant. *Biology of the Neonate, 3,* 65–119.

Bruetsch, W. L. (1949). Why malaria cures general paralysis. *Journal of the Indiana State Medical Association Journal, 42,* 211–216.

Brunelli, M., Castellucci, V., & Kandel, E. R. (1976). Synaptic facilitation and behavioral sensitization in *Aplysia:* Possible role of serotonin and cyclic AMP. *Science, 194*(4270), 1178–1181.

Bruni, O., Galli, F., & Guidetti, V. (1999). Sleep hygiene and migraine in children and adolescents. *Cephalalgia, 19,* 57–59.

Bruno, B. A. (2008). Obesity and brain disorder. *American Journal of Psychiatry, 165,* 138.

Bryden, M. P. (1982). *Laterality: Functional asymmetry in the intact brain.* New York: Academic Press.

Bryden, M. P. (1988). An overview of the dichotic listening procedure and its relation to cerebral organization. In K. Hugdahl (Ed.), *Handbook of dichotic listening* (pp. 1–44). Chichester, England: John Wiley.

Buck, L. B., & Axel, R. (1991). A novel multigene family may encode odorant receptors: A molecular basis for odor recognition. *Cell, 65,* 175–187.

Buitelaar, J. K. (2003). Why have drug treatments been so disappointing? *Novartis Foundation Symposium,* 251, 235–244; discussion 245–239, 281–297.

Burger, J. M. S., Kolss, M., Pont, J., & Kawecki, T. J. (2008). Learning ability and longevity: A symmetrical evolutionary trade-off in *Drosophila. Evolution, 62*(6), 1294–1304.

Burke, R. (1978). Motor units: Physiological histochemical profiles, neural connectivity and functional specialization. *American Zoologist, 18,* 127–134.

Burr, D. (2005). Vision: In the blink of an eye. *Current Biology, 15*(14), R554–556.

Buscemi, N., Vandermeer, B., Friesen, C., Bialy, L., Tubman, M., Ospina, M., et al. (2007). The efficacy and safety of drug treatments for chronic insomnia in adults: A meta-analysis of RCTs. *Journal of General Internal Medicine, 22*(9), 1335–1350.

Busey, T. A., & Loftus, G. R. (2007). Cognitive science and the law. *Trends in Cognitive Science, 11*(3), 111–117.

Bushman, B. J. (2002). Does venting anger feed or extinguish the flame? Catharsis, rumination, distraction, anger and aggressive responding. *Personality & Social Psychology Bulletin, 28*(6), 724–731.

Butuzova, M. V., & Kitchigina, V. F. (2008). Repeated blockade of GABA(A) receptors in the medial septal region induces epileptiform activity in the hippocampus. *Neuroscience Letters, 434*(1), 133–138.

Buxbaum, J. D., Silverman, J. M., Smith, C. J., Greenberg, D. A., Kilifarski, M., Reichert, J., et al. (2002). Association between a GABRB3 polymorphism and autism. *Molecular Psychiatry, 7,* 311–316.

Byer, C. O., & Shainberg, L. W. (1995). *Living well: Health in your hands* (2nd ed.). New York: HarperCollins.

Byne, W., Lasco, M. S., Kemether, E., Shinwari, A., Edgar, M. A., Morgello, S., Jones, L. B., & Tobet, S. (2000). The interstitial nuclei of the human anterior hypothalamus: An investigation of sexual variation in volume and cell size, number and density. *Brain Research, 856,* 254–258.

Byrne, J. H., & Kandel, E. R. (1996). Presynaptic facilitation revisited: State and time dependence. *Journal of Neuroscience, 16*(2), 425–435.

Bystritsky, A., Pontillo, D., Powers, M., Sabb, F. W., Craske, M. G., & Bookheimer, S. Y. (2001). Functional MRI changes during panic anticipation and imagery exposure. *Neuroreport, 12,* 3953–3957.

Cacioppo, J. T., Berntson, G. G., & Klein, D. J. (1992). What is an emotion? The role of somatovisceral afference, with special emphasis on somatovisceral "illusions." *Review of Personality and Social Psychology, 14,* 63–98.

Cacioppo, J. T., Berntson, G. G., Larsen, J. T., Poehlmann, K. M., & Ito, T. A. (2000). The psychophysiology of emotion. In M. Lewis & J. M. Haviland-Jones

(Eds.), *Handbook of emotions* (Vol. 2, pp. 173–191). New York: Guilford Press.

Cain, W. S., & Gent, J. F. (1991). Olfactory sensitivity: Reliability, generality, and association with aging. *Journal of Experimental Psychology: Human Perception and Performance, 17,* 382–391.

Caldwell, D. F., & Caldwell, M. C. (1976). Cetaceans. In T. A. Sebeok (Ed.), *How animals communicate* (pp. 794–808). Bloomington: Indiana University.

Caldwell, J. A., Caldwell, J. L., Smythe, N. K., III, & Hall, K. K. (2000). A double-blind, placebo-controlled investigation of the efficacy of modafinil for sustaining the alertness and performance of aviators: A helicopter simulator study. *Psychopharmacology, 150,* 272–282.

Caligiuri, M. P., Brown, G. G., Meloy, M. J., Eberson, S. C., Kindermann, S. S., Frank, L. R., et al. (2003). An fMRI study of affective state and medication on cortical and subcortical brain regions during motor performance in bipolar disorder. *Psychiatry Research, 123,* 171–182.

Calle, E. E., Thun, M. J., Petrelli, J. M., Rodriguez, C., & Heath, C. W. (1999). Body-mass index and mortality in a prospective cohort of U.S. adults. *New England Journal of Medicine, 341*(15), 1097–1105.

Calvin, W. H. (2004). *A brief history of the mind: From apes to intellect and beyond.* Oxford, UK: Oxford University Press.

Cannon, M., Jones, P. B., & Murray, R. M. (2002). Obstetric complications and schizophrenia: Historical and meta-analytic review. *American Journal of Psychiatry, 159,* 1080–1092.

Cannon, M., Kendell, R., Susser, E., & Jones, P. (2003). Prenatal and perinatal risk factors for schizophrenia. In R. M. Murray, P. B. Jones, E. Susser, J. van Os, & M. Cannon (Eds.), *The epidemiology of schizophrenia* (pp. 74–99). Cambridge, UK: Cambridge University Press.

Cannon, W. (1927). The James-Lange theory of emotions: A critical examination and an alternative theory. *American Journal of Psychology, 39,* 106–124.

Cannon, W. (1929). *Bodily changes in pain, hunger, fear and rage* (2nd ed.). New York: Harper & Row.

Cannon, W. (1932). *The wisdom of the body.* New York: Norton.

Cannon, W. B. (1957). "Voodoo" death. *Psychosomatic Medicine, 19,* 182–190. (Original work published 1942)

Cannon, W., & Washburn, A. L. (1912). An explanation of hunger. *American Journal of Physiology, 29,* 441–454.

Cantalupo, C., & Hopkins, W. D. (2001). Asymmetric Broca's area in great apes. *Nature, 414,* 505.

Cantor, J. M., Blanchard, R., Paterson, A. D., & Bogaert, A. F. (2002). How many gay men owe their sexual orientation to fraternal birth order? *Archives of Sexual Behavior, 31*(1), 63–71.

Cao, X., Cui, Z., Feng, R., Tang, Y. P., Qin, Z., Mei, B., et al. (2007). Maintenance of superior learning and memory function in NR2B transgenic mice during ageing. *European Journal of Neuroscience, 25*(6), 1815–1822.

Cao, X., Wang, H., Mei, B., An, S., Yin, L., Wang, L. P., et al. (2008). Inducible and selective erasure of memories in the mouse brain via chemical-genetic manipulation. *Neuron, 60*(2), 353–366.

Capela, J. P., Fernandes, E., Remião, F., Bastos, M. L., Meisel, A., & Carvalho, F. (2007). Ecstasy induces apoptosis via 5-HT(2A)-receptor stimulation in cortical neurons. *Neurotoxicology, 28*(4), 868–875.

Cappuccino, A. (2008). Moderate hypothermia as treatment for spinal cord injury. *Orthopedics, 31*(3), 243–246.

Carew, T. J., & Kandel, E. R. (1973). Acquisition and retention of long-term habituation in *Aplysia:* Correlation of behavioral and cellular processes. *Science, 182*(4117), 1158–1160.

Carpenter, M. (1976). *Human neuroanatomy* (7th ed.). Baltimore, MD: Williams & Wilkins.

Carpenter, W. T., Jr., Conley, R. R., Buchanan, R. W., Breier, A., & Tamminga, C. A. (1995). Patient response and resource management: Another view of clozapine treatment of schizophrenia. *American Journal of Psychiatry, 152,* 827–832.

Carroll, B. J., Feinberg, M., Greden, J. F., Haskett, R. F., James, N. M., Steiner, M., et al. (1980). Diagnosis of endogenous depression: Comparison of clinical, research, and neuroendocrine criteria. *Journal of Affective Disorders, 2,* 177–194.

Carskadon, M. A., Acebo, C., & Jenni, O. G. (2004). Regulation of adolescent sleep: Implications for behavior. *Annals of the New York Academy of Sciences, 1021*(1), 276–291.

Carskadon, M. A., Harvey, K., Duke, P., Andres, T. F., Litt, I. F., & Dement, W. C. (1980). Pubertal changes in daytime sleepiness. *Sleep, 2,* 453–460.

Carskadon, M. A., Vieira, C., & Acebo, C. (1993). Association between puberty and delayed phase preference. *Sleep, 16,* 258–262.

Carskadon, M. A., Wolfson, A. R., Acebo, C., Tzischinsky, O., & Seifer, R. (1998). Adolescent sleep patterns, circadian timing, and sleepiness at a transition to early school days. *Sleep, 21,* 871–881.

Carter, C. S. (1992). Oxytocin and sexual behavior. *Neuroscience and Biobehavioral Reviews, 16,* 131–144.

Carter, R., 3rd, Cheuvront, S. N., & Sawka, M. N. (2007). A case report of idiosyncratic hyperthermia and review of U.S. Army heat stroke hospitalizations. *Journal of Sport Rehabilitation, 16*(3), 238–243.

Cartwright, R. D. (1978). *A primer on sleep and dreaming.* Reading, MA: Addison-Wesley.

Casanova, M. F., Switala, A. E., Trippe, J., & Fitzgerald, M. (2007). Comparative minicolumnar morphometry of three distinguished scientists. *Autism, 11*(6), 557–569.

Casanova, M. F., van Kooten, I. A., Switala, A. E., van Engeland, H., Heinsen, H., Steinbusch, H. W., et al. (2006). Minicolumnar abnormalities in autism. *Acta Neuropathologica, 112*(3), 287–303.

Casey, M. D., Segall, L. J., Street, D. R., & Blank, C. E. (1966). Sex chromosome abnormalities in two state hospitals for patients requiring special security. *Nature, 209,* 641–642.

Caspi, A., McClay, J., Moffitt, T. E., Mill, J., Martin, J., Craig, I. W., et al. (2002). Role of genotype in the cycle of violence in maltreated children. *Science, 297*(5582), 851–854.

Caspi, A., Sugden, K., Moffitt, T. E., Taylor, A., Craig, I. W., Harrington, H., et al. (2003). Influence of life stress on depression: Moderation by a polymorphism in the 5-HTT gene. *Science, 301*(5631), 386–389.

Caspi, A., Williams, B., Kim-Cohen, J., Craig, I. W., Milne, B. J., Poulton, R., et al. (2007). Moderation of breastfeeding effects on the IQ by genetic variation in fatty acid metabolism. *Proceedings of the National Academy of Sciences of the United States of America (PNAS),* 104, 18860–18865.

Casson, I. (2002). Boxing and Parkinson disease. Retrieved June 2, 2002, from http://www.parkinson.org/boxing.htm.

Castellanos, F. X., Giedd, J. N., Eckburg, P., Marsh, W. L., Vaituzia, A. C., Kaysen, D., et al. (1994). Quantitative morphology of the caudate nucleus in attention deficit hyperactivity disorder. *American Journal of Psychiatry, 151,* 1791–1796.

Castellanos, F. X., Lee, P. P., Sharp, W., Jeffries, N. O., Greenstein, D. K., Clasen, L. S., et al. (2002). Developmental trajectories of brain volume abnormalities in children and adolescents with attention-deficit/hyperactivity disorder. *Journal of the American Medical Association, 288,* 1740–1748.

Castelucci, V. F., Carew, T. J., & Kandel, E. R. (1978). Cellular analysis of long-term habituation of the gill-withdrawal reflex in *Aplysia californica. Science, 202,* 1306–1308.

Caterina, M. J., Leffler, A., Malmberg, A. B., Martin, W. J., Trafton, J., Petersen-Zeitz, K. R., et al. (2000). Impaired nociception and pain sensation in mice lacking the capsaicin receptor. *Science, 220,* 306–313.

Caterina, M. J., Schumacher, M. A., Tominaga, M., Rosen, T. A., Levine, J. D., & Julius, D. (1997). The capsaicin receptor: A heatactivated ion channel in the pain pathway. *Nature, 389,* 816–824.

Center for Science, Technology, and Congress. (2001, June). NBAC proposes human subjects reforms. Retrieved June 9, 2002, from the American Association for the Advancement of Science Web site: http://www.aaas.org/spp/cstc/stc/stc01/01-06/nbac.htm.

Centers for Disease Control (CDC). (1993). Cigarette smoking–attributable mortality and years of potential life lost—United States, 1990. *Morbidity and Mortality Weekly Report [serial online], 42*(33), 645–649.

Centers for Disease Control (CDC). (2004). *West Nile virus.* Retrieved June 25, 2004, from the Centers for Disease Control Web site: http://www.cdc.gov/ncidod/dvbid/westnile/index.htm.

Centers for Disease Control (CDC). (2005). Mental health in the United States: Prevalence of diagnosis and medication treatment for attention deficit/hyperactivity disorder—United States, 2003. Retrieved October 1, 2005, from http://www.cdc.gov/mmwr/preview/mmwrhtml/mm5434a2.htm.

Centers for Disease Control (CDC). (2007). Global polio eradication. Retrieved on October 14, 2008 from http://www.cdc.gov/vaccines/vpd-vac/polio/global.htm

Centers for Disease Control (CDC). (2007). Prevalence of autism spectrum disorders--autism and developmental disabilities monitoring network, six sites, United States, 2000. *MMWR Surveillance Summaries, 56*(1), 1–11.

Centers for Disease Control (CDC). (2008). BSE (Bovine Spongiform Encephalopathy, or Mad Cow Disease). Retrieved November 7, 2008, from the Centers for Disease Control Web site: http://www.cdc.gov/ncidod/dvrd/bse/.

Centers for Disease Control (CDC). (2008). Prevalence of self-reported postpartum depressive symptoms: 17 states, 2004–2005. *Morbidity and Mortality Weekly Report, 57*(14), 361–366.

Centers for Disease Control (CDC; 2007). vCJD (Variant Creutzfeldt-Jakob Disease): Risk for travelers. Retrieved on October 28, 2008 from http://www.cdc.gov/ncidod/dvrd/vcjd/risk_travelers.htm

Cervilla, J. A., Prince, M., Lovestone, S., & Mann, A. (2000). Longterm predictors of cognitive outcome in a cohort of older people with hypertension. *The British Journal of Psychiatry, 177,* 66–71.

Chade, A. R., Kasten, M., & Tanner, C. M. (2006). Nongenetic causes of Parkinson's disease. *Journal of Neural Transmission. Supplementum,* (70), 147–151.

Chakravarthy, M. V., & Booth, F. W. (2004). Eating, exercise, and "thrifty" genotypes: Connecting the dots toward an evolutionary understanding of modern chronic diseases. *Journal of Applied Physiology, 96*(1), 3–10.

Chamberlain, S. R., Menzies, L. A., Hampshire, A., Fineberg, N. A., del Campo, N., Craig, K., et al. (2008). Orbitofrontal dysfunction in patients with obsessive-compulsive disorder and their unaffected relatives. *Science, 321,* 3131.

Chan, W. Y., Lorke, D. E., Tiu, S. C., & Yew, D. T. (2002). Proliferation and apoptosis in the developing human neocortex. *Anatomical Record, 267,* 261–276.

Chandana, S. R., Movva, S., Arora, M., & Singh, T. (2008). Primary brain tumors in adults. *American Family Physician, 77*(10), 1423–1430.

Changeux, J. P., & Danchin, A. (1976). Selective stabilisation of developing synapses as a mechanism for the specification of neuronal networks. *Nature, 264,* 705–712.

Changizi, M. A., Zhang, Q., & Shimojo, S. (2006). Bare skin, blood and the evolution of primate colour vision. *Biology Letters, 2*(2), 217–221.

Charbonneau, S., Scherzer, B. P., Aspirot, D., & Cohen, H. (2003). Perception and production of facial and prosodic emotions by chronic CVA patients. *Neuropsychologia, 41,* 605–613.

Chaudhari, N., Landlin, A. M., & Roper, S. D. (2000). A metabotropic glutamate receptor variant functions as a taste receptor. *Nature Neuroscience, 3,* 113–119.

Chen, D., Buchanan, G. F., Ding, J. M., Hannibal, J., & Gillette, M. U. (1999). Pituitary adenylyl cyclase-activating peptide: A pivotal modulator of glutamatergic regulation of the suprachiasmatic circadian clock. *Proceedings of the National Academy of Sciences of the United States of America, 96,* 13468–13473.

Chen, J., Marmur, R., Pulles, A., Paredes, W., & Gardner, E. L. (1993). Ventral tegmental microinjection of delta 9-tetrahydrocannabinol enhances ventral tegmental somatodendritic dopamine levels but not forebrain dopamine levels: Evidence for local neural action by marijuana's psychoactive ingredient. *Brain Research, 621,* 65–70.

Chen, J.-F., Xu, K., Petzer, J. P., Staal, R., Xu, Y.-H., Beilstein, M., et al. (2001). Neuroprotection by caffeine and A2A adenosine receptor inactivation in a model of Parkinson's disease. *Journal of Neuroscience, 21,* RC143.4

Chen, M., Ona, V. O., Li, M., Ferrante, R. J., Fink, K. B., Zhu, S., et al. (2000). Minocycline inhibits caspase-1 and caspase-3 expression and delays mortality in a transgenic mouse model of Huntington disease. *Nature Medicine, 6,* 797–801.

Chervin, R. (2000). Sleepiness, fatigue, tiredness, and lack of energy in obstructive sleep apnea. *Chest, 118,* 372–379.

Cheung, Z. H., Gong, K., & Ip, N. Y. (2008). Cyclin-dependent kinase 5 supports neuronal survival through phosphorylation of Bcl-2. *Journal of Neuroscience, 28*(19), 4872–4877.

Chio, A., Benzi, G., Dossena, M., Mutani, R., & Mora, G. (2005). Severely increased risk of amyotrophic lateral sclerosis among Italian professional football players. *Brain: A Journal of Neurology, 128,* 472–476.

Cho, K., Ennaceur, A., Cole, J. C., & Suh, C. K. (2000). Chronic jet lag produces cognitive deficits. *Journal of Neuroscience, 20,* RC66.

Cho, M. K., & Bero, L. A. (1996). The quality of drug studies published in symposium proceedings. *Annals of Internal Medicine, 124,* 485–489.

Choi, D. W., & Rothman, S. M. (1990). The role of glutamate neurotoxicity in hypoxic-ischemic neuronal death. *Annual Review of Neuroscience, 13,* 171–182.

Chomsky, N. (1957). *Syntactic structures.* The Hague, Netherlands: Mouton.

Christakis, N., & Fowler, J. (2007). The spread of obesity in a large social network over 32 years. *New England Journal of Medicine, 357,* 370–379.

Christian, K. M., & Thompson, R. F. (2003). Neural substrates of eyeblink conditioning: Acquisition and retention. *Learning and Memory, 10*(6), 427–455.

Christman, S. D., & Propper, R. E. (2001). Superior episodic memory is associated with interhemispheric processing. *Neuropsychology, 15,* 607–616.

Christos, G. (1996). Investigation of the Crick-Mitchison reverselearning dream sleep hypothesis in a dynamic setting. *Neural Networks, 9,* 427–434.

Chua, H. F., Boland, J. E., & Nisbett, R. E. (2005). Cultural variation in eye movements during scene perception. *Proceedings of the National Academy of Sciences of the United States of America, 102*(35), 12629–12633.

Chung, J. H., Des Roches, C. M., Meunier, J., & Eavey, R. D. (2005). Evaluation of noise-induced hearing loss in young people using a web-based survey technique. *Pediatrics, 115*(4), 861–867.

Chung, Y., Klimanskaya, I., Becker, S., Li, T., Maserati, M., Lu, S.-J., et al. (2008). Human embryonic stem cell lines generated without embryo destruction. *Cell Stem Cell, 2,* 113–117.

Cingolani, L. A., & Goda, Y. (2008). Actin in action: The interplay between the actin cytoskeleton and synaptic efficacy. Nature Reviews. *Neuroscience, 9*(5), 344–356.

Cinzano, P., Falchi, F., & Elvidge, C. D. (2001). The first World Atlas of the artificial night sky brightness. *Monthly Notices of the Royal Astronomical Society, 328*(3), 689–707.

Clark, A., & Burn, J. (1991). Sweat testing to identify female carriers of X linked hypohidrotic ectodermal dysplasia. *Journal of Medical Genetics, 28,* 330–333.

Clark, R. E., Manns, J. R., & Squire, L. R. (2001). Trace and delay eyeblink conditioning: Contrasting phenomena of declarative and nondeclarative memory. *Psychological Science, 12*(4). 304–308.

Claustrat, B., Brun, J., & Chazot, G. (2005). The basic physiology and pathophysiology of melatonin. *Sleep Medicine Reviews, 9*(1), 11–24.

Cleckley, H. (1950). *The mask of sanity.* St. Louis, MO: Mosby.

Clower, W. T., & Finger, S. (2001). Discovering trepanation: the contribution of Paul Broca. *Neurosurgery, 49*(6), 1417–1425; discussion 1425–1416.

CNN.com (2001). Vikings football player dies of heat stroke. Retrieved October 15, 2008 from http://archives.cnn.com/2001/US/08/01/vikings.death/

Coccaro, E. F., Bergeman, C. S., Kavoussi, R. J., & Seroczynski, A. D. (1997). Heritability of aggression and irritability: A twin study of the Buss-Durkee aggression scales in adult male subjects. *Biological Psychiatry, 41*(3), 273–284.

Coffey, S., Dansky, B. S., Carrigan, M. H., & Brady, K. T. (2000). Acute and protracted cocaine abstinence in an outpatient population: A prospective study of mood, sleep and withdrawal symptoms. *Drug and Alcohol Dependence, 59,* 277–286.

Cohen, D. (1972). Magnetoencephalography: detection of the brain's electrical activity with a superconducting magnetometer. *Science, 175*(22), 664–666.

Cohen, M. S., & Bookheimer, S. Y. (1994). Localization of brain function using magnetic resonance imaging. *Techniques in Neuroscience, 17,* 268–277.

Cohen, S. (1988). Psychosocial models of the role of social support in the etiology of physical disease. *Health Psychology, 7,* 269–297.

Cohen, S., & Herbert, T. B. (1996). Health psychology: Psychological factors and physical disease from the perspective of human psychoneuroimmunology. *Annual Review of Psychology, 47,* 113–142.

Cohen, S., Levi-Montalcini, R., & Hamburger, V. (1954). A nerve growth-stimulating factor isolated from sarcomas 37 and 180. *Proceedings of the National Academy of Sciences of the United States of America, 40,* 1014–1018.

Cohen-Kettenis, P. T. (2005). Gender change in 46,XY persons with 5α-reductase-2 deficiency and 17β-hydroxysteroid dehydrogenase-3 deficiency. *Archives of Sexual Behavior, 34*(4), 399–410.

Cohen-Tannoudji, M., Babinet, C., & Wassef, M. (1994). Early determination of a mouse somatosensory cortex marker. *Nature, 368,* 460–463.

Colapinto, J. (2001). *As nature made him: The boy who was raised as a girl.* New York: Perennial.

Colburn, R., Lubin, M., Stone, J., D., Wang, Y., Lawrence, D., D'Andrea, M., et al. (2007). Attenuated cold sensitivity in TRPM8 null mice. *Neuron, 54*(3), 379–386.

Coleman, R. M. (1986). *Wide awake at 3:00 a.m. by choice or by chance?* New York: W.H. Freeman.

Colicos, M. A., Collins, B. E., Sailor, M. J., & Goda, Y. (2001). Remodeling of synaptic actin induced by photoconductive stimulation. *Cell, 107,* 605–616.

Colom, R., Lluis-Font, J. M., & Andrés-Pueyo, A. (2005). The generational intelligence gains are caused by decreasing variance in the lower half of the distribution: Supporting evidence for the nutrition hypothesis. *Intelligence, 33,* 83–91.

Comings, D. E., & Blum, K. (2000). Reward deficiency syndrome: Genetic aspects of behavioral disorders. *Progress in Brain Research, 126,* 325–341.

Committee on Animal Research and Ethics (CARE, 2008). Guidelines for the ethical use and care of animals. Retrieved on October 11, 2008 from http://www.apa.org/science/anguide.html

Compton, M. T., McKenzie Mack, L., Esterberg, M. L., Bercu, Z., Kryda, A. D., Quintero, L., et al. (2006). Associations between olfactory identification and verbal memory in patients with schizophrenia, first-degree relatives, and non-psychiatric controls. *Schizophrenia Research, 86*(1–3), 154–166.

Connolly, M., & Van Essen, D. (1984). The representation of the visual field in parvocellular and magnocellular layers of the lateral geniculate nucleus in the macaque monkey. *Journal of Comparative Neurology, 226,* 544–565.

Cook, E. H., & Leventhal, B. L. (1996). The serotonin system in autism. *Current Opinion in Pediatrics, 8,* 348–354.

Cook, E. H., Courchesne, R., Lord, C., Cox, N. J., Yan, S., Lincoln, A., et al. (1997). Evidence of linkage between the serotonin transporter and autistic disorder. *Molecular Psychiatry, 2,* 247–250.

Cooke, S. F., & Bliss, T. V. P. (2006). Plasticity in the human central nervous system. *Brain, 129*(7), 1659–1673.

Cooper, J., & Mackie, D. (1986). Video games and aggression in children. *Journal of Applied Social Psychology, 16,* 726–744.

Cooper, S. J., & Dourish, C. T. (1990). Multiple cholecystokinin (CCK) receptors and CCK-monoamine interactions are instrumental in the control of feeding. *Physiology and Behavior, 48,* 849–857.

Corazza, R., Bon, L., & Inchingolo, P. (1976). Eye movement patterns during REM sleep in the "encephale isole" cat. *Archives Internationales de Physiologie et de Biochimie, 84,* 327–331.

Corballis, M. C. (1997). The genetics and evolution of handedness. *Psychologica Reviews, 104*(4), 714–727.

Corballis, M. C. (2003). From mouth to hand: Gesture, speech, and the evolution of right-handedness. *Behavioral & Brain Sciences, 26*(2), 199–260.

Corballis, M. C. (2004). FOXP2 and the mirror system. *Trends in Cognitive Science, 8*(3), 95–96.

Corballis, M. C. (2004). The origins of modernity: Was autonomous speech the critical factor? *Psychological Review, 111*, 543–552.

Corballis, M. C., Hattie, J., & Fletcher, R. (2008). Handedness and intellectual achievement: An even-handed look. *Neuropsychologia, 46*(1), 374–378.

Corbit, J. D. (1973). Voluntary control of hypothalamic temperature. *Journal of Comparative and Physiological Psychology, 83*, 394–411.

Coren, S. (1996a). *Sleep thieves*. New York: Free Press.

Coren, S. (1996b). Daylight savings time and traffic accidents. *New England Journal of Medicine, 334*, 924.

Corina, D., Chiu, Y.-S., Knapp, H., Greenwald, R., San Jose-Robertson, L., & Braun, A. (2007). Neural correlates of human action observation in hearing and deaf subjects. *Brain Research, 1152*, 111–129.

Corkin, S., Amaral, D. G., Gonzalez, R. G., Johnson, K. A., & Hyman, B. T. (1997). H. M.'s medial temporal lobe lesion: Findings from magnetic resonance imaging. *Journal of Neuroscience, 17*, 3964–3979.

Corkin, S., Milner, B., & Rasmussen, T. (1970). Somatosensory thresholds. *Archives of Neurology, 23*, 41–58.

Cotran, R. S., Kumar, V., Fausto, N., Robbins, S. L., & Abbas, A. K. (2005). *Robbins and Cotran pathologic basis of disease*. St. Louis: Elsevier Saunders.

Coulter, J. D., & Lester, B. K. (1971). Reserpine and sleep. *Psychopharmacology, 19*, 134–147.

Courchesne, E. (1997). Brainstem, cerebellar and limbic neuroanatomical abnormalities in autism. *Current Opinion in Neurobiology, 7*, 269–278.

Cousins, N. (1989). *Head first: The biology of hope*. New York: Dutton.

Coutinho, E. (1999). *Is menstruation obsolete? How suppressing menstruation can help women who suffer from anemia, endometriosis, or PMS*. New York: Oxford University Press.

Cowey, A., & Stoerig, P. (1991). The neurobiology of blindsight. *Trends in Neurosciences, 14*, 140–145.

Cramer, S. C. (2008). Repairing the human brain after stroke. II. Restorative therapies. *Annals of Neurology, 63*(5), 549–560.

Cravatt, B. F., Prospero-Garcia, O., Siuzdak, G., Gilula, N. B., Henriksen, S. J., Boger, D. L., et al. (1995). Chemical characterization of a family of brain lipids that induce sleep. *Science, 268*, 1506–1509.

Crespo-Facorro, B., Paradiso, S., Andreasen, N. C., O'Leary, D. S., Watkins, G. L., Ponto, L. L., et al. (2001). Neural mechanisms of anhedonia in schizophrenia: A PET study of response to unpleasant and pleasant odors. *Journal of the American Medical Association, 286*, 427–435.

Crestani, F., Lorez, M., Baer, K., Essrich, C., Benke, D., Laurent, J. P., et al. (1999). Decreased GABAA-receptor clustering results in enhanced anxiety and a bias for threat cues. *Nature Neuroscience, 2*(9), 833–839.

Creutzfeldt, H. G. (1920). Über eine eigenartige herdförnige erkrankung des zentralnervensystems. [On a particular focal disease of the central nervous system.]vorläufige mitteilung [A preliminary report]. *Zeitschrift für die gesamte Neurologie und Psychiatrie, 57*, 1–18.

Crick, F., & Mitchison, G. (1983). The function of dream sleep. *Nature, 304*, 111–114.

Cropley, J. E., Suter, C. M., Beckman, K. B., & Martin, D. I. (2006). Germ-line epigenetic modification of the murine A vy allele by nutritional supplementation. *Proceeding of the National Academy of Sciences of the United States of America (PNAS), 103*(46), 17308–17312.

Crow, T. J. (1997). Schizophrenia as failure of hemispheric dominance for language. *Trends in Neurosciences, 20*(8), 339–343.

Crow, T. J., Crow, L. R., Done, D. J., & Leask, S. (1998). Relative hand skill predicts academic ability: Global deficits at the point of hemispheric indecision. *Neuropsychologia, 36*, 1275–1282.

Crow, T. J., Paez, P., & Chance, S. A. (2007). Callosal misconnectivity and the sex difference in psychosis. *International Review of Psychiatry, 19*(4), 449–457.

Crowley, K., Trinder, J., Kim, Y., Carrington, M., & Colrain, I. M. (2002). The effects of normal aging on sleep spindle and K complex production. *Clinical Neurophysiology, 113*, 1615–1622.

Crowley, S. J., Acebo, C., & Carskadon, M. A. (2007). Sleep, circadian rhythms, and delayed phase in adolescence. *Sleep Medicine, 8*(6), 602–612.

Culbertson, F. M. (1997). Depression and gender: An international review. *American Psychologist, 52*, 25–31.

Culebras, A., & Moore, J. T. (1989). Magnetic resonance findings in REM sleep behavior disorder. *Neurology, 39*, 1519–1523.

Cunnane, S. C. (2006). [Survival of the fattest: The key to human brain evolution] [Article in French]. *Médecine sciences, 22*, 659–663.

Cursiefen, C., Chen, L., Saint-Geniez, M., Hamrah, P., Jin, Y., Rashid, S., et al. (2006). Nonvascular VEGF receptor 3 expression by corneal epithelium maintains avascularity and vision. *Proceeding of the National Academy of Sciences of the United States of America, 103*(30), 11405–11410.

Curtiss, S., de Bode, S., & Mathern, G. W. (2001). Spoken language outcomes after hemispherectomy: Factoring in etiology. *Brain and Language, 79*(3), 379–396.

Czeisler, C. A., & Gooley, J. J. (2007). Sleep and circadian rhythms in humans. *Cold Spring Harbor Symposia on Quantitative Biology, 72*(1), 579–597.

Dabbs, J. M., Jr., & Morris, R. (1990). Testosterone, social class, and antisocial behavior in a sample of 4,462 men. *Psychological Science, 1*, 209–211.

Dahl, R. (1996). The regulation of sleep and arousal: Development and psychopathology. *Development and Psychopathology, 8*, 3–27.

Dahl, R. E., Holttum, J., & Trubnick, L. (1994). A clinical picture of child and adolescent narcolepsy. *Journal of the American Academy of Child and Adolescent Psychiatry, 33*, 834–841.

Dallos, P. (1981). Cochlear physiology. *Annual Review of Psychology, 32*, 153–190.

Dallos, P. (1984). Peripheral mechanisms of hearing. In I. Darian-Smith (Ed.), *Handbook of physiology* (Vol. 3, Part 2, pp. 595–637). Bethesda, MD: American Physiological Society.

Damasio, A. R. (1989). Time-locked multiregional retroactivation: A systems-level proposal for the neural substrates of recall and recognition. *Cognition, 33*(1–2), 25–62.

Damasio, A. R. (1994). *Descartes' error: Emotion, reason, and the human brain*. New York: G.P. Putnam's Sons.

Damasio, A. R., Grabowski, T. J., Bechara, A., Damasio, H., Ponto, L. L., Parvizi, J., et al. (2000). Subcortical and cortical brain activity during the feeling of self-generated emotions. *Nature Neuroscience, 3*, 1049–1056.

Damasio, A., Bellugi, U., Damasio, H., Poizner, H., & Gilder, J. V. (1986). Sign language aphasia during left-hemisphere amytal injection. *Nature, 322*, 363–365.

Damsma, G., Day, J., & Fibiger, H. C. (1989). Lack of tolerance to nicotine-induced dopamine release in the nucleus accumbens. *European Journal of Pharmacology, 168*, 363–368.

Dani, J. (2001). Overview of nicotinic receptors and their roles in the central nervous system. *Biological Psychiatry, 49*, 166–174.

Dapretto, M., Davies, M. S., Pfeifer, J. H., Scott, A. A., Sigman, M., Bookheimer, S. Y., et al. (2006). Understanding emotions in others: Mirror neuron dysfunction in children with autism spectrum disorders. *Nature Neuroscience, 9*(1), 28–30.

Dark, J., Forger, N. G., Stern, J. S., & Zucker, I. (1984). Recovery of lipid mass after removal of adipose tissue in ground squirrels. *American Journal of Physiology, 249* (Pt. 2), R73–R78.

Dartnall, H. J. A., Bowmaker, J. K., & Mollon, J. D. (1983). Human visual pigments: Microspectro-photometric results from the eyes of seven persons. *Proceedings of the Royal Society of London, 220B*, 115–130.

Darwin, C. (1872). *The expression of emotions in man and animals*. London: Murray.

Darwin, C. (1875). *The variation of animals and plants under domestication*. London: Murray.

Dasgupta, A. (2008). Herbal supplements and therapeutic drug monitoring: Focus on digoxin immunoassays and interactions with St. John's Wort. *Therapeutic Drug Monitoring, 30*(2), 212–217.

Davidson, R. J. (1998). Anterior electrophysiological asymmetries, emotion, and depression: Conceptual and methodological conundrums. *Psychophysiology, 35*(5), 607–614.

Davidson, R. J., & Irwin, W. (1999). The functional neuroanatomy of emotion and affective style. *Trends in Cognitive Sciences, 3*(1), 11–21.

Davidson, R. J., Putnam, K. M., & Larson, C. L. (2000). Dysfunction in the neural circuitry of emotion regulation: A possible prelude to violence. *Science, 289*, 591–594.

Davies, G., Welham, J., Chant, D., Torrey, E. F., & McGrath, J. (2003). A systematic review and meta-analysis of Northern Hemisphere season of birth studies in schizophrenia. *Schizophrenia Bulletin, 29*(3), 587–593.

Davis, M., & Whalen, P. J. (2001). The amygdala: Vigilance and emotion. *Molecular Psychiatry, 6*(1), 13–34.

Davis, S., & Mirick, D. K. (2006). Circadian disruption, shift work and the risk of cancer: A summary of the evidence and studies in Seattle. *Cancer Causes Control, 17*(4), 539–545.

Dawkins, R. (1982). *The extended phenotype: The long reach of the gene*. Oxford: Oxford University Press.

Dawson, V. L., Dawson, T. M., London, E. D., Bredt, D. S., & Snyder, S. H. (1991). Nitric oxide mediates glutamate neurotoxicity in primary cortical cultures. *Proceedings of the National Academy of Sciences of the United States of America, 88*, 6368–6371.

de Gelder, B., Snyder, J., Greve, D., Gerard, G., & Hadjikhani, N. (2004). Fear fosters flight: A mechanism for fear contagion when perceiving emotion expressed by a whole body. *Proceedings of the National Academy of Science of the United States of America (PNAS), 101*(47), 16701–16706.

de Grouchy, J., & Turleau, C. (1990). Autosomal disorders. In A. E. H. Emery & D. L. Rimoin (Eds.), *Principles and practice of medical genetics* (pp. 247–272). Edinburgh, UK: Churchill-Livingstone.

De Jonge, F. H., Louwerse, A. L., Ooms, M. P., Evers, P., Endert, E., & van de Poll, N. E. (1989). Lesions of the SDN-POA inhibit sexual behavior of male Wistar rats. *Brain Research Bulletin, 23,* 483–492.

de Kloet, E. R., Oitzl, M. S., & Joels, M. (1993). Functional implications of brain corticosteroid receptor diversity. *Cellular and Molecular Neurobiology, 13,* 433–455.

De la Fuente-Fernandez, R., & Stoessl, A. J. (2004). The biochemical bases of the placebo effect. *Science and Engineering Ethics, 10,* 143–150.

de Lecea, L., Kilduff, T. S., Peyron, C., Gao, X. B., Foye, P. E., Danielson, P. E., et al. (1998). The hypocretins: Hypothalamus-specific peptides with neuroexcitatory activity. *Proceedings of the National Academy of Sciences of the United States of America (PNAS), 95*(1), 322–327.

De Nil, L. F. (1999). Stuttering: A neurophysiological perspective. In N. B. Ratner & C. Healey (Eds.), *Current perspectives in stuttering: Nature and treatment* (pp. 85–102). Mahwah, NJ: Erlbaum.

De Renzi, E., & Vignolo, L. A. (1962). The Token Test: A sensitive test to detect receptive disturbances in aphasics. *Brain, 84,* 665–678.

De Valois, R. L., & De Valois, K. K. (1980). Spatial vision. *Annual Review of Psychology, 31,* 309–341.

de Vries, A. P., Kassam-Adams, N., Cnaan, A., Sherman-Slate, E., Gallagher, P. R., & Winston, F. K. (1999). Looking beyond the physical injury: Posttraumatic stress disorder in children and parents after pediatric traffic injury. *Pediatrics, 104,* 1293–1299.

DeBow, S. B., Davies, M. L., Clarke, H. L., & Colbourne, F. (2003). Constraint-induced movement therapy and rehabilitation exercises lessen motor deficits and volume of brain injury after striatal hemorrhagic stroke in rats. *Stroke, 34,* 1021–1026.

Deems, D. A., Doty, R. L., Settle, R. G., Moore-Gillon, V., Shaman, P., Mester, A. F., et al. (1991). Smell and taste disorders, a study of 750 patients from the University of Pennsylvania Smell and Taste Center. *Archives of Otolaryngology—Head and Neck Surgery, 117,* 519–528.

Dei, M., Verni, A., Bigozzi, L., & Bruni, V. (1997). Sex steroids and libido. *The European Journal of Contraception and Reproductive Health Care, 2,* 253–258.

Deiber, M.-P., Honda, M., Ibanez, V., Sadato, N., & Hallett, M. (1999). Mesial motor areas in self-initiated versus externally triggered movements examined with fMRI: Effect of movement type and rate. *Journal of Neurophysiology, 81*(6), 3065–3077.

DeLisi, L. E., Mirsky, A. F., Buchsbaum, M. S., van Kammen, D. P., Berman, K. F., Phelps, B. H., et al. (1984). The Genain quadruplets 25 years later: A diagnostic and biochemical follow-up. *Psychiatry Research, 13,* 59–76.

Dement, W. (1960). The effect of dream deprivation. *Science, 131,* 1705–1707.

Dement, W. (1974). *Some must watch while some must sleep.* San Francisco: Freeman.

Dement, W. (2000, February 21). *Sleep deprivation: The national nightmare.* Retrieved December 26, 2000, from the WebMD Web site: http://my.webmd.com/content/article/1707.50296.

Dement, W., & Kleitman, N. (1957). The relation of eye movements during sleep to dream activity: An objective method for the study of dreaming. *Journal of Experimental Psychology, 53,* 339–346.

Dement, W., & Vaughan, C. (1999). *The promise of sleep: A pioneer in sleep medicine explains the vital connection between health, happiness, and a good night's sleep.* New York: Delacourt Press.

Demet, M. M., Ozmen, B., Deveci, A., Boyvada, S., Adiguzel, H., & Aydemir, O. (2002). Depression and anxiety in hyperthyroidism. *Archives of Medical Research, 33,* 552–556.

Deutsch, J. E., & Mirelman, A. (2007). Virtual reality–based approaches to enable walking for people poststroke. *Topics in Stroke Rehabilitation, 14*(6), 45–53.

Devane, W. A., Hanus, L., Breuer, A., Pertwee, R. G., Stevenson, L. A., Griffin, G., et al. (1992). Isolation and structure of a brain constituent that binds the cannabinoid receptor. *Science, 258,* 1946–1949.

Dhaka, A., Murray, J., Mathur, J., Earley, T., Petrus, M., & Patapoutian, A. (2007). TRPM8 is required for cold sensation in mice. *Neuron, 54*(3), 371–378.

Dhurandhar, N. (2000). Increased adiposity in animals due to a human virus. *International Journal of Obesity, 24,* 989–996.

Diamond, A. (2007). Consequences of variations in genes that affect dopamine in prefrontal cortex. *Cerebral Cortex, 17,* 1161–1170.

Diamond, A., & Goldman-Rakic, P. S. (1989). Comparison of human infants and rhesus monkeys on Piaget's AB task: Evidence for dependence on dorsolateral prefrontal cortex. *Experimental Brain Research, 74,* 24–40.

Diamond, D. M., Campbell, A. M., Park, C. R., Halonen, J., & Zoladz, P. R. (2007). The temporal dynamics model of emotional memory processing: A synthesis on the neurobiological basis of stress-induced amnesia, flashbulb and traumatic memories, and the Yerkes-Dodson law. *Neural Plasticity, 2007,* 60803.

Diamond, L. M. (2004). Emerging perspectives on distinctions between romantic love and sexual desire. *Current Directions in Psychological Science, 13*(3), 116–119.

Diamond, M., & Sigmundson, H. K. (1997). Sex reassignment at birth: Long-term review and clinical implications. *Archives of Pediatric and Adolescent Medicine, 151,* 298–304.

Dickens, W. T., & Flynn, J. R. (2001). Heritability estimates versus large environmental effects: The IQ paradox resolved. *Psychological Review, 108,* 346–369.

Diereck, H. A., & Greenspan, R. J. (2006). Molecular analysis of flies selected for aggressive behavior. *Nature Genetics, 38,* 1023–1031.

Dierks, T., Linden, D. E., Jandl, M., Formisano, E., Goebel, R., Lanfermann, H., et al. (1999). Activation of Heschl's gyrus during auditory hallucinations. *Neuron, 22,* 615–621.

DiGrande, L., Perrin, M. A., Thorpe, L. E., Thalji, L., Murphy, J., Wu, D., et al. (2008). Posttraumatic stress symptoms, PTSD, and risk factors among lower Manhattan residents 2–3 years after the September 11, 2001, terrorist attacks. *Journal of Traumatic Stress, 21*(3), 264–273.

Dijk, D. J., & Lockley, S. W. (2002). Integration of human sleep-wake regulation and circadian rhythmicity. *Journal of Applied Physiology, 92*(2), 852–862.

DiLalla, L. F., Kagan, J., & Reznick, J. S. (1994). Genetic etiology of behavioral inhibition among 2-year-old children. *Infant Behavior and Development, 17,* 405–412.

DiLella, A., & Woo, S. L. C. (1987). Molecular basis of phenylketonuria and its clinical applications. *Biology and Medicine, 4,* 183–192.

Ding, J. M., Chen, D., Weber, E. T., Faiman, L. E., Rea, M. A., & Gillette, M. U. (1994). Resetting the biological clock: Mediation of nocturnal circadian shifts by glutamate and NO. *Science, 266,* 1713–1717.

Dobelle, W. (2000). Artificial vision for the blind by connecting a television camera to the visual cortex. *American Society of Artificial Internal Organs Journal, 46,* 3–9.

Doig, P., Lloyd-Smith, R., Prior, J. C., & Sinclair, D. (1997). *Sex testing (gender verification) in sport.* Retrieved February 21, 2003, from the Canadian Academy of Sport Medicine Web site: http://www.casm-acms.org/PositionStatements/GendereVerifEng.pdf.

Donnan, G. A., Fisher, M., Macleod, M., & Davis, S. M. (2008). Stroke. *Lancet, 371*(9624), 1612–1623.

Dooldeniya, M. D., Khafagy, R., Mashaly, H., Browning, A. J., Sundaram, S. K., & Biyani, C. S. (2007). Lower abdominal pain in women after binge drinking. *British Medical Journal, 335*(7627), 992–993.

Dopfel, R. P., Schulmeister, K., & Schernhammer, E. S. (2007). Nutritional and lifestyle correlates of the cancer-protective hormone melatonin. *Cancer Detection and Prevention, 31*(2), 140–148.

Doty, R. L., Yousem, D. M., Pham, L. T., Kreshak, A. A., Geckle, R., & Lee, W. W. (1997). Olfactory dysfunction in patients with head trauma. *Archives of Neurology, 54*(9), 1131–1140.

Doumin, C. (2004). The external environment. Retrieved 2/13/04 from http://webusers.xula.edu/cdoumen/CAP/Environment.html.

Drachman, D. A., & Leavitt, J. (1972). Memory impairment in the aged: Storage versus retrieval deficit. *Journal of Experimental Psychology, 93,* 302–308.

Drain, P., Folkers, E., & Quinn, W. G. (1991). CAMP-dependent protein kinase and the disruption of learning in transgenic flies. *Neuron, 7,* 71–82.

Drevets, W. C., Price, J. L., Bardgett, M. E., Reich, T., Todd, R. D., & Raichle, M. E. (2002). Glucose metabolism in the amygdala in depression: Relationship to diagnostic subtype and plasma cortisol levels. *Pharmacology, Biochemistry, and Behavior, 71*(3), 431–447.

Drevets, W. C., Videen, T. O., Price, J. L., Preskorn, S. H., Carmichael, S. T., & Raichle, M. E. (1992). A functional anatomical study of unipolar depression. *Journal of Neuroscience, 12*(9), 3628–3641.

Driessen, M., Herrmann, J., Stahl, K., Zwaan, M., Meier, S., Hill, A., et al. (2000). Magnetic resonance imaging volume of the hippocampus and the amygdala in women with borderline personality disorder and early traumatization. *Archives of General Psychiatry, 57,* 1115–1122.

Driscoll, H. C., Serody, L., Patrick, S., Maurer, J., Bensasi, S., Houck, P. R., et al. (2008). Sleeping well, aging well: A descriptive and cross-sectional study of sleep in "successful agers" 75 and older. *American Journal of Geriatric Psychiatry, 16*(1), 74–82.

Dronkers, N. F., Pinker, S., & Damasio, A. (2000). Language and the aphasias. In E. R. Kandel, J. H. Schwartz, & T. M. Jessell (Eds.), *Principles of neural science* (4th ed., pp. 1169–1185). New York: McGraw-Hill.

Dronkers, N. F., Plaisant, O., Iba-Zizen, M. T., & Cabanis, E. A. (2007). Paul Broca's historic cases: High resolution MR imaging of the brains of Leborgne and Lelong. *Brain, 130*(Pt) 5, 1432–1441.

DuBose, C. N., Cardello, A. V., & Maller, O. (1980). Effects of colorants and flavorants on identification, perceived flavor intensity, and hedonic quality of fruit-flavored beverages and cake. *Journal of Food Science, 45,* 1393–1400.

Dubovsky, S. L., & Buzan, R. (1999). Mood disorders. In R. E. Hales, S. C. Yudofsky, & J. A. Talbott (Eds.), *Textbook of psychiatry* (pp. 479–565). Washington, DC: American Psychiatric Press.

Duclaux, R., & Kenshalo, D. R. (1980). Response characteristics of cutaneous warm fibers in the monkey. *Journal of Neurophysiology, 43,* 1–157.

Dudai, Y. (1989). *The neurobiology of memory: Concepts, findings, trends.* Oxford, UK: Oxford University Press.

Duffy, J. F., & Wright, K. P., Jr. (2005). Entrainment of the human circadian system by light. *Journal of Biological Rhythms, 20*(4), 326–338.

Dunwiddie, T. V., & Masino, S. A. (2001). The role and regulation of adenosine in the central nervous system. *Annual Review of Neuroscience, 24,* 31–55.

Durand, J. B., Nelissen, K., Joly, O., Wardak, C., Todd, J. T., Norman, J. F., et al. (2007). Anterior regions of monkey parietal cortex process visual 3D shape. *Neuron, 55*(3), 493–505.

Dutton, D. G., & Aron, A. P. (1974). Some evidence for heightened sexual attraction under conditions of high anxiety. *Journal of Personality and Social Psychology, 30,* 510–517.

Duval, J., Dumont, M., Braun, C. M., & Montour-Proulx, I. (2002). Recovery of intellectual function after a brain injury: A comparison of longitudinal and cross-sectional approaches. *Brain and Cognition, 48,* 337–342.

Dyer, J. E., Roth, B., & Hyma, B. A. (2001). Gamma-hydroxybutyrate withdrawal syndrome. *Annals of Emergency Medicine, 37,* 147–153.

Eaton, W. W., Shao, H., Nestadt, G., Lee, B. H., Bienvenu, O. J., & Zandi, P. (2008). Population-based study of first onset and chronicity in major depressive disorder. *Archives of General Psychiatry, 65*(5), 513–520.

Ebstein, R. P., Novick, O., Umansky, R., Priel, B., Osher, Y., Blaine, D., et al. (1996). Dopamine D4 receptor (D4DR) exon III polymorphism associated with the human personality trait of novelty seeking. *Nature Genetics, 12,* 78–80.

Edelman, A. B., Gallo, M. F., Jensen, J. T., Nichols, M. D., Schulz, K. F., & Grimes, D. A. (2005). Continuous or extended cycle vs. cyclic use of combined oral contraceptives for contraception. *Cochrane Database of Systematic Reviews, 20*(3), CD004695.

Edin, B. (2001). Cutaneous afferents provide information about knee joint movements in humans. *Journal of Physiology, 531,* 289–297.

Edvardsen, J., Torgersen, S., Røysamb, E., Lygren, S., Skre, I., Onstad, S., et al. (2008). Heritability of bipolar spectrum disorders. Unity or heterogeneity. *Journal of Affective Disorders, 106*(3), 229–240.

Edwards, J., & Booth, A. (1994). Sexuality, marriage, and well-being: The middle years. In A. Rossi (Ed.), *Sexuality across the life course* (pp. 233–259). Chicago: University of Chicago Press.

Eglinton, E., & Annett, M. (1994). Handedness and dyslexia: A meta-analysis. *Perceptual Motor Skills, 79,* 1611–1616.

Ehlert, F. J., Roeske, W. R., & Yamamura, H. I. (1995). Molecular biology, pharmacology, and brain distribution of subtypes of the muscarinic receptor. In F. E. Bloom & D. J. Kupfer (Eds.), *Psychopharmacology: The fourth generation of progress* (pp. 111–124) Baltimore, MD: Lippincott, Williams, & Wilkins.

Eiberg, H., Berendt, I., & Mohr, J. (1995). Assignment of dominant inherited nocturnal enuresis (ENUR1) to chromosome 13q. *Nature Genetics, 10,* 354–356.

Eisenberger, N. I., Lieberman, M. D., & Williams, K. D. (2003). Does rejection hurt? An fMRI study of social exclusion. *Science, 302,* 290–292.

Ekman, P. (1996). Why don't we catch liars? *Social Research, 63,* 801–817.

Ekman, P., Friesen, W. V., & Ellsworth, P. (1972). *Emotion in the human face: Guidelines for research and an integration of findings.* London: Pergamon Press.

Elbert, T., Pantev, C., Weinbruch, C., Rockstroh, B., & Taub, E. (1995). Increased cortical representation of the fingers of the left hand in string players. *Science, 270,* 305–307.

Emery, N. J., Capitanio, J. P., Mason, W. A., Machado, C. J., Mendoza, S. P., & Amaral, D. G. (2001). The effects of bilateral lesions of the amygdala on dyadic social interactions in rhesus monkeys (*Macaca mulatta*). *Behavioral Neuroscience, 115,* 515–544.

Enard, W., Khaitovich, P., Klose, J., Zollner, S., Heissig, F., Giavalisco, P., et al. (2002). Intra- and interspecific variation in primate gene expression patterns. *Science, 296*(5566), 340–343.

Engel, A. (1984). Myasthenia gravis and myasthenic syndromes. *Annals of Neurology, 16,* 529–535.

Epilepsy Foundation. (2002). *Photosensitivity and seizures.* Retrieved June 4, 2002, from the Epilepsy Foundation Web site: http://www.efa.org/answerplace/factsheets/photo.html.

Eslinger, P. J., & Damasio, A. R. (1985). Severe disturbance of higher cognition after bilateral frontal lobe ablation: Patient EVR. *Neurology, 35,* 1731–1741.

Ettinger, U., Kumari, V., Crawford, T. J., Corr, P. J., Das, M., Zachariah, E., et al. (2004). Smooth pursuit and antisaccade eye movements in siblings discordant for schizophrenia. *Journal of Psychiatric Research, 38,* 177–184.

Evans, A. H., Lawrence, A. D., Potts, J., MacGregor, L., Katzenschlager, R., Shaw, K., et al. (2006). Relationship between impulsive sensation seeking traits, smoking, alcohol and caffeine intake, and Parkinson's disease. *Journal of Neurology, Neurosurgery, and Psychiatry, 77*(3), 317–321.

Evans, E. (1982). Functional anatomy of the auditory system. In H. B. Barlow and J. D. Mollon (Eds.), *The senses.* (pp. 251–306). Cambridge, England: Cambridge University Press.

Ezzeddine, Y., & Glanzman, D. L. (2003). Prolonged habituation of the gill-withdrawal reflex in *Aplysia* depends on protein synthesis, protein phosphatase activity, and postsynaptic glutamate receptors. *Journal of Neuroscience, 23*(29), 9585–9594.

Falck, R. S., Wang, J., & Carlson, R. G. (2008). Depressive symptomatology in young adults with a history of MDMA use: A longitunidal analysis. *Journal of Psychopharmacology, 22*(1), 47–54.

Falls, J. G., Pulford, D. J., Wylie, A. A., & Jirtle, R. L. (1999). Genomic imprinting: Implications for human disease. *The American Journal of Pathology, 154*(3), 635–647.

Fanselow, M. S., & LeDoux, J. E. (1999). Why we think plasticity underlying Pavlovian fear conditioning occurs in the basolateral amygdala. *Neuron, 23,* 229–232.

Farah, M. J., Illes, J., Cook-Degan, R., Gardner, H., Kandel, E., King, P., et al. (2004). Neurocognitive enhancement: What can we do and what should we do? *Nature Reviews Neuroscience, 5,* 421–425.

Faraone, S. V., & Biederman, J. (1998). Neurobiology of attention-deficit hyperactivity disorder. *Biological Psychiatry, 44*(10), 951–958.

Faraone, S. V., Biderman, J., & Milberger, S. (1996). An exploratory study of ADHD among second degree relatives of ADHD children. *Society of Biological Psychiatry, 35,* 398–402.

Farber, N. B., Newcomer, J. W., & Olney, J. W. (1998). The glutamate synapse in neuropsychiatric disorders: Focus on schizophrenia and Alzheimer's disease. *Progress in Brain Research, 116,* 421–437.

Farooqi, I., & O'Rahilly, S. (2000). Recent advances in the genetics of severe childhood obesity. *Archives of Disease in Childhood, 83,* 31–34.

Farrer, C., Franck, N., Frith, C. D., Decety, J., Georgieff, N., d'Amato, T., & Jeannerod, M. (2004). Neural correlates of action attribution in schizophrenia. *Psychiatry Research, 131*(1), 31–44.

Farwell, L. (2002). *Executive summary.* Retrieved May 26, 2002, from http://www.brainwavescience.com/ExecutiveSummary.php.

Fasano, C., Tercé, F., Niel, J.-P., Nguyen, H. T. T., Hiol, A., Bertrand-Michel, J., et al. (2007). Neuronal conduction of excitation without action potentials based on ceramide production. *PLoS ONE, 2*(7), e612.

Faurie, C., & Raymond, M. (2004). Handedness frequency over more than ten thousand years. *Proceedings: Biological Sciences/The Royal Society, 271*(Suppl 3), S43–45.

Favre, J., Burchiel, K. J., Taha, J. M., & Hammerstad, J. (2000). Outcome of unilateral and bilateral pallidotomy for Parkinson's disease: Patient assessment. *Neurosurgery, 46,* 344–353.

Feder, H. H., & Whalen, R. E. (1965). Feminine behavior in neonatally castrated and estrogen-treated male rats. *Science, 147,* 306–307.

Feldman, R., Weller, A., Zagoory-Sharon, O., & Levine, A. (2007). Evidence for a neuroendocrinological foundation of human affiliation: Plasma oxytocin levels across pregnancy and the postpartum period predict mother–infant bonding. *Psychological Science, 18*(11), 965–970.

Fellin, T., Sul, J. Y., D'Ascenzo, M., Takano, H., Pascual, O., & Haydon, P. G. (2006). Bidirectional astrocyte-neuron communication: the many roles of glutamate and ATP. *Novartis Found Symp, 276,* 208–217; discussion 217–221, 233–207, 275–281.

Fergusson, D. M., Horwood, L. J., & Ridder, E. M. (2005). Tests of causal linkages between cannabis use and psychotic symptoms. *Addiction Research and Theory, 100,* 354–366.

Fesenko, E. E., Kolesnikov, S. S., & Lyubarsky, A. L. (1985). Induction by cyclic GMP of cationic conductance in plasma membrane of retinal rod outer segment. *Nature, 313,* 310–313.

Fiala, C., & Gemzel-Danielsson, K. (2006). Review of medical abortion using mifepristone in combination with a prostaglandin analogue. *Contraception, 74*(1), 66–86.

Fibiger, H. C., & Lloyd, K. G. (1984). The neurobiological substrates of tardive dyskinesia: The GABA hypothesis. *Trends in Neuroscience, 8,* 462.

Field, T. M., & Walden, T. (1982). Perception and production of facial expressions in infancy and early childhood. In H. W. Reese & L. P. Lipsitt (Eds.), *Advances in child development and behavior* (Vol. 16, pp. 169–211). New York: Academic Press.

Filiano, J. J., & Kinney, H. C. (1994). A perspective on neuropathologic findings in victims of the sudden infant death syndrome: The triple-risk model. *Biology of the Neonate, 65*(3–4), 194–197.

Filipek, P. A., Semrud-Clikeman, M., Steingard, J. F., Renshaw, P. F., Kennedy, D. N., & Beiderman, J. (1997). Volumetric MRI analysis comparing subjects having attention-deficit hyperactivity disorder with controls. *Neurology, 48,* 589–601.

Fine, H. A., Kim, L., Albert, P. S., Duic, J. P., Ma, H., Zhang, W., et al. (2007). A phase I trial of lenalidomide in patients with recurrent primary central nervous system tumors. *Clinical Cancer Research, 13*(23), 7101–7106.

Fink, G. R., Markowitsch, H. J., Reinkemeier, M., Bruckbauer, T., Kessler, J., & Heiss, W. D. (1996). Cerebral representation of one's own past: Neural networks involved in autobiographical memory. *Journal of Neuroscience, 16,* 4275–4282.

Finlay, B. L., & Darlington, R. B. (1995). Linked regularities in the development and evolution of mammalian brains. *Science, 268,* 1578–1584.

Finucci, J. M., & Childs, B. (1981). Are there really more dyslexic boys than girls? In A. Ansara, N. Geschwind, A. Galaburda, M. Albert, & N. Gartrell (Eds.), *Sex differences in dyslexia* (pp. 1-9) Towson, MD: Orton Dyslexia Society.

Fitzpatrick, R. C., Butler, J. E., & Day, B. L. (2006). Resolving head rotation for human bipedalism. *Current Biology, 16*(15), 1509–1514.

Fitzsimons, J. T. (1961). Drinking by rats depleted of body fluid without increase in osmotic pressure. *Journal of Physiology (London), 159,* 297–309.

Flaten, M. A., & Friborg, O. (2005). Impaired classical eyeblink conditioning in elderly human subjects: The role of unconditioned response magnitude. *Aging Clinical and Experimental Research, 17*(6), 449–457.

Flint, J., & Yule, W. (1994). Behavioural phenotypes. In M. Rutter, E. Taylor, & L. Hersov (Eds.), *Child and adolescent psychiatry: Modern approaches* (3rd ed., pp. 666–687). Oxford, UK: Blackwell.

Flynn, J. P. (1967). The neural basis of aggression in cats. In D. C. Glass (Ed.), *Neurophysiology and emotion* (pp. 40–60). New York: Rockefeller University Press.

Flynn, J. R. (1999). Searching for justice: The discovery of IQ gains over time. *American Psychologist, 54,* 5–20.

Folstein, S. E., Santangelo, S. L., Gilman, S. E., Piven, J., Landa, R., Lainhart, J., et al. (1999). Predictors of cognitive test patterns in autism families. *Journal of Child Psychology and Psychiatry, 40,* 1117–1128.

Fournier, A. E., GrandPre, T., & Strittmatter, S. M. (2001). Identification of a receptor mediating Nogo-66 inhibition of axonal regeneration. *Nature, 409,* 341–346.

Fouts, R. S., & Bodamer, M. (1987). Chimpanzee intrapersonal signing. *Friends of Washoe, 7,* 4–12.

Foutz, A. S., Mitler, M. N., Cavalli-Sforva, G. L., & Dement, W. C. (1979). Genetic factors in canine narcolepsy. *Sleep, 1,* 413–421.

Fox, R., Aslin, R. N., Shea, S. L., & Dumais, S. T. (1980). Stereopsis in human infants. *Science, 207,* 323–324.

Francks, C., Maegawa, S., Laurén, J., Abrahams, B. S., Velayos-Baeza, A., Medland, S. E., et al. (2007). LRRTM1 on chromosome 2p12 is a maternally suppressed gene that is associated paternally with handedness and schizophrenia. *Molecular Psychiatry, 12*(12), 1129–1139, 1057.

Frangos, J. E., Alavian, C. N., & Kimball, A. B. (2008). Acne and oral contraceptives: update on women's health screening guidelines. *Journal of the American Academy of Dermatology, 58*(5), 781–786.

Frankel, M. S., & Siang, S. (1999, November). Ethic and legal aspects of human subjects research on the Internet. Retrieved June 12, 2002, from the American Association for the Advancement of Science Web site: http://www.aaas.org/spp/dspp/sfrl/projects/intres/main.htm.

Freedman, D. G. (1964). Smiling in blind infants and the issue of innate vs. acquired. *Journal of Child Psychology and Psychiatry, 47,* 171–184.

Freedman, D. G. (1974). *Human infancy: An evolutionary perspective.* Hillsdale, NJ: Erlbaum.

Freud, S. (1885). *Über Coca.* Vienna, Austria: Verlag von Moritz Perles.

Frey, W. H., DeSota-Johnson, D., Hoffman, C., & McCall, J. T. (1981). Effect of stimulus on the chemical composition of human tears. *American Journal of Ophthalmology, 92*(4), 559–567.

Friedland, R. P., Fritsch, T., Smyth, K. A., Koss, E., Lerner, A. J., Chen, C. H., et al. (2001). Patients with Alzheimer's disease have reduced activities in midlife compared with healthy control-group members. *Proceedings of the National Academy of Sciences of the United States of America, 98,* 3440–3445.

Friedman, J. M., & Halaas, J. L. (1998). Leptin and the regulation of body weight in mammals. *Nature, 395*(6704), 673–770.

Friedman, M., & Rosenman, R. H. (1959). Association of specific overt behavior patterns with blood and cardiovascular findings: Blood cholesterol level, blood clotting time, incidence of arcus senilis, and clinical coronary artery disease. *Journal of the American Medical Association, 169,* 1286–1296.

Friedman, M., & Rosenman, R. H. (1974). *Type A behavior and your heart.* New York: Knopf.

Frisch, R. E. (1983). Fatness, menarche, and fertility. In S. Golub (Ed.), *Menarche: The transition from girl to woman* (pp. 5–20). Lexington, MA: Lexington Books.

Frith, C., & Frith, U. (1996). A biological marker for dyslexia. *Nature, 382,* 19–20.

Fritsch, G., & Hitzig, E. (1960). On the electrical excitability of the cerebrum. In G. von Bonin (Trans.), *Some papers on the cerebral cortex* (pp. 73–96). Springfield, IL: Thomas. (Original work published 1870)

Froelich, J., Harts, J., Lumeng, L., & Li, T. (1990). Naloxone attenuates voluntary ethanol intake in rats selectively bred for high ethanol preference. *Pharmacology, Biochemistry and Behavior, 35,* 385–390.

Frost, P. (2006). European hair and eye color. *Evolution and Human Behavior, 27,* 85–103.

Fukumitsu, N., Tsuchida, D., Ogi, S., Uchiyama, M., & Mori, Y. (2002). 125I-iomazenil-benzodiazepine receptor binding during psychological stress in rats. *Annals of Nuclear Medicine, 16,* 231–235.

Fulop, T., & Smith, C. (2006). Physiological stimulation regulates the exocytic mode through calcium activation of protein kinase C in mouse chromaffin cells. *The Biochemical Journal, 399*(1), 111–119.

Furchgott, R. F. (1999). Endothelium-derived relaxing factor: Discovery, early studies, and identification as nitric oxide. *Bioscience Reports, 19,* 235–251.

Fuster, J. M. (1997). *The prefrontal cortex: Anatomy, physiology, and neuropsychology of the frontal lobe.* New York: Raven Press.

Gabuzda, D. (1996). Nerve cell "suicide" in AIDS dementia [Electronic version]. *Harvard Mahoney Neuroscience Institute Letter, 5*(1). Retrieved May 30, 2002, from http://www.med.harvard.edu/publications/On_The_Brain/Volume5/Numberl/AIDS.html.

Gadjusek, D. C. (1973). Kuru and Creutzfeldt-Jakob disease: Experimental models of noninflammatory degenerative slow virus disease of the central nervous system. *Annals of Clinical Research, 5,* 254–261.

Gadjusek, D. C., & Zigas, V. (1957). Degenerative disease of the central nervous system in New Guinea: The endemic occurrence of kuru in the native population. *New England Journal of Medicine, 257,* 974–978.

Gadjusek, D. C., Gibbs, C. J., & Alpers, M. (1966). Experimental transmission of a kuru-like syndrome to chimpanzees. *Nature, 209,* 794–796.

Gage, F. (2000, November). *Neurogenesis in the adult brain and spinal cord.* Paper presented at the meeting of the Society for Neuroscience, New Orleans, LA.

Gaillard, R. C., & Spinedi, E. (1998). Sex-and stress-steroids interactions and the immune system: Evidence for a neuroendocrine-immunological sexual dimorphism. *Domestic Animal Endocrinology, 15,* 345–352.

Gainotti, G. (1972). Emotional behavior and hemispheric side of lesion. *Cortex, 8,* 41–55.

Gais, S., & Born, J. (2004). Declarative memory consolidation: mechanisms acting during human sleep. *Learning and Memory, 11*(6), 679–685.

Galaburda, A. M., Sherman, G. F., Rosen, G. D., Aboitiz, F., & Geschwind, N. (1985). Developmental dyslexia: Four consecutive patients with cortical anomalies. *Annals of Neurology, 18,* 222–233.

Galati, D., Scherer, K. R., & Ricci-Bitti, P. E. (1997). Voluntary facial expression of emotion: Comparing congenitally blind with normally sighted encoders. *Journal of Personality and Social Psychology, 73,* 1363–1380.

Gallant, S. J., Popiel, D. A., Hoffman, D. M., Chakraborty, P. K., & Hamilton, J. A. (1992a). Using daily ratings to confirm premenstrual syndrome/late luteal phase dysphoric disorder: Part I. Effects of demand characteristics and expectations. *Psychosomatic Medicine, 54,* 149–166.

Gallant, S. J., Popiel, D. A., Hoffman, D. M., Chakraborty, P. K., & Hamilton, J. A. (1992b). Using daily ratings to confirm premenstrual syndrome/late luteal phase dysphoric disorder: Part II. What makes a "real" difference? *Psychosomatic Medicine, 54,* 167–181.

Gallassi, R., Morreale, A., Montagna, P., Cortelli, P., Avoni, P., Castellani, R., et al. (1996). Fatal familial insomnia: Behavioral and cognitive features. *Neurology, 46,* 935–939.

Gallopin, T., Fort, P., Eggermann, E., Cauli, B., Luppi, P., Rossier, J., et al. (2000). Identification of sleep-promoting neurons in vitro. *Nature, 404,* 992–995.

Gallup, G. G., Jr. (1977). Self-recognition in primates: A comparative approach to the bidirectional properties of consciousness. *American Psychologist, 32,* 329–337.

Galyer, K. T., Conaglen, H. M., Hare, A., & Conaglen, J. V. (1999). The effect of gynecological surgery on sexual desire. *Journal of Sex and Marital Therapy, 25,* 81–88.

Gannon, P. J., Holloway, R. L., Broadfield, D. C., & Braun, A. R. (1998). Asymmetry of chimapnzee planum temporale: Humanlike pattern of Wernicke's brain language area homolog. *Science, 279,* 220–222.

Garakani, A., Mathew, S. J., & Charney, D. S. (2006). Neurobiology of anxiety disorders and implications for treatment. *Mt. Sinai Journal of Medicine, 73*(7), 941–949.

García, H. H., González, A. E., Del Brutto, O. H., Tsang, V. C., Llanos-Zavalaga, F., Gonzalvez, G., et al. (2007). Strategies for the elimination of taeniasis/cysticercosis. *Journal of the Neurological Sciences, 262*(1–2), 153–157.

Gardner, H. (1968). *Fundamentals of neurology.* Philadelphia: Saunders.

Gardner, H. (1976). *The shattered mind: The person after brain damage.* New York: Knopf.

Gardner, H. (1983). *Frames of mind: The theory of multiple intelligences.* New York: Basic Books.

Gardner, R. A., & Gardner, B. I. (1969). Teaching sign language to a chimpanzee. *Science, 165,* 664–672.

Garstecki, D. (2005). Possible perils of mp3 player headphones. Retrieved on October 4, 2008 from http://www.northwestern.edu/univ-relations/broadcast/2005/12/players.html

Gauthier, I., Skudlarski, P., Gore, J. C., & Anderson, A. W. (2000). Expertise for cars and birds recruits brain areas involved in face recognition. *Nature Neuroscience, 3,* 191–197.

Gauthier, L. V., Taub, E., Perkins, C., Ortmann, M., Mark, V. W., & Uswatte, G. (2008). Remodeling the brain: Plastic structural brain changes produced by different motor therapies after stroke. *Stroke, 39*(5), 1520–1525.

Gawne, T., & Martin, J. (2000). Activity of primate V1 cortical neurons during blinks. *Journal of Neurophysiology, 84,* 2691–2694.

Gazzaniga, M. S. (1967). The split brain in man. *Scientific American, 217,* 24–29.

Gazzaniga, M. S. (1970). *The bisected brain.* New York: Appleton-Century-Crofts.

Gazzaniga, M. S. (1983). Right hemisphere language following brain bisection: A 20-year perspective. *American Psychologist, 38,* 525–537.

Gazzaniga, M. S. (1988). *Mind matters.* Boston: Houghton Mifflin.

Ge, R.-S., Chen, G.-R., Dong, Q., Akingbemi, B., Sottas, C. M., Santos, M., et al. (2007). Biphasic effects of postnatal exposure to diethylhexylphthalate on the timing of puberty in male rats. *Journal of Andrology, 28*(4), 513–520.

Gelisse, P., & Crespel, A. (2008). Slow alpha variant during REM sleep. *Neurophysiologie Clinique, 38*(1), 3–8.

Geller, B., & Luby, J. (1997). Child and adolescent bipolar disorder: A review of the past 10 years. *Journal of the American Academy of Child and Adolescent Psychiatry, 36,* 1168–1176.

Gelsinger, P. (2002). Jesse's intent. *Bulletin of Medical Ethics, 179,* 13–20.

Georgieva, S. S., Todd, J. T., Peeters, R., & Orban, G. A. (2008). The extraction of 3D shape from texture and shading in the human brain. *Cerebral Cortex, 18*(10), 2416–2438.

Georgopoulos, A. P., Taira, M., & Lukashin, A. (1993). Cognitive neurophysiology of the motor cortex. *Science, 260,* 47–52.

Gerberding, J. L. (2007). Diabetes: Disabling disease to double by 2050. Retrieved April 18, 2008, from http://www.cdc.gov/print.do?url=http://www.cdc.gov/nccdphp/publications/aag/ddt.htm.

Gerwig, M., Eßer, A., Guberina, H., Frings, M., Kolb, F., Forsting, M., et al. (2008). Trace eyeblink conditioning in patients with cerebellar degeneration: Comparison of short and long trace intervals. *Experimental Brain Research, 187*(1), 85–96.

Gerwig, M., Haerter, K., Hajjar, K., Dimitrova, A., Maschke, M., Kolb, F., et al. (2006). Trace eyeblink conditioning in human subjects with cerebellar lesions. *Experimental Brain Research, 170*(1), 7–21.

Geschwind, N. (1970). The organization of language and the brain. *Science, 170,* 940–944.

Geschwind, N. (1972). Language and the brain. *Scientific American, 226,* 76–83.

Geschwind, N., & Galaburda, A. (1987). *Cerebral lateralization: The genetical theory of natural selection.* Oxford, UK: Clarendon Press.

Geuze, E., van Berckel, B. N., Lammertsma, A. A., Boellaard, R., de Kloet, C. S., Vermetten, E., et al. (2008). Reduced GABAA benzodiazepine receptor binding in veterans with post-traumatic stress disorder. *Molecular Psychiatry, 13*(1), 74–83, 73.

Gewirtz, J. C., & Davis, M. (1997). Second-order fear conditioning prevented by blocking NMDA receptors in amygdala. *Nature, 388,* 471–474.

Ghani, A. C., Ferguson, N. M., Donnelly, C. A., Hagenaars, T. J., & Anderson, R. M. (1998). Epidemiological determinants of the pattern and magnitude of the vCJD epidemic in Great Britain. *Proceedings of the Royal Society of London B, Biological Science, 265,* 2443–2452.

Gibson, J. (1966). *The senses considered as perceptual systems.* Boston: Houghton-Mifflin.

Giedd, J. N., Blumenthal, J., Jeffries, N. O., Castellanos, F. X., Liu, H., Zijdenbos, A., et al. (1999). Brain development during childhood and adolescence: A longitudinal MRI study. *Nature Neuroscience, 2*(10), 861–863.

Gilbert, S. J., Spengler, S., Simons, J. S., Steele, J. D., Lawrie, S. M., Frith, C. D., et al. (2006). Functional specialization within rostral prefrontal cortex (area 10): A meta-analysis. *Journal of Cognitive Neuroscience, 18*(6), 932–948.

Gilbertson, M. W., Shenton, M. E., Ciszewski, A., Kasai, K., Lasko, N. B., Orr, S. P., & Pitman, R. K. (2002). Smaller hippocampal volume predicts pathologic vulnerability to psychological trauma. *Nature Neuroscience, 5,* 1242–1247.

Gilbertson, T. A., Fontenot, D. T., Liu, L., Zhang, H., & Monroe, W. T. (1997). Fatty acid modulation of K+ channels in taste receptor cells: Gustatory cues for dietary fat. *American Journal of Physiology, 272*(4 Pt 1), C1203–1210.

Gilger, J. W., Hanebuth, E., Smith, S. D., & Pennington, B. F. (1996). Differential risk for developmental reading disorders in the offspring of compensated versus noncompensated parents. *Reading and Writing, 8*(5), 407–417.

Gill, M., Daly, G., Heron, S., Hawi, Z., & Fitzgerald, M. (1997). Confirmation of a dissociation between attention deficit hyperactivity disorder and a dopamine transporter polymorphism. *Biological Psychiatry, 2,* 311–313.

Gillihan, S. J., & Farah, M. J. (2005). Is self special? A critical review of evidence from experimental psychology and cognitive neuroscience. *Psychological Bulletin, 131*(1), 76–97.

Gillin, J. C., & Borbely, A. A.(1985). Sleep: a neurobiological window on affective disorders. *Trends in Neurosciences, 8,* S. 537–542.

Giraud, A. L., Neumann, K., Bachoud-Levi, A. C., von Gudenberg, A. W., Euler, H. A., Lanfermann, H., et al. (2008). Severity of dysfluency correlates with basal ganglia activity in persistent developmental stuttering. *Brain and Language, 104*(2), 190–199.

Glantz, L. A., & Lewis, D. A. (2000). Decreased dendritic spine density on prefrontal cortical pyramidal neurons in schizophrenia. *Archives of General Psychiatry, 57,* 65.

Glanzman, D. L. (2006). The cellular mechanisms of learning in *Aplysia:* Of blind men and elephants. *The Biological Bulletin, 210*(3), 271–279.

Glickman, S. E., Frank, L. G., Licht, P., Yalcinkaya, T., Siiteri, P. K., & Davidson, J. (1992). Sexual differentiation of the female spotted hyena: One of nature's experiments. *Annals of the New York Academy of Sciences, 662,* 135–159.

Glosser, G., Grugan, P., & Friedman, R. B. (1999). Comparison of reading and spelling in patients with probable Alzheimer's disease. *Neuropsychology, 13,* 350–358.

Godemont, P., Wang, L. C., & Mason, C. A. (1994). Retinal axon divergence in the optic chiasm: Dynamics of growth cone behavior at the midline. *Journal of Neuroscience, 14,* 7024–7039.

Goetz, C. G., Leurgans, S., Pappert, E. J., Raman, R., & Stemer, A. B. (2001). Prospective longitudinal assessment of hallucinations in Parkinson's disease. *Neurology, 57,* 2078–2082.

Gogos, J. A., Santha, M., Takacs, Z., Beck, K. D., Luine, V., Lucas, L. R., Nadler, J. V., & Karayiorgou, M. (1999). The gene encoding proline dehydrogenase modulates sensorimotor gating in mice. *Nature Genetics, 21,* 434–439.

Gold, J. J., & Squire, L. R. (2006). The anatomy of amnesia: Neurohistological analysis of three new cases. *Learning and Memory, 13*(6), 699–710.

Goldberg, I. I., Harel, M., & Malach, R. (2006). When the brain loses its self: Prefrontal inactivation during sensorimotor processing. *Neuron, 50*(2), 329–339.

Goldman-Rakic, P. S., & Rakic, P. (1984). Experimentally modified convolutional patterns in nonhuman primates: Possible relevance of connections to cerebral dominance in humans. In N. S. Geschwind & A. M. Galaburda (Eds.), *Cerebral dominance: The biological foundations* (pp. 179–194). Cambridge, MA: Harvard University Press.

Goldstein, A. P., Glick, B., & Gibbs, J. C. (1998). *Aggression replacement training: A comprehensive intervention for aggressive youth.* Champaign, IL: Research Press.

Goldstein, D. S., Holmes, C. S., Dendi, R., Bruce, S. R., & Li, S.-T. (2002). Orthostatic hypotension from sympathetic denervation in Parkinson's disease. *Neurology, 58,* 1247–1255.

Goldstein, D. S., Holmes, C., Li, S.-T., Bruce, S., Metman, L. V., & Cannon, R. O. (2000). Cardiac sympathetic denervation in Parkinson's disease. *Annals of Internal Medicine, 133,* 338–347.

Golomb, J., de Leon, M. J., George, A. E., Kluger, A., Convit, A., Rusinek, H., de Santi, S., Litt, A., Foo, S. H., & Ferris, S. H. (1994). Hippocampal atrophy correlates with severe cognitive impairment in elderly patients with suspected normal pressure hydrocephalus. *Journal of Neurology, Neurosurgery, and Psychiatry, 57,* 590–593.

Gonzaga, G. C., Turner, R. A., Keltner, D., Campos, B., & Altemus, M. (2006). Romantic love and sexual desire in close relationships. *Emotion, 6*(2), 163–179.

Gonzalez-Maeso, J., Ang, R. L., Yuen, T., Chan, P., Weisstaub, N. V., Lopez-Gimenez, J. F., et al. (2008). Identification of a serotonin/glutamate recetor complex implicated in psychosis. *Nature, 452*(7183), 93–97.

Gonzalez-Maeso, J., Weisstaub, N. V., Zhou, M., Chan, P., Ivic, L., Ang, R., et al. (2007). Hallucinogens recruit specific cortical 5-HT(2A) receptor-mediated signaling pathways to affect behavior. *Neuron, 53*(3), 439–452.

Goodale, M. A., & Humphrey, G. K. (2001). Separate visual systems for action and perception. In E. B. Goldstein (Ed.), *Blackwell handbook of perception* (pp. 311–343). Oxford, UK: Blackwell.

Goodale, M. A., & Milner, A. D. (1992). Separate visual pathways for perception and action. *Trends in Neurosciences, 15*(1), 20–25.

Goodfellow, P. N., & Lovell-Badge, R. (1993). *SRY* and sex determination in mammals. *Annual Review of Genetics, 27,* 71–92.

Goodman, E., & Capitman, J. (2000). Depressive symptoms and cigarette smoking among teens. *Pediatrics, 106,* 748–755.

Goodwin, D. W., & Guze, S. B. (1984). *Psychiatric diagnosis* (3rd ed.). New York: Oxford University Press.

Gordon, I. T., & Whelan, P. J. (2006). Deciphering the organization and modulation of spinal locomotor central pattern generators. *The Journal of Experimental Biology, 209,* 2007–2014.

Gordon, I., Zagoory-Sharon, O., Schneiderman, I., Leckman, J. F., Weller, A., & Feldman, R. (2008). Oxytocin and cortisol in romantically unattached young adults: Associations with bonding and psychological distress. *Psychophysiology, 45*(3), 349–352.

Gorelick, D. A., & Balster, R. L. (1995). Phencyclidine. In F. E. Bloom & D. J. Kupfer (Eds.), *Psychopharmacology: The fourth generation of progress* (pp. 1767–1776). New York: Raven Press.

Gorski, R. (1980). Sexual differentiation in the brain. In D. T. Krieger & J. C. Hughes (Eds.), *Neuroendocrinology* (pp. 215–222). Sunderland, MA: Sinauer.

Gorski, R. A., Gordon, J. H., Shryne, J. E., & Southam, A. M. (1978). Evidence for a morphological sex difference within the medial preoptic area of the rat brain. *Brain Research, 148,* 333–346.

Gotlib, I. H., Joormann, J., Minor, K. L., & Hallmayer, J. (2008). HPA axis reactivity: A mechanism underlying the associations among 5-HTTLPR, stress, and depression. *Biological Psychiatry, 63*(9), 847–851.

Gottesman, I. I. (1991). Schizophrenia genesis: The origins of madness. New York: Freeman.

Gottlieb, B., Pinsky, L., Beitel, L. K., & Trifiro, M. (1999). Androgen insensitivity. *American Journal of Medical Genetics, 89,* 210–217.

Gottlieb, D. J., O'Connor, G. T., & Wilk, J. B. (2007). Genome-wide association of sleep and circadian phenotypes. *BMC Medical Genetics, 8*(Suppl 1), S9.

Gotz, M. J., Johnstone, E. C., & Ratcliffe, S. G. (1999). Criminality and antisocial behaviour in unselected men with sex chromosome abnormalities. *Psychological Medicine, 29,* 953–962.

Gould, E., Reeves, A. J., Graziano, M. S., & Gross, C. G. (1999). Neurogenesis in the neocortex of adult primates. *Science, 286,* 548–552.

Gould, S. J. (1981). *The mismeasure of man.* New York: Norton.

Grafman, J., Schwab, K., Warden, D., Pridgen, A., Brown, H. R., & Salazar, A. M. (1996). Frontal lobe injuries, violence, and aggression: A report of the Vietnam Head Injury Study. *Neurology, 46*(5), 1231–1238.

Graham, R. K., Deng, Y., Slow, E. J., Haigh, B., Bissada, N., Lu, G., et al. (2006). Cleavage at the caspase-6 site is required for neuronal dysfunction and degeneration due to mutant huntingtin. *Cell, 125*(6), 1179–1191.

Gray, P. B., Singh, A. B., Woodhouse, L. J., Storer, T. W., Casaburi, R., Dzekov, J., et al. (2005). Dose-dependent effects of testosterone on sexual function, mood, and visuospatial cognition in older men. *Journal of Clinical Endocrinology and Metabolism, 90*(7), 3838–3846.

Gray, R. H., Campbell, O. M., Apelo, R., Eslami, S. S., Zacur, H., Ramos, R. M., et al. (1990). Risk of ovulation during lactation. *Lancet, 335*(8680), 25–29.

Greer, D. M. (2006). Hypothermia for cardiac arrest. *Current Neurology and Neuroscience Reports, 6*(6), 518–524.

Gregg, A. P. (2007). When vying reveals lying: The Timed Antagonistic Response Alethiometer. *Applied Cognitive Psychology, 21,* 621–647.

Gregorian, R. S., Golden, K. A., Bahce, A., Goodman, C., Kwong, W. J., & Khan, Z. M. (2002). Antidepressant-induced sexual dysfunction. *Annals of Pharmacotherapy, 36,* 1577–1589.

Gresch, P. J., Smith, R. L., Barrett, R. J., & Sanders-Bush, E. (2005). Behavioral tolerance to lysergic acid diethylamide is associated with reduced serotonin-2A receptor signaling in rat cortex. *Neuropsychopharmacology, 30*(9), 1693–1702.

Griffin, D. (1959). *Echoes of bats and men.* New York: Doubleday/Anchor.

Griffy, L. (2006). Suspect's words won't be considered. *The Tribune,* B1.

Grillner, S., Ekeberg, O., El Manira, A., Lansner, A., Parker, D., Tegnér, J., & Wallén, P. (1998). Intrinsic function of a neuronal network: A vertebrate central pattern generator. *Brain Research Reviews, 26,* 184–197.

Grisham, J. R., Anderson, T. M., & Sachdev, P. S. (2008). Genetic and environmental influences on obsessive-compulsive disorder. *European Archives of Psychiatry and Clinical Neuroscience, 258*(2), 107–116.

Grossenbacher, P. G., & Lovelace, C. T. (2001). Mechanisms of synesthesia: Cognitive and physiological constraints. *Trends in Cognitive Sciences, 5*(1), 36–41.

Grossman, A. W., Elisseou, N. M., McKinney, B. C., & Greenough, W. T. (2006). Hippocampal pyramidal cells in adult Fmrl knockout mice exhibit an immature-appearing profile of dendritic spines. *Brain Research, 1084*(1), 158–164.

Grossman, M. (2007). *Unprotected.* New York: Sentinel.

Guehl, D., Benazzouz, A., Aouizerate, B., Cuny, E., Rotgé, J. Y., Rougier, A., et al. (2008). Neuronal correlates of obsessions in the caudate nucleus. *Biological Psychiatry, 63*(6), 557–562.

Gugger, J. J., & Wagner, M. L. (2007). Rapid eye movement sleep behavior disorder. *Annals of Pharmacotherapy, 41*(11), 1833–1841.

Guinan, J. J. (1996). Physiology of olivocochlear efferents. In A. P. P. Dallos & R. R. Fay (Eds.), *The cochlea* (pp. 435–502). New York: Springer.

Guler, A. D., Ecker, J. L., Lall, G. S., Haq, S., Altimus, C. M., Liao, H.-W., et al. (2008). Melanopsin cells are the principal conduits for rod-cone input to non-image-forming vision. *Nature, 453*(7191), 102–105.

Gumbel, A. (2005). California idyll shocked by "skateboard murder" of 87-year-old. Retrieved July 5, 2008, from http://www.independent.co.uk/news/world/americas/californian-idyll-shocked-by-skateboard-murder-of-87yearold-527617.html.

Gusella, J. F., & McDonald, M. E. (1993). Hunting for Huntington's disease. *Molecular Genetic Medicine, 3,* 139–158.

Gusella, J. F., McNeil, S., Persichetti, F., Srinidhi, J., Novelletto, A., Bird, E., Faber, P., Vonsattel, J.-P., Myers, R. H., & MacDonald, M. E. (1996). Huntington's disease. *Cold Spring Harbor Symposia on Quantitative Biology, 61,* 615–626.

Guskiewicz, K. M., McCrea, M., Marshall, S. W., Cantu, R. C., Randolph, C., Barr, W., et al. (2003). Cumulative effects associated with recurrent concussion in collegiate football players: The NCAA Concussion Study. *Journal of the American Medical Association (JAMA), 290*(19), 2549–2555.

Guyton, A. (1991). *Textbook of medical physiology* (8th ed.). Philadelphia: Saunders.

Haddad, P. M., & Dursun, S. M. (2008). Neurological complications of psychiatric drugs: Clinical features and management. *Human Psychopharmacology, 23* (Suppl.1), 15–26.

Haekel, E. (1896). *Evolution of man: A popular exposition of the principal points of human ontogeny and phylogeny.* New York: Appleton.

Hagoort, P. (2005). On Broca, brain, and binding: A new framework. *Trends in Cognitive Sciences, 9*(9), 416–423.

Hagoort, P., Hald, L., Bastiaansen, M., & Petersson, K. M. (2004). Integration of word meaning and world knowledge in language comprehension. *Science, 304*(5669), 438–441.

Hague, J. F., Gilbert, S. S., Burgess, H. J., Ferguson, S. A., & Dawson, D. (2003). A sedentary day: Effects on subsequent sleep and body temperatures in trained athletes. *Physiology and Behavior, 78,* 261–267.

Haimov, I., & Lavie, P. (1996). Melatonin: A soporific hormone. *Current Directions in Psychological Science, 5,* 106–111.

Hakimi, P., Yang, J., Casadesus, G., Massillon, D., Tolentino-Silva, F., Nye, C. K., et al. (2007). Overexpression of the cytosolic form of phosphoenolpyruvate carboxykinase (GTP) in skeletal muscle repatterns energy metabolism in the mouse. *Journal of Biological Chemistry, 282*(45), 32844–32855.

Halaas, J. L., Gajiwala, K. S., Maffei, M., Cohen, S. L., Chait, B. T., Rabinowitz, D., et al. (1995). Weight-reducing effects of the plasma protein encoded by the obese gene. *Science, 269,* 543–546.

Halberda, J., Sires, S. F., & Feigenson, L. (2006). Multiple spatially overlapping sets can be enumerated in parallel. *Psychological Science, 17*(7), 572–576.

Haldane, J. B. S. (1932). *The causes of evolution.* London: Longmans, Green.

Haldane, J. B. S. (1949). *What is life?* London: Alcuin Press.

Hall, C. (1951). What people dream about. *Scientific American, 184,* 60–63.

Hall, C., & Van de Castle, R. (1966). *The content analysis of dreams.* New York: Appleton-Century-Crofts.

Halpern, D. F. (1992). *Sex differences in cognitive abilities.* Hillsdale, NJ: Erlbaum.

Halpern, J. H., & Pope, H. G., Jr. (2003). Hallucinogen persisting perception disorder: What do we know after 50 years? *Drug and Alcohol Dependence, 69*(2), 109–119.

Hamburger, V. (1975). Cell death in the development of the lateral motor column of the chick embryo. *Journal of Comparative Neurology, 169,* 535–546.

Hamel, E. (2007). Serotonin and migraine: Biology and clinical implications. *Cephalalgia, 27*(11), 1293–1300.

Hammel, H. T. (1965). Neurones and temperature regulation. *Aerospace Medical Research Laboratories,* 1–32.

Hampson, R. E., & Deadwyler, S. A. (1999). Cannabinoids, hippocampal function and memory. *Life Sciences, 65,* 715–723.

Hancock, D. B., Martin, E. R., Mayhew, G. M., Stajich, J. M., Jewett, R., Stacy, M. A., et al. (2008). Pesticide exposure and risk of Parkinson's disease: A family-based case-control study. *BMC Neurology, 8,* 6.

Hänecke, K., Tiedemann, S., Nachreiner, F., & Grzech-Sukalo, H. (1998). Accident risk as a function of hour at work and time of day as determined from accident data and exposure models for the German working population. *Scandinavian Journal of Work, Environment and Health, 24,* 43–48.

Hankin, B. L., Abramson, L. Y., Moffitt, T. E., Silva, P. A., McGee, R., & Andell, K. E. (1998). Development of depression from preadolescence to young adulthood: Emerging gender differences in a 10-year longitudinal study. *Journal of Abnormal Psychology, 107,* 128–140.

Hanson, D. R., & Fearn, R. W. (1975). Hearing acuity in young people exposed to pop music and other noise. *Lancet, 2,* 203–205.

Happe, F., Ronald, A., & Plomin, R. (2006). Time to give up on a single explanation for autism. *Nature Neuroscience, 9*(10), 1218–1220.

Harata, N. C., Aravanis, A. M., & Tsien, R. W. (2006). Kiss-and-run and full-collapse fusion as modes of exo-endocytosis in neurosecretion. *Journal of Neurochemistry, 97*(6), 1546–1570.

Harata, N., Pyle, J. L., Aravanis, A. M., Mozhayeva, M., Kavalali, E. T., & Tsien, R. W. (2001). Limited numbers of recycling vesicles in small CNS nerve terminals: Implications for neural signaling and vesicular cycling. *Trends in Neurosciences, 24,* 637–643.

Harbeck-Weber, C., & Peterson, L. (1996). Health-related disorders. In E. J. Mash & R. A. Barkley (Eds.), *Child psychopathology* (pp. 572–601). New York: Guilford Press.

Hardeland, R., Poeggeler, B., Srinivasan, V., Trakht, I., Pandi-Perumal, S. R., & Cardinali, D. P. (2008). Melatonergic drugs in clinical practice. *Arzneimittel-forschung, 58*(1), 1–10.

Hardy, J., Cai, H., Cookson, M. R., Gwinn-Hardy, K., & Singleton, A. (2006). Genetics of Parkinson's disease and parkinsonism. *Annals of Neurology, 60*(4), 389–398.

Hare, R. D. (1993). *Without conscience: The disturbing world of psychopaths among us.* New York: Pocket Books.

Harper, C., & Matsumoto, I. (2005). Ethanol and brain damage. *Current Opinion in Pharmacology, 5*(1), 73–78.

Harper, J. (2008). Breakthrough claimed in male contraceptives. Retrieved April 27, 2008, from http://www.washingtontimes.com/apps/pbcs.dll/article?AID=/20080326/NATION/657226903/1002

Harris, L. J. (1980). Lateralised sex differences: Substrate and significance. *Behavioural Brain Science, 3,* 236–237.

Hartlage, S. A., Arduino, K. E., & Gehlert, S. (2001). Premenstrual dysphoric disorder and risk for major depressive disorder: A preliminary study. *Journal of Clinical Psychology, 57,* 1571–1578.

Hartline, H. (1938). The response of single optic nerve fibers of the vertebrate eye to illumination of the retina. *American Journal of Physiology, 121,* 400–415.

Hashimoto, I., Suzuki, A., Kimura, T., Iguchi, Y., Tanosaki, M., Takino, R., et al. (2004). Is there training-dependent reorganization of digit representations in area 3b of string players? *Clinical Neurophysiology, 115*(2), 435–447.

Hassett, J. M., Siebert, E. R., & Wallen, K. (2008). Sex differences in rhesus monkey toy preferences parallel those of children. *Hormones and Behavior, 54*(3), 359–364.

Hasson, U., Nir, Y., Levy, I., Fuhrman, G., & Malach, R. (2004). Intersubject synchronization of cortical activity during natural vision. *Science, 303,* 1634–1640.

Hattori, E., Liu, C., Badner, J. A., Bonner, T. I., Christian, S. L., Maheshwari, M., et al. (2003). Polymorphisms at the g72/g30 gene locus, on 13q33, are associated with bipolar disorder in two independent pedigree series. *American Journal of Human Genetics, 72,* 1131–1140.

Hauri, P. (1982). *The sleep disorders.* Kalamazoo, MI: Upjohn.

Hauser, W. A., & Beghi, E. (2008). First seizure definitions and worldwide incidence and mortality. *Epilepsia, 49*(Supplement 1), 8–12.

Hausmann, M., Slabbekoorn, D., Van Goozen, S. H. M., Cohen-Kettenis, P. T., & Güntürkun, O. (2000). Sex hormones affect spatial abilities during the menstrual cycle. *Behavioral Neuroscience, 114,* 1245–1250.

Hawasli, A. H., Benavides, D. R., Nguyen, C., Kansy, J. W., Hayashi, K., Chambon, P., et al. (2007). Cyclin-dependent kinase 5 governs learning and synaptic plasticity via control of NMDAR degradation. *Nature Neuroscience, 10*(7), 880–886.

Hayak, Y., Walker, J. R., Li, C., Wong, W. H., Davis, L., Buxbaum, J. D., et al. (2001). Genome-wide expression analysis reveals disregulation of myelination-related genes in chronic schizophrenia. *Proceedings of the National Academy of Sciences of the United States of America, 48,* 4746–4751.

Haynes, J.-D., & Rees, G. (2006). Decoding mental states from brain activity in humans. *Nature Reviews Neuroscience, 7,* 523–534.

Heath, R. G. (1963). Electrical self-stimulation of the brain in man. *American Journal of Psychiatry, 120,* 571–577.

Hebb, D. O. (1949). *The organization of behavior: A neuropsychological theory.* New York: Wiley.

Hecht, S., Shlaer, S., & Pirenne, M. H. (1942). Energy, quanta, and vision. *Journal of General Physiology, 25,* 819–840.

Heidelberger, R., Heinemann, C., Neher, E., & Matthews, G. (1994). Calcium dependence of the rate of exocytosis in a synaptic terminal. *Nature, 371,* 513–515.

Heilbronn, L. K., de Jonge, L., Frisard, M. I., DeLany, J. P., Larson-Meyer, D. E., Rood, J., et al. (2006). Effect of 6-month calorie restriction on biomarkers of longevity, metabolic adaptation, and oxidative stress in overweight individuals: A randomized controlled trial. *Journal of the American Medical Association (JAMA), 295*(13), 1539–1548.

Hembree, E. A., Riggs, D. S., Kozak, M. J., Franklin, M. E., & Foa, E. B. (2003). Cognitive-behavioral therapy for panic disorder: A review of treatment elements, strategies, and outcomes. *CNS Spectrums, 8,* 363–371.

Henderson, D. C. (2008). Managing weight gain and metabolic issues in patients treated with atypical antipsychotics. *Journal of Clinical Psychiatry, 69*(2), e4.

Hendrickson, A. E., Wagoner, N., & Cowan, W. M. (1972). Autoradiographic and electron microscopic study of retinhypothalamic connections. *Zeitschrift fur Zellforschung und Mikroskopische Anatomie, 125,* 1–26.

Hendry, S. H., & Reid, R. C. (2000). The koniocellular pathway in primate vision. *Annual Review of Neuroscience, 23,* 127–153.

Hening, W., Allen, R. P., Tenzer, P., & Winkelman, J. W. (2007). Restless legs syndrome: Demographics, presentation, and differential diagnosis. *Geriatrics, 62*(9), 26–29.

Henneman, E. (1991). The size principle and its relation to transmission failure in Ia projections to spinal motoneurons. *Annals of the New York Academy of Sciences, 627,* 165–168.

Henquet, C., Krabbendam, L., Spauwen, J., Kaplan, C., Lieb, R., Wittchen, H. U., et al. (2005). Prospective cohort study of cannabis use, predisposition for psychosis, and psychotic symptoms in young people. *British Medical Journal, 330,* 11.

Hering, E. (1878). *On the theory of sensibility to light. (Zur Lehre vom Lichtsinn)* Vienna: G.A. Agoston.

Herman-Giddens, M. E., Slora, E. J., Wasserman, R. C., Bourdony, C. J., Bhapkar, M. V., Koch, G. G., et al. (1997). Secondary sexual characteristics and menses in young girls seen in office practice: A study from the pediatric research in office settings network. *Pediatrics, 99,* 505–512.

Hermans, E. J., Ramsey, N. F., & van Honk, J. (2008). Exogenous testosterone enhances responsiveness to social threat in the neural circuitry of social aggression in humans. *Biological Psychiatry, 63*(3), 263–270.

Hernandez, A. E., Martinez, A., & Kohnert, K. (2000). In search of the language switch: An fMRI study of picture naming in Spanish-English bilinguals. *Brain and Language, 73,* 421–431.

Herpertz, S. C., Werth, U., Lukas, G., Qunaibi, M., Schuerkens, A., Kunert, H. J., et al. (2001). Emotion in criminal offenders with psychopathy and borderline personality disorder. *Archives of General Psychiatry, 58,* 737–745.

Herrera, D. G., & Robertson, H. A. (1996). Activation of c-fos in the brain. *Progress in Neurobiology, 50*(2–3), 83–107.

Herrnstein, R. J., & Boring, E. G. (1965). *A source book in the history of psychology.* Cambridge, MA: Harvard University Press.

Hervias, I., Beal, M. F., & Manfredi, G. (2006). Mitochondrial dysfunction and amyotrophic lateral sclerosis. *Muscle and Nerve, 33*(5), 598–608.

Herxheimer, A., & Petrie, K. J. (2002). Melatonin for the prevention and treatment of jet lag. *The Cochrane Review* (The Cochrane Library, Disk Issue 4, CD001520). Chichester, UK: Wiley.

Herxheimer, A., & Waterhouse, J. (2003). The prevention and treatment of jet lag. *British Medical Journal, 326,* 296–297.

Hess, W. R. (1928). Stammganglian-reizversuche, 10 tagung der deutschen physiologischen gesellschaft. Frankfurt am Main. *Berichte uber die Gesamte Physiologie, 42,* 554–555.

Hill, A. F., Desbruslais, M., Joiner, S., Sidle, K. C., Gowland, I., Collinge, J., Doey, L. J., & Lantos, P. (1997). The same prion strain causes vCJD and BSE. *Nature, 389,* 448–450, 526.

Hill, J. O., & Peters, J. C. (1998). Environmental contributions to the obesity epidemic. *Science, 280*(5368), 1371–1374.

Hiller, W. D. (1989). Dehydration and hyponatremia during triathlons. *Medicine and Science in Sports and Exercise, 21,* S219–S221.

Hilz, M. J., Dutsch, M., Perrine, K., Nelson, P. K., Rauhut, U., & Devinsky, O. (2001). Hemispheric influence on autonomic modulation and baroreflex sensitivity. *Annals of Neurology, 49,* 575–584.

Hines, M. (1990). Gonadal hormones and human cognitive development. In J. Balthazart (Ed.), *Comparative Physiology: Vol. 8. Hormones, brain, and behavior in vertebrates: I. Sexual differentiation, neuroanatomical aspects, neurotransmitters and neuropeptides* (pp. 51–63). Basel, Switzerland: Karger.

Hines, M., & Shipley, C. (1984). Prenatal exposure to diethylstilbestrol and development of sexually dimorphic cognitive abilities and cerebral lateralization. *Developmental Review of Psychiatry, 20,* 81–94.

Hines, M., Brook, C., & Conway, G. S. (2004). Androgen and psychosexual development: Core gender identity, sexual orientation and recalled childhood gender role behavior in women and men with congenital adrenal hyperplasia (CAH). *Journal of Sex Research, 41*(1), 75–81.

Hines, M., Golombok, S., Rust, J., Johnston, K. J., & Golding, J. (2002). Testosterone during pregnancy and gender role behavior of preschool children: A longitudinal population study. *Child Development, 73,* 1678–1687.

Hirota, T., & Fukada, Y. (2004). Resetting mechanism of central and peripheral circadian clocks in mammals. *Zoological Science, 21,* 359–368.

Hirsch, J., De La Paz, R., Relkin, N., Victor, J., Li, T., Kim, K., Olyarchuk, J., & Georgakakos, B. (1994). Single voxel analysis of functional magnetic resonance images (fMRI) obtained during human visual stimulation. *Supplement to Investigative Ophthalmology and Visual Science, 35,* 1438.

Hirshkowitz, M., & Moore, C. A. (1996). Sleep-related erectile activity. *Neurological Clinics, 14,* 721–737.

Hjerrild, B. E., Mortensen, K. H., & Gravholt, C. H. (2008). Turner syndrome and clinical treatment. *British Medical Bulletin, 86,* 77–93.

Ho, H. N., Yang, Y. S., Hsieh, R. P, Lin, H. R., Chen, S. U., Huang, S. C., et al. (1994). Sharing of human leukocyte antigens in couples with unexplained infertility affects the success of in vitro fertilization and tubal embryo transfer. *American Journal of Obstetrics and Gynecology, 170,* 63–71.

Hobson, J., &. McCarley, R. W. (1977). The brain as a dream state generator: An activation-synthesis hypothesis of the dream process. *American Journal of Psychiatry, 134,* 1335–1348.

Hochgeschwender, U., Costa, J. L., Reed, P., Bui, S., & Brennan, M. B. (2003). Altered glucose homeostasis in proopiomelanocortinnull mouse mutants lacking central and peripheral melanocortin. *Endocrinology, 144,* 5194–5202.

Hodgkin, A. L. (1992). *Chance and design: Reminiscences of science in peace and war.* Cambridge, UK: Cambridge University Press.

Hodgkin, A. L., & Huxley, A. F. (1952) A quantitative description of membrane current and its application to conduction and excitation in nerve. *Journal of Physiology, 117,* 500–544.

Hodgman, J. E. (2002). Commentary: Effect of sleep position on apnea and brachycardia in high-risk infants. *Journal of Perinatology, 22,* 163–164.

Hoebel, B. G., & Teitelbaum, P. (1966). Effects of forcefeeding and starvation on food intake and body weight in a rat with ventromedial hypothalamic lesions. *Journal of Comparative and Physiological Psychology, 61,* 189–193.

Hoebel, B. G., Patten, C. S., Colantuoni, C., & Rada, P. V. (2000, November). *Sugar withdrawal causes symptoms of anxiety and acetylcholine release in the nucleus accumbens.* Paper presented at the meeting of the Society for Neuroscience, New Orleans, LA.

Hoekstra, R. A., Bartels, M., Verweij, C. J. H., & Boomsma, D. I. (2007). Heritability of autistic traits in the general population. *Archives of Pediatric and Adolescent Medicine, 161*(4), 372–377.

Hoffman, E., Phelps, M., Mullani, N., Higgins, C., & Ter-Pogossian, M. (1976). Design and performance characteristics of a whole body transaxial tomograph. *Journal of Nuclear Medicine, 17,* 493–503.

Hoffman, R. E., Gueorguieva, R., Hawkins, K. A., Varanko, M., Boutros, N. N., Wu, Y. T., et al. (2005). Temporoparietal transcranial magnetic stimulation for auditory hallucinations: safety, efficacy and moderators in a fifty patient sample. *Biological Psychiatry, 58*(2), 97–104.

Hoffman, R. E., Hawkins, K. A., Gueorguieva, R., Boutros, N. N., Rachid, F., Carroll, K., et al. (2003). Transcranial magnetic stimulation of left temporoparietal cortex and medicationresistant auditory hallucinations. *Archives of General Psychiatry, 60,* 49–56.

Hofman, P., Van Riswick, J. G. A., & Van Opstal, J. A. (1998). Relearning sound localization with new ears. *Nature Neuroscience, 1,* 417–421.

Hoge, C. W., Terhakopian, A., Castro, C. A., Messer, S. C., & Engel, C. C. (2007). Association of posttraumatic stress disorder with somatic symptoms, health care visits, and absenteeism among Iraq war veterans. *American Journal of Psychiatry, 164*(1), 150–153.

Holden, C. (1986). Days may be numbered for polygraphs in the private sector. *Science, 232,* 705.

Holden, C. (1991). Is "gender gap" narrowing? *Science, 253,* 959–960.

Holden, C. (2001). Panel seeks truth in lie detector debate. *Science, 291,* 967.

Holgers, K. M., & Pettersson, B. (2005). Noise exposure and subjective hearing symptoms among school children in Sweden. *Noise Health, 7*(27), 27–37.

Hollander, L. E., Freeman, E. W., Sammel, M. D., Berlin, J. A., Grisso, J. A., & Battistini, M. (2001). Sleep quality, estradiol levels, and behavioral factors in late reproductive age women. *Obstetrics and Gynecology, 98,* 391–397.

Holloway, M. (2000). The female hurt. *Scientific American, 11,* 32–37.

Holt, L. H., Lotto, A. J., & Kluender, K. R. (1998). Incorporating principles of general learning in theories of language acquisition. In M. Gruber, C. Derrick Higgins, K. S. Olson, & T. Wysocki (Eds.), *Chicago Linguistic Society: Vol. 34. The panels* (pp. 253–268). Chicago: Chicago Linguistic Society.

Holzman, P., Levy, D., & Proctor, L. (1976). Smooth pursuit eye movements, attention, and schizophrenia. *Archives of General Psychiatry, 33,* 1415–1420.

Hopfield, J., Feinstein, D. I., & Palmer, R. G. (1985). "Unlearning" has a stabilizing effect in collective memories. *Nature, 304,* 158–159.

Horne, J. (1988). *Why We Sleep.* NY: Oxford University Press.

Hornsveld, R. H., Nijman, H. L., Hollin, C. R., & Kraaimaat, F. W. (2008). Aggression control therapy for violent forensic psychiatric patients: Method and clinical practice. *International Journal of Offender Therapy and Comparative Criminology, 52*(2), 222–233.

Horridge, G. (1962). Learning of leg position by the ventral nerve cord in headless insects. *Proceedings of the Royal Society of London, B, Biological Science, 157,* 33–52.

Hoschl, C., & Hajek, T. (2001). Hippocampal damage mediated by corticosteroids: A neuropsychiatric research challenge. *European Archives of Psychiatry and Clinical Neuroscience, 251*(Suppl. 2), II81–88.

Houts, A. C., Berman, J. S., & Abramson, H. (1994). Effectiveness of psychological and pharmacological treatments for nocturnal enuresis. *Journal of Consulting and Clinical Psychology, 62,* 737–745.

Howard, R., Rabins, P. V., Seeman, M. V., Jeste, D. V., & the International Late-Onset Schizophrenia Group. (2000). Late-onset schizophrenia and very-late-onset schizophrenia-like psychosis: An international consensus. *American Journal of Psychiatry, 157,* 172–178.

Howlett, R. (1996). Prime time for neuropeptide Y. *Nature, 382,* 113.

Hoyt, J. (2002). Medical group warns about concussions and youth soccer. *The Nando Times.* Retrieved May 31, 2002, from http://www.nandotimes.com/sports/story/387710p-3083747c.html.

Hoza, B., Waschbusch, D. A., Pelham, W. E., Molina, B. S. G., & Milich, R. (2000). Attention-deficit/hyperactivity disordered and control boys' responses to social success and failure. *Child Development, 71,* 432–447.

Hrobjartsson, A., & Gotzsche, P. C. (2001). Is the placebo powerless? An analysis of clinical trials comparing placebo with no treatment. *New England Journal of Medicine, 344,* 1594–1602.

Hsiao, K., Baker, H. F., Crow, T. J., Poulter, M., Owen, F., Terwilliger, J. D., et al. (1988). Linkage of a prion protein missense variant to Gerstmann-Straussler syndrome. *Nature, 338,* 342–345.

Hsu, J. L., Leemans, A., Bai, C. H., Lee, C. H., Tsai, Y. F., Chiu, H. C., et al. (2008). Gender differences and age-related white matter changes of the human brain: a diffusion tensor imaging study. *Neuroimage, 39*(2), 566–577.

Hsu, L. K. G., Chesler, B. E., & Santhouse, R. (1990). Bulimia nervosa in eleven sets of twins: A clinical report. *International Journal of Eating Disorders, 9,* 275–282.

Hu, F., & Strittmatter, S. M. (2008). The N-terminal domain of Nogo-A inhibits cell adhesion and axonal outgrowth by an integrin-specific mechanism. *The Journal of Neuroscience, 28*(5), 1262–1269.

Huang, A. L., Chen, X., Hoon, M. A., Chandrashekar, J., Guo, W., Trankner, D., et al. (2006). The cells and logic for mammalian sour taste detection. *Nature, 442*(7105), 934–938.

Hubel, D. H., & Livingstone, M. S. (1987). Segregation of form, color, and stereopsis in primate area 18. *Journal of Neuroscience, 7,* 3378–3415.

Hubel, D. H., & Wiesel, T. N. (1959). Receptive fields of single neurons in the cat's striate cortex. *Journal of Physiology, 148,* 574–591.

Hubel, D. H., & Wiesel, T. N. (1962). Receptive fields, binocular interaction, and functional architecture in the cat's visual cortex. *Journal of Physiology, 160,* 106–154.

Hubel, D. H., & Wiesel, T. N. (1965). Binocular interaction in striate cortex kittens reared with artificial squint. *Journal of Neurophysiology, 288,* 1041–1059. (Figure 5.29)

Hubel, D. H., & Wiesel, T. N. (1977). Ferrier lecture: Functional architecture of macaque monkey visual cortex. *Proceedings of the Royal Society of London, B, Biological Science, 198,* 1–59.

Hublin, C., Kaprio, J., Partinen, M., & Koskenvu, M. (2001). Parasomnias: Co-occurrence and genetics. *Psychiatric Genetics, 11*(2), 65–70.

Hudspeth, A. (1983). The hair cells of the inner ear. *Scientific American, 248,* 54–64.

Hughes, J., Kosterlitz, H. W., & Smith, T. W. (1977). The distribution of methionine-enkephalin and leucine-enkephalin in the brain and peripheral tissues. *British Journal of Pharmacology, 61,* 639–647.

Hughes, J., Smith, T. W., Kosterlitz, H., Fothergill, L. A., Morgan, B. A., & Morris, H. R. (1975). Identification of two related pentapeptides from the brain with potent opiate agonist activity. *Nature, 258,* 577–579.

Hulka, B. S., & Moorman, P. G. (2002). Breast cancer: Hormones and other risk factors. *Maturitas, 42* (Suppl. 1), S95–105.

Hultman, C. M., Sparen, P., Takei, N., Murray, R. M., & Cnattingius, S. (1999). Prenatal and perinatal risk factors for schizophrenia, affective psychosis, and reactive psychosis of early onset: Case control study. *British Medical Journal, 318,* 421–426.

Human Rights Watch. (2006). Lethal injection drugs. Retrieved March 24, 2008, from http://hrw.org/reports/2006/us0406/4.htm#_Toc133042054.

Humphreys, G. W., & Riddoch, M. J. (1987). *To see but not to see: A case of visual agnosia.* London: Erlbaum.

Hung, R. J., McKay, J. D., Gaborieau, V., Boffetta, P., Hashibe, M., Zaridze, D., et al. (2008). A susceptibility locus for lung cancer maps to nicotinic acetylcholine receptor subunit genes on 15q25. *Nature, 452*(7187), 633–637.

Hunt, H. T. (1989). *The multiplicity of dreams.* New Haven, CT: Yale University Press.

Hurvich, L. (1981). *Color vision.* Sunderland, MA: Sinauer.

Husky, M. M., Mazure, C. M., Paliwal, P., & McKee, S. A. (2008). Gender differences in the comorbidity of smoking behavior and major depression. *Drug and Alcohol Dependence, 93*(1–2), 176–179.

Huttenlocher, P. (1994). Synaptogenesis in human cerebral cortex. In G. Dawson & K. W. Fischer (Eds.), *Human behavior and the developing brain* (pp. 137–152). New York: Guilford Press.

Huxley, A. (1954). *The doors of perception.* New York: Harper.

Iacoboni, M., & Dapretto, M. (2006). The mirror neuron system and the consequences of its dysfunction. *Nature Reviews Neuroscience, 7*(12), 942–951.

Iacoboni, M., & Mazziotta, J. C. (2007). Mirror neuron system: Basic findings and clinical applications. *Annals of Neurology, 62*(3), 213–218.

Imaizumi, Y. (2003). A comparative study of zygotic twinning and triplet rates in eight countries, 1972–1999. *Journal of Biosocial Science, 35,* 287–302.

Imperato-McGinley, J., Guerrero, L., Gautier, T., & Peterson, R. E. (1974). Steroid 5alpha-reductase deficiency in man: an inherited form of male pseudohermaphroditism. *Science, 186*(4170), 1213–1215.

Imperato-McGinley, J., Peterson, R. E., Gautier, T., & Sturla, E. (1979). Male pseudohermaphroditism secondary to 5 alpha-reductase deficiency--a model for the role of androgens in both the development of the male phenotype and the evolution of a male gender identity. *Journal of Steroid Biochemistry, 11*(1B), 637–645.

Ingersoll, B., Lewis, E., & Kroman, E. (2007). Teaching the imitation and spontaneous use of descriptive gestures in young children with autism using a naturalistic behavioral intervention. *Journal of Autism and Developmental Disorders, 37*(8), 1446–1456.

Ingram, J. L., Stodgell, C. J., Hyman, S. L., Figlewicz, D. A., Weitkamp, L. R., & Rodier, P. M. (2000). Discovery of allelic variants of HOXA1 and HOXB1: Genetic susceptibility to autism spectrum disorders. *Teratology, 62,* 393–405.

Inoue, M., Koyanagi, T., Nakahara, H., Hara, K., Hori, E., & Nakano, H. (1986). Functional development of human eye movement in utero assessed quantitatively with real time ultrasound. *American Journal of Obstetrics and Gynecology, 155,* 170–174.

Institute of Medicine. (1989). *Behavioral influences on the endocrine and immune systems.* Washington, DC: National Academy Press.

International Human Genome Sequencing Consortium. (2004). Finishing the euchromatic sequence of the human genome. *Nature, 431*(7011), 931–945.

International League Against Epilepsy (ILAE). (2008). Seizure types. Retrieved July 10, 2008, from http://www.ilae-epilepsy.org/Visitors/Centre/ctf/seizure_types.cfm.

Inui, A., Asakawa, A., Bowers, C. Y., Mantovani, G., Laviano, A., Meguid, M. M., et al. (2004). Ghrelin, appetite, and gastric motility: The emerging role of the stomach as an endocrine organ. *The FASEB Journal, 18*(3), 439–456.

Irwin, W., Anderle, M. J., Abercrombie, H. C., Schaefer, S. M., Kalin, N. H., & Davidson, R. J. (2004). Amygdalar interhemispheric functional connectivity differs between the non-depressed and depressed human brain. *Neuroimage, 21*(2), 674–686.

Ishunina, T. A., & Swaab, D. F. (1999). Vasopressin and oxytocin neurons of the human supraoptic and paraventricular nucleus; Size changes in relation to age and sex. *Journal of Clinical Endocrinology & Metabolism, 84*(12), 4637–4644.

Islam, T., Gauderman, W. J., Cozen, W., & Mack, T. M. (2007). Childhood sun exposure influences risk of multiple sclerosis in monozygotic twins. *Neurology, 69*(4), 381–388.

Ito, M. (1984). *The cerebellum and neural control.* New York: Raven.

Izard, C. E. (1972). *Patterns of emotions: A new analysis of anxiety and depression.* New York: Academic Press.

Izard, C. E. (1977). *Human emotions.* New York: Plenum.

Izard, C. E. (1982). *Measuring emotions in infants and children.* New York: Cambridge University Press.

Izquierdo, A., Suda, R. K., & Murray, E. A. (2005). Comparison of the effects of bilateral orbital prefrontal cortex lesions and amygdala lesions on emotional responses in rhesus monkeys. *Journal of Neuroscience, 25*(37), 8534–8542.

Jacob, T. C., Moss, S. J., & Jurd, R. (2008). GABA(A) receptor trafficking and its role in the dynamic modulation of neuronal inhibition. *Nature Reviews Neuroscience, 9*(5), 331–343.

Jacobs, P. A., Price, W., Court Brown, M., Brittain, R. P., & Whatmore, P. B. (1968). Chromosome studies on men in a maximum security hospital. *Annals of Human Genetics, 31,* 339.

Jaffe, J. (1984). Evaluating drug abuse treatment: A comment on the state of the art. *NIDA Research Monograph, 51,* 13–28.

Jäger, R. J., Anvret, M., Hall, K., & Scherer, G. (1990). A human XY female with a frame shift mutation in the candidate testisdetermining gene SRY. *Nature, 348,* 452–454.

Jakob, A. (1921). Über eigenartige Erkrankungen des Zentralnervernsystems mit bemerkenswerten anatomischen Befunde (spastische Pseudosklerose-Encephalomyelopathie mit disseminierten Denerationsherden). Vorläufige Mitteilung.[About strange illnesses of the central nervous system with remarkable anatomical findings (spastic pseudosclerosis-encephalomyopathy with disseminated (Denerationsherden) A preliminary report] *Deutsche Zeitschrift für Nervenheilkunde, 70,* 132–146.

James, W. (1890). *The principles of psychology.* New York: Holt.

Jameson, K. A., Highnote, S. M., & Wasserman, L. M. (2001). Richer color experience in observers with multiple photopigment opsin genes. *Psychonomic Bulletin & Review, 8*(2), 244–261.

Jamison, K. (1993). *Touched with fire: Manic-depressive illness and the artistic temperament.* New York: Free Press.

Jan, J. E., & O'Donnell, M. E. (1996). Use of melatonin in the treatment of paediatric sleep disorders. *Journal of Pineal Research, 21,* 193–199.

Jancke, L., & Kaufmann, N. (1994). Facial EMG responses to odors in solitude and with an audience. *Chemical Senses, 19,* 99–111.

Janowsky, J. S., Oviatt, S. K., & Orwell, E. S. (1994). Testosterone influences spatial cognition in older men. *Behavioral Neuroscience, 108,* 325–332.

Janson, P. A. (2002). *Kuru.* Retrieved May 30, 2002, from http://www.emedicine.com/med/topic1248.htm.

Jean, A., Conductier, G., Manrique, C., Bouras, C., Berta, P., Hen, R., et al. (2007). Anorexia induced by activation of serotonin 5-HT4 receptors is mediated by increases in CART in the nucleus accumbens. *Proceedings of the National Academy of Sciences of the United States of America (PNAS), 104*(41), 16335–16340.

Jefferson, T., Price, D., Demicheli, V., & Bianco, E. (2003). Unintended events following immunization with MMR: A systematic review. *Vaccine, 21,* 3954–3960.

Jeffries, K. J., Fritz, J. B., & Braun, A. R. (2003). Words in melody: An H215O PET study of brain activation during singing and speaking. *Neuroreport, 14,* 749–754.

Jegalian, K., & Lahn, B. T. (2001). Why the Y is so weird. *Scientific American, 284,* 56–61.

Jellies, J. (1981). *Associative olfactory conditioning in* Drosophila melanogaster *and memory retention through metamorphosis.* Illinois State University, Normal, IL. Master's thesis.

Jemmott, J. B., III, & Magloire, K. (1988). Academic stress, social support, and secretory immunoglobulin A. *Journal of Personality and Social Psychology, 55,* 803–810.

Jensen, A. R. (1998). *The g factor: The science of mental ability.* Westport, CT: Praeger.

Jentsch, J. D., & Roth, R. H. (1999). The neuropsychopharmacology of phencyclidine: From NMDA receptor hypofunction to the dopamine hypothesis of schizophrenia. *Neuropsychopharmacology, 20,* 201–225.

Jentsch, J. D., Redmond, D. E., Jr., Elsworth, J. D., Taylor, J. R., Youngren, K. D., & Roth, R. H. (1997). Enduring cognitive deficits and cortical dopamine dysfunction in monkeys after longterm administration of phencyclidine. *Science, 277,* 953–955.

Jepson, T., Ernst, M. E., & Kelly, M. W. (1999). Perspectives on the management of seasonal affective disorder. *Journal of the American Pharmaceutical Association, 39,* 822–829.

Jerison, H. (1973). *The evolution of the brain and intelligence.* New York: Academic Press.

Jerome, L., & Segal A. (2000). ADHD, executive function, and problem driving. *ADHD Reports, 8,* 7–11.

Jessell, T. M., & Sanes, J. R. (2000). The induction and patterning of the nervous system. In E. R. Kandel, J. H. Schwartz, & T. M. Jessell (Eds.), *Principles of neural science* (4th ed., pp. 1019–1040). New York: McGraw-Hill.

Jiang, S., Hemann, M. A., Lee, M. P., & Feinberg, A. P. (1998). Strain-dependent developmental relaxation of imprinting of an endogenous mouse gene, *Kvlqt1. Genomics, 53,* 395–399.

Jin, Y. H., Nishioka, H., Wakabayashi, K., Fujita, T., & Yonehara, N. (2006). Effect of morphine on the release of excitatory amino acids in the rat hind instep: Pain is modulated by the interaction between the peripheral opioid and glutamate systems. *Neuroscience, 138*(4), 1329–1339.

Joghataie, M. T., Roghani, M., Negahdar, F., & Hashemi, L. (2004). Protective effect of caffeine against neurodegeneration in a model of Parkinson's disease in rat: Behavioral and histochemical evidence. *Parkinsonism & Related Disorders, 10*(8), 465–468.

Johns, M. W. (1991). A new method for measuring daytime sleepiness: The Epworth sleepiness scale. *Sleep, 14*(6), 540–545.

Johnson, B. W., McKenzie, K. J., & Hamm, J. P. (2002). Cerebral asymmetry for mental rotation: Effects of response hand, handedness and gender. *Neuroreport, 13,* 1929–1932.

Johnson, E., Jr., & Deckwerth, T. L. (1993). Molecular mechanisms of developmental neuronal death. *Annual Review of Neuroscience, 16,* 31–46.

Johnson, P. L., Truitt, W. A., Fitz, S. D., Lowry, C. A., & Shekhar, A. (2008). Neural pathways underlying lactate-induced panic. *Neuropsychopharmacology, 33*(9), 2093–2107.

Johnson, W. G., Tsoh, J. Y., & Vanrado, P. J. (1996). Eating disorders: Efficacy of pharmacological and psychological interventions. *Clinical Psychology Review, 16,* 457–478.

Johnsrude, I. S., Owen, A. M., White, N. M., Zhao, W. V., & Bohbot, V. (2000). Impaired preference conditioning after anterior temporal lobe resection in humans. *Journal of Neuroscience, 20*(7), 2649–2656.

Johnston, V. (2000). Female facial beauty: The fertility hypothesis. *Pragmatics and Cognition, 8,* 107–122.

Jones, B. E. (1991). Paradoxical sleep and its chemical/structural substrates in the brain. *Neuroscience, 40,* 637–656.

Jones, E. G. (1999). Golgi, Cajal, and the neuron doctrine. *Journal of the History of the Neurosciences, 8,* 170–178.

Jope, R. S. (1999). Anti-bipolar therapy: Mechanism of action of lithium. *Molecular Psychiatry, 4,* 117–128.

Jordan, B. D. (1998). Genetic susceptibility to brain injury in sports: A role for genetic testing in athletes. *The Physician and Sports Medicine, 26*(2). Retrieved June 2, 2002, from http://www.physsportsmed.com/issues/1998/02feb/jordan.htm.

Jordan, B. D. (2000). Chronic traumatic brain injury associated with boxing. *Seminars in Neurology, 20*(2), 179–185.

Jordan, B. D., Relkin, N. R., Ravdin, L. D., Jacobs, A. R., Bennett, A., & Gandy, S. (1997). Apolipoprotein E epsilon4 associated with chronic traumatic brain injury in boxing. *Journal of the American Medical Association, 278,* 136–140.

Jordan, G., & Mollon, J. D. (1993). A study of women heterozygous for colour deficiencies. *Vision Research, 33,* 1495–1508.

Jouvet, M. (1967). Neurophysiology of the states of sleep. In T. M. G. C. Quarton & F. O. Schmitt (Eds.), *The neurosciences* (pp. 529–544). New York: Rockefeller University.

Jouvet, M. (1972). The role of monoamines and acetylcholinecontaining neurons in the regulation of the sleep-waking cycle. *Ergebnesse der Physiologie, 64,* 166–307.

Julesz, B. (1971). *Foundations of cyclopean perception.* Chicago: University of Chicago Press.

Julien, R. M. (1995). *A Primer of Drug Action.* New York: WH Freeman.

Jung, H., Cárdenas, G., Sciutto, E., & Fleury, A. (2008). Medical treatment for neurocysticercosis: Drugs, indications and perspectives. *Current Topics in Medicinal Chemistry, 8*(5), 424–433.

Juranek, J., Filipek, P. A., Berenji, G. R., Modahl, C., Osann, K., & Spence, M. A. (2006). Association between amygdala volume and anxiety level: Magnetic resonance imaging (MRI) study in autistic children. *Journal of Child Neurology, 21*(12), 1051–1058.

Jurynec, M. J., Riley, C. P., Gupta, D. K., Nguyen, T. D., McKeon, R. J., & Buck, C. R. (2003). TIGR is upregulated in the chronic glial scar in response to central nervous system injury and inhibits neurite outgrowth. *Molecular and Cellular Neurosciences, 23,* 69–80.

Jyonouchi, H., Sun, S., & Itokazu, N. (2002). Innate immunity associated with inflammatory responses and cytokine production against common dietary proteins in patients with autism spectrum disorder. *Neuropsychobiology, 46,* 76–84.

Kaas, S. H., Nelson, R. H., Sur, M., & Merzenich, M. M. (1981). Organization of somatosensory cortex in primates. In F. O. Schmitt, F. G. Worden, G. Adelman, & S. G. Dennis (Eds.), *The organization of the cerebral cortex* (pp. 237–262). Cambridge, MA: MIT Press.

Kadekaro, M., Cohen, S., Terrell, M. L., Lekan, H., Gary, J., & Eisenberg, H. M. (1989). Independent activation of subfornical organ and hypothalamo-neurohypophysial system during administration of angiotensin II. *Peptides, 10,* 423–429.

Kagan, J. (1994). *Galen's prophecy: Temperament in human nature.* New York: Basic Books.

Kagan, J. (1997). Temperament and the reactions to unfamiliarity. *Child Development, 68,* 139–143.

Kagan, J., Kearsley, R. B., & Zelazo, P. R. (1978). *Infancy: Its place in human development.* Cambridge, MA: Harvard University Press.

Kahkonen, M., Alitalo, T., Airaksinen, E., Matilamen, R., Laumiala, K., Auno, S., & Leisti, J. (1987). Prevalence of Fragile X syndrome in four birth cohorts of children of school age. *Human Genetics, 30,* 234–238.

Kaiser, D. A., & Sterman, M. B. (1994, September 16–21). *Periodicity of standardized EEG spectral measures across the waking day.* Paper presented at the 7th annual Summer Sleep Workshop Multi-Site Training Program for Basic Sleep Research, Lake Arrowhead, CA.

Kalin, N. H., Dawson, G., Tariot, P., Shelton, S., Barksdale, C., Weiler, S., & Thienemann, M. (1987). Function of the adrenal cortex in patients with major depression. *Psychiatry Research, 22,* 117–125.

Kalinowski, J. (2003). Self-reported efficacy of an all in-the-ear-canal prosthetic device to inhibit stuttering during one hundred hours of university teaching: A case study. *Disability and Rehabilitation, 21,* 107–111.

Kalueff, A. V., & Nutt, D. J. (2007). Role of GABA in anxiety and depression. *Depression and Anxiety, 24*(7), 495–517.

Kamboh, M. (1995). Apolipoprotein E polymorphism and susceptibility to Alzheimer's disease. *Human Biology, 67,* 195–215.

Kamischke, A., & Nieschlag, E. (2004). Progress towards hormonal male contraception. *Trends in Pharmacological Science, 25,* 49–57.

Kandel, E. R. (1995). Synaptic integration. In E. R. Kandel, J. H. Schwartz, & T. M. Jessel (Eds.), *Essentials of neural science and behavior* (pp. 219–242). Norwalk, CT: Appleton & Lange. (Figure 3.23)

Kandel, E. R. (2000). Cellular mechanisms of learning and the biological basis of individuality. In E. R. Kandel, J. H. Schwartz, & T. M. Jessell (Eds.), *Principles of neural science* (4th ed., pp. 1247–1279). New York: McGraw-Hill.

Kandel, E. R., & Siegelbaum, S. (1995). An introduction to synaptic transmission. In E. R. Kandel, J. H. Schwartz, & T. M. Jessell (Eds.), *Essentials of neural science and behavior* (pp. 161–178). Norwalk, CT: Appleton & Lange.

Kane, J. M., & Freeman, H. L. (1994). Towards more effective antipsychotic treatment. *British Journal of Psychiatry, 165,* 22–31.

Kaneda, M., & Osaka, N. (2008). Role of anterior cingulate cortex during semantic coding in verbal working memory. *Neuroscience Letters, 436*(1), 57–61.

Kant, I. (1978). *Anthropology from a pragmatic point of view* (H. H. Rudnick, Ed.; V. L. Dodwell, Trans.). Carbondale, IL: Southern Illinois University Press. (Original work published 1798)

Karimi-Abdolrezaee, S., Eftekharpour, E., Wang, J., Morshead, C. M., & Fehlings, M. G. (2006). Delayed transplantation of adult neural precursor cells promotes remyelination and functional neurological recovery after spinal cord injury. *The Journal of Neuroscience, 26,* 3377–3389.

Kasai, K., Yamasue, H., Gilbertson, M. W., Shenton, M. E., Rauch, S. L., & Pitman, R. K. (2008). Evidence for acquired pregenual anterior cingulate gray matter loss from a twin study of combat-related posttraumatic stress disorder. *Biological Psychiatry, 63*(6), 550–556.

Kasper, S., & Dienel, A. (2002). Cluster analysis of symptoms during antidepressant treatment with Hypericum extract in mildly to moderately depressed out-patients: A meta-analysis of data from three randomized, placebo-controlled trials. *Psychopharmacology, 164,* 301–308.

Kasper, S., & Wehr, T. A. (1992). The role of sleep and wakefulness in the genesis of depression and mania. *L'Encephale, 18,* 45–50.

Katoh-Semba, R., Wakako, R., Komori, T., Shigemi, H., Miyazaki, N., Ito, H., et al. (2007). Age-related changes in BDNF protein levels in human serum: Differences between autism cases and normal controls. *International Journal of Developmental Neuroscience, 25*(6), 367–372.

Katzenberg, D., Young, T., Finn, L., Lin, L., & Mignot, E. (1998). A CLOCK polymorphism associated with human diurnal preference. *Sleep, 21,* 569–576.

Kawase, T., Delgutte, B., & Liberman, M. C. (1993). Anti-masking effects of the olivocochlear reflex: II. Enhancement of auditorynerve response to masked tones. *Journal of Neurophysiology, 70,* 2533–2549.

Kay, K. N., Naselaris, T., Prenger, R. J., & Gallant, J. L. (2008). Identifying natural images from human brain activity. *Nature, 452*(7185), 352–355.

Kayser, C., Petkov, C. I., Augath, M., & Logothetis, N. K. (2007). Functional imaging reveals visual modulation of specific fields in auditory cortex. *Journal of Neuroscience, 27*(8), 1824–1835.

Kearney, C. A., Albano, A. M., Eisen, A. R., Allan, W. D., & Barlow, D. H. (1997). The phenomenology of panic disorder in youngsters: An empirical study of a clinical sample. *Journal of Anxiety Disorders, 11,* 49–62.

Keightley, P., & Eyre-Walker, A. (2000). Deleterious mutations and the evolution of sex. *Science, 290,* 331–333.

Kelly, D., & Jessell, T. (1995). Sex and the brain. In E. R. Kandel, J. H. Schwartz, & T. M. Jessell (Eds.), *Essentials of neural science and behavior* (pp. 579–594). Norwalk, CT: Appleton & Lange.

Kelly, T. L., Gomez, S. A., Ryman, D. H., Schlangen, K., & Elsmore, T. (1995). The effects of pemoline on performance and mood during sleep deprivation. *Military Psychology, 9,* 213–225.

Kelly, T. L., Neri, D. F., Grill, J. T., Ryman, D., Hunt, P. D., Dijk, D. J., et al. (1999). Nonentrained circadian rhythms of melatonin in submariners scheduled to an 18-hour day. *Journal of Biological Rhythms, 14,* 190–196.

Kelso, W. M., Nicholls, M. E., Warne, G. L., & Zacharin, M. (2000). Cerebral lateralization and cognitive functioning in patients with congenital adrenal hyperplasia. *Neuropsychology, 14,* 370–378.

Keltner, D., & Ekman, P. (2000). Facial expression of emotion. In M. Lewis & J. M. Haviland-Jones (Eds.), *Handbook of emotions* (2nd ed., pp. 236–250). New York: Guilford Press.

Kemppainen, N. V., Aalto, S., Karrasch, M., Någren, K., Savisto, N., Oikonen, V., et al. (2008). Cognitive reserve hypothesis: Pittsburgh Compound B and fluorodeoxyglucose positron emission tomography in relation to education in mild Alzheimer's disease. *Annals of Neurology, 63*(1), 1128–1118.

Kendler, K. S., Gatz, M., Gardner, C. O., & Pedersen, N. L. (2006). A Swedish national twin study of lifetime major depression. *American Journal of Psychiatry, 163*(1), 109–114.

Kendler, K. S., Gatz, M., Gardner, C. O., & Pedersen, N. L. (2006). A Swedish national twin study of lifetime major depression. *American Journal of Psychiatry, 163*(1), 109–114.

Kennard, M. A. (1936). Age and other factors in motor recovery from precentral lesions in monkeys. *Journal of Neurophysiology, 1,* 477–496.

Kennard, M. A. (1942). Cortical reorganization of motor function. *Archives of Neurological Psychiatry, 48,* 227–240.

Kennedy, G. C. (1953). The role of depot fat in the hypothalamic control of food intake in the rat. *Proceedings of the Royal Society of London, B, Biological Science, 140,* 578–592.

Kennedy-Moore, E., & Watson, J. C. (1999). *Expressing emotion: Myths, realities, and therapeutic strategies.* New York: The Guilford Press.

Kennerknecht, I., Grueter, T., Welling, B., Wentzek, S., Horst, J., Edwards, S., et al. (2006). First report of prevalence of non-syndromic hereditary prosopagnosia (HPA). *American Journal of Medical Genetics, Part A, 140*(15), 1617–1622.

Kerr, D. A., Maragakis, N., O'Brien, R., Snyder, E., Gearhart, J., & Rothstein, J. (2000, November). *Neural stem cell engraftment as a potential therapeutic strategy for motor neuron disease.* Paper presented at the meeting of the Society for Neuroscience, New Orleans, LA.

Kerr, S., Campbell, L. W., Thibault, O., & Langfield, P. (1992). Hippocampal glucocorticoid receptor activation enhances voltage-dependent Ca2+ conductances: Relevance to brain aging. *Proceedings of the National Academy of Sciences of the United States of America, 89,* 8527–8531.

Kessler, R. C., Angermeyer, M., Anthony, J. C., De Graaf, R., Demyttenaere, K., Gasquet, I., et al. (2007). Lifetime prevalence and age-of-onset distributions of mental disorders in the World Health Organization's World Mental Health Survey Initiative. *World Psychiatry, 6*(3), 168–176.

Kessler, R. C., Berglund, P., Demler, O., Jin, R., Koretz, D., Merikangas, K. R., et al. (2003). The epidemiology of major depressive disorder: Results from the National Comorbidity Survey Replication (NCS-R). *Journal of the American Medical Association (JAMA), 289*(23), 3095–3105.

Kessler, R. C., Chiu, W. T., Demler, O., & Walters, E. E. (2005). Prevalence, severity, and comorbidity of twelve-month DSM-IV disorders in the National Comorbidity Survey Replication. *Archives of General Psychiatry, 62*(6), 617–627.

Kessler, R. C., Sonnega, A., Bromet, E., Hughes, M., & Nelson, C. B. (1996). Posttraumatic stress disorder in the National Comorbidity Survey. *Archives of General Psychiatry, 52,* 1048–1060.

Kety, S. S., Rosenthal, D., Wender, P. H., & Schulsinger, F. (1968). The types and prevalence of mental illness in the biological and adoptive families of adopted schizophrenics. In D. Rosenthal & S. S. Kety (Eds.), *The transmission of schizophrenia* (pp. 345–362). Oxford, UK: Pergamon Press.

Kety, S. S., Wender, P. H., Jacobsen, B., Ingraham, L. J., Jansson, L., Faber, B., et al. (1994). Mental illness in the biological and adoptive relatives of schizophrenic adoptees: Replication of the Copenhagen Study in the rest of Denmark. *Archives of General Psychiatry, 51,* 442–455.

Keuning, J. (1968). On the nasal cycle. *International Rhinology, 6,* 99–136.

Kiehl, K. A., Smith, A. M., Hare, R. D., Mendrek, A., Forster, B. B., Brink, J., et al. (2001). Limbic abnormalities in affective processing by criminal psychopaths as revealed by functional magnetic resonance imaging. *Biological Psychiatry, 50*(9), 677–684.

Kieler, H., Cnattingius, S., Haglund, B., Palmgren, J., & Axelsson, O. (2001). Sinistrality—a side effect of prenatal sonography: A comparative study of young men. *Epidemiology, 12,* 618–623.

Kienast, T., & Heinz, A. (2006). Dopamine and the diseased brain. *CNS Neurol Disord Drug Targets, 5*(1), 109–131.

Kieseppä, T., Partonen, T., Haukka, J., Kaprio, J., & Lönnqvist, J. (2004). High concordance of bipolar I disorder in a nationwide sample of twins. *American Journal of Psychiatry, 161*(10), 1814–1821.

Kim, H. J., Chu, K., Lee, K. M., Kim, D. W., & Park, S. H. (2002). Phonological agraphia after superior temporal gyrus infarction. *Archives of Neurology, 59,* 1314–1316.

Kim, K. H., Relkin, N. R., Lee, K. M., & Hirsch, J. (1998). Distinct cortical areas associated with native and second languages. *Nature, 388,* 171–174.

Kim, Y. S., & Joh, T. H. (2006). Microglia, major player in the brain inflammation: their roles in the pathogenesis of Parkinson's disease. *Experimental and Molecular Medicine, 38*(4), 333–347.

Kimura, D. (1973). The asymmetry of the human brain. *Scientific American, 228,* 70–78.

Kimura, D. (1992). Sex differences in the brain. *Scientific American, 267,* 119–125.

Kimura, D., & Hampson, E. (1994). Cognitive pattern in men and women is influenced by fluctuations in sex hormones. *Current Directions in Psychological Science, 3,* 57–61.

King, D. S., Sharp, R. L., Vukovich, M. D., Brown, G. A., Reifenrath, T. A., Uhl, N. L., et al. (1999). Effect of oral androstenedione on serum testosterone and adaptations to resistance training in young men: A randomized controlled trial. *Journal of the American Medical Association, 281,* 2020–2028.

King, M. E., Kan, H.-M., Baas, P., Erisir, A., Glabe, C. G., & Bloom, G. S. (2006). Tau-dependent microtubule disassembly induced by pre-fibrillar ß-amyloid. *Journal of Cell Biology, 175,* 541–546.

Kingsberg, S., Shifren, J., Wekselman, K., Rodenberg, C., Koochaki, P., & DeRogatis, L. (2007). Evaluation of the clinical relevance of benefits associated with transdermal testosterone treatment in postmenopausal women with hypoactive sexual desire disorder. *The Journal of Sexual Medicine, 4*(4i), 1001–1008.

Kirik, D., Georgievska, B., Burger, C., Winkler, C., Muzyczka, N., Mandel, R. J., et al. (2002). Reversal of motor impairments in parkinsonian rats by continuous intrastriatal delivery of L-dopa using rAAV-mediated gene transfer. *Proceedings of the National Academy of Sciences of the United States of America, 99,* 4708–4713.

Kirk, K. M., Bailey, J. M., & Martin, N. G. (2000). Etiology of male sexual orientation in an Australian twin sample. *Psychology, Evolution & Gender, 2*(3), 301–311.

Kirsch, I., & Sapirstein, G. (1998). Listening to Prozac but hearing placebo: A meta-analysis of antidepressant medication. *Prevention and Treatment, 1,* Article 0002a. Retrieved May 26, 2003, from journals.apa.org/prevention/volume-1/toc-jun26-98.html.

Kishimoto, Y., Fujimichi, R., Araishi, K., Kawahara, S., Kano, M., Aiba, A., et al. (2002). mGluR1 in cerebellar Purkinje cells is required for normal association of temporally contiguous stimuli in classical conditioning. *European Journal of Neuroscience, 16*(12), 2416–2424.

Kishimoto, Y., Hirono, M., Sugiyama, T., Kawahara, S., Nakao, K., Kishio, M., et al. (2001). Impaired delay but normal trace eyeblink conditioning in PLCbeta4 mutant mice. *Neuroreport, 12*(13), 2919–2922.

Kishimoto, Y., Kawahara, S., Fujimichi, R., Mori, H., Mishina, M., & Kirino, Y. (2001). Impairment of eyeblink conditioning in GluRdelta2-mutant mice depends on the temporal overlap between conditioned and unconditioned stimuli. *European Journal of Neuroscience, 14*(9), 1515–1521.

Klein, W. L., Krafft, G. A., & Finch, C. E. (2001). Targeting small A ß-oligomers: The solution to an Alzheimer's disease conundrum? *Trends in Neurosciences, 24,* 219–224.

Kleinmuntz, B., & Szucko, J. J. (1984). A field study of the fallibility of polygraph lie detection. *Nature, 308,* 449–450.

Klimanskaya, I., Chung, Y., Becker, S., Lu, S. J., & Lanza, R. (2006). Human embryonic stem cell lines derived from single blastomeres. *Nature, 444*(7118), 481–485.

Klimanskaya, I., Chung, Y., Becker, S., Lu, S. J., & Lanza, R. (2006). Human embryonic stem cell lines derived from single blastomeres. *Nature, 444*(7118), 481–485.

Kloner, R. A., & Rezkalla, S. H. (2007). To drink or not to drink? That is the question. *Circulation, 116*(11), 1306–1317.

Klonoff-Cohen, H. S., Edelstein, S. L., & Lefkowitz, E. S. (1995). The effect of passive smoking and tobacco exposure through breast milk on sudden infant death syndrome. *Journal of the American Medical Association, 273,* 795.

Klonsky, E. D. (2007). The functions of deliberate self-injury: A review of the evidence. *Clinical Psychological Review, 27,* 226–239.

Klonsky, E. D., & Muehlenkamp, J. J. (2007). Self-injury: A research review for the practitioner. *Journal of Clinical Psychology, 63*(11), 1045–1056.

Kluger, M. J. (1991). Fever: Role of pyrogens and cryogens. *Physiological Reviews, 71*(1), 93–127.

Klüver, H., & Bucy, P. C. (1939). Preliminary analysis of functions of the temporal lobes in monkeys. *Archives of Neurological Psychology, 42,* 979–1000.

Knight, A., Underhill, P. A., Mortensen, H. M., Lin, A. A., Louis, D., Ruhlen, M., et al. (2001). Y chromosome and mtDNA variation in linguistically diverse peoples of Tanzania: Ancient roots and ancient clicks. *American Journal of Human Genetics, 69,* 180.

Knight, C. A., & Kamen, G. (2007). Modulation of motor unit firing rates during a complex sinusoidal force task in young and older adults. *Journal of Applied Physiology, 102*(1), 122–129.

Koelega, H. S., & Koster, E. P. (1974). Some experiments on sex differences in odor perception. *Annals of the New York Academy of Sciences, 237,* 234–246.

Koenigsberg, H. W., Teicher, M. H., Mitropoulou, V., Navalta, C., New, A. S., Trestman, R., et al. (2004). 24-h monitoring of plasma norepinephrine, MHPG, cortisol, growth hormone and prolactin in depression. *Journal of Psychiatric Research, 38*(5), 503–511.

Koff, E., Borod, J., & Strauss, E. (1985). Development of hemiface size asymmetry. *Cortex, 21*(1), 153–156.

Kolstad, H. A. (2008). Nightshift work and risk of breast cancer and other cancers: A critical review of the epidemiologic evidence. *Scandinavian Journal of Work, Environment, and Health, 34*(1), 5–22.

Kondziolka, D., Wechsler, L., Gebel, J., DeCesare, S., Elder, E., & Meltzer, C. C. (2003). Neuronal transplantation for motor stroke: From the laboratory to the clinic. *Physical and Medical Rehabilitation Clinics of North America, 14,* S153–160, xi.

Konopka, R. J., & Benzer, S. (1971). Clock mutants of *Drosophila melanogaster. Proceedings of the National Academy of Sciences of the United States of America, 68,* 2112–2116.

Konradi, C., & Heckers, S. (2003). Molecular aspects of glutamate dysregulation: Implications for schizophrenia and its treatment. *Pharmacology and Therapeutics, 97*(2), 153–179.

Kordower, J. H., Emborg, M. E., Bloch, J., Ma, S. Y., Chu, Y., Leventhal, L., et al. (2000). Neurodegeneration prevented by lentiviral vector delivery of GDNF in primate models of Parkinson's disease. *Science, 290,* 767–773.

Kosambi, D. D. (1967). Living prehistory in India. *Scientific American, 216,* 105.

Kossoff, E. H. (2001). *Neurocysticercosis.* Retrieved June 2, 2002, from http://www.emedicine.com/ped/topic1573.htm.

Kossut, M. (1992). Plasticity of the barrel cortex neurons. *Progress in Neurobiology, 39,* 389–442.

Kosten, T. R., Rosen, M., Bond, J., Settles, M., Roberts, J. S., Shields, J., et al. (2002). Human therapeutic cocaine vaccine: Safety and immunogenicity. *Vaccine, 20,* 1196–1204.

Koster, A., Leitzmann, M. F., Schatzkin, A., Mouw, T., Adams, K. F., van Eijk, J. T. M., et al. (2008). Waist circumference and mortality. *American Journal of Epidemiology, 167*(12), 1465– 1475.

Kovelman, I., Baker, S. A., & Petitto, L. A. (2008). Bilingual and monolingual brains compared: A functional magnetic resonance imaging investigation of syntactic processing and a possible "neural signature" of bilingualism. *Journal of Cognitive Neuroscience, 20*(1), 153–169.

Kovelman, J., & Scheibel, A. B. (1984). A neurohistological correlate of schizophrenia. *Biological Psychiatry, 19,* 1601.

Kozel, F. A., Johnson, K. A., Mu, Q., Grenesko, E. L., Laken, S. J., & George, M. S. (2005). Detecting deception using functional magnetic resonance imaging. *Biological Psychiatry, 58*(8), 605–613.

Kraemer, B., Noll, T., Delsignore, A., Milos, G., Schnyder, U., & Hepp, U. (2006). Finger length ratio (2D:4D) and dimensions of sexual orientation. *Neuropsychobiology, 53*(4), 210–214.

Krain, A. L., & Castellanos, F. X. (2006). Brain development and ADHD. *Clinical Psychology Review, 26*(4), 433–444.

Krause, J., Lalueza-Fox, C., Orlando, L., Enard, W., Green, R. E., Burbano, H. A., et al. (2007). The derived FOXP2 variant of modern humans was shared with Neandertals. *Current Biology, 17*(21), 1908–1912.

Kraut, R., Olson, J., Banaji, M., Bruckman, A., Cohen, J, & Couper, M. (2004). Psychological research online: Opportunities and challenges. *American Psychologist, 59*(2), 105–117.

Kravitz, H. M., Haywood, T. W., Kelly, J., Wahlstrom, C., Liles, S., & Cavanaugh, J. L., Jr. (1995). Medroxyprogesterone treatment for paraphiliacs. *Bulletin of the American Academy of Psychiatry and the Law, 23,* 19–33.

Kreisel, S. H., Hennerici, M. G., & Bäzner, H. (2007). Pathophysiology of stroke rehabilitation: The natural course of clinical recovery, use-dependent plasticity and rehabilitative outcome. *Cerebrovascular Diseases, 23*(4), 243–255.

Kril, J., Halliday, G., Svoboda, M., & Cartwright, H. (1997). The cerebral cortex is damaged in chronic alcoholics. *Neuroscience, 79,* 983–998.

Krimsky, S., Rothenberg, L., Stott, P., & Kyle, G. (1996). Financial interests of authors in scientific journals: A pilot study of 14 publications. *Science and Engineering Ethics, 2,* 395–410.

Kruijver, F. P., & Swaab, D. F. (2002). Sex hormone receptors are present in the human suprachiasmatic nucleus. *Neuroendocrinology, 75,* 296–305.

Krupa, D. J., Thompson, J. K., & Thompson, R. F. (1993). Localization of a memory trace in the mammalian brain. *Science, 260,* 989–991.

Kryger, M. H., Roth, T., & Dement, W. C. (1994). *Principles and practice of sleep medicine* (2nd ed.). Philadelphia: Saunders.

Kuhn, C. M. (2002). Anabolic steroids. *Recent Progress in Hormone Research, 57*(1), 411–434.

Kulkarni, S. K., & Naidu, P. S. (2003). Pathophysiology and drug therapy of tardive dyskinesia: Current concepts and future perspectives. *Drugs of Today, 39*(1), 19–49.

Kumari, V., Soni, W., Mathew, V. M., & Sharma, T. (2000). Prepulse inhibition of the startle response in men with schizophrenia. *Archives of General Psychiatry, 57,* 609–614.

Kuo, L. E., Kitlinska, J. B., Tilan, J. U., Li, L., Baker, S. B., Johnson, M. D., et al. (2007). Neuropeptide Y acts directly in the periphery on fat tissue and mediates stress-induced obesity and metabolic syndrome. *Nature Medicine, 13*(7), 803–811.

Kupfermann, I., Kandel, E. R., & Iverson, S. (2000). Motivational and addictive states. In E. R. Kandel, J. H. Schwartz, & T. M. Jessell (Eds.), *Principles of neural science* (4th ed., pp. 998–1013). New York: McGraw-Hill.

Kupka, R. W., Nolen, W. A., Post, R. M., McElroy, S. L., Altshuler, L. L., Denicoff, K. D., et al. (2002). High rate of autoimmune thyroiditis in bipolar disorder: Lack of association with lithium exposure. *Biological Psychiatry, 51,* 305–311.

Kurzman, D. (1987). *A killing wind: Inside Union Carbide and the Bhopal catastrophe.* New York: McGraw-Hill.

Kushner, D. S. (2001). Concussion in sports: Minimizing the risk for complications. *American Family Physician, 64*(6), 1007–1014.

Kwiecien, M., Edelman, A., Nichols, M. D., & Jensen, J. T. (2003). Bleeding patterns and patient acceptability of standard or continuous dosing regimens of a low-dose oral contraceptive: A randomized trial. *Contraception, 67,* 9–13.

Kyle, U. G., & Pichard, C. (2006). The Dutch Famine of 1944–1945: A pathophysiological model of long-term consequences of wasting disease. *Current Opinion in Clinical Nutrition and Metabolic Care, 9*(4), 388–394.

La Barre, W. (1975). Anthropological perspectives on hallucination and hallucinogens. In L. J. West & R. K. Siegel (Eds.), *Hallucinations* (pp. 9–52). New York: Wiley.

Lafer, B., Sachs, G. S., Labbate, L. A., Thibault, A., & Rosenbaum, J. F. (1994). Phototherapy for seasonal affective disorder: A blind comparison of three different schedules. *American Journal of Psychiatry, 151,* 1081–1083.

Lagerspetz, K. M. J., & Lagerspetz, K. Y. H. (1983). Genes and aggression. In E. C. Simmel, M. E. Hahn, & J. K. Walters (Eds.), *Aggressive behavior: Genetic and neural approaches* (pp. 89–102). Hillsdale, NJ: Erlbaum.

Lai, C. S., Fisher, S. E., Hurst, J. A., Vargha-Khadem, F., & Monaco, A. P. (2001). A forkhead-domain gene is mutated in a severe speech and language disorder. *Nature, 413,* 519–523.

Lai, Y. Y., & Siegel, J. M. (1990). Muscle tone suppression and stepping produced by stimulation of midbrain and rostral pontine reticular formation. *Journal of Neuroscience, 10,* 2727–2734.

Land, E. (1959). Experiments in color vision. *Scientific American, 200,* 84–94, 96, 99.

Landisman, C. E., Long, M. A., Beierlein, M., Deans, M. R., Paul, D. L., & Connors, B. W. (2002). Electrical synapses in the thalamic reticular nucleus. *The Journal of Neuroscience, 22*(3), 1002–1009.

Lange, C. (1912). The mechanisms of the emotions. In B. Rand (Ed.), *The classical psychologists* (pp. 672–684). Boston: Houghton Mifflin. (Original work published 1885)

Langleben, D. D., Loughead, J. W., Bilker, W. B., Ruparel, K., Childress, A. R., Busch, S. I., et al. (2005). Telling truth from lie in individual subjects with fast event-related fMRI. *Human Brain Mapping, 26*(4), 262–272.

Langley, J. (1921). *The autonomic nervous system.* Cambridge, UK: Heffer & Sons.

Langlois, J. H., Roggman, L. A., & Rieser-Danner, L. A. (1990). Infants' differential social responses to attractive and unattractive faces. *Developmental Psychology, 26,* 153–160.

Langston, J. W. (1985). MPTP and Parkinson's disease. *Trends in Neurosciences, 8,* 79–83.

Lapish, C. C., Seamans, J. K., & Judson Chandler, L. (2006). Glutamate-dopamine cotransmission and reward processing in addiction. *Alcoholism, Clinical and Experimental Research, 30*(9), 1451–1465.

Laposky, A. D., Bass, J., Kohsaka, A., & Turek, F. W. (2008). Sleep and circadian rhythms: Key components in the regulation of energy metabolism. *FEBS Letters, 582*(1), 142–151.

Larkin, K., Resko, J. A., Stormshak, F., Stellflug, J. N., & Roselli, C. E. (2002, November). Neuroanatomical correlates of sex and sexual partner preference in sheep. (Program No. 383.1). Retrieved March 5, 2003, from Society for Neuroscience, *2002 Abstract Viewer/Itinerary Planner* Web site: http://sfn.scholarone.com/itin2002/index.html.

Larkin, M. (1997a). *What causes head pain in migraine.* Retrieved June 4, 2002, from the American Medical Association Web site: http://www.ama-assn.org/special/migraine/newsline/briefing/pain.htm.

Larkin, M. (1997b). *The role of serotonin in migraine.* Retrieved June 4, 2002, from the American Medical Association Web site: http://www.ama-assn.org/special/migraine/newsline/briefing/serotoni.htm.

Lashley, K. (1929). *Brain mechanisms and intelligence.* Chicago: University of Chicago Press.

Lasser, K., Boyd, J. W., Woolhandler, S., Himmelstein, D. U., McCormick, D., & Bor, D. H. (2000). Smoking and mental illness: A population-based prevalence study. *Journal of the American Medical Association, 284,* 2606.

Laumann, E. O., Paik, A., Glasser, D. B., Kang, J.–H., Wang, T., Levinson, B., et al. (2006). A cross-national study of subjective sexual well-being among older women and men: Findings from the global study of sexual attitudes and behaviors. *Archives of Sexual Behavior, 35*(2), 145–161(117).

Lavie, P. (1998). *The enchanted world of sleep.* New Haven, CT: Yale University Press.

Lavie, P., & Kripke, D. F. (1981). Ultradian circa 1.5-hour rhythms: A multioscillatory system. *Life Sciences, 29,* 2445–2450.

Lawrie, S. M., Whalley, H. C., Job, D. E., & Johnstone, E. C. (2003). Structural and functional abnormalities of the amygdala in schizophrenia. *Annals of the New York Academy of Sciences, 985,* 445–460.

Le Courteur, A., Bailey, A., Goode, S., Pickles, A., Robertson, S., Gottesman, I., et al. (1996). A broader phenotype of autism: The clinical spectrum in twins. *Journal of Child Psychology and Psychiatry, 37,* 785–801.

Lean, M. E., James, W. P., Jennings, G., & Trayhurn, P. (1986). Brown adipose tissue uncoupling protein content in human infants, children and adults. *Clinical Science, 71,* 291–297.

LeBlanc, S. A. (2003). Constant battles: The myth of the peaceful, noble savage. New York: St. Martin's Press.

LeDoux, J. (1993). Emotional memory systems in the brain. *Behavioral Brain Research, 58,* 69–79.

LeDoux, J. (1994). Emotion, memory and the brain. *Scientific American, 270,* 50–57.

LeDoux, J. E. (2000). Emotion circuits in the brain. *Annual Review of Neuroscience, 23,* 155–184.

LeDoux, J. E., Iwata, J., Pearl, D., & Reis, D. J. (1986). Disruption of auditory but not visual learning by destruction of intrinsic neurons in the rat medial geniculate body. *Brain Research, 371,* 395–399.

LeDoux, J. E., Ruggiero, D. A., Forest, R., Stornetta, R., & Reis, D. J. (1987). Topographic organization of convergent projections to the thalamus from the inferior colliculus and spinal cord in the rat. *Journal of Comparative Neurology, 264,* 123–146.

Lee, C.-K., Weindruch, R., & Prolla, T. A. (2000). Gene-expression profile of the ageing brain in mice. *Nature Genetics, 25,* 294–297.

Lee, G. P., Meador, K. J., Loring, D. W., Allison, J. D., Brown, W. S., Paul, L. K., et al. (2004). Neural substrates of emotion as revealed by functional magnetic resonance imaging. *Cognitive and Behavioral Neurology, 17*(1), 9–17.

Lee, K. H., & Thompson, R. F. (2006). Multiple memory mechanisms in the cerebellum? *Neuron, 51*(6), 680–682.

Lehman, A. F., & Steinwachs, D. M. (1998). Patterns of usual care for schizophrenia: Initial results from the Schizophrenia Patient Outcomes Research Team (PORT) Client Survey. *Schizophrenia Bulletin, 24,* 11–20.

Leirer, V. O., Yesavage, J. A., & Morrow, D. G. (1991). Marijuana carry-over effects on aircraft pilot performance. *Journal of the American Medical Association, 265,* 2796.

Leonard, B. E. (1992). Sub-types of serotonin receptors: Biochemical changes and pharmacological consequences. *International Clinical Psychopharmacology, 7*(1), 13–21.

Lepage, M., Habib, R., & Tulving, E. (1998). Hippocampal PET activations of memory encoding and retrieval: The HIPER model. *Hippocampus, 8,* 313–322.

Leranth, C., Roth, R. H., Elswoth, J. D., Naftolin, F., Horvath, T. L., & Redmond, D. E. (2000). Estrogen is essential for maintaining nigrostriatal dopamine neurons in primates: Implications for Parkinson's disease and memory. *Journal of Neuroscience, 20,* 8604–8609.

LeVay, S. (1991). A difference in hypothalamic structure between heterosexual and homosexual men. *Science, 253,* 1034–1037.

LeVay, S. (2000). *Sexual orientation: The science and its social impact.* Retrieved January 25, 2001, from http://hometown.aol.com/slevay/page6.html.

Levenson, J., Weeber, E., Selcher, J. C., Kategaya, L. S., Sweatt, J. D., & Eskin, A. (2002). Long-term potentiation and contextual fear conditioning increase neuronal glutamate uptake. *Nature Neuroscience, 5,* 155–161.

Levenson, R. W., & Ruef, A. M. (1992). Empathy: A physiological substrate. *Journal of Personality and Social Psychology, 63,* 234–246.

Levenson, R. W., Ekman, P., & Friesen, W. V. (1990). Voluntary facial action generates emotion-specific autonomic nervous system activity. *Psychophysiology, 27,* 363–384.

Levin, E. D., & Rose, J. E. (1995). Acute and chronic nicotine interactions with dopamine systems and working memory performance. *Annals of the New York Academy of Sciences, 757,* 245–252.

Levin, H. S., Gary, H. E., High, W. M., Mattis, S., Ruff, R. M., Eisenberg, H. M., et al. (1987). Minor head injury and the postconcussional syndrome: Methodological issues in outcome studies. In H. S. Levin, J. Grafman, & H. M. Eisenberg (Eds.), *Neurobehavioral recovery from head injury* (pp. 262–275). New York: Oxford University Press.

Levin, L. I., Munger, K. L., Rubertone, M. V., Peck, C. A., Lennette, E. T., Spiegelman, D., et al. (2005). Temporal relationship between elevation of Epstein-Barr virus antibody titers and initial onset of neurological symptoms in multiple sclerosis. *Journal of the American Medical Association (JAMA), 293*(20), 2496–2500.

Levin, M. (2002). *Chemotherapy for brain tumors.* Retrieved June 3, 2002, from http://virtualtrials.com/levin1.cfm.

Levitan, R. D. (2007). The chronobiology and neurobiology of winter seasonal affective disorder. *Dialogues in Clinical Neuroscience, 9*(3), 315–324.

Levy-Lahad, E., Wasco, W., Poorkaj, P., Romano, D. M., Oshima, J., Pettingell, W. H., et al. (1995). Candidate gene for the chromosome 1 familial Alzheimer's disease locus. *Science, 269,* 973–977.

Lewinsohn, P. M., Klein, D. N., & Seeley, J. R. (1995). Bipolar disorders in a community sample of older adolescents: Prevalence, phenomenology, comorbidity, and course. *Journal of the American Academy of Child and Adolescent Psychiatry, 34,* 454–463.

Lewy, A. J. (2007). Melatonin and human chronobiology. *Cold Spring Harbor Symposia on Quantitative Biology, 72,* 623–636.

Lewy, A. J., Wehr, T. A., Goodwin, F. K., Newsome, D. A., & Markey, S. P. (1980). Light suppresses melatonin secretion in humans. *Science, 210*(4475), 1267–1269.

Ley, R. E., Turnbaugh, P. J., Klein, S., & Gordon, J. I. (2006). Microbial ecology: Human gut microbes associated with obesity. *Nature, 444*(7122), 1022–1023.

Ley, R., & Bryden, M. P. (1982). A dissociation of right and left hemispheric effects for recognizing emotional tone and verbal content. *Brain and Cognition, 1,* 3–9.

Li, B., Nolte, L. A., Ju, J.-S., Han, D. H., Coleman, T., Holloszy, J. O., et al. (2000). Skeletal muscle respiratory uncoupling prevents diet-induced obesity and insulin resistance in mice. *Nature Medicine, 6,* 1115–1120.

Li, M., Ona, V. O., Guégan, C., Chen, M., Jackson-Lewis, V., Andrews, L. J., et al. (2000). Functional role of caspase-1 and caspase-3 in an ALS transgenic mouse model. *Science, 288,* 335–339.

Li, S., & Tator, C. H. (2000). Action of locally administered NMDA and AMPA/kainate receptor antagonists in spinal cord injury. *Neurological Research, 22,* 171–180.

Li, W., & Qiu, Y. (2007). Relation of supplementary feeding to resumptions of menstruation and ovulation in lactating postpartum women. *Chinese Medical Journal, 120*(10), 868–870.

Li, W., Moallem, I., Paller, K. A., & Gottfried, J. A. (2007). Subliminal smells can guide social preferences. *Psychological Science, 18*(12), 1044–1049.

Li, Y., Field, P. M., & Raisman, G. (1997). Repair of adult rat corticospinal tract by transplants of olfactory ensheathing cells. *Science, 277,* 2000–2002.

Liao, R. M., & Yeh, C. C. (2000). Influences on water intake in the rat after lesions of the septal subareas. *Proceedings of the National Science Council of the Republic of China, B, 24,* 26–32.

Liben, L. S., & Golbeck, S. L. (1980). Sex differences in performance on Piagetian spatial tasks: Differences in competence or performance. *Child Development, 51,* 594–597.

Liberatore, G. T., Samson, A., Bladin, C., Schleuning, W. D., & Medcalf, R. L. (2003). Vampire bat salivary plasminogen activator (desmoteplase): A unique fibrinolytic enzyme that does not promote neurodegeneration. *Stroke, 34,* 537–543.

Liberles, S. D., & Buck, L. B. (2006). A second class of chemosensory receptors in the olfactory epithelium. *Nature, 442*(7103), 645–650.

Liberski, P. (2008). The tubulovesicular structures: The ultrastructural hallmark for all prion diseases [Review]. *Acta Neurobiologiae Experimentalis, 68*(1), 113–121.

Liederman, J., Kantrowitz, L., & Flannery, K. (2005). Male vulnerability to reading disability is not likely to be a myth: A call for new data. *Journal of Learning Disabilities, 38*(2), 109–129.

Light, K. C., Grewen, K. M., & Amico, J. A. (2005). More frequent partner hugs and higher oxytocin levels are linked to lower blood pressure and heart rate in premenopausal women. *Biological Psychology, 69*(1), 5–21.

Lilenfeld, L., Ringham, R., Kalarchian, M., & Marcus, M. (2008). A family history study of binge-eating disorder. *Comprehensive Psychiatry, 49*(3), 247–254.

Lilly, I. C. (1967). *The mind of the dolphin.* New York: Doubleday.

Lim, C. L., & Mackinnon, L. T. (2006). The roles of exercise-induced immune system disturbances in the pathology of heat stroke: The dual pathway model of heat stroke. *Sports Medicine, 36*(1), 39–64.

Lima, D. P., Simão Filho, C., Abib Sde, C., & de Figueiredo, L. F. (2008). Quality of life and neuropsychological changes in mild head trauma. Late analysis and correlation with S100B protein and cranial CT scan performed at hospital admission. *Injury, 39*(5), 604–611.

Lin, J. S., Hou, Y., & Jouvet, M. (1996). Potential brain neuronal targets for amphetamine-, methylphenidate-, and modafinil-induced wakefulness, evidenced by c-fos immunocytochemistry in the cat. *Proceedings of the National Academy of Sciences of the United States of America, 93,* 14128–14133.

Lin, Y., Shea, S. D., & Katz, L. C. (2006). Representation of natural stimuli in the rodent main olfactory bulb. *Neuron, 50*(6), 937–949.

Lind, R. W., & Johnson, A. K. (1982). Central and peripheral mechanisms mediating angiotensin-induced thirst. In E. Ganten, M. Printz, M. I. Phillips, & B. A. Schölkens (Eds.), *The renin angiotensin system in the brain* (pp. 353–364). Berlin: Springer-Verlag.

Linden, M. G., Bender, B. G., & Robinson, A. (1996). Intrauterine diagnosis of sex chromosome aneuploidy. *Obstetrics and Gynecology, 87,* 468–475.

Lindstrom, H. A., Fritsch, T., Petot, G., Smyth, K. A., Chen, C. H., Debanne, S. M., et al. (2005). The relationships between television viewing in midlife and the development of Alzheimer's disease in a case-control study. *Brain and Cognition, 58,* 157–165.

Lindvall, O., Widner, H., Rehncrona, S., Brundin, P., Odin, P., Gustavii, B., et al. (1992). Transplantation of fetal dopamine neurons in Parkinson's disease: One-year clinical and neurophysiological observations in two patients with putaminal implants. *Annals of Neurology, 31,* 155–165.

Ling, W. Y., Robichaud, A., Zayid, I., Wrixon, W., & MacLeod, S. C. (1979). Mode of action of dl-norgestrel and ethinylestradiol combination in postcoital contraception. *Fertility and Sterility, 32,* 297–302.

Ling, W. Y., Wrixon, W., Zayid, I., Acorn, T., Popat, R., & Wilson, E. (1983). Mode of action of dl-norgestrel and ethinylestradiol combination in postcoital contraception: II. Effect of postovulatory administration on ovarian function and endometrium. *Fertility and Sterility, 39,* 292–297.

Linnoila, V. M., & Virkkunen, M. (1992). Aggression, suicidality, and serotonin. *Journal of Clinical Psychiatry, 53,* 46–51.

Linszen, D. H., Dingemans, P. M., & Lenior, M. E. (1994). Cannabis abuse and the course of recent-onset schizophrenic disorders. *Archives of General Psychiatry, 51,* 273–279.

Liu, Y., Gao, J.-H., Liu, H.-L., & Fox, P. T. (2000). The temporal response of the brain after eating revealed by functional MRI. *Nature, 405,* 1058–1062.

Livingstone, M. S., & Hubel, D. H. (1984). Anatomy and physiology of a color system in the primate visual cortex. *Journal of Neuroscience, 4,* 309–356.

Livshits, G., Kato, B. S., Wilson, S. G., & Spector, T. D. (2007). Linkage of genes to total lean body mass in normal women. *Journal of Clinical Endocrinology and Metabolism, 92*(8), 3171–3176.

Lloyd-Richardson, E., Perrine, N., Dierker, L., & Kelley, M. L. (2007). Characteristics and functions of non-suicidal self-injury in a community sample of adolescents. *Psychological Medicine, 37,* 1183–1192.

Lockwood, D. R., Kwon, B., Smith, J. C., & Houpt, T. A. (2003). Behavioral effects of static high magnetic fields on unrestrained and restrained mice. *Physiology and Behavior, 78,* 635–640.

Loeb, G. E., & Ghez, C. (2000). The motor unit and muscle action. In E. R. Kandel, J. H. Schwartz, & T. M. Jessell (Eds.), *Principles of neural science* (4th ed., pp. 674–694). New York: McGraw-Hill.

Loftus, E. F., & Davis, D. (2006). Recovered memories. *Annual Review of Clinical Psychology, 2,* 469–498.

Loftus, E. F., & Polage, D. C. (1999). Repressed memories. When are they real? How are they false? *The Psychiatric Clinics of North America, 22*(1), 61–70.

Loftus, T. M., Jaworsky, D. E., Frehywot, G. L., Townsend, C. A., Ronnett, G. V., Lane, M. D., et al. (2000). Reduced food intake and body weight in mice treated with fatty acid synthase inhibitors. *Science, 288,* 2379–2381.

Logan, C. G., & Grafton, S. T. (1995). Functional anatomy of human eyeblink conditioning determined with regional cerebral glucose metabolism and positron-emission tomography. *Proceedings of the National Academy of Sciences of the United States of America, 92,* 7500–7504.

Lombion-Pouthier, S., Vandel, P., Nezelof, S., Haffen, E., & Millot, J. L. (2006). Odor perception in patients with mood disorders. *Journal of Affective Disorders, 90*(2–3), 187–191.

London, R. S. (1993). A comparison of levonorgestrel implants with depo-medroxyprogesterone acetate injections for contraception. *Journal of the Society of Obstetricians and Gynaecologists, 15,* 925–928.

Lonsdorf, E. V., & Hopkins, W. D. (2005). Wild chimpanzees show population-level handedness for tool use. *Proceedings of the National Academy of Sciences of the United States of America (PNAS), 102*(35), 12634–12638.

Lorenz, K. (1952). *King Solomon's ring.* New York: Crowell.

Ludwig, D. S., & Ebbeling, C. B. (2001). Type 2 diabetes mellitus in children: Primary care and public health considerations. *Journal of the American Medical Association, 286*(12), 1427–1430.

Luria, A. R. (1968). *The mind of a mnemonist.* New York: Avon Books.

Lykken, D. T. (1982). Fearlessness: Its carefree charm and deadly risks. *Psychology Today, 16,* 20–28.

Maas, J. B., Wherry, M. L., Axelrod, D. J., Hogan, B. R., & Bloomin, J. (1998). *Power sleep: The revolutionary program that prepares your mind for peak performance.* New York: Villard.

MacArthur, D. G., & North, K. N. (2007). ACTN3: A genetic influence on muscle function and athletic performance. *Exercise and Sport Sciences Reviews, 35*(1), 30–34.

Mackowiak, P. A., & Boulant, J. A. (1996). Fever's glass ceiling. *Clinical Infectious Diseases, 22*(3), 525–536.

MacLean, P. (1949). Psychosomatic disease and the "visceral brain": Recent developments bearing on the Papez theory of emotion. *Psychosomatic Medicine, 11,* 338–353.

Macleod, J., Davey Smith, G., Heslop, P., Metcalfe, C., Carroll, D., & Hart, C. (2002). Psychological stress and cardiovascular disease: Empirical demonstration of bias in a prospective observational study of Scottish men. *British Medical Journal, 324,* 1247.

Maggard, M. A., Shugarman, L. R., Suttorp, M., Maglione, M., Sugerman, H. J., Livingston, E. H., et al. (2005). Meta-analysis: Surgical treatment of obesity. *Annals of Internal Medicine, 142*(7), 547–559.

Magnusson, A., Axelsson, J., Karlsson, M. M., & Oskarsson, H. (2000). Lack of seasonal mood change in the Icelandic population: Results of a cross-sectional study. *American Journal of Psychiatry, 157,* 234–238.

Maguire, E. A., Frackowiak, R. S., & Frith, C. D. (1996). Learning to find your way: A role for the human hippocampal formation. *Proceedings of the Royal Society of London, B, Biological Science, 263,* 1745–1750.

Maher, B. (2008). Poll results: Look who's doping. *Nature, 452,* 674–675.

Mair, W. G. P., Warrington, E. K., & Wieskrantz, L. (1979). Memory disorder in Korsakoff's psychosis. *Brain, 102,* 749–783.

Malatesta, G. Z. (1982). The expression and regulation of emotion: A lifespan perspective. In T. Field & A. Fogel (Eds.), *Emotion and early interaction* (pp. 1–24). Hillsdale, NJ: Erlbaum.

Malatesta, G. Z., & Haviland, J. (1982). Learning display rules: The socialization of emotional expression in infancy. *Child Development, 53,* 991–1003.

Malatesta, G. Z., & Haviland, J. (1985). Signals, symbols, and socialization. In M. Lewis & C. Saarni (Eds.), *The socialization of emotions* (pp. 89–116). New York: Plenum.

Malberg, J. E., Eisch, A. J., Nestler, E. J., & Duman, R. S. (2000). Chronic antidepressant treatment increases neurogenesis in adult rat hippocampus. *The Journal of Neuroscience, 20*(24), 9104–9110.

Malloy, M. H., & Freeman, D. H. (2004). Age at death, season, and day of death as indicators of the effect of the back to sleep program on sudden infant death syndrome in the United States, 1992–1999. *Archives of Pediatric and Adolescent Medicine, 158,* 359–365.

Mantyh, P. W., Rogers, S. D., Honore, P., Allen, B. J., Ghilardi, J. R., Li, J., et al. (1997). Inhibition of hyperalgesia by ablation of lamina I spinal neurons expressing the substance P receptor. *Science, 278,* 275–279.

Maquet, P. (1999). Brain mechanisms of sleep: Contribution of neuroimaging techniques. *Journal of Psychopharmacology, 13(4) Suppl 1,* S25–28.

Marazziti, D., & Dell'osso, M. C. (2008). The role of oxytocin in neuropsychiatric disorders. *Current Medicinal Chemistry, 15*(7), 698–704.

Mark, V. H., & Ervin, F. R. (1970). *Violence and the brain.* New York: Harper & Row.

Marr, D. (1969). A theory of cerebellar cortex. *J. Physiol. (Lond.) 202,* 437–471.

Martin, A., Wiggs, C. L., Ungerleider, L. G., & Haxby, J. V. (1996). Neural correlates of category-specific knowledge. *Nature, 379,* 649–652.

Martins, R. S., Siqueira, M. G., Santos, M. T., Zanon-Collange, N., & Moraes, O. J. (2003). Prognostic factors and treatment of penetrating gunshot wounds to the head. *Surgical Neurology, 60*(2), 98–104; discussion, 104.

Martland, H. W. (1928). Punch drunk. *Journal of the American Medical Association, 91,* 1103–1107.

Mason, W. A., Capitanio, J. P., Machado, C. J., Mendoza, S. P., & Amaral, D. G. (2006). Amygdalectomy and responsiveness to novelty in rhesus monkeys (Macaca mulatta): generality and individual consistency of effects. *Emotion, 6*(1), 73–81.

Massachusetts General Hospital/Harvard Medical School. (2002). *Malignant brain tumors and neuro-oncology resources.* Retrieved June 3, 2002, from http://neurosurgery.mgh.harvard.edu/nonc-hp.htm.

Masters, W. H., & Johnson, V. E. (1970). *Human sexual inadequacy.* Boston: Little, Brown.

Mataro, M. (1997). Magnetic resonance imaging measurement of the caudate nucleus in adolescents with attention-deficit hyperactivity disorder and its relationship with neuropsychological and behavioral measures. *Journal of the American Medical Association, 278,* 1720.

Mathews, G. A., Fane, B. A., Pasterski, V. L., Conway, G. S., Brook, C., & Hines, M. (2004). Androgenic influences on neural asymmetry: Handedness and language lateralization in individuals with congenital adrenal hyperplasia. *Psychoneuroendocrinology, 29*(6), 810–822.

Matser, E. J. T., Kessels, A. G., Jordan, B. D., Lezak, M. D., & Troost, J. (1998). Chronic traumatic brain injury in professional soccer players. *Neurology, 51,* 791–796.

Matser, E. J. T., Kessels, A. G., Lezak, M. D., Jordan, B. D., & Troost, J. (1999). Neuropsychological impairment in amateur soccer players. *Journal of the American Medical Association, 282,* 971–973.

Matthes, H. W., Maldonalo, R., Simonin, R., Valverde, O., Slowe, S., Kitchen, I., et al. (1996). Loss of morphineinduced analgesia, reward effect and withdrawal symptoms in mice lacking the mu-opioid-receptor gene. *Nature, 383,* 819–823.

Matuszczyk, J. V., Fernandez-Guasti, A., & Larsen, K. (1988). Sexual orientation, proceptivity, and receptivity in the male rat as a function of neonatal hormonal manipulation. *Hormones and Behavior, 22,* 362–378.

Maxwell, J. S., & Davidson, R. J. (2007). Emotion as motion: Asymmetries in approach and avoidant actions. *Psychological Science, 18*(12), 1113–1119.

Mayer, J. (1955). Regulation of energy intake and the body weight: The glucostatic theory and the lipostatic hypothesis. *Annals of the New York Academy of Sciences, 63,* 15–43.

Mayford, M., Bach, M. E., Huang, Y.-Y., Wang, L., Hawkins, R. D., & Kandel, E. R. (1996). Control of memory formation through regulated expression of a CaMKII transgene. *Science, 274,* 1678–1683.

Mayo Clinic. (2001). *What is encephalitis?* Retrieved May 31, 2002, from the Mayo Clinic Web site: http://www.mayoclinic.com/invoke.cfm?id=DS00226.

Mazer, N. A. (2002). Testosterone deficiency in women: Etiologies, diagnosis, and emerging treatments. *International Journal of Fertility and Women's Medicine, 47,* 77–86.

Mazur, A., & Booth, A. (1998). Testosterone and dominance in men. *Behavioral and Brain Sciences, 21,* 353–363.

Mazur, A., & Michalek, J. (1998). Marriage, divorce and male testosterone. *Social Forces, 77,* 315–331.

Mazur, A., & Mueller, E. (1996). Facial dominance. In A. Somit & S. Peterson (Eds.), *Research in biopolitics* (Vol. 4, pp. 99–111). London: JAI Press.

McCabe, S. E., Brower, K. J., West, B. T., Nelson, T. F., & Wechsler, H. (2007). Trends in non-medical use of anabolic steroids by U.S. college students: results from four national surveys. *Drug and Alcohol Dependence, 90*(2–3), 243–251.

McCann, J. (2000, September 18). Movement disorders: Less of a black box. *Scientist, 14,* 14.

McCann, L., & Holmes, D. (1984). Influence of aerobic exercise on depression. *Journal of Personality and Social Psychology, 46,* 1142–1147.

McCann, U. D., Szabo, Z., Scheffel, U., Dannals, R. F., & Ricaurte, G. A. (1999). Positron emission tomographic evidence of toxic effect of MDMA ("Ecstasy") on brain serotonin neurons in human beings. *Lancet, 352,* 1433–1437.

McCarley, R. W. (2007). Neurobiology of REM and NREM sleep. *Sleep Medicine, 8*(4), 302–330.

McCarthy, R. A., & Warrington, E. K. (1990). *Cognitive neuropsychology: A clinical introduction.* San Diego, CA: Academic Press.

McClung, C. A. (2007). Circadian genes, rhythms and the biology of mood disorders. *Pharmacology and Therapeutics, 114*(2), 222–232.

McCoy, N., & Pitino, L. (2002). Pheromonal influences on sociosexual behavior in young women. *Physiology and Behavior, 75,* 367–375.

McCrory, P. (2003). Super athletes or gene cheats? *British Journal of Sports Medicine, 37,* 192–193.

McEwen, B. S., Luine, V. N., & Fischette, C. T. (1988). Developmental actions of hormones: From receptors to function. In S. S. Easter, Jr., K. F. Barald, & B. M. Carlson (Eds.), *From message to mind: Directions in developmental neurobiology* (pp. 272–287). Sunderland, MA: Sinauer.

McFadden, D., & Pasanen, E. G. (1999). Spontaneous otoacoustic emissions in heterosexuals, homosexuals, and bisexuals. *Journal of the Acoustical Society of America, 105,* 2403–2413.

McGaugh, J. L. (1992). Neuromodulatory regulation of memory: Role of the amygdaloid complex. *International Journal of Psychology, 27,* 403.

McGee, A. M., & Skinner, M. (1987). Facial asymmetry and the attribution of personality traits. *British Journal of Social Psychology, 26,* 181–184.

McGuckin, C. P., Forraz, N., Baradez, M. O., Navran, S., Zhao, J., Urban, R., et al. (2005). Production of stem cells with embryonic characteristics from human umbilical cord blood. *Cell Proliferation, 38*(4), 245–255.

McGuffin, P., Reveley, A., & Holland, A. (1982). Identical triplets: Non-identical psychosis? *British Journal of Psychiatry, 140,* 1–6.

McGuire, P. (2000). New hope for people with schizophrenia. *APA Monitor, 31*(2). Retrieved December 15, 2000, from http://www.apa.org/monitor/feb00/schizophrenia.html.

McGuire, P. K., Silbersweig, D. A., & Frith, C. D. (1996). Functional neuroanatomy of verbal self-monitoring. *Brain: A journal of neurology, 119,* 907–917.

McKetin, R., McLaren, J., Lubman, D. I., & Hides, L. (2006). The prevalence of psychotic symptoms among methamphetamine users. *Addiction, 101*(10), 1473–1478.

McLachlan, R. I., Robertson, D. M., Pruysers, E., Ugoni, A., Matsumoto, A. M., Anawalt, B. D., et al. (2004). Relationship between serum gonadotropins and spermatogenic suppression in men undergoing steroidal contraceptive treatment. *Journal of Clinical Endocrinology and Metabolism, 89,* 142–149.

McManus, C. (1999). Handedness, cerebral lateralization, and the evolution of handedness. In M. C. Corballis & S. E. G. Lea (Eds.), *The descent of mind* (pp. 194–217). Oxford, UK: Oxford University Press.

McManus, I. C. (1985). Handedness, language dominance and aphasia: A genetic model. *Psychological Medicine. Monograph Supplement, 8,* 1–40.

McNeil, T. F., Cantor-Graae, E., & Weinberger, D. R. (2000). Relationship of obstetric complications and differences in size of brain structures in monozygotic twin pairs discordant for schizophrenia. *American Journal of Psychiatry, 157,* 203–212.

McNeilly, A. S. (2001). Neuroendocrine changes and fertility in breast-feeding women. *Progress in Brain Research, 133,* 207–214.

McNeilly, A. S., Glasier, A., Jonassen, J., & Howeic, P. W. (1982). Evidence for a direct inhibition of ovarian function by PRL. *Journal of Reproduction and Fertility, 65,* 559–569.

McNulty, J. K., Neff, L. A., & Karney, B. R. (2008). Beyond initial attraction: Physical attractiveness in newlywed marriage. *Journal of Family Psychology, 22*(1), 135–143.

Meddis, R., Pearson, A., & Langford, G. (1973). An extreme case of healthy insomnia. *Electroencephalography and Clinical Neurophysiology, 35,* 213–214.

Meldrum, B. S., & Rogawski, M. A. (2007). Molecular targets for antiepileptic drug development. *Neurotherapeutics, 4*(1), 18–61.

Melke, J., Goubran Botros, H., Chaste, P., Betancur, C., Nygren, G., Anckarsater, H., et al. (2007). Abnormal melatonin synthesis in autism spectrum disorders. *Molecular Psychiatry, 13*(1), 90–98.

Meltzer, C. C., Kondziolka, D., Villemagne, V. L., Wechsler, L., Goldstein, S., Thulborn, K. R., et al. (2001). Serial [18F] fluorodeoxyglucose positron emission tomography after human neuronal implantation for stroke. *Neurosurgery, 49,* 586–591.

Meltzer, H. Y. (2000). Side effects of antipsychotic medications: Physician's choice of medication and patient compliance. *Journal of Clinical Psychiatry, 61,* 3–4.

Melzack, R. (1992). Phantom limbs. *Scientific American, 266,* 120–126.

Melzack, R., & Wall, P. D. (1965). Pain mechanisms: A new history. *Science, 150,* 971–979.

Mendoza, J. (2007). Circadian clocks: Setting time by food. *Journal of Neuroendocrinology, 19*(2), 127–137.

Meningitis Foundation of America. (2002). *Meningococcal meningitis in college students.* Retrieved May 31, 2002, from the Meningitis Foundation of America Web site: http://www.musa.org/men_coll.html.

Meningitis Trust. (2002). *What is meningitis?* Retrieved May 31, 2002, from the Meningitis Trust Web site: http://www.meningitis-trust.org.uk/frame.htm.

Mennella, J. A., & Beauchamp, G. K. (2005). Understanding the origin of flavor preferences. *Chemical Senses, 30, Supplement 1,* i242–i243.

Mennella, J. A., Jagnow, C. P., & Beauchamp, G. K. (2001). Prenatal and postnatal flavor learning by human infants. *Pediatrics, 107,* E88.

Mental Health Research Institute of Victoria. (2003). *Auditory Hallucinations Project.* Retrieved May 26, 2003, from the Applied Schizophrenia Division Web site: http://www.mhri.edu.au/asd/.

Menzies, L., Chamberlain, S. R., Laird, A. R., Thelen, S. M., Sahakian, B. J., & Bullmore, E. T. (2008). Integrating evidence from neuroimaging and neuropsychological studies of obsessive-compulsive disorder: The orbitofronto-striatal model revisited. *Neuroscience and Biobehavioral Reviews, 32*(3), 525–549.

Merims, D., & Giladi, N. (2008). Dopamine dysregulation syndrome, addiction and behavioral changes in Parkinson's disease. *Parkinsonism & Related Disorders, 14*(4), 273–280.

Merrick, J., Kandel, I., & Morad, M. (2004). Trends in autism. *International Journal of Adolescent Medicine and Health, 16,* 75–78.

Merritt, L. L., Martin, B. R., Walters, C., Lichtman, A. H., & Damaj, M. I. (2008). The endogenous cannabinoid system modulates nicotine reward and dependence. *Journal of Pharmacology and Expermental Therapeutics, 326*(2), 483–492.

Merzenich, M. M., & Jenkins, W. M. (1993). Reorganization of cortical representations of the hand following alterations of skin inputs induced by nerve injury, skin island transfers, and experience. *Journal of Hand Therapy, 6,* 89–104.

Merzenich, M. M., Jenkins, W. M., Johnston, P., Schreiner, C., Miller, S. L., & Tallal, P. (1996). Temporal processing deficits of language-learning impaired children ameliorated by training. *Science, 271,* 77–81.

Meyer, W. J., III, Cole, C., & Emory, E. (1992). Depo Provera treatment for sex offending behavior: An evaluation of outcome. *Bulletin of the American Academy of Psychiatry and the Law, 20,* 249–259.

Meyer-Bahlburg, H. F., Dolezal, C., Baker, S. W., & New, M. I. (2008). Sexual orientation in women with classical or non-classical congenital adrenal hyperplasia as a function of degree of prenatal androgen excess. *Archives of Sexual Behavior, 37*(1), 85–99.

Migraine as a women's issue: Will research and new treatments help? (1998). *Journal of the American Medical Association.* Retrieved June 4, 2002, from the American Medical Association Web site: http://www.ama-assn.org/special/migraine/newline/special/jmn80154.htm.

Milgram, S. (1963). Behavioral study of obedience. *Journal of Abnormal and Social Psychology, 67,* 371–378.

Milin, R., Manion, I., Dare, G., & Walker, S. (2008). Prospective assessment of cannabis withdrawal in adolescents with cannabis dependence: A pilot study. *Journal of the American Academy of Child & Adolescent Psychiatry, 47*(2), 174–178.

Millar, J. K., Wilson-Annan, J. C., Anderson, S., Christie, S., Taylor, M. S., Semple, C. A. M., et al. (2000). Disruption of two novel genes by a translocation cosegregating with schizophrenia. *Human Molecular Genetics, 9,* 1415–1423.

Millecamps, M., Centeno, M., Berra, H., Rudick, C., Lavarello, S., Tkatch, T., et al. (2007). d-Cycloserine reduces neuropathic pain behavior through limbic NMDA-mediated circuitry. *Pain, 132*(1–2), 108–128.

Miller, A., & Adeli, K. (2008). Dietary fructose and the metabolic syndrome. *Current Opinion in Gastroenterology, 24*(2), 204–209.

Miller, B. L., Cummings, J., Mishkin, F., Boone, K., Prince, F., Ponton, M., et al. (1998). Emergence of artistic talent in frontotemporal dementia. *Neurology, 51,* 978–982.

Miller, G. (2004). Forgetting and remembering. Learning to forget. *Science, 304*(5667), 34–36.

Miller, G. A. (1956). The magical number seven, plus or minus two: Some limits on our capacity for processing information. *Psychological Review, 63,* 81–97.

Miller, G. A., & Gildea, P. M. (1987). How children learn words. *Scientific American, 257,* 94–99.

Miller, I. J., Jr., & Reedy, F. E. (1990). Variations in human taste bud density and taste intensity perception. *Physiology and Behavior, 47,* 1213–1219.

Miller, J. J. (2003, May 20). War of all against all. *The Wall Street Journal.* Retrieved May28,2003,fromhttp://online.wsj.com/article_email/0,,SB10533961275571 6900-H9jeoNplaZ2m52tZH6I baWHm4,00.html.

Millward, C., Ferriter, M., Calver, S., & Connell-Jones, G. (2008). Gluten- and casein-free diets for autistic spectrum disorder. Cochrane database of systematic reviews (Online) (2): CD003498.

Milner, A. D., & Goodale, M. A. (1995). *The visual brain in action.* New York: Oxford University Press.

Milner, B. (1966). Amnesia following operation on the temporal lobes. In C. W. M. Whitty & O. L. Zangwill (Eds.), *Amnesia* (pp. 109–133). London: Butterworth.

Milunsky, A. (2004). *Genetic disorders and the fetus: Diagnosis, prevention and treatment* (5th ed.). Baltimore, MD: The Johns Hopkins University Press.

Mirnics, K., Middleton, F. A., Marquez, A., Lewis, D. A., & Levitt, P. (2000). Molecular characterization of schizophrenia viewed by microarray analysis of gene expression in prefrontal cortex. *Neuron, 28,* 53.

Mirsky, A. F., DeLisi, L. E., Buchsbaum, M. S., Quinn, O. W., Schwerdt, P., Siever, L. J., et al. (1984). The Genain quadruplets: Psychological studies. *Psychiatry Research, 13,* 77–93.

Mishkin, M., & Appenzeller, T. (1987). The anatomy of memory. *Scientific American, 256,* 80–89.

Mobbs, D., Lau, H. C., Jones, O. D., & Frith, C. D. (2007). Law, responsibility, and the brain. *PLOS Biology, 5*(4), 0693–0700.

Modell, J. G., Rosenthal, N. E., Harriett, A. E., Krishen, A., Asgharian, A., Foster, V. J., et al. (2005). Seasonal affective disorder and its prevention by anticipatory treatment with bupropion XL. *Biological Psychiatry, 58*(8), 658–667.

Moffitt, T. E. (2005). The new look of behavioral genetics in developmental psychopathology: Gene-environment interplay in antisocial behaviors. *Psychological Bulletin, 131*(4), 533–554.

Moghaddam, B., & Adams, B. W. (1998). Reversal of phencyclidine effects by a group II metabotropic glutamate receptor agonist in rats. *Science, 281,* 1349–1352.

Mokdad, A. H., Ford, E. S., Bowman, B. A., Dietz, W. H., Vinicor, F., Bales, V. S., & Marks, J. S. (2003). Prevalence of obesity, diabetes, and obesity related health risk factors, 2001. *Journal of the American Medical Association, 289,* 76–79.

Moldofsky, H., & Scarisbrick, P. (1976). Induction of neurasthenic musculoskeletal pain syndrome by selective sleep stage deprivation. *Psychosomatic Medicine, 38,* 35–44.

Molina-Carballo, A., Fernandez-Tardaquila, E., Uberos-Fernandez, J., Seiquer, I., Contreras-Chova, F., & Munoz-Hoyos, A. (2007). Longitudinal study of the simultaneous secretion of melatonin and leptin during normal puberty. *Hormone Research, 68*(1), 11–19.

Møller, A. L., Hjaltason, O., Ivarsson, O., & Stefansson, S. B. (2006). The effects of repetitive transcranial magnetic stimulation on depressive symptoms and the P300 event-related potential. *Nordic Journal of Psychiatry, 60*(4), 282–285.

Møller, A. R. (2006). History of cochlear implants and auditory brainstem implants. *Advances in Otorhinolaryngology, 64,* 1–10.

Money, J. (1972). *Man and woman, boy and girl.* Baltimore, MD: Johns Hopkins.

Money, J., Schwartz, M., & Lewis, V. G. (1984). Adult erotosexual status and fetal hormonal masculinization and demasculinization: 46,XX congenital virilizing adrenal hyperplasia and 46,XY androgen–insensitivity syndrome compared. *Psychoneuroendocrinology, 9,* 405–414.

Moore, R., & Eichler, V. B. (1972). Loss of circadian adrenal corticosterone rhythm following suprachiasmatic lesions in the rat. *Brain Research, 42,* 201–206.

Morecraft, R. J., Louie, J. L., Herrick, J. L., & Stilwell-Morecraft, K. S. (2001). Cortical innervation of the facial nucleus in the non-human primate: A new interpretation of the effects of stroke and related subtotal brain trauma on the muscles of facial expression. *Brain, 124(Pt. 1),* 176–208.

Morgan, K. D., Dazzan, P., Orr, K. G., Hutchinson, G., Chitnis, X., Suckling, J., et al. (2007). Grey matter abnormalities in first-episode schizophrenia and affective psychosis. *British Journal of Psychiatry,* Supplement, 51, s111–116.

Morris, J. K., Alberman, E., Scott, C., & Jacobs, P. (2007). Is the prevalence of Klinefelter syndrome increasing? *European Journal of Human Genetics, 16*(2), 163–170.

Morris, J. M. (1953). The syndrome of testicular feminization in male pseudohermaphrodites. *American Journal of Obstetric Gynecology, 65,* 1192–1211.

Morris, J. S., Frith, C. D., Perrett, D. I., Rowland, D., Yong, A. N., Calder, A. J., et al. (1996). A different neural response in the human amygdala to fearful and happy facial expressions. *Nature, 383,* 812–815.

Morris, R. G., Anderson, E., Lynch, G. S., & Baudry, M. (1986). Selective impairment of learning and blockade of long-term potentiation by an N-methyl-D-aspartate receptor antagonist, AP5. *Nature, 319*(6056), 774–776.

Moruzzi, G., & Magoun, H. W. (1949). Brain stem reticular formation and activation of the EEG. *Electroencephalography and Clinical Neurophysiology, 1,* 455–473.

Moser, H. W., Ramey, C. T., & Leonard, C. O. (1990). Mental retardation. In A. E. H. Emery & D. L. Rimion (Eds.), *Principles and practice of medical genetics* (2nd ed., pp. 495–511). Edinburgh, UK: Churchill-Livingstone.

Mosso, A. (1881). *Ueber den Kreislauf des Blutes im menschlichen Gehirn.* Leipzig: Viet.

Mothet, J.-P., Parent, A. T., Wolosker, H., Brady, R. O., Linden, D. J., Ferris, C. D., et al. (2000). D-serine is an endogenous ligand for the glycine site of the N-methyl-d-aspartate receptor. *Proceedings of the National Academy of Sciences of the United States of America, 97,* 4926–4931.

Mountcastle, V. (1978). An organizing principle for cerebral function: The unit model and the distributed system. In G. M. Edelman & V. B. Mountcastle (Ed.), *The Mindful Brain.* Cambridge, MA: MIT Press.

Mueller, A. D., Pollock, M. S., Lieblich, S. E., Epp, J. R., Galea, L. A. M., & Mistlberger, R. E. (2008). Sleep deprivation can inhibit adult hippocampal neurogenesis independent of adrenal stress hormones. *American Journal of Physiology. Regulatory, Integrative and Comparative Physiology, 294*(5), R1693–1703.

Munson, J., Dawson, G., Abbott, R., Faja, S., Webb, S. J., Friedman, S. D., et al. (2006). Amygdalar volume and behavioral development in autism. *Archives of General Psychiatry, 63*(6), 686–693.

Murphy, K. D., Rose, M. W., Chinkes, D. L., Meyer, W. J., 3rd, Herndon, D. N., Hawkins, H. K., et al. (2007). The effects of gammahydroxybutyrate on hypermetabolism and wound healing in a rat model of large thermal injury. *Journal of Trauma, 63*(5), 1099–1107.

Murphy, S., Wylie, A. A., & Jirtle, R. (2001). Imprinting of *PEG3,* the human homologue of a mouse gene involved in nurturing behavior. *Genomics, 71,* 110–117.

Murray, E. A. (2007). The amygdala, reward and emotion. *Trends in Cognitive Sciences, 11*(11), 489–497.

Murray, E. A., & Izquierdo, A. (2007). Orbitofrontal cortex and amygdala contributions to affect and action in primates. *Annals of the New York Academy of Sciences, 1121,* 273–296.

Musso, M., Weiller, C., Kiebel, S., Muller, S. P., Bulau, P., & Rijntjes, M. (1999). Training-induced brain plasticity in aphasia. *Brain, 122,* 1781–1790.

Myers, D. (2001). *Psychology* (6th ed.). New York: Worth.

Myers, R. D., Wooten, M. H., Ames, C. D., & Nyce, J. W. (1995). Anorexic action of a new potential neuropeptide Y antagonist [D-Tyr27, 36, D-Thr32]-NPY (27–36) infused into the hypothalamus of the rat. *Brain Research Bulletin, 37,* 237–245.

Nabi, H., Kivimäki, M., Zins, M., Elovainio, M., Consoli, S. M., Cordier, S., et al. (2008). Does personality predict mortality? Results from the GAZEL French prospective cohort study. *International Journal of Epidemiology, 37*(2), 386–396.

Narr, K. L., Woods, R. P., Thompson, P. M., Szeszko, P., Robinson, D., Dimtcheva, T., et al. (2007). Relationships between IQ and regional cortical gray matter thickness in healthy adults. *Cerebral Cortex, 17*(9), 2163–2171.

Narumi, J., Miyazawa, S., Miyata, H., Suzuki, A., Kohsaka, S., & Kosugi, H. (1999). Analysis of human error in nursing care. *Accident: Analysis and Prevention, 31,* 625–629.

Nathans, J. (1989). The genes for color vision. *Scientific American, 260,* 42–49.

Nathanson, N. (1982). Eradication of poliomyelitis in the United States. *Reviews of Infectious Diseases, 4,* 940–945.

National Institute of Child Health and Human Development. (2000). *Clinical features of Turner syndrome.* Retrieved February 18, 2003, from the National Institutes of Health Web site: http://turners.nichd.nih.gov/ClinFrIntro.html.

National Institute of Child Health and Human Development. (2002). *Babies sleep safest on their backs: Reduce the risk of sudden infant death syndrome.* Retrieved April 24, 2003, from the National Institutes of Health Web site: http://www.nichd.nih.gov/sids/reduce_infant_risk.htm.

National Institute of Diabetes and Digestive and Kidney Diseases, National Institutes of Health. (2002). *Diabetes.* Retrieved February 6, 2003, from the National Insitutes of Health Web site: http://www.niddk.nih.gov/health/diabetes/diabetes.htm.

National Institute of Mental Health. (1994). *Attention deficit hyperactivity disorder: Decade of the brain* (NIMH Publication No. 94-3572). Washington, DC: Author.

National Institute of Mental Health. (2000). *Anxiety disorders.* Bethesda, MD: U.S. Department of Health and Human Services.

National Institute on Aging. (1989). *Hypothermia: A hot weather hazard for older people.* Retrieved February 3, 2003, from the National Institutes of Health Web site: http://www.nia.nih.gov/health/agepages/hyperthe.htm.

National Institute on Deafness and Other Communication Disorders (NIDCD). (2006). Healthy Hearing 2010. Retrieved October 8, 2006, from the National Institutes of Health Web site: http://www.nidcd.nih.gov/health/inside/spr05/pg1.asp.

National Institute on Drug Abuse (NIDA) (2007). NIDA infofacts: High school and youth trends. Retrieved March 25, 2008 from http://www.nida.nih.gov/Infofacts/HSYouthtrends.html

National Institutes of Health (NIH). (2000). National Institutes of Health Consensus Development Conference statement: Diagnosis and treatment of attention-deficit/hyperactivity disorder (ADHD). *Journal of the American Academy of Child and Adolescent Psychiatry, 32,* 182–193.

National Institutes of Health (NIH). (2004). Clinical features of Turner syndrome. Retrieved April 21, 2008, from http://turners.nichd.nih.gov/ClinFrIntro.html

National Sleep Foundation. (2000). *2000 Omnibus Sleep in America poll.* Retrieved December 26, 2000, from the National Sleep Foundation Web site: http://www.sleepfoundation.org/publications/2000poll.html.

Navara, K. J., & Nelson, R. J. (2007). The dark side of light at night: Physiological, epidemiological, and ecological consequences. *Journal of Pineal Research, 43,* 215–224.

Neary, W. (2002, January). *Individual neurons reveal complexity of memory within the brain.* Retrieved April 24, 2002, from http://www.eurekalert.org/pub_releases/2002-01/uow-inr010302.php.

Neher, E., & Sakmann, B. (1976). Single-channel currents recorded from membrane of denervated frog muscle fibres. *Nature, 260,* 799–802.

Neher, E., & Sakmann, B. (1992). The patch clamp technique. *Scientific American, 266,* 44–51.

Neitz, M., Kraft, T. W., & Neitz, J. (1998). Expression of L-cone pigment gene subtypes in females. *Vision Research,* **38**, 3221–3225.

Nelson, K. B., Grether, J. K., Croen, L. A., Dambrosia, J. M., Dickens, B. F., Jelliffe, L. L., Hansen, R. L., & Phillips, T. M. (2001). Neuropeptides and neurotrophins in neonatal blood of children with autism or mental retardation. *Annals of Neurology, 49,* 597–606.

Neuroethics needed. (2006). *Nature, 441*(7096), 907–907.

Neville, H. J., Bavelier, D., Corina, D., Rauschecker, J., Karni, A., Lalwani, A., et al. (1998). Cerebral organization for language in deaf and hearing subjects: Biological constraints and effects of experience. *Proceedings of the National Academy of Sciences of the United States of America, 95,* 922–929.

Newman, E. A., & Zahs, K. R. (1998). Modulation of neuronal activity by glial cells in the retina. *Journal of Neuroscience, 18,* 4022–4028.

Newsom, C. (1998). Autistic disorder. In E. J. Mash & R. A. Barkley (Eds.), *Treatment of childhood disorders* (pp. 416–467). New York: Guilford Press.

Niehoff, D. L., & Kuhar, M. J. (1983). Benzodiazepine receptors: Localization in rat amygdala. *Journal of Neuroscience, 3*(10), 2091–2097.

Nielsen, J., & Wohlert, M. (1991). Sex chromosome abnormalities among 34, 910 newborn children: Results from a 13-year incidence study in Århus, Denmark. *Birth Defects: Original Article Series, 26*(4), 209–223. Retrieved February 19, 2003, from the Turner Center Web site at http://www.aaa.dk/TURNER/ENGELSK/incidence.htm.

Nielsen, J., Pelsen, B., & Sørensen, K. (1988). Follow-up of 30 Klinefelter males treated with testosterone. *Clinical Genetics 33,* 262–269.

Nieschlag, E., Zitzmann, M., & Kamischke, A. (2003). Use of progestins in male contraception. *Steroids, 68,* 965–972.

Nietzel, M. T. (2000). Police psychology. In A. E. Kazdin (Ed.), *Encyclopedia of psychology* (Vol. 6, pp. 224–226). Washington, DC: American Psychological Association.

Nimchinsky, E. A., et al. (1999). A neuronal morphologic type unique to humans and great apes. *Proceedings of the National Academy of Sciences of the United States of America, 96,* 5268–5273.

Nimmerjahn, A., Kirchhoff, F., & Helmchen, F. (2005). Resting microglial cells are highly dynamic surveillants of brain parenchyma in vivo. *Science, 308*(5726), 1314–1318.

Nisbett, R. E. & Masuda, T. (2003). Culture and point of view. *Proceedings of the National Academy of Sciences of the United States of America, 100,* 11163–11170.

Nisbett, R. E., Peng, K., Choi, I. & Norenzayan, A. (2001). Culture and systems of thought: Holistic vs. analytic cognition. *Psychological Review, 2,* 291–310.

Nishimura, K., Nakamura, K., Anitha, A., Yamada, K., Tsujii, M., Iwayama, Y., et al. (2007). Genetic analyses of the brain-derived neurotrophic factor (BDNF) gene in autism. *Biochemical and Biophysical Research Communications, 356*(1), 200–206.

Nissen, R., Bourque, C. W., & Renaud, L. P. (1993). Membrane properties of organum vasculosum lamina terminalis neurons recorded in vitro. *American Journal of Physiology, 264,* R811–R815.

Noaghiul, S., & Hibbeln, J. R. (2003). Cross-national comparisons of seafood consumption and rates of bipolar disorders. *American Journal of Psychiatry, 160,* 2222–2227.

Noakes, T. (1993). Fluid replacement during exercise. *Exercise and Sport Sciences Reviews, 21,* 297–330.

Nolan, J. P., Morley, P. T., Vanden Hoek, T. L., Hickey, R. W., Kloeck, W. G. J., Billi, J., et al. (2003). Therapeutic hypothermia after cardiac arrest: An advisory statement by the advanced life support task force of the International Liaison Committee on Resuscitation, *108,* 118–121.

Nolen-Hoeksema, S., & Girgus, J. S. (1994). The emergence of gender differences in depression during adolescence. *Psychological Bulletin, 115,* 424–443.

Nunez, C., Beyer, J., Strain, G., Zumoff, B., Kovera, A., Gallagher, D., & Heymsfield, S. D. (1997). *Composition of weight-loss while dieting: A comparison of research and clinically based methods.* Retrieved February 14, 2003, from http://www.healthchecksystems.com/tdiet.htm.

Nussmeier, N. A., Arlund, C., & Slogoff, S. (1986). Neuropsychiatric complications after cardiopulmonary bypass: Cerebral protection by a barbiturate. *Anesthesia, 64,* 165–170.

O'Connor, D. B., Archer, J., & Wu, F. C. W. (2000). Does testosterone affect cognitive function in normal men? *Proceedings of the British Psychological Society, 8,* 40–41.

O'Hara, C. (1988). Emotional adjustment following minor head injury. *Cognitive Rehabilitation, 6,* 26–33.

O'Keefe, J., & Dostrovsky, J. (1971). The hippocampus as a spatial map: Preliminary evidence from unit activity in the freely-moving rat. *Brain Research, 34,* 171–175.

Ogawa, S., Lee, T. M., Kay, A. R., & Tank, D. W. (1990). Brain magnetic resonance imaging with contrast dependent on blood oxygenation. *Proceedings of the National Academy of Sciences of the United States of America, 87,* 9868–9872.

Ogden, C. L., Carroll, M. D., Curtin, L. R., McDowell, M. A., Tabak, C. J., & Flegal, K. M. (2006). Prevalence of overweight and obesity in the United States, 1999–2004. *Journal of the American Medical Association, 295*(13), 1549–1555.

Ogloff, J. R. (2006). Psychopathy/antisocial personality disorder conundrum. *The Australian and New Zealand Journal of Psychiatry, 40*(6–7), 519–528.

Ohno, K., & Sakurai, T. (2008). Orexin neuronal circuitry: Role in the regulation of sleep and wakefulness. *Frontiers in Neuroendocrinology, 29*(1), 70–87.

Ojemann, G., Schoenfield-McNeill, J., & Corina, D. P. (2002). Anatomic subdivisions in human temporal cortical neuronal activity related to recent verbal memory. *Nature Neuroscience, 5,* 64–71.

Oksenberg, J. R., Baranzini, S. E., Sawcer, S., & Hauser, S. L. (2008). The genetics of multiple sclerosis: SNPs to pathways to pathogenesis. *Nature Reviews Genetics, 9*(7), 516–526.

Olds, J., & Milner, P. (1954). Positive reinforcement produced by electrical stimulation of septal areas and other regions of the rat brain. *Journal of Comparative and Physiological Psychology, 47,* 419–427.

Olds, M. E., & Olds, J. (1963). Approach-avoidance analysis of rat diencephalon. *Journal of Comparative and Physiological Psychology, 120,* 259–295.

Olney, J. W. (1969). Brain lesion, obesity and other disturbances in mice treated with monosodium glutamate. *Science, 164,* 719–721.

Olney, J. W. (1994). New mechanisms of excitatory transmitter neurotoxicity. *Journal of Neural Transmission. Supplementum, 43,* 47–51.

Olney, J. W., Labruyere, J., Wang, G., Wozniak, D. F., Price, M. T., Sesma, M. A., et al. (1991). NMDA antagonist neurotoxicity: Mechanism and prevention. *Science, 254,* 1515–1518.

Olson, R. K., Datta, H., Gayan, J., DeFries, J. C., Klein, R. M., & McMullen, P. A. (1999). A behavioral-genetic analysis of reading disabilities and component processes. In *Converging methods for understanding reading and dyslexia.* (pp. 133–151). Cambridge, MA: MIT Press.

Olszewski, P. K., Schiöth, H. B., & Levine, A. S. (2008). Ghrelin in the CNS: From hunger to a rewarding and memorable meal? *Brain Research Reviews, 58*(1), 160–170.

Online Medical Dictionary. (2000). Retrieved June 9, 2002, from http://cancerweb.ncl.ac.uk/omd/.

Oquendo, M. A., Placidi, G. P., Malone, K. M., Campbell, C., Keilp, J., Brodsky, B., et al. (2003). Positron emission tomography of regional brain metabolic responses to a serotonergic challenge and lethality of suicide attempts in major depression. *Archives of General Psychiatry, 60,* 14–22.

Orfinger, B. (2000). *Red Cross joins pledge to eradicate polio worldwide by 2005.* Retrieved March 21, 2004, from http://www.disasterrelief.org/Disasters/000929polio/.

Ornstein, R. (1977). *The psychology of consciousness* (2nd ed.). New York: Harcourt Brace Jovanovich.

Orson, F. M., Kinsey, B. M., Singh, R. A., Wu, Y., Gardner, T., & Kosten, T. R. (2007). The future of vaccines in the management of addictive disorders. *Current Psychiatry Reports, 9*(5), 381–387.

Osaka, M., Osaka, N., Kondo, H., Morishita, M., Fukuyama, H., Aso, T., et al. (2003). The neural basis of individual differences in working memory capacity: An fMRI study. *Neuroimage, 18*(3), 789–797.

Owen, M. J., Craddock, N., & Jablensky, A. (2007). The genetic deconstruction of psychosis. *Schizophrenia Bulletin, 33*(4), 905–911.

Pääbo, S. (2001, April 25). *A comparative approach to human origins.* Paper presented at the Human Genome Meeting, Edinburgh, Scotland.

Pace-Schott, E. F., Gersh, T., Silvestri, R., Stickgold, R., Salzman, C., & Hobson, J. A. (2001). SSRI treatment suppresses dream recall frequency but increases subjective dream intensity in normal subjects. *Journal of Sleep Research, 10*(2), 129–142.

Packard, M. G., Hirsh, R., & White, N. M. (1989). Differential effects of fornix and caudate nucleus lesions on two radial maze tasks: Evidence for multiple memory systems. *Journal of Neuroscience, 9,* 1465–1472.

Pagel, J. (2000). Nightmares and disorders of dreaming. *American Family Physician, 61,* 2037–2042.

Palmer, R. F., Blanchard, S., Stein, Z., Mandell, D., & Miller, C. (2005). Environmental mercury release, special education rates, and autism disorder: An ecological study of Texas. *Health & Place, 12*(2), 203–209.

Pan, H.-L., Wu, Z.-Z., Zhou, H.-Y., Chen, S.-R., Zhang, H.-M., & Li, D.-P. (2008). Modulation of pain transmission by G-protein-coupled receptors. *Pharmacology & Therapeutics, 117*(1), 141–161.

Panesar, N. S. (2008). What caused lymphopenia in SARS and how reliable is the lymphokine status in glucocorticoid-treated patients? *Medical Hypotheses, 71*(2), 298–301.

Papez, J. W. (1937). A proposed mechanism of emotion. *Archives of Neurology and Psychiatry, 38,* 725–744.

Papp, L. A., Klein, D. F., Martinez, J., Schneier, F., Cole, R., Liebowitz, M. R., et al. (1993). Diagnostic and substance specificity of carbon-dioxideinduced panic. *American Journal of Psychiatry, 150,* 250–257.

Paquet, E. R., Rey, G., & Naef, F. (2008). Modeling an evolutionary conserved circadian cis-element. *PLoS Computational Biology, 4*(2), e38.

Pardo, C. A., & Eberhart, C. G. (2007). The neurobiology of autism. *Brain Pathology, 17*(4), 434–447.

Park, N. W., & Ingles, J. L. (2001). Effectiveness of attention rehabilitation after an acquired brain injury: A meta-analysis. *Neuropsychology, 15,* 199–210.

Parker, A., Eacott, M. J., & Gaffan, D. (1997). The recognition memory deficit caused by mediodorsal thalamic lesion in non-human primates: A comparison with rhinal cortex lesion. *European Journal of Neuroscience, 9*(11), 2423–2431.

Parnas, H., Segel, L., Dudel, J., & Parnas, I. (2000). Autoreceptors, membrane potential and the regulation of transmitter release. *Trends in Neurosciences, 23,* 60–68.

Parpura, V., & Haydon, P. G. (2000). Physiological astrocytic calcium levels stimulate glutamate release to modulate adjacent neurons. *Proceedings of the National Academy of Sciences of the United States of America, 97,* 8629–8634.

Parrilla, L. (2006). O'Malley killer begins his sentence. *The Tribune,* p. B2.

Parrott, A. C. (2007). The psychotherapeutic potential of MDMA (3,4-methylenedioxymethamphetamine): An evidence-based review. *Psychopharmacology (Berl), 191*(2), 181–198.

Pascual-Leone, A., & Torres, F. (1993). Plasticity of sensorimotor cortex representation of the reading finger in Braille readers. *Brain, 116,* 39–52.

Paterson, D. S., Trachtenberg, F. L., Thompson, E. G., Belliveau, R. A., Beggs, A. H., Darnall, R., et al. (2006). Multiple serotonergic brainstem abnormalities in sudden infant death syndrome. *The Journal of the American Medical Association (JAMA), 296*(17), 2124–2132.

Patterson, F. (1978, October). Conversations with a gorilla. *National Geographic,* 438–465.

Patterson, G. R. (1986). Performance models for antisocial boys. *American Psychologist, 41,* 432–444.

Paulesu, E., Harrison, J., Baron-Cohen, S., Watson, J. D. G., Goldstein, L., Heather, J., et al. (1995). The physiology of colored hearing. *Brain, 118,* 661–676.

Pauley, S. M. (2004). Lighting for the human circadian clock: Recent research indicates lighting has become a public health issue. *Medical Hypotheses, 63,* 588–596.

Paulus, M. P., & Stein, M. B. (2006). An insular view of anxiety. *Biological Psychiatry, 60*(4), 383–387.

Pavlov, I. P. (1927). *Conditioned reflexes* (G. V. Annep, Trans.). London: Oxford University Press.

Pawlowski, B. (1998). Why are human newborns so big and fat? *Human Evolution, 13*(1), 65–72.

Payne, J. D., Jackson, E. D., Hoscheidt, S., Ryan, L., Jacobs, W. J., & Nadel, L. (2007). Stress administered prior to encoding impairs neutral but enhances emotional long-term episodic memories. *Learning and Memory, 14*(12), 861–868.

Pelham, W. (1993). Pharmacotherapy for children with attentiondeficit hyperactivity disorder. *School Psychology Review, 22,* 199–227.

Penfield, W. (1958). *The excitable cortex in conscious man.* Springfield, IL: Thomas.

Penfield, W., & Rasmussen, T. (1950). *The cerebral cortex of man: A clinical study of localization.* Boston: Little, Brown.

Pennebaker, J. (1990). *Opening up: The healing power of confiding in others.* New York: Morrow.

Penner, J. D., & Brown, A. S. (2007). Prenatal infectious and nutritional factors and risk of adult schizophrenia. *Expert Review of Neurotherapeutics, 7*(7), 797–805.

Penton-voak, I. S., Cahill, S., Pound, N., Kempe, V., Schaeffler, S., & Schaeffler, F. (2007). Male facial attractiveness, perceived personality, and child-directed speech. *Evolution and Human Behavior, 28*(4), 253–259.

Pepperberg, I. M. (1990). An investigation into the cognitive capacities of an African grey parrot (*Psittacus erithacus*). In P. J. B. Slater, J. R. Rosenblatt, & C. Beer (Eds.), *Advances in the study of behavior* (pp. 357–409). New York: Academic Press.

Perani, D., Paulesu, E., Galles, N. S., Dupoux, E., Dehaene, S., Bettinardi, V., et al. (1998). The bilingual brain: Proficiency and age of acquisition of the second language. *Brain, 121,* 1841–1852.

Perera, T. D., Coplan, J. D., Lisanby, S. H., Lipira, C. M., Arif, M., Carpio, C., et al. (2007). Antidepressant-induced neurogenesis in the hippocampus of adult nonhuman primates. *Journal of Neuroscience, 27*(18), 4894–4901.

Pert, C. B., Snowman, A. M., & Snyder, S. H. (1974). Localization of opiate receptor binding in synaptic membranes of rat brain. *Brain Research, 70,* 184–188.

Peters, A., Palay, S. L., & Webster, H. de F. (1991). *The fine structure of the nervous system: Neurons and their supporting cells.* New York: Oxford University Press.

Petersen, S. E., Fox, P. T., Snyder, A. Z., & Raichle, M. E. (1990). Activation of extrastriate and frontal cortical areas by visual words and word-like stimuli. *Science, 249,* 1041–1044.

Peterson, L. R., & Peterson, M. J. (1959). Short-term retention of individual verbal items. *Journal of Experimental Psychology, 58,* 193–198.

Petit, F., Minns, A. B., Dubernard, J. M., Hettiaratchy, S., & Lee, W. P. (2003). Composite tissue allotransplantation and reconstructive surgery: First clinical applications. *Annals of Surgery, 237,* 19–25.

Petrie, K., Dawson, A. G., Thompson, L., & Brook, R. (1993). A double-blind trial of melatonin as a treatment for jet lag in international cabin crew. *Biological Psychiatry, 33,* 526–530.

Petty, R. G. (1999). Structural asymmetries of the human brain and their disturbance in schizophrenia. *Schizophrenia Bulletin, 25,* 121–139.

Pezzoli, G., Canesi, M., Antonini, A., Righini, A., Perbellini, L., Barichella, M., et al. (2000). Hydrocarbon exposure and Parkinson's disease. *Neurology, 55,* 667–673.

Pfizer, Inc. (2002). *Mechanism of action and PDE5 selectivity of Viagra.* Retrieved February 28, 2003, from the Pfizer, Inc. Web site at http://www.viagra.com/professional/clinicalInfo/moa.asp.

Pfrieger, F. W., & Barres, B. A. (1997). Synaptic efficacy enhanced by glial cells in vitro. *Science, 277,* 1684–1687.

Phelps, E. A. (2004). Human emotion and memory: Interactions of the amygdala and hippocampal complex. *Current Opinion in Neurobiology, 14,* 198–202.

Phelps, M. E., Hoffman, E., Mullani, N., Higgins, C., & Ter-Pogossian, M. (1976). Design considerations for a positron emission transaxial tomograph (PET III). *I.E.E.E. Transactions on Biomedical Engineering, NS-23,* 516–522.

Phillips, A. G., Coury, A., Fiorino, D., LePiane, F. G., Brown, E., & Fibiger, H. C. (1992). Self-stimulation of the ventral tegmental area enhances dopamine release in the nucleus accumbens: A microdialysis study. *Annals of the New York Academy of Sciences, 654,* 199–206.

Phillips, K. A., & Gunderson, J. G. (1999). Personality disorders. In R. E. Hales, S. C. Yudofsky, & J. A. Talbott (Eds.), *Textbook of psychiatry* (pp. 795–823). Washington, DC: American Psychiatric Press.

Phillips, M. L., Drevets, W. C., Rauch, S. L., & Lane, R. (2003). Neurobiology of emotion perception II: Implications for major psychiatric disorders. *Biological Psychiatry, 54*(5), 515–528.

Piacentini, J., & Graae, F. (1997). Childhood OCD. In E. Hollander & D. Stein (Eds.), *Obsessive-compulsive disorders: Diagnosis, etiology, treatment* (pp. 23–46). New York: Dekker.

Picard, N., & Strick, P. L. (1997). Activation on the medial wall during remembered sequences of reaching movements in monkeys. *Journal of Neurophysiology, 77*(4), 2197–2201.

Piccini, P., Brooks, D. J., Bjorklund, A., Gunn, R. N., Grasby, P. M., Rimoldi, O., et al. (1999). Dopamine release from nigral transplants visualized in vivo in a Parkinson's patient. *Nature Neuroscience, 2,* 1137–1140.

Pickett, J. P., et al. (2000). The American Heritage dictionary of the English language (4th ed.) Retrieved September 7, 2006, from http://www.bartleby.com/br/61.html

Pinker, S. (1994). *Language is to us as flying is to geese.* New York: Morrow.

Pitman, R. K., & Delahanty, D. L. (2005). Conceptually driven pharmacologic approaches to acute trauma. *CNS Spectrums, 10*(2), 99–106.

Pitman, R. K., Sanders, K. M., Zusman, R. M., Healy, A. R., Cheema, F., Lasko, N. B., et al. (2002). Pilot study of secondary prevention of posttraumatic stress disorder with propranolol. *Biological Psychiatry, 51*(2), 189–192.

Plomin, R., Hill, L., Craig, I. W., McGuffin, P., Purcell, S., Sham, P., et al. (2001). A genome-wide scan of 1842 DNA markers for allelic associations with general cognitive ability: A five-stage design using DNA pooling and extreme selected groups. *Behavioral Genetics, 31,* 497–509.

Plomin, R., Turic, D. M., Hill, L., Turic, D. E., Stephens, M., Williams, J., et al. (2004). A functional polymorphism in the succinate-semialdehyde dehydrogenase (aldehyde dehydrogenase 5 family, member A1) gene is associated with cognitive ability. *Molecular Psychiatry, 9*(6), 582–586.

Plotnik, J. M., de Waal, F. B. M., & Reiss, D. (2006). From the Cover: Self-recognition in an Asian elephant. *Proceedings of the National Academy of Sciences, USA (PNAS), 103*(45), 17053–17057.

Poldrack, R. A., Clark, J., Paré-Blagoev, E. J., Shohamy, D., Creso Moyano, J., Myers, C., et al. (2001). Interactive memory systems in the human brain. *Nature, 414,* 546–550.

Pollard, C. D., Braun, B., & Hamill, J. (2006). Influence of gender, estrogen and exercise on anterior knee laxity. *Clinical Biomechanics, 21*(10), 1060–1066.

Popper, C. W. (1993). Psychopharmacologic treatment of anxiety disorders in adolescents and children. *Journal of Clinical Psychiatry, 54,* 52–63.

Porkka-Heiskanen, T. (1999). Adenosine in sleep and wakefulness. *Annals of Medicine, 31,* 125–129.

Prasad, S., & Steer, C. (2008). Switching from neurostimulant therapy to atomoxetine in children and adolescents with attention-deficit hyperactivity disorder : Clinical approaches and review of current available evidence. *Paediatric Drugs, 10*(1), 39–47.

Pressman, M. R. (2007). Factors that predispose, prime and precipitate NREM parasomnias in adults: Clinical and forensic implications. *Sleep Medicine Reviews, 11*(1), 5–30; discussion 31–33.

Price, R. W., & Spudich, S. (2008). Antiretroviral therapy and central nervous system HIV type 1 infection. *Journal of Infectious Diseases, 197* Suppl 3, S294–306.

Prior, B. M., Modlesky, C. M., Evans, E. M., Sloniger, M. A., Saunders, M. J., Lewis, R. D., et al. (2001). Muscularity and the density of the fat-free mass in athletes. *Journal of Applied Physiology, 90,* 1523–1531.

Prusiner, S. B. (1982). Novel proteinaceous infectious particles cause scrapie. *Science, 216,* 136–144.

Prusiner, S. B. (1995). The prion diseases. *Scientific American, 272,* 48–56.

Prusiner, S. B., Groth, D. F., Bolton, D. C., Kent, S. B., & Hood, L. E. (1984). Purification and structural studies of a major scrapie prion protein. *Cell, 38,* 127–134.

Purpura, D. P. (1974). Dendritic spine "dysgenesis" and mental retardation. *Science, 186,* 1126–1128.

Quirk, G. J., Repa, J. C., & LeDoux, J. E. (1995). Fear conditioning enhances short-latency auditory responses of lateral amygdala neurons: Parallel recordings in the freely behaving rat. *Neuron, 15,* 1029–1039.

Quiroga, R. Q., Reddy, L., Kreiman, G., Koch, C., & Fried, I. (2005). Invariant visual representation by single neurons in the human brain. *Nature, 435*(7045), 1102–1107.

Quitkin, F. M., Petkova, E., McGrath, P. J., Taylor, B., Beasley, C., Stewart, J., Amsterdam, J., Fava, M., Rosenbaum, J., Reimherr, F., Fawcett, J., Chen, Y., & Klein, D. (2003). When should a trial of fluoxetine for major depression be declared failed? *American Journal of Psychiatry, 160,* 734–740.

Qu-Peterson, Z., Deasy, B., Jankowski, R., Ikezawa, M., Cummins, J., Pruchnic, R., et al. (2002). Identification of a novel population of muscle stem cells in mice: Potential for muscle regeneration. *Journal of Cell Biology, 157,* 851–864.

Radulovacki, M. (1985). Role of adenosine in sleep in rats. *Reviews in Clinical and Basic Pharmacology, 5*(3–4), 327–339.

Raine, A., Ishikawa, S. S., Arce, E., Lencz, T., Knuth, K. H., Bihrle, S., et al. (2004). Hippocampal structural asymmetry in unsuccessful psychopaths. *Biological Psychiatry, 55*(2), 185–191.

Raine, A., Meloy, J. R., Bihrle, S., Stoddard, J., LaCasse, L., & Buchsbaum, M. S. (1998). Reduced prefrontal and increased subcortical brain functioning assessed using positron emission tomography in predatory and affective murderers. *Behavioral Sciences and the Law, 16*(3), 319–332.

Raine, A., Stoddard, J., Bihrle, S., & Buchsbaum, M. S. (1998). Prefrontal glucose deficits in murderers lacking psychosocial deprivation. *Neuropsychiatry, Neuropsychology, and Behavioral Neurology, 11,* 1–7.

Rainville, P., Duncan, H. G., Price, D. D., Carrier, B., & Bushnell, M. C. (1997). Pain affect encoded in human anterior cingulate but not somatosensory cortex. *Science, 277,* 968–971.

Rajnicek, A. M., Foubister, L. E., & McCaig, C. D. (2006). Growth cone steering by a physiological electric field requires dynamic microtubules, microfilaments and Rac-mediated filopodial asymmetry. *Journal of Cell Science, 119,* 1736–1745.

Rakic, P. (1988). Specification of cerebral cortical areas. *Science, 241,* 170–176.

Raleigh, M. J., Brammer, G. L., McGuire, M. T., Pollack, D. B., & Yuwiler, A. (1992). Individual differences in basal cisternal cerebrospinal fluid F0HIAA and HVA in monkeys: The effects of gender, age, physical characteristics, and matrilineal influences. *Neuropsychopharmacology, 7,* 295–304.

Ralph, M. R., Foster, R. G., Davis, F. C., & Menaker, M. (1990). Transplanted suprachiasmatic nucleus determines circadian period. *Science, 247,* 975–978.

Ramachandran, V. S. (2005). Plasticity and functional recovery in neurology. *Clinical Medicine, 5*(4), 368–373.

Ramachandran, V. S., & Hubbard, E. M. (2001). Synaesthesia: A window into perception, thought and language. *Journal of Consciousness Studies, 8*(12), 3–34.

Ramachandran, V. S., & Rogers-Ramachandran, D. (2000). Phantom limbs and neural plasticity. *Archives of Neurology, 57,* 317–320.

Ramaekers, J. G., Moeller, M. R., van Ruitenbeek, P., Theunissen, E. L., Schneider, E., & Kauert, G. (2006). Cognition and motor control as a function of [Delta]9-THC concentration in serum and oral fluid: Limits of impairment. *Drug and Alcohol Dependence, 85*(2), 114–122.

Rand, M. N., & Breedlove, S. M. (1987). Ontogeny of functional innervation of bulbocavernosus muscles in male and female rats. *Brain Research, 430,* 150–152.

Rapkin, A. J., Mikacich, J. A., Moatakef-Imani, B., & Rasgon, N. (2002). The clinical nature and formal diagnosis of premenstrual, postpartum, and perimenopausal affective disorders. *Current Psychiatry Reports, 4,* 419–428.

Rapoport, J. (1989). *The boy who couldn't stop washing: The experience and treatment of obsessive-compulsive disorder.* New York: Dutton.

Rapoport, J. L., Giedd, J. N., Blumenthal, J., Hamburger, S., Jeffries, N., Fernandez, T., et al. (1999). Progressive cortical change during adolescence in childhood-onset schizophrenia: A longitudinal magnetic resonance imaging study. *Archives of General Psychiatry, 56*(7), 649–654.

Rasband, M. N., & Shrager, P. (2000). Ion channel sequestration in central nervous system axons. *Journal of Physiology, 525,* 63–73.

Rasmussen, T., & Milner, B. (1977). The role of early left-brain injury in determining lateralization of cerebral speech functions. *Annals of the New York Academy of Sciences, 299,* 355–369.

Rauschecker, J. P., Ian, B., & Hauser, M. (1995). Processing of complex sounds in the macaque nonprimary auditory cortex. *Science, 268,* 111–114.

Ravits, J. (2005). Sporadic amyotrophic lateral sclerosis: A hypothesis of persistent (non-lytic) enteroviral infection. *Amyotrophic lateral sclerosis and other motor neuron disorders: Official publication of the World Federation of Neurology, Research Group on Motor Neuron Diseases, 6*(2), 77–87.

Rawson, N. E. (2006). Olfactory loss in aging. *Science of Aging Knowledge Environment, 2006*(5), pe6.

Records, R. (1979). Eyebrows and eyelids. In R. E. Records (Ed.), *Physiology of the human eye and visual system* (pp. 1–24). New York: Harper & Row.

Reed, G. M., Kemeny, M. E., Taylor, S. E., Wang, H.-Y., & Visscher, B. R. (1994). "Realistic acceptance" as a predictor of decreased survival time in gay men with AIDS. *Health Psychology, 13,* 299–307.

Reed, S. C., Levin, F. R., & Evans, S. M. (2008). Changes in mood, cognitive performance and appetite in the late luteal and follicular phases of the menstrual cycle in women with and without PMDD (premenstrual dysphoric disorder). *Hormones and Behavior, 54*(1), 185–193.

Regan, C. (2000). *Intoxicating minds.* London: Weidenfeld & Nicolson.

Regan, D., Beverley, K. I., & Cynader, M. (1979). The visual perception of motion in depth. *Scientific American, 241,* 136–151.

Reiche, E. M., Morimoto, H. K., & Nunes, S. M. (2005). Stress and depression-induced immune dysfunction: implications for the development and progression of cancer. *International Review of Psychiatry, 17*(6), 515–527.

Reinholz, M. M., Merkle, C. M., & Poduslo, J. F. (1999). Therapeutic benefits of putrescine-modified catalase in a transgenic mouse model of familial amyotrophic lateral sclerosis. *Experimental Neurology, 159,* 204–216.

Reinisch, J. M., Ziemba-Davis, M., & Sanders, S. A. (1991). Hormonal contributions to sexually dimorphic behavioral development in humans. *Psychoneuroendocrinology, 16,* 213–278.

Reis, D. J., & LeDoux, J. E. (1987). Some central neural mechanisms governing resting and behaviorally coupled control of blood pressure. *Circulation, 76,* 12–19.

Rescorla, R. A., & Freberg, L. (1978). Extinction of withincompound flavor associations. *Learning and Motivation, 9,* 411–427.

Reuter, B., & Kathmann, N. (2004). Using saccade tasks as a tool to analyze executive dysfunctions in schizophrenia. *Acta Psychologia, 115*(2–3), 255–269.

Revonsuo, A. (2000). The reinterpretation of dreams: An evolutionary hypothesis of the function of dreaming. *The Behavioral and Brain Sciences, 23*(6), 877–901; discussion 904–1121.

Reznick, J. S. (1999). Can prenatal caffeine exposure affect behavioral inhibition? *Review of General Psychology, 3*(2), 118–132.

Ribeiro, S., & Nicolelis, M. A. (2004). Reverberation, storage, and postsynaptic propagation of memories during sleep. *Learning and Memory, 11*(6), 686–696.

Ricardo, J. A. (1981). Efferent connections of the subthalamic region in the rat: II. The zona incerta. *Brain Research, 214,* 43–60.

Rice, M. J., & Chippindale, A. K. (2001). Sexual recombination and the power of natural selection. *Science, 294,* 555–559.

Ridgway, S. H. (2002). Asymmetry and symmetry in brain waves from dolphin left and right hemispheres: Some observations after anesthesia, during quiescent hanging behavior, and during visual obstruction. *Brain, Behavior, and Evolution, 60,* 265–274.

Ridley, M. (1999). *Genome: The autobiography of a species in 23 chapters.* New York: HarperCollins.

Ridley, M. (2003). *Nature via nurture: Genes, experience, & what makes us human.* New York: HarperCollins.

Riedel, G., & Davies, S. N. (2005). Cannabinoid function in learning, memory and plasticity. *Handbook of Experimental Pharmacology, 168,* 445–477.

Riggs, L. A., Ratliff, F., Cornsweet, J. C., & Cornsweet, T. N. (1981). Suppression of the blackout due to blinks. *Vision Research, 21,* 1075–1079.

Rinn, W. E. (1984). The neuropsychology of facial expression: A review of the neurological and psychological mechanisms for producing facial expressions. *Psychological Bulletin, 95*(1), 52–77.

Ritvo, J. I., & Park, C. (2007). The psychiatric management of patients with alcohol dependence. *Current Treatment Options in Neurology, 9*(5), 381–392.

Rivas-Vazquez, R. A., Blais, M. A., Rey, G. J., & Rivas-Vazquez, A. (2000). Atypical antipsychotic medications: Pharmacological profiles and psychological implications. *Professional Psychology: Research and Practice, 31,* 628–640.

Rives, N., Siméon, N., Milazzo, J. P., Barthélémy, C., & Macé, B. (2003). Meiotic segregation of sex chromosomes in mosaic and non-mosaic XYY males: Case reports and review of the literature. *International Journal of Andrology, 26*(4), 242–249.

Rivkin, M. J., Davis, P. E., Lemaster, J. L., Cabral, H. J., Warfield, S. K., Mulkern, R. V., et al. (2008). Volumetric MRI study of brain in children with intrauterine exposure to cocaine, alcohol, tobacco, and marijuana. *Pediatrics, 121*(4), 741–750.

Rizzolatti, G., Fadiga, L., Gallese, V., & Fogassi, L. (1996). Premotor cortex and the recognition of motor actions. *Brain Research. Cognitive Brain Research, 3*(2), 131–141.

Rizzolatti, G., Fadiga, L., Gallese, V., & Fogassi, L. (1996). Premotor cortex and the recognition of motor actions. *Cognitive Brain Research, 3,* 131–141.

Roberson, E. D., Scearce-Levie, K., Palop, J. J., Yan, F., Cheng, I. H., Wu, T., et al. (2007). Reducing endogenous tau ameliorates amyloid beta-induced deficits in an Alzheimer's disease mouse model. *Science, 316*(5825), 750–754.

Roberts, A. C., & Glanzman, D. L. (2003). Learning in *Aplysia:* Looking at synaptic plasticity from both sides. *Trends in Neurosciences, 26*(12), 662–670.

Roberts, M., & Scanlan, L. (1999). *The man who listens to horses.* New York: Ballantine Books.

Robins, L. N., & Regier, D. A. (Eds.). (1991). *Psychiatric disorders in America: The Epidemiologic Catchment Area Study.* New York: The Free Press.

Robins, L. N., Helzer, J. E., & Davis, D. H. (1975). Narcotic use in Southeast Asia and afterward. *Archives of General Psychiatry, 41,* 955–961.

Robinson, R. G., Kubos, K. L., Starr, L. B., Rao, K., & Price, T. R. (1984). Mood disorders in stroke patients: Importance of location of lesion. *Brain, 107*(1), 81–93.

Robleto, K., & Thompson, R. F. (2008). Extinction of a classically conditioned response: Red nucleus and interpositus. *Journal of Neuroscience, 28*(10), 2651–2658.

Rodin, J. (1986). Aging and health: Effects of the sense of control. *Science, 233,* 1271–1276.

Rogawski, M. A. (2005). Update on the neurobiology of alcohol withdrawal seizures. *Epilepsy Currents, 5*(6), 225–230.

Rogers, L. J. (2000). Evolution of hemispheric specialization: Advantages and disadvantages. *Brain and Language, 73,* 236–253.

Rogers, L. J., Andrew, R. J., & Johnston, A. N. B. (2007). Light experience and the development of behavioural lateralization in chicks: III. Learning to distinguish pebbles from grains. *Behavioural Brain Research, 177*(1), 61–69.

Rojansky, N., Brzezinski, A., & Schenker, J. G. (1992). Seasonality in human reproduction: An update. *Human Reproduction, 7,* 735–745.

Roland, P. (1993). *Brain activation.* New York: Wiley-Liss.

Rolls, E. T. (2004). The functions of the orbitofrontal cortex. *Brain and Cognition, 55*(1), 11–29.

Román, G. C. (2007). Autism: Transient in utero hypothyroxinemia related to maternal flavonoid ingestion during pregnancy and to other environmental antithyroid agents. *Journal of the Neurological Sciences, 262*(1–2), 15–26.

Roney, J. R., Hanson, K. N., Durante, K. M., & Maestripieri, D. (2006). Reading men's faces: women's mate attractiveness judgments track men's testosterone and interest in infants. *Proceedings of the Royal Society, B: Biological Sciences, 273*(1598), 2169–2175.

Rose, F. D., Attree, E. A., Brooks, B. M., & Johnson, D. A. (1998). Virtual environments in brain damage rehabilitation: A rationale from basic neuroscience. In G. Riva, B. K. Wiederhold, & E. Molinari (Eds.), *Virtual environments in clinical psychology and neuroscience: Methods and techniques in advanced patient–therapist interaction* (pp. 233–242). Amsterdam: Ios Press.

Rosen, D. R., Siddique, T., Patterson, D., Figlewicz, D. A., Sapp, P., Hentati, A., et al. (1993). Mutations in Cu/Zn superoxide dismutase gene are associated with familial amyotrophic lateral sclerosis. *Nature, 362,* 59–62.

Rosen, J. C., Leitenberg, H., Fisher, C., & Khazam, C. (1986). Binge-eating episodes in bulimia nervosa: The amount and type of food consumed. *International Journal of Eating Disorders, 5,* 255–257.

Rosenbaum, R. S., Priselac, S., Köhler S., Black, S. E., Gao, F., Nadel, L., & Moscovitch, M. (2000). Remote spatial memory in an amnesic person with extensive bilateral hippocampal lesions. *Nature Neuroscience, 3,* 1044–1048.

Rosenzweig, M. R., Leiman, A. L., & Breedlove, S. M. (1999). *Biological Psychology* (2nd ed.). Sunderland, MA: Sinauer Associates, Inc.

Ross, G. W., & Petrovitch, H. (2001). Current evidence for neuroprotective effects of nicotine and caffeine against Parkinson's disease. *Drugs and Aging, 18*(11), 797–806.

Ross, G. W., Abbott, R. D., Petrovitch, H., Morens, D. M., Grandinetti, A., Tung, K. H., et al. (2000). Association of coffee and caffeine intake with the risk of Parkinson disease. *Journal of the American Medical Association, 283,* 2674–2679.

Ross, J. L., Roeltgen, D. P., Stefanatos, G., Benecke, R., Zeger, M. P. D., Kushner, H., et al. (2008). Cognitive and motor development during childhood in boys with Klinefelter syndrome. *American Journal of Medical Genetics, 146A*(6), 708–719.

Rosvold, H. E., Mirsky, A. F., & Pribram, K. (1954). Influence of amygdalectomy on social behavior in monkeys. *Journal of Comparative Physiology and Psychology, 47,* 173–178.

Roth, J. (2006). Endogenous antipyretics. *Clinica Chimica Acta, 371*(1–2), 13–24.

Rothman, S. M. (1984). Synaptic release of excitatory amino acid neurotransmitter mediates anoxic neuronal death. *Journal of Neuroscience, 4,* 1884–1891.

Routtenberg, A., & Lindy, J. (1965). Effects of the availability of rewarding septal and hypothalamic stimulation on bar-pressing for food under conditions of deprivation. *Journal of Comparative and Physiological Psychology, 60,* 158–161.

Roy, N. S., Cleren, C., Singh, S. K., Yang, L., Beal, M. F., & Goldman, S. A. (2006). Functional engraftment of human ES cell-derived dopaminergic neurons enriched by coculture with telomerase-immortalized midbrain astrocytes. *Nature Medicine, 12*(11), 1259–1268.

Rozin, P., & Pelchat, M. L. (1988). Memories of mammaries: Adaptations to weaning from milk. *Progress in Psychobiology and Physiological Psychology, 13,* 1–29.

Rubin, J., Provenzano, F., & Luria, Z. (1974). The eye of the beholder: Parents' views on sex of newborns. *American Journal of Orthopsychiatry, 44,* 512–519.

Ruby, P., & Decety, J. (2001). Effect of subjective perspective taking during simulation of action: A PET investigation of agency. *Nature Neuroscience, 4,* 546–550.

Rucker, D., Padwal, R., Li, S. K., Curioni, C., & Lau, D. C. (2007). Long term pharmacotherapy for obesity and overweight: Updated meta-analysis. *British Medical Journal, 335*(7631), 1194–1199.

Rudebeck, P. H., Walton, M. E., Smyth, A. N., Bannerman, D. M., & Rushworth, M. F. (2006). Separate neural pathways process different decision costs. *Nature Neuroscience, 9*(9), 1161–1168.

Rushton, D. H., Dover, R., Sainsbury, A. W., Norris, M. J., Gilkes, J. J., & Ramsey, I. D. (2001). Why should women have lower reference limits for haemoglobin and ferritin concentrations than men? *British Medical Journal, 322,* 1355–1357.

Rushton, J. P., Fulker, D. W., Neale, M. C., Nias, D. K. B., & Eysenck, H. J. (1986). Altruism and aggression: The heritability of individual differences. *Journal of Personality and Social Psychology, 50,* 1192–1198.

Rushton, W. A. H. (1961). Rhodopsin measurement and dark adaptation in a subject deficient in cone vision. *Journal of Physiology, 156,* 193–205.

Rushworth, M. F. (2008). Intention, choice, and the medial frontal cortex. *Annals of the New York Academy of Sciences, 1124,* 181–207.

Rushworth, M. F., Behrens, T. E., Rudebeck, P. H., & Walton, M. E. (2007). Contrasting roles for cingulate and orbitofrontal cortex in decisions and social behaviour. *Trends in Cognitive Sciences, 11*(4), 168–176.

Rutter, M., Moffitt, T., & Caspi, A. (2006). Gene-environment interplay and psychopathology: Multiple varieties but real effects. *Journal of Child Psychology and Psychiatry, 47*(3), 226–261.

Rutter, N. (1996). The immature skin. *European Journal of Pediatrics, 155*(Suppl. 2), S18–S20.

Sacco, K. A., Termine, A., & Seyal, A. (2005). Effects of Cigarette Smoking on Spatial Working Memory and Attentional Deficits in Schizophrenia: Involvement of Nicotinic Receptor Mechanisms. *Archives of General Psychiatry, 62*(6), 649–659.

Sachar, E. J., & Baron, M. (1979). The biology of affective disorders. *Annual Review of Neuroscience, 2,* 505–517.

Sack, R. L., Brandes, R. W., Kendall, A. R., & Lewy, A. J. (2000). Entrainment of free-running circadian rhythms by melatonin in blind people. *New England Journal of Medicine, 343*(15), 1070–1077.

Sackeim, H. A., Greenberg, M. S., Weiman, A. L., Gur, R. C., Hungerbuhler, J. P., & Geschwind, N. (1982). Hemispheric asymmetry in the expression of positive and negative emotions: Neurologic evidence. *Archives of Neurology, 39,* 210–218.

Sackett, G. P. (1966). Monkeys reared in isolation with pictures as visual input: Evidence for an innate releasing mechanism. *Science, 154,* 1468–1473.

Sackheim, H. A., Gur, R. C., & Saucy, M. C. (1978). Emotions are expressed more intensely on the left side of the face. *Science, 202,* 434–436.

Sacks, O. (1985). *The man who mistook his wife for a hat, and other clinical tales.* New York: Summit Books.

Safar, P. (1980). Amelioration of post-ischemic brain damage with barbiturate. *Stroke, 2,* 565–568.

Sahu, A., Kalra, P. S., & Kalra, S. P. (1988). Food deprivation and ingestion induce reciprocal changes in neuropeptide Y concentration in the paraventricular nucleus. *Peptides, 9,* 83–86.

Sakai, Y., Dobson, C., Diksic, M., Aubé, M., & Hamel, E. (2008). Sumatriptan normalizes the migraine attack-related increase in brain serotonin synthesis. *Neurology, 70*(6), 431–439.

Sakurai, T. (2002). Roles of orexins in feeding and wakefulness. *Neuroreport, 13,* 987–995.

Sakurai, T., Amemiya, A., Ishii, M., Matsuzaki, I., Chemelli, R. M., Tanaka, H., et al. (1998). Orexins and orexin receptors: A family of hypothalamic neuropeptides and G protein-coupled receptors that regulate feeding behavior. *Cell, 92,* 573–585.

Salamone, J. D., Cousins, M. S., & Bucher, S. (1994). Anhedonia or anergia? Effects of haloperidol and nucleus accumbens dopamine depletion on instrumental response selection in a T-maze cost/benefit procedure. *Behavioral Brain Research, 65*(2), 221–229.

Salio, C., Lossi, L., Ferrini, F., & Merighi, A. (2006). Neuropeptides as synaptic transmitters. *Cell Tissue Research, 326*(2), 583–598.

Sallee, R., & Greenawald, J. (1995). Neurobiology. In J. S. March (Ed.), *Anxiety disorders in children and adolescents* (pp. 3–34). New York: Guilford Press.

Salmon, S. (2004). The PEACE curriculum: Expanded aggression replacement training. In A. P. Goldstein, R. Nensén, B. Daleflod, & M. Kalt (Eds.), *New perspectives on aggression replacement training* (pp. 171–188). Chichester, UK: Wiley.

Salvesen, K. A. (2002). EFSUMB: Safety tutorial: Epidemiology of diagnostic ultrasound exposure during pregnancy. *European Journal of Ultrasound, 15,* 165–171.

Salvesen, K. A. (2007). Epidemiological prenatal ultrasound studies. *Progress in Biophysics and Molecular Biology, 93,* 295–300.

Sample, I. (2001). Sound defense. *New Scientist, 172,* 24. Retrieved January 13, 2003, from the New Scientist Web site: http://archive.newscientist.com/secure/article/article.jsp?rp=1&id=mg17223173.200.

Samson, S., & Zatorre, R. J. (1994). Contribution of the right temporal lobe to musical timbre discrimination. *Neuropsychologia, 32,* 231–240.

Sandberg, A. A., Koepf, G. F., Ishiara, T., & Hauschka, T. S. (1961). An XYY human male. *Lancet, 2,* 488–489.

Sanes, J. R., & Jessell, T. M. (2000). The guidance of axons to their targets. In E. R. Kandel, J. H. Schwartz, & T. M. Jessell (Eds.), *Principles of neural science* (4th ed., pp. 1063–1086). New York: McGraw-Hill.

Santosa, C. M., Strong, C. M., Nowakowska, C., Wang, P. W., Rennicke, C. M., & Ketter, T. A. (2007). Enhanced creativity in bipolar disorder patients: A controlled study. *Journal of Affective Disorders, 100*(1–3), 31–39.

Sapolsky, R. (2001). *A primate's memoir.* New York: Scribner.

Sapolsky, R. M. (2002). Chickens, eggs and hippocampal atrophy. *Nature Neuroscience, 5,* 1111–1113.

Sapolsky, R. M., Krey, L. C., & McEwen, B. S. (1985). Prolonged glucocorticoid exposure reduces hippocampal neuron number: Implications for aging. *Journal of Neuroscience, 5,* 1222–1227.

Sartorius, N., Jablensky, A., Korten, A., Ernberg, G., Anker, M., Cooper, J. E., et al. (1986). Early manifestations and first-contact incidence of schizophrenia in different cultures. A preliminary report on the initial evaluation phase of the WHO Collaborative Study on determinants of outcome of severe mental disorders. *Psychological Medicine, 16,* 909–928.

Sathyanarayana, S., Karr, C. J., Lozano, P., Brown, E., Calafat, A. M., Liu, F., et al. (2008). Baby Care Products: Possible Sources of Infant Phthalate Exposure. *Pediatrics, 121*(2), e260–268.

Satinoff, E. (1964). Behavioral thermoregulation in response to local cooling of the rat brain. *American Journal of Physiology, 206,* 1389–1394.

Satinoff, E. (1978). Neural organization and evolution of thermal regulation in mammals. *Science, 201,* 16–22.

Savage-Rumbaugh, S., Shanker, S. G., & Taylor, T. J. (1998). *Apes, language, and the human mind.* New York: Oxford University Press.

Savine, R., & Sonksen, P. (2000). Growth hormone: Hormone replacement for the somatopause? *Hormone Research, 53*(Suppl. 3), 37–41.

Saxena, S. (2003). Neuroimaging and the pathophysiology of obsessive compulsive disorder (OCD). In C. H. Y. Fu, C. Senior, T. Russell, D. Weinberger, & R. Murray (Eds.), *Neuroimaging in psychiatry* (pp. 191–224). London, UK: Martin Dunitz.

Sayer, F. T., Kronvall, E., & Nilsson, O. G. (2006). Methylprednisolone treatment in acute spinal cord injury: The myth challenged through a structured analysis of published literature. *The Spine Journal: Official Journal of the North American Spine Society, 6,* 335–343.

Sbordone, R. J., Liter, J. C., & Pettler-Jennings, P. (1995). Recovery of function following severe traumatic brain injury: A retrospective 10-year follow-up. *Brain Injury, 9,* 285–299.

Scarmeas, N., Shih, T., Stern, Y., Ottman, R., & Rowland, L. P. (2002). Premorbid weight, body mass, and varsity athletics in ALS. *Neurology, 59*(5), 773–775.

Schachter, S., & Singer, J. (1962). Cognitive, social and physiological determinants of emotional state. *Psychological Review, 69,* 379–399.

Schaffer, C. E., Davidson, R. J., & Saron, C. (1983). Frontal and parietal electroencephalogram asymmetry in depressed and nondepressed subjects. *Biological Psychiatry, 18,* 753–762.

Schaffir, J. (2006). Hormonal contraception and sexual desire: A critical review. *Journal of Sex and Marital Therapy, 32*(4), 305–314.

Schaie, K. W. (1994). The course of adult intellectual development. *American Psychologist, 49,* 304–313.

Schechter, R., & Grether, J. K. (2008). Continuing increases in autism reported to California's developmental services system: Mercury in retrograde. *Archives of General Psychiatry, 65*(1), 19–24.

Schellenberg, E. G., & Trehub, S. (1996). Children's discrimination of melodic intervals. *Developmental Psychology, 32,* 1039–1051.

Schenck, C. H., Bundlie, S. R., Ettinger, M. G., & Mahowald, M. W. (1986). Chronic behavioral disorders of human REM sleep: A new category of parasomnia. *Sleep, 9,* 293–308.

Schernhammer, E. S., & Schulmeister, K. (2004). Melatonin and cancer risk: Does light at night compromise physiologic cancer protection by lowering serum melatonin levels? *British Journal of Cancer, 90*(5), 941–943.

Schernhammer, E. S., Kroenke, C. H., Dowsett, M., Folkerd, E., & Hankinson, S. E. (2006). Urinary 6-sulfatoxymelatonin levels and their correlations with lifestyle factors and steroid hormone levels. *Journal of Pineal Research, 40*(2), 116–124.

Schiffito, G., Sacktor, N., Marder, K., McDermott, M. P., McArthur, J. C., Kieburtz, K., et al. (1999). Randomized trial of the platelet-activating factor antagonist lexipafant in HIVassociated cognitive impairment. *Neurology, 53,* 391–396.

Schiller, P. H., & Carvey, C. E. (2005). The Hermann grid illusion revisited. *Perception, 34*(11), 1375–1397.

Schlagger, B. L., & O'Leary, D. D. (1991). Potential of visual cortex to develop an array of functional units unique to somatosensory cortex. *Science, 252,* 1556–1560.

Schlaug, G., & Christian, G. (2001, May). *Musical training during childhood may influence regional brain growth.* Paper presented at the annual meeting of the American Academy of Neurology, Philadelphia, PA.

Schlaug, G., Jancke, L., Huang, Y., & Steinmetz, H. (1995). In vivo evidence of structural brain asymmetry in musicians. *Science, 267,* 699–701.

Schlessinger, D., Herrera, L., Crisponi, L., Mumm, S., Percesepe, A., Pellegrini, M., et al. (2002). Genes and translocations involved in POF. *American Journal of Medical Genetics, 111*(3), 328–333.

Schmolesky, M. T., Wang, Y., Pu, M., & Leventhal, A. G. (2000). Degradation of stimulus selectivity of visual cortical cells in senescent rhesus monkeys. *Nature Neuroscience, 3,* 384–390.

Schneider, J. S., Stone, M. K., Wynne-Edwards, K. E., Horton, T. E., Lydon, J., O'Malley, B., & Levine, J. E. (2003). Progesterone receptors mediate male aggression toward infants. *Proceedings of the National Academy of Sciences of the United States of America, 100,* 2951–2956.

Schredl, M., Ciric, P., Götz, S., & Wittmann, L. (2004). Typical dreams: Stability and gender differences. *Journal of Psychology, 138*(6), 485–494.

Schuckit, M. A., & Smith, T. L. (1997). Assessing the risk for alcoholism among sons of alcoholics. *Journal of Studies on Alcohol, 58,* 141–145.

Schultz, R. T. (2005). Developmental deficits in social perception in autism: The role of the amygdala and fusiform face area. *International Journal of Developmental Neuroscience, 23,* 125–141.

Schulze, K., McDonald, C., Frangou, S., Sham, P., Grech, A., Toulopoulou, T., et al. (2003). Hippocampal volume in familial and nonfamilial schizophrenic probands and their unaffected relatives. *Biological Psychiatry, 53,* 562–570.

Schumann, C. M., Hamstra, J., Goodlin-Jones, B. L., Lotspeich, L. J., Kwon, H., Buonocore, M. H., et al. (2004). The amygdala is enlarged in children but not adolescents with autism; the hippocampus is enlarged at all ages. *Journal of Neuroscience, 24,* 6392–6401.

Schuurman, P. R., Bosch, D. A., Bossuyt, P. M. M., Bonsel, G. J., van Someren, E. J. W., de Bie, R. M. A., et al. (2000). A comparison of continuous thalamic stimulation and thalamotomy for suppression of severe tremor. *New England Journal of Medicine, 342,* 461–468.

Schwab, M. E., Suda, K., & Thoenen, H. (1979). Selective retrograde transsynaptic transfer of a protein, tetanus toxin, subsequent to its retrograde axonal transport. *Journal of Cell Biology, 82*(3), 798–810.

Schwartz, J. H. (2000). Neurotransmitters. In E. R. Kandel, J. H. Schwartz, and T. M. Jessell (Eds.), *Principles of neural science,* (4th ed, pp. 280–297). New York: McGraw-Hill.

Schwartz, S. (1994). *Visual perception: A clinical orientation.* Norwalk, CT: Appleton & Lange.

Schwartz, W., & Gainer, H. (1977). Suprachiasmatic nucleus: Use of 14C-labelled deoxyglucose uptake as a functional marker. *Science, 197,* 1089–1091.

Schwartz, W., Reppert, S. M., Eagan, S. M., & Moore-Ede, M. C. (1983). In vivo metabolic activity of the suprachiasmatic nuclei: A comparative study. *Brain Research, 274,* 184–187.

Scientific American. (1999). *The Scientific American book of the brain.* New York: Author.

Sclafani, A., Springer, D., & Kluge, L. (1976). Effects of quinine adulteration on the food intake and body weight of obese and nonobese hypothalamic hyperphagic rats. *Physiology and Behavior, 16,* 631–640.

Scott, V., & Gijsbers, K. (1981). Pain perception in competitive swimmers. *British Medical Journal* [Clinical research ed.], *283,* 91–93.

Search and Rescue Society of British Columbia. (1995). *Hypothermia: Physiology, signs, symptoms, and treatment considerations.* Retrieved February 3, 2003, from the Search and Rescue Society of British Columbia Web site: http://www.sarbc.org/hypo1.html.

Sears, C. L. (2005). A dynamic partnership: Celebrating our gut flora. *Anaerobe, 11*(5), 247–251.

Sebrechts, M. M., Marsh, R. L., & Seamon, J. G. (1989). Secondary memory and very rapid forgetting. *Memory & Cognition, 17,* 693–700.

Seeman, P., Schwarz, J., Chen, J. F., Szechtman, H., Perreault, M., McKnight, G. S., et al. (2006). Psychosis pathways converge via D2high dopamine receptors. *Synapse, 60*(4), 319–346.

Segerstrom, S. C., & Miller, G. E. (2004). Psychological stress and the human immune system: A meta-analytic study of 30 years of inquiry. *Psychological Bulletin, 130,* 601–630.

Sehgal, A., Price, J. L., Man, B., & Young, M. W. (1994). Loss of circadian behavioral rhythms and per RNA oscillations in the Drosophila mutant timeless. *Science, 263,* 1603–1606.

Sehic, E., Ungar, A. L., & Blatteis, C. M. (1996). Interaction between norepinephrine and prostaglandin E2 in the preoptic area of guinea pigs. *American Journal of Physiology, 271,* R528–536.

Seidenbecher, T., Balschun, D., & Reymann, K. G. (1995). Drinking after water deprivation prolongs "unsaturated" LTP in the dentate gyrus of rats. *Physiology and Behavior, 57*(5), 1001–1004.

Seksel, K., & Lindeman, M. J. (2001). Use of clomipramine in treatment of obsessive-compulsive disorder, separation anxiety and noise phobia in dogs: A preliminary, clinical study. *Australian Veterinary Journal, 79,* 252–256.

Sekuler, R., & Blake, R. (2002). *Perception* (4th ed.). Boston: McGraw-Hill.

Selverstone, V. J., Doucette, P. A., & Zittin, P. S. (2005). Copper-zinc superoxide dismutase and amyotrophic lateral sclerosis. *Annual Review of Biochemistry, 74,* 563–593.

Selye, H. (1936). A syndrome produced by diverse nocuous agents. *Nature, 138,* 32.

Selye, H. (1946). The general adaptation syndrome and the diseases of adaptation. *Journal of Clinical Endocrinology, 6,* 177–231.

Selye, H. (1976). *The stress of life.* New York: McGraw-Hill.

Serbin, L. A., Poulin-Dubois, Colburne, K. A., Sen, M. G., & Eichstedt, J. A. (2001). Gender stereotyping in infancy: Visual preferences for and knowledge of gender-stereotyped toys in the second year. *International Journal of Behavioral Development, 25*(1), 7–15.

Sergent, J., Zuck, E., Terriah, S., & MacDonald, B. (1992). Distributed neural network underlying musical sight-reading and keyboard performance. *Science, 256,* 106–109.

Seroczynski, A. D., Bergeman, C. S., & Coccaro, E. F. (1999). Etiology of the impulsivity/aggression relationship: Genes or environment? *Psychiatry Research, 86*(1), 41–57.

Shaner, A., Miller, G., & Mintz, J. (2004). Schizophrenia as one extreme of a sexually selected fitness indicator. *Schizophrenia Research, 70,* 101–109.

Shapira, M., Thompson, C. K., Soreq, H., & Robinson, G. E. (2001). Changes in neuronal acetylcholinesterase gene expression and division of labor in honeybee colonies. *Journal of Molecular Neuroscience, 17,* 1–12.

Shapley, R., & Perry, V. H. (1986). Cat and monkey retinal ganglion cells and their visual functional roles. *Trends in Neurosciences, 9,* 229–235.

Shaw, P. J., Cirelli, C., Greenspan, R. J., & Giulio Tononi, G. (2000). Correlates of sleep and waking in *Drosophila melanogaster. Science, 287,* 1834–1837.

Shaw, P., Eckstrand, K., Sharp, W., Blumenthal, J., Lerch, J. P., Greenstein, D., et al. (2007). Attention-deficit/hyperactivity disorder is characterized by a delay in cortical maturation. *Proceedings of the National Academy of Sciences of the United States of America (PNAS), 104*(49), 19649–19654.

Shaywitz, S. (1996). Dyslexia. *Scientific American, 275,* 98–105.

Shaywitz, S. E., Morris, R., & Shaywitz, B. A. (2008). The education of dyslexic children from childhood to young adulthood. *Annual Review of Psychology, 59,* 451–475.

Shaywitz, S., Shaywitz, B. A., Pugh, K. R., Fulbright, R. K., Constable, R. T., Mencl, W. E., et al. (1998). Functional disruption in the organization of the brain for reading in dyslexia. *Proceedings of the National Academy of Sciences of the United States of America, 95,* 2636–2641.

Shearman, L. P., Sriram, S., Weaver, D. R., Maywood, E. S., Chaves, I., Zheng, B., et al. (2000). Interacting molecular loops in the mammalian circadian clock, *Science, 288,* 1013–1019.

Sheline, Y. I., Barch, D. M., Donnelly, J. M., Ollinger, J. M., Snyder, A. Z., & Mintun, M. A. (2001). Increased amygdala response to masked emotional faces in depressed subjects resolves with antidepressant treatment: An fMRI study. *Biological Psychiatry, 50*(9), 651–658.

Shelton, R. C., Keller, M. B., Gelenberg, A., Dunner, D. L., Hirschfeld, R., & Thase, M. E. (2001). Effectiveness of St. John's Wort in major depression: A randomized controlled trial. *Journal of the American Medical Association, 285,* 1978.

Shema, R., Sacktor, T. C., & Dudai, Y. (2007). Rapid erasure of long-term memory associations in the cortex by an inhibitor of PKM zeta. *Science, 317*(5840), 951–953.

Sheng, H.-W. (2000). Sodium, chloride, and potassium. In M. Stipanuk (Ed.), *Biochemical and physiological aspects of human nutrition* (pp. 686–710). Philadelphia: Saunders.

Shepherd, S., & Martin, J. M. (2002). *Submersion injury, near drowning.* Retrieved February 5, 2003, from http://www.emedicine.com/emerg/topic744.htm.

Sherman, C. (2000). Treatment for psychopaths is likely to make them worse. *Clinical Psychiatry News, 28,* 38.

Sherwin, B. B., & Henry, J. F. (2008). Brain aging modulates the neuroprotective effects of estrogen on selective aspects of cognition in women: A critical review. *Frontiers in Neuroendocrinology, 29*(1), 88–113.

Shi, L., Fatemi, S. H., Sidwell, R. W., & Patterson, P. H. (2003). Maternal influenza infection causes marked behavioral and pharmacological changes in the offspring. *Journal of Neuroscience, 23,* 297–302.

Shibata, D., & Zhong, J. (2001, November). *Tactile vibrations are heard in auditory cortex in the deaf: Study with FMRI.* Paper presented at the 87th annual convention of the Radiological Society of North America, Chicago, IL.

Shibata, S., & Moore, R. Y. (1988). Development of a fetal circadian rhythm after disruption of the maternal circadian system. *Brain Research, 469,* 313–317.

Shifren, J. L., Braunstein, G. D., Simon, J. A., Casson, P. R., Buster, J. E., Redmond, G. P., et al. (2000). Transdermal testosterone treatment in women with impaired sexual function after oophorectomy. *New England Journal of Medicine, 343*(10), 682–688.

Shih, R. A., Belmonte, P. L., & Zandi, P. P. (2004). A review of the evidence from family, twin and adoption studies for a genetic contribution to adult psychiatric disorders. *International Review of Psychiatry, 16*(4), 260–283.

Shima, K., & Tanji, J. (1998). Role for cingulate motor area cells in voluntary movement selection based on reward. *Science, 282*(5392), 1335–1338.

Shimada, M., Tritos, N. A., Lowell, B. B., Flier, J. S., & Maratos-Flier, E. (1999). Mice lacking melanin-concentrating hormone are hypophagic and lean. *Nature, 396,* 670–674.

Shimoda, K., & Robinson, R. G. (1999). The relationship between poststroke depression and lesion location in long-term follow-up. *Biological Psychiatry, 45,* 187–192.

Shirota, A., Tanaka, H., Nittono, H., Hayashi, M., Shirakawa, S., & Hori, T. (2002). Volitional lifestyle in healthy elderly: Its relevance to rest–activity cycle, nocturnal sleep, and daytime napping. *Perceptual and Motor Skills, 95,* 101–108.

Shute, N. (2000, June 5). A maddening disconnect: Unraveling the mysteries of autism. *U.S. News & World Report.* Retrieved December 16, 2000, from http://www.usnews.com/usnews/issue/000605/autism.htm.

Si, K., Giustetto, M., Etkin, A., Hsu, R., Janisiewicz, A. M., Miniaci, M. C., et al. (2003). A neuronal isoform of CPEB regulates local protein synthesis and stabilizes synapse-specific long-term facilitation in *Aplysia. Cell, 115,* 893–904.

Si, K., Lindquist, S., & Kandel, E. R. (2003). A neuronal isoform of the *Aplysia* CPEB has prion-like properties. *Cell, 115,* 879–891.

Siegel, J. (1995). Phylogeny and the function of REM sleep. *Behavioural Brain Research, 69,* 29–34.

Siegel, J. M. (1999). Narcolepsy: A key role for hypocretins (orexins). *Cell, 98*(4), 409–412.

Siegel, J. M. (2004). Hypocretin (orexin): Role in normal behavior and neuropathology. *Annual Review of Psychology, 55,* 125–148.

Siegel, J. M. (2005). Clues to the functions of mammalian sleep. *Nature, 437*(7063), 1264–1271.

Siegel, J. M. (2008). Do all animals sleep? *Trends in Neurosciences, 31*(4), 208–213.

Siegel, J. M., & Rogawski, M. A. (1988). A function for REM sleep: Regulation of noradrenergic receptor sensitivity. *Brain Research Review, 13,* 213–233.

Siegel, R. K. (1989). *Intoxication: Life in pursuit of artificial paradise.* New York: Dutton.

Siegel, S., Hinson, R. E., Krank, M. D., & McCully, J. (1982). Heroin "overdose" death: Contribution of drug-associated environmental cues. *Science, 216,* 436–437.

Siever, L. J. (2008). Neurobiology of aggression and violence. *The American Journal of Psychiatry, 165*(4), 429–442.

Sievert, L. L., Obermeyer, C. M., & Price, K. (2006). Determinants of hot flashes and night sweats. *Annals of Human Biology, 33*(1), 4–16.

Sillito, A. 1995. *The Artful Eye.* Oxford: Oxford University Press.

Silvanto, J. (2008). A re-evaluation of blindsight and the role of striate cortex (V1) in visual awareness. *Neuropsychologia, 46*(12), 2869–2871.

Silventoinen, K., Magnusson, P. K., Tynelius, P., Kaprio, J., & Rasmussen, F. (2008). Heritability of body size and muscle strength in young adulthood: A study of one million Swedish men. *Genetic Epidemiology, 32*(4), 341–349.

Simmons, A., Matthews, S. C., Feinstein, J. S., Hitchcock, C., Paulus, M. P., & Stein, M. B. (2008). Anxiety vulnerability is associated with altered anterior cingulate response to an affective appraisal task. *Neuroreport, 19*(10), 1033–1037.

Simner, J., & Hubbard, E. M. (2006). Variants of synesthesia interact in cognitive tasks: Evidence for implicit associations and late connectivity in cross-talk theories. *Neuroscience, 143*(3), 805–814.

Simon, R. P., Swan, J. H., Griffiths, T., & Meldrum, B. S. (1984). Blockage of N-methyl-D-aspartate receptors may protect against ischemic damage in the brain. *Science, 226,* 850–852.

Simpson, J. B., Epstein, A. N., & Camardo, J. S. (1978). The localization of dipsogenic receptors for angiotensin II in the subfornical organ. *Journal of Comparative and Physiological Psychology, 92,* 581–608.

Sinclair, A. H., Berta, P., Palmer, M. S., Hawkins, J. R., Griffiths, B. L., Smith, M. J., et al. (1990). A gene from the human sex-determining region encodes a protein with homology to a conserved DNA binding motif. *Nature, 346,* 240–244.

Sinclair, R. C., Hoffman, C., Mark, M. M., Martin, L. L., & Pickering, T. L. (1994). Construct accessibility and the misattribution of arousal. *Psychological Science, 5,* 15–19.

Sinden, J. D., Hodges, H., & Gray, J. A. (1995). Neural transplantation and recovery of cognitive function. *Behavioral and Brain Sciences, 18,* 10–35.

Singh, D. (1993). Adaptive significance of female physical attractiveness: Role of waist-to-hip ratio. *Journal of Personality and Social Psychology, 65,* 293–307.

Sitaram, N., Moore, A. M., & Gillan, J. C. (1978). Experimental acceleration and slowing of REM ultradian rhythm by cholinergic agonist and antagonist. *Nature, 274,* 490–492.

Skene, D. J., Lockley, S. W., & Arendt, J. (1999). Use of melatonin in the treatment of phase shift and sleep disorders. *Advances in Experimental Medicine and Biology, 467,* 79–84.

Slagboom, P. E., Droog, S., & Boomsma, D. I. (1994). Genetic determination of telomere size in humans: A twin study of three age groups. *American Journal of Human Genetics, 55,* 876–882.

Sloane, P. D., Zimmerman, S., Suchindran, C., Reed, P., Wang, L., Boustani, M., et al. (2002). The public health impact of Alzheimer's disease, 2000–2050: Potential implication of treatment advances. *Annual Review of Public Health, 23,* 213–231.

Slob, A. K., Bax, C. M., Hop, W. C., Rowland, D. L., & van der Werff ten Bosch, J. J. (1996). Sexual arousability and the menstrual cycle. *Psychoneuroendocrinology, 21,* 545–558.

Smirniotopoulos, J. (2002). Intracranial vascular malformations. Retrieved June 1, 2002, from http://rad.usuhs.mil/rad/home/vascmalf/malf0.html.

Smith, A., & Sugar, O. (1975). Development of above normal language and intelligence 21 years after left hemispherectomy. *Neurology, 25*(9), 813–818.

Smith, C., & Fazekas, A. (1997). Amounts of REM sleep and stage 2 sleep required for efficient learning. *Sleep Research, 26,* 960.

Smith, C., & MacNeill, C. (1994) Impaired motor memory for a pursuit rotor task following Stage 2 sleep loss in college students. Journal of Sleep Research,3(4), 206–213.

Smith, L., & Byers, J. F. (2002). Gene therapy in the post-Gelsinger era. *JONAS Healthcare Law, Ethics and Regulation, 4*(4), 104–110.

Smith, P. M., Beninger, R. J., & Ferguson, A. V. (1995). Subfornical organ stimulation elicits drinking. *Brain Research Bulletin, 38,* 209–213.

Smith, T. W. (1992). Hostility and health: Current status of a psychosomatic hypothesis. *Health Psychology, 11,* 139–150.

Smith, T. W. (1998, December). *American sexual behavior: Trends, socio-demographic differences, and risk behavior* (GSS Topical Report No. 25). National Opinion Research Center, University of Chicago.

Smith, T., & Lovaas, I. (1998). Intensive early behavioral intervention with autism: The UCLA Young Autism Project. *Infants and Young Children, 10,* 67–78.

Smock, T. K. (1999). *Physiological Psychology: A neuroscience Approach.* Upper Saddle River, NJ: Prentice-Hall.

Snapinn, K. W., Holmes, E. C., Young, D. S., Bernard, K. A., Kramer, L. D., & Ebel, G. D. (2007). Declining growth rate of West Nile virus in North America. *Journal of Virology, 81*(5), 2531–2534.

Sneed, D. (2006). Teen murder suspect's judgment could be impaired, says doctor. *The Tribune,* p. B1.

Snow, C. E. (1993). Bilingualism and second language acquisition. In J. B. Gleason & N. B. Ratner (Eds.), *Psycholinguistics* (pp. 391–416). Fort Worth, TX: Harcourt Brace Jovanovich.

Snowdon, D. (1997). Aging and Alzheimer's disease: Lessons from the nun study. *Gerontologist, 37,* 150–156.

Snyder, A., Bahramali, H., Hawker, T., & Mitchell, D. J. (2006). Savant-like numerosity skills revealed in normal people by magnetic pulses. *Perception, 35*(6), 837–845.

Snyder, S. H., & Dawson, T. M. (2000). Nitric oxide and related substance as neural messengers. In *Psychopharmacology: The fourth generation of progress.* Nashville, TN: American College of Neuropsychopharmacology.

Snyderman, M., & Rothman, S. (1987). Survey of expert opinion on intelligence and aptitude testing. *American Psychologist, 42,* 137–144.

Sobel, N., Prabhakaran, V., Zhao, Z., Desmond, J. E., Glover, G. H., Sullivan, E. V., et al. (2000). Time course of odorantinduced activation in the human primary olfactory cortex. *Journal of Neurophysiology, 83,* 537–551.

Society for Neuroscience. (2008). About membership. Retrieved May 21, 2008, from http://www.sfn.org/index.cfm?pagename=membership_AboutMembership§ion=membership

Sohal, R. S., & Weindruch, R. (1996). Oxidative stress, caloric restriction, and aging. *Science, 273,* 59–68.

Sokoll, G. R., & Mynatt, C. R. (May 1984). *Arousal and free throw shooting.* Paper presented at the meeting of the Midwestern Psychological Association. Chicago.

Solomons, N. W. (2007). Food fortification with folic acid: Has the other shoe dropped? *Nutrition Reviews, 65*(11), 512–515.

Somerville, L. H., Wig, G. S., Whalen, P. J., & Kelley, W. M. (2006). Dissociable medial temporal lobe contributions to social memory. *Journal of Cognitive Neuroscience, 18*(8), 1253–1265.

Sommer, I. E., Aleman, A., Somers, M., Boks, M. P., & Kahn, R. S. (2008). Sex differences in handedness, asymmetry of the planum temporale and functional language lateralization. *Brain Research, 1206,* 76–88.

Sommer, I., Ramsey, N., Kahn, R., Aleman, A., & Bouma, A. (2001). Handedness, language lateralisation and anatomical asymmetry in schizophrenia: Meta-analysis. *British Journal of Psychiatry, 178*(4), 344–351.

Soomro, G. M., Altman, D., Rajagopal, S., & Oakley-Browne, M. (2008). Selective serotonin re-uptake inhibitors (SSRIs) versus placebo for obsessive compulsive disorder (OCD). Cochrane database of systematic reviews (Online) (Cochrane Database Syst Rev) 2008(1): CD001765.

Sørensen, K. (1987). *Klinefelter's syndrome in childhood, adolescence and youth: A genetic, clinical, developmental, psychiatric and psychological study.* Chippenham, Wiltshire, UK: Parthenon.

Sorenson, J. M., Wheless, J. W., Baumgartner, J. E., Thomas, A. B., Brookshire, B. L., Clifton, G. L., & Willmore, L. J. (1997). Corpus callosotomy for medically intractable seizures. *Pediatric Neurosurgery, 27,* 260–267.

Sortland, O., & Tysvaer, A. T. (1989). Brain damage in former association football players: An evaluation by cerebral computed tomography. *Neuroradiology, 31,* 44–48.

Sowell, E. R., Thompson, P. M., Holmes, C. J., Jernigan, T. L., & Toga, A. W. (1999). In vivo evidence for post-adolescent brain maturation in frontal and striatal regions. *Nature Neuroscience, 2*(10), 859–861.

Sparing, R., Meister, I. G., Wienemann, M., Buelte, D., Staedtgen, M., & Boroojerdi, B. (2007). Task-dependent modulation of functional connectivity between hand motor cortices and neuronal networks underlying language and music: A transcranial magnetic stimulation study in humans. *European Journal of Neuroscience, 25*(1), 319–323.

Spear, P. D., Kim, C. B.-Y., Ahmad, A., & Tom, B. W. (1996). Relationship between numbers of retinal ganglion cells and lateral geniculate neurons in the rhesus monkey. *Visual Neuroscience, 13,* 199–203.

Spence, S. A., Kaylor-Hughes, C., Farrow, T. F., & Wilkinson, I. D. (2008). Speaking of secrets and lies: The contribution of ventrolateral prefrontal cortex to vocal deception. *Neuroimage, 40*(3), 1411–1418.

Sperling, R. (2007). Functional MRI studies of associative encoding in normal aging, mild cognitive impairment, and Alzheimer's disease. *Annals of the New York Academy of Sciences, 1097,* 146–155.

Sperry, R. (1945). The problem of central nervous reorganization after nerve regeneration and muscle transposition. *Quarterly Review of Biology, 20,* 311–369.

Sperry, R. W. (1974). Lateral specialization in the surgically separated hemispheres. In F. O. Schmitt & F. G. Worden (Eds.), *The neurosciences: Third study program* (pp. 5–20). Cambridge, MA: MIT Press.

Sperry, R. W. (1982). Some effects of disconnecting the cerebral hemispheres. *Science, 217,* 1223–1226.

Sperry, R. W., Gazzaniga, M. S., & Bogen, J. E. (1969). Interhemispheric relationships: The neocortical commissures; syndromes of hemisphere disconnection. In P. J. Vinken & G. W. Bruyn (Eds.), *Handbook of clinical neurology* (Vol. 4, pp. 273–290). New York: Wiley.

Spiegel, K., Leproult, R., & Van Cauter, E. (1999). Impact of sleep debt on metabolic and endocrine function. *Lancet, 354*(9188), 1435–1439.

Spiegel, K., Tasali, E., Penev, P., & Van Cauter, E. (2004). Brief communication: Sleep curtailment in healthy young men is associated with decreased leptin levels, elevated ghrelin levels, and increased hunger and appetite. *Annals of Internal Medicine, 141*(11), 846–850.

Spieker, L. E., Sudano, I., Hürlimann, D., Lerch, P. G., Lang, M. G., Binggeli, C., Corti, R., Ruschitzka, F., Lüscher, T. F., & Noll, G. (2002). High-density lipoprotein restores endothelial function in hypercholesterolemic men. *Circulation, 105,* 1399–1402.

Spina Bifida Association of America. (2001). *Facts about spina bifida.* Retrieved April 18, 2001, from the Spina Bifida Association of America Web site: http://www.sbaa.org/html/sbaa_facts.html.

Spires, T. L., Grote, H. E., Varshney, N. K., Cordery, P. M., van Dellen, A., Blakemore, C., et al. (2004). Environmental enrichment rescues protein deficits in a mouse model of Huntington's disease, indicating a possible disease mechanism. *Journal of Neuroscience, 24,* 2270–2276.

Spiteri, E., Konopka, G., Coppola, G., Bomar, J., Oldham, M., Ou, J., et al. (2007). Identification of the transcriptional targets of FOXP2, a gene linked to speech and language, in developing human brain. *American Journal of Human Genetics, 81*(6), 1144–1157.

Spoormaker, V. I., & van den Bout, J. (2006). Lucid dreaming treatment for nightmares: A pilot study. *Psychotherapy and Psychosomatics, 75*(6), 389–394.

Spreen, O., & Benton, A. L. (1969). *Neurosensory Center Comprehensive Examination for aphasia.* Victoria, British Columbia: University of Victoria Neuropsychology Laboratory.

Springer, S. P., & Deutsch, G. (1998). *Left brain, right brain* (5th ed.). New York: Freeman.

Squire, L. R. (1987). *Memory and the brain.* New York: Oxford University Press.

Squire, L. R., & Moore, R. Y. (1979). Dorsal thalamic lesion in a noted case of chronic memory dysfunction. *Annals of Neurology, 6,* 503–506.

Squire, L. R., Amaral, D. G., Zola-Morgan, S., & Kritchevsky, M. P. G. (1989). Description of brain injury in the amnesic patient N. A. based on magnetic resonance imaging. *Experimental Neurology, 105,* 23–35.

Squire, L. R., Zola-Morgan, S., Cave, C. B., Haist, F., Musen, G., & Suzuki, W. A. (1990). Memory: Organization of brain systems and cognition. *Cold Spring Harbor Symposium on Quantitative Biology, 55,* 1007–1023.

Stacher, G. (1986). Effects of cholecystokinin and caerulein on human eating behavior and pain sensation: A review. *Psychoneuroendocrinology, 11,* 39–48.

Stader, S. R., & Hokanson, J. E. (1998). Psychosocial antecedents of depressive symptoms: An evaluation using daily experiences methodology. *Journal of Abnormal Psychology, 107,* 17–26.

Stahl, L. A., Begg, D. P., Weisinger, R. S., & Sinclair, A. J. (2008). The role of omega-3 fatty acids in mood disorders. *Current Opinion in Investigational Drugs,* 9(1), 57–64.

Stanley, B. G., Magdalin, W., Seirafi, A., Thomas, W. J., & Leibowitz, S. F. (1993). The perifornical area: The major focus of (a) patchily distributed hypothalamic neuropeptide Y-sensitive feeding system(s). *Brain Research, 604,* 304–317.

Stanley, S. A., Connan, F., Small, C. J., Murphy, K. G., Todd, J. F., Ghatei, M., et al. (2003). Elevated circulating levels of cocaine-and amphetamine-regulated transcript (CART) in anorexia nervosa. *Endocrine Abstracts, 5,* OC30.

Stark, E. (1984, October 16). To sleep, perchance to dream. *Psychology Today, 18,* 16.

Stearns, V., Ullmer, L., Lopez, J. F., Smith, Y., Isaacs, C., & Hayes, D. (2002). Hot flushes. *Lancet, 360,* 1851–1861.

Steele, C. M., & Josephs, R. A. (1990). Alcohol myopia: Its prized and dangerous effects. *American Psychologist, 45,* 921–934.

Stein, M. B., Simmons, A. N., Feinstein, J. S., & Paulus, M. P. (2007). Increased amygdala and insula activation during emotion processing in anxiety-prone subjects. *American Journal of Psychiatry, 164*(2), 318–327.

Stein-Behrens, B., Mattson, M. P., Chang, I., Yeh, M., & Sapolsky, R. (1994). Stress exacerbates neuron loss and cytoskeletal pathology in the hippocampus. *Journal of Neuroscience, 14,* 5373–5380.

Steiner, M., Brown, E., Trzepacz, P., Dillon, J., Berger, C., Carter, D., et al. (2003). Fluoxetine improves functional work capacity in women with premenstrual dysphoric disorder. *Archives of Women's Mental Health, 6,* 71–77.

Steinhausen, H. C., Willms, J., & Spohr, H. (1994). Correlates of psychopathology and intelligence in children with fetal alcohol syndrome. *Journal of Child Psychology and Psychiatry, 37,* 339–343.

Steinschneider, A. (1972). Prolonged apnea and the sudden infant death syndrome: Clinical and laboratory observations. *Pediatrics, 197,* 646–654.

Stella, N., Schweitzer, P., & Piomelli, D. (1997). A second endogenous cannabinoid that modulates long-term potentiation. *Nature, 388,* 773–778.

Stellar, J. R., Kelley, A. E., & Corbett, D. (1983). Effects of peripheral and central dopamine blockade on lateral hypothalamic self-stimulation: Evidence for both reward and motor deficits. *Pharmacology, Biochemistry, and Behavior, 18,* 433–442.

Stephan, F. K., & Zucker, I. (1972). Circadian rhythms in drinking behavior and locomotor activity of rats are eliminated by hypothalamic lesions. *Proceedings of the National Academy of Sciences of the United States of America, 69,* 1583–1586.

Stephan, K. E., Fink, G. R., & Marshall, J. C. (2007). Mechanisms of hemispheric specialization: Insights from analyses of connectivity. *Neuropsychologia, 45*(2), 209–228.

Steriade, M., & McCarley, R. W. (2005). *Brain control of sleep and wakefulness.* New York: Kluwer Academic Press.

Sterman, M. B., & Clemente, C. D. (1962). Forebrain inhibitory mechanisms: Cortical synchronization induced by basal forebrain stimulation. *Experimental Neurology, 6,* 91–102.

Sternberg, R. J., & Salter, W. (1982). Conceptions of intelligence. In R. J. Sternberg (Ed.), *Handbook of human intelligence* (pp. 3–28). New York: Cambridge University Press.

Sternberg, W. F., Bailin, D., Grant, M., & Gracely, R. H. (1998). Competition alters the perception of noxious stimuli in male and female athletes. *Pain, 76*(1–2), 231–238.

Sterr, A., Herron, K. A., Hayward, C., & Montaldi, D. (2006). Are mild head injuries as mild as we think? Neurobehavioral concomitants of chronic post-concussion syndrome. *BMC Neurology, 6,* 7.

Stevens, S. S. (1960). Psychophysics of sensory function. *American Scientist, 48,* 226–252.

Stewart, W. K., & Fleming, L. W. (1973). Features of a successful therapeutic fast of 382 days' duration. *Postgraduate Medical Journal, 49,* 203–209.

Stickgold, R., & Walker, M. P. (2007). Sleep-dependent memory consolidation and reconsolidation. *Sleep Medicine, 8*(4), 331–343.

Stickgold, R., James, L., & Hobson, J. A. (2000). Visual discrimination learning requires sleep after training. *Nature Neuroscience, 3,* 1237–1238.

Stiefel Laboratories. (2001). *Excessive perspiration.* Retrieved February 5, 2003, from the Stiefel Laboratories Web site: http://www.oilatum.co.uk/consumer/perspiration/about.html.

Stoil, M. J. (1987–1988). The case of the missing gene: Hereditary protection against alcoholism. *Alcohol Health and Research World, 12,* 130–136.

Stoller, R. J., & Herdt, G. H. (1985). Theories of origins of male homosexuality. A cross-cultural look. *Archives of General Psychiatry, 42,* 399–404.

Stone, A. C., Starrs, J. E., & Stoneking, M. (2001). Mitochondrial DNA analysis of the presumptive remains of Jesse James. *Journal of Forensic Science, 46*(1), 173–176.

Stone, V. E., Nisenson, L., Eliassen, J. C., & Gazzaniga, M. S. (1996). Left hemisphere representations of emotional facial expressions. *Neuropsychologia, 34,* 23–29.

Stovner, L. J., Zwart, J. A., Hagen, K., Terwindt, G. M., & Pascual, J. (2006). Epidemiology of headache in Europe. *European Journal of Neurology, 13*(4), 333–345.

Streissguth, A. P., Aase, J. M., Clarren, S. K., Randels, S. P., LaDue, R. A., & Smith, D. F. (1991). Fetal alcohol syndrome in adolescents and adults. *Journal of the American Medical Association, 264,* 1961–1967.

Strickland, B. R. (1992). Women and depression. *Current Directions in Psychological Science, 1,* 132–135.

Substance Abuse and Mental Health Services Administration (SAMHSA). (2007). *Results from the 2006 National Survey on Drug Use and Health: National findings.* Retrieved March 25, 2008. from http://oas.samhsa.gov/nsduh/2k6nsduh/2k6results.pdf.

Sumner, P., & Mollon, J. D. (2000). Catarrhine photopigments are optimised for detecting targets against a foliage background. *Journal of Experimental Biology, 203,* 1963–1986.

Sun, T., & Walsh, C. A. (2006). Molecular approaches to brain asymmetry and handedness. *Nature Reviews Neuroscience, 7,* 655–662.

Sun, T., Patoine, C., Abu-Khalil, A., Visvader, J., Sum, E., Cherry, T. J., et al. (2005). Early asymmetry of gene transcription in embryonic human left and right cerebral cortex. *Science, 308*(5729), 1794–1798.

Svensson, E. C., Black, H. B., Dugger, D. L., Tripathy, S. K., Goldwasser, E., Hao, Z., et al. (1997). Longterm erythropoietin expression in rodents and non-human primates following intramuscular injection of a replication-defective adenoviral vector. *Human Gene Therapy, 8,* 1797–1806.

Swanson, J. M., McBurnett, K., Christian, D. L., & Wigal, T. (1995). Stimulant medications and the treatment of children with ADHD. In T. Ollendick & R. J. Prinz (Eds.), *Advances in clinical child psychology* (pp. 265–322). New York: Plenum Press.

Swanson, J., Castellanos, F. X., Murias, M., LaHoste, G., & Kennedy, J. (1998). Cognitive neuroscience of attention deficit hyperactivity disorder and hyperkinetic disorder. *Current Opinion in Neurobiology, 8,* 263–271.

Swedo, S. E., Leonard, H. L., Mittleman, B. B., Allen, A. J., Rapoport, J. L., Dow, S. P., et al. (1997). Identification of children with pediatric autoimmune neuropsychiatric disorders associated with streptococcal infections by a marker associated with rheumatic fever. *American Journal of Psychiatry, 154,* 110–112.

Sweeney, H. L. (2004). Gene doping. *Scientific American, 291*(1), 62–69.

Symons, D. (1995). Beauty is in the adaptation of the beholder: The evolutionary psychology of human female sexual attractiveness. In P. R. Abramson & S. D. Pinkerton (Eds.), *Sexual nature/sexual culture* (pp. 80–120). Chicago: University of Chicago Press.

Syvalahti, E. K. G. (April 1994). I. The theory of schizophrenia: Biological factors in schizophrenia. *British Journal of Psychiatry Supplement, 164,* 9–14.

Szeszko, P. R., MacMillan, S., McMeniman, M., Chen, S., Baribault, K., Lim, K. O., et al. (2004). Brain structural abnormalities in psychotropic drug-naive pediatric patients with obsessive-compulsive disorder. *American Journal of Psychiatry, 161*(6), 1049–1056.

Szyf, M., McGowan, P., & Meaney, M. J. (2008). The social environment and the epigenome. *Environmental and Molecular Mutagenesis, 49*(1), 46–60.

Szymusiak, R., & McGinty, D. (1986). Sleep-related neuronal discharge in the basal forebrain of cats. *Brain Research, 370,* 82–92.

Tafet, G. E., & Bernardini, R. (2003). Psychoneuroendocrinological links between chronic stress and depression. *Progress in Neuropsychopharmacology and Biological Psychiatry, 27,* 893–903.

Tainturier, M. J., Moreaud, O., David, D., Leek, E. C., & Pellat, J. (2001). Superior written over spoken picture naming in a case of frontotemporal dementia. *Neurocase, 7,* 89–96.

Takahashi, K., Tanabe, K., Ohnuki, M., Narita, M., Ichisaka, T., Tomoda, K., et al. (2007). Induction of pluripotent stem cells from adult human fibroblasts by defined factors. *Cell, 131,* 861–872.

Tallal, P. (1991). Hormonal influences in developmental learning disabilities. *Psychoneuroendocrinology, 16,* 203–211.

Tallal, P., Ross, R., & Curtiss, S. (1989). Familial aggregation in Specific Language Impairment. *Journal of Speech and Hearing Disorders, 54,* 167–171.

Tamminga, C., & Schulz, S. C. (1991). *Schizophrenia research.* New York: Raven Press.

Tanaka, K., & Saito, H. (1989). Analysis of motion of the visual field by direction, expansion/contraction, and rotation cells clustered in the dorsal part of the medial superior temporal area of the macaque monkey. *Journal of Neurophysiology, 62,* 626–641.

Tang, Y. P., Shimizu, E., Dube, G. R., Rampon, C., Kerchner, G. A., Zhuo, M., et al. (1999). Genetic enhancement of learning and memory in mice. *Nature, 401*(6748), 63–69.

Tanji, J., & Evarts, E. V. (1976). Anticipatory activity of motor cortex neurons in relation to direction of an intended movement. *Journal of Neurophysiology, 39,* 1062–1068.

Tannock, R. (1998). Attention deficit hyperactivity disorder: Advances in cognitive, neurobiological, and genetic research. *Journal of Child Psychology and Psychiatry, 39,* 65–99.

Taubes, G. (2000). Toward molecular talent scounting. *Scientific American, 11,* 26–31.

Tausk, F., Elenkov, I., & Moynihan, J. (2008). Psychoneuroimmunology. *Dermatologic Therapy, 21*(1), 22–31.

Tavris, D. (1989). *Anger: The misunderstood emotion.* New York: Simon & Schuster.

Taylor, C., Fricker, A. D., Devi, L. A., & Gomes, I. (2005). Mechanisms of action of antidepressants: From neurotransmitter systems to signaling pathways. *Cellular Signaling, 17*(5), 549–557.

Taylor, D. J., Jenni, O. G., Acebo, C., & Carskadon, M. A. (2005). Sleep tendency during extended wakefulness: Insights into adolescent sleep regulation and behavior. *Journal of Sleep Research, 14*(3), 239–244.

Taylor, L., Faraone, S. V., & Tsuang, M. T. (2002). Family, twin, and adoption studies of bipolar disease. *Current Psychiatry Reports, 4,* 130–133.

Taylor, S. F., Martis, B., Fitzgerald, K. D., Welsh, R. C., Abelson, J. L., Liberzon, I., et al. (2006). Medial frontal cortex activity and loss-related responses to errors. *Journal of Neuroscience, 26*(15), 4063–4070.

Teasdale, G. M., Nicoll, J. A. R., Murray, G., & Fiddes, M. (1997). Association of apolipoprotein E polymorphism with outcome after head injury. *Lancet, 350,* 1069–1071.

Terman, L. (1916). *The measurement of intelligence.* Boston: Houghton Mifflin.

Terp, I. M., & Mortensen, P. B. (1998). Post-partum psychoses: Clinical diagnoses and relative risk of admission after parturition. *British Journal of Psychiatry, 172,* 521–526.

Terrace, H. S. (1979, November). How Nim Chimpsky changed my mind. *Psychology Today,* 65–76.

Tetrault, J. M., Crothers, K., Moore, B. A., Mehra, R., Concato, J., & Fiellin, D. A. (2007). Effects of marijuana smoking on pulmonary function and respiratory complications: A systematic review. *Archives of Internal Medicine, 167*(3), 221–228.

Tetrud, J. W., Langston, J. W., Irwin, I., & Snow, B. (1994). Parkinsonism caused by petroleum waste ingestion. *Neurology, 44,* 1051–1054.

Teuber, H. L., & Rudel, R. G. (1962). Behavior after cerebral lesions in children and adults. *Developmental Medicine and Child Neurology, 3,* 3–20.

Thacher, P. V. (2008). University students and "the all nighter": Correlates and patterns of students' engagement in a single night of total sleep deprivation. *Behavioral Sleep Medicine, 6*(1), 16031.

Thannickal, T. C., Moore, R. Y., Nienhuis, R., Ramanathan, L., Gulyani, S., Aldrich, M., et al. (2000). Reduced number of hypocretin neurons in human narcolepsy. *Neuron, 27,* 469–474.

Thase, M. E. (2002). Antidepressant effects: The suit may be small, but the fabric is real. *Prevention and Treatment, 5,* Article 32. Retrieved May 26, 2003, from journals.apa.org/prevention/volume5/ toc-jul15-02.html.

The science of gender and science: Pinker vs. Spelke, a debate. (2005). Retrieved April 27, 2008, from http://www.edge.org/3rd_culture/debate05/debate05_index.html

Thiboudot, D., & Chen, W. (2003). Update and future of hormonal therapy in acne. *Dermatology, 206,* 57–67.

Thiruchelvan, M., Richfield, E., Baggs, R., Tank, A. W., & Cory-Slechta, D. (2000). The nigrostriatal dopaminergic system as a preferential target of repeated exposures to combined paraquat and maneb: Implications for Parkinson's disease. *Journal of Neuroscience, 20,* 9207–9214.

Thomas, K. G. F., Laurance, H. E., Jacobs, W. J., & Nadel, L. (1995). Memory for traumatic events: Formulating hypotheses and critical experiments. *Traumatology, 1.* Retrieved May 14, 2004, from http://www.greenhouse.ort/_Research/Vol1-2.asp.

Thompson, M. A., Callaghan, P. D., Hunt, G. E., Cornish, J. L., & McGregor, I. S. (2007). A role for oxytocin and 5-HT(1A) receptors in the prosocial effects of 3,4 methylenedioxymethamphetamine ("ecstasy"). *Neuroscience, 146*(2), 509–514.

Thompson, P. M., Cannon, T. D., Narr, K. L., van Erp, T., Poutanen, V.-P., Huttunen, M., et al. (2001). Genetic influences on brain structure. *Nature Neuroscience, 4,* 1253–1258.

Thompson, P. M., Giedd, J. N., Woods, R. P., MacDonald, D., Evans, A. C., & Toga, A. W. (2000). Growth patterns in the developing brain detected by using continuum mechanical tensor maps. *Nature, 404*(6774), 190–193.

Thompson, P. M., Vidal, C., Giedd, J. N., Gochman, P., Blumenthal, J., Nicolson, R., et al. (2001). Mapping adolescent brain change reveals dynamic wave of accelerated gray matter loss in very early-onset schizophrenia. *Proceedings of the National Academy of Science of the United States of America (PNAS), 98,* 11650–11655.

Thompson, R. F. (1986). The neurobiology of learning and memory. *Science, 233,* 941–947.

Thompson, R. F., Thompson, J. K., Kim, J. J., Krupa, D. J., & Shinkman, P. G. (1998). The nature of reinforcement in cerebellar learning. *Neurobiology of Learning and Memory, 70*(1–2), 150–176.

Thorgeirsson, T. E., Geller, F., Sulem, P., Rafnar, T., Wiste, A., Magnusson, K. P., et al. (2008). A variant associated with nicotine dependence, lung cancer and peripheral arterial disease. *Nature, 452*(7187), 638–642.

Thornhill, R., & Gangestad, S. W. (1994). Fluctuating asymmetry correlates with lifetime sex partner numbers and age at first sex in *Homo sapiens. Psychological Science, 5,* 297–303.

Tinbergen, N. (1951). *The study of instinct.* Oxford, UK: Clarendon Press.

Tinson, D. J. (1989). How stroke patients spend their days: An observational study of the treatment regimen offered to patients with movement disorders in hospitals following stroke. *International Disability Studies, 11,* 45–49.

Tishkoff, S. A., Gonder, M. K., Henn, B. M., Mortensen, H., Knight, A., Gignoux, C., et al. (2007). History of click-speaking populations of Africa inferred from mtDNA and Y chromosome genetic variation. *Molecular Biology and Evolution, 24*(10), 2180–2195.

Tisserand, D. J., Bosma, H., Van Boxtel, M. P. J., & Jolles, J. (2001). Head size and cognitive ability in nondemented older adults are related. *Neurology, 56,* 969–971.

Titus-Ernstoff, L., Perez, K., Hatch, E. E., Troisi, R., Palmer, J. R., Hartge, P., et al. (2003). Psychosexual characteristics of men and women exposed prenatally to diethylstilbestrol. *Epidemiology, 14,* 155–160.

Toot, J., Dunphry, G., & Ely, D. (2001, October). *Sex differences in brain monoamines and aggression.* Paper presented at the meeting of the American Physiological Society, Pittsburgh, PA.

Tosini, G., & Fukuhara, C. (2003). Photic and circadian regulation of retinal melatonin in mammals. *Journal of Neuroendocrinology, 15,* 364–369.

Tovée, M. J., Reinhardt, S., Emery, J. L., & Cornelissen, P. L. (1998). Optimum body-mass index and maximum sexual attractiveness. *Lancet, 352,* 548.

Traub, S. J., Hoffman, R. S., & Nelson, L. S. (2002). The "ecstasy" hangover: Hyponatremia due to 3,4-methylenedioxymethamphetamine. *Journal of Urban Health, 79*(4), 549–555.

Treffert, D. A., & Wallace, G. L. (2002). Islands of genius. *Scientific American, 286,* 76–85.

Trimble, B. K., & Baird, P. A. (1978). Maternal age and Down syndrome: Age specific incidence rates by single year intervals. *Journal of Medical Genetics, 2,* 1.

Trivedi, M. H., Greer, T. L., Grannemann, B. D., Church, T. S., Galper, D. I., Sunderajan, P., et al. (2006). TREAD: TReatment with Exercise Augmentation for Depression: Study rationale and design. *Clinical Trials, 3*(3), 291–305.

Trivers, R., & Burt, A. (1999). Kinship and genomic imprinting. *Results and Problems in Cell Differentiation, 25,* 1–21.

Trotti, D., Rolfs, A., Danbolt, N. C., Brown, R. H., & Hediger, M. A. (1999). SOD1 mutants linked to amyotrophic lateral sclerosis selectively inactivate a glial glutamate transporter. *Nature Neuroscience, 2,* 427–433.

Trujillo, K. Q., & Akil, H. (1991). Opiate tolerance and dependence: Recent findings and synthesis. *New Biologist, 3,* 915–923.

Trulson, M. E., & Crisp, T. (1986). Do serotonin-containing dorsal raphe neurons possess autoreceptors? *Experimental Brain Research, 62,* 579–586.

Trussell, J., Ellertson, C., Stewart, F., Raymond, E. G., & Shochet, T. (2004). The role of emergency contraception. *American Journal of Obstetrics and Gynecology, 190*(4, Supplement 1), S30–S38.

Tsai, S. J. (2005). Is autism caused by early hyperactivity of brain-derived neurotrophic factor? *Medical Hypotheses, 65*(1), 79–82.

Tsien, J. Z., Huerta, P. T., & Tonegawa, S. (1996). The essential role of hippocampal CA1 NMDA receptor-dependent synaptic plasticity in spatial memory. *Cell, 87,* 1327–1338.

Tuba, Z., Maho, S., & Vizi, E. S. (2002). Synthesis and structure-activity relationships of neuromuscular blocking agents. *Current Medicinal Chemistry, 9*(16), 1507–1536.

Tulving, E. (1972). Episodic and semantic memory. In E. Tulving & W. Donaldson (Eds.), *Organization and memory.* New York: Academic Press.

Tulving, E. (1985). How many memory systems are there? *American Psychologist, 40,* 385–398.

Tulving, E. (1987). Multiple memory systems and consciousness. *Human Neurobiology, 6,* 67–80.

Tulving, E. (1989). Memory: Performance, knowledge, and experience. *European Journal of Cognitive Psychology, 1,* 3–26.

Tulving, E. (1995). Organization of memory: Quo vadis? In M. S. Gazzaniga (Ed.), *The cognitive neurosciences* (pp. 839–853). Cambridge, MA: MIT Press.

Tulving, E. (1998). Brain/mind correlates of human memory. In M. Sabourin, F. Craik, & M. Robert (Eds.), *Advances in psychological science: Vol. 2. Biological and cognitive aspects* (pp. 441–460). Hove, East Sussex, UK: Psychology Press.

Turek, F. W., Joshu, C., Kohsaka, A., Lin, E., Ivanova, G., McDearmon, E., et al. (2005). Obesity and metabolic syndrome in circadian Clock mutant mice. *Science, 308*(5724), 1043–1045.

Turley-Ames, K. J., & Whitfield, M. M. (2003). Strategy training and working memory task performance. *Journal of Memory and Language, 49,* 446–468.

Turnbaugh, P. J., Ley, R. E., Mahowald, M. A., Magrini, V., Mardis, E. R., & Gordon, J. I. (2006). An obesity-associated gut microbiome with increased capacity for energy harvest. *Nature, 444*(7122), 1027–1031.

Turner, S. M., Beidel, D. C., & Nathan, R. S. (1985). Biological factors in obsessive-compulsive disorders. *Psychological Bulletin, 97,* 430–450.

Tysvaer, A. T., & Storli, O. V. (1989). Soccer injuries to the brain: A neurologic and encephalographic study of active football players. *American Journal of Sports Medicine, 17,* 573–578.

U.S. Department of Agriculture. (2002). *Bovine spongiform encephalopathy (BSE).* Retrieved May 29, 2002, from the U.S. Department of Agriculture Web site: http://www.aphis.usda.gov/oa/bse/.

U.S. Department of Health and Human Services (SAMHSA) Office of Applied Studies (2006). Results from the 2006 National Survey on Drug Use and Health: National results. Retrieved on October 29, 2008 from http://www.oas.samhsa.gov/NSDUH/2k6NSDUH/2k6results.cfm#8.1.5

U.S. Department of Health and Human Services. (1999, December). *Draft National Institutes of Health guidelines for research involving human pluripotent stem cells.* Retrieved June 9, 2002, from the National Institutes of Health Web site: http://www.nih.gov/news/stemcell/draftguidelines.htm.

U.S. Department of Health and Human Services. (2003). *What are the purposes and background of the Privacy Rule?* Retrieved July 1, 2003, from the National Institutes of Health Web site: http://privacyruleandresearch.nih.gov/pr_04.asp.

U.S. Food and Drug Administration (FDA). (2006). Inter-agency advisory regarding claims that smoked marijuana is a medicine. Retrieved April 3, 2008, from http://www.fda.gov/bbs/topics/NEWS/2006/NEW01362.html.

U.S. Food and Drug Administration (FDA; 2002). What can I expect before, during and after liposuction? Retrieved on October 15, 2008 from http://www.fda.gov/cdrh/liposuction/expect.html#2

U.S. Food and Drug Administration. (1993). 3-month contraceptive injection approved. *FDA Medical Bulletin, 23,* 6–7.

U.S. Food and Drug Administration. (1995, August 31). *Monosodium glutamate.* Retrieved November 24, 2002, from the U.S. Food and Drug Administration Web site: http://www.fda.gov/opacom/backgrounders/msg.html.

U.S. Food and Drug Administration. (2002). Liposuction information. Retrieved February 12, 2003, from the U.S. Food and Drug Administration Web site: http://www.fda.gov/cdrh/liposuction/alternatives.html.

U.S. Food and Drug Administration. (2004). Black box warning added concerning long-term use of Depo-Provera contraceptive injection. Retrieved April 21, 2008, from http://www.fda.gov/bbs/topics/ANSWERS/2004/ANS01325.html

U.S. Institute of Medicine. (1979). *Sleeping pills, insomnia, and medical practice.* Washington, DC: National Academy of Sciences.

Udry, J. R. (1970). The effect of the great blackout of 1965 on births in New York City. *Demography, 7,* 325–327.

UK Creutzfeldt-Jakob Disease Surveillance Unit. (2002). *Creutzfeldt-Jakob disease.* Retrieved May 30, 2002, from http://www.cjd.ed.ac.uk/intro.htm.

UK ECT Review Group. (2003). Efficacy and safety of electroconvulsive therapy in depressive disorders: A systematic review and meta-analysis. *Lancet, 361,* 799–808.

Ullian, E. M., Sapperstein, S. K., Christopherson, K. S., & Barres, B. A. (2001). Control of synapse number by glia. *Science, 291,* 657–661.

Umhau, J., George, D. T., Reed, S., Petrulis, S. G., Rawlings, R., & Porges, S. W. (2002). Atypical autonomic regulation in perpetrators of violent domestic abuse. *Psychophysiology, 39,* 117–123.

Ungerleider, L. G., & Mishkin, M. (1982). Two cortical visual systems. In D. J. Ingle, M. A. Goodale, & R. J. Mansfield (Eds.), *Analysis of visual behavior* (pp. 549–580). Cambridge, MA: MIT Press.

Ungless, M. A., Whistler, J. L., Malenka, R. C., & Bonci, A. (2001). Single cocaine exposure in vivo induces long-term potentiation in dopamine neurons. *Nature, 411,* 583–587.

United Nations Office on Drugs and Crime. (2001). The seventh United Nations survey on crime trends and the operations of criminal justice systems (1998–2000). Retrieved October 7, 2007, from http://www.unodc.org/unodc/crime_cicp_survey_seventh.html.

University of Pennsylvania. (2001, July). Bionic ear implanted by Penn surgeons to give hearing to the deaf [Press release]. Philadelphia: University of Pennsylvania, Office of Public Affairs.

University of Washington PKU Clinic. (2000). *What is the diet for PKU?* Retrieved December 15, 2002, from the University of Washington Web site: http://depts.washington.edu/pku/diet.html.

Valenstein, E. S. (1986). *Great and desperate cures.* New York: Basic Books.

Valla, J., Berndt, J. D., & Gonzalez-Lima, F. (2001). Energy hypometabolism in posterior cingulate cortex of Alzheimer's patients: Superficial laminar cytochrome oxidase associated with disease duration. *Journal of Neuroscience, 21*(13), 4923–4930.

Valla, J., Berndt, J. D., & Gonzalez-Lima, F. (2001). Energy hypometabolism in posterior cingulate cortex of Alzheimer's patients: Superficial laminar cytochrome oxidase associated with disease duration. *Journal of Neuroscience, 21*(13), 4923–4930.

van Anders, S. M., & Watson, N. V. (2006). Relationship status and testosterone in North American heterosexual and non-heterosexual men and women: Cross-sectional and longitudinal data. *Psychoneuroendocrinology, 31*(6), 715–723.

van Anders, S. M., Hamilton, L. D., & Watson, N. V. (2007). Multiple partners are associated with higher testosterone in North American men and women. *Hormones and Behavior, 51*(3), 454–459.

van Apeldoorn, F. J., van Hout, W. J., Mersch, P. P., Huisman, M., Slaap, B. R., Hale, W. W., 3rd, et al. (2008). Is a combined therapy more effective than either CBT or SSRI alone? Results of a multicenter trial on panic disorder with or without agoraphobia. *Acta Psychiatrica Scandinavica, 117*(4), 260–270.

Van Borsel, J., Achten, E., Santens, P., Lahorte, P., & Voet, T. (2003). fMRI of developmental stuttering: A pilot study. *Brain and Language, 85,* 369–376.

Van Cauter, E., Leproult, R., & Plat, L. (2000). Age-related changes in slow wave sleep and REM sleep and relationship with growth hormone and cortisol levels in healthy men. *Journal of the American Medical Association, 284,* 861.

Van Dongen, H. P., Maislin, G., Mullington, J. M., & Dinges, D. F. (2003). The cumulative cost of additional wakefulness: Dose-response effects on neurobehavioral functions and sleep physiology from chronic sleep restriction and total sleep deprivation. *Sleep, 26*(2), 117–126.

Van Essen, D. C., & Anderson, C. H. (1995). Information processing strategies and pathways in the primate visual system. In S. F. Zornetzer, J. L. Davis, & C. Lau (Eds.), *An introduction to neural and electronic networks* (2nd ed., pp. 45–75). San Diego, CA: Academic Press.

van Londen, L., Goekoop, J. G., van Kempen, G. M. J., Frankhuijzen-Sierevogel, A. C., Wiegant, V. M., van der Velde, E. A., et al. (1997). Plasma levels of arginine vasopressin elevated in patients with major depression. *Neuropsychopharmacology, 17,* 284–292.

Van Os, J. (2004). Does the urban environment cause psychosis? *British Journal of Psychiatry, 184*(4), 287–288.

Van Someren, E. J., & Riemersma-Van Der Lek, R. F. (2007). Live to the rhythm, slave to the rhythm. *Sleep Medicine Reviews, 11*(6), 465–484.

Vandenburgh, H., Chromiak, J., Shansky, J., Del Tatto, M., & Lemaire, J. (1999). Space travel directly induces skeletal muscle atrophy. *FASEB Journal, 13,* 1031–1038.

Vanderbeek, R. D., & Emonson, D. L. (1995). The use of amphetamines in U.S. Air Force tactical operations during Desert Shield and Storm. *Aviation Space and Environmental Medicine, 66,* 230.

Vanni-Mercier, G., & Debilly, G. (1998). A key role for the caudoventral pontine tegmentum in the simultaneous generation of eye saccades in bursts and associated ponto-geniculo-occipital waves during paradoxical sleep in the cat. *Neuroscience, 86,* 571–585.

Vawter, M. P., Freed, W. J., & Kleinman, J. E. (2000). Neuropathology of bipolar disorder. *Biological Psychiatry, 48*(6), 486–504.

Vazquez, J., & Baghdoyan, H. A. (2001). Basal forebrain acetylcholine release during REM sleep is significantly greater than during waking. *American Journal of Physiology. Regulatory, Integrative and Comparative Physiology, 280*(2), R598–601.

Vellaichamy, M. (2001). Hyponatremia. *eMedicine Journal, 4*(1). Retrieved February 6, 2003, from http://author.emedicine.com/PED/topic1124.htm.

Velosa, J. F., & Riddle, M. A. (2000). Pharmacologic treatment of anxiety disorders in children and adolescents. *Child and Adolescent Psychiatry Clinics of North America, 9,* 119–133.

Venkatesh, B., Lu, S. Q., Dandona, N., See, S. L., Brenner, S., & Soong, T. W. (2005). Genetic basis of tetrodotoxin resistance in pufferfishes. *Current Biology, 15*(22), 2069–2072.

Verheyden, S. L., Hadfield, J., Calin, T., & Curran, H. V. (2002). Sub-acute effects of MDMA (+/-3, 4-methylenedioxymethamphetamine, "ecstasy") on mood: Evidence of gender differences. *Psychopharmacology, 161,* 23–31.

Verney, E. B. (1947). The antidiuretic hormone and the factors which determine its release. *Proceedings of the Royal Society of London, B, Biological Science, 135,* 25–106.

Videbech, P., & Ravnkilde, B. (2004). Hippocampal volume and depression: A meta-analysis of MRI studies. *American Journal of Psychiatry, 161*(11), 1957–1966.

Vijande, M., Lopez-Sela, P., Brime, J. I., Bernardo, R., Diaz, F., Costales, M., & Marin, B. (1990). Insulin stimulation of water intake in humans. *Appetite, 15,* 81–87.

Vince, G. (2006). Watching the brain "switch off" self-awareness. Retrieved August 18, 2006, from http://www.newscientist.com/article.ns?id=dn9019&feedId=online-news_rss20

Vining, E. P., Freeman, J. M., Pillas, D. J., Uematsu, S., Carson, B. S., Brandt, J., et al. (1997). Why would you remove half a brain? The outcome of 58 children after hemispherectomy: The Johns Hopkins experience: 1968 to 1996. *Pediatrics, 100*(2) Pt 1, 163–171.

Vinokur, R. (2004). Acoustic noise as a non-lethal weapon. *Sound and Vibration, 38,* 19–23.

Viscusi, E. R., & Schechter, L. N. (2006). Patient-controlled analgesia: Finding a balance between cost and comfort. *American Journal of Health-System Pharmacy, 63*(8 Suppl 1), S3–13; quiz S15–16.

Vitaterna, M. H., King, D. P., Chang, A. M., Kornhauser, J. M., Lowrey, P. L., McDonald, J. D., et al. (1994). Mutagenesis and mapping of a mouse gene, Clock, essential for circadian behavior. *Science, 278,* 38–39.

Vogel, G. W., Vogel, F., McAbee, R. S., & Thurmond, A. J. (1980). Improvement of depression by REM sleep deprivation: New findings and a theory. *Archives of General Psychiatry, 37,* 247–253.

Vogt, B. A., Finch, D. M., & Olson, C. R. (1992). Functional heterogeneity in cingulate cortex: The anterior executive and posterior evaluative regions. *Cerebral Cortex, 2*(6), 435–443.

Volkow, N. D., Fowler, J. S., & Wang, G.-J. (2004). Dopamine in drug abuse and addiction: Results from imaging studies and treatment implications. *Molecular Psychiatry, 9*(9), 557–569.

Volkow, N., & O'Brien, C. (2008). Drs. Volkow and O'Brien reply. *American Journal of Psychiatry, 165,* 139.

Vollenweider, F. X., Vollenweider-Sherpenhuyzen, M. F., Bäbler, A., Vogel, H., & Hell, D. (1998). Psilocybin induces schizophrenia-like psychosis in humans via a serotonin-2 agonist action. *Neuroreport, 9,* 3897–3902.

Von Economo, C., & Koskinas, G. N. (1929). *The cytoarchitectonics of the human cerebral cortex.* London: Oxford University Press.

von Gersdorff, H., & Matthews, G. (1994). Dynamics of synaptic vesicle fusion and membrane retrieval in synaptic terminals. *Nature, 367,* 735–739.

Von Helmholtz, H. (1856–1866). *Handbuch der physiologischen Optik.* Leipzig: Voss.

Vorel, S. R., Liu, X., Hayes, R. J., Spector, J. A., & Gardner, E. L. (2001). Relapse to cocaine-seeking after hippocampal theta burst stimulation. *Science, 292,* 1175–1178.

Wade, T. D., Bulik, C. M., Neale, M., & Kendler, K. S. (2000). Anorexia nervosa and major depression: Shared genetic and environmental risk factors. *American Journal of Psychiatry, 157*(3), 469–471.

Wager, T. D., Rilling, J. K., Smith, E. E., Sokolik, A., Casey, K. L., Davidson, R. J., et al. (2004). Placebo-induced changes in FMRI in the anticipation and experience of pain. *Science, 303,* 1162–1167.

Wagner, D. R. (1996). Disorders of the circadian sleep-wake cycle. *Neurological Clinics, 14,* 651–670.

Wagner, G. C., Beuving, L. J., & Hutchinson, R. R. (1980). The effects of gonadal hormone manipulations on aggressive target-biting in mice. *Aggressive Behavior, 6,* 1–7.

Wagner, G., Koch, K., Schachtzabel, C., Reichenbach, J. R., Sauer, H., & Schlösser Md, R. G. (2008). Enhanced rostral anterior cingulate cortex activation during cognitive control is related to orbitofrontal volume reduction in unipolar depression. *Journal of Psychiatry and Neuroscience, 33*(3), 199–208.

Wagner, M. L., Walters, A. S., & Fisher, B. C. (2004). Symptoms of attention-deficit/hyperactivity disorder in adults with restless legs syndrome. *Sleep, 27*(8), 1499–1504.

Wagner, U., Fischer, S., & Born, J. (2002). Changes in emotional responses to aversive pictures across periods rich in slow-wave sleep versus rapid eye movement sleep. *Psychosomatic Medicine, 64*(4), 627–634.

Wagner, U., Gais, S., & Born, J. (2001). Emotional memory formation is enhanced across sleep intervals with high amounts of rapid eye movement sleep. *Learning and Memory, 8*(2), 112–119.

Wahlstrom, K. L. (2003). Changing times: Findings from the first longitudinal study of later high school start times. *Bulletin of the National Association of Secondary School Principals (NASSP), 86,* 3–21.

Wald, G., & Brown, P. K. (1958). Human rhodopsin. *Science, 127,* 222–226.

Wallace, D. (1997, August). Mitochondrial DNA in aging and disease. *Scientific American, 277,* 40–47.

Walter, G., Cordier, L., Bloy, D., & Sweeney, H. L. (2005). Noninvasive monitoring of gene correction in dystrophic muscle. *Magnetic Resonance in Medicine, 54*(6), 1369–1376.

Wang, J., Horlick, M., Thornton, J. C., Levine, L. S., Heymsfield, S. B., & Pearson, R. S., Jr. (1999). Correlations between skeletal muscle mass and bone mass in children 6–18 years: Influences of sex, ethnicity, and pubertal status. *Growth, Development, and Aging: GDA, 63,* 99–109.

Wang, Z. X., Ferris, C. F., & De Vries, G. J. (1994). Role of septal vasopressin innervation in paternal behavior in prairie voles (*Michrotus ochrogaster*). *Proceedings of the National Academy of Sciences of the United States of America, 91,* 400–404.

Wansink, B., & Huckabee, M. (2005). De-marketing obesity. *California Management Review, 47*(4), 6–18.

Ward, J., Hall, K., & Haslam, C. (2006). Patterns of memory dysfunction in current and 2-year abstinent MDMA users. *Journal of Clinical and Experimental Neuropsychology, 28*(3), 306–324.

Waterland, R. A., Travisano, M., Tabiliani, K. G., Rached, M. T., & Mirza, S. (2008). Methyl donor supplementation prevents transgenerational amplification of obesity. *International Journal of Obesity, 32*(9), 1373–1379.

Watkins, K. E., Smith, S. M., Davis, S., & Howell, P. (2008). Structural and functional abnormalities of the motor system in developmental stuttering. *Brain, 131*(1), 50–59.

Watkins, K. E., Vargha-Khadem, F., Ashburner, J., Passingham, R. E., Connelly, A., Friston, K. J., et al. (2002). MRI analysis of an inherited speech and language disorder: Structural brain abnormalities. *Brain, 127,* 465–478.

Watson, K. K., Jones, T. K., & Allman, J. M. (2006). Dendritic architecture of the von Economo neurons. *Neuroscience, 141,* 1107–1112.

Weaver, I. C., Cervoni, N., Champagne, F. A., D'Alessio, A. C., Sharma, S., Seckl, J. R., et al. (2004). Epigenetic programming by maternal behavior. *Nature Neuroscience, 7*(8), 847–854.

Webb, S. J., Nalty, T., Munson, J., Brock, C., Abbott, R., & Dawson, G. (2007). Rate of head circumference growth as a function of autism diagnosis and history of autistic regression. *Journal of Child Neurology, 22*(10), 1182–1190.

Webster, J., & Koch, H. F. (1996). Aspects of tolerability of centrally acting antihypertensive drugs. *Journal of Cardiovascular Pharmacology, 27* (Suppl. 3), S49–54.

Wederkind, C., & Füri, S. (1997). Body odour preferences in men and women: Do they aim for specific MHC combinations or simple heterogeneity? *Proceedings of the Royal Society of London, B, Biological Science, 264,* 1471–1479.

Wehr, T., Sack, D., Rosenthal, N., Duncan, W., & Gillin, J. C. (1983). Circadian rhythm disturbances in manic-depressive illness. *Federation Proceedings, 42,* 2809–2814.

Weiller, C., May, A., Limmroth, V., Jüptner, M., Kaube, H., Schayck, R. V., et al. (1995). Brainstem activation in spontaneous human migraine attacks. *Nature Medicine, 1,* 658–660.

Weinberger, D. R., Aloia, M. S., Goldberg, T. E., & Berman, K. F. (1994). The frontal lobes and schizophrenia. *Journal of Neuropsychiatry and Clinical Neurosciences, 6,* 419–427.

Weindruch, R., Walford, R. L., Fligiel, S., & Guthrie, D. (1986). The retardation of aging in mice by dietary restriction: Longevity, cancer, immunity, and lifetime energy intake. *Journal of Nutrition, 116,* 641–654.

Weiner, R. D. (1984). Does ECT cause brain damage? *Brain and Behavior Science, 7,* 153.

Weinmann, M. (2003). Hot on the inside. *Emergency Medical Services, 32*(7), 34.

Weinrich, M., & Wise, S. P. (1982). The premotor cortex of the monkey. *Journal of Neuroscience, 2,* 1329–1345.

Weissman, M. M., Warner, V., Wickramaratne, P., Moreau, D., & Olfson, M. (1997). Offspring of depressed parents: 10 years later. *Journal of Affective Disorders, 15,* 269–277.

Weissman, T., Noctor, S. C., Clinton, B. K., Honig, L. S., & Kriegstein, A. R. (2003). Neurogenic radial glial cells in reptile, rodent and human: From mitosis to migration. *Cerebral Cortex, 13,* 550–559.

Wells, A. S., Read, N. W., Laugharne, J. D., & Ahluwalia, N. S. (1998). Alterations in mood after changing to a low-fat diet. *British Journal of Nutrition, 79,* 23–30.

Wender, P. H., Kety, S. S., Rosenthal, D., Schulsinger, F., Ortmann, J., & Lunde, I. (1986). Psychiatric disorders in the biological and adoptive families of adopted individuals with affective disorders. *Archives of General Psychiatry, 43,* 923–929.

Wentorf, F. A., Sudoh, K., Moses, C., Arendt, E. A., & Carlson, C. S. (2006). The effects of estrogen on material and mechanical properties of the intra- and extra-articular knee structures. *American Journal of Sports Medicine, 34*(12), 1948–1952.

Werner, E., & Dawson, G. (2005). Validation of the phenomenon of autistic regression using home videotapes. *Archives of General Psychiatry, 62*(8), 889–895.

Wernicke, C. (1874). *Der aphasische symptomenkomplex.* Breslau, Germany: Cohn & Weigart.

Wessely, S., & Kerwin, R. (2004). Suicide risk and the SSRIs. *Journal of the American Medical Association, 292,* 379–381.

Westbrook, G. (2000). Seizures and epilepsy. In E. R. Kandel, J. H. Schwartz, & T. M. Jessell (Eds.), *Principles of neural science* (pp. 910–935). New York: McGraw-Hill.

Whalley, L. J., Starr, J. M., Athawes, R., Hunter, D., Pattie, A., & Deary, I. J. (2000). Childhood mental ability and dementia. *Neurology, 55,* 1455–1459.

White, G. L. (1980). Physical attractiveness and courtship progress. *Journal of Personality and Social Psychology, 39,* 660–668.

Whitley, R. J. (2006). Herpes simplex encephalitis: Adolescents and adults. *Antiviral Research, 71,* 141–148.

Whittington, C. J., Kendall, T., Fonagy, P., Cottrell, D., Cotgrove, A., & Boddington, E. (2004). Selective serotonin reuptake inhibitors in childhood depression: Systematic review of published vs. unpublished data. *Lancet, 363,* 1341–1345.

Widom, C. (1978). A methodology for studying non-institutionalized psychopaths. In R. D. Hare & D. Schalling (Eds.), *Psychopathic behaviour: Approaches to research* (pp. 71–84). Chichester, UK: Wiley.

Wiersma, D., Nienhuis, F. J., Slooff, C. J., & Giel, R. (1998). Natural course of schizophrenic disorders: A 15-year follow-up of a Dutch incidence cohort. *Schizophrenia Bulletin, 24,* 75–85.

Wildgruber, D., Ackermann, H., Kreifelts, B., & Ethofer, T. (2006). Cerebral processing of linguistic and emotional prosody: fMRI studies. *Progress in Brain Research, 156,* 249–268.

Wildgruber, D., Riecker, A., Hertrich, I., Erb, M., Grodd, W., Ethofer, T., et al. (2005). Identification of emotional intonation evaluated by fMRI. *Neuroimage, 24*(4), 1233–1241.

Wilensky, A. E., Schafe, G. E., Kristensen, M. P., & LeDoux, J. E. (2006). Rethinking the fear circuit: The central nucleus of the amygdala is required for the acquisition, consolidation, and expression of Pavlovian fear conditioning. *Journal of Neuroscience, 26*(48), 12387–12396.

Williams, S. (2006). Direct-to-consumer genetic testing: Empowering or endangering the public? Retrieved April 5, 2008, from http://www.dnapolicy.org/policy.issue.php?action=detail&issuebrief_id=32.

Williams, T. J., Pepitone, M. E., Christensen, S. E., Cooke, B. M., Huberman, A. D., Breedlove, N. J., et al. (2000). Finger-length ratios and sexual orientation. *Nature, 404,* 455–456.

Williamson, A. M., & Feyer, A. (2000). Moderate sleep deprivation produces impairments in cognitive and motor performance equivalent to legally prescribed levels of alcohol intoxication. *Occupational and Environmental Medicine, 57,* 649–655.

Wills, S. (1997). *Drugs of abuse.* Cambridge, UK: Pharmaceutical Press.

Wilton, P. (2002). A rule of thumb. *Canadian Medical Association Journal, 167,* 1367.

Wing, R. R., & Phelan, S. (2005). Long-term weight loss maintenance. *The American Journal of Clinical Nutrition, 82*(1), 222S–225.

Wingard, D. L., & Berkman, L. F. (1983). Mortality risk associated with sleeping patterns among adults. *Sleep, 6,* 102–107.

Winson, J. (1985). *Brain and psyche.* Garden City, NY: Anchor Press/Doubleday.

Winters, W. D. (1975). The continuum of CNS excitatory states and hallucinosis. In L. J. West & R. K. Siegel (Eds.), *Hallucinations* (pp. 53–70). New York: Wiley.

Wirth, T., & Ylä-Herttuala, S. (2006). Gene technology based therapies in the brain. *Advances and Technical Standards in Neurosurgery, 31,* 3–32.

Wirz-Justice, A. (2006). Biological rhyth*m disturbances in mood disorders. International Clinical Psychopharmacology,* 21(Suppl. 1), s11–15.

Wise, M. S., Arand, D. L., Auger, R. R., Brooks, S. N., & Watson, N. F. (2007). Treatment of narcolepsy and other hypersomnias of central origin. *Sleep, 30*(12), 1712–1727.

Witelson, S. F., Kigar, D. L., & Harvey, T. (1999). The exceptional brain of Albert Einstein. *Lancet, 353*(9170), 2149–2153.

Witkin, H., Mednick, S., Schulsinger, F., Bakkestrom, E., Christiansen, K., Goodenough, D., et al. (1976). Criminality in XYY and XXY men. *Science, 193,* 147–155.

Witt, D. M., Carter, C. S., Lederhendler, I. I., & Kirkpatrick, B. (1997). Regulatory mechanisms of oxytocin-mediated sociosexual behavior. In *The integrative neurobiology of affiliation.* (pp. 287–301). New York, NY, US: New York Academy of Sciences.

Wittling, W., Block, A., Genzel, S., & Schweiger, E. (1998). Hemisphere asymmetry in parasympathetic control of the heart. *Neuropsychologia, 36,* 461–468.

Wojtys, E. M., Huston, L. J., Lindenfeld, T. N., Hewett, T. E., & Greenfield, M. L. (1998). Association between the menstrual cycle and anterior cruciate ligament injuries in female athletes. *The American Journal of Sports Medicine, 26,* 614–619.

Wolfe, J., Erickson, D. J., Sharkansky, E. J., King, D. W., & King, L. A. (1999). Course and predictors of posttraumatic stress disorder among Gulf War veterans: A prospective analysis. *Journal of Consulting and Clinical Psychology, 67,* 520–528.

Wolff, K., Tsapakis, E. M., Winstock, A. R., Hartley, D., Holt, D., Forsling, M. L., et al. (2006). Vasopressin and oxytocin secretion in response to the consumption of ecstasy in a clubbing population. *Journal of Psychopharmacology, 20*(3), 400–410.

Wolfson, S., & Neave, N. (2002). Testosterone surge linked to sports home advantage. *New Scientist.* Retrieved May 26, 2002, from the New Scientist Web site: http://www.newscientist.com/news/news.jsp?id=ns99992050.

Wong-Riley, M. T. (1989). Cytochrome oxidase: an endogenous metabolic marker for neuronal activity. *Trends in Neurosciences, 12*(3), 94–101.

Wood, C. J., & Aggleton, J. P. (1989). Handedness in 'fast ball' sports: Do left-handers have an innate advantage? *British Journal of Psychology, 80*(2), 227–240.

Wood, J. M., Bootzin, R. R., Kihlstrom, J. F., & Schacter, D. L. (1992). Implicit and explicit memory for verbal information presented during sleep. *Psychological Science, 3,* 236–239.

Woodruff-Pak, D. S., & Disterhoft, J. F. (2008). Where is the trace in trace conditioning? *Trends in Neurosciences, 31*(2), 105–112.

Woodruff-Pak, D. S., Papka, M., & Ivry, R. B. (1996). Cerebellar involvement in eyeblink classical conditioning in humans. *Neuropsychology, 10,* 443–458.

Woodruff-Pak, D. S., Vogel, R. W., 3rd, Ewers, M., Coffey, J., Boyko, O. B., & Lemieux, S. K. (2001). MRI-assessed volume of cerebellum correlates with associative learning. *Neurobiology of Learning and Memory, 76*(3), 342–357.

Woods, B. T., & Teuber, H. L. (1973). Early onset of complementary specialization of cerebral hemispheres in man. *Transactions of the American Neurological Association, 98,* 113–117.

World Health Organization. (1993). *The management of fever in young children with acute respiratory infections in developing countries.* Retrieved February 3, 2003, from the World Health Organization Web site: http://www.who.int/childadolescent-health/New_Publications/CHILD_HEALTH/WHO_ARI_93.30.htm-2.%20UNDERSTANDING%20FEVER.

Wrangham, R. W., & Peterson, D. (1996). *Demonic males: Apes and the origins of human violence.* Boston: Houghton Mifflin.

Wright, R. (1994). *The moral animal: The new science of evolutionary psychology.* New York: Pantheon Books.

Wurtman, R. J. (2005). Genes, stress, and depression. *Metabolism, 54*(5), Supplement 1, 16–19.

Wurtman, R. J., Wurtman, J. J., Regan, M. M., McDermott, J. M., Tsay, R. H., & Breu, J. J. (2003). Effects of normal meals rich in carbohydrates or proteins on plasma tryptophan and tyrosine ratios. *American Journal of Clinical Nutrition, 77*(1), 128–132.

Xiao, Y., Richter, J. A., & Hurley, J. H. (2008). Release of glutamate and CGRP from trigeminal ganglion neurons: Role of calcium channels and 5-HT1 receptor signaling. *Molecular Pain, 4,* 12.

Yamazaki, S. (2000). Resetting central and peripheral circadian oscillators in transgenic rats. *Science, 288,* 682–685.

Yang, M. S., & Gill, M. (2007). A review of gene linkage, association and expression studies in autism and an assessment of convergent evidence. *International Journal of Developmental Neuroscience, 25*(2), 69–85.

Yang, Y., Hentati, A., Deng, H. X., Dabbagh, O., Sasaki, T., Hirano, M., et al. (2001). The gene encoding alsin, a protein with three guanine-nucleotide exchange factor domains, is mutated in a form of recessive amyotrophic lateral sclerosis. *Nature Genetics, 29,* 160–165.

Yates, W. R., Perry, P., & Murray, S. (1992). Aggression and hostility in anabolic steroid users. *Biological Psychiatry, 31,* 1232–1234.

Yerkes, R. M., & Dodson, J. D. (1908). The relation of strength of stimulus to rapidity of habit-formation. *Journal of Comparative Neurology and Psychology, 18,* 459–482.

Yin, J. C. P., Wallach, J. S., Del Vecchio, M., Wilder, E. L., Zhuo, H., Quinn, W. G., et al. (1994). Induction of a dominant negative CREB transgene specifically blocks long-term memory in Drosophila. *Cell, 79,* 49–58.

Yolken, R. H., Karlsson, H., Yee, F., Johnston-Wilson, N. L., & Torrey, E. F. (2000). Endogenous retroviruses and schizophrenia. *Brain Research Review, 31,* 193–199.

Yonkers, K., O'Brien, P., & Eriksson, E. (2008). Premenstrual syndrome. *The Lancet, 371*(9619), 1200–1210.

Yotsutsuji, T., Saitoh, O., Suzuki, M., Hagino, H., Mori, K., Takahashi, T., et al. (2003). Quantification of lateral ventricular subdivisions in schizophrenia by high-resolution three-dimensional magnetic resonance imaging. *Psychiatry Research, 122,* 1–12.

Young, A. S., Sullivan, G., Burnam, M. A., & Brook, R. H. (1998). Measuring the quality of outpatient treatment for schizophrenia. *Archives of General Psychiatry, 55,* 611–617.

Young, L. J., Wang, Z., & Insel, T. R. (1998). Neuroendocrine bases of monogamy. *Trends in Neurosciences, 21,* 71–75.

Yu, J., Vodyanik, M. A., Smuga-Otto, K., Antosiewicz-Bourget, J., Frane, J. L., Tian, S., et al. (2007). Induced pluripotent stem cell lines derived from human somatic cells. *Science, 318,* 1917–1920.

Yu, Y. W., Chen, T. J., Wang, Y. C., Liou, Y. J., Hong, C. J., & Tsai, S. J. (2003). Association analysis for neuronal nitric oxide synthase gene polymorphism with major depression and fluoxetine response. *Neuropsychobiology, 47,* 137–140.

Yun, A. J., Bazar, K. A., & Lee, P. Y. (2004). Pineal attrition, loss of cognitive plasticity, and onset of puberty during the teen years: Is it a modern maladaptation exposed by evolutionary displacement? *Medical Hypotheses, 63*(6), 939–950.

Zadra, A. L., & Pihl, R. O. (1997). Lucid dreaming as a treatment for recurrent nightmares. *Psychotherapy and Psychosomatics, 66,* 50–55.

Zager, A., Andersen, M. L., Ruiz, F. S., Antunes, I. B., & Tufik, S. (2007). Effects of acute and chronic sleep loss on immune modulation of rats. *American Journal of Physiology. Regulatory, Integrative and Comparative Physiology, 293*(1), R504–509.

Zaidel, D. (2001). Neuron soma size in the left and right hippocampus of a genius. *Proceedings of the Society for Neuroscience, 27.* Retrieved May 11, 2002, from http://cogprints.soton.ac.uk/documents/disk0/00/00/19/27/index.html.

Zambelli, H., Carelli, E., Honorato, D., Marba, S., Coelho, G., Carnevalle, A., et al. (2007). Assessment of neurosurgical outcome in children prenatally diagnosed with myelomeningocele and development of a protocol for fetal surgery to prevent hydrocephalus. *Child's Nervous System, 23*(4), 421–425.

Zambrano, A., Solis, L., Salvadores, N., Cortés, M., Lerchundi, R., & Otth, C. (2008). Neuronal cytoskeletal dynamic modification and neurodegeneration induced by infection with herpes simplex virus type 1. *Journal of Alzheimer's Disease, 14*(3), 259–269.

Zammitt, S., Allebeck, P., Andreasson, S., Lundberg, I., & Lewis, G. (2002). Self reported cannabis use as a risk factor for schizophrenia in Swedish conscripts of 1969: Historical cohort study. *British Medical Journal, 325,* 1199–1201.

Zatorre, R. J., Evans, A. C., & Meyer, E. (1994). Neural mechanisms underlying melodic perception and memory for pitch. *Journal of Neuroscience, 14,* 1908–1919.

Zatorre, R. J., Evans, A. C., Meyer, E., & Gjedde, A. (1992). Lateralization of phonetic and pitch discrimination in speech processing. *Science, 256,* 846–849.

Zeis, T., & Schaeren-Wiemers, N. (2008). Lame ducks or fierce creatures? The role of oligodendrocytes in multiple sclerosis. *Journal of Molecular Neuroscience, 35*(1), 91–100.

Zeki, S. (1983). Color coding in the cerebral cortex: The responses of wavelength-selective and color coded cells in monkey visual cortex to changes in wavelength composition. *Neuroscience, 9,* 767–781.

Zelman, S. (1973). Correlation of smoking history with hearing loss. *Journal of the American Medical Association, 223,* 920.

Zenhausen, R. (1978). Imagery, cerebral dominance and style of thinking: A unified field model. *Bulletin of the Psychonomic Society, 12,* 381–384.

Zerjal, T., Xue, Y., Bertorelle, G., Wells, R. S., Bao, W., Zhu, S., et al. (2003). The genetic legacy of the Mongols. *American Journal of Human Genetics, 72*(3), 717–721.

Zhang, Y., Proenca, R., Maffei, M., Barone, M., Leopold, L., & Friedman, J. M. (1994). Positional cloning of the mouse obese gene and its human homologue. *Nature, 372,* 425–432.

Zhang, Z. F., Morgenstern, H., Spitz, M. R., Tashkin, D. P., Yu, G. P., Marshall, J. R., et al. (1999). Marijuana use and increased risk of squamous cell carcinoma of the head and neck. *Cancer Epidemiology, Biomarkers & Prevention, 8,* 1071–1078.

Zhao, Y., & Klein, M. (2002). Modulation of the readily releasable pool of transmitter and of excitation-secretion coupling by activity and by serotonin at *Aplysia* sensorimotor synapses in culture. *Journal of Neuroscience, 22*(24), 10671–10679.

Zimmermann, K., Leffler, A., Babes, A., Cendan, C. M., Carr, R. W., Kobayashi, J.-i., et al. (2007). Sensory neuron sodium channel Nav1.8 is essential for pain at low temperatures. *Nature, 447*(7146), 856–859.

Zito, K. A., Vickers, G., & Robert, D. C. (1985). Disruption of cocaine and heroin self-administration following kainic acid lesions of the nucleus accumbens. *Pharmacology, Biochemistry, and Behavior, 23,* 1029–1036.

Zivin, J. A., & Choi, D. W. (1991). Stroke therapy. *Scientific American, 265,* 56–63.

Zmarzty, S. A., Wells, A. S., & Read, N. W. (1997). The influence of food on pain perception in healthy human volunteers. *Physiology of Behavior, 62,* 185–191.

Zou, Z., Horowitz, L. F., Montmayeur, J. P., Snapper, S., & Buck, L. (2001). Genetic tracing reveals a stereotyped sensory map in the olfactory cortex. *Nature, 414,* 173–179.

Zubieta, J. K., Bueller, J. A., Jackson, L. R., Scott, D. J., Xu, Y., Koeppe, R. A., et al. (2005). Placebo effects mediated by endogenous opioid activity on mu-opioid receptors. *Journal of Neuroscience, 25*(34), 7754–7762.

Zubieta, J.-K, Huguelet, P., Ohl, L. E., Koeppe, R. A., Kilbourn, M. R., Carr, J. M., et al. (2000). High vesicular monoamine transporter binding in asymptomatic Bipolar I Disorder: Sex differences and cognitive correlates. *American Journal of Psychiatry, 157,* 1619–1628.

Zubieta, J.-K., Smith, Y. R., Bueller, J. A., Xu, Y., Kilbourn, M. R., Jewett, D. M., et al. (2001). Regional mu opioid receptor regulation of sensory and affective dimensions of pain. *Science, 293,* 311–315.

Zuloaga, D. G., Puts, D. A., Jordan, C. L., & Breedlove, S. M. (2008). The role of androgen receptors in the masculinization of brain and behavior: What we've learned from the testicular feminization mutation. *Hormones and Behavior, 53*(5), 613–626.

Zuscho, H. (1983). Posttraumatic anosmia. *Archives of Otolaryngology, 4,* 252–256.

Zyzak, D. R., Otto, T., Eichenbaum, H., & Gallagher, M. (1995). Cognitive decline associated with normal aging in rats: A neuropsychological approach. *Learning and Memory, 2,* 1–16.

Name Index

Subject Index/Glossary

AAAS. *See* American Association for the Advancement of Science

Abducens nerve (VI) (ab-DOO-sens) A cranial nerve that controls the muscles of the eye., 46, 48f

Abilities, intelligence and, 397–398

Ablation (uh-BLAY-shun) The surgical removal of tissue., 17

Absolute refractory period The period in which an action potential will not occur in a particular location of an axon regardless of input., 78

Absorption The ability to retain something rather than reflect or transmit it to another location., 156

ACC. *See* Anterior cingulate cortex

Accidental spinal cord damage, 246–247

Accommodation The ability of the lens to change shape to adjust to the distance of the visual stimulus., 160

Acetyl CoA. *See* Acetyl coenzyme A

Acetyl coenzyme A (Acetyl CoA), 97

Acetylcholine (ACh) (ah-see-til-COE-leen) A major small-molecule neurotransmitter used at the neuromuscular junction, in the autonomic nervous system, and in the central nervous system., 50, 97, 97f, 106, 225, 245, 333t

Acetylcholinesterase (AChE) (ah-seetil-cole-in-ES-ter-aze) An enzyme that breaks down the neurotransmitter acetylcholine., 97

ACh. *See* Acetylcholine

AChE. *See* Acetylcholinesterase

Acoustic reflex The protective restriction of the movement of the tympanic membrane and the ossicles, resulting in a reduction of sound to the inner ear by a factor of 30 dB., 192–193

Acquired immune deficiency syndrome (AIDS) A disease of the human immune system caused by the human immunodeficiency virus (HIV) that renders the subject highly vulnerable to life-threatening conditions., 442–443

ACTH. *See* Adrenocorticotropic hormone

Actin A protein that makes up the thin filaments of the myofibril., 226

Action potential The nerve impulse arising in an axon., 61, 73, 78f, 89t
- channels open/close during, 77–78
- propagation of, 79–80f, 79–81
- refractory periods of, 78–79

ACTN3 gene, 229

Aδ (alpha-delta) fiber A myelinated fiber that carries information about cold and sharp pain to the central nervous system., 206, 207f

ADC. *See* AIDS dementia complex

Adderall A combination of amphetamine salts prescribed to treat attention deficit/hyperactivity disorder., 479

Addiction A compulsive craving for drug effects or other experience., 98-111
- to drugs, causes, 111–112
- to drugs, treatment, 112–113
- *See also* **Psychoactive drug**

Adenosine (ah-DEN-oh-seen) A byproduct of adenosine triphosphate (ATP) that functions as a neurotransmitter., 65, 102, 333t

Adenosine triphosphate (ATP), 102

ADH. *See* Antidiuretic hormone

ADHD. *See* Attention deficit/hyperactivity disorder

Adoption studies, 19, 143, 144f, 467, 471, 473

Adrenaline, 99

Adrenocorticotropic hormone (ACTH) (uh-DREE-noh-kore-ti-koh-TROE-pik) A pituitary hormone that stimulates the adrenal glands., 275

Adulthood, 149

Aerobic metabolism A chemical processes that requires oxygen., 228–229

Afferent nerve (AF-er-ent) A nerve that carries sensory information to the CNS., 48–49

Aggression The intentional initiation of a hostile or destructive act., 421
- biochemistry and, 423–425, 424f
- brain structures and, 421–423, 423f
- genetics and, 421
- structural/biochemical correlates of, 428
- testosterone and, 3, 424f

Aging
- behavior and, 148
- of brain, 148
- cataracts and, 183, 183f
- hearing and, 200–201
- memory and, 370–371
- muscles and, 230, 230f
- of nervous system, 148–151
- reflexes and, 237–238
- sleep and, 323–324, 324f
- technology for prevention of, 149
- vision and, 182–183

Agonist Substance that promotes the activity of a neurotransmitter., 105

Agouti-related protein (AgRP) A small protein secreted by the arcuate nucleus that initiates eating., 274–276

Agraphia, 394

AgRP. *See* Agouti-related protein

AIDS. *See* Acquired immune deficiency syndrome

AIDS dementia complex (ADC) A collection of neurological symptoms that result either directly from the actions of the HIV virus itself or from other opportunistic infections overlooked by the impaired immune system of the HIV patient., 442–443, 443f, 448

AIS. *See* Androgen insensitivity syndrome

Aitchison's ten criteria for language, 385t

Alarm reaction The first stage of Selye's General Adaptation Syndrome, characterized by activation of the sympathetic nervous system and mental alertness., 425, 425f

Alcohol, 107, 113
- as drug, 121
- *See also* **Fetal alcohol syndrome**

Aldosterone (al-DOS-ter-one) A hormone that signals the kidneys to retain sodium., 267, 267f

Alexia, 394

Allele (uh-LEEL) Alternative version of a particular gene., 125–126, 126f

All-trans The form taken by retinal after light is absorbed by the rod outer segment., 163, 164f

Alpha fetoprotein (fee-toe-PRO-teen) A substance circulated by rats that deactivates estradiol and prevents maternal estradiol from masculinizing female pups., 302, 302f

Alpha melanocyte-stimulating hormone (αMSH) A neurochemical originating in the arcuate nucleus, believed to inhibit feeding behavior., 277

Alpha motor neuron A spinal motor neuron directly responsible for signaling a muscle fiber to contract., 232

Alpha wave A brain waveform having 9 to 12 cycles per second, associated with less alertness and more relaxation than beta activity during wakefulness., 320, 320f

ALS. *See* Amyotrophic lateral sclerosis

Alzheimer's disease A degenerative, ultimately fatal condition marked initially by memory loss., 63–64, 64f, 97, 130, 149–151, 150f, 371

Amacrine cell (AM-uh-krin) A retinal interneuron in the inner nuclear layer that integrates signals across adjacent segments of the retina., 160, 167

Amanita muscaria, 120

Amblyopia (am-blee-OH-pee-uh) A condition also known as lazy eye, in which one eye does not track visual stimuli., 183

American Association for the Advancement of Science (AAAS), 24

American Sign Language (ASL) A language of signs, produced by the hands and arms, that is used by people with hearing impairments., 389

Amino acid An essential component of proteins., 96

Distal A directional term meaning farther away from another structure, usually in reference to limbs., 28, 28f
Disulfiram, 113, 113f
Diversity, genetic, 126–130, 128f
Dizygotic twins (DZ), 130
DNA. *See* Deoxyribonucleic acid
Dogs, vision of, 155f
Dominant allele A gene that produces its phenotype regardless of whether its paired allele is heterozygous or homozygous., 126
The Doors of Perception (Huxley), 120
Dopamine A major monoamine and catecholamine neurotransmitter implicated in motor control, reward, and psychosis., 98–99, 98f, 107f, 249, 462, 463f
  reward system, 111–112
  subtypes of, 99
Dopaminergic synapse, 107
Dopaminergic systems, 99f
Dorsal. *See* **Superior / dorsal**
Dorsal column The spinal pathway that carries information about touch and position to the medulla., 208, 208f
Dorsal column-medial lemniscus pathway, 208, 208f
Dorsal horns Gray matter in the spinal cord that contains sensory neurons., 34
Dorsal stream A pathway leading from the primary visual cortex in a dorsal direction thought to participate in the perception of movement., 174–175, 175f
Dorsolateral prefrontal cortex An area located at the top and sides of the frontal lobe that participates in executive functions such as attention and the planning of behavior., 44–45, 45f
Double-blind experiment A research design in which neither the participant nor the experimenter knows whether the participant is receiving a drug or a placebo until after the research is concluded., 21, 109
Down syndrome An abnormal genetic condition resulting from a genotype with three copies of chromosome 21, responsible for moderate mental retardation and a characteristic physical appearance., 145, 288
Dreaming, 324–327
  See also specific types
Drinking
  brain and, 270
  cessation of, 268–269
  initiation of, 268
Drosophila, 368
Drugs
  addiction to, 111–113
  administration of, 108, 109f
  alcohol as, 121
  cognition and, 480
  common, 122
  compensation and, 110f
  "designer," 111
  effects of, 108–113
  interactions of, 106–108f
  placebo effects of, 109
  receptor effects and, 106–107
  responses to, 109
  reuptake and, 107–108
  at synapse, 105–108, 106f
  tolerance and, 110f
  withdrawal and, 109–111, 110f
  See also specific drugs
Dura mater (DO-ruh MAH-ter) The outermost of the three layers of meninges, found in both the central and peripheral nervous systems., 29
Dyslexia A condition characterized by difficulty learning to read in spite of normal intelligence and exposure to standard instruction., 394–396, 395f
Dyssomnia (dis-SOM-nee-ah) A sleep disorder that involves difficulty initiating or maintaining sleep., 334–336
DZ. *See* Dizygotic twins

Ear, 192, 193f
  See also Auditory system; Hearing; specific parts
Eating
  disorders, 254, 278–282
  initiation of, 273–276
  satiety and, 276–277
Echidna, 329f
Echolocation, 190, 190f
Ecstasy (MDMA) A close relative of amphetamine that produces its behavioral effects by stimulating the release of serotonin., 108, 111, 115, 117, 117f
ECT. *See* Electroconvulsive shock therapy
Ectoderm One of the initial three germ layers of the embryo, the source of skin and neural tissue., 134
Ectotherm An animal that relies on external methods, such as moving into the sun or shade, for maintaining body temperature., 257
Edwin Smith Surgical Papyrus, 3–4
EEG. *See* Electroencephalogram
Efferent nerve (EE-fer-ent) A nerve that carries motor commands away from the CNS., 48–49
Electrical force The force that moves molecules with like electrical charges apart and molecules with opposite electrical charges together., 75–76, 75f
Electrical self-stimulation of the brain (ESB) A behavior engaged in willingly by research subjects that leads to electrical stimulation of certain parts of the brain., 419
Electrical signaling, 81
Electrical synapse A type of synapse in which a neuron directly affects an adjacent neuron through the movement of ions from one cell to the other., 82–84, 83f, 83t
  See also **Chemical synapse**; **Neuron**; Synapse
Electricity, in neural communication, 5, 5f
Electroconvulsive shock therapy (ECT) A treatment of mood disorders in which convulsions are produced by the passage of an electric current through the brain., 470, 470f
Electrodes, implanted in rats, 15, 16f
Electroencephalogram (EEG) (eelek-troh-en-SEF-uh-loh-gram) A technology for studying the activity of the brain through recordings from electrodes placed on the scalp., 12–13, 12f, 321–323, 321f
Electrolyte A substance that has broken up into ions in solution., 262
Electromagnetic radiation Radiation emitted in the form of energy waves., 155, 155f
Electromagnetic spectrum, 156, 156f
Electron microscopes, 8–9
11-cis The form taken by retinal while it is bound to opsin in the absence of light., 163
Embolism A blood vessel blockage that originated elsewhere and traveled to its current location., 432
Embryo An organism in its early stage of development; in humans, the developing individual is referred to as an embryo between two and eight weeks following conception., 21, 134, 134f
Emergency contraception, 297
Emotion A combination of physical sensations and the conscious experience of a feeling., 403–419
  activation and, 419
  amygdala and, 413–415, 414–415f
  autonomic nervous system and, 413
  biology and, 405–407, 406f
  brain damage and, 418
  cerebral cortex and, 416–418, 416–418f
  cingulate cortex and, 416
  detecting, 12
  environment and, 407
  evolution of, 403
  expression/recognition of, 403–408, 404–406f
  limbic system and, 419–420
  lying and, 407–408, 408f
  theories of, 408–413
  See also **Aggression**; Pleasure, and reward; Reward; **Stress**; Violence
Empathy The ability to relate to the feelings of another person., 410–411
Encapsulated receptor A mechanoreceptor in which the axon fibers are surrounded by a fluid-filled capsule formed of connective tissue., 205, 205t
Encephalitis (en-sef-uhl-EYE-tis) A condition characterized by inflammation of the brain., 441–442, 448
Encephalization quotient (EQ), 57, 57f
Endoderm One of the initial three germ layers of the embryo, the source of many internal organs., 134
Endolymph (EN-doh-limf) The fluid found in the cochlear duct., 193, 194f
Endoplasmic reticulum (en-doh-PLAZ-mik reh-TIK-you-lum) An organelle in the cell body that participates in protein synthesis., 65
Endorphin (en-DOR-fin) A naturally occurring neuropeptide that is very closely related to opioids., 19, 117
Endotherm An animal that can use internal methods, such as perspiration or shivering, to maintain body temperature., 257
Engram A physical memory trace in the brain., 354

Inferior / ventral A directional term meaning toward the belly of a four-legged animal., 27, 28f
Inferior colliculi A pair of bumps on the dorsal surface of the midbrain that process auditory information., 38
Information processing models theories of memory that seek to explain the management of information by the brain, from detection to storage to retrieval., 352–353, 353f
Infrasound Sound at frequencies below the range of human hearing, or lower than about 20 Hz., 192
Inhibition In neural communication, a hyperpolarizing influence on the postsynaptic neuron., 84
Inhibitory postsynaptic potential (IPSP) A small hyperpolarization produced in the postsynaptic cell as a result of input from the presynaptic cell., 88–89, 89f, 89t
Inner ear, 193–197, 193f, 194, 194f, 197, 197f, 203f
Inner hair cell An auditory receptor cell located near the connection between the tectorial membrane and cochlear duct., 194
Inner nuclear layer The layer of retinal interneurons containing amacrine, bipolar, and horizontal cells., 161, 161f
Inner plexiform layer The location in the retina containing axons and dendrites that connect the ganglion, bipolar, and amacrine cells., 161, 161f
Insomnia The inability to sleep a normal amount of time., 334–335
  See also Onset insomnia
Instinct A stereotyped pattern of behavior elicited by particular environmental stimuli., 341, 341f
Institutional Review Boards (IRBs), 21
Insular cortex An area of cortex found with the lateral fissure separating the frontal and temporal lobes., 393
Insulin A pancreatic hormone that facilitates the movement of sugars from the blood supply into the body's tissues., 272, 273f
Intellect. *See* Intelligence
Intelligence
  abilities and, 397–398
  assessing, 396–397
  biological correlates of, 399
  enhancing, 398
  genetics and, 398–399, 399f
Intensity, of sound, 190, 191t
Internal clocks, 315–317
Internet, research ethics and, 24
Interneuron A neuron that serves as a bridge between sensory and motor neurons., 68
Interpositus nucleus A cerebellar nucleus thought to be essential to classical conditioning in vertebrates., 348–349, 348f
Intersex A condition in which elements of both male and female development occur in the same fetus., 288
Interstitial fluid (in-ter-STI-shul) A type of extracellular fluid surrounding the body's cells., 262
Interstitial nuclei of the anterior hypothalamus (INAH) (in-ter-STISH-uhl) A collection of four small nuclei in the anterior hypothalamus, two of which (INAH-2 and INAH-3) appear to be sexually dimorphic. The size of INAH-3 might be associated with male sexual orientation., 301
Intracellular fluid The fluid inside a cell., 62, 62f, 262–263, 263f
  ionic composition of, 73–74, 73f
Intrafusal muscle fiber (in-truh-FEW- suhl) One of the fibers that make up a muscle spindle., 233, 234f
Intralaminar nucleus (in-truh-LAM- in-ar) One of many nuclei in the thalamus that receive some pain and temperature input., 213, 213f
Invertebrates, 54
  learning and, 342–347
Ion An electrically charged particle in solution., 62
  movement of, 74–76
  See also Chloride ion; Potassium ion; Sodium ion
Ion channel The protein structure embedded in a cell membrane that allows ions to pass without the use of additional energy., 62, 86
Ion pump A protein structure embedded in a cell membrane that uses energy to move ions across the membrane., 62
Ionic composition, 73–74, 74f
  See also **Resting potential**
Ionotropic receptor (eye-on-oh-TROE-pik) A receptor protein in the postsynaptic membrane in which the recognition site is located in the same structure as the ion channel., 86–87, 87f, 100
Ipsilateral A directional term referring to structures on the same side of the midline., 28, 28f
IPSP. *See* Inhibitory postsynaptic potential
IQ scores, distribution of, 400
IRBs. *See* Institutional Review Boards
Iris The circular muscle in the front of the eye that controls the opening of the pupil., 159–160, 159f
Ischemia (iss-KEE-mee-uh) A condition in which inadequate blood flow results in insufficient quantities of oxygen being delivered to tissue., 431–432
Isotonic Having the same concentration of solutes as a reference solution., 263
IVF. *See* In vitro fertilization

Jacksonian march During some simple partial seizures, the progression of convulsions or twitches from body part to body part related to the organization of the primary motor cortex., 437
Jacksonian seizure A type of simple partial seizure originating in the motor cortex., 437
James-Lange theory A theory of emotion in which a person's physical state provides cues for the identification of an emotional state., 408–411, 409f, 412f
Jet lag Fatigue, irritability, and sleepiness resulting from travel across time zones., 314–315, 315f
Joints, 231, 231f, 235, 235f

K cells A small percentage of ganglion cells that do not fit the criteria for P or M cells exactly and respond to blue and yellow light., 168, 169t, 179–180
K-complex A brief burst of brain activity occurring during Stage 2 slow-wave sleep., 322–323
Kidney One of a pair of structures located in the lower back responsible for maintaining fluid balance and for producing urine., 263
  See also Sodium
Klinefelter syndrome A condition in males caused by an XXY genotype, characterized by frequent problems with fertility, secondary sex characteristics, and verbal skills., 287–288
Klüver-Bucy syndrome (KLOO-ver BYEW-see) A collection of symptoms, including tameness, extreme sexual behavior, and oral exploration, that results from damage to the temporal lobes, and the amygdala in particular., 414
Knockout genes Genes that take the place of normal genes but that fail to produce the specific protein produced by the normal genes., 19
Koniocellular layers (cone-ee-oh-CELL-ue-ler) Layers of very small neurons between the larger six layers of the lateral geniculate nucleus that receive input from K cells in the ganglion layer of the retina., 170–171, 171f
Korsakoff's syndrome (KORE-suh-koffs) Anterograde amnesia resulting from thiamine deficiency, typically found in chronic alcoholics., 362
Kuru (KER-oo) A human TSE identified among the Fore of New Guinea, related to their practice of cannibalism., 445, 445f

Lactose intolerance, 271, 271f
Lamellipodia (lah-mel-oh-POH-dee-uh) Flat, sheetlike extensions from the core of growth cones, located between the filopodia., 137
Language, 384–396
  Aitchison's ten criteria for, 385t
  Animals and, 387–388, 388f
  brain mechanisms for, 389–396
  click, 386, 386f
  hemisphere differences in, 378–379, 378f
  origins of, 384–386
  schizophrenia and, 386
  systems, 393, 394f
  See also **American Sign Language; Bilingual**
Lateral A directional term meaning away from the midline., 28, 28f
Lateral geniculate nucleus (LGN) The nucleus within the thalamus that receives input from the optic tracts., 141–142, 143f, 169–171, 171f
Lateral hypothalamus (LH) A part of the hypothalamus that participates in behavioral responses to thirst and in the initiation of feeding behavior., 268
Lateral inhibition The process in which active cells limit the activity of neighboring, less active cells., 168, 169f
Lateral pathway A large collection of axons that originates in the cerebral cortex,

synapses on either the red nucleus or alpha motor neurons, and controls voluntary movements., 238–239, 239f
Lateral sulcus The fissure separating the temporal and frontal lobes of the cortex., 43–44
Lateralization The localization of a function in one hemisphere or the other., 376–384
behavior and, 379–384
development of, 379–380
gender differences in, 383–384
hemispheres and, 381
prosody/musical abilities and, 382–383
schizophrenia and, 386
L-dopa A substance produced during the synthesis of catecholamines that is also administered as a treatment for Parkinson's disease., 98–99, 249
Learning A relatively permanent change in behavior or the capacity for behavior due to experience., 341
cost of, 347
improving, 361
invertebrates for studying, 342–347
types of, 341–342, 352
Left hemisphere, 377–379, 378f
Lens The clear structure behind the pupil and iris that focuses light on the retina., 159f, 160
Leptin A substance secreted by fat cells that helps the body regulate its fat stores., 274
Lesbians. *See* Sexual orientation
Lesion (LEE-zhun) Pathological or traumatic damage to tissue., 16–17, 17f
Lethal injection, 76
LGN. *See* Lateral geniculate nucleus
LH. *See* Lateral hypothalamus; Luteinizing hormone
Lie detectors, 12
Ligand-gated channel (LIE-gend) An ion channel in the neural membrane that responds to chemical messengers., 63
Light
characteristics of, 155–157
environment and, 156f
pollution, 319
as stimulus, 155
Limbic system (LIM-bik) A collection of forebrain structures that participate in emotional behavior and learning., 39–41, 40f
emotion and, 419–420
smell and, 218
structures of, 42t
See also Mesolimbic system
Linear acceleration The force perceived when our rate of movement changes., 202–203
Linkage The characteristic of genes located adjacent to one another to be passed along as a group., 126
Lipostatic theory, 273
Lithium (LITH-ee-um) A simple salt that appears to stabilize serotonin and norepinephrine levels in cases of bipolar disorder., 472
Lobe One of the four major areas of the cerebral cortex: frontal, parietal, temporal, and occipital., 42–43
of cerebral cortex, 45f
See also **Frontal lobe; Occipital lobe; Parietal lobe; Temporal lobe**
Local circuit neuron A neuron that communicates with neurons in its immediate vicinity., 67
Localization, in hemispheres, 384
Localization of function, 6
Localization of sound, 199–200, 200f
Locus coeruleus (LOW-kuss se-ROOlee-us) A structure in the pons that participates in arousal., 36, 36f
Longitudinal fissure The major fissure dividing the two cerebral hemispheres on the dorsal side of the brain., 43–44
Long-term depression (LTD) A type of synaptic plasticity in which postsynaptic potentials in target cells are reduced., 351
Long-term memory A memory store in which apparently unlimited amounts of data can be held for an unlimited amount of time., 353–354f
biochemistry and, 366–368, 367–368f
Long-term potentiation (LTP) A type of synaptic plasticity in which the application of a rapid series of electrical shocks to an input pathway increases the postsynaptic potentials recorded in target neurons.
memory and, 358–360
NMDA glutamate receptors and, 359–360, 360f
spatial memory and, 360–361, 361f
Loudness, 198–199, 199f
Love, 308–310, 309f
LSD. *See* Lysergic acid diethylamide
LTD. *See* Long term depression
LTP. *See* Long-term potentiation
Lucid dreaming Thoughtful dreaming; the dreamer is aware that he or she is dreaming and can manipulate the experience., 325
Lumbar nerve One of the five spinal nerves serving the lower back and legs., 34
Lung cancer, 98
Luteinizing hormone (LH) (LOO-tin-eye-zing) A hormone released by the anterior pituitary that signals the male testes to produce testosterone and that regulates the menstrual cycle in females., 291–292, 294, 295f
Lying, 407–408, 408f
Lymphocyte (LIMF-oh-site) A white blood cell; an important feature of the immune system., 427–428
Lysergic acid diethylamide (LSD) A hallucinogenic drug that resembles serotonin., 111, 120–121

M cell Large ganglion cell that responds to all wavelengths regardless of color, subtle differences in contrast, and stimuli that come and go rapidly., 168, 169t
Macroglia Large glial cells, including astrocytes, oligodendrocytes, and Schwann cells., 68, 70–72, 70t
Macula (MACK-you-luh) A 6 mm round area in the retina that is not covered by blood vessels and that is specialized for detailed vision., 160–161
Magnetic resonance imaging (MRI) An imaging technique that provides very high resolution structural images., 10–11, 11f
Magnetoencephalography (MEG) (mag-nee-toh-en-seh-fuhl-AW-graf-ee) A technology for recording the magnetic output of the brain., 13–14, 14f
Magnocellular layers (mag-noh-CELL-ue-ler) The two ventral layers of the LGN that receive input from M cells in the ganglion layer of the retina., 170–171, 171f
Maintenance insomnia Insomnia in which the individual cannot stay asleep during the night., 334–335
Major depressive disorder (MDD) A disorder in which intense feelings of sadness, hopelessness, and worthlessness persist a minimum of two weeks., 466–470
Major histocompatibility complex (MHC) gene A gene that encodes our immune system's ability to recognize intruders; might account for female human preferences for male odors., 308
Males
contraception and, 300
sex hormones and behavior of, 299–300
See also Gender
Malignant tumor A type of abnormal cell growth that, lacking boundaries, invades the surrounding tissue and is very likely to recur following surgical removal., 434
Malleus (MALL-ee-us) The first of three ossicles in the middle ear., 192, 193f
Mammillary body (MAM-i-laree) One of two bumps on the ventral surface of the brain that participate in memory and are included in the limbic system., 41, 42t
Mania An emotional state characterized by abnormally elevated, expansive, or irritable mood., 471
MAO. *See* Monoamine oxidase
MAOA gene, 480–481
Marijuana, 117–119, 118–119f
Marijuana Medical Papers 1839–1972 (Mikuriya), 119
Massa intermedia (MASS-uh in-ter-MEE-dee-uh) The connection between the right and left thalamic nuclei., 377, 377f
Mating, assortative, 307
MCH. *See* Melanin-concentrating hormone
MDD. *See* Major depressive disorder
MDMA. *See* Ecstasy
Mechanoreceptor A skin receptor that senses touch, pressure, or vibration., 204f, 205, 205t, 207–208f
Medial A directional term meaning toward the midline., 28, 28f
Medial forebrain bundle (MFB) A fiber pathway that is a major site for electrical self-stimulation. The MFB connects the substantia nigra and ventral tegmental area with higher forebrain structures, including the hypothalamus and nucleus accumbens., 419, 420f
Medial geniculate nucleus Nucleus of the thalamus that receives auditory input., 198
Medial lemniscus (lem-NIS-us) The pathway originating in the dorsal column nuclei and synapsing in the ventral posterior (VP) nucleus of the thalamus that is responsible for carrying information about touch and position., 208, 208f

Otolith organ (OH-toh-lith) A structure in the inner ear vestibular system that provides information about the angle of the head relative to the ground and about linear acceleration., 202–203, 203f
Outer ear, 192, 193f, 194–195, 194f
Outer hair cell An auditory receptor cell located on the organ of Corti that may serve to amplify sounds., 194
Outer nuclear area The location in the retina containing the cell bodies of the photoreceptors., 161f, 162
Outer plexiform layer The retinal layer containing axons and dendrites forming connections between bipolar cells, horizontal cells, and the photoreceptors., 161–162, 161f
Outer segment The portion of a photoreceptor containing photopigments., 162, 162f
Oval window A membrane that forms the boundary between the middle and inner ears., 192, 193f
Ovaries Female gonads; the source of ova and sex hormones., 288, 289f
OVLT. *See* Organum vasculosum of the lamina terminalis
Ovulation The process of releasing a mature egg from the ovary., 295
Ovum A female reproductive cell, or egg., 294–295
Oxytocin (ok-see-TOE-sin) A hormone, released by the posterior pituitary gland, that stimulates uterine contractions, releases milk, and participates in social bonding, including romantic love and parenting behavior., 308–310

P cell Retinal ganglion cell that is small and responds to high contrast and color., 168, 169t, 179–180
Pacinian corpuscle (puh-CHIN-ee-uhn) An encapsulated, rapidly adapting mechanoreceptor with large receptive field that provides information about pressure and vibration., 205–206, 205t
Pain
  brain, pathways of, 212–213, 213f
  chronic, 215
  managing, 214–215, 214–215f
  phantom, 210–211
  purpose for, 212
  receptors for, 212
  sensitivity to, 202f
Pancreatic hormones, 272–273
Panic attack The experience of intense feelings of impending doom and the need to escape accompanied by strong sympathetic arousal, including heart palpitations, sweating, trembling, and shortness of breath., 475
Panic disorder A condition characterized by repeated panic attacks and worries about having panic attacks., 475
Papillae (PAP-i-lie) Bumps on the tongue containing taste buds and taste receptors., 220, 220f
Parahippocampal cortex (pear-uh-hip-oh-KAM-puhl) An area of cortex just ventral to the hippocampus., 41, 358
Parahippocampal gyrus (pear-uh-hip-oh-KAMP-uhl JIE-rus) A fold of tissue near the hippocampus that is often included in the limbic system., 41t
Parahippocampal place area (PPA), 12
Parallel fiber A fiber originating in the granule cells of the cerebellum that synapses on the Purkinje cells., 350, 350f
Parasites, 440–441, 441f
Parasomnia (pear-uh-SOM-nee-ah) A sleep disorder that involves the intrusion of unusual behaviors into sleep., 334, 336–338
  See also Sleep
Parasympathetic nervous system (pear-uh-sim-puh-THET-ik) The division of the autonomic nervous system responsible for rest and energy storage., 50, 51f, 52
Paraventricular nucleus (PVN) (pear-ah-ven-TRI-cu-lar) A portion of the hypothalamus involved with the regulation of hunger., 274, 275f
Parenting, 308–309, 311
Parietal lobe (puh-RIE-et-uhl) One of the four lobes of the cerebral cortex; located between the frontal and occipital lobes., 43
Parkinson's disease A degenerative disease characterized by difficulty in moving, muscular tremors, and frozen facial expressions., 38, 99, 112, 248–249, 249–250f
Paroxysmal depolarizing shift (PDS) A characteristic electrical pattern that occurs in neurons within a focus during a partial seizure., 437
Partial seizure A seizure that has a clear area of origin, or focus., 436, 437f
  characteristics of, 439
Parvocellular layers (par-voh-CELL-ue-ler) The four dorsal layers of the LGN that receive input from P cells in the ganglion layer of the retina., 170–171, 171f
Passive conduction The movement of an action potential down the length of an unmyelinated axon., 80–81, 80f
Patellar reflex (puh-TEL-er) The knee-jerk reflex; a spinal reflex in which tapping below the knee produces a reflexive contraction of the quadriceps muscle of the thigh, causing the foot to kick., 34–35
Pathways. *See* specific types
PCC. *See* Posterior cingulate cortex
PCP. *See* Phencyclidine
PCS. *See* Postconcussion syndrome
PDS. *See* Paroxysmal depolarizing shift
Peacocks, 341f
Penumbra The area of tissue surrounding an infarct., 432–433
Perception The process of interpreting sensory signals sent to the brain., 176, 188–189
  auditory, 198–200
  culture's effect on, 186, 186f
  depth, 178–179
  visual, 176–181
Perforant pathway A pathway made up of axons originating in the rhinal cortex that form synapses in the dentate gyrus of the hippocampus., 358, 359f
Periaqueductal gray (pear-ee-AHkweh-duk-tuhl) Gray matter surrounding the cerebral aqueduct of the midbrain that is believed to play a role in the sensation of pain., 37, 37f, 214, 214f
Perilymph (PEAR-ee-limf) Fluid found in the vestibular and tympanic canals of the inner ear., 193, 194f
Peripheral nervous system (PNS) The nerves exiting the brain and spinal cord that serve sensory and motor functions for the rest of the body., 30, 33, 33f
Peripheral vision The ability to perceive visual stimuli that are off to the side while looking straight ahead., 161
Perirhinal cortex (pear-ee-RINE-uhl) A substructure of the rhinal cortex., 358, 359f
Permeability A property of a substance that determines the extent to which other substances may pass through it., 62
PET. *See* Positron emission tomography
Petit mal seizure A mild type of generalized seizure in which the patient experiences a brief period of unconsciousness., 437–438
PGO spike An electrical waveform observed during REM sleep, originating in the pons and traveling to the thalamus and occipital cortex. Each PGO wave is associated with an eye movement., 331, 332f
Phantom pain, 210–211
Pharmalogical therapies, 453
Phencyclidine (PCP) (fen-SIE-klideen) A hallucinogen that acts as an antagonist at the NMDA glutamate receptor, 120
Phenothiazine (feen-oh-THIE-uh-zeen) One of a major group of dopamine antagonists used in the treatment of psychosis., 463
Phenotype The observable appearance of an organism., 125
Phenylketonuria (PKU) (fee-nil-key-tone-UR-ee-uh) A heritable condition in which the individual does not produce enzymes necessary for the breakdown of phenylalanine; left untreated, the condition produces mental retardation., 146
Phonological agraphia The inability to write by sounding out words., 394
Phonological awareness The ability to discriminate between rapidly presented speech sounds., 394–395
Photons Individual, indivisible, very small particles that form waves of electromagnetic energy., 155
Photopic vision (foe-TOP-ik) The ability to perceive visual stimuli under bright light conditions due to the activity of cones., 162–163, 163t
Photopigment A pigment contained in the photoreceptors of the eye that absorbs light., 162
Photoreceptor Specialized sensory cell in the retina that responds to light., 160, 162–163, 163t
Phrenology The pseudoscientific notion that skull contours indicate personality and character traits., 6, 6f, 26–27
Phthalates, 291
Pia mater (PEE-ah MAH-ter) The innermost of the layers of meninges, found in both